HARROD'S LIBRARIANS' GLOSSARY
AND REFERENCE BOOK

A Directory of Over 10,200 Terms,
Organizations, Projects and Acronyms
in the Areas of Information
Management, Library Science,
Publishing and Archive Management

HARROD'S LIBRARIANS' GLOSSARY

AND REFERENCE BOOK

A Directory of Over 10,200 Terms,
Organizations, Projects and Acronyms
in the Areas of Information
Management, Library Science,
Publishing and Archive Management

Tenth Edition

Compiled

by

RAY PRYTHERCH

ASHGATE

Published by
Ashgate Publishing Limited
Gower House
Croft Road
Aldershot
Hants GU11 3HR
England

Ashgate Publishing Company
Suite 420
101 Cherry Street
Burlington, VT 05401-4405
USA

Ashgate website: http://www.ashgate.com

British Library Cataloguing in Publication Data
Harrod's librarians' glossary and reference book : a
   directory of over 10,200 terms, organizations, projects and
   acronyms in the areas of information management, library
   science, publishing and archive management. - 10th ed.
   1.Library science - Dictionaries 2.Information science -
   Dictionaries 3.Publishers and publishing - Dictionaries
   4. Book industries and trade - Dictionaries 5.Archives -
   Administration - Dictionaries
   I.Prytherch, Raymond John II.Harrod, Leonard Montague
   III.Librarians' glossary and reference book
   020.3

Library of Congress Cataloging-in-Publication Data
Prytherch, Raymond John.
   Harrod's librarians' glossary and reference book : a dictionary of over 10,200 terms,
organizations, projects and acronyms in the areas of information management, library
science, publishing and archive management / by Ray Prytherch.--10th ed.
      p. cm.
   ISBN 0-7546-4038-8
   1. Library science--Dictionaries. 2. Information science--Dictionaries. 3.
Publishers and publishing--Dictionaries. 4. Book industries and trade--Dictionaries.
5. Archives--Administration--Dictionaries. 6. Bibliography--Dictionaries. I. Title:
Librarians' glossary and reference book. II. Title.

   Z1006. H32 2005
   020'.3--dc22
                                                                    2004026891
ISBN 0 7546 4038 8

Typeset by P. Stubley, Sheffield

Printed and bound in Great Britain by MPG Books Ltd, Bodmin, Cornwall

Contents

Preface to the tenth edition

The first edition of *Harrod's Librarians' Glossary* was published in 1938, and consisted of 176 pages; a second edition was not needed until 1959 and increased in size to 350 pages. Leonard Montague Harrod had originally decided to compile the work after the Library Association (now CILIP) proposed an examination paper in library terminology. Although the proposal never came to fruition, it appeared that the *Glossary* filled a need, and further editions were published in 1971 and 1977. The text of the fourth edition covered over 900 pages.

The Gower Publishing Company took over the title in 1981. I was approached at that time to consider revision with the view to one further edition. L. M. Harrod acted as advisory editor for that fifth edition which was published in 1984 – the year of his death. Since that edition, I have revised the work on five more occasions at intervals of around five years.

Obviously the information professions have changed thoroughly over the last two or three decades. Most noticeably in the last ten years the appearance of the World Wide Web as an information resource is having a profound effect on paper-based services. Digital technology has opened up lines of development that could not have been foreseen. As the technology has matured, the impact it has on society has become pervasive. The Information Society concept, with its permutations of e-government, e-publishing, e-learning, e-commerce and more, and the policies of many national governments to empower citizens to exploit new resources, has led to the creation of an information labyrinth; Freedom of Information legislation should increase our access to formerly closed areas.

However, information professionals will look with concern at this cornucopia of information: where is the assurance of quality? If the professions have a future, it must centre on their judgement of the worthiness of the 'facts' that are presented with such apparent authority on our screens. The challenges of the Internet and the Web are key professional concerns: questions of access, quality, and evaluation. And to balance these: the protection of intellectual property, copyright, privacy, and the threat of piracy.

The *Glossary* has developed to reflect these changes in the professions. A major focus of the tenth edition is the explanation of terms associated with the Information Society concept and the other technological offshoots that have sprouted from it. Information itself, which used to be the core material of the subject we called librarianship, has now expanded with a new life of its own. Instead of a traditional world of publishing, reviewing, selection, acquisition, cataloguing and classification, storing and conserving, we have in its place a completely open system where end-users help themselves to whatever they can find – and need no assistance. The very role of the information professional could vanish at the moment when information is everywhere.

This glut of raw material will become a greater problem and the professions will need to find ways to systematize its lack of pattern – unless we are to let Google and its rivals do it for us in their own way. The current responses have included the rise of Information Management as a discipline in its own right; it has come to stand as a reasonable term for the range of new information tasks. Other terms, such as Knowledge Management and Content Management, are perhaps less convincing as permanent additions to our vocabulary.

The *Glossary* therefore serves still to offer a guide through the maze of terminology. Technical terms are covered only so far as they are essential for information professionals to understand, but terms within the core areas of digitization and electronic products are explained comprehensively. A large proportion of the text is taken up with organizations – libraries, associations, networks, consortia, institutions and government bodies. Entries for these include a website address: a novelty in the ninth edition but now a matter of routine. This has enabled some reduction in the extent of organizational entries as users can check the website if more information is needed.

Projects and programmes are covered extensively; in the ninth edition the UK eLib programme formed a focus area with every project included and explained; for the tenth edition these projects has been removed as they are no longer current and have been replaced with other projects from different sources. European Union projects have been similarly treated; as with most reference sources, users may turn to previous editions to check completed projects.

This leads to the *Glossary*'s most important feature: terminology relevant to the information professions is not confined to the last ten years. The business of the publishing and organization of books and serials remains a central part of many professionals' lives. Thus the *Glossary* includes printing and binding terminology, earlier printing methods, paper sizes and similar entries, together with the terminology of classification and cataloguing, reprography, conservation and preservation. The basic terminology of Records Management and Archive Management are included as before. Historical perspective is retained by the inclusion of official reports of enduring value.

The international aspect continues as in previous editions: the *Glossary* is of UK origin but reflects global trends and concerns. The central criterion for inclusion is that a term or name might be encountered in the English-language professional literature.

The tenth edition of the *Glossary* contains over 10,250 entries; this figure includes the separate parts of subdivided entries. Around 1,700 entries are new or have been completely rewritten. At least 3,000 entries from the ninth edition have been improved or upgraded for this edition. As part of the revision process, every website address was checked in the period from April to June of 2004; where no URL is given for an organization it indicates that none could be located or that the site had not been updated for two years or more.

I am indebted for assistance and support in revising this edition to Priscilla Schlicke and to Peter Stubley; Graham Cornish and Gill Goddard have offered specialist advice. In previous editions advice was received from Angela Abell, Professor Charles Oppenheim, Professor M P Satija, Colin Steele and others; some of their input is still reflected in these pages. Overall, the errors and omissions are mine.

Ray Prytherch
rprytherch@aol.com
August 2004.

Advice on using the *Glossary*

The word-by-word method of filing is used; acronyms and abbreviations, whether pronounceable or not, are treated as words and filed in the alphabetical sequence in their appropriate place. Words separated by a hyphen are treated as a single word.

Where there is a choice between a full term and an acronym, the entry appears under whichever is likely to be more commonly found in the literature, with a reference from the alternative expression.

In the text of entries, words beginning with a capital letter appear as entry words elsewhere in the *Glossary*.

Glossary

@lis. <europa.eu.int/comm/europeaid/projects/alis/index_en.htm> Alliance for the Information Society, an EU programme in co-operation with Latin America aiming to promote the Information Society and fight the digital divide throughout Latin America. Adopted in 2001 with a total budget of 77.5 million Euros, @lis covers a wide spectrum of objectives aiming at creating a long-term partnership between the two regions in the field of the Information Society. It focuses on a dialogue on policy and regulatory aspects, the development of standards, the implementation of demonstration projects in favour of the Civil Society, a network of regulators and the interconnection of research centres.

3G. In mobile telephony, third-generation protocols and products of wireless communications technology, the first generation having been analogue cellular, and the second generation digital cellular networks. An initiative of the International Telecommunication Union and regional standards bodies, 3G aims to provide universal, high-speed, high-bandwidth (up to 4 Mbps) wireless services supporting a variety of advanced applications.

A2A. <www.a2a.org.uk> Access to Archives, the English strand of the UK Archives Network permitting a search through archives catalogues in England, dating from the 900s to the present day. These archives are cared for in local record offices and libraries, universities, museums and national and specialist institutions across England, where they are made available to the public.

A4 size. A European standard size of paper, 210 x 297 mm (8.27 x 11.69 inches). *See also* DIN, Paper sizes for a complete table of sizes.

A5 size. A European standard size of paper, 148 x 210 mm (5.83 x 8.27 inches). *See also* DIN, Paper sizes for a complete table of sizes.

A6 size microfiche. A standard size of microfiche for several layout formats; BS/ISO 9923:1994 gives specifications.

A7 library card. Standard size card of 74 x 105 mm (2.91 x 4.13 inches), eight of which can be cut from a DIN A4 sheet of 210 x 297 mm (8.27 x 11.69 inches). Also called 'A7 size card'. *See also* Card, DIN, Paper sizes for a complete table of sizes.

AAA. Authentication, Authorization and Accounting, a programme area for JISC running for two years from October 2002 designed to advance practical understanding of the latest developments in these areas on behalf of the UK academic and research community. The intention was to address both the general needs for access management to electronic library materials and learning objects, and also the more specialized needs of the e-Science research programme. *See also* Middleware.

AACR. <www.facetpublishing.co.uk> Acronym for Anglo-American Cataloguing Rules; the first edition appeared in 1966 (North America) and 1967 (UK). A second edition (AACR 2) published in 1978, was the product of a Revision Committee including representatives from the

British Library, the Library of Congress, the British and American Library Associations and the Canadian Committee on Cataloguing. AACR is published by CILIP's Facet Publishing, the ALA and Canadian LA. The latest revision was published in October 2002 (ISBN: 1 85604 469 6) and is regularly updated in loose-leaf format and electronically.

AAD. *See* Access to Archival Databases.

AAL. *See* Association of Assistant Librarians.

AALL. *See* American Association of Law Libraries.

AAP. *See* Association of American Publishers, Inc.

AARNet. *See* Australian Academic and Research Network.

AASL. *See* American Association of School Librarians.

ABACUS. Acronym for Association of Bibliographic Agencies of Britain, Australia, Canada and the United States.

ABC. *Abridged Building Classification for architects, builders and civil engineers.* *See* International Council for Research and Innovation in Building and Construction (CIB).

Aberrant copy. One in which binding or machining errors, and not merely defects, occur, and the correct state of which can be recognized.

ABES. Agence Bibliographique de l'Enseignement Supérieur; the French National Bibliographic Service, responsible for the French Collective Catalogue of Books.

ABF. *See* Association des Bibliothécaires Français.

ABHB. Acronym for *Annual Bibliography of the History of the Printed Book and Libraries*; a series of annual volumes covering output from 1970, issued under the auspices of the IFLA Committee on Rare and Precious Books and Documents. Volume 17A is a cumulated subject index covering 1970–1986. From volume 27 onwards a database *Book History Online (BHO)* is also produced. *BHO* currently contains all *ABHB* records from volume 21 (1989) onwards. The present publisher is Kluwer Academic (ISSN: 0305 5964).

Abilene. <abilene.internet2.edu> An Internet2 high-performance backbone network that enables the development of advanced Internet applications and the deployment of leading-edge network services to Internet2 universities and research laboratories. The Abilene Network supports the development of applications such as virtual laboratories, digital libraries, distance education and tele-immersion, as well as the advanced networking capabilities that are the focus of Internet2. Abilene complements and peers with other high-performance research networks in the US and internationally. It connects regional network aggregation points – GigaPoPs – to provide advanced network services to over 220 Internet2 university, corporate, and affiliate member institutions in all US states, the District of Columbia, and Puerto Rico. The current network is a 10 Gbps backbone employing optical transport technology and advanced high-performance routers. *See also* SuperJANET.

ABN. Australian Bibliographic Network; a national online bibliographic database which became an operational system within the National Library of Australia in 1980 and became a publicly available service in 1981. *See now* Kinetica.

Abridged Decimal Classification. An abridgement of the Dewey Decimal Classification, it was first published in 1894; intended for use in schools and small libraries having collections up to 20,000 books. Latest edition is Abridged DDC-13 (1997).

Abridged edition. An edition in which the author's text is reduced in length, or which summarizes the original text of a work. *See also* Expurgated edition.

Abridgement. *See* Epitome.

Absolute location. *See* Fixed location.

Absolute size. *See* Exact size.

Absorbency. The ability of paper to absorb printing ink. This quality varies widely between different papers.

Abstract. 1. A form of current bibliography in which sometimes books, but mainly contributions to periodicals, are summarized: they are accompanied by adequate bibliographical descriptions to enable the publications or articles to be traced, and are frequently arranged in classified order. They may be in the language of the original or be translated. Periodicals which contain only abstracts are known as journals of abstracts or abstract journals. Abstracts may be *indicative*, mainly directing to the original; *informative*, giving much information about the original, summarizing the principal arguments and giving the principal data; or *evaluative*, when they comment on the worth of the original. A *general* abstract is one which covers all essential points in an article, and is provided where the interests of readers are varied and known to the abstractor only in general terms. A *selective* abstract contains a condensation of such parts of an article known to be pertinent to the needs of the clientele and is prepared (i) for the executives, research workers and specialists within the organization or those normally making use of library services, (ii) in response to a request for a literature search, or (iii) to keep the staff of the organization or users of the services informed of developments in their field as revealed in the daily or periodical press, documents or reports. An *author* abstract is one written by the author of the original article. A *comprehensive abstracting service* endeavours to abstract every publication and article appearing in its subject field, whereas a *selective abstracting service* selects only those publications and articles which it considers are likely to be of use to a specific class of reader. *See also* Head (5), Metadata, Synopsis. 2. The individual entry in an abstract journal. 3. In law libraries two further types of abstract are found: a *locative* abstract, which specifies where the original document can be traced, and an *illative* abstract which specifies the general nature of the material in the document. 4. Printers' type, the design of the face of which is based on mechanical drawing, with more or less straight edges and lines of uniform thickness, having no serifs (Sans serif) or square serifs of the same weight as the letter (block serif). Futura, Lydian and Optima are examples of sans serif, and Beton, Cairo, Karnak and Memphis of block serif.

Abstracting service.   The preparation of abstracts, usually in a limited field, by an individual, an industrial organization for restricted use, or a commercial organization; the abstracts being published and supplied regularly to subscribers. Also the organization producing the abstracts. Such services may be either comprehensive or selective. Also called 'Secondary service'.

Abstraction.   The mental process of dividing and grouping which is involved in classifying.

ABTAPL.   <www.abtapl.org.uk> Association of British Theological and Philosophical Libraries; set up in 1954 to be the UK member of the International Association of Theological Libraries after a meeting of the World Council of Churches under the auspices of Unesco. An Organization in Liaison (OiL) with CILIP.

Academic libraries.   Libraries in educational establishments at any level – universities, colleges, research associations etc., although the term is less often associated with school libraries. Such libraries have a role in the educative process far beyond the provision of materials; student-centred and self-programming methods throw a heavy demand on libraries, and staff will be part of faculty teams to plan learning processes and participate in the roll-out of electronic developments such as VLEs. Academic libraries are increasingly the location for IT resources for student use, and there may be Convergence between management of the library and computing facilities.

Acanthus.   An ornament, representing two acanthus leaves pointing different ways, used in tooling book-bindings.

ACARM.   <www.comnet.mt/acarm/index.html> Association of Commonwealth Archivists and Records Managers; also the title of its *Newsletter* (3 p.a.). Established 1984, ACARM is a professional organization linking archivists, archival institutions and records managers across the Commonwealth.

Accent.   A mark used in typesetting to indicate a stress or pitch in spoken language.

Acceptable Use Policy.   Any statement that defines the acceptable conduct – and warns against what is unacceptable conduct – to be followed when using networks and services, generally those that are connected to the Internet but also covering Intranets and Extranets. The specification of unacceptable use varies but can include: the creation or transmission of offensive, obscene, indecent or defamatory material; the transmission of unsolicited commercial or advertising material; corrupting or destroying data; violating the privacy of other users. As examples, the JANET Acceptable Use Policy can be found at: <www.ja.net/documents/

use.html> and that for JISCmail at <www.jiscmail.ac.uk/help/policy /index.htm>.

Access. 1. (*Information retrieval*) (i) a device or method whereby a document may be found; (ii) permission and opportunity to use a document; (iii) the approach to any means of storing information, e.g. index, bibliography, catalogue, computer terminal. 2. (*Archives*) Availability of government archives to the general public; such documents are subject to restrictions of confidentiality for a specified number of years. Similar restrictions are also sometimes applied to donations or bequests of other kinds of documents to archive deposit-ories or libraries. Such documents are said to be 'closed' until their access date is reached and 'open' when the period of restriction has expired. There are other types of access restrictions. Uniform conditions of access are in the process of being agreed by the European Union.

Access codes. A system of indicating standards of disabled access to buildings and facilities in the UK. The codes are:

E   Hearing loop system installed. Check with venue whether in operation.

W   Venue with un-stepped access via main or side door, wheelchair spaces and adapted toilet.

X   Venue with flat or one-step access to event/meeting area.

A   Venue with 2–5 steps to event/meeting area, or split-level access.

S   Venue with many unavoidable steps and/or other obstacles for wheelchair users.

G   Provision made for guide dogs.

Access courses. Preliminary courses of study, recognized by universities or other educational institutions as suitable preparation for admission to their courses.

Access management. The combination of Authentication and Authorization services required for sharing and licensing access to information resources in large-scale networked environments at the organizational and inter-institutional level. A background document on the issues can be found at <www.cni.org/projects/authentication/ authentication-wp.html>. *See also* Middleware.

Access Network. <gaynorb@sloughlibrary.org.uk> Previously known as the Community Care Network (part of the Health Libraries Group of the former Library Association); works to support disabled people, the housebound, and carers. An Organization in Liaison (OiL) with CILIP.

Access point. (*Indexing*) Any unique heading in an index. An element used as a means of entry to a file.

Access to Archival Databases (AAD). <www.archives.gov/aad> A research tool launched in 2003 by the (US) National Archives and Records Administration to make easier the selection of records over the Internet. Over 350 databases from 20 Federal Agencies are included.

Access to Archives. *See* A2A.

Access to Learning Award. <www.clir.org/fellowships/gates> An annual award of up to $1 million made by the Bill and Melinda Gates Foundation to a library, library agency or comparable organization outside the USA that has been innovative in providing free public access to information. The award is administered by the Council on Library and Information Resources.

Accessible and Personalised Local Authority Websites Project. *See* Aplaws Project.

Accession. 1. To enter in an Accessions record or register particulars of each item in the order of its acquisition. 2. (*Archives*) The act of taking documents into physical custody in an archival agency, records centre, or manuscript repository, and recording same. In some cases transfer of legal title may also be involved.

Accession number/code. (*Archives*) A number or code allocated to an accession on arrival in the repository, to identify it for control purposes. The number is recorded in an accessions register, and used until replaced by a permanent Reference code.

Accession order. The arrangement of items on the shelves according to the order of their addition to a class; a numerical and chronological, as distinguished from a classified, arrangement.

Accessions. A group term indicating additions to the stock of a library or archives service.

Accessions record/register. 1. The chief record of the stock added to a library. Items are numbered progressively as they are added to stock. 2. (*Archives*) The formal record of accessions of archival material received by an Archives service, in which information on the immediate source and the broader provenance of the material is preserved permanently. In such cases the accessions register is an essential record, since it preserves evidence of the provenance of material received.

Accident. *See* Predicables, five.

Accompanying material. (*Cataloguing*) Material such as an atlas, portfolio of plates, videotape, software, etc., which is intended to be kept in physical conjunction with a publication, and to be used with it.

Accordion fold. Computer paper used on older types of printer (before the almost universal use of the Laser printer) may be stored in page lengths that are folded so that each fold is in the opposite direction to the previous fold, in the manner of the bellows of an accordion. Also termed 'Zigzag fold', 'Concertina fold'.

Accreditation. A process of recognition for academic courses, usually involving evaluation of the providing institution; especially the procedure operated by the American Library Association for approval of schools running courses in library science.

Accrual. (*Archives*) New materials received by an archives service that must be assimilated into a series already held by that service. This situation frequently arises in government archives, where departments transfer materials at intervals.

Achieve Award. <www.cilip.org.uk> An annual award made by CILIP and learndirect to recognize adult learners who have used e-learning methods in a library or information centre.

Achievement in European Information. An award made by the European Information Association (EIA) and sponsored by Chadwyck-Healey; it recognizes contributions to promoting access to information about the European Union and wider Europe, and is open to authors, publishers and those within organizations promoting EU sources.

ACHLIS. *See* Australian Clearing House for Library and Information Science.

Acid blast. The spraying of half-tone and zinc plates with acid as part of the etching process. This results in a sharper image.

Acid resist. An acid-proof protective coating which is applied to metal plates before etching.

Acid-free paper. In principle, paper which contains no free acid, or which has a pH value (determined by the standard method) of 7.0 or more. Commercial practice permits a limited amount of acid under the designation 'acid-free', provided that the paper is essentially chemically inert. Acid, as a residue of the manufacturing process, causes paper to decay, turn brown, become brittle and eventually disintegrate. In proper storage conditions, acid-free paper should be virtually permanent. *See also* Alkaline paper, Permanent paper, pH value.

ACLA. *See* African-Caribbean Library Association.

ACLIP. Affiliate of CILIP. Proposed new post-nominal letters for a category of CILIP members.

ACLIS. Australian Council of Library and Information Services. Founded in 1988 to focus attention on strategic issues; wound up in 1998 and merged into ALIA.

ACLS. *See* American Council of Learned Societies.

ACM. *See* Association for Computing Machinery.

Acoustic coupler. In the early days of online searching, this device was used for connecting a terminal to a remote computer when a dedicated data line was not available: a standard telephone line was used, and the handset fitted into the acoustic coupler to receive and transmit sound tones. Now largely replaced by direct data lines and Modems.

Acquisition. The processes of obtaining books and other items for a library, documentation centre or archive.

Acquisition record. A record of all books and other material added or in process of being added to a collection.

Acquisitions policy. (*Archives*) The stated policy of an archives service, particularly in central government, explaining how its Appraisal and selection procedures are to be applied. The *Standard for Record Repositories* applies to this activity.

ACRL. *See* Association of College and Research Libraries.

Acrography. A method of producing relief surfaces on metal or stone by means of tracing with chalk, for making electrotype or stereotype plates.

Acronym. A word formed from the initial letter or letters of each of the successive parts of the name of an organization, group or term, e.g. Unesco (United Nations Educational Scientific and Cultural Organization).

Acrophony. In pictographic writing, the principle that the value of each consonant is the value of the first letter of its name, as the *b* of *beta*, the *g* of *gamma*, and the *d* of *delta*.

ACSI. Association Canadienne des Sciences de l'Information. *See* Canadian Association for Information Science.

Acting edition. An edition of a play which gives directions concerning exits, entrances, properties, etc. It is intended for actors and is often published in a limp cover, usually of paper.

Active records. *See* Current records.

Activity. (*Information retrieval*) A term which indicates that a record in a file is used, referred to or altered.

Activity ratio. (*Information retrieval*) The ratio of the number of records in a file which have Activity to the total number of records in that file.

ACURIL. *See* Association of Caribbean University, Research and Institute Libraries.

Ad loc. Abbreviation for *ad locum* (Lat. 'At the place cited').

Adams Report. The 'Report on library provision and policy' by Professor W. G. S. Adams to the Carnegie United Kingdom Trustees (CUKT, 1915). The Report, which contained much statistical information, related especially to grants made by Andrew Carnegie to develop public libraries, and presented a view of future policy.

Adaptation. A book that has been re-written or edited, wholly or in part, for a particular purpose such as for reading by children when the original was intended for adults, or a novel adapted for dramatic presentation. Not to be confused with an abridgement or Epitome.

Adaptive hypermedia. Hypertext and hypermedia systems which reflect some features of the user and which are adaptive to user needs. The systems can adapt the content of a hypermedia page to a particular user's knowledge and goals – instead of providing the same links for everyone – or to suggest the most relevant links to follow for a particular context. Also known as the Adaptive Web. (Reference: Brusilovsky, P. (1996) Methods and techniques of adaptive hypermedia. *User modeling and user-adapted interaction*, vol. 6, pp. 87–129 <www.contrib.andrew.cmu.edu/~plb/UMUAI.ps>)

Adaptive Web. *See* Adaptive hypermedia.

ADBS. *See* Association des Documentalistes et Bibliothécaires Spécialisés.

Add instructions. From the 18th edition of the Dewey Decimal Classification, 'add instructions' which specify exactly what digits should be added to a base number, replaced the 'divide-like' notes. *See also* Divide like the classification.

Added copies. Duplicate copies of titles already in stock. Not to be confused with Added edition.

Added edition.   A different edition from the one already in the library.

Added entry.   1. A secondary catalogue entry, i.e. any other than the Main entry with the addition of a heading for subject, title, editor, series, or translator, and in the case of music, for arranger, librettist, title, medium, form, etc. It must not be confused with a Cross reference.

Added title entry.   An entry, not being a main entry, made under the title for books with distinctive titles or in cases where title entries would be an advantage, such as anonymous works.

Added title-page.   A title-page additional to the one from which a main entry for a catalogue entry is made. It may precede or follow the one chosen and may be more general, such as a series title-page, or may be equally general, as a title-page in another language, and placed either at the beginning or end of a book. *See also* Parallel title.

Addendum (*Pl.* Addenda)   1. Matter included in a book after the text has been set. It is printed separately and is inserted at the beginning or end of the text; it is less extensive than a Supplement.   2. A slip added to a printed book. *See also* Corrigenda.

Addition.   1. (*Classification*) The simple extension of an existing Array, either by interpolation or extrapolation.   2. (*Noun*) A book or other item that has been obtained for addition to the stock of the library. This term is sometimes used to refer to such items before they have been accessioned.

Additional designation.   (*Cataloguing*) Explanatory information, e.g. dates, place of birth, residence or an Honorific title added to a name for purposes of distinguishing it from other identical names. *See also* Descriptor.

Adequate description, principle of.   The provision of enough information in a catalogue entry to enable a user to make a sensible decision on the suitability of the item described. *See also* Cataloguing, principles of.

Adhesive binding.   A method of binding in which the leaves are attached to one another by some form of strong but flexible adhesive rather than by sewing. Double fan adhesive binding is an example.

Adjacency.   The proximity of two or more words specified as a requirement in an online search statement; thus a phrase can be sought, where individual words by themselves would be irrelevant.

Adjustable classification.   A scheme of classification designed by James Duff Brown in 1897. It was superseded by his Subject classification.

Adopt a Book Appeal.   Launched 1987 by the National Preservation Office of the British Library to raise funds for conservation treatment of stock. Major sponsors receive an illuminated scroll, and the conserved item carries a bookplate with the sponsor's name.

Adoption of the Public Libraries Acts.   The decision of the local authority to take the necessary administrative and legal steps to provide library facilities as permitted by law.

ADP.   1. Abbreviation for automatic (or automated) data processing.   2. *See* Association of Database Producers.

ADSL.   Asymmetric Digital Subscriber Line, pseudo-Broadband technology allowing the simultaneous transmission of voice and data and which for the most part is both cheaper and faster than ISDN. One direction of data transmission has comparatively high Bandwidth (up to 8Mbps) with low bandwidth in the other, making it suitable for World Wide Web surfing and the delivery of Streaming Multimedia. *See also* SDSL.

Adult department.   The department of a library which provides books for the use of adults.

Adult independent learners.   *See* Adult learners.

Adult learners.   People who are following organized or independent courses of study, but who are not enrolled in an educational establishment. Usually, but not always, people who are older than the conventional 'student' age group. The term Adult independent learners (AIL) is also used.

Adult Learners' Week.   <alw@niace.org.uk> An annual UK-wide festival to encourage participation in adult learning. Dates in 2004 were May 15–21, and the week included presentation of the New Learning Opportunities Awards. The week is organized by the National Institute of Adult Continuing Education.

Advance copy (sheet).   A copy of a book, usually bound, but sometimes in sheets, to serve as a proof of the binder's work, for review, notice, advertising or other purposes.

Advancement of Librarianship Programme (ALP).   One of the core programmes of IFLA. *See* International Federation of Library Associations and Institutions.

Advancement of Literacy Award.   An annual award of the Public Library Association of the American Library Association to an American publisher or bookseller who has made a significant contribution to literacy advancement.

Advances in Librarianship.   A well-established annual review series, started in 1977, which remains committed to the traditional areas of librarianship. Coverage of public, academic, school libraries, and some special topics are examined in each volume, with substantial bibliographies. Published by Academic Press (US).

Advice centre.   An area in a central, branch or mobile library, or in non-library premises, devoted to the provision of advice, usually on social issues.

Advisory Council on Libraries (UK).   Re-constituted in 2003, the Council comprises a group of senior public librarians appointed by the Department of Culture, Media and Sport (DCMS) as (unpaid) statutory advisors. The Council will issue an *Annual Report on Libraries*. There are two working parties: on Best Value Performance Indicators, and on Public Library Standards. The Council aims to play a leading role in moving forward the DCMS strategy paper *Framework for the Future*.

Advocates' Library, Edinburgh.   *See* National Library of Scotland.

Aerial map.   A map made from one or more photographs taken from above the surface of the earth.

Aerograph.   An instrument, which by means of compressed air, blows a fine spray of liquid colour onto a lithograph stone or drawing, or when re-touching photographs.

AETLTA.   Acronym for the Association for the Education and Training of Library Technicians and Assistants. Formed in 1981 from the Library Assistants' Certificate Tutors' Group. United those actively concerned with the development of sub-professional qualifications. Disbanded in 2003.

Affiliated library.   One which is part of a library system, but has its own board of management and is not administered as part of the system.

Affiliated Members' Group.   A membership group of CILIP, formed for those who are non-qualified library or information workers.

Affiliation of Local Government Information Specialists (ALGIS). <janeinman@warwickshire.gov.uk> An association of information professionals in UK local government, including website managers, knowledge managers, e-government workers and librarians. Previously a part of the Institute of Information Scientists, ALGIS is now affiliated to LARIA, the Local Authority Research and Intelligence Association.

Afghan Library Association.   Suspended in 1982; currently the Iranian Library Association and others are trying to re-launch. *See* National Library of Iran.

AFNOR.   Acronym for Association Français de Normalisation, the French equivalent of the British Standards Institution.

African Library Association of South Africa.   *See* Library and Information Association of South Africa (LIASA).

African-Caribbean Library Association (ACLA).   <libraryannie@ yahoo.co.uk> (Waltham Forest Central Library, High Street, London E17 9JN, UK) Formed in 1981, ACLA combats racism in library services, employment and publishing. An Organization in Liaison (OiL) with CILIP.

Against the grain.   Said of paper which has been folded at right angles to the direction in which the fibres tend to lie. In a well-printed book the back fold of the paper is never 'against the grain'; the grain direction should run from head to tail in the finished book in order that the pages will lie flat when the book is opened. *See also* Cross direction, Grain direction, With the grain.

AGAMEMNON.   <www.cordis.lu/ist/directorate_e/digicult/ agamemnon.htm> An FP6 project which plans to exploit 3G mobile phones equipped with embedded cameras as the input/output device making use of graphical interfaces and voice-based commands for visitors to archaeological sites and museums.

Agate.   1. (*Binding*) A bloodstone or agate used in hand binding to burnish gold or coloured edges.   2. (*Printing*) Used to denote $5^{1}/_{2}$ point type.

Agate line.   An American standard of measurement for the depth of columns of advertising space in a newspaper. Fourteen agate lines make one column inch.

Agence Bibliographique de l'Enseignement Supérieur. *See* ABES.

Agence pour la Diffusion de l'Information Technologique. <www.adit.fr> (2 rue Brulée, 67000 Strasbourg, France) An agency responsible for disseminating scientific information to French companies.

Agency. In the UK certain government departments and research stations are now termed agencies; this reflects their semi-privatized status. *See also* Government library.

Agent. An individual or firm acting as a middleman between librarian and publisher in the acquisition of material. An agent is commonly used in connection with periodical subscriptions, back numbers of periodicals, and foreign publications. *See also* Literary agent, Managing agent, Subscription agent.

Agglutinative symbol. A symbol, in a system of Notation in a classification scheme, two or more parts of which have a constant and inflexible core.

AGI. (Block C, Morelands, 5–23 Old Street, London EC1V 9HL, UK) Set up following the recommendations of the Chorley Committee in 1987, the Association for Geographic Information is a focus for the geographic information service community, active in promoting GIS initiatives and policies, international standards, and awareness programmes. Membership is open to every sector of government, business and commerce. Activities include conferences, special interest groups. There are currently 18 sponsoring members including the Ordnance Survey, Environment Agency, and HM Land Registry.

AGLINET. Agricultural Libraries Information Network, established within the framework of the International Association of Agricultural Librarians and Documentalists (IAALD) for the purpose of organizing co-operation among agricultural libraries at regional and international levels.

AgNIC. <www.agnic.org> Agriculture Network Information Center, a distributed network that provides access to agriculture-related information, subject area experts, and other resources. Established by an alliance of the (US) National Agricultural Library, land-grant universities, and other organizations committed to facilitating public access to agricultural and related information.

AGORA. <www.aginternetwork.org> Access to Global Online Research in Agriculture. An initiative of the United Nations Food and Agriculture Organization (FAO) to help students, researchers and scientists in developing countries gain free or low-cost access to scientific literature. The portal covers some 400 journals.

AGRA. *See* Association of Genealogists and Record Agents.

AGRICOLA. *See* National Agricultural Library.

Agricultural Librarians in Colleges and Universities (ALCU). *See* ALLCU.

Agricultural Libraries Information Network. *See* AGLINET.

Agriculture Network Information Center. *See* AgNIC.

AgriFor. <agrifor.ac.uk> A subject gateway providing access to Internet resources on agriculture, food and forestry; part of the BIOME Hub of the (UK) RDN.

AGRIS. <www.fao.org/agris> Abbreviation for International Information System for the Agricultural Sciences and Technology, which was adopted in November 1971 at the 16th Conference of the Food and Agricultural Organization (FAO) of the United Nations. Collects information on the agricultural literature of the world through 120 national, regional and international centres co-ordinated by the AGRIS Centre at FAO Headquarters, Rome.

AHDS. <ahds.ac.uk> (AHDS Executive, King's College London, 75–79 York Road, 8th Floor, Waterloo, London, SE1 7AW) The Arts and Humanities Data Service is a national UK service funded by JISC and the Arts and Humanities Research Board to aid the discovery, creation and preservation of digital collections in the arts and humanities. The AHDS web site acts as an integrated access point to the five subject-specific sections: AHDS Archaeology (formerly Archaeology Data Service) hosted by the University of York; AHDS History (formerly the History Data Service) hosted by the University of Essex; AHDS Literature, Languages and Linguistics hosted by the Oxford Text Archive, University of Oxford; AHDS Performing Arts (formerly the Performing Arts Data Service) hosted by the University of Glasgow; and AHDS Visual Arts (formerly the Visual Arts Data Service) hosted by The Surrey Institute of Art & Design.

AHIP. Art History Information Program. *See* Getty Information Institute.

AI. *See* Artificial intelligence.

AIB. <www.aib.it> Associazione Italiana Biblioteche (CP 2461, 00100 Rome, Italy) Founded in 1930 and now with 3,000 members, AIB is a principal professional organization in Italy. Publishes *Bollettino d'Informazioni* (q.) and *AIB Notizie* (m.).

AIDBA. Association Internationale pour le Développement de la Documentation des Bibliothèques et des Archives en Afrique. *See* International Association for the Development of Documentation, Libraries and Archives in Africa.

AIIM. *See* Association for Information and Image Management.

AIInfSc. Associate of the Institute of Information Scientists. *See* CILIP.

AIIP. <www.aiip.org> (8550 United Plaza Blvd., Suite 1001, Baton Rouge, LA 70809, USA) The (US) Association of Independent Information Professionals; founded in 1987 and now with 700 members in 20 countries. Membership open to people owning their own businesses providing research services, consultancy, library support and development, abstracting, writing. Operates vendor discount programmes, mentoring service, public relations support, industry surveys, referral service. In 2003 AIIP and SCIP announced that they would form a strategic alliance.

AIL. 1. Adult independent learners. *See* Adult learners. 2. *See* Association of International Libraries.

AIM25. <www.aim25.ac.uk> A project to provide electronic access to collection level descriptions of the archives of over 50 higher education institutions and learned societies within the greater London area. Initially funded by the Research Support Libraries Programme.

AIOPI. <www.aiopi.org.uk> Association of Information Officers in the Pharmaceutical Industry. An independent professional group for those in the fields of medical and pharmaceutical research. Publishes *AIOPI Newsletter*.

Air brush. *See* Aerograph.

Air-dried. Hand-made, or good machine-made paper or brown paper which is hung over lines and dried slowly in air at a uniform temperature, as distinct from paper which is machine-dried in heat.

Aisle. The passageway between two parallel runs of shelving.

AJL. *See* Association of Jewish Libraries.

Ajouré binding. A style of binding practised in the last third of the fifteenth century in Venice. It was in the traditional Eastern manner with arabesques, gilding, and cut-out leather, over a coloured background.

A.L. *See* A.L.S.

ALA. 1. Asociación Latinoamericana de Archivos: the Latin American Branch of the International Council on Archives. 2. *See* American Library Association. 3. *See* Associateship (UK).

ALAG. *See* Asian Librarians and Advisers Group.

ALASA. *See* Library and Information Association of South Africa (LIASA).

Alaska seal. Sheepskin or cowhide made to imitate sealskin.

Albertype. A process of making pictures with a gelatine-covered plate, the printing being a variety of photogravure.

Albion Press. Invented in 1823 by R. W. Cope of London; it was an improvement on the Stanhope Press and enabled sufficient pressure for printing to be achieved with a single pull on the spindle bar. It was simple in construction, durable, cheap, and easy to work. Its American counterpart was the Washington Press, and its German one, the Hagar Press. The Albion and Columbian presses were used commercially well into the twentieth century; several British private presses used the Albion.

Album. A book of blank leaves in which literary extracts, quotations, poems, drawings, photographs, autographs, newspaper cuttings, stamps, etc. are written, inserted or fixed.

Albumen process. The most commonly used sensitizer for coating photo offset plates.

ALCL. Association of London Chief Librarians. *See* Society of Chief Librarians.

Alcophoto. A photo-mechanical process for making zinc, aluminium or other litho plates.

Alcove. A recess formed by placing two Presses at right angles to a wall, and touching it at one end.

Alcove mark. In an old library, the mark used to indicate in which alcove any particular book may be found. Books in such libraries are arranged according to location and not classification. *See also* Fixed location.

ALCS. *See* Authors' Licensing and Collecting Society.

ALCTS. *See* Association for Library Collections and Technical Services.

ALCU. *See* ALLCU.

Aldine leaves. Small binders' stamps bearing a leaf and stem design; used on books bound for Aldus *c.* 1510.

Aldine Press. An Italian publishing firm founded at Venice in 1495 by Teobaldo Manucci (Aldus Pius Manutius; Aldo Manuzio) 1450–1515. Aldus specialized in small-size editions of Greek and Latin classics which were published between 1494 and 1515, and the first Italic type (1501), which was cut for Aldus by Griffi, was first used for a small format edition of the classics. Aldus's printer's device of anchor and dolphin has frequently been used by other printers, e.g. William Pickering for the Chiswick Press in the late nineteenth century. Between 1515 and 1533 the press was managed by his brothers-in-law, the Asolani, during which time the work of the press deteriorated. In 1533 his youngest son Paulius Manutius (1512–74) took over the press and concentrated on Latin classics.

Aldine style/Italian style. 1. (*Printing*) Ornaments of solid face without any shading whatever, used by Aldus and other early Italian printers. The ornaments are Arabic in character. 2. (*Binding*) Late fifteenth and early sixteenth century Venetian bindings in brown or red morocco carried out for Aldus Manutius. They had the title, or the author's name in a simple panel in the middle of the front cover of a book so that it could be seen when the book lay on a shelf or table. Early examples were decorated in blind with an outer frame and a central device. It is assumed that as Aldus was the leading printer in Venice he would supervise the binding of his books which was done by the Greek binders he employed.

ALEBCI. Asociación Latinamericana de Escuelas de Bibliotecologia y Ciencias de la Información, established in 1970 at Buenos Aires to further library education in Latin America.

ALEX. <www.infomotions.com/alex> The Alex Catalogue of Electronic Texts is a collection of digital documents whose scope includes items from American literature, English literature, and Western philosophy. The catalogue's purpose is to provide value-added access to some of the world's literature through a number of unique features such as the ability to carry out word searches across the content of texts.

Alexandria Digital Library. <alexandria.sdc.ucsb.edu> One of the US Digital Libraries Initiative projects created during the first phase of funding to provide online access to over six million items of geospatial information based around the holdings of the Davidson Library at the University of California, Santa Barbara.

Alexandrian Library. <www.bibalex.org> or <www.bibalex.gov.eg> (Biblioteca Alexandrina, El-Shatby, Alexandria 21516, Egypt) The greatest library of the ancient classical world; founded in the fourth century BC at Alexandria which was then a pre-eminent international meeting point for trade and culture. By the first century BC the library held over 500,000 manuscripts, catalogued in the 'Pinakes' of Callimachus – a form of bibliography giving names of author and a summary of the text. The materials were lost and the library destroyed during the civil wars of the third and fourth century AD. In 1987 Unesco launched an appeal to re-establish a library at Alexandria, to be operated by the government of Egypt as part of an Arab and Middle Eastern research centre. The architects of the striking, modern building are Snohetta A/S of Norway. The new library opened in 2002.

Alfa. An alternative name for esparto grass. *See* Esparto.

ALGIS. *See* Affiliation of Local Government Information Specialists.

Algorithm. (*Indexing*) Instructions for carrying out a series of logical procedural steps in a specified order.

Algorithmic code. One that has rules for converting source (i.e. common language) words into code equivalents.

Algraphy. The process of printing from aluminium plates by lithographic and offset printing. Also called 'Aluminography'.

ALIA. *See* Australian Library and Information Association.

ALICE. <www.dante.net/server/show/conWebDoc.156> America Latina Interconectada Con Europa, a DANTE project set up in 2003 to develop an IP research network infrastructure within the Latin American region and towards Europe. It addresses the infrastructure objectives of the European Commission's @lis programme, which aims to promote the Information Society and fight the digital divide throughout Latin America.

Alienation. (*Archives*) The act of transferring, or losing, custody or ownership of documents to an agency or person not officially connected with the organization whose documents are involved.

Alignment. 1. The exact correspondence in a straight line of the top and bottom of the letters and characters in a font. 2. The arrangement of type in straight lines. 3. The setting of lines of type so that ends appear even at the margins.

ALISA. <www.library.auckland.ac.nz/databases/learn_database> *Australian Library and Information Science Abstracts. ALISA* indexes and abstracts articles in the fields of librarianship and information science, attempting to cover Australian literature comprehensively; it includes children's literature, education, training, information technology, networking, electronic publishing, and telecommunications. Sources include monographs, research reports, conference papers, periodical articles and unpublished material. Work by Australian authors or on Australian libraries published in overseas sources is also covered. The database is compiled by ACHLIS (Australian Clearing House for Library and Information Science).

ALISE. *See* Association for Library and Information Science Education.

ALJH.　*See* Association of Libraries of Judaica and Hebraica in Europe.

Alkaline paper.　An acid-free paper with a residual reserve or buffer of extra alkalinity; synthetic, neutral sizes are typically used, and the fillers or coatings are chalk (alkaline calcium carbonate) rather than clay.

All along.　The method of sewing by hand the sections (usually on cords or tapes) of a book, when the thread goes 'all along', or from Kettle stitch to kettle stitch in each section. Also used to describe machine book-sewing when each section is sewn with the full number of stitches. *See also* Two sheets (sections) on.

All published.　Used in a catalogue entry and in other connotations, concerning a work, the publication of which has been started but is not completed. Also relates to all the issues of a periodical, publication of which has ceased. *See also* Ceased publication.

All rights reserved.　A phrase placed in a book usually on the back of the title-page, signifying that the Copyright is reserved, and that action may be taken against any person infringing that copyright.

All through.　Letter by letter alphabetization. *See* Alphabetization.

ALLCU.　<www.allcu.org.uk> (Library, Wiltshire College Lackham, Lacock, Chippenham SN15 2NY, UK) Association of Land-based Librarians in Colleges and Universities, originally formed in 1978 as Agricultural Librarians in Colleges and Universities (ALCU). An Organization in Liaison (OiL) with CILIP.

Alliances.　*See* Consortia.

Allonym.　A false name, especially the name of some person assumed by an author to conceal identity or gain credit; an alias; a pseudonym.

All-over style.　The style of book decoration which covers the whole of the side of a binding, as distinct from a corner, centre or border design, whether made up of a single motif, different motifs, or a repeated motif.

All-Union Institute of Scientific and Technical Information.　*See* Viniti.

Allusion book.　A collection of contemporary allusions to a famous writer.

ALM London.　*See* Museums, Libraries and Archives Council (MLA).

Almanac(k).　A publication, usually an annual, containing a variety of useful facts of a miscellaneous nature, and statistical information. It was originally a projection of the coming year by days, months, holidays, etc.

ALP.　*See* Advancement of Librarianship Programme.

Alpha testing.　The testing of new Applications software or new 'versions' of existing applications 'in house' by the developers themselves and before carrying out any Beta testing.

Alphabet length.　(*Printing*) The length, usually stated in points, of the twenty-six letters of the alphabet. The relative compactness of a typeface is determined by the comparison of alphabet lengths. The alphabet length in points, divided into 341, gives the number of 'characters per pica'. *See also* Typeface.

Alphabet mark.　A mark, such as the Cutter Author Mark, which is incorporated in the call number of a book to enable alphabetic order to be maintained on the shelves without the use of abnormally long symbols.

Alphabet of symbols. A set of distinct recognizable and repeatable characters or symbols which are used for identifying documents, as the notation used in a scheme of classification, e.g. the figures, capital letters and lower case letters used in Bliss's Bibliographic Classification, or the 10 numerals, 26 capital letters, 26 lower case letters, 8 Greek letters and 9 punctuation marks used in the Colon Classification. Also called 'Base of symbolism'.

Alphabetic writing. The third, and final, stage in the development of writing, in which a single symbol was used to represent a single distinctive sound feature in the spoken language, rather than ideas or syllables. *See also* Phonetic writing, Pictography.

Alphabetical arrangement. The systematic arrangement of entries in a catalogue, index, bibliography or other list of items, or of books on the shelves of a library in alphabetical order of authors, subjects, titles or other distinguishing characteristics. *See also* Alphabetization.

Alphabetical catalogue. One in which the author, title, and/or subject entries are arranged alphabetically.

Alphabetical subject index. An alphabetical list of all subjects named, or dealt with, in a classification scheme, or classified catalogue, together with reference to the place(s) where each subject occurs.

Alphabetico-classed catalogue. An alphabetical subject catalogue, in which entries are not made under specific subjects, as in the dictionary form, but under broad subjects arranged alphabetically, and each sub-divided alphabetically by subject to cite more specific sub-divisions. Author and title entries may be included in the same alphabet under the appropriate subject headings.

Alphabetico-direct catalogue. One in which 'direct' headings, i.e. consisting of natural language and the natural form of phrases, as 'stamp collecting', 'subject cataloguing', are used, the headings being arranged in alphabetical order. Also called Alphabetico-specific catalogue.

Alphabetization. Arranging a list of words, names, or phrases according to the letters of the alphabet. In the main there are two methods in use: 1, 'word by word', or 'nothing before something'; 2, 'letter by letter' strictly according to the letters irrespective of their division into words, or of punctuation. The first method would give an order:

N.S.W.	Newcastle (NSW, Australia)
New Castle (Ps., U.S.A.)	Newels
New Haven (Conn., U.S.A.)	Newhaven (England)
New Testament	News-room
New York	Newton
Newark	

the second method would give an order:

Newark	News-room
Newcastle (NSW, Australia)	New Testament
New Castle (Pa., U.S.A.)	Newton
Newels	New York
New Haven (Conn., U.S.A.)	N.S.W.
Newhaven (England)	

ALPSP. <www.alpsp.org.uk> (South House, The Street, Clapham, Worthing BN13 3UU, UK) Association of Learned and Professional Society Publishers, founded in 1972, an association of those involved in the publishing of academic and professional books and journals; has committees on copyright, marketing, professional education, electronic developments. Recent work has included policies and practice in online publishing, and a Learned Journals Collection scheme to assist smaller members to sell packages of titles.

A.L.S. (Autograph letter signed). A letter entirely in the handwriting of the signer. If unsigned it is referred to by the letters 'A.L.'; if written by someone else but signed, by 'L.S.'; if typed and signed by hand, by 'T.L.S.'.

ALSC. *See* Association for Library Service to Children.

alt. A collection of Usenet news groups that discuss alternative ways of looking at things'. They range from the bizarre to the useful.

ALT. <www.alt.ac.uk> Association for Learning Technology; a UK organization for learning-technology practitioners in further and higher education – teachers, trainers, researchers, developers, service providers, librarians, computer professionals, software companies, publishers. Activities include an annual conference, workshops, awards, and a journal (q.).

ALTA. *See* Association for Library Trustees and Advocates.

Alternative title. 1. A secondary title following the words 'or', 'a', or 'an'. More commonly known as the Subtitle. 2. One of several titles, which in particular circumstances (e.g. in multi-language publications with titles in the languages of the text) could be used as the Main title.

ALTIS. <www.altis.ac.uk> A Hub of the (UK) RDN which aims to provide a trusted source of selected, high quality Internet information for students, lecturers, researchers and practitioners in the areas of hospitality, leisure, sport and tourism. Based at the University of Birmingham.

Aluminium plates. Extremely flexible plates used in Offset printing.

Aluminography. *See* Algraphy.

Alvey Programme. The Alvey Committee (chairman John Alvey, of British Telecom) was established in 1982 by Kenneth Baker, the then Minister for Information Technology. Its report – *Programme for Advanced Information Technology* (HMSO, 1982) – the 'Alvey Report', proposed a programme of collaborative research in four main areas: software engineering; man-machine interfaces; intelligent knowledge-based systems; very large-scale integration. The British Government devoted some £350 million to the programme over a five-year period.

Ambiguous title. One which is so vague that it may be misunderstood. In a catalogue, amplification may be made in brackets immediately following the title, or in a note.

Ambrogal printing. An offset printing process invented by Ambrosius Galetzka; it is reminiscent of American aquatone printing. Sheets of celluloid are prepared for lithographic printing. *See also* Aquatone.

AMC. Archives and Manuscripts Control: a version of USMARC developed by the Society of American Archivists to enable archivists to use MARC formats for archival description.

AMDECL (UK). Association of Metropolitan District Education and Children's Librarians; one of the three professional groups which in 1995/96 merged to become the Association of Senior Children's and Education Librarians (ASCEL).

American Association of Law Libraries (AALL). <www.aallnet.org> (53 W Jackson Blvd, Chicago, IL 60604, USA) Established 1906. Aims 'to promote librarianship, to develop and increase the usefulness of law libraries, to cultivate the science of law librarianship and to foster a spirit of co-operation among members of the profession'. Operates ALLNET – American Association of Law Libraries Information System. Publishes *Law Library Journal* (q.).

American Association of School Librarians (AASL). A Division of the American Library Association since 1 January 1951; became an associated organization of the National Education Association in 1969. It is concerned with the improvement and extension of library services in elementary and secondary schools. Publishes *School Media Quarterly*.

American Booksellers Association. <www.bookweb.org> (828 South Broadway, Tarrytown, NY 10591, USA) Founded in 1900, the ABA has a core membership of independently-owned book stores with store front locations. Actively supports free speech, literacy, and programmes to encourage children's reading. Publishes research reports and statistics on the book industry.

American Braille. An obsolete variation of Braille.

American Council of Learned Societies. <www.acls.org> (633 Third Avenue, New York, NY 10017-6795, USA) ACLS is a private non-profit federation of 52 national scholarly organizations. The purpose of the Council, as set forth in its constitution, is 'the advancement of humanistic studies and the maintenance and strengthening of relations among the national societies devoted to such studies'. Included in the programmes of the Council are awards to individual scholars to advance research in the humanities and humanistic aspects of the social sciences; support for international scholarly research and exchanges; activities concerned with the identification of present and future needs of humanistic scholarship, and planning and development to meet these needs; and organizational functions. In addition, the Council has fiscal and administrative oversight for the Council for International Exchange of Scholars (CIES) which administers the Fulbright program. Organized in 1919 and incorporated in the District of Columbia in 1924, ACLS was granted a federal charter through the United States Congress in 1982.

American finish. *See* Paper finishes.

American Library Association (ALA). <www.ala.org> (50 East Huron Street, Chicago, IL 60611-2795, USA) The American Library Association, founded in 1876, is the oldest and largest national library association in the world. Its concern spans all types of libraries: state, public, school and academic libraries; special libraries serving persons in government, commerce and industry, the arts, the armed services, hospitals, prisons, and other institutions. With a membership of libraries, librarians, library trustees, and other interested persons from every state and many countries of the world, the Association is a focus in the search for high quality services. It maintains close relationships with similar organizations world-wide, and with cognate bodies in education, research and cultural development such as the Freedom to Read Foundation, the Merritt Humanitarian Fund, the National Coalition for Literacy, and the National Forum for Information Literacy. There are 64,000 members (2004). There are 11 divisions: American Association of School Librarians (AASL), Association for Library Collections and Technical Services (ALCTS), Association for Library Service to Children (ALSC), Association for Library Trustees and Advocates (ALTA), Association of College and Research Libraries (ACRL), Association of Specialized and Cooperative Library Agencies (ASCLA), Library Administration and Management Association (LAMA), Library and Information Technology Association (LITA), Public Library Association (PLA), Reference and User Services Association (RUSA), Young Adult Library Services Association (YALSA). In addition there are regional chapters, discussion groups, round tables; an extensive publishing programme includes *American Libraries* (12 p.a), monographs, and many well-respected titles from the divisions.

American Library Trustee Association (ALTA). *See* Association for Library Trustees and Advocates.

American National Standards Institute, Inc (ANSI). <www.ansi.org> (25 West 43rd Street, New York, NY 10036, USA) The US organization for issuing recommendations as to the production, distribution and consumption of goods and services; it is the United States member of the International Organization for Standardization. Standards issued by the Institute are known as American National Standards. From 1918, when it was founded, until 1966 it was known as the American Standards Association (ASA) and from then until October 1969 as the United States of America Standards Institute (USASI), its Standards being known as USA Standards. *See also* International standards, NSSN, Z39.

American Russia. Cow-hide used for bookbinding.

American Society for Information Science and Technology (ASIS&T). <www.asis.org> (1320 Fenwick Lane, Suite 510, Silver Spring, MD 20910, USA) Founded in 1937 as the American Documentation Institute; expanded in 1952 to permit personal membership; changed its name to American Society for Information Science (ASIS) in 1968, and to its present title in 2000. There are 4,000 members (2004). It aims to encourage good practice and development opportunities for information professionals and organizations. There are 24 special interest groups. Publications include *Journal* (12 p.a.), *Annual Review of Information Science and Technology* (*ARIST*), conference proceedings and monographs. Co-sponsor of *Information Science Abstracts*.

American Society of Indexers (ASI). <www.asindexing.org> (10200 West 44th Street, Suite 304, Wheat Ridge, CO 80033, USA) Founded 1968 with the objectives to: (a) improve the quality of indexing and to secure useful standards for the field; (b) act as an advisory body on the qualification and remuneration of indexers to which authors, editors, publishers and others may apply for guidance. Members' activities include indexing books, databases and periodicals, teaching indexing courses and conducting research on indexing problems. Increasingly involved in the preparation of metadata. Publishes guidelines and various bulletins. Co-sponsor of *Information Science Abstracts*.

American Standard Code for Information Interchange. *See* ASCII.

American Theological Library Association (ATLA). <www.atla.com> (250 South Wacker Drive, Suite 1600, Chicago, IL 60606-5889, USA) Founded 1947 to bring its members into closer working relations with each other and with the American Association of Theological Schools; to study the distinctive problems of theological seminary libraries; to increase the professional competence of the membership; and to improve the library service to theological education.

American Trust for the British Library. Formed 1979 primarily to fill the gaps in the British Library's collections of American materials during the period 1880–1950 when funds were small. Encourages private donations and sales, and liaises with American booksellers.

Americana. Material relating to the Americas, whether printed about or in, the Americas, or written by Americans or not.

AMIA. *See* Association of Moving Image Archivists.

AMICO. *See* Art Museum Image Consortium.

AMIGOS Library Services, Inc. <www.amigos.org> A US network consortium of 320 member libraries; covers Texas, Oklahoma, New Mexico, Arkansas, Arizona, and Mexico, with additional members in Louisiana, Kansas and Nevada. An OCLC Network Affiliate.

Ampersand. The abbreviation, sign or character for the word 'and', thus: &. Also called 'Short and'.

AMPS. Advanced mobile phone service, Cellular communications using sophisticated switching between mobile units and mobile switching centres to track and monitor mobile units, control the radio transmission link, and perform real-time transfers from one cell to another. *See also* GSM.

A.Ms.S. (*Pl.* A.Mss.S.) (autograph manuscript signed). A manuscript wholly in the handwriting of the signer.

-ana. (often with the euphonic *i* added: iana) A suffix to names of persons or places, denoting a collection of books, anecdotes, literary gossip, or other facts or pieces of information, e.g. Americana, Johnsoniana, Lincolniana.

Analects. A collection of literary fragments, gleanings or other miscellaneous written passages.

Analet. A 'small analysis' or statement of the (*classification*) steps taken to analyse a complex subject.

Analysis. 1. (*Cataloguing*) A book is said to be 'analysed' when any part of it is recorded separately in a catalogue by means of an Analytical entry. 2. (*Classification*) Breaking down a subject into its facets and other aspects of a document. *See* Facet. 3. (*Information retrieval*) (i) The perusal of source materials and the selection of analytics (e.g. index entries, subject headings, keywords and descriptors) that are considered to be of sufficient probable importance to justify the effort of rendering them searchable in an information-retrieval system. (ii) A detailed examination of a document to determine and state its characteristics, including abstracting, classifying and indexing. 4. (*Management*) The separation of problems and situations into common elements and basic principles; a detailed examination of the essential components then yields a framework for the implementation of management ideas on efficiency and productivity.

Analytical bibliography. The kind of bibliography which determines facts and data concerning a publication by examining the Signatures, Catchwords, Cancels and Watermarks, and making a record in an approved form of the results. Also called 'critical' or 'historical bibliography'. *See also* Bibliography, Descriptive bibliography.

Analytical entry. An entry in a catalogue for part of a book, periodical or other publication, article or contribution of separate authorship in a collection (volume of essays, Festschrift, serial, volume of musical compositions, etc.). The entry includes a reference to the work containing it. Such entries, called 'Analytics', may be made under authors, subjects or titles. In special libraries they are often made for significant paragraphs, sections, tables, etc., and occasionally for particular facts or figures, in addition to parts or chapters of books, units of a series and of a collection.

Analytical index. 1. An index in which the entries are not arranged in one straightforward alphabetical sequence, but the subject of the work is divided into a number of main headings and these in turn are subdivided as necessary, each sequence of entries being arranged alphabetically. The abstracts (or papers) included in the volume to be indexed are then classified according to these main headings and so placed in their appropriate places in the analytical index.   2. An alphabetical subject index to information in articles of broader connotation than the subject index headings, as in an encyclopaedia.   3. A classified index to material under specific subjects, as in a reference book.

Analytical method.   In classification, the breaking down of a specific subject into constituent elements according to a given formula, these elements then being reassembled in a predetermined order designed to give the most useful arrangement.

Analytico-synthetic classification.   A scheme of classification involving analysis of a subject into its facets and synthesis into class number. An analytico-synthetic classification is always a faceted classification, but not vice versa. It affords autonomy in constructing numbers for new specific subjects not enumerated in the schedules. Ranganathan's Colon Classification (1933) was the first scheme of this kind.

Anastatic printing.   A process or method of obtaining facsimile impressions of any printed design or engraving by transferring it to a plate of zinc, which, on being subjected to the action of an acid, is etched or eaten away, with the exception of the parts covered with ink. These parts are left in relief and can be printed from readily.

Anastatic reprint.   An unaltered reprint made in the mid nineteenth century, especially in France, by making an inked offset of the type of metal plates which were etched in relief.

And others.   When there are more than three joint authors, collaborators, etc., a catalogue entry may be made only under the first to be mentioned followed by *and others*, or by *et al.*

Andersen (Hans Christian) Medals.   In full, the International Hans Christian Andersen Youth Book Awards. First awarded in 1956 (to Eleanor Farjeon for *The Little Book Room*), now awarded to a living author, and to an illustrator, whose complete work has made 'a lasting contribution to literature for children and young people'. The Awards take the form of medals and are made every two years by the International Board on Books for Young People. *See* IBBY.

Anderson Report (UK).   In the wake of the Follett Report, the Higher Education Funding Councils established a Working Group, under the chairmanship of Professor M. Anderson of Edinburgh University, to consider the development of a national strategy for the provision of library support for research. The Group's report – generally known as the Anderson Report – was issued in 1995 and made recommendations regarding a national retention policy, devolution of some collection responsibilities, local schemes for co-operation, and the preservation of local research collections and non-print materials. A Task Force was set up, also under Professor Anderson, to progress matters and led to the Research Support Libraries Programme in late 1998.

Anepigraphon. A publication whose title-page is missing.

Angle brackets. *See* Brackets.

Anglo-American Cataloguing Rules. *See* AACR.

Angular marks. *See* Brackets.

Anhydrous. Water-free, with reference to chemical salts and solvents.

Animal tub-sized. *See* Tub-sizing.

Animals in foliage panel. A panel in a book-binding decoration which is divided vertically into two, each half containing curving foliage with an animal within each curve. It is the characteristic Netherlands design.

Animation software. Software running on a PC which is used to produce animations i.e. the creation of the illusion of movement through the rapid viewing of individual frames. Can be used to animate not only figures but also text elements and can incorporate sound and graphics. In addition to its use in desktop Multimedia systems, this software can also be used to create movement on Web pages.

Annalistic arrangement. A bibliography of an author's writings arranged in order of publication.

Annals. A record of events arranged in chronological order.

Annexe. 1. Supporting contributions to a main report, thesis, or other work. 2. A document usually attached to, but not physically a part of, that to which it is attached.

Annotation. A note added to an entry in a catalogue, reading list or bibliography, to elucidate, evaluate or describe the subject and contents of a book; it sometimes gives particulars of the author

Annual. A serial publication, e.g. a report, year book or directory issued once a year. *See also* Biannual, Year book.

Annual Bibliography of the History of the Printed Book and Libraries. *See* ABHB.

Anonym. 1. An anonymous publication. 2. An anonymous person or writer. 3. A pseudonym.

Anonymous. A publication is said to be anonymous when the author's name does not appear anywhere in it, either on the title-page or cover, or in the preface, introduction or foreword. According to some authorities, if the authorship can be traced in catalogues or bibliographies it may be considered not to be anonymous. The opposite of onymous.

Anonymous classic. A work of unknown or doubtful authorship, commonly designated by title, which may have appeared in the course of time in many editions, versions, and/or translations.

Anonymous ftp. *See* ftp.

Anopisthographic printing. The manner of printing early block books, using writing ink and printing on only one side of the leaf. *See also* Block books, Opisthographic.

ANRT <www.anrt.asso.fr> (41 boulevard des Capucines, 75002 Paris, France) Association Nationale de la Recherche Technique; a body which aims to link research and industry, and to support research and development activities.

ANSI.   *See* American National Standards Institute, Inc.

Ante-dated.   A book which bears a date of publication which is earlier than the actual date. The opposite of 'Post-dated'.

Anterior numeral classes.   The first group of the main classes of Bliss's Bibliographic Classification. They are bibliothetic in character and conform to the generalia classes of other schemes. Three of the nine divisions accommodate general works (2 bibliography, 6 periodicals, 7 miscellanea); the remainder provide for special collections of books which for some reason it is preferred to shelve apart from the main collection. *See also* Systematic auxiliary schedules.

Anteriorizing value.   (*Classification*) Said to be possessed by a digit which, when added to a class number (and which is then said to be the 'host class number'), causes the resulting class number to have precedence over the host number. For example, in the Colon Classification, class numbers containing lower case roman letters, or arrows, have precedence over class numbers without them, as: X*a*, precedes X, B63*a* precedes B63, L23: 45*a* precedes L23: 45.

Anthology.   A collection of choice extracts, usually of poetry, or on one subject, from the writings of one author, or various authors, and having a common characteristic such as subject matter or literary form.

Antiphonary/Antiphoner.   A liturgical book intended for use in a choir. Generically it includes antiphons and antiphonal chants sung at Mass and at the canonical Hours, but now refers only to the sung portions of the Breviary.

Antiqua.   A German name for roman types. A small Book hand based on the Caroline minuscule, called *lettera rotonda* or *lettre ronde* (round letter) in Italy and France. Type based on this writing is now known as roman, and is the usual kind of type (as distinct from *italic*) used for book work.

Antiquarian bookseller.   One who deals in old books, which are rare enough to command higher prices than ordinary second-hand books.

Antiquarian Booksellers' Association (UK).   <awww.aba.org.uk> Founded in 1906, the Association represents large numbers of antiquarian booksellers and holds regular bookfairs.

Antique.   1. (*Paper*) The name given to printing papers made from esparto grass. They usually have a rough surface, and the poorer qualities are called *featherweight*, so loosely woven that 75 per cent of the bulk is air space. The term originally referred to machine-made paper made in imitation of hand-made paper. Antique papers have a matt or dull finish and are neither calendered nor coated. They are suitable for printing type and line engravings, but not for half-tones. 2. (*Binding*) Designates blind tooling. *See* Tooling.

Antique gold edges.   *See* Gilt edges.

Antique laid.   Originally, paper made on moulds of which the chain wires were laced or sewn direct to the wooden ribs or supports of the Mould, thus causing the pulp to lie thicker along each side of every chain line in the sheet of paper. Now, any rough-surfaced laid paper.

Antique tooling.   A form of blind tooling.

Antonym.   A word having the opposite meaning of another. The opposite of synonym.

ANW.   *See* Archives Network Wales.

AP.   Abbreviation for Author's proof.

Aperture card.   A card with one or more openings (the number depending on the amount of space required for identifying stored document images) into each of which is mounted a 'frame' cut from a strip of microfilm. The identification on the card can consist of written information, punched holes, or characters on film.

API.   Application Program Interface (also Application Programming Interface), an interface between an application program and an IT resource or service, such as an operating system, database or another application which enables specific functionality to be provided.

APIN.   <www.unesco.org/webworld/portal_bib/groups/networks> The Asia Pacific Information Network; formed by the merger of ASTINFO, the Regional Information Network for South East Asia and the Pacific (RINSEAP) and the Regional Information Network for South and Central Asia (RINSCA). Members are: India. Pakistan, Iran, Indonesia, Malaysia, Papua New Guinea, Korea, Sri Lanka, Thailand, Vietnam and the National Library of Australia.

Aplaws Project.   <www.aplaws.org.uk> The Accessible and Personalised Local Authorities Websites Project has created tools for the implementation of Electronic Government Metadata Standards (e-GMS) on local authority websites to ensure compatibility of activity under e-GIF.

Apoconym.   A name changed by the cutting off or elision of letters or syllables.

Apocryphal.   Of unknown authorship or doubtful authenticity.

Apograph.   A copy of an original manuscript.

Apostil (Apostille).   An annotation, or marginal note (*archaic*).

app.   Abbreviation for Appendix.

Apparatus criticus.   The sources of information and the existence of manuscripts, letters and other material used by an author, and enumerated in footnotes, marginalia and commentary in support of a text, and thus associated with the preparation of the definitive edition of a work. Includes particularly information concerning variant readings, doubtful texts and obscurities. *See* Critical edition, Definitive edition.

Appendix.   Matter which comes at the end of the text of a book and contains notes which are too long for footnotes, tables of statistics, or other items for which there is no room in the body of the book, which, from the nature of the information, is more suitably placed at the end of the text.

Applet.   A small Java program that can be included in a Web page. When the page is viewed via a Java-compatible browser, the applet's code is transferred to the user's system and the program is run. Used to enhance Web pages with special effects or greater interactivity.

Application.   Software program written to perform a particular function and increasingly used to refer to software packages in general. For example, Microsoft Word, Microsoft Excel, Quark XPress, are all applications written with particular tasks in mind. Also referred to as 'applications software'.

Application Program Interface.   *See* API.

Applied bibliography.   *See* Historical bibliography.

Appraisal.   1. An estimate of the value of a book as a contribution to a subject. *See also* Intrinsic value.   2. (*Archives, Records management*) The process of analysing and selecting records in order to determine which are suitable for retention as archives. No materials should be accepted by an archives service except as a result of appraisal.   3. (*Management*) An estimation of value or quality, especially an assessment of the quality of work performed by an employee, linked to future tasks planning, and the overall quality of an organization's performance. *See also* Continuing professional development.

Approach term.   The word which a catalogue-user seeks in a catalogue, in anticipation that it will lead to a statement in Subject heading language of a required compound subject.

Appropriate copy.   The copy of a journal article that might be available on the Internet from a range of suppliers, in different formats and at varying prices, which most satisfies the criteria specified by a requesting library or individual. Particularly used in relation to OpenURL transactions.

Aquatint.   1. A process of etching on copper or steel plates by means of nitric acid, producing an effect resembling a fine drawing in water colours, sepia or India ink. It is used to render tonal effects rather than lines. Now supplanted commercially by lithography.   2. A print made by this method.

Aquatone.   A photographic printing process which is similar to collotype, but is used with offset presses.

Arabesque.   A species of decoration consisting of interlaced lines and convoluted curves arranged in more or less geometrical patterns; so-called because it was brought to its highest perfection by Arabian or kindred artists. Also applied to a fanciful mixture of animals, birds, and insects, and of plants, fruit and foliage, involved and twisted.

Arabic figures.   The numerical characters 1, 2, 3, etc., as distinct from roman numerals I, II, III, etc., so called from having been introduced into Europe from Arab use: they have been used for foliation since the last quarter of the fifteenth century. Arabic numerals first appeared in European MSS. in the twelfth century, although the Arabs probably brought them from India in the eighth century. Arabic is used for numbering the text pages of books. *See also* Foliation, Hanging figures, Lining figures, Pagination, Roman numerals.

Arbeitgemeinschaft der Spezialbibliotheken.   <www.ubka.uni.karlsruhe. de/hylib/aspb> (University Library, Postfach 6920, 76049 Karlsruhe,

Germany) Founded in 1946, an organization providing services to specialized libraries in the private and public sectors. There are over 650 members. Publishes *Arbeitgemeinschaft der Spezialbibliotheken* (a.).

ARBICA. Arab Regional Branch of the International Council on Archives. *See* International Council on Archives.

Arbitrary symbol. (*Classification*) A symbol, e.g. a punctuation mark, used in a Notation as a Facet indicator.

Arbuthnot (May Hill) Honor Lecture. An endowed annual lecture, established by Scott, Foresman and Company in tribute to May Hill Arbuthnot, one of the foremost authorities on literature for children. The Association for Library Service to Children of the ALA administers the selection of the lecture series.

Archaeology Data Service. *See* AHDS.

Archetypal novel. Commonly used to describe the earliest romances, tales and works of fiction; the forerunner of the modern novel.

Architects' brief. See Brief (4).

Architectural binding. A sixteenth-century style of book cover decoration which consisted of columns supporting an arch under which was a panel to contain the title. The contents of the books so decorated seldom related to architecture.

Architecture. A general term used to refer to the structure of all or part of a computer system. Computer architecture incorporates computer systems, chips, circuits and system programs but does not refer to Applications software. *See also* Information architecture.

Architecture Librarians Group. *See* ARCLIB.

Archival Description. The equivalent for archives of cataloguing in librarianship. The most common standards in use are *MAD* and *RAD*.

Archival Description Project. *See Manual of Archival Description.*

Archival order. The order or sequence of components of a Group or Class of Archives, arising from or demonstrating the original system under which they were created.

Archival quality. Characteristics possessed by records that qualify them for selection as Archives during the course of appraisal.

Archival relationships. The relationships between components of a set of Archives, arising from the original system under which they were created.

Archival Resource Key. *See* ARK.

Archive administration. As an academic discipline, also termed archivistics or archivology.

Archive group. *See* Group (*Archives*).

Archives. 1. Public Records or selected materials kept in a recognized archival repository. The British government published a policy on archives in 1999 (Cm. 4516) and this has led to an Action Plan (2002) and a lengthy period of public consultation. 2. Records in any medium which were compiled for the purpose of, or used during, a public or private business transaction of which they themselves formed a part; and which were selected for preservation by the persons concerned with the transaction, or their successors or delegates, for their own use and as material for research or reference.   3. An accumulation of original records assembled in the course of the activities of a person or persons, or of a public or private organization; or such records from a number of different sources; and kept together to ensure their preservation and to promote their use.   4. The archival repository itself.   5. Those materials in any information service that have been selected for long-term or permanent retention because of the retrospective or archival values they are perceived to possess.   6. In the Eprints community synonymous with repositories of scholarly papers. *See* Eprints, Open Archives Initiative, Repository. *See also* Records, Public Records (UK).

Archives.   Journal published by the British Records Association.

Archives and Manuscripts.   Journal of the Australian Society of Archivists.

Archives Council Wales.   <www.llgc.org.uk/cac> Established in 1995, represents institutions and organizations from all parts of Wales involved in the administration of archives and aims to influence policy on archives in Wales, to bring to the attention of the public, government and other institutions matters of concern in the field of archives in Wales, and to provide a focus for collaborative projects. *See also* Archives Network Wales (ANW).

Archives Hub.   <www.archiveshub.ac.uk> Provides a single point of access to descriptions of archives held in UK universities and colleges. At present these are primarily at collection-level, although where possible they are linked to complete catalogue descriptions. The Archives Hub forms one part of the UK's National Archives Network, alongside related networking projects. A Steering Committee which includes representatives of the Public Record Office, the Historical Manuscripts Commission and the other archive networks guides the progress of the project. The service is funded by JISC and hosted at MIMAS on behalf of CURL.

Archives Libraries Museums London (ALM London).   *See* Museums, Libraries and Archives Council (MLA).

Archives Network Wales (ANW).   <www.archivesnetworkwales.info> A project of the Archives Council Wales to create a web resource to allow the searching of collections of documents held by record offices, universities, museums and libraries in Wales.

Archives New Zealand.   *See* National Archives of New Zealand.

Archives service.   An organization, for example a record office, which is responsible for the management of archives. The term is broader than Repository, which refers to an archives service only in its role as the physical holder or custodian of archival materials.

Archiving colours.   *See* ROMEO.

Archivist.   A person who is responsible for the management of archives. *See also* Registered Archivist, Society of Archivists.

Archivum. The principal journal of the International Council on Archives (a.). Commenced 1951, publishes proceedings of International Congresses on Archives, but also texts of international interest, e.g. archival legislation, studies of professional practice.

ARCHON. <www.nationalarchives.gov.uk/archon> An online database that is the principal information gateway for UK archivists and users of manuscript sources for British history. It also includes information on archival repositories world-wide that have entries in the National Register of Archives.

ARCLIB. <www.arclib.org.uk> The (UK) Architecture Librarians Group; an independent professional organization for those interested in architecture and the built environment. A major activity is an annual conference.

Area. 1. (*Public libraries*) A geographical part of the Library system, not as extensive as a region, served by a number of branches and/or centres, and forming a library unit for administrative purposes. 2. (*Cataloguing*) A major section of a bibliographic description (forming a part of a catalogue entry) which comprises data of a particular category or set of categories.

Area search. Examination of a large group of documents to segregate those documents pertaining to a general class, category or topic. Screening.

Area table. A common geographical facet based on the geographical numbers used in the Dewey Decimal Classification in order to provide geographical arrangement of material classified primarily by subject.

Ariadne. <www.ariadne.ac.uk> A magazine aimed at librarians and information service professionals in academic libraries with the principal goal of reporting on information service developments and information networking issues worldwide, keeping the busy practitioner abreast of current digital library initiatives. Started in January 1996 funded by the UK eLib programme and published in parallel hard copy and electronic format until issue 18 (November 1998). The web version continues as a quarterly publication.

Ariane Programme. An EU programme that ran until 1999 and covered activities in the areas of books and reading, and access to literature and history.

Ariel. <www.infotrieve.com/ariel/index.html> Software used for document delivery that enables the sending and receiving of documents electronically. Ariel transmits over the Internet using both the FTP and MIME e-mail standards, scans and sends greyscale and colour images and provides higher resolution and superior graphic image quality when compared to facsimile transmission.

ARIST. Annual Review of Information Science and Technology. <www.asis. org> A well established title, first published 1966, which concentrates on the information science area of professional activity. Currently published by Information Today, Inc. on behalf of the American Society for Information Science and Technology (ASIS&T) – there have been different publishers at various times. Eight to ten chapters in each volume are divided into planning of services, basic techniques, applications, and the professions. Substantial bibliographies are a key feature.

Aristo paper. A photographic copying paper, the colloid being gelatine.

Aristonym. A title of nobility converted into, or used as, a surname.

Arithmetical notation. *See* Integral notation.

ARK. <www.cdlib.org/inside/diglib/ark> Archival Resource Key, a naming scheme that provides an identifier for persistent access to digital objects (including images, texts, datasets, and finding aids), tested and implemented by the California Digital Library for the collections that it manages. *See also* Digital Object Identifier, Persistence, PURL.

ARL. *See* Association of Research Libraries.

ARLIS. <www.arlis.org.uk> (c/o 18 College Road, Bromsgrove, Worcester B60 2NE, UK) Abbreviation for The Art Libraries Society founded in 1969; this Society exists to promote art librarianship, particularly by acting as a forum for the interchange of information and materials. ARLIS is affiliated to its American counterpart ARLIS/NA. An Organization in Liaison (OiL) with CILIP.

ARLIS/NA. <www.arlisna.org> (329 March Road, Suite 232, Box 11, Kanata, Ontario K2K 2E1, Canada) The Art Libraries Society of North America; founded 1972 and now having 1,350 members world-wide, comprising individuals, institutions, and business affiliates. ARLIS/NA has similar objectives to ARLIS, and functions via regional chapters and special interest groups. Publishes *ARLIS/NA Update Newsletter* (6 p.a.); *Art Documentation* (2 p.a.), handbook, occasional papers, etc. Sponsors two annual awards: George Wittenborn Award (for an outstanding art publication) and the Gerd Muehsam Award (for an exceptional student paper in the field).

Arm. The projecting, or unclosed, horizontal or upward-sloping stroke of a type of letter.

ARMA. *See* Association of Records Managers and Administrators International.

Armaria. *See* Armarium.

Armarian. A worker in a monastic library whose duty it was to prevent the books under his charge from being injured by insects, to look after bindings, and keep a correct catalogue. He presided over a Scriptorium and supplied the scribes with parchment, pens, ink, knives, awls and rulers. Also called an 'Armarius'.

Armarium. A wardrobe, or cupboard, possibly a separate piece of furniture in which scrolls, or subsequently books, were kept. Closed armaria apparently developed in Imperial times and survived in monastic libraries until the Renaissance or later.

Armenian bole. A bright-red clay which is used as a colouring material and also to dust on to the edges of books before gilding to act as a base for the gold, to which it gives a greater depth and lustre. It is obtained mainly from Bohemia, Italy and Silesia.

Arming press.   A hand blocking press used now only for short runs but originally for impressing armorial bearings.

Armorial binding.   One decorated with the arms or other device of royalty or nobility. Generally applied to bindings earlier than the mid nineteenth century.

Arms block.   An engraved brass block or binder's Zinco made by a line-block maker and used in an arming or blocking press to impress a coat of arms on leather bindings.

Arrangement.   1. The adaptation of a whole musical work, or an integral part of a musical work, to a medium of performance other than that for which it was originally written, e.g. the casting of a song as a piano piece, or of an orchestral overture as an organ piece. Sometimes also, a simplification or amplification, when the musical structure and the medium of performance remain the same.   2. (*Archives*) The intellectual and physical operations involved in the analysis and organization of archives.

Array.   1. In classification, the series of co-ordinate subdivisions which are obtained by dividing a class or a division according to a single characteristic: e.g. Literature divided according to characteristic Form gives the array Poetry, Drama, Novel, Essay. Each co-ordinate division in an array should exclude all of the others, and the whole array should be exhaustive of the contents of the class. The order of the divisions in an array should be that deemed most helpful to users.   2. A set of co-ordinate terms (i.e. terms subordinate to the same genus). Also used in information retrieval for a sequence of headings in a file and as a set of search terms. An ordinal arrangement of informational materials.   3. A set of mutually exclusive co-ordinate subclasses arranged in a logical sequence totally exhaustive of a class, derived by its division according to some one characteristic.

Art.   The name given to papers coated on one or both sides after the paper is made by brushing on China clay, sulphate or barium, or sulphate of lime and alumina (the last for the 'satin-white' finish) and afterwards polished. In imitation art the paper is 'loaded' (i.e. the China clay is mixed in with the fibre) not 'coated'. Matt art is unglazed coated paper with a smooth, soft, egg-shell finish.

Art canvas.   A cloth for bookbinding, also known as light-weight buckram.

Art History Information Program.   *See* Getty Information Institute.

Art Libraries Society.   *See* ARLIS.

Art Museum Image Consortium (AMICO).   <www.amico.org> Formed in 1997 by the Association of Art Museum Directors, AMICO is a not-for-profit digital educational resource, giving access to images of over 100,000 works of art.

Art paper.   *See* Art.

Art parchment.   *See* Vellum parchment.

Art vellum.   1. A brand name for a lightweight book cloth.   2. A fabric used for classes of works which do not require a very strong cloth.

Art work.   A term covering all forms of illustrative matter (line drawings, photographs, paintings, diagrams, hand lettering, etc.) used in a printed publication to distinguish it from type-set matter. In America the term is used to distinguish any material prepared by hand as camera copy.

Artefact.   1. Something made or prepared by man, such as a tool or a work of art. The term is often used for archaeological finds and for man-made objects in a museum. The US spelling is artifact.   2. (*Classification*) Man-made entities which are 'concrete' (such as chairs or houses), and which are to be distinguished from their abstract equivalents – Mentefacts.

Artefactual value.   A volume or document that is important as a physical object, instead of or in addition to the importance of the information it contains, is considered to have value and significance as an artefact. Where artefactual value is present, any preservation or conservation treatment should aim to restore the item as nearly as possible to its original state.

Article.   A contribution written by one or more persons for publication in a Periodical; such a contribution when so published. *See also* Work.

Article Numbering Association (ANA).   *See* e-centre.

Articulated indexing.   A method of producing computer-generated subject indexes from a sentence-like title statement without complex subject analysis.

Artifact.   <www.artifact.ac.uk> A Hub of the (UK) RDN providing access to quality-controlled Internet services in the arts and creative industries – architecture; art; communications and media; culture; design; fashion and beauty; and the performing arts. Based at Manchester Metropolitan University.

Artificial characteristic.   *See* Characteristic of a classification.

Artificial classification.   1. One in which some accidental thing is adopted as the 'difference', for example, the size of a book. *See* Predicables, five.   2. Classification by analogy, i.e. by external or accidental likeness, unlikeness, or apparent purpose. *See* Characteristic of a classification.

Artificial indexing language.   (*Information retrieval, Indexing*) A group of signs, symbols or digits (or of phrases, or words arranged in an inverted order according to rules and so becoming 'controlled' language) to represent facts and ideas. An index language. The opposite of Natural language. *See also* Indexing language.

Artificial intelligence (AI).   The branch of computer science involved in the replication of aspects of human intelligence such as problem solving, deduction and speech recognition and utilizing computer programs that learn by experience. Applications software packages that utilize Artificial intelligence are known as Expert systems. *See also* Neural network.

Artistic manuscript.   A record or document produced by hand, and decorated or illustrated in such a way as to achieve distinction as a work of artistic merit. Illuminated manuscripts are the most important examples. *See also* Literary manuscript.

Artistic map. One made by an artist rather than by a cartographer; such maps consequently appeal to the eye and are often not correct cartographically. They are used as illustrations, endpapers, and for advertisement.

Artist's proof. A proof of an engraving or etching, usually with the signature of the artist in pencil, and sometimes with a small sketch, known as a remarque, in the margin. Used as a model or sample. Also called 'Remarque proof'.

Artotek. A picture and art library.

Artotype. A photo-engraved picture made by one of the gelatine processes.

Arts and Humanities Data Service *See* AHDS.

Arts and Humanities Initiative. <arts.internet2.edu> An Initiative of Internet2 to assist members in enabling and advancing collaborations between high performance networking technologies and applications in the arts and humanities.

ARTstor. <www.artstor.org> A non-profit initiative, founded by the Andrew W. Mellon Foundation, with a mission to use digital technology to enhance scholarship, teaching and learning in the arts and associated fields. The aim of the project is to digitize 300,000 images, with particular strengths in Asian and American art, architecture and modern design. The roots of ARTstor, as well as its name, can be traced to the Foundation's creation of JSTOR.

ArXiv. <arxiv.org> An Eprint service in the fields of physics, mathematics, non-linear science, computer science, and quantitative biology owned, operated and funded by Cornell University and the National Science Foundation. Formerly the Los Alamos Eprint Archive.

'As if' filing. The filing alphabetically of abbreviations as if they were spelled out, e.g. St. as Saint, Mr. as Mister, 1001 as One thousand and one.

As issued. Indicates that a book offered for sale secondhand is in its original format.

As new. Used in secondhand booksellers' catalogues to indicate that the physical condition of a book offered for sale is 'almost indistinguishable from the condition of newness'.

ASA. 1. American Standards Association. *See* American National Standards Institute, Inc.   2. *See* Australian Society of Archivists, Inc.

ASCEL. <www.ascel.org.uk> Association of Senior Children's and Education Librarians; a UK body formed in 1995/96 by the amalgamation of three groups previously working in the children's and education services sector – SOCCEL (for counties), AMDECL (for metropolitan areas) and YELL (for London). The amalgamation was one of the recommendations of the LISC report *Investing in Children*. ASCEL covers both public and school library services, and is made up of librarians with managerial responsibility for the delivery of services to children in England and Wales.

Ascender.   The vertical ascending stem of lower-case letters such as b, d, k, etc.; that part which extends above the x-height. *See also* Descender.

Ascender line.   (*Printing*) The imaginary line which runs along the top of ascenders. This will be above the Cap line in the case of types the capitals of which are lower than the ascenders. *See also* Ascender, Base line, Cap line, Mean line.

Ascetonym.   The name of a saint used as a proper name.

ASCII.   American Standard Code for Information Interchange; a character coding system widely used as a a means of transferring documents between otherwise incompatible computer systems or Applications. It cannot be used to transmit formatted documents but all word processors provide the ability to save in ascii code via a 'save as text' option. Of less importance with the improved ability of computers to handle multiple coding systems. Pronounced 'askee'.

ASCLA.   *See* Association of Specialized and Co-operative Library Agencies.

ASD.   <www.svd-asd.org> Association Suisse de Documentation. The Swiss Association for Documentation; it was formed in 1939 after having been in existence as a study group since 1930. Publishes *Kleine Mitteilungen/Petites Communications* (irr.).

ASEDIE.   Asociación Española de Distribuidores de Información Electronica <www.asedie.es> (C/ Victor de la Sema 8-1B, 28016 Madrid, Spain.) An umbrella organization co-ordinating the activities of publishers of databases in law, social sciences, humanities, science and technology, and acting as representative for international hosts.

Ashendene Press.   One of the most distinguished British private presses. It was founded in 1895 by C. H. St. John Hornby, a partner in the firm of W. H. Smith & Son, and undertook fine printing at the request of Sydney Cockerell in 1900.

ASHSL.   *See* Association of Scottish Health Sciences Librarians.

ASI.   *See* American Society of Indexers.

Asia Pacific Information Network.   *See* APIN.

Asian Librarians and Advisers Group (ALAG).   (Southall Library, Osterley Park Road, Southall UB2 4BL, UK) Formed in 1988, ALAG encourages participation from any individuals or organizations active in the cultural life of the UK Asian community. An Organization in Liaison (OiL) with CILIP.

ASIDIC.   <www.asidic.org> (PO Box 3212, Maple Glen, PA 19002, USA) Association of Information and Dissemination Centers. Founded 1968. Promotes applied technology of information storage and retrieval as related to large databases; recommends standards for data elements, formats and codes; and promotes research and development for more efficient use of varied databases. Digital publishing is now a focus of its activities. Publishes *ASIDIC Newsletter* (2 p.a.). Formerly Association of Scientific Information Dissemination Centers.

Asilomar Institute for Information Architecture (AIFIA).   <www.aifia. org> Formed as a not-for-profit organization in the USA in 2002. It has become one of the leading centres for the discussion of Information architecture.

ASIS&T.   *See* American Society for Information Science and Technology.

Ask-a-Librarian.   <www.ask-a-librarian.org.uk> A UK-based electronic reference service operated by some 75 public libraries. Enquiries via e-mail are routed to participating reference libraries for answer. The service is available 24 hours every day.

Aslib.   <www.aslib.co.uk> (Temple Chambers, 3–7 Temple Avenue, London EC4Y 0HP, UK) Aslib – subtitled the Association for Information Management – was formed in 1924 as a corporate member organization promoting best practice in the management of information resources, and representing its members in all aspects of the management of information at local, national and international levels, and in legislation concerning information. It has over 2,000 members in 70 countries. There is a regional structure, and twelve special interest groups. A range of professional services is offered to members. Publications include *Managing Information* (m.), *Handbook of Special Librarianship and Information Work*, and *Directory of Libraries and Information Services*.

Asociación Latinamericana de Escuelas de Bibliotecologia y Ciencias de la Informacion.   *See* ALEBCI.

Assembler.   (*Information retrieval*) The program which converts the symbolic language program, written by the programmer, to a machine-language program.

Assertiveness.   The positive realization, confirmation and declaration of one's rights in a given situation; implies an awareness and command of one's position, and needs total clarity of communication.

Assessment.   In management, the calculation of value or quality of an operation, an employee's work, or overall performance of an organization. Usually involves a close scrutiny, based on comparison with objective guidelines or standards.

Associação Portuguesa de Bibliotecários, Arquivistas e Documentalistas.   <www.apbad.pt> (43C-1 DTD, 1900 Lisbon, Portugal) The Portuguese Association of Librarians, Archivists and Documentalists is the principal professional association in that country.

Associate librarian.   American term for a deputy librarian.

Associated book.   As used in connection with the Colon Classification, a book which is written about another book, as e.g. a criticism of, or reply to, it. The book which is the subject of the criticism or reply is called a 'Host book'.

Associateship (UK).   Formerly the basic stage in professional qualification. Associates were admitted to the Register of Chartered Librarians maintained by the Library Association and used the post-nominal letters ALA. *See* CILIP.

Association book.   One having an autograph inscription or notes by the author, or which was in any way intimately connected with a prominent person who may have owned or presented it, or which had belonged to someone connected with its contents. Evidence in or on the book of the association is essential. If there is no signature or presentation inscription there should be a bookplate, or binding stamp, or marginal or other notes to indicate the association.

Association Canadienne des Sciences de l'Information. *See* Canadian Association for Information Science.

Association copy. *See* Association book.

Association des Bibliothécaires d'Expression Française. *See* Belgian library associations.

Association des Bibliothécaires Français (ABF). <www.abf.asso.fr> (31 rue Chabrol, 75010 Paris, France) Founded in 1906, the Association is concerned in all aspects of librarianship; its membership is drawn principally from the public library sector. Publishes *ABF Bulletin de l'Information* (q.).

Association des Bibliothèques de Recherche du Canada. *See* Canadian Association of Research Libraries.

Association des Documentalistes et Bibliothécaires Spécialisés (ADBS). <www.adbs.fr> (25 rue Claude Tillier, 75012 Paris, France) A major French professional association of documentation staff, working mainly in the private sector, and with many regional groups and subject divisions. Publications include *ADBS Informations* (m.). Also known by the title 'Association des Professionnels de l'Information et de la Documentation'.

Association des Professionnels de l'Information et de la Documentation. *See* Association des Documentalistes et Bibliothécaires Spécialisés.

Association for Computing Machinery (ACM). <www.acm.org> (1515 Broadway, 17th floor, New York, NY 10036-5701 USA) Established 1947, now having 80,000 members in industry, education, and government; concerns are software engineering, interfaces, multimedia, graphics, artificial intelligence, object-oriented technology. Operates over 100 technical conferences each year; extensive proceedings publishing programme. Other publications include: *Communications* (m.), *Journal* (q.), *Computing Reviews* (m.), *Computing Surveys* (q.), *Computing Archive* (CD-ROM).

Association for Geographic Information. *See* AGI.

Association for Information and Image Management International (AIIM). <www.aiim.org> (8 Canalside, Lowesmoor Wharf, Worcester WR1 2RR, UK) AIIM is a document management association, with over 14,000 members in 150 countries. There are forty local chapters. Imaging and micrographics are key concerns, and the Association is much involved in standards development.

Association for Learning Technology. *See* ALT.

Association for Library and Information Science Education (ALISE). <www.alise.org> (1009 Commerce Park Drive, Suite 150, PO Box 4219, Oak Ridge, TN 37839, USA) Formed in 1981 as a development of the Association of American Library Schools; seeks to promote excellence in professional education, provide a forum for the interchange of ideas, promote research and formulate policy. There are 70 institutional members and over 500 personal members. Publishes *Journal of Education for Library and Information Science* (q.).

Association for Library Collections and Technical Services (ALCTS). A division of the American Library Association, until 1989 known as Resources and Technical Services Division (RTSD). Major concerns include collection development, acquisition, cataloguing, automation, preservation, etc.

Association for Library Service to Children (ALSC). Division of the American Library Association. Founded 1957, present title 1977. Aims to improve and extend library services to children in all types of libraries. Publishes *Journal of Youth Services in Libraries* (q.) jointly with the Young Adult Services Division. Operates several award systems: Newbery-Caldecott, M. L. Batchelder, Laura Ingalls Wilder.

Association for Library Trustees and Advocates (ALTA). A division of the American Library Association, until 2001 known as American Library Trustee Association. Offers a focus for those seeking to support the role of libraries in the wider community.

Association Nationale de la Recherche Technique. *See* ANRT.

Association of American Publishers, Inc (AAP). <www.publishers.org> (71 5th Avenue, New York, NY 10003-3004) Formed in May 1970 by a merger of the American Book Publishers Council and the American Educational Publishers Institute. The Association aims to promote and expand the market for American books, journals, software, databases, audio-visual materials etc., and has a membership of some 250 firms. Divisions include general publishing, trade and mass market paperbacks, elementary and secondary instructional materials, higher education publications, professional and scholarly publications, international marketplace. Core programmes feature communications and public affairs, government relations, international freedom to publish, literacy, statistics.

Association of Assistant Librarians (AAL). Formerly a Group of the (UK) Library Association, it catered for members of a particular status rather than, as in the case of other groups, those engaged in a particular branch of librarianship. It was organized in Divisions which operated at local level. Originally known as the Library Assistants Association, it was formed on 3 July 1895 at a meeting convened by Mr. W. W. Fortune; the name was changed to the Association of Assistant Librarians in June 1922. It was an independent association until 1 January 1930 when it became a Section of the Library Association. Published *Assistant Librarian* (11 p.a.). In 1998 it was retitled the Career Development Group. *See* CILIP.

Association of British Theological and Philosophical Libraries. *See* ABTAPL.

Association of Canadian Archivists (ACA). *See* Libraries and Archives Canada.

Association of Caribbean University Research and Institute Libraries (ACURIL). Formed in 1968 to foster and improve contact and collaboration between members; holds conferences and seminars, encourages co-operative initiatives, and exchanges of staff. There are currently 50 members. Publishes *Caribbean Education Bulletin* (q.).

Association of Chief Librarians of Education and Library Boards. (c/o Belfast Central libraries, Royal Avenue, Belfast BT1 1EA, UK) An association of the five chief librarians of the Northern Ireland boards. *See* Association of Northern Ireland Education and Library Boards, Education and Library Boards.

Association of College and Research Libraries (ACRL). A Division of the American Library Association since 1938; founded in 1889 to represent and promote 'libraries of higher education (institutions supporting formal education above the secondary school level), independent research libraries, and specialized libraries'. Has 13 sections. Publishes *College and Research Libraries* (17 issues p.a., 11 being *C&RL News*).

Association of Commonwealth Archivists and Records Managers. *See* ACARM.

Association of County Archivists. Founded in 1980 to create a voice to speak on behalf of the UK County archives services on issues of urgency or importance. The ACA maintains liaison with the National Council for Archives, other professional groups, and the Association of County Councils.

Association of Database Producers. A UK trade organization aiming to represent the interests of commercial and non-commercial organizations developing and selling databases.

Association of European Documentation Centre Librarians. *See* European Information Association.

Association of Genealogists and Record Agents (AGRA). (29 Badgers Close, Horsham, RH12 5RU, UK) Founded in 1968 to promote and maintain high standards of professional conduct and expertise within the spheres of genealogy, heraldry and record searching and to safeguard the interests of members and clients. Members are subject to a Code of Practice. This is open to well-qualified professional researchers who have been engaged as genealogists or record agents for a number of years. The Association does not undertake research but publishes an informative booklet listing members with details of their special interests and the areas where they work. Publishes *Newsletter* (3 p.a.).

Association of Independent Information Professionals. *See* AIIP.

Association of Independent Libraries. <www.independentlibraries.co.uk> (Leeds Library, 18 Commercial Street, Leeds LS1 6AL, UK) An association of UK subscription libraries, all of which date from before

1841 and the creation of the public library service. There are currently 27 members.

Association of Information and Dissemination Centers. *See* ASIDIC.

Association of Information Officers in the Pharmaceutical Industry. *See* AIOPI.

Association of International Libraries (AIL). Founded in September 1963 at the Sofia meeting of the International Federation of Library Associations and Institutions, of which it is a Section. Aims to facilitate co-operation between international libraries. Membership is open to (a) individuals capable of promoting co-operation between international libraries, (b) libraries of international organizations, in particular the libraries of inter-governmental organizations, (c) all other libraries whose international character is recognized by the Executive Committee. It is financed by members' dues.

Association of Jewish Libraries (AJL). <www.jewishlibraries.org> Formed in 1965 by the amalgamation of the Jewish Librarians Association and the Jewish Library Association 'to promote and improve library services and professional standards in all Jewish libraries; to serve as a centre of dissemination of Jewish library information and guidance; to encourage the establishment of Jewish libraries; to promote publication of literature which will be of assistance to Jewish librarianship; to encourage people to enter the field of librarianship'. Publishes *AJL Newsletter* (q.). Runs numerous awards and scholarship schemes.

Association of Land-based Librarians in Colleges and Universities. *See* ALLCU.

Association of Learned and Professional Society Publishers. *See* ALPSP.

Association of Libraries of Judaica and Hebraica in Europe (ALJH). Founded in Paris, 28 April 1955, to facilitate the use of literature on Judaica and Hebraica in European libraries; to create a catalogue of such literature in Europe; to give bibliographical and other help to affiliated libraries and others. Has an information bureau and arranges training courses in Jewish librarianship.

Association of London Chief Librarians. *See* Society of Chief Librarians.

Association of Metropolitan District Chief Librarians. *See* Society of Chief Librarians.

Association of Metropolitan District Education and Children's Librarians. *See* AMDECL.

Association of Moving Image Archivists (AMIA). <www.amianet.org> Incorporated in 1991, AMIA was established to advance the field of moving image archiving by fostering co-operation among those concerned with the acquisition, preservation, exhibition and use of moving image materials. With an international membership of over 750, individuals and organizations from a wide variety of constituencies are represented. In addition to its publication and education activities, AMIA holds an annual conference, develops and promotes standards, encourages communication through its Listserv, honors the work of archivists and archival organizations, administers a scholarship and fellowship programme and collaborates with other institutions and organizations to design, promote and implement national moving image preservation policies and plans. Publishes *The Moving Image*, (biannual) *AMIA Newsletter* (q.) and *AMIA Membership Directory* (a.).

Association of Northern Ireland Education and Library Boards. (40 Academy Street, Belfast BT1 2NQ, UK) Formed on 24 October 1973 to: (a) seek to achieve the highest standards in education and library services for all the people of Northern Ireland, and to co-ordinate the efforts of the Education and Library Boards to that end; (b) promote and encourage the interchange of ideas on questions relating to the education and library services and to provide a forum for debate on such matters; (c) supply information and advice to member Boards on education and library matters; (d) exercise vigilance in relation to all proposed legislation, regulations and administrative arrangements affecting education and library services and to take action, where deemed necessary, for the safeguarding or improvement of standards in the services affected; (e) provide a collective voice for the education and library services in relations with the government and the community. Financed by the Department of Education (NI) and controlled by the five Area Boards in membership.

Association of Online Publishers (AOP). <www.ukaop.org.uk> (Queen's House, 28 Kingsway, London WC2B 6JR, UK). A UK industry body formed in 2002 to present a unified voice to industry and government. Its main aims are to drive standards and revenues, raise the credibility of online publishing, and collect trade statistics.

Association of Records Managers and Administrators International (ARMA). <www.arma.org> Based in the US but with international Chapters, the mission of ARMA International is to provide education, research and networking opportunities to information professionals, to enable them to use their skills and experience to leverage the value of records, information and knowledge as corporate assets and as contributors to organizational success. Publishes *Records Management Quarterly* (4 p.a.).

Association of Regional Information Society Initiatives. Formed in 1997, the Association was set up by the European Commission to ensure that the less-favoured regions of Europe integrate the Information Society initiative into their regional development policies.

Association of Research Libraries (ARL). <www.arl.org> (21 Dupont Circle NW, Suite 800, Washington DC 20036, USA) Formed in 1932, ARL is a not-for-profit membership organization for North American research libraries that aims to shape and influence forces affecting the future of research libraries in the process of scholarly communication. It monitors concerns, forms coalitions, makes policy, encourages innovation. Current activities and programmes include Access services,

Global resources, Coalition for Networked Information, Diversity, Federal relations and policy, Leadership and management, Scholarly communication, Preservation, SPARC, Statistics and measurement. There are 123 members.

Association of Scottish Health Sciences Librarians (ASHSL). The principal Scottish organization of library and information workers in health care disciplines. It acts as a single, authoritative and independent voice for the views of this group of health care staff; offers opportunities for conference and discussion; and provides services which promote the efficient flow of information in the health sciences. ASHSL started informally in 1970 and became a formally constituted body in 1974. Membership includes those working in Colleges of Nursing and Midwifery, Postgraduate Medical Centres, University Medical Schools, the Royal Colleges, the National Library of Scotland, the Scottish Office, the Health Boards and the Common Services Agency. Publishes *Interim* (2 p.a.), *Union List of Periodicals*, and *Directory.*

Association of Senior Children's and Education Librarians. *See* ASCEL.

Association of Specialized and Co-operative Library Agencies (ASCLA). Division of the American Library Association. Founded in 1977 by the merger of the Association of State Library Agencies and the Health and Rehabilitative Library Services Division. The Association represents the interests of state library agencies, specialized library agencies, and multi-type library co-operatives. Publishes *Interface* (q.).

Association of Swiss Librarians. <www.bbs.ch> (Hallerstrasse 58, CH 3012, Berne, Switzerland). Founded 1897, based in Berne, the Association has 2,200 members. Publishes *ARBIDO-Bulletin, ARBIDO-Revue,* and various professional documents.

Association of UK Media Librarians (AUKML). <www.aukml.org.uk> Formed in 1986, the AUKML expanded in 1988 by merging with the National Association of News Librarians. Aims to create links between people working in media libraries (newspapers, broadcasting, etc.) and develop international comparisons. Publishes *Deadline* (q.).

Association of Welsh Health Librarians. (c/o Institute of Health Care Studies, University Hospital of Wales, Cardiff CF4 4XW, UK) A forum for discussion and staff development; compiles a *Union List of Journals in Welsh Health Libraries*; publishes *AWHL Newsletter.*

Association pour l'Avancement des Sciences et des Techniques de la Documentation. *See* ASTED.

Association Professionelle des Bibliothécaires et Documentalistes. *See* Belgian library associations.

Association Suisse de Documentation. *See* ASD.

Associative indexing. Automatic (i.e. computer) indexing, which records associations between terms, or words in a text, without there necessarily being a specified functional relationship between them.

Associazione Italiana Biblioteche. *See* AIB.

ASTED. <www.asted.org> (3414 Avenue du Parc, Bureau 202, Montréal, Québec H2X 2H5, Canada) Association Pour l'Avancement des Sciences et des Techniques de la Documentation; founded in 1943 as l'Association Canadienne des Bibliothécaires de Langue Française, principally to meet the needs of French-speaking professionals. It adopted its current name in 1974. Publishes *Bulletin de Nouvelles* (6 p.a.); *Documentation et Bibliothèques* (q.v.).

Asterisk (*). The first and most frequently used reference mark for footnotes, technically known as a 'Star'. *See also* Reference marks.

Asterism. 1. A group of asterisks, as in a triangle, *** or *** drawing attention to a following remark, passage or paragraph. 2. The use of a number of asterisks instead of a proper name, as Mr. T******; a form of pseudonym.

ASTINFO. A co-operative programme in science and technology among countries of the Asia/Pacific region. Formed in 1983, the organization had over 80 national and regional members in 18 states. *See now* APIN.

Astronomical map. One showing the stars. Also called a 'star map'.

Asymmetric Digital Subscriber Line. *See* ADSL.

Asynchronous transfer mode. *See* ATM.

Asyndetic. Without cross-references. The reverse of Syndetic. *See also* Syndetic catalogue.

Athens. <www.athensams.net> Fully, the Athens Access Management System which provides Single sign-on and manages access to web-based subscription services. The service was designed and developed in 1994 and has been in active use since 1996 in the UK higher education community, providing access to many centrally-funded web-based services. In August 2000 a contract was awarded by JISC for the provision of authentication services to its communities and this contract has now been extended to 2006. Athens has also been adopted by the National Health Service Information Authority to control access to the National electronic Library for Health (NeLH). Athens is administered by Eduserv Athens.

Atkinson (Hugh C.) Memorial Award. An award to recognize outstanding accomplishments by academic libraries that have advanced library automation, management, or research. Administered by ACRL, LITA, LAMA and ALCTS divisions of the American Library Association.

Atkinson Report (UK). The report *Capital Provision for University Libraries*, prepared by a working party of the University Grants Committee (HMSO, 1976) Chairman: Prof. R. Atkinson. *See also* Self-renewing library.

ATLA. *See* American Theological Library Association.

Atlas. A volume of maps, with or without descriptive letterpress. It may be issued to supplement or accompany a text, or be published independently. Also, a volume of plates, engravings, etc., illustrating any subject; a large size of drawing paper measuring 26½ x 34 inches; a large folio volume, resembling a volume of maps, sometimes called

'Atlas folio'. The word 'atlas' was first used in the title of the first collection of maps – Gerardus Mercator's *Atlas sive cosmographicae meditationes de fabrica mundi,* Düsseldorf, [1585]–1595, which was composed in three parts in 1585, 1590 and 1594, and issued after his death by his son Rumold Mercator in 1595.

Atlas folio. The largest size folio. About 25 inches by 16 inches. *See also* Elephant folio.

ATM. Asynchronous transfer mode. A data Switching technology particularly suitable for handling the high data rates required for transmitting audio and video. One of the key technologies in the implementation of high Bandwidth networks.

Atom. A news feed format proposed by the Internet Engineering Task Force for representing, and a protocol for editing, Web resources such as Blogs, online journals and similar content. The feed format enables syndication, that is, provision of a channel of information by representing multiple resources in a single document. The editing protocol enables agents to interact with resources by nominating a way of using existing Web standards in a pattern. *See also* RSS.

ATS. Abbreviation for Animal Tub-sized. *See* Tub-sizing.

ATS-1. <www.loc.gov/z3950/agency/profiles/ats.html> An Attribute set for Z39.50 searching based on Author-Title-Subject access points. The text of the profile has remained unchanged since January 1997 and other more recent profiles should be considered in preference. *See also* Bib-1.

Attaching. (*Binding*) The process of attaching the boards to the sewn sections after rounding and backing. The attaching joint is a strip of tough paper pasted on to the outside of the end leaf to serve as a connecting link with the boards. Not to be confused with Casing.

Attachment. Any electronic document such as a word processed file, a digital image, a presentation, transmitted along with an E-mail message. *See also* MIME.

Attention note. A note, sometimes combined with a Routeing slip, attached to a periodical in order to draw the attention of users to specific articles or items of information in which they may be interested.

Attribute. 1. A characteristic that defines an object for a particular purpose. For example, within Z39.50, an attribute is a qualifier applied to a search term keyed in by an end user so that the term becomes a valid access point in the bibliographic database. More than a single attribute can be applied and the full group is termed an 'attribute set', the most common being Bib-1. In Access management systems, a name or identity has attributes associated with it such as an undergraduate student on a particular course. In HTML, formatting elements can take attributes that further define the element, e.g. assigning centred justification to a heading. 2. In co-ordinate indexing, a characteristic mentioned as subject-matter. *See also* Characteristic of a classification.

Attributed author. The person to whom a book is attributed, because of doubt as to the authorship. *See also* Supposed author.

Audio library.   A collection of sound recordings, including compact discs, tapes and records.

Audiotape.   A generic term designating a sound recording on magnetic tape. Also called 'phonotape'. *See also* DAT.

Audio-visual area.   Space within a library building equipped with apparatus for screening or listening, and for storing related materials. Now less common due to the integration of different formats within the library.

Audio-visual materials.   Non-book materials such as records, tapes, slides, filmstrips and video-tapes. *See also* Non-book materials.

Audit.   Checking accounts for accuracy and to see that expenditure is authorized by the appropriate authority. *See also* Information audit.

Audit Commission (UK).   <www.audit-commission.gov.uk> (1 Vincent Square, London SW1P 2PN, UK) An independent public body sponsored by the Office of the Deputy Prime Minister with the Department of Health and the National Assembly for Wales. Its task is to ensure that public money in England and Wales is spent economically, efficiently and effectively in the areas of local government, housing, health and criminal justice services. Its local government role covers culture and leisure services and thus includes library and information services.

AUKML.   *See* Association of UK Media Librarians.

Australian Academic and Research Network (AARNet).   <www. avcc.edu.au/avcc/aarnet> Inaugurated in 1990 by the Australian Vice-Chancellor's Committee to provide a high performance communications system linking users, both academic and commercial, within Australia and providing a link to global networks. In 1995 the AVCC entered into a deal with Telstra, which took over management of the backbone and the commercial customers; this led to restructuring and further agreements with the private sector for technical upgrades. In 1998 AVCC announced that AARNet would become an independent company.

Australian Archives.   *See* National Archives of Australia.

Australian Bibliographic Network.   *See now* Kinetica.

Australian Book Publishers Association.   *See now* Australian Publishers Association.

Australian Booksellers Association.   <www.aba.org.au> (Unit 9, 828 High Street, Kew East, Vic 3102, Australia) The ABA represents booksellers in Australia from the largest chain to the small independent bookseller in a country town, newsagents with large book holdings and specialist booksellers such as library suppliers or foreign language booksellers.

Australian Clearing House for Library and Information Science (ACHLIS).   <www.library.unisa.edu.au/about/achlis> ACHLIS was established in 1982 by A. L. Bundy at the Footscray Institute of Technology, Melbourne, as a response to the poor coverage of Australian documentation in *Library and Information Science Abstracts* (*LISA*). ACHLIS aims to identify, collect, abstract and index all

Australian documentation, published and unpublished, in library and information science. *See also ALISA.*

Australian Library and Information Association (ALIA). <www. alia.org.au> (PO Box 6335, Kingston, ACT 2604, Australia) The professional association for the library and information sector in Australia. Its main aims are to empower the profession in the development, promotion and delivery of high-quality library and information services to the nation, through leadership, advocacy and mutual support. There is a regional structure, and special interest groups. A major activity is a biennial conference. Publishes *Australian Library Journal*, and *InCite* – a members' newsletter.

Australian Library and Information Science Abstracts. *See ALISA.*

Australian Publishers Association. <www.publishers.asn.au> Formed in 1948 as the Australian Book Publishers Association; current name adopted 1996. The Association represents a wide cross-section of the Australian publishing industry.

Australian School Library Association (ASLA). <www.asla.org.au> ASLA is a national authority, a peak forum in the field of teacher librarianship and school library resource services in Australia as well as a federation of school library associations in the states and territories. Founded in 1967, the first biennial conference was held in Canberra in 1968 and the Association was inaugurated at a meeting held in Melbourne which was attended by representatives from New South Wales, Queensland and Victoria. Member associations subscribe to ASLA with an annual fee. *ACCESS* is the official journal of the Association.

Australian Society of Archivists. <www.archivists.org.au> (PO Box 77, Dickson, ACT 2602, Australia) Founded in 1975, the principal professional body for archivists in Australia. Publishes *Archives and Manuscripts* (2 p.a.).

Austrian National Library. See Österreichische Nationalbibliothek.

Authentication. 1. (*Archives*) The act of determining that a document, or a reproduction of a document, is what it purports to be. *See also* Certification. 2. Confirmation that a record entered on a database is of the approved standard. 3. A component of core Middleware in networking systems, the process where a user establishes a right to an identity; can be thought of as, 'Is the person who they say they are?'. *See also* Access management, Authorization.

Author. The person, persons or corporate body, responsible for the writing or compilation of a book or other publication not a periodical. Usually to be distinguished from an editor, translator, compiler, etc., although, failing any alternative, these may be regarded as authors for purposes of cataloguing. In a wider sense, an artist, a composer of a musical work, and a photographer are authors to whom would be attributed work which they had created.

Author abstract. *See* Abstract.

Author affiliation. The organizations with which an author is affiliated, as indicated on the title-page, or in a periodical article or proceedings, and sometimes appearing after the author's name in a library catalogue.

Author bibliography. One listing books, articles, or other contributions to knowledge made by, or by and about, a particular author. It may include biographies and criticisms.

Author catalogue. A catalogue of author entries arranged alphabetically under authors' names; it usually includes entries under editors, translators, composite authors, corporate bodies, first words of titles, or any other words or names used as headings for the main entries.

Author entry. A catalogue entry under the name of the person or body responsible for the writing, or compilation, of a published work. Failing one or more real names, the author entry may have to be made under a pseudonym, initials, or some other heading. For music, it is generally an added entry under the name of the author of the text accompanying a musical work, e.g. librettist, or author whose work served as the basis or inspiration for a musical work, the main entry being made under the composer's name.

Author mark. Symbols (letters, figures, or other signs) used to represent authors and so individualize books having the same class, subject, or shelf number, in order to subarrange documents or catalogue entries. It is part of the Call number. *See also* Book number, Call number, Cutter Author Marks, Merrill alphabeting (book) numbers.

Author order. Sequence of books, or of entries relating to books, which are arranged in alphabetical order of authors' names.

Author statement. That part of a catalogue entry which mentions the author when transcribing the title. It is usually omitted unless it contributes data which is essential in some way to the entry, e.g. it would be given for joint authors.

Author table. *See* Author mark.

Authoritative edition. *See* Definitive edition.

Authorities. *See* Primary sources, Secondary sources.

Authority list. 1. A list of all personal and corporate names, names of anonymous classics and sacred books, the titles of anonymous books and the headings for series, which are used as headings in the catalogue; sometimes references are given to books in which each name and its variants are found, and in the case of corporate entries, sources, a brief history and particulars as to changes of name. The entries are made when a heading is first decided upon. It gives the cataloguer a record in the forms used in the public catalogues. 2. A list in classified order of classification symbols or numbers which have been allocated to books, with their corresponding index entries. Also called 'Authority file'. *See also* Authority record, Chain indexing, Name authority file, Subject authority file. 3. Also called, in the context of indexing documents, Closed indexing system; Controlled term list. *See also* Open ended term list, Term, Thesaurus.

Authority practice.   The current definitive listing of Anglo-American standards, names and uniform headings is R. L. Maxwell: *Maxwells' Guide to Authority Work*. Chicago: ALA, 2002. (ISBN: 0 8389 0822 5).

Authority record.   1. A record which gives the form selected for a heading in a catalogue. If a personal name is used as a heading, references to sources and records of variant forms are given; if a corporate name, sources, brief history and any changes of name are given.   2. A record which bears the classification number given by the classifiers to a subject, and also the subject index headings for entries made out for it. Where chain indexing is undertaken, a separate entry would be made for each step taken in determining the number. *See also* Authority list, Chain indexing, Name authority file, Subject authority file.   3. In acquisition work, a term sometimes used to denote a request, requisition or recommendation document, so named because it bears the signature or authority for an acquisition transaction.

Authorization.   A component of core Middleware in networking systems, the process of determining whether an identity is permitted to perform an action such as accessing a resource. Ideally, authorization services should be able to manage the life cycle of access so that as a user moves from undergraduate to postgraduate to academic, access rights are easily updated. *See also* Access management, Authentication, PERMIS.

Authorized edition.   An edition issued with the consent of the author, or of his/her representative.

Author-publisher.   The writer of a work who is his or her own publisher.

Author's agent.   *See* Literary agent.

Author's alterations.   *See* Author's corrections.

Author's binding.   A superior binding used on a few copies of a book as presentation copies from the author.

Author's copies.   The complimentary copies of a book, usually six in number, presented on publication to its author by the publisher.

Author's corrections.   Deviations from the original copy, as distinct from corrections by the author of printer's errors marked on a printer's proof. *See also* Author's revise.

Author's edition.   1. The collected or complete edition of an author's works, uniformly bound, and indicating on the title-page that it is the complete works of the author.   2. An edition the publication of which has been authorized by the author. *See also* Definitive edition.

Authors' Licensing and Collecting Society (ALCS).   <www.alcs.co.uk> (Marlborough Court, 14–18 Holborn, London EC1N 2LE, UK) The main collecting society for authors in the UK; its directors together with the Publishers' Licensing Society (PLS) make up the board of the Copyright Licensing Agency (CLA). ALCS secures mandates from rights owners, and CLA offers licences to institutions and individuals wishing to copy copyright works. ALCS has details of over 100,000 authors and is therefore a valuable source of information. *See also* Copyright Licensing Agency; Publishers' Licensing Society.

Author's proof (AP). The clean proof sent to an author after the compositor's errors have been corrected.

Author's revise. A proof bearing the author's or editor's corrections as distinct from one corrected by the printer.

Author's rights. Those secured to an author under a copyright act.

Author-title index. One which has entries under authors' names and under titles, either in one or in two alphabetical sequences.

Autobiography. The life of a person written by himself/herself.

Autograph. A person's signature. In the book trade, a description of cards, documents, letters, manuscripts, etc., written or signed with the writer's own hand.

Autographed edition. An edition of a work, copies of which are signed by the author. *See also* Limited edition.

Autography. 1. The author's own handwriting. 2. Reproductions of the form or outline of anything by an impression from the thing itself. 3. A lithographic process of reproducing writing, drawing, etc., in facsimile. 4. That branch of diplomatics which is concerned with autographs. *See* Diplomatic.

Autokerning. In Computer typesetting, and Desktop publishing the automatic reformatting of text to remove unsightly white spaces between characters. Based on 'kerning tables' which vary with Typeface. *See also* Kern.

Auto-lithography. A lithographic method in which the artist draws in reverse directly on to the stone or medium.

Automated systems librarian. *See* Systems librarian.

Automatic data processing. *See* Data processing.

Automatic format recognition. (*Information retrieval*) The automatic recognition by a computer of the structure of a record in terms of fields, element, etc., without the need for Tagging.

Automatic indexing. 1. The selection of keywords from a document by a machine method in order to develop index entries. 2. The use of machines to extract and assign index terms without human intervention once programmes or procedural rules have been established.

Automation. A generic term to represent the use of computer-based systems in libraries. Automated systems are used in a wide variety of tasks and contexts from Circulation control, acquisitions and cataloguing to the provision of web services and electronic databases. The term can also be used to include general purpose PCs used by library staff. *See also* Integrated library system, Online public access catalogue.

Automation librarian. *See* Systems librarian.

Autonym. The real name of an author.

Autotype reproduction. One reproduced by the autotype process, which is a variety of the collotype process, in which the plate is coated with a light-sensitive resin instead of a gelatine.

Auxiliary number. One placed after the class number in order to group the books by some method, such as alphabetically or chronologically. The

Olin book number and Cutter Author Marks are auxiliary numbers. *See also* Author mark.

Auxiliary publication.   The process of making data available by means of specially ordered microfilm or photocopies. Auxiliary publication usually presupposes that the materials have not been published before, although it is sometimes applied to publication of microcard copies of out-of-print books.

Auxiliary schedules and tables.   Tables of subdivisions which are appended to schedules of all schemes of Classification. They consist of items of relationship, time, locality, languages, groups of people, external and internal forms of documents, etc. and the symbols of the different items can be added to book classification numbers. Broadly, they fall into four groups: those which (a) are common and can be used with the same meaning throughout the classification, e.g., the common subdivisions of the Dewey Decimal Classification; (b) are common to, and may only be applied to, certain subjects, e.g. the Systematic and Auxiliary Schedules of Bliss's Bibliographic Classification; (c) can be applied in only one place as in most of the Library of Congress Classification Schedules, (d) in the Universal Decimal Classification, are tables of secondary aspects of subjects which may be applied to primary aspects to qualify them, and are distinguished by a special symbol, or 'facet indicator'. *See also* Systematic auxiliary schedules.

Auxiliary syndesis.   The accessory apparatus, e.g. cross reference, which is used to supplement indexing sequence so as to reveal other relations.

AVC.   *See* H.264 Advanced Video Codec.

Average slope map.   One which indicates the average steepness of land slopes.

Azerty.   The standard typewriter keyboard arrangement used in continental Europe, placing the letters a.z.e.r.t.y. from the left on the top row. *See also* Qwerty.

Azured tool.   A bookbinder's tool with close parallel lines running diagonally across its surface. Derived from the use of thin horizontal lines used in heraldry to indicate blue.

Baber (Carroll Preston) Award.   An annual cash award presented for the encouragement of research in library science, improvement in services to specific user groups, and new uses for technology. Administered by the American Library Association Awards Committee. First awarded in 1986.

Back.   1. The 'back' or inside margins of pages.   2. *See* Spine.   3. The surface of a piece of movable type parallel to the Belly.

Back board.   The piece of millboard or strawboard which is used for the back cover of a book.

Back cornering.   (*Binding*) The cutting off of a small portion of the inner corners of the boards near the headcaps in order to improve their setting.

Back cover.   *See* Reverse cover.

Back file.   The file of 'back numbers' or 'back issues' (i.e. those preceding the current issue) of a periodical.

Back fold.   *See* Bolt.

Back issue.   *See* Back file.

Back lining.   A piece of material (paper, cloth, calf skin) glued to the back sections of a book after sewing, before securing the cover.

Back list.   The titles which a publisher keeps in print.

Back margin.   The margin of a printed page which is nearest the fold of the section. Also called: 'Gutter', 'Gutter margin', 'Inner margin', 'Inside margin'.

Back mark.   A small oblong block or number printed in such a position on the sheet that when the sheets of a book are folded and placed together for casing, the oblongs or numbers will follow each other in a slanting and/or numerical sequence down the spine and thus show if any section has been duplicated, misplaced or omitted. Also called 'Collating mark', 'Quad mark'. *See also* Black step.

Back matter.   Matter which is published at the end of the text, e.g. addenda, appendix, author's notes, bibliography, glossary, index, reference matter. Also called 'End-matter', 'Subsidiaries'. *See also* Preliminaries (prelims).

Back number.   *See* Back file.

Back order.   An uncompleted order which is held back for future delivery.

Back page.   The verso, even-numbered, side of a leaf of a book or sheet of printed paper or manuscript. The back of a page.

Back title.   The title which is placed on the spine, or back, of a book. *See also* Binder's title, Cover title.

Backbone.   1. *See* Spine.   2. (*Networking*) Central large capacity, high-speed networks in an area or for particular groups of users to which mid-level networks are connected. *See also* Internet, Local area networks, Metropolitan area networks, Wide area networks.

Backed.   1. A damaged leaf of a book, whether text or plate, which has been 'laid down' on, or pasted on, to paper, gauze or linen.   2. The spine of a book which is covered with a different material to the sides, as 'marbled boards backed with leather'.   3. The spine of a book which has been re-covered with a different material to the original, a 're-backed' one having been re-covered with similar material to the original.

Backing.   The bookbinding operation whereby the sewn sections of a book, after glueing, are placed securely between backing boards after Rounding, and hammered to splay them outwards from the centre of the book. It adds permanence to the rounding, and forms an abutment, or ridge, into which to fit the boards: the ridge so formed is called a 'joint'. This operation is carried out in Britain and America after Rounding: in most Western European countries rounding only is done. *See also* Flat back, Round back.

Backing boards.   Boards used when backing and forming the groove or joint. They are made of very hard wood and sometimes faced with iron.

The edge intended to form the groove is thicker than that which goes towards the fore-edge, so that when placed on either side of the book in the lying press the power of the press is directed towards the back.

Backing machine. A machine for backing books, generally used for publishers' binding and cheap work.

Backing up. *See* Perfecting, Back-up.

Backless binding. A volume which is bound in such a way that the spine is flat or concave, covered with paper and gilt, and probably tooled, so as to look like the fore-edge which is itself finished in a similar manner.

Backlining. The material, usually paper, pasted on the inside of the Spine of a book.

Backslide. The block which is placed behind the cards in a catalogue drawer, and is moved backwards and forwards according to the quantity of cards in the drawer to prevent them from falling out of an upright position. It is usually made with its front sloping back at the top to permit of easy consultation.

Backstage. <www.backstage.ac.uk> A single point of entry for finding and searching performing arts collections in the UK funded originally by the Research Support Libraries Programme.

Backstrip. *See* Spine.

Back-up. 1. To print the second side of a sheet after the first has been printed. 2. A copy of an electronic file usually made and maintained for Computer security purposes.

Back-up services. 1. The services provided by libraries in support of a central loan collection. 2. Those providing documents, or substitutes for documents, in support of a literature survey, reading list or some similar information service.

Baconian Classification. The scheme propounded by Francis Bacon (1561–1626) in his *Advancement of learning* (1605), which more than any other philosophical scheme of thought, or classification of knowledge, has had the greatest influence on library classification. It was based on the three faculties of mind – Memory, Imagination, and Reason – and these produced the three main headings, History, Poesy and Philosophy. The scheme was used for the arrangement of books, and its inversion is the basis of Dewey's Decimal Classification.

Bad break. Incorrect line end hyphenation, or the start of a page of text with a Widow or the end of a hyphenated word.

Bad copy. 'Copy' which is difficult to read. This reduces the speed, and increases the cost, of typesetting. *See also* Copy (1).

Bad letter. *See* Damaged letter.

BAILER. <www.bailer.ac.uk> The British Association for Information and Library Education and Research was formed in 1992 as a forum for all lecturers and researchers in the UK schools and departments of librarianship or information studies. It replaces ABLISS, which was confined to heads of schools. BAILER is the general focus for contact in education and research, and maintains international links.

Baker Report. The Report of the Working Party appointed by the Minister of Education in March 1961, *Inter-Library Co-operation in England and Wales,* 1962. E. B. H. Baker was Chairman of the Working Party. *See also* Bourdillon Report.

Ball. 1. *See* Ink ball. 2. In typography, the finishing element at the top of the strokes of the type letters 'a' and 'c'.

Ball Local History Awards. The Alan Ball Local History Awards, were instituted in 1985 by Library Services Trust, a charity formed by the London and Home Counties Branch of the Library Association (now CILIP). Alan Ball, Chief Librarian of the London Borough of Harrow, had been active in the Branch for over 20 years. The Awards are to encourage UK activity in the area of local history publications.

BALLOTS. Acronym of Bibliographic Automation of Large Library Operations using a Time-sharing System, the online interactive library automation system that supported the acquisition and cataloguing functions of the Stanford University libraries' technical processing operations. A grant from the Council on Library Resources, Inc. in 1975, enabled new development toward a California automation network to be undertaken. This project eventually formed the basis for RLIN.

Bands. The cords or strings whereon the sheets of a book are sewed. With Flexible sewing, the bands appear upon the back. When books are sewn so as to embed the cord in the back, or in modern books sewn on tapes, the appearance of raised bands is sometimes produced by narrow strips of leather or cardboard glued across the back before the volume is covered. The space between the bands is called 'between bands'.

Bandwidth. In communications, the difference between the highest and the lowest frequencies which can be carried. In networking, the transmission capacity of a computer or a communications channel, stated in bits per second; the higher the number, the faster the data transmission rate.

Bangemann Challenge. *See* Stockholm Challenge.

Bangladesh National Scientific and Technical Documentation Centre. *See* BANSDOC.

Banned. Prohibited from sale by ecclesiastical or secular authority.

BANSDOC. Abbreviation for the Bangladesh National Scientific and Technical Documentation Centre which developed in Dacca from the East Pakistan branch office of PANSDOC and is now a part of the Bangladesh Council of Scientific and Industrial Research (BCSIR). BANSDOC operates from the premises of the Bangladesh Council of Scientific and Industrial Research, based in Dacca, and functions 'to serve as an infrastructure for an effective research and development programme as a part of the overall development of the country'. *See now* APIN.

BAOL. *See* British Association for Open Learning.

BAPLA. <www.bapla.org.uk> (18 Vine Hill, London EC1R 5DZ, UK) The British Association of Picture Libraries and Agencies. A trade association formed in 1975 that represents UK picture libraries and agencies holding stock photographs. Each of the 320 members is a commercial library or agency and together they handle more than 300 million images. Electronic delivery of images over the Internet is routine. The membership embraces almost all the major commercial libraries and agencies and many of the smaller, specialist ones. Members are asked to adhere to a Code of Conduct which ensures that the membership acts in an ethical manner. BAPLA maintains close contact with other trade associations with similar aims, such as the Association of Photographers (AFAEP), British Institute of Professional Photographers (BIPP), Society for Picture Researchers and Editors (SPREd), Professional Sports Photographers Association (PSPA), American Society of Magazine Photographers (ASMP), Picture Council Agency of America (PACA), German BVPA and Italian GADEF. BAPLA has also been an active member of the Committee on Photographic Copyright. Publishes *BAPLA Journal* (q.) and a *Directory* (a.). *See also* CEPIC.

Bar. The horizontal stroke of letters; e.g. A, H and e.

Bar code. A code arranged in a series of parallel lines or bars, representing data that is transferred by a *bar code scanner* or Light pen into digital signals for computer use. *See also* RFID.

Barnard (Cyril) Memorial Prize. This Prize was established by the Medical Section of the (UK) Library Association (now CILIP) in 1960 to commemorate one of the founders of the Section.

Barnes Report (UK). The Report of the Commission on the Supply of and Demand for Qualified Librarians. The Chairman was M. P. K. Barnes, and the Report was published by the (UK) Library Association in 1977.

Barrow Process. A process of document repair and restoration which involves de-acidification, the use of tissue to strengthen the original, and thermoplastic lamination. It is named after William J. Barrow (1904–67), a pioneer investigator into the deterioration of library materials. From studying the chemical composition of paper and effects of some inks, he was one of the first to document the condition of brittle paper and identify causes and treatments for it. Among the treatments were a stronger yet more flexible laminate material and the calcium hydroxide/calcium bicarbonate deacidification process. He also worked on the development of performance standards for library binding. Some of his research was carried out in the British Museum Library in the 1950s, but the bulk was done at the Barrow Research Laboratory in Virginia, US, and was funded by the Council on Library Resources (CLR).

Baryta paper. A form of metallic paper, consisting of a suitable body paper coated with barium sulphate; marks can be made on this with a metal point or stylus. It is used in some types of automatic recording apparatus and also for text impressions on photocomposing machines.

Basan skin. Sheepskin tanned with the bark of oak or larch.

Base. The range of characters of a Notation (1). The total number of such characters is known as the base length.

Base line. (*Printing*) The lowest limit of the body of a piece of type; the imaginary line on which the bases of capitals rest. *See also* Cap line, Mean line.

Base map. One on which additional information may be plotted for a particular purpose.

Base of a notation. (*Classification*) Total number of symbols used in a notation of a classification system. In the Dewey Decimal Classification it is ten – the ten arabic numerals, in Bliss's Bibliographic Classification it is thirty-five – the twenty-six letters of the English alphabet combined with the nine arabic numerals. The Colon Classification has the largest base of 74 digits.

Base of symbolism. *See* Alphabet of symbols.

Base of type. The feet, or lowest part, on which the base of a capital letter rests.

Base paper. *See* Body paper, or board.

Base stock. The material, such as plastic, paper or cloth, used as carrier for a photosensitive emulsion.

Basic analysis. The citation in upward hierarchical order of the constituent elements of a composite subject. It is the first stage in converting a classification symbol into a verbal subject heading. The second stage is producing the Qualified list.

Basic stock. Standard books which it may be considered should form the basis of a well-balanced and authoritative book stock.

Basic weight. (*Paper*) The substance of paper is expressed as the weight of a given superficial area, the units most commonly used being either pounds per ream or grammes per square metre. For example '20 x 30 inches 36 lb 480s' means that if the paper were cut into sheets measuring 20 x 30 inches, then 480 sheets would weigh 36 lb.

Basil. A thin sheepskin not suitable for library bookbinding. It is mostly used for binding account books.

Baskerville. A Typeface named after John Baskerville (1706–75) of Birmingham, famous printer and type-founder who was printer of Bibles and prayer books to the University of Cambridge 1758–68. His folio Bible of 1763 was his masterpiece. The type is a modification of Caslon. *See* Transitional.

Basket deal. An offer made to libraries by publishers whereby a large number of (primarily electronic) journals from related subject areas, or the complete collection of journals, are offered at a rate discounted from the sum of their individual subscriptions but usually at a price higher than the library is paying for the currently-subscribed journals from that particular publisher. An economic model derived by publishers in transferring from paper-based journals to the supply of electronic full text. The system is generally disliked by libraries as little or no choice is provided in the content of the basket. Also known as Big deal, Bundling.

Bas-relief printing. *See* Embossing.

Basso continuo. Italian for continued bass. *See* Figured bass.

Bastard title. *See* Half-title.

Bastard type. Type having the face larger or smaller than the size proper to the body, as a nonpareil face on a brevier body, or 10 point face on 12 point body, used to give the appearance of being leaded. *See also* Gothic type.

Bastarda. *See* Gothic type.

Batch processing. A technique by which items to be processed in a data processing machine must be collected into groups prior to their processing; contrasted to online processing.

Batchelder (Mildred L.) Award. Awarded, for the first time in 1968, to an American publisher for the most outstanding of those books originally published in a foreign language in a foreign country, and subsequently published in English in the United States during the calendar year preceding the appointment of the Mildred L. Batchelder Award Committee which is appointed annually. This Committee nominates from three to five books, the final choice is made by the membership of the Association for Library Services to Children.

Bath Profile. <www.collectionscanada.ca/bath/ap-bath-e.htm> An international Z39.50 specification supporting library applications and resource discovery. The Profile defines searching across multiple servers to improve international and extra-national search and retrieval among library catalogues, union catalogues, and other electronic resources worldwide. The Profile also describes and specifies a subset to allow basic cross-domain search and retrieval of networked resources including library catalogues, government information, museum systems, and archives. Release 2.0 of the Profile was issued in 2004. Libraries and Archives Canada acts as the Bath Profile Maintenance Agency. *See also* Interoperability.

Batten system. A method of indexing, invented by W. E. Batten, utilizing the co-ordination of single attributes to identify specific documents. Sometimes called the 'peek-a-boo' system because of its method of punching holes in cards, then superimposing them and checking the coincidence of holes.

Battered. Type matter or Electros when accidentally injured, or so worn that they give defective impressions, are said to be battered.

Battered letter. *See* Damaged letter.

Battledore. *See* Horn book.

Baud rate. Used as a meaure of the data transmission speed of Modems. Generally assumed to be the measurement in bits per second, but more accurately it is the number of events or signal changes per second. At low speeds (300 baud) the two are the same but at high speeds one baud can represent two or more bits.

Bay. A section of library shelving bounded by uprights of any width and height irrespective of the number of shelves. A row of shelving can consist of several bays or a single one, depending on library space and configuration. *See also* Press (1), Stack, Tier.

Bay Psalm Book. *The Whole Book of Psalms faithfully translated into English metre*; the first book printed in Cambridge, Mass., in what is now the US, in 1640 by Stephen Day, on the first press introduced into English-speaking America in 1638.

B.Bibl. Bachelier en Bibliothéconomie et en Bibliographie. A degree of librarianship awarded in Canada.

BBK. Bibliotechno-bibliograficheskaya Klassifikatsiya; the principal classification scheme used by libraries in Russia.

BBS. *See* Bulletin board (1).

BBSLG. *See* British Business Schools Librarians Group.

BC2. *See* Bibliographic Classification.

BCM. *See British Catalogue of Music.*

BCR. <www.bcr.org> (14394 East Evans Avenue, Aurora, CO 80014-1478, USA) Bibliographical Center for Research, a US network consortium with members in Colorado, Idaho, Iowa, Kansas, Montana, Nevada, Utah and Wyoming. An OCLC Network Affiliate.

BDB. *See* Bundesvereinigung Deutscher Bibliotheksverbände.

Beacon Award. *See* Council for Learning Resources in Colleges (CoLRiC).

Beard. That part of the shoulder of a piece of movable type that slopes down from the 'face', or bottom of the printing surface of the letter to the front of the 'body', but more particularly that portion sloping from the bottom serifs of the face to the 'belly'. It consists of the Bevel and the Shoulder.

Bearers. (*Printing*) Type-high strips of metal placed around pages of type when locked in formes from which electrotype plates are to be made. They appear as black borders on proofs. *See also* Forme.

Beater. *See* Breaker.

BECTa. <www.becta.org.uk> The UK government's lead agency for Information and Communication Technology in education. Its strategic aims include improving learning and teaching through effective and embedded use of ICT, increasing the number of organizations and institutions making effective and sustained use of ICT, improving the availability and use of high-quality educational content, and developing a coherent and sustainable ICT infrastructure within education. Active in promoting the National Grid for Learning (NGfL).

Bed. The flat steel table of a printing machine or press on which the Forme of type is placed for printing. When the forme has been secured, it is described as having been 'put to bed'. *See also* Chase.

Bedford Bindings. Bindings by Francis Bedford (1799–1883) an Englishman who succeeded to the business of Charles Lewis. He was the greatest English binder of his time, but his work has little artistic merit and little originality. He attained good results by imitating early Venetian work, with twisted or Saracenic ornament, as well as the later Veneto-Lyonese style, practised in England in Queen Elizabeth's time.

Beirut Agreement. The 'Agreement for facilitating the international circulation of visual and auditory materials of an educational, scientific and cultural character' was intended essentially to promote social and cultural progress in all countries. The purpose of the Agreement is to facilitate the despatch from country to country of (i) films, filmstrips and microfilms; (ii) sound recordings; (iii) glass slides, models, wall charts, maps and posters. At a meeting of international experts held at Geneva in 1967 (the Agreement had been adopted at the Third Session of Unesco held at Beirut in 1948 and came into force on 12 August 1954) it was agreed that the term 'audio-visual' should be liberally interpreted to include the various types of such equipment which had been introduced in the intervening years.

Belgian library associations. There are currently two functioning associations in Belgium: Vlaamse Vereniging voor Biblioteek-, Archief en Dokumentatiewezen <www.vvbad.be> founded in 1921 and L'Association Professionelle des Bibliothécaires et Documentalistes <www.apbd.bc>.

Belgian national library. *See* Bibliothèque Royale Albert 1er.

Belles lettres. Polite literature, or works of literary art showing grace and imagination, as poetry, drama, criticism, fiction and essays. From the French; literally 'beautiful letters'.

Bellows press. A small flat-bed platen press used for jobbing work, e.g. envelopes, broadsides, cards, hand bills, etc.

Belly. The front of the part of a piece of movable type called the body.

Bembo. A roman typeface cut originally by Francesco Griffi for Aldus and first used by him in Cardinal Pietro Bembo's *Aetna*, 1495–6. It was the model followed by Garamond and was re-cut by the Monotype Corporation in 1929. It is regarded by many as the most beautiful of the old-face designs; the modern 'Monotype' Bembo is relatively condensed, a good space saver, and having long ascenders, is legible and pleasant even when set solid. *See also* Typeface.

Ben Day process. A process invented by Ben Day to produce shaded tints or mottled effects by transferring various inked designs in relief on a gelatine film to the metal plate which is later etched.

Bench press. A small press, resting on a work bench and used by bookbinders to press cased books. *See also* Standing press.

Benchmark (Bench-test). An examination and assessment of performance, usually by comparison with agreed requirements of performance or other points of reference. The process of comparing local performance with comparators, either by sector or by function. Especially used in quality assessment, and in the consideration of the speed, reliability, accuracy etc. of software or equipment.

Beneventan handwriting. A beautiful minuscule handwriting used in Southern Italy and Dalmatia which survived in a number of national varieties developed from the Italian semi-cursive minuscule, itself a descendant of the roman cursive. *See also* Cursive, Handwriting.

Berghoeffer system. A filing system first used by Prof. Dr. Christian W. Berghoeffer who compiled the Frankfurter Sammelkatalog in 1891. *See also* Finding list.

Berlin Declaration. <www.zim.mpg.de/openaccess-berlin/berlin declaration.html> Fully, the Berlin Declaration on Open Access to Knowledge in the Sciences and Humanities, a statement published from the Max Planck Society in October 2003 to promote the Internet as a functional instrument for storing and disseminating global scientific knowledge through Open access publishing and Self archiving. *See also* Bethesda Statement on Open Access Publishing, Budapest Open Access Initiative.

Berne Convention. In full, Berne International Convention for the Protection of Literary and Artistic Works. *See* Berne Copyright Covention.

Berne Copyright Convention. The International Convention for the Protection of Literary and Artistic Works, known as the 'Berne Convention' or 'Berne Copyright Union', was adopted by an international conference held at Berne in 1886. Designed to protect effectively, and in as uniform a manner as possible, the rights of authors in their literary and artistic works, the Berne Convention was originally signed on 9 September 1886, and completed in Paris on 4 May 1896; it was revised in Berlin on 13 November 1908, completed in Berne on 20 March 1914, revised in Rome on 2 June 1928, in Brussels on 26 June 1948, in Stockholm on 13 July 1967, and in Paris on 24 July 1971. The United Kingdom has been a party to the Convention from 5 December 1887, but the USA, although bound by the Universal Copyright Convention since 16 September 1955, joined only in 1988. The protection of the Berne Convention applies to authors who are nationals of one of the countries of the Union established by that Convention, for their works whether published or not, and to authors who are nationals of non-Union countries, for their works first published in one of those countries, or simultaneously in a country outside the Union and in a country of the Union. The duration of the protection provided by the 'Paris Act' of the Berne Convention is for the author's life and fifty years after death. The Convention in its various forms has been ratified by most countries throughout the world. It has also been updated by the WIPO Copyright Treaty. *See also* Copyright, International, IGC.

Berufsverband Information Bibliothek (BIB). <www.bib-info.de> German library organization; one of the partners in Bundesvereinigung Deutscher Bibliotheksverbande (BDB).

Bespoke books. *See* On-demand publishing.

Best matched. *See* Nearest neighbour.

Best seller. A book which is so popular that unusually large numbers are sold.

Besterman Medal. <www.cilip.org.uk> Part of the CILIP/Nielsen Bookdata Awards series; two awards are made annually for outstanding bibliographies or literature guides in print and electronic formats.

Beta Phi Mu.   International Library and Information Science Honor Society. Founded in 1948, the society recognizes high scholarship in the study of librarianship, and sponsors professional and scholarly projects. The society is open to all graduates of ALA accredited library and information science programmes.

Beta Phi Mu Award.   A cash award presented to a library school faculty member, or anyone making an important contribution to education for librarianship. Administered by the American Library Association Awards Committee.

Beta testing.   The testing of new Applications software or new 'versions' of existing Applications, usually by selected End users to identify problems before the package is finally released to the public at large. *See also* Alpha testing.

Bethesda Statement on Open Access Publishing.   <www.earlham.edu/~peters/fos/bethesda.htm> A statement published in June 2003 to stimulate discussion within the biomedical research community on how to proceed, as rapidly as possible, to the goal of providing Open access to the primary scientific literature. The intention was to agree on significant, concrete steps that all relevant parties could take to promote the rapid and efficient transition to open access publishing. *See also* Berlin Declaration, Budapest Open Access Initiative.

Better Connected Website Awards.   *See* Society of Public Information Networks (SpiN).

Between bands.   *See* Bands.

Bevel.   The part of the shoulder of a piece of movable type immediately sloping down from the 'face'. The distance from the face to the bottom of the bevel is known as the 'depth of strike'. Also called 'Neck'.

Bevelled boards.   Heavy boards with bevelled edges principally used for large books in imitation of antique work.

b.f.   Abbreviation for Bold face type.

BI.   *See* Bibliographical instruction.

BIALL.   *See* British and Irish Association of Law Librarians.

Biannual.   A publication which is issued twice a year. This word is sometimes used synonymously with *Biennial* which strictly means 'published every two years'. To avoid misunderstanding, the terms 'Half-yearly' or 'Twice a year' are tending to be used instead of Bi-annual. *See also* Bi-monthly.

Bias phase.   1. In classification, where one topic is described (usually in a relatively elementary manner) for the benefit of those working in, or concerned with, another field, a document is classified under the topic introduced, not under the persons for whom it is written, e.g. anatomy for speech therapists would go under anatomy, not speech therapists. 2. The treatment of a subject generally and fairly completely, if concisely, from the point of view of a class of users whose primary interest is in another subject. It is one of Ranganathan's six 'phase relations'. Lately, Dewey Decimal Classification and Bibliographic

Classification-2 have also recognized this phase. It can be a useful tool for Reader-interest classification.

BIB. *See* Biennale of Illustrations Bratislava.

Bib-1. <www.loc.gov/z3950/agency/defns/bib1.html> The Attribute set designed for searching databases of bibliographic records registered as a standard by the Z39.50 Maintenance Agency. There are six types of attributes: use; relation; position; structure; truncation and completeness. The use attribute identifies a set of access points against which the term is to be matched, for example, author, title, subject. A sub-set of attributes from the many comprising Bib-1 and that represent practical access points for particular systems are denoted as a 'profile'.

Bibelot. An unusually small book, valuable as a curiosity because of its format or rarity. Also called 'Dwarf book', 'Thumb book'.

Bible paper. A very thin tough opaque paper used for Bibles or other lengthy books which are required to have little bulk. It is made from new cotton or linen rags. Often erroneously referred to as India paper. Also called 'Bible printing'. *See also* Cambridge India paper, Oxford India paper.

Bible printing. *See* Bible paper.

Bibles. Manuscript versions of the Bible include the *Book of Kells*, an illuminated copy of the Latin gospels found in the Abbey of Kells, Ireland, and thought to date from the eighth century (now in Trinity College, Dublin); the *Book of Armagh*, a manuscript in the Irish pointed hand of portions of the New Testament, copied by the scribe Ferdomnach who died in 844; the *Book of Cerne*, part of the gospels copied at Cerne Abbey, Dorset, (now in Cambridge University Library); and the *Lindisfarne Gospels* (also known as the *Durham Book*) written in English half-uncials around 700.

Celebrated printed versions include the *42-line Bible*, in Latin, printed by Johann Gutenberg, Johann Fust and Peter Schoeffer in Mainz between 1450–55 which is one of the earliest books to be printed from moveable type (48 copies are known, one of which is the *Mazarin Bible*, owned by Cardinal Mazarin, 1602–61; the British Library possesses two copies, one on vellum, one paper; also known as the *Gutenberg Bible*); the *36-line Bible* printed in Bamberg about 1460, probably by Heinrich Keffer; and the *48-line Bible* (Fust and Schoeffer, Mainz, 1462). The *Complutensian Polyglot* in six volumes, printed by Arnald Guillen de Brocar between 1514 and1517 at Alcala de Henares near Madrid, is the first great multi-lingual Bible (*See* Polyglot) and is a landmark in Spanish printing; the text is in Hebrew, Aramaic, Greek and Latin (Complutum is the Roman name for the town of Alcala de Henares). The *Geneva Bible*, 1560, was produced by Marian exiles, but was openly printed in London from 1576; it was the first to be divided into verses. It is sometimes referred to as the *Breeches Bible* ('made themselves breeches', Genesis iii,7) and the *Whig Bible* ('blessed are the place makers', Matthew 5,9.). The *Oxford Folio* (John Baskett,

Oxford, 1716–17) has many errors, of which one (Luke 20) gives it the nickname *Vinegar Bible* (instead of 'vineyard').

Biblia Pauperum. A type of mediaeval picture book of scriptural subjects, with descriptive vernacular text. Very popular among clergy and laity in continental countries before the Reformation. Many manuscript copies are preserved in different languages. It was one of the first books printed in the Netherlands and Germany, originally from blocks and then from type. It was reprinted several times in later years, most recently in 1884, with a preface by Dean Stanley.

Biblio. The bibliographical note and/or imprint which is placed on the back of the title-page. *See also* Preliminaries (prelims).

Biblioclasm. The destruction of books, or of the Bible.

Biblioclast. A destroyer of books.

Bibliogenesis. The production of books.

Bibliognost. One versed in knowledge about books and in bibliography.

Bibliogony. The production of books.

Bibliograph. A bibliographer.

Bibliographee. A person concerning whom a bibliography has been made.

Bibliographer. 1. A person who is able to describe the physical characteristics of books by recognized methods. 2. One able to prepare bibliographies by recognized principles.

Bibliographic. *Synonymous with* Bibliographical. [This latter term is used in this glossary except where it forms a part of the title of an organization or publication.]

Bibliographic Automation of Large Library Operations using a Time-sharing System. *See* BALLOTS.

Bibliographic Classification. A scholarly and detailed scheme devised by H. E. Bliss (1870–1955) and first applied in the College of the City of New York where he was librarian in 1902. Following the publication of two massive theoretical works on the organization of knowledge, the full scheme was published in four volumes over the period 1940–1953. Its main feature was the carefully designed main class order, reflecting the Comptean principle of gradation in speciality. It contained numerous Systematic Auxiliary Schedules for the building of detailed classmarks; four of these were applicable to all classes (form; time; place; language) and the others to particular subjects. The Scheme had some success in Britain and the Commonwealth, with some 80 libraries eventually applying it. Work on a radical revision, incorporating the advances in logical facet analysis initiated by Ranganathan and developed by the Classification Research Group (CRG) in Britain, began in the early 1970s and this revision (BC2) has now superseded the earlier Scheme. BC2 is virtually a new system, using only the broad outline developed by Bliss; the vocabulary is very much greater, the number of enumerated terms is ten times as great – and far more if the synthesis possible is considered. The main features of BC2 are: main-class order based on closely-argued theoretical principles; each main-class, and sub-classes where necessary, are fully faceted; a comprehensive and consistent citation order is observed throughout all classes; the filing order consistently maintains general-before-special; the notation is fully faceted and synthetic; fully detailed alphabetical indexes to all classes are provided. The new system began publication in 1977 (originally Butterworth, now Bowker-Saur) and will be completed in 22 volumes. *See also* Bliss Classification Association.

Bibliographic Index. <www.hwwilson.com> A subject index to current bibliographies, whether published separately as books, or pamphlets, or bibliographies appearing in books and pamphlets, or as periodical articles. Published by the H.W.Wilson Company and from 2002 available on WilsonWeb. Over 250,000 bibliographies in English, German and the Romance languages from 1984 can be searched digitally.

Bibliographical. Of, or relating to, or dealing with, bibliography.

Bibliographical Center for Research. *See* BCR.

Bibliographical centre. A place where bibliographies and catalogues of libraries, and those issued by publishers, are assembled, and information on books is given. They are usually associated with book-lending agencies, co-operative book stores, or national libraries, and may or may not be intimately connected with the lending of books. In the US they also serve as bureaux organizing the inter-lending of books between libraries.

Bibliographical classification. One designed for the Classification of books and other literary material, and for the entries in bibliographies and catalogues. The Universal Decimal Classification was the first such classification. *See also* Knowledge classification.

Bibliographical control. The creation, development, organization, management and exploitation of records prepared firstly to describe items held in libraries or on databases, and secondly to facilitate user access to such items.

Bibliographical coupling. Comparison of articles and books cited in references and bibliographies appended to documents, as an indication of likely overlap or identity of subject coverage in the documents.

Bibliographical database. A database containing records made up of Bibliographical information and designed to identify and locate relevant items.

Bibliographical description. The description of a published work of literary or musical composition, giving particulars of authorship, of others who have contributed to the presentation of the text (editor, translator, illustrator, arranger, etc.), title, edition, date, particulars of publication (place and name of publisher and possibly of printer), format, etc. In the case of music it may relate to a single recording or to an album of the same, as well as to printed music, and is concerned only with the publication *per se*, not its musical content, and is different from Musical description.

Bibliographical index. 1. A systematic list of writings or publications (e.g. of books or periodical articles) with or without annotations. 2. An index of publications or articles which contains no material descriptive of their contents other than bibliographical references.

Bibliographical information. Details concerning a publication which are sufficient to identify it for the purpose of ordering. They may include the following: author, title, publisher, place of publication, edition, series note, number of volumes, parts and/or supplements, and price; editor, translator or illustrator may also be necessary in the case of certain books. Sometimes called 'trade information'.

Bibliographical instruction. The process whereby library staff help users to gain access to information, both by formal instructional methods and training on the spot. A variety of techniques will be used, including Multimedia and interactive systems.

Bibliographical item. An article in a periodical, a technical report, a patent, a monograph, or a chapter in a symposium, which is capable of being given a separate bibliographical entry in a catalogue or bibliography.

Bibliographical note. 1. A note, often a footnote, containing a reference to one or more books or periodical articles, etc., as sources for the work. 2. A note in a catalogue or in a bibliography relating to the bibliographical history of, or describing, a book. 3. A note, often a footnote or annotation, in a catalogue, mentioning a bibliography contained in a book.

Bibliographical references. References to books and parts of books (including articles in books), to periodicals and other serials, and to articles in periodicals.

Bibliographical scatter. The appearance of an article on one subject in a periodical devoted to a totally different subject. *See* Law of scattering.

Bibliographical service. The facilities, procedures and devices which are employed to produce a bibliography consisting of a continuing series of publications, or bibliographical information as requested.

Bibliographical Society. <www.bibsoc.org.uk> (Institute of English Studies, Room 3, Senate House, Malet Street, London WC1E 7HU, UK) Formed in 1892 to promote and encourage study and research in the fields of historical, analytical, descriptive and textual bibliography, and the history of printing, publishing, bookselling, bibliography and collecting. Awards grants and bursaries, occasional medals for services to bibliography, maintains a library. Publishes *The Library* (q.).

Bibliographical Society of America (BSA). <www.bibsocamer.org> (Box 1537, Lenox Hill Station, New York, NY 10021, USA) The leading bibliographical society in America. It was founded in 1904 to promote bibliographical research and to issue bibliographical publications. Publishes *Papers* (q. to members).

Bibliographical Society of Australia and New Zealand. <www.csu.edu.au/community/BSANZ> The Society was founded in 1969, modelled on the UK and American counterparts. It is concerned with all aspects of physical bibliography in all parts of the world. It publishes a quarterly *Bulletin*, an irregular newsletter (the *Broadsheet*) and an Occasional Publications series and holds an annual two-day conference.

Bibliographical Society of Canada. <www.library.utoronto.ca/~bsc> (Box 575, Postal Station P, Toronto, Ontario M5S 2T1, Canada) Founded in May 1946 to promote bibliographical publication, encourage the preservation of printed works and manuscripts, and extend knowledge of them, particularly those relating to Canada, and facilitate the exchange of bibliographical information. Membership is open to individuals and to institutions. Publishes *Papers* (a.), and a six-monthly *Bulletin*.

Bibliographical tool. A publication, such as a list of books, which is used by a bibliographer in the course of his or her work.

Bibliographical unit. 1. Any document, part of a document, or several documents, forming a bibliographic whole which is treated as a single entity in a system of bibliographical description. A Bibliographical item. 2. More commonly, a group of people working together as a team in some bibliographic work.

Bibliographical volume. A unit of publication distinguishable from other units by having its own title-page, half title, cover title, or portfolio title. If a periodical, all the parts which comprise the publisher's volume.

Bibliography. 1. The compilation of *systematic* or *enumerative* bibliographies – books, MSS, audio-visual formats and other publications arranged in a logical order giving author, title, date and place of publication, publisher, details of edition, pagination, series and literary/information contents. Such a bibliography might be of works by one author, or on one subject, or printed by one printer, or in one place, or during one period. The term is also applied to the whole of the literature on a subject. A bibliography may be complete/general/universal (i.e. including all formats, periods, subjects, etc.) or national (material emanating from one country), or select (rated by quality or relevance to a purpose) or special (limited to one aspect) or trade (compiled for commerical purposes in the booktrade). 2. The art or science of describing books, especially their physical make-up or literary contents; consideration of books as physical objects, and the history of book production. Often in this sense the terms *critical, analytical, historical,* or *physical* bibliography are used. *See also* Bio-bibliography, Cartobibliography, Textual bibliography.

Bibliography of bibliographies. An extensive list of bibliographies.

Bibliokleptomaniac. A book-thief whose activities are not rational.

Bibliolatry. Book-worship.

Bibliology. The scientific description of books, dealing with their construction from the beginnings to the present day, including paper and other materials, typography, illustration and binding. Also called *analytical, critical, descriptive* or *historical* bibliography. *See also* Bibliography.

Bibliomancy.   Divination by books, generally by verses of the Bible.

Bibliomane.   An indiscriminate collector of books.

Bibliomania.   A mania for collecting and possessing books. Also called 'Bibliomanianism', 'Bibliomanism'.

Bibliometrics.   The application of mathematical and statistical methods to the study of the use made of books and other media within and between library systems. *See also* Metrics.

Bibliomining.   <www.bibliomining.com> The combination of Data mining, Bibliometrics, statistics, and reporting tools used to extract behaviour-based patterns from library systems. *See also* Text mining.

Bibliopegy.   The art of bookbinding.

Bibliophagist.   One who 'devours' books.

Bibliophegus.   The name used in early Christian times for a bookbinder.

Bibliophile.   A lover of books who knows how to discriminate between good and bad editions. Also called 'Bibliophilist'.

Bibliophile binding.   A special binding such as might be used by a bibliophile.

Bibliophile edition.   A specially printed and bound edition of a book which is published for sale to bibliophiles. *See also* Fine paper copy.

Bibliophily.   A love of books; a taste for books.

Bibliophobia.   A dislike, or dread, of books; an aversion to books.

Bibliopoesy.   The making of books.

Bibliopolar.   Of, or belonging to, booksellers. Also called 'Bibliopolic', 'Bibliopolical'.

Bibliopole.   One who deals in books, especially rare or curious ones.

Bibliopolism.   The principles, or trade, of bookselling.

Bibliopoly.   The selling of books. Also called 'Bibliopolery'.

Bibliopsychology.   The study of books, readers and authors and their mutual relationships. It was formulated by Nicholas Rubakin in his Institute of Bibliopsychology in Switzerland, 1916–46.

Bibliosoph.   One who knows, or knows about, books.

Bibliotaph.   One who keeps his books under lock and key. Also called 'Bibliotaphist'.

Biblioteca Alexandrina.   *See* Alexandrian Library.

Biblioteca Nacional.   1. <www.bn.pt> (Rua Ocidental do Campo Grande 83, 1751 Lisbon, Portugal) The national library of Portugal, founded in 1796.   2. <www.bne.es> (Paseo de Recoletos 20, 28071 Madrid, Spain) The national library of Spain, founded in 1712.

Biblioteca Nazionale.   There are a number of 'national libraries' in Italy, reflecting the former separate states. The four generally now included as such are: Biblioteca Nazionale Centrale (Piazza dei Cavalleggeri 1B, 50122 Florence) founded in 1747; Biblioteca Nazionale Vittorio Emanuele III (Piazza dei Plebiscito, Palazzo Reale, 80132 Naples) founded in 1804; Biblioteca Nazionale Vittorio Emanuele II (Viale Castro Pretorio 105, 00185 Rome) founded in 1876; and Biblioteca Nazionale Marciana (San Marco 7, 30124 Venice) originally founded in

1468. In 2004 the catalogue of the first of these libraries was combined with the Italian National Bibliography and made available as a very full source of Italian book titles <www.ie-online.it>.

Biblioteca Universalis. <www.kb.nl/gabriel/biblioteca-universalis> An international project that offers the major works and artefacts of the world cultural and scientific heritage via multimedia technologies. The goal is to foster cross-border dialogue and enhance services to end users by providing a practical framework for international co-operation.

Bibliotekarforbundet. *See* Danish library associations.

Bibliotekstjänst (BTJ). <www.btj.com> (P.O. Box 200, 22100 Lund, Sweden) The Swedish library supply agency (a company since 1960) which developed from a central selling agency founded in 1936 by the Swedish Library Association (Sveriges Allmanna Biblioteksforening). It develops and sells products, services and technology in the fields of media and information. Its operations extend over several Scandinavian countries and the USA.

Bibliotheca. 1. A library. 2. A bibliographer's catalogue.

Bibliothecal. Belonging to a library.

Bibliothecarian. 1. A librarian. 2. Of, or belonging to, a library, or a librarian. Also, Bibliothecary.

Bibliothek & Information International (BII). [Library and Information International] A project operated by Bundesvereinigung Deutscher Bibliotheksverbande (BDB) and its partners, focusing on the international transfer of library and information science knowledge.

Bibliothek und Information Deutschland (BID). New German umbrella organization for library associations to be launched late in 2004, formed by the merger of Bundesvereinigung Deutscher Bibliotheksverbände (BDB) and Deutsche Gesellschaft für Informationswissenschaft und Informationpraxis (DGI).

Bibliothèque Nationale de France (BNF). <www.bnf.fr> The French National Library which opened in new premises ('François Mitterand' Building) located in the Tolbiac suburb of eastern Paris in October 1998; holdings in the new building total over 11 million volumes and are generally post-1945 – material before that date remains in the former Bibliothèque Nationale (BN), which has existed in Paris from the fourteenth century, initially as the library of the sovereigns. A network of back-up libraries (CADISTs) in universities and major public collections supports the Library.

Bibliothèque Nationale du Canada. *See* National Library of Canada.

Bibliothèque Nationale du Québec . *See* National Library of Québec.

Bibliothèque Royale Albert 1er. <www.kbr.be> (Bd. de l'Empereur 4, 1000 Brussels, Belgium) The national library (Royal Library) of Belgium; originally founded in 1559.

Bibliothèques et Archives Canada. *See* Libraries and Archives Canada.

Bibliotherapy. The use of selected reading and related materials for therapeutic purposes in physical medicine and in mental health. As an aspect of hospital and institution librarianship it requires an acquaintance with a wide range of literature and a knowledge of the techniques of group leadership and individual guidance.

Bibliothetic. Pertaining to, or based on, the placing or arrangement of books.

BIBOS. Bibliotheksverbund; library bibliographic network, based in Vienna.

Bibsys. <www.bibsys.no> Bibliographic network for Norwegian university libraries.

BIC. *See* Book Industry Communication.

BICI. Book Item and Component Identifier; designed to follow the pattern of SICI and identify chapters, indexes etc., within a book for document delivery purposes, rights information, database records etc. A draft NISO standard was drawn up <www.niso.org/pdfs/BICI-DS.pdf> and made available for comments up to January 2002 but was not progressed. *See also* Digital Object Identifier, Metadata, SICI.

BID. *See* Bibliothek und Information Deutschland.

BIDS. <www.bids.ac.uk> Provider of bibliographic services for the UK higher education and research community, also providing access to the IngentaJournals full text service, directly and through links from database search results. BIDS is managed by Ingenta on a fully accountable and not-for-profit basis.

Biennale of Illustrations Bratislava (BIB). An international exposition of children's book illustrations which, with the co-operation of the Unesco national commissions, seeks to develop this art-form by creating a suitable environment for their evaluation. The first BIB was held in Bratislava in September 1967.

Biennial. A publication issued every two years; but *see also* Biannual.

Bifurcate classification. 1. A classification branching in pairs, positive and negative, such as the Tree of Porphyry. Also called classification by dichotomy. 2. The bifurcate division of a genus by a single significant difference into a species and a residuum, which may or may not be disregarded in further division.

Big Blue. <www.library.mmu.ac.uk/bigblue> A JISC-funded project that surveyed practice in Information skills training for students in further and higher education and made recommendations towards the development of an information literate student population in the UK. It was managed jointly by Manchester Metropolitan University Library and Leeds University Library. The project ended in July 2002.

Big deal. *See* Basket deal.

Bigram. Any group of two successive letters.

Bill. 1. A written complaint at law. 2. A draft of a proposed law introduced in a legislative body.

Bill and Melinda Gates Foundation. *See* Gates Library Foundation.

Bill Book. A book in which invoices or bills (accounts) are entered as received. The entries are usually arranged alphabetically under the suppliers' names (American).

Bill of Middlesex. A precept having the same force as a writ, but with the formal opening omitted.

Bill of type. 1. A complete assortment of any Font of type. 2. The plan or ratio by which fonts of type are made up by type founders in order to provide the correct proportion of each letter or character, as ascertained by experience as to probable requirements. Also called 'Font Scheme', 'Scheme'.

BIMA. *See* British Interactive Multimedia Association.

Bi-monthly. A serial publication issued in alternate months.

Binary. 1. A number system using only two symbols, the digits one and zero. 2. A number system where quantities are represented in base 2 rather than base 10.

Binary number system. A system, used in many computers and in information theory, which has only one digit, 1, and a zero. Thus the first ten whole numbers of this system, together with their decimal equivalents, which consist of nine digits and a zero, in parentheses, are: 0 (0), 1 (1), 10 (2), 11 (3), 100 (4), 101 (5), 110 (6), 111 (7), 1000 (8), 1001 (9), 1010 (10).

Binary search. (*Information retrieval*) A search in which a set of items is divided into two parts, where one part being rejected, the process is repeated on the accepted part until the item having the required property is found. *See also* Fractional scanning.

Bind. To assemble and fasten securely printed or manuscript Sheets within a cover which may be made of wood or board covered with leather or cloth, plastic, stiff card (board) or paper. *See also* Boards (1), Sheets.

Bind in. To fasten supplementary material securely into a bound book.

Binder. 1. A person who binds books. 2. A case, or detachable cover, for filing magazines, pamphlets, etc., usually on wires or cords, one for each publication.

Binder's block. *See* Binder's brass.

Binder's board. *See* Millboard, Strawboard.

Binder's brass. A design, or letters of the alphabet, cut in brass and used by a bookbinder's finisher in lettering book covers. When a Block is used it is called a 'Binder's block'. *See also* Arms block, Zinco.

Binder's dies. (*Binding*) Lettering or designs cut in brass and used for decorating book covers by stamping or embossing them. Also called 'Panel stamps'.

Binder's ticket. A small engraved or printed label, usually fixed to the top outside corner of one of the front end papers between about 1750 and 1825, and giving the name of the binder. These tickets were superseded by the binder's name stamped in gilt, ink, or blind, on one of the inside boards, usually on the extreme lower edge: this is called a 'name pallet'.

Binder's title. The title lettered on the back of a book when re-bound, to distinguish it from the publisher's title on the cover or title-page. *See also* Back title, Cover title.

Binder's waste. Printed sheets which are surplus to a bookbinder's needs and which are sometimes used in bookbinding for lining purposes.

Bindery. A place in which books are bound or re-bound.

Binding. 1. The cover of a volume. 2. The finished work resulting from the processes involved in binding a book. 3. Colloquially, a number of books in a library which are waiting to be re-bound, or those which have been re-bound. *See also* Bookbinding.

Binding book. A book in which are entered particulars of books sent to a binder for re-binding.

Binding cloth. *See* Book cloth.

Binding copy. A book which is so worn as to need rebinding.

Binding department. The department of a library or printing establishment in which books are bound or re-bound.

Binding edge. A back edge of a volume, or the folded edge of a section; the edge opposite the Fore-edge. *See also* Ridge.

Binding from sheets. Purchasing books in unfolded sheets and having them bound by the library binder.

Binding margin. *See* Back margin.

Binding record. A record of books sent to the binder.

Binding rub. *See* Rub.

Binding slip (sheet). The form on which instructions for binding are written for the binders' guidance. A slip relates to one book only and is usually inserted in a book before it leaves the library and remains in it throughout all the binding processes.

Binding variations. The bindings of books, which, although published in the same edition, vary in colour or type of book cloth, tooling, etc. This may arise through a number of manufacturing causes, especially if the whole of an edition is not bound at the same time, or through storage under unsatisfactory conditions, e.g. dampness.

Binomial. *(Classification)* A name which consists of two, and occasionally three, terms.

Bio-bibliography. A bibliography which contains brief biographical details about the authors.

Biographee. A person who is the subject of biography.

Biographer. A person who writes a biography of another.

Biographical dictionary. A collection of lives of people arranged in alphabetical order.

Biography. 1. A written account of a person's life. 2. The branch of literature concerned with the lives of people.

Biography file. A file of records, or of cuttings, giving information about individuals. Also called a 'Who's who' file.

BIOME. <biome.ac.uk> A Hub of the (UK) RDN, a collection of gateways which provides access to evaluated, quality Internet resources in the health and life sciences, aimed at students, researchers, academics and practitioners. The subject specific gateways comprising BIOME are: OMNI (health and medicine); VETGATE (animal health); BIORES (biological and biomedical sciences); Natural Selection (the natural world); and AgriFor (agriculture, food and forestry). Based at the University of Nottingham.

BioMed Image Archive. <www.brisbio.ac.uk> A JISC-funded project to build a national repository for biomedical images that are copyright-cleared and free for use in learning, teaching and research. It builds on the Bristol BioMed Image Archive which has been established for 10 years and originally comprised a collection of 8,500 images from the medical, dentistry and veterinary sciences, supplied by Bristol University and other academics. The new resource will allow users from other institutions to add images and metadata to the archive for the purpose of sharing: all images will be copyright-cleared for use in further and higher education.

BioMedCentral. <www.biomedcentral.com> A commercial publisher producing a range of Open access journals in the biomedical sciences. *See also* Public Library of Science, PubMed Central.

BIORES. <bioresearch.ac.uk> A subject gateway providing access to Internet resources in the biological and biomedical sciences; part of the BIOME Hub of the (UK) RDN.

BIPA. *See* British Internet Publishers Alliance.

Birmingham notation. *See* GKD notation.

BIRS. British Institute of Recorded Sound Ltd. *See* National Sound Archive.

Biscoe Time Numbers (Biscoe Date Table). A table designed by W. S. Biscoe (1853–1933) which allocated letters and numerals to year periods in order to sub-arrange books in chronological, rather than alphabetical, order both on the shelves and in the catalogue. First published in 1885, it was initially intended to be used with the Dewey Decimal Classification. The full table was:

A	B.C.	J	1830–1839	S	1920–1929
B	0–999	K	1840–1849	T	1930–1939
C	1000–1499	L	1850–1859	U	1940–1949
D	1500–1599	M	1860–1869	V	1950–1959
E	1600–1699	N	1870–1879	W	1960–1969
F	1700–1799	O	1880–1889	X	1970–1979
G	1800–1809	P	1890–1899	Y	1980–1989
H	1810–1819	Q	1900–1909	Z	1990–1999
I	1820–1829	R	1910–1919		

Examples of use: a book published in 1676 would be lettered E76, in 1916 R6.

BISG. *See* Book Industry Study Group, Inc.

Bishop's Rules. A set of rules for abbreviating periodical titles: (1) if the journal title consists of a single word, the first four letters are taken; (2) if of two words, the first two letters of each word; (3) if of three words, the first letter of each of the first two words and the first two letters of the last word; (4) if of more than four words, usually the first letter of each of the first four words. *See also* Coden (2).

Bit. A contraction of 'binary digit'. The smallest unit of information; a zero or a one; a 'yes' or 'no'.

Bit map. A collection of bits that represents, in computer memory, an image to be displayed on screen. The image is constructed from pixels arranged in rows and columns with each pixel represented by either 1 bit (simple black and white) or up to 32 bits (high-definition color). Text can be stored as a bit map by using a Scanner and saving in a format such as TIFF or EPS but the individual letters and words of text do not then exist as separate entities and cannot be manipulated in a word processor or searched via text retrieval.

Bite. The term given to the action of acid eating into metal in the process of block making or plate engraving.

Bitnet. *See* Internet.

Bi-weekly. Also 'Semi-monthly'. *See* Fortnightly.

BL. *See* British Library.

Black. A mark made unintentionally on a sheet of paper by a Lead, Space or piece of Furniture which has risen. Also called 'Work up'.

Black face. *See* Bold face.

'Black' headings. Headings, other than subject headings, in a dictionary catalogue. The term has its origin in the fact that it was the practice in many libraries to use red for the subject headings and black for all the others.

Black letter. A term used to indicate old English, text, or church type, which was based on the writing in mediaeval manuscripts. *See also* Gothic type.

Black step. A rule about 6 points thick and up to 24 points long printed between the first and last pages of a section so as to show on the spine of the section when folded. In the first Forme it is positioned opposite the top line of text, and about 24 points lower in each successive forme, so that when all the sections of a book have been gathered and placed together a diagonal line is seen across the spine. Any error in gathering is immediately apparent. Also called 'Back mark', 'Collating mark', 'Quad mark'.

Blackwell/North America Scholarship Award. An annual award administered by the Association for Library Collections and Technical Services of the ALA for an outstanding book or paper on acquisition or collection development.

Blad. A mock-up of a book used for advertising purposes, including covers, wrappers and maybe preliminaries to give an idea of the finished appearance.

BLAISE. The British Library's Automated Information Service, provided access to a range of databases, including *British National Bibliography*, *British Books in Print, The Stationery Office database, ISSN UK Centre* *records, British Library Catalogues*. The service closed in January 2002 being replaced by free access to the British Library OPAC.

Blank. An unprinted page which is part of a Signature and is consequently recorded when making a bibliographical description of a book in the form 'bl.' following the unprinted signature or page number in [].

Blank book. A bound book consisting of blank leaves only; used for notes, records, accounts, etc.

Blank cover. The cover of a bound book which is devoid of lettering or ornamentation.

Blank leaves. The unprinted leaves to be found at each end of a book. If these are conjugate with printed leaves they should be included in a bibliographical description of the book, but if only binder's fly-leaves, ignored.

Blank page. A page of a book on which nothing has been printed.

Blanket. 1. The packing used on the impression cylinder of a printing machine; it may consist of cloth, rubber or paper. 2. The resilient rubber sheet attached to a cylinder on to which the image to be printed is transferred, or offset, from the inked lithographic plate, and then offset on to the paper.

Blanket cylinder. *See* Offset printing.

Blanking. (*Binding*) An impression made on the cloth cover of a book with a heated brass stamp as a base for lettering or decorative stamping.

BLDSC. British Library Document Supply Centre, the former title of the Library's West Yorkshire site.

Bleach. The process of whitening pulp or cellulose, usually with a solution of chlorine.

Bleached Kraft. A white paper made from bleached sulphate wood pulp and used for a variety of purposes when strength is required, e.g. as a body paper for coating. *See also* Kraft Paper.

Bled. A book the letterpress or plates of which have been cut into by the binder is said to have been 'bled'. *See also* Cropped (1).

Bled off. Said of a book when the illustrations have been intentionally printed across the normal margins so that the final trim has brought some of the illustrations to the outside edges of the page.

Bleed. 1. To trim printed matter so close that the text or plates are cut into. *See also* Cropped (1), Cut, Trimmed, Uncut. 2. In the Diazotype process of reproduction, the dye image which has run or spread.

Bleeding. The diffusion of printing inks or colours into surrounding areas.

BLEND. Acronym for Birmingham and Loughborough Electronic Network Development. In 1980 the British Library made grants to both Birmingham and Loughborough Universities to facilitate a programme of research into communication through electronic networks. *See* Project Quartet.

Blind. Lettering on a book or other article without using gold leaf or colour.

Blind embossing. Raising paper in a pattern, or in the shape of letters, by means of dies but not using ink on the raised (i.e. embossed) parts. *See also* Embossing.

Blind P. The paragraph mark ¶. *See also* Paragraph mark, Reference marks.

Blind page. An unnumbered, and usually blank, page which is included in the overall pagination. These usually occur in the Preliminaries.

Blind reference. A reference in an index to a Catchword which does not occur in the index, or a reference in a catalogue or bibliography to a heading under which no entry will be found.

Blind stamping. Embossing lettering or a design on to book covers, whether by hand or in a press, without using gold leaf or colour. Also called 'Antique', 'Blind blocking' and 'Blind tooling'.

Blind tooling. *See* Tooling.

Blind-blocked. Lettering on book covers not inked or gilt, only embossed or impressed.

Blinded-in. A design which is impressed on a book cover with heated tools but not coloured or gilt.

BLISS. The British Library Information Sciences Services; a title adopted in 1988 for the library formerly known as the Library Association Library. The library was started in 1933, and financial responsibility passed to the BL in 1974. In 1997 the collection was moved, and merged into the stock of the BL at its St. Pancras site.

Bliss Bibliographic Classification. *See* Bibliographic Classification.

Bliss Classification Association. <www.sid.cam.ac.uk/bca/bcahome.htm> (BCA Secretary, Sidney Sussex College, Cambridge CB2 3HU, UK) Formed in May 1967 to replace the former British Committee for the Bliss Classification consequent upon the receipt of the copyright of the BC from the H. W. Wilson Company. Publishes *BC Bulletin* (a.). An Organization in Liaison (OiL) with CILIP. *See also* Bibliographic Classification.

Block. 1. To print with a solid shading at the bottom or sides, as a second impression in a different colour and in a projecting position. 2. In bookbinding, to emboss or letter book covers with a block or frame containing the entire device, and at one operation, as distinguished from die stamping. 3. A large stamp without a handle used in a blocking press by bookbinders for impressing a design on a book cover. 4. A type-high piece of wood, plastic or metal, bearing a design from which an impression can be made. A general term which includes line-blocks, half-tones, Electros, etc. 5. To secure a plate to its proper position for printing. 6. A piece of wood or metal on which a stereotype, electrotype or other plate is mounted to make it type high. 7. A piece of hard wood used by engravers. 8. The core of a roller on a lithographing press. 9. In photography, to paint over a part of a negative to prevent or modify its printing. 10. A stop in a catalogue drawer (Backslide).

Block books. Those printed from engraved blocks of wood. Block books originated in the Netherlands and in Germany after about 1410; most are dateable from 1460 to 1480. They were printed on one side of the leaf in a thin brownish ink. Generally they may be divided into three groups: 1. those which have pictures and words descriptive of the pictures engraved at the foot of the picture or in cartouches proceeding from the mouths of the principal figures; 2. those which have pictures on one page and a full page of explanatory text opposite, or form distinct and separate units on the same page; 3. those with xylographic text only. The *Biblia pauperum* and *Apocalypse of St. John* are well-known examples of Group 1; *Ars memorandi, Ars moriendi* and *Speculum humanae salvationis* of Group 2; and the *Donatus de Octo Partibus Orationis* of Group 3. Block books continued to be printed well into the sixteenth century and several of the later ones were printed on a press with printer's ink, in such instances often on both sides of the paper. Those printed on one side only of the paper are called 'anopisthographic'. Books printed from engraved wood blocks, are called 'xylographic' books. *See also* Opisthographic, Wood block, Woodcut, Xylography.

Block printing.   Making an illustration, or printing a design on paper or material, from wood or metal blocks with the design in relief.

Blocking.   The impressing of a gold leaf, metal foil, or other graphic medium into a book-cover by means of a stamp, 'brass' or Block (3) having a raised surface. The term is also applied to the impressing of type, blocks, etc., without any intervening media, this operation being known as 'blind-stamping'. Called 'Stamping' in the US.

Blocking foil.   A paper foil coated with gold, white metal or coloured pigment which is transferred to the leather or cloth cover of a book by means of a heated die used in a blocking press. The process using these materials is known as 'foil blocking'.

Blocking press.   A press using heated blocks to impress, or stamp, lettering, designs, etc., on the book covers and cases. In machine bookbinding, ribbons of blocking foil of varying widths are used; these contain their own glair or adhesive. The press is also used for blind or ink blocking, no heat being necessary for the latter process.

Block-pull.   A proof of an illustration or text engraved on a block as distinct from type.

Blog.   Truncation of web log or weblog, a frequently-updated and generally chronological listing of personal thoughts, activities and Web links. A blog is often a mixture of what is happening in a person's life and what is happening on the web, a kind of hybrid diary/guide site, although there is no one, fixed, approach. The trend gained momentum with the introduction of automated publishing systems such as Blogger <www.blogger.com>. The activity of updating a blog is blogging and one who keeps a blog is a blogger.

Blow up.   1. A photograph, jacket, book review, specimen page of a book, etc., greatly enlarged for exhibition or advertising purposes. *See also* Giant book.   2. In documentary reproduction a copy having a larger scale than the original; an enlargement or Projection print.

BLPES.   *See* British Library of Political and Economic Science.

Blue Book. A more lengthy British Government official publication of similar character to a White Paper printed with a blue paper cover. (The traditional blue cover is now used principally for Select Committee Reports and for certain Accounts and Papers presented to Parliament under statute.) The French colour is yellow; German, white; Italian, green. *See also* Green Paper, Parliamentary publications, White Paper.

Blue publisher. A publisher, as defined by the ROMEO project, that permits authors to Self archive only the post-print of their academic paper.

Blue-line print. 1. A positive print made by the Diazotype process. 2. A blue-print with blue lines on a white field, made by printing from a negative master.

Blueprint. A blue on white, or white on blue, print submitted by a block-maker as a rough proof before blocks are supplied. Also, a print produced by the Blueprint process.

Blueprint process. A method of reproducing documents whereby a sheet of paper, which has been treated with a preparation mainly consisting of ferro prussiate, together with the document, are exposed to powerful arc lamps. The paper is then developed by placing it in running water. A blue and white negative results and this can be used to produce a blue and white positive. Only single-sided documents which are perfect (having no creases or alterations) are suitable for reproduction by this process.

Bluetooth. <www.bluetooth.com> An open specification for seamless wireless short-range communications of data and voice between both mobile and stationary devices. The specification defines how mobile phones, computers and Personal digital assistants interconnect with each other, with computers, and with office or home telephones. The first generation of Bluetooth permits exchange of data at up to 1 Mbps.

Blurb. The publisher's description and recommendation of a book, usually found on the front flap of a book jacket. *See also* Puff.

BN. *See* Bibliothèque Nationale de France.

BNB. See British National Bibliography.

BNF. *See* Bibliothèque Nationale de France.

BOAI. *See* Budapest Open Access Initiative.

Board label. The label pasted on the inside of the front board of a library book to show ownership, and usually bearing a few of the more important rules. Also called a 'Book plate' or 'Book label'.

Board paper. *See* Paste down.

Boards. 1. The sheets of millboard, pasteboard or strawboard used for bookcovers. When covered with paper, a book so bound is said to be bound in 'paper boards', when covered with cloth, in 'cloth boards'. 2. The wooden boards used as covers in early binding. 3. A general term which includes pulp, index, paste, ivory and other forms of card used for printing. *See also* Bristol Board, Ivory Board. 4. The pieces of wooden board used by a binder to grip a book when pressing, cutting, backing, burnishing, etc.

Boar's Head Press. A private printing press founded 1931 by Christopher Sandford who afterwards acquired the Golden Cockerel Press.

BOBCATSSS. A series of conferences organized since 1992 by European higher education institutions teaching librarianship and information science. The acronym is formed from the initial letters of the city names of the founding organizations: Budapest, Oslo, Barcelona, Copenhagen, Amsterdam, Tampere, Stuttgart, Szombathely, Sheffield. From 1999, the conferences have been held under the auspices of EUCLID.

Bodleian Library. <www.bodley.ox.ac.uk> (Oxford OX1 3BG, UK) Originally founded in 1327, the Library passed to the University of Oxford in 1410; Humphrey, Duke of Gloucester, gave substantial sums of money for its expansion in the years 1411–1447. The library was partly dismantled as the college libraries grew, but Sir Thomas Bodley oversaw its restoration and it re-opened in 1602. From 1610 it has benefited from copyright deposit, confirmed by the Press Licensing Act of 1662. It holds over 6 million printed books, with fine collections of incunabula, manuscripts, and oriental manuscripts. The present Library consists of the Old Library, the Radcliffe Camera, the New Library, and seven dependent libraries.

Bodoni. An early Modern face roman type designed in 1790 by Giambattista Bodoni (1740–1813) of Parma, the most celebrated printer of his day. It was re-cut for contemporary printing in 1921. Characteristics are vertical stress, long ascenders and descenders, fine straight-line serifs, and thin hair lines.

Body. 1. (*Printing*) (i) The measurement (or thickness) from back to front of a type letter, slug, rule, lead etc. (ii) The part of a piece of movable type from the foot to the flat surface at the upper end, above which is the 'Shoulder' and from which the moulded letter rises. It comprises the 'Belly', 'Back', 'Feet', 'Sides', 'Pin mark', 'Nick' and 'Grooves'. Also called the 'Shank' or 'Stem'. 2. (*Paper*) The apparent weight of a sheet of paper.

Body matter. (*Printing*) The text, as distinct from display matter, or illustrations.

Body paper, or board. The foundation for art, chromo, coated, blueprint, gummed, photographic and other papers which are made by coating or treating with a composition of any kind. Also called 'base' or 'raw' paper.

Body size. *See* Type size.

Body type. Type, of 14 point or less, used for the main body of a composition, as distinguished from the display type used in headings, etc. It also includes sizes of type up to 24 point which may be used in book work. Display type may begin at 18 point.

Bogle International Library Travel Fund Award. An award made by the International Relations Committee of the American Library Association to enable an ALA member to attend an international conference for the first time.

Boiler. The part of paper-making machinery in which the raw material is boiled in water before it goes into the Breaker. Also called 'Kier'. *See also* Digester.

Bold face. Heavy-faced type, also called 'Full face' and 'Black face'. **This is bold face**, and is indicated in a MS. by wavy underlining. Bold face is usually used to give emphasis to certain words, and for headings. Most Fonts have a bold face based on the same design as the medium weight as well as the roman and italic. Bold face developed from the Clarendon face which has only slight contrast in the up and down strokes and was used, with other typefaces, for emphasis. Clarendon grew out of the Antique face, cut by Vincent Figgins prior to 1815, believed to be the earliest of the designs now generally known as Egyptian. It is peculiar in giving equal emphasis to the up and down strokes and serifs. *See also* Typeface.

Bole. (*Printing*) To reduce the height of type by shaving the feet. *See also* Armenian bole.

Bolognese letters. Manuscript lettering which originated at the legal school of the University of Bologna and was used as the basis for the Gothic types known as 'Rotunda'. It was introduced into Germany from Venice and was consequently often called 'Litterae Venetae' by the early German printers.

Bolt. The folded or doubled edge of paper at the head, tail or fore-edge of a sheet in an uncut or unopened book. These are known as head bolts, tail bolts or fore-edge bolts. The folded edge at the back of a sheet is referred to, not as a 'bolt', but as the 'last fold' or 'back fold'. *See also* Fold to paper, Fold to print, Open edge.

Bom proof. A proof which is specially printed and bound for submission to a book club.

Bone folder. A flat piece of bone 6 to 9 inches (15 to 23 cms) long, about 1 inch (2.5 cms) wide and 1/8 inch (3 mm) thick with rounded corners and edges which is used for rubbing along the fold of a sheet of paper to bend the fibres of the paper firmly into position, and in book repairing. *See also* Folding stick.

Book. 1. A set of sheets of paper bound along one edge and enclosed within protective covers to form a volume, especially a written or printed literary composition presented in this way. 2. A division of a literary work, which is separately published and has an independent physical existence, although its pagination may be continuous with other volumes. 3. At a Unesco conference in 1964 a book was defined as 'a non-periodical printed publication of at least forty-nine pages, exclusive of cover pages'. *See also* Pamphlet. 4. A collection (Fr. *assemblage*) of manuscript or printed leaves fastened together to form a volume or volumes, forming a Bibliographical unit. It is distinct from periodicals, and from other forms of material, such as films, prints, maps, etc. *See also* Adaptation, Document, Fascicle, Part, Printed book, Publication, Version, Volume, Work.

Book Aid International. <www.bookaid.org> (39–41 Coldharbour Lane, London SE5 9NR, UK) Formerly the Ranfurly Library Service; the new name was adopted in 1994 in an effort to raise its profile and expand its work. The charity has been combating the lack of books in developing countries for 50 years, and currently sends over 750,000 books each year to some 65 countries – mainly in sub-Saharan Africa – benefiting schools, colleges and libraries. Ranfurly Library Service was founded by Lady Ranfurly in the early 1950s when her husband was Governor General of the Bahamas.

Book auction sale. A method of selling second-hand books; it dates from the early seventeenth century, and is the usual method of selling large libraries or individual copies of rare or valuable books. The prices realized are recorded in *Book auction records* or the American *Book prices current*.

Book availability. A measure of library performance based on the actual finding of a required item on the library shelves. Problems experienced range from library/system malfunctions to patron misunderstandings.

Book band. A narrow strip, or band, of printed paper placed round a jacketed book to draw attention to it through, e.g. its cheap price, an award which had been made in respect of it, the 'book of the film', etc.

Book card. A piece of card or plastic material on which are written the means of identifying a particular book (usually some or all of the following: charging symbol, accession number, class number, author, title) and which is used in charging (i.e. recording) the loan of the book. Book cards are usually made of manilla, of different colours for different departments or classes of books, but plastic is often used because of its better handling properties and greater durability. Also called 'Charging card', and in America 'Book slip', 'Charge slip' and 'Charging slip'.

Book catalogue. A catalogue produced in book form. Also used as a synonym for Printed catalogue. Sometimes used synonymously for Page catalogue and 'Book form catalogue'.

Book classification. A general term covering bibliographical and bibliothecal classifications. Mostly refers to library classification for arrangements of books and documents on the shelves. Usually a broad classification.

Book cloth. Cotton or linen cloth (usually coloured) used for book covers.

Book Club. A publishing activity issuing to subscribing members, specially, and cheaply, printed books. The subjects of the books published may be restricted to one subject; the books have usually been published before, although in some cases very recently, and are limited in number in any one year.

Book Club edition. A book sold by a Book Club to its members. Such books may not be the same edition, reprint, issue or impression as are normally available through trade channels to the public; they are usually specially printed and bound.

Book collecting. The assembling of books which because of their bibliographical interest, their contents (historic or factual), the history of the individual copies, or their rarity, have some permanent interest to the collector.

Book coupon. *See* Unesco coupons.

Book cover. *See* Cover.

Book cradle. A device intended to support an open volume while being exhibited or used. The cradle is made of foam rubber blocks which can be arranged on a flat plane where the book is on display and open at a particular page, or placed together at angles of about 45°. Cradles help to prevent damage to the spine of fragile books.

Book crafts. The operations which are carried out in producing books and which require varying degrees of skill in their performance; these include paper-making, printing, design of books, design and production of illustrations, and binding.

Book decoration. The impressing of a design on the cover of a book, often by gold (but sometimes blind) tooling. The design so impressed.

Book detection system. Equipment, normally consisting of two upright panels through which all library users must exit, which detects whether books and other library materials have been issued before being removed. Each item is fitted with a Trigger which is 'de-sensitized' at issue and then 're-sensitized' on return to stock. Items which are not de-sensitized sound an alarm when passing through the system and can also lock a security gate or exit door. Also referred to as 'security system'.

Book drop. A box or chute provided so that readers can return books when a library is closed or where drive-in facilities are available.

Book end. *See* Book support.

Book fair. 1. An event, festival or exhibition in which books play a prominent role, maybe including readings, book signings by authors, trade stands, or promotional activities. 2. Trade exhibitions of books with the object of selling and exchanging books. Some, particularly those held at Frankfurt and Leipzig before the Second World War, became world famous. The Frankfurt Book Fair has in recent years developed into an important international means of selling books and encouraging translation of books into other languages.

Book form. Said of a work published as a book but which has been issued previously in serial form, usually in a periodical.

Book fund. The fund, or amount of money, which is available for the purchase of books and other stock for a library.

Book hand. A style of artificial, calligraphic handwriting used for books (as distinct from the cursive styles used by individuals for records, memoranda, correspondence, etc.), before the introduction of printing. Uncial, Caroline minuscule, Gothic, and Humanistic are book hands. Bastard, and Chancery are not.

Book History Online (BHO). *See* ABHB.

Book holder.   (*Reprography*) A device for holding open a bound volume in a level or near-level plane so that all parts of the image are in focus during reproduction.

Book hunter.   One whose occupation is the tracing of specific titles in the second-hand market, sometimes at the request of a would-be purchaser.

Book illustration.   The making of drawings or paintings to illustrate the text of a book. The resulting illustration.

Book Industry Communication (BIC).   <www.bic.org.uk> (39–41 North Road, London N7 9DP, UK) Set up in 1991, with sponsorship from the Publishers Association, the Booksellers Association, the Library Association (now CILIP), the British Library and the main system suppliers and individual book trade companies. The brief is to facilitate communication throughout the industry, and promote standards for the format and transmission of bibliographical data and related commercial messages. BIC is the British partner in EDItEUR.

Book Industry Study Group, Inc (BISG).   (160 Fifth Avenue, New York, NY 10010, USA) A voluntary research organization with some 250 members from all sectors of the US book trade. Aims to increase readership, improve distribution of books, and examine the market. Promotes and supports research into reading and the book and publishing industries. Major trade and professional organizations are members.

Book Item and Component Identifier.   *See* BICI.

Book jacket.   The paper wrapping covering a book as issued by the publisher. It serves the purposes of protecting the book, and if illustrated (as it usually is), of attracting attention. It bears the name of the author, the title, and usually has a Blurb on the first flap, and elsewhere, particulars of other books by the same author or issued by the same publisher. Also called 'Dust cover', 'Dust jacket', 'Dust wrapper', 'Jacket', 'Wrapper'.

Book label.   *See* Board label, Book plate.

Book list.   A list of books, usually on some specific subject and arranged in classified or author order.

Book number.   1. The number, letter, or other symbol or combination of symbols used to distinguish an individual book from every other book in the same class, and at the same time to arrange books bearing the same class number in the desired order on the shelves, by author, title, edition, date of publication, etc. It usually consists of the (a) Author mark, (b) Title mark, (c) Volume number, (d) Edition mark. Also called 'Book mark'. *See also* Call number.   2. In the Colon Classification it follows the Collection number and precedes the class number to form the Call number; it is the symbol used to fix the position of a book in relation to other books having the same Ultimate class. *See also* Associated book, Author mark.

Book of Armagh.   *See* Bibles.

Book of Cerne.   *See* Bibles.

Book of Hours. The name given to books of private devotions designed for the laity; they were very popular and in general use throughout the Catholic Church from the fourteenth to the sixteenth centuries. Both before and after the discovery of printing they were often beautifully illuminated, and fine examples of them are today much coveted by collectors. Great personages were fond of having these books made specially for themselves, with decorations and illustrations of an individual appeal.

Book of Kells. *See* Bibles.

Book paper. A name given to paper manufactured for books to distinguish it from newsprint, cover paper and writing paper.

Book plate. A label pasted in a book to mark its ownership and sometimes to indicate its location in a library. Private book plates are often ornate or artistic: simpler and smaller ones bearing merely the owner's name are called 'book labels'.

Book pocket. The strong paper receptacle like the corner of an envelope pasted on the inside of the board of a book to take the book card.

Book preparation. *See* Processing.

Book press. 1. A press, usually of wood or steel, into which books are placed during binding or repairing processes. 2. *See* Bay, Book stack, Bookcase, Press (1), Tier.

Book processing. *See* Processing.

Book processing center (US). A co-operative organization operated for a group of libraries where the ordering and processing of books (cataloguing, preparation) is undertaken for all the participants, whether as a separate service or as one of other services.

Book production. The art and craft of making books including designing, choice and use of materials, illustration, printing and binding.

Book rest. A portable fitting similar to the music rest of a piano which is placed at a convenient angle for reading on a table or desk to hold a book when notes are being made from it.

Book review. An evaluation or personal opinion of a book published in a periodical or newspaper, broadcast on radio or television, or appearing on the Internet.

Book sale. A sale organized by a library to dispose of surplus and out-of-date stock.

Book satchel. A bag used in mediaeval times for carrying books. It frequently hung from a cleric's habit cord or on a warrior's belt.

Book security system. *See* Book detection system.

Book selection. The process of choosing books for inclusion in a library with a view to providing a balanced stock.

Book shrine. A box or chest, usually ornamented, in which valuable books were placed in mediaeval times. *See also* Cumdach.

Book sizes. Book sizes nowadays are expressed in metric terms (*see* Metric book sizes) but the traditional British sizes, in inches, are listed below:

	Octavos			Quartos		
Pott	$6^{1}/_{4}$	x	4	8	x	$6^{1}/_{4}$
Foolscap	$6^{3}/_{4}$	x	$4^{1}/_{4}$	$8^{1}/_{2}$	x	$6^{3}/_{4}$
Crown	$7^{1}/_{2}$	x	5	10	x	$7^{1}/_{2}$
Large Crown	8	x	$5^{1}/_{4}$	$10^{1}/_{2}$	x	8
Large Post	$8^{1}/_{4}$	x	$5^{1}/_{4}$	$10^{1}/_{2}$	x	$8^{1}/_{4}$
Demy	$8^{3}/_{4}$	x	$5^{5}/_{8}$	$11^{1}/_{4}$	x	$8^{3}/_{4}$
Post	8	x	5	10	x	8
Small Demy	$8^{1}/_{2}$	x	$5^{5}/_{8}$	$11^{1}/_{4}$	x	$8^{1}/_{2}$
Medium	9	x	$5^{3}/_{4}$	$11^{1}/_{2}$	x	9
Small Royal	$9^{1}/_{4}$	x	$6^{1}/_{8}$	$12^{1}/_{2}$	x	10
Royal	10	x	$6^{1}/_{4}$	$12^{1}/_{2}$	x	10
Super Royal	$10^{1}/_{4}$	x	$6^{3}/_{4}$	$13^{1}/_{2}$	x	$10^{1}/_{4}$
Imperial	11	x	$7^{1}/_{2}$	15	x	11

See also Octavo, Paper sizes, Size.

American book sizes are given below: in several instances there are minor differences between these and the British sizes with a common name. The sizes are not absolute.

Name	*inches*		
Thirty-sixmo	4	x	$3^{1}/_{3}$
Medium thirty-twomo	$4^{3}/_{4}$	x	3
Medium twenty-fourmo	$5^{1}/_{2}$	x	$3^{5}/_{8}$
Medium eighteenmo	$6^{2}/_{3}$	x	4
Medium sixteenmo	$6^{3}/_{4}$	x	$4^{1}/_{2}$
Cap octavo	7	x	$7^{1}/_{4}$
Duodecimo	$7^{1}/_{2}$	x	$4^{1}/_{2}$
Crown octavo	$7^{1}/_{6}$	x	5
Post octavo	$7^{1}/_{2}$	x	$5^{1}/_{2}$
Medium duodecimo	$7^{2}/_{3}$	x	$5^{1}/_{8}$
Demy octavo	8	x	$5^{1}/_{2}$
Small quarto (usually less)	$8^{1}/_{2}$	x	7
Broad quarto (varies up to 13 x 10)	$8^{1}/_{2}$	x	7
Medium octavo	$9^{1}/_{2}$	x	6
Royal octavo	10	x	$6^{1}/_{2}$
Super Royal octavo	$10^{1}/_{2}$	x	7
Imperial quarto	11	x	15
Imperial octavo	$11^{1}/_{2}$	x	$8^{1}/_{4}$

(The first column gives the vertical height.)

See also Metric book sizes.

Book slip. *See* Book card.

Book stack. A room which is equipped to shelve large numbers of little-used books in as small a space as possible. *See also* Book press, Bookcase, Compact storage, Press (1), Tier.

Book stamp.   An ownership mark made by means of an ink impression from a metal or rubber stamp, embossed, on the title-page, cover or end-paper of a book.

Book stock.   The whole of the books comprising a library.

Book store.   1. A room or stack in which books are kept.   2. A book shop.

Book support.   A sliding metal 'V' or similar integral to library shelving and which can be moved along the shelf as books are added or removed to keep the row upright. Also called 'Book end'.

Book token.   A greetings card to which stamps of various values can be attached; the stamps are purchased from, and exchanged at, bookshops for books of the appropriate value.

Book trade.   The organized business of selling books. The term usually relates to the whole national organization involving booksellers and their organizations together with the publishers and their organizations.

Book trolley.   A wheeled trolley about 3 feet long, with two or three shelves accessible from each side which is used for conveying books to different parts of a building. Special adaptations are made for taking books to patients in hospital wards. Also known as 'book truck'.

Book trough.   A short V-shaped shelf for displaying books on a flat surface.

Book truck.   See Book trolley.

Book Trust.   <www.booktrust.org.uk> (Book House, 45 East Hill, London SW18 2QZ, UK) The National Book League, founded as the National Book Council in 1924, was reconstituted as Book Trust in 1986. It is an independent body that promotes books and reading, supported by the book trade, the Arts Council and subscription income. Operates an information service, library, reference collection of recent children's books, organizes exhibitions, issues booklists and guides, and administers several literary prizes. Administers the BookStart programme.

Book Week.   A local or national event in which librarians, often with the co-operation of booksellers and publishers, arrange book displays and lectures, with the object of stimulating interest in books, particularly amongst children. These are arranged on a national scale more frequently in the US, where in addition to the general book week, others dealing with a particular type of book are arranged, as Religious Book Week, Catholic Book Week.

Bookbinder.   A person whose occupation is the binding of books.

Bookbinding.   1. The act or process of binding a book, whereby the sheets are sewn or otherwise fastened into a permanent cover of book-binder's board, the sides and back of which are covered with leather or cloth, or other suitable material.   2. The strong covering of the book.

Bookbinding board.   A board (*See* Boards) used as a component in making covers of hardback books.

Bookbinding stamp.   A tool with an embossed design which is used to impress a design on the cover of a book.

Bookcase. A case with shelves for books; it may or may not have doors. *See also* Bay, Book press, Book stack, Press (1), Tier.

Booker Prize. *See* Man Booker Prize.

Bookform index. An index having the physical form of a book, the terms, or headings, followed by their appropriate references, being printed and bound up in the form of a book.

Booklet. A small book in a paper cover or in very light binding.

Bookmark. 1. A piece of paper or other material placed between the leaves of a book to mark a place. Bookmarks are frequently used as a means of advertising. It may take the form of a piece of ribbon fastened in the 'hollow' back of a book, i.e. between the back folds of the sections and the spine. Also called 'Book marker'. 2. An electronic marker – also known as 'Favourite' – placed in an Application, Web browser or Client to permit an End user to move quickly to frequently used information sources or sections of a package.

Bookmark list. A list of books printed in the form of a bookmark.

Bookmobile. A large van, equipped with shelves and a book-issuing desk, which the public may enter to select books for home reading. Also called a 'Mobile library' or 'Travelling library'.

Books for All. A Unesco/IFLA project established in 1973 to help support libraries in developing countries; fundraising efforts are held world-wide. A high-profile anniversary event was held at the 1998 IFLA Conference in Amsterdam.

Bookseller. A retail dealer having a varied selection of books covering a wide range of subjects. Sometimes second-hand or antiquarian books may be stocked.

Booksellers Association of Great Britain and Ireland. <www.booksellers. org.uk> (272 Vauxhall Bridge Road, London SW1V 1BA, UK) Founded in 1895, the Association exists to promote and protect the interests of bookselling businesses of all sizes, including independent, chain and multiple bookshops. The Association aims to help book-sellers become more profitable and efficient by assisting them to increase sales and develop the market; by helping them to reduce costs, by fighting for better distribution in the trade; by giving advice on all aspects of bookselling, including training, trade practice, marketing and starting a bookselling business. It provides a forum for booksellers and represents their interests on a national and international level. There is a sub-group for Library Booksellers.

Bookshelf. *See* Shelf.

Bookshop. A retail outlet specializing in books.

Bookstall. A 'stand', of temporary or permanent design, at which books are sold, the vendor usually being on the inside and the purchaser on the outside of the stand.

BookStart. Originally an initiative of the Book Trust in 1992 to encourage parents to share books with children from a very early age, the programme ran in Birmingham (UK) with 300 participants. In 1998 commercial sponsorship became available and the scheme was extended nationwide; at the 8-month health check almost all UK babies receive a bag of new books and a library membership card. Over 560,000 babies each year are now covered by the scheme; from 2004 British government funding of £1.8 million from the Sure Start Unit has been added to the book industry's support of £5.6 million.

Bookwork. The branch of the printing industry, particularly typesetting, which is concerned with book production.

Bookworm. 1. The larva of a moth or beetle which burrows into the covers and pages of books. 2. A person who reads voraciously.

Boolean logic. A technique of using the most basic conceivable forms of expression to represent any logical possibility, i.e. a thing either exists or does not exist, is either present or not present, operative or not operative, etc. It was first developed and codified by the English mathematician George Frederick Boole (1815–1864). The use of the terms 'and', 'or', 'not' in formulating online search commands is based on Boolean logic. *See also* Reverse Polish Notation.

Boot. The operation of powering-up a computer, derived from the expression 'to pull up by one's bootstraps'.

BOPCAS. <www.soton.ac.uk/~bopcas> British Official Publications Current Awareness Service, BOPCAS was inaugurated in July 1995 from a grant awarded as part of the NFF Programme following the Follett Report. Until December 1998 all services were free of charge but after this date subscription value-added services – keyword searching, abstracting service, hypertext linking, browsing by category and e-mail alerting services – were introduced. Previously known as NUKOP (New UK Official Publications), the site is operated by the Ford Collection of British Official Publications in the Hartley Library at the University of Southampton, and by Aslib.

BOPCRIS. <www.bopcris.ac.uk> British Official Publications Collaborative Reader Information Service provides a searchable and browsable web-based bibliographic database on British Official Publications covering the period 1688–1995. In addition to abstracts and locations of the original documents, digitized full text of a limited number of documents is provided.

Border. 1. (*Bibliography*) An ornamental enclosure of a title-page or a substantial part of it, or of a page of type, illuminated manuscript or body of printed matter; or merely an ornamental design placed on one or more sides of the above. *See also* Block (4), Compartment, Frame, Rule border. 2. (*Binding*) Ornamentation placed close to the edges of the sides of a book-cover or the spine of a volume. To be distinguished from Frame. 3. (*Printing*) A continuous decorative design arranged around matter. It can consist of continuous cast strips of plain or patterned rule, or be made up of repeated units of Flowers.

Born digital. Used to describe a document for which no previous version exists in traditional (e.g. paper, film, slide) analogue format.

Borrower.   *See* Reader (2).

Borrower's ticket (card).   The membership card entitling the holder to borrow books from a library.

Borrowers' register.   A list of members of a library. Also called Borrowers' index.

Boss.   A metal knob, often ornamented, fixed upon the covers of books, usually at the corners and centre, for protection and embellishment.

Bottom edge.   The Tail of a book. Also called 'Lower edge', 'Tail edge'.

Bottom margin.   *See* Tail margin.

Bottom note.   *See* Footnote.

Bound.   A book which is sewn or otherwise fastened into stiff boards.

Bound term.   (*Indexing*) A heading, or term, consisting of more than one word. *See also* Collateral term, Generic term.

Bound volume.   Any book that is bound; usually a number of issues of a periodical comprising a volume and bound.

Bound with.   A term used by cataloguers when referring to books published separately but subsequently bound together.

Boundary straps.   *See* Deckle straps.

Bound-to-Stay-Bound Scholarships.   Two annual awards to support students of library work with children; administered by the Association for Library Service to Children.

Bourdillon Report.   The Report of the Working Party appointed by the (UK) Minister of Education in March 1961, *Standards of public library service in England and Wales*, 1962. H. T. Bourdillon was Chairman of the Working Party. This, together with the Baker Report, formed the basis of parliamentary discussions and the framing of the Public Libraries and Museums Act of 1964.

Bourgeois.   An obsolete name for a size of type equal to 9 pt.

Boustrophedon writing.   Derived from *boustrophedon*, Greek for 'as the ox ploughs'; refers to primitive writing in which alternate lines run from left to right and then from right to left – the pattern that would be made by an ox ploughing a field. The letters in the lines commencing at the right are reversed as if mirrored.

Bow bracket.   *See* Brace.

Bowdlerized.   A text which is altered by changing or omitting words or passages considered offensive or indelicate: after Thomas Bowdler who in 1818 published an expurgated edition of Shakespeare.

Bowker/Ulrich Serials Librarianship Award.   An annual award instituted in 1985 by the R. R. Bowker Company and presented under the auspices of the American Library Association. Rewards outstanding service in the field of serials librarianship.

Bowl.   The full rounded and entirely enclosed portion of a type letter as in O, B, D, b, a; the part enclosing a closed Counter.

Box.   (*Printing*) 1. An area within a larger type area, or within or between type columns, formed by rules or white spaces with the object of emphasizing what is printed within.   2. A rectangular or square border of one or more lines placed around type matter, and made up of rules which may be mitred or butted.

Box file. A container made to stand on a shelf, and intended primarily to contain flimsy material such as correspondence or newspaper cuttings. The most durable kinds are those with wooden sides, board base and hinged lid, the whole being covered with cloth and/or paper and lined with paper. A spring clip is usually provided to keep the contents in position. *See also* Pamphlet box, Solander case.

Box in. To place rules around type matter so that the characters when printed appear in a frame or box.

Box library. Boxes containing standard sets of books catering for different tastes and supplied in developing countries by community development organizations to community centres in rural areas for circulation from village to village.

Boxed. A work in two or three volumes inserted into a container to display them, keep them together, or protect them.

Boxhead. 1. A series of printed or ruled lines for headings in a ruled table. 2. A cut-in head with a frame around it. Also called 'Box heading'.

Boxhead ruling. The space at the top of a ruled column for the insertion of hand-written headings for each column.

Boyet style. A style of book decoration practised by Luc Antoine Boyet, who worked in France in the eighteenth century for Count Hoym. It is characterized by a plain border, ornamental corners and edges, and a central monogram or device. Boyet is sometimes credited with introducing Doublures.

Boys and Girls House, Toronto. Established in 1922 by the Toronto Public Library as a library for children, it is now an international centre for those concerned with library work for children. It includes the Osborne and Lillian H. Smith Collections.

BRA. *See* British Records Association.

Brace. (*Printing*) A bracket } cast on its own body, usually to a definite number of ems. Formerly called 'Vinculum'. A *sectional brace* is made of several parts which can be assembled to the length required; the middle position is called a Cock.

Bracket shelf. A shelf secured temporarily or permanently for display purposes at the end of a bookcase.

Bracket shelving. Adjustable shelving where the shelves rest, or are fixed, on brackets, which are secured to the rear upright stanchions of steel shelving fixtures, and which also serve as book supports. Also called 'Suspension shelving'. Sometimes the brackets simply support the shelves from underneath; this type is also called 'Cantilever shelving'.

Brackets. Rectangular enclosing marks [ ]. Used in cataloguing to indicate something which does not appear in the original but is added by the cataloguer. To be distinguished from Curves ( ). Angle brackets < > are used to enclose matter which itself appears in [ ] on the title-page; with the advent of electronic communication, angle brackets have also come to be used for identifying e-mail addresses and urls in text passages. Also called 'Angular marks', 'Square brackets'. *See also* Curves.

Bradel binding. A type of temporary binding said to have originated in Germany, and first adopted in France by a binder named Bradel.

Bradford's Law of Scattering. *See* Law of Scattering.

Braille. A system of reading and writing for the blind in which the letters are formed by raised dots embossed into the paper in groups of six, three high and two wide. Named after the inventor Louis Braille (1809–52), a blind Frenchman.

Braille Book Bank. *See* NBA.

Branch. *See* Branch library.

Branch and Mobile Libraries Group. A membership group of CILIP, first formed in 1966.

Branch library. 1. A library other than the main one in a system. It usually comprises adult lending and children's departments, a quick-reference collection and possibly a news-room, and is intended to meet the library needs of the surrounding population, particularly in the matter of books for home-reading. It is housed in premises set aside for the purpose, is specially equipped and furnished, and staffed by trained assistants. The book stock is a permanent one. 2. In a college or university, a collection of books and other materials housed in a separate area and serviced by its own staff. It is centrally administered and can be on the same campus as the main library.

Branching classification. A classification with two or more sub-classes, or main branches, each subdivided again, and perhaps again and again. It may be converted into a Tabular classification. Also called a 'Ramifying classification'.

Branching Out. <www.branching-out.net> An online public library outreach and reader development programme. Staff development, stock development, reading groups and similar initiatives are in progress. The Society of Chief Librarians is the organizer of the programme, and 'Opening the Book' is the contractor; funded by the Arts Council England, which has provided £190,000 in 2003/2004 and indicated ongoing support for two further years.

Brand name. *See* Trademark.

Brass rule. *See* Rule.

Brayer. Formerly a wooden pestle, round in shape and flat at one end with a handle on the other, used to spread ink on the block to an even depth and consistency before being taken up by the ink balls. Later, a hand-roller for distributing the ink before it is taken up by forme rollers. Also used when making a galley proof.

Break (Break up). (*Printing*) To dispose of a Forme of printing matter by separating material to be re-melted from furniture, blocks, rules, foundry type, etc. *See also* Distributing.

Breaker. A part of the machinery used to make paper; it is a tub-like vessel into which the raw material is placed after boiling in the 'boiler' or 'kier' in order that it may be washed and further broken to reduce and separate the fibres. Also called 'Beater' or 'Hollander'.

Break-line. The last line of a paragraph where quads are needed to fill out the last space. In good typesetting it does not begin a new page. *See also* End a Break, End even, Run on.

Breviary. The book of daily Divine Office used in the Roman Catholic Church. It contains: 1. Calendar; 2. Psalter; 3. Proprium de Tempore (collects and lessons); 4. Proprium Sanctorum (collects, etc., for Saints' Days); 5. Commune Sanctorum (collects, etc., for Saints without special services); 6. Hours of the Virgin, burial services, etc., i.e. Small Offices. It contains neither the Communion Service nor the Mass.

Brevier. An obsolete name for a size of type equal to about 8 pt.

BRICKS. <www.cordis.lu/ist/directorate_e/digicult/bricks.htm> An FP6 project that aims to establish the organizational and technological foundations of a digital library at the level of a European Digital Memory: a networked system of services over globally available collections of multimedia digital documents, providing different knowledge layers for a variety of users and access modes.

Brief. 1. A letter of authority. 2. A letter of the pope to a religious community, or an individual upon matters of discipline, and differing from a Bull by being less solemn and ample, and in the form in which it is written. 3. A letter patent which used to be issued by the sovereign as head of the church, licensing a collection to be made in churches for a specified object or charity 4 A written description of the requirements for a building to be designed, and supplied to an architect so that plans may be prepared. It sets out the purpose of the building and its various rooms or departments, indicating their size, shape and juxta-position, and any special features to be provided.

Brief cataloguing. Simplified cataloguing, especially in respect of details after the imprint, for books that are likely to go into a storage centre, for pamphlets, and for other special categories. *See also* Limited cataloguing, Simplified cataloguing.

Brieflisting. (*Cataloguing*) A method of briefly cataloguing books which pose problems for the cataloguer, as a means of temporarily reducing a backlog of cataloguing arrears.

Brilliant. An obsolete name for a size of type about 4 pt.

Bring up. To bring a block up to the correct printing height by using underlay or interlay.

Briquet. A conventional representation on a bookbinding of a steel used with tinder for striking a light.

Bristol board. A fine quality board made from rags and used for drawings or paintings. It is made by pasting two or more sheets of paper together, the substance being determined by the number of sheets.

Britain in Print. <www.britaininprint.net> A participative project involving eight CURL libraries with the Edinburgh Royal College of Physicians and the Mitchell Library in Glasgow to enhance electronic access to significant collections of pre-1700 British books which were not previously catalogued in electronic form. Work will also embrace the creation of a subject-based interpretative resource to add value to the discovery information for special interest groups such as school-age learners, local history groups, genealogical societies and life-long learners. The project is supported by the Heritage Lottery Fund.

British and Irish Association of Law Librarians (BIALL). <www.biall. org.uk> Founded 1969; the principal aim of the Association is to promote the better administration and exploitation of law libraries and legal information units, by further education and training, through the organization of meetings and conferences, the publication of useful information, the encouragement of bibliographical study and research in law and librarianship, and co-operation with other organizations and societies. The Association holds meetings and conferences, publishes a newsletter, a journal *Law Librarian, Manual of Law Librarianship, Directory of Law Libraries*.

British Architectural Library. <www.architecture.com/go/architecture/ reference/library> A national collection maintained by the Royal Institute of British Architects (RIBA).

British Archives. Foster, J. and Sheppard, J. (eds.) *British archives: a guide to archive resources in the United Kingdom.* 4th ed., Palgrave, 2002. (ISBN: 0 333 73536 6).

British Association for Information and Library Education and Research. *See* BAILER.

British Association for Open Learning (BOAL). <www.baol.co.uk> (Suite 12, Pixmore House, Pixmore Avenue, Letchworth SG6 1JG, UK) BAOL promotes quality and best practice in open, flexible and distance learning throughout the education and training sectors in the UK and overseas. Membership is drawn from corporate users, government agencies, consultants, research organizations, business support organizations. It collaborated with the (UK) Library Association (now CILIP) in the 'Open for Learning' programme which enabled library services and others to set up open learning centres.

British Association of Picture Libraries and Agencies. *See* BAPLA.

British Book Design and Production Awards. Various annual prizes awarded by the British Printing Industries Federation.

British Business Schools Librarians Group (BBSLG). <www.bham.ac. uk/is/BBSLG> An independent group, open to librarians specializing in business information and working in universities or colleges which offer courses in business or management at postgraduate level.

British Catalogue of Music (BCM). <www.csa.com/csa/journals. britmuzcat> A catalogue of music and books about music published in Great Britain and consisting of entries made from material deposited under the Copyright Acts at the Copyright Receipt Office at the British Library. Publication began in 1957 under the auspices of the Council of the British National Bibliography. Publication is now commercially handled by Cambridge Scientific Abstracts. A faceted scheme of classification, drawn up by E. J. Coates, former Editor of the *Catalogue*, was used for arranging entries until 1981. From 1982 arranged by the Dewey Decimal Classification *Revision of 780 Music* (Forest Press, 1980). Originally published quarterly, now three times p.a.

British Catalogue of Music Classification. The scheme, drawn up by E. J. Coates, which was used to classify the entries in the *British Catalogue of Music*.

British Copyright Council. <www.britishcopyright.org.uk> (Copyright House, 29–33 Berners Street, London W1T 3AB, UK) An umbrella organization for those who create or hold rights in literary, dramatic, musical and artistic works and for those who perform such works. Its aims are to foster the principles of copyright, act as a forum for liaison, to monitor the law and to act as a pressure group for improvements in British, European and international copyright legislation. The Council strongly promotes the Copyright Licensing Agency.

British Council. <www.britishcouncil.org> (Bridgewater House, 58 Whitworth Street, Manchester M1 6BB, UK) Established in 1934, and incorporated by Royal Charter in 1940, the Council promotes a wider knowledge of Britain abroad, develops cultural relations with other countries, and administers educational aid programmes. It maintains some 200 libraries or knowledge and learning centres overseas and operates support schemes for book purchasing and library development. It is currently promoting the concept of the Information Society in developing countries.

British Educational Communications and Technology agency. *See* BECTa.

British Film Institute. <www.bfi.org.uk> (21 Stephen Street, London W1N 1LN, UK) The British Film Institute is a grant-aided cultural and educational organization founded in 1933, and its aims include the stimulation of appreciation and study of the cinema and television as art, and entertainment, and as a record of contemporary society. A further aim is to maintain and preserve a national repository of films of permanent value and this has now been extended to include television. The BFI maintains the National Film Archive, and operates the BFI National Film Library, a research collection with an emphasis on film and television in the UK.

British Institute of Recorded Sound Ltd. *See* National Sound Archive.

British Interactive Multimedia Association (BIMA). <www.bima. co.uk> (Briarlea House, Southend Road, South Green, Billericay CM11 2PR, UK) BIMA was established in 1985 as the British Interactive Video Association. It was the first organization in Europe to create a professional body to represent commercial interests. BIMA is dedicated to the idea of attracting the full range of specialist services in the multimedia industry in a single organization to allow for free exchange of information and to initiate activity. Members include end-users, application developers, distributors, lawyers, publishers, hardware manufacturers, etc.

British Internet Publishers Alliance (BIPA). <www.bipa.co.uk> Founded in 1998, BIPA has in membership publishers and broadcasters with an interest in Internet publishing, and Internet businesses. Its main aims include the growth and development of the sector, copyright issues and data protection.

British Library. <www.bl.uk> (96 Euston Road, London NW1 2DB, UK; Boston Spa, Wetherby, West Yorkshire LS23 7BQ, UK) The national library of the UK, funded by government through the Department for Culture, Media and Sport. It is the national deposit library and has benefited under the Copyright Acts since the Royal Library (which had enjoyed the right since 1662) was transferred to the British Museum in 1757. The British Library was formed in 1973 following the recommendations of the Dainton Report and the passing of the British Library Act 1972, amalgamating the former British Museum Library, National Central Library, National Lending Library for Science and Technology, and the British National Bibliography. The Library's London site was opened in 1998, and contains the reference collections except for the Newspaper Library in Colindale.

The Library is organized into six directorates under a Chief Executive; these are Human Resources, Operations and Services, Finance and Corporate Resources, Strategic Marketing and Communications, Scholarship and Collections, and Electronic Information Services. Services are grouped as follows: Bibliographic Service, Conference Centre, Copy Services (including Patents), Current Awareness, Images Online, Information Services, Learning, National Preservation Office, Publishing and Bookshop, Reading Rooms. There has been substantial investment in digital library services. A nationwide initiative is currently highlighted – the Co-operation and Partnership Programme (CPP) involving many libraries throughout the country. In addition to books and journals, the collections comprise manuscripts, maps, music, newspapers, patents, reports, conferences and theses, philatelic, sound archive. There are substantial collections of early printed books and other national treasures. The British Library Public Catalogue contains over 10 million items and there are catalogues for special materials. An Integrated Library System is currently in process of implementation and the switch from various legacy systems will continue through 2004 and 2005.

British Library of Political and Economic Science. <www.lse.ac.uk/library> (London School of Economics, 10 Portugal Street, London WC2A 2HD, UK) Founded in 1896, BLPES holds over 4 million bibliographic items with strong collections in economics, political science, law (especially international law), sociology, history, geography, legislative and administrative reports. It is an important depository of official documents, and maintains many special collections. Publishes *International Bibliography of the Social Sciences*.

British Museum Library (BML). This Library ceased to exist as a part of the British Museum on its incorporation as a major part of the British Library. The British Museum (Natural History) Library was not so transferred.

British National Bibliographic Service. The title given to the range of bibliographic publications and aids produced by the Bibliographic Services of the British Library.

British National Bibliography (BNB). <www.bl.uk/services/bibliographic/natbib.html> Originally an organization which in 1950 began issuing a weekly printed list of books published in the UK; incorporated into the British Library in 1974. Full catalogue entries in accordance with AACR2 are made from books received at the Legal Deposit Office, classified by DC21 and with LCSH headings. Records are included for items in advance of publication (CIP) and from 2003 records have been made for electronic resources. Entries are now prepared in partnership with the Copyright Libraries Shared Cataloguing Programme. *BNB* is issued weekly on paper and monthly on CD-ROM; there are plans to change publication methods.

British National Bibliography for Report Literature. Monthly companion publication to *BNB*; lists newly-acquired non-trade publications – technical and other reports published in the UK by research organiz ations, universities, charities, pressure groups, etc. Published by the British Library National Bibliographic Service.

British National Committee on Palaeography. A sub-committee on manuscripts of the Standing Conference of National and University Libraries (SCONUL). *See also* SCONUL.

British National Film and Video Guide. Published by the British Library National Bibliographic Service from information supplied by the British Film Institute. The Catalogue ceased publication after the 2002 annual volume.

British Official Publications Collaborative Reader Information Service. *See* BOPCRIS.

British Official Publications Current Awareness Service. *See* BOPCAS.

British Phonographic Industry Ltd. <www.bpi.co.uk> (Riverside Building, County Hall, Westminster Bridge Road, London SE1 7JA, UK) The trade association for record companies in the UK, it was formally incorporated in 1973 but had its beginnings in the early 1930s when a few record companies then in existence formed the British Record Producers Association to deal with common problems in the legal and copyright areas. BPI also acts as a focal point both for its members and for individuals and organizations having dealings with the record industry. It provides regulatory, conciliation and co-ordinating services, deals with Government departments, and negotiates with a wide variety of organizations.

British Printing Industries Federation. <www.bpif.org.uk> Founded in 1903. Promotes and represents the interests of the printing industry in the UK and offers technical and legal consulting services. Publishes *Printing Industries* (12 p.a.).

British Record Society. <members.lycos.co.uk/carolyn_busfield/ brshome.html> (College of Arms, Queen Victoria Street, London EC4V 4BT, UK) Formed in 1889 with the object of preserving records and making them accessible to scholars by the publication of indexes in a series known as the *Index Library*. Over 80 volumes have been published relating to various categories of record, and in the last few decades they have been concerned almost exclusively with indexing testamentary records.

British Records Association (BRA). <www.hmc.gov.uk/bra> (Finsbury Library, 245 St. John's Street, London EC1 4NB, UK) Established 1932 to co-ordinate and encourage the preservation and use of all types of archives; to act as a forum for users, custodians and owners of archives, and to campaign on archival issues. The Records Preservation Section is largely funded by grants and donations, including a grant-in-aid from HM Treasury (administered through the Royal Commission on Historical Manuscripts). The Association has about 800 members, organizes an annual conference, publishes *Archives* (2 p.a.), *Newsletter* (2 p.a.) and various other pamphlets and guides.

British Standards Institution (BSI). <www.bsi.org.uk> (389 Chiswick High Road, London W4 4AL, UK) BSI was the first standards body to be formed; now there are over 100 similar organizations belonging to the International Organization for Standardization (ISO) and the International Electrotechnical Commission (IEC). BSI co-ordinates the views of British industry on world bodies in seeking to harmonize international standards; it performs the same function at European level in the European standards organizations CEN and CENELEC, where standards are developed that are critical to the completion of the single market. There are over 17,000 British Standard publications, and 2,000 are added or revised each year (published on paper, on fiche and on CD-ROM); they are drawn up by users, manufacturers, research organizations, government departments and consumers. All are made available for public comment before publication. *See also* Standards.

British Talking Book Service for the Blind. *See* NTBL.

British Theatre Association Library. <theatremuseum.vam.ac.uk> (Theatre Museum, Russell Street, Covent Garden, London WC2E 7PA, UK) An international centre for theatre research; founded in 1919 as the British Drama League, and containing the largest collection of play texts in Europe. The libraries of many theatrical families are represented in its holdings. The Library has recently been passed to the Theatre Museum.

British Universities Film and Video Council (BUFVC). <www.bufvc.ac.uk> (77 Wells Street, London W1T 3QJ, UK) Exists to encourage the use, production and study of audio-visual media, materials and techniques for teaching and research in higher education. It provides a forum for the exchange of information and experience in this field. Founded 1948 (as the British Universities Film Council). In 2003 BUFVC acquired over 3,000 hours of ITV News archives and this collection will be digitized as 'Newsfilm Online' with JISC support; it has also acquired British Pathé news content with some 12 million images.

Brittle books.   A phrase used to describe books whose paper has become so acidic and brittle that they are crumbling into dust. Such books cannot be handled as the paper is literally disintegrating.

Broad.   Applies to a sheet of paper which is divided by halving the long side (i.e. across the narrow way). This is the regular or common way of dividing a sheet. Hence a Broad folio, quarto, or octavo. The opposite of Oblong. A broad fold is a sheet folded so that the longest dimension is horizontal; the grain then runs with the shorter dimension of the paper.

Broad classification.   1. Use of only the more inclusive classes of a classification scheme, omitting detailed subdivision. Also called 'Reduction of numbers'.   2. A classification scheme which does not provide for minute subdivision of topics.   3. An arrangement of books in main classes with little or no sub-division. *See also* Close classification (2).

Broad folio.   *See* Folio.

Broad System of Ordering.   *See* BSO.

Broadband.   A transmission facility having a bandwidth sufficient to carry multiple voice, video or data channels simultaneously. *See also* ADSL, ISDN, SDSL.

Broader term.   (*Information retrieval*) A term which denotes a concept which is broader than one with a more specific meaning, e.g. Science is broader than Anthropology. *See also* Narrower term, Related term.

Broadsheet.   A long, narrow advertising leaflet; usually the long quarto of the sheet of paper from which it is cut. It may be printed on both sides. Sometimes used synonymously with Broadside.

Broadside.   A large sheet of paper printed on one side right across the sheet, for sheet distribution, and usually intended to be posted up, e.g. proclamations, ballad sheets, news-sheets, sheet calendars, etc. *See also* Broadsheet. Also used of a poster of which the width is greater than the depth.

Broadside page.   *See* Landscape page.

Brochure.   Literally 'a stitched work' (from the French *brocher*, to stitch). A short printed work of a few leaves, merely stitched together (or these days stapled/'wire-bound'), and not otherwise bound, a pamphlet.

Broken back.   A book whose back has broken open from head to tail. Also called 'Broken binding'.

Broken letter.   One, the face of which is damaged and cannot give a complete impression. Indicated in a proof by placing a small x in the margin. Also called 'Bad letter', 'Battered letter', 'Damaged letter', 'Spoiled letter'.

Broken order. The removal of a section, or sections, of the book stock from its proper sequence in the classification in order to facilitate use.

Broken-over. A Plate or other separate sheet which is to be inserted in a book, and is given a narrow fold near the back, or binding, edge before sewing, etc., to ensure that it will lie flat and turn easily when the book is bound.

Broker. A Gateway that provides access to information or data from a range of sources and presents them to the end user in a co-ordinated, organized and balanced manner. *See also* Information broker.

Bromide. The Camera ready output from an Imagesetter, printed onto special 'bromide' paper.

Bronzing. Dusting with a fine metallic powder over a sheet freshly printed with ink, varnish or size to give a brilliant, lustrous effect.

Brothers of the Common Life. Monks who maintained monasteries in various parts of Germany and the Low Countries in the last quarter of the fifteenth century and set up printing presses in about sixty of them between 1475 and 1490. Their first dated book was issued in 1476 from the 'Nazareth' Monastery at Brussels.

Brown Classification. The familiar name for James Duff Brown's Subject Classification. *See also* Adjustable classification, Subject classification.

Brown (John Carter) Library. <www.brown.edu/facilities> A collection of 30,000 books dealing with the discovery and settlement of America to 1800; assembled by John Carter Brown (1797–1874) who was one of America's best-known book collectors. The library was passed on to Brown University, Providence, Rhode Island, USA, in 1900, since when it has grown considerably and is one of the finest collections of Americana in existence.

Brown mechanical woodpulp. A woodpulp for papermaking obtained by grinding steamed or boiled logs.

Browne book charging system. A system of book charging which is attributed to Nina E. Browne, an American librarian, who described it in 1895. It is, however, very little different from the method adopted about 1873 by L. G. Virgo, Librarian of Bradford Public Library, UK. The reader has a limited number of tickets, each of which is available for one book only at a time, and which are given up when books are borrowed and handed back when the books are returned. This simple, reliable and speedy method was replaced in America by the Newark and Detroit methods and others based on them, but, until photo-charging and computerized methods were introduced, was the most universally used method in Great Britain. 'Reverse Browne' uses a pocket book-card and a card ticket: this was described by Jacob Schwartz in 1897 and had been in use for a number of years. *See also* Charging methods/systems, Token charging.

Browsability. The ability of an indexing system to lend itself to unsystematic or random searches. This ability is of interest or use to the searcher even though it may not produce a logical answer to the search question.

Browse. To investigate, without design, the contents of a collection of books or documents.

Browser. (*Networking*) Another name for a Client, the Application which resides on the End users' PC to permit access to networked information sources; especially used to describe the clients – Web browsers – used in the World Wide Web.

Brush coated. Paper given a smooth printing surface by applying the clay, or other, coating substance as a separate and later operation to the actual paper making, in order to make it perfectly smooth so as to take a high degree of finish. *See also* Art, Coated paper, Machine coated.

Brush-pen. A pen, with a fibrous point, made of reed, used for writing on papyrus.

Brussels Convention. Popular name for the revision (signed on 26 June 1948) of the Berne Copyright Convention. *See also* Copyright, International.

Brussels expansion. A familiar name for the Universal Decimal Classification.

Bryant (E. T.) Memorial Prize. An award made by the Music Libraries Trust and the UK Branch of IAML, to a student or young professional for a significant contribution to the literature of music librarianship.

BS. British Standard. *See* British Standards Institution.

BSA. *See* Bibliographical Society of America.

BSI. *See* British Standards Institution.

BSO. Broad System of Ordering, a system (within the UNISIST programme) being developed to serve as a switching mechanism between individual classifications and thesauri in the process of information transfer, rather than as a new classification system. It will be an essential tool for systems interconnection and will play an essential part in ISDS.

BTJ. *See* Bibliotekstjänst.

Bubble jet printer. A type of Inkjet printer which uses thermally generated bubbles of ink to create the printout.

BUBL. <bubl.ac.uk> (Centre for Digital Library Research, Strathclyde University, 101 St James Road, Glasgow G4 0NS, Scotland) An information service which aims to 'provide value-added access to Internet resources and services of academic, research, and professional significance to the UK higher education community'. It has a special focus on library and information science and includes, for example, a directory of UK organizations and institutions, and links to current LIS journals and newsletters.

Buckle-folder. A machine which folds printed sheets by passing them between two continuously revolving rollers placed one above the other until the leading edge touches a stop bar. The rollers continue to impel the rear half of the sheet until it is folded and so carried down between the lower revolving roller and a third one which is parallel to it. *See also* Knife-folder.

Buckles. (*Binding*) Severe wrinkles near the head and back of the folded sections. *See also* Section (1).

Buckram. A strong textile, either of linen or cotton, used for covering books. *See also* Art canvas.

Budapest Open Access Initiative (BOAI). <www.soros.org/openaccess/ index.shtml> Published in February 2002 with the goal of achieving Open access to the peer-reviewed journal literature, the Initiative stresses that this can be achieved through two complementary strategies: Self archiving; and the creation of a new generation of Open access journals. The Initiative has been influential in moving forward the discussion of these issues internationally and led to further statements such as the Berlin Declaration.

Budget. The total amount of money which is available for library purposes after the estimate of anticipated needs has been approved by the appropriate authority.

Buds. In bookbinding, an ornament filling a small panel on some rolls: it is a conventionalized form of a spray bearing buds.

Buffer. 1. A substance, or mixture of substances, which in document preservation is used to control the acidity or alkalinity of a solution or paper at a pre-determined level, e.g. the use of chalk in the manufacture of paper. 2. A temporary memory data store, typically between two devices when input and output speeds differ.

BUFVC. *See* British Universities Film and Video Council.

Bug. A software problem, allegedly named after a moth that caused the failure of an early digital computer at Harvard University.

Building the New Library Network. *See New Library: the People's Network.*

Building-in machine. A machine which, in book production, dries cased books in a matter of seconds by means of several applications of heat and pressure. This is an alternative to the slower method of the Standing press.

Bulk. 1. The thickness of a book exclusive of its covers; this will be less after, than before, binding. Book papers are measured by the thickness of a number of pages. The extremes between which papers of the same weight, but of a different class, vary in bulk may be seen from the figures below , based on 320 pp. of quad crown 100 lb.

Featherweight	53/32 in.	Pure super – calendered	22/32 in.
Esparto M.F.	29/32 in.	Coated art	21/32 in.
Pure M.F.	24/32 in.	Imitation art	20/32 in.

2. The thickness of a sheet of paper related to its weight and measured

in thousandths of an inch. 3. To 'bulk' a book is to make it appear bigger than it need be by using a thick but lightweight paper.

Bull. A formal papal letter under the leaden seal (Bulla).

Bulletin. 1. A publication, generally a pamphlet, issued by a government, society or other organization at regular intervals and in serial form. 2. A periodical or occasional publication containing lists of books added to a library, and other library information.

Bulletin board. 1. An online asynchronous messaging facility on which discussions can be read by all subscribers and responses posted. It is asynchronous because discussions do not occur in real time, in contrast to a Chat room. Also known as 'BBS', 'bulletin board systems', and 'electronic bulletin boards' *See also* BUBL, Mailbase, Usenet. 2. A notice board in a library on which are exhibited lists of books, announcements of forthcoming events, jackets of new books added to the library, and miscellaneous library information.

Bullock Report. *A language for life, report of the Committee of Inquiry appointed by the Secretary of State for Education and Science under the Chairmanship of Sir Alan Bullock* published in 1975. The Committee was set up by Margaret Thatcher in 1972 when Secretary of State for Education and Science, to inquire into the teaching of reading and the other uses of English in UK Schools.

Bumped out. (*Printing*) 1. Matter which is widely leaded. 2. A line of characters in which extra spacing has been inserted to square it up with the measure of a longer line.

Bumper. A machine used to compact the sections of a book after they have been sewn together. Also called a 'Nipper' or 'Smasher'.

Bundesvereinigung Deutscher Bibliotheksverbände (BDB). <www.bdb-dachverband.de> (Strasse des 17 Juni 114, 10623 Berlin, Germany) Federal Union of German Library Associations; members include: Deutscher Bibliotheksverband (DBV), Berufsverband Information Bibliothek (BIB), Verein Deutscher Bibliothekare (VDB). Operates Bibliothek & Information International (BII); publishes *Bibliotheks-dienst* (m.). In 2004 it was announced that BDB would merge with Deutsche Gesellschaft für Informationwissenschaft und Information-praxis (DGI) to form Bibliothek und Information Deutschland. (BID).

Bundling. *See* Basket deal.

Burin. An engraver's tool.

Burn. The act of transferring data files (text, images, audio, video) onto a recordable medium such as CD-R. The equivalent of copying to a floppy disc but, unless CD-RW discs are used, the data cannot be changed once it has been burnt. The equipment used to carry out this operation, the CD-writer, is frequently referred to as a 'burner'.

Burn-in. *See* Screen saver.

Burning Issues Group. *See* Sexuality Issues in Libraries Group.

Burnished edges. Coloured or gilt edges which have been made smooth and bright by a polishing tool.

Bursting strain. The measurement, expressed in pounds per square inch, of pressure required to rupture paper when being tested on a Mullen or Ashcroft machine.

Bus network. A topology for a Local area network in which all devices are connected to a main communications line, the bus. *See also* Ring network, Star network.

Business Archives Council (BAC). A UK-based charitable organization supported by subscriptions, aims to promote the efficient management, preservation and use of business records. Originating in 1934 as the Council for the Preservation of Business Archives, the BAC now supports the maintenance and use of archives generated by all parts of the private sector. It has carried out a series of surveys into the survival of many types of these materials, including archives of banking, insurance, railways, pharmaceuticals, veterinary medicine and others. BAC is currently not functioning; for temporary access consult the National Register of Archives.

Business Archives Council of Scotland. <www.archives.gla.ac.uk/bacs> (77–81 Dumbarton Road, Glasgow G11 6PP, UK) Established in 1960 as an independent archive body concerned with the active preservation of Scottish business records.

Business Link. <www.businesslink.gov.uk> A UK business advice service organized by the Department of Trade and Industry and delivered by a network of online and local operators. In addition to legal, financial, health and safety, and personnel advice the service also offers support in ICT and Knowledge Management.

Business performance management. A combination of metrics, processes and systems used to monitor and manage strategy; BPM includes scorecards, measures of added value and customer perceptions.

Business plan. A financial and strategic framework for the efficient operation of a commercial service. Libraries and information units need to prepare such a plan for viable services in a free-market environment.

Business process engineering. The use of information management and document handling procedures in the corporate environment, to enhance accuracy, efficiency, productivity and customer service. BPE typically involves analysis and redesign of management systems and organizational structures. The introduction of such systems into existing offices may be termed Business process re-engineering (BPR).

Butt splice. *See* Splice.

Butted. (*Printing*) Lines of type, or rules, placed end to end to make larger lines. Also called 'Butted slugs'.

Buying in. The process of purchasing the services of outside consultants, specialists and contractors to provide those parts of an operation that an organization does not wish to provide from its own internal resources. Economies may be made as fewer employees are needed, and specialist providers should offer greater expertise.

Bye-laws. Bye-laws may be made under the provisions of the (UK) Public

Libraries and Museums Act 1964, s. 19, regulating the use of facilities provided by the authority under this Act and the conduct of persons in premises where those facilities are provided. Bye-laws may include provisions enabling officers of a local authority to exclude or remove from premises maintained by the authority any person who contravenes the bye-laws. A set of model bye-laws has been prepared. Before bye-laws can be effective they must be submitted by local authorities in England and Wales to the Secretary of State for confirmation. Bye-laws must be displayed in any premises maintained under the Act to which the public has access. The provisions in Northern Ireland and in Scotland are slightly different.

Byline. The line of type at the head of a newspaper or magazine article indicating its authorship. *See also* Masthead.

Byname. *See* Nickname.

Byte. Abbreviation for binary term; the space occupied in a computer memory by one character or by one space; and which consists of eight Bits. Strictly a kilobyte is 1024 bytes, and a megabyte is 1,048,576 bytes, but they are commonly assumed to be 1000 bytes and 1,000,000 bytes respectively.

Byzantine bindings. Book covers, rather than true bindings, finely wrought in gold and silver, and often inlaid with precious stones. They date from the foundation of Byzantium by Constantine the Great in the fourth century.

c. Abbreviation for Chapter, caput or *circa*. Also for the word 'copyright' when used in descriptive notes, though not legally valid in a copyright notice when © should be used.

©. The symbol claiming copyright under Article III (1) of the Universal Copyright Convention (*see* Copyright, International); for those countries which have signed only the Universal Copyright Convention, it is required by law to be placed before the name of the copyright proprietor and the year of first publication. The Intergovernmental Copyright Committee, meeting in Washington in October 1957, recommended positions in various kinds of publication where the symbol might be placed: amongst these was the title-page or the page immediately following, or at the end of a book or pamphlet; under the main title or the Masthead of a newspaper, magazine or other periodical; on the face side of a map, print or photograph, either on the actual map or picture (but near the title or the margin) or on the margin.

C&IT. Communications and Information Technology, an expression particularly used in the 1997 UK Dearing Report to indicate the importance that a combination of computing power and communications facilities could play in improving the quality, flexibility and effectiveness of higher education. Current use favours 'ICT'.

ca. Abbreviation for *circa*.

Cabinet.   1. An enclosed rack or frame for holding type cases, galleys, etc.; made formerly of wood but now also of pressed sheet steel.   2. A standard size of card, 4¹/₄ x 6¹/₂ inches.

Cabinet edition.   *See* Library edition.

Cabinet size.   *See* Oblong.

Cable systems.   Hard-wired systems between transmitter and end user, usually using Fibre optic cable, and introduced initially to provide dedicated one-way entertainment to domestic televisions. Fibre optic has the capacity to transmit large quantities of data efficiently, enabling the layering onto the video stream of new products for domestic users and online information services for business users.

Cache.   In networking, the use of intermediate storage for holding copies of electronic resources that have been requested and retrieved on previous occasions. The cache can provide improved responsiveness and reduce networking charges, although the actual savings will be determined by the size available for the cache and the number of repeated requests to the same resources. *See also* Mirror.

CACL.   *See* Canadian Association of Children's Librarians (a Section of the Canadian Association of Public Libraries).

CACUL.   *See* Canadian Association of College and University Libraries (a Division of the Canadian Library Association).

Cadastral map.   One drawn on a large scale to show ownership, extent and value of land for purposes of taxation.

CADP.   *See* Coalition Against Database Piracy.

Caillet Commission.   A commission held in France in 1979 into the state of preservation of library materials. The report led to the adoption of the Plan de Sauvegarde of the Bibliothèque Nationale. The plan included a programme of microfilming and chemical treatment of documents as well as the establishment of a conservation centre at Sable and a centre for the filming and treatment of newspapers at Provins.

CAIN.   <cain.ulst.ac.uk> Conflict Archive on the Internet, a regularly-updated web site that provides a wide range of information and source material on 'the Troubles' in Northern Ireland from 1968 to the present. The site also contains information on Northern Ireland society and politics in the region.

CAIRNS.   <cairns.lib.gla.ac.uk> Co-operative Academic Information Retrieval Network for Scotland, an initiative that aims to integrate 25 Z39.50-compliant catalogues or information services across Scotland into a functional and user-adaptive test-bed service. Began as an eLib Clump project and extended into CC-Interop.

CAIS.   *See* Canadian Association for Information Science.

Calcography.   *See* Chalk drawing.

Caldecott (Randolph) Medal.   This medal is awarded annually under the auspices of the Association for Library Services to Children of the American Library Association. The award is made each January to the illustrator of the most distinguished picture book for children published in the United States during the previous year. Donated by the Frederic G. Melcher family, the medal has been awarded since 1938 and recipients must be citizens of or resident in the United States. *See also* Newbery (John) Medal.

Calendar. 1. A chronological list of documents in a given collection, e.g. charters, state papers, rolls, etc., giving the date, and with annotations indicating or summarizing the contents of each. 2. An almanack giving lists of days, months, saints' days, etc., for a given year, or a special list of important days for certain purposes throughout the year, e.g. a university or gardening calendar.

Calender. A machine consisting mainly of metal rollers between which paper is passed to give it a smooth surface. The degree of smoothness depends on the pressure of the rollers and the extent to which they close the pores.

Calendered paper. Paper that is given a smooth surface by rolling, when newly-made, between smooth cylinders under pressure. Paper which receives a minimum of calendering emerges as an antique. With more calendering it acquires a machine finish, then an English finish, and it finally becomes a super-calendered, glossy sheet.

Calf. A bookbinding leather made from calfskin and so used since at least 1450. It may have a rough or a smooth (the more usual) finish. Books which are full-bound can be further described as being diced, grained, marbled, mottled, scored, sprinkled, stained, or tree, according to the form of decoration used. Special styles are known as antique, divinity, law, reversed or roughened.

California Digital Library (CDL). <www.cdlib.org> Opened to the public in 1999, CDL is a partnership with the 10 University of California campuses in a continuing commitment to apply innovative technology to managing scholarly information. CDL provides a centralized framework for sharing materials, gives wider and easier access to digital content, and supports researchers in developing new tools and innovations for scholarly communication.

CALIM. *See now* NoWAL.

CALIMERA. <www.cordis.lu/ist/directorate_e/digicult/calimera.htm> An FP6 project co-ordinated by the Libraries and Archives Department of the Municipality of Lisbon, to build upon the achievements of the Pulman Network for promoting best practice for co-operation among local institutions (libraries, archives, museums) throughout Europe.

CALL. *See* Canadian Association of Law Libraries.

Call card. *See* Call slip.

Call number. The number by which a reader requisitions a book. Usually the classification number (or in fixed location, shelf number) followed by the Book number or simply the Author mark. It is used to identify a particular book, and to indicate both its position on the shelves and its position relative to other books; it is marked on the spine of a book as well as on catalogue and other records.

Call slip. A printed blank on which are entered the author, title and call number for books requested by readers from closed access collections. Also called 'Call card', 'Readers' slip', 'Requisition form'.

Calligraphic initial. An initial in a mediaeval illuminated manuscript made by a scribe rather than an artist. Such initials are in ink, and rarely brushed with colour or touched with gold.

Calligraphy. The art of fine handwriting: penmanship. Calligraphic types are those designed in close sympathy with the spirit of good handwriting.

Calotype. An early photographic process invented (c. 1839) by W. H. Fox Talbot. Paper sensitized with silver iodide was brushed over with a solution of silver nitrate, acetic acid or gallic acid and exposed while wet. Translucent paper permitted a positive to be printed and led to the use of the glass plate. Also called 'Talbotype'.

Cambridge History of the Book in Britain. A major publishing venture by Cambridge University Press, under the editorship of J. Barnard and O. F. McKenzie. To date volume 2 (1557–1695) and volume 3 (1400–1557) have appeared. Each volume comprises a substantial introduction and specialized essays; treatment is authoritative and scholarly, and there are extensive bibliographies and efficient indexes.

Cambridge India paper. Trade name for a grade of paper used for Bibles; made by James R. Compton & Bros. Ltd., Bury, Lancashire, UK. So named to distinguish it from Oxford India Paper. *See also* India paper.

Cambridge style. The English style of book decoration characterized by double panels with a flower tool at each of the outer four corners.

Cambridge University Library. <www.cam.ac.uk> (Park Road, Cambridge CB3 9DR, UK) Founded in 1424, the Library occupies a huge 1930s building designed by Sir Giles Scott. It holds over 6 million printed books and has extensive collections of maps, manuscripts, etc. There are numerous special collections. The Library benefits from copyright deposit.

Cameo. A die-stamping process which results in the design being in plain relief on a coloured background.

Cameo binding. A binding having the centre of the boards stamped in relief, in imitation of antique gems or medals. Also called 'Plaquette binding'.

Cameo stamp. The earliest form of tool for blind tooling used between the eleventh and early sixteenth centuries. It was oval in shape and engraved with a pictorial design; when impressed on the side of a book it resembled a cameo.

Cameo-coated paper. An American dull-finished coated paper suitable for printing half-tones with a non-lustrous surface: it is particularly suitable for artistic engravings. The English equivalent is matt-finished art paper. *See also* Art.

Camera copy. Material (e.g. table, diagram, photograph, etc.) which is ready for photographing for reproduction, usually by lithography, in a publication.

Camera ready.   Printed pages comprising typescript and graphics which are ready to be photographed as part of the book production process. Also know as camera ready copy or crc.

Campaign for America's Libraries.   <www.ala.org/@yourlibrary> A campaign launched in 2001 by the American Library Association to explain the value of libraries and librarians, and the vital roles of public, school, academic and special libraries. The trademark logo "@yourlibrary" has now extended to several other countries.

Campaign for Freedom of Information.   <www.cfoi.org.uk> The Campaign is a UK-based non-profit organization that is very active in monitoring the progress of Freedom of Information legislation, and offers advice and training to public authorities. It is supported by some 90 national charities and other bodies. *See also* Freedom of Information.

Campbell (Francis Joseph) Citation.   A citation and medal awarded by the American Library Association for outstanding contributions to library services for the blind.

Campbell (John) Trust Award.   An award made by CILIP (and formerly by the Institute of Information Scientists) to support students. Part of the award is a bursary for conference attendance or travel; the second part is a dissertation bursary.

Campus information service.   *See* CWIS (1).

Campus Wide Information Service.   *See* CWIS (1).

Canada Institute for Scientific and Technical Information.   *See* CISTI.

Canadian Association for Information Science/Association Canadienne des Sciences de l'Information (CAIS/ACSI).   <www.cais-acsi.ca> (McGill Graduate School of Library and Information Studies, 3459 McTavish Street, Montreal, Quebec H3A 1Y1, Canada) Formed in 1970 to promote the development of information science in Canada by bringing together persons in the many disciplines engaged in the production, storage, retrieval, and transmission of scientific and other information. Financed by membership dues, annual conferences of the Association, and publications. Publishes *Newsletter* (q.), *Canadian Journal of Information Science* (a.).

Canadian Association of Children's Librarians (CACL).   Formed 1939. Agreed, consequent upon the restructuring of the Canadian Library Association, to become a Section of the Canadian Association of Public Libraries. Publishes *CACL Bulletin.*

Canadian Association of College and University Libraries (CACUL).   A Division of the Canadian Library Association. Exists to further the interests of librarians and libraries in institutions which offer formal education above secondary level, and to support the highest aims of education and librarianship. There are three sections: Small University Libraries, Community and Technical Colleges, and Canadian Academic Research Libraries (CARL). Publishes *CACUL Newsletter* (6 p.a.) and reports.

Canadian Association of Law Libraries (CALL). <www.callacbd.ca> (PO Box 1570, 4 Cataraqui Street, Suite 310, Kingston, Ontario K7L 5C8, Canada) Founded in July 1962 as a Chapter of the American Association of Law Libraries with the objects of fostering a spirit of co-operation among Canadian law libraries and increasing their usefulness and efficiency. Publishes *CALL newsletter, Index to Canadian legal periodical literature.*

Canadian Association of Public Libraries (CAPL). A Division of the Canadian Library Association. Founded in June 1972 at the Canadian Library Association's annual conference; it incorporates three former sections of the Canadian Library Association – Adult Services, Canadian Association of Children's Librarians, and Young People's, and aims to further public library service to all Canadians. Provides sections and committees to encourage interchange among public librarians who serve various groups. Publishes a newsletter.

Canadian Association of Research Libraries/Association des Bibliothèques de Recherche du Canada (CARL/ABRC). <www.carl-abrc.ca> CARL/ABRC is mainly concerned with aspects of co-operation and resource sharing betweeen libraries in Canada.

Canadian Association of Special Libraries and Information Services (CASLIS). A Division of the Canadian Library Association. Membership is open to special librarians, librarians from subject divisions of academic and public libraries, and specialists in information science. Publishes a newsletter *Agora* (q.) and directories, etc.

Canadian Council of Archives. <www.CdnCouncilArchives.ca> Founded 1985, represents principal agents in the archival community and supports programmes of research, promotion of standards and positive projects for the preservation and use of archival resources in Canada.

Canadian Initiative on Digital Libraries. <www.nlc-bnc/cidl> An alliance formed in 1997 by 20 major Canadian libraries to work together to improve access to digital resources. *See also* vCUC.

Canadian Library Association (CLA). <www.cla.ca> (328 Frank Street, Ottawa, Ontario K2P 0X8, Canada) Formed in 1946 and incorporated in 1947, CLA works to improve the quality of Canadian library and information services, encourage professional conduct, and promote public support for libraries. There are five divisions: Canadian Association of College and University Libraries (CACUL); Canadian Association of Public Libraries (CAPL); Canadian Association of Special Libraries and Information Services (CASLIS); Canadian Library Trustees' Association (CLTA); Canadian School Library Association (CSLA). There are also 30 special interest groups; current membership is 2,750.

Canadian Library Trustees' Association (CLTA). A Division of the Canadian Library Association. Its main objective is to educate members in the principles of trusteeship; membership is open to all library trustees interested in promoting better public library services. Publishes a *Newsletter* (4 p.a.).

Canadian School Library Association (CSLA). Founded in 1961; became a Division of the Canadian Library Association in 1973. Aims: to improve the quality of school library service by stimulating interest at all levels of the education system. Publishes a newsletter – *Moccasin Telegraph* (3 p.a.).

Cancel. This term is loosely given to a part of a book (leaf, part of a leaf or leaves) on which there is a major error which cannot be allowed to remain, and to the leaf which is printed to take the place of the original. The original leaf, which would be more accurately described as the 'cancelled leaf' (cancelland, cancellandum), is cut out by the binder and the corrected one (cancel, cancelling leaf, cancellans) pasted to its stub. Occasionally both leaves are found in a book, the binder having omitted to remove the cancelled leaf.

Cancel title. A reprinted title-page to replace one cut out.

Cancellation. 1. The removal of a leaf of a section of a book because of textual error, or for some other reason, leaving a portion of the leaf in the form of a stub. The portion left is known as a disjunct leaf. 2. An instruction to a publisher or other supplier to cease provision of items, periodical titles, series etc. previously supplied to a library on a regular subscription basis.

Cancellation mark. *See* Deletion mark.

CanCore. <www.cancore.ca> The Canadian Core Learning Object Metadata Application Profile, intended to facilitate the interchange of records describing educational resources and the discovery of these resources both in Canada and beyond its borders. CanCore is based on and fully compatible with the IEEE Learning Object Metadata standard and the IMS Learning Resource Metadata specification.

Canevari binding. A style of binding named after Demetrio Canevari (1539–1625), physician to Pope Urban VII, and usually consisting of a blind-tooled centre panel enclosing a sunken portion bearing a large cameo either glued to the leather or impressed on it.

Canon. An obsolete name for a size of type equal to about 48 pt. The name is probably derived from the use by early printers of this size of type for printing the Canon of the Mass.

Canonical class. (*Classification*) Traditional sub-class of a main class, enumerated as such in a scheme of classification, and not derived on the basis of definite characteristics.

Canonical order. 1. (*Cataloguing*) An order for arranging a group of entries, other than by alphabetical sequence, which derives from a convention associated with the material to which the entries refer, as for example, the order of the books of the Bible. 2. (*Classification*) A possible order for terms in an array forming a series of co-ordinate classes. Order by means of a notation. *See* Mathematical order.

Cantilever shelving. Shelving in which the shelves rest on cantilever brackets having lugs at the back which engage in slots in the upright. No uprights support the shelves at the front, all the weight being carried on the brackets. *See also* Bracket shelving, Shelving.

Caoutchouc binding. A method of binding which was introduced in about 1840 whereby the spine folds of a book were cut off and the resulting separate leaves attached to each other and to a backing strip by a coating of flexible rubber solution and cased in the ordinary way. The rubber solution eventually perished and the leaves fell out. The process was abandoned about 1870, the method being revived in the late 1940s when the so-called Perfect method was used.

Cap. 1. Abbreviation for capital. 2. (*Binding*) Protection given to the leaves of a book while being tooled by hand, by wrapping and pasting brown paper around all the book except the boards. When so protected, the book is said to be capped.

Cap line. (*Printing*) 1. A line of type which is set in capital letters. 2. An imaginary line which runs along the top of capital letters. *See also* Ascender line, Base line, Mean line.

CAPCON Library Network. <www.capcon.net> (1990 M Street NW, Suite 200, Washington, DC 20036-3430, USA) US bibliographic network based in Washington DC, and having member libraries in Washington DC, Maryland and Virginia. An OCLC Network Affiliate.

Capitales quadrata. *See* Square capitals.

Capitalization. The use of capital letters.

Capitals (caps). The largest letters of any size of type: those kept in the upper of the two cases of printer's type. Sometimes called 'full capitals' to distinguish them from Small capitals. THIS IS AN EXAMPLE. The use of capitals is indicated in a MS. or proof by a treble underlining. *See also* Lower case letters, Small capitals, Upper case letters.

CAPL. *See* Canadian Association of Public Libraries.

CAPP. *See* Council of Academic and Professional Publishers.

Capped. *See* Cap.

Capsa. A cylindrical box used in Roman libraries to hold one or more rolls standing upright.

Capstan. (*Binding*) An ornament, roughly resembling a capstan, which was common on English and French heads-in-medallions rolls.

Caption. 1. The heading at the beginning of text or of a chapter, section, etc. 2. The wording which appears immediately underneath, or adjacent and relating to, an illustration. This is sometimes called 'Cut line', 'Legend', or 'Underline'.

Caption title. The title printed at the beginning of a chapter or section, or at the top of a page. Where the title-page of a book is missing, this may be used to provide a title for the entry in a catalogue or bibliography; in such case a note 'caption title' is normally used. Also called 'Head title', 'Drop-down title', 'Text title'.

CARBICA. Caribbean Regional Branch of the International Council on Archives.

Card.   A rectangular piece of card (*see* Boards (3)) of international standard size, usually 5 x 3 inches, 12.5 cm x 7.5 cm (7.5 cm x 12.5 cm in continental countries), having a surface suitable for writing or typing on, and used for entries in catalogues and similar records. *See also* A7 Library card.

Card catalogue.   A catalogue, the entries of which are made on cards of uniform size and quality, and stored in any desired order on their edges in drawers or other form of container, each card being restricted to a single entry and with details of class number or call number to enable the item to be found. *See also* A7 Library card, Main entry, Online public access catalogue.

Card charging.   The recording of issues of books by means of book-cards associated with readers' tickets or identification cards.

Card font.   The smallest complete font of type stocked and sold by a typefounder.

Card index.   An index made on cards usually of standard size (5 x 3 inches) and kept on their edges in a drawer. *See also* Card.

Card number.   A symbol consisting of numbers, or a combination of letters and numbers, and possibly the date, used to identify particular entries on centrally produced printed catalogue cards.

Card stock.   A 'board', or heavy weight paper, usually over .006 inch in thickness made to withstand heavy wear.

Career Development Group (CDG).   A membership group of CILIP; the current title was adopted in 1998 by the former Association of Assistant Librarians (AAL) to reflect changes in personnel terminology.

Caret.   (Lat.: 'it needs'). The mark (ʌ) used in a MS. or proof to signify that something is omitted and indicate where an addition or insertion is to be made. Also called 'Insertion mark'.

Carey Award.   An occasional award made by the Society of Indexers for outstanding services to indexing, and named in honour of Gordon V. Carey, the Society's first president.

CARL.   *See* Canadian Association of Research Libraries.

Carnegie Library.   A library built with the financial assistance of funds given by Andrew Carnegie. *See* Carnegie United Kingdom Trust.

Carnegie Medal.   <www.carnegiegreenaway.org.uk> <www.cilip.org.uk/practice/awards.html> An award made by CILIP to the author of an outstanding book for children published in the UK. It was first awarded in 1936.

Carnegie United Kingdom Trust.   The Carnegie United Kingdom Trust was inaugurated under the auspices of Andrew Carnegie in 1913 and incorporated by Royal Charter in 1917. Its aim is the improvement of the well-being of the masses of the people of Great Britain and Ireland by such means as are embraced within the meaning of the word 'charitable' according to Scottish or English law. The work of the Trust operates on a five-yearly cycle and is particularly concerned with innovatory schemes in community service, amateur participation in the arts and nature conservation. Grants are not normally made to individuals. The Trust initially continued Carnegie's own policy of giving library buildings to local communities; these were once-and-for-all gifts, requiring the community to stock the building with books and pay for the maintenance. Although several hundred such buildings are still to be found in use in the United Kingdom, the Trust's work has now largely moved into other community projects for which there is no clear statutory provision.

CARNet.   <www.carnet.hr/CUC> Croatian Academic Research Network.

Carolingian.   A minuscule book hand developed in France in the eighth century from the roman cursive, much influenced by the English half uncial. The Carolingian minuscule is the prototype of the modern styles of penmanship, and of lower case roman type. It belongs to the second dynasty of French Kings founded by Charlemagne and much of its success was due to Alcuin of York, a distinguished English scholar, churchman and poet, who took charge of the Abbey of St. Martin at Tours at his invitation. It was the dominant book hand for nearly three centuries.

Carrel.   A small room connected with a reference library, which is set aside for continuous research work by one reader and in which books, note-books, etc., may be securely locked during the temporary absence of the reader. This word is now used to indicate any table or other space reserved for one reader which provides by means of front and side screening a more or less secluded study and writing area, whether or not facilities are provided for locking up books. *Closed carrels* are cubicles which give complete seclusion. *Open carrels* give partial seclusion.

Carriage.   A flat frame bearing the guide rails on which the plank (supporting the stone on which rests the forme) of a hand printing machine moves to its printing position.

Cart.   A small book box, not on wheels, but divided into sections to display children's books face up (American). Called in Europe a Kinderbox.

Cartobibliography.   A bibliography of maps.

Cartogram.   A highly abstracted, simplified map the purpose of which is to demonstrate a single idea in a diagrammatic way. In order to do this outlines of land or the exact locations of other features are often altered.

Cartographer.   A maker of maps.

Cartography.   The science and art of making maps.

Cartouche.   1. A frame, either simple or decorative, or a scroll, in which the title, name of the cartographer, and other particulars relating to a map are placed. The cartouche usually appears in a corner of the map, and in old maps was frequently adorned with country scenes, animals, human figures, armorial or architectural designs, etc.   2. A drawn framing of an engraving, etc.   3. (*Binding*) A small rectangular ornament formed on blind rolls by one or more lines, generally with a plain centre.

Cartouche title.   The title which appears within the cartouche or scroll-like design on a map or engraving.

Cartridge. 1. A single-core container enclosing processed microforms, for insertion into readers, reader-printers and retrieval devices, the film requiring no threading or rewinding. 2. A plastic box containing a continuous loop of sound tape for insertion into a sound reproducing machine, thus providing continuous playback without rewinding. 3. The ink-reservoir of a printer. *See* Printer (2).

Cartridge paper. A hard, tough paper made with a rough surface and in a number of grades; used for drawing upon. Also a grade of paper used as an Endpaper.

Cartulary. *See* Chartulary.

CASBAH. <www.casbah.ac.uk> Carribean Studies Black and Asian History, a pilot web site for research resources relating to Caribbean Studies and the history of Black and Asian peoples in the UK. The database contains information from a UK-wide sample of relevant archives, printed and audio-visual resources held in academic, public and special libraries and repositories and comprises a demonstrator sample of approximately 400 records. Originally financed by the Research Support Libraries Programme, the Public Record Office announced the intention of taking over the database in 2002 though this had not happened by mid-2004.

Cascading Style Sheets (CSS). <www.w3.org/Style/CSS> A Style sheet mechanism that allows designers to attach style (for example, Fonts, colours and spacing) to Web pages without having this information coded into each document: a second document – the CSS – contains the formatting data and applies it at the time of display. Many documents can use the same CSS so that the look and feel of a Web site can be changed with little re-writing of HTML.

Case. 1. (*Binding*) The cover for a book which is made completely before being attached to a book by means of the endpapers and sometimes tapes in addition. 2. (*Printing*) In hand composition, a tray divided by 'bars' into compartments in which printer's individual letters, numerals and spaces are kept and which is placed on the Frame when in use, and in a cabinet when idle. The arrangement of the compartments is the same for all types and sizes. Cases may be in pairs, an upper and a lower containing respectively the capitals and small letters (hence *upper* case (u.c.) and *lower* case (l.c.)) or the whole font may be in a double unit. *See also* Casing.

Case binding. *See* Case (1).

Case book. A book bearing a cloth cover, as originally issued by the publisher. Thus 'cased'.

CAS-IAS. Current Awareness Services, combined with Individual Article Supply; integrated systems which offer listings of journal articles from core research journals with an associated document delivery service.

Casing. The operation of inserting a sewn book into its case, or cover, which is made separately from the book, and pasted to the book by means of endpapers.

CASLIS. *See* Canadian Association of Special Libraries and Information Services.

Caslon. A typeface designed and cut in 1722 by William Caslon (1692–1766). It is an Old face type and is one of the most widely used of all typefaces in American and British printing.

Cassette. 1. A double-core container enclosing processed roll microfilm for insertion into readers, micro-printers and retrieval devices. 2. A container for videotape or audiotape for insertion into a camera, projector, reader, recorder or play-back unit. *See* Tape cassette, Videotape recording.

Cassie. An old term, derived from the Fr. *cassé* (broken), for the outside and frequently damaged sheets of a ream of good paper. 'Cassie quires' are the two outside quires of a ream, also called 'Coding quires'.

Cast coated paper. A very expensive American art paper with an exceptionally soft, absorbent and uniformly flat surface.

Casting box. (*Printing*) A machine, or device, for casting stereotypes.

Casting off. The process of estimating the amount of space Copy will occupy when set up in a given size of type.

Cast-up. To calculate the cost of composing type.

Casual mnemonics. Characters used mnemonically in a scheme of classification where letters in the notation are used to indicate subjects, the notation letter being the same as the first letter of the name of the subject. They are used in particular circumstances and not as part of the normal method of notation. *See also* Mnemonics.

CAT. Computer-aided translation, or computer-assisted translation. *See* Machine translation.

Catalogue. 1. (*Noun*) A list of books, maps, or other items, arranged in some definite order. It records, describes and indexes (usually completely) the resources of a collection, a library or a group of libraries. To be distinguished from (i) a list, which may or may not be in any particular order and may be incomplete, and (ii) a bibliography, which may not be confined to any one collection or to a particular group of libraries. Each entry bears details of class number or call number to enable the item to be found, as well as sufficient details (such as author, title, date of publication, editorship, illustrations, pagination and edition) to identify and describe the item. 2. (*Verb*) To compile a list of documents according to a set of rules so as to enable the consulter to know what items are available, and from the class number, call number or other means of identification, where they may be found. In a special library, in addition to entries under authors, subjects, and possibly titles, it may include: (a) analytical entries; (b) abstracts – especially in scientific and technical libraries; (c) annotations indicating the treatment or coverage of the subject; (d) entries under subjects for work in progress and for individuals who are authoritative sources of information on specific subjects; (e) entries for pertinent information material in other parts of the organization or in other libraries. 3. (*Archives*) A set of descriptions which includes all the components of one or more related management group, or collection, at all the different levels of Description, and with an index. Also colloquially used for archival description generally.

Catalogue card. 1. A plain or ruled card on which catalogue entries may be made. 2. A card containing such an entry. *See also* A7 library card.

Catalogue code. A set of rules for guidance of cataloguers in preparing entries for catalogues so as to ensure uniformity in treatment. Such codes may include rules for subject cataloguing, and for filing and arranging entries.

Catalogue raisonné. A catalogue of an author's work, especially of an artist's pictures, engravings, etc., usually arranged by subjects, with comments, elucidations, appraisals, and bibliographical details.

Cataloguing, principles of. There may be said to be seven basic principles of cataloguing; five (Inevitable association, Multiple approach, Probable association, Specific entry, Unique entry) common to all types of entry, and two (Adequate description, Concise description) relating to book description. *See* under the names of the various principles.

Cataloguing and Indexing Group (CIG). A membership group of CILIP; formed in 1965 to unite members concerned with the production of catalogues, bibliographies and indexes.

Cataloguing department. The department of a library which deals with the cataloguing and classification of stock, and can include processing, i.e. preparation for issue to library users. Where there is no Order department, the work relating to acquisition is also undertaken here.

Cataloguing in Publication (CIP). CIP was pioneered in the Library of Congress in 1971, and the British programme which closely resembles the US system became fully operational in 1977. The aim of the programme is to provide bibliographic data for new books in advance of publication, and it depends heavily on the voluntary co-operation of publishers. Records are compiled from information supplied by publishers on a standard data sheet. The record also appears in the book itself, usually on the verso of the title-page.

Cataloguing in source. Cataloguing books before they are published, the entries being compiled from proof copies made available by the publishers, and the work being carried out by a centralized agency so that full cataloguing information is printed in the books concerned. *See also* Cataloguing in Publication.

Cataloguing rules. *See* Catalogue code.

Catch. A metal plate secured to a book cover and having a bar, over which the clasp fits. Sometimes a pin is used instead of there being a bar.

Catch letters. Groups of letters (usually three in a group) appearing in dictionaries, gazetteers, etc., at the tops of pages to indicate the first or last words of a page or column. Those on *verso* pages represent the first three letters of the first word on that page, those on the *recto* represent the first three of the last word on that page. Sometimes two groups of letters joined by a hyphen indicate the first and last words on a page.

Catch stitch. *See* Kettle stitch. Also a stitch made when sewing on tapes by passing the needle (after it comes out of the right side of the tape and before it goes across the tape) eye-end down under three or four threads below it and then into the loop so formed. The thread is then pulled up tight to form a knot in the centre of the tape before being drawn back into the middle of the section. This is done to avoid too great looseness.

Catch title. *See* Catchword title.

Catchline. A line of type inserted temporarily at the top of matter by the compositor in order to identify it, and so printed on proofs. Also the name given to a short line of type in between two large displayed lines.

Catchment area. In library planning, denotes the area from which readers may be expected to be drawn to a given library service point.

Catchword. 1. The word occurring at the bottom of a page after the last line, such word being the first on the following page. Catchwords originally appeared at the last page of a quire of a MS. and served as a guide to the binder. Later, they appeared at the foot of every verso, sometimes every page, but in conjunction with the signature served no useful purpose and were discontinued in the nineteenth century. Also called 'Direction word'. 2. A word at the top of a page or column in encyclopaedias and works of a similar nature, denoting the first or last heading dealt with on the page. 3. In indexing, the word or words which govern the position of an entry in the index.

Catchword entry. An entry in a catalogue, bibliography or index under some striking word in a book's title, other than the first, which is likely to be remembered, and so selected as entry word.

Catchword title. A Partial title consisting of some striking or easily remembered word or phrase. It may be the same as a sub-title or the Alternative title. Also called 'Catch title'.

Categorical tables. In J. D. Brown's Subject Classification, tables representing forms, standpoints, qualifications and other modes of dividing subjects. Each term in the tables is given a number (0 to 975). These are added (after a point which is used as a separating device) to subject numbers in any part of the classification:

> e.g. .1 Bibliography.
> .2 Dictionaries.
> .10 History.
> .33 Travel.
> .57 Museums.

Category. (*Classification*) 1. A 'point of view' according to which a subject can be divided. Considered by some to be synonymous with Facet. 2. A concept of high generality and wide application which can be used to group other concepts. 3. A comprehensive class or description of things. 4. A logical grouping of associated documents. 5. A class or

division formed for purposes of a given classification. In faceted classification, special distinctions are made between categories, classes,
facets and phases. *See also* Fundamental categories.

Catena.   A series of extracts from the writings of the Fathers of the Church,
arranged with independent additions to elucidate scripture and provide a
commentary thereon.

Catenati.   Chained books.

Cater-cornered.   Paper which is cut diagonally, not square.

Cathedral binding.   One decorated with Gothic architectural motifs, often
including a rose window, done between 1815 and 1840 in England and
France. In England the decoration was sometimes built up of large
single tools; in France it was normally stamped on the covers. This was
a revival by the nineteenth century binder Thouvenin of the Architectural binding style.

Cathedral Libraries and Archives Association.   <www.blackburn.
anglican.org> (Westminster Abbey Chapter Library, East Cloister,
London SW1P 3PA, UK) Specialist group concerned with collection
policies, archive management, preservation; holds a triennial conference.

Catholic Archives Society.   Founded in 1979 to promote the care and
preservation of the archives of the dioceses, religious foundations,
institutions and societies of the Roman Catholic Church in the UK and
Ireland, in order that these may be of greater administrative service to
the organizations they concern and may become accessible for
academic research and cultural purposes. Publishes *Catholic Archives*
(a.) and *CAS Bulletin* (2 p.a.).

Catholic Library Association (CLA).   <www.cathla.org> Founded 1921 in
the US to initiate, foster, and encourage any movement toward the
development of Catholic literature and Catholic library work. Publishes
Catholic Library World (10 p.a.); *Catholic Periodical and Literature
Index* (6 p.a.); *Handbook and Membership Directory* (a.).

Cat's paw calf.   *(Binding)* An acid strain pattern on a calf binding which
resembles the paw marks of a cat.

Caucus.   A short-term interest group set up within an organization to
respond to pressing needs without establishing a permanent group or
committee.

CAUSE.   A US association for the management and use of information
resources and technology in higher education; membership comprised
1,400 colleges and universities and over 80 other corporations. One of
the organizations behind the founding of the Coalition for Networked
Information. Merged with EDUCOM in 1997 to form Educause.

CBC.   *See* Children's Book Council.

CCC.   *See* Copyright Clearance Center.

CC-Interop.   <ccinterop.cdlr.strath.ac.uk> A two-year project funded by
JISC from May 2002 arising from the UKNUC Feasibility Study which
investigated interoperability issues such as the inter-linking between
union catalogues, both physical and virtual, and the use of collection

level description schemas. A user behaviour study was also undertaken. Partners were the London School of Economics, the University of Strathclyde and MIMAS.

CCITT. Comité Consultatif International Télégraphique et Téléphonique (International Consultative Committee for Telephones and Telegraph) was formed in 1956, and was one of the members of the International Telecommunication Union. In 1993 CCITT was superseded by ITU-T.

CCT. *See* Competitive tendering.

CD. Compact disc, a 12-centimetre diameter polished metal disc with protective plastic coating scanned by a laser beam. Commercial sound recordings were introduced in this format in March 1983. Very occasionally referred to as CD-DA (Compact Disc Digital Audio) to differentiate it from other CD-ROM formats. *See also* DVD.

CD Extra. A format developed by Sony, Microsoft and Philips to provide interactive CDs containing audio, graphics and Interleaved data. The CD Extra disc is a multi-session CD which contains two sessions, the first consisting of pure audio tracks and the second a data track. Also known as Enhanced CD.

CDG. *See* Career Development Group.

CD-i. Compact disc interactive, a consumer Multimedia format developed by Philips, Sony and Matsushita.

CDLR. *See* Centre for Digital Library Research.

CDNL. *See* Conference of Directors of National Libraries.

CD-R. Compact disc recordable. A format that permits audio CDs and CD-ROM discs to be produced or 'burnt' from cheap 'blanks' on desktop equipment directly from data stored on a PC's hard Disk. This eliminates the mastering process and is attractive for small runs of discs. Also used to Back-up large files that will not fit onto smaller media such as floppy discs. *See also* Burn, CD-ROM, CD-RW.

CD-ROM. Compact disc read-only memory, a 12-centimetre diameter high-capacity storage and transfer medium shipped with data that cannot be changed. The capacity of a single disc is 550–680 megabytes and the data is read by a laser beam. Linked to PCs, CD-ROM rapidly became a major publishing medium for distributing databases, directories, catalogues and software though the early advantages have largely been superceded by the World Wide Web. Extensions to the technology saw a range of formats appear since the High Sierra, ISO 9660, standard in 1986, including CD Extra, CD-R, CD-RW, CDV and Video CD. *See also* DVD, Optical disc.

CD-RW. CD-rewritable, a disc that can be written to, erased and re-recorded many times.

CDV. Compact disc video, a combination of CD and Laserdisc. Part of the disc contains 20 minutes of digital audio playable on any CD or DVD player while the other part contains 5 minutes of analog video and digital audio in laserdisc format, playable only on a CDV-compatible laserdisc player.

Ceased publication. A work in several volumes, the publication of which was not completed, or a periodical, the publication of which has been discontinued.

CEC. Commission of the European Community. *See* European Union.

CECILIA. <www.cecilia-uk.org> An online guide to music collections in archives, libraries and museums in the UK and Ireland. The database includes printed and audio resources, concert programmes, scores, performing sets for all types of music. Developed by the UK branch of IAML with support from the British Library and MLA; available via AHDS Performing Arts.

CEDAR. 1. Computer Enhanced Digital Audio Restoration; a low-cost digital signal processing software package which allows old audio recordings to be re-mastered without extraneous noises, scratches and crackling. Developed for the National Sound Archive. 2. Centre for Educational Development Appraisal and Research; based at the University of Warwick, UK, the Centre was responsible for the document package *Role of Libraries in a Learning Society* (1998) which was funded by the Library and Information Commission (LIC) to investigate the potential for the participation of libraries in lifelong learning initiatives. 3. CeDAR. *See* Centre for Database Access Research.

CEDARS. <www.curl.ac.uk/projects/cedars.html> CURL Exemplars for Digital Archives, an eLib project that investigated the requirements for preservation of electronic resources and ended in 2002.

Cedilla. The mark under the letter ç to indicate that it has a sound other than that of k; in French it has the sound of *s* and in Spanish of *th*.

CEEFAX. The Teletext service provided by the British Broadcasting Corporation.

Cel. Generally a sheet of transparent acetate on which letters, characters or objects are printed or painted. They are used as overlays on top of an opaque background, and can be exchanged for other cels over the same background.

Cell. An area in a library formed by placing two free-standing bookcases against wall shelving. This arrangement was used by Sir Christopher Wren at Trinity College, Cambridge, in 1676. Usually called 'Alcove'.

Cellulose. The common term for chemical wood pulp, the basic substance of paper manufacture. It is the predominating constituent of plant tissues from which it must be separated before it can be used.

Cellulose acetate. *See* Film base.

Cellulose triacetate. *See* Film base.

CEN. <www.cenorm.be> European Committee for Standardization whose mission is to promote voluntary technical harmonization in Europe in conjunction with world-wide bodies and its partners in Europe.

CENL. *See* Conference of European National Librarians.

Censorship. Prohibition of the production, distribution, circulation or sale of material considered to be objectionable for reasons of politics, religion, obscenity or blasphemy. This action is usually taken by persons empowered to act by federal, national, state or local laws, and takes the forms of preventing publications passing through the Customs or through the post, or of action in a law court to prevent their sale. *See also* Index Librorum Prohibitorum.

Center for Networked Information Discovery and Retrieval (CNIDR). <www. mcnc.org/rdi/index.cfm?fuseaction=page&filename=network_ information_systems_overview.html> (MCNC, Information Technologies Division, 3021 Cornwallis Road, Research Triangle Park, NC 27709-2889, USA) CNIDR focuses on the design and implementation of distributed information management systems. It originated as a research project funded by the National Science Foundation. In October 1992, MCNC entered into a three-year co-operative agreement with NSF to create the Clearinghouse for Networked Information Discovery and Retrieval, a research and development group specializing in distributed information systems. The Clearinghouse project has since produced and contributed to several prototype systems built around internationally accepted open communications standards for Client-server applications.

Center for Paper Permanency. Formed 1988 at the New York Public Library as a clearinghouse for information about the efforts of various bodies and agencies advocating the use of permanent/durable, alkaline paper.

Center for Research Libraries (CRL). <wwwcrl.uchicago.edu> (6050 South Kenwood Avenue, Chicago, IL 60637, USA) A North American co-operative scheme to acquire and preserve traditional and digital resources and make them available to member libraries by inter-library loan or electronically. Originally formed in 1949 as the Midwest Inter-Library Center (MILC) to house little used material and eliminate duplication; the name was changed in 1965.

Center for the Book. Established 1977 in the Library of Congress to organize, focus, and dramatize the US's interest in books, reading and the printed word. The Center involves authors, publishers, booksellers, librarians, scholars, readers and educators in improving the quality of book production, encouraging the international flow of printed material, encouraging the study of books, promoting books and reading, and generally raising 'book awareness'. *See also* Centre for the Book.

Centesimal device. A method used in the Universal Decimal Classification to lengthen arrays where nine divisions are inadequate; the digits 11–99 are used to represent co-ordinate subjects instead of 1–9.

Central and Eastern Europe Online Library. <www.ceeol.com> An online library and document shop offering content from Central and Eastern European countries and digital publications. It also functions as a portal to resources for academics and researchers.

Central catalogue. 1. A catalogue placed in the central library of a library system but containing entries for books in all the libraries. 2. A catalogue of the central library of a library system.

Central library. The chief library in a system, maybe containing the office of the chief librarian, the administrative department, and the largest collections of books. Sometimes called the 'Main library'.

Central processing unit (CPU). The centre of a digital computer system which co-ordinates and controls the activities of all other units and performs the logical and arithmetic processes to be applied to data.

Central shelf list. 1. A shelf list recording all the books in the central library of a system of libraries. 2. A combined shelf list, housed in the central library, but recording all books in all the libraries of a library system.

Centralized cataloguing. 1. The cataloguing of books by some central bureau, and the distribution therefrom of entries. 2. The cataloguing at one library of all the books of a library system comprising more than one library, thus achieving uniformity throughout the system.

Centralized processing. In the USA, centres for the purchase, cataloguing, classifying and processing of books, audio-visual and other material for a number of libraries.

Centralized registration. The registering of readers at one library in a system, comprising several libraries, rather than at those at which the application forms are handed in.

Centre. 1. In the rural areas of the UK, a small static library service point, provided in premises which may at times be used for other purposes, open less than ten hours a week, having a stock which is changed from time to time, and staffed by voluntary or paid librarians. 2. An organization, with or without a building for its exclusive use, which makes available at one central point a pool of specialized personnel and information, or services for the benefit of other organizations or individuals. *See also* Advice centre, Referral centre, Research library.

Centre for Bibliographic Management. Name adopted 1987 by the Centre for Catalogue Research; funded by British Library grants from 1977, it was the focal point in the United Kingdom for research, information and instruction in the field of bibliographic record research and development. *Now see* UKOLN.

Centre for Database Access Research (CeDAR). <www.hud.ac.uk/schools/cedar> (University of Huddersfield, HD1 3DH, UK) Based in the School of Computing and Mathematics, CeDAR conducts research into software efficiency and accuracy in database searching.

Centre for Digital Library Research. <cdlr.strath.ac.uk> Formed in 1999 at the University of Strathclyde, Scotland, CDLR seeks to combine theory with practice in innovative ways with the aim of being a centre of excellence on digital library issues ranging from information policy and information retrieval to document storage technologies and standards.

Centre for Educational Development Appraisal and Research. *See* CEDAR (2).

Centre for Episcopal Acta. Established at the Borthwick Institute of the University of York, UK; the Centre has taken over a central index of English episcopal *acta* relating to the twelfth and thirteenth centuries which had been established at the Institute, and with the assistance of The British Academy is publishing volumes of bishops' *acta*.

Centre for Information Management and Technology. *See* CIMTECH.

Centre for Information Quality Management (CIQM). <www.i-a-l.co. uk/ciqm> (Penbryn, Bronant, Aberystwyth SY23 4TJ, UK) Formed in conjunction with the Library Association (now CILIP) and the UK Online User Group in 1993, CIQM is a clearinghouse for database quality, passing on problems to hosts, providers, or publishers and routing replies to users. It is funded by the information industry.

Centre for Research in Library and Information Management. *See* CERLIM.

Centre for the Book. 'To promote the significance of the book in all its forms, as a vital part of the cultural, commercial and scientific life of the country' the British Library opened a Centre in autumn 1990. The Centre has exhibition space at the new British Library building, and operates a number of lectures, new technology seminars, and a fellowship programme. *See also* Center for the Book.

Centre for the Children's Book. <www.centreforthechildrensbook.org.uk> A UK initiative to form an archive, exhibition centre, education programme and library. Premises near Ouseburn, Newcastle-upon-Tyne were offered for the Centre in 1998, and fund-raising has continued steadily. In December 2003 it was reported that £6 million had been raised and that the Centre was scheduled to open towards the end of 2004.

Centre for the Study of Early English Women's Writing. *See* Chawton House Library.

Centre National de la Recherche Scientifique et Technique. *See* CNRS.

Centre note. (*Printing*) A note, or reference, placed between columns of text as in a Bible. *See also* Incut note.

Centred dot. (*Printing*) A period placed higher than the base line of a piece of type, as, c·e·n·t·r·e·d, to show multiplication (1·2 = 2), or to separate roman capitals in the classic form of inscriptions (M·A·R·C·V·S). Also called 'Space dot'.

Centred heading. (*Classification*) A typographical device used in the Dewey Decimal classification. It consists of a range of notation numbers and a heading, which are centred on the page instead of the numbers being in the usual column, and represents a concept for which there is no specific number in the hierarchy of notation, and which therefore covers a span of numbers.

Centrepiece. (*Binding*) An ornament, usually Arabesque, placed in the centre of the cover of a bound book and often used with cornerpieces, or cornerstamps. It was a favourite style of binding in the late sixteenth and early seventeenth centuries. Also used of a piece of metal usually embossed and engraved, and fastened on to the cover. Also called 'Centrestamp'.

Centroid. A summary of the contents of a server that can be used to indicate whether or not that server may provide relevant search results for a particular query. Essentially an inverted index of the information in a database and a number of centroids can be accumulated and integrated to form a single inverted index of a number of servers, making searching more efficient and reducing network load.

CEPIC. <www.cepic.org> (Teutonenstr. 22, 14129 Berlin, Germany) Co-ordination of European Picture Agencies Press and Stock; an organization representing the interests of photo libraries and photo press agencies across Europe. Formed 1993 as a European Economic Interest Group, CEPIC comprises 10 national agencies (the UK member agency is BAPLA). Priorities of CEPIC are to consolidate copyright protection, support information exchange, fight for comparable trade regulations, and to develop ethical standards.

CEPIS. <www.cepis.org> (7 Mansfield Mews, London W1M 9FJ, UK) The Council of European Professional Informatics Societies; an umbrella organization for leading computing societies in Europe – over 20 members in 17 countries, and with affiliated international partners in North America and Japan. International co-operation is directed particularly at issues such as electronic publishing, networking, legal issues, professional licensing and certification *See also* EUCIP, European Computer Driving Licence.

CERL. *See* Consortium of European Research Libraries.

CERLIM. <www.cerlim.ac.uk> (Manchester Metropolitan University, Department of Information and Communications, Geoffrey Manton Building, Rosamund Street West, Manchester M15 6LL, UK) Centre for Research in Library and Information Management – based at the University of Central Lancashire 1993–1998 – focuses its research on supporting operational work in all kinds of library and information services and collaborates with partners across the UK and overseas.

CERNET. *See* Zhong Guo Jiao Yu Huo Ke Yan Ji Suan Ji Wang.

CERNIC. *See* Zhong Guo Jiao Yu Huo Ke Yan Ji Suan Ji Wang.

Cerograph. A wax engraving process usually used for making maps. A drawing is made direct on wax spread over a copper plate which is then used as a mould from which an electrotype is made. Also called 'Cerotype'.

Certificate of issue. The statement, printed in a Limited edition, certifying the number of copies printed and sometimes bearing the autograph of the author and/or illustrator.

Certification. (*Archives*) 1. The act of attesting that a document, or a repro-duction of a document, is what it purports to be. 2. The document containing such an attestation. *See also* Authentication.

CETIS. <www.cetis.ac.uk> Centre for Educational Technology Interoperability Standards which advises UK Universities and Colleges on the strategic, technical and pedagogic implications of educational technology standards and represents UK higher and further education on international educational standards initiatives such as the IMS Global Learning Consortium. *See also* Learning Object Metadata, UK LOM Core.

cf.   Abbreviation for *confer* (Lat., meaning 'compare').

CGI.   Common Gateway Interface: a standard interface between web server software and other programs running on the same machine that makes it possible for users to interact with World Wide Web pages by, for example, searching databases and retrieving specific information.

ch.   Abbreviation for Chapter.

Chain.   (*Classification*) The succession of divisions subordinate one to another expressing the relation 'A includes B, which in turn includes C' (or, conversely, 'C is part of B, which is part of A'), e.g. Literature, English Literature, English Poetry, Shakespeare's Poetry, *Adonis*, constitute a chain of divisions in the class Literature. A hierarchy of terms, each containing or including all which follow it in the same series: a hierarchy of sub-classes of decreasing extension and increasing intension, devised by successive division. The chain of progression in a hierarchical scheme of classification from general to specific may be:

780	Music
782	Dramatic music
782.1	Opera
782.15	Scores and parts
782.154	Wagner *Die Meistersinger*

The indexer, using the principle of chain indexing, works back from the most specific step to more general terms, and in this case would provide these entries:

Operas by individual composers	782.154
Scores and parts: opera	782.15
Opera	782.1
Music: dramatic	782
Music	780

Chain indexing.   An alphabetical subject indexing system, originally devised in 1938 by S. R. Ranganathan (1892–1972), wherein a heading is provided for each term, or link for all the terms, used in a subject heading or classification. Each term represented by a given part of the classification symbol, followed by the term for each other part, appears as a heading in the reverse order of the symbol, so that the last term in the symbol becomes the first. If the symbol is comprised of four parts, there will be four entries: the first consisting of four terms; the second, of three after the first term of the previous entry has been omitted; the third, of two, and so on. The final one is the heading for the symbol with the widest connotation, and the most extension, relating to the subject in question. *See also* Correlative index, Relative index.

Chain line. *See* Laid paper.

Chain mark. *See* Laid paper.

Chain procedure. 1. (*Cataloguing*) A mechanical method of constructing subject headings, without permutation of components, from a class number. *See also* Chain. 2. (*Classification*) The procedure for determining the class index entries, the specific subject entries, the *See also* subject entries for a document from its class number and the class numbers of the cross-reference entries provided for it. *See also* Chain indexing.

Chain stitch. *See* Kettle stitch.

Chained books. Books chained to shelves or reading desks in libraries of the fifteenth to early eighteenth centuries to prevent theft. The practice began to die out by the middle of the seventeenth century when it became customary to shelve books upright.

Chained library. One in which the books were chained to shelves or reading desks.

Chalcography. Engraving on copper or brass.

Chalk drawing. One executed in crayon or paste. The art of drawing with chalks or pastels is called calcography.

Chalk engraving. *See* Crayon engraving.

Chalk overlay. A method of overlaying whereby an impression is taken on paper having a thin coating of chalk. This coating is then washed off the non-inked parts with dilute acid, leaving the inked design in relief. The resulting outline is then fitted as an overlay to the cylinder or platen so as to decrease or increase pressure. Also called 'Mechanical overlay'.

Champlevé. Enamelled bindings made by craftsmen between the eleventh and thirteenth centuries. Designs were cut into a thin sheet of gold or copper which formed the cover, the cavities being filled with enamel. On other bindings the enamel was limited to the decoration of borders and corners. This kind of binding was mainly carried out at Limoges. *See also Cloisonné.*

Chancery. The department of the Lord Chancellor, from which issue documents under the Great Seal, such as Charters, Letters Patent, writs and the like, also the place where Charters, Letters Patent and documents of a like nature are enrolled.

Chancery Liberate. *See* Liberate Roll.

Chap. Abbreviation for Chapter.

Chap-book. A small, cheap book, in a paper binding, and of a popular, sensational, juvenile, moral or educational character. These were popular in the seventeenth and eighteenth centuries, and contained tales, ballads, historical incidents, biographies, tracts, interpretations of dreams, palmistry, astrology, etc. They were sold by chapmen, i.e., pedlars, hawkers. The word comes from the Anglo-Saxon root *ceap* (trade).

Chapel. An association of journeymen in the printing and binding trades. Chapels usually exist in printing works of medium and larger size. The secretary, or leader, called the Father of the Chapel, is appointed by the members and one of his duties is to collect and forward trade union dues. To 'call a chapel' is to hold a chapel meeting of the journeymen.

Chapman codes. Two- or three- letter code abbreviations for British county and regional names; issued by the Federation of Family History Societies, 1980.

Chapter. 1. A division of a book, usually being complete in itself in subject matter but related to the preceding and following ones. 2. An autonomous unit of the American Library Association, responsible for the promotion of library service within a geographical region.

Chapter heading (head, headline). The heading placed at the text beginning a chapter. It is usually set below the normal top of the type area of the other pages; the type used is normally larger than that used for running titles, and is of a uniform size and position for each chapter.

Character. 1. A letter of the alphabet, numeral, punctuation mark, or any other symbol cast as a type. Also called 'Sort'. 2. A personage, real or fictitious, figuring in an opera or work of imaginative literature, especially a novel or play. 3. A style of handwriting. 4. (*Information retrieval*) A symbol which is used in a data processing system; it may be a numeral, a letter of the alphabet, punctuation mark or space.

Character count. A count of every letter, number, punctuation mark, word or sentence space, etc., in a piece of prose copy.

Character recognition. *See* Optical character recognition.

Character significance sequence. An order applied to symbols forming headings which are used as filing media and indicating the precedence each symbol is to have in the filing sequence. Thus the letters of the alphabet are normally arranged in their conventional order in the character significance sequence, but numerals and other non-alphabetic symbols may be arranged in their own conventional order (or if contractions or abbreviations, to be filed as if in full) or be arranged to precede or follow the alphabetic sequence.

Characteristic of a classification. A distinctive property, element, or feature, inherent in an entity by which a class is defined. A *typical characteristic* is one by which an individual of a class is representative of that class. A *type* is a typical individual, one that has most distinctly the typical characteristic, or characteristics, distinctive of the class. A class may be a type, or *typical class*, if it is representative of a *class of classes* (Bliss). The attribute which forms the basis of division. Language, form, and historical period are common characteristics in the classification of literature. A term used to express the principles by which a group is divided (as, genus into species), e.g. the characteristic that divides the animal kingdom into two parts is the absence or presence of a backbone. The characteristic is said to be 'natural' when it exhibits the inherent properties of the things classified. When it does not affect the structure, purpose, or intrinsic character of the things to be divided, but separates according to an accidental quality it is said to be 'artificial'. Thus, in zoology, the presence of a backbone is a natural characteristic. The characteristics chosen as the basis of arrangement must be essential (i.e., the most useful) to the purpose of the classification. They must be used consistently, i.e. it is impossible to classify a subject by two characteristics at once. *See* Cross classification (1). Ranganathan's characteristics are: differentiation, concomitance, relevance, ascertainability, permanence, relevant sequence, consistency. Also called a 'Principle of division'.

Characters in pica.   *See* Alphabet length.

Charcoal drawing.   One made with a charcoal crayon on paper with a rough surface. Such drawings are easily smudged, and to prevent this they are sprayed with a fixative.

Charcoal paper.   A soft, rough-surfaced paper used for making charcoal drawings.

Charge.   1. Financial arrangements made between libraries to support Co-operation; methods of charging might include barter/exchange, bulk/subscription payments, deliberate subsidies, transaction-based fees, levies for shared services. *See also* Costs.   2. A payment made to a library or information service for the use of its stock or facilities; charges are particularly levied for the use of non-traditional services, for example the searching of online databases. Public libraries in the UK may only make a charge for services under Section 8 of the Public Libraries and Museums Act 1964.   3. The record of a loan, giving particulars of the item lent and the borrower's details.   4. The process of issuing an item for loan is also termed 'charging'.

Charge slip.   *See* Book card.

Charging card.   *See* Book card.

Charging methods/systems.   The methods by which loans of books are recorded.

Chart.   1. A map for the use of marine navigators showing the coastline, the position of rocks, sandbanks, channels, anchorages, and the depths of water in different parts of the sea expressed in feet or fathoms.   2. A graphical representation by means of curves, or the like, of the fluctuation of statistical records of such items as population, prices, production, barometric pressure, temperature, etc.   3. Information of any kind arranged in tabular form, or graphically by means of curves. 4. A map designed for aeronautical navigation.

Chart paper.   A hard, tub-sized paper which must be strong, tough, pliable and subject to folding without cracking. It should be liable to stretch as little as possible during printing, smooth without gloss, suitable for pen and ink charting and therefore able to withstand erasure. *See also* Plan paper.

Charter.   1. An instrument whereby a sovereign or legislature grants rights to a person or corporation.   2. A statement of rights, typically prepared by an organization to indicate the standards of service its customers should expect; student charters, for example, give details to students of the basis of their relationship with the academic institution.

Charter bookseller. A retail bookseller who satisfies certain conditions laid down by the (UK) Booksellers Association with regard to service to the public.

Charter for the Reader. Adopted in 1992 by the International Book Committee, the Charter consists of five articles: Article 1 – the right to read, for cultural and scientific purposes, social role, economic need, democratic right, and individual creativity; Article 2 – opportunities for reading, from early encounters, access to books in schools, extra-curricular youth education; Article 3 – support and encouragement for reading, from governments, writers and translators, publishers, illustrators, booksellers, libraries, the media; Article 4 – information and co-operation on reading; Article 5 – concluding statement 'books deserve universal interest and support'.

Charter of the Book. A declaration of the principles which should guide the treatment of books both nationally and internationally, was approved in 1971 by the international professional organizations of authors, publishers, librarians, booksellers and documentalists, in association with Unesco and in connection with International Book Year, 1972. The theme of each of the articles was: (1) everyone has the right to read; (2) books are essential to education; (3) society has a special obligation to establish the conditions in which authors can exercise their creative role; (4) a sound publishing industry is essential to national development; (5) book manufacturing facilities are necessary to the development of publishing; (6) booksellers provide a fundamental service as a link between publishers and the reading public; (7) libraries are national resources for the transfer of information and knowledge, and for the enjoyment of wisdom and beauty; (8) documentation serves books by preserving and making available essential background material; (9) the free flow of books between countries is an essential supplement to national supplies and promotes international understanding; (10) books serve international understanding and peaceful co-operation. The full text of each article is given in *Unesco Bulletin for Libraries*, vol. 26, no. 5, (September–October), 1972, pp. 238–40. *See also* Charter for the reader, London Declaration.

Charter roll. A parchment roll upon which charters were enrolled at the Chancery.

Chartered Institute of Library and Information Professionals. *See* CILIP.

Chartered Institute of Public Finance and Accountancy. *See* Cipfa.

Chartered Librarian (UK). One who has become fully qualified professionally, and been admitted to the Register of Chartered Librarians maintained by CILIP.

Chartulary. 1. A keeper of archives. 2. A place in which records or charters relating to a religious, civil or private state are kept. 3. The book in which they are listed or copied. Also called 'Cartulary'.

Chase. (*Printing*) A rectangular iron frame in which, by means of wedges, composed matter is secured and rendered portable. The wedges are called side- and foot-sticks and quoins. When they are adjusted, between the type matter and the chase, the whole becomes a forme, and is said to be 'locked up'. In Sheet work the forme which contains the text which will be on the inside pages of a printed sheet when folded, is called the 'inner forme' and that which contains those on the outside, the 'outer forme'.

Chased edges. *See* Gauffered edges.

Chat room. A place on the Internet where people can communicate synchronously, in real time, and view the conversations taking place between all participants without the in-built delay of E-mail. Private chat rooms are also available where only a small number of agreed participants are involved. *See also* Instant messaging.

Chaucer type. A re-cutting, in 12 point, of the Troy type designed by William Morris. It was first used in 1892. *See also* Golden type.

Chawton House Library. <www.chawton.org> Opened in 2003 in an Elizabethan mansion that once belonged to Jane Austen's brother, the library contains some 9,000 books enabling readers to have access to texts in the appropriate setting of a 17th/18th century country house and working manor farm. The library is the first part of an international project to establish a Centre for the Study of Early English Women's Writing, 1600–1830.

Cheap edition. An edition of a book issued at a cheaper price. Usually it is a reprint of an earlier edition, printed on poorer paper and bound in a cheaper cover.

Check digit. A digit added to a sequence of digits intended for computer input purely to check the accuracy of the main sequence; it is related arithmetically to the sequence and thus an error is automatically noticed. The final single digit of an ISBN is a check digit.

Check marks. Pencilled indications made by cataloguers on title-pages of books, as a guide to assistant cataloguers or data input staff, of items to be included or omitted in the entries.

Check-list. 1. A record on which is noted each number, or part, of a work 'in progress' as it is received. 2. A list of items giving brief information sufficient only for identification. 3. An enumeration of documentary holdings with a minimum of organization and bibliographic information.

Checkout routine. The necessary procedures demanded before removing a document from a collection.

Cheltenham. A typeface designed by Bertram G. Goodhue (1869–1924) in 1896 and widely used by jobbing printers as it is a Founders' type.

Cheltenham Classification. A system devised for the library of the Ladies' College, Cheltenham, and used in a number of schools. The tables were published under the editorship of Miss E. S. Fegan and Miss M. Cant who were successive librarians of the College. Being aligned closely with the school curriculum, the contents of the main classes correspond with the traditional coverage of subjects as taught.

Chemac. A kind of copper line block used for blocking. *See also* Block (2).

Chemical wood. Wood reduced to pulp by a chemical process, cooking in acid (sulphite process), or an alkaline liquor (soda process), for use in the manufacture of paper. This produces a purer pulp than that obtained by the Mechanical wood process. A combined chemical and mechanical wood process results in a paper which is intermediate in quality between the two.

Chemise. A loose cover for a book with pockets for boards. These were sometimes used in the Middle Ages instead of binding.

Cheque book charging method. An adaptation of the Browne book charging system to enable it to deal more rapidly with great pressure at the entrance side of the circulation desk. With this system a reader is issued with a small book of perforated slips of paper, similar to a small cheque book, and each bearing the same number. When a book is borrowed, a slip torn from the cheque book by an assistant is placed with the book card to form a Charge. Delayed discharging (i.e. cancelling the loan record at a less busy time) is possible with this method.

Chequering. (*Binding*) To divide a surface into squares of alternately different ornament or colours, by equidistant vertical and horizontal lines like a chess-board.

Chesire II. <sca.lib.liv.ac.uk/cheshire> A collaborative JISC/NSF project undertaken by the University of Berkeley (US) and the University of Liverpool (UK) to develop a next-generation online catalogue and full-text information retrieval system using advanced techniques. The system is being deployed in a working library environment and its use and acceptance by local library patrons and remote network users are being evaluated. The system incorporates a client/server architecture with implementations of standards including Z39.50 and SGML.

CHEST. The Combined Higher Education Software Team acted as a focal point for the supply of software, data, information, training materials and other IT related products to higher and further education in the UK. Combined with NISS in 1999 to form EduServ.

chi. (*Bibliography*) The Greek letter χ used to denote an unsigned gathering or leaf in respect of which no signature can be inferred and which is not the first gathering. *See also* pi.

Chiaroscuro. 1. A black and white sketch. 2. A method of printing engravings, usually wood-engravings, from blocks representing lighter and darker shades, used especially in the fifteenth and sixteenth centuries. 3. A print produced by this means. 4. The earliest form of colour printing. It was a woodcut method, the colours being successively printed in register from separate blocks after an impression from the master block had been made.

CHIC. *See* Consumer Health Information Consortium.

Chicago Style. A citation method in which each paper is given a running number at the end of the sentence in which reference is made, normally in superscript, and a corresponding note of the full reference appears below the main text on the same page. In some implementations, the notes are gathered together at the end of the paper. Also known as Turabian Style. *See also* Harvard Style, Vancouver Style.

Chiffon silk. A thin, strong and durable silk material which can be used for mending and strengthening paper, especially of valuable books.

Children's Book Award. An award founded in 1980 and given to authors of fiction for children under the age of 14 by the Federation of Children's Book Groups.

Children's Book Circle. <www.booktrusted.co.uk> (27 Wrights Lane, London W8 5TZ, UK) An informal group of children's book editors and those who work in publishers' children's book departments. It was started in 1962 to provide an opportunity to exchange ideas on the publication of, and publicity for, children's books. The Eleanor Farjeon Award 'for distinguished services to children's books in the past year' was first made in 1966 in memory of Eleanor Farjeon, one of the greatest children's writers, who died in 1965. Anyone doing outstanding work for children's books, whether librarian, teacher, author, artist, publisher, reviewer, television producer is eligible for the award.

Children's Book Council (CBC). <www.cbcbooks.org> (12 W37th Street, New York, NY 10018-7480, USA) A not-for-profit organization, encouraging the reading and enjoyment of children's books. The Council consists of American publishers of trade books for children. It organized the first National Children's Book Week in 1945 and has continued to do so each year since; it is also concerned with projects involving the annual Children's Book Showcase. The Council acts as the US section of the International Board on Books for Young People (IBBY) and participates in this connection by making an annual donation of a selection of children's books to twelve repositories throughout the world. Publishes *CBC Features*. *See also* Book Week, Trade book.

Children's Book Council of Australia. <www.cbc.org.au> The main objective of the Council is to foster children's enjoyment of books and to encourage them to be skilful and discerning readers. It was established in 1945 in New South Wales and by 1959 it had become a national organization. Publishes *Reading Time* (q.), which aims to review all books for children and young people published in Australia.

Children's Book Group. A specialist publishers' group of the Publishers Association; regular meetings of members are held for the common interest of the kind of publishing with which they are concerned.

Children's Book Groups. Unofficial groups of persons concerned with furthering the use of books for children by means of story telling, children's activities, talks, book exhibitions and book sales, co-operation with public libraries and with schools and booksellers. The usefulness of the groups was recognized in the Bullock Report. *See also* Federation of Children's Book Groups.

Children's Book History Society. <cbhs@abcgarrett.demon.co.uk> (25 Field Way, Hoddesdon, EN11 0QN, UK) An association for those interested in the history of children's books and literature; publishes a newsletter. An Organization in Liaison (OiL) with CILIP.

Children's Book Trust (UK). *See* Young Book Trust.

Children's library. A department reserved for the use of children.

Children's Literature Association (ChLA). <ebbs.english.vt.edu/chla> (PO Box 138, Battle Creek MI 49016, USA) Essentially a university-oriented organization, formed in 1972 in the US to advance the scholarly and critical teaching of children's literature, especially at college level. Works in conjunction with other organizations, with publishers and with the public to disseminate information about children's literature. Membership (currently 750) is open to anyone interested in children's books. Publishes *Children's Literature Association Quarterly* (q.) and an annual book *Children's Literature*.

China clay. A substance (SiO_2) found in large quantities in Cornwall and used in paper making to obtain finish, consistency and opacity, it is also used for coating papers.

China Education and Research Network. *See* Zhong Guo Jiao Yu Huo Ke Yan Ji Suan Ji Wang.

China paper. Very thin, silky and costly, waterleaf paper used for proofs for woodcuts and for woodcuts to be mounted on stronger paper. Also called 'Chinese paper' and 'Indian proof paper'.

China Society for Library Science (CSLS). *See* Zhong Guo Tu Shu Guan Xue Hui.

Chinese American Librarians Association (CALA). <www.cala-web.org> 500 members. Formerly Mid-West Chinese American Librarians Association; in 1983 incorporated the Chinese Librarians Association. Publishes *Chinese American Librarians Association–Newsletter* (irreg.), *Journal of Library and Information Science* (in Chinese and English, 2 p.a.).

Chinese Science and Technology Information Association. Founded 1978 in Beijing. Aims to sponsor exchanges of information at national and international level. Publishes *Library and Information Service* (6 p.a.) with English contents page.

Chinese style. A book printed on double leaves, i.e. with unopened folds at the fore-edges and the interior pages blank. 'Japanese style' refers to a Japanese book printed in the same manner.

Chip. A term denoting a single integrated electronic circuit, also called a 'microchip', or 'silicon chip'. Single-chip central processing units – microprocessors – were the foundation of PCs.

Chip board. (*Binding*) A less expensive material than Millboard or Strawboard used for covering books.

Chirograph. A formal handwritten document.

Chiroxylographic. A mediaeval block book in which the illustrations are printed from blocks and the text added by hand.

Chiswick Press. The printing press founded by Charles Whittingham the Elder (1767–1840) in 1811, and continued even more successfully by his nephew of the same name (1795–1876) who controlled the Press from 1840. The elder Whittingham was famous for his attractive, popularly priced classics and for his handling of woodcuts; the nephew was well known for his association with the publisher William Pickering, whose printing he did after 1830. The name of the Press was first used in an imprint in 1811 and persisted for 150 years.

ChLA. *See* Children's Literature Association.

Chloride paper. Sensitized photographic paper with an emulsion of gelatin-silver chloride of medium sensitivity. Mainly used for contact printing.

Chomhairle Leabharlanna (Ireland). *See* Library Council.

Chorochromatic map. One in which distribution by area is shown by distinctive colours or tints. This method is used for most geological, soil or political maps.

Chorographic map. One representing a large region, country, or continent, on a small scale.

Choropleth map. One showing 'quantity in area' calculated on a basis of average numbers per unit of area, such as population in a country, by tinting civil divisions by graduated lines or colours, the degree of darkness of which is proportionate to the value represented.

Choroschematic map. One in which small semi-pictorial symbols such as dots or lines of various shapes, sizes and density are used over the area of the map to represent distribution without indication of quantity, of land utilization or vegetation.

Chorus score. *See* Score.

Chrestomathy. A collection of excerpts and choice selections, especially from a foreign language, with notes of explanation and instruction.

Chromium-faced plates. Printing plates upon which chromium has been deposited electrolytically.

Chromo. Pertaining to colours. 1. In colour printing there are many terms prefixed by this word, the combining word often giving the particular definition, such as chromo-collotype, chromo-lithography, chromo-xylography. 2. (*Paper*) A heavily coated paper used for chromo-lithography; it is more heavily coated than art paper.

Chromography. A reproduction of a coloured illustration by lithography, or one of the many photo-mechanical processes.

Chromo-lithography. *See* Colour lithography.

Chromo-xylography. Coloured woodcuts. *See also* Chiaroscuro (4).

Chronicles. These differ from annals in being more connected and full; though like annals, the events are treated in the order of time.

Chronogram. A phrase, sentence or inscription, in which certain letters (usually distinguished by size or otherwise from the rest) express by their numerical values a date or epoch, e.g. stVLtVM est DIffICILes habere nVgas, which is:

V	L	V	M	D	I	I	C	I	L	V		
5	50	5	1000	500	1	1	100	1	50	5	=	1718.

See also Roman numerals.

Chronological device. One of the distinctive principles for determining the sequence of subjects in the Colon Classification. It is a notational device which ensures chronological order by using a symbol to represent a date of origin.

Chronological order. Arrangement in order of date. Applies to order of entries in a catalogue (date of publication – imprint or copyright) or of the material itself.

Chrysography. The art of writing in gold letters, as practised by mediaeval writers of manuscripts.

Church and Synagogue Library Association (CSLA). <www. worldaccessnet.com/~csla> (P.O. Box 19357, Portland, OR 97280, USA) Formed 1967 in Philadelphia for librarians of all church and synagogue libraries. Membership (currently 1,900) is open to voluntary and professional librarians, to library committee members, ministers, priests, rabbis, directors of Christian education, principals of synagogue schools, Sunday school superintendents, churches, publishers, booksellers and others interested in church and synagogue libraries. It is an ecumenical association, having Chapters based on geographic areas. Publishes *Church and Synagogue Libraries* (6 p.a.), and guides to practice.

CIA. Conseil International des Archives. *See entry under* International Council on Archives.

CIB. Conseil International du Bâtiment pour la Recherche, l'Étude et la Documentation. *See now* International Council for Research and Innovation in Building and Construction (CIB).

CIC. <www.cic.uiuc.edu> Committee on Institutional Cooperation, established in 1958, is the academic consortium of twelve major teaching and research universities in the US with programmes and activities extending to virtually all aspects of university activity. The member university libraries completed a large-scale study of the implementation of Z39.50 and subsequently created the CIC Virtual Electronic Library (VEL). *See also* Clump, vCUC.

Cicero. A continental unit for measuring the width of a line of type. One Cicero equals 4.511 mm, or 12 Didot points. The name is said to be derived from the size of type used in Schoeffer's edition of Cicero's *De Oratore* in the late fifteenth century. *See also* Didot system, Measure, Point.

CICIREPATO. Committee for International Co-operation in Information Retrieval among Examining Patent Offices; a committee of ICIREPAT.

cIDf. <www.cidf.org> Content ID Forum, an organization supported by approximately 200 Japanese companies, working to standardize a unique identifier for digital content in order to provide a copyright management framework for Internet use, combining Digital watermarking technology with the Handle System. The 'Content ID', or handle, is located by watermarking technology in a piece of content, and the handle is then resolved to identify the rights holder.

CIE. *See* Common information environment.

CIIG. *See* Construction Industry Information Group.

CILIP. <www.cilip.org.uk> (7 Ridgmount Street, London WC1E 7AE, UK) The Chartered Institute of Library and Information Professionals was formed in April 2002 by the merger of the Library Association (founded 1877) and the Institute of Information Scientists (founded 1958). CILIP is the professional body in the UK for those working in libraries and information services. It covers all sectors of the profession, and operates a qualification system which allows the use of post-nominal letters ACLIP (Affiliate member), MCLIP (Chartered member) and FCLIP (Fellow). During the period 2003–2005 transitional arrangements are in place following the merger; these cover the structure of qualifications, regional branches, code of conduct and ethics, subscription framework and website. Also currently subject to scrutiny are the 28 special interest groups: Affiliated Members; Branch and Mobile Libraries; Career Development; Cataloguing and Indexing; Colleges of Further and Higher Education; Community Services; Diversity; Education Librarians; Government Libraries; Health Libraries; Industrial and Commercial Libraries; Information Services; International Library and Information; Library and Information History; Library and Information Research; Local Studies; Multimedia and Information Technology; Patent and Trademark; Personnel Training and Education; Prison Libraries; Public Libraries; Publicity and Public Relations; Rare Books; Retired Members; School Libraries; UK Online User Group (UKOLOG); University College and Research; Youth Libraries. CILIP is responsible for several professional awards and medals including the Carnegie Medal, the Greenaway Medal, and Libraries Change Lives Awards. CILIP's main publication is *Update* (10 p.a.) and (from 2004) the *Library + Information Gazette* (fortnightly) which contains membership and events news.

CILIP Cymru. <www.cilip.org.uk> The regional organization of CILIP in Wales.

CILIP/Emerald Public Relations and Publicity Awards. <www.cilip.org. uk> A series of awards recognizing good examples of work in the field; administered by CILIP.

CILIP/English Speaking Union Award. <www.cilip.org.uk> An annual travel grant for self-directed CPD, administered through CILIP.

CILIP/FreePint Community Award. *See* Online Community Award.

CILIP/Nielsen BookData Reference Awards. <www.cilip.org.uk> A series of awards for outstanding reference works in print and electronic formats. The series includes the Besterman Medal, the McColvin Medal, the Walford Award, and the Wheatley Medal.

CILIP/Online Information Personal Development Award. <www.cilip. org.uk> An award to honour commitment to CPD on the part of recent Chartered Members of CILIP.

CILIPS. <www.cilip.org.uk> CILIP Scotland – the regional organization of CILIP in Scotland.

CILLA. <oclcpica.org> Originally an acronym for Co-operative of Indic Language LASER Libraries, set up by five London public library services to acquire and exploit materials in five languages: Bengali, Gujarati, Hindi, Panjabi, Tamil and Urdu. After the winding-up of LASER, activity passed in 2002 to OCLC-PICA in Birmingham, UK.

CIMI. <www.cimi.org> The consortium for the Computer Interchange of Museum Information explored how emerging technical standards could be applied to problems that restricted electronic interchange of museum information. It ceased operations in December 2003 though the website still exists.

CIMTECH. <www.cimtech.co.uk> (University of Hertfordshire, Hatfield AL10 9AD, UK) Centre for Information Management and Technology which specializes in advising organizations on information and document management strategies. This includes studying clients' existing systems, providing an impartial analysis of needs and preparing functional requirements documents. All forms of storage media, indexing and retrieval techniques, hardware and software are impartially assessed. Publishes *Information Management and Technology* (q.) and *Document Content and Record Management Guide* (a.).

CIO Connect. <www.ncc.co.uk> UK-based networking organization for Chief Information Officers formed in 1998; merged with the National Computing Centre in 2003.

CIP. 1. *See* Cataloguing in Publication. 2. *See* Common Indexing Protocol.

Cipfa. <www.cipfastats.net> The Chartered Institute of Public Finance and Accountancy is a highly-regarded UK organization that monitors the financial performance of local authorities. It publishes an annual report on library performance, based in part on information collected by PLUS – the Cipfa Public Library User Survey.

Cipher. 1. The initials of a name, or the arrangement of its letters in an ornamental manner, but disposed in such a way that it becomes a kind of private mark. 2. In data storage, a Code or an Encoded character.

CIQM. *See* Centre for Information Quality Management.

circa. (Lat. 'about') Used to indicate uncertainty in a date, as *c*. 1934, about 1934. Usually abbreviated to *c*. or *ca*.

Circle of Officers of National and Regional Library Systems. *See* CONARLS.

Circle of State Librarians (CSL). <www.circleofstatelibrarians.co.uk> The organization to which those employed in British government libraries and information bureaux may belong. It had its beginnings in 1914 when the Panizzi Club, named after Sir Anthony (Antonio) Panizzi who was Director of the British Museum, was formed. Government librarians were only a minority of the membership of the Club, the objects of which were 'to provide opportunities for social intercourse between the Senior Officers of Reference and Research Libraries and to promote all measures tending to their higher efficiency'. After the First World War the Club was revived and the name 'Circle of State Librarians' was used; it was an informal organization limited to officers-in-charge of Government libraries. The circle was revived in 1946 and membership was widened. In 1953 the function of the Circle was again widened 'to cultivate a common interest in bibliographical problems arising in Government service' and the membership opened 'to all members of the Government service who are interested in the activities of the Circle'. Now functions in a semi-informal manner as a social facility arranging visits and courses. Publishes *State Librarian* (3 p.a.).

Circuit edges. The edges of a book-cover which overlap the edges of the book. Used mostly for Bibles. Also called 'Divinity circuit', 'Divinity edges', 'Yapp edges'.

Circulating library. A library which lends books. In England, the term usually indicates a commercial library where payment has to be made for the use of the books. *See also* Subscription library.

Circulation. The total number of books issued from a library in a given period.

Circulation control system. An automated package available to libraries for the routines of the circulation system. Software will record loans using a stock database and a user database, generate overdues warnings and fines, trap reserved items, and provide relevant management information. *See also* Integrated library system.

Circulation department. The American term for the department of a public library which lends books for home-reading. Called a 'Lending department' in the UK.

Circulation desk. The area of a library in which the staff handle the loans procedures. Also called 'Counter', 'Issue desk'.

Circumflex. An accent, shaped like an inverted 'v' or 'u' and placed above the appropriate letter.

CIS. 1. *See* Cataloguing in source. 2. *See* CWIS (1).

CISTI. <www.nrc.ca/cisti> (NRC Canada, Montreal Road, Ottawa, Ontario K1A 0S2, Canada) Canada Institute for Scientific and Technical Information which was formed in Ottawa in 1974 by combining the National Science Library (NSL) and the Technical Information Service (TIS). Funded by the Canadian government through the National Research Council, CISTI promotes the use of scientific and technical information by the people and government of Canada to meet economic, regional and social development. CISTI is Canada's largest publisher of scientific journals, and one of OCLC's major interlibrary loan suppliers.

CISTIP. Committee on International Scientific and Technical Information Programs, established within the Commission on International Relations of the National Academy of Sciences – National Research Council. Its function is to provide continuing reviews, analyses and information to the Academy, the National Science Foundation and other bodies on issues and activities relating to US participation in the planning, development, co-ordination, operation and financing of international scientific and technical information programmes.

Citation. A reference to a text or part of a text identifying the document in which it may be found. *See also* References.

Citation index. A list of articles that, subsequent to the appearance of the original article, refer to, or cite, that article. This method is particularly applicable to scientific literature and allows easy tracing of similar research.

Citation order. The order of application of principles of division in determining an appropriate class number for a document. Also called 'Facet formula'.

CITED. Copyright in Transmitted Electronic Documents; an EU ESPRIT II project to devise a mechanism to monitor use and make payments for electronic publications. The partners in the project came from several European countries and included electronic publishers, computer manufacturers, libraries, security and software specialists, legal experts, and database and network specialists. Although the project was completed in 1996, it laid the foundation for considerable research in this field. *See also* COPYSMART, SEDODEL.

CITRA. *See* Round Table on Archives.

City Legal Information Group (CLIG). <www.clig.org> UK-based organization formed in the 1970s as the City Law Librarians Group; present title adopted in 2000. The Group operates seminars and courses, information exchanges and a social network. There are 300 members.

Civilité. A group of gothic cursive printing typefaces, the earliest and best of which was cut by Robert Granjon in the mid sixteenth century. They were based on a relatively informal hand, closely related to the English 'secretary'.

CIX. Commercial Internet eXchange, a non-profit, trade association of public data Internet service providers which disbanded in 2002 and was replaced by the US Internet Service Provider Association.

CJK. Chinese, Japanese, Korean; abbreviation registered by RLG to indicate East Asian language materials in the RLIN database.

CLA. 1. *See* Canadian Library Association. 2. *See* Catholic Library Association. 3. *See* Copyright Licensing Agency.

Claim. 1. Any communication sent to a bookseller or other supplier to hasten the delivery of overdue material. 2. CLAIM: Centre for Library and Information Management, based at Loughborough

University of Technology, UK. A research organization that specialized in the field of library management. *Now see* Library and Information Statistics Unit.

Clandestine literature.   Publications which are printed, published, and circulated secretly. They are usually of a political nature and seek to overthrow the government, or in time of war, act against the power in authority. Also called 'Secret literature', 'Underground literature'.

Clandestine press.   A printing press which operates secretly.

Clapp-Jordan Formulae.   Formulae devised by Verner Clapp and Robert T. Jordan, and stated in 'Quantitative criteria for adequacy of academic library collections' (*College and Research Libraries*, vol. 26, no. 5, 1965). They attempt to identify the principal factors affecting the academic needs for books and to ascribe suitable weights to each.

Clarendon.   The name of a particular typeface, and also of a group of faces characterized by little difference between thick and thin strokes, narrowness, and angular semi-Egyptian serifs. 'Consort' and 'Fortune' are of this kind. They were originally designed to give bold emphasis, particularly for dictionaries so that the word defined stood out clearly, and although still used for this purpose are now being used in their own right.

Clarendon Press.   Edward Hyde, first Earl of Clarendon (1609–74), gave the profits of the copyright of his *History of the Rebellion* to the University of Oxford to erect the first building in which the University's business of printing was wholly carried on – hence the name Clarendon Press. The business was transferred from the Sheldonian Theatre to this new building in 1713.

Clark (Daphne) Award.   Daphne Clark was a founder member of the Library and Information Research Group, and was its Chair at the time of her death, in September 1983. LIRG agreed to make an annual award in her memory towards the research expenses of an approved project, the first award being made in 1985.

Clasp.   A metal fastening hinged to one board and made to clip or lock into a loop or bar on the other board of a bound book or album. *See also* Catch.

Class.   (*Classification*) (*Noun*) 1. A group of entities, i.e. concepts or things, assembled by some shared likeness which unifies them. This likeness is called the 'Characteristic of a classification'. A class consists of all the things that are alike in essentials, characters, properties and relations, by which it is defined.   2. A group having the same or similar characteristics.   3. A major division of a Category. *See also* Form classes, Main class, Summum genus.   4. (*Verb*) To classify entities or books according to a scheme of classification.   5. (*Archives*) A set of archival materials which result from the same original compiling or filing process, are of broadly similar physical shape and informational content, and are referred to collectively by a specific title. Level 3 in the *MAD* taxonomy of levels of description. Known internationally as

'Series'. In some archives services, particularly the Public Record Office, and in the *Manual of Archival Description*, a level of archival description, equivalent to the international 'series'.

Class entry.   An entry in a catalogue under the name of a class, as distinct from one under a specific subject.

Class guide.   A guide to the shelves which gives the main class symbol and subject, and perhaps the same information for the main divisions of the class. A shelf guide.

Class library.   The classroom library in a primary school, so called to distinguish it from the 'general' or 'central' library provided in the same school for all to use. *See also* Classroom collection.

Class list.   A list of the books in a particular class, usually arranged in classified order. In archive administration, a list of the documents in a Class (*See* Class (5)), the entries being arranged in numerical order with enough detail to distinguish one document from another.

Class mark.   *See* Class number.

Class number.   One or more characters showing the class to which a book or other item belongs in the scheme of classification in use. In a Relative location, this number also shows the place of the item on the shelves and in relation to other subjects. It translates the name of its specific subject into the artificial language of the notation of the scheme of classification. The class number may be compounded of a variety of symbols used in a specific sequence, and followed by certain signs or symbols the purpose of which is to separate the constituent parts of the Class number and/or to indicate the characteristic of the following symbol. A key constituent of the Call number in library classification.

Classed catalogue.   *See* Classified catalogue. Also called 'Class catalogue'.

Classic.   An outstanding work, usually appearing in several versions and in translation, and sometimes adapted, being the subject of commentaries and other writings, and continuing in print even long after first publication.

Classic device.   (*Classification*) In the Colon Classification, the digit *x* which is put after the class number to which a Classic should be assigned and which precedes a Work facet or Author facet. This is done to bring together the different editions of a classic in a class, also the different editions of each of its commentaries, and to keep a classic and the commentaries thereon in juxtaposition.

Classical author.   For the purposes of the Colon Classification, an author, one at least of whose works is a classic.

Classification.   1. The arrangement of things in logical order according to their degrees of likeness, especially the assignment of books or other items to their proper places in a scheme of classification.   2. A scheme for the arrangement of books and other material in a logical sequence according to subject or form.   3. A 'coding' system within which the series of symbols indicating a concept, or semantemes, are subject to certain order relationships.   4. 'Any method of recognizing relations, generic or other, between items of information, regardless of the degree of hierarchy used and of whether those methods are applied in connection with traditional or computerized information systems' – the definition adopted in recommendations of the 2nd International Study Conference on Classification Research (1964, Elsinore). *See also* Broad classification, Close classification, Enumerative classification, Hierarchical classification, Summum genus.

Classification code.   A scheme of classification.

Classification Decimale Universelle.   *See* Universal Decimal Classification.

Classification for Social Sciences.   A Faceted classification compiled by Barbara Kyle for the Unesco Social Science bibliographies at the request of the International Committee for Social Sciences Documentation. Referred to as the KC (Kyle Classification).

Classification mark.   *See* Class number.

Classification of Library Science.   A faceted scheme which was prepared by the Classification Research Group (UK) and published in 1965. The Scheme is in two sections; the first (sections A/Z) contains the 'core' subjects of library science, while the second (classes 1/8) contains 'fringe' subjects which are disciplines in their own right but are of concern to librarians and information scientists. A revised version of this scheme was used in *Library and Information Science Abstracts* till 1992. A second edition appeared in 1975.

Classification Research Group (CRG).   An unattached, unofficial group of British volunteer librarians who have been meeting since February 1952 to discuss the theory and practice of classification. *See also* Classification of Library Science.

Classification schedule.   The printed scheme of a system of classification.

Classification scheme.   A scheme by which books or other items are classified or arranged in systematic order. The better known schemes are: Bibliographic Classification (Bliss); Colon Classification (Ranganathan); Decimal Classification (Dewey); Expansive Classification (Cutter); International Classification (Fremont Rider); Library of Congress Classification; Subject Classification (Brown); Universal Decimal Classification.

Classification system.   *See* Classification scheme.

Classified arrangement.   The arrangement of stock in a library according to some scheme of classification.

Classified catalogue.   A catalogue in which the entries are arranged in classified order of subjects. It is usually in two parts: the classified file of entries in systematic order, and the alphabetical subject index to the classified file. Also called 'Classed catalogue', 'Classified subject catalogue'.

Classified Catalogue Code.   The code of practice for assembling classified catalogues, with rules to apply to dictionary catalogue compilation. Formulated by S. R. Ranganathan and first published in 1934.

Classified file.   The entries, in systematic order, of the Classified catalogue. This is one (the main) part of this kind of catalogue, the other part being the alphabetical subject index. Also called 'Systematic file'. *See also* Feature heading.

Classified index.   1. One in which entries are not arranged in one strict alphabetical sequence, but under general headings, e.g. the names of binders would be arranged alphabetically, under the heading 'binders' and not in their correct places in the alphabetical sequence.   2. An index characterized by sub-divisions of hierarchic structure. An index using or displaying genus-species (class-sub-class) relationships. *See also* Classified catalogue, Correlative index.

Classified library.   A library in which the stock is arranged according to a recognized scheme of classification. Also called a 'Classed library'.

Classified material.   Memoranda, reports and other documents emanating from government departments, industrial and other corporations, research associations, etc., which are of a secret and confidential nature. They are classified as 'top secret', 'secret', 'confidential' and 'restricted' in a descending order of secrecy. Also called 'Classified information'.

Classified order.   The arrangement of books and other materials, or of entries in a catalogue, in order according to a scheme of classification.

Classified subject catalogue.   *See* Classified catalogue.

Classifier.   One who operates a system of classification.

Classify.   To bring individual items or persons with the same or similar characteristics together actually, or mentally, that is, conceptually. Also, in a secondary sense, to arrange classes in a classification, and to allocate the appropriate Class number to a book or other document according to a scheme of classification. *See also* Class (4).

Classifying.   The act of fitting books or other material into an existing scheme of classification.

Classroom collection.   1. A temporary, or semi-permanent, collection of books deposited in a schoolroom by a public, or a school, library.   2. A number of books sent by a college library to a classroom for use by students and teachers (US).

Clay tablets.   Cuneiform clay tablets were the earliest form of books, and were protected by an outer shell of clay which was inscribed with a copy, abstract, or title, of the contents.

CLCSP.   Copyright Libraries Shared Cataloguing Programme. *See* British National Bibliography.

Clean electrical supply.   A supply taken directly from the mains and which will not be subject to wide fluctuations in load caused by other equipment connected to the same circuit. *See also* Dedicated line.

Clean proof.   One having very few, or no, printer's errors.

Clear base.   *See* Film base.

Clearinghouse.   An organization that collects and maintains records of research, development, and other activities being planned, currently in progress, or completed; it provides documents derived from these activities, and referral services to other sources for information relating to these activities. Also clearing house.

Clements (William L.) Library. In 1923 William L. Clements deposited the library of Americana which he had been collecting for over twenty years with the University of Michigan, Ann Arbor. It is primarily a 'collection of the sources of American history' and has been extended over the years by the addition of books and documents which promote that study.

Clerical assistant. A person who performs work requiring ability in routines, but not knowledge of the theoretical or scientific aspects of library work. *See also* Library clerk.

Cliché. 1. A common and stereotyped journalistic or literary phrase. 2. An electrotype or stereotype plate.

Clichograph. *See* Klischograph.

Client/server. A computer architecture used to share data, Applications software and services among users on a network. Both the server and the client are stand-alone computers and this architecture is used particularly for communicating over the Internet. The 'client', the local PC or terminal, uses locally-mounted software, e.g. the Web browser, to communicate with databases and other software held on the remote computer, the 'server', which controls access and delivery of information back to the client. The client normally has significant computing capacity so that local processing can occur without placing undue load on the server. 'Client' and 'server' are also used to describe the software used at the local and remote ends. In the implementation of SR/Z39.50 'origin' and 'target' replace the client/server terminology. *See also* Peer to peer, Thin client.

Clift (David H.) Scholarship. An award made by the American Library Association Office for Library Personnel Resources.

CLIG. *See* City Legal Information Group.

Clinical librarian. A person who, by aptitude, training and experience, is qualified to participate in the remedial, therapeutic and rehabilitative care of individuals in hospitals and institutions.

Clip. The metal eye, of whatever form, fixed to one of the covers of a book in a mediaeval chained library, and to which the book's chain was fastened.

Clipping. A piece clipped, or cut from a newspaper or periodical (American). Called in the UK a 'Cutting', 'Press cutting'.

Clipping bureau. A commercial organization which clips, or cuts, items from newspapers and periodicals on specific subjects and sends them to subscribers (American). Called in the UK a 'Cuttings bureau'.

Clippings file. A collection of cuttings from newspapers and periodicals. Also called 'Cuttings file'.

CLIR. *See* Council on Library and Information Resources.

CLM. *See* Committee on Copyright and Other Legal Matters.

Cloaking. The act of hiding true web page content from either a human visitor or, more generally, a Web crawler or spider. The technique is used to camouflage actual page content from page thieves and to mislead search engines, thereby increasing the number of listings and providing better rankings for targeted keywords. Cloaking is considered an unacceptable practice by the major search engines and can be cause for banning. *See also* Spam.

Clogged. A half-tone, or line block, the impression from which has become smudged by the spaces between the dots or lines of the block becoming filled with ink. It may be due to dirty ink, dust, over-inking or the incorrect damping of a lithographic plate. Also known as 'filling in'.

Cloisonné. Enamelled bindings made during the eleventh century, mainly by Greek and Italian craftsmen. The design was first outlined by soldering thin strips of metal on to a metal plate and then filling the compartments so formed with coloured enamels. *See also Champlevé.*

Close. The second of a pair of punctuation marks, e.g.')]. *See also* Brackets, Curves, Square brackets.

Close classification. 1. The arrangement of books or other items in a classification system in as minute sub-divisions as possible; i.e. the full application of a scheme. Also called 'Exact classification', 'Depth classification', 'Minute classification'. Bibliographic classification is usually a close classification. 2. Arrangement of works in conformity with the provisions of such a scheme. *See also* Broad classification.

Close matter. Lines of type set without leads, or thinly spaced.

Close roll. A parchment roll upon which Letters close were enrolled at the Chancery.

Close score. A musical score in which the music of more than one part or instrument is written on one stave. Also called 'Short score', 'Compressed score', 'Condensed score'.

Close up. (*Printing*) To place lines or characters together by removing spacing-out leads or intervening letters.

Closed access. The obsolete method of keeping readers from the book shelves; this necessitated the provision in lending libraries of printed catalogues and indicators to inform readers which books were 'in' or 'out'. Also called 'Closed shelves', and 'Closed library'. In archive administration, archives which are not available to the general public due to the existence of a confidentiality restriction. They are said to be 'open' when the period of restriction has expired. *See also* Access.

Closed bibliography. One which has been completed. The opposite of Periodical bibliography. *See* Retrospective bibliography; *see also* Bibliography, Current bibliography.

Closed entry. 1. The catalogue entry for all the parts or volumes of a serial publication or work in several volumes, containing complete bibliographical information. Until the library has acquired a complete set, the bibliographical details are recorded in an Open entry. 2. A catalogue entry in which blank spaces are not left in the body of the entry or in the collation so that additional particulars of holdings may be entered subsequently.

Closed file.   1. One containing documents on which action has been finalized and to which further material is unlikely to be added.   2. One to which access is limited or denied because of the confidential nature of its contents.

Closed indexing system.   One in which the terms comprising the Authority list or File, or Controlled term list may not be added to when new knowledge, or the indexing of a new document, would make the addition of new terms appear appropriate. A new edition of the approved list or an amendment sheet must be awaited. An Open indexing system permits the addition of terms as necessary. *See also* Open ended term list.

Closed joint.   (*Bookbinding*) The type of joint which is obtained when cover boards are laced on. Also called 'Tight joint'. *See also* French joint.

Closed library.   *See* Closed access.

Closed shelves.   *See* Closed access.

Closed up.   When typesetting is divided between several compositors and each has completed the allocation, the Matter is closed up.

Closed user group.   A group, usually associated with a Mailing list or a particular resource, whose participation is restricted to members or approved subscribers.

Cloth.   A generic term applied to material which is not leather or paper used for covering books. It was originally a material made of natural fibres of some kind. It was first used for this purpose in about 1820. *See also* Cloth binding.

Cloth binding.   Used to describe a book which is bound entirely in cloth. A book so bound is called 'Cloth bound'.

Cloth boards.   *See* Boards.

Cloth joint.   Piece of cloth used to cover the joints on the inside of very heavy or large books.

Cloth sides.   A book which has cloth sides but leather at the spine and possibly at the corners as well.

Cloth-centred.   A duplex board or paper having a core, or centre, of muslin, linen or canvas (i.e. a cloth with paper on both sides), and used for maps, tables, etc. Cloth-faced, -lined, or -mounted paper or card indicates that the cloth is not a core but is pasted on one side only, and is termed linen- or canvas-lined (-backed) according to the kind of cloth used.

Cloth-lined paper (board).   Paper or board which is reinforced with muslin or cloth affixed to one side. *Cloth centred paper,* or *board,* is made up of two sheets or furnish layers with muslin or cloth between them.

CLR.   *See* Council on Library Resources, Inc.

CLTA.   *See* Canadian Library Trustees' Association.

Club line.   (*Printing*) The last line of type on a page when it begins a new paragraph. Printers try to avoid this, as they do a Widow, because of its unsightliness.

Clump. 1. An aggregation of catalogues, a term popular for a number of years following its introduction in the UK at the 3rd MODELS Workshop in 1996 <www.ukoln.ac.uk/dlis/models/models3>. The clump was seen as being 'physical' – in traditional terminology a union catalogue – or 'virtual', being created at the time of search from, for example, the catalogues of libraries having related subject collections, being in the same geographical area, or serving similar types of user. 2. A thick piece of type metal, ranging in width from 5 pt. upwards, but usually 6 pt. or 12 pt., and of the height of leads. Clumps are used in whiting out, and as footlines at the bottoms of columns and pages.

Cluster. (*Information retrieval*) A group of related documents.

CMS. *See* Content Management System.

CMYK. Cyan, magenta, yellow, and key (black), the four subtractive colours used in colour printing, each colour requiring a separate pass through the printing press using one colour at a time. The subtractive system starts with white and subtracts percentages of the other colours to yield the desired final effect. Subtracting 100 per cent results in black, subtracting no colour produces white. *See also* RGB.

CNI. *See* Coalition for Networked Information.

CNIDR. *See* Center for Networked Information Discovery and Retrieval.

CNRS. Centre National de la Recherche Scientifique [et Technique]. <www.cnrs.fr> (3–5 rue Michel Ange, 75794 Paris, France) Founded in 1939 and controlling 1,370 laboratories and research centres, CNRS plays a major role in scientific documentation in France. *See also* INIST.

Coalition Against Database Piracy. <www.cadp.net> An alliance of US database providers, including the American Medical Association, Information Industry Association, McGraw-Hill Companies, Reed Elsevier Inc., Thompson Corporation etc., formed to secure passage by Congress of legislation that deters database piracy without causing unintended difficulties for scientists, educators and other legitimate users.

Coalition for Networked Information (CNI). <www.cni.org> (21 Dupont Circle, Washington, DC 20036, USA) Founded in 1990, the Coalition is sponsored by the Association of Research Libraries and Educause who recognized the need to broaden the community's thinking beyond issues of network connectivity and bandwidth to encompass networked information content and applications. The work of the Coalition is structured around three central themes: developing and managing networked information content; transforming organizations, professions and individuals; and building technology, standards and infrastructure. It comprises around 200 member institutions representing higher education and library institutions, professional and scholarly organizations, and publishing and information technology companies. In addition to semi-annual Task Force Meetings the Coalition also hosts a variety of networked information projects.

Coarse screen. *See* Screen (1).

Coated paper.   1. A general term for papers such as chromo, art, enamel, which have been prepared for different printing processes by applying a mineral such as china clay after the body paper has been made. Also called 'Surface paper'.   2. Any paper whose surface is coated with a mixture of clay and glue made of casein to give it a smooth surface. The term is used to distinguish it from loaded papers in which the clay is mixed with the pulp during manufacture. *See also* Art.

Coating.   A thin layer of light-sensitive chemical applied to a base material such as cloth, paper, or transparent plastic, or a mineral such as china clay to a printing paper. *See also* Coated paper.

Coaxial cable.   A cable formed from two concentric wires, the inner signal-carrying wire being protected from radio interference by the outer, grounded, 'shield'. The two wires are separated by insulation.

Cock.   The middle portion of a Brace, when cast in three pieces.

Cockle.   (*Paper*) A puckered effect on paper, produced either naturally or artificially during the drying process. Paper and board will cockle and get out of shape with excessive heat or moisture; to prevent this these materials must be kept under temperature- and humidity-controlled conditions.

Cock-up initial.   An initial letter that extends above the first line of text but aligns with the foot of it.

COCOREES.   Collaborative Collection Management for Russian and East European Studies. *See now* CoFoR.

COCRIL.   Council of City Research and Information Libraries. The Council evolved from the Group of City Librarians which was formed after the 1955 (UK) Library Association Conference. Represents the interests of large city libraries with research and large-scale information provision responsibilities. Currently very low level of activity.

cod.   Abbreviation for Codex.

codd.   Abbreviation for codices. *See* Codex.

Code.   1. A standardized system of symbols, which may be visual, acoustic, magnetic, etc. by which information in a normal, common, source language can be converted into an artificial format for a specific purpose; typically such a system would be used to convert information into a format that could be accepted and handled by a computer.   2. A set of rules for carrying out a function in a standardized manner, for example, a code of cataloguing rules. *See also* Algorithmic code, Description, Non-semantic code, Semantic code.

Code mark.   An indication of purchase made in code on the back of a title-page.

Code of ethics.   *See* Professional Ethics, Code of.

Codec.   Compressor/decompressor, an algorithm used to ease the storage and transfer of large data files, particularly audio and video in desktop video systems and for Multimedia use across the Internet. The codec is used to compress files for storage and transfer (using an encoder) and then provides automatic decompression on playback (via a decoder).

Coden. 1. A code classification assigned to a document or other library item consisting of four capital letters followed by two hyphenated groups of arabic numerals, or of two arabic numerals followed by two capital letters or of some similar combination. 2. The combination of letters, numbers and symbols assigned as a result of applying coding rules in order to produce a bibliographical citation. *See also* Bishop's Rules. The *ASTM Coden for periodical titles* uses five-letter codes for the titles of periodicals and serials; the first four letters of each coden have some mnemonic relation to the title, and the fifth letter is arbitrary and will assist in maintaining as many mnemonic relationships as possible for similar periodical titles. The *ASTM Coden* system was transferred on 1 January 1975 by the American Society for Testing Materials (ASTM), which had sponsored the system since 1955, to Chemical Abstracts Service (CAS). The *Coden* serves as a unique and unambiguous permanent identifier for a specific title, and is used in lieu of full or abbreviated titles of publications in processing and storing bibliographical data in many computer-based information handling systems. *See also* ISSN.

Codex. (*Pl.* Codices) An ancient book composed of pieces of writing material fastened so as to open like a modern book as distinct from the Scroll or Volumen which it superseded. The name was originally given to two or more tablets of metal, wood or ivory, hinged together with rings; the inner sides were covered with wax and these were written on with a stylus. Later 'Codex' was given to books of this type made of papyrus, vellum or parchment, and later still to volumes consisting of many leaves of parchment or vellum, e.g. *Codex Alexandrinus.* Codices became general for law-books in classical Rome, and were used largely for MS. copies of the scriptures and classics. Codex means a block of wood, probably from the wooden covers. When a codex of the original form consisted of two leaves, it was called a Diptych, of three, a Triptych, and of more, a Polyptych. Abbreviated cod. (*Pl.* codd.). There are a number of codices of the Bible, and these are often named after the place of discovery. The four most important of these are *Codex Sinaiticus* (4th or beginning of the 5th century – in the British Library), *Codex Vaticanus* (4th Century – in the Vatican), *Codex Alexandrinus* (5th century – in the British Library) and the palimpsest *Codex Ephraemi* (5th century Greek text overwritten in a 12th-century hand – in the Bibliothèque Nationale de France, Paris). These originally contained the whole Greek text of the Old and New Testaments, but are now incomplete. The *Codex Bezae* (5th or 6th century – at Cambridge University Library) containing only the *Gospels* and *Acts* is another important early copy of the *Bible.* All were written in uncials (i.e. capitals) and without breaks between words. The term 'codex' was also used for a collection of Roman laws; these included *Codex Theodosianus* and *Codex Justinianeus.*

Coding quires. *See* Cassie.

Co-extensiveness.   Intensive classification to coincide with the specific nature of the subject of a book.

Coffee table book.   A sumptuously produced illustrated book, intended to be browsed through at leisure rather than purposefully read. *See also* Table book (3).

Coffin.   A square frame in a hand printing press in which is bedded a stone on which the Forme is placed.

CoFHE.   *See* Colleges of Further and Higher Education Group.

CoFoR.   <www.cocorees.ac.uk> Collaboration For Research, a CURL project to promote collaborative collection management, set up to provide research libraries with practical tools (templates, guidelines and recommendations) for collaborative acquisition and retention. It also gave special attention to techniques for serial de-duplication and to the mapping of relationships between research activity and library provision. Built on the earlier COCOREES project.

CogPrints.   <cogprints.ecs.soton.ac.uk> Cognitive science E-prints archive, an electronic archive for self-archived papers in any area of psychology, neuroscience, and linguistics, and many areas of computer science, philosophy, biology as well as any other portions of the physical, social and mathematical sciences that are pertinent to the study of cognition. Started life as an eLib project.

Coiled Binding.   *See* Spiral binding.

COINE.   <www.coine.org> Cultural Objects in Networked Environments, an EU-funded project aimed at empowering European citizens to tell their own stories, provide personal histories and recollections, display photographs and pictures, publish sound recordings, or mix all these together. COINE provided the tools to enable even those without previous computer skills to become writers and creators and to publish their work on the World Wide Web. The project was completed in September 2004.

Cold composition.   (*Printing*) Any method of composition which does not involve the casting of metal type. Typewriter, filmsetting and photographic methods are included. 'Cold type' is sometimes used to distinguish this method from 'hot metal' typesetting.

Cold type.   Composition by a composing machine which does not require hot metal, such as photographically, on a typewriter, or by computer keyboard.

Cole size card.   A graduated card for determining the sizes of books (not by measurement but by bibliographical description) when writing catalogue and bibliography entries. The card, which was first issued in 1889 by the Library Bureau, was based on the size rules of the American Library Association, the more uniform and accurate use of which the size card was intended to achieve. The card was named after its designer, Dr. George Watson Cole (1850–1939), who was Librarian of the Huntington Library from 1915 to 1924. A description of the card may be read in *The Library Journal*, vol. 14, 1889, pp. 485–486.

COLICO. <www.librarycouncil.ie/colico> Committee on Library Co-operation in Ireland; established in 1977, COLICO advises the Library Council and the Library and Information Services Council (Northern Ireland) on all matters relating to library co-operation and interlending.

Collaborator. One who is associated with another, or others, especially in the writing of books, being responsible for some aspect of, or contribution to, a work, but not responsible for the content as a whole.

Collage. A picture or visual arrangement made partly or entirely of pieces of paper, wallpaper, illustrations, photographs or any other textured or figured material.

Collate. *See* Collation.

Collateral arrays. (*Classification*) Arrays of the same order. *See also* Array (1).

Collateral classes. (*Classification*) Classes of the same order but not belonging to the same array. *See also* Array (3).

Collateral reference. One which in an alphabetico-direct subject catalogue links two headings belonging to the same hierarchical level under a common generic term, and which would stand side-by-side if arranged in a classification scheme.

Collateral term. (*Indexing*) A word which forms a constituent part of a Bound term and which is also found in association with another word, both being used as a heading in a subject index. *See also* Generic term.

Collating mark. A quad mark having a printing surface about 12 point deep by 5 point wide, which is printed so that after folding and gathering, the marks appear in descending order on the back of each section in such a way that the omission or duplication of a section becomes immediately apparent. Also called Back mark, Black step, Quad mark.

Collation. 1. That part of a description of a book, apart from the contents, which describes the book as a physical object by specifying the number of volumes, pages, columns, leaves, illustrations, photographs, maps, format, size, etc. In a bibliographical description of an old book the number, which is expressed by the signature letters (*see* Signature (2)), and composition of the sections is important. A *collation by gatherings* records the make-up of a book by stating the signature letters, e.g. A^4, $*^2$, $B-2A^4$, etc.; a *collation by pagination* records the make-up by the page numbers, e.g. [1]–[12], 1–374, etc. 2. The process of examining a new book to check its completeness, presence of all the illustrations, etc. 3. To check that a book is complete before binding or re-binding. 4. To compare two or more texts, either (a) to ascertain which is the first edition of a printed work, or (b) to establish a definitive or standard text. 5. To merge and combine two or more similarly ordered sets of items to produce an ordered set.

Collectanea. Passages selected from one or more authors, generally for instruction. A collection or miscellany.

Collected edition. An edition of an author's works published in one volume or in a number of volumes in a uniform style of binding.

Collected works. All the writings of an author, including those which have not been printed previously, published in one volume or a number of volumes in a uniform style of binding, usually with an inclusive title.

Collecting drum. A revolving drum which is fitted to a high-speed printing press or paper-making machine to catch the sheets of paper coming out of the machine and collect them in groups of from five to ten so that final delivery can be at a slower speed.

Collection. 1. A number of books or other items on one subject, or of one kind, or collected by one person or organization. 2. (*Bibliography*) A number of works, or parts of them, not forming a treatise or monograph on a single subject, and regarded as constituting a single whole, as a collection of plays, essays, etc. 3. (*Cataloguing*) If written by one author, three or more independent works, or parts of works, published together; if written by more than one author, two or more independent works, or parts of works, published together but not written for the same occasion or for the same publication. 4. (*Archives*) An artificial accumulation of manuscript or archive material related to a theme, interest, type of document or person, or compiled by an individual. Used colloquially and in manuscript libraries instead of 'Group'.

Collection Description Focus. <www.ukoln.ac.uk/cd-focus> A post jointly funded by the British Library, JISC and the Museums, Libraries and Archives Council (MLA) to improve co-ordination of work on collection description methods, schemas and tools, with the goal of ensuring consistency and compatibility of approaches across projects, disciplines, institutions, domains and sectors. The Focus provides support for projects actively involved in collection description work and for those planning such work. *See also* Collection level description.

Collection development. The process of planning a stock acquisition programme not simply to cater for immediate needs, but to build a coherent and reliable collection over a number of years, to meet the objectives of the service. The term demands a depth and quality of stock, and includes associated activity towards exploitation of the collection through publicity, staff training, etc.

Collection evaluation. Similar to Collection management; maintaining the stock of a library by examining its use (for example via circulation system data) and by physical inspection of age and condition.

Collection level description. <www.ukoln.ac.uk/cd-focus/cdfocus-tutorial/intro.html> A description of a collection only at the collection level i.e. information about the collection as a whole and not information about individual items within the collection. It can be used to assist the location of searchable databases, particularly in a networked environment. The collections described can be library, museum and archival catalogues, Internet catalogues, and physical items, among other things. The basis for collection description implementations in the UK is the RSLP Collection Description Schema, a set of metadata attributes which was created for describing collections within the Research Support Libraries Programme. A Dublin Core-based schema also exists, see for example <dublincore.org/groups/collections>. Sometimes abbreviated to Collection description. *See also* Collection Description Focus, Conspectus.

Collection management. The organization and maintenance of library stock, starting from Collection development principles, keeping the needs of users a priority objective, and considering alternative means of document and information supply to supplement local holdings.

Collective biography. A volume, or volumes, consisting of separate accounts of the lives of people.

Collective cataloguing. The cataloguing of minor and fugitive material by (a) assembling a group of such items and assigning it a heading and a collective title; (b) cataloguing it by form but stating the corporate or personal authorship and giving the class number or other retrieval identification. *See also* Form entry, Form heading.

Collective entries. In selective cataloguing, several entries in one place for pamphlets on the same or related subjects. They may be either author or subject entries.

Collective title. 1. A title under which articles written separately by several authors are published together. If there is no recognized author, compiler, or editing body, the main catalogue entry appears under the title of the work. 2. The title given to a work as a whole when that work consists of several works, each with its own title.

Collectives. *See* Consortia.

College library. A library established, maintained, and administered by a college to meet the needs of its students and faculty.

Colleges of Further and Higher Education Group (CoFHE). A membership group of CILIP. Originally formed in 1970 as the Colleges of Technology and Further Education Group; name changed in 1979.

Collocation. The arrangement of sub-classes of a classification by degrees of likeness.

Collocative *v.* direct cataloguing. The principle of entering books written by one author using several pseudonyms under the real name (collocative) or under the name used for each individual title (direct).

Collography. A similar production process to collotype except that a film base wrapped around a cylinder is used instead of a flat glass plate.

Colloplas. Trade name for a process for making non-etched gravure cylinders in which a rubber surface on which the printing image is impressed hydraulically is substituted for the copper-coated etched cylinders used in photogravure.

Collotype. A variety of photogravure. A print which gives accurate gradation of tone; it is made by a photo-mechanical process directly from a hardened emulsion of bichromated gelatine on glass. Phototype, Albertype, Artotype, Heliotype and Lichtdruck are forms of collotype. William Henry Fox Talbot, an English pioneer of photography, discovered in 1852 that a chromate gelatine layer was case-hardened by exposure to light, and the first person to employ this process for the production of printing plates was Alphonse Louis Poitevin in 1855. By coating a plate with chromated gelatine and printing and developing a photographic image on it, a surface could be obtained which, when damped, responds to ink in the same way as a lithographic stone. Also called a 'gelatine print'.

Colombier. Drawing and plate paper size 24 x 34$^{1/2}$ inches. Also spelled 'Columbier'.

Colon. 1. A device used in the Universal Decimal Classification to link related class terms. 2. A device initially used in the Colon Classification to separate successive foci. Later, in the Colon Classification, a device to introduce only the energy facet. 3. A punctuation symbol.

Colon book number. A book number used in connection with the Colon Classification. Based on a lengthy facet formula, it sub-arranges books within an ultimate class by their year of publication.

Colon Classification. A pioneer faceted classification authored by S. R. Ranganathan (1892–1972) and published in 1933. It is based on scientific principles and literary warrant. Unlike earlier schemes it does not provide ready-made class numbers; it has to be synthesized. But like other schemes it first divides knowledge traditionally into main classes denoted by 1/9 and A/Z: A/M Sciences; N/S Humanities; T/Z Social Sciences. Between M and N is interposed a main class 'Mysticism and Spiritual Experience' denoted by Δ (Delta). 1/9 denote newly recognized main classes. Under each of these main classes are listed concepts (termed Isolates) pertaining to that subject. The isolates arranged in arrays and chains are grouped under facets, and facets belong to any of the five fundamental categories – personality, matter, energy, space, time (PMEST) – postulated by Ranganathan. Isolate numbers preceded by the main class digit are arranged in the PMEST order, which is of decreasing concreteness. In the facet formula each category has its own indicator digit which acts as a signpost to identify back the category of a particular isolate number. In addition there are common schedules for languages, space and time; and a schedule of common isolates representing viewpoints, or document formats applicable to all main classes. A category may be manifested in more than one facet. All the facets within a category or in the overall facet formula are arranged by objectively-stated principles of facet sequence such as wall/picture, or cow/calf. Complex and multi-disciplinary subjects are classified by phase analysis. The notation is highly mixed and hospitable to new concepts at their logical places. It comprises 26 Roman capitals, 23 Roman lower-case letters, 0/9 used decimally, and one Greek letter. There are 14 indicator digits, namely ()&':;,-=→←+*". The scheme has very slim schedules, and has contributed many seminal ideas and techniques to the theory and practice of library classification. Although in its 7th. edition (1987), it is endangered by lack of maintenance.

Colophon. (Gr. 'finishing, end') 1. Particulars of printer, place and date of printing, title, name of author, and publisher's or printer's device, found at the end of early printed books. It was first used in printed books by Fust and Schoeffer in the 'Mainz Psalter' of 1457, and gradually became common, but was superseded towards 1600 by the Publisher's Imprint. Its use in MSS. was occasional; it then gave the scribe's name and the date. *See also* Imprint. 2. A current, but incorrect, meaning is the publisher's device, e.g. Benn's *horse*, Heinemann's *windmill* or Thames and Hudson's *dolphins*.

Colophon date. The date given in the Colophon, and so described when used in a catalogue and bibliography.

Colour gravure. The process of producing coloured illustrations by Photogravure. This method is used principally for mass circulation colour magazines and packaging materials. The colour picture is usually of almost continuous tone, the dark and light shades being obtained by varying depths of the etched cells.

Colour lithography. A method of printing in colour by lithography using separate stones or plates for each colour.

Colour printing. The art of producing pictures, designs, etc., in a variety of colours, shades and tones by means of printing from plates, or by lithography; chromatic printing.

Colour process. A set of two or more half-tones made by colour separation. Half-tone colour printing is commonly called process colour work.

Colour separation. The process by which colours of an original work of art or colour print are analysed into the basic colours in such a way that printing plates may be prepared in order to print in succession and finally yield a print of correct colouring. This is done by placing filters in front of the camera lens when making negatives.

Colour transparency. A positive colour photograph on a transparent support, usually film.

Colour under gilt. The edges of a book coloured (usually red) before gilding. Usually found in Bible binding. *See also* Edges, Red under gold edges.

Colour work. Printing processes used to print in two or more colours, such as two-, or four-colour half-tone, planographic and intaglio work in colour. Often called according to the number of plates used, 'Three-colour process', 'Four-colour process'.

Coloured edges. *See* Sprinkled edges.

Coloured plate. A whole-page coloured illustration produced by any process.

Coloured printings. A cheap paper, having a high content of mechanical wood pulp; it is used, among other purposes, for the covers of pamphlets.

Colporteur. A travelling bookseller or agent, usually of a religious group or society, who sells tracts and copies of the scriptures at low prices.

CoLRiC. *See* Council for Learning Resources in Colleges.

Columbian. An out-of-date name for a size of type equal to about 16 point.

Columbian Press. A printing press designed by George Clymer of Philadelphia and brought to England in 1817 where it became more successful than in the United States. The press derived its power from a system of levers which converted the lateral movement of the bar to the vertical movement of the iron beam from which the platen was suspended. The most conspicuous feature of the press was a cast-iron eagle which acted as an adjustable counter weight.

Columbier. *See* Colombier.

Column. 1. A narrow division of a page of a book formed by vertical lines or spaces to form two or three columns of type. 2. A narrow block of letterpress arranged in the form of a column. 3. (*Printing*) A vertical line or square bracket.

Column inch. (*Printing*) *See* Agate line.

Column picture. Picture in a mediaeval illuminated manuscript the width of a column of text, whether at the head of a page, or interrupting the text at intervals.

Column rule. (*Printing*) A metal rule used to separate columns of type in the text or in tables. *See also* Rule.

Columnar. A series or classification in which the terms, or classes, are arranged in a column. The classes may be co-ordinate, or they may be regarded as subordinate, each to that above it. *See* Horizontal, Tabular classification.

COM. Computer output microfilm/microfiche, output from a computer produced directly in a microformat instead of in printed form.

Comb pattern. A pattern produced on marbled papers or other surfaces from a vat in which colours have been combed to form a pattern. *See also* Marbled paper.

Combination order. (*Cataloguing, Classification, Information retrieval*) The order in which facets in a compound subject heading are to be arranged, e.g. the order of Decreasing concreteness. *See also* Distributed facets.

Combination plate. One in which both half-tone and line methods have been used.

Combined Regions (The). <www.thecombinedregions.com> A UK consortium that manages the Unity Combined Regions Database and Unityweb. *See also* CONARLS, Unityweb.

Comedia Report. A national study into the future of the UK public library service, carried out by the cultural planning consultants Comedia and the Gulbenkian Foundation (UK). Topics covered include statutory obligations, the changing range of services, charges, demographic factors, and wider cultural issues. The report was published in 1993.

COMLA. *See* Commonwealth Library Association.

Comma. A punctuation mark. *See also* Quotes, Turned comma.

Command Papers. *See* Parliamentary Papers.

Command-driven. An early method of User interface for a PC in which the end user typed in command line strings – sets of characters in fixed arrangement – to carry out operations. Largely replaced by GUI/ WIMPS.

Commentary. 1. Explanatory or critical notes on an Act of Parliament, a literary text or some other work. It may accompany the text or be issued separately. 2. A spoken script to a film, videotape, or tape/slide presentation.

Commercial Internet Exchange. *See* CIX.

Commercial library. A subject department within a library system, or an independent unit, specializing in business, financial, trade and commercial information.

Commission of the European Community. *See* European Union.

Commission on Preservation and Access. Set up in 1986 in the USA and funded by the Council on Library Resources Inc., the H.W.Wilson Foundation, the Mellon Foundation, the Hewlett Foundation, the Getty Grant Program and several major research libraries; a high profile body whose purpose was to foster, develop and support systematic collaboration among libraries in order to ensure the preservation of published and documentary records in all formats and to provide enhanced public access to preserved materials through an open distribution system. It was advised by the National Advisory Council on Preservation. In 1997 the Commission merged with the Council on Library Resources to form the Council on Library and Information Resources.

Committee on Copyright and Other Legal Matters (CLM). <wtabb@ jhu.edu> (Chair: Winston Tabb, The Sheridan Libraries, 3400 N Charles Street, Baltimore, MD 21218-2683, USA) Set up by IFLA in 1997 and became operational in 1998. Monitors legal issues relating to library matters, especially copyright but also trade barriers, ownership disputes, privacy, education and training, and customs and excise laws.

Committee on Institutional Cooperation. *See* CIC.

Committee on Library Co-operation in Ireland. *See* COLICO.

Common auxiliaries. *See* Universal Decimal Classification.

Common carrier. A company regulated by government to provide a communications service to the general public. Common carriers should not exercise any control over content of the messages they carry.

Common facets. Facets or terms which may occur in more than one field in a general classification.

Common folio. *See* Folio.

Common Indexing Protocol. A standard Internet protocol defined by the Internet Engineering Task Force and used between servers in a network to facilitate query routing – directing queries towards the servers holding the actual results via reference to indexing information. The Common Indexing Protocol is based upon the concept of index summaries: summaries of the structured information in a given server.

Common information environment (CIE). <www.jisc.ac.uk/cie> A vision of a future in which electronic content would be more widely available as a result of collaborative cross-sectoral partnerships. One immediate example in the UK is for JISC-funded materials to be made available outside the academic community. A CIE Group has been formed to develop this vision and lobby for progress. (Reference: Pothen, P. Building a CIE. *Update* vol. 2, no. 12, (December) 2003: pp. 46–47)

Common isolates. Symbols attached to many classes in the Colon Classification and indicating literary form, e.g. *a* bibliography; *c* concordance; *v* history; *y*2 syllabus, P*v* history of linguistics; Plll*v* history of English linguistics. When attached to a host class number without a connecting symbol, as in the examples given, they are called *Anteriorising common isolates*, but when needing a connecting symbol *Posteriorising common isolates*.

Common ruling. Term used to denote the vertical lines (rules) printed on account-book paper. *See also* Feint ruling.

Common subdivisions. Form divisions which are used throughout a classification to sub-divide any subject. These have distinctive names in different classifications, e.g.Auxiliary tables in Dewey and the Universal Decimal Classification; Categorical tables in Brown's Subject Classification, and Systematic schedules in Bliss's Bibliographic Classification.

Commonwealth Library Association (COMLA). <mona.uwi.edu/library> <www.thecommonwealth.org> <nkpodo@uwi.edu.jm> (P.O. Box 144, Mona, Kingston 7, Jamaica, WI) Founded in 1972 with a membership of 20 national library associations in Commonwealth countries. It is one of more than 25 Commonwealth Professional Associations sponsored by the Commonwealth Foundation since 1966, when this agency was established by the Commonwealth Heads of Government for the 'nurturing of professional activity throughout the Commonwealth as an important component of the developmental process'. Aims of COMLA are: to support and encourage library associations in the Commonwealth; to forge, maintain and strengthen professional links between librarians; to promote the status and education of librarians and the reciprocal recognition of qualifications in librarianship; to improve libraries; and to initiate research projects designed to promote library provision and to further technical development of libraries in the Commonwealth. Publishes *COMLA Newsletter* (q.).

Communication. The transfer of information or data from one place to another, particularly in the electronic context. *See* ICT. Communication is also an interpersonal skill important in customer relations, training and human resource management.

Communication to the Public Right. A new right established by the European Union giving the owner of the copyright in a work the exclusive right to make it available via the Internet.

Communications and Information Technology. *See* C&IT.

Communications protocol. *See* Protocol.

Communities of practice. The formation of formal or informal groups of those with similar concerns; it is within the model of Knowledge management that the term has become most used. Knowledge can be deepened and extended by interaction within the domain or community, and ideas are generated. (Reference: Wenger, E. *et al. Cultivating communities of practice: a guide to managing knowledge.* Boston: Harvard Business School, 2002)

Community information. Material collected to provide a local information service to a small geographical area; the information will relate to any topics that affect the life of the community, for example social, domestic, health or educational facilities, details of local cultural activities, clubs and societies, and the range of local authority or governmental services. Material is usually in pamphlet or loose-leaf format; such a service may be provided in a public branch library, or via a special unit set up by a local authority, voluntary agency or advice group.

Community Initiative Award. A UK award offered annually to public libraries to highlight their pivotal role in local communities. *See now* Libraries Change Lives Award.

Community library. Usually a branch library (although maybe a central or mobile service) intended to provide advice-centre functions and local information for the whole of its community, rather than only offering a bookstock to readers.

Community profile. A demographic study of the community served by a library, including information on social, economic and educational factors, average ages, levels of employment, numbers of children, old-peoples homes, etc., that the service should take account of in planning, and in purchasing stock.

Community Research and Development Information Service. *See* CORDIS.

Community Services Group. A membership group of CILIP, formed in 1982 as a forum for those who wish to promote library and information services to the wider community; ethnic communities and disadvantaged people have been priority interests.

Compact disc. *See* CD, CD-ROM.

Compact disc recordable. *See* CD-R.

Compact disc rewritable. *See* CD-RW.

Compact disc video. *See* CDV.

Compact storage. The storing of books on rolling or swinging stacks which have to be moved into another position to permit consultation, or of books or other material placed in drawers built into shelving and opening into a stack aisle. Such shelving is used normally in stack rooms. *See also* Draw-out shelves, Rolling bookcase, Swinging bookcase.

Company file. A file, kept especially in commercial, industrial, research and learned or professional association libraries, containing information relating to individual firms. The type of information kept depends on the type of library and the needs of its users but may include reports, company reports, house journals, catalogues, booklets, cuttings, advertisements, stock exchange listings, etc. Also called 'Corporation file'.

Comparative librarianship. The study of library services in various countries, reflecting differing national, cultural, political or societal environments. The comparison of similarities and analysis of differences leads to a better understanding of the general principles involved, and mature consideration of the success of varying approaches.

Compartment. 1. In a book stack, sets of shelves arranged vertically between two uprights and placed back to back (US). *Compare* Bay. 2. (*Bibliography*) A group of decorative borders comprising (a) a single carved or engraved piece with the centre portion cut out so as to resemble a picture frame into which the letterpress of a title or other matter is set; (b) a piece originally carved or engraved as (a) but later cut into four or more pieces; (c) four or more pieces cut or engraved separately but intended to form a single design when assembled; (d) such borders made from four pieces of cast type-ornaments but with ends cut obliquely to help form a border. *See also* Frame.

Compartment picture. An illumination, in a mediaeval illuminated manuscript, divided into sections each of which contains a picture.

Compass map. *See* Portolan chart.

Compend. A subject treated briefly, or in outline only.

Compendium. A work containing in a small compass the substance or general principles of a larger work; a brief, comprehensive summary.

Compensation guards. Short stubs bound into a volume to balance the space taken up by folded maps or other bulky material so that this can be incorporated without distorting the shape of the book. Also called 'Filling-in guards'. *See also* Guard, Stub.

Competencies. The mix of skills, expertise and experience needed to fill a role at the required level, and achieved through identifiable outcomes; they may be defined in terms of 'behaviours'. A framework of competencies is a foundation to define and assess the capability needed in a workforce and to develop a strategy to fill gaps. *Compare* Literacy.

Competitive intelligence. The systematic scanning and monitoring of external trends and events in order to gather, analyze and manage information that can affect the future of an organization. The focus would be on the activities and intentions of competitors. CI includes aspects of economics, market research, information science and strategic management.

Competitive tendering (CT). The process of Contracting out library services, with the effect that new suppliers and existing providers need to make bids (tenders) in competition with others to operate services. In the UK, it has been an obligation in certain sectors to require that such tenders be sought, and thus the phrase Compulsory competitive tendering (CCT) has been frequently used.

Compilation. A work compiled by assembling material from other books.

Compiler.   1. A collector or editor of written or printed material gleaned from various sources or from one or more authors; and who arranges it for publication.   2. One who produces a musical work by collecting and putting together written or printed matter from the work of several composers. Also, one who chooses and combines into one work selections and excerpts from one or more composers.

Compiler entry.   A catalogue entry for the compiler of a work.

Complete bibliography.   *See* Bibliography.

Complete specification.   *See* Patent, Specification.

Completion.   *See* Continuation.

Complex subject.   In classification, one which reflects more than one distinct conventional class.

Component.   An individual constituent word in a compound subject heading.

Compose.   To set type-matter ready for printing.

Composer.   One who composes, especially music.

Composer entry.   An entry in a catalogue for a musical composition under the name of the composer as the heading.

Composing room.   A room in which printing type is set, or composed, and made up into formes for printing. *See also* Compositor.

Composing rule.   A flat strip of steel or brass placed by the Compositor between each line of type in the composing stick when setting type. Rules provide a flat surface for each line of type and facilitate the handling of the composed type. Also called 'Setting rule'.

Composing stick.   *See* Stick.

Composite authors.   Name given to the several authors contributing to one work. Not to be confused with Joint author.

Composite book.   1. A book of a composite nature, where an editor has brought together several works by different authors into one volume. 2. A book on more than one subject.   3. A Composite work.

Composite classification.   A method of classifying whereby specific subjects are represented by coupling two or more elementary terms from the classification schedules. Also known as Faceted classification.

Composite heading.   (*Cataloguing*) A heading consisting of more than one element each of which is to be distinguished by punctuation, or typographically, for filing purposes.

Composite subject.   (*Classification*) One which consists of more than one element, e.g. the design of furniture for children's libraries.

Composite work.   1. A literary production on a single subject written by two or more authors in collaboration, the contribution by each forming a distinct section or part of the complete work.   2. A musical composition in which two or more composers collaborate similarly, each contribution forming a distinct section or part of the complete work.

Composition.   Type setting: hence Compositor.

Composition font.   Loosely used to indicate any Typeface of a size of 14 point or less, used for book printing and 'tapped' on a type-composing machine.

Compositor. One who sets printer's type. A typesetter.

Compound catchword. In indexing, a hyphenated word which must be treated as if the hyphen did not exist.

Compound heading. (*Information retrieval*) A number of general terms arranged together in a co-ordinate relationship to designate a complex idea. *See also* Main heading.

Compound name. A name made of two or more proper names, generally connected by a hyphen, conjunction or preposition.

Compound subject. 1. (*Cataloguing*) One which requires more than one word in the subject heading to express its meaning. A compound subject may consist of a phrase or a combination, the separate words of which are divided by punctuation. 2. (*Classification*) One which reflects more than one facet within a conventional class, for example, within the class Building, *wooden floor* is a compound, reflecting both a material and a part.

Compound subject heading. A heading which consists of (a) two words joined by a conjunction, as 'Punch and Judy'; (b) a phrase, as 'Council of Trent'; (c) words which are always associated together, e.g. 'Capital punishment'; 'Political economy'.

Comprehensive bibliography. One which lists, as far as possible, everything published on the subject.

Compresence. A linked set of Features describing a given Item, or of items defining a given feature.

Compressed full score. *See* Score.

Compressed score. *See* Close score. *See also* Score.

Compression. The conversion of digital data to a more compact form for storage and transmission. Particular benefits are seen in the compression of video, graphics and sound files, especially when transferring these across the Internet. *See also* Codec, JPEG, MPEG.

Compulsory competitive tendering. *See* Competitive tendering.

Computer. An electronic machine, operating in Stand-alone mode or connected to other computers on a Network, which can accept data, store it, manipulate it as instructed in a program, retrieve it and convey the results to a user. As miniaturization has increased and the technology developed, the terminology of mainframes, mini-computers and micro-computers, based on difference in performance and which held good in the early 1980s, has been replaced by the virtually ubiquitous 'PC'. Smaller machines can now carry out functions that could be handled previously only by very large installations, and most libraries now use more powerful workstations for housekeeping systems and PCs with networking capability for other tasks.

Computer Output Microfiche/Microfilm. *See* COM.

Computer security/data security. In its broadest sense, the prevention of unauthorized access to individual computers or the machines on a network. Measures have to be taken to prevent the Hacker getting access to networks of a sensitive nature (defence systems or those containing personal details) but also to prevent the infiltration of Viruses and Worms that can spread to all organizational PCs. At the local level, security can be used to limit access to particular files on individual machines. Personal security software can limit access by locking hard Disks, directories, folders, or individual files and Encryption can also be applied. Most systems are Password-controlled. Software protection is of little use if the computer itself is stolen and methods of physically binding machines to desktops may have to be considered, in addition to preventing access to the internals of machines to prevent the removal of memory chips and hard drives. Regular Back-ups of important files should be made, the back-up disks or tapes stored in a location remote from the computers themselves. *See also* Access management, Firewall, Spam.

Computer translation. *See* Machine translation.

Computer typesetting. Use of a computer to set up a page of printing; the operator can set the text on a display screen, adjust the layout, incorporate graphic material, insert page numbers, running headlines, etc., and the final product can be stored by the computer for output when required either onto printing plates or via an Imagesetter. *See also* Desktop publishing.

Computers in Teaching Initiative. *See* CTI.

Computing Services and Software Association (CSSA). *See* Intellect.

CONARLS. <www.nls.uk/professional/interlibraryservices/services/conarls> (Stella Pilling <sp35@york.ac.uk>) The Circle of Officers of National and Regional Library Systems, an informal group which reviews current issues in interlending and library co-operation and endeavours to give practical support to the effective development and operation of co-operative services. *See also* Regional library co-operation (UK), Unityweb.

Concept co-ordination. 1. A system of multi-dimensional indexing with single concepts to define a document uniquely. 2. A system of co-ordinate indexing for information retrieval. *See also* Uniterm concept co-ordinate indexing.

Concept indexing. 1. The process of deciding which are the concepts in a particular document that are of sufficient importance to be included in the Subject index. 2. The use of a standard description for each concept (whether it has been used by the author of the text or not) and using it as a subject heading whenever appropriate.

Concertina fold. A method of folding paper, first to the right and then to the left, so that it opens and closes in the manner of a concertina. Also called 'Zig-zag fold'. *See also* Accordian fold.

Concilium Bibliographicum. A bibliographical work begun by Herbert Haviland Field at Zurich in 1895. Cards were printed and distributed as soon as published for all publications (primarily periodical articles, with some books and pamphlets) on zoology, palaeontology, general biology, microscopy, anatomy, physiology and kindred subjects, from all countries. It thus formed a complete bibliography. After the death of the founder in 1921, the Rockefeller Foundation made a grant for five years, hoping that the organization would receive finance internationally. The enterprise continued on subscriptions alone until 1940 when it ceased to function. It is often referred to as the Zurich Index.

Concise description, principle of. The avoidance of duplication or unessential information in a catalogue entry. *See also* Cataloguing, principles of.

Concord. <www.bl.uk/about/cooperation/concord> The website maintained by the British Library Co-operation and Partnership Programme to publicize and co-ordinate activity.

Concordance. 1. A book arranged so as to form an alphabetical index of all passages, or of all the more important words, in any work, with indications of the context of such passages and phrases in the text. 2. In machine indexing, an alphabetical index of words in a document, each word present in the text being an index entry.

Concreteness, principle of decreasing. *See* Decreasing concreteness, principle of.

Condensed score. *See* Close score. *See also* Score.

Condensed type. Type which is narrow in proportion to its height.

Condition survey. An examination of books or other documents in a library or a collection to gather data on their physical condition. Usually a random sample of items is identified and inspected with regard to paper, binding, boards and covers, foxing, insect damage etc. The results of a survey can help a library to plan its programme of preservation and conservation.

Conditioning. The maturing of paper, carried out in the paper mill by drying out or adding moisture to it so as to bring it 'into balance' with what is accepted as normal printing-room atmosphere and to enable it to be used on fast-running machines without danger of cockling. The process is carried out in a temperature of 60°–65°F, and a relative humidity of 65 per cent; the paper will then contain about 7 per cent moisture evenly distributed over the sheet, and the fibres will remain stable during printing.

Conductor's part. The printed music for an instrumentalist who also simultaneously conducts a work. Also called 'Conductor's score'. *See also* Score.

Conduit. U-shaped metal or plastic Trunking set into the floor screed or attached to building walls to enable the efficient and controlled distribution of data cables.

confer. (Lat. 'compare'.) To compare or refer to. Usually used in the abbreviated form (cf.).

Conference of Directors of National Libraries (CDNL). <jcameron@nla.gov.au> Formed 1975 as an adjunct to the IFLA Section of National

Libraries, and meets during IFLA Conferences; it nevertheless has a life of its own and initiates research in a number of areas. Directors from over 160 countries are in membership. *See also* ICABS.

Conference of European National Librarians (CENL). <www.bl.uk/gabriel> An independent association of chief executives of the national libraries of the member states of the Council of Europe. Holds an annual meeting, manages several collaborative projects, supports research and development activity. CENL is concerned with harmonization policies, standardization of networks, and preservation and conservation issues.

Confidential file. Material in a library which is kept securely, and apart from other material, and is only used under certain conditions. *See also* Classified material.

Conger. A group of from ten to twenty wholesale booksellers who combined to share the publishing and selling of books, and to protect the sale of their books from undercutting and piracy. Congers were a feature of the London book trade in the late seventeenth and early eighteenth centuries.

Congress, Library of, Classification. *See* Library of Congress Classification.

Congress of Southeast Asian Librarians. *See* CONSAL.

Conjoint authorship. *See* Joint author.

Conjugate. (*Bibliography*) This term is applied to two leaves which can be traced into and out of the back of a book and found to be one piece of paper.

Conjunction. (*Classification*) In the Colon Classification, a symbol used to couple two substantives.

Conjunctive. Pertaining to the joining or coupling of two documents, words, phrases, or elements of information in order to express a unity. Being neither disjunctive nor collateral.

Connecting symbols. *See* Class number, Fundamental categories.

Connotation. A term in classification indicative of all the qualities conveyed by, or comprised in, a class name; e.g. 'man' in connotation means the qualities (mammalian structure, upright gait, reason, etc.) that go to make up man, as opposed to *denotation*, where the term merely marks down or indicates. The phrase: 'That man is really a man' shows the denotative followed by the connotative use of the word. Connotation and denotation may be considered synonymous with intension and Extension.

Connotative. *See* Connotation.

Conover-Porter Award. <lcweb.loc.gov/rr/amed> A prize given by the (UK) African Studies Association; established in 1980 and honouring two pioneers of African Studies librarianship – Helen Conover and Dorothy Porter. The award recognizes achievement in Africana bibliography and reference works.

CONSAL. <www.consal.org.sg> The Congress of Southeast Asian

Librarians was formed in 1970 and its main activity is the operation of a triennial conference. The organization is open to libraries, library schools and library associations and there are currently ten member countries: Brunei, Cambodia, Indonesia, Laos, Malaysia, Myanmar, The Philippines, Singapore, Thailand and Vietnam. CONSAL is supported by Unesco, IFLA, the Commonwealth Foundation and the National Library of Australia.

CONSER. <lcweb.loc.gov/acq/conser> The Co-operative Online Serials Program, originally planned in 1973 as the Co-operative Conversion of Serials Program. There are 50 participating members including the Library of Congress, National Agricultural Library, National Library of Canada, National Library of Medicine, National Serials Data Program, Center for Research Libraries and several major US university libraries. A newsletter – *CONSERline* – is issued in electronic format. Produces *CD-MARC Serials* which contains the complete CONSER database. *See now* PCC.

Conservation. According to IFLA, a term which denotes those specific policies and practices involved in protecting library and archive materials from deterioration, damage and decay; it includes the methods and techniques devised and undertaken by technical staff. Common conservation techniques include deacidification, encapsulation or lamination, preservation microfilming, and digitization and electronic storage.

Consistent characteristics. *See* Characteristic of a classification.

Console. *See* Terminal.

Consolidated index. An index, in one sequence, to several volumes, a long run of a periodical or other serial publication, or to several independent works or serial publications.

Consolidated system. A system of libraries established by the decision of several municipal governing bodies, or by the action of voters, and governed by the Board of Trustees of the system. The individual library units operate as branches of the system (US).

Consortia. Resource sharing organizations formed by libraries; also termed co-operatives, networks, collectives, alliances, or partnerships. Services covered may vary, but often comprise co-operative collection development, education and training, preservation, centralized services, and network alliances featuring library automation services, systems support, consultation, and administrative support needed for cataloguing, inter-library lending, union listing, retrospective conversion, and co-operative purchasing. Discounts may be arranged with information suppliers. Consortia members may include any type of library, and may be regionally-based, or subject-based over a large area. Numbers of members may be from two or three libraries to several hundred.

Consortium of European Research Libraries (CERL). <www.cerl.org> The Consortium was formed in 1992 with the primary objective of establishing a database of European printing of the hand-press period (c.1455–1830). Its members are the major research collections in Europe, and its aims are to share resources and expertise, and secure the preservation of the European printed heritage with good access. Early in 1994 the Consortium contracted with the Research Libraries Group as the database supplier. The Hand Press Book Database (HPB) contains 4.5 million entries. The Consortium secretariat is at the British Library.

Consortium of University Research Libraries. CURL. *See* Curl (1).

Consortium of Welsh Library and Information Services. *See* CWLIS.

Conspectus. Conspectus is an instrument for libraries to describe their existing collection strengths and current collecting intensities by assigning a set of simple alpha-numeric codes, within the basic framework of the Library of Congress subject classification. Conspectus was conceived in 1979 to support the efforts of the Research Libraries Group (RLG) in the United States to co-operate and share resources in a more comprehensive way than had previously been attempted. As members gathered information about their collections and submitted it to the RLG, the data was made available through the Research Libraries Information Network. In 1983 the RLG and the Association of Research Libraries joined forces to work on the North American Collections Inventory Project (NCIP), a co-operative effort intended to provide data online about the collections of a large number of libraries throughout North America, using Conspectus as the basis for collection assessment. Conspectus effectively ended in 1997. *See also* Collection level description.

Constant mnemonics. *See* Mnemonics.

Construction Industry Information Group (CIIG). <www.ciig.org.uk> Formed in 1962 from the earlier Building Industry Libraries Group, CIIG aims to promote good practice in libraries and information services, to provide a forum for discussion of common problems by arranging meetings, visits and social events, improving liaison between members and aiding the flow of information at national and local levels. It also promotes conferences, seminars etc., and the publication of material on documentation in the construction industry. An Organization in Liaison (OiL) with CILIP.

Consultant. *See* Information consultant, Library consultant.

Consumer Health Information Consortium (CHIC). <omni.ac.uk/chic> (Patients Library, St Thomas' Hospital, Lambeth Palace Road, London SE1 7EH, UK) A forum for information exchange for those concerned with public access to health information. An Organization in Liaison (OiL) with CILIP.

Contact copying. A non-optical copying process whereby the original and the material of reproduction are brought into close contact during exposure. The resulting copy can be described as a 'contact copy' or 'contact print'. The opposite of Optical copying. *See also* Contact printing, Reflex copying, Transmission copying.

Contact printing.   Any form of photographic or other copying in which a sheet of sensitized material is held in firm and even contact with the original photographic negative or original document during exposure. The copying may be done by the direct or transmission method, or by the reflex method; the resulting print may be termed a 'contact copy'. *See also* Contact copying, Reflex copying, Transmission copying.

Container library service.   A service for providing library facilities in small urban communities as an alternative to a small static branch library or visits from mobile libraries or trailers. The containers are special portable buildings 36' 6" long and 8' wide which are built to International Container Standards to withstand frequent loading and unloading. *See also* Mobile library.

Contemporary binding.   One that is contemporary with the printing of the book.

Contemporary Medical Archives Centre (UK).   <library.wellcome.ac.uk> Established 1979 as part of the Wellcome Institute for the History of Medicine, as a repository of archives relevant to twentieth century medicine and health services. Publishes a *Guide*.

Contemporary Scientific Archives Centre.   *See* National Cataloguing Unit for the Archives of Contemporary Scientists.

Content.   The intrinsic information and data stored in and communicated by any document – printed or electronic – that make it useful and usable to End users. It is distinguished from the printed format, distribution channel or network that carries it. Content can include all forms of textual material and manuscripts, sound, moving and still images, bibliographic datasets, statistical and other forms of data.

Content ID Forum.   *See* cIDf.

Content management (CM).   With the growth in volume of content on Intranets, often as a result of Knowledge management procedures, and the development of sophisticated Portals, the need arises to structure information to make it usable. Other terms are in use for similar activities, such as Document management, Digital asset management, Digital rights management, Web content management, Enterprise content management. Content management makes use of the technologies, tools and methods used to capture, store, manage, preserve and deliver information content across an organization. It seeks to integrate external and internal information, to match information to user requirements, and to organize materials by grouping them into a pre-determined structure controlled by effective classification or taxonomies. It is of the greatest use in handling unstructured information such as reports and e-mails rather than databases or accounting systems that are already structured. As well as text, information content will include images, Web pages, video and audio resources, graphics and rich media assets. Content management is also essential as a part of the preparation when migrating to new systems, and in the corporate context for making transparent governance audit trails for content such as text files, e-mails, attachments, and scanned-in documents. *See also* Information architecture.

Content Management System (CMS). Software used to manage Web site content and which typically comprises two elements: content management application (CMA) and content delivery application (CDA). The CMA allows the content manager or author, who may not know HTML, to manage the creation, modification, and removal of content; the CDA uses and compiles that information to update the site. The features of a CMS system vary, but most include Web-based publishing, format management, revision control, and indexing, search, and retrieval.

Contents. Strictly, a 'table of contents' but seldom used in this form. 1. A list of the Preliminaries and chapter headings of a book in their correct order, or of articles in a periodical, with the numbers of the pages on which they begin. 2. A list of the musical works contained in a printed collection of music or in an album of recordings or of those recorded on a single record or cassette. 3. A list of items recorded on videotape.

Contents list. The contents page of a periodical, or other publication.

Contents list bulletin. A periodical bulletin consisting of reproductions of copies of the contents pages of selected periodicals, and assembled under some form of cover. *See also* Current awareness journal.

Contents note. A note appearing after the catalogue entry giving the headings of the chapters, parts, or volumes. In a descriptive bibliography it will indicate what is printed on each page included in the collation by gatherings.

Contents page. The page, usually in the Preliminaries of a book, on which the table of contents is printed.

Context. (*Indexing*) The parts of a title or text that precede or follow the Keyword, usually influencing its meaning.

Continuation. 1. A book only partly written by the original author and continued or completed by someone else. 2. A work issued as a supplement to one already published. 3. A part issued in continuance of a serial, series or book. An order to supply subsequent parts as issued is called a 'Continuation order'.

Continuing professional development (CPD). A career-long process of improving and updating the skills, abilities and competencies of staff by regular in-service training and education, supported by external courses. In the UK, CILIP will implement in 2005 a new qualification structure that involves regular re-accreditation through CPD. *See also* Staff development, Training.

Continuity file. (*Archives*) *See* Reading file.

Continuous feed. The action of an automatic sheet feeder attached to a printing press, folding, or other machine, so that the supply of sheets can be replenished without interrupting the operation of the machine.

Continuous flow camera. Apparatus for taking photographs, which automatically moves the originals and the film to be exposed after each exposure. Also called 'Flow camera', 'Rotary camera'.

Continuous pagination. The use of one sequence of page numbering throughout a book or several parts or volumes.

Continuous processing. Processing photographs or films in machines which automatically transport the photographic material through the required solutions, finally drying the product.

Continuous revision. A multi-volume work, such as an extensive encyclopaedia, which is not completely revised and published as a new edition. Minor alterations or extensive additions or revisions are carried out for each printing, replacement and additional pages being inserted within the existing pagination by the addition of 'A, B, C,' etc. to the page numbers.

Continuous stationery. Computer print-out paper usually supplied many metres in length, folded and perforated at intervals.

Contours. Lines drawn on a map to join all places at the same height above sea level. The intervals between contours represent height differences. On physical maps the areas between contours are often shown in different colours progressing from various shades of green for lowlands through browns to red and finally white. Depths of the sea bed are indicated by Isobaths.

Contract. 1. An agreement between an organization and an employee setting out the terms, conditions, policies of employment etc. 2. An agreement made under a Contracting out procedure, whereby an outside organization supplies goods or services; also termed a 'service contract'.

Contracting out. The process whereby libraries concentrate on core activities and invite outside agencies to tender for the supply of certain services. Advantages might include economic gain, improved efficiency, flexibility, additional expertise, added credibility. The UK government has particularly fostered such concepts under its commitment to Competitive tendering. *See also* Outsourcing.

Contraries. Any impurities in the waste paper, rags or other materials such as silk, feathers, wool, string, bones, pins, rubber, etc., to be used for paper- or board-making, and which are likely to be injurious.

Contrast. The difference between the high and low densities in a print, negative, or television picture.

Control field. A Field in a machine-readable record which identifies a particular part of the data within that record. It may contain a Tag.

Controlled circulation. *See* Routeing.

Controlled circulation serial. A serial publication which is usually issued without charge and is only available to those whom the author or those responsible for its publication specify.

Controlled indexing. Implies a careful selection of terminology so as to avoid, as far as possible, the scattering of related subjects under different headings. *See also* Word indexing.

Controlled term list. A term used in the indexing aspects of information retrieval which is equivalent to the Authority list in cataloguing; it is a list of terms which have a fixed and unalterable meaning, and from which a selection is made when indexing data or items in documents. The list may not be altered or extended. *See also* Controlled indexing, Open ended term list, Term.

Convenience file.   (*Archives*) Duplicates of documents, Personal papers, or books, assembled for easy access and reference.

Convention application.   A patent application filed within ten months of the first application, and made for protection of the invention in any one of the countries signatory to the Paris Convention of 1883, and claiming priority accordingly. *See also* Patent of addition, Priority date.

Convention Concerning the Exchange of Official Publications and Government Documents Between States.   A multilateral convention which was adopted by the General Conference of Unesco in December 1958, and came into force on 30 May 1961.

Convention country.   A country which is a signatory to the 1883 Paris Convention for the Protection of Industrial Property, and which is thereby bound to observe the international rules for protecting patents.

Convention date.   The date on which disclosure is made in an application for patent protection in any Convention country and therefore the date for which priority can subsequently be claimed when application is made in any other of the convention countries.

Conventional foliage.   A bookbinding ornament which is often quite unrealistic but obviously suggested by foliage.

Conventional name.   A name, other than the real or official name, by which a person, corporate body, thing or place has come to be familiarly known.

Conventional title.   A Uniform title which is constructed from terms describing the form or subject of a work, and arranged in a generally accepted sequence. It is used mostly in cataloguing music, where, e.g. terms are arranged in the order given to describe the musical form of the composition, its instrumentation (sonata, concerto, trio, piano quartet, etc.), its position in a sequence of the composer's works, its key, its opus (or equivalent) number, and descriptive title or soubriquet.

Convergence.   1. In general terms the combination of telecommunications, computing, and television to produce a new integrated technology such as Multimedia.   2. In higher and further education (particularly in the UK) the name given to the process of bringing academic services such as library, computing services and audio-visual services under one umbrella, usually in terms of line management.

Conversion.   The process of changing the representation of information to a form which is usable by a computer, e.g. converting it to machine 'language'.

Co-operation.   Collaborative arrangements made between libraries to fulfil a number of functions, such as: inter-library lending, co-ordinated collection management, shared storage, co-operative cataloguing, automation facilities, network access, user access, staff training, lobbying etc. *See also* Co-operative.

Co-operation and Partnership Programme (CPP). An initiative of the British Library to foster collaboration with library services of all types throughout the UK. The Concord website <www.bl.uk/about/ cooperation/concord> is the principal means of communication.

Co-operative. An association of libraries and similar institutions formed for mutual assistance and undertaking functions where the sharing of resources or division of costs can be advantageous and efficient. *See also* Consortia, Co-operative training, Network (3), Regional library co-operation (UK).

Co-operative acquisition. A system for organizing and co-ordinating acquisitions between two or more documentary organizations (library, archive or documentation centre) at a local, regional, national or international level to ensure that one copy of each publication is held in the geographical area concerned.

Co-operative cataloguing. The sharing by a number of libraries of the cost and/or labour of cataloguing to avoid the duplication of effort common to each. Not to be confused with Centralized cataloguing.

Cooperative Online Serials Program. *See* CONSER.

Co-operative training. Schemes of co-operation between various types of libraries in a region, or similar libraries in a wider area, in the provision of Training. Co-operative training may be one function within the activities of a Co-operative. *See also* Regional library co-operation (UK), Training.

Co-ordinate classes. (*Classification*) 1. Classes which are correlated so that classes leading up to a subject come before it and those which develop from it, or are next in likeness or character, come after it.   2. Classes which are of the same order of Specification and grade of division in a classification (Bliss).   3. Classes belonging to the same Array.

Co-ordinate indexing. 1. An indexing scheme whereby the inter-relations of terms are shown by coupling individual words.   2. A system of information retrieval in which the indexing or recording of information in, or characteristics of, a document are accomplished by entering a reference number (page number, report number, etc.) on a card (or a column of a card) which is reserved for, and bears the heading of, an individual term to which it is devoted. Also called 'Concept co-ordination', 'Correlative indexing'. *See also* Free indexing, Uniterm concept co-ordination indexing.

Co-ordinate relation. (*Information retrieval*) The relation between terms which are subordinate to the same term.

Co-ordination of terms. The modulation from one term to another by gradual steps in order that the process of evolving a classification may exhibit its hierarchy or schedule.

COPAC. <www.copac.ac.uk> The 'CURL OPAC' that provides free online access to the unified catalogues of the members of CURL, the major research libraries in the UK as well as the British Library, the National Library of Scotland, and special collections from a small number of non-CURL libraries. Based at the University of Manchester and funded by JISC.

Copal. A resinous substance obtained from various tropical trees, and used in the manufacture of varnish and printing inks.

COPANT. <www.copant.org> (Instituto Argentino de Normalización (IRAM), Chile 1192, 1098 Buenos Aires, Argentina) Pan American Standards Commission, founded in 1961; it comprises national standards bodies in the USA and Latin American countries with 35 members representing 24 countries. It is a co-ordinating organization concerned with the regional implementation of International Standards Organization recommendations.

COPOL. Council of Polytechnic Librarians. *See* SCONUL, with which body COPOL merged in 1993.

Copper engraving. *See* Engraving.

Copper plate. A plate used for Engraving in which the drawing is incised with a burin.

Copperplate. A carefully written cursive script often used when inscribing the captions under engravings and used by writing masters as models for their pupils to copy.

Copy. 1. Matter for the printer to set up in type. 2. A single specimen of a printed book. 3. The material to be reproduced by photographic or other means; also the result of a reproduction process.

Copy edit. The checking of a MS. by a publisher or printer before marking it up for the typesetter, for accuracy of facts, grammatical construction, possible libel, House style, etc.

Copy fitting. (*Printing*) Adjusting 'copy' to the space available by changing the space allotment, the length of copy, or the size of type. *See also* Copy (1).

Copy number (or Copy letter). A figure or letter added to the Author mark or Book number of a book to distinguish different copies of the same book. *See also* Book number, Call number, Volume number, Work mark.

Copy preparation. (*Printing*) The act of preparing for the compositor a MS. which has been 'copy edited', by making the MS. legible and accurate, indicating printing style, type to be used, etc.

Copy reader. An employee at a printing works whose task was to prepare the copy for composition by marking the measure, sizes of type to be used for text, quotations, footnotes, etc. and checking the author's consistency in the use of capitals, citation, spelling, punctuation and sentence structure.

Copy slip. *See* Process slip.

Copyholder. 1. A device attached to composing machines or used in conjunction with a typewriter to hold a MS. or 'copy'. 2. An assistant who reads the 'copy' to a proof reader. 3. A device which may be a simple board or an elaborate vacuum frame designed to hold the copy before the camera.

Copying process. A process for making copies of documents on sensitized material.

Copyist. A person who transcribed MSS. prior to the introduction of printing.

Copyleft. A method for treating a program as free software and requiring all modified and extended versions of the program to be similarly treated. The simplest way to achieve this is to put it in the public domain, uncopyrighted.

Copyright. 1. A procedure whereby the originator of a piece of intellectual property (book, article, piece of music, etc.) acquires a series of rights over the work created, including copying, publishing, performing, broadcasting and adaptation. In England copyright was originally used by the Stationers' Company to protect publications issued by one member from piracy by another; it was a marketable commodity and could be traded or assigned between members. An author usually sold rights to a publisher. In the US the right of the author was given greater emphasis. The changing world and multiplicity of items led to substantial changes in copyright legislation and international agreements; current technological advances (databases, video-recordings, web sites) have put copyright law under stress again. Four interests are now recognized: that of the creator; the publisher/distributor; the consumer; and society at large. The Universal Declaration of Human Rights (Article 27, 2) states: 'Everyone has the right to protection of the moral and material interests resulting from any scientific, literary or artistic production of which he is the author'. The European viewpoint grants copyright to the creator by natural right only; Anglo-American law treats it as a privilege that can be passed on to successors in ownership; Eastern Europe saw the state as the ultimate beneficiary and minimized the special interest of the creator. International regulation between these groups and with the special needs of developing countries poses great difficultues. *See* Copyright, International, Creative Commons, Electronic copyright. 2. (*Archives, Manuscripts*) The application of copyright law in the case of archive and manuscript material is unusually complicated as the material is not published, and sets of archives usually contain items with varying copyright status. Guidelines are published by the Society of Archivists.

Copyright, International. International copyright is regulated by a number of agreements which include: (a) Berne Convention (The International Convention for the Protection of Literary and Artistic Works) concluded in 1886. Revised 1948 (Brussels) and 1967 (Stockholm); the latter conference helped to integrate the system into the World Intellectual Property Organization (WIPO). *See also* Berne Copyright Union. (b) Inter-American Conventions (Montevideo 1889, Mexico City 1902, Rio de Janeiro 1906, Buenos Aires 1910, Havana 1928, Washington

1946). (c) Universal Copyright Convention; convened by Unesco in 1952, came into effect in 1955. UCC agreed that copyright should be secured by the simple procedure of a single notice comprising the symbol ©, the name of the copyright proprietor, and the year of first publication. (d) Paris revision (1971) A reworking of (c) that came into effect in 1974. A further treaty, the WIPO Copyright Treaty was signed in 1996 and became effective in 2000. *See also* IGC, ICIC.

Copyright Agency Ltd. <www.copyright.com.au> CAL was formed in Australia in 1974 as a non-profit company to act as an agent for its member publishers and authors; it is authorized by the Federal Attorney-General to administer the statutory licenses contained in the Copyright Act 1968. CAL has reciprocal agreements with collecting societies in many other countries.

Copyright Clearance Center (CCC). <www.copyright.com> (222 Rosewood Drive, Danvers, MA 01923, USA) The Center was established in 1977 in response to the (US) Copyright Act of 1976 by a group of authors, publishers and users of copyright material. The Center acts as a mechanism so that authorizations to photocopy copyright material can be readily obtained from copyright owners. A digital rights management solution – "Rightslink" – has been developed.

Copyright date. The date copyright was granted for an individual work. This is usually printed on the verso of the title page of books. If several dates are given, they signify changes in the text, or renewals of copyright (USA only). The first copyright date indicates the date of the first edition of a book and corresponds to the imprint date of the original edition. *See also* Berne Copyright Convention, Copyright, Copyright, International.

Copyright deposit. A system by which publishers deposit free copies of their publications with, usually, a national library. It rarely has any link now to copyright law and is more correctly called Legal deposit.

Copyright fee. Fee paid to the holder of a copyright for the right to use material for a particular purpose, e.g. to include a poem in an anthology or to read it in public, or to play a piece of music, or a recording of the same, in public.

Copyright Libraries Shared Cataloguing Programme (CLSCP). *See* British National Bibliography.

Copyright library. A term still used in the UK for the six libraries which are entitled to receive free copies of published works under Legal deposit legislation. The term is now misleading as there is no link between copyright and legal deposit. A new Legal Deposit Act came into force in the UK in 2003 replacing the former clauses of the Copyright Act 1911 that led to the confusion.

Copyright Licensing Agency. <www.cla.co.uk> (90 Tottenham Court Road, London W1P 9HE, UK) The CLA is the UK's reproduction rights organization. A non-profit making organization, it was formed in 1982 by the Authors' Licensing and Collecting Society and the

Publishers' Licensing Society to promote and enforce the intellectual property rights of British authors and their publishers, both at home and abroad. Its role is to license educational establishments, government departments, public bodies and commercial organizations to photocopy extracts from books, journals and periodicals. The CLA collects fees on behalf of publishers and authors in the UK and in over 20 other countries for reproduction of their texts. Licences are now available for all sectors of society in view of the changes to definitions of Fair dealing in UK law. *See also* Educational Recording Agency Ltd.

Copyright list. A list of the books deposited in a library under the copyright laws.

COPYSMART. An EU-funded project using Smartcard technology to manage copyright use and payments. The project was tested satisfactorily in library use. Based on the CITED model, it is being implemented through project SEDODEL.

Copy-tax. Another term for Legal deposit.

Copy-text. The text used as the basis for a critical work or for a critical edition, for example of Chaucer or Shakespeare; it is usually the extant text most likely to represent what the author wrote. Also used as an alternative term for Printer's copy.

Copywriter. A writer of advertisements.

Coranto. 1. The earliest form of newspaper, consisting of one leaf in small folio, the text being in two columns on each side of the leaf. Published first in Holland and Germany, and in England in 1620 and 1621, such publications were known by the name *coranto*, whether published in England or on the continent. They were issued at least once a week and only foreign news was printed. 2. Sometimes the word *coranto* is used to include Newsbooks which were published until 1642. *See also* Newsbook, Relation. Nathaniel Butter began a *Newes* on 2 August 1622, and in October 1622 commenced publishing with Nicholas Bourne and William Sheffard *A Coranto*; these were numbered serially.

CORBA. <www.omg.org/gettingstarted> Common Object Request Broker Architecture, a set of Interoperability specifications published by the Object Management Group (OMG) for an open, vendor-independent architecture and infrastructure that computer applications use to work together over networks. A CORBA-based program from any vendor, on almost any computer, operating system, programming language, and network, can interoperate with a CORBA-based program from the same or another vendor, on almost any other computer, operating system, programming language, and network.

Cording quires. *See* Cassie.

CORDIS. <www.cordis.lu> Community Research and Development Information Service; a current awareness bulletin published on the Web, and fortnightly in print, by the Communication and Awareness Unit of the Enterprise Directorate-General. It gives news of European Union research and research-related programmes and policies.

Cordovan leather. Goatskin, originally tanned and dressed at Cordova, Spain. Used for Mudéjar bindings, and often dyed red. The English name is 'Cordwain'.

Cords. Heavy strings to which the sections of large and heavy books are bound. Sometimes called Bands. *See also* Tapes.

Cordwain. *See* Cordovan leather.

Core journal. A leading journal in a particular discipline, considered as essential reading.

Core middleware. 1. *See* Middleware. 2. Core Middleware Programme, two programmes funded by JISC, April 2004–March 2007, to investigate core Middleware via two streams: technology development; and infrastructure.

Core support service. Activities carried out by an organization in pursuance of its central purpose; usually implies in-house operations as opposed to activities operated under a Contracting out procedure.

Corner-fold. A crude test for brittle paper which involves bending the corner of a page over on itself. A double-corner-fold consists of repeating the action once. Brittle paper breaks after two double-corner-folds. *See* Brittle books.

Cornerpiece. 1. (*Binding*) An ornament, usually arabesque, designed to be used at the corners of a bound book, usually to match a centre-piece or other decoration. Also used of metal corners attached to the binding. Also called 'Cornerstamp'. 2. (*Bibliography*) Interlacing bars, 'cusping' or other separate ornament at the corner of a border around type, or lettering of an illuminated manuscript.

Corners. 1. The leather over the corners of a book in 'half' binding. *See also* Library corner, Mitred corner, Square corner. 2. In printing, ornamental type metal connecting borders. 3. Pieces of metal or pasteboard to slip over the corners of a book to protect them in the post. Also called 'Cornerpieces'.

Cornerstamp. *See* Cornerpiece.

Corporate author. A corporate body such as a government or government department, a society (learned, social, etc.), or an institution which authorizes the publication of documents, and under the name of which, as the author, the documents will be entered in a catalogue. In certain kinds of corporate authorship, entries are made under the *place* followed by the *name* of the body.

Corporate body. An institution, organized body, or assembly of persons known by a corporate or collective name.

Corporate entry. A catalogue entry made under a government, government department, society or institution or other body, of a work issued by that body, or under its authority.

Corporate name. The name by which a corporate body is known.

Corporation file. *See* Company file.

Corrected edition. A new edition of a book in which errors, etc., have been corrected.

Corrected proof. A printer's proof on which errors in typesetting have been marked, using the generally accepted code of correction-marks. *See also* Proof, Proof corrections.

Correction marks. The signs used on a printer's proof to mark errors in typesetting. These are set out in British Standard 5261: Part 2: 1976 *Copy preparation and proof correction*. *See* Proof corrections.

Correlation. A systematic or reciprocal connection – sometimes, the establishment of a mutual or reciprocal relation.

Correlation of properties. In classification the likeness between the various qualities which are common to all the things comprised by a genus.

Correlative index. An index enabling selection of documents or of references to them by correlation of words, numbers, or other symbols which are usually unrelated by hierarchic organization. *See also* Classified index, Co-ordinate indexing.

Correspondence management. (*Archives*) The application of the techniques of archive administration to correspondence.

Corrigenda. (*Sing.* Corrigendum) A printed list of corrections of errors which were noticed after matter was printed. It is usually printed on a slip and inserted among the Preliminaries but sometimes a blank page is used. Also called 'Errata'. *See also* Paste-in.

Corrupt a text. To tamper with a text by omission, addition, or alteration in order to convey a meaning which was not intended by the original author. This is sometimes done to standard or modern works for political propaganda.

Cost benefit. The measurement of the positive effect on an operation that can be attributed to a particular cost.

Cost centre. A department or other well-defined unit which has the responsibility for controlling its finances and to which is devolved financial allocations which previously had been maintained by the central administration of the organization.

Cost-effectiveness. The measurement of the impact made on an operation by a specified cost; usually only used as a positive indicator of success.

Costeriana. Fragments of books, having the appearance of early printing and asserted to have been printed before 1473, and consisting mostly of editions of the *Donatus*, or the *Doctrinale*. These were supposed to have been printed by Laurens Janszoon Coster of Haarlem (1405–84) who was thought at one time to have invented printing with movable types in or about 1440.

Costs. The financial outpayments made by an organization in support of its activities; in constructing a business plan it is important to separate various types of cost. An arbitrary attribution must be made from *overheads* and *capital costs*; *direct costs* are those directly attributable to a particular activity; *marginal costs* or *indirect costs* are those which are incurred in whole or in part in support of an activity; *opportunity costs* are those made in pursuit of further business and future plans, bringing no immediate returns; *external costs* are payments made to outside organizations or individuals whose services are bought in under a Contracting out procedure.

Cottage binding.   *See* Cottage style.

Cottage style.   A decorative binding in which the centre panel was often given a gable at head and foot, and the spaces filled with a variety of interlacings, sprays, and small 'tools'. Although this style may have originated in France, it is most characteristic of English bindings of the late seventeenth century to 1710. Also called 'Cottage binding'. *See also* Mearne style.

Cotton linters.   The short fibres adhering to the cotton seed after ginning (separating the seeds from the fibre), and also obtained as 'recovered' fibres from the cotton seed oil and cake factories. When purified it is used for paper-making. It can be used to replace 5–35 per cent of the rag content of fine papers without lessening the strength of the paper; it improves uniformity and the colour properties of the paper, and provides a cleaner, bulkier sheet. It is also used in the cheaper kinds of blotting paper used for interleaving diaries and account books.

Couch roll.   That part of a Fourdrinier paper making machine which removes some of the moisture from the sheet of paper during manufacture.

Council for Learning Resources in Colleges (CoLRiC).   <www.colric.org.uk> (122 Preston New Road, Blackburn BB2 6BU, UK) The Council is an independent support agency established to help libraries and learning resource units provide quality services, based on national standards, throughout the further education sector (including sixth form colleges) in the United Kingdom. Makes the annual Beacon Award for the effective integration of libraries or learning resource centres in curriculum delivery. An Organization in Liaison (OiL) with CILIP.

Council of Academic and Professional Publishers.   *See* Publishers Association.

Council of Australian University Librarians (CAUL).   <www.caul.edu.au> The representative body for tertiary libraries in Australia which had its origins in a meeting of representatives of Australian university libraries in 1928 but was formally established in its present form as the Committee of Australian University Librarians in 1965. It changed to its present title in 1992 to reflect a more pro-active role in Australian library initiatives. Its mission is to advance teaching, learning and research through planned co-operative endeavours; it is a forum for discussion of major issues and a mechanism for co-ordination. CAUL has close working relationships with the Australian Vice-Chancellors' Committee, the Department of Employment, Education and Training, the National Library of Australia, and many other relevant bodies. CAUL meets twice yearly and its subscription revenue supports research projects, produces issues papers, and overviews the yearly statistics of the thirty-seven university libraries published in *Australian Academic and Research Libraries*.

Council of City Research and Information Libraries.   *See* COCRIL.

Council of Europe. <www.coe.int> Founded in 1949 and based in Strasbourg, the Council of Europe has in membership 45 countries – including 21 from Central and Eastern Europe. Observer status has been granted to the USA, Canada and Japan. The Council's main role is to be a political anchor for the security of democracy in Europe, and to further this role it concentrates on human rights and political, economic and constitutional reform. The Council is a completely separate organization from the European Union (EU).

Council of European Professional Informatics Societies. *See* CEPIS.

Council of National Library and Information Associations (CNLIA). Formed in 1942, the Council played a major role in co-operative activities throughout the USA and Canada; its work was particularly evident in standards and copyright practice. In 1996 the membership decided that the Council had served its purpose and voted for dissolution. The archives are housed with the Special Libraries Association.

Council of Planning Librarians (CPL). Founded in 1960 as a special interest group for city and regional planning librarians. CPL's archive has been made available at <web.library.uiuc.edu/ahx/cplarchives>.

Council of Polytechnic Librarians. *See* SCONUL, with which COPOL merged in 1993.

Council on Library and Information Resources (CLIR). <www.clir.org> (1755 Massachusetts Ave. NW, Suite 500, Washington DC 20036, USA) Formed in 1997 by the merger of the Council on Library Resources, Inc. and the Commission on Preservation and Access. Its purpose is to identify the critical issues that affect the welfare and prospects of libraries and archives and their users, to engage and respond to these issues and to encourage collaboration to achieve and manage change. CLIR aims to overcome barriers to wider information access and use, and to help society understand what is at risk in the changing information environment. There are six areas of work: preservation awareness; resources for scholarship; digital libraries; leadership; economics of information; international developments. Its agenda is enhanced by the Digital Library Federation.

Council on Library Resources, Inc. CLR was founded in 1956 with support from the Ford Foundation to aid in the solution of the problems of libraries generally, and research libraries particularly, by putting emerging technologies to use to improve operating performance and expand services. In 1997 merged with the Commission on Preservation and Access to form the Council on Library and Information Resources.

Counselling. Support of employees by management through a process of individual assessment and advice, in pursuit of individual and corporate aims.

Counter. 1. *See* Circulation desk. 2. (*Printing*) The interior 'white' of a letter; it may be entirely enclosed by a bowl as in 'O' or it may be the sunken part of the face as 'M' 'E' 'n'. The angular corner is known as the 'crotch'. The distance from the face to the bottom of the counter is known as the 'depth of counter'. 3. Counting Online Usage of Networked Electronic Resources <www.projectcounter.org> Launched in 2002 by UK publishers and libraries in alliance, but now spreading internationally. The project is a code of practice for the measurement of use of journals and databases; from 2004 vendors' figures are to be independently audited.

Countermark. A smaller and subsidiary Watermark found in antique papers, usually in the centre, or lower centre of the second half of a sheet and opposite the watermark. Border or corner positions are not uncommon. It usually comprises the name or initials of the maker (in the UK), and in later times, the mill number and the date (first in 1545) and place of making, although small devices such as a small post-horn or cabalistic signs have been found.

Countersunk. A binding having a panel sunk or depressed below the normal level of the binding to take a label, inlay or decoration.

Country House Libraries Campaign. <www.royal-oak.org> (Royal Oak Foundation, 285 West Broadway, Suite 400, New York NY 10013, USA) The current focus for the fundraising efforts of the Royal Oak Foundation – the American support organization of the (UK) National Trust; the Campaign was launched in 1995 and seeks to raise funds for two full-time posts (Librarian and Conservator), equipment, and for a catalogue in electronic format of the Trust's 500,000 volumes in its stately homes.

County library. A library provided to supply the reading needs of people dwelling in a county. In America, a free public library service provided for county residents and financed from county tax funds; it may be administered as an independent agency or in co-operation with another library agency.

County Record Office (UK). *See* Record Office.

County schools library. An instructional materials library maintained in America by a county superintendent of schools who provides materials and services to contracting schools.

Courants. Dutch news publications, related but not numbered, known to have existed since the year 1607. *See also* Coranto, Newsbook.

Course pack. *See* Study pack.

Course reserve collection. *See* Reserve collection (2). *Compare* Electronic course reserve collection.

Court. A standard size for cards, 3½ x 4½ inches; envelopes are 3¾ x 4¾ inches.

Court Baron. Court held by the Lord of a Manor in virtue of his right as a land holder, in which offences against the customs of the manor could be published but no punishments involving the life or limbs of the subject could be inflicted.

Court hand. 1. Style of writing used in legal and other public documents. Generally used of 'hands' from about 1100 to the end of the sixteenth century.   2. Sometimes used to mean legal hands of the same period only.

Court Leet.   Court of Record to punish all offences under High treason, not incidental to a manor, but frequently held by a Lord of a Manor by virtue of a special grant.

Court roll.   A roll on which records of cases in private courts such as a Court Baron or Court Leet were kept.

Courtesy storage.   *See* Deposit.

Cover.   1. That which is placed securely on a sewn or stapled publication to protect it in use; it may be of paper or cloth, or board covered with paper, cloth or leather. The cover of a 'hard cover' book (as distinct from a 'paperback') is known as a 'case' or 'publisher's case'.   2. The outside sheet of a pamphlet, or the case of a book, used to protect the body of the work. 'Front cover' and 'back cover' relate to the side pieces or outsides of the boards of the cover.

Cover date.   The date which appears on the cover of a publication, usually a pamphlet.

Cover paper.   A generic term usually indicative of a strong, coloured paper with good folding qualities suitable for brochure, booklet, pamphlet and price-list covers. Cover papers are available in a variety of embossings as well as plain. Sizes:

	inches		
Cover Double Crown	$20^{1/2}$	x	$30^{1/2}$
Cover Medium	$18^{1/2}$	x	$23^{1/2}$
Cover Royal	$20^{1/2}$	x	$25^{1/2}$
Double Crown	20	x	30
Double Medium	23	x	36
Double Royal	25	x	40
Imperial	22	x	30
Quad Crown	30	x	40

Cover pocket.   *See* Pocket.

Cover title.   The title of a book placed on a publisher's case, or as distinguished from that printed on the title-page. Not to be confused with the Binder's title. *See also* Back title.

Cover to cover translation.   A serial publication which contains in each issue a translation of the whole, or a major part, of an issue of a serial publication in another language.

Covers bound in.   The original covers of a publication bound in, or to be bound in, when a book is re-bound.

CPD.   *See* Continuing professional development.

CPL.   *See* Council of Planning Librarians.

CPP.   *See* Co-operation and Partnership Programme.

CPU.   *See* Central Processing Unit.

CQL.   Common Query Language, the query language for SRW (Search/Retrieve Web Service) and which may be used by other protocols. It is designed to be human readable and writable, while maintaining the expressiveness of more complex languages. Part of the ZING initiative.

Crabs. Books returned to a publisher by a bookseller because they had remained unsold. Also called 'Returns'.

Crackle. *See* Rattle.

Cradle books. *See* Incunabula.

Crash. 1. The sudden failure of a computer system, generally used to describe the failure of a program or a Disk drive. *See also* Hang. 2. Synonymous with Mull.

Crash finish. A cover paper which is similar to Linen finish but has a coarser texture.

Crawler. *See* Web crawler.

Crayon drawing. A drawing made with a soft, black crayon, usually for strong or impressionistic effects. It is suitable for illustrations, portraits, etc., and may be reproduced by half-tone.

Crayon engraving. A similar process to Stipple but aiming to produce the effect of a chalk drawing. Various specially grained roulettes, etching needles, and a *mattoir* (a form of miniature cudgel) are used through the etching ground to prepare the printing plate for biting with acid. The graver and roulette may be used afterwards directly on the surface of the plate. Also called 'Chalk engraving'.

CRC. Camera ready copy. *See* Camera ready.

Creasing. 1. A linear indentation made by machine in a card or thick paper. By compressing the fibres it provides a hinge and increases the number of times the paper can be flexed at the crease before breaking. *See also* Scoring. 2. A printing fault, seen as deep creases; it may result from storing the paper at an incorrect humidity, or from other causes.

Creative Commons. <www.creativecommons.org> Founded in 2001 by Lawrence Lessig as a reaction against extended periods of copyright embodied in the Digital Millennium Copyright Act and other legislation; supported by the Center for the Public Domain and housed at the Stanford Law School. The organization aims to use private rights to create public goods, protecting work while encouraging use and building a layer of reasonable, flexible copyright in the face of increasingly restrictive default rules. A set of new licences free for public use was designed in 2003; these are not for software but for web sites, scholarship, music, film, photography, literature and courseware. There is also development of Metadata to ensure works are linked to their licence status, and an international dimension (icommons).

Credit. A statement of the authorship, cast, and those associated with the production of a radio, television, film or videotape programme.

Credit line. A statement giving the name of an artist, photographer, author, agency, or owner of an original or of copyright, and printed under a photograph, drawing, article or quotation which is reproduced or published.

Cresting roll. A Roll which has, on one side of the design, a series of crests or tufts, the other side being approximately straight. *See also* Heraldic cresting.

CRG. *See* Classification Research Group.

Criblé initial. A decorated initial used at the beginning of a chapter, specially by the sixteenth-century French printer Geoffrey Tory, in which the capital appears on an all-over ground of small dots, or sieve-like pattern.

Criblé metal cut. A soft metal used late in the fifteenth century for block printing instead of wood, the metal being punched with holes (criblé) to relieve the black mass. *See also* Manière criblée.

CRILIS. *See Current Research in Library and Information Science.*

Crime Writers' Association. <www.thecwa.co.uk> (PO Box 26473, London SE10 8XF, UK) A UK organization responsible for several annual literary awards, viz: Cartier Diamond Dagger Award (outstanding title), John Creasey Memorial Award (best crime novel by an unpublished author), Gold and Silver Dagger Awards for Fiction (best crime novels published in the UK), and Sunday Express Magazine/Veuve Cliquot Short Story Competition (best unpublished short story). A recent new award is titled: Dagger in the Library.

Critical apparatus. *See Apparatus criticus.*

Critical bibliography. 1. The comparative and historical study of the make-up of books 2. The science of the material transmission of literary texts. Also called 'Analytical' or 'Historical' bibliography. *See also* Bibliography.

Critical edition. A scholarly text of a work, established by an editor after original research, and the comparison of manuscripts, documents, letters and earlier texts. This editorial work is considerable, especially in textual criticism. The edition is characterized by the *Apparatus criticus* included. *See also* Standard edition, Variorum edition, Definitive edition.

Critical success factors. In the assessment of performance, the identification of crucial targets or incidents which give a clear signal of positive outcomes.

CRL. *See* Center for Research Libraries.

CRLIS. *See Current Research in Library and Information Science.*

Crocketed cresting. (*Binding*) A frame formed by roughly rectangular stamps ornamented with crockets (small curved designs) or with roughly triangular stamps, which, placed together and pointing outwards, give a cresting effect.

Crop marks. Marks which indicate to a printer which sections of a photograph are to be reproduced in a document.

Cropped. 1. In bookbinding, a term applied to a book when too much of its margin, especially the head-margin, has been trimmed off and the type area mutilated. *See also* Bled, Cut, Shaved, Trimmed, Uncut. 2. A photograph of which a part of the top, bottom or sides is omitted from its reproduction, in order to bring it into proper proportions for the space it is to occupy.

Cropper. A small printing machine working on the platen principle; so named after the English manufacturer H. S. Cropper & Co. who produced the 'Minerva' machine in 1867; this was similar to the 'Franklin Press' manufactured by George Phineas Gordon, a small master printer of New York.

Cropping. (*Printing*) Masking, or trimming off portions of an illustration to eliminate unimportant detail and to obtain desired proportion.

Cross classification. 1. The action of dividing when forming a scheme of classification by more than one characteristic in a single process of division, leading to confusion of ideas and terms and resulting in the parts having no real relationship to one another, and in placing related subjects in different divisions or unrelated subjects in a given array of classes. 2. A Tabular classification, or one that is reducible to tabular form, in which the classes or sub-classes of each series are crossed by the terms of a secondary series of specifications, so that the resulting sub-classes have the specifications of both series and are therefore common to both.

Cross direction. Said of paper which is cut across, that is, cut at right angles to the direction in which the web of a paper machine moves. The cross direction of the paper is much weaker, and expands more, than in the direction parallel to the flow of the pulp on the machine. *See also* Against the grain, Grain direction, With the grain.

Cross hatching. (*Binding*) Two sets of parallel lines executed in opposite directions so that the lines cross.

Cross-bars. Metal bars used to divide a Chase into sections of equal size, each of which contains the same number of pages. They enable the pages to be locked up more securely, and also make corrections in one section easier while not disturbing the others.

Cross-head. A short descriptive heading placed in the centre of a type line to divide the sections of a work, or the chapters of a book. Cross-heads are separated from the text by one or more lines of space, and normally indicate primary sub-divisions of a chapter. Subsequent sub-divisions are: shoulder-heads and side-heads. *See also* Heading (4), Shoulder head, Side head.

Cross-index. To make an index entry under several headings, where appropriate, for the same item.

CrossRef. <www.crossref.org> Launched by the Publishers International Linking Association in 2000 with the general purpose of promoting the development and co-operative use of new and innovative technologies to speed and facilitate scholarly research. The specific CrossRef mission is to be the citation linking backbone for all scholarly information in electronic form. The organization holds no full text content, but effects linkages through the Digital Object Identifier which is tagged to article Metadata supplied by participating publishers. The end result is a scalable linking system through which a researcher can click on a reference citation in a journal and access the cited article. The CrossRef implementation remains the largest user of the Digital Object Identifier. *See also* OpenURL.

Cross-reference, general. *See* General reference.

Cross-references. In indexing and cataloguing, references or directions from one heading to another. 1. *Single* (*see* —) An instruction to look elsewhere for *all* items relating to the subject matter which is sought. 2. *Reciprocal* (*see also* —) An instruction to look elsewhere for *other* items relating to the subject matter sought. 3. *Multiple* (*see also* —) An instruction to refer to several other places, usually to more specific entries. 4. References in the text of a book to other parts of the same book. *See also* General reference.

Crotch. (*Printing*) The angular corner of the Counter of a type letter.

Crown. A sheet of printing paper measuring 15 x 20 inches.

Crown copyright. Copyright that is vested in the British Crown when any work, whether published or unpublished, has been made by, or under the direction or control of, the Sovereign or any Government department. A White paper *The Future Management of Crown Copyright* was issued in 1999; this introduces the concept of the Information Asset Register (IAR) – a single point of entry to government information. Much crown copyright material can now be freely copied, re-used and published without permission, and much central government material can now be used with only the need to register to use it.

Crown Octavo. A book size, 7½ x 5 inches. *See also* Book sizes.

Crown Quarto. A book size 10 x 7½ inches. *See also* Book sizes.

Crushed Levant. A large-grained Levant leather binding with a smooth, polished surface, caused by crushing down the natural grain.

Crushed Morocco. Morocco, the grain of which has been smoothed by hand. *See also* Glazed Morocco.

Cryptography. Writing in cipher.

Cryptonym. A secret name.

Cryptonymous book. One in which the name of the author is concealed under an anagram or similar device, e.g. Mesrat Merligogels (Master George Mills).

CSL. *See* Circle of State Librarians.

CSLA. 1. *See* Church and Synagogue Library Association. 2. *See* Canadian School Library Association.

CSS. *See* Cascading Style Sheets.

CSSA. *See* Intellect.

CT. 1. *See* Machine translation. 2. *See* Competitive tendering.

CTI. Computers in Teaching Initiative, established in the UK in 1984 to encourage the development, evaluate the potential, and promote the awareness of information technology for teaching in higher education. Funded by the Higher Education Funding Councils, 24 centres were supported. It was co-ordinated and supported by CTISS, the Computers in Teaching Initiative Support Service. The Computers in Teaching Initiative handed over, in 2000, to the Learning and Teaching Support Network (LTSN).

Cuban Libraries Solidarity Group.   <www.cubanlibrariessolidaritygroup. org.uk> Established in 1999, the Group supports Cuban libraries as centres of social change.

Cuir Bouilli.   Book decoration in which the leather cover is soaked in hot water, modelled and hammered to raise the design in relief; it sets very hard, and in the ninth century it was found to be so hard that boards were unnecessary.

Cuir-Ciselé **binding.**   A binding with a design cut into dampened leather instead of being stamped or tooled on it. A relief effect was then obtained by punching the leather around the design. Hammering from the back gave an embossed effect. A widely-practised method in fifteenth-century Germany.

CUKT.   *See* Carnegie United Kingdom Trust.

Cul-de-lampe.   A form of decorative printing practised in the sixteenth century which used arabesque title-borders and tail-pieces strongly suggestive of metal lantern-supports. A tail-piece. J. B. M. Papillon (1698–1776), the most distinguished member of a family of French wood-engravers, was renowned for the delicacy in his minute floral head- and tail-pieces (*culs-de-lampe*), which decorate many mid-eighteenth-century French books.

Cultural consortia (UK).   In 2000 the Department for Culture, Media and Sport (DCMS) set up 8 regional cultural consortia to provide a voice for arts, sports, tourism, heritage, libraries, museums, local government and creative businesses.

Cultural diversity.   *See* Diversity.

Cultural Materials Alliance.   <www.rlg.org> A subset of members of the Research Libraries Group who joined together to establish best practices for making digitized cultural heritage collections – images, objects, published and unpublished texts, and artefacts of many types – accessible via RLG Cultural Materials.

Culture 2000.   <www.culture2000.info> EU project launched in 2000 to drive forward cultural activity within Europe; proposals for actions are called for annually. In 2004, the priority sector was libraries and archives. In 2003 the European Parliament accepted a decision to extend the Culture 2000 programme to include 2005 and 2006, and the European Commission is expected to propose a new cultural programme for 2007–2013. The UK link organization is EUCLID.

Culture Online (UK).   <www.cultureonline.gov.uk> A project of the Department of Culture, Media and Sport (DCMS), launched 2002, to develop e-content; the focus is on encouraging sustainable ICT-based resources in innovative contexts. The aim is to forge new partnerships and new experiences, and to integrate the virtual and online world with real activities for the public at large.

Cum Licentia.   *See Cum Privilegio.*

Cum Privilegio.   (Lat. 'with permission') Printed by authority, either secular or ecclesiastical. Sole authority for printing.

Cumdach.   A rectangular box (usually of bronze, brass or wood, and plated with ornamented silver or gold), which was made for the preservation of precious books. Also called 'Book shrine'.

Cumulated volume.   A publication consisting of entries for a bibliography, catalogue, index, etc., which have previously appeared in periodically published parts, and re-assembled into one sequence.

Cumulation.   The progressive inter-filing of items arranged in a predetermined order and usually published in periodical form, the same order of arrangement being maintained.

Cumulative index.   One which is built up from time to time by combining separately published indexes into one sequence.

Cuneiform writing.   Wedge-shaped letters in which Old Persian and Babylonian inscriptions were written, so termed from their wedge-like appearance made by pressing the end of a stick or reed into the soft clay of the tablet at an angle and continuing the stroke in a straight line with constantly diminishing pressure.

Cunningham Memorial Fellowship.   A fellowship offered by the Medical Library Association (US) to qualified medical librarians outside North America to enable them to spend a six-month period in the USA or Canada.

Curator.   The superintendent of a museum, art gallery, etc.

Curators.   Name given to boards of people responsible for managing the various institutions of Oxford University. The Curators of the Bodleian Library, for example, number eighteen, namely, the Vice-Chancellor, the Proctors or their deputies, seven members of Congregation elected by that House, six professors elected by the professors of the various faculties, and two members of Congregation elected by Council, one of whom must be a Curator of the Chest; these are elected to serve for ten years, and are entrusted with the general control of the affairs of the library, including the appointment of a librarian, and of other officers, subject to the approval of Convocation, and are responsible for the expenditure of all sums accruing to them through the University Chest or otherwise.

Curia Regis.   Under feudal organization a court of justice, or administration was called a 'curia'; *Curia Regis* was the Court of the Norman Kings of England.

Curiosa.   Term used in describing books of curious and unusual subject matter. Sometimes used euphemistically as a classification for *erotica*.

Curl.   1. CURL <www.curl.ac.uk> (1211 Muirhead Tower, University of Birmingham, Birmingham B15 2TT, UK) Consortium of University Research Libraries; a grouping of very large academic libraries formed in 1982 to facilitate development of their common interests. CURL aims to increase the abilities of research libraries to share resources, to develop the concept of the distributed and hybrid library of the future, and to offer leadership and support. There is a strategic plan 2003–2006. The CURL database contains over 38 million records and is the basis of COPAC.   2. A deformation of a sheet of paper or board over its whole surface so that it tends to roll up into the form of a cylinder.

Current awareness.   A system, and often a publication, for notifying current documents to users of libraries and information services, for example, through selective dissemination of information, indexing services, etc. The term is sometimes used synonymously for SDI. *See also* Push technology.

Current awareness journal.   A periodical consisting of reproductions in facsimile of contents tables of individual journals.

Current bibliography.   A list of books which is compiled at the same time as the books are published. It is usually published as a periodical. Sometimes called 'Open bibliography'.

Current complete national bibliography.   A complete list of published or issued records of a nation; such a list can be complete only to a specified date. A current national bibliography is a listing of publications compiled at the time of publication and falling within the definition of a National bibliography.

Current number.   The last-issued number of a newspaper or serial publication and bearing the most recent issue number and/or date. Also called 'Current issue'.

Current publication survey.   *See* Literature survey (2).

Current records.   (*Records management*) The records which are necessary for conducting the day-to-day business of an organization, and which must therefore be kept accessible in current systems.

Current Research in Library and Information Science.   *CRLIS* (or *CRILIS*) was originally published by the (UK) Library Association in 1983 and continued the earlier *RADIALS Bulletin* (1978–1982). From 1990 it was commercially published – initially by Bowker Saur, then by Cambridge Scientific Abstracts. It is currently continued as *Information Research Watch International* (*IRWI*).

Curriculum materials center.   A centre, usually located in a US school central administration building, in which are kept professional books, current and back numbers of teaching professional periodicals, and other materials.

Cursive.   1. Running writing, letters within words being joined.   2. Sometimes used to differentiate smaller 'hands' from uncial.   3. A class of typeface which is based on handwriting. It may be Italic in which there is a version of almost every named typeface or script which is drawn to look as though handwritten. *See also* Typeface.

Cursor.   In a Command-driven system, the entry point for data or instructions on a VDU screen; in a GUI or WIMPS interface the Mouse-controlled pointer can also be referred to as the cursor.

Curves.   ( ) Signs used to denote inserted explanatory or qualifying words, phrases, clauses or remarks. To be distinguished from Brackets. Also called Round brackets or Parentheses.

Custodian. A person in charge of a special collection or of a building in which exhibits are displayed.

Custom-bound. (*Binding*) A book which is bound to specific instructions, not in accordance with general instructions.

Customer. The user of a service; in particular the term implies that a financial transaction is taking place whereby a service or commodity is transferred to a purchaser.

Customer care. Processes to enhance the status of the customer in a transaction; staff training programmes in commercial settings have proved highly successful and the concept is now commonly found in organizations dealing with users who have a choice of supplier.

Customized publishing. *See* On-demand publishing.

Cut. (*Noun*) 1. A design cut or engraved on wood, copper, or steel from which a print is made. 2. The impression from such a printing block. 3. An engraving, or plate, printed on the text page. 4. (*Verb*) To trim the edges of a book. 5. (*Adjective*) Of a book having cut edges. *See also* Cut edges, Opened, Plate.

Cut and paste. A software facility which allows text, graphics and video elements to be transferred easily from one location to another within the same document, from one document to another or between Applications.

Cut corner pamphlet file. A free-standing box file which has the upper back corners of the sides cut away to half the height of the box; the upper half of the back as well as the top are unenclosed. Such boxes are used for containing pamphlets on shelves.

Cut dummy. Complete proofs of the illustrations of a book, arranged in proper sequence and containing the figure and galley numbers.

Cut edges. (*Binding*) The top, fore, and tail edges of a book cut solid by a guillotine. When gilt they are known as 'gilt edges'. *See also* Edges.

Cut flush. A book having its cover and edges quite even, the cutting operation having been done after the cover (usually paper-boards or limp cloth) had been attached to the book. Also called 'Stiffened and cut flush'. A book so made is described as with 'flush boards'.

Cut in-boards. A book which has had the head, tail and fore-edge trimmed after the boards have been secured. *See also* Cut out-of-boards.

Cut line. Matter appearing below an illustration. More often called a 'Caption'.

Cut out-of-boards. A book which has had its edges cut or trimmed before the boards are affixed. This method is used for books with a hollow back, the boards of which are not laced on but fit closely in the grooves. *See also* Cut in-boards, Lacing-in.

Cut to register. Watermarked paper which has been so cut that the watermark appears in the same position in each sheet.

Cut-in heading. A paragraph or section heading set in a bold or otherwise distinguishing type in a space made available against the outer margin but within the normal type area. Also called 'Incut heading'. *See also* Incut note.

Cut-in index. *See* Thumb index.

Cut-in letter. One of a large size, and occupying the depth of two or more lines of type as at the beginning of a chapter or paragraph. *See also* Cock-up initial, Drop letter.

Cut-in note. *See* Incut note.

Cut-in side note. *See* Incut note.

Cut-out half-tone. *See* Half tone.

Cutter Author Marks. A system of author marks devised in 1880 by C. A. Cutter, (1837–1903) and consisting of from one to three letters at the beginning of an author's name, followed by numbers which increase as the names proceed along the alphabet. Author's names beginning with a consonant other than S have one letter, with S or a vowel have two letters, and Sc have three letters, followed in each case by a number, e.g.:

AB2	Abbot	G42	Gilman	SA1	Saint
AL12	Aldridge	SCH51	Schneider	SW1	Swain
G16	Gardiner	SCH86	Schwarts		

Their purpose is to enable books to be arranged alphabetically by using a relatively brief and easy to arrange symbol. In 1969 a revision was issued; in 1998 OCLC issued a four-figure table with software for automated 'cuttering'. *See also* Author mark, Book number, Cutter-Sanborn Three-figure Table.

Cutter Classification. *See* Expansive classification.

Cutter numbers. *See* Cutter Author Marks.

Cutter's objects. The 'objects' of a dictionary catalogue as adumbrated by Charles Ammi Cutter in his *Rules for a dictionary catalogue*, in 1875, are: (i) to enable a person to find a book of which either (a) the author, (b) the title, (c) the subject is known; (ii) to show what the library has (d) by a given author, (e) on a given subject, (f) in a given kind of literature; (iii) to assist in the choice of a book (g) as to its edition (bibliographically), (h) as to its character (literary or topical).

Cutter-Sanborn Three-figure Table. An extension, by Kate E. Sanborn, of the Cutter Author Marks for individualizing authors by using a combination of letters and three numbers (two for J, K, Y, Z, E, I, U, O; one for Q and X) in numerical order. For example:

Rol 744	Roli 748	Roman 758
Role 745	Roll 749	Romani 759
Rolf 746	Rolle 751	
Rolfe 747	Rollo 755	

In 1969 a revision of this and of the Cutter Author Marks was issued; in

1998 OCLC issued a four-figure table with software for automated 'cuttering'.

Cutting.   A piece cut from a newspaper or periodical. Also called 'Clipping' (American), 'Press cutting'. *See also* Clipping bureau, Clippings file.

CWIS.   1. Also CIS, Campus-Wide Information Service/System, an electronic system on which is maintained much information of interest to a local community of users. The term had a level of popularity in the early 1990s – before the take-off of the World Wide Web – but then became largely superseded by 'Web site' or 'Web pages'. *See also* Portal.   2. Collection Workflow Integration System, software to assemble, organize, and share collections of data about resources, like Yahoo or Google Directory but conforming to international and academic standards for Metadata. CWIS was specifically created to help build collections of Science, Technology, Engineering, and Mathematics resources and connect them into the National Science Foundation's National Science Digital Library. More information can be found at <scout.wisc.edu/Projects/CWIS>.

CWLIS.   <www.dils.aber.ac.uk.holi> Consortium of Welsh Library and Information Services; formed 1996 with the support of Interlending Wales and the Library and Information Plan Wales. Its functions are to facilitate development of services, instigate research and innovation, propose initiatives, and influence policy in the library and information sector.

Cyberinfrastructure.   A concept developed through the Blue Ribbon Advisory Panel on Cyberinfrastructure commissioned by the (US) National Science Foundation (NSF) to consider the computing and technological requirements of new research environments for the future. In its January 2003 report <www.cise.nsf.gov/sci/reports/toc.cfm>, the Panel recommended that the NSF should establish and lead a large-scale, inter-agency and internationally co-ordinated Advanced Cyber-infrastructure Program to create, deploy and apply cyberinfrastructure in ways that radically empower all scientific and engineering research and allied education (at $1billion per year). 'The emerging vision is to use cyberinfrastructure to build more ubiquitous, comprehensive digital environments that become interactive and functionally complete for research communities in terms of people, data, information, tools and instruments and that operate at unprecedented levels of computational storage and data transfer capacity'.

Cybernetics.   (Greek, steersman) The science of control and communication processes in animals and their replication in computerized systems.

Cyberspace.   Credited to the novelist William Gibson, cyberspace can be thought of as the ether-world (as opposed to nether-world) occupied by the messages, files and data that circulate around the Internet.

Cybrarian Project.   <www.dfes.gov.uk/cybrarianproject> Launched in 2004 by the (UK) Department for Education and Skills, the project aims to help the hardest-to-reach potential users of ICT who are currently held back by lack of skills or confidence or because of physical or cognitive disabilities.

Cyclopaedia. *See* Encyclopaedia.

Cydfenthyca Cymru. *See* Interlending Wales.

Cylinder dried. Paper which has been dried on the papermaking machine by being passed over steam-heated cylinders, as distinct from other methods of drying. Also called 'Machine-dried'.

Cylinder press. A printing press which makes the impression by cylinder as opposed to platen. It has a revolving impression cylinder under which is a flat bed containing the plates of type which moves backwards and forwards. These presses can be of two types; the Wharfedale or stop-cylinder press in which for every sheet printed, the cylinder makes almost one complete revolution and stops while the bed returns, an opening in the cylinder allowing the bed to return freely, and the Miehle or two-revolution press in which a smaller and continuously revolving cylinder revolves once to print one sheet then rises and revolves once more while the type bed slides back into position. This type of machine is the best letterpress machine for colour-printing and book-work. *See also* Flat-bed press, Platen press, Rotary press.

CyMAL. Museums, Archives and Libraries Wales was launched in 2004 as a division of the Welsh Assembly and will develop and implement policy in the sector. It is the equivalent of the Museums, Libraries and Archives Council (MLA) in England.

Cymru Ar-lein. Partner with UKOnline, ELFNI, and Digital Scotland in the People's Network (PN).

Cyngor Llyfrau Cymru. *See* Welsh Books Council.

Cyrillic Alphabet. The form of writing used for the Russian language. Originally used by the Eastern Church and supposedly devised by St. Cyril.

DACS. <www.dacs.co.uk> (Parchment House, 13 Northburgh Street, London EC1V 0AH, UK) Design and Artists Copyright Society, the main copyright collecting society for designers and artists in the UK. It licenses the use of appropriate materials for publication and educational purposes. Offers a licensing scheme for slide collections in academic institutions.

Daedalus. <www.lib.gla.ac.uk/daedalus> A JISC FAIR project which established a network of freely accessible digital collections – published and peer reviewed academic papers; pre-prints and grey literature; theses; research resource finding aids – at the University of Glasgow.

Dagger. (†) The second reference mark in footnotes, coming after the asterisk. When placed before an English, or after a German, person's name, it signifies 'dead' or 'died'. *See also* Reference marks.

Dagger in the Library Award (UK). <www.thecwa.co.uk> An award of the Crime Writers' Association for crime fiction selected by library staff.

Daguerreotype. A means of making a photographic image on a copper plate coated with a light-sensitive layer of silver. The process was invented by Louis Jacques Mandé Daguerre (1789–1851) in 1833 following the death of J. N. Niepce, with whom he had been in partnership, but not made public until 1839. The earliest daguerreotypes are unique in that they cannot be copied, but the process was superseded in the 1850s by a negative positive process by which an unlimited number of copies may be made. The process is considered to be the first really practicable photographic method. Daguerre was a French scene-painter who became well known as a result of the diorama he built in Paris in 1822; after 1826 he devoted himself to developing photographic processes.

Daily. A serial publication issued every day, except perhaps on Sunday.

Dainton Lecture. Initiated by the British Library in honour of Lord Dainton, who himself gave the first of the annual series in 1987.

Dainton Report. The report of the (UK) National Libraries Committee, published in 1969; the Chairman was the late Lord Dainton (at the time Dr. F. S. Dainton; later Sir Frederick Dainton). The main recommendations were incorporated in a White Paper, entitled *The British Library*, and published on 13 January 1971. The subsequent *British Library Bill* implemented these proposals, which were mainly: (i) a Board comprising a Chairman and up to 13 members would be created to manage and develop the British Library resulting from the amalgamation of the library departments of the British Museum, including the National Reference Library of Science and Invention, with the National Central Library, the National Lending Library for Science and Technology, and the *British National Bibliography*; (ii) councils would be appointed to advise on the needs of the Library's users. *See also* British Library.

Damaged letter. A piece of type, the printing surface of which has been damaged. When appearing in a printer's proof it is marked by an X in the margin. Also called 'Bad letter', 'Battered letter', 'Broken letter', 'Spoiled letter'.

Dampers. The damping rollers which are part of lithographic printing presses; they damp the printing plate after each impression with a fluid, known as a damping mixture, the composition of which varies according to the material used for the forme (stone, zinc, steel, aluminium), in order to prevent the ink adhering to the plate, which it would do if the plate became too dry. In a hand-press done with a sponge.

Dana (John Cotton) Award. An award made by the (US) Special Libraries Association to recognize exceptional service to special librarianship.

Dandy roll. A cylinder of wire gauze which presses upon the drained but still moist pulp just before it leaves the wire cloth of the paper-making machine for the rollers. The weaving of the wire of the dandy roll leaves its impression on the paper and determines whether it is to be wove paper (with the impression of fine, even gauze) or laid paper (with the impression of parallel lines). When devices or monograms are worked into the fine wire of the roll, 'watermarks' are produced.

Daniel Press. A private printing press established by the Rev. C. H. O. Daniel at Frome in 1846, revived at Worcester College, Oxford, in 1874 and used until he died in 1919 for the private publication of family verses as well as small pamphlets and books. In 1877 he discovered the punches, matrices and types which had been used by Dr. Fell at the University Press between 1667–74 and used them at his press. *See also* Fell types.

Danish Electronic Research Library. *See* DEF.

Danish library associations. There are several library associations in Denmark, serving different types of library. The most significant are Danmarks Biblioteksforening <www.dfb.dk> (Telegrafvej 5, 2750 Ballerup) founded in 1905 which serves the library community generally and publishes *Bogens Verden* (10 p.a.), and Bibliotekarforbundet (Danish Librarians Union) <www.bf.dk> (Lindevangs Alle 2, 2000 Frederiksburg) founded in 1923 with over 5,000 members, which represents the interests of individual librarians.

Danish Library Centre. [Dansk Bibliotheks Center] <www.dbc. bib.dk> (Tempovej 7–9, DK-2750 Ballerup, Denmark) The Centre provides data, information services and promotional materials to Danish libraries; it operates the DanBib national union catalogue system and the network for Danish libraries.

Danmarks Biblioteksforening. *See* Danish library associations.

DANTE. <www.dante.net> (Francis House, 112 Hills Road, Cambridge CB2 1PQ, UK) Delivery of Advanced Network Technology to Europe, DANTE, a not-for-profit company, was established in July 1993 by the European National Research and Education Networks to provide advanced international computer network services for the European research community. Projects include ALICE, EUMEDCONNECT and GÉANT.

DARE. <www.darenet.nl> Digital Academic Repositories, a joint initiative by Dutch universities, the National Library of the Netherlands, the Royal Netherlands Academy of Arts and Sciences and the Netherlands Organization for Scientific Research with the aim of storing the results of all Dutch research in a network of repositories, thereby facilitating access. *See also* Eprints, Open Archives Initiative, Repository (1), SHERPA.

DAREnet. <www.darenet.nl> The infrastructure of repositories that brings together the local collections of digital documentation held by all the Dutch universities and related institutions as part of the DARE initiative in the Netherlands.

DARPA Internet. *See* Internet.

Dartmouth Medal. An annual award for achievement in creating new reference works of outstanding quality and significance. Presented under the auspices of the American Library Association. First awarded 1974.

Dash. A short strip of rule cast in the following lengths, and used for punctuation: the two-em dash ——; the one-em dash —; the en rule –;

and the hyphen -. These may be used for decoration or for the clearer laying out of printed matter, but usually longer rules or ornamental rules are more often used for these purposes. *See also* Border, French rule, Rule, Swung dash.

Dash entry. Said of an entry for a book – following one or two long dashes (one for the author, the second for the title) – which continues, indexes, or supplements a monograph. Such an entry follows the entry for the main work in a printed bibliography or catalogue.

DAT. Digital audio tape, a magnetic tape onto which the sound is recorded digitally. Standard DAT cassettes were designed to store 1.3 Gbytes of data, are 4mm deep and approximately the size of a credit card. Also used for computer Back-up.

Data. A general term for information; particularly used for information stored in a database.

Data Archive. *See* UK Data Archive.

Data archives. Sets of data compiled and held in machine-readable form and available as primary sources for research. *See also* UK Data Archive.

Data element. (*Archives*) In *MAD*, the basic unit of information in the structured table of data elements. The elements in the table are structured into sectors, areas and sub-areas.

Data integrity. *See* Integrity.

Data mining. The process of extracting information from databases and datasets, particularly using techniques to discover otherwise hidden information with the goal of analyzing patterns and relationships. *See also* Bibliomining, Text mining.

Data processing. The handling or manipulation of data by computerized means to achieve a desired end result. Abbreviated DP, ADP (automatic data processing) and EDP (electronic data processing).

Data projector. Hardware which re-directs or duplicates a PC screen display, enabling it to be projected onto an external screen so that all activity is shown to a large group or audience. Particularly used with Presentation software.

Data protection. The threat to privacy posed by the collection of personal information in computerized databases has made legislation necessary, to ensure that certain fundamental principles of security and confidentiality are observed. In the UK, the Office of the Data Protection Registrar was created by the *Data Protection Act 1984*; the Registrar was renamed Data Protection Commissioner under the *Data Protection Act 1998* <www.hmso.gov.uk/acts/acts1998/19980029.htm>; and more recently renamed again as the Information Commissioner <www.informationcommissioner.gov.uk> (Wycliffe House, Water Lane, Wilmslow SK9 5AF, UK). The 1998 Act implemented the EU Data Protection Directive in the UK. It is the Commissioner's duty to compile and maintain the register of data users and computer bureaux and to provide facilities for members of the public to examine the register, to promote observance of data protection principles, to disseminate information about the Act, to encourage trade associations and others to introduce codes of practice, and to co-operate with other parties to the Council of Europe Convention on Data Protection (1981). *See also* European Data Protection Directive, Freedom of Information.

Data security. *See* Computer security.

Data validation. The checking of data for its validity, consistency and accuracy.

Data warehouse. For companies of all sizes, but especially larger organizations, problems in planning strategies occur because huge quantities of data are available about the business but there is no adequate means of bringing it all into one coherent focus. Data on sales, inventories, cost profiles, sales force feedback etc. can be integrated with external data (such as market reports, regulatory body specifications, or material drawn from customer or supplier Extranets) and mounted in a data warehouse. All data can be placed in one common resource which can be used to provide a company with a consistent and reliable view of its activity overall. Such factors as customer base, buying behaviours, commercial opportunities, new product ranges can be tested against the warehouse, using all available data to measure likely outcomes. Commercial providers of data warehouse services have proliferated. *See also* Knowledge management.

Databank. Usually synonymous with Database but sometimes used to specify collections of numeric data only.

Database. Any grouping of data for a particular purpose or for the use of a particular set of End users, usually organized via Fields, and providing tools to enable manipulation of the data such as sorting, grouping, extraction and reporting. A database might contain bibliographic data, or numerical, statistical material, and may be assembled and marketed commercially, or by an organization, library, or individual. Access to an online database may be obtained via a Host. A database is now defined in law as 'a collection of works, data or other materials which: (a) are arranged in a systematic or methodical way and (b) are individually accessible by electronic or other means'. This definition is much wider than the usual concept of a database as a collection of facts organized in a meaningful or useful order. *See also* Data mining, Data protection.

Database management systems (DBMS). Software packages for the creation and maintenance of databases.

Database Promotion Center. *See* Detabesu Shinko Senta.

Database right. In the EU, the right of the owner of the intellectual property in a database to prevent anyone else extracting or re-using the content of the database.

Dataset. A collection of data records having a particular subject, organizational or formatting focus and managed as a single entity. These can be bibliographic databases, full-text services or computer readable data; thus Compendex, JSTOR and Beilstein are all considered datasets in this context.

Date. 1. The statement in a book, either at the foot of the title-page, or on the reverse thereof, of the year in which the book was published. 2. (*Cataloguing*) A filing element appearing in a heading and consisting of the date(s) of birth and/or death of a person whose name is the main element in the name heading. *See also* Colophon, Copyright date, False date, Imprint date.

Date card. *See* Date label.

Date due. The date on which a book is due for return to a library.

Date guide. A guide bearing numerals representing the dates on which books are due for return and placed in front of the appropriate charges in the issue trays, when using the Browne system.

Date label. The label placed in a lending library book and dated to indicate when it is due for return. In a few libraries dates of issue are used instead. Also called in America a 'Date slip' or 'Dating slip'. Sometimes a loose card, called a 'date card', is used. *See also* Transaction card charging.

Date line. The line in any paper or magazine on which the date of issue appears.

Date of publication. 1. The year in which a book was published. It is usually printed at the foot of, or on the back of, the title-page. In old books a date often formed part of the Colophon. 2. The day and/or month and year of publication in the case of a newspaper or other periodical. 3. The exact date a document was released to the public. *See also* Copyright date.

Date stamp. 1. The date a library book is due for return (or of issue) which is stamped on a transaction card or date label. 2. The machine or dater used to make the impression.

Datum. (*Information retrieval*) The smallest element of information.

Dawson Award for Innovation in Academic Librarianship. A biennial award open to professional staff in academic libraries for any aspect of library activity. Sponsored by Wm. Dawson and Sons Ltd., and first presented in 1988.

Day of publication. *See* Publication day.

DBI. *See* Deutsches Bibliotheksinstitut.

DBMS. *See* Database management systems.

DC. 1. *See* Decimal Classification. 2. *See* Dublin Core Metadata Element Set. 3. *d.c.* Abbreviation for a page of printed matter set in Double column; Double Crown (paper 20 x 30 inches); Double cap (i.e. double foolscap) printing paper, 17 x 27 inches.

DCC. 1. Digital compact cassette, an audio tape format that permits digital recording. 2. *See* Digital Curation Centre.

DC-dot. <www.ukoln.ac.uk/metadata/dcdot> A Web-based tool developed by UKOLN for creating Dublin Core metadata in a variety of different formats.

DCF. *See* Digital Content Forum.

DCMS (UK). <www.dcms.gov.uk> (2–4 Cockspur Street, London SW1Y 5DH, UK) Department for Culture, Media and Sport; previously Department of National Heritage (DNH), Office of Arts and Libraries, etc. The central UK government department responsible for policy on the arts, sport, recreation, the National Lottery, libraries, museums, galleries, export licensing of cultural goods, broadcasting, film, press freedom and regulation, the built heritage, the royal estate, and tourism. It is responsible for English public libraries under the Public Libraries and Museums Act of 1964, and for the People's Network.

DDC. *See* Dewey Decimal Classification.

De luxe binding. A fine leather binding, lettered and tooled by hand. So-called de luxe bindings are often machine products.

De luxe edition. An edition of a book in which especially good materials and fine workmanship have been used.

De Vinne. A Typeface cut for Theodore Low De Vinne, 1828–1914, a distinguished American printer. He was a co-founder with Robert Hoe in 1884 of the Grolier Club and printed its first publication, a reprint of the *Star Chamber Decree*, 1637. He encouraged New York printing house owners to form a union which, when combined with similar groups from other cities, became known in 1887 as the United Typothetae.

Deacidification. A general term for a variety of processes which raise the pH value of paper documents to a minimum of 7.0 to assist in their preservation. Deacidification stabilizes the paper and inhibits further deterioration, but does not return brittle paper to its original condition. Treated documents can be laminated or encapsulated to extend their useful life. Sprays are available to deacidify single sheets or volumes, and methods for deacidification on a mass scale have been developed. *See* DEZ, pH value, Wei T'o.

Dead file. In acquisition work, a file containing (1) records for books received and catalogued, (2) records for books not available as gifts or by purchase despite considerable correspondence, (3) completed or filled records for serial publications.

Dead matter. (*Printing*) Type matter or plates which have been used for printing but are not to be used again and may therefore be distributed or melted. *See also* Kill, Live matter, Matter.

Dearing Report (UK). <www.leeds.ac.uk/educol/ncihe> The Report of the National Committee of Inquiry into Higher Education *Higher Education in the Learning Society* (Chair: Sir Ron Dearing) issued in 1997; the Report stresses collaboration and strategic partnerships, and examines diversity, widening participation, expansion, franchising, quality assurance, effectiveness, communication and information technologies, research, copyright, fees, key skills and staff roles.

Debug. Remove problem areas – Bugs – from computer programs so that they run accurately and maintain data Integrity.

Decalcomania (Decal).   1. A transfer or design printed on special paper for transfer to pottery or some other permanent base.   2. The paper for printing such transfers on.   3. The process of printing illustrations on glass, wood, pottery, etc.

Decimal Classification (DC).   There have been several schemes which have employed decimals in some way but the one usually referred to by this name is that compiled by Melvil Dewey (1851–1931) and published in 1876, in which it is the notation that is used decimally. *See also* Abridged Decimal Classification, Dewey Decimal Classification, Universal Decimal Classification.

Decimal notation.   A Notation used to identify subjects in a scheme of classification; it consists of numerals used decimally so as to permit the logical subdivision of subjects, or a chain of classes, indefinitely. Most current classification schemes use this type of notation.

Decimo-octavo.   Synonymous with Octodecimo. *See* Eighteen-mo.

Decimo-sexto.   *See* Sexto-decimo.

Decision making.   The management process of systematic analysis and consideration of all relevant factors, necessary before embarking on a strategy. Assessment of performance and evaluation of progress would be key components in the process.

Decision support system (DSS).   Considered by some to be a branch of Management information systems, decision support systems attempt to aid the manager to examine data in a way which helps to draw conclusions. The major components of a system are: the end user or decision maker; a database relevant to the topic under consideration; models and procedures to simulate the effects of decision making; and computer software to manage and integrate these issues.

Deck.   One floor of a stack containing book shelves and workrooms (American).

Deckle.   1. Abbreviation for Deckle edge, and for deckle strap.   2. The frame or border, usually of wood, which confines the paper pulp to the mould when making paper by hand.   3. In the paper-making machine, the distance between the two deckle straps.

Deckle edge.   The feathery edge at the borders of a sheet of handmade or mould-made paper; it is caused by the deckle or frame which confines the paper pulp to the mould. It is also found in machine-made papers, being caused in these by the rubber deckle straps at the sides of the paper machine, or by artificial means such as a jet of water. Also called 'Feather-edge'.

Deckle straps.   Endless rubber bands which run on both sides of the wire cloth of a paper-making machine in order to keep the wet pulp within the desired limits of width. Also called 'Boundary straps'.

Declassify.   To remove a secret or confidential document from a security classification under proper authorization. *See also* Downgrade.

Decorated cover.   The front cover of a book which bears distinctive lettering or an illustration or design.

Decorative.   A class of typefaces which have exaggerated characteristics of the other three classes, Abstract, Cursive and Roman, or distinctive features which preclude them from being included in those classes. They are usually fussily ornamental, but included in this group is Old English.

Decreasing concreteness, principle of.   A general principle for choosing an order of application of the Characteristics of a classification. Ranganathan developed a general facet formula which reflects this principle and is popularly known by the abbreviation PMEST standing for the five 'fundamental categories' Personality, Matter, Energy, Space and Time. *See* Fundamental categories.

Dedicated line.   A power or data line which provides for the special requirements of particular pieces of computer or communications equipment, in particular to prevent degradation of data.

Dedication.   The author's inscription to a person or persons testifying respect, and often recommending the work to special protection and favour, it usually appears on the recto of the leaf following the title-page. In sixteenth- and seventeenth-century books the dedication often took the form of a dedicatory letter written by the author to a patron.

Dedication copy.   A copy of a book presented by the author, and so inscribed, to the person to whom the work is dedicated.

Deep etched half-tone.   *See* Half-tone.

Deep etching.   In photo-engraving, additional etching made necessary to secure proper printing depth where this cannot be accomplished by routing, as in places where dense black lines are used, or where line negatives and half-tone negatives are combined in the same place. *See also* Etching.

Deep Web.   That proportion of the World Wide Web that is dynamic in content, is not readily retrieved by a Web crawler, and, as a result, is not displayed by Web search engines. The part of the Web that does not exist as fixed pages written in html resides in databases and is delivered 'on the fly' in response to particular requests. It has been estimated that the deep web is 500 times the size of the fixed web. Also referred to as the Invisible Web.

DEF.   <www.deflink.dk/eng/default.asp> Danish Electronic Research Library, a project that began in 1998 to support Danish research and education by strengthening the development of the Danish research libraries and creating a coherent and simple access to the information resources of these libraries. The seven DEF programme areas are: user facilities; digitization; e-learning; e-publishing; licenses; portals; and system architecture.

Defaulter.   A reader who fails to return a book or pay a fine.

Defense Technical Information Center (DTIC).   <www.dtic.mil> (8725 John J. Kingman Road, Suite 0944, Fort Belvoir, VA 22060, USA) The Center plays a major role in information transfer and holds vast collections of scientific and technical reports. Access is available to citations of unclassified, unlimited documents and many other technical resources.

Deferred cataloguing. The postponement by a library of the full cataloguing of less important material, brief catalogue entries being made and possibly separately arranged temporarily to serve as a finding medium.

Definition. (*Classification*) Concise description in distinct terms for essentials and characteristics.

Definitive edition. The final authoritative text of the complete works of an author – the nearest possible approach to what the author intended – edited usually after the author's death. It is characterized by its editorial introduction, notes and sometimes *Apparatus criticus*. Not to be confused with a Variorum edition. Applies also to the works of a composer of music.

del, delt. Abbreviation for *delineavit* (Lat. 'he or she drew it'). Used on engravings, maps, etc. and followed by the name of the artist or cartographer responsible for the original drawings. *See also fecit, sculpt.*

Delayed discharging. Delaying the cancellation of a loan until after the reader returning a book has left the counter. This is done as a normal part of the routine in some libraries, but in others discharging is only delayed during very busy periods, it being the usual practice to discharge books immediately they are returned. *See also* Cheque book charging method, Transaction card charging.

dele. *See* Delete.

deleatur. (Lat. 'delete'). *See* Delete.

Delete. To blot out, to erase, to omit. A mark, like the Greek letter δ, used in correcting proofs, is put in the margin to show that certain letters or words crossed through are to be deleted. Often abbreviated 'del', 'dele', or d (representing the lower case initial letter of the Latin *deleatur*).

Deletion mark. The mark used in correcting a proof to indicate matter to be omitted. Also called 'Cancellation mark'. *See also* Delete.

DeLiberations on Learning and Teaching in Higher Education. <www.city.londonmet.ac.uk/deliberations> DeLiberations (ISSN 1363-6715) is an international website on issues of learning and teaching for the higher education community. It was set up in 1995 with funding from the eLib Programme and is designed to act as a resource and an interactive forum to support staff concerned with the innovative design and delivery of courses, particularly those with substantial electronic input. It is based in the Educational and Staff Development Unit at London Guildhall University.

Delimiter. (*Information retrieval*) A symbol (i) separating data elements within a Field or (ii) separating fields.

Deliquescence. Tendency to absorb atmospheric moisture.

DELOS. <www.cordis.lu/ist/directorate_e/digicult/delos.htm> An FP6 project to create a 'Network of Excellence on Digital Libraries' through a joint programme of activities aimed at integrating and co-ordinating the ongoing research activities of the major European research teams in the field of digital libraries. The DELOS 10-year grand vision is that 'Digital Libraries should enable any citizen to access all human knowledge any time and anywhere, in a friendly, multi-modal, efficient and effective way, by overcoming barriers of distance, language, and culture and by using multiple Internet-connected devices'.

Delphi. In contemporary operations research, a prophetic method of forecasting technique whereby experts solicit the opinions of a group of advisers through a series of carefully designed questionnaires. The experts reply to the questionnaires, receive statistical feedback and resubmit their estimates. The process is repeated more than once. This Delphi approach has been used to predict trends for periods as far as fifty years ahead, e.g. an environmental forecast for research libraries in Sweden. The name originates from the Delphic Oracle of classical times, presided over by Apollo, the god of the sun, prophecy, music, medicine and poetry.

Demonym. A popular or ordinary qualification used as a pseudonym, as 'An Amateur', 'A Bibliophile'.

Demopleth map. A type of Choropleth map which shows distribution by civil divisions.

Demy. A standard size of printing paper, $17^{1}/_{2}$ x $22^{1}/_{2}$ inches, and of writing and drawing paper (also called 'small demy') $15^{1}/_{2}$ x 20 inches. *See also* Octavo, Paper sizes.

Demy Octavo. A book size, $8^{3}/_{4}$ x $5^{5}/_{8}$ inches. *See also* Book sizes.

DENET. <www.denet.dk> Danish Academic Network.

DENI. *See* Department of Education, Northern Ireland.

Denotation. *See* Connotation.

Densitometer. A photoelectric instrument for measuring the density, or degree of blackness, of a photographic image. A reflection-densitometer is used to measure the density of an opaque surface (print) before setting the camera and screen for half-tone exposure. Optical density of ink films during printing is measured with a similar instrument.

Density. In documentary reproduction, the degree of photographic opacity. The degree of opacity of films and blackness of prints (the light-absorbing quality of a photographic image); it is usually expressed as the logarithm of opacity.

Dentelle. Lace-like tooling on the borders of a book cover, placed near the edges and pointing towards the centre. The most notable binders working in this style were the Derome family and Pierre-Paul Dubuisson who was appointed binder to Louis XV in 1758.

Dentelle à l'oiseau. Dentelle bindings in which birds are introduced into the design of the borders; chief executant was N. D. Derome. *See also* Derome style.

Denudation. (*Classification*) The formation of a chain of classes by the application of successive characteristics of division. A Fission mode of formation of new subjects discovered by Ranganathan.

Department.   1. A section of a library devoted to one subject, or to one kind of service, as a 'Reference library'.   2. An administrative section of a library which has one function or series of functions, such as 'Cataloguing department'. In America sometimes called a 'Division'.

Department for Culture, Media and Sport.   *See* DCMS.

Department for Education and Skills (DfES).   <www.dfes.gov.uk> (Sanctuary Buildings, Great Smith Street, London SW1P 3BT, UK) The department of UK government that is responsible for education services at all levels, and for the promotion of skills attainment.

Department of Education, Northern Ireland (DENI).   <www.deni.gov. uk> (Rathgael House, Balloo Road, Bangor, Co Down, BT19 7PR, Northern Ireland) The Department of the Northern Ireland Civil Service with responsibility for policy matters affecting the provision of library and information services in Northern Ireland. Day-to-day responsibility for public library services is devolved to the five Education and Library Boards.

Department of Trade and Industry (DTI).   <www.dti.gov.uk> (1 Victoria Street, London SW1H 0ET, UK) The department of UK government which supports businesses through policies to encourage competitiveness, industrial sponsorship, trade policy, consumer protection etc. It is responsible for several executive agencies, including the Patent Office, and incorporates the Office for Science and Technology. DTI is responsible for policy on information security, for Broadband initiatives, and is working with the Digital Content Forum on a digital content overview.

Departmental library.   A library in a college or university which is apart from the main library and restricted to one subject or group of subjects. Also called 'Branch library', 'Faculty library', 'Laboratory collection', 'Office collection', 'Seminar collection'.

Departmental publications.   Non-Parliamentary Publications published and made available from the Departments of the British Central Government.

Dependent work.   A term used by cataloguers to indicate a work which is related in some way to a work by another author already published. It may be a modification, adaptation or amplification of the earlier work; the term includes such writings as abridgements, commentaries, continuations, dramatizations, librettos, parodies, revisions, selections, sequels and supplements.

Deposit.   (*Archives*) The system whereby owners of archives may lend them to an archives service on a long-term basis, so as to provide conservation and user facilities for them. There are legal and practical difficulties: the Society of Archivists publishes guidelines.

Deposit collection.   A collection of materials from a single publisher, or owner, placed in a library organization as a collection and so that they may be made available to the public. The depositor often prescribes regulations for access.

Deposit copy. A copy of a newly published book, pamphlet or periodical, etc., which is sent to one or more libraries, as required by law, and sometimes to complete copyright protection in the country. *See* Depository library.

Deposit library. 1. (*Archives*) A library in which documents are deposited under special conditions. 2. A library to which books and other publications are sent by the publishers for permanent preservation under the provisions of national copyright or legal deposit legislation; also called a Copyright library, Depository library. *See also* Legal deposit.

Depositors. (*Archives*) 1. People or institutions who place their archives on deposit with an archives service. 2. Owners of archives who have deposited them in an archives service or record office.

Depository library. In the UK, a library which is entitled by law to receive a free copy of every book published. In America, a library which is entitled to receive all, or selected, United States government publications. *See also* Copyright library, Deposit library.

Depth classification. Classifying so minutely that the most specific subject in all its aspects is identified and dealt with fully and accurately. *See also* Close classification.

Depth indexing. Indexing as fully as possible by making specific entries for all the subjects, persons, places, books, etc. mentioned in the text.

Depth of strike. *See* Bevel.

Deputy librarian. The chief assistant librarian. One who becomes acting chief librarian in all absences of the principal. Sometimes called 'Associate librarian'.

Dequeker system. (*Information retrieval*) The first information searching system to be introduced. It consisted of cards with rows of holes punched in the body of the cards and filed on their edges in a cabinet. Rods were inserted through the holes corresponding to the codes for the subject of an enquiry, and a half-turn of a handle operated a mechanism to raise slightly above the level of the remainder of the cards those bearing the codes required. *See also* Edge-notched cards, Marginal-hole punched cards, Punched card.

Derivative work. A Work, e.g. extracts, anthology, abridgement, adaptation, translation, revision, compilation, arrangement of a musical work, which is the result of adapting, arranging, translating or transforming an Intellectual work. The copyright of a derived work is protected without affecting the copyright of the original, provided that the choice, the presentation, or the form, represents the personal work of the author.

Derome style. A style of book decoration practised by the Derome family in France in the eighteenth century. It is mainly confined to symmetrical corner tooling of a very richly engraved floreated scroll work. Nicholas Denis Derome (1731–88) who worked for Count Hoym is famous for his Dentelle borders. *See also* Dentelle.

Descender. The vertical descending stem of lower-case letters such as j, p, q, etc.; that part which extends below the 'X'-height. *See also* Ascender.

Description.   (*Archives*) The activity corresponding to cataloguing in libraries. As a noun, the representation of archival materials for retrieval or management purposes.

Descriptive bibliography.   The area of bibliography which makes known precisely the material conditions of books, that is, the full name of the author, the exact title of the work, the date and place of publication, the publisher's and printer's names, the format, the pagination, typographical particulars, illustrations and the price, and for old books, other characteristics such as the kind of paper, binding. Also called 'Analytical bibliography', 'Physical bibliography'. *See also* Historical bibliography.

Descriptive cataloguing.   That part of the cataloguing process which is concerned with the choice and form of entries, transcription of title-page details, collation, etc. The term was coined by the survey committee at the Library of Congress in 1940. *See also* Subject cataloguing.

Descriptive list.   (*Archives*) A list of documents, with a brief description of the contents of each, sufficient to enable the researcher to determine whether it is likely to provide the information needed.

Descriptive metadata.   *See* Metadata.

Descriptor.   (*Information retrieval*) 1. An elementary term used to identify a subject.   2. A simple word or phrase used as a subject.   3. A word, translatable into a code, or symbol, which is given to a document to describe it and by means of which it can be discovered when required Also called 'Code', 'Semantic factor'. It may be a subject heading or a class number.   4. (*Cataloguing, Indexing*) A descriptive designation added to a heading in a catalogue entry or index entry to distinguish otherwise identical headings. A type of Additional designation. *See also* Subject heading, Thesaurus, Unit record.

Desensitization.   Applying a solution, called an 'etch' (of nitric acid and gum arabic for stone; gum arabic, chromic acid and phosphoric acid for zinc; gum arabic and phosphoric acid for aluminium) to a lithographic printing plate after an image has been transferred to it, to desensitize the non-image areas, remove stray traces of grease from them, and increase the moisture-retaining capacity.

Desiderata.   1. A list of subjects on which the author of a book requires information. If only one is required the singular form 'desideratum' is used.   2. A list of books required.

Design.   (*Verb*) To plan the entire format of a book. (*Noun*) The specification for the format of a book.

Design and Artists Copyright Society.   *See* DACS.

Designation mark.   Letters corresponding to the initial letters of the title of a book, and the volume number (if any), which are sometimes printed alongside the Signature mark on each section to help the binder identify the sections belonging to a particular title. *See also* Direction line.

Desktop publishing (DTP).   A term generally credited to Paul Brainerd of Aldus Corporation; desktop publishing began through a combination of a computer with a new concept in screen display (the Apple Macintosh), innovative software (Aldus PageMaker) and the first mass market laser printer incorporating PostScript. This combination permitted the mixing of text and graphics anywhere on the printed page, accurate scaling and high quality printing of the displayed results. Since then the concept has expanded to all hardware platforms and produced a wide range of software to be used by individuals, through libraries, to professional publishing houses. Professional desktop publishing systems are frequently connected to Imagesetters to produce the highest quality output. Word processing packages have gradually increased in sophistication to incorporate desktop publishing features. Not to be confused with Electronic publishing.

Dessicant drying. A method for drying documents undertaken with the wet materials left on the shelves. Moist air is pumped out of the areas and hot, dry air introduced. A procedure appropriate for damp rather than sodden materials, and one which should be started quickly, before mould develops. *See also* Freeze drying, Vacuum drying.

Destination slips. Pieces of paper which project from books in the Order Department or Cataloguing Department to indicate by their colour or marking to which libraries they are allocated.

Destruction schedule. A list of documents, or of types of document, which may be destroyed as of no further value after the expiry of a specified term of years, the promulgation of the list being authority to destroy. *See also* Schedule (6).

Detabesu Shinko Senta. [Database Promotion Center] <www.dpc.or.jp> (5th fl, Shimbashi Towa Bldg, 2-13-8 Shimbashi, Minato-ku, Tokyo 105-0004, Japan) Established in 1984 under an initiative from the Japanese Ministry of Trade and Industry (MITI), now Ministry of Economy, Trade and Industry (METI), the DPC's operations include the promotion of integrated database production and technical development through research, training and international co-operation. Publishes *Database Hakusho* [*Database White Paper*] (a.) and *Database Daicho Soran* [*Database Directory*] (a.), *Newsletter* (q.), *Databases in Japan* (a.), as well as on-line directories.

Detection system. *See* Book detection system.

Deutsche Bibliothek. <www.ddb.de> (Adickesalice 1, 60322 Frankfurt a.M., Germany) Formed in 1990 by the union of the earlier Deutsche Bibliothek in Frankfurt a.M. with the Deutsche Bücherei in Leipzig. Deposit library functions date back to 1913, and the new organization acts as the German National Library with appropriate bibliographic information provision. There are many special collections. The Frankfurt premises contain some 6 million volumes, and the Library incorporates another 8 million at the Leipzig site (Deutsche Bücherei, Deutscher Platz, 04103 Leipzig). The Deutsches Musikarchiv in Berlin is also incorporated in the Library. Publishes *Deutsche National-bibliographie* (weekly and cumulations), special lists of theses, music.

Deutsche Bücherei. *See* Deutsche Bibliothek.

Deutsche Forschungsgemeinschaft (DFG). <www.dfg.de/lis> The German Research Foundation, a non-profit organization for science research. Members include research universities, research institutes and science associations. DFG funds special projects in libraries, archives, computing centres, and promotes co-operative actions such as the German National Database of Journals. Co-operates with the (US) National Science Foundation in the Internet Digital Library Research Program.

Deutsche Gesellschaft für Informationswissenschaft und Informationpraxis (DGI). <www.dgi-info.de> (Ostbahnhofstr. 13, 60314 Frankfurt a.M., Germany) Founded in 1948; 2,100 members comprise authors, publishers and other information suppliers, archives, libraries, documentation departments, hosts, information agencies, software producers, information and system consulting agencies, organizers of education and training, and all other participants in the field of knowledge processing. DGI promotes research in documentation, development of methods and tools, and promotes education and training of information specialists. Specialized committees cover classification and thesaurus research, artificial intelligence, patent documentation, terminology, technical communication, economic efficiency, etc. Publishes *Nachrickten für Dokumentation* (6 p.a.) and reports of conferences and meetings. In 2004 it was announced that DGI would merge with Bundesvereinigung Deutscher Bibliotheksverbände (BDB) to form Bibliothek und Information Deutschland (BID).

Deutscher Bibliotheksverband (DVB). <www.bibliotheksverband.de> (Alt-Moabit 101A, 10559 Berlin, Germany) German professional organization covering all sectors; particular attention is given to co-operation and collaboration, political lobbying on library issues, and a programme of lectures, conferences, publications and research. Founded in 1949, DVB absorbed the Bibliotheksverband der Deutschen Demokratik Republik (the professional association of the former GDR) in 1992. It plays a key role in the Bundesvereinigung Deutscher Bibliotheksverbände (BDB), the umbrella organization for library associations in Germany.

Deutsches Biblioheksinstitut (BDI). BDI was a service institution for libraries in Germany; the service closed in 2003.

Deutsches Forschungsnetz. *See* DFN.

Deutsches Institut für Medizinische Dokumentation und Information. *See* DIMDI.

Device. An emblem or monogram used by a printer or publisher to identify work. It is usually used as part of the printer's Imprint or publisher's name on the title-page or spine.

Devil. *See* Willow.

Devolution. The process of delegating the provision of local services to local organizations or service points, whose interest and knowledge of a community will be more acute.

Dewey Decimal Classification (DDC). The classification devised by Melvil Dewey (1851–1931) in 1873, and first published anonymously in 1876. Knowledge is divided into the following main classes: 0, General works; 1, Philosophy; 2, Religion; 3, Sociology; 4, Philology; 5, Natural Science; 6, Useful Arts; 7, Fine Arts; 8, Literature; 9, History. The notation is a pure one, being based on three figures and used decimally. Sub-division by form is facilitated by the use of a table of common sub-divisions; the linguistic numbers from 420–499 and the geographical numbers from 940–999 are used mnemonically to subdivide by language and place. The relative index is original, and shows the relation of each subject indexed to a larger subject (or class or division), or after the entry word the phase of the subject is indicated. The schedules were considerably extended in each successive edition until the fifteenth 'Standard' Edition (1951) which was published after Dewey's death and was a much attenuated edition, being designed for a small library. In this, the simplified spelling which Dewey had always used was discontinued. The current edition is the 22nd (2003). DDC is published by Forest Press which was acquired by OCLC in 1988. Translations of DDC are available in Arabic, French, Italian, Persian, Spanish, Turkish and work is in progress on versions in Chinese and Russian. An electronic version – WebDewey <www.oclc.org/dewey> – has been available from 1996 and is updated continuously. An abridged version is also available (14th, ed., 2000).

Dewey (Melvil) Medal. Donated by Forest Press, Inc., this annual award, consisting of a medal and citation of achievement, is made to an individual or a group for recent creative professional achievement of a high order, particularly in those fields in which Melvil Dewey was so actively interested, notably library management, library training, cataloguing and classification, and the tools and techniques of librarianship. The award is administered by the ALA Awards Committee which appoints a jury of five to make the selection. The Medal was first awarded (in 1953) to Ralph R. Shaw.

DEZ. An abbreviation for the chemical substance diethyl zinc. A method for the mass deacidification of books developed by the Library of Congress. The books (up to 5,000) are placed in a large chamber which is flooded with DEZ gas, thus neutralizing acids and forming alkaline reserves and buffering the paper. DEZ gas is highly unstable and early experiments with the technique resulted in some serious explosions. (Reference: Unesco, *Study on mass conservation techniques for the treatment of library archives and material*. Paris, 1989. PGI-89/W5/14.)

DfES. *See* Department for Education and Skills.

DFN. <www.dfn.de> (DFN-Verein, Pariser Str. 44, 10707 Berlin, Germany) Deutsches Forschungsnetz; the German Research Network.

DG XIII. *See* Directorate General XIII.

DGI. *See* Deutsche Gesellschaft für Informationswisenschaft und Informationpraxis.

DHTML. *See* Dynamic HTML.

Diachronous. In user and citation studies, referring to changes that occur with the passage of time as revealed by observations made on two or more separate occasions. *See also* Synchronous.

Diacritical mark. A mark, such as an accent, placed over or under a letter to express some special phonetic value.

Diaeresis. Two dots placed over the second of two consecutive vowels to show that they are to be pronounced separately, as Chloë, coöperate. In English it is now an obsolescent symbol, having been replaced by the hyphen (co-operate).

Diagonal fraction. The separation of the numerator from the denominator by an oblique stroke instead of a horizontal one, e.g. 1/2.

diagr. (*Pl.* diagrs.) Abbreviation for Diagram.

Diagram. As distinct from an illustration proper, a diagram gives only the general outline or plan of the thing represented. Abbreviated diagr.

DialogPlus. <www.dialogplus.org> Subtitled Digital Libraries in Support of Innovative Approaches to Learning and Teaching in Geography, the DialogPlus project develops and deploys reusable digital learning nuggets through the Alexandria Digital Library. The project combines the efforts of geographers, education specialists, and computer scientists at Pennsylvania State University, University of California, Santa Barbara, University of Southampton and the University of Leeds. It is funded jointly by the National Science Foundation and JISC, as part of the Digital Libraries in the Classroom initiative.

Dial-up access. Access from local PC to remote server via the public telephone system, using a Modem to convert the signals.

Diamond. An out-of-date name for a size of type equal to approximately 4$\frac{1}{2}$ point.

Diaper. A binding pattern consisting of a simple figure constantly repeated in geometrical form: the pattern may consist of figures separated by the background only, or of compartments constantly succeeding one another, and filled with a design. The design is done with a 'diaper roll'.

Diapositive. A positive copy (of a document) made on transparent material. *See also* Negative, Positive.

Diazo. A contraction of diazonium, the chemical compound used in ammonia-developing reproduction papers, cloths and films which will reproduce anything printed, drawn, or written on a translucent or transparent material when exposed to ultra-violet light and developed in ammonia fumes. *See also* Diazotype process.

Diazotype process. A copying process whereby paper treated with a diazo compound is placed against the document to be copied and an exposure made by means of powerful arc lamps. The exposed paper is developed by passing it through a chamber containing ammonia fumes or over rollers damped with a specially prepared solution.

Diced. Binding with tooling to resemble dice or small diamond squares.

Dichotomy, classification by. *See* Bifurcate classification.

Dictionary. 1. A book explaining the words of a language, the words being arranged in alphabetical order; it usually gives the orthography, pronunciation and meaning of each word. A dictionary of the words in a restricted field of knowledge usually gives only the meaning. 2. In information retrieval, *synonymous with* Thesaurus.

Dictionary catalogue. A catalogue in which all the entries (author, title, subject, series, etc.) and references are arranged in a single alphabet – like a dictionary. As distinct from other alphabetical catalogues, subject entries are made under specific subjects. In some instances, the arrangement of sub-entries may depart from a strictly alphabetical order to provide a logical, or other convenient, arrangement, the main headings still retaining the alphabetical order. For the 'objects' of a dictionary catalogue, *See* Cutter's objects.

Dictionary code. The use, as a code, of words and terms in the alphabetical order of a dictionary.

Dictionary index. A series of entries with verbal headings arranged in alphabetical order.

Didone. A category of Typeface having a sharp contrast between the thick and thin strokes. The axis of the curves is vertical, the serifs of the lower-case ascenders are horizontal and there are no brackets to the serifs. Examples are Bodoni, Corvinus, Extended and Modern. The term Didone has replaced Modern face.

Didot. A Modern-face type cut in 1784 by Firmin Didot (1764–1836) the most famous of a French family important in the history of printing. Most eminent as a typefounder, he was mainly responsible for developing the type which is now familiar. He revived and developed the stereotyping process, and produced singularly perfect editions of many classical English and French works. He and other members of his family fixed the standard for book types in France in the nineteenth century.

Didot normal. The standard on the Continent of Europe for the height of type from the feet to the printing surface. It is 0.9278 inches. *See also* Type height.

Didot point. *See* Didot system.

Didot system. A system of type measurement originated by François Ambroise Didot (1730–1804), the French typefounder, in 1775. One Didot point equals 0.0148 inches; one English point equals 0.013837 inches. The Didot System was generally adopted in France early in the nineteenth century and by German typefounders between 1840 and 1879. *See also* Cicero, Point.

Die. An engraved stamp used for stamping a design.

Die sinking. The process of making dies; die cutting.

Die stamping. A printing process that gives a raised effect. Sometimes the die does not carry the ink, and the raised paper alone makes the letter discernible. *See also* Embossing.

Die sunk. A depression produced by the application of a heated die or block.

Dieper. <www.sub.uni-goettingen.de/gdz/dieper> Digitized European Periodicals, an EU project in which partners from ten countries joined to build a virtual network for retrospectively digitized periodicals. The central access point is devised as a register built on the model of the European Register of Microform Masters. Records of the register will be linked to reliable and comprehensive archives of periodical literature working at different sites thoughout Europe.

Diethyl zinc. *See* DEZ.

Difference. *See* Predicables, five.

Diffuse facets. (*Information retrieval*) Facets representing very general and abstract subjects without specification of primary substance.

Digest. A methodically arranged compendium or summary of literary, historical, legal, scientific, or other written matter.

Digester. (*Paper*) The vessel in which rags, esparto or wood are boiled, with chemicals, often caustic soda, to break down the fibres. *See also* Boiler.

DigiCULT. <www.cordis.lu/ist/directorate_e> <digicult@cec.eu.int> Digital Heritage and Cultural Content; a programme promoting access to cultural heritage. DigiCULT is part of the IST priority area in the EU's Sixth Framework programme (FP6) for the period 2002–2006.

Digimap. <edina.ac.uk/digimap> A service from EDINA that delivers Ordnance Survey Map Data to UK higher education. Data is available either to download to use with appropriate application software such as GIS, or as maps generated by Digimap online. Users can view and print maps of any location in Great Britain at a series of predefined scales. The service has been available since January 2000, based on the trial service run as part of the Digimap Project.

Digit. 1. Each of the symbols comprising a Book number in the Colon Classification. 2. In classification, a distinctively recognizable config-uration of marks (e.g. letters – both capital and lower case – numbers, punctuation marks and any other symbols), or code elements, included in a notation, therefore synonymous with 'sort'. 3. The printers' symbol ☞. Also known as 'Fist', 'Hand' or 'Index'.

Digital. 1. Representation of data or information in combinations of separate groups of digits suitable for processing by a computer. 2. An indicator, in general terms, of the influence of computerized systems in all walks of life e.g. the digital world.

Digital Asset Management. The process of itemizing, understanding and evaluating the intellectual assets held in electronic formats by an organization. *Compare* Content management.

Digital audio tape. *See* DAT.

Digital camera. Camera which captures images on a charge coupled device in place of traditional film. Once the image is captured in digital form it can be transferred to a PC, manipulated, and then transmitted as an Attachment or incorporated into Applications.

Digital certificate. An electronic document used to authenticate web transactions and related communications such as secure E-mail.

Authentication is based on public key cryptography (also referred to as public key infrastructure, PKI) where each participant is issued with a public key and a private key: anything encrypted with the public key requires the private key to decrypt it and *vice versa*. A certificate contains the certificate holder's public key together with some identifying information such as the individual's name, organization, a serial number and expiration dates. Digital certificates can be kept in registries so that authenticating users can look up other users' public keys. ITU-T Recommendation X.509 *Public-key and attribute certificate frameworks* relates. *See also* Digital signature, Digital watermarking.

Digital compact cassette. *See* DCC.

Digital content. Information content from any source and in any format that has been transferred into a digital format for loading onto electronic sources of information. As early technology tended to stress systems rather than content, digital content has been slower to grow in quantity and quality than was foreseen. Several initiatives are now addressing this issue. *See also* e-Content.

Digital Content Forum (DCF). <www.dcf.org.uk> A UK industry body that is currently charged by the Department of Trade and Industry with investigating new initiatives to expand and improve the range of publicly-accessible e-content.

Digital copyright. *See* Electronic copyright.

Digital Curation Centre (DCC). <www.dcc.ac.uk> A Centre established on 1 March 2004 and jointly funded by JISC and the e-Science Core Programme to support expertise and practice in data curation and preservation, prompting collaboration between the universities and the Research Councils to ensure that there is continuing access to data of scholarly interest. The initial focus will be on research data, but the policy intention is to also address the preservation needs of e-learning and scholarly communication. The DCC is run by a consortium comprising the Universities of Edinburgh and Glasgow, which together host the National e-Science Centre, UKOLN, and CCLRC, which manages the Rutherford Appleton and Daresbury Laboratories.

Digital divide. <europa.eu.int/information_society/eeurope> The concept of the digital divide recognizes that access to digital services is very different in various areas of the world. In the developed world, home use of the Internet is available to around 60% of the population in the USA and the Netherlands; in Greece the figure is 10%, and in less-developed countries is far lower than this. The Digital divide programme is an EU initiative under the e-Europe Action Plan 2005, and seeks to spread access more equally.

Digital Learning Alliance (DLA). <www.literacytmst.org.uk/database/electronic> A consortium of UK educational software and book publishers; currently negotiating with government over e-learning issues to create public/private partnerships and improve standards.

Digital Libraries in the Classroom. <www.jisc.ac.uk/index.cfm?name=programme_dlitc> A JISC programme from 2003 to 2006 funded in conjunction with the National Science Foundation which was developed to bring about significant improvements in the learning and teaching process, through bringing emerging technologies and readily available digital content into mainstream educational use. The programme aims to examine how integrating recent technical developments with digital content will improve the learning experience of students and provide new models for the classroom including the impact of integration on student achievement, retention, recruitment and on institutional structures and practices.

Digital Libraries Initiative. <www.dli2.nsf.gov> A joint initiative in the US of the National Science Foundation, the Department of Defense Advanced Research Projects Agency (DARPA), and the National Aeronautics and Space Administration that ran in two phases. Phase 1 (1994–1998) funded six research projects developing new technologies for digital libraries to dramatically advance the means to collect, store, and organize information in digital forms, and make it available for searching, retrieval, and processing via communication networks. DLI2 projects began in 1999 with the majority being completed by mid-2004. A number of initiatives into 'International Digital Libraries' were announced, particularly through partnership with Deutsche Forschungs-gemeinschaft (DFG), the EU and JISC.

Digital Libraries Network (DLnet). An informal network of librarians, trainers and other professionals, formed 2003 within the (UK) National Electronic Library for Health (*see* NeLH) to raise awareness of digital library resources across the health community.

Digital library. An umbrella term a) for conceptual models of libraries of the future that focus on the provision of services associated almost totally with digital content and b) used to describe those aspects of existing library services that have a significant digital component. Also referred to as 'electronic library'. *See also* Hybrid library.

Digital Library Federation (DLF). <www.dglib.org> Founded in 1995 to establish the conditions for creating, maintaining, expanding, and pre-serving a distributed collection of digital materials accessible to scholars, students, and a wider public. The Federation is a leadership organization operating under the umbrella of the Council on Library and Information Resources. It comprises 28 libraries and related agencies pioneering the use of digital technologies to extend collections and services. In 2004 the British Library was the first non-US partner.

Digital Library Forum. <www.dl-forum.de> Collates information on the subject of digital libraries with particular focus on the funding activities of the Bundesministerium für Bildung und Forschung (German Ministry of Education and Research), the Deutsche Forschungs-gemeinschaft (German Research Institute), individual German federal states and other research institutes.

Digital Millennium Copyright Act. <www.loc.gov/legislation/dmca> Passed late in 1998, US legislation that is aimed at encouraging electronic commerce while protecting creative work. It includes fair use rights for libraries and educational institutions, but there is no provision for copyright protection of databases. The Act also serves as the instrument by which the USA becomes signatory to major WIPO treaties. The Act adds twenty further years to the Duration of copyright protection afforded to copyright holders; it is against this provision that Creative Commons and other organizations seek to protest.

Digital Object Identifier (DOI). <www.doi.org> A system for identifying and exchanging intellectual property in the digital environment launched at the Frankfurt Book Fair in October 1997. Developed by the International DOI Foundation on behalf of the publishing industry, its goals are to provide a framework for managing intellectual content, link customers with content suppliers, facilitate electronic commerce, and enable automated copyright management. The DOI is of no fixed length yet is a unique and persistent identification code, based on the Handle system, included in both the print and electronic versions of a document. The identifier is made up of two components: a prefix and a suffix. The prefix is assigned to the publisher by a registration agency; the suffix is a designation assigned by the publisher to the specific content being identified. The DOI can be used to identify any item at any granularity and not simply print-based media but also audio, images and software; it can also be used to identify free materials and transactions as well as entities of commercial value. One of the largest implementations is via CrossRef. There are DOI agencies in the US, Australasia and Europe. *See also* indecs, OpenURL, Persistence.

Digital optical disc. *See* Optical disc.

Digital preservation. 1. Use of Digitization as a preservation technique. 2. The methods of keeping digital materials 'alive' so that they remain usable as technological advances render original hardware and software specifications obsolete. *See also* Preservation metadata.

Digital Preservation Coalition (DPC). <www.dpconline.org.uk> A UK pressure group of some 20 organizations including the British Library and CURL; formed in 2001, it has succeeded in putting digital issues onto the political agenda and has a role in implementation of the Legal Deposit Libraries Act 2003.

Digital Preservation Program. *See* National Digital Infrastructure and Preservation Program.

Digital Rights Management (DRM). Systems devised for the automated handling of copyright permissions and fees in the electronic environment. *See also* Electronic Copyright Management Systems (ECMS).

Digital Scotland. Partner with UKOnline, Cymru Ar-lein and ELFNI in the People's Network (PN).

Digital signal processor (DSP). An integrated circuit incorporated in PCs to handle multimedia Applications.

Digital signature.   An encrypted digest of an electronic document verifying to a recipient that the contents originated from the sender. To apply a digital signature to a document involves transforming it into a unique digital fingerprint which is then encrypted with the sender's private key. The encrypted fingerprint is referred to as the digital signature. *See also* Digital certificate, Digital watermarking.

Digital Solidarity Fund Initiative.   Established at the World Summit on the Information Society in 2003, the Fund will seek to break down barriers to equal access to digital resources. The founding partners are the Cities of Geneva, Lyon and the region of Torino.

Digital superhighway.   *See* Information superhighway.

Digital TV.   A broadcast medium that uses MPEG2 for compression and, when played back on an analogue television set, requires a Set-top box to decode transmissions. There are three key levels of digital television: Standard Definition TV (SDTV), Enhanced Definition TV (EDTV), and High Definition TV (HDTV). *See also* HDTV.

Digital Versatile Disk.   *See* DVD.

Digital Video.   *See* DV.

Digital Video Disk.   *See* DVD.

Digital Video Initiative (DVI).   <dv.internet2.edu> An Initiative of Internet2, a distributed organization which seeks to build upon the efforts of other digital video groups and individuals and which provides an organizational structure for joint projects, dissemination and sharing of information, and the promotion of digital video in general.

Digital Video Interactive.   *See* DVI.

Digital watermarking.   A methodology for permanently indicating the provenance of electronic documents that provides the evidence of, but does not necessarily prevent, copying. *Fragile watermarking* provides integrity and authenticity control; *robust watermarking* enables tracking and policing.

Digitization.   The process of transferring information content from a traditional format into a digitally-readable version. Typically a Scanner would be used for this purpose when digitizing a printed book; digital imaging of manuscripts, paintings, prints etc. is also covered by this term. Digitization is now much favoured as part of the drive to improve preservation techniques, as fragile originals need not be handled afterwards except in specialized circumstances. Access is greatly improved as digitized texts can be readily searched, and digital images of faded or difficult originals can be computer-enhanced. Several national libraries have started digitization programmes for Brittle books, delicate or rare materials. *See also* MINERVA.

Digraph.   *See* Diphthong.

DIMDI.   <www.dimdi.de> (Waisenhausgasse 36-38, 50676 Köln, Germany) Deutsches Institut für Medizinische Dokumentation und Information, a major host organization specializing in the biosciences field; founded in 1969 it is an institute within the German Federal Ministry of Health.

Dime novel.   An American term for a type of paper-covered fiction which was popular during the second half of the nineteenth century. A cheap, sensational novel.

DIN.   The characters used before figures to identify standards issued by the Deutscher Normenausschuss (DNA), the German standards institution. The DIN standards for sizes of paper were later adopted by the International Standards Organization.

DIP.   *See* Document image processing.

Diphthong.   Two letters joined together and representing one sound, as æ, Æ, œ, Œ. Also called 'Digraph'.

Diplomatic.   The science of the critical study of official as opposed to literary sources of history, i.e. of charters, acts, treaties, contracts, judicial records, rolls, chartularies, registers and kindred documents.

Diptych.   *See* Codex.

Direct cataloguing.   *See* Collocative v. direct cataloguing.

Direct contact copying.   A process for documentary copying which requires the action of light on a sensitized coating on paper.

Direct costs.   *See* Costs.

Direct entry.   (*Indexing*) An entry for a multi-word subject in its normal word order, as opposed to inverted word sequence.

Direct printing.   Printing in which the impression is made direct from forme to paper, as in letterpress, and is not offset on to the paper from another medium. *See also* Letterpress (3), Offset (1).

Direct sub-division.   When determining subject headings for a dictionary catalogue in respect of a book limited to one locality, the heading is sub-divided by the name of a county, province, city or other locality without the interposition of the name of the country; e.g. Geology – Surrey. Indirect sub-division interposes the name of the country; e.g. Geology – England – Surrey.

Direction line.   Used to indicate the line of characters when the abbreviated title of a book, called Designation mark, follows the signature mark, or letter, which is printed at the foot of the first page of each sheet, to guide the binder when gathering. Originally, the line on which a Catchword was printed. Also called 'Signature line', 'Title signature'. *See also* Designation mark, Signature and catchword line.

Direction number.   The number which appears on the Direction line at the bottom of a leaf of an old book, i.e. below the lowest line of type.

Direction word.   *See* Catchword.

Directorate General XIII.   <europa.eu.int/comm/dg13> The section of the Commission of the European Union concerned with library matters; its coverage is defined as 'telecommunications, information industries and innovation'.

Directory.   A book containing lists of names of residents, organizations or business houses in a town, a group of towns or a country, in alphabetical order, and/or in order of situation in roads, or of firms in trade classifications arranged in alphabetical order; or of professional people, manufacturers or business houses in a particular trade or profession. *See also* Trade directory.

Directory of Open Access Journals. <www.doaj.org> Produced and maintained by Lund University Library with the aim of increasing the visibility and ease of use of Open access journals and so promoting their increased usage and impact. The Directory aims to be comprehensive and cover all open access scientific and scholarly journals that use a quality control system to guarantee the content. All subject areas and languages are covered.

Directory Publishers Association. <www.directory-publisher.co.uk> Formed 1970 to promote the interests of directory publishers, avoid fraudulent practice, encourage high standards, quality and integrity. Publishes *DPA Newsletter* (6 p.a.), *Code of professional practice*, *Directory* (including lists of publications of member organizations).

Directory services. Software tools providing lookup capabilities for locating information about individuals – 'White Pages' – or services and service providers (including, for example, OPACs) – 'Yellow Pages'. In spite of considerable efforts there is still no single White Pages directory service for the entire Internet. *See also* Domain Name System, Information lookup, LDAP, Whois, Whois++.

DIRS. DIMDI Information Retrieval Service. *See* DIMDI.

Dirty proof. A proof containing many errors or typographical imperfections; a proof that has been returned to the printer with many corrections.

Dis. *See* Distributing.

Disability Discrimination Act (DDA). <www.hmso.gov.uk/acts/acts1995> UK legislation that came fully into force in October 2004; it requires the removal generally of all "physical barriers" to access of buildings and services, or for services to be provided in alternative ways. The Museums, Libraries and Archives Council (MLA) has produced a series of Guides to assist museums, archives and libraries in meeting the provisions of the Act and operates a disability database. The organization Disability Rights <www.drc-gb.com> is active in this area; it has recently (2003) investigated web accessibility.

Disaster plan. A plan, developed and written, to enable a library to ensure the protection of its collections. Disasters can be natural or man-made and usually involve damage by fire, water, wind and/or earthquake. A plan to deal with disasters effectively will vary depending upon the size and scope of the collection, but should cover six stages: the formation of a disaster action team; education and training; a survey of the library premises and collections; an analysis of the survey; establishment of authority and responsibilities; recovery procedures. A plan should cover all media and materials in the library; computer-based electronic files can also be at risk from viruses or other technological threats.

Disc. 1. Note: current conventions suggest that the spelling 'disc' be applied to optical media such as CD-ROM and DVD and the spelling 'disk' used in all other cases. *See* Disk.　2. DISC <www.bsi.org.uk/disc> The department within the British Standards Institution that manages IT and telecommunication standardization activities in the UK, and participates in European and international standards bodies. It publishes a series of guides which include titles on Electronic Document Management Systems, Good Practice in Information Management, and Information Security Management.

Disc inking.　The inking system which is found particularly in some platen printing machines. A round disc revolves on its own gearing at the head of the machine and the inking rollers pass over the disc before descending on the type-forme. *See also* Platen press.

Discard.　A book that is withdrawn from circulation in a library.

Discharge.　(*Verb*) The act of cancelling the record of the loan of a book or other item on its return to the library. *See also* Charge (4).

Discography.　A catalogue or similar listing of sound recordings in any format (cylinder, roll, disk, tape, CD etc.) giving full details of the item recorded (title, composer/author, performers, date etc.) and manufacturer's product number.

Discontinued number.　(*Classification*) A number from a preceding edition of a scheme of classification vacated because its content has been moved back to a more general number.

Discourse.　*See* Relation.

Discussion group.　An electronic forum for the world-wide discussion of a particular subject or topic accessible via Usenet. Not to be confused with Discussion lists (more frequently known as Mailing lists).

Discussion lists.　*See* Mailing lists.

Disjoined hand.　Handwriting in which the letters are not connected to one another. Also called 'Script writing'. The opposite of Joined hand.

Disjunct leaf.　The stub which remains in a book after the removal of the remainder of the leaf because it contained matter which could not be allowed to remain. *See also* Cancel.

Disk.　(Current conventions suggest that the spelling 'disc' be used for optical media such as CD-ROM and DVD but that for all other uses the spelling used here is correct.) A form of magnetic storage for PCs which can vary from *floppy disks* or *diskettes* of around 1.4 Mbytes capacity to the 80 Gbytes or greater capacity of *hard disks*; Removable storage is also available. CD-ROM and DVD are popular implementations of Optical storage. Audio recordings (gramophone/ phonograph records), initially produced on black vinyl, were substantially replaced by Compact discs in the early 1990s but continue to provide for a niche market.

Disk drive.　That part of a computer system that manipulates the Disk and inputs and extracts data from it.

Diskette.　*See* Disk.

Display.　The presentation of data from a PC, Online or Videotex system via a Visual display unit or Monitor.

Display type.   Large or heavy-faced type used for headings, title-pages, posters or advertisements. They may include sizes between 18 and 24 point but usually comprise 30, 36, 42, 48, 60, 72 and more exceptionally 84 and 96 point.

Display work.   The setting of short lines in varying faces and sizes of type, as distinct from a solid area of type. Advertisements, titles and headings are 'display' work.

Displayed.   (*Printing*) Matter which has been set on separate lines and distinguished from the remainder of the text by being set in a smaller or larger size of type, or by its position in relation to the margin (by being full out, indented or centred). Such matter is normally further emphasized by being preceded and followed by additional space. Long quotations, mathematical equations and headings are examples of displayed matter.

Disposal list.   In archives management, a list of types of document with instructions for their disposal, i.e. destruction or permanent preservation. *See also* Retention schedule.

Disposal schedule.   *See* Schedule.

Disposition.   (*Archives*) The action taken after the Appraisal of non-current documents. This may include transfer to a records centre or archive depository for temporary or permanent storage, reproduction on microfilm, or destruction. The term 'disposal' is more common outside North America.

Dissection.   (*Classification*) The formation of an array of co-ordinate classes.

Dissemination of information.   The distribution, or sending, of information whether specifically requested or not, to members of an organization by a librarian or information officer. *See also* SDI.

Dissertation.   A thesis or treatise prepared as a condition for the award of a degree or diploma.

Distance learning.   *See* Open learning.

Distinctive title.   One that is peculiar to a particular publication.

Distributed computing.   The transfer of computing provision for an organization away from a system based on a single main computer to one based on networked PCs.

Distributed facets.   (*Classification, Information retrieval*) In a compound subject, facets which are scattered throughout a classification consequent upon the Combination order applied. Also called 'Distributed terms'.

Distributed National Collection (Australia).   Resolution AA1 of the 1988 Australian Libraries Summit formalized the concept of the Distributed National Collection in stating the notion that the following principles of a national collection be accepted: a) aggregation of all library collections in Australia whether in the public or private sector; b) comprehensive in relation to Australia; c) selective in relation to the rest of the world; d) adequately recorded and readily accessible. The origins can be traced to a meeting of the Australian Humanities Research Council in 1965; while the Summit refined the idea, there has been little conceptual development over the last three decades, as there is still an emphasis on printed materials and self-sufficiency at a local or national level.

Distributed National Electronic Resource (UK). *See* DNER.

Distributed relatives. A secondary aspect of a subject which is used to show a relationship when classifying a document, and which will not be used as the main, but as a subordinate, subject when determining the class number. The same sub-heading may be used to subdivide many headings.

Distributed terms. *See* Distributed facets.

Distributing. 1. Putting loose type back into their respective boxes and cases after use, or for melting, after use in the forme. This was done after machining and when type was not to be kept standing for reprints. Commonly called 'dissing'. Abbreviated 'dis'. *See also* Break. 2. In presswork, the uniform spreading of ink on the face of the printing forme.

Distribution imprint. The statement on the verso of the title-page of a book, which names the branches or representatives through which the publisher's books are distributed.

Distributor rollers. The rollers on a printing press which spread ink on the ink slab, roll it to the correct consistency and transfer it to the rollers which ink the type-forme. They are made wholly of metal, or of rubber or composition on a metal core. Also called 'Distributing rollers'.

District. (*Public libraries*) A part of the Library area other than a Region or Area and usually comprising a town and its adjacent rural area organized as a library unit.

Dittogram. A printed character, or group of printed characters, repeated in error.

Diurnal. A periodical which is published or issued every day.

DiVA. <www.diva-portal.org> Digital Scientific Archive [Digitala Vetenskapliga Arkivet], a document archive repository holding theses, dissertations and other fulltext documents developed at Uppsala University Library and progressed in co-operation with University libraries in Stockholm, Umeå, Örebro and Södertörn. In 2003 the first member outside Sweden was the State and University Library of Århus in Denmark.

Diversity. The term now in common use to describe the cosmopolitan, multicultural society of the western world. The diverse nature of populations is recognized as an asset in cultural, social and religious contexts.

Diversity awards. <www.cilip.org.uk> A series of awards operated by CILIP; the awards are designed to break down barriers to access for non-traditional communities, and recognize organizational change and personal achievement in this field.

Diversity Group.   A membership group of CILIP, formed 2003 to cater for members concerned with diversity and multi-cultural issues.

Divide like the classification.   Instruction for expanding a given class number by various parts of a classification schedule or from any of the Auxiliary tables in order to sub-divide a subject, as e.g. in 016 of the Dewey Decimal Classification (DDC):

016	Bibliography	of special subjects
016.1	„	of philosophy
016.17	„	of ethics
016.22	„	of the Bible
016.54	„	of chemistry

The 'divide-like' notes which were used in the 17th and earlier editions of the DDC were replaced in later editions by 'Add to...' instructions. A major device for synthesis of numbers in the DDC.

Divided catalogue.   A catalogue in which the entries are separated into two or more sequences in order to simplify filing and consultation, which may become complicated in a large dictionary catalogue. All subject and form entries and their necessary references may form an alphabetical subject catalogue and the remaining entries form an author-title catalogue. *See also* Split catalogue.

Dividing stroke.   *See* Line division mark.

Divinity calf.   A plain dark brown calf binding often used in the mid-nineteenth century for theological or devotional books. The boards were sometimes bevelled and the edges red.

Divinity circuit.   The US equivalent of Yapp, or Circuit edges.

Divinity edges.   *See* Circuit edges.

Division.   1. The process of dividing classes or groups of a classification scheme into their more minute parts.   2. The result so formed.   3. A subject or topic which is subordinate to a class.   4. Breaking down a Facet into its foci. In the Dewey Decimal Classification, each of the ten main classes is divided into 10 divisions, hence there are 100 divisions in all which form the second summary of the scheme. *See* Focus. *See also* Exhaustive division, Main class.   5. A Department or a section of a department in a library.   6. A unit in a library system which is concerned with a particular function, as a 'Catalogue division', or with a definite subject, as 'Science division'.   7. In professional associations, certain groupings of members. *See also* Branch, Group, Section.

Division library.   In a US university or college, a collection of books attached to, and administered by, a division or a group of related departments, usually with some form of co-operative arrangement with the general library, or as a part of the library system.

Divisional title.   A page preceding a section or division of a book, and bearing the name or number of the section or division. The reverse is usually blank.

Divisional title-pages.   *See* General title.

DLA.   *See* Digital Learning Alliance.

DLI2.   *See* Digital Libraries Initiative.

D-Lib.   <www.dlib.org> A solely electronic publication with a primary focus on digital library research and development, including but not limited to new technologies, applications, and contextual social and economic issues. The magazine is published eleven times a year and the full contents, including all back issues, are available free of charge at the web site as well as multiple mirror sites around the world. It is produced by the Corporation for National Research Initiatives.

DLnet.   *See* Digital Libraries Network.

DNER.   Distributed National Electronic Resource, an integrated information environment formulated in 1998 for the UK higher education community. The name is no longer used and the work is continued in the JISC Information Environment. *See* Information Environment.

DNS.   *See* Domain Name System.

do.   Abbreviation for ditto, the same.

DocDel.   Abbreviation for Document delivery.

Doctoral Dissertation Fellowship.   An award of the Association of College and Research Libraries.

Document.   1. A record which conveys information; originally an inscribed or written record, but now considered to include any form of information – graphic, acoustic, alphanumeric, etc. (e.g. maps, manuscripts, tape, videotapes, computer software).   2. (*Archives*) A single component or entity in a set of archival materials, usually a physically indivisible object. In *MAD*, a piece. *See* Archives.

Document address.   (*Information retrieval*) A class number or other symbol indicating the whereabouts of a document in a Store. *See also* Unit record.

Document case.   A container, usually made of stout card and approximately 15 x 10 x 3 inches, for the filing flat of archives or manuscripts.

Document delivery.   The provision of a required item to a user; originally only the physical supply of a book or journal, but now document delivery may be more efficiently performed by photocopy, fax, E-mail, network message etc. *See also* Electronic document delivery, Interlending.

Document image processing (DIP).   The capture, storage, distribution and display of paper documents into digital form on a large scale i.e. on a departmental or company-wide basis. DIP was a major concern when ICT was introduced into organizations, as huge amounts of information needed to be captured in digital formats and scanning technology was primitive.

Document management.   The creation, handling, storage and disposal of records needed in a business context. Electronic technologies allow such information to be collected and exploited in an integrated system featuring internal and external databases, available instantly to managers and other staff, and which can be manipulated as necessary, and output in any appropriate format. *See also* Information management, Intranet.

Document Object Model (DOM). <www.w3.org/DOM> A platform- and language-neutral interface that will allow programs and scripts to dynamically access and update the content, structure and style of documents, particularly HTML-based documents. The document can be further processed and the results of that processing can be incorporated back into the presented page. The W3C DOM activity is working to ensure that interoperable and scripting-language neutral solutions are available for what is described by some vendors as Dynamic HTML.

Document retrieval system. One which provides a complete copy of a required document instead of merely a citation or reference. An aspect of Information retrieval.

Document store. In information retrieval, a place where documents are kept.

Document supply centre. That part of a large library or similar organization that handles the actual delivery of materials to clients.

Document Type Definition. *See* DTD.

Documentalist. One who practises documentation. An information officer or intelligence officer who is concerned with the collection and dissemination of knowledge, rather than the librarian who is concerned with the techniques of handling records of knowledge, making them available and possibly exploiting them. One concerned with assembling information contained within documents together with data from other sources to form a new compilation.

Documentary information. Information about documents, or information recorded in documents. Either kind of information may be 'retrieved' according as to whether the purpose of the retrieval is to indicate where the needed information can be found, or what it is. *See also* Metadata.

Documentary reproduction. The copying of documents or pages of books by photographic or non-photographic means so that the copy has the appearance of the original.

Documentation. The study of the acquisition, handling, and communication of information, particularly relating to scientific reports, semi-published material, statistics, etc. *See also* Informatics.

Documentation centre. A place where publications are received, processed, preserved, summarized, abstracted and indexed; where bulletins relating to such material are prepared for distribution to those interested; where research is undertaken, bibliographies prepared, and copies or translations made.

Documents depository (US). A library which is legally designated to receive without charge copies of all or selected US government publications.

Dog-eared Said of a book, portfolio, or similar article having the corners of the leaves turned down and soiled by careless or long continued usage.

DOI. *See* Digital Object Identifier.

DOM. *See* Document Object Model.

Domain Name System (DNS). The system that designates names and addresses to computers connected to the Internet to ensure the accurate transmission and receipt of data world-wide. Names are constructed hierarchically starting with 'Top-Level Domains' that are of two types: generic (gTLD) and country code (ccTLD). In the 1980s seven generic domains were created (.com, .edu, .gov, .int, .mil, .net, and .org) to be followed, in November 2000, by a further seven (.aero, .biz, .coop, .info, ..museum, .name, .pro). Country codes are, in general, two letter codes, such as: .us, .jp, .uk. Management of the Domain Name System is carried out on behalf of ICANN by IANA. Internationalized Domain Names (IDNs) are under development to make domain names available in character sets other than ASCII.

Donation. A book or other item given to a library, maybe by its author or publisher, or by an unconnected person or organization. Such items need close inspection to determine relevance to the library's collection policies, age and physical condition, and whether the contents represent an unacceptably extreme point of view. Donations may have a special bookplate or identification label attached, and may be recorded in a separate file in addition to normal cataloguing. Also known as 'gift'.

Donation record. A record of gifts.

Dormitory library. A collection of books placed in a dormitory of a US college or university. The books are usually intended for recreational reading but may also be recommended texts.

Dorse. The reverse side of a Membrane.

DOS. Disk Operating System; the program that controls a computer's inputs and outputs. Also called system software, or by type e.g. MS-DOS.

Dos-à-dos binding. Two or more books – usually small ones – bound back to back so that the back cover of one serves as the back cover of the other and the fore-edges of one are next to the spine of the other.

Dot etching. *See* Retouching.

Dot map. One which shows density of distribution by dots of uniform size, each dot representing a given quantity.

Dot-matrix printer. A printer that produces characters composed of individual dots using a wire-pin print head. Usually characterized by the number of pins in the print head: e.g. 9, 18, 24. Largely superceded by the Inkjet printer and the Laser printer.

Dotted rule. A strip of metal of type height with a face showing a dotted line which may vary from fine dots close together to a sequence of short dashes. *See also* Rule.

Dotting wheels. Small hand-tools of varying shapes used by artists when engraving metal plates.

Double. 1. In printing, a word, etc., erroneously repeated. 2. A sheet of paper twice the unit size, e.g. Double crown (20 x 30 inches), Ordinary crown being 15 x 20 inches. *See also* Paper sizes.

Double book.   A book printed on half sheets.

Double click.   A method of selecting data on a computer screen or opening an Application, by quickly clicking the Mouse button twice.

Double columned.   A page of printed matter set to half the width of a normal page line, with an em or more space, or a Rule, between the columns. Abbreviated d.c. Also said to be set in 'Half-measure'. Double columns are used in such works as dictionaries, encyclopaedias and Bibles.

Double crown.   A sheet of paper measuring 20 x 30 inches.

Double dagger (‡).   The third reference mark for footnotes, coming after the Dagger. Sometimes called a 'Double obelisk'. *See also* Reference marks.

Double elephant.   *See* Elephant.

Double entry.   Entry in a catalogue under more than one subject, or under subject and place, and under the names of subordinate contributors such as joint authors, editors, illustrators, translators, etc., using the same form of entry with suitable headings added. Also, entry for a pseudonymous work under the real name of the author as well as under the pseudonym.

Double fan adhesive binding.   A method of adhesive binding in which the milled pages are fanned and passed over a glue roller, and the process repeated. The adhesive penetrates between the leaves and effectively tips one page to another. After gluing, a stretch cloth back is applied to the spine. One advantage of this method is the facility to open the book completely flat.

Double leaded.   *See* Leaded matter.

Double leaves.   The leaves of Chinese style books. These are recorded in a catalogue entry in the form '18 double l' or '36 pp. (on double leaves)'. Should the leaves be unnumbered, each is counted as two pages, as: [36] pp. (on double leaves).

Double letter.   *See* Ligature.

Double numeration.   A system of numbering whereby illustrations, charts, etc., are related to the chapter, the numbers of which are the key numbers, e.g. Fig. 7.5 indicates the fifth figure in the seventh chapter.

Double obelisk.   *See* Double dagger.

Double pica.   An out-of-date name for a type size equal to about 22 points.

Double plate.   An illustration which stretches across two pages of a book when open. *See also* Folding plate.

Double printing.   Two impressions on the same sheet.

Double quotes.   Pairs of superior commas ". . ." used to indicate quoted matter. *See also* Single quotes, Turned comma.

Double register.   Two ribbons fastened in a book to serve as book-markers.

Double rule.   A Rule having two lines of different thickness of face. *See also* Parallel rule.

Double spread.   Two facing pages on which printed matter is spread across as if they were one page. When printing an illustration this way two blocks must be used unless the spread comes in the middle of a Section. *See also* Conjugate, Opening.

Double title-page.   Used where a work has both a right-hand and a left-hand title-page. Usually one of these serves for the series or the complete volumes of a set, and the other is limited to the individual volume.

Double weight paper.   Sensitized photographic paper between 0.0112 and 0.0190 inches inclusive. *See also* Photographic papers.

Doublette.   *See* Replica.

Doublure.   1. An ornamental inside lining of a book cover of leather or silk, usually with a leather hinge, and often elaborately decorated.   2. Ornamental end-paper. Also called 'Ornamental inside lining'.

Doubtful authorship.   Authorship ascribed to one or more persons with no convincing proof. *See also* Attributed author.

Doves Press.   One of the most famous British private presses. It was directed by T. J. Cobden-Sanderson, who founded it with Sir Emery Walker, at Hammersmith, London, in 1900. Their partnership was dissolved in 1909 but Cobden-Sanderson continued to operate until 1916. The most important publication was the Doves Bible, published in five volumes between 1903–5. The name 'Doves' was taken from Doves Place, a passage off the Upper Mall, Hammersmith. The name was first used for the Doves Bindery which Cobden-Sanderson started in 1893 at 15 Upper Mall.

Dow Jones 21st Century Competencies Award.   An award made by the (US) Special Libraries Association (first awarded 1998), to recognize an individual who has demonstrated leadership through personal and professional competencies.

Down.   A term used to signify that a computer system is out of operation.

Down time.   Time when a computer or system is out of operation.

Downgrade.   To assign a secret or confidential document to a less restricted security classification under proper authorization. *See also* Declassify.

Downloading.   The transfer of data from a remote computer to a desktop PC.

Downward reference.   A direction from a more- to a less-comprehensive heading in an alphabetico-direct subject catalogue. The reverse of Upward reference.

dpi.   Dots per inch, a measure of image resolution, particularly associated with the output of Laser printers and Imagesetters. Early Laser printers produced output at 300 dpi but many now print to 1,200 dpi. By comparison, Imagesetters print at 1,000 to 5,000 dpi.

Drag and drop.   The ability, within some software applications, to highlight a range of characters and move them to another location by dragging to this location and dropping them into place.

Dragon's blood.   Any of several resinous substances, mostly dark red in colour. It is used in powdered form in photo-engraving for etching line plates. Dragon's blood powder is brushed up against the slightly raised lines of the image or design on the metal plate from four sides, and 'burned in', thus protecting these lines against the action of the etching solution or acid.

Dramatic work.   An Intellectual work which expresses dramatic action. Copyright in performance arises when the work is staged for presentation before the public.

Drawer handle.   A tool of a Corinthian volute which was commonly used in English Restoration book decoration. So called from its similarity to the handle of a small drawer.

Draw-on covers.   The binding of square-backed magazines and paperbacks, the cover being attached by glueing to the spine of the book. When the end-papers are pasted down, it is said to be *drawn-on solid*.

Draw-out shelves.   A form of compact storage consisting of shelves wide enough to take two rows of books, one facing each way, fixed across, or in place of, ordinary shelves. When it is desired to consult the books these shelves are drawn out, as if they were drawers, into the gangway.

Dressed forme.   A forme of pages of type with Furniture between and around them, the page-cord having been removed. *See also* Forme, Naked forme.

Dressing.   1. Fitting the Furniture between and around the pages in a chase prior to locking up the Forme.   2. Fitting an illustration block into type so that text and illustration can be printed together.

Drive out.   (*Printing*) 1. Said of type-matter which is spaced widely between the words so as to occupy more lines.   2. An instruction to the compositor to insert wide spaces between words. *See also* Keep in.

DRM.   *See* Digital Rights Management.

Drop.   (*Printing*) To unlock a forme and remove the furniture and chase after printing, the type then being either distributed or 'kept standing', i.e. tied up and stored.

Drop capital.   *See* Drop letter.

Drop folio.   A folio number or page number at the bottom of a page.

Drop guides.   *See* Feed guides.

Drop initials.   *See* Drop letter.

Drop letter.   Large initial used at the beginning of a chapter or article, and running down two lines or more. Also called 'drop capital', 'drop cap'. *See also* Cock-up initial, Cut-in letter.

Drop-down title.   The short title on the first page of text. It should be the same as the Running title. *See also* Caption title.

Drop-out.   (*Printing*) A Half-tone from which all, or some, of the dots have been removed. Also called a 'Highlight'.

Dropped head.   The first page of a chapter or book where the first line commences a third or more down the page.

Dropped letter.   A character which becomes removed during the course of printing and drops out of the forme causing an omission in the matter when printed.

Drum scanner.   A scanner where printed or transparency art is mounted on a rotating drum. As the drum spins, light from the image enters a lens, allowing the image to be recorded in data in a series of fine lines. Used by printers to create high quality digital graphics for incorporation into Desktop published documents.

Dry ammonia process. The ammonia process of reprography. Also called Dry process.

Dry end. *See* Drying end.

Dry flong. *See* Flong.

Dry offset. 1. Printing by letterpress onto a rubber cylinder from which the impression is offset on to paper. The resulting advantages are reduced Make-ready, the possibility of using uncoated paper for fine half-tones, etc. The process is not lithographic and no water need be used. 2. A printing process by which photo-engraved plates are printed by the offset transfer principle, the inked impression from a relief-etched magnesium plate being made on a rubber blanket cylinder and offset from this on to the paper as this is carried round the impression cylinder.

Dry process. A method for producing copies of documents which does not employ wet chemicals. Some Diazotype prints are made by a dry process. The usual developing process used in electro-photography is dry. *See also* Documentary reproduction, Dust development.

Dry silver. A silver halide copying process in which the latent image is made visible by the application of heat rather than the use of chemicals. *See also* Silver processes.

Drying end. The end of a paper-making machine where there are the steam-heated drying cylinders over which the damp web of paper (containing about 70 per cent water) is passed before it reaches the calender rolls. The other end is known as the Wet end.

Drypoint etching. An etching made directly on copper by means of a sharp needle called a point. In drypoint work, the etching is all done by hand and not by a mordant applied to a wax-covered plate in which the design has been cut, as is the rule in ordinary etching. Etchings often have drypoint lines, which have been added after the acid etching has taken place. The beauty of this method is due to the burr caused by the point on each side of the channel being left and not removed as in an engraving. The effect of this in printing is to produce the velvety line which is characteristic of a drypoint.

D.S. Document signed, a document in which only the signature is autographic.

DSP. *See* Digital signal processor.

DSpace. <www.dspace.org> A digital library system developed jointly by MIT (Massachusetts Institute of Technology) Libraries and Hewlett-Packard to capture, store, index, preserve, and redistribute the intellectual output of a university's research faculty in digital formats. The software is Open Archives Initiative-compliant and is freely available as an open source system that can be customized and extended.

DSS. *See* Decision Support System.

DTD. Document Type Definition, a file comprising a formal definition of the elements, structures and rules associated with SGML and XML documents that defines how Markup is interpreted by the application that will display the document.

DTIC. *See* Defense Technical Information Center.

DTP. *See* Desktop publishing.

Dual-use libraries. Library premises that offer services to more than one community; typically such a library might be located in a school but also function as a public library branch, jointly funded, staffed and managed. This is rare in the UK, but more common in the US and Australia. (Reference: S. McNicol, Dual-use libraries. *Update* vol. 2, no. 10, (October) 2003: pp. 52–53)

Dublin Core Metadata Element Set. <dublincore.org/documents/dces> Fifteen metadata elements agreed at the 1995 Online Computer Library Center (OCLC) and National Center for Supercomputing Applications (NCSA) Metadata Workshop as key descriptors for networked resources. Version 1.1 was released in 2003. Frequently abbreviated to Dublin Core. *See also* Dublin Core Metadata Initiative.

Dublin Core Metadata Initiative. <dublincore.org> An organization dedicated to promoting the widespread adoption of interoperable metadata standards and developing specialized metadata vocabularies for describing resources that enable more intelligent information discovery systems. *See also* Dublin Core Metadata Element Set.

Ducali bindings. Venetian bindings of the decrees of the Doges which are decorated with a combination of Oriental and Western techniques. The method was to cover the board with a paper composition, the centre and corners being recessed, then to paste on thinly pared leather and add a coating of colour lacquer to complete the background. Gold-painted arabesques provided the final decoration.

Duck-foot quotes. The common name for Continental quotes or inverted commas. The form « » is used by French printers, but the Swiss and German printers use them in reverse, i.e. » «. They were first used in 1546 by Guillaume Le Bé of Paris, and are consequently also known as 'Guillemets'.

Dudley (Miriam) Award for Bibliographic Instruction. An award for contribution to the advancement of bibliographic instruction; administered by the Association of College and Research Libraries.

Due for Renewal. A report on the public library service in England and Wales, published 1997 by the Audit Commission (ISBN: 1 86240 0504). In the face of declining lending figures, reduced access hours, and increasing staff costs, the Report includes a range of recommendations on partnership arrangements, use of technologies, service costing, stock management, and service planning.

Duirnall. *See* Newsbook.

Dull finish. *See* Dull-coated.

Dull-coated. Paper which is coated but not polished: it is suitable for fine half-tones, being smooth but having no gloss. The term 'dull finish' is sometimes applied to the low or natural finish of Coated paper or uncoated papers which have not been glazed; practically identical with 'matt art' paper. *See also* Art.

Dummy. 1. A copy, generally made up of blank leaves, trimmed and sewn but not bound, to represent the actual bulk of a book about to be published.   2. A complete layout of a job showing the arrangement of matter to be printed on every page, and giving particulars of type, illustrations, etc. *See also* Shelf dummy.

Dummy bands. Imitation raised bands on the spine of a book. Also called 'False bands'.

Dunn and Wilson/National Preservation Office Conservation Competition. <www.rdw.co.uk> An annual award first made in 1988 for a policy statement on conservation/preservation, relevant to an organization and capable of realistic implementation. The title 'Keeping our words' is sometimes used for the competition.

Dunn and Wilson Prizes. <www.rdw.co.uk> A sum of money presented annually by the library binding firm of Dunn & Wilson Ltd., to each of the British Schools of Librarianship, to be used at the Schools' discretion as prizes to students.

Duodecimo. (12 mo) 1. A sheet of paper folded four times to form a section of twelve leaves (24 pp.). As a sheet cannot be folded for binding without a portion being cut, the smaller cut-off portion has to be inserted after folding into the larger folded portion to provide the page sequence. Alternatively a sheet and a half sheet can be used. If the printer lays down two rows of six pages the result is known as 'Long twelves', but if three by four pages, 'short' or 'square' twelves. Where the width of the pages is greater than the height, the term 'broad twelves' is used. Also called 'Twelvemo'.   2. A book printed on paper folded to form sections of twelve leaves. *See also* Oblong.

Duotone. Two-colour half-tone printing.

Duotype. Two half-tone plates of the same black and white original, both made from the same half-tone negative, but etched separately so as to give different colour values when superimposed during printing.

Duplex. 1. A communications link between a computer and a remote terminal operating in both directions simultaneously; also known as *full-duplex*. A link operating alternately in one direction or the other, but not both simultaneously is termed *Half-duplex. See also* Simplex. 2. Photographic paper which has a coating of emulsion on both sides. 3. An image-positioning technique used in rotary camera microfilming, whereby the use of mirrors or prisms enables an image of the front side of a document to be photographed on one half of the film, while an image of the back of the same document is photographed simultaneously on the other half of the film.   4. Any make of camera which will copy as described in 3.

Duplex half-tone.   A screen reproduction in two printings from half-tone blocks made from a monochrome original, one being used as a colour tone. The method is used in both letterpress and offset work to give the impression of a mellow monochrome picture, being richer and better toned than is possible from a single-colour half-tone block.

Duplex ledger.   *See* Ledger weight.

Duplex paper.   1. Paper having two different coloured surfaces.   2. Any paper composed of two sheets pasted together. Duplex papers are usually made by bringing the two layers, generally of different colours or quality, together in the wet state and pressing or rolling them together, thus forming a homogeneous mass. *See also* Twin wire paper. If three papers are brought together in the way described the resulting paper is known as Triplex.

Duplicate.   A second, or subsequent, copy of a book already in stock. Strictly it should be identical in edition, imprint, etc., but the kind of library and the intrinsic value placed on variations of bibliographical details or contents determines the exact meaning of 'duplicate' in specific libraries.

Duplicate entry.   Entry in an index or other form of record of the same subject matter under two or more distinct aspects of it or under two headings.

Duplicate paging.   Description of a book which has paging in duplicate, as e.g. a book with the original text on the verso and the translation on the recto.

Duplicate title.   Used of a reprint which has a reproduction of the original title-page in addition to its own.

Duplicated signatures.   Two sets of Signatures which are identical.

Durable paper.   *See* Permanent paper.

Duration of copyright.   The period through which copyright extends. It may be measured from the death of the creator, the year the work was created or when it was published. Various types of printed or electronic publication may have different periods of duration.

Durham Book.   *See* Bibles.

Dust cover.   *See* Book jacket.

Dust development.   A development process used in document copying by which latent electrostatic images are made visible by treatment with a developing powder. *See also* Xerography.

Dust jacket.   *See* Book jacket.

Dust wrapper.   *See* Book jacket.

Duster.   *See* Willow.

Dutch gold.   *See* Dutch leaf.

Dutch leaf.   A thin sheet obtained by beating an alloy of copper and zinc; it is sometimes used in tooling as a substitute for gold leaf. It quickly discolours. Also called 'Dutch gold'.

Dutch library associations.   The most significant associations in the Netherlands are Vereniging Openbare Bibliotheken (Netherlands Public

Library Association, formerly Nederlands Bibliothek en Lectuur Centrum – NBLC) <www.debibliotken.nl>, and NVB (Nederlandse Vereniging van Bibliothecarissen, Documentalisten en Literatuur Onderzoekers) <www.kb.nl/infolev/bmi>.

Dutch national library. *See* Koninklijke Bibliotheek (KB).

Dutch paper. *See* Van Gelder paper.

DV. Digital Video, a consumer digital video format developed in the early 1990s by an international consortium of 10 companies led by Sony, Panasonic, JVC, Toshiba and Hitachi subsequently expanding to over 60 companics. Originally known as DVC for Digital Video Cassette. *See also* HDV.

DVB. *See* Deutscher Bibliotheksverband.

DVD. Digital Versatile Disk, in appearance identical to CD-ROM but with a capacity between 4.7 Gbytes and 17 Gbytes, compared to the 650 Mbyte capacity of CD-ROM. DVD is most usually interpreted as the abbreviation for DVD-Video, the consumer electronics format which holds movie files on disc for playback on a DVD-Video player or a PC with a DVD drive. Using MPEG-2 video compression, a full-length movie fits onto a single DVD Video disc and the capacity allows for multi-channel audio effects, multi-language versions and additional information. The base format that holds data is known as DVD-ROM. *See also* DVD-R.

DVD Alliance. A voluntary organization of approximately 100 members – largely leading PC, Optical storage, software, electronics, and blank media manufacturers (including Hewlett-Packard, Philips, Sony, Yamaha, Vertatim, Ricoh, Dell and Microsoft) – whose mission is to develop, maintain and support the DVD+R and DVD+RW formats. *See also* DVD Forum.

DVD Forum. An industry group of primarily consumer electronics and computer equipment companies (including Pioneer, NEC, Sharp, Thomson) largely responsible for developing DVD formats since the mid-1990s. *See also* DVD Alliance.

DVD-R. Recordable DVD of which there are five main formats: DVD-R, DVD+R, DVD-RAM, DVD-RW, DVD+RW, incompatible formats supported by the competing commercial interests of the DVD Forum and the DVD Alliance. DVD-R appeared in 1997 and is the equivalent of CD-R, the 'write-once' format. It can store 4.7 Gbytes of data, is compatible with most DVD writers and is recognised by most DVD-ROM drives and domestic players. There are two variations: DVD-R for General and DVD-R for Authoring. Further information on formats and DVD issues can be found at <www.dvddemystified.com>.

DVD+R. Recordable 'write-once' DVD format released in 2002 and developed by the DVD Alliance. The format can only be written by a compatible writer though the DVD Alliance claims the discs are compatible with most commercial DVD-ROM and DVD players. *See also* DVD-R.

DVD-RAM. Recordable/re-writable DVD released in 1998 and supported by the DVD Forum as well as being additionally endorsed by Hitachi, Toshiba, Panasonic and Samsung. The format is more of a removable storage device for computer data Back-up than a video recording format, permitting re-writes of up to 100,000 times. It was the first format to be used in PC drives as well as commercial DVD recorders; capacities vary from 2.6 Gbytes to 9.4 Gbytes. Discs are not compatible with commercial players or most DVD-ROM drives though DVD-RAM writers can write to DVD-R discs which function in most commercial DVD home players. *See also* DVD-R.

DVD-RW. Recordable/re-writable DVD released in Japan in 1999 (later in the rest of the world) and endorsed by the DVD Forum. Storage capacity is 4.7 Gbytes and the discs can be used up to 1,000 times. *See also* DVD-R.

DVD+RW. Recordable/re-writable DVD released in 2001 and endorsed by the DVD Alliance. Storage capacity is 4.7 Gbytes and includes built-in defect management to deal with interruptions on a PC that can occur when burning discs. See also DVD-R.

DVI. 1. *See* Digital Video Initiative. 2. Digital Video Interactive, an initiative by RCA, General Electric and Intel to develop a programmable chip to act as a Codec for full screen full motion video for Multimedia applications. Supplanted by software-only codecs such as MPEG.

d.w. Abbreviation for dust wrapper. *See* Book jacket.

Dwarf book. *See* Bibelot.

Dye-line process. *See* Diazotype process.

Dynamic HTML (DHTML). A term used by some vendors to describe the combination of HTML, style sheets and scripts that allows documents to be animated. DHTML is not an agreed standard, though it does not introduce new tags to HTML. The W3C is attempting to create an interoperable solution via the Document Object Model.

Dynamic map. One which expresses movement such as transport, migration, or military manoeuvres. The symbols used are mainly flow lines and arrows but change is sometimes expressed by isopleths or choropleths.

e. As a prefix, used widely to signify electronic or digital services, or delivery of services by electronic means. Examples include e-government, e-democracy, e-health, e-library, e-society and many others.

E2Epi. *See* End-to-End Performance Initiative.

EAD. <www.loc.gov/ead> Encoded Archival Description, a format for adapting SGML to archives, to assist in the creation of electronic finding aids. Developed at University of California (Berkeley), it is now maintained and supported as a standard by the Library of Congress and sponsored by the Society of American Archivists. The EAD can be used to represent complete archival structures, including hierarchies and associations. The functionality can also be implemented using Dublin Core, and it is also possible to migrate records from Dublin Core into the EAD format.

EAGLE. *See* European Association for Grey Literature Exploitation.

EAHIL. *See* European Association for Health Information and Libraries.

EAN International. <www.ean-int.org> Established in 1977, EAN is the supervisory organization for international article numbering; it has 700,000 member organizations in 87 countries. *See* e-centre.

EARL. Elcctronic Access to Resources in London (EARL) was a consortium of UK public libraries and associated organizations established in 1995, and located with LASER. It ceased to function in 2001 with the launch of alternative London-based services, and its Networked Services Policy Task Group passed to Resource (now MLA). There was discussion on the possible formation of an EARL Fellowship.

Early English Books Online (EEBO). <www.jisc.ac.uk/coll_eebo.html> A database of some 125,000 titles published 1473–1700; reproduces the content of STC and STC-Wing together with the Thomason Tracts.

Early map. *See* Map.

EASTICA. East Asian Regional Branch of the International Council on Archives.

EBLIDA. <www.eblida.org> The European Bureau of Library, Information and Documentation Associations was founded in 1992; over 30 associations in the EU are members, together with a number of associations from countries outside the EU, and several individual libraries which are associate members. EBLIDA fosters consultation between members, acts as a channel of communication with the EU, the European Parliament, and other European bodies. It is a collective representative voice in international affairs, and promotes the interests of the LIS profession in Europe. There is a Council, an Executive Committee, and a permanent Secretariat.

EBONI Project. <ebooks.strath.ac.uk/eboni> The Electronic Books On-Screen Interface Project is working on guidelines for design and usability requirements for electronic books.

EBSLG. *See* European Business Schools Librarians Group.

EC. European Community. *See* European Union (EU).

ECA. *See* e-centre.

ECDL. *See* European Computer Driving Licence.

e-centre. <www.e-centre.org.uk> Formed 1998 by the merger of the Article Numbering Association (ANA) and the Electronic Commerce Association (ECA). The organization is a member of EAN International which with the US Uniform Code Council sets standards for business data and best practices for electronic commerce, including directing the use of article numbers – the EAN.UCC codes – worldwide.

ECHO. The European Commission Host Organization, based in Luxembourg, and offering online access to EU databases. Set up in

1980, it was considered to have done its work and was decommissioned at the end of 1998.

ECIA.   *See* European Council of Information Associations.

e-Citizen (UK).   <www.e-citizen.gov.uk> A national programme organized by the Office of the Deputy Prime Minister to persuade local authorities to make e-government a normal part of their activities. The programme will also conduct research into e-services, and public perceptions of e-government.

ECMS.   *See* Electronic Copyright Management Systems.

Ecole Nationale Supérieure des Sciences de l'Information et des Bibliothèques (ENSSIB).   <www.enssib.fr> (17/18 blvd. de 11 Novembre 1918, 69623 Villeurbanne, France) The French Higher National School of Librarianship; founded in 1963 it provides courses for professional librarians seeking to work in the education and municipal sectors, and advanced courses in information sciences. Publishes *Bulletin des Bibliothèques de France* (6 p.a.).

e-Commerce.   *See* Electronic Commerce.

Economy.   A generic term for the housekeeping arrangements needed for the efficient functioning of an organization; in this overall sense it is perhaps an old-fashioned term, but it is now reappearing in the modern context of library management where efficient action is closely related to cost measurement and control.

e Content.   <www.cordis.lu/econtent> An EU programme scheduled 2001 2004 to improve the competitiveness of the European digital content sectors. The aim was to improve access to public service information, to enhance information with multilingual and multicultural features and increase dynamism. *See also* e-Contentplus, Digital content.

e-Contentplus.   <www.cordis.lu/ist/directorate_e> An EU programme (2005–2008) designed to follow on from the e-Content programme; it is expected to increase demand for broadband access, and will highlight three main content areas: geographical data, educational material, and cultural content.

ECPA.   *See* European Commission on Preservation and Access.

Écrasé leather.   Leather which has been crushed mechanically to give it a grained appearance.

Ed. (edit.).   Abbreviation for Edited, Edition, Editor.

EDC.   *See* European Documentation Centres.

Edge decoration.   The application of ink, coloured (sprayed, sprinkled or marbled), or gold leaf to the edges of a book.

Edge fog.   Light or dark areas along the edge of a developed film or print, caused either by the unintentional admission of light to the sensitive material, or to the effects of age or unsatisfactory storage conditions.

Edge-notched cards.   Punched cards which have up to four rows of holes drilled round the edges. These are punched out to record information; one edge-notched card is allocated to each document and each punchable position is reserved for one feature. Also called 'Edge-punched cards'. *See also* Feature card system, Marginal-hole punched cards.

Edge-rolled.   Said of leather-bound books the broad edges of which have been tooled 'blind' or 'gold' with a Fillet. *See also* Tooling.

Edges.   (*Binding*) The three outer edges of the leaves of a book; they may be finished in a number of ways. *See also* Cut edges, Edge-rolled, Gauffered edges, Gilt edges, Gilt top, Marbled edges, Red edges, Red under gold edges, Sprinkled edges, Tooled edges, Trimmed (2), Uncut, White edges.

EDI.   Electronic data interchange; the development of standards to permit rapid exchange of data between organizations and companies. EDI should improve the speed and efficiency of all business communications, from production, stock control, to sales and marketing. National administrations will need to adapt their procedures, particularly in their relationship with industry. At present there are a number of standards used in the transmission of data in different geographical and industrial market areas.

EDIFACT.   Electronic Data Interchange for Administration, Commerce and Transport: an international programme to oversee the development of standards for companies and organizations. Interested bodies include the United Nations, and Directorate General XIII of the Commission of the European Union. *See also* EDI.

EDILIBE.   Electronic Data Interchange between Libraries and Booksellers in Europe; supported by Directorate General XIII of the EU Commission, and initiated in 1990 by a consortium of booksellers and libraries in Germany, Italy, the Netherlands and the UK. The project is targeted at producing and implementing EDIFACT-based standards for the European library sector. EDILIBE II continues the work.

EDINA.   <www.edina.ac.uk> A JISC-funded national data centre based at Edinburgh University Data Library providing online access to a range of specialist bibliographic and geo-spatial services (e.g. Digimap). *See also* MIMAS.

Edit.   1. To amend a computer record or programme; especially to amend or upgrade a computerized bibliographic record.   2. To prepare or arrange a document for publication.   3. EDIT. *See* NMI-EDIT.

Edited.   1. A literary work by one author, or several authors, which has been prepared for publication by one or more persons other than the author of the whole work.   2. A work consisting of separate items, often written by different people, which has been assembled or prepared for publication by an Editor.

EDItEUR.   <www.editeur.org> (Book Industry Communication, 39/41 North Road, London N7 9DP, UK) EDItEUR is the Pan-European Book Industry EDI Group, and is engaged in harmonizing EDI standards.

Editio minor.   A lesser, but important, edition of a book or work previously printed, but sometimes the first separate printing of a work previously included in a larger volume. *See also Editio princeps.*

Editio princeps.   1. The first edition of a book printed from the old manuscript, when printing first began. *See also Editio minor.*   2. The first
edition of any new work, but for this the term 'first edition' is more
commonly used.

Edition.   1. All the copies of a work published in one typographical format,
printed from the same type or plates, and issued at one time or at
intervals. An edition may comprise a number of impressions.   2. One
of the various versions of a newspaper printed at different times on the
same day, or periodically summarizing the news of the period since the
previous edition was issued, or to celebrate some particular event.
3. One of the successive forms in which a musical composition is issued
and in which alterations have been incorporated either by the composer
or by an editor. *See also* Abridged edition, Autographed edition,
Definitive edition, Expurgated edition, Fine paper copy, First edition,
Grangerizing, Impression, Issue (3), Large paper copy, or edition,
Library edition, Limited edition, New edition, Numbered and signed
edition, Parallel edition, Polyglot, Reprint, Revised edition,
Subscribers' edition, Title leaf, Unexpurgated edition, Variorum edition.

Edition bindery.   A bindery in which books are bound for publishers; one in
which Edition binding is undertaken. *See also* Case, Publisher's cover.

Edition binding.   A binding, usually a casing, ordered and paid for by the
publisher as a part of the normal publishing of trade editions, and used
for all the copies of a title so published, as distinct from individual
binding carried out for the bookseller or purchaser. Also called
'Publisher's binding'.

Edition de luxe.   A special edition of a book containing extras not in ordinary editions, such as additional plates, or printed on large paper, etc.

Edition statement.   That part of a catalogue entry which relates to the
edition of the book catalogued, as: 2nd rev. ed.

Editor.   1. A person, employed by a publisher, who prepares someone else's
work for publication. The editorial work may be limited to mere
preparation of the matter for printing, or may involve considerable
revisionary and elucidatory work, including an introduction, notes and
other critical matter.   2. A person who is responsible for the contents
of a newspaper, journal, or periodical and sometimes its publication.

Editor reference.   A reference in a catalogue from the name of an editor, or
from an entry under an editor's name to another entry where more
complete information is to be found.

Editorial.   An article expressing a paper's own policy and beliefs on current
matters.

Editorial copies.   Copies of a new publication sent out by the publisher for
review, notice, or record. *See also* Advance copy (sheet), Review copy.

EDMS.   *See* Electronic Document Management Systems.

EDP.   Electronic data processing. *See* Data processing.

Education Aid.   <info@educationaid.org.uk> (PO Box 3855, London NW9
9LZ, UK) A UK charity which obtains surplus books and journals from

libraries, publishers and booksellers to send to school, college and university libraries in developing countries.

Education and Library Boards. The five bodies that oversee the public library services of Northern Ireland; they are: Belfast; North Eastern; South Eastern; Southern; Western. *See* Association of Northern Ireland Education and Library Boards.

Education Image Library. <edina.ac.uk/eig> A collection of 50,000 images specifically designed for use in UK higher and further education and based on the resources of the Hulton Archive, Photodisc and the Getty Images News Service. The large variety of images covers key events and multiple subject areas including history, entertainment, sport, science, fashion, politics, music, conflict, film, art, leisure and women's studies. The images are copyright-cleared and available for downloading in screen-resolution format.

Education Librarians Group (ELG). A membership group of CILIP, formed in 1981; formerly the Colleges, Institutes and Schools of Education Group. Publishes *ELG News* (2 p.a.).

Education Library Service/Department. *See* School Libraries Department.

Education Media OnLine. <www.emol.ac.uk> A JISC-funded set of collections of film and video, hosted by EDINA and cleared and digitized through MAAS who are also producing associated metadata. Initially 300 hours of non-fiction films and video were freely available for download for use in learning, teaching and research. The films come from a diverse set of collections and are of interest to teachers and students in many different study areas, from British and European history through media studies, archaeology, performing arts and music to the medical, health and life sciences.

Educational Copyright Users Forum. A body set up under the terms of the (UK) Copyright, Designs and Patents Act, 1988, to monitor existing and future licensing arrangements and to provide advice and guidance to educational users and to rights owners on licensing matters. The members include local authorities, universities and teaching unions, and the members collectively have considerable experience of negotiating and applying licensing schemes. It is hoped that reference to the Forum at an early stage will help to ensure that licensing schemes are relevant, fair and workable.

Educational Low-priced Books Scheme. Title of a recent development of the English Language Book Society, which preserves the same acronym – ELBS.

Educational Publishers Council. *See* Publishers Association.

Educational Recording Agency Ltd (ERA). <www.era.org.uk> (Marlborough Court, 14–18 Holborn, London EC1N 2LE, UK) ERA is the UK body formed in 1990 to provide educational establishments with licences to record off-air for educational purposes a wide range of radio and television broadcasts, following the recommendations of the

Copyright Designs and Patents Act, 1988. ERA represents the major broadcasting organizations and the copyright collection agencies such as the Authors' Licensing and Collecting Society and the Musicians' Union. *See also* Copyright Licensing Agency.

Educational Resources Information Center. *See* ERIC.

Education-line. <www.leeds.ac.uk/educol/index.html> An Eprint archive with the focus on texts which are relevant to the study, practice and administration of education at a professional level. Texts in the archive include presentations made at conferences.

Educause. <www.educause.edu> (1150 18th Street NW, Suite 1010, Washington, DC 20036, USA) Formed as a result of a merger between CAUSE and Educom in 1998, Educause focuses 'on the management and use of computational, networks and information resources in support of higher education's missions of scholarship, instruction, service, and administration'. In 2002 the US government gave control of the .edu domain to Educause.

Educom. A US consortium of colleges, universities and other organizations with a mission to further the use of information technology in higher education; there were 600 institutional members and 100 corporate associates. It was active in the Networking and Telecommunications Taskforce and the National Learning Infrastructure Initiative. It was associated with CAUSE in the formation of the Coalition for Networked Information, and in 1997 CAUSE and Educom merged to form Educause.

EduServ. <www.eduserv.org.uk> Created from the merger of CHEST and NISS in 1999, Eduserv is an independent not-for-profit company and registered charity that provides information and communication technology services to universities and colleges. Established with the support of the UK higher education funding bodies, Eduserv provides the corporate structure for the operation of three well established educational services: Eduserv Athens; Eduserv Chest; and Eduserv Internet (formerly NISS).

Edwards of Halifax. *See* Etruscan style, Fore-edge painting.

EEMA. <www.eema.org> (Alexander House, High Street, Inkberrow, Worcester WR7 4DT, UK) Formed in 1987 and previously titled the European Electronic Messaging Association, EEMA now uses its acronym alone and is a proponent of all aspects of electronic business. There are over 300 members in 30 countries.

EEMLAC. *See* Museums, Libraries and Archives Council (MLA).

e-Envoy. <www.e-envoy.gov.uk> A UK government official whose role was to increase awareness of the possibilities of electronic delivery of government services. In 2004 this position was re-titled 'Head of e-Government'.

e-Europe. <europa.eu.int/information_society/eeurope> Originally titled e-Europe 2002, the current version of this EU programme is the e-Europe Action Plan 2005. The strategic aim is for Europe to become the most competitive knowledge-based economy in the world by 2010; current targets include wider broadband access to counter the Digital divide, and enhancement of online public services. *See also* Information Society, PULMAN.

EEVL. <www.eevl.ac.uk> The Internet Guide to Engineering, Mathematics and Computing, a Hub of the (UK) RDN. Originally, the 'Edinburgh Engineering Virtual Library', the name changed in September 2001 to represent the inclusion of mathematics and computing information. The acronym now nominally stands for Enhanced and Evaluated Virtual Library though EEVL is preferred. A partnership between Heriot-Watt University (the lead site), the University of Birmingham, Cranfield University and the University of Ulster.

EFF. *See* Electronic Frontier Foundation.

Effectiveness. The measure of how successfully an organization carries out its role and fulfils its objectives, seen from the standpoint of the users of the service.

Efficiency. The measure of the speed, accuracy and cost consciousness with which an organization manages its internal affairs in order to provide the best service at an economical price.

e.g. Abbreviation for *exempli gratia* (Lat. 'for example'). Also for 'edges gilt'.

Eggshell. A paper with a non-glossy, soft, smooth finish. Most antique papers have an eggshell finish.

e-GIF. <www.egifcompliance.org> The UK electronic-Government Interoperability Framework; adherence to the specifications and policies of the framework is mandatory for systems that are to be used to deliver public service information. e-GIF regulates the exchange of information between systems and interactions between government and citizens, government and businesses, and between government organizations.

e-GMS. *See* Electronic Government Metadata Standard.

e-Government. Delivery of government services by electronic means. In the UK, there is a target to ensure that all national and local government services can be accessed and delivered online by the end of 2005; the Head of e-Government (formerly the e-Envoy) is responsible for monitoring this target. The current position is shown at <www.localegov.gov.uk> and <www.socitm.gov.uk>. In the USA, the E-Government Act (S.803) of 2002 created an Office of Electronic Government within the Office of Management and Budget; the intention is to move towards a single government portal. In the EU, an Observatory on Interoperable e-Government Services has been set up, and will operate until 2007.

Egyptian. A group of display faces having slab-serifs and little contrast in the thickness of the strokes. They developed from the Antique face cut by Vincent Figgins prior to 1815 and were extensively used by jobbing printers in the nineteenth century. Early Sans serif types were also known as Egyptians but the name gradually became limited to slab-serif types, 'grotesque' being given to sans serifs. Modern Egyptian faces are Beton, Cairo, Karnak, Luxor, Playbill, Rockwell, etc.; these are also called block-serif abstract faces. *See also* Bold face, Clarendon.

e-Health. <europa.eu.int/information_society/eeurope/ehealth> There are several EU initiatives that aim to improve access and delivery of health information and solutions to medical professionals and to the general public.

EIA. *See* European Information Association.

EIC. *See* European Information Centres.

Eichner dry copy. A method of producing facsimile copies of single-sheet documents by feeding them through a machine in contact with copying paper. *See also* Thermography.

Eighteen-mo. 1. A book in which the sections are folded four times so that each leaf is an eighteenth of the sheet. Also called 'Octodecimo'. 2. A sheet of paper so folded.

Eighteenth Century Short-title Catalogue. *See* ESTC.

EIRENE. <www.eirene.com> The European Information Researchers Network is a professional organization representing information brokers throughout Europe; it seeks to promote contacts, improve access to information, develop brokerage as a commercial activity, and raise the quality of service to clients. There are 30 information brokers currently in membership, from the EU and eastern European countries.

EIS. Electronic information services.

Ejector. In the Linotype and Intertype casting machines, the mechanism for ejecting cast lines.

e-Journal. *See* Electronic journal.

ELBS. *See* English Language Book Society.

Eleanor Farjeon Award. *See* Children's Book Circle.

e-Learning. <europa.eu.int/comm/education/elearning> A blanket term used to describe educational initiatives that use electronic means for delivery of services. These may include online learning, computer-based learning, web-based learning, networked collaborative learning, VLEs and similar schemes. The EU priorities are to use the Internet to disseminate interactive learning packages, and to use ICT to support collaborative learning through discussion groups and conference rooms.

Electric stylus. An electrically heated stylus used over a strip of metallic foil to impress the Call number on to the spine of a book.

Electro. Abbreviation for Electrotype.

Electrographic process. *See* Xerography.

Electronic book. A generic term for products of Electronic and Multimedia publishing, available directly from the Web or in physical format on Optical disc. Increasingly, key texts for undergraduates are being made available by publishers and handled by libraries in ways similar to those for the more established electronic journals.

Electronic bulletin board. *See* Bulletin board.

Electronic commerce. Conducting business activities by electronic means; the use of EDI in particular is typical of e-commerce, but Intranets, Extranets and Web sites are all part of a wider definition. 'Internet shopping' is another manifestation that falls loosely into this category of business.

Electronic Commerce Association (ECA). *See* e-centre.

Electronic copyright. The extension of Copyright to electronic formats. Copyright issues will include the use of software, material on the Internet or on an intranet (such as web pages, diagrams etc), e-mail messages, electronic databases in all formats, and all manner of digitized content. Copyright legislation for conventional materials is automatically extended to cover digital and electronic materials, but there are many problems as national laws may not apply internationally. Permission should always be sought when re-using or passing on electronic materials.

Electronic Copyright Management Systems (ECMS). Systems through which various aspects of the rights existing in electronic documents can be managed. They usually include one or more of the following elements: (a) facilitating and controlling access; (b) controlling use; (c) managing re-transmissions; (d) monitoring use; (e) collecting royalties; (f) guaranteeing the integrity of the document in terms of both content and authorship. *See also* CITED, IMPRIMATUR. *Compare* Digital Rights Management.

Electronic course reserve collection. Library materials such as individual journal papers and chapters from books which are in heavy demand and which, after obtaining the requisite permissions, are digitized and made available to registered users over a network. *See also* HERON, Reserve collection (2).

Electronic data processing. *See* Data processing.

Electronic document delivery. The transfer of information from publisher or library to user by electronic means; paper versions of the 'documents' involved may or may not exist. *See also* Document delivery.

Electronic Document Management Systems (EDMS). Business processes are transferring rapidly from paper to electronic forms; the need to organize these electronic 'documents' so that they can be easily stored, combined with other documents as required, readily retrieved, read, updated, maybe used as legal evidence etc., has led to the development of software packages of various levels of sophistication. For small companies simple applications are sufficient, but larger firms may need the techniques of Data warehousing to achieve adequate management results. *See also* Knowledge Management.

Electronic Frontier Foundation (EFF). <eff.org> (454 Shotwell Street, San Francisco, CA 94110) A non-profit, non-partisan organization founded in 1990 working in the public interest to protect fundamental civil liberties, including privacy and freedom of expression, in the arena of computers, the Internet and the World Wide Web. The EFF comprises a group of lawyers, technologists, volunteers, and visionaries working to protect the rights of web surfers everywhere by challenging legislation that threatens to put a price on what is invaluable. Publishes a bi-weekly electronic newsletter, *EFFector*.

Electronic Government Interoperability Framework. *See* e-GIF.

Electronic Government Metadata Standard (e-GMS). <www.govtalk.gov.uk/schemasstandards/metadata_document> A UK government guide to the categories of metadata that should be used in public sector applications and websites. It is based on the Dublin Core Metadata Element Set. The Standard was first issued in 2002 and is currently (2004) in version 3. It contains 25 elements of metadata with over 90 refinements (qualifiers) together with encoding schemes and entry formats. e-GMS is recommended by the Aplaws Project.

Electronic journal. A journal which is available in electronic format; a physical, printed version may also be available. *See also* Basket deal, Electronic publishing.

Electronic Libraries Programme. *See* eLib.

Electronic library. *See* Digital library.

Electronic mail. *See* E-mail.

Electronic office. *See* Paper-less office.

Electronic photo-engraving machines. Machines which produce half-tone plates automatically. The engraving is done on metal or plastic by a cutting or burning stylus used in conjunction with a scanning device which traces the original by means of a photographic cell.

Electronic Privacy Regulations. An EU Directive (2002/58/EC) that was intended to reduce Spam. The Directive came into force in the UK in December 2003.

Electronic Publishers Forum. *See* Publishers Association.

Electronic publishing. e-Publishing is the blanket term for a range of publishing processes by electronic means. Earlier initiatives have included CD-ROM and Optical discs, but the current area of activity is the publication and dissemination of information via the Internet. Although take-up was initially slow, new formats are now regularly appearing and sales are rising sharply. The (US) Open-eBook Forum is a trade and standards body that monitors growth. *See also* Electronic document delivery, Electronic journal, Multimedia publishing, Parallel publishing. Not to be confused with Desktop publishing.

Electronic Rights Management Systems. *See* Electronic Copyright Management Systems.

Electronic service delivery (ESD). As a part of e-Government, the essential action of moving all services to digital and electronic methods of provision.

Electrophotographic process. *See* Xerography.

Electrostatic processes. *See* Xerography.

Electrotype (Electro). A facsimile plate of a type forme or another plate, produced by taking an impression in wax, lead or plastic, depositing in this mould a thin shell of copper and other metal by an electro-plating process, backing it with type metal, and mounting it type high on wood. Half-tones (except the very coarsest) demand electros, which may also be made from line blocks and composed type.

Element. (*Cataloguing*) 1. A unit of data appearing in a record which can be, or needs to be, distinguished for filing purposes, or which, representing a distinct item of bibliographic information, forms part of an area of a bibliographical description within a catalogue entry. 2. A portion of an Area of a catalogue entry, e.g. a parallel title.

Elephant. A size of paper varying from 28 x 23 inches to 34 x 28 inches. 'Double elephant' printing and writing papers vary from 36 x 24 inches to 46 x 31 inches; drawing papers are 26³/₄ x 40 inches (not an exact multiple of 'Elephant'). 'Long elephant' is a term employed for wallpaper 12 yards long and usually 22, 22¹/₂ or 30 inches wide.

Elephant folio. A folio volume larger than an ordinary folio but not so large as Atlas folio, about 14 x 23 inches, and formerly used for service books, maps, etc.

ELFNI. <ni-libraries.net> The Electronic Libraries in Northern Ireland project is a ten-year programme of the five Education and Library Boards to ensure that all citizens can use any public library without restriction, that all stock items would be traceable from any service point, and that the public library in every community would be the gateway to e-government and other electronic services. The People's Network initiative has been a catalyst for the project. Partner with UKOnline, Cymru Ar-lein, and Digital Scotland in the People's Network (PN).

eLib. <www.ukoln.ac.uk/services/elib> The Electronic Libraries Programme of UK higher education which ran from 1995 to 2000. Funded by JISC, the main aim was to engage the community in developing and shaping the implementation of the electronic library. *See also* Digital Libraries Initiative.

Eliot (Ida and George) Prize Essay Award. Offered by the (US) Medical Library Association for the essay published in any journal during the previous year which has done most to further medical librarianship.

Eliot (T. S.) Centenary Fund. A memorial fund set up in 1988 by the London Library to raise revenue to enable needy students and scholars to pay their library subscriptions at a reduced rate. T. S. Eliot was President of the London Library 1952–1964, and championed the cause of those who needed to be library members but found the subscription burdensome.

Elision. The contraction of pairs of numbers, e.g. 93–98 becomes 93–8; 1974–1975 becomes 1974–5.

Elision marks. *See* Omission marks.

Elite. The smaller of the two common sizes of typewriter type, having twelve characters to the inch as against ten for the larger 'pica' size.

E-literacy. The skills required for an individual to operate with maximum effectiveness in a global, electronic and information-rich environment. *See also* Competencies, Information literacy, Literacy.

Ellipsis.   *See* Omission marks.

Ellis Prize.   Prize offered annually by the Society of Archivists in honour of the late Roger Ellis, to mark outstanding contributions to the archival profession.

Elrod.   *See* Ludlow.

Elsevier/LIRG Research Award.   Sponsored by Elsevier Science, an award to encourage research and innovation in retrieval, access and use of information, presented annually by the Library and Information Research Group (LIRG).

ELVIL.   <elvil.sub.su.se> The European Legislative Virtual Library is an academic portal to European law and politics. It also offers citizens access to legal and political information from parliaments and related organizations.

Elzevier.   Name of the house of Elzevier, Dutch booksellers and printers; founded by Lodewijck (Louis) Elzevier (1542–1617) at Leyden in 1583 it continued until 1791, being directed by members of the Elzevier family. Of the books emanating from this firm, the most famous are the 32 mo. pocket-sized editions of the Latin classics begun in 1629. Books of this size printed elsewhere were known as 'Elzevirs'. Also spelled Elsevier and Elzevir. The distinctive typeface they used had a great influence on book design.

Em.   The square of the body of any size of type; the printer's unit of square measure. A standard unit of typographic measurement, for which a 12 point em is the basis. This equals 0.166 inch, and there are approximately six 12-point ems to one inch. Sometimes called 'Pica'. This unit is used for computing the area of a printed page no matter what size of type is to be used for setting the text; thus if the area is 20 ems wide and 30 ems deep, the width is 240-point and the depth 360-point. It is also used to indicate the amount of indenting required. So called because the space taken up by the letter m is usually square. If the printer is instructed to indent paragraphs one, two or three ems, the indention will be approximately the width of one, two or three lower-case *m*'s of the type used. *See also* En, Pica.

Em quadrat.   A square of metal used to fill out short lines of type to the required length; its width is equal to the Body. It is a type body cast less than type height, and is always the square of the size of type it accompanies, e.g. an em quadrat of 12-point type is 12 x 12 points. Em quadrats are often made in multiple. Used normally before the first of a new paragraph. Usually called 'Em quad' or 'Mutton' (slang). *See also* En quadrat.

Em rule.   A Dash used in punctuation; strictly its length should be the same as that occupied by the letter 'm'. Also known as em dash.

Emage.   The area of a block of text, or of a text page, measured in terms of ems of its type size.

E-mail. Electronic mail, a method of sending messages, information, files and data rapidly and globally from a PC using networking/telecommunications hardware and dedicated software. *See also* Attachment, MIME, Spam.

Emblem book. A type of book in which designs or pictures called emblems, expressing some thought or moral idea, were printed with accompanying proverbs, mottoes, or explanatory writing; or in which verses are arranged in symbolic shapes such as crosses.

Embossed. 1. (*Binding*) A design which is raised in relief. 2. (*Printing*) Lettering, or a design, which is raised above the surface of the paper.

Embossed book. A book in which the text is printed in embossed characters, such as Braille, for the use of the blind.

Embossing. Relief printing by the use of a sunken die and a raised counterpart, called female and male, the surface of the paper being raised in relief. It may also be done by the use of certain substances dusted on the printed surface and caused to be raised by heating. Also called 'Process embossing', 'Relief printing', 'Bas relief printing'. *See also* Die stamping, Thermography.

Embossing plate. A plate cut or etched below its surface and used for producing a design, usually lettering, in relief on a sheet of paper. *See also* Embossing.

Embossing press. A machine used in binderies for impressing lettering and designs on book covers.

Embroidered binding. Binding in which the covering material is embroidered cloth. Also called 'Needlework binding'.

e-Metrics. *See* Metrics.

Emil Award. An award organized by the Book Trust and given annually for the children's book 'in which text and illustration are both excellent and perfectly harmonious'; now combined with the Maschler (Kurt) Award.

EMMLAC. *See* Museums, Libraries and Archives Council (MLA).

Empowerment. The raising of the awareness of individuals and groups so that they are able to make more effective use of their own resources through understanding of their abilities. In many cases empowerment comes through increased political awareness of employees, or through greater access to information resulting from technological developments.

Empty digits. (*Classification*) 1. Symbols, e.g. punctuation marks used in a notation solely to separate meaningful characters (or groups of characters) forming part of a composite notation, which themselves have no meaning but merely convey structure. 2. A digit (*see* Digit (1)) having ordinal value but without representing any specific idea.

Emulsion. The chemicals with which a photographic film or paper is coated.

En. A unit of printer's measurement that is half of the Em in width but the same as the em in depth; thus a 12 point en quad is 12 by 6 points, a 10 point en is 10 by 5 points, and an 8 point en is 8 by 4 points.

En point.   A point, i.e. dot, set midway along a piece of printer's type as wide as an en, so that when printed it will appear with space on either side of it. It may be on, or above, the Base line.

En quadrat.   A square of metal half the width of the body of a type, and half an Em quadrat, usually inserted after a punctuation mark when not ending a sentence. Usually called 'En quad' or 'Nut' (slang).

En rule.   A Dash the width of an en space; also known as 'en dash'.

Enamel paper.   A highly finished paper coated on one side.

Enamelled bindings.   *See Champlevé, Cloisonné.*

Encapsulated PostScript.   *See* EPS.

Encapsulation.   A method for protecting a fragile document by enclosing it within sheets of chemically stable, clear polyester film and sealing the edges by heat. The film serves to protect the document and helps to prevent damage and disintegration. Highly acidic paper should be deacidified before encapsulation.

Enchiridion.   (*Pl.*, – ons or – a). A hand-book, specifically a manual of devotions.

Encode.   1. (*Computer security*) To make a file or the contents of a storage medium accessible only to authorized users by means of Encryption. 2. In computer programming to change into Code.

Encoding.   (*Information retrieval*) A process whereby a message is transformed into signals that can be carried by a communication channel.

ENCORE!   <www.iaml-uk-irl.org> Launched by IAML (UK) in 2001, ENCORE! is an online catalogue of musical performance sets in UK libraries. It gives details of some 80,000 sets.

Encryption.   The mechanism of coding data so that only authorized users may have access to it. Can be applied to data transmitted over telecommunication systems and utilized for sensitive information (for example, drug data to pharmacists) or to ensure that only those paying for a certain service can obtain it (e.g. satellite television channels) but also to prevent access to data on local or networked machines.

Encyclopaedia.   A work containing information on all subjects, or limited to a special field or subject, arranged in systematic (usually alphabetical), order. Encyclopaedias may be in one volume, in which case very brief information will be given, or they may be in many volumes in which the various matters will be comprehensive, usually written by experts, and sometimes containing bibliographies and illustrations. The term was first used in a book title in Johann Henrich Alsted's *Encyclopaedia cursus philosophici*, Herborn, 1608. The first to be published in English was John Harris's *Lexicon technicum, or, An universal English dictionary of the arts and sciences*, London, 1704. One of the earliest encyclopaedias was the Spanish Archbishop Isidore of Seville's *Etymologiarum sive originum libri XX* which was completed in 623. More than a thousand manuscripts of this have survived, and in printed form it had an undiminished appeal as late as the seventeenth century.

End a break. An instruction to the compositor that the last line of a Take or section of copy is to be filled out with quad spacing after setting the last word. *See also* Break-line, End even, Run on.

End even. An instruction to the compositor that the last line of type in a Take or section of copy is to be spaced out so that the last word is at the end of a line. *See also* Break-line, End a break, Run on.

End leaf. The piece of paper covering the turned-in covering material and the joint, or hinge reinforcement, of a re-bound book (US).

End user searching. Information retrieval carried out by End users – non-library staff – by directly accessing networked resources or Online services. As distinct from Mediated searching.

End users. Those who actually make use of products and services, as distinct from intermediaries.

End-matter. The items which follow the text of a printed book. These include appendices, bibliography, notes, supplements, indexes, glossary, imprint or collation, advertisements. *See also* Back matter.

Endnotes. Notes printed at the end of a chapter or end of a book.

Endpaper. A sheet of paper at each end of a book which is inserted by the binder to help fasten the sewn sections to the cover. One half, the 'paste-down endpaper', is pasted on to a cover of the book (with the tapes between); the other, the 'free endpaper' or 'fly-leaf' is pasted with a narrow strip of paste at the fold to the end leaf of a section. *See also* Doublure, Map endpapers.

End-to-End Performance Initiative (E2Epi). <e2epi.internet2.edu> An Initiative of Internet2 to create a predictable, and well-supported, environment in which campus network users have routinely successful experiences in their development and use of advanced Internet applications by focusing resources and efforts on improving performance problem detection and resolution throughout campus, regional, and national networking infrastructures. *See also* Quality of service.

Engine-sizing. Hardening paper by adding a moisture-resistant substance such as casein, starch or resin to the pulp before the Stuff flows on to the machine wire. This is the usual method of sizing the cheaper papers and produces a weaker paper than Tub-sizing. Engine-sized paper is abbreviated ES. *See also* Surface sizing.

English. An out-of-date name for a size of type equal to about 14 point.

English finish paper. A calendered paper with a smooth but not highly glossy finish.

English Language Bibliography 1945 to the present. Issued in 2003 as a single database (online and DVD) the Bibliography comprises over 12 million titles taken from British Library and Library of Congress records, and includes the complete British Library General Catalogue of Printed Books to 1975. As well as BNB records, there are several specialist catalogues from the BL; LC records include English books from 1968 and serials from 1978. Updated weekly online and quarterly on DVD; records are in MARC21 format and can be downloaded.

English Language Book Society (ELBS). A non-profit making publishing organization financed by the UK Government and administered by the British Council with the object of making books of an educational nature – provided both publisher and author are British – available through the usual trade channels. Since 1960 when the scheme was launched more than 15,000,000 books have been sold at a third or sometimes less of their normal price in seventy-nine scheduled developing countries of Asia, Africa, the West Indies and the Pacific. These editions cannot be purchased except in the scheduled countries. The Society also now uses its acronym to designate its Educational Low-priced Book Scheme.

English Short Title Catalogue. *See* ESTC.

English Speaking Union Travelling Librarian Award. *See* Wrench (Sir Evelyn) Travelling Librarian Award.

English stock. A group of publications of which the Stationers' Company held the sole rights of printing and distributing. Perpetual rights were given in a patent granted in 1603 by James I to the Master, Wardens and Assistants of the Company. The publications included almanacs, ABC primers, prognostications, psalters, psalms in metre and catechisms and were sold in large numbers.

Engraved title-page. A supplementary title-page usually wholly engraved on copper which faces the usual printed title-page. These were popular in the seventeenth century and were frequently elaborate allegorical pictures or symbolic designs.

Engraver's proofs. Proofs of engravings used for verifying the quality of the work and for dummying up in pages.

Engraving. 1. The art or process of making letters or designs on wood, metal or other substances, by cutting or etching, for the purpose of printing or stamping by an Intaglio or Recess process on paper or other material. 2. An engraved plate, or an impression made from an engraved plate. 3. An engraved inscription. 4. The act of taking an impression from an engraved plate. *See also* Aquatint, Etching, Line engraving, Mezzotint, Wood engraving.

Enhanced CD. *See* CD Extra.

ENISA. *See* European Network and Information Security Agency.

Enlarged edition. *See* Revised edition.

Enlargement. A copy, usually of a photograph or microphotograph, having a larger scale than the original. Also called 'Blowup', 'Projection print'.

Enosis Hellenicon Bibliothekarion. (Skouleniou 4, 10561 Athens, Greece) The principal Greek library association; all types of library services are included.

Enright Report. The report *Selection for Survival: a Review of Acquisition and Retention Policies* (British Library, 1989) by B. Enright *et al.* The report was an internal review of British Library policies, and concluded that the BL could no longer be a universal library: many issues such as preservation and access needed thorough examination.

Enrolled account.   An account which has been entered on a roll, usually for audit.

Enrolment.   Entry of a document upon a roll.

ENSSIB.   *See* Ecole Nationale Supérieure des Sciences de l'Information et des Bibliothèques.

Enterprise Content Management (ECM).   An umbrella term that embraces Content management, Document management, Web content management, Records management, Digital asset management, Digital rights management.

Entropy.   The unavailable information in a group of documents. The degree of disorganization in an informational assemblage.

Entry.   1. The record of a book publication, or other item in a catalogue or other library record. In a catalogue it may be the main entry or an entry under subject, or an Added entry or an Index entry. It may give a description of the item and also the location.   2. Sometimes used to indicate the cataloguing process which is concerned with determining the headings to be used for the Body of the entry or that part of the description of an item which follows a heading.   3. (*a*) A unit of an index consisting of a heading (and qualifying expression, if any) with at least one reference to the location of the item in the text or with a 'See' cross-reference. (*b*) In a complex entry, when references are numerous enough for systematic grouping sub-headings are used to introduce sub-entries, each with the relevant reference(s).   4. An item in an index to a literary composition (MS., book, periodical, etc.) which refers to a single specific place in the text, and possibly indicates the nature of the material to be found there.   5. The physical form of record on which entries are made; in information retrieval sometimes called a Tally.   6. (*Classification*) In schedules and tables, a self-contained unit of the text consisting of a number or span of numbers, a heading, and often one or more notes. *See also* Added entry, Analytical entry, General secondary, Heading, Main entry, Reference, Series entry, Title entry.

Entry word.   1. The first word, other than an article, of a heading in a catalogue; the one by which the entry is arranged. *See also* Heading. 2. The word determining the place of an entry or group of related entries in the catalogue.

Enumerative bibliography.   A list of items compiled within limits set by the compiler; these may be geographical, chronological or topical.

Enumerative classification.   A classification which attempts to list all specific subjects and provide ready-made class numbers. Owing to the difficulty of enumerating all possible specific subjects, most of such classifications are necessarily selective. The Library of Congress Classification is of this kind.

Enumerative indexing language.   Subject terms used as headings for both single and composite concepts and providing a closed system (i.e. a list of terms allowing of no insertions) which the classifier could use. *See also* Synthetic indexing language.

EPC. Educational Publishers Council. *See* Publishers Association.

EPF. Electronic Publishers Forum. *See* Publishers Association.

Ephemera. 1. Pamphlets, cuttings and other material, of ephemeral interest and value. 2. Such material of earlier periods which has acquired literary or historical importance.

Ephemera Society. <www.ephemera-society.org.uk> A UK association devoted to the preservation of ephemera, particularly the organization of collections of ephemera in museums and libraries. Awards the *Samuel Pepys Medal* for outstanding contributions to ephemera studies.

Ephemeris. (*Pl.* Ephemerides) 1. An almanac or calendar. 2. An obsolete term for a diary. 3. A title-word of many seventeenth and eighteenth century periodicals. 4. An astronomical almanac giving the daily positions of stars and other heavenly bodies.

Epigraph. A quotation in the preliminary pages or at the commencement of the chapter of a book to indicate the sentiment or idea.

Epistemology. The science of organized ideas in their exact correspondence with outward things, or knowledge.

Epistolaria. A liturgical book containing the Epistles.

Epithalamium. A poem or song in honour of a wedding, or of a bride and bridegroom.

Epithet. A descriptive, significant name; an additional name or title expressing an attribute of the person referred to, and used to distinguish from others of the same name. In catalogue entries, the epithet follows the personal name under which the entry is made.

Epitome. A work that has been abridged or summarized from some larger work for a particular purpose, the essential matter of the original being retained. To be distinguished from an Adaptation.

EPOCH. <www.cordis.lu/ist/directorate_e/digicult/epoch.htm> Excellence in Processing Open Cultural Heritage, an EU FP6 project being progressed by 86 European cultural institutions interested in integrating the currently fragmented efforts in research and development of intelligent Information Society technologies towards sustainable cultural heritage applications.

Eponym. 1. One who gives, or is supposed to give, his name to a people, place or institution; also the name of that personage. 2. A distinguishing title formed from the name of a person to designate a period, people or place, e.g. Victorian era.

Epopee. An epic poem. Epic poetry.

Eprint archive. A Repository – of electronic pre-prints and/or post-prints – available both for authors to submit new materials and the academic community to locate up-to-the-minute scientific papers of interest. Can be international and subject-focused – e.g. ArXiv – or an institutional repository to make the reports of research from a single university openly available. *See also* Eprints (2).

Eprints. 1. The electronic Full texts of peer-reviewed journal articles, before and after refereeing. Before refereeing and publication, the draft is called a pre-print; the refereed, published final draft is called a post-print. Eprints can include both pre-prints and post-prints (as well as any significant drafts in between, and any post-publication updates). 2. <www.eprints.org> EPrints: Open Archives Initiative-compliant software developed at the University of Southampton, UK to enable the setting up of an Eprints repository, together with a web site dedicated to opening access to refereed research literature online through author Self archiving.

EPS. Encapsulated PostScript, a PostScript format for images recognizable by computer graphics Applications, Desktop publishing programs and Scanners.

e-Publishing. *See* Electronic publishing.

Equal opportunities policy. A recruitment and promotion procedure in an organization to ensure that there is no discrimination in dealings with staff or job applicants in respect of gender, colour, race, religion etc.

ERA. *See* Educational Recording Agency.

Erasable optical disc. *See* Optical disc.

ERCIM. <www.ercim.org> European Research Consortium for Informatics and Mathematics which aims to foster collaborative work within the European research community and to increase co-operation with European industry. Leading research institutes from eighteen European countries are members. Acts as the European host for W3C.

ERIC. <eric.ed.gov> Educational Resources Information Center, a national organization supported financially by the Office of Educational Research and Improvement of the US Department of Education. ERIC acquires, selects, catalogues, abstracts, and indexes educational research documents in the widest sense. In 2004 ERIC began a re-engineering plan of its services; when complete this will add free fulltext links to commercial sources.

ERMS. Electronic Rights Management Systems. *See* Electronic Copyright Management Systems.

Ermuli Trust. (Barbican Music Library, Barbican Centre, London EC2Y 8DS, UK) A trust fund that supports education and research in music libraries and music bibliography. Bursaries are also available for conference attendance.

EROMM. *See* European Register of Microform Masters.

Erotica. Literary or artistic works intended to stimulate sexual interests. *See also* Curiosa, Facetiae.

ERPANET. <www.erpanet.org> The Electronic Resources Preservation and Access Network is an EU funded clearinghouse and state-of-the-art knowledge base maintained by Glasgow University in the UK with partners in the Netherlands and Italy. Funding covered 2002–2004.

Errata. (*Sing.* Erratum) *See* Corrigenda.

E.S. Abbreviation for engine-sized. *See* Engine-sizing.

ESARBICA. Eastern and Southern Africa Regional Branch of the International Council on Archives.

Escapist literature. Light literature such as thrillers, adventure stories and romances which are read for entertainment, as a relief from more serious reading, and as a distraction.

e-Science. Large-scale science that will increasingly be carried out through distributed global collaborations enabled by the Internet. A feature of such collaborative enterprises is that they will require access to very large data collections, very large scale computing resources and high performance visualization back to individual users. A much more powerful infrastructure than the Web is needed to support e-Science for, besides information stored in Web pages, scientists will need easy access to expensive remote facilities, to computing resources – either as dedicated Teraflop computers or cheap collections of PCs – and to information stored in dedicated databases. For more information, see, for example, the National e-Science Centre <www.nesc.ac.uk>. In November 2000 funding for a new UK e-Science programme was announced, with allocations to programmes within each of the Research Councils: <www.rcuk.ac.uk/escience>. There have been calls for librarians to be involved in a curation role for the products of e-Science, e.g. Hey, Tony, Why engage in e-science. *Update* vol. 3, no. 3, 2004: pp. 25–27. *See also* Global Grid Forum, Globus, Grid, NCeSS.

ESD. *See* Electronic service delivery.

Esdaile (Arundell) Memorial Fund. A Fund opened in 1958 in memory of a former Secretary of the British Museum and a Past President of the (UK) Library Association, in order to endow a lecture to be given periodically as a memorial to the late Dr. Arundell Esdaile in commemoration of his unique services to librarianship and bibliography.

ESDS. <www.esds.ac.uk> The Economic and Social Data Service is a UK national project launched in 2003 and operated by MIMAS and the UK Data Archive at the University of Essex.. The service includes national and international data sets, and support materials for training.

e-Society. Another way of expressing the concept of the Information Society; in the UK this version has been recently favoured by the Museums, Libraries and Archives Council (MLA).

Esparto. A coarse grass, also termed 'Alfa', growing in countries around the Mediterranean, particularly southern Spain and northern Africa, which is used for making the better (but not the best) grades of book paper, featherweight and coating papers. The best grade is known as 'Spanish', the cheaper grades as 'Tripoli'. Esparto papers are distinguished by their refined silky texture and bulk, and their close uniform surface or finish. Their finish is their chief characteristic; this together with their bulkiness makes them eminently suitable for fine printings and other papers required to take a good impression from plates.

ESPRIT. <www.cordis.lu/esprit/home.html> (CEC, DG XIII-A, Rue de la Loi 200, B-1049 Brussels, Belgium) The European Strategic Programme of Research and Development in Information Technology. Began in pilot phase in 1983; the main programme 1984–89 aimed to improve Europe's IT capability, to reinforce technological co-operation and pave the way to internationally accepted standards. The programme ceased at the end of the fourth period of work (1994–1998).

ESRC Data Archive. *See* UK Data Archive.

Essay periodical. A periodical publication, prevalent in the fifteenth century, each issue of which usually consisted of a single essay. The *Spectator* and the *Rambler* are examples.

Essential characteristics. *See* Characteristic of a classification.

ESTC. <www.rlg.org/estc> The English Short Title Catalogue is a retrospective cataloguing project involving 1,500 libraries world-wide and the American Antiquarian Society; the British Library is a principal participant, and there is an editorial centre at the University of California at Riverside. ESTC is a comprehensive bibliography covering the output of the hand-press era, from the beginning of English printing in 1473 to 1800; coverage is of items printed in the British Isles or governed territories in any language, relevant items printed in Colonial America, the United States (1776–1800) and Canada in any language, and all relevant items printed wholly or partly in English or other British vernaculars in any other part of the world. For many years the abbreviation ESTC stood only for the *Eighteenth Century Short Title Catalogue*; this publication remains available. See <www.bl.uk/ collections/early/holdingsenglish> for details of the relationship.

Esther J. Piercy Award. *See* Piercy (Esther J) Award.

Estienne, Robert. Born 1503 and son of Henry Estienne who founded in 1501 the famous firm of Parisian scholar-printers. Founded his own business in 1524, and was appointed in 1539 and 1540 printer to the king in Latin, Greek and Hebrew. The fine press-work of his books matches the careful editing of the classical texts, dictionaries and translations. From 1550 until his death in 1559 he worked at Geneva, where he printed several of Calvin's works. The most important member of the greatest family of scholar-printers of all ages, his chief and most secure claim of many to immortality, is that based on his Thesaurus, *Dictionarius sive Latinae thesaurus,* Paris, 1531. He established the principle, contrary to his mediaeval predecessors, that a Latin dictionary must be based on classical authorities. He undertook the compilation of a series of Latin-French and French-Latin dictionaries which helped to create the classical French language: these were translated into German, Dutch and English, and were the progenitors of all bilingual dictionaries.

Estimates. Calculations of amounts of money needed to provide a service.

Estray. (*Archives*) The legal term applying to a document not in the custody of the original records creator or its legal successor. *See also* Replevin.

et al. Abbreviation for *et alii* (Lat. 'and other people'). Used in footnotes in a second or subsequent reference to a work. It follows the name of the first of three or more collaborators whose work has previously been cited. Also for *et alia* 'and other things', *et alibi* 'and elsewhere'.

et infra. (Lat. 'and below') Used to indicate that something which follows may be of smaller size, as '24 vols., 8vo. *et infra*', meaning that the largest is 8vo. *See also infra.*

et seq. Abbreviation for *et sequens* (Lat. 'and the following one'). *Pl. et seqq.* abbreviation for *et sequentes, et sequentia* 'and those that follow'. *See also seq.*

etc. Abbreviation for *et cetera* (Lat. 'and the other, the rest'). Also abbreviated '&c'.

Etching. 1. The process of producing a design upon a plate of steel, copper or zinc by means of drawing lines with an etching needle through an acid-resisting wax coating upon the polished surface of the plate, and then submerging the plate in an acid which corrodes the metal in the lines thus laid bare. (A different method is used for glass etching.) 2. A plate with an etched design upon its surface. 3. The art of producing impressions on paper or other material from an etched plate. 4. The impression produced by 3. *See also* Deep etching, Drypoint etching, Intaglio, Intaglio printing.

ETD. Electronic Thesis or Dissertation, the digital version of a thesis or dissertation whose initiation is generally credited to Virginia Polytechnic Institute (Virginia Tech) who started creating ETDs in 1994. *See also* NDLTD, Theses alive!.

eTEN. <europa.eu.int/information_society/programme/eten> <www.ten-telecom.org> Formed in 1997, the European Telecommunications Network is an initiative of the EU, active in encouraging further development of electronic service delivery in e-government, public services, healthcare, the information society, learning and business. One of its action lines concerns access to Europe's cultural heritage, including communication projects arising from co-operation between libraries, museums and archives.

Ethernet. A local-area network protocol developed by Xerox Corporation in co-operation with DEC and Intel in 1976. The Ethernet specification served as the basis for the IEEE 802.3 standard, which specifies the physical and lower software layers; the original data transfer rate was 10 Mbps. It is one of the most widely implemented LAN standards and network nodes are connected by Coaxial cable – in 'thick' or 'thin' varieties – or Twisted pair wiring. A later version, called 100Base-T (or Fast Ethernet), supports data transfer rates of 100 Mbps while the newest version, Gigabit Ethernet introduced in 1998, supports data rates of 1 Gbps (1,000 Mbps).

Ethics. *See* Professional Ethics, Code of.

Ethnic numbers. Numbers added to a classification symbol so as to arrange books by language or race. They are usually applicable throughout a classification scheme. Also called 'Linguistic numbers'.

Ethniki Vivliotiki tis Ellados. <forum-kithara.gr/yabbse/index> (Odos El Benizelou 32, 10679 Athens, Greece) The Greek National Library, founded in 1828.

Ethnomusicology. The study of the native music of a people or of a race.

ETOCs. Electronic table of contents. The provision, for network access, of the contents of a wide range of journal titles immediately on publication. Keyword searching by subject or journal title might be provided enabling current awareness to be carried out by library staff or End users. *See also* TOCS, Zetoc.

Etruscan alphabet. The most significant offshoot from the Greek alphabet and adapted to the language of the Etruscans. It developed, probably in the eighth century B.C. and lasted until the first century A.D. The Latin alphabet was derived from it.

Etruscan style. A calfskin binding style, so called becuse of the contrasting colours or shades of leather (light brown or terracotta) and decoration (dark brown or black tooling); the terracotta shades and decoration combined represent Greek and Etruscan vases. Such bindings usually have a rectangular central panel on each cover, or occasionally a plain oval with a classical urn in the middle and are tooled in black, surrounded by a border of Greek palmated leaves in black, with outer borders of classical design (Grecian key or Doric entablature) tooled in gold. The spines also are decorated with classical ornaments. This style was used by and probably originated by William Edwards of Halifax towards the end of the eighteenth century, and was practised until about 1820.

EU. *See* European Union.

EUCIP. <www.bcs.org/eucip> European Certification for Informatics Professionals; the IT equivalent of the European Computer Driving Licence (ECDL). In 2003 the British Computer Society and CEPIS began to set up a network of accredited training providers and testing centres.

EUCLID. <www.jbi.hio.no/bibin/euclid> Acronym for the 'European Conference of Library and Information Science Deans, Directors and Deputies', to which is appended the sub-title 'European Association for Library and Information Education and Research'. EUCLID is an independent, non-profit organization whose purposes are to promote European co-operation within library and information education and research, and to provide a body through which it can be represented in matters of European interest. *See also* BOBCATSSS.

EUDISED. European Documentation and Information System for Education, a programme of the Council of Europe. It has been in existence since 1970, and has produced a number of reports and technical studies.

EUMEDCONNECT. <www.dante.net/server/show/conWebDoc.155> A DANTE project to develop an IP research network infrastructure within the Mediterranean region, and link this to the pan-European GÉANT network. The infrastructure will provide an international backbone dedicated to research and other non-commercial purposes.

EURASICA. The Eurasian branch of the International Council on Archives.

EURASLIC. *See* European Association of Aquatic Sciences Libraries and Information Centres.

EURBICA. The European Branch of the International Council on Archives.

Euro Info Centres (EICs). *See* European Information Centres.

EUROGUIDE. <www.euroguide.org> A subject gateway to Web sites containing information about the European Union developed by Essex County Libraries with input from members of the EARL European Task Group; access is via 60 subject categories and a search engine.

EuroISPA. <www.euroispa.org> European Internet Services Providers' Association, the largest association of ISPs in the world comprising ten members and one associate member. The organization is assisted by a secretariat in Brussels. The EuroISPA Council meets at least four times each year to discuss policy, matters of importance to the EU Internet industry and the administration of the organization. *See also* Internet Service Providers' Association.

Europa. <europa.eu.int> Official portal for news, policies, and institutions of the European Union; contributing bodies include the European Parliament, the Council, the Commission, the Court of Justice, the Court of Auditors. The Web site functions in the Union's eleven official languages.

European Association for Grey Literature Exploitation. <www.cas.org/online/DBS/sigle> <stneasy.fiz-karlsruhe.de> EAGLE is the co-ordinating body responsible for SIGLE (System for Information on Grey Literature in Europe). Members are generally leading information and document supply centres in each country.

European Association for Health Information and Libraries (EAHIL). <www.eahil.org> Formed in 1986 and now having 400 members from 25 countries, EAHIL represents information professionals in medical libraries, health services, hospitals and the pharmaceutical industry.

European Association for Library and Information Education and Research. *See* EUCLID.

European Association of Aquatic Sciences Libraries and Information Centres (EURASLIC). <www.euraslic.org> A network linking marine and freshwater sciences libraries, information centres and documentation centres in 28 countries. Formed in 1988, EURASLIC runs conferences, publishes a newsletter and a directory of member libraries.

European Association of Research Libraries. *See* LIBER.

European Association of Scientific Information Dissemination Centres. *See* EUSIDIC.

European Bureau of Library, Information and Documentation Associations. *See* EBLIDA.

European Business Schools Librarians Group (EBSLG). <www.ebslg.org> EBSLG is a pan-European forum for discussion and exchange of ideas and information, and hopes to promote a network of co-operation and assistance throughout European business schools' libraries.

European Commission. *See* European Union.

European Commission Host Organization. *See* ECHO.

European Commission on Preservation and Access (ECPA). <www. knaw.nl/ecpa> (PO Box 19121, 100GC, Amsterdam, Netherlands) Established in 1994 with the aim of raising public awareness about the problems of preserving books and documents so that they remain accessible. There are five constituencies: universities, academies and learned societies, libraries, archives, and publishers. Activities include consultation and co-ordination, exchange of views, training, research and development, information dissemination to specialists and to the wider public.

European Community. *See* European Union.

European Computer Driving Licence (ECDL). Launched in 1997 by CEPIS and adopted by the EU, ECDL is a general purpose qualification framework to demonstrate computer literacy. The qualification – operated by the non-profit ECDL Foundation – is now very widely recognized and an international version is also marketed (as International CDL); a US franchise was awarded in 2001.

European Conference of Library and Information Science Deans, Directors and Deputies. *See* EUCLID.

European Council of Information Associations (ECIA). <www.aslib. co.uk/ecia> Formed in 1994 and with secretariat services provided by Aslib, ECIA is a successor to WERTID – the Western European Round Table for Information and Documentation – and represents the interests of its members (national associations and federations) to international governmental bodies, particularly the Commission of the European Union.

European Data Protection Directive. <europa.eu.int/comm/dg15/ en/media/dataprot/index.htm> Guidelines on the electronic collection of personal details and the way in which they can be used; promulgated as Document 95/46/EC, the Directive was introduced in November 1998 and sets out guidelines which are stricter and tighter than those previously applied, and more comprehensive than current US legislation. *See also* Data protection.

European Documentation Centres (EDC). Depository libraries entitled to receive a full range of European Union publications. Forty-five UK sites are so designated. An Association of EDC Librarians was formed in 1981. *See also* European Information Association.

European Electronic Messaging Association. *See* EEMA.

European Information Association (EIA). <www.eia.org.uk> (Manchester Central Library, St. Peter's Square, Manchester M2 5PD, UK) Formed in 1991 as successor to the Association of European Documentation Centre Librarians, EIA's main purpose is to improve access to EU information and documents by focusing on the development and co-ordination of their provision. It also acts as a lobbying body, and is a forum for the exchange of experience, the development of expertise, and the dissemination of information at a regional, national and international level. EIA makes awards to recognize contributions to promoting access to European information; the EIA/Chadwyck-Healey Achievement in European Information Award was launched in 1997, and the Helen Greer Memorial Prize is presented annually to a European Documentation Centre librarian. EIA has also instituted a series of awards for European information sources.

European Information Centres (EICs). <www.euro-info.org.uk> A network of EU-sponsored centres in all member countries, intended to provide Small and Medium-sized Enterprises (SMEs) with advice and information on legislation, finance, research, etc. EICs frequently work in partnership with other support organizations. There are 300 EICs across Europe, of which 24 are in the UK.

European Information Researchers Network. *See* EIRENE.

European Library. <www.europeanlibrary.org> Scheduled for launch at the end of 2004, the Library is a collaborative venture of 42 European National Libraries under the auspices of CENL. Mainly funded by the EU, the Library is developing open standards, methods and practices, interoperability, metadata, and business models. There will be a single access point to a range of holdings in all partner libraries. The acronym TEL is preferred ('The European Library'). The British Library is the co-ordinating partner <www.bl.uk/about/coop/tel>.

European Network and Information Security Agency (ENISA). The Agency was agreed in principle in 2003 by the EU Telecommunications Council and the European Parliament; a launch date in 2004 was scheduled. The Agency will be based in Brussels and will act as an advisory body to member states on information exchange and security issues.

European Parliament. *See* European Union.

European Register of Microform Masters (EROMM). A European Community initiative to facilitate the preservation of rare books in European libraries. Initial work began in 1989 with much support from LIBER; currently thirty major European libraries are adding records. EROMM contains records of any microfilmed item originally printed on paper from the invention of printing, but it is strongest in ninteenth- and twentieth-century material. *See also* Dieper.

European Union (EU). <europa.eu.int> (European Commission, 200 rue de la Loi, B-1049 Brussels, Belgium) The union of European countries that has grown out of the European Coal and Steel Community (founded 1951), the European Atomic Energy Community and the European Economic Community (both founded 1957). The first countries in the Community were Belgium, France, Germany, Italy, Luxembourg and the Netherlands; in 1973 they were joined by the UK, Ireland and Denmark; in 1981 by Greece; in 1986 by Spain and Portugal. In 1990 the former East German territory was added. The Treaty of Maastricht (1993) extended the range and depth of activities and changed the title from European Community to European Union. In 1995 Austria, Finland and Sweden joined. A further ten countries joined in 2004 – Czech Republic, Estonia, Latvia, Lithuania, Hungary, Poland, Slovenia, Slovakia, Cyprus and Malta. Bulgaria and Romania are scheduled to join in 2007, and in the longer term Croatia and Turkey. The principal institutions are the European Parliament (626 members elected every five years by direct, universal suffrage), the European Commission (the executive arm), the Council of the EU (formerly the Council of Ministers), the Court of Justice, the Court of Auditors, the European Central Bank, the European Investment Bank, the Economic and Social Committee, and the Committee of the Regions. The EU highlights the Information Society concept, and is heavily involved in research activity through its Sixth Framework Programme (FP6). The European Commission is represented in every member state – the UK representation is at <www.cec.org.uk>.

Eurostat. The Statistical Office of the European Union is located in Luxembourg. Its task is to collect and process statistical data on the EU Member States and their main trading partners to serve as a basis for the policy decisions that have to be taken.

Eurotra. An automatic translation system, designed to work between several languages, using a central pivot language. The system is under development by the EU and is intended to facilitate rapid publication of official papers in all necessary languages.

EUSIDIC. <www.eusidic.org> Originally an acronym for European Scientific Information Dissemination Centres, founded 1970, but now used as a name in its own right. Currently the largest association in the European electronic information sector with members active in production, distribution, and use of information services. Acts as a forum for discussion, advice, exchange of experience, and opinion. Holds two major conferences each year.

Evaluation. The process of measuring the effectiveness of an organization in meeting its aims and objectives; would normally include judgements on the overall success of the organization in a wider context.

Evaluative abstract. *See* Abstract.

Eve style. *See* Fanfare style.

Even page. A page of a book bearing an even number; usually the Verso.

Even right-hand margin. Said of matter where the lines have been justified and all have the same length, thus giving an even right-hand margin as well as the usual even left-hand margin.

Even small caps. An instruction to the compositor that all the copy so marked is to be set in small capitals without any large capitals as would be done in 'caps and smalls'. Abbreviated even s. caps, or even s.c. Also called 'Level small caps'.

Even working. The setting of Copy so that it will occupy a full sheet of, say, 32 pages. If an additional portion of a sheet is required for completion, this is called 'uneven working'. *See also* Oddments.

Evidence-based Management in Action. <www.lboro.ac.uk/departments/dis/lisu> An initiative of LISU and Lancashire County Library and Information Service in the UK to improve data quality and collection for library and information services. Funded by Resource (now Museums, Libraries and Archives Council (MLA)) 2003–2005.

Evidence-based practice (EBP). The (UK) Department of Culture, Media and Sport (DCMS) in its Strategy for Research 2003–2006 recommends the use of evidence-based procedures to justify spending on areas where conventional measures of performance are difficult to administer. The gathering of non-traditional statistics and measures is held to be illuminating in non-technical or non-scientific areas. Reflecting on and reviewing professional practice by examining previous research, and seeking more evidence to answer questions, will lead to the formulation of the most creative answers and solutions. *See also* Metrics.

Evolutionary order. (*Classification*) The method by which subjects are shown in the order of their history or development, 'in natural history putting the parts of each subject in the order which that theory assigns to their appearance in creation. As science proceeds from the molecular to the molar, from number and space through matter and force to matter and life, etc., etc.' (*Cutter*). Cutter's Expansive Classification follows this order, as also in a rough way does Brown's Subject Classification. No scheme is, or can be, evolutionary throughout.

ex libris. 1. Latin phrase, meaning *from the books* (i.e. from the library of); frequently used on book plates, the owner's name being written or printed after 'ex libris'. 2. Surplus books from a subscription or other library.

Exact classification. *See* Close classification.

Exact size. The measured size of a book expressed by centimetres or inches rather than by a signature symbol. Also called 'Absolute size'.

Excerpt. A verbatim extract from a book, or piece of music, whether printed or manuscript. An extract or selection.

Exchange. 1. The exchange by barter or trade of duplicate material with other libraries. 2. An arrangement whereby an organization exchanges its publications for those of another organization.

Exchange for Learning. *See* X4L.

Exchequer series. *See* Liberate roll.

Exhausted edition. An edition which has become out-of-print.

Exhaustive division. Dividing as exhaustively and minutely as possible in order to give specific places in a scheme of classification.

Exit counter. 1. The side of an issue desk at which readers leave a library and have books issued or 'charged' to them. 2. A sensor, frequently part of a Book detection system, that records the number of users exiting the library.

Ex-library copy. A catalogue description of a book originally in a library.

Exotics. A general name used in the printing industry for Cyrillic, Arabic and other non-Latin letter-forms.

Expansion. (*Classification*) The development of a concept or series of concepts in the schedules or tables to provide for more minute subdivision.

Expansion board/card. An integrated circuit card which can be added to a PC to provide improved performance or connectivity.

Expansive Classification. The scheme of classification devised by C. A. Cutter (1837–1903), which began to appear in 1891; it is one of the most minute and scholarly of schemes for a general library, but it is now out-of-date. It consists of seven expansions (the seventh, uncompleted, being very detailed and suitable for a very large library) each of which covers the whole field of knowledge but in varying detail, and can be used according to the size of the library. Later expansions cannot be used in the same library, however, without re-classifying a number of the books, as the fundamental symbols had to be altered as the expansions progressed. The order of the schedules is evolutionary, the main classes being given below:

A	General works	N	Botany
B	Philosophy	O	Zoology
BR	Religion	Q	Medicine
C	Christian and Jewish Religions	R	Useful arts (technology)
D	Ecclesiastical history	S	Engineering; Building
E	Biography	T	Manufactures; Handicrafts
F	History	U	Defensive/preservative arts
G	Geography and travels	V	Recreative arts; Sports
H	Social sciences	VV	Music
I	Sociology	W	Fine arts
J	Government; Politics	X	Language
K	Legislation; Woman; Societies	Y	Literature
L	Sciences	Z	Book arts
M	Natural history		

The intervening letters in the above schedule are given to the more important divisions. The notation is a pure alphabetical one, permitting sub-division at any point in the scheme by the use of the alphabet, but form divisions and the Local List for sub-dividing geographically have numerical notations which can be used mnemonically.

Expert system. An Application program that uses Artificial intelligence techniques and thereby in part replicates human decision-making when applied to a particular field of endeavour. Expert systems rely on a knowledge base – including specific facts and rules – from the subject in hand and are sometimes known as 'knowledge-based systems'.

Explain. A feature introduced in Version 3 of the Z39.50 standard that allows a Client to discover information about a server such as available databases, supported Attribute sets and record syntaxes.

Explicit. The closing phrase of a manuscript or early printed book indicating its completion and sometimes giving the author's name and the title of the work. It is the author's or scribe's Colophon taken over from the manuscript, and may appear instead of, or in conjunction with, the printer's colophon. It is a contraction for *explicitus est* 'it is unfolded'.

Expressive notation. One of Ranganathan's canons of notation – that the notation should be designed to show that two terms are in the same array, or the same chain.

Expurgated edition. An edition with those parts left out that might be objected to on moral or other grounds. *See also* Abridged edition, Bowdlerized, Unexpurgated edition.

Extended copyright. When copyright protection was extended from 50 to 70 years after the creator's death, many works acquired a longer period of protection than had been the case when the creator died. This longer period is called extended copyright.

Extended score. *See* Open score, Score.

Extender. That part of a type letter which projects above or below the main body of the letter. Also called 'Extruder'. *See also* Ascender, Descender.

Extensible HyperText Markup Language. *See* XHTML.

Extensible Markup Language. *See* XML.

Extension. (*Classification*) The extension of a term or class indicates all the different items included in the term; in other words, the compass of the term. The intension indicates their *qualities*. Extension and intension vary conversely; when one is great the other is small

Extension work. Activities which are undertaken with the object of reaching groups of people who might otherwise be unaware of the library, such as lecture societies, reading circles, discussion groups; and the provision of books for prisons, clubs, hospitals, literary societies, etc. *See also* Outreach.

Extent. (*Publishing*) The length of a book expressed in terms of the number of pages.

External bibliography. *See* Historical bibliography.

External costs. *See* Costs.

External reader. A person who is permitted to use a library provided primarily for the use of a defined community, such as a professional body, an association or an institution of higher education.

Extra binder. A craftsman who uses the best materials and employs the soundest methods of construction; he or she usually decorates each binding with a design specially made for it.

Extra binding. In binding, a trade term for the best work. Applicable to any book well 'forwarded', lined with marbled or other special paper, silk head-bands, and gilt with a narrow roll round the sides and inside the 'squares'.

Extra lightweight paper. Sensitized photographic paper between 0.0023 and 0.0031 inches inclusive. Also called 'Ultra thin paper'.

Extra thin paper. Sensitized photographic paper between 0.0032 and 0.0037 inches inclusive. *See also* Photographic papers.

Extract type. Type which is different from that used for the text, normally being smaller, and used to enable quoted (or extracted) material such as poems, bibliographies, extracts, etc., to be easily distinguished from the text itself.

Extracted article. *See* Separate.

Extra-illustrated. A book which has had additional illustrations and printed matter inserted since publication. *See also* Grangerizing.

Extranet. An Intranet that has been extended to allow some access to external users; in a commercial organization, for example, customers or suppliers would have access to certain areas, but sensitive data would be protected to ensure security.

Extrapolation. (*Classification*) The addition of new subjects to the end of an Array. This flexible aspect of notation is facilitated by the Octave device. *See also* Interpolation.

Extruder. *See* Extender.

Exxon Awards Preservation Grant. An award of $1.5 million given to the Council on Library Resources, Inc. to establish long-term research projects to preserve the holdings of American research libraries. CLR received the award early in 1985 and formed a Preservation Committee to co-ordinate the work.

f. Abbreviation for 'following'. *Pl.* ff.

F4F. *See* Framework for the Future.

Fabriano paper. An Italian paper used for special and fine editions.

Fabric binding. One in which a fabric has been used instead of leather and vellum. Velvet, silk, satin, and canvas have been the most popular materials, and have been used more frequently in England than elsewhere. Velvet, a most extensively used fabric, was plain, embroidered, or even gilt-tooled. Embroidered bindings, in a form of split-stitch work known as *opus anglicanum* on satin, were popular in the fifteenth century.

fac. Abbreviation for Facsimile and Factotum.

Face. 1. The entire unbroken front of shelving on one side of a double case or on one side of a room or gallery. 2. (*Printing*) The printing surface of type. It comprises Stem, Bowl, Serif, Counter, Crotch and Kern. Measured set-wise, i.e. left to right, a face may be condensed (compressed) or extended (expanded); measured body-wise, it may be small, ordinary, medium or large, according to the actual size of the short and long letters. Also, the printing surface of any kind of printing plate. 3. (*Printing*) A particular design or style of a font of type. *See also* Typeface.

Face up. (*Printing*) Said of full-page illustrations which are printed on the right-hand side of an opening, i.e. on the recto of a leaf.

Facet. In classification, the whole group of divisions or foci (*see* Focus (*Noun*)), produced when a subject is divided according to a single characteristic. Each division of a facet is said to be an Isolate focus, or simply an Isolate. Sometimes used to denote any single Isolate or any basic class. Also called divisions of a 'Category'. *See also* Characteristic of a classification, Subordination. 2. An aspect, or orientation, of a topic.

Facet analysis. (*Classification*) The analysis of any subject into Categories and Facets for synthesis of class numbers. The process of subject analysis of a document. *See also* Facet, Fundamental categories.

Facet formula. (*Classification*) A formula for the application of division; used so that the order of applying characteristics may be consistently maintained. *See also* Citation order.

Facet indicator. A symbol which separates parts of a notation of a scheme of classification and indicates exactly what facet is to follow. Facet indicators were made possible in the Colon Classification by adopting the five Fundamental categories, each of which is introduced by its own symbol. It may be a different kind of character in a mixed notation, e.g. a letter or a punctuation mark whereas other characters in the notation are figures, in which case every letter would indicate a facet. Also known as Indicator digit. *See also* Notation.

Faceted classification. 1. A scheme of classification which reflects in its structure the analysis of subjects according to a number of fundamental concepts, particularly those denominated say: Personality, Matter, Energy, Space, Time. It lists constituent parts of specific subjects to be assembled in a predetermined order to express the specific subjects. Almost all modern schemes of classification are faceted to a certain degree: e.g. they provide tables of constant numbers for divisions relating to time and to space and other recurring concepts. A classification scheme which allows the classifier to build up the notation for a particular book from various unit schedules is called a 'faceted', 'synthetic' or 'analytico-synthetic' classification. 2. Classification schemes whose terms are grouped by conceptual categories and ordered so as to display their generic relations. These categories or 'facets' are standard unit-schedules and the terms, or rather the notation for the terms from these various unit-schedules, are combined at will in accordance with a prescribed order of combination.

Faceted initial. In a mediaeval illuminated manuscript, an initial letter given the appearance of being faceted, that is cut like a gem.

Faceted notation. (*Classification*) A Notation representing the classification in which distinctive symbols are used to separate the facets which comprise it.

Facetiae. Coarsely witty books; objectionable or indecent works collectively. *See also* Curiosa, Erotica.

Facing pages. The two pages which are visible when a book is open. An Opening.

facsim. Abbreviation for Facsimile. Also abbreviated 'fs.', 'fac.'.

Facsimile. 1. A copy of an original, reproduced in its exact form and style. 2. Used in cataloguing to indicate that the book catalogued contains a facsimile. Abbreviated 'facsim.', 'facsims.' (*pl.*) and sometimes 'fs.', 'fac.'. 3. An electronic system for transmitting pictures and graphic materials. *See* Facsimile transmission.

Facsimile binding. A binding which closely resembles an older binding.

Facsimile catalogue. One which incorporates facsimiles of maps, pictures, designs, etc., as part of each catalogue entry which is made on larger cards than the normal size, or in loose leaf binders.

Facsimile edition. An exact copy of a book made photographically, by xerography, or by an offset process. Used to avoid the cost of setting up type in order to produce a new edition of an out-of-print book. Previously, a copy, as near the original as possible typographically, published to make widely available a book which existed only as an incunabulum or as a manuscript.

Facsimile reprint. A reproduction of a work, however printed, and reproducing exactly the appearance of the original.

Facsimile transmission. A process whereby a representation of a document in its entirety can be transmitted over a telecommunications link. Expansion cards enable facsimile transmission to be carried out directly from a PC. The abbreviation fax is commonly used.

Factotum (fac). An ornament of wood or metal having a space in the centre for the insertion of a capital letter of an ordinary font of type; used to print ornamental initial letters at the commencement of a chapter. It is sometimes called a 'Factotum initial'.

Faculty library. *See* Departmental library.

Faculty of Advocates, Edinburgh. *See* National Library of Scotland.

FAFLRT. *See* Federal and Armed Forces Librarians Round Table.

FAIFE. *See* Freedom of Access to Information and Freedom of Expression.

FAIR. Focus on Access to Institutional Resources, a JISC programme which aimed to evaluate and explore mechanisms for the disclosure and sharing of content to fulfil the vision of a web of resources built by groups with a long term stake in the future of those resources, and made available to the whole community of learning. Specific objectives included the exploration of the Open Archives Initiative.

Fair calf. *See* Law calf.

Fair copy. A carefully made typescript or manuscript without mistakes or corrections, made after examining a draft.

Fair dealing. In UK copyright law, privileges given to individuals to copy or use copyright material within certain limits and for specified purposes without the need for a licence or permission from the copyright owner. In the US a similar facility exists, and is termed 'Fair use'.

Fair use. *See* Fair dealing.

Fall-out ratio. (*Information retrieval*) In the testing of an information retrieval system, a measure expressing the ratio of the number of non-relevant documents retrieved to the total number of non-relevant documents in the file.

False bands. *See* Dummy bands.

False combinations.   (*Information retrieval*) Noise which is produced by simple correlation of descriptors. Also called 'False sorts'.

False date.   A date given wrongly, either intentionally or in error. In a catalogue entry the correct date is given in brackets following 'i.e.'.

False drop.   (*Information retrieval*) 1. Citation that does not pertain to the subject sought.   2. An irrelevant reference made in indexing documents for concept co-ordinate indexing. Also called 'False co-ordination'. *See also* Uniterm concept co-ordination indexing.

'False first' edition.   An edition of a book said to be the first when in fact there had been an edition published previously by another publisher.

False hyphen.   One placed by the printer between two parts of a word which is broken at the line end. In Desktop publishing, known as 'discretionary hyphen' or 'soft hyphen'.

False imprint.   *See* Fictitious imprint.

False link.   (*Classification*) In chain indexing, a step in the notational hierarchy where the notational chain is lengthened by a symbol without an appropriate term being supplied. In the Dewey Decimal Classification, for example, where a zero is needed to introduce a standard sub-division or geographical table number, the zero having no verbal equivalent, but being merely an indicator that a form or geographical division is about to be employed. *See also* Unsought link.

Falstaff.   A fat face type. *See* Fat faces.

Family.   The complete group or collection of all the sizes and styles of type of the same design: they have common characteristics and differ only in size, set or thickness of lines.

Family name.   A surname.

Fan.   A book decoration style characteristic of Italian bindings in the seventeenth century, and of Scottish bindings, in which a design like a fan is tooled on the sides making a full circle in the centre, and often quarter circles in the corners. It is a development of the centre and Cornerpiece bindings.

Fancy type.   Printing type of various sizes, ornamental in design; usually used for display purposes.

Fanfare style.   The later Eve style of decorating bookcovers, being a complication of geometrical interlacings and a multitude of scrolls, wreaths, sprays and flowers, filling all available space on back and sides of the book. It was practised in the late sixteenth century. Also called 'Flourish style'.

Fanzines.   Uncommercial, non-professional, small-circulation magazines which deal with fantasy literature, popular crazes etc.

FAQs.   Frequently asked questions, those that are asked regularly, particularly by new users to a service, accompanied by detailed answers. Originated with Usenet groups and Mailing lists in an attempt to prevent the clogging up of discussion but now a feature on many Web sites giving explanations of services or background details.

Farjeon (Eleanor) Award.   *See* Children's Book Circle.

Farmington Plan. A scheme whereby over sixty American research libraries agreed co-operatively to purchase books published in foreign countries in order to ensure that at least one copy of new books and pamphlets likely to interest research workers was acquired by an American library. Such books were promptly listed in the Union Catalogue at the Library of Congress and made available by inter-library loan or photographic reproduction. The plan was drawn up at Farmington, Connecticut, by K. D. Metcalf, J. P. Boyd and Archibald Macleish, and began to operate in January 1948.

FARNET. <www.cni.org/docs/farnet> The Federation of American Research Networks was launched in 1993 to raise awareness of the possibilities of networking. It is now almost inactive.

Farradane (Jason) Award. An award offered by CILIP (formerly by the Institute of Information Scientists) to recognize outstanding work in the information field.

Fascicle. Parts of a work which for convenience of publishing or printing, is issued in small instalments. They are usually incomplete in themselves and do not necessarily coincide with the formal division of the work into parts. They usually consist of sections, or groups of plates, protected by temporary wrappers, and may or may not be numbered or designated as a 'part', 'fascicule', 'Lieferung', etc. Also called 'Fascicule', 'Fasciculus'.

Fast back. *See* Tight back.

Fat faces. Typefaces which have extra thick perpendicular strokes whether straight or curved, such as Elephant, Ultra Bodoni, and Falstaff.

Fat matter. Copy which can be set up in type easily since many lines of type will not be full. Novels which are largely dialogue are 'fat'. This is the opposite to difficult copy which is known as 'lean matter'. *See also* Matter.

Fathom.com. An important higher education e-project that operated 2000–2003. The experimental service involved Columbia University with several partners including the British Library, London School of Economics, University of Cambridge, New York Public Library and the Smithsonian Institution. The aim was to put authenticated knowledge onto the Internet for business and individual users in an online education market.

Faulty margin. An unequal margin due to imperfect registering.

Fawcett Library. *See now* Women's Library.

Fax. *See* Facsimile transmission.

Faxon (F. W.) Scholarship. An award to cover the cost of an internship for a student; administered by the American Library Association Office for Library Personnel Resources.

FCLIP. *See* CILIP.

FDDI. Fibre distributed data interface, a set of standards developed by ANSI in response to the growing need for high-speed, high bandwidth transmission over reasonable distances. FDDI bandwidth enables transmission speeds of 100 Mbps and is generally implemented in Backbone networks.

FDLP. The Federal Depository Library Program provides US government publications to a network of 1,400 geographically scattered libraries for comprehensive, no-fee, local access. Increasingly distribution is accomplished by electronic media.

Feather edge. *See* Deckle edge.

Feather ornament. (*Binding*) Engraved ornament which resembles feathers, on clasps or catches.

Feathering. 1. A fault in printing which results in a feathering effect visible when ink spreads beyond the printed impression via the fibres of the paper. It is caused by an excess of solvent in the ink, or an unsuitable paper. 2. Thinning down the overlapping edges of two pieces of paper which are to be joined when repairing a book.

Featherweight paper. Light, bulky, printing paper with 75 per cent air space; it is made largely from Esparto and has little or no calendering. It is slightly porous and not easy to handle. *See also* Antique.

Featherwork. A type of book decoration which originated in Irish eighteenth century bindings, in which curved lines formed freehand with a gouge radiate from one point to produce a delicate and very rich pattern resembling feathers.

Feature. A characteristic of a thing indexed. *See also* Characteristic of a classification, Compresence, Item, Term.

Feature card system. A method of information retrieval in which a card is reserved for a feature (variously called 'aspect', 'dimension', 'facet'), characteristic, or piece of information. Each card is printed with the same grid of punchable positions, which are numbered, and each of these corresponds to a particular document. *See also* Edge-notched cards, Marginal-hole punched cards.

Feature heading. The verbal part of a subject heading used in the systematic file of a Classified catalogue, i.e. that part which is a translation into words of the last element of a classification symbol. The verbal part usually follows the symbol, and may be utilized to specify subjects for which no exact notation is provided in the scheme of classification.

fecit. (Lat. 'he or she made (did) this') Frequently added after the artist's name on a drawing, engraving or sculpture. *See also del., sculpt.*

Federal and Armed Forces Libraries Round Table (FAFLRT). <www. ala.org/ala/faflrt> Established by the Council of ALA in 1972 as the Federal Librarians Round Table; promotes federal and armed forces services, better resources, and staff networking.

Federal Depository Library Program. *See* FDLP.

Federal Library and Information Center Committee (FLICC). <www. loc.gov/flicc> Founded in 1965 as the Federal Library Committee, a US body that co-ordinates activity and makes recommendations on and for the 2,500 libraries and information centres in the federal sector. *See also* FEDLINK.

Fédération Internationale des Archives de Télévision.   *See* FIAT/IFTA.

Fédération Internationale des Archives du Film.   *See* FIAF.

Fédération Internationale d'Information et de Documentation.   *See* International Federation for Information and Documentation.

Federation of Children's Book Groups.   Formed in the UK in 1968 the Federation exists to promote an awareness of children's literature, principally among parents, and to encourage the wider distribution and availability of a large range of books for children. It also acts as a channel for negotiations with publishers, libraries and any other official body concerned with children and books.

Federation of Local Authority Chief Librarians.   *See* Society of Chief Librarians (SCL).

FEDLINK.   <www.loc.gov/flicc/fedlink> US nationwide federal government network having members in each state, and libraries in Germany and Saudi Arabia. Formed in 1977, and operated by the Federal Library and Information Center Committee, Washington, DC. Affiliated with OCLC; there are over 800 members.

Fedora.   <www.fedora.info> Flexible Extensible Digital Object and Repository Architecture, a project funded by the Andrew W. Mellon Foundation to build an open-source digital object repository management system and to demonstrate how distributed digital library architecture can be deployed using web-based technologies. Jointly developed by the University of Virginia and Cornell University, the system can be used to support the creation of institutional repositories, and in areas of Content management, Digital Asset Management, scholarly publishing, and Digital preservation.

Feed board.   The platform on a printing machine on to which single sheets of paper are passed from the pile on the stock table and from which they are passed to the impression cylinder.

Feed guides.   One, or more, of several kinds of device for holding a sheet of paper in a uniformly straight position before it is taken, possibly by the grippers, to the place at which it will come into contact with the printing surface. On a cylinder press these are called 'Drop guides'.

Feedback.   The process of using the outcome of an operation as a monitoring tool of its efficiency; for example, user comments and suggestions on the success of a service could be assimilated by management and staff, and improvements or amendments incorporated as necessary. The process can also be used to refine the performance of a retrieval system by assessing the relevance of retrieved items and adjusting the search criteria to produce improved results.

Feeder.   The various pieces of automatic apparatus by means of which sheets of paper are fed to, and positioned on, printing presses and paper processing machines of various kinds.

Feet.   The base of a piece of movable type formed by the 'groove' or 'heel-nick' which runs set-wise across the bottom surface of the body. Type not standing squarely is said to be 'off its feet'.

Feet of fine. In law, the foot of a fine was that one of the parts of a tripartite indenture recording the particulars of a fine, which remained with the court, the other two being retained by the parties. When the undivided sheet was placed so that this counterfoil could be read, it was actually at the foot of the parchment.

Feint ruling. Term used to indicate the horizontal lines (rules), or cross-rules, printed on account-book paper or exercise books. *See also* Common ruling.

Fell types. Types cut by the Dutch typefounder Walpergen between 1667 and 1672 and introduced by Dr. John Fell to Oxford University Press during and after 1671 when this press was revived. Dr. Fell was Dean of Christ Church and later Bishop of Oxford. The beautiful Fell types which are used by the OUP for books requiring an Old Style type are still cast from the collection of type-punches and matrices made by Dr. Fell, having been re-discovered by the Rev. C. H. O. Daniel in 1877, and used by him on his private press at Worcester College. Dr. Fell was the second of the Press's great patrons, the first being Archbishop Laud. He took charge of printing and publishing on behalf of the University from 1672 until his death in 1686.

Fellowship. The highest professional qualification awarded by CILIP; various routes are available for attainment. The post-nominal letters FCLIP can be used.

Felt mark. An imprint left on paper by the felt of the papermaking machine due to the pressure of the felt on it.

Felt side. The side of a sheet or roll of paper which has not come in contact with the wire during manufacture; therefore the smooth side of a sheet instead of the Wire side. Also known as the 'Top side'.

Feminist Library. <feministlibrary@beeb.net> (5, Westminster Bridge Road, London SE1 7XW, UK) A resource and information centre run by volunteers, and containing the largest contemporary collection of feminist material in Britain. Established in 1975, the library has been in a difficult financial position since 1988 when grants ran out; currently it receives temporary support from Southwark Council.

Fere-Humanistica. *See* Black letter, Gothic type.

FESABID. <www.fesabid.org> Federación Española de Sociedades de Archivística, Biblioteconomía, Documentación y Museística/Spanish Federation of Archives, Libraries and Museums Societies (Joaquin Costa 22, 28002 Madrid, Spain) A forum for Spanish information professionals to meet and discuss common concerns and projects; encourages collaboration and international action. Member organizations (a full list is on the web site) include Andalucían Librarians Association, Asturian Librarians Association, Catalonia College of Librarians and Documentalists, Catalonia Society of Information and Documentation, Guipuzcoan Librarians Association, Librarians of the Balearic Islands, Spanish Scientific Information and Documentation Society.

Festoon drying. A method of drying paper in a drying chamber in which warm air is circulated. The paper is hung in loops over rods which travel slowly through the chamber.

Festschrift. A memorial or complimentary volume usually consisting of a number of contributions by distinguished persons, often students and colleagues of a person and issued in his or her honour. The subject matter of the various contributions is usually concerned with the subject in which the individual was distinguished. It may also honour an institution or society especially on the occasion of an anniversary. Also called 'Memorial volume'. *Pl.* Festschriften.

ff. Abbreviation for *folgende Seiten* (Ger. 'following pages'); for a proper name (e.g. ffolkes); for *fecerunt* (Lat. 'they made it'); for folios (e.g. 200ff., i.e. 200 leaves, not pages) and foliation.

FIAB. Fédération Internationale des Associations de Bibliothécaires. *See* entry under International Federation of Library Associations and Institutions.

FIAF. <www.fiafnet.org> (1, Rue Defacqz, B-1000 Brussels, Belgium) The Fédération Internationale des Archives du Film (FIAF) was founded in 1938 to promote the preservation of the film as art and historical document throughout the world and to bring together all organizations devoted to this end; to facilitate the collection and international exchange of films and documents related to cinematographic history and art for the purpose of making them as widely accessible as possible; to develop co-operation between its members; and to promote the development of cinema art and culture. The word 'film' in FIAF's name was later broadened to include all forms of the moving image, in concurrence with developments in the media. The founding members were the Department of Film of the Museum of Modern Art (New York), the National Film Archive (London), the Cinémathèque Française (Paris) and the Reichsfilmarchiv (Berlin). The first general assembly was held in 1939 in New York.

FIAT/IFTA. <www.fiatifta.org> The International Federation of Television Archives/Fédération Internationale des Archives de Télévision is a professional association established to provide a means for co-operation among television archives, multimedia and audiovisual archives and libraries concerned with the collection, preservation and exploitation of moving image and recorded sound materials and associated documentation. It was established in Rome in 1977, by ARD (Germany), BBC (UK), INA (France) and RAI (Italy). With 180 members from over 70 countries, FIAT/IFTA is presently the most important professional organization in the field of broadcasting archives. Its membership is drawn from public and commercial broadcasters, national audiovisual archives and technical companies catering to the broadcasting industry.

Fibre optics. Thin strands of glass or other transparent material manufactured into high capacity cables which carry information via light beams. They can be used over long distances as the signal degrades slowly, are ideal for high speed transmissions due to high Bandwidth, and they suffer no degradation as a result of electrically noisy environments.

Fibres. The plant cells, largely composed of cellulose, which are contained in the rag, grass, wood or other vegetable matter from which paper is made. The length and strength of these fibres, and the way in which they are interwoven, determine the quality and strength of the paper.

Fiche. A card. *See also* Microfiche.

Fiction. Prose novels and stories, of which the action and/or characters are the product of the writer's imagination.

Fiction reserve. *See* Joint Fiction Reserve.

Fictitious imprint. An imprint that is misleading with the object of evading legal or other restrictions, concealing the identity of the author, or concealing a piracy publication, etc. Also called 'False imprint'. Fictitious and imaginary imprints may be given in catalogue entries as given, or in the conventional form. When the real imprint is known, it is given in [ ] after the fictitious one.

FID. *See* International Federation for Information and Documentation.

Fidler (Kathleen) Award. An annual award administered by Book Trust Scotland for a children's novel by a new author.

Field. 1. (*Cataloguing*) Normally considered to mean an Element or a group of elements. Used in some systems, e.g. MARC, to mean a group of one or more subfields. *See also* Filing code. 2. (*Classification*) A group of things, or concepts, or their representations, having one or more characteristics in common. Sometimes used in contradiction to Class when class is defined as a group formed by consideration of characteristics used in drawing up a strictly conventional hierarchy, then 'field' is defined as a group formed in Array by consideration of secondary characteristics. In this sense, a field is a group formed by consideration of characteristics other than those used in drawing up a classification schedule. 3. A broad group of related subjects. 4. (*Information retrieval*) In machine-readable records, the position of a data element, or a set of data elements, regarded as a single descriptive element; it may be allocated a unique identification symbol in the record format. 5. A particular section of a computer record, e.g. in a bibliographic record, the author, or the publication date, of a document. Fields may be of fixed or of variable length.

Fielden Report. The report *Supporting expansion: a report on human resource management in academic libraries*, 1993. Prepared by the John Fielden Consultancy as a contribution to the Follett Report, the document proved controversial, particularly in its suggestion of an integrated grading system for all library staff which was supposed to 'remove the barriers to promotion and flexible movement'. There was also particular attention given to Learner support.

FIG. *See* Fire Information Group.

FIGARO. <www.figaro-europe.net> A European-based project focused on the creation of an effective and affordable communication and publishing environment for scholars. It consists of a network of partners who provide e-publishing services and support to the European academic community based on a common technical and organizational infrastructure. The project is the product of two earlier initiatives – Roquade and GAP – and the project name is an acronym for the Federated Initiative of GAP and Roquade.

Figure. 1. An illustration, map, chart, graph, etc., forming part of a page of text with which it is printed from a block imposed with the type, as distinct from a Plate. Figures are usually numbered consecutively by means of Arabic numerals. 2. A graphic symbol or character to represent a number. *See also* Marginal figure.

Figure initial. In a mediaeval illuminated manuscript, an initial letter which is made by representations of the bodies of human beings or animals.

Figured bass. On a music score, a line of bass notes with figures under or over them from which indications the player of a harpischord or organ could tell what chords the composer intended to be used, and could construct the accompaniment. This is known as realization. Also called 'Basso continuo', 'Thorough bass'.

Figures, Old style. *See* Hanging figures, Old style, Ranging figures.

FIL. *See* Forum for Interlending.

File. (*Noun*) 1. A collection of written, typed, printed or machine-readable material or information arranged in some systematic order. 2. A holder or cabinet designed to hold such material. 3. A homogeneous collection of a single type of file items. *See also* Biography file, Company file, Confidential file, Geographic filing method, Lateral filing, Legal file, Map file, Media file, Open back file, Organization file, Patent file, Suspension file, Transfer file, Vertical file. (*Verb*) To arrange written, typed or printed material in order. 4. (*Archives*). A level of archival arrangement and description. In ISAD(G) the file is the item, or unit of handling, of archive materials.

File item. The smallest element to be handled as a unit in a file.

File server. A computer on a Local area network providing file storage accessible to all registered users when using networked versions of Applications software and for providing some workspace and storage space. The file server manages the files on the network and organizes the requests for files as they are received.

File transfer. The action of connecting to a remote computer host, the identification of relevant files (e.g. electronic texts, programs, graphics files) and their subsequent Downloading to the local machine. Not to be confused with Remote login. *See also* ftp.

File transfer protocol. *See* ftp.

File-as-if. An instruction to file an entry consisting of, or beginning with, a symbol, an abbreviation, or a numeral, as if that which is represented by the filing element were spelled out in the letters of the alphabet.

Filigree.   Initials and borders decorated with fine lines around the edges.

Filigree letter.   An initial letter with a decorated or filigree outline or background.

Filing.   The action of arranging papers, non-book materials and other documents, and records of such, or other, items, into predetermined sequences; also the subsequent insertion of additional items in their correct places.

Filing code.   A code of rules for arranging entries in a catalogue, or other material in a file. Such codes may cover manual sorting, or may be intended for computer sorting. Alphabetization will be included, and the order of other data elements, for example punctuation symbols used in UDC. Terms used in filing codes may comprise the following: *Filing entry* – all of the fields that may be considered in determining the filing position of an item in a catalogue (e.g. an author heading, title and imprint date); *Field* – a major component of a filing entry that comprises one or more elements (e.g. a heading; a title); *Element* – one or more words that make up an integral part of a field (e.g. the surname in a personal name heading). An element and a field are identical when the field contains only one element (e.g. a title). The first element in a field is called the *leading element*, the others are called *subordinate elements*. For example, in a heading consisting of a surname, forename and birth and death dates, the surname is the leading element, the forename and the dates are subordinate elements; *Word* – one or more characters forming a meaningful group and separated from others by spaces and/or marks of significant punctuation; *Character* – a letter, digit, symbol, or mark of punctuation. *Significant punctuation* is a mark of punctuation that marks the end of an element.

Filing epithet.   An Epithet which is added to a personal name to assist in the filing sequence as well as to distinguish between persons whose names would otherwise be identical. A kind of Descriptor. *See* Honorific epithet.

Filing order.   The order (usually alphabetical, but also by classification notation, or some other appropriate sequence such as makers' catalogue number) for arranging books, documents, records, including catalogue entries. *See also* Simplified filing.

Filing rules.   Explicit directions, preferably based on a recognized code, and provided in written or printed form, for the filing of entries in catalogues. *See* Filing code.

Filing significance.   (*Cataloguing*) 1. An attribute of an element of data which makes it necessary to take account of the data when filing entries.   2. The sum of the attributes of one or more elements of data, which determines the position in a filing order of the entry or record which contains them.

Filing title.   1. The title under which are filed catalogue, or bibliography, entries for work known by a number of different titles.   2. The portion of a title which is longer than an essential part by which the book is well known, and under which the catalogue entry is filed, e.g. *David Copperfield*, the full title of which is *The personal history of David Copperfield*. Augmented headings and conventional titles in the entries for music scores are forms of filing title. *See also* Uniform title.

Fillet. 1. A plain line or lines impressed upon the back or side of a book-cover. A 'French fillet' is three gilt lines unevenly spaced. 2. The wheel-shaped tool, with which lines are impressed. Also called 'Roulette' or 'Roll'. *See also* Tooling.

Filling in. A printing fault in which the spaces in type characters, or the spaces between the dots of a half-tone block, fill with ink. This may be caused by using too much, or an unsuitable, ink, the forme being too high or the rollers incorrectly set, or by using an unsuitable paper, especially one which gives off fluff. *See also* Clogged.

Filling-in guards. *See* Compensation guards.

Film Archive Forum. <www.bufvc.ac.uk/faf> A forum that represents all of the public sector film and television archives which care for the UK's moving image heritage. Members include the National Film and Television Archive, the Imperial War Museum Film and Video Archive, the Scottish Screen Archive, the National Screen and Sound Archive of Wales, and the eight English regional film archives.

Film base. The plastic material which is coated with chemicals to make it sensitive to light. Called 'Clear base' before being coated with photographic emulsion. *See also* Base stock.

Film clip. A strip of film cut specially to illustrate something specific.

Film jacket. A transparent holder into which individual frames, or strips, of 16 or 35 mm microfilm may be inserted for storage.

Film library. A collection of films and video recordings; preservation of older film bases is a particular problem in such libraries.

Filmsetting. The setting of type by photographic means using film as a medium. Each key on a filmsetting machine operated the placing of a negative of a letter of the alphabet (or other character) in position to be printed photographically in its correct order on a sheet of film. This sheet of film represented whole pages which could then be imposed in the proper position and printed down on to the lithographic printing plate. *See also* Computer typesetting.

Filmstrip. A strip of 16 mm or 35 mm film varying in length up to about fifty frames and bearing pictures, text or captions. The positive images, in black and white or in colour, and usually on 35 mm film, are projected one at a time by means of a film strip projector. Some film strips are equipped with a tape or a recording that contains not only the narration but also a subsonic signal that activates a solenoid to advance the filmstrip to the next frame on being given a cue.

Filter. A software mechanism for identifying and blocking unwanted data transmissions. A filter might be applied by an organization or an Internet Service Provider to reduce Spam freely passing from the

Internet but it might also limit access to pornographic and other undesirable content from within the organization. *See also* PICS.

Final proof.   Also called 'Page proof'. *See* Proof.

Final title strip.   The wording at the end of a film which indicates its contents.

Finding aids.   Classification schemes, catalogues, indexes of various kinds and of different varieties of library materials, etc., which have been devised to enable stored material, or information, to be obtained (retrieved) when required. In Archives, the term generally covers all the descriptions, indexes etc. provided for readers in a record office.

Finding list.   A very brief list of books and documents in a library system, usually limited to author, title and class mark or location symbol. *See also* Berghoeffer System.

Fine.   A charge made for retaining a book longer than the time allowed.

Fine copy.   Used to describe a second-hand book the condition of which is better than 'good' but poorer than Mint.

Fine edition.   *See* De luxe edition.

Fine paper copy.   Name applied to a book printed on better and larger paper than the ordinary edition.

Fine Press Book Association (FPBA).   <www.fpba.com> (Four Rivers Books Ltd., 7228 Four Rivers Road, Boulder CO 80301, USA) Formed 1998 to promote the fine art of printing and the appreciation of beautiful books; members in the UK and USA. FPBA aims to be a distribution centre for news, events information, seminars, and publications.

Fine screen.   A screen with ruling above 120 lines per inch. *See also* Screen.

Fine-face rule.   A printer's brass Rule of hair-line thickness.

FinELib.   <www.lib.helsinki.fi/finelib/english> The Finnish National Electronic Library acquires Finnish and international resources to support teaching, learning and research and negotiates user-rights agreements for electronic resources on a centralized basis for its member organizations. The National Library of Finland is responsible for FinELib operations and development and co-ordinates the service with member universities, polytechnics, research institutes and public libraries.

Finis.   (Lat.) The end, conclusion. Frequently printed at the end of a book.

Finish.   1. (*Paper*) The degree of smoothness of the surface of paper; printing papers may be described as, e.g. antique or supercalendered, writing and drawing papers as vellum or rough. 'Hot pressed' (H.P.) means plate glazed finish. *See also* Not, Paper finishes.   2. (*Block-making*) The treatment of the outer edges of blocks as e.g. squared up, vignetted.   3. (*Binding*) Ornamenting and lettering a bound book.

Finisher.   1. A bookbinding craftsman who performs the processes (polishing the leather, lettering, embellishing) which are carried out on a hand-bound book after the sections have been secured within the case. 2. A machine which applies varnish, lacquer, liquid plastic or other fluid to cover materials by spraying, by roller, or by a printing plate.

Finishing.   That branch of binding concerned with the book after it has been put into its cover. Includes tooling, lettering, polishing. The person who does this is called a 'finisher'. *See also* Forwarding.

Finishing house/room.   *See* Salle.

Finnish library associations.   There are several library associations in Finland; the most significant are Suomen Kirjastoseura/Finnish Library Association <www.fla.fi> (Vuorikatu 22, A18, FIN-00100 Helsinki, Finland) founded in 1910 with 2,000 members, which serves librarians in general; Finnish Association of Library and Information Science (University of Tampere Department of Information Studies, PO Box 607, 33101 Tampere, Finland) founded in 1979; and the Finnish Research Library Association <www.pro.tsv.fi/stks> founded in 1929. There are separate associations for medical librarians and those speaking primarily Swedish.

Fire Information Group.   <www.figuk.org.uk> (London Fire & Emergency Planning Authority, Library Room 520, Hampton House, 20 Albert Embankment, London SE1 7SD, UK) An informal group of information professionals in the fire and loss prevention industries.

Firewall.   Hardware or software installed on a network or Intranet, particularly at the Gateway to the Internet, to provide security internally and protect all machines and users from Spam, Viruses or unauthorized access.

Firewire.   A Hot pluggable serial data transfer protocol and interconnection system, used to connect Peripherals and consumer devices such as digital camcorders to PCs. Firewire was originally developed by Apple Computer, Inc. and in 1995 was standardized by the Institute of Electrical and Electronic Engineers as IEEE 1394-1995. The original Firewire speed of 400 Mbps (IEEE 1394a) has been doubled in Firewire 800 (IEEE 1394b). *See also* USB.

Firmware.   Software routines stored in ROM and which remain intact when the computer is powered down. Start-up routines are stored in firmware.

FIRN.   <www.firn.edu> Florida Information Resources Network.

First edition.   The whole number of copies first printed from the same type and issued at the same time. Later printings from the same type are known as Reprints. Sometimes small typographical errors in a first edition are corrected during the printing, qualifying the later printings for the classification 'Corrected edition', 'New edition' or 'Revised edition', but described as 'First issue of the first edition'. *See also* Edition, Impression, Issue, New edition, Reprint, Revised edition.

First English edition.   The first edition published in England of a book written in English and which had already been published abroad.

First impression.   All the copies of a book printed at the first printing and before any alterations or additions have been made to the text. Subsequent printings made soon after the first, and before a reprint is made after a lapse of time, are called 'Second impression', 'Third impression', etc.

First line index. An index in which the first lines of poems, hymns, songs are arranged in alphabetical order.

First lining. The piece of mull which is glued with a flexible glue to a book after it is sewn and nipped; it extends to within 1/4 in. from the head and tail of the book and projects 1 1/4 in. on either side for affixing to the end-papers to give strength and firmness to the book. A strip of brown paper, the full size of the spine, is then stuck over it; this is known as the 'second lining'.

First name. The first of the forenames or Christian names; a personal name as distinct from family or clan name.

First printing. The first quantity of a book to be printed; equivalent to First impression.

First proof. A proof of type-set matter which is read by the printer's reader and corrected before the galley proof is made. *See also* Proof.

First published edition. The first edition published for sale to the public, and implying that it was preceded by an edition printed for private, official or otherwise restricted, circulation.

First separate edition. The first edition to be printed within its own covers, of a publication which had previously been published with other matter.

First word entry. Entry under the first word of a book's title other than an article.

Firsts. First editions.

Fission. A method of forming a chain of classes in classification by repeated division into successive characteristics. *See also* Denudation.

Fist. *See* Hand.

Five Laws of Library Science. (*S. R. Ranganathan*) 1. Books are for use. 2. Every reader his book. 3. Every book its reader. 4. Save the time of the reader. 5. A library is a growing organism.

Five predicables. *See* Predicables, five.

Fixed field coding. (*Cataloguing, Information retrieval*) In computer cataloguing, the allocation of as many areas of the record as there are particular parts of a catalogue entry, including the classification notation. With 'fixed symbol', or 'variable field' coding each part of the entry is 'tagged' with a special symbol (e.g. a punctuation mark) to indicate which part of the entry is to follow. *See also* Tag.

Fixed fields. In information retrieval, locations on a search medium that are reserved for information of a particular type, form or length. *See also* Free fields.

Fixed function planning. Planning a building in such a way that each room or department is designed and constructed for its specific purpose. Walls dividing the rooms are permanent, and normally an essential part of the structure. The opposite of Modular planning.

Fixed location. An antiquated method of arrangement by marking a book with shelf and other marks so that its position on a particular shelf should always be the same. The bookcases, tiers and shelves are each marked distinctly to make finding easy and these markings are often incorporated in the book number. Also called 'Absolute location'. The opposite of Relative location.

Fixed symbol coding. Variable field coding. *See* Fixed field coding.

fl. Abbreviation for *flores* (Lat. 'flowers'), *floruit*.

Flag. *See* Masthead.

FLAI. *See* Library Association of Ireland.

Flame. A Posting to a Mailing list, Usenet Discussion group or similar which is intended to insult or provoke or which is abusive and aimed at a particular person or people.

Flange. The margin round a half-tone plate or line block to provide for fixing to the block.

Flat. (*Printing*) The sheet containing offset negatives or positives in the proper arrangement, from which the printing plate is made. Also, a flat printing plate.

Flat back. A book which has not been rounded before being placed inside its Case, its back being at right angles to the sides. Also called 'Square back'. *See also* Backing, Round back, Rounding.

Flat copy. A photograph having no contrast and therefore normally unsuitable for process work. *See also* Process engraving.

Flat display. A book display which features the front covers rather than the spines of the books.

Flat file database. A database which utilizes a single record structure and which does not enable the relationships between objects to be established or notated, as is possible in a Relational database.

Flat proof. A print made from each plate in a colour series, using the colour in which that plate is to be printed in the series. *See also* Proof, Progressive proof.

Flat pull (Rough pull). The proof taken on the machine without Underlay or Overlay.

Flat stitched. A publication which is sewn by the Flat stitching method.

Flat stitching. Sewing a pamphlet or book, which must have a flat back, in such a way that the wire or linen thread used passes through the inner margins as close to the folds of the sections as possible from the front right through to the back. *See also* Saddle stitching, Side-stitch.

Flat-bed camera. *See* Planetary camera.

Flat-bed cylinder press. A printing machine with a flat bed on which the forme is placed under a rotating cylinder.

Flat-bed press. A printing machine having the printing forme on a bed with a flat surface, as distinct from a press with a curved surface.

Flat-bed web press. A machine for printing from a flat forme on to an endless roll of paper.

Flatness. A condition of paper or board when it has no Cockle, Curl or wave.

Fletcher (*Sir* Bannister) Award. An annual UK prize of the Society of Authors for the best book on architecture or the arts.

Fleur-de-lis lozenge. A lozenge stamp consisting of a flower with fleur-de-lis, or a variation of this design, filling the corners.

Fleuron. A conventional flower or an anomalous type of ornament of floral or foliage character, generally of roughly lozenge shape, used in decorating book-bindings. *See also* Flowers.

Flexible binding. A binding that allows the book to lie flat when open. This is largely achieved by using a Flexible sewing and flexible glue.

Flexible notation. A Notation which has the quality of allowing, by the addition of one or more symbols, the insertion of any new subject into any place in the classification without dislocating the sequence of either the notation or the classification schedule. Popularly known as Hospitality, it is the chief quality of a notational system.

Flexible plate. A plastic or rubber printing plate.

Flexible sewing. Sewing a book on raised bands or cords, passing the thread entirely round all the bands which are then laced through the boards. It is the strongest form of sewing. A style of binding which allows the book to lie quite flat when open.

Flexitime. Arrangements of employees' working hours to allow for early or late starting times and finishing times. Provided that adequate staffing is available at stated core times, staff may chose their actual hours of work to fit in with travel convenience, domestic needs etc., scoring up a total of hours which would be balanced with their contracted hours at the end of each month or other agreed interval.

FLICC. *See* Federal Library and Information Center Committee.

Flong. A pulp like board used for making the moulds for casting stereotypes. *Wet flong* is made (usually in the foundry of a printing establishment) from layers of tissue paper and blotting paper pasted together with a special paste and beaten onto the type or blocks in the forme and then dried. *Dry flong* is a similar material which, either in a completely dry state, or damp, is placed together with the forme in a hydraulic press. The use of paper in place of plaster of Paris for moulding was introduced by Genoux of Lyons in 1829; a British patent, based on this method, was taken out by Moses Poole in 1839.

Floor case. *See* Island stack.

Floppy disk. *See* Disk.

Florence Agreement. The 'Agreement on the importation of educational, scientific and cultural material' covering: 1. books, publications and documents; 2. works of art and collectors' pieces of an educational, scientific or cultural character; 3. visual and auditory materials of an educational, scientific or cultural character; 4. scientific instruments or apparatus; 5. articles for the blind. Contracting states undertake not to apply customs duties on any of the materials covered by the Agreement; they also undertake, *unconditionally*, to grant licences and/ or foreign exchange for a variety of categories of books and publications. The Agreement, which was adopted unanimously by the General Conference of Unesco at its Fifth Session held in Florence in July 1950, was brought into force on 21 May 1952. It is of major interest to libraries, making it easier to import such materials, reducing tariff and trade obstacles to the international circulation of these materials and permitting organizations and individuals to obtain them from abroad with less difficulty and at less cost.

Florentine repair. A method of repairing damaged documents developed after the devastating floods of the River Arno in Florence in 1966.

Florentine woodcuts. These are often characterized by the combination of black-line and white-line methods in the same block; e.g. black is used as the colour of the ground, any stones, plants or other objects being represented by white lines on a black ground, while the upper part of the illustration follows the Venetian style of black lines on a white ground.

Floret. 1. A binder's finishing tool with a flower or leaf design. 2. A flower or leaf-shape type used to separate sentences or paragraphs.

floruit. (Lat. 'he or she flourished') The period during which a person, whose birth and death dates were not exactly known, was believed to have been alive or flourished. Indicated by '*fl.*' before the dates or period.

Flourish. 1. A mark or flourish after a signature, often made as a protection against forgery. Also called a 'Paraph'. 2. A curved line or ornament, made of brass or cast metal, and used with lines of type.

Flourish style. *See* Fanfare style.

Flow camera. *See* Continuous flow camera.

Flower-headed rivet. (*Binding*) A rivet with an ornamental head with a design resembling a daisy.

Flowers. Printer's ornaments which can be made up into decorative borders, strips, head and tail pieces. They may be floral, arabesque, geometric or pictorial in design. The best of them derive from bookbinders' arabesque stamps. *See also* Fleuron, Type flowers, Type ornaments.

Flow-line map. One which shows movement, the direction or route followed being indicated by a line representing the railway or waterway concerned, while the width of the line represents the quantity of material conveyed.

Flush. (*Printing*) Denotes the absence of Indention. The instruction 'set flush on left' means that the matter is to be set evenly at the left margin, 'flush right' that all lines align at the right margin.

Flush binding. A binding in which the covers do not project beyond the leaves, the whole having been placed in a guillotine and trimmed after the covers were secured.

Flush boards. A style of binding in which boards are glued to the pastedowns and a paper cover glued to the boards. The whole is then put into a guillotine and Cut flush. *See also* Flush trim.

Flush paragraph. A paragraph having no indention, spacing being used to separate paragraphs.

Flush trim. A style of binding in which the top, fore and bottom edges are cut after the paper, board or lining cloth covers have been put on. The covers are thus flush with the edges and do not overlap. Such books are said to be 'cut flush'. Also called 'Flush work'. *See also* Flush boards.

Fly-leaf. A blank leaf at the beginning or end of a book, being the half of an Endpaper, which is not stuck down to the board, or cover, of a book. Also called 'Free endpaper'. The half which is stuck down to the board, is called a Paste-down. If there are other blank leaves, these are parts of the end sections – not fly-leaves although they are sometimes known as such.

Fly-sheet. 1. A two- or four-page tract.   2. An endpaper.

Fly-title. *See* Half-title.

fo. Abbreviation for Folio.

Focal point. In international projects, it is useful to offer a network of national support and information centres so that assistance and publicity can be managed on a country-by-country basis. Such centres are often termed focal points, as they are intended to be the initial point of scrutiny.

Focus. (*Classification*) (*Noun*) 1. A generic term used to denote an Isolate or a class or any of its equivalents in the other Planes.   2. Any specific division of the subject according to one characteristic, i.e. any single division of a Facet. (*Verb*) To decrease the Extension and increase the intension within any facet, and so to arrive at a specific division of a facet. *See also* Classifying, Facet, Phase.

Fol. *See* Freedom of Information.

Foil. Metal or pigment forming a very thin film on a thin backing material which is used with a stylus of a block when lettering or Blocking a book.

Foil blocking. *See* Blocking foil.

fol. Abbreviation for Folio. Less usual than '*fo.*', or '*Fo.*'.

FOLACL. *See* Society of Chief Librarians (SCL).

Fold. *See* Bolt.

Fold symbols. The symbols used to indicate the way the paper of which a book is made is folded, and consequently the number of leaves in the section. These are F., Fo (Folio); 4to (Quarto); 6to (Sexto); 8vo (Octavo); 12mo (Duodecimo, Twelve-mo); 16mo (Sextodecimo, Sixteen-mo); 18mo (Octodecimo, Eighteen-mo); 24mo (Vicesimo-quarto, Twenty-fourmo); 32mo (Trigesimo-secundo, Thirty-twomo); 64mo (Sexagesimo-quarto, Sixty-fourmo). They are often used to indicate the size of modern books.

Fold to paper. An instruction that a sheet of printed paper is to be folded so that the edges of the leaves and the bolts are all level. *See also* Bolt, Fold to print.

Fold to print. An instruction that a printed sheet is to be folded in register, i.e. the edges of the printed areas are to be placed over one another exactly before the sheet is folded. *See also* Fold to paper.

Folded book. One consisting of a long strip of paper folded like a sheet map, concertina fashion, the ends being attached to stiff covers. Used commonly in the Orient, but in the rest of the world mainly for books of a pictorial character giving views of places or panoramas. Also called 'Folding book'.

Folded leaf. A leaf of a bound book which is so large that it has to be folded one or more times to keep it within the area of the page size. The abbreviation *fold.* is added to the appropriate term in the collation to indicate that illustrative matter is folded, as: 80 *l.* (*3 fold.*); *fold.frontis*; 2 *fold.family trees*; 60 *maps* (2 *fold. in pocket*). *See also* Folding plate, Gatefold, Throw out.

Folder. 1. A publication consisting of one sheet of paper folded to make two or more leaves but neither stitched nor cut. 2. A large sheet of stout paper, usually manilla, folded once, and having a projection or tag for a heading at the top of the back portion, into which papers are placed for storage in a filing box or cabinet.

Folding. The folding of flat printed sheets into sections. The number of pages in a folded sheet is always a multiple of four (i.e. two leaves). After the last folding all the sections are secured by Sewing or stapling.

Folding book. *See* Folded book.

Folding guides. Short lines printed on imposed sheets to indicate where they are to be folded.

Folding machine. A machine for folding printed sheets to make sections for bookbinding. *See also* Buckle-folder, Knife-folder.

Folding plate. An illustration bound into a book but folded so as not to project beyond the pages of the book. Called a 'folded plate' by cataloguers. *See also* Double plate.

Folding stick. A strip of white bone used when folding paper by hand to crease the paper without damaging it. *See also* Bone folder.

Foldings. A general term referring to printed sheets which have been folded to form sections. The following table gives the usual foldings.

Folio	(fo)	Folded	once	giving	2	leaves	4	pages
Quarto	(4to)	„	twice	„	4	„	8	„
Sexto	(6to)	„	three times	„	6	„	12	„
Octavo	(8vo)	„	three	„	8	„	16	„
Duodecimo	(12mo)	„	four	„	12	„	24	„
Sextodecimo,	(16mo)	„	four	„	16	„	32	„
Octodecimo,	(18mo)	„	five	„	18	„	36	„
Vicesimo-quarto	(24mo)	„	five	„	24	„	48	„
Trigesimo-secundo	(32mo)	„	five	„	32	„	64	„
Trigesimo-sexto	(36mo)	„	six	„	36	„	72	„
Quadrigesimo-octavo	(48mo)	„	six	„	48	„	96	„
Sexagesimo-quarto	(64mo)	„	six	„	64	„	128	„

Foldout. *See* Throw out.

Folger Shakespeare Library. <www.folger.edu> Research centre for advanced scholars opened in Washington, DC in 1932. It contains the world's largest collection of research materials on William Shakespeare and one of the Western Hemisphere's finest collections of materials on the British civilization of the sixteenth and seventeenth centuries. The stock numbers 250,000 volumes. Henry Clay Folger, an American industrialist and his wife Emily Jordan Folger selected the material forming the original collection. The collection was bequeathed to the American people, together with an endowment which was sufficient to maintain and expand it. The trust is administered by the Trustees of Amherst College, Folger's alma mater. The library is a modern building on Capitol Hill although the interior preserves the architectural conventions of the Tudor period.

Foliaged staff. A bookbinding ornament consisting of a staff or branch entwined with foliage.

Foliate. To number the leaves of a book.

Foliate initial. In a mediaeval illuminated manuscript, an initial letter decorated with, or composed of, foliage.

Foliated. Used to describe the marking of every leaf – not page – of a manuscript or printed book with a consecutive number, or foliation.

Foliation. (*Verb*) Allotting folio or section numbers or other markings to pages. (*Noun*) The numbering of leaves of a MS. or book. Foliation was comparatively rare until the last quarter of the fifteenth century: it consisted originally of the word 'Folio', or an abbreviation thereof, followed by a Roman numeral. Arabic figures were used in Italy between 1475 and 1500, and outside Italy after 1500. Eventually the Arabic figures stood alone. Sometimes columns of print were numbered instead of leaves. The numbering of pages (pagination) began to replace foliation towards the end of the sixteenth century but was not finally established until the eighteenth century. Abbreviated ff.

Folio. 1. Relates to the format of a book; a book printed on sheets of paper folded once, each sheet making two leaves or four pages. For an accurate indication, the paper size should also be stated, e.g. *crown folio*. In practice, a double-size sheet could be used and folded twice, or a quad-size sheet folded three times to give the same size pages. *See* Foldings.   2. The individual leaf of a book. A sheet is usually folded into two parallel with the narrow way (i.e. halving the long side) and when so folded is called 'regular', 'common', or 'broad' folio.   3. An indication of the size of a book, usually 30 cm. The actual size depends on the size of the sheet of paper and on the way it is folded. Abbreviated *Fo., fo., fol., or* 2°. *See also* Book sizes, Elephant folio.   4. A sheet of paper in its full size, i.e. flat unfolded, hence a folio ream is a ream of paper supplied flat.   5. The number of a leaf written or printed at the top or more usually, the bottom of the Recto.   6. One sheet of MS. (which should be written, typed or printed on one side only) supplied to a printer's compositor for setting. Folios are numbered consecutively from 1 with arabic numerals to indicate correct sequence, and bear no relation to subsequent page numbering of the resultant print.

Folio edition.   One issued in Folio form.

Follett Report.   The (UK) *Joint Funding Councils' Libraries Review Group: Report*; the Group, chaired by Professor Sir Brian Follett, produced its findings in December 1993. The Report revealed that libraries were struggling to meet the increased demand for their services, that students needed more space and were using libraries more intensively, while resources for books and journals had failed to keep pace with rising student numbers. Also discussed the issues relating to Convergence, Performance indicators and recommended that each institution draw up an Information strategy. The section on IT gave rise to the eLib initiative.

Follow copy.   When written on a MS. this is a direction to the compositor to follow precisely the spelling and punctuation, however incorrect it may appear. When written on printed matter it indicates that the style and setting of the original are to be followed as closely as possible.

Follow through.   *See* Alphabetization (the 'letter-by-letter' system).

FOLUSA.   *See* Friends of Libraries USA.

Fonds (*Fonds d'archives*).   The total body of records and archives, in whatever medium, generated by a particular individual, institution or organization in the exercise of their activities and functions. In *MAD*, equivalent to a Group; in ISAD(G), a level of archival description corresponding to the total archive of an organization. *See Manual of Archival Description*.

Font.   A full set of type of one style and size containing the correct number of the various characters, i.e. upper and lower case, numerals, punctuation marks, accents, ligatures, etc. A type family includes fonts of roman, italic, semi-bold, semi-bold condensed, and Sans serif. In Desktop publishing, 'font' is understood to be simply the Typeface. Spelling formerly 'fount' but latterly almost universally replaced by 'font'. *See also* Sort, Typeface (2).

Font scheme.   *See* Bill of type.

Foolscap.   A sheet of printing paper measuring $13\frac{1}{2}$ x 17 inches, usually folded to give a size of $13\frac{1}{2}$ x $8\frac{1}{2}$ inches. Formerly known as 'large foolscap'.

Foolscap Folio.   A book size $13\frac{1}{2}$ x $8\frac{1}{2}$ inches. *See also* Book sizes.

Foolscap Octavo.   A book size $6\frac{3}{4}$ x $4\frac{1}{4}$ inches. *See also* Book sizes.

Foolscap Quarto.   A book size $8\frac{1}{2}$ x $6\frac{3}{4}$ inches. *See also* Book sizes.

Foot.   1. The bottom edge of a book. *See also* Head.   2. The margin at the bottom of a page of type.   3. The under-surface of type. The plane, parallel to the face on which the Body rests. *See also* Feet.

Footline.   1. The line at the bottom of a page, especially the blank line or Direction line i.e. the line containing the folio, signature, or page number just below the lowest line of type.   2. The horizontal ruled line near the bottom of a ruled page or sheet.   3. Supplementary material at the bottom of a page to be used in connection with matter appearing above it.

Footnote.   A note at the foot of a page, usually in smaller type than the text, giving a reference, an authority, or an elucidation of matter in the text above. Footnotes are usually referred to by Superior figures or symbols in the text. *See also* Reference marks. Also called 'Bottom note'.

Footstick.   *See* Chase.

Fore-edge.   The front edge of a sheet of paper or of the sections of a book opposite the folded edge through which the sewing passes. Also called 'Front edge'.

Fore-edge fold.   *See* Bolt.

Fore-edge margin.   The space between the type matter and the fore-edge of a book or periodical. Also called 'Outside margin'. *See also* Margin.

Fore-edge painting.   A picture painted on the fore-edges of a book which is seen to the best advantage when the pages are splayed out. A 'double fore-edge' has two paintings which can be seen singly by fanning the leaves first one way, and then the other. Gold is usually applied after the paintings have been done. A 'triple fore-edge' has a visible painting in addition. This form of decoration is particularly associated with William Edwards of Halifax, a binder who opened a bookshop in London for his sons James and John in 1785, although the earliest known *dated* disappearing fore-edge painting is on a Bible dated 1651, where the painting of the Leigh arms is signed 'Lewis fecit, Anno Dom. 1653'. Edwards pioneered the idea of painting landscapes on fore-edges, first of all in brown or grey monochrome, and later in a full range of colours.

Fore-edge title.   A title hand-written on the fore-edge of a book so that it could be identified when standing on a shelf with its fore-edge outwards, the normal position in the sixteenth century.

Forel.   1. Heavy, rough parchment used for covering old books. Also called 'Forrel', 'Forril'. 2. A case or cover in which a book or MS. is kept for protection, or into which it is sewn.

Forel binding.   English book-bindings in which oak boards were covered with roughly dressed deerskins. They were made by monks in the eighth and ninth centuries.

Forename.   A name that precedes the family name, clan name, or surname. A Christian, or personal, name. It is a name or part of a name which designates a person as an individual and distinguishes her/him from others bearing the same family name, surname or clan name. Also called Given name, personal name.

Forename entry.   The entry in a catalogue for a book under the author's forename or personal name instead of the surname or family name as is usual. Books by the following are so entered: saints, popes, persons known by the first name only, sovereigns, ruling princes and members of the immediate families of sovereigns.

Foresight programme.   <www.foresight.gov.uk> A UK government programme to improve the competitiveness of the UK economy, and enhance the quality of life, by bringing together business, the science base, and government to identify and respond to emerging opportunities in markets and technologies. Launched in 1994/95, it has been regularly reviewed and the current round began in 2002. There are several panels for various economic sectors.

Foreword. *See* Preface.

Form. 1. A classification term applied to the manner in which the text of a book is arranged, as a dictionary, or the literary form in which it is written, as drama, poetry, etc. *See also* Form classes, Form divisions. 2. In music indicates the structure of a musical composition which may be indicated by 'sonata', 'symphony', etc. 3. US spelling for Forme.

Form classes. Those parts of a classification in which the books are arranged according to the form in which they are written, e.g. poetry, drama, fiction, essays, etc., the subjects of the books being ignored.

Form divisions. Adjuncts to a classification which enable books to be arranged (within their subject) according to the form in which they are written. They usually have a mnemonic notation which can be applied to any part of a scheme. There are two kinds of form division. Outer form indicates books of which the contents are arranged in a particular way, such as in classified or alphabetical order as in dictionaries, or according to the form of writing or presentation, as essay, bibliography, periodical. Subjective, or Inner form, indicates modes of approach such as the theory, history, or philosophy of a subject.

Form entry. An entry in a catalogue under (1) the name of the form in which a book is written, e.g. Poetry, Drama, Fiction, or (2) the form in which the subject material is presented, e.g. Periodicals.

Form heading. 1. A heading used in a catalogue for a Form entry, e.g. 'Encyclopaedias'. Also called 'Form subject heading'. 2. A heading derived from and describing the category of document entered under it rather than its author, title or subject, e.g. Encyclopaedias.

Form number. (*Classification*) A symbol used to indicate the literary form in which a work is written. It is obtained in connection with the Colon Classification by translating the name of the form of exposition into appropriate symbols in accordance with the Scheme's Form schedule, and may be used as part of the Book number.

Form subheading. 1. A subheading used for sub-arranging in a catalogue entries for books on the same subject by their literary or practical form, e.g. Electronics – Bibliography. 2. A subheading, not consisting of an author's name or of a title, designed to delimit a group of entries according to some common characteristic of form, e.g. Laws, Treaties, under the name of a country.

Formal anonyma. Works, like periodicals, which do not involve the idea of concealed authorship. *See also* True anonyma.

Format. 1. A term used to describe the appearance and make-up of a book; its size, shape, paper, type, binding, illustrations, etc. 2. Strictly, the number of times a sheet of paper has been folded to form a section of a book, e.g. quarto (folded twice giving four leaves). 3. The layout or presentation of items in machine-readable form according to hardware and software requirements. 4. The physical type of an audio-visual item, e.g. a slide transparency, or a particular specification in any given type, e.g. a *VHS* video tape. 5. The general style, or make-up, or the general plan of physical organization, or arrangement, of an index. *See also* Foldings, Folio. 6. (*Verb*) To prepare a Disk for use with specific computer hardware.

Forme. The combination of chase, furniture and type when 'locked up' ready for machining; i.e. the pages imposed in a chase. The forme containing the text, which will be on the inside pages of a printed sheet when folded, is called the 'inner forme' and that which contains those on the outside, the 'outer forme'. Spelt in America without the 'e'. *See also* Dressed forme, Naked forme.

Forme gauge. *See* Gauge.

Forrel/Forril. *See* Forel.

Fortnightly. A serial publication issued every second week. Also called 'Bi-weekly', 'Semi-monthly'.

Forty-eightmo. (48mo) A sheet of paper folded six times to form a section of forty-eight leaves (96 pp). Also called 'Quadrigesimo-octavo'.

Forum for Interlending. <www.cilip.org.uk/groups/fil> The Forum is an independent organization in the UK established to enable ideas and viewpoints on interlending and document supply to be discussed and explored. Charging, copyright, protocols, management systems, international interlending, cross-sectoral co-operation, and training are amongst the current priority issues.

Forwarding. The processes of binding a book after it is sewn until it is about to be placed in its cover ready for Finishing.

Fotosetter. A machine for typesetting by photography, constructed by the Intertype company and introduced in 1947. A keyboard releases matrices from the magazines in which they are stored. A matrix, known as a *Fotomat*, has a photographic negative character embedded in its side; type lines are made up of separately photographed characters, justification being pre-arranged and automatic, and interlinear spacing obtained by adjusting the film feed dial as necessary.

Foul case. A case of type in which some of the separate pieces of type have been put into wrong compartments.

Foul proof. One with many corrections marked on it. A proof pulled after corrections have been made (US).

Foundation for Information Policy Research. <www.fipr.org> An independent organization that monitors governments' policy moves that relate to the information world.

Founder's type. Type cast by a type-founder as distinct from type cast by the printer on such machines as the Monotype, Linotype, Ludlow or Intertype.

Foundry. The department of a printing works where matrices are made from the type-formes and blocks, and where stereo plates are cast.

Other operations concerned with the casting or fabricating of type and other printing surfaces are also carried out here; the casting and routing machines, type-metal, stereo-metal and similar materials and the necessary tools are to be found here.

Foundry proof. A proof pulled before the forme is sent to the foundry to be stereotyped.

Foundry type. *See* Founders' type.

Fount. 1. *See* Font. 2. The whole collection of tools used by a binder's finisher.

Four-colour process. An extension of the *Three-colour process*, by adding black or grey to give greater depth or solidarity. Also called 'Full colour'.

Fourdrinier machine. The first machine for making a continuous roll of printing paper. It was invented by Nicolas Louis Robert in 1797, developed in England by Bryan Donkin on behalf of Henry and Sealy Fourdrinier but not perfected until 1804. The principle of this machine is the basis for contemporary machines. The fluid pulp flows from a tank to a moving wire mesh belt during which it is strained and the fibres shaken into a web by agitation. This web of pulp then passes between couch rolls which give it enough strength to be transferred from the wire-cloth to an endless felt on which it passes through successive pairs of press rolls and so to drying cylinders. All the separate processes carried out in the vat, mould, couch and press are combined in one machine. Originally the paper was then cut into sheets and loft-dried in the traditional way, but later additions to the Fourdrinier machine enabled the web of paper to be passed round a series of heated drums and so dried before being drawn through the rolls of a calender to impart the desired finish.

Fournier. A typeface cut about 1730 by the French engraver and type-founder Pierre Simon Fournier *the younger* (1712–68). A Modern face type which is characterized by its very fine hair-line serifs.

Fournier point. A unit of type measurement, one point being 0.0137 inch, established by P. S. Fournier in 1737. It was superseded by the Didot point. *See also* Didot system.

Foxed. 1. Prints and pages of old books with yellowish-brown spots caused by dampness. 2. A mechanical gluing technique sometimes used to make up shortrun multiple snap-apart forms.

Foxing. *See* Foxed.

FP6. <www.cordis.lu/fp6> The research and technology development activity of the European Union has been channelled through a series of Framework Programmes; FP6 (Sixth Framework Programme) has a budget of some 3.6 billion Euros and covers the years 2002–2006. Key areas of work include IT, and there are several sub-programmes that highlight Information Society technologies in the fields of cultural heritage, access to information, and preservation. A fabric of research infrastructures is also under development <www.cordis.lu/infrastructures>.

FPBA. *See* Fine Press Book Association.

Fractional scanning. (*Information retrieval*) Scanning a file by a series of stages. *See also* Binary search.

Fragmenting. (*Information retrieval*) Determining a number of appropriate terms or descriptors, to indicate adequately the various aspects of a document.

Fraktur. (*Printing*) The group name for German blackface type or bold face type. *See also* Bold face.

Frame. 1. A wooden stand with a sloped top on which cases of type are placed for the compositor's use. 2. (*Binding*) Ornamentation consisting of a simple hollow rectangle placed some distance from the edges of the cover of a book. To be distinguished from Border. 3. (*Bibliography*) The complete borders which are not Compartments. They comprise (a) enclosures made up of separate cuts or ornaments which show no evidence of having been carved or engraved for use together as a border; (b) those made up of separate cast type-ornaments, commonly used for book decoration. 4. (*Reprography*) An area containing an image in a film or microprint. 5. A geometric subdivision of the microfiche grid. A micro-image and its margins are contained within a frame. The standard size of a microfiche frame is 11.25 mm x 16 mm (single) or 23 mm x 16 mm (double). 6. In microcopying, cinematography, and videotaping, portion of film exposed to light through the camera optical system for one image. 7. A single still image in a film or video sequence. 8. (*World Wide Web*) A feature of HTML that allows a page on a Web site to be divided into sections that inter-relate; particularly useful for incorporating indexes and tables of contents into Web pages. Frames can have disadvantages, not always working in predicted ways with all browsers, and potentially causing difficulties for visually-impaired users who employ screen readers to dictate page conent and for navigation.

Framed-cut. A completely carved decorative full-page cut except for a small panel into which is set a letterpress title. Also called 'compartment', 'title-cut' or 'woodcut title-page with panel'.

Framework for the Future (F4F). <www.dcms.gov.uk> A strategic report issued in 2003 by the (UK) Department of Culture, Media and Sport (DCMS) outlining future developments for public libraries; there are three main themes: books, reading and learning; digital citizenship; community and civic values. The report also highlights management innovation. An implementation group has been formed; members include DCMS, CILIP, MLA, Society of Chief Librarians. A substantial agenda for 2004–2006 has been drawn up.

Framework Programme (EU). *See* FP6.

Franchised courses. Academic courses packaged by an educational establishment and 'sold' under contract to another institution, whose students may then spend part of their time on the francise operator's premises.

Francis Joseph Campbell Citation. *See* Campbell (Francis Joseph) Citation.

Fraternity library. A library in a fraternity on a US college or university campus. It may be one of a circulating collection from the main library, or it may be owned by the fraternity.

FRBR. *See* Functional Requirements for Bibliographic Records.

Free. 1. (*Binding*) Said of a stamp, of whatever form, which has no boundary line, or frame, round it; such stamps may be in intaglio or relief.

Free endpaper. That portion of an endpaper which is not pasted down to the cover but adhered to the end section of a book. Also called 'Fly-leaf'. *See also* Endpaper.

Free field coding. (*Information retrieval*) The use of a complete coding field, the entry of codes not being restricted to fixed positions.

Free fields. In information retrieval, location on a search medium which is not reserved for information of a particular type, form or length. *See also* Fixed fields.

Free hand. Writing of any period not conforming to definite rules such as the regular use of set abbreviations.

Free indexing. In Co-ordinate indexing, the assignment as index terms for a given document, of words or phrases chosen from a set of words or phrases considered by the indexer to be appropriate indexing terms even though they may not appear in the document.

Free software. Software that comes with permission for anyone to use, copy, and distribute, either verbatim or with modifications, either free or for a fee. In particular, this means that source code must be available. *See also* Free Software Foundation, Open Source software, Public domain software, Shareware.

Free Software Foundation. <www.gnu.org/fsf> Founded in 1985 and dedicated to promoting computer users' rights to use, study, copy, modify, and redistribute computer programs. The Foundation promotes the development and use of Free software and free documentation and helps to spread awareness of the ethical and political issues of freedom in the use of software.

Free term list. (*Information retrieval*) A list of terms or descriptors not rigidly defined, and to which other terms or descriptors can be freely added.

Free text searching. Online searching in which all aspects of the records may be used as sought terms; natural language is used rather than a controlled vocabulary.

Freedley (George) Memorial Award. Established in 1968 by the Theatre Library Association to honour the late founder of the Association, theatre historian and first curator of the Theatre Collection of the New York Public Library. The award, in the form of a plaque, is made on the basis of scholarship, readability, and general contribution to knowledge. It was first awarded (in 1969) to Louis Sheaffer for his *O'Neill, son and playwright*.

Freedom of Access to Information and Freedom of Expression (FAIFE). <www.ifla.org/faife> (Birketinget 6, DK-2300, Copenhagen, Denmark) An Initiative of IFLA to defend and promote basic human rights. It monitors the state of intellectual freedom with the library and information community worldwide, responds to violations of freedom of access to information and freedom of expression. Issues a 'World Report' every two years; in 2003 this covered 88 countries and focused on libraries and the Internet.

Freedom of Information (FoI). <www.lcd.gov.uk/foi> or <www.dataprotection.gov.uk/dpr/foi> A right of public access to all types of 'recorded' information held by local or national governments or public authorities. Legislation exists in many countries, such as Sweden (1766), Finland (1919), Australia, New Zealand and Canada (1980s), USA (1996; see <www.usdoj/oip.foia>). In the UK, The Freedom of Information Act was passed in 2000 <www.hmso.gov.uk/acts/acts2000/20000036> and comes fully into force in 2005. 'Public authorities' will include schools, colleges, universities, police, health services; all authorities have to issue a 'publication scheme' – a guide to the information they hold – and this scheme must be approved by the Information Commissioner <www.informationcommissioner.gov.uk>. The Act covers England, Wales, and Northern Ireland; in Scotland there is a separate Act (2002).

Freedom to Read Foundation (FTRF). <www.ftrf.org> Founded in 1969 by the American Library Association, the Foundation has a two-part objective: to (a) support and defend librarians whose jobs are jeopardized because they challenge violations of intellectual freedom; (b) provide a means through which librarians and others can set legal precedent for the freedom to read. As a non-profit group, it is supported entirely by membership contributions: there are no special criteria for membership. Publishes *Freedom to Read Foundation News* (q.).

Freelance. Term used to indicate a style of self-employment in which the individual sells a service to a number of different agencies for a fee. Journalists, photographers or information workers may operate on this basis. *Compare also* Information broker, Information consultant, Library consultant.

Freenets. Non-profit organizations that provide networking services and sometimes free Internet access to individuals within a geographical region. They are often compared to community Bulletin boards where citizens can find community information. Freenets depend greatly on volunteers and sponsors for assistance in maintaining the service.

Freeze drying. A method of treating books that have been severely damaged by water. Frozen books are placed in a vacuum chamber, and the temperature is raised to release water vapour without causing a change from solid to liquid. The vapour molecules are attracted to a cryogenic panel within the chamber where they revert to a solid state. Books dried in this way may need to be humidified before any further treatment is undertaken. *See also* Dessicant drying, Vacuum drying.

French fillet.   *See* Fillet.

French fold.   A sheet printed on one side only and then folded into a section, the bolts being left uncut. *See also* Orihon.

French Japon.   *See* Japanese paper.

French joint.   A joint formed by keeping boards a short distance from the back, splitting the boards and placing tapes between, thus allowing greater play at the hinge and permitting the use of a much thicker leather or cloth than otherwise. *See also* Closed joint.

French library associations.   *See* Association des Bibliothécaires Français, Association des Documentalistes et Bibliothécaires Spécialisés, GFII.

French rule.   (*Printing*) A rule made of brass or type metal and widening to a diamond shape in the middle.

French sewing.   (*Binding*) Sewing without tapes.

Frequency-division multiplexing.   *See* Multiplexer.

Frequently asked questions.   *See* FAQs.

Fret.   A continuous border pattern made up of interlaced bands or fillets. Such patterns may be used for the decoration of pages or tooled on book covers.

Friar.   A light patch left on a forme or printed sheet due to imperfect inking. *See also* Monk.

Friends of Libraries.   <www.libdex.com/fol> A UK charitable trust set up in 1987 which aims to build up a permanent fund from which it will give grants to help libraries in the public and academic domain. The Board of Trustees includes eminent figures from the fields of libraries, bookselling and finance.

Friends of Libraries USA (FOLUSA).   <www.folusa.org> An association to encourage and support volunteer action and sponsorship for libraries. Operates from American Library Association Headquarters and makes awards each year for State Friends Organization; Large Public Library Friends; Small Public Library Friends; Academic Library Friends.

Friends of the British Library.   <www.bl.uk> (British Library, 96 Euston Road, London NW1 2DB, UK) An organization established in 1989 to widen public awareness of the British Library and encourage special relationships for fund-raising and joint ventures. Publishes a *Newsletter* (3 p.a.).

Friends of the National Libraries.   <www.bl.uk> (c/o British Library, 96 Euston Road, London NW1 2DB, UK) Formed in 1931 to aid the UK's libraries and record offices; its aim was to ensure that books and documents of national importance were retained in the UK in suitable institutions, conserved, and accessible.

Friends of the National Library of Wales.   <www.llgc.org.uk/cyfellion/friends.html> (National Library of Wales, Aberystwyth SY23 3BU, UK) The organization seeks to support the work of the Library by maintaining a fund for special purchases, stimulating gifts and bequests. Publishes a newsletter, holds open days.

Fringed foliage ornament. (*Binding*) A finisher's ornament of roughly lozenge shape, with a design of conventional foliage, the characteristic feature of which is a shallow fringe round its edge.

Frisket. A light rectangular iron frame about the size of a Tympan which is covered with brown paper and attached to the upper part of the tympan. The frisket sheet is folded over the tympan, the centre part of the brown paper which would otherwise cover the printing surface being cut out, before the tympan is turned over the forme. Its purpose is to prevent the sheet of paper being dirtied or blackened by the Chase, and Furniture, to hold the sheet to the tympan, and to lift the sheet from the Forme after printing.

front. Also 'frontis.'; abbreviation for Frontispiece.

Front board. The piece of millboard or strawboard which is used for the front cover of a book.

Front cover. *See* Obverse cover.

Front edge. *See* Fore-edge.

Front matter. *See* Preliminaries.

Frontispiece. Any pictorial representation at the front of a book, usually facing the title-page, and as a rule unnumbered and unpaged. *See also* Illustrations.

Front-projection reader. A reader in which an enlargement of a microform is projected onto the front of an opaque screen and read by reflected light.

fs. Abbreviation for Facsimile.

ftp. File transfer protocol, a function that permits the logging on to a remote computer host and the uploading or downloading of files. Anonymous ftp signifies that one does not need a registered account on the remote host, and the word 'anonymous' is used at Login for Username; convention suggests that the Password should be one's E-mail address.

FTR. *See* Full text retrieval.

FTRF. *See* Freedom to Read Foundation.

Fugitive colours. Coloured printing inks which change or fade when exposed to normal light. Reds, greens and blues are particularly susceptible to fading.

Fugitive facts file. A file of facts which it has been difficult to obtain in answer to readers' enquiries, and which are likely to be asked for again (US).

Fugitive material. Such publications as pamphlets, programmes and duplicated material produced in small quantities and of immediate, transitory or local interest.

Full binding. A binding in which the covering material covers back and sides. Usually applied to a leather bound book. A book so bound is described as 'full bound' or 'whole bound'. *See also* Half leather, Quarter leather, Three-quarter leather.

Full bound. A book wholly covered with leather.

Full cataloguing. The style of cataloguing in which the entries give all the information provided for by the rules of the code adopted.

Full colour.   When an ample amount of ink has been used in printing; in distinction from grey colour, when only a small quantity of ink is used.

Full face.   Sometimes used synonymously with Bold face. Also used to denote Full on the body.

Full leather.   *See* Full binding.

Full measure.   Type set throughout the whole length of a line, whether of type column or page. *See also* Measure.

Full music edition.   *See* Score.

Full name note.   The full name of an author which is given in the bottom right-hand corner of Library of Congress catalogue cards when a short form of the name (e.g. omitting an indication of a Christian name or giving only the initials) is used for the heading. Similar notes are given in the same position for the name in religion, the original name, a pseudonym which covers joint authors, the real name, secular name, or stage name.

Full on the body.   A font of capitals designed to occupy the complete Body area. Also called 'Full face'.

Full out.   (*Printing*) To commence printed matter flush without indention.

Full point.   The punctuation mark used at the end of a sentence, between figures to mark decimals, and elsewhere in typography. Also called a 'Full stop'.

Full score.   *See* Score.

Full stop.   *See* Full point.

Full term co-ordination.   A Permuted title index in which all significant words in the title are co-ordinated with every other significant word.

Full text.   Primarily used in relation to electronic versions of documents such as journal papers when the complete article is available online, either through subscription-based services or via Open access.

Full text retrieval/searching.   Online searching in which every word of the source documents is on the record and can be retrieved.

Full title.   *See* Main title.

Full-gilt.   A book with all edges gilded.

Function.   The tasks actually performed by an individual or an organization; to be distinguished from Role.

Function key.   A key on a computer keyboard – normally marked F1 to F12 – that can be programmed to provide ready access to a Macro or prepared text strings or provide specific functionality in software applications.

Functional Requirements for Bibliographic Records (FRBR).   <www.ilfa.org/VII/S13/frbr> Proposed by IFLA in 1998, FRBR is an initiative to supply Metadata for information objects, drawing together all versions of the same work. The system is becoming widely used, and OCLC has developed an algorithm for converting bibliographic databases to the FRBR model. OCLC has calculated that the 47 million records in its WorldCat database can be traced to 32 million works – FRBR would aid efficient searching by avoiding duplication.

Fundamental categories. (*Classification*) Personality, Matter, Energy, Space, and Time (PMEST) are the five fundamental categories of facets which Ranganathan has developed into a general facet formula which represents the Principle of Decreasing Concreteness, Personality being regarded as the most concrete category and Time as the most abstract. *See also* Category. 'Each facet of any subject, as well as each division of a facet, is considered as a manifestation of one of the five fundamental categories' (*Ranganathan*). The indicator digits and Symbols of the Facet are as follows:

Fundamental category (FC)	Indicator digit (ID)	Symbol for the Facet
Personality	, (comma)	[P]
Matter	; (semicolon)	[M]
Energy	: (colon)	[E]
Space	. (dot)	[S]
Time	' (apostrophe)	[T]

See also Colon Classification, Decreasing concreteness, principle of.

Furnish. The materials from which a paper is made, e.g. the furnish of a litho paper might be: esparto, 60 per cent; chemical wood, 30 per cent; loading, 10 per cent.

Furnish layer. Paper or board made up of one or more plies of the same furnish, combined while still moist, without the use of adhesive. Two, three, or more furnish layers similarly combined are known as 'Two-layer, Three-layer, or Multi-layer paper or board' (in some countries as 'Biplex' or 'Duplex', 'Triplex', or 'Multiplex' respectively) according to the number of layers. The external furnish layers of the three-layer papers may be of the same composition, while the multi-layer papers may have two or more furnish layers of the same composition.

Furniture. The wood or metal material used by the printer to form margins and to fill in large gaps between the type matter especially where there is a small amount of type to a page as on a dedication or title-page, and to help secure the printing material in the Chase.

Futhark. *See* Runes.

Fuzzy logic. A component of Artificial intelligence; although computers cannot 'think', they can now be programmed to make certain assumptions – for example, that 'warm' exists between 'hot' and 'cold'. This recognition facility shows characteristics of 'thinking' and can be incorporated into information systems and decision support systems.

GABRIEL. <www.bl.uk/gabriel> The GAteway and BRIdge to Europe's national Libraries; launched in 1995/1996, the Web portal service was renovated in 2002. The participants are the 41 national libraries from 39 countries represented in CENL.

Gale Research Financial Development Award. An award presented to a library organization for outstanding achievement in securing and carrying out a library financial development project. Administered by the American Library Association Awards Committee.

Galley. A long narrow and shallow steel tray about 22 inches long and open at one end, into which type is transferred from the compositor's stick or from the typesetting machine to await making up into pages. It is from the type in this galley that the galley proof (also called a 'galley') was taken. *See also* Proof.

Galley press. A printing press made up for the pulling of galley proofs. *See also* Proof.

Galley proof. *See* Proof.

GAP. <www.ubka.uni-karlsruhe.de/gap-c> German Academic Publishers, a project begun in 2001 and run by three German universities (Hamburg, Karlsruhe, Oldenburg) and funded by the Deutsche Forschungs-gemeinschaft. The aim was to develop an innovative model for the dynamic design and administration of electronic publications, applicable to articles published in electronic journals and books published in the traditional way. Continued as part of FIGARO.

Garalde. A category of Typeface in which the axis of the curves is inclined towards the left. There is generally more contrast between the relative thickness of the strokes than in the Humanist designs (*See* Humanist (1)), the serifs are bracketed, the bar of the lower-case 'e' is horizontal, and the serifs of the lower-case ascenders are oblique. These designs are based on those of Aldus and Garamond, and were formerly called Old face or Old style. Bembo, Caslon and Vendôme are garalde faces.

Garamond. An elegant Old face type named after Claude Garamond (d. *circa* 1561), a pupil of Geoffroy Tory, and the first, and perhaps the finest, of the French letter-cutters and typefounders. Garamond types are very legible and unusually pleasing; the face is of light and clean design, showing a very slight difference between the thick and thin strokes.

Gascon. *See* Le Gascon style.

GASHE. <www.gashe.archives.gla.ac.uk> Gateway to Archives of Scottish Higher Education providing electronic access to descriptions of the archives produced by ten higher education institutions and their predecessors in Scotland, dating from 1215 to the present. Funded by the Research Support Libraries Programme and ended in October 2002, though the web site is still operational.

Gatefold. An illustration, map, or other insert which is larger than the page of the publication into which it is bound, so that it must be unfolded for viewing (US). *See also* Folded leaf, Folding plate, Throw out.

Gates Library Foundation. <www.glf.org> Bill Gates of the Microsoft Corporation set up a programme in collaboration with the American Library Association to assist US public libraries in deprived areas in 1995, with the title *Libraries Online!* In 2000 the Foundation was re-named the Bill and Melinda Gates Foundation, merging with the Gates Learning Foundation and the William H Gates Foundation. The Foundation has an endowment of $26 billion; the aim is to improve equity in global health and learning. A libraries program remains part of the Foundation's work. *See also* People's Network (PN).

Gateway. 1. (*Internet*) A single point of access for a wide range of services with a particular subject, commercial or user focus. *See also* Hub, Portal. 2. A device connecting networks running different protocols that enables the transfer of data without loss of Integrity.

Gateway to Archives of Scottish Higher Education. *See* GASHE.

Gathering. (*Verb*) The process of assembling and arranging in correct order the various sections which go to make up a book, preparatory to Sewing. (*Noun*) *See* Section (1).

GATS. <www.libr.org/GATS> The General Agreement on Trade and Services was negotiated by the World Trade Organization in 1994 and is moving slowly into effect; all aspects are scheduled to be in place in 2005. There are many implications for library services, and the Website links to statements from several national and international library and information science bodies. *See also* TRIPS.

Gauffered edges. The gilt edges of the leaves of a book which have been decorated by impressing heated engraved tools to indent a small repeating pattern. This style was popular in the sixteenth and seventeenth centuries. Also called 'Chased', 'Gauffred', 'Goffered'.

Gauge. (*Printing*) A strip of metal or wood with a notch which is used during Make-up to denote the exact lengths of pages or widths of margins. Also called 'Forme gauge'.

Gazette. A record of public events which is published periodically. A journal or newsheet. A publication issued by a government or university to convey official information, decisions or statements.

Gazetteer. A geographical dictionary with a varying amount of descriptive, geographical, historical or statistical information.

GBC. General Books Council. *See* Publishers Association.

Gbps. Gigabits per second, a measure of data transfer rate.

Gbyte. Abbreviation for gigabyte. *See also* Byte.

g.e. Abbreviation for Gilt edges.

GÉANT. <www.dante.net/server.php?show=nav.007> The name given to both a project and the network that emerged from it. The GÉANT project is a collaboration between 26 National Research and Education Networks representing 30 countries across Europe, the European Commission, and DANTE. Its principal purpose has been to develop the GÉANT network, a multi-gigabit pan-European data communications network, reserved specifically for research and education use and which replaced TEN-155.

Gelatine print. Another name for Collotype.

Genealogical table. A representation of the lineage of a person or persons in tabular or diagrammatical form.

General Books Council.　*See* Publishers Association.

General classification.　A classification which arranges the whole field of knowledge – the visible and invisible universe – in logical order.

General cross-reference.　*See* General reference.

General Information Programme.　A programme sponsored by Unesco to provide news of activities in the fields of scientific and technological information, and of documentation, libraries and archives by and for member states. Part of the programme is the UNISIST project, for the development and co-ordination of scientific and technological information. *See also* ISORID, Office of Information Programmes and Services, UNISIST.

General reference.　A *See also* reference in an index or catalogue which directs the user to a number of headings under which entries on specific subjects may be found. These are often used to avoid bulking out the catalogue with a number of specific references. Also called 'General cross-reference', 'Information entry', 'Multiple reference'. *See also* Cross-references, Specific reference.

General secondary.　An entry for a person or a corporate body whose connection with the publication catalogued cannot be indicated in the heading by the use of some specific designation as arranger, editor, etc.

General title.　One which is provided for a book consisting of several works which have previously been published separately and whose title-pages are called 'Divisional title-pages'.

General works.　A group name, sometimes used as a heading in a scheme of classification, for books of a general nature, i.e. dealing with many different subjects. Sometimes called a Generalia class.

Generalia class.　The main class of a classification which is reserved for books on many subjects such as encyclopaedias.

Generation.　(*Reprography*) An indication of the remoteness of a copy from the original document. The original picture of the document is called a 'first generation' microfilm (camera microfilm); copies made from this are called 'second generation', and copies made from this, 'third generation', etc.

Generic.　Pertaining to a genus or class of related things.

Generic coding.　(*Classification*) The encoding of descriptors in such a way as to preserve generic relations, e.g. encoding by hierarchical class numbers, or with characteristics, replacing each descriptor by a compound of its characteristics.

Generic relation.　(*Classification*) 1. The relationship between *Genus* and *Species*.　2. The relationship between a class term and the members of that class, where all the members have certain characteristics defined by the class term.　3. The relation between classes in a chain of subordinate classes, where each foregoing member includes all the following members of the chain.　4. (*Information retrieval*) The relationship between two concepts or classes of a classification where one is the genus and one the species. *See also* Relation.

Generic term. (*Indexing*) A single word which is a constituent part of a Bound term. *See also* Collateral term.

Generic Top Level Domain. *See* Domain Name System.

Genesis. <www.genesis.ac.uk> A mapping initiative, funded by the Research Support Libraries Programme, to identify and develop access to women's history sources based on collections from libraries, archives and museums from around the British Isles.

Geneva Convention. Popular name for the Universal Copyright Convention. *See* Copyright, International.

GeNii. Global Environment for Networked Intellectual Information. *See* Kokuritsu Johogaku Kenkyujo.

Genre. In the writing of fiction, various categories which are distiguishable from general fiction, such as *adventure stories*, *romances*, *thrillers*, *detective stories*, *war stories*. The American Library Association has issued *Guidelines on Subject Access to Individual Works of Fiction, Drama, etc.* (*GSAFD*). In 1997, BNB began to index catalogue entries with forms and genres taken from the *GSAFD*.

Genus. *See* Predicables, five.

Geographic division. Sub-division in classification or in subject headings by country, region or locality. *See also* Area table.

Geographic filing method. Arranging material, or entries in a catalogue, list or bibliography, according to place, either by place-names or by a geographic classification scheme. Also sub-arrangement by place (either alphabetically by place-name or by classification) in any method of filing. Alphabetical filing may be by specific place.

Geographical Information System. *See* GIS.

Geographical numbers. Numbers added to a classification symbol to arrange documents geographically. They are usually applicable throughout a classification scheme. *See also* Area table.

Geological Survey. <www.bgs.ac.uk> (Kingsley Dunham Centre, Keyworth, Nottingham, NG12 5GG, UK) A UK organization that produces geological maps and various series of reports on geological matters.

Geometric. A group of Lineale typefaces which are based on a circle, a triangle or on geometric shapes. They are usually Monoline.

George Freedley Memorial Award. *See* Freedley, (George) Memorial Award.

GeoScience Information Group. *See* GIG.

German library associations. *See* Arbeitgemeinschaft der Spezialbibliotheken, Bibliothek und Information Deutschland, Bundesvereinigung Deutscher Bibliotheksverbände, Deutsche Gesellschaft für Informationswissenschaft und Informationpraxis, Deutscher Bibliotheksverband, Gesellschaft für Informatik, Gesellschaft für Klassification, Verein Deutscher Bibliothekare.

German national library. *See* Deutsche Bibliothek. Other recognized national libraries are the German National Library of Medicine

(ZBMed) <www.zbmed.de>, German National Library of Science and Technology (TIB) <www.tib.uni-hannover.de>, and the German National Library of Economics (ZBW) <www.zbw-kiel.de>.

German Research Network.   *See* DFN.

Germanic handwriting.   A pre-Carolingian, or pre-Caroline handwriting, which was greatly limited in time and space (eighth to ninth centuries A.D.). A 'national' style of handwriting which developed after the dissolution of the Roman Empire, and was a development of the Latin cursive. *See also* Cursive, Handwriting.

Gesellschaft für Informatik.   <www.gi-ev.de> Founded in 1969 and now with 20,000 members, this organization promotes informatics in research and education.

Gesellschaft für Klassifikation.   <www.gfkl.de> The German Classification Society was founded in 1977 to develop research activities relating to classification and ordering of data, processing of statistical and conceptual information, and the construction of databases. There are 340 members; several special interest groups have been formed.

GEsource.   <www.gesource.ac.uk> A Hub of the (UK) RDN which provides access to high quality Internet resources for students, researchers and practitioners in geography and the environment through five distinct subject gateways: Environment; General Geography; Human Geography; Physical Geography; and Techniques and approaches.

Get en mol.   *See Jeté en moule.*

Get in.   1. To set 'copy' in less space than estimated.   2. To set type very close, or to set it so that it will fit within a required area by using thin spacing.

Getty Information Institute.   Originally titled the Getty Art History Information Program (AHIP), the Institute was formed in 1996 and was a major sponsor of various initiatives to make art history information more accessible through digital technologies. After a re-appraisal of its roles, the Institute closed in 1999.

GFII.   <www.gfii.asso.fr> (25 rue Claude Tillier, 75012 Paris, France) Groupement Français de l'Industrie de l'Information; an association of producers, publishers, intermediaries, information distributors in the public and private sectors. Its role is to offer a discussion forum, assist quality assurance in electronic information, promote professional status.

GGF.   *See* Global Grid Forum.

Ghost writer.   One who writes or prepares a book such as an autobiography, or articles for, and in the name of, another (usually well-known) person.

Giant book.   A three-dimensional cardboard blow-up of the outside of a book for purposes of display. *See also* Blow-up.

GIF.   Graphics Interchange Format, developed by CompuServe for the compression of graphics images to permit their more efficient transfer over the Internet. The format is especially suitable for images containing large areas of the same colour though not as effective as the JPEG format for photographic images.

Gift. *See* Donation.

Gift binding. Any book bound in leather for presentation such as a school prize, or part of an edition bound in leather at the publisher's order for the gift market.

Gift book. *See* Keepsake.

GIG. <www.gig-uk.org> GeoScience Information Group. An affiliated group of the Geological Society, GIG aims to promote best practice in the use and management of geoscience information. An electronic newsletter is available on the web site.

Giga. Prefix denoting one thousand million, as in gigabyte.

GigaPOP. A technology for providing advanced communications services over Internet2. GigaPOP is a complex of technologies developed over the first decade of the Internet integrated with new technologies developed by vendors and the Internet Engineering community. It acts as the point of interconnection and service delivery between one or more institutional members of Internet2 and one or more service providers. *See also* Abilene.

Giggering. Polishing a blind impression on a leather binding by rubbing a small hot tool on it.

GII. *See* Global Information Infrastructure.

Giles (Louise) Minority Scholarship. An award made by the American Library Association Office for Library Personnel Resources, to a student from an ethnic minority community.

Gill. A typeface named after Eric Gill (1882–1940) the English sculptor, artist and type designer, it is characterized by the absence of serifs and is therefore known as 'Gill Sans'. Although excellent for display captions it is not wholly suitable for book work as it becomes tiring to read after a time but is often used for children's books. Gill designed two typefaces which are appropriate for book work: 'Joanna' (1930) and 'Perpetua' (1929–30), the last being his most widely-used type. This most pleasing type is used for display as well as for text. In 1934 he designed a special type for Sterne's *Sentimental journey* published by the Limited Editions Club of New York. This was the basis for Linotype's 'Pilgrim' which appeared in 1953.

GILS. <www.gils.net> Global Information Locator Service, a Metadata format influenced by MARC, designed for Z39.50 systems and which has a core element set much larger than Dublin Core. Previously Government Information Locator Service.

Gilt edges. (*Binding*) The edges of a book which have been trimmed by a guillotine, covered with gold leaf and burnished. 'Antique gold edges' are those which have an unburnished gilt finish. Edges are sometimes tooled with a diapered pattern after binding. *See also* Edges.

Gilt extra. (*Binding*) A binding with more than the normal amount of gilt ornamentation.

Gilt in the round. A book, the fore-edges of which have been gilded after rounding, the fore-edge appearing as a solid gilt surface.

Gilt in the square.   A book, the fore-edges of which have been gilded before rounding with the result that there is a tendency for the sections at the beginning and the end of the book to show a white edge.

Gilt on the rough.   Gilding on the uncut edge of a book, or on one that has not been cut solid. It provides the elegance of gold without any sacrifice of margin but does not, like smooth gilt edges, keep the dust out. This was a popular style in France in the nineteenth century and continues to be found. *See also* Marbling under gilt, Rough gilt edges, Solid gilt.

Gilt top.   The top edge of a book trimmed smooth and gilded, the remaining edges being trimmed only. Also called 'Top edges gilt'. Abbreviated g.t., g.t.e., or t.e.g. *See also* Edges, Gauffered edges, Solid gilt.

Girdle book.   A book used in the middle ages and early Renaissance which had secured to it an extra protective cover of soft leather made in such a way that the book could be hung from the girdle or habit cord of a cleric.

GIS.   Geographical Information Systems, which offer sophisticated storage, manipulation, analysis and display of maps and other geographic data, have been widely introduced into many aspects of government, professions, and business; examples now abound in health services, highway management, transport, insurance, marketing, retailing, farming, public utilities, police forces, planning authorities, etc.

Given name.   The personal name (in Western races the 'Christian' name) given to an individual to distinguish him or her from other members of the family or clan.

GKD Notation.   An abbreviation for the Gordon-Kendall-Davison notation which is used to describe structural formulae in chemistry. Also called the 'Birmingham notation'. *See also* Wiswesser Line Notation.

Glaire.   An adhesive substance (made by heating up the white of eggs and vinegar or water) used as a size to retain gold in 'finishing' and edge-gilding books.

Glasgow Declaration.   <www.ifla.org> A declaration of principles on libraries, information services and intellectual freedom made by IFLA at its conference in Glasgow, Scotland in 2002.

GLASS.   Greater London Audio Specialization System, a subject specialization scheme, with inter-lending facilities, for audio materials. The scheme became operational on 1 April 1972. Recordings of classical music, jazz and spoken word are covered. The purchase and collection of classical music is allocated to the libraries by composer, and of jazz by performer; recordings by these composers/performers withdrawn from stock in other libraries in the Scheme may be sent to the 'specializing' libraries for preservation. GLASS does not have a Website, but is mentioned in the sites of several of its members – for example <www.lbhf.gov.uk/council_services/education/libraries/music>.

Glass plate negatives.   Photographic negatives held within glass plates; they are very fragile and easily cracked. For preservation purposes they should be enclosed in individual acid-free envelopes and stored vertically on edge for good air circulation.

Glassine. A transparent glossy-surfaced paper obtained by excessive beating of the Stock, or by acid treatment. It is made in white and a variety of colours, and is used for panels for window-envelopes, as jackets to protect new books, and for general wrapping purposes.

Glazed Morocco. Morocco, the grain of which has been smoothed by calendering to impart a polished appearance. *See also* Crushed Morocco.

Glenerin Declaration. A tri-national statement resulting from a series of meetings of information specialists from Canada, UK and USA, convened by the Institute for Research on Public Policy (Canada), British Library, and National Commission on Libraries and Information Service (USA). (The relevant meeting was held at the Glenerin Inn, Mississauga, Ontario, Canada, in 1988.) The Declaration aims to foster understanding of the role of information in the economy and society, and develop an agenda to maximize the benefits to society of the changing role of information and the information industry. The text can be found in *FID News Bulletin*, 1988, vol. 38, no. 5, pp. 37–38.

GLG. *See* Government Libraries Group.

Global Grid Forum (GGF). <www.ggf.org> A community-initiated forum of individuals from industry and research leading the global standardization effort for Grid computing. Primary objectives are to promote and support the development, deployment, and implementation of grid technologies and applications via the creation and documentation of best practices.

Global Information Infrastructure (GII). <www.giic.org> An initiative in which many countries world-wide share a common objective to ensure that the full potential benefit of advances in information and communications technologies are realized for all citizens. Governments around the globe have come to recognize that the ICT sectors are not only dynamic growth areas themselves, but are also engines of development and economic growth throughout the economy. With this realization, governments have sharply focused their public policy debates and initiatives on the capabilities of their underlying information infrastructures. The GII is a vehicle for expanding the scope of these benefits on a global scale. By interconnecting local, national, regional, and global networks, the GII can increase economic growth, create jobs, and improve infrastructures. Taken as a whole, this world-wide 'network of networks' will create a global information marketplace, encouraging broad-based social discourse within and among all countries. *See also* National Information Infrastructure.

Globus. <www.globus.org> The Globus Alliance conducts research and development to create fundamental technologies behind the Grid to enable the sharing of computing power, databases, and other online tools securely across corporate, institutional, and geographic boundaries without sacrificing local autonomy. The alliance produces Open source software and is developing the Open Grid Services Architecture (OGSA).

Gloss. In ancient MSS. an explanation or interpretation of a word or expression, placed in the margin or above the line, often in a more familiar language. Also used for an explanation inserted in the margin or text of a book to clarify a foreign or difficult passage. *See also* Side note.

Gloss ink. A printing ink consisting of a synthetic resin base and drying oils; this composition ensures that penetration and absorption into the paper is retarded and that it dries with a brilliant, glossy surface. Specially suitable for use with coated papers and for printing by letterpress or lithographic methods.

Glossarial index. An index to a book which gives a description or definition of the word indexed as well as its page number.

Glossary. 1. An alphabetical list of abstruse, obsolete, unusual, specialist, technical, dialectical or other, terms concerned with a subject field, together with definitions. 2. A collection of equivalent synonyms in more than one language.

Glossator. A writer of glosses to texts; a commentator; especially a mediaeval commentator on the texts of civil and canon law.

Glossographer. A writer of glosses to a text, or of commentaries on a text; an annotator. Also called a glossarist, glossist, glottographer.

Glossy print. A photographic print with a shiny surface. These are necessary for the making of satisfactory half-tone blocks.

Gluing off. The process of applying glue to the spine of a book, either after sewing, or instead of sewing, and just prior to placing it within its case.

Glyphic. Styles of Typeface which are chiselled, rather than calligraphic, in form. Of such are Albertus, Augustea and Latin.

Glyphography. A process of making printing plates by engraving on a copper plate covered with a wax film, then dusting with powdered graphite, producing a surface that is used to make an Electrotype.

Go list. (*Indexing, Information retrieval*) A list of terms or characters which one wishes to include in a printout. A Go list makes it possible to select specific items from a very large number forming a group. The opposite of a Stop list.

Goal area. *See* Performance.

Goatskin. Leather manufactured from the skins of goats; the best skins come from the River Niger, the Levant or Morocco, and are named after the places from which they come.

Godfrey Award. <www.cartography.org.uk> (BCS, 16 Emmett Road, Rownhams, Southampton SO16 8JB, UK) Started in 1994, an award made by the British Cartographic Society with the support of Alan Godfrey Maps (Newcastle, UK). The award recognizes a librarian or archivist who has furthered the use, appreciation and understanding of maps.

GODORT. *See* Government Documents Round Table.

Goffered edges. *See* Gauffered edges.

Gold.   Used in the form of thin leaves or foil for lettering or tooling books.

Gold cushion.   A pad, used by binders' finishers, to which a sheet of gold leaf adheres and from which the finisher takes the small pieces required for each book. The pad is usually filled with blotting paper, felt, or similar material, and covered with leather.

Gold knife.   A knife used by binders' finishers, to cut gold leaf while on the gold cushion. It has a long, flat blade, and is sharpened on both sides.

Gold stamped.   A book with a design stamped in gold on the binding. *See also* Block (3), Panel stamp, Tooling.

Gold tooling.   *See* Tooling.

Golden Cockerel Press.   An English private press, founded in December 1920 by Harold Midgely Taylor at Waltham Saint Lawrence, Berkshire, to print and publish (in a co-operative manner, and under the conditions of a 'village industry') new works of literary significance by young authors; and to print and publish fine editions of books of established worth. When Mr. Taylor retired in January 1924 owing to illness, the Press was purchased by Robert Gibbings, illustrator and woodcutter who operated it until 1933. The press is still active. Most of the printing is done in Caslon Old Face.

Golden type.   The first of three types cut by William Morris for his Kelmscott Press. It was a 14 point roman based on an early font used by Nicholas Jenson. *See also* Kelmscott Press.

Gone to bed.   *See* Gone to press

Gone to press.   A term used to indicate that formes or plates have been sent for machining and that it is too late to make any but vital corrections or alterations. Any which occur at this stage are often included in corrigenda. In a newspaper office the term 'Gone to bed' is generally used.

Gooey.   *See* GUI.

Gore.   A triangular piece of paper or thin card on which is printed a section of a map of the world, bounded by meridians and tapering to the Poles; twelve or twenty-four of these can be stuck to a sphere and so make a complete printed globe.

Gothic minuscule.   The style of handwriting which, by the end of the twelfth century, had degenerated from the Carolingian Minuscule into a hand consisting of long, angular pointed letters. It was on this that most of the early European printers based their first types.

Gothic type.   Type resembling the Gothic script used as a book hand in the later middle ages. Gothic types are usually divided into four groups: (1) *Text, Lettre de forme* (Lat. *textura*), or (pointed) church type; (2) *Gothico-antiqua, lettre de somme* (Lat. *fere-humanistica*), the simple round gothic; (3) *Rotunda*, the ordinary round text-type; (4) *Bastard, lettre bâtarde* (Lat. *bastarda*), or cursive type. It is now loosely used to include all bold sans serif and grotesque typefaces. Also called 'Black letter type'.

Gothico-antiqua.   *See* Gothic type.

Gottlieb (Murray) Prize.   Offered by the (American) Medical Library Association for the best essay submitted on some phase of medical history.

Goudy.   A typeface named after the American type designer, Frederic W. Goudy who flourished in the early years of the twentieth century. Probably his most famous type is Kennerley.

Gouffered.   *See* Gauffered edges.

Gouge.   A bookbinder's finishing tool for producing a curved line on a book cover at a single application. It has a set of arcs of concentric circles.

Governance.   A term that gained popularity in the corporate area, and is now spreading into the public service area; as it spreads, it seems to become an alternative term for 'government', but its original, specific meaning covers issues of control and government that relate particularly to identification, analysis, assessment, evaluation, monitoring and management of risk in business. Clear audit trails are therefore a necessary part of governance, and must be monitored as Knowledge management and Content management programmes are introduced. At the World Summit on the Information Society, no way forward was found on Internet governance and the United Nations agreed to form a Task Force to discuss a definition of Internet governance and identify relevant public policy issues and the roles and responsibilities of different stakeholders.

Government document.   A publication issued at government expense or published by authority of a governmental body. As used in the US, any publication in book, serial or non-book form bearing an imprint of a government, whether federal, state, local, or foreign, and of inter-governmental organizations, such as Unesco. *See also* Government publications, Official publication.

Government Documents Round Table (GODORT).   A discussion group permanently sponsored by the American Library Association.

Government Libraries Group.   A membership group of CILIP, first formed 1977 and representing those employed in central government department libraries, national libraries, museums and galleries.

Government library.   A library maintained out of central government funds. Government libraries normally fall into three broad groups: National libraries, departmental libraries and the libraries of research stations. *See also* Agency.

Government publications.   Publications of an official character, or of an instructional, descriptive, or historical nature, which are published by the government publishing department for parliament or one of the government departments. *See also* Government document, Parliamentary Publications.

GPRS.   General Packet Radio Service, a radio technology for Global System for Mobile Communications (GSM) networks. It incorporates packet-switching protocols, has shorter set-up time for Internet Service Provider connections, and offers the possibility to charge by the amount of data sent rather than connect time. It is designed to support flexible data transmission rates typically up to 20 or 30 Kbps (with a theoretical maximum of 171.2 Kbps), as well as continuous connection to the network. The higher data rates allow users to take part in video conferences and interact with multimedia Web sites and similar applications using mobile handheld devices as well as notebook computers. *See also* GSM, MMS, SMS.

Grabhorn Press.   Founded by the Grabhorn brothers, Edwin and Robert, of San Francisco, this press has established a leading reputation for gifted and original work since the first commission from the Book Club of California in 1921. The Grabhorns are particularly skilful in colour-printing, especially from wood-blocks.

Grain direction.   The direction in which the majority of the fibres in a sheet of paper lie. The moving web of a paper-making machine causes the fibres in the pulp to lie parallel with one another in the direction of the web movement. Also called 'Machine direction'. It is important to determine the 'direction' of paper used for lithography, postage stamps, account books or close register work, to avoid differences in expansion. Hand-made papers expand or shrink equally in all directions due to the shaking which occurs during manufacture and which felts the fibres in all directions. *See also* Against the grain, With the grain.

Grained leather.   A tanned skin on which the natural grain (visible on the side on which the hair grew) has been worked up to raise and accentuate it. Graining is also artificially produced by stamping a skin with engraved metal plates.

Gramophone record.   A sound recording made on a flat, black vinyl disk; the US term is 'phonograph record'. *See also* Disk.

Grand People's Study House, Democratic People's Republic of Korea. *See* Inmin Taehak Suptang.

Grangerizing.   The practice of inserting in a bound volume illustrations, letters, documents, etc., not issued as part of the volume but referred to in the text. Such additional matter is mounted or inlaid on sheets of good quality paper and inserted in the appropriate parts of the book which is usually re-bound. The practice dates from 1769, when James Granger published a *Bibliographical History of England* with blank leaves for the reception of illustrations. Such a volume is said to be 'Extra-illustrated' or 'Grangerized'.

Granularity.   The level of detail expressed in a search term and an information resource that influences the relevance of retrieved data to the end user. The end user can move along an information granularity spectrum, beginning with coarse granularity criteria (broad terms) that lead to large results, subsequently narrowing these to a finer granularity that reduces the size of the result set.

Graph.   A pictorial representation of numerical data. Graphs may take various forms and are described as pictograms or as bar, line, broken-line or circular, graphs.

Graphic. Styles of typefaces which suggest that the characters have not been written but drawn. Of such are Cartoon, Libra and Old English (Monotype).

Graphical user interface. *See* GUI.

Graphics. Non-textual material, e.g. diagrams, drawings, photographs, graphs.

Graphics tablet. *See* Tablet (2).

Graticule. A system of lines representing meridians and parallels on a map. Not to be confused with grid which is a network of parallel lines drawn at right angles on a map to represent fixed distances.

Graver. *See* Burin.

Gravure. A French word, meaning cutting or engraving; used to denote various illustration processes such as Photogravure, Rotogravure, etc.

Great primer. An out-of-date name for a size of type equal to about 18 point.

Greek fashion. Book bindings with raised Headbands i.e. those which project beyond the boards at the head and tail of the spine. The Greek technique of forwarding was used in the West only for Greek books.

Greek Library Association. *See* Enosis Hellenikon Bibliothekarion.

Greek National Library. *See* Ethniki Vivliotiki tis Ellados.

Green Book. An official report published by the Italian government; so called because bound in a green paper cover. *See also* Blue Book.

Green Paper. A document issued by any Department or Ministry of the British Government. It has green covers, and sets out government propositions so that full consultation and public discussion may take place while policy is still in a formative stage. Green Papers are intended to meet the need for better communication between Government and public rather than to present proposals as in a White Paper. *See also* Blue Book, Parliamentary papers, White Paper.

Green publisher. A publisher, as defined by the ROMEO project, that permits authors to Self archive both the pre-print and the post-print of their academic papers.

Greenaway (Kate) Medal. <www.carnegiegreenaway.org.uk> <www.cilip. org/practice/awards.html> An award made by CILIP to recognize the importance of illustrations in children's books. It was first awarded in 1956.

Greer (Helen) Memorial Prize. Presented annually to a European Documentation Centre librarian by the European Information Association (EIA).

Gregynog Press. A private press founded in 1922 within the cultural centre formed by the Misses Gwendoline and Margaret Davies at Newtown, Montgomeryshire (now Powys), Wales. The press ran from 1923–40 under a succession of controllers; wood engraving was a speciality, and Kennerley, Bembo, and Poliphilus types were much used. Bindings were varied in style. The press was willed to the University of Wales, and re-started operation in 1978.

Grey literature. 'Semi-published' material, for example reports, internal documents, theses etc. not formally published or available commercially, and consequently difficult to trace bibliographically. *See also* System for Information on Grey Literature in Europe.

Greyscale. The number of shades of grey ranging between black and white that can be displayed or produced by a computer graphics system. Generally used in relation to non-colour images generated by a Scanner and to the capabilities of computer displays. An eight-bit greyscale image could have 256 greys between black and white. *See also* Half-tone.

Grid. 1. A technology for linking high-performance computers, data resources, scientific instruments and visualization environments using high bandwidth networks through co-ordinated resource sharing. The Grid is initially finding application in advanced scientific research projects as exemplified by a section of the UK e-Science programme and via the Global Grid Forum. *See also* Globus, GRIDS, Open Grid Services Architecture, NCess, Virtual organizations. 2. (*Binding*) An ornament which is frequently used on heads-in-medallions rolls, and consists of two horizontal lines with a few short vertical bars between them, the sides having a foliage character. 3. (*Cartography*) A referencing system using distances measured on a chosen projection. Not to be confused with Graticule.

Grid reference. The position of a point on a map expressed in grid letters and co-ordinates, or co-ordinates alone. *See also* Grid (3).

GRIDS. <www.grids-center.org> Grid Research Integration Development and Support Center, created through the NSF Middleware Initiative to define, develop and deploy an integrated national middleware infrastructure in support of 21st Century science and engineering applications. GRIDS is a partnership of the University of Southern California's Information Sciences Institute, the National Center for Supercomputing Applications, the University of Chicago, the San Diego Supercomputer Center, and the University of Wisconsin-Madison.

Grievance. The term used when an employee has a complaint against an employer relating to allegedly unfair disciplinary action, discrimination, dismissal etc.

Griffin Poetry Prize. <www.griffinpoetryprize.com> Two awards made by the Griffin Trust, for published poetry: one is for a Canadian poet, the other is awarded internationally.

Grigg Committee. Popular name of the (UK) Committee on Departmental Records of which Sir James Grigg was Chairman. It was set up in 1952 by the Master of the Rolls and the Chancellor of the Exchequer to review the arrangements for the preservation of Government Departments' records and to make recommendations. The Committee's report was presented in 1954, and the recommendations it contained were accepted by Government in principle; the Public Records Act 1958 which came into force on 1 January 1959 repealed the former acts of 1838, 1877 and 1898. This Act transferred the direction of the Public Record Office from the Master of the Rolls to a Minister of the Crown, the Lord Chancellor, who was given a general responsibility for public records. *See also* Modern Public Records, Public Records, Wilson Committee.

Gripper edge.   *See* Lay edges.

Grolier Americana Scholarships.   Donated by the Grolier Foundation, and made to two library schools, one of which is a graduate library school and the other with a programme of library education at undergraduate level, for scholarships for a student in each institution who is in training for school librarianship. It is awarded annually, and administered by the American Association of School Librarians.

Grolier Foundation Award.   This award is made annually to a librarian in a community or in a school who has made an unusual contribution to the stimulation and guidance of reading by children and young people. Selection of the recipient is made by a jury appointed by the American Library Association Awards Committee.

Grolieresque.   The style of binding which is associated with Jean Grolier (1479–1565). It depends for its effect on light and graceful geometrical 'strapwork' (interlaced double fillets), and influenced ornate binding for two centuries. *See also* Maioli Style.

Groove.   The cut-out portion of the base of a piece of movable type. Also called 'Heel-nick'. It has no particular purpose in printing. *See also* Feet.

Grooves.   (*Binding*) 1. The shoulders formed on the sides of books in backing, to allow the boards to lie even with the back when secured. 2. Incisions in the back edge of a board to take the cords on which the sections are sewn.

Grotesque.   Sans serif display types of unconventional design. A name given at the beginning of the nineteenth century to the earliest Sans serif types, which have been revived and come into favour for display work. During the 1920s and 1930s the following sans serif faces became popular: Futura, Gill, Granby, Vogue. These are a group of Lineale typefaces with nineteenth-century origins. Some contrast in the thickness of the strokes exists, and there is a squareness in the curves. The ends of the curved strokes are usually horizontal. The G is spurred and the R usually has a curled leg. *See also* Neo-grotesque.

Ground.   An acid-resisting compound used on etching plates to protect the non-image-bearing portions from the action of the acid. It is composed of beeswax, asphaltum, gum mastic and pitch.

Groundwood pulp.   *See* Mechanical wood.

Group.   1. A section of the membership of CILIP concerned with a particular special interest.   2. A section of the membership of the Society of Archivists devoted to a special form of archive materials or a professional specialism.   3. (*Archives*) The archives of a distinct organization, body or person, considered as a whole. A level of archival arrangement and description, used in *MAD* as an alternative (for the UK) to the international 'Fonds'. Sometimes also (erroneously) referred to as 'collection'.

Groupement Français de l'Industrie de l'Information.   *See* GFII.

Groupware.   Applications software that permits members of a workgroup connected to a LAN or Intranet to work on a single document or group of documents simultaneously and co-operatively.

Growing flower.   A common ornament on bookbinders' finishers' rolls, consisting usually of a flattened elliptical base from which springs a stem bearing leaves and at the top two flowers, the tops of which curl outwards.

Grub Street.   An expression for the world of less-successful authors. According to Dr. Johnson, 'originally the name of a street near Moorfields, much inhabited by writers of small histories, dictionaries, and occasional poems...'.

GSAFD.   Guidelines on Subject Access to Individual Works of Fiction, Drama, etc. *See* Genre.

GSM.   Global System for Mobile Communications, the pan-European standard for digital cellular telephone services. GSM networks were built as an alternative to AMPS systems and support enhanced data applications. GSM was designed for European markets to provide the advantage of automatic, international roaming in multiple countries. The SIM (Subscriber Identification Module) card is a vital component, enabling the user to store all relevant data for the phone on a removable plastic card. The card can be plugged into any GSM compatible phone and the phone is instantly personalized to the user. *See also* GPRS.

g.t. (or g.t.e.).   Abbreviation for Gilt top.

gTLD.   Generic Top Level Domain; *see* Domain Name System.

Guard.   1. A strip of linen or paper pasted by a binder (a) onto or into the sections of a book to prevent the sewing tearing through the paper, (b) on the inner edge of an illustration, the guard being sewn through. 2. One or more pieces of paper or linen placed together to equalize the space taken by a folded map or other insert or by material pasted to the pages of cuttings book. Also to enable additional illustrations, maps or leaves to be added after binding. Also called 'Stub'.

Guard book catalogue.   *See* Page catalogue.

Guard sheet.   A sheet of paper, usually thinner (and often transparent) than that on which the book is printed, bearing a letterpress description or an outline drawing to protect and/or elucidate the illustration which it accompanies. The guard sheet is not normally included in the pagination.

Guarding.   Fixing a guard to a section, map or illustration, etc. Strengthening the fold between two conjugate leaves with an adhesive, pasted, or glued-on strip of paper.

GUI.   Graphical user interface, a method of interacting with a computer using a Mouse, Icons, and Windows in place of Command driven systems. A WIMPS interface provides the same features. Often pronounced 'gooey'.

Guide. (*Archives*) A published finding aid which summarizes the holdings of a repository, usually at group or group/class levels, as a help to users.

Guide card. A card with a projecting tab used in a card catalogue or file to indicate the arrangement and to facilitate reference.

Guide letter. A letter printed in the space to be filled by the rubrisher or illuminator of an early printed book as a guide to prevent the insertion of a wrong letter.

Guide slip. *See* Process slip.

Guidelines on Subject Access to Individual Works of Fiction, Drama, etc. *See* Genre.

Guiding. A system of signs, signpostings, maps, plans, shelf-labels or symbols devised to assist a user in finding services, categories of stock etc., in a library.

Guillemets. *See* Duck-foot quotes, Quotes.

Gum Arabic. A solution used to preserve offset plates, and in lithographic printing. *See also* Desensitization.

Gumming up. Applying a solution of gum arabic to an offset plate to protect it from grease and oxidation.

Gutenberg. *See* Project Gutenberg.

Gutenberg-Gesellschaft [Gutenberg Society]. <www.gutenberg-gesellscheft.uni-mainz.de> (Liebfrauenplatz 5, 55116 Mainz, Germany). Founded in 1901, the Society has 1,700 members and encourages research in the art of printing and books from Gutenberg to the present. Publishes *Gutenberg-Jahrbuch* (a.).

Gutter. 1. The adjoining inner margins of two facing pages of type; the margins at the sewn fold of a section. 2. (*Binding*) The trough between the edge of the board and the backed spine of a bound book. *See also* Backing, Groove, Joint (3), Spine. 3. In a permuted title, index, or similar mechanically-produced listing, a vertical column of one or more spaces at which point the index words are positioned to provide a readily-viewable alphabetical order.

Gutter margin. *See* Back margin.

Guttering. The ridges that sometimes occur (as a result of use) along the spine of a binding which has a tight or a flexible back.

Guust van Wesermael Prize. *See* Wesermael (Guust van) Prize.

Gypsographic print. *See* Seal print.

H & J. Abbreviation for hyphenation and justification, combined features that affect the spacing between words and the general appearance of paragraphs in a printed document. Justification of text can give rise to white space and Rivers when long words have to be transferred to the next line and hyphenation enables these words to be broken at syllable (or user-defined) breaks to avoid the unsightliness. Desktop publishing programs generally allow close control over H and J.

H.264 Advanced Video Codec (AVC).   The Codec to be included in the 'next generation' High Definition DVD format jointly developed by MPEG and the International Telecommunication Union and ratified into the MPEG-4 specification. H.264/AVC is based on open standards and designed to deliver excellent quality across the entire bandwidth spectrum, from high definition television to video conferencing and 3G mobile multimedia.

Hachures.   Vertical and horizontal lines used on a map to indicate by their length and closeness the direction and steepness of variations in height of the earth's surface, the lines being crowded together to represent the steepest slopes. *See also* Hatching.

Hacker.   One who gains unregistered – and thereby generally unlawful – access to a remote networked computer system.

Hagar Press.   The German counterpart of the Albion Press.

Hagionym.   The name of a saint taken as a proper name.

Hague Scheme.   A scheme of book classification compiled by Dr. Greve. *See also* SISO.

Hair line.   A thin stroke of a letter or type character.

Hair space.   (*Printing*) The thinnest spacing material. It is cast less than type height and is used between letters or words. Hair spaces vary in thickness from eight to twelve to an em, according to body size, thus in 6pt. the hair space is $1/2$ pt.; in 12 pt. it is $1 1/2$ pts.; in 18 pt. it is 2 pts.; and in 24 pt. it is 3 pts.

Half bands.   Ridges on the spine of a bound book, at the top and bottom, smaller than bands. They usually mark the position of the Kettle stitch.

Half binding.   *See* Quarter binding.

Half bound.   *See* Half leather.

Half cloth.   A book with a cloth spine, usually with the title printed on a paper label, and having paper covered 'board' (i.e. strawboard) sides. May also be called 'Half linen'.

Half frame.   The use of a mask in the gate of a camera to reduce the image to half size.

Half leather.   A term used to describe a book with a leather spine and corners, but with the rest of the sides covered in cloth. *See also* Leather bound, Quarter leather.

Half monthly.   A periodical issued twice a month, or fortnightly.

Half see safe.   An expression used by a bookseller when ordering copies of a book from a publisher to indicate that, while all copies will be paid for, he may ask the publisher to take back half of them in exchange for copies of another title. *See also* See safe.

Half uncial.   The last stage in the development of the Roman period of Latin manuscript handwriting, being a somewhat informal kind of letter based on minuscule forms and used from the fifth to the ninth centuries. It is specially associated with the calligraphic revival by Alcuin in the ninth century. Most of the letters were minuscules, only a few of the capitals, such as N and F, remaining.

Half yearly. A periodical which is issued at six-monthly intervals. Also called 'Semi-annual'. *See also* Bi-annual.

Half-dark type. *See* Medium face.

Half-duplex. *See* Duplex.

Half-line block. A printing block made by interposing a half-line screen (i.e. parallel lines without cross-lines) between the original line drawing and the negative. The result is lighter in tone than the original.

Half-linen. *See* Half cloth.

Half-measure. *See* Double columned.

Half-sheet work. Printing (with two machinings) a sheet of paper on both sides with the same Forme, laid out in such a way that the paper may then be cut in half to give two copies. *See also* Sheet work. Also called 'Half-sheet imposition'.

Half-stamp. (*Binding*) A finisher's stamp the design of which is the same as, or similar to, one half of a fleuron, pineapple, etc. It is generally used for the compartments at the edges of the frame in lozenge compartment bindings. Sometimes used back to back to form the lozenges in the centre.

Half-stuff. (*Paper*) Partially broken and washed Stock which has been reduced to a fibrous pulp, usually before it is bleached. The finished pulp, ready for the vat or paper machine is termed 'whole-stuff'. *See also* Pulp, Stock, Stuff, Whole-stuff.

Half-title. The brief title of a book appearing on the recto of the leaf preceding the title-page. It serves to protect the title-page and help the printer to identify the book to which the first sheet belongs. The wording of long titles is often abbreviated. The use of such a page dates from the latter half of the seventeenth century although a blank sheet had been used to protect title-pages for a very long time. It is often abbreviated h.t. Also called 'Bastard title', 'Fly-title'. *See also* Second half-title.

Half-tone. The name given to the process by means of which photographs, drawings, designs, etc., are reproduced in tone as opposed to solid black and white: also to the actual prints made by it. The printing plate is of copper or zinc and the image is reduced to a series of dots varying in intensity with the tone values of the original. This is done photographically in conjunction with a mechanically ruled screen which is coarse with few dots to the square inch for printing on coarse papers, and many to the square inch for fine, smooth papers. Etching removes the background, leaving the dots representing the image to be printed by relief process. A *Squared-up half-tone* is one finished with straight sides at right angles. Half-tones are also finished as Circles or Ovals. A *Vignetted half-tone* is one which has no sharp edge to the design, and 'fades' out. A *Cut-out half-tone* is one from which the background is entirely removed. A *Deep-etched half-tone* is one from highlights of which the dots characteristic of a half-tone are entirely removed, leaving the paper virgin white in the reproduction. A *Highlight,* or *Drop-out*, is one from which the dots have been removed.

Half-tone paper. An Art, imitation art, or other super-calendered or coated paper suitable for the printing of half-tones.

Half-tone screens. Transparent plates of glass used for making half-tone blocks. They are ruled diagonally with opaque lines usually, but not necessarily, at right angles to each other, the thickness of the lines and of the intervening spaces being approximately equal. The number of lines to the inch varies, 'fine' screens having more than 'coarse' ones. The smoother the paper used, the finer must be the half-tone block. *See also* Screen.

Hand. The printers' symbol ☞. Used to attract attention. Also called 'Digit', 'Fist', 'Index'.

Hand composition. The setting up of printer's type by hand as distinct from machine setting.

Hand gravure. A method of copperplate printing. After inking and before each impression is taken, the surface is wiped by hand.

Hand press. A press in which the forme is inked, the paper fed and removed, and the pressure applied, by hand; used to distinguish it from one worked by power; often used in printing offices to pull proofs by hand and for short runs on small sheets of paper. It is the direct descendant of the earliest type of printing press.

Hand Press Book Database. *See* Consortium of European Research Libraries.

Hand roller. *See* Brayer.

Hand set. Type which has been set by hand, as opposed to type set by machine.

Hand sewing. The sewing by hand through the folds of sections of a book, using a sewing frame. *See also* Sewn.

Hand stamp. A brass letter, or motif, set in a wooden handle, and used by a binder's finisher in lettering the cover of a hand-bound book.

Handbill. A poster, or placard, printed by hand.

Handbook. A treatise on a special subject; often nowadays a simple but all-embracing treatment, containing concise information, and being small enough to be held in the hand; but strictly, a book written primarily for practitioners and serving for constant revision or reference. Also called a 'Manual'.

Handle system. <www.handle.net> A distributed system developed by the Corporation for National Research Initiatives which stores names of digital objects and resolves the names into the information necessary to locate and access resources. Use of the system is intended to ensure stability in the names of digital objects so that even if a URL changes, the handle remains the same. The handle system is implemented in the Digital Object Identifier.

Hand-made paper. Paper made by dipping a mould into the pulp vat and taking up sufficient 'stuff' to form a sheet of paper of the required substance. A shaking movement causes the fibres to mix together. The pulp is composed of rag fibres; when the best linen rags are used the resulting paper is the most durable obtainable. Also called 'Vat paper'.

Hand-shaking. In telecommunications, the process of affirming that data transfer can take place by an exchange of signals. Handshakes can be software or hardware controlled.

Handwriting. Books were produced by writing by hand before the use of wood blocks early in the fifteenth century (*see* Block books). After European countries had shaken off the political authority of the Roman empire, and the educated communities had been scattered and dissolved, the Latin 'cursive' or 'running' script changed and several 'national' hands or style of the Latin cursive minuscule developed. The five principal national hands are South Italian or Beneventan, Merovingian (in France), Visigothic (in Spain), Germanic pre-Carolingian, and Insular (in Ireland and England). The earliest of the five periods into which Latin manuscript handwriting can be divided is the Roman period (second to eighth centuries) and this can be divided into five groups: *Quadrata*, or *Square capital*, hand; *Rustic capital* hand; *Uncial* hand; *Later cursive* hand; and *Half uncial* hand.

Hang. An unexpected freezing of a computer system, the only usual recourse being the powering down and powering up of the machine. Hangs cannot always be replicated and can (seemingly) depend on one-off situations. *See also* Crash.

Hanging figures. The numerals of certain type-designs which range within the limits of the Extruders. Old face types usually have hanging figures, although in some, e.g. Plantin, Ranging figures are available as an alternative. *See* Old Style figures.

Hanging indention. A paragraph of which the first line is set to the full width of the measure, the second and all subsequent lines of the paragraph being indented one or more ems from the left-hand margin as for this definition. *See also* Em, Paragraph indention. Also called 'Hanging paragraph'.

Han'guk Kwahak Kisul Chongbo Yongu-won. [Korea Institute of Science and Technology Information (KISTI)] <www.kisti.re.kr> (Eoeun-dong 52, Yuseong-gu, Daejeon-si, 122, S. Korea). A government organization with a key role to promote a nationwide infrastructure for knowledge and information. Hosts the Korean Library and Information Science Society. KISTI provides a nationwide information service via its KINITI-IR service, offering 10 foreign databases in the English language and over 25 domestic bibliographic databases.

Han'guk Tosogwan Chongbo Hakhoe. [Korean Library and Information Science Society] *See* Han'guk Kwahak Kisul Chongbo Yongu-won.

Han'guk Tosogwan Hyophoe. [Korean Library Association (KLA)] <www.korla.or.kr> (3-60-1 Panpo-dong, Seocho-gu, Seoul, 137-702, S. Korea) Founded in 1955, and based at the National Library of Korea, its function is to contribute to cultural advancement through development of the library service. Its aims are to develop standards and to encourage education and research in library management, and to co-operate with international professional organizations. It represents Korea at IFLA. Publishes *KLA Bulletin* (m.), plus subject guides and bibliographies.

'Hansard'.   *See* Parliamentary Publications.

Hard bound.   Bound in cloth- or paper-covered boards. Also called 'Hard cover'.

Hard copy.   A document or record output from a computer system to a printer rather than read directly on screen.

Hard cover.   *See* Hard bound.

Hard disk.   *See* Disk.

Hard packing.   Thin card, or hard or stiff paper, used to cover the cylinder of a printing press in order to obtain a sharp impression, with little indentation of the paper, when printing on smooth hard paper.

Hardback.   A book published in stiff covers. The opposite of Paperback.

Hardware.   In general, a term that can be applied to any equipment. More specifically applied to equipment used in ICT and particularly to computer equipment i.e. the display unit and the box that holds the Central Processing Unit, hard Disk, etc, together with all Peripherals. *See also* Software.

Harleian Style.   An English style of book decoration with a centre motif composed of small tools usually arranged in a lozenge-shaped design, and having an elaborate if sometimes rather narrow border decorated by means of one or more rolls. These 'Harleian' bindings were made by Thomas Elliott for Robert and Edward Harley, the First and Second Earls of Oxford.

Harris (John) Award.   Offered by the New Zealand Library and Information Association (now LIANZA) 'for the written record of notable library work, whether in the bibliographical, critical, historical or administrative fields, which will be a contribution to New Zealand librarianship'. It was first made to W. J. McEldowney in 1963.

Hart's Rules.   A classic rule book for compositors and proofreaders, compiled in 1903 by Horace Hart.

Harvard Style.   A method of citing papers from scientific books and periodicals. The items making up a reference are as follows: (i) author's name and initials; (ii) year of publication, in parentheses, with *a, b,* etc. if more than one paper in the year is cited; (iii) full title of paper (roman type); (iv) name of periodical, maybe contracted as in the *World list of scientific periodicals* (italic type); (v) volume number (in bold arabic figures, or preceded by 'vol.'); (vi) part number, maybe in parentheses with date; (vii) pagination; e.g.

Weng, C. G., Tam, M. T. and Lin, G. C. (1992), Acoustic emission characteristics of mortar under compression. *Cement and Concrete Research*, vol. 22, no. 4, (July), pp. 641–652.

One of the chief advantages of this system is that footnotes can be dispensed with, a list of references being printed at the end of the article in alphabetical order of authors' names. In the text, references are given by printing the author's name and the date of publication in parentheses as (Weng, Tam and Lin, 1992), but if the author's name is part of the text the date only is given in (). When three or more authors have collaborated in a paper, all the names are given in the first citation, but subsequently only the first name followed by ' *et al.* ' need be used. *See also* Chicago Style, Vancouver Style.

Harvest. A system providing a software architecture for gathering, indexing and accessing Internet information. *See*, for example, Open Archives Initiative Protocol for Metadata Harvesting. *See also* Web harvesting.

Hash. The sign # commonly found on alphanumeric keyboards for computer or viewdata use.

Hatching. A row of parallel, diagonal lines. Often found on the half bands or on the heads and tails of the spines of bindings from the sixteenth century onwards. Also used for the 'azured' shading on the centres of finishers' tools. *See also* Cross hatching, Hachures.

HATRICS – Southern Information Network. <www.hants.gov.uk/hatrics> (Hampshire County Libraries, 81 North Walls, Winchester SO23 8BY, UK) A co-operative organization of libraries, industrial and commercial firms. Founded to develop industry and commerce through an information network, and to assist members in their information needs.

Hawley Committee. The body responsible for *Information as an Asset: the Board Agenda; a Consultative Report* (Chairman Dr. Robert Hawley) which was issued in 1995 by the KPMG IMPACT Programme. The programme is a club of major organizations seeking to share experience in information management; the Committee was examining how information should be valued as an asset of business. The Report was widely regarded as a significant move towards higher regard for information.

Hawnt Report. The Report on *The public library service in Northern Ireland*, 1966, (Belfast HMSO, Cmd. 494), so named after Dr. J. S. Hawnt, the Chairman of the Advisory Committee appointed in September 1964 by the Minister of Education, Government of Northern Ireland, 'to consider the public library service... and make recommendations for its development, having regard to the relationship of public libraries to other libraries'.

HDTV. High definition television, broadcast television that provides a screen resolution of up to 1,080 lines, compared to the 625 lines for a PAL analogue set. The standard can also include hifi audio to allow for surround sound. Standards and implementations vary throughout the world with Japan having used analogue HDTV for a number of years, the US launching digital HDTV around 1999, while there has been no substantial take-up of the technology in Europe. *See also* HDV.

HDV. High Definition Video, a specification agreed in September 2003 by a consortium of companies including Sony, Canon, JVC and Sharp. HDV writes digital data to a tape cassette in a camcorder and compresses using MPEG-2, resulting in much higher resolution at the same file sizes when compared to standard-definition DV.

Head. 1. The margin at the top of a page. 2. The top of a book or of a page. 3. The top of the spine of a book where the headband is placed. 4. The top edge of a book. *See also* Foot. 5. In a document record, the primary identification field containing the author, title, citation and brief abstract.

Head and tail. The top and bottom edges of a book.

Head margin. The blank space above the top line of printed matter. 'Heads' relates to the top margins.

Head ornament. An ornament specially designed for the top of a page: it may incorporate the lettering of the chapter heading, or provide an *island space* in which to print it. It is sometimes called a 'Headband' or 'Head piece'. *See also* Tail ornament.

Head piece. *See* Head ornament.

Head title. The title, even in abbreviated form, given as a heading above a page or on the first page of a piece of music. *See also* Headline.

Headband. (*Binding*) The band, usually of coloured silk threads, at the head of a book, sewn or glued to the folds of sections, placed between the sections and the cover, and projecting slightly beyond the head. Originally it was a cord or leather thong similar to the ordinary bands, around which the ends of the threads were twisted, and laced in to the boards. Nowadays headbands are usually made of coloured silks and are sewn on after the book has been forwarded thus having no purpose other than decoration. The two were formerly distinguished as 'headband' and 'tailband' but both are now called 'headbands' or 'heads'. *See also* Tailband. 2. (*Printing*) A printed or engraved decorative band at the head of a page or chapter. Also called 'Head piece', 'Head ornament'.

Headcap. The thickened end of the spine at head and tail of the leather spine of a book; this is caused by placing a piece of sized Italian hemp inside the turn-in at the head and tail of the spine after the leather has been fitted to the book. If headbands are used, they are left visible. *See also* Headband, Tailcap.

Heading. 1. (*Cataloguing*) The first sequence of characters (forming a number, name, word or phrase) at the beginning of a catalogue entry to (a) determine the exact position of an entry in a catalogue, (b) keep group-related entries together in a catalogue. A third function of a heading is to display entries either singly or in groups. This function has become more important in the various forms of printed catalogues. The heading is generally the author, subject, or first word not an article, of the title, but may be the class number. *See also* Entry word, Form heading, Form sub-heading, Subheading, Uniform heading.

2. (*Information retrieval*) The word, name or phrase at the beginning of an entry to indicate some special aspect of the document (authorship, subject content, series, title, etc.).   3. (*Indexing*) The word(s) or symbol(s) selected from, or based on, an item in the text, used as an additional part of an entry; this includes any qualifying expression or epithet. Such words or symbols express the subject or idea to which reference is given and appear at the beginning of the entry.   4. The entry word followed by any other (or others) necessary for its meaning. 5. The word or words at the top of a page, chapter or section. 6. (*Book production, Printing*) Sub-headings which divide chapters and comprise Cross-heads, Incut note, Marginal notes, Shoulder-heads, Sideheads.

Headline. The heading at the top of the page giving the title of the book (usually on the verso) or the subject of the chapter or of the page (usually on the recto). Also called 'Page head'. *See also* Caption title, Half-title, Page headline, Running title, Section headline. When giving the title of the book, even in abbreviated or different form, it may be called 'Head title'.

Headnote. (*Archives*) In *MAD* used to designate a block of text set at the head of a list of archive materials, in which information is given relating to provenance.

Heads. *See* Head, Head margin.

Health care libraries. A generic term covering medical, nursing, and hospital library services, together with specialized resources in ancillary fields.

Health Libraries Group. A membership group of CILIP, originally formed in 1978 by the merger of the Hospital Libraries and Handicapped Readers Group and the Medical Section, and previously titled the Medical, Health and Welfare Libraries Group.

HEAnet. <www.heanet.ie> The Higher Education Network implemented for academic institutions in Ireland.

HEDS. <heds.herts.ac.uk> Originally Higher Education Digitisation Service, HEDS provides advice, consultancy, and a complete production service for digitization and digital resource development and management. It serves the higher education sector, museums, public and national libraries, archives and other not-for-profit organizations.

Heel-nick. *See* Groove.

HEFC. *See* Higher Education Funding Councils.

Heidelberg. The name of a fully automatic printing press made by the Schnellpressenfabrik A.G., Heidelberg. The first press was a platen press made in 1914, in which the paper was fed by revolving wings. The Cylinder Heidelberg, first marketed in 1936, is a single-revolution machine in which the cylinder, moving at a constant speed, makes one revolution for each impression.

Height to paper. The exact height of type from the bottom (or feet) of the type to the printing surface. Types of the exact height will print evenly;

those which are too high receive too much pressure while those too low receive little or no pressure. Also called Type height.

Heiligenbilder. *See* Helgen.

HEIRNET. <www.britarch.ac.uk/HEIRNET> Historic Environment Information Resources Network, formed by a group of organizations with an interest in information relating to archaeology and the historic environment. HEIRNET enables access to information resources for conservation, research, learning and general interest through promotional activities and by offering technical advice.

Helgen. Woodcuts printed on paper at the end of the fourteenth century and beginning of the fifteenth. They were usually very simple black-line pictures, often hand-coloured, with little or no shading, and consisted of pictures of the saints or other religious subjects. They were intended to illustrate the teachings of the wandering monks who distributed them to the illiterate peasantry. Also called 'Heiligenbilder'.

HELICON. <www.lib.jr2.ox.ac.uk/linchealth> The (UK) Health Library and Information Confederation; a strategy group originally functioning as the LINC Health Panel until the demise of that body in 2001.

HELIN. <library.uri.edu> Higher Education Library Information Network (Rhode Island).

Heliograph. A print made by Albrecht Breyer of Berlin who used the Reflex copying process in 1839. He placed silver chloride papers in contact with the printed pages to be copied.

Heliography. 1. An obsolete name for photography. 2. In photo-engraving, the art of fixing the images produced by the *camera obscura*.

Heliogravure. Any photo-engraving process by which intaglio engravings are made.

Hellbox. (*Printing*) The box into which damaged or broken type made on a casting machine is thrown for melting down and re-casting.

Helpful order. The order of items in a classification schedule which displays the subjects in such a way that the order itself leads the user to the specific subject needed.

Hemi-celluloses. (*Paper*) Impure forms of cellulose consisting of organic substances, comprising, in the main, sugars, starches and carbohydrates. These are associated with cellulose (which is formed from the elements carbon, hydrogen and oxygen, and obtained from the atmosphere by the process known as photo-synthesis) in plant fibres. A high hemi-cellulose content in pulp is desirable as this provides a paper with good bonding and folding qualities.

Hemp. A fibre derived from the tissue of an annual plant which is grown extensively in America, Asia and many parts of Europe. Hemp, hemp refuse, twines and old ropes are used to make brown wrapping paper and cable insulating paper.

Henne (Frances) Award. An award to enable a young school library media specialist to attend an American Association of School Librarians conference, or an American Library Association Conference.

HENSA.   Higher Education National Software Archive, transferred to the UK Mirror Service in 1999.

Her Majesty's Stationery Office.   <www.tso.co.uk> The government publisher in Britain, variously named 'Her Majesty's' or 'His Majesty's' according to whether the ruling monarch was a queen or king. HMSO printed all Parliamentary Publications and many others but arranged with commercial printers to print much that was published. The printing of stationery and the purchase of books was undertaken for government departments and libraries as well as the publishing for all government departments. It was also the agency in the United Kingdom for publications of Unesco, the United Nations, OECD, and some other international bodies and governments. In 1996 HMSO was privatized, and much government publishing is now carried out by departments themselves or by commercial companies. Certain residual functions are still in the hands of the HMSO, which now uses the title 'The Stationery Office' (TSO).

Heraldic cresting.   Cresting on bindings, the projections of which terminate in heraldic (usually Tudor) emblems. *See also* Cresting roll.

Heritage Lottery Fund.   <www.hlf.org.uk> (7 Holbein Place, London SW1W 8NR, UK) Administered by the National Heritage Memorial Fund, and funded from the UK National Lottery, the Fund is used to support projects that help preserve or restore access to land, buildings, objects or collections of interest to the local, regional or national heritage. Several grants have been made to libraries.

HERO.   <www.hero.ac.uk> Higher Education and Research Opportunities in the United Kingdom, the primary Internet portal for academic research and higher education in the UK. In the 'Resources' section of its web site <www.hero.ac.uk/reference_resources/index.cfm>, it includes a list of OPACs in Britain and Ireland (not just academic libraries), previously available through NISS.

HERON.   <www.heron.ingenta.com> Higher Education Resources ON-demand, originally an eLib project that investigated the problems associated with online publishing and electronic reserves, particularly those associated with copyright clearance. HERON operates a national resource bank of digitized extracts and acts as a one-stop-shop for copyright clearance and digitization on behalf of universities and colleges. In March 2002, HERON was acquired by Ingenta.

HERTIS Information and Research.   Originally conceived in 1956 as a technical information co-operative based on Hatfield Polytechnic; now merged into CIMTECH.

HESA.   <www.hesa.ac.uk> Higher Education Statistics Agency, set up in 1993 to collect, analyse and report on HE statistics as the basis of a comprehensive management information system for publicly funded HE in the UK. HESA collects five main data sets: student; student first destinations; staff; finance and the non-credit-bearing course records.

Heures.   *See* Book of Hours.

Heuristic searching.   The search for information using Heuristic techniques, the search being modified as it progresses, each piece of information or document found tending to influence the user's continuing search.

Heuristic techniques.   Problem-solving methodologies and programs based on successive applications of trial and error to achieve the final result.

Hierarchical classification.   1. A scheme of classification in which the schedules are developed systematically, every term, descriptor, or isolate (*See* Isolate (3)) showing a logical relationship to each preceding and following term.   2. A scheme of classification in which the terms are arranged according to a genus-species, or whole-part principle and are consequently arranged in subordination to other terms. The Dewey Decimal Classification is of this kind.

Hierarchical force.   (*Classification*) The property by which headings and certain notes apply to all subdivisions of the topic described and defined. What is true of genus is also true of its species.

Hierarchical notation.   (*Classification*) A Notation which is designed to show the subordination of terms. The chains and arrays of symbols reflect the hierarchy of terms. All main classes are represented by symbols of equal length, and new main classes are inserted by the introduction of new digits. Also called 'Expressive notation', 'Structural notation'.

Hierarchy.   The order of precedence in which subjects are set out in the schedule of a scheme of classification. Where each element in a sequence of terms has a unique predecessor, this is known as *strong hierarchy*; in a *weak hierarchy* an element may have more than one predecessor; a given descriptor may be immediately subordinate to more than one generic descriptor.

Hieroglyph.   A character, originally in the form of picture-writing engraved in stone by the ancient Egyptians, to convey thoughts or information. Any symbol or character used in any form of picture-writing. The meaning of the ancient Egyptian symbols was discovered in 1799 by Champollion when he deciphered the Rosetta Stone, now in the British Museum, on which was a parallel text in hieroglyphics, demotic script and Greek.

Hieroglyphics.   The form of communicating information or ideas by hieroglyphs.

Hierogram.   A sacred character or written symbol.

Hierographic.   Pertaining to sacred writing.

Hieronym.   A sacred name used as a surname.

High definition television.   *See* HDTV.

High Definition Video.   *See* HDV.

High Sierra.   The location (a hotel on Lake Tahoe) of a meeting in November 1985 which gave its name to the standard format specification developed for CD-ROM systems. The original members were Hitachi, Apple Computer, Microsoft, Philips, Sony and 3M. The High Sierra specification formed the basis of ISO 9660.

Higher Education Funding Councils. The group of four resource channelling bodies which support higher education in the UK. They are the three funding councils for England <www.hefce.ac.uk>, Wales <www.elwa.ac.uk>, and Scotland <www.shefc.ac.uk>, and the Department of Education for Northern Ireland <www.deni.gov.uk>.

Higher Education Statistics Agency. *See* HESA.

Highlight. The white, or light, parts of a photograph, drawing or half-tone block. Also called 'Drop-out half-tone'.

HILT. <hilt.cdlr.strath.ac.uk> High-Level Thesaurus, a one year project jointly funded by JISC and the Research Support Libraries Programme to study the issues of cross-searching and browsing by subject across a range of communities, services, and service or resource types (Libraries, Museums, Archives, Clumps, the RDN, bibliographic databases, numeric data, and others). HILT II, completed in September 2003, built a pilot system.

Hinge. *(Binding)* A strip of paper or fabric, placed between the two halves of an endpaper, where the body of the book is fixed to the covers, to give strength. In America this term is used to indicate the part of the book identified by the groove along the front and back covers when they join the back strip or spine, allowing the book to be opened easily. *See also* Joint.

Hinged. Plates, maps or other separate sheets to be inserted in a book, which have been given a narrow fold on the inner edges so that there is little chance of the sheets tearing away from those to which they are attached; also so that they will lie flat, and turn easily in use, when bound.

Hinged and jointed plates. Two adjoining plates from which a strip has been cut away at the binding edge and then joined together by means of a common strip of linen or paper to form a hinge and joints.

Historiated initial. An initial, capital or border of a mediaeval MS. or early book decorated with figures of people and/or animals, rather than illuminated with flowers or conventional designs; a representation of a person or scene, illustrating the text it introduces. *See also* Inhabited initial.

Historic Libraries Forum. <p.hoare@virgin.net> (21, Oundle Drive, Nottingham, NG8 1BN, UK) A UK group of libraries which have interesting or unusual historical features, such as important buildings, valuable collections etc. Mainly, these are privately-funded libraries belonging to professional associations, learned societies and similar bodies, and older subscription libraries. Informally organized, the Forum offers members an opportunity to exchange information on common problems, and discuss matters of concern in fields of security, conservation and related issues. An Organization in Liaison (OiL) with CILIP.

Historical bibliography. Dealing with the history and methods of book production – printing, binding, paper making, illustrating and publishing.

Also called 'analytical', 'applied', 'critical', 'descriptive', 'external', or 'material' bibliography.

Historical Manuscripts Commission (HMC). *See* National Archives (UK).

History Data Service. *See* AHDS.

History entry. An entry in a catalogue which gives changes of name, affiliations, etc., concerning a person or corporate body, or in the wording of a title, together with significant dates.

Hit. In searching a computer database, a hit is the successful location of a relevant item.

HMSO. *See* Her Majesty's Stationery Office.

Holding area. (*Archives*) Space assigned for storing semi-current records temporarily.

Holdings. 1. The stock (books, pamphlets, periodicals, audio-visual items, micro-records, software and other material) possessed by a library. 2. Specifically, the volumes, or parts of serial publications, possessed by a library.

Holing. The drilling, or punching, of holes in the boards of a book to take the slips or cords ready for lacing. Also called 'Holing out'.

Hollander. (*Paper*) A beater or beating engine of the type made in Holland towards the end of the seventeenth century.

Hollow. The space between the back of a book itself (i.e. the folded and sewn sheets) and the spine of a Hollow back book.

Hollow back. A binding in which there is a space between the back of the book itself and the cover, caused by the leather, cloth or other material being attached at the joints, and not glued to the back of the book itself. Also called 'Loose back', 'Open back'. Sometimes a tube of thin card or paper is flattened and pasted between section folds and spine-covering. A publisher's case binding is of this type. *See also* Case (1). When the cover is glued to the back it is known as a Tight back.

Hollow quads. Large quads which are cast with hollow parts to make them lighter and save metal. Also used of type which is occasionally cast similarly for the same reason.

Hologram. Alternative term for Holograph (2).

Holograph. 1. A document or manuscript wholly in the handwriting of its author. Hence, holograph reprint, a reproduction of a MS. by mechanical means. 2. A recording on photo-sensitive film, made without the use of lenses, by combining two or more laser beams of different colour to form a single beam. When the holograph is viewed in white light a three-dimensional, multicolour picture is revealed.

Home bindery. 1. A binding department maintained by a library. 2. A method of developing the book-buying habit in Asia. It is run by a single publisher who has a strong and varied list of publications, or by a wholesale bookseller, and incorporates features of book clubs in the West.

Home page. *See* Web pages.

Home reading department.   *See* Lending department.

Homograph.   One of several words having the same spelling but a different meaning, e.g. Birmingham (Alabama), Birmingham (England); skate (fish), skate (sport); game (sport), game (fowl). These should be avoided in subject headings and indexes where possible, but when unavoidable, a qualifying, or defining word or phrase should be added to each in order to clarify the meanings and to separate entries on different subjects. *See also* Homonym, Homophone.

Homology.   The principle used in forming schedules in a classification which uses the similarity of essential characteristics as a basis of division.

Homonym.   1. An identical name (surname and forenames) for two or more people. A namesake. Also an identical corporate, or other, name. 2. One of several words which may have a different origin and meaning but the same sound and possibly a different spelling, e.g. pail (bucket), pale (stake), pale (wan).

Homonymic, Homonymous.   Having the same name.

Homophone.   A word with a different spelling and meaning as another but with the same pronunciation, e.g. rough, ruff.

Homotopic abstract.   An abstract of an article published in the same issue of a journal as the article abstracted.

Honorific epithet.   (*Cataloguing, Indexing*) A title of honour or of rank which is appended to a heading (and so becomes part of it) for identification but which may or may not be used as a Filing epithet.

Honorific title.   A title conferred on a person to indicate royalty, nobility, rank, or an honour. The whole name is sometimes incorporated with that of an organization or activity with which the person was associated. Examples: John XXIV, *Pope*; Mountbatten *Earl, Field-Marshal*; Princess Mary Home; Bishop Creighton House; Sir Halley Stewart Trust; Lord Roberts Workshops. A 'title of honour'.

Hooked on own guard.   The method of securing a single-leaf illustration by folding its binding edge, so as to form a guard, around the fold of the section before sewing. *See also* Guard (1 (b)), Plate guarded and hooked.

Horae.   *See* Book of Hours.

Horizontal.   A series or classification in which the terms, or classes, are arranged in a horizontal line. The several classes are then usually regarded as co-ordinate; but a series of successively subordinate classes and sub-classes might also be so arranged, instead of in a column. *See also* Columnar, Tabular classification.

Horn book.   A children's primer which appeared towards the end of the sixteenth century. It consisted of a thin sheet of vellum or paper mounted on an oblong piece of wood and covered with transparent horn. The wooden frame had a handle by which it was hung from the child's girdle. The sheet bore the alphabet, the vowels in a line followed by the vowels combined with consonants in tabular form, the Roman numerals, the Lord's Prayer, and the exorcism 'in the name of the Father and of the Sonne and of the Holy Ghost, Amen!' A simpler and later form of Horn book, consisting of the tablet without the horn covering, or a piece of varnished cardboard, and resembling a horn book without the handle, was called a battledore.

Hors texte.   Illustrations to a book which are without text matter. A plate. They are usually numbered with Roman numerals to avoid confusion with numbered illustrations in the text (which are usually in line) and with the pagination of a book.

Hospital library.   A library provided for the use of hospital patients and sometimes the staff, either by the hospital authority, a voluntary organization, or another local library service.

Hospitality.   (*Classification*) The quality of a notation which enables new subjects to be inserted in their appropriate place.

Host.   1. A commercial enterprise that makes available access to any number of databases via its own computer, and using a common command language.   2. Any computer connected to a network which makes files available to remote users. *See also* Client/server.

Host book.   As used in connection with the Colon Classification, a book about which another is written, as e.g. a criticism or a reply; the latter is called an Associated book.

Hot melt.   In bookbinding, a glue which is applied hot and sets immediately when used on a cool surface.

Hot pluggable.   A Peripheral that uses a Firewire or USB connection and which can be connected and disconnected to a PC at any time, even with the power on. Also known as hot swappable.

Hot-metal typesetting.   A method of typesetting which uses a process for casting type from molten metal (e.g. Intertype, Monotype, Linotype) as distinct from Cold composition.

Hot-pressed (HP).   Good quality rag paper which is given a glazed, smooth finish by being pressed with hot metal plates. *See also* Finish, Not, Rough.

Hotspot.   An area in a Multimedia or Hypermedia document from which a Link is made enabling branching to related information or providing feedback to the user such as initiation of an animation.

House corrections.   Corrections, or alterations, made to a script or proof by the publisher or printer's proof reader, as distinct from those made by the author.

House journal.   A periodical produced by a commercial or industrial organization, either for internal distribution amongst the staff and employees or externally to customers.

House magazine.   *See* House journal.

House of Commons Bills.   Public Bills, printed by HMSO on pale green paper for consideration in the House of Commons. *See also* Private Bills.

House of Commons Papers.   Reports and returns which have to be presented to the House under the provisions of various Acts of

Parliament, reports from government departments compiled by direct order of the House, and reports of the Standing Committees and Select Committees of the House.

House of Commons Science and Technology Committee. <www.publications.parliament.uk/pa/cm/cmsctech.htm> The Committee's inquiry into 'Scientific publications' was announced in December 2003 and was published in July 2004 as *Scientific Publications: Free for all?* (HC 399). It took aural evidence from a range of commercial and professional society publishers, academics, libraries and JISC. The Report recommended that all UK higher education institutions establish institutional repositories on which their published output can be stored and from which it can be read, free of charge, online. It also recommended that Research Councils and other Government funders mandate their funded researchers to deposit a copy of all of their articles in this way. It was recognized that the Government will need to appoint a central body to oversee the implementation of the repositories, to help with networking, and to ensure compliance with the technical standards needed to provide maximum functionality. *See also* Eprints, Repository.

House of Lords Papers and Bills. A series of publications consisting almost entirely of Public Bills but also a few Papers. Public Bills are printed by HMSO on pale green paper.

House of Lords Record Office. Contains over 1,500,000 records of Parliament as a whole dating back to 1497. They are in the custody of the Clerk of the Parliaments. The Search Room is open to the public who may also be granted access to the Journals of the House of Commons (from 1547), and to the other surviving records of the Commons (from 1572). Records of Parliament prior to 1497 are preserved in the Public Record Office, now National Archives (UK).

'House' papers. *See* Parliamentary Papers.

House style. The typesetting style normally used in a printing establishment or publishing house. *See also* Style manual, Style sheet.

Housekeeping. Routine and continuing library operations, such as book ordering, accessioning, cataloguing, processing, and the circulation, etc. of documents and other library materials. In computer operations, it is generally contrasted with information retrieval.

Housekeeping system. *See* Integrated library system.

HPB. Hand Press Book Database; *see* Consortium of European Research Libraries.

HRM. *See* Human resources management.

h.t. Abbreviation for Half-title.

HTML. <www.w3.org/MarkUp> HyperText Markup Language, the standard formatting mechanism for publishing documents on the World Wide Web. It is a non-proprietary format based on Standard Generalized Markup Language (SGML), and can be created and processed by a wide range of tools, from simple plain text editors, to sophisticated WYSIWYG authoring tools. Guidance on the use of Web

Markup languages is provided by W3C and HTML 4.01 – released in 1997 with subsequent fixes of minor errors – was the current W3C recommendation in 2004. The next generation of HTML is under development by a Working Group of W3C and is expected to be a suite of XML tag sets with a clean migration path from HTML 4. Some of the expected benefits include: reduced authoring costs, an improved match to database and workflow applications, a modular solution to the increasingly disparate capabilities of browsers, and the ability to cleanly integrate HTML with other XML applications. *See also* XHTML.

Http. HyperText Transport Protocol, the communications protocol for moving hypertext documents over the Internet. For details of the specification, see <www.w3.org/Protocols>.

Hub. An individual organization or, more frequently, a consortium of library, academic, research and professional organizations that provide data for a centralized service provider such as the RDN. Hubs are also services in their own right, providing Gateways to Internet resources in their subject areas and other electronic services. Key activities, such as the selection and evaluation of resources, are carried out locally by persons with the appropriate expertise and subject knowledge. Current hubs of the RDN are: ALTIS; Artifact; BIOME; EEVL; GEsource; Humbul; PSIgate; and SOSIG. *See also* Archives Hub, Portal.

Hulton Getty Picture Collection. Housed in London, an enormous collection of photojournalism comprising over 15 million photographs, prints and engravings; holdings include images from *Picture Post*, Mirror Syndication International etc. The Reuters News Picture Service has been digitally archived; several CD-ROMs are published.

Human computer interface. *See* User interface.

Human resources management. People are an organization's most valuable resource; the skills of planning and managing human resources ('staff', 'employees') are complex, and will include such features and tasks as job analysis, job description, job specification, selection, recruitment, assessment, appraisal, motivation, mentoring, training, team building, career planning, promotion criteria, personal development, industrial relations legislation, trade union negotiation, communication, corporate culture, change management, etc.

Humanist. 1. A group of typefaces, formerly known as 'Venetian' and derived from the fifteenth-century style of minuscule handwriting characterized by a varying stroke thickness achieved by means of an obliquely-held broad pen. In faces in this group the cross stroke of the lower case 'e' is oblique, the axis of the curves is inclined to the left, there is little contrast between thin and thick strokes, the serifs are bracketed, and the serifs of the ascenders of the lower case letters are oblique. 2. Also a group of Lineale typefaces based on the proportions of roman capitals and Humanist or Garalde lower-case letters, rather than on the early grotesques which are another group of Lineales. They have some contrast between the thick and thin strokes.

Humanistic hand. A mediaeval handwriting less angular than Gothic, based on Old Roman capitals and the Carolingian minuscule. It was a result of the Renaissance in the fifteenth century which brought a general awakening of interest in classic, and pre-Christian literature. Also called 'Neo-Caroline'.

Humbul. <www.humbul.ac.uk> A Hub of the (UK) RDN providing access to evaluated online resources in the humanities such as American studies; archaeology; classics; history; linguistics; manuscript studies; philosophy; religion and theology; English studies; French studies; German studies; and Slavonic studies. Based at the University of Oxford.

Humphrey (John Ames)/OCLC/Forest Press Award. An annual award for a significant contribution to international librarianship, made by the International Relations Committee of the American Library Association.

Hundred Rolls. Fully, Hundred Rolls of A.D. 1274. Public records of great importance for local history, containing an inquisition into the state of every hundred (a division of a county) and answers, on oath, to questions relating to the public exchequer.

Huntington Library. <www.huntington.org> One of the most famous of scholars' libraries of Americana and English literature. It is situated in San Marino, California, USA, and is surpassed only by the British Library and the Bodleian in the quality and importance of its British books. The library is in a building which was opened in 1920 and was especially designed to protect and preserve the valuable collection of books in the grounds of Huntington House (formerly the home of Henry Edwards Huntington, 1850–1927). The collections contain 2.2 million manuscripts, 336,000 rare books and 253,000 reference books, concentrated in the fields of British and American history, literature and art, and stretching in time from the eleventh century to the present. The R. Stanton Avery Conservation Center, completed in 1981, has up-to-date equipment for the repair and preservation of rare books, manuscripts and photographs in the Huntington collections. There are also magnificent art collections and botanical gardens.

Hybrid library. A library that provides services in a mixed-mode, electronic and paper, environment, particularly in a co-ordinated way. Derived from a strand of eLib which explored the issues surrounding the retrieval and delivery of information in these types of environments but also investigated the integration of different electronic services so that a single search approach could be offered to the End user.

Hydrographic chart. A chart of coasts and harbours.

Hypermedia A method of presenting electronic information in a way that is intended to encourage exploration. Hypermedia documents incorporate links, created in HTML, from terms in the original to related information anywhere, either in the same document, to files on the same Local area network, or to documents on the Internet. In this way users can work interactively, following links and building up their own perspectives on a topic. Links can be made to other text documents but also to graphics, and video and sound clips. The World Wide Web is the most successful implementation of a hypermedia system. *See also* Adaptive hypermedia, Multimedia.

Hypertext.   Text systems using links; *see* Hypermedia.

HyperText Markup Language.   *See* HTML.

HyperText Transport Protocol.   *See* Http.

Hyphen.   The shortest rule used for punctuation. It is used to join compound words, or as the link at the end of a line to join the parts of a word which cannot be set in one line. *See also* Dash.

Hyphen stringing.   *(Indexing)* The process of using hyphens to bind terms in order to convey more information, as well as for filing purposes.

Hyphenation and justification.   *See* H & J.

Hypo.   Abbreviation for hyposulphite of soda (formerly known as sodium thiosulphate) which is used in photography for fixing prints.

Hypsometric map.   One on which the successive altitudes are indicated by the system of colour tints.

Hytelnet.   <www.lights.com/hytelnet> An archive of Telnet sites, Hytelnet was the first online, hypertext Internet directory, compiled in 1990. It is no longer being maintained and none of the links are active (though the web page stated here is still available).

Hytime.   A time-based structuring language detailed in ISO 10744: 1997, 2nd edition and based on Standard Generalized Markup Language for representing the structure of Multimedia, Hypertext, Hypermedia, time- and space-based documents. A User Group web page, though not updated since 1998, provides useful information at <www.hytime.org>.

IA.   *See* Information architecture.

IAAA.   *See* International Alliance on Access for All.

IAB.   *See* Internet Architecture Board.

IACODLA.   International Advisory Committee on Documentation Libraries and Archives, established in 1967 to advise the Director-General of Unesco at his request, on questions of documentation in general, and in particular on those related to subject fields of interest to Unesco.

IAFA/whois++ templates.   <www.ukoln.ac.uk/metadata/desire/overview/rev_11.htm> A Metadata format, the templates were designed by the IAFA (Internet Anonymous FTP Archive) working group of the Internet Engineering Taskforce to facilitate effective access to ftp archives by describing the contents and services available from the archive. The template format has been developed for use with the Whois++ protocol. Supporters of IAFA templates have widened the original aim, and the intention is to devise a record format simple enough to be generated by the wide variety of individuals and organizations involved with creating resources on the Internet, whether on web servers or ftp archives.

IALL.   *See* International Association of Law Libraries.

IAML.   *See* International Association of Music Libraries, Archives and Documentation Centres.

IANA.   <www.iana.org> Internet Assigned Numbers Authority 'dedicated to preserving the central co-ordinating functions of the global Internet for the public good'. IANA was the original co-ordinator for the Internet address system operating under a US government contract awarded to the Information Sciences Institute at the University of Southern California's School of Engineering, but was required in a government plan in 1997 to transfer its responsibilities to a new not-for-profit corporation with an international Board of Directors. The web site still exists but most functions have been transferred to ICANN. Under ICANN, the IANA continues to distribute addresses to the Regional Internet Registries, co-ordinate with the IETF and others to assign protocol parameters, and oversee the operation of the Domain Name System.

IAOL.   *See* International Association of Orientalist Librarians.

IAR.   *See* Information Asset Register.

IASA.   *See* International Association of Sound and Audiovisual Archives.

IASL.   *See* International Association of School Librarianship.

IASLIC.   <www.iaslic.org> (P-291, CIT Scheme no. 6M, Kankurgachi, Calcutta-700054, India) Indian Association of Special Libraries and Information Centres. Founded in September 1955 with the following aims: to encourage and promote the systematic acquisition, organization and dissemination of knowledge; to improve the quality of library and information services and documentation work; to co-ordinate the activities of, and to foster mutual co-operation and assistance among, special libraries, scientific, technological and research institutions, learned societies, commercial organizations, industrial research establishments, as well as other information and documentation centres.

IATUL.   *See* International Association of Technological University Libraries.

ib., ibid.   Abbreviation for *ibidem* (Lat. 'in the same place', 'the same reference'). Used in a footnote reference to avoid repeating the title of a work referred to immediately above. It can be used in successive references to the same work.

IBBY.   <www.ibby.org> International Board on Books for Young People. Founded by Jella Lepman in 1953 in Zurich to promote international understanding through children's books. It is composed of national Sections from many countries which work to promote children's books. Awards the Hans Christian Andersen Medal for important contributions to children's literature. International Children's Book Day (ICBD), originated by Jella Lepman, is a well-known activity of the Board observed each year throughout the world on 2 April which is Hans Christian Andersen's birth date. The Board's secretariat is at Basle, Switzerland. The IBBY Documentation Centre of Books for Disabled

Young People was established in 1985 at the Norwegian Institute of Special Education. IBBY has links with Unesco and Unicef, and is a member of IFLA and the International Book Committee. Publishes *Bookbird* (q.) in co-operation with the International Institute for Children's Literature and Reading Research.

IBSS. *See International Bibliography of the Social Sciences.*

IBY. International Book Year, organized by Unesco and held on a world-wide basis in 1972 to promote books and encourage reading. *See also* International Book Award, International Book Committee.

ICA. *See* International Council on Archives.

ICABS. <www.ifla.org/VI/7/icabs.htm> (Deutsche Bibliothek Office for Library Standards, Adickesalee 1, D-60322 Frankfurt am Main, Germany) The IFLA-CDNL Alliance for Bibliographic Standards was established in 2003 to continue the work of the previous IFLA core programmes UBCIM and UDT, with the active support of the Conference of Directors of National Libraries (CDNL) Committee on Digital Issues. Participants in ICABS include the British Library, Library of Congress, National Library of Australia, Koninklijke Bibliotheek, Deutsche Bibliothek, and the Biblioteca Nacional (Portugal). The Alliance seeks to maintain, promote and harmonize international bibliographic standards, develop strategies for future needs and promote new conventions for such issues as the archiving of electronic resources. Maintenance and monitoring of ISBD, MARC21, UNIMARC, Web harvesting and Z39.50/ZING are included in its functions.

ICAE. <www.web.net/icae> International Council for Adult Education, a non-governmental organization whose chief function is to facilitate development and exchange of experience in adult education, including associated fields such as functional literacy, publishing and libraries, manpower training, labour education and 'learning at a distance'. The Council does not duplicate the work of existing institutions but works with and through them in order to build upon and support their activities. The Secretariat is in Toronto.

ICANN. <www.icann.org> Internet Corporation for Assigned Names and Numbers, an internationally organized, non-profit corporation that has responsibility for Internet Protocol address space allocation, protocol identifier assignment, generic and country code top-level Domain Name System management, and root server system management functions. These services were originally delivered under US Government contract by the IANA and other entities but ICANN now performs the IANA function.

ICBA. *See* International Community of Booksellers' Associations.

ICBD. International Children's Book Day. *See* entry under IBBY.

ICCP. *See* International Conference on Cataloguing Principles.

ICCU. <www.iccu.sbn.it> The National Centre for the Union Catalogue, set up in 1951 with the task of cataloguing the whole of the Italian national bibliographic heritage, became the Central Institute for the Union Catalogue of Italian Libraries and for Bibliographic Information (ICCU) [Istituto Centrale per il Catalogo Unico delle Biblioteche Italiane e per le Informazioni Bibliografiche] in 1975 following the establishment of the Ministry for Cultural and Environmental Heritage. The Institute promotes and co-ordinates national censuses of manuscripts, of 16th century Italian editions, and of Italian libraries, and supports the cataloguing activity of libraries in Italy by setting guidelines and disseminating standard cataloguing rules. The Institute reports to the Central Office for Libraries, Cultural Institutes and Publishing, acts as co-ordinator of the National Library Service (SBN) and for cataloguing projects utilizing information technology.

Icelandic Library Association. *See* Information – the Icelandic Library and Information Association.

ICIC. <portal.unesco.org/culture> International Copyright Information Centre, based at Unesco Headquarters, Paris; approved at the 16th Session of Unesco in 1970. Functions to: (a) collect copyright information on books that can be made available to developing countries on terms as favourable to them as possible; (b) arrange for the transfer to developing countries of rights ceded by copyright holders; (c) help in the development of simple model forms of contracts for translation, reprint and other rights required by developing countries; (d) study ways and means of securing copyright and other rights as well as methods of financing the rights required where foreign currency is not available; (e) promote arrangements for the adaptation and publication of works, particularly those of a technical and educational nature; (f) encourage the formation of national copyright information centres in both developed and developing countries, and act as a link between them; (g) provide assistance to developing countries for the organization of training courses for translators and covering all aspects of the publishing industry, for the provision of fellowships and equipment, for the joint publication of technical works, and for bringing together pedagogical authorities to develop adaptations of works. Publishes *Information Bulletin* (irreg.) which gives information on the centre and serves as a link for the exchange of information and ideas on copyright activities.

ICOLC. <www.library.yale.edu/consortia> The International Coalition of Library Consortia was formed in 1997 to be a 'forum to work with information providers to find common ground'. A priority is to begin discussions with the publishing community to advance the use and availability of electronic information resources in educational and research institutions. ICOLC advocates a new economic model to break the cycle in which libraries spend more on serials each year but can buy fewer of them. ICOLC has been active in producing guidelines for the collection of statistics on electronic usage – these were issued in 1998 and are currently under revision (*see* Metrics). In 2002 there were 150 library consortia in membership from around the world. A European chapter (E-ICOLC) has been formed and runs occasional conferences.

icommons. *See* Creative Commons.

Icon. Symbolic representation of a software application or a file on a computer display that avoids the use of command statements. In this way a component of GUI and WIMPS interfaces such as used on the Apple Macintosh and in Windows.

Iconography. 1. The study of the portraits, statues, coins, and other illustrative material relating to a person, place or thing. 2. The detailed listing of such material. 3. The art of illustrating, or representing, by figures, images, diagrams, etc.

ICSSD. *See* International Committee for Social Sciences Documentation.

ICSTI. *See* 1. International Centre for Scientific and Technical Information. 2. International Council for Scientific and Technical Information.

ICSU. *See* International Council of Science.

ICT. Information and Communications Technology, replacing the older 'IT' and the alternative 'C&IT' to express the combination of computing hardware and software with the capabilities of communications networks that provides new opportunities for teaching, learning and training through the delivery of digital content. The expression arose from an educational context but has since expanded into other sectors and its use is now widespread. *See also* ILT.

id. Abbreviation for *idem* (Lat. 'the same [author or publication]'). Used in footnotes to avoid repeating an author's name, or other identity of a book or periodical when being referred to successively.

Ida and George Eliot Prize Essay. *See* Eliot (Ida and George) Prize Essay Award.

Identification. (*Bibliography*) The discovery of the date of an undated book, or the determination of the precise edition, impression, issue or state of a given copy or series of copies of a book. (*Information retrieval*) A classification number, code number or code name which identifies a record, file, document or other unit of information.

Identification caption. (*Reprography*) The identification symbol or phrase, both on the document and on the frame of microfilm or fiche, which is visible to the unaided eye.

Identifier. *See* Digital Object Identifier.

Identifiers. (*Information retrieval*) Terms, such as acronyms, projects, proper names of persons, geographical locations, the number of a patents specification or of a national 'standard', or any part of a bibliographical description, test names, and trade names which provide subject indexing, in addition to descriptors. Also called 'Identifying factors'.

Identity management. A component of core Middleware in networking systems whereby a user is identified by a unique string of characters, a Username. Identity management systems enable the different identities associated with various services (E-mail, library, access to electronic journals, etc.) to be cross-mapped and synchronized to a single username and Password.

Ideogram.   *See* Ideograph (2).

Ideograph.   1. An individual signature or trademark.   2. A symbol or picture used in writing, e.g. in Chinese, to represent an object or an idea, and not, as in the phonetic system, the sounds which make up the name of these.

Ideography.   The representation of ideas by graphic symbols ('ideograms'). A highly developed form of picture-writing in which ideas are conveyed by pictorial representation.

IDNs.   Internationalized Domain Names. *See* Domain Name System.

IEEE 1394.   *See* Firewire.

IETF.   *See* Internet Engineering Task Force.

IFD.   *See* International Federation for Information and Documentation.

IFEG.   <www.petroleum.co.uk/index> (Institute of Petroleum, 61 New Cavendish Street, London W1M 8AR, UK) Information for Energy Group, a UK forum for information professionals with interests in the energy industries. Organizes conferences, and publishes a directory of members.

IFIP.   *See* International Federation for Information Processing.

IFLA.   *See* International Federation of Library Associations and Institutions.

IFLA-CDNL Alliance for Bibliographic Standards.   *See* ICABS.

IFOBS.   *See* International Forum on Open Bibliographic Systems.

IFRRO.   <www.ifrro.org> International Federation of Reproduction Rights Organizations; an independent, non-profit organization focused on an international collective approach to administering reproduction and related copyright rights through the co-operation of pertinent organizations. It also promotes the establishment of new RROs.

IFRT.   *See* Intellectual Freedom Round Table.

IGC.   Abbreviation for Intergovernmental Copyright Committee which was established in Geneva on 6 September 1952; it is administered by Unesco. Aims: to study the problems concerning the operation of the Universal Copyright Convention of 1952; make preparations for periodic revisions thereof; study any other problems concerning the international protection of copyright (or which may affect copyright) in co-operation with the various interested international organizations. It works jointly with the Berne Convention. *See also* Copyright, International.

IIDR.   *See* Institute for Image Data Research.

IKBS.   Intelligent knowledge-based system. *See* Expert system.

ILA.   *See* 1. Indian Library Association.   2. Inspiring Learning for All.

ILDS.   Abbreviation for Interlending and Document Supply.

ILIAC.   <www.iliac.ru> (1776 Massachusetts Avenue NW, Suite 700, Washington DC 20036, USA/12 Kuznetsky Most, Moscow 107996, Russia) International Library Information and Analytical Center; a non-profit US-based corporation facilitating access to the services and products of libraries, information centres, universities and other academic institutions of Russia and other eastern European countries to the users in the USA and world-wide. Also operates an International School of Librarianship, IT, and Cultural Studies.

ILL.   Abbreviation for Inter-library loan.

ill. (illus.).   Abbreviation for illustrated, Illustrations.

ILL Protocol Standards.   As Open Systems Interconnection standards, the suite of Interlibrary Loan (ILL) application standards has been designed to allow, with a minimum of technical agreements outside the standards, the interconnection of computer systems from different manufacturers, under different management, of different levels of complexity, and of different ages. In addition, the protocol provides support for the control and management of ILL transactions for both lending and borrowing activities. There are three individual standards in the suite of ILL application standards: ISO 10160:1997 *Information and Documentation – Open Systems Interconnection – Interlibrary Loan Application Service Definition*; ISO 10161-1:1997 *Information and Documentation – Open Systems Interconnection – Interlibrary Loan Application Protocol Specification – Part 1: Protocol Specification*; and *Part 2: PICS Proforma*. In April 2004 new drafts were submitted to ISO of ISO 10161 *Information and documentation – Interlibrary loan application: Part 1: Service definition and protocol specification*; and *Part 2: Protocol implementation conformance statement (PICS)*. *See also* Interlibrary Loan Application Standards Maintenance Agency.

Illative abstract.   *See* Abstract (3).

ILLINET Online.   <www.ilcso.uiuc.edu> A network consortium formed in 1976, and now offering 21 million records from the catalogues of the 56 members. An OCLC Network Affiliate.

Illuminated binding.   A term used for all bindings which included extra colours, but particularly to those where a design was blocked in blind and the outline afterwards filled in with colour. Originally a French innovation, this style was practised in Britain from about 1830 to 1860.

Illuminated book.   A book or manuscript, usually on vellum, decorated by hand, with designs and pictures in gold, silver and bright colours, not primarily to illustrate the text, but to make with it a unified whole.

Illuminated initial.   A first letter of a word or paragraph decorated with colours, especially gold.

Illumination.   1. The painting of initial letters at the commencement of a chapter of a MS. in gold, silver, or colour.   2. The system for lighting in libraries. *See* Lux.

illus.   Abbreviation for illustrated, illustration, illustrator.

Illustrations.   Photographs, drawings, portraits, maps, plans, plates, tables, facsimiles, diagrams, etc., placed in a book to elucidate the text.

Illustrations collection.   A collection of photographs, prints, drawings or reproductions of pictures assembled either for general use in public libraries or in institutions as an aid to their work. *See also* Picture collection, Picture file.

ILT. Information Learning Technology, the use of ICT to support learning and skills uptake as used by the (UK) National Learning Network.

ILY. *See* International Literacy Year.

IM. *See* Information management.

IMAC. *See* International Marc Network Advisory Committee.

Image. 1. A design or picture to be reproduced by a printing process as an illustration. 2. (*Reprography*) That area within the frame (*see also* Frame (4)) which, after exposure and processing, contains the whole of the representation of the original.

Image manipulation software. Software for the modification of any aspect of an image, normally applied to line art, half-tones and full colour photographs imported via a Scanner or to images imported from a digital camera.

Imagesetter. The piece of equipment used to produce the Camera ready output from Computer typesetting or Desktop publishing systems. Such hardware provides resolutions up to 5,000 dots per inch, compared to 300–1,200 dots per inch from Laser printers. Though beyond the budget of most libraries, organizations purchase imagesetters for their internal publishing operations. Now used in preference to the terms Typesetter, Photosetter.

IMAP. Internet Message Access Protocol, an E-mail standard that allows e-mail programs to access messages on a remote machine as if they were local, in other words, all messages stay on the remote machine and are not downloaded to the user's desktop. Useful for people who need to read their e-mail from more than a single computer.

Imbrication. A style of book decoration in which the pattern consists of overlapping leaves or scales.

IMC. *See* Irish Manuscripts Commission.

IMCE. International Meeting of Cataloguing Experts which met in Copenhagen in 1969 (prior to the IFLA Conference) to examine closely *inter alia* an annotated edition, in a provisional form, of the *Statement of principles* with a view to the preparation of a definitive edition. Another working party was formed to prepare the International Standard Bibliographic Description to serve the needs of catalogues and national bibliographies, and which would include all the bibliographical data required for catalogues, bibliographies and other records, e.g. book orders. *See also* International Conference on Cataloguing Principles, ISBD, Paris Principles.

Imitation art. *See* Art.

Imitation binding. A modern binding made to represent an old style.

Imitation embossing. *See* Thermography.

Imitation leather. Paper or cloth embossed or finished to represent leather.

Imitation parchment. A variety of tough paper first made by W. E. Gaine in 1857. It may be (a) rendered transparent, strong, grease-proof, and sometimes water-proof, by prolonged beating of the pulp, or (b) passed through a bath of sulphuric acid which 'toughens' the fibres.

IMLS. *See* Institute for Museum and Library Services.

Immroth (John Phillip) Memorial Award. An annual award to honour intellectual freedom fighters, made by the Intellectual Freedom Round Table of the American Library Association.

IMP. *See* International MARC Programme.

Impac Dublin Literary Prize. <www.impacdublinaward.ie> Established in 1996 by Impac, an international management-productivity company, with the support of the City of Dublin; the award is given for an outstanding work of contemporary fiction selected from nominations made by public libraries in the capital cities of 170 countries, co-ordinated by Dublin City Library.

Impact. The effect that is made on the public at large or on clients by a process or service; a measure of the effectiveness of organizational outputs. In the evaluation of library services, 'impact' has become an important factor. Libraries are part of the cultural infrastructure of a country and need to be able to demonstrate their 'value' in ways that will secure respect and support. Libraries will have an impact on education, the economy, social life and culture. Impact studies show that libraries are trusted and popular, that they assist in community cohesion, in complementing educational services, in providing social capital, in combating social exclusion, and in supporting employment as they attract knowledge-based industries.

impensis. (Lat. 'at the expense of') Used in an Imprint or Colophon of an early printed book to indicate the publisher, or bookseller or patron who was financially responsible for its publication.

Imperfect. A book which is found to have pages or sections omitted, duplicated, misplaced or inserted upside down, damaged or missing.

Imperfections. Printed sheets rejected by the binder as being in some respect imperfect, and for which others are required to make the work complete.

Imperial. A sheet of printing and drawing paper measuring 22 x 30 inches.

Import. 1. A book published in one country and imported into another. The importer may act as one of several importers or may have sole distribution rights over a given area. 2. (*Verb*) Open a computer file in a software Application not used for its creation. Thus, a word processed file may be imported into a Desktop publishing package for subsequent format modification.

Imposing stone. *See* Stone.

Imposition. The arrangement of the pages of type in the chase so that they will read consecutively when the printed sheet is folded. On correct imposition depends not only the right order of the pages but also Register.

Impressed watermark. A watermark produced, not by the usual method, but by placing a stereo, in bronze, rubber, or other substance, on the press roll of the paper-making machine, and so leaving a design in the paper where it was more compressed. *See also* Watermark.

Impression.   1. (*Printing*) The copies of a book printed at the same time from the same type or plates. A *new impression* is one taken from the same standing type, or stereotype, as the original. An edition may consist of several impressions providing no alterations are made. Also called a 'Printing'.   2. All those copies of an edition printed at one time. *See also* Edition, First edition, Issue, Reprint, Revised edition. 3. The pressure applied to a forme of type by the cylinder or platen. 4. (*Binding*) The effect of impressing a block or type into the cover of a book.   5. A single copy of a print or map.   6. (*Illustration*) A print taken, by means of the special engraving press, from an engraved plate. *See also* State.

Impression cylinder.   The roller of an offset printing press which presses the paper into contact with the blanket cylinder; or any cylinder around which the paper is carried during its contact with type or plates.

Imprimatur.   1. *imprimatur* (Lat. 'let it be printed') The licence for publication, granted by a secular or ecclesiastical authority, carrying the name of the licenser, and the date (which may differ from that of the imprint). Usually printed at the beginning of a book: when on a separate leaf this is called a 'licence leaf'. Now rarely found except in the form of the words 'permissu superiorum' on works by Roman Catholic priests. This is distinct from copyright. Where state or church censorship exists, the imprimatur becomes an approval of what has been published.   2. IMPRIMATUR <www.imprimatur.alcs.co.uk> Intellectual Multimedia Property Rights Model And Terminology for Universal Reference, an extremely large EU funded project to facilitate trading Intellectual Property Rights (IPRs) in a digital age. The project aimed to build a world-wide consensus on how this should be achieved and built a business model to be mapped on to various situations such as broadcasting, use of music on Web sites, library use of CD-ROMs, copying news clippings and syndicating material for newspapers and journals. Many of the participants are now carrying on the ideas behind IMPRIMATUR through a company named Rights.com <www.rightscom.com>.

Imprint.   1. The statement in a book concerning the publication or printing of a book. Also called 'Biblio'. The *publisher's imprint* is the name of the publisher and the date and place of publication, it usually appears at the foot of the title-page, and sometimes more completely on the back. The *printer's imprint* gives the printer's name and the place of printing, it usually appears on the back of the title-page, on the last page of text, or on the page following. *See also* Colophon, Distribution imprint.   2. (*Cataloguing*) That part of an entry which gives the above particulars, though it is customary to omit the *place* of publication if it is the capital city of the country. When the imprint is covered by a label (usually giving the name of a publisher or agent in a country other than that of origin) the date for the catalogue entry is taken from the label. 3. (*Binding*) The name of (a) the owner; (b) the publisher appearing at the bottom of the spine; (c) the binder stamped on the cover of a book, usually at the bottom of the inside of the back board. 4. (*Printing*) The name of an Old Face type which is much used for book work.

Imprint date. The year of publication as specified on the title-page. *See also* Date of publication.

IMS. 1. <www.imsglobal.org> IMS Global Learning Consortium, a worldwide non-profit organization that includes more than 50 contributing members and affiliates which develops and promotes the adoption of open technical specifications for interoperable learning technology, or instructional management systems. Several IMS specifications have become worldwide *de facto* standards for delivering learning products and services, one example being the IMS Learning Resource Metadata Specification. 2. *See* International Musicological Society.

In boards. 1. When a book is cut after the mill-boards are attached, it is said to be cut in boards. *See also* Boards. 2. A cheap style of binding common in the eighteenth and early nineteenth centuries, consisting of pasteboards covered with paper (usually blue sides and white spine). It was superseded by cloth. Occasionally used in the early twentieth century.

In galley. Type which has been set and is in a galley awaiting correction and making up into pages.

In pendentive. (*Printing*) Typesetting in which successive lines are set in decreasing width, the first (and possibly second) line being set to the full measure, the subsequent ones being indented left and right of a central axis so that the last line of a page or paragraph is only a single word. It has the effect of a triangle resting on its apex.

In print. Said of a book which is available from the publisher.

In progress. A term used in catalogues and elsewhere to indicate that a work in several volumes is not complete but still in course of publication. *See also* Check-list (1).

In quires. A book in unbound sheets. *See also* In sheets.

In sheets. Printed sheets of a book, either flat or folded, but unbound. This term is replacing 'in quires' with which it is synonymous. *See also* Sheets.

In slip. Matter set up and proof-pulled on galleys before being made up into pages.

In stock. Said of a book, copies of which are held by a bookseller for sale.

In the press. A book which is in the actual process of being printed.

In the trade. Books published by, and obtainable from, commercial publishing firms rather than from government or private presses.

INASP. *See* International Network for the Availability of Scientific Publications.

Incidental music.   Music written for performance during the presentation of a theatrical play or film whether it has an essential connection with the plot, or story, or not.

Incipit.   1. *incipit* (Lat. 'here begins') The commencement of a mediaeval MS. or early printed book. The identity of the work and of the author may be found here if it is not given on the title-page or in the colophon. 2. INCIPIT <www.cordis.lu/libraries/en/projects/incipit> Sub-titled 'Bibliographic records and images: a CD-ROM of incunabula editions', the objective of this EU-funded project was the creation of tools for the identification and differentiation of incunabula editions and the provision of widespread access to them. Three CD-ROMs were produced, the final one including 28,000 ISTC records and 5,000 images.

INCOLSA.   <www.incolsa.net> Indiana Cooperative Library Services Authority, a US network consortium formed in 1974 having currently 2,200 member libraries. An OCLC Network Affiliate.

Income generation.   The making of a charge for certain library and information services in order to recover some of the costs. Generally used in the context of publicly funded libraries where the scope for charging may be limited to additional services such as the reservation of specific items, the borrowing of audio-visual items, or imposition of fines. In a commercial context, an information service would expect to recoup its costs by charging an economic rate for its work.

Incomplete.   Said of a book from which a part has been omitted during manufacture.

Incunabula.   (*Sing.*, Incunabulum; Anglicized, Incunable) Books printed before 1500, this date limitation probably deriving from the earliest known catalogue of incunabula: an appendix to Johann Saubert's *Historia bibliothecae Noribergensis ... catalogus librorum proximis ab inventione annis usque ad a. Chr. 1500 editorum,* 1643. 'Incunabula' derives from the Latin 'cunae' (cradle) and indicates books produced in the infancy of printing; more specifically those which were printed before the use of loose type was common.

Incunabula Short Title Catalogue.   *See* ISTC.

Incunabulist.   One who is well versed in a knowledge of incunabula.

Incut heading.   *See* Cut-in heading.

Incut note.   A side note which is let into the outer edge of a paragraph of text instead of appearing in the margin. Usually set in smaller and heavier type than the text. Also called 'Cut-in note', 'Cut-in side note', 'Let-in note'. *See also* Centre note.

indecs.   <www.indecs.org> Interoperability of data in e-commerce systems, a project established in 1998 with support from the European Commission's Info 2000 Programme to investigate whether Metadata developed in different contexts could interoperate effectively and permit automated e-commerce in intellectual property in the network environment. The project ended in March 2000 but <indecs>

Framework Ltd was established by the partners as a not-for-profit company to own the intellectual property rights created. The name is normally presented in angle bracks and in lower case: <in*decs*>. The DOI Metadata System is based on the <in*decs*> framework.

Indent. To begin a line of type a little way in, as at the beginning of a fresh paragraph.

Indented style. In book indexes, the typographical setting which allows subheadings to be indented, usually one em, the main heading being set flush to the lefthand margin. Sub-subheadings are further indented. *See also* Run-on style.

Indention. (*Printing*) The leaving of a blank space at the beginning of a line or a new paragraph. *See also* Em, Hanging indention.

Indenture. A document drawn up in duplicate and divided so as to leave a tooth-like edge on each part.

Independent Research Libraries Association. *See* IRLA.

Independents. Books or pamphlets published separately and afterwards bound together.

Index. 1. A detailed alphabetical list or table of topics, names of persons, places, etc., treated or mentioned in a book or series of books, pointing out their exact positions in the volume, usually by page number (sometimes with an additional symbol indicating a portion of a page) but often by section, or entry, number. 2. A much broader connotation is now given to this term due to contemporary practices of compiling finding-guides to the contents of, and shelved position of, material in a library collection, sometimes using mechanical methods for this purpose. From many points of view an index is synonymous with a catalogue, the principles of analysis used being identical, but whereas an index entry merely locates a subject, a catalogue entry includes descriptive specification of a document concerned with the subject. 3. (*Information retrieval*) That which specifics, indicates or designates the information, contents or topics of a document or a group of documents. Also a list of the names or subjects referring to a document or group of documents. 4. (*Verb*) To prepare an organized or systematic list which specifies, indicates or designates the information, contents or topics in a document or group of documents. 5. The printer's symbol ☛. Also called 'Digit', 'Fist', 'Hand'.

Index board. A quality of single- or twin-wire pulp board, white or coloured, used for cutting into standard sizes for index cards and record work generally. They may be described as pulp board with a good, even and well-finished surface suitable for writing. They are smooth, hard-sized and of even Look through. Sizes: Index Royal $20^{1}/_{2}$ x $25^{1}/_{2}$ inches, Index Royal and a half $25^{1}/_{2}$ x $30^{1}/_{2}$ inches.

Index entry. The entry which is included in an index.

Index Expurgatorius. An index to passages to be expunged or altered in works which are otherwise permitted. This term is loosely used for the list of books that the Roman Catholic Church forbade its members to read, or permitted them to read only in expurgated form – the Index Librorum Prohibitorum.

Index language. The language that is used in the subject index which is part of an information retrieval system. It may be an alphabetical or classified arrangement of terms, or a variation of these. Each term or heading actually used in the index language, of whatever kind, is called an 'index term'. Also called 'Descriptor language'. Its 'vocabulary' is the complete collection of sought terms in the natural language.

Index Librorum Prohibitorum. A list of books which Roman Catholics were prohibited by ecclesiastical authority from reading or keeping without permission. Such books could not be imported into countries where Roman Catholic control was considerable. The list was commonly called the 'Index' or 'Roman Index', and was also known as 'Index Expurgatorius'. The *Index* was printed first by Antonio Blado in Rome in 1559 and is the classic example of censorship. From late Roman times there had been censorship of books considered to be dangerous to religion and morals, and although bishops, universities and inquisitions had circulated lists of prohibited books this was the first really effective means of censorship. The 'Congregation' which was first set up in 1558 to prepare the *Index* continued to be responsible for its publication. The *Index* was last brought up to date in 1947; Cardinal Ottaviani, pro-prefect of the Doctrinal Congregation declared in April 1965 that no more books would be put on the Index. On 14 June 1966 the Vatican announced that it had been abolished; although it ceased to be legally binding, Roman Catholics were reminded of their duty to avoid reading books dangerous to faith and morals.

Index map. A small-scale key map to an atlas or series of maps, which shows how the total area has been divided up by the individual maps.

Index tab. A small piece of paper, card or fabric attached to, and projecting from, the fore-edge of a leaf and bearing in progressive order from top to bottom letters or words. Its purpose is to assist the speedy finding of the information required. *See also* Thumb index.

Index term. *See* Index language.

Indexing. The art of compiling an Index. *See also* American Society of Indexers, Society of Indexers.

Indexing at source. The publication of indexing data simultaneously with (often at the head of) a periodical article.

Indexing by exclusion. A system of automatic indexing based on the isolation and exclusion of non-significant or meaningless words. All words which have not been so excluded are processed as indexing words.

Indexing language. A set of indexing terms as used in a particular retrieval system. The 'language' can be 'natural' (the language of the documents indexed) or 'structured' or 'controlled' (classified or having classificatory features). *See also* Artificial indexing language, Natural language, Thesaurus.

Indexing service. A periodical publication which regularly and systematically indexes the contents of periodicals and sometimes other forms of publication, either of a general nature or within specified subject fields.

India Office Library and Records (IOLR). <www.bl.uk/collections> The IOLR comprises the records of the East India Company (1600–1858), the Board of Control (1784–1858), the India Office, and the Burma Office, together with the Library which was founded in 1801. The collection includes books, prints, drawings, paintings, sculpture, furniture, stamps, coins, maps, medals and photographs. In April 1982 responsibility for IOLR passed from the Foreign and Commonwealth Office to the British Library.

India paper. Originally a soft absorbent paper, cream or buff in colour, imported from China for proofs of engravings. In 1875 the name was used for a thin opaque paper made from hemp or rag. *See also* Bible paper, Cambridge India paper, Oxford India paper.

India proof. A proof of an engraving taken on India or other fine paper. Sometimes wrongly applied to the whole first edition.

India proof paper. *See* China paper.

Indian Association for Special Libraries and Information Centres. *See* IASLIC.

Indian ink. A very black waterproof writing and drawing fluid having great density, used for drawings designed for reproduction and for records where permanence is desired.

Indian Library Association. <www.ilaindia.org> (Ansal Buildings, A40/41 Mukherjee Nagar, Delhi 110009, India) Founded in 1933, with the following objects: the furtherance of the library movement in India, the promotion of the training of librarians, and the improvement of the status of librarians. Publishes *ILA Bulletin* (q.), *ILA Newsletter* (bi-monthly), proceedings of its annual conferences.

Indicative abstract. *See* Abstract (1).

Indicator. 1. A frame, glazed on the public side, which indicated the numbers of the books 'in' and 'out' in a closed access library. 2. A dye used to evaluate the active acidity of paper. 3. (*Printing*) A 'superior' number or symbol in the text which indicates a foot-note at the bottom of the page (or at the end of the chapter, or at the end of the textual matter) to the word or sentence. *See also* Superior figures (Letters). 4. A data element associated with a field supplying further information about the contents of the field, the relationship between the field and other fields in the record, or the action required in certain data manipulation processes.

Indicator digit. A symbol used in the notation of a scheme of classification to announce a change of method of division. *See also* Division, Facet indicator.

Indicography. The compilation of an index.

Indirect costs. *See* Costs.

Indirect subdivision. *See* Direct sub-division.

Indirect subject heading. (*Indexing*) A subject heading which merely refers to another subject heading by means of a 'See' reference. *See also* Mixed subject heading.

Individual entry. Entry in a catalogue under a person or place as subject.

Industrial and Commercial Libraries Group (ICLG). A membership group of CILIP, originally formed in 1971 as the Industrial Group; changed to present title in 1995. It aims to represent information workers in industry and commercial environments.

Industrial libraries. Libraries provided by, and in, industrial firms.

Inedita. Unpublished works.

Inedited. A work published without editorial changes; it may contain indelicate passages which might have been altered or omitted in editing.

Inevitable association, principle of. In descriptive cataloguing, the principle that applies to any name, whether it be of person, book (title), corporate body, periodical, etc., that contains a word that will inevitably be remembered by anyone who asks for that person, book, subject, corporate body or periodical. The principle dictates that the entry chosen for that name will be the word inevitably remembered. *See also* Cataloguing, principles of.

Inferior characters. Small figures and letters cast below the level of the base line, as in chemical formulae, thus: H_2SO_4. Also called 'Subscript'. *See also* Base line, Superior figures (letters).

Infima species. The class with which the division of a classification ends. *See also* Subaltern genera, Summum genus.

Influence phase. One of Ranganathan's three main 'phase relations'; it is the relationship of one subject influencing another. The other two are Bias phase and Tool phase. The process of determining the appropriate class for a document; where one thing influences another, the document is classified under the thing influenced. *See also* Phase.

INFOMINE. <infomine.ucr.edu> Subtitled 'Scholarly Internet Resource Collections', INFOMINE is a Gateway to 140,000 Internet resources – including databases, Electronic journals, Electronic books, Bulletin boards, Mailing lists, OPACs, articles and directories of researchers – organized into nine broad subject areas and accessible via a Search engine. Started in January 1994 as a project of the Library of the University of California, Riverside and was one of the first web-based, academic virtual libraries.

InforM25. <www.m25lib.ac.uk> A virtual union catalogue – based on the eLib project, M25 Link – that enables simultaneous access to over 140 college and university library catalogues in the London area.

Informatics. 1. The processes, methods and laws relating to the recording, analytical-synthetical processing, storage, retrieval and dissemination of scholarly information, but not the scholarly information as such which is the attribute of the respective science or discipline. 2. The study of the structure of knowledge and of its embodiment in information-handling systems.   3. The study of the handling and communication of information, particularly by automated and electronic methods.

Information.   An assemblage of data in a comprehensible form capable of communication. This may range from Content in any format – written or printed on paper, stored in electronic databases, collected on the Internet etc. – to the personal knowledge of the staff of an organization. As terms below demonstrate (especially Information engineering, Information management, Information science), information is a term that covers many inter-related activities which use the skills of librarianship. Content Management and Knowledge Management are recent manifestations of the extent of the value and power of information.

Information and Communications Technology.   *See* ICT.

Information architecture (IA).   In an increasingly complex digital environment, organization of resources becomes a critical issue. Although IA does not yet have an agreed definition, its intention is clear: to reduce the time-wasting chaos that can arise from navigating through vast quantities of information globally. Its main features are therefore likely to be overall design of a shared/common information environment, organizing and structuring information resources (Web sites etc.) through formalization and manipulation of metadata, creating efficient methods of linking resources, designing structures for future generations so that anticipated needs can be met. The Asilomar Institute for Information Architecture (AIFIA) <www.aifia.org> has emerged as a leading forum for discussion of IA. *See also* Information enviroment.

Information Asset Register (IAR).   <www.inforoute.hmso.gov.uk/inforoute> Access to the information resources of very large organizations and governments is hampered by the multiplicity of paths that a user might try to use; the IAR is a suggested solution whereby each such organization would set up one single entry point with comprehensive knowledge of pathways to deeper information. *See also* Crown copyright.

Information audit.   The examination and evaluation of existing information sources, services and products in an organization, with a view to developing a strategy for their more efficient and effective preparation, promotion, use or marketing.

Information broker.   An information worker who sells a personal service on a commercial basis, probably operating as a Freelance self-employed individual, offering information gathering, research, and information-marketing services. *See also* Broker.

Information centre.   Usually an office, or a section of a bibliographical centre, research bureau or documentation centre, which gives inform-ation on a subject with which the organization providing the facilities of the centre is concerned. Staffing varies, but may include any or all of the following: research officers, librarians, bibliographers or trained information officers. It may include the functions of a Special library and extend its activities to include collateral functions such as abstracting, SDI, and research for clients.

Information clearinghouse. A name sometimes given to a special library possessing a limited amount of published material, but which collects and disseminates information.

Information Commissioner. <www.informationcommissioner.gov.uk> A UK government-appointed independent champion of public openness and personal privacy, with various specific responsibilities set out in the Data Protection Act (1998) and the Freedom of Information Act (2000).

Information commons. Collaborative facilities providing extended opening hours and integration of a range of student-centred services such as library, computing, multimedia, learning development, educational technology, tutoring and advice, thereby enhancing support for learning, teaching and research within institutions (particularly in higher education). *See also* Learning resources.

Information consultant. A generic term used by self-employed Freelance individuals operating on a commercial basis in the areas of information handling, research, data handling and related fields. *See also* Library consultant.

Information department. The department of an organization, the primary function of which is to give information when requested.

Information engineering. The process of transforming information into products and services which people can use; involves the design, construction and maintenance of objects and systems. Closely identified with multimedia and electronic publishing.

Information Environment. One of the strategic activities of JISC, the creation of an Information Environment is intended to provide a range of services, tools and mechanisms for colleges and universities to exploit fully the value of online resources and services. The environment will enable presentation, delivery and use of online resources in ways tailored to support individual and institutional requirements in learning, teaching and research. Achieving a managed, coherent and shared information environment in contrast to a wide range of potential sources of electronic information, each with its own name, its own interface, features and search facilities is a key challenge and is being progressed in four strands: i) doorways to the future – accessing online resources through portals; ii) making the most of our wares – building and sharing community resources; iii) joining up delivery – developing shared services; and iv) from libraries to learning – digital resources in practice. The Environment needs to be compatible with the many developments that are taking place within colleges and universities, such as the growth of institutional Web sites, Portals, Intranets, VLEs and MLEs and its creation will be furthered by engaging and collaborating with key organizations and agencies in the UK and worldwide. *See also* Information architecture.

Information file. 1. A list of sources of information which is not readily found and which may in the first instance have been difficult to obtain. 2. Extracts, illustrations, pamphlets, and articles taken from periodicals and other fugitive material filed in a systematic order for ready reference.

Information Focus for Health. <www.tavi-port.org> (Royal School of Speech and Language Therapists, 2 White Hart Yard, London SE1 1NX, UK) An Organization in Liaison (OiL) with CILIP.

Information for Energy Group. *See* IFEG.

Information for Social Change. <libr.org/ISC> (32 Petten Grove, Orpington, BN5 4DU, UK) An activist organization concerned with censorship, freedom of information, and ethics. An Organization in Liaison (OiL) with CILIP.

Information handling. The processes of acquiring, organizing, storing, retrieving, analyzing, disseminating, explaining, and marketing of information in any format.

Information industry. A loosely defined term for information-based activity: library automation systems and services, bibliographic agencies, publishers and database producers, specialist software houses and computer companies, web site developers, intranet specialists, online vendors, hosts and gateways, CD-ROM publishers and vendors, business information providers, consultants, conference organizers, and professional associations.

Information Industry Association. *See* SIIA.

Information Learning Technology. *See* ILT.

Information literacy. The ability to identify, locate, evaluate, organize and use information – particularly from electronic sources – to address an issue or solve a problem, whether for personal, social, cultural or business purposes. Also to communicate such information to others. It is seen as a basic human right; an essential component in the acquisition of life-long learning; a means to help in the eradication of inequality of access to information and the encouragement of tolerance. *See also* Prague Declaration.

Information lookup. A component of core Middleware in networking systems comprising a specialized database tuned for fast look-ups by applications and users. The data stored include a person's unique identifier mapped to their system-dependent identifiers, together with related Authentication and Authorization information. Also known as Directory services. *See also* Identity management.

Information management (IM). IM is becoming the most generally accepted term for a range of information-related activities. Broadly, it covers all aspects of the production, co-ordination, storage, retrieval and dissemination of information – regardless of format or source – and suggests an organizational aspect that will impart some degree of added value to the information. The shift towards acceptance of the term in a wider context is due to its increasing use as a parallel with librarianship, implying that the traditional skills of the librarian and those of the IM professional are related. The term was initially used in the corporate context but has spread into mainstream areas of librarianship. The growing role of end users in finding and arranging their own information via the Internet and intranets has given further impetus to this term, and incidentally hugely increased the number of people who consider themselves as information managers. *See also* Content management, Knowledge management.

Information mapping. A technique for the analysis, organization and presentation of information in an organization, in such a way that its content can be more readily and quickly assimilated by managers and staff. The methodology can usefully address intranet implementation and can aid information design and corporate communication.

Information North. A development agency for library and information services in the UK Northern Region; it was set up in 1988/89 and grew out of the LIP for the area. It achieved great success and initiated an Internet-based public library network. Now merged into NEMLAC. *See* Museums, Libraries and Archives Council (MLA).

Information officer. A member of the staff of an organization responsible for the acquisition, arrangement, exploitation, interpretation, and marketing of information in all formats. The materials may be generated within the organization, or purchased from outside.

Information Policy. *See* National Information Strategy.

Information Processing Society of Japan. *See* Joho Shori Gakkai.

Information provider. The individual or organization responsible for preparing the information content of a database, directory, or other source item. Now widely used as a description of companies that build content for intranets, etc.

Information Research Watch International (***IRWI***). <www.csa.com/primaryjournals> Published commercially by Cambridge Scientific Abstracts (searchable database or printed issues 6 p.a.), *IWRI* continues *Current Research in Library and Information Science* (*CRLIS*). The main part of the publication consists of Research Records with a brief abstract in a broad subject arrangement, with name and subject indexes.

Information resource management (IRM). Generally synonymous with Information management, but with a clear emphasis on the value of information as an organizational asset. Integrates such fields as Records management, data processing management, database management, and specialist information science skills.

Information retrieval. The finding and recall of information from a store; earlier methods included comprehensive classification and cataloguing, and searching databases by various mechanical means. Electronic methods have now generally replaced these systems, and modern retrieval depends on searching full-text databases, locating items from bibliographic databases, and document supply via a network.

Information science. The study of the use of information, its sources and development; usually taken to refer to the role of scientific, industrial and specialized libraries and information units in the handling and dissemination of information.

Information Science Abstracts (ISA). <www.infotoday.com> First published in 1969, an abstract service for library and information science publications, currently adding some 10,000 abstracts annually to its database, taken from world-wide sources covering journals, books, proceedings, reports and patents. There is now good coverage of e-journals. Its early publishing history was confused and publishers included Plenum Publishing Corporation and Documentation Abstracts, Inc. In 1998 Information Today, Inc. acquired the service. Founded by the American Society for Information Science, the Division of Chemical Information of the American Chemical Society, and the Special Libraries Association. Currently guided also by the American Library Association (ALA), the American Society of Indexers (ASI), Association of Information and Dissemination Centers (ASIDIC), Association of Library and Information Science Education (ALISE) and the Medical Library Association (MLA).

Information Science and Technology Association. *See* Joho Kagaku Gijutsu Kyokai.

Information scientist. A professional member of the staff of an information service or special library, skilled in the use and exploitation of specialist subject sources, and their interpretation to the user community.

Information service. A generic term for a library or other organization of which a main role is the collection, analysis, dissemination and presentation of information. Such information may be held by the organization, assembled on demand, or distributed for publicity purposes.

Information Services Group (ISG). A membership group of CILIP; previously the Reference, Special and Information Section (RSIS), it adopted its current title in 1985. Unites information professionals involved in the provision of reference and information services.

Information Services National Training Organization. *See* ISNTO.

Information Society. The overall concept that the convergence of communication and information technologies will have a profound effect on all aspects of our lives; there are social, economic, political, educational, medical, legal implications of emerging electronic services that can only be addressed by a holistic approach. The prominent features of the Information Society include Internet access to enable e-government, e-health, e-learning, electronic commerce and citizen empowerment. Many issues remain to be resolved in the introduction of such services – especially privacy, security and legal questions. Clearly some countries will have better access to such services than others in the developing world; this issue of the Digital divide is receiving increasing attention. The term e-Society can be used synonymously.

Information Society Directorate General. <europa.eu.int/information_ society> The administrative driver of the EU Information Society plans. The starting point is the e-Europe Action Plan which aims to increase understanding, development and updating of ICTs and their applications. The programmes, which cover research, standards and regulatory activity, impact on many areas of life including citizenship, education, culture, business, health, environment and transport.

Information Society Standardization System. *See* ISSS.

Information strategy. A strategy to ensure that investment in information, information technology, systems and services is efficient and effective; and that information produced within an institution is exploited to the benefit of the institution. An information strategy provides a focus for these issues and a forum for a wide range of people to consider the institution's information needs; it must flow from the strategic plan of the institution and help to achieve its mission. In UK higher education, JISC has been pre-eminent in encouraging the development of strategies and case studies can be downloaded from JISC infoNET: <www.jiscinfonet.ac.uk/Resources>. *See also* National Information Strategy.

Information superhighway. A (concept of a) network to link organizations, businesses, individuals, universities, colleges, governments etc., to allow the free flow of information; usually an alternative term for the Internet on which the idea is based. *See also* National Information Infrastructure.

Information system. An organized procedure for collecting, processing, storing, and retrieving information to satisfy a variety of needs.

Information technology. *See* IT.

Information Technology Group. (*Archives*) An interest group of the Society of Archivists, formed from the earlier Computer Applications Committee in 1989.

Information – the Icelandic Library and Information Association. <www.bokis.is> Formed 2001 as a successor organization to four earlier Icelandic library and information bodies.

Information work. The collection, evaluation and organized dissemination of information; it may include abstracting, translation, editing, indexing, literature searching, preparation of bibliographies, creation of databases, and general subject advice and support. *See also* Information science.

Informative abstract. *See* Abstract (1).

INFOSTA. *See* Joho Kagaku Gijutsu Kyokai.

INFOTERM. <linux.infoterm.org> (Aichholzgasse 6/12, A-1120 Vienna, Austria) International Information Centre for Terminology. Established in 1972 within the framework of UNISIST with the assistance of Unesco, and affiliated to the Austrian Standards Institute in Vienna, this Centre has as its main objective to enhance and co-ordinate terminological work. Its principal function is the maintenance and operation of the TERMNET database.

INFOTERRA. <www.infoterra-global.com> The International Referral System for Sources of Environmental Information, initiated at the UN Conference on the Human Environment, Stockholm, 1972. A world-wide network designed by experts from various countries under the auspices of the UN Environment Programme (UNEP), which began operating in 1975 and is a decentralized system based on existing environmental information services; the central UNEP Headquarters in Nairobi, Kenya co-ordinates activities with an international system of national, regional and sectoral focal points.

infra. (Lat. 'below') Used in footnotes and sometimes in the text to refer to an item mentioned subsequently. *See also supra.*

Ingenta. *See* BIDS.

Ingrain. A rough and shaggy quality of tinted paper used for pamphlet covers and wall hangings.

Inhabited initial. In a mediaeval illuminated manuscript, an initial letter containing figures of human beings, beasts, or both. *See also* Historiated initial.

In-house. The system of provision of particular services or activities within a company or organization from its own resources, rather than from outside agents or contractors.

In-house bids. Where contracts are awarded for the supply of services, existing suppliers (for example library services or other traditional agencies) may make bids to continue the present arrangements in competition with outside contractors. Such in-house bids will be treated on an equal footing with external bids.

INIST. <www.inist.fr> (2 allee du Parc de Brabois, F-54514 Vandoeuvre-les-Nancy, France) Institut de l'Information Scientifique et Technique; created 1988 to replace the Centre de Documentation Scientifique et Technique (CDST) and the Centre de Documentation Sciences Humaines (CDSH). INIST is directly attached to the CNRS Direction de l'Information Scientifique et Technique. Aims to disseminate scientific knowledge by database development, document delivery systems, and research programmes. It is the leading French document delivery centre for scientific and technical literature.

Initial letter. A capital letter, being the first letter of a word, sentence or paragraph, larger than the subsequent letters, and so set to give emphasis or for decoration. In typography, its size is indicated by the number of lines of body type it occupies, as '3-line initial'. Sometimes called 'Ornamental initial'. *See also* Factotum.

Initialism. *See* Acronym.

Ink ball. A large, round sheepskin or buckskin pad stuffed with wool, or horsehair and cotton, and fastened to a wooden handle. It was used from the fifteenth century until about 1820 (when superseded by rollers) for inking set-up type in the forme. The pressman used them in pairs holding one in each hand.

Ink block. A piece of beech wood fastened to the hind-rail of a printing press and used for spreading the ink. *See also* Ink slab.

Ink slab. The part of some printing machines, consisting of a large, flat, steel bed, on to which the ink is placed and from which the distributing rollers take, mix and spread it, before transferring it to the forme. *See also* Ink block.

InkCor Project. <www.infosrvr.nuk.uni.lj.si/jana/inkcor> An EU project involving Germany, France, the Netherlands and Slovenia; the aim is to address the problem of the preservation of paper documents endangered by the corrosive properties of old ink recipes.

Inkjet printer. A non-impact printer that produces the characters by squirting tiny drops of ink at the paper. Inkjet printers are seen as a way of achieving near-laser printer quality at a much reduced price, but they are slower machines, their output cost per page is significantly greater and they are less robust.

Inlaid. 1. A piece of printing, a MS., or an illustration, which is inset in a frame or border of paper, the overlapping edges having first been shaved thin in order to prevent bulkiness at the joints. 2. A leather binding with leather of another colour or kind set in the cover.

Inlay. 1. The paper used to stiffen the spine of a book when being re-bound. 2. A picture or decoration inlaid in the cover of a book. *See also* Onlay. 3. A MS., letter, leaf, plate or document mounted in a cut-out frame to protect it and permit both sides to be read.

Inlaying. In bookbinding, pasting down a differently coloured leather to that of the cover as part of the decoration; usually within an outlined tool form, border or panel. *See also* Onlay.

Inline letters. Jobbing and display work letters in which hand-tooling of the main strokes results in a white line forming their central part when printed. This gives the effect of blackness relieved by white. *See also* Open letters.

Inmin Taehak Suptang. [Grand People's Study House, Democratic People's Republic of Korea] (PO Box 200, Kim Il Sung Square, Pyongyang, N. Korea). The house, opened in 1982, is the national library of North Korea, and has space for 30 million items, 15 reading rooms, including Q&A rooms, where specialist academics answer the people's questions. It maintains an active social educational role, and provides services to factories, enterprises, and rural areas. Its homepage is on Kwangmyong, the nationwide government-established intranet which links universities, ministries and similar establishments. Through this network, limited e-mail is available to some users, although the network is not believed to be interconnected to the Internet and normal library visitors do not get e-mail access.

Inner form. *See* Form divisions.

Inner forme. A Forme containing the pages of type which will, when printed, become the inside of a printed sheet in Sheet work. The reverse of 'outer forme'.

Inner margin. *See* Back margin.

INPADOC. <www.european-patent-office.org/inpadoc> International Patent Documentation Centre. Established by the Austrian Government in collaboration with WIPO in 1972, and as a result of the signing (at a Diplomatic Conference held in Washington in 1970) of the Patent Co-operation Treaty (PCT). It aims to furnish to national or regional patent offices, and also to make available to industry, bibliographic data concerning patent documentation in machine-readable form, as well as services identifying patent documents relating to the same invention or to a given branch of technology. It is now closely merged into the general functions of the European Patent Office.

Input. That which is put into a computer system, either from external storage or committed directly to digital format, e.g. via a word processor.

Input devices. Equipment that provides the means by which data is entered into a computer; includes various devices such as keyboard, optical character equipment, light pen, Scanner, etc.

Input standards. *See* Performance.

Inscribed Copy. *See* Presentation Copy.

INSDOC. <www.icast.org.in> (14 Satsang Vihar Merg, New Delhi -110067, India) Indian National Scientific Documentation Centre, established in 1952 as a national laboratory under the Council of Scientific and Industrial Research to provide information, documentation and translation services at national and international levels. Major objectives are: to meet the information needs of research organizations, universities, government establishments, industry, to harness information technology applications in information management; to act as a single access point for scientific and technological information generated in India.

Insert. An additional sentence or a paragraph added to a proof to be inserted in a revise or final proof.

Insertion mark. *See* Caret.

Insertion motif. An ornament such as a pillar or a bar, etc., dividing two columns of text, or one scene from another, in a mediaeval illuminated manuscript.

In-service training. A scheme whereby trainees or the more junior members of a staff are given instruction in the routines carried out in the library and on wider and more general aspects of library and information work. *See also* Training.

Inset. 1. An illustration, map or other item, not part of the printed sheets, included when binding a pamphlet or book. They may or may not be sewn in. 2. A folded sheet laid inside another. It may be part of a printed sheet cut off before folding and inserted in the middle of the folded sheet to complete the succession of the pages. If so, it is also called 'offcut'. 3. An advertisement or separate leaf, not an integral part of the publication inserted in a magazine or booklet. 4. An extra page or set of pages inserted in a proof, or a book. 5. A small map, illustration, etc., set within the border of a larger one.

Inset map.   A small map printed within the border of a larger one.

Inside lining, ornamental.   *See* Doublure.

Inside margin.   *See* Back margin.

INSPEC.   <www.iee.org.uk/publish/inspec> The abstracting and indexing service of the (UK) Institution of Electrical Engineers (originally an acronym of Information Services for the Physics and Engineering Communities). Services are available in printed form, online and CD-ROM, and centre on four areas: physics; electrical engineering and electronics; computers/computing and control technology (including software engineering and desktop publishing); and information technology.

INSPIRE.   <www.inspire.gov.uk> Information Sharing Partners in Resources for Education, a UK national referral and access scheme working to link across 875 higher education, 4,610 public and three national libraries, interweaving the existing network of successful access partnerships into a single pathway. The ambition is to provide managed reciprocal access and referral to other libraries with relevant collections. Inspire England is directly funded by the Department for Education and Skills; partners include SCONUL, the Society of Chief Librarians, the British Library, the Learning and Skills Council, the Museums, Libraries and Archives Council (MLA), the Scottish Library and Information Council, and the National Libraries of Scotland and Wales.

Inspiring Learning for All (ILA).   <www.inspiringlearningforall.gov.uk> A set of resources issued in the UK in 2004 by the Museums, Libraries and Archives Council (MLA) designed to help libraries, museums, galleries and archives achieve transformational change – diversifying activities so that education and learning become core functions alongside collection management and preservation. The involvement of the Department of Education and Skills with MLA is an example of cross-departmental working in government. The ILA toolkit stresses 'generic learning outcomes' grouped into five areas: knowledge and understanding; skills; values, attitudes and feelings; enjoyment, creativity and inspiration; behaviour (activity, modification, progression). It has been piloted in seven library services.

inst.   Abbreviation for instant, and meaning 'of the current month' when following a date. *See also ult.*

Instalment.   A part of a literary work, published serially in a periodical; sometimes a portion of a work which is published in 'parts' or 'numbers'.

Instant messaging.   A web-based service – a combination of Chat room and E-mail – that enables users to see whether a chosen friend or co-worker is connected to the Internet and, if they are, to exchange messages. Instant messaging differs from e-mail in the immediacy of the message exchange and also makes a continued exchange simpler than sending e-mail back and forth. Most exchanges are text-only but some services allow attachments.

Institut de l'Information Scientifique et Technique. *See* INIST.

Institut International de Documentation. Formerly the Institut International de Bibliographie. Now the Fédération Internationale de L'Information et Documentation. *See* International Federation for Information and Documentation, Universal Decimal Classification.

Institut National des Techniques de la Documentation (INTD). (2 rue Conté, 75141 Paris, France) French school for the training of information scientists; based at the Conservatoire National des Arts et Métiers, Paris.

Institute for Image Data Research (IIDR). <www.unn.ac.uk/iidr> A multidisciplinary research centre founded at the University of Northumbria, UK, in 1998. The Institute will concentrate on the investigation of the role of electronic images in human communication; an early development is Artisan, a shape retrieval system for trademark images.

Institute for Learning and Research Technology (ILRT). <www.ilrt.bristol.ac.uk> A UK centre of excellence in the development and use of ICT – particularly Web technology – to support learning and research. The Institute has training, advisory and consultative roles.

Institute for Museum and Library Services (IMLS). <www.imls.gov> Established by US legislation late in 1996, IMLS consolidates federal support programmes for museums previously administered by the Institute of Museum Services, and programmes supporting libraries previously administered by the Department of Education. The National Commission on Libraries and Information Science (NCLIS) is responsible for advising the Institute on general policy related to financial assistance for libraries and information services. IMLS administers the Library Services and Technology Act, and awards grants for projects and programmes. Digitization is a current priority.

Institute of Arab Manuscripts. <www.alecso.org.tn/anglais/pages/ alecsostre10> Founded in April 1946 by the Arab League to make more widely known the Arab contribution to universal culture which is to be found in more than three million volumes scattered in public and private libraries throughout the world. Microfilms and enlargements have been made of over 15,000 rare and valuable manuscripts. These are available for consultation at the Institute in Cairo, through inter-library loans or by providing enlargements.

Institute of Information Scientists. *See* CILIP.

Institute of Librarians (IOL). A national voluntary organization of professional librarians in India which was formed in 1975; the Institute is located at the Department of Library Science, University of Calcutta. Publishes *Indian Journal of Library Science* (q.).

Institute of Paper Conservation (IPC). <www.ipc.org.uk> (Bridge House, Waterside, Upton upon Severn, WR8 0HG, UK) A UK professional organization concerned with books and archives, their storage and display, protective measures, safe handling, preventive conservation, and emergency salvage. Holds an annual international conference (proceedings published) and various courses and workshops. Publishes *The Paper Conservator* (2 p.a.).

Institutional repository. *See* Repository.

Instituto de Documentación e Información Cientifica y Tecnica. A national documentation centre established in 1963, with the technical assistance of Unesco, at Havana, Cuba, being attached to the Comisión Nacional de la Academia de Ciencias de la República de Cuba. Publishes a *Boletín*.

Instruction note. (*Classification*) A note directing the user to take some specific step which is not obvious from the heading and its context or from the general notes.

Instructional Management System. *See* IMS (1).

Instructional materials center. A room, in an American elementary or high school, in which all learning materials (books, periodicals, vertical file materials, slides, films, filmstrips, transparencies, tapes, models, art reproductions, etc., and any necessary machinery to operate them) are kept and from which they may be borrowed, or used, by teachers or pupils. Also called 'Learning resources center'. *See also* Curriculum materials center.

Instrumental cues. Abbreviations and/or thematic indications in a music score or Part and serving as a guide to the instrumentation, or as an entry signal, for the performer. These are common in 'parts' of concerted music and essential in the scores for piano-conductor. *See also* Score.

Insular handwriting. The beautiful national style of handwriting which developed from the semi-uncial book hand of the early Christian missionaries to the British Isles and, unlike the Continental styles, from the cursive minuscule. The two principal varieties of this script are (a) the Irish hand which was used from the sixth century to the Middle Ages and developed into the modern Irish script, and (b) the Anglo-Saxon semi-uncial style which developed from (a) in the seventh and eighth centuries. *See also* Cursive, Handwriting.

Intaglio. 1. (*Printing*) A design engraved or incised in the surface of a hard plate. An intaglio plate for printing is usually of copper and has the design engraved with a graver or etched by acid. Photogravure is an intaglio process. 2. (*Binding*) The impression of a Roll in which the sunk part of the leather forms the design.

Intaglio printing. Printing done from an intaglio (incised) plate, into which the design or image is countersunk or depressed; after being inked and wiped, leaving ink only in the engraved parts, it is placed with a damp sheet of printing paper on the press, layers of felt are added, and pressure applied. The thickness of the ink transferred to the paper varies with the depth of the incisions on the plate; this ink being layered on the plate can be felt on the resulting print (as distinct from the planographic and letterpress methods) and is a means of identifying the method of printing. Copperplate printing, steel die embossing and impressions taken from dry-point plates are forms of intaglio printing, as are etchings, line engravings, mezzotints, aquatints, photogravures and dry-point etchings. The opposite of Letterpress and Relief printing.

INTAMEL. <www.ifla.org/VII/rt3/rtiamcl> The International Association of Metropolitan Libraries is a network for exchange of information and professional communication for public library services of cities of 400,000 population and above. Formed in 1968, it became a Round Table of IFLA in 1976. In 2000 membership was widened to include regional libraries of similar size. There are 90 members from 32 countries.

Integer notation. One in which the notation of a scheme of classification consists of whole numbers as opposed to decimal *fraction notation*. There is no method of allowing for interpolation of new subjects in an integer notation except by leaving gaps where it is estimated that future expansion might take place.

Integral. A leaf which is part of a section, as distinct from one which is printed independently from a section but inserted in it.

Integral notation. The Notation of a scheme of classification which uses numbers arithmetically (as does the Library of Congress scheme) and not decimally. Also called an 'arithmetical' notation.

Integrated document management. *See* Document management.

Integrated library system. Software (though in early incarnations a software/hardware combination) that provides housekeeping activities and management information in relation to library services. Modules available can include cataloguing, acquisitions, circulation, OPAC, inter-library loans, periodicals control and reading list organization. It is becoming increasingly important that elements from these systems interoperate with wider institutional systems such as Portals and VLEs.

Integrated Services Digital Network. *See* ISDN.

Integrity. The accuracy and completeness of data, particularly after it has undergone transmission from one system to another.

Integrity of numbers. The view that the numbers or other symbols used to denote items in a scheme of classification should not be drastically altered in later revisions of the scheme. The policy was first proposed by M. Dewey in the second edition of the Dewey Decimal Classif-ication (1885); since then all new editions of the scheme have had to balance between stability and keeping pace with change.

Intellect. <www.intellectUK.org> (Russell Square House, 10/12 Russell Square, London WC1B 5EE, UK) A trade body for the UK-based IT, telecommunications and electronics industry. It has about 1,000 members, and was formerly known as CSSA – Computing Services and Software Association.

Intellectual Freedom Award. An award made by the American Association of School Librarians to recognize a school library media specialist who has upheld the principles of academic freedom.

Intellectual Freedom Round Table (IFRT). A part of the American Library Association.

Intellectual level. An indication of the presumed age-range and intelligence of the potential readers of a book; such information could be included in code form in a bibliographical description, to avoid confusion for example between a children's book, general monograph, or specialized treatise with similar titles. The development of such a code was investigated by Unesco in the late 1970s.

Intellectual property (IP). The asset value of intellectual activity, such as the writing of a novel, formulation of a patent, or the compilation of a glossary. In the increasingly commercial world of information management, the financial value of intellectual activity has become more obvious. Copyright protection and various other tradable rights are a normal part of any contract for publication in conventional or electronic formats, and there has been much legal activity to clarify the intellectual property rights inherent in the publication of databases and for material published on the World Wide Web. The term carries more legal weight than 'intellectual work'. *See also* IPR.

Intellectual Property Rights. *See* IPR.

Intellectual work. (*Copyright*) A creation resulting from intellectual activity covering all forms of expression, and possessing the characteristics of Novelty or Originality.

Intelligent agent. Software that displays autonomy, intelligence, communications capabilities and mobility, enabling it to travel across networks. An agent's role is to act without the user having to do anything: it reacts to events and takes the initiative. The current impact in information retrieval relates to filtering, reducing the effects of information overload by focusing on just those topics of interest to the searcher, and on the development of the Semantic Web. *See also* Knowbot.

Intelligent building. A building that incorporates sensing equipment to enable the adjustment of all aspects of its internal environment by computer control.

Intelligent documents. Documents (generally electronic, including multimedia documents) that act like Intelligent agents – automatically performing functions such as translation, indexing, linkage to other documents. In workflow applications, such documents may automatically perform routeing, life cycle, deadline or default actions.

Intelligent knowledge-based system. *See* Expert system.

Intension. *See* Extension.

Interactive video. The combination of computing and video technologies where the video is controlled by a computer program enabling the End user to progress through the material at their own speed. The techniques were the forerunner of Multimedia systems and have been incorporated into Web-based training.

Interest-profile. A list of terms selected from a thesaurus indicating the area of interest of the user of an information service; it is used in the selection of documents in a Selective Dissemination of Information System. Also called User-profile. *See also* SDI.

Interface. *See* User interface.

Intergovernmental Copyright Committee. *See* IGC.

Interlacing. 1. Ornament composed of bands, etc., woven together. 2. A method used in some Monitors and televisions whereby only alternate lines of display are refreshed in each sweep of the screen while still giving the impression of a continuous picture. This is achieved by taking advantage of the screen phosphor's ability to maintain an image for a short time before fading.

Interlay. An Underlay consisting of a sheet of paper or other material placed between a printing plate and its mount in order to raise the plate to its proper height for good printing.

Interleaf. An extra leaf, usually blank, inserted between the regular leaves of a book. The blank leaves may be provided for the writing of notes, or if they are thin tissues, to prevent the text and illustrations from rubbing. The latter may be pasted to the inner margins, or they may be loose. The plates so protected are known as tissued plates. Such a book is said to be interleaved.

Interleave. The arrangement of data in a storage device or of memory in RAM to enable its quick and efficient retrieval at the precise time it is required, of particular importance when handling high-volume data types such as audio and video.

Interlending. Schemes whereby users of one library or information system may request their service point to borrow from other library systems materials not held in their own library. Most libraries participate in interlending schemes, which may be locally, regionally, nationally or internationally organized. Many requests will be lodged with library services set up to act as interlending bases. *See also* Document delivery.

Inter-library co-operation. *See* Co-operation.

Interlibrary loan. A book or other item lent between libraries. *See* Interlending.

Interlibrary Loan Application Standards Maintenance Agency. <www.lac-bac.gc.ca/iso/ill> Based at Library and Archives Canada and having responsibility for preparing and maintaining defect reports, for developing amendments, and for updating the Interlibrary Loan Application standards (ISO 10160, ISO 10161-1 and ISO 10161-2). *See also* ISO ILL Protocol Standards.

Interlinear blank. *See* Interlinear space.

Interlinear matter. Characters providing explanations, translations or subsidiary matter, written or printed in smaller characters between the ordinary lines of text to which they relate.

Interlinear space. Space between lines of type. Also called 'Interlinear blank'.

Interlinear translation. A translation printed between the lines of the original text to which it relates.

Intermediate storage. (*Records management*) Alternative term for Records centre.

Intern. In America, a graduate who works in a library full-time while attending a school of librarianship.

International Advisory Committee on Documentation, Libraries and Archives. *See* IACODLA.

International Alliance on Access for All (IAAA). <www.unesco.org/webworld> A Unesco initiative launched in 2001 to promote more equitable access to information and develop an action plan for achieving this.

International Association for the Development of Documentation, Libraries and Archives in Africa (AIDBA). Founded in 1960 and known as the International Association for the Development of Libraries in Africa until 1967 when the name was changed to indicate the expanded aims of promoting and establishing in all African countries a public archives service, a national system of libraries, documentation centres and museums. Membership is open to individuals. It has national sections in four countries. Abbreviated AIDBA (Association Internationale pour le Développement de la Documentation des Bibliothèques et des Archives en Afrique). There is no evidence of recent activity.

International Association of Law Libraries (IALL). <www.iall.org> (PO Box 5709, Washington, DC 20016-1309, USA) Founded in New York in 1959 'to promote on a co-operative, non-profit and fraternal basis the work of individuals, libraries, and other institutions and agencies concerned with the acquisition and bibliographic processing of legal materials collected on a multinational basis, and to facilitate the research and other uses of such materials on a world-wide basis'. Publishes *International Journal of Law Libraries* (3 p.a.) formerly *IALL Bulletin*.

International Association of Metropolitan City Libraries. *See* INTAMEL.

International Association of Music Libraries, Archives and Documentation Centres (IAML). <www.iaml.info> Founded in Paris in 1951, the object being 'to constitute a representative international organization charged with stimulating and co-ordinating all the activities, national and international, of music libraries, and to study and facilitate the realization of all projects dealing with music bibliography and music library science'. The British branch of the Association <www.iaml-uk-irl.org> was founded in 1953 and was primarily responsible for the British Catalogue of Music and currently for CECILIA. It is an Organization in Liaison (OiL) with CILIP. *See also* RISM.

International Association of Orientalist Librarians (IAOL). <www.library.cornell.edu/wason/iaol> Founded in 1967 to promote better communication between orientalist librarians and researchers worldwide. With over 250 members, it maintains a discussion list, holds annual conferences, and publishes *IAOL Bulletin* (2 p.a.), plus conference proceedings.

International Association of Scholarly Publishers (IASP). <www.iasp.at> Formed in 1970 to associate university presses with other publishers of scholarly works, and encourage efficient production and dissemination of scholarship and research. Affiliated to the International Publishers Association. Headquarters in Vienna.

International Association of School Librarianship (IASL). <www.iasp-slo.org> (PMB 292, 1903 W 8th Street, Erie, PA 16505, USA) Founded in 1969 (originally as a Committee of the World Confederation of Organizations of the Teaching Profession) to promote school library provision all over the world. Financed by the subscriptions of individual members and associations. Publishes *Newsletter* (4 p.a.).

International Association of Schools of Information Science (AIESI). <www.aiesi.refer.org> Founded 1977, sponsors workshops and conferences. Secretariat at the University of Montréal. Abbreviated AIESI, from the French title.

International Association of Sound and Audiovisual Archives. <www.iasa-web.org> A non-governmental Unesco affiliated organization. It was established in 1969 in Amsterdam to function as a medium for international co-operation between archives which preserve recorded sound documents. The Association is actively involved in the preservation, organization and use of sound recordings, techniques of recording and methods of reproducing sound in all fields in which the audio medium is used; in the exchange of recordings between archives and of related literature and information; and in all subjects relating to the professional work of sound archives and archivists including acquisition, documentation, copyright, access, distribution, preservation, and the technical aspects of recording and playback. The Association extended its title from the 'International Association of Sound Archives' in 2000.

International Association of Technological University Libraries (IATUL). <www.iatul.org> A voluntary international non-governmental organization represented by their library directors or university managers who have responsability for information services and resource management. It is small enough for individual members to be able to develop a close relationship, yet widespread enough to cover the interests of libraries operating in virtually all modern social, economic and political situations.

International Bibliography of the Social Sciences. <www.ibss.ac.uk> (BLPES, 10 Portugal Street, London WC2A 2HD, UK) Originally set up by the International Committee for Social Science Information and Documentation under the auspices of Unesco, *IBSS* was started in 1951 and now indexes over 2,700 journals from 100 countries and languages. The total size of the file is now over 2 million items and is growing by 100,000 items each year.

International Board on Books for Young People. *See* IBBY.

International Book Award. Instituted at the first meeting of the International Book Committee held at Bogatá, Colombia, in 1973, the Award is designed to accord recognition for outstanding services rendered by a person or institution to the cause of books in such fields as authorship, publishing, production, translation, bookselling, encouragement of the reading habit and promotion of international co-operation. It was first awarded to Mr Herman Liebaers, Royal Librarian of Belgium, President of IFLA, and Chairman of the Preparatory Meeting, the Planning Committee and the Support Committee which organized IBY 'in recognition of his outstanding contribution to International Book Year, 1972'.

International Book Committee. The Committee was originally organized in 1971 in Paris as a support body for Unesco's International Book Year, 1972 (*see* IBY). It collaborates with other international bodies and experts concerned with books and reading. In 2004/2005, a priority is co-operation with the IFLA Reading Section <www.ifla.org/VII/s33/annual>.

International Book Year. *See* IBY.

International catalogue card. The size of card which has been adopted internationally for use in card catalogues: it is 5 x 3 inches (7.5 x 12.5 centimetres).

International Centre for Scientific and Technical Information (ICSTI). <www.icsti.su> (21-b, Kuuinen Street, 125252 Moscow, Russia) Originally founded in 1969, ICSTI provides various information services to its member countries: Bulgaria, Byelorus, Cuba, Estonia, Georgia, Hungary, India, Korea Democratic Peoples Republic, Latvia, Moldova, Mongolia, Poland, Romania, Russia, Sri Lanka, Turkey, Ukraine and Vietnam. Its main aim is to provide information, analytical, consultative and organizational support for international co-operation in science, technology and business. Its 200 staff in Moscow enjoy diplomatic status; there are several grant schemes and publications.

International Children's Book Day. *See* IBBY.

International Classification. The brief name for Fremont Rider's scheme of classification for a general library, *International classification for the arrangement of books on the shelves of general libraries*, first published in 1961. Its main outline is similar to the Library of Congress classification; form and geographical sub-divisions are enumerated in each main class; the notation consists of three letters and can be extended by 'book numbers' which are a combination of letters from the Biscoe Date Table plus the initial letter of the author's name; no auxiliary tables are provided, neither are alternative locations. The schedules have 17,500 places approximately. It is now a dead classification.

International Coalition of Library Consortia. *See* ICOLC.

International Committee for Social Sciences Documentation (ICSSD). Founded in November 1950 in Paris at a meeting called by Unesco following recommendations of two committees of experts in 1948 and 1949. Registered in accordance with French law. Collects, keeps up-to-date and disseminates information on the different documentation services in the social sciences, and helps establish bibliographies and documentary tools which its surveys show to be necessary. It initiated, with the help of the Nuffield Foundation, investigation into the need for, and production of, a scheme of classification for the four Unesco bibliographies dealing with sociology, political science, economics, and social anthropology. The Kyle Classification for Social Sciences was the result.

International Committee of the Blue Shield. <www.ifla.org/blueshield> <christiane.logie@kbr.be> (ICBS Secretariat, Boulevard de l'Empereur 4, 1000-Brussels, Belgium) The Committee was set up by IFLA, ICA (International Council on Archives), ICOM (International Council of Museums), ICOMOS (International Council on Monuments and Sites); it operates under the Hague Convention for the Protection of Cultural Property in the Event of Armed Conflict, and aims to collect and disseminate information and to co-ordinate action in emergency situations.

International commons. An expression that envisages a range of information and related services that should be available easily and without charge to the greatest number of people, as a fundamental right that enriches human life and that should be subject to minimal legal protection. *See also* Creative commons, Public goods.

International Community of Booksellers Associations (ICBA). Founded in 1956. Aims: co-operation between all booksellers and associations of booksellers of countries which enjoy freedom of thought and expression with a view to the exchange of experience and the discussion of common commercial problems.

International Conference on Cataloguing Principles (ICCP). A conference of cataloguers, bibliographers and library officers with cataloguing expertise was held in Paris, 9–18 October 1961, consequent upon a proposal made by the council of IFLA in 1957 to seek agreement on certain basic cataloguing principles. It was sponsored by IFLA with the object of reaching 'agreement on basic principles governing the choice and form of entry in the alphabetical catalogue of authors and titles'. The definitive annotated edition of the *Statement of principles*, known as the Paris Principles, which was an outcome of this Conference and was mainly written by Dr Eva Verona, was published by the IFLA Committee on Cataloguing, London, in 1971. *See also* IMCE.

International Copyright. *See* Copyright, international.

International Copyright Information Centre. *See* ICIC.

International Council for Research and Innovation in Building and Construction (CIB). <www.cibworld.nl> (Postbox 1837, 3000 BV Rotterdam, Netherlands) The new name, adopted in 1998, for the International Council for Building Research, Studies and Documentation, which was founded in 1953 and superseded the International Council for Building Documentation formed in 1950. The abbreviation CIB remains in use. The Council, which has over 500 organizational members, aims to encourage and develop international co-operation in all aspects of the building and construction industries, and has an extensive publications programme including *ABC: abridged building classification for architects, builders and civil engineers* (several language editions), directories, scientific and technical analyses, international state-of-the-art reports, proceedings of conferences, workshops, symposia, conferences.

International Council for Scientific and Technical Information (ICSTI). <www.icsti.org> (51 Bvd. de Montmorency, F75016 Paris, France) Established 1984 as successor to the International Council of Scientific Unions Abstracts Board (ICSU/AB). Exists to widen access to and awareness of scientific and technical information. In 1985 its scope was extended to cover electronic publishing and document delivery.

International Council of Science. <www.icsu.org> (51 Bvd. de Montmorency, F75016 Paris, France) Formerly known as the International Council of Scientific Unions (ICSU), which was established in 1931 from an earlier International Research Council (created in 1919). The organization now comprises 101 national science bodies and 27 international scientific unions. The main objectives are to encourage international scientific activity which will serve scientific and technological development and so help to promote the cause of peace and international security throughout the world; to facilitate and co-ordinate the activities of the International Scientific Unions; to stimulate, design and co-ordinate international interdisciplinary scientific research projects, and scientific education; to facilitate the co-ordination of the international scientific activities of its National Members. *See also* International Council for Scientific and Technical Information.

International Council on Archives. <www.ica.org> (60, Rue de Francs-Bourgeois, 75003 Paris, France) Also Conseil International des Archives. Founded in 1948 by professional archivists meeting in Paris under the auspices of Unesco. The professional organization for the world archival community, bringing together national archives, professional associations, regional and local archives, and archives of other organizations as well as individual archivists. ICA has more than 1,700 members in 174 countries. It is a non-governmental organization (NGO), and normally acts as agency for Unesco in archival matters. It holds international Congresses every four years (Beijing 1996; Seville 2000; Vienna 2004), and meetings of the Round Table on Archives every year in which there is no Congress. There are 11 regional branches: ALA (see ALA 1); ARBICA; CARBICA; EASTICA; ESARBICA; EURICA; EURASICA; PARBICA; SARBICA; SWARBICA; WARBICA.

International DOI Foundation. <www.doi.org/welcome.html> Created in 1998 to support the needs of the intellectual property community in the digital environment, by the development and promotion of the Digital Object Identifier system as a common infrastructure for content management. The Foundation is a registered not-for-profit organization.

International Encyclopaedia of Information and Library Science. A major reference source published in 1996 (2nd ed., 2003) that contains authoritative articles on a wide range of professional topics from 150 contributors. Published by Routledge in the UK (ISBN 0 415 25901 0).

International Federation for Information and Documentation (FID). The English title of the Fédération Internationale d'Information et de Documentation (FID). FID began its existence as the Institut International de Bibliographie (Brussels, 1895); in 1931 it became the Institut International de Documentation (IID); in 1937 the International Federation for Documentation; final name adopted in 1986. It was a highly-regarded professional association for organizations and individuals involved in information systems, products and methods; in 2001/2, FID took a decision to close down. Although there were discussions with IFLA during 2000 and 2001, no deal was reached. The 105-year archive of FID will be located at the Royal Library of the Netherlands <www.kb.nl>.

International Federation for Information Processing (IFIP). <www.ifip. or.at> (Hofstrasse 3, A 2361 Laxenburg, Austria) Formerly the International Federation of Information Processing Societies which was set up as a result of an international congress on information processing organized by Unesco and held in Paris in 1959. The members of the Federation are national societies, the adhering society in the United Kingdom being the British Computer Society. Aims: to sponsor international conferences and symposia on information processing; to establish international committees to undertake special tasks falling within the scope of member societies; to advance the interests of member societies in international co-operation in the field of information processing.

International Federation of Film Archives. *See* FIAF.

International Federation of Library Associations and Institutions (IFLA). <www.ifla.org> (Box 95312, 2509 CH The Hague, Netherlands) Founded in Edinburgh in 1927, IFLA is the leading international body representing the interests of library and information services and their users. It aims to improve understanding and promote awareness of the importance of ready and unfettered access to information. It is represented on many international bodies and is active in a huge range of areas. There are eight divisions:

1. General Research Libraries (includes National Libraries, University Libraries and other General Research Libraries, and Library and Research Services for Parliaments)

2. Special Libraries (includes Government Libraries, Social Science

Libraries, Geography and Map Libraries, Science and Technology Libraries, Biological and Medical Science Libraries, and Art Libraries)

3. Libraries serving the general public (includes Public Libraries, Libraries Serving Disadvantaged Persons, Libraries for Children and Young Adults, School Libraries and Resource Centres, Libraries for the Blind, Library Services to Multicultural Populations, and Round Tables for National Centres for Library Services, INTAMEL and Mobile Libraries)

4. Bibliographic Control (includes Classification and Indexing)

5. Collections and Services (includes Acquisition and Collection Development, Document Delivery and Interlending, Serial Publications, Government Information and Official Publications, Rare Books and Manuscripts, and a Round Table on Newspapers)

6. Management and Technology (includes Preservation and Conservation, Library Buildings and Equipment, Information Technology, Statistics, Management and Marketing, and Round Tables on Audiovisual and Multimedia, Management of Library Associations and Women' s Issues)

7. Education and Research (includes Education and Training, Library Theory and Research, Reading and Round Tables on Continuing Professional Development, Library History, Editors of Library Journals and User Education)

8. Regional Activities (includes groups for Africa, Asia and Oceania, and Latin America and Caribbean).

Five Discussions Groups focus on Corporate and For-Profit Libraries, the Internet, Friends and Advocates of Libraries, Reference Work, and Social Responsibilities. There are also two working committees: Copyright and Other Legal Matters (CLM) and Freedom of Access to Information and Freedom of Expression (FAIFE). For information on the former IFLA core programmes UBCIM and UDT, *see now* ICABS.

International Federation of Reproduction Rights Organizations. *See* IFRRO.

International Federation of Television Archives. *See* FIAT/IFTA.

International Forum on Open Bibliographic Systems (IFOBS). (National Library of Canada, 395 Wellington Street, Ottawa, Ontario K1A 0NA, Canada) IFOBS aimed to facilitate the international use of OSI protocols for bibliographic applications; it is now inactive.

International Group. A membership group of CILIP, originally formed in 1968 as the International and Comparative Librarianship Group (ICLG). Encourages international perspectives and links with libraries outside the UK.

International Information Centre for Standards in Information and Documentation. *See* ISODOC.

International Information Centre for Terminology. *See* INFOTERM.

International Information System on Research in Documentation. *See* ISORID.

International Institute for Children's Literature and Reading Research. <www.jugendliteratur.net> (Mayerhofgasse 6, 1040 Vienna, Austria) The Institute is a non-profit-making association; it also serves as the office of the Austrian Section of the International Board on Books for Young People (IBBY). Founded in 1965, it endeavours to create an international centre of work and co-ordination in the field of children's literature and to take over documentation in this area.

International Library Information and Analytical Center. *See* ILIAC.

International Literacy Year. 1990 was so designated by the United Nations; the lead organization for activity was Unesco, which used the year to launch a Plan of Action to eradicate illiteracy by 2000.

International MARC Network Advisory Committee (IMAC). A consultative body of libraries using MARC for national bibliographic networks; members include British Library, Bibliothèque Nationale de France, Library of Congress, etc.

International MARC Programme (IMP). A core programme of IFLA responsible for the testing and development of UNIMARC. Later combined into the UBC programme; *see* Universal Bibliographic Control and International MARC (UBCIM).

International Meeting of Cataloguing Experts. *See* IMCE.

International Musicological Society (IMS). <www.ims-online.ch> (P.O. Box 1561, CH-40011, Basle, Switzerland) Founded in Basle, 1927, by amalgamating the *Internationale Musikgesellschaft* and the *Union Musicologique*. Reconstituted in 1949, the Society aims to establish relations between musicologists in different countries; serves as a central information and bibliographical office. Publishes *Acta Musicologica* (q.), and congress reports. *See also* RISM.

International Network for the Availability of Scientific Publications (INASP). <www.inasp.info> (PO Box 516, Oxford OX1 1WG, UK) Formed 1992 as a result of efforts by the International Council for Scientific Unions (ICSU) in co-operation with Unesco and other organizations such as the Third World Academy of Science (TWAS) and the American Association for the Advancement of Science. The general objective is to create a co-operative network of donors and partners and to expand programmes that distribute scientific books and journals to institutions, mainly in the developing world. Current priorities are health information, library services in Africa, local publication and improved access, and in-country capacity building.

International Organization for Standardization (ISO). <www.iso.ch> (P.O. Box 56, rue de Varembé 1, CH-1211 Geneva, Switzerland) Constituted in London under its present statutes in October 1946 to replace the pre-war International Federation of National Standardizing Associations (ISA) and the United Nations Standards Co-ordinating Committee. Aims to promote development of standards in the world with a view to facilitating international exchange of goods and services, and to develop mutual co-operation in the sphere of intellectual, scientific, technological and economic activity. Over 2,850 technical committees of experts appointed by national standards bodies who are members formulate recommendations to national member associations. Operates ISONET, the ISO Information Network.

International paper sizes. The international 'A' series of paper sizes, now widely used throughout the world. Originally specified by Deutsche Industrie Normen (DIN), there is a British Standard (BS 4000) and an international recommendation (ISO/R 216) covering them. *See* Paper sizes, for details of dimensions.

International Patent Documentation Centre. *See* INPADOC.

International public goods. *See* International commons, Public goods.

International Publishers Association (IPA). <www.ipa-uie.org> (Avenue de Miremont 3, CH-1206 Geneva, Switzerland) Founded in Paris in 1896 as International Publishers Congress to consider problems common to the publishing and bookselling trades, and to uphold and defend the right to publish and distribute in complete freedom, both within the frontiers of each country and among the nations; to secure international co-operation among themselves and to overcome illiteracy, the lack of books and other means of education. Congresses are held periodically in different countries. A permanent office is maintained at Geneva. Membership is open to professional book and music publishers associations. Activities include help to secure signatories to the Berne Convention and Universal Copyright Convention and to keep the flow of books between countries free of tariffs and other obstacles, provision of aid to emerging countries, and consideration of international copyright and translation rights.

International Reading Association (IRA). <www.reading.org> Founded in the US on 1 January 1956 to encourage the study of reading problems at all levels, and also to stimulate and promote research in developmental, corrective and remedial reading. Membership ranges over 99 countries. There is an extensive publishing programme. *See also* United Kingdom Literacy Association.

International Records Management Trust (IRMT). <www.irmt.org> Founded in 1990 with support from major funding agencies, seeks to promote efficiency in records management as an essential aspect of the accountability of government to its people. Several projects are in hand, principally in the British Commonwealth. Offers a public sector records study programme.

International Scholarly Communications Alliance. <www.curl.ac.uk/about/isca> Formed in 2002 by research library associations in Australia, Canada, Europe, Japan, Hong Kong, New Zealand, the United Kingdom and the United States, the Alliance is a global network that collaborates with scholars and publishers to establish equitable access to scholarly and research publications.

Members engage in a series of activities that focus the scholarly publishing process on the primary goals of the academic research community, advancing the discovery of new knowledge and facilitating its dissemination, and on ways to ensure open and affordable access to scholarship across national boundaries. Its essential partnership is with the scholar-author.

International Serials Data System. *See* ISDS.

International SGML/XML Users' Group (ISUG). <www.isgmlug.org> A federation of user groups and individuals formed in 1984 to support users through sharing knowledge of Markup technologies and influencing the development of related standards.

International Society for Knowledge Organization (ISKO). <isko2004@ucl.ac.uk> Founded July 1989 in Frankfurt/Main, Germany, to unite personal and institutional members interested in 'research, development and application of all methods for the organization of knowledge in general or of particular fields by integrating especially the conceptual approaches of classification research and artificial intelligence'. There is a small publishing programme, and regular conferences are held (e.g. London, 2004.)

International Society for Performing Arts Libraries and Museums. Founded in September 1954 at Zagreb with the object of developing co-operation among libraries, as well as museums, public, private and specialized collections concerned with the theatre, dance, cinema, marionettes, mime, festivals, *son et lumière*, radio and television. *Now see* SIBMAS.

International Standard Bibliographic Description. *See* ISBD.

International Standard Book Number. *See* ISBN, Standard Book Number.

International Standard Music Number. *See* ISMN.

International Standard Recording Code. *See* ISRC.

International Standard Serial Number. *See* ISSN.

International Standard Technical Report Number. *See* ISRN.

International Standard Work Code. *See* ISWC.

International Telecommunication Union (ITU). <www.itu.int> (Place des Nations, CH-1211, Geneva, Switzerland) An international organization within the United Nations System of Organizations where governments and the private sector co-ordinate global telecommunications networks and services. Its concerns range over all aspects of world-wide telecommunications development, policy, strategy, and regulation. The Union is structured into three Sectors: Radiocommunication (ITU-R), Telecommunication Standardization (ITU-T), and Telecommunication Development (ITU-D). ITU was a prime mover of the World Summit on the Information Society. *See also* ITU–T.

International Translations Centre. The Centre, formerly known as the European Translations Centre, was founded in 1961 and was best known for publishing *World Translations Index*. This ceased to appear in 1997.

International Union for the Protection of Literary and Artistic Works.
Founded 9 September 1886 to ensure effective protection to authors of
literary and artistic works, and to ensure and develop the international
protection of literacy and artistic works. Membership is open to
governments. Organizes diplomatic conferences. Publishes *Le Droit
d'Auteur* (m.), *Copyright* (m.).

International Youth Library (IYL). <www.ijb.de> An associated project
of Unesco; founded 1949 in Munich out of the first post-war exhibition
of international children's books organized 1946 by Jella Lepman
(1891–1970). From 1982 housed in Schloss Blutenburg, near Munich.
The objects of the Library are to encourage international exchange and
co-operation in children's book publishing and research, to provide
information and advice, and to organize exhibitions. The Library is
reckoned the largest collection of children's literature in the world, and
holds over 470,000 volumes in 100 languages.

Internationalized Domain Names. *See* Domain Name System.

Interne. *See* Intern.

Internet. An amalgamation of inter-related computer networks using the
TCP/IP protocol, permitting electronic communication on a global
scale. It started in 1969 as a single US network, ARPAnet (the
Department of Defense Advanced Research Projects Agency
Network), to allow researchers in defence-related areas to share
distributed hardware and software resources. In the early 1980s the
original ARPAnet was split into two and, somewhat expanded, became
known as the DARPA (Defense Advanced Research Projects Agency)
Internet, subsequently 'the Internet'. Gradually, links were made
between the Internet and existing networks for the wider research and
academic communities (CSNET (Computer Science Network), Bitnet
(Because its time network)) and then, in 1986, came the establishment
of the NSFnet (National Science Foundation Network) Backbone.
Linking researchers across the US to supercomputing facilities, this
rapidly grew to encompass the growing needs of universities and
research consortia and eventually replaced the ARPAnet (dismantled in
1990) and CSNET (ceased in 1991). In 1994 the NSF awarded
contracts to enable commercial telecommunications companies to
operate on the high speed backbone previously reserved for education
and research, and in April 1995 the NSFnet backbone was
decommissioned, replacing the government-sponsored service with a
fully commercial system of backbones. The growth of similar
initiatives in other countries (e.g. JANET and SuperJANET in the UK;
SURFNet in the Netherlands; UNINETT in Norway), coupled with the
extraordinary impact of the World Wide Web as a universal
information exchange, established the infrastructure for the rapid
increase in communication and information transfer across the Internet
experienced since the mid-1990s. The Internet today is a complex
interconnection of networks provided by public and private interests

used for education, leading edge research, shopping, commerce and leisure, continuing to see rapid growth and at the same time offering concerns to society. *See also* Abilene, Electronic Frontier Foundation, GÉANT, Grid (1), Internet2, National Information Infrastructure, Next Generation Internet, PICS, Usenet, W3C, Worm (1).

Internet Architecture Board (IAB). <www.iab.org/iab> A committee of the Internet Engineering Task Force whose responsibilities include architectural oversight of IETF activities, Internet standards process oversight and appeal, management of publication of the Request for Comment (RFC) Series, and management of the IETF protocol parameter registry, operated by the IANA.

Internet Archive. <www.archive.org> An initiative to collect and store public materials from the Internet going back to 1996 to provide historians, researchers, scholars, and others access to a vast collection of data and ensure the longevity of this information. Resources covered include moving images, audio and texts and a 'Wayback Machine' allows users to visit archived versions of Web sites by inputting a URL and a date range.

Internet Assigned Numbers Authority. *See* IANA.

Internet Corporation for Assigned Names and Numbers. *See* ICANN.

Internet Engineering Task Force (IETF). <www.ietf.org> A large open international community of network designers, operators, vendors, and researchers concerned with the evolution of the Internet architecture and the smooth operation of the Internet. It is open to any interested individual. A number of working groups are organized by topic into areas such as routeing, transport and security with much of the work handled via mailing lists. The IETF holds meetings three times per year.

Internet governance. *See* Governance.

Internet Protocol. *See* IP (2).

Internet Scout Project. <scout.wisc.edu> Located at the University of Wisconsin-Madison, and funded in part by the National Science Foundation, the Scout Project focuses on developing better tools and services for finding, filtering, and presenting online information and metadata. Open source software tools (such as a Portal) have been created, though the Project is perhaps best known for its *NSDL Scout Reports* which offer high quality information about online resources. Part of the NSDL.

Internet service provider (ISP). A company or organization that provides connections to the Internet via its own Backbone.

Internet Service Providers' Association (ISPA). <www.ispa.org.uk> (23 Palace Street, London SW1E 5HW, UK) The UK Trade Association for providers of Internet services established in 1995 to promote competition, self-regulation and the development of the Internet industry. Main activity is in making representations on behalf of the industry to Government bodies, such as the Home Office, the Department of Trade and Industry and Oftel. Members (over 100 companies in the UK) observe a Code of Practice and co-operate with the Internet Watch Foundation. Publishes *Hardcopy* (bi-annually). *See also* EuroISPA.

Internet Society.   <www.isoc.org> (1775 Wiehle Avenue, Suite 102, Reston, VA 20190-5108, USA) A professional membership society with more than 150 organizational and 16,000 individual members in over 180 countries. It provides leadership in addressing issues that confront the future of the Internet, and is the organizational home for the groups responsible for Internet infrastructure standards, including the Internet Engineering Task Force and the Internet Architecture Board. Publishes *OnTheInternet* (paper, twice-yearly) and *e-OnTheInternet* (electronic, updated regularly).

Internet Watch Foundation (IWF).   <www.iwf.org.uk> (5 Coles Lane, Oakington, Cambridgeshire, CB4 5BA, UK) Established in the UK in 1996 following an agreement between the government, police and the Internet service provider industry that a partnership approach was needed to tackle the distribution of child abuse images (often referred to as child pornography) online. The IWF provides a hotline for the public to report their inadvertent exposure to illegal content on the Internet, and works with law enforcement agencies at home and abroad to have the content removed and the potential offenders traced.

Internet2.   <www.internet2.edu> A US consortium of 206 universities working in partnership with industry and government to develop and deploy advanced network applications and technologies, accelerating the creation of tomorrow's Internet. The primary goals of Internet2 are to create a leading edge network capability for the national research community, enable revolutionary Internet applications, and to ensure the rapid transfer of new network services and applications to the broader Internet community. Initiatives include Middleware, End-to End Performance, K20, Arts and Humanities, Digital Video, and Internet2 Commons. *See also* Abilene, Next Generation Internet.

Internet2 Commons.   <commons.internet2.edu> An Initiative of Internet2, a large-scale, distributed, collaborative environment for the research and education community. The Commons is a framework for collaboration throughout the research and education community that will encourage large scale deployment of tools for one-to-one, one-to-group, and group-to-group collaborations. These interactive communications include meetings, conferences, and activities related to teaching and learning.

Interoperability.   Initiatives to create, and to encourage the take-up by systems suppliers, of standards, protocols and recommendations that facilitate the working together of computer systems, or the perception of their integration when seen from the perspective of the end user. One of the key starting points was Open Systems Interconnection and the World Wide Web – itself a major contributor to interoperability – has provided further incentive to develop systems, particularly for the interchange of Metadata (*see for example*, RDF). Interoperability of library catalogue data has been a feature of the Bath Profile and Z39.50; in learning systems and VLEs, IMS and SCORM are prominent. *See also* Interoperability Focus.

Interoperability Focus (UK). <www.ukoln.ac.uk/interop-focus> A post jointly funded by JISC and the Museums, Libraries and Archives Council (MLA) and located at UKOLN. Established in January 1999, the post is responsible for exploring, publicizing and mobilizing the benefits and practice of effective interoperability across diverse information sectors, including libraries and the cultural heritage and archival communities. Issues under consideration include metadata, distributed systems and public library networking.

Interpolated note. An explanation or description added to an entry by the compiler of a catalogue or bibliography to clarify the original material. Such information is inserted within Square brackets.

Interpolation. (*Classification*) The insertion of a new topic at any point in an array of classes in a scheme of classification. A non-structural type of notation renders this readily possible. The Dewey Decimal Classification achieves this by leaving gaps in the array. *See also* Extrapolation.

Inter-regional subject coverage scheme. Under this scheme each of the British Regional Bureaux became responsible on 1 January 1959 for seeing that one library in its area purchases every new book and pamphlet published in the United Kingdom, which is included in the *British National Bibliography*; the allocation of sections of the Dewey Classification is as follows:

000–099	Northern	400–499	East Midlands
100–199	Wales	500–599	West Midlands
200–299	South-Western	600–699	North-Western
300–349	Yorkshire	700–799	London
350–399	Scotland	800–899	East Midlands
		900–999	South-Eastern

The books purchased under this scheme are intended primarily for preservation. *Compare* Joint Fiction Reserve.

Interrogation mark. A punctuation sign (?) placed at the end of a direct question. Also used between parentheses to indicate an author's questioning the accuracy of a statement. Also called 'Interrogation point', 'Mark of interrogation', 'Question mark'.

Intersecting frame. (*Binding*) One or more decorative frames, the sides of which (or some of them) are extended, where they meet each other, to the edges of the cover.

Interspacing. *See* Letter spacing.

Intertype. A typesetting machine casting type in a slug, similar to, but differing in detail from, the Linotype.

Intra-facet relation. *See* Phase.

Intranet. An in-house network, usually constructed on the same model as the Internet, operating within a company or other organization; the use of Web browsers allows easy access and searching, as users apply standard Internet techniques. An intranet that allows some access to external users – customers or suppliers for example – is termed an Extranet.

Intrinsic value. (*Archives*) In the appraisal of manuscripts, the worth of a document as affected by some unique factor such as its age, an attached seal, a signature or the handwriting of a distinguished person, or the circumstances regarding its creation. *See also* Appraisal.

Introduction. 1. A short essay or statement, usually being a general survey of the subject preparing the reader for the treatment to follow, of a commendatory nature, and written by an authority in the field with which the book deals. Its order in the Preliminaries, is after the Preface and immediately before the first page of text. Sometimes it is the first chapter. 2. Included in the title of a book, it indicates that it is an introductory book on the subject, intended for students, and possibly a popular treatment, but not as elementary as a Primer.

Introduction date. The date given at the beginning or end of an Introduction.

Inventory. (*Archives*) Often used as a synonym for List, a finding aid for archival materials, usually at class or item level.

Inversion, principle of. In classification, placing the facets in schedule order in such a way that the most concrete, intensive or significant is last.

Inversion of title. The turning about of a title to bring a particular word to the front. This practice is frequently adopted in dictionary catalogues.

Inverted Baconian Scheme. A scheme of classification in which the order of the main classes in Francis Bacon's philosophical system outlined in his *The advancement of learning* (1605) – History, Poesy, Philosophy – are inverted, as in the Dewey Decimal Classification and the Universal Decimal Classification.

Inverted commas. Pairs of superior commas, or sometimes single commas, placed at the beginning and end of quotations. *See also* Quotes.

Inverted entry. An index entry which has been re-arranged to bring the most important word or words to the front. For example, 'Co-efficient of expansion, apparent'. The opposite of Direct entry.

Inverted heading. A catalogue heading which has had the order of the words inverted to bring the most important word to the front, as Chemistry, Organic. Also called 'Indirect heading'.

Inverted title. *See* Inversion of title.

Investing in Children: the Future of Library Services for Children and Young People. A key UK report published by HMSO in 1995.

Investing in Knowledge. An advocacy campaign launched in the UK in 2003 by Resource (now MLA) to demonstrate the present and future value of the information sector to the whole of society for education, creativity, community and economy. From this initiative, a workforce development strategy was scheduled to be issued in 2004. The Knowledge for All vision is set to run over five years.

Invisible Web. *See* Deep Web.

IOLR. *See* India Office Library and Records.

Ionometer. *See* pH value.

IP. 1. *See* Information provider. 2. Internet Protocol, the communications protocol underlying the Internet that allows large, geographically diverse networks of computers to communicate with each other quickly and economically over a variety of physical links. Currently there are two types of Internet Protocol address in active use: IP version 4 (IPv4) and IP version 6 (IPv6). IPv4 was initially deployed on 1 January 1983 and is still the most commonly used version. IPv4 addresses are 32-bit numbers often expressed as 4 octets in 'dotted decimal' notation (for example, 192.0.32.67). Deployment of the IPv6 protocol began in 1999. IPv6 addresses are 128-bit numbers and are conventionally expressed using hexadecimal strings (for example, 1080:0:0:0:8:800:200C:417A). *See also* TCP/IP. 3. *See* Intellectual property.

IPA. *See* International Publishers Association.

IPC. *See* Institute of Paper Conservation.

IPIG. ILL Protocol Implementors' Group. *See* ILL Protocol Standards, Interlibrary Loan Application Standards Maintenance Agency.

IPR. Abbreviation for 'Intellectual Property Rights', the bundle of rights which include copyright, patents, trademarks, performing rights, and rights held by makers of sound recordings and videos.

IPS. *See* Office of Information Programmes and Services.

i.q. Abbreviation for *idem quod* (Lat. 'the same as').

IR. *See* Information retrieval.

IRA. *See* International Reading Association.

Iranian Library Association. Currently involved with the National Library of Iran in re-building the library service in Afghanistan. *See* National Library of Iran.

Irish Central Library. Founded by the Carnegie United Kingdom Trust in 1923 as the Irish Central Library for Students; control was passed to An Chomhairle Leabharlanna (The Library Council) in 1948. Supplements the regular library services of local authorities, educational institutions and learned societies, and the services of public and special libraries generally, by providing books for study and research both from its own stock and by means of inter-library loans. *See also* Library Council/An Chomhairle Leabharlanna.

Irish Library Council. *See* Library Council/An Chomhairle Leabharlanna.

Irish Manuscripts Commission (IMC). Set up in October 1928 (under a warrant of the President of the Executive Council of Saorstát Éireann) to report on collections of manuscripts and papers of literary, historical and general interest, relating to Ireland, whether in private or public ownership, and also to arrange for and supervise the execution of programmes of publication. Since September 1970, the Commission has been responsible for a Survey of Business Records throughout the Republic of Ireland. Financed by government vote under the Department of Education. Publishes *Analecta Hibernica* (irreg.) and many books of calendars, abstracts, reports etc.

Irish Society for Archives [Cumann Cartlannaiochta Eirann] (ISA). <www.ucd.ie/archives/isa> Founded in December 1970 'to stimulate, encourage and co-ordinate the work of the many individuals, authorities and societies interested in the conservation and use of archives in Ireland'. Membership is available to students, individuals and organizations. Financed by members' subscriptions. Publishes *Irish Archives Bulletin* (a.).

Irish style. An eighteenth-century style of book decoration distinguished by a large centre lozenge of inlaid fawn leather.

IRLA. <irla.lindahall.org> Independent Research Libraries Association; an association of major US research collections, formed in 1972 to safeguard the interests of members, and promote their development. Members are: American Antiquarian Society, American Philosophical Society, Folger Shakespeare Library, Hagley Museum and Library, Linda Hall Library, Historical Society of Pennsylvania, Huntington Library, Library Company of Philadelphia, Massachusetts Historical Society, Pierpont Morgan Library, Newberry Library, New York Academy of Medicine, New York Historical Society, New York Public Library, Virginia Historical Society.

IRM. *See* Information resource management.

IRWI. *See Information Research Watch International.*

ISA. *See Information Science Abstracts.*

ISAAR (CPF). <www.ica.org/biblio/isaar> International Standard Archival Authority Record for Corporate Bodies, Persons and Families. Adopted by the International Council on Archives in 1996 after wide consultation. *See also* ISAD(G), NNAF.

ISAD. The International Council on Archives set up an Ad Hoc Commission on Archival Description in 1990. At a meeting in Madrid in 1992 this Commission produced the *Statement of Principles regarding Archival Description* (the Madrid Principles). This was adopted by the general session of the ICA at the XII International Congress on Archives held in Montréal, 1992. In 1993, at a meeting in Stockholm, the Commission produced a revised draft General International Standard Archival Description (ISAD(G)). The Commission's secretariat is at the National Archives of Canada.

ISAD(G). <www.ica.org/biblio/cds/isad_g_2e.pdf> General International Standard Archive Description. Adopted by the International Council on Archives in 1992 after wide consultation, this is now the normal standard for archival data being exchanged internationally (a second edition was adopted in 1999). Most national groups of archivists have adopted it as the basis for their national standards and formats: the (UK)

Society of Archivists formally adopted it in 1997 at a general meeting. See also ISAAR(CPF).

Isadore Gilbert Mudge Citation. *See* Mudge (Isadore Gilbert) Citation.

Isarithms. *See* Isopleths.

ISBD. The International Meeting of Cataloguing Experts (Copenhagen 1969), organized by IFLA, established a basis for internationally uniform descriptive cataloguing practices and set up a Working Group to develop an International Standard Bibliographic Description (ISBD). The first edition of this appeared in 1971, and in subsequent years further specialist groups were formed. The ISBD programme has been IFLA's major contribution to bibliographic standardization, and was a central part of the programme for Universal Bibliographic Control. Published ISBDs are:

ISBD(M) (Monographs) 1987 (revised edition)
ISBD(S) (Serials)1988 (revised edition)
ISBD(G) (General) 1992 (revised edition)
ISBD(CM) (Cartographic Material) 1987 (revised edition)
ISBD(NBM) (Non-Book Materials) 1987 (revised edition)
ISBD(A) (Antiquarian) 1991 (2nd revised edition)
ISBD(PM) (Printed Music) 1991 (2nd revised edition)
ISBD(CP) (Component Parts) 1988
ISBD(ER) (Electronic Resources) 1997 (revised from ISBD(CF) (Computer Files))

Each ISBD specifies the requirements for the description and identification of the material it covers, assigns an order to the elements of the description, and specifies a system of punctuation for the description. The use of the ISBDs promotes production of bibliographic records that can be more economically exchanged and more easily interpreted internationally. As a result, they have been widely translated and incorporated into all major cataloguing codes. In order to maintain the ISBDs the IFLA Section on Cataloguing has established an ISBD Review Group which monitors developments and initiates projects to revise them when appropriate.

ISBN. <www.isbn.org> <www.niso.org> International Standard Book Number. A number which is given to every book or edition of a book before publication to identify the publisher, the title, the edition and volume number. The ISBN consists of ten digits (arabic 0 to 9) the first group of which is a group identifier and indicates a national geographical, language or other convenient group. The other digits are grouped to indicate the publisher, title or edition of a title; the final digit serves as a check digit. Between 2005 and 2007 a new style of ISBN is being introduced; this will extend the number to 13 digits and incorporate the EAN.UCC prefix which is used to form article barcodes. A core set of Metadata elements associated with the ISBN will be required from publishers. There will be some major changes to ISBN control and administration. *See also* ISSN, Standard Book Numbering Agency.

ISDN. Integrated Services Digital Network; a system based on ITU-T recommendations to create a totally digital public telecommunications network. With full ISDN, high quality rapid data transmission is achieved, together with services such as video-conferencing. There are two types of ISDN: Basic Rate Interface (BRI) and Primary Rate Interface (PRI). BRI ISDN – also known as ISDN-2 – consists of two 64Kbps channels for data transmission and one hidden 16Kbps channel for control information; the two 64Kbps channels can be bonded together to provide a single channel of 128Kbps. BRI ISDN is suitable for home and small business. PRI ISDN, for larger installations, consists of thirty 64Kbps channels and one 64Kbps control channel. *See also* ADSL, SDSL.

ISDS. International Serials Data System. An international network of operational centres (established in 1973 within the framework of the UNISIST programme) which are jointly responsible for the creation and maintenance of computer-based data banks. Objects: to (a) develop and maintain an international register of serial publications containing all the necessary information for identifying the serials; (b) define and promote the use of a standard code (ISSN) for identifying each serial; (c) facilitate retrieval of scientific and technical information in serials; (d) make this information currently available to all countries, organizations or individual users; (e) establish a network of communication between libraries, secondary information services, publishers of serial literature and international organizations; (f) promote international standards for bibliographic description, communication formats, and information exchange in the area of serial publications. The system has an International Centre (IC) in Paris and also national and regional centres. *See also* ISSN.

Isephodic map. One which shows the equal cost of travel, places of equal freight rates being connected by isephodes similar to isochrones.

ISKO. *See* International Society for Knowledge Organization.

Island bookcase. *See* Island stack.

Island stack. A book Stack which is placed away from the wall so that readers can walk all round it. Also called 'Island bookcase'. *See also* Bay.

ISLIC. *See* Israel Society of Special Libraries and Information Centers.

ISMN. <www.ismn.org> International Standard Music Number; a consultative document was issued in August 1986 by the International Association of Music Libraries (UK) as a draft standard. In 1983 the Trade and Copyright Sub-committee of IAML (UK) had begun a full investigation of ISBNs applied to music, and found there was no possibility of complete coverage of music; plans for the ISMN followed from this investigation. ISMN was introduced in Europe in 1992; it was launched in the US by R R Bowker in 2002.

ISNTO. The (UK) Information Services National Training Organization was formed in the late 1990s as part of a national network of similar training organizations (NTOs) designed to promote workforce development in its area of concern, by identifying skills needs, recommending action, and formulating strategic plans. It was the successor to the Information and Library Services Lead Body which had been operated through the Library Association (now CILIP) in the late 1990s to co-ordinate qualifications routes via external agencies. ISNTO was recognized by the Secretary of State for Education and Skills in 2000. Shortly after this date, the government decided to replace the NTOs by Sector Skills Councils (SSC) – larger in scale and broader in scope, with government funding and greater influence. Negotiation towards a suitable SSC into which information services could be fitted is ongoing; this is expected to be a Lifelong Learning SSC.

ISO. *See* International Organization for Standardization.

ISO 9660. The international format standard for CD-ROM, following the recommendations (with some modifications) of the High Sierra Group.

ISO ILL protocol. *See* ILL Protocol Standards.

Isobars. Lines on a map which connect places with the same barometric pressure.

Isobaths. Lines on a map joining points on the sea bed which have an equal depth. Such lines show the relief of the sea bed, just as Contours show the relief of the land by joining places of equal altitude. Areas between isobaths are coloured in varying shades of blue.

Isochronic map. One which shows possible progress of travel in all directions from a given centre in certain specified time intervals.

Isocrymes. Lines on a map which connect places with the same degree of frost.

ISODOC. <www.iso.org/iso> International Information Centre for Standards in Information and Documentation which was established by agreement between Unesco and ISO and is located at the Secretariat of ISO/TC 46. The Centre is designed to facilitate and promote the availability and application of standards in the area of information and documentation and related fields by (a) collecting, evaluating and storing information on standards, (b) disseminating this information.

Isogones. Lines on a map which connect places with equal angles of magnetic variation. Also called 'Isogonic lines'.

Isograms. *See* Isopleths.

Isohalines. Lines on a map joining points in the oceans which have equal salinity.

Isohels. Lines on a map which connect places with the same amount of sunshine over a certain period.

Isohyets. Lines on a map which connect places with the same amount of rainfall over a certain period.

Isohypses. Lines on a map which connect places with the same elevation.

Isolate. (*Classification*) 1. A generic term applicable to all the three planes – Idea, Notation, Verbal – in the Colon Classification, and indicating a division of a Facet. Also called 'Isolate focus'. In addition to Common isolates, there are Time, Space and Language isolates used to indicate periods of time, geographical division, and languages respectively. 2. The name of anything that can exist and behave as a unit or a word expressing its behaviour. Isolates are taken from the literature of a subject. 3. A single component ('ingredient') of a compound subject. 4. Ultimate division of knowledge in a scheme of classification.

Isonephs. Lines on a map which connect places with the same amount of cloud over a certain period.

Isopleths. Lines on a map which connect places of equal density or value of distribution of any specific element. Also called 'Isarithms' and 'Isograms'. If they connect places of equal temperature they are called 'isotherms'; of equal rainfall, 'isohyets'; of barometric pressure, 'isobars'; of magnetic variation, 'isogones'; of sunshine, 'isohels'; of frost, 'isocrymes'; of clouds, 'isonephs'; of equal elevation, 'isohypses'. They connect an average number of individual units. Lines which connect a continuous value, such as temperature, are called 'isarithms'.

ISORID. <www.unesco.org> The International Information System on Research in Documentation established by Unesco in co-operation with FID, is charged with collecting, organizing, analyzing, storing and diffusing information on research and development in the fields of information, documentation, libraries and archival records management. There is only a low level of current activity.

Isoseismal lines. Lines on a map which connect places with the same temperature at a particular instant or having the same average temperature over a certain period.

ISP. *See* Internet Service Provider.

ISPA. *See* Internet Service Providers' Association.

Israel Society of Special Libraries and Information Centers (ISLIC). <www.asmi.org.il> (2, Dvora Haneviah Street, Tel Aviv 61430, Israel) Registered in August 1966 to encourage and promote efficient utilization of knowledge through special libraries and information centres, to facilitate written and oral communication among its members, and to co-operate with other bodies with similar or allied interests in Israel and abroad. Publishes *Bulletin* (3 p.a.), *Contributions to Information Science* (irreg.).

ISRC. <www.ifpi.org/isrc> International Standard Recording Code; developed by the International Organization for Standardization (ISO) for the more efficient identification of sound and audio/visual recordings. Published as ISO 3901.

ISRN. International Standard Technical Report Number; in December 1994 the first edition appeared of ISO 10444 *Information and Document-ation: International Standard Technical Report Number*. ISRNs complement ISBN and ISSN; they consist of an alphabetical segment representing the organization or corporate body issuing the report and a sequential number assigned by the issuing agency. ISRNs apply to in-house technical reports as well as publicly distributed reports and those issued in non-print media. FIZ (Karlshuhe, Germany) was the ISRN Agency, but resigned from this role in 2003: *see* <stn.permcnti.ru/fiz/services/isrn>.

ISSN. <www.issn.org> International Standard Serial Number – an internationally accepted code for the identification of serial publications; it is precise, concise, unique and unambiguous. The ISSN consists of seven arabic digits with an eighth which serves to verify the number in computer processing. A letter code indicating the country of publication may precede as an additional identifier; this is optional. The International Organization for Standardization Technical Committee 46 (ISO/TC46) is the agency responsible for the development of the ISSN and the relevant standard is ISO 3297. The US standard is ANSI/NISO Z39.9. The organization responsible for the administration and assignment of ISSN is the International Centre (IC) of the International Serials Data System (ISDS); this is supported by the French government and Unesco, and is situated in Paris. There are over 900,000 serials from 180 countries in the system; 67 national centres worldwide register and number serials and the IC co-ordinates the process and registers the publications of international organizations etc. Electronic journals are included, and the whole system has been available on the Web from 1998. *See also* ISBN, ISDS.

ISSS. <www.cenorm.be/ISSS> Information Society Standardization System, part of CEN that came into force during the second half of 1997 and which operates open workshops to produce quickly the standards specifications needed by the market in a range of areas associated with the implementation of ICT.

Issue. 1. All the charges or other records representing books and other items on loan. 2. The number of items so issued. 3. The copies of a book in which the original sheets are used but which differ in some respects from copies previously issued (e.g. a new title-page, an additional appendix, the inclusion of a list of publisher's announcements, or different format paper edition). 4. The number of impressions (copies) of an old map or print made at a given time without any change being made in the plate. 5. A particular publication, complete in itself, of a serial or periodical which is issued at intervals or in parts. *See also* Edition, First edition, Impression, New edition, Reprint, Revised edition.

Issue date. 1. The date on which a publication was issued to a reader. 2. (*Publishing*) The specified day, date, month or period by which the date of publication of a particular issue of a serial may be identified.

Issue desk. *See* Circulation desk.

Issue guides. Pieces of card, plastic or metal which project above the Issue (1) (the projection being numbered or lettered according to the method of arrangement) to facilitate the finding of records of books on loan in certain manual charging systems.

Issue number. The number given to a separately issued part of a serial to distinguish it from other issues. Numbers may run consecutively from the first issue onwards, but if the issues are divided into volumes, a new sequence of issue numbers commences with each volume.

Issue systems. *See* Charging methods, Circulation control system.

Issue tray. A tray containing the Issue (1) in certain manual charging systems.

IST. Information Society Technologies; most frequently encountered in the European context to describe the infrastructures of research and the Information Society under the Sixth Framework Programme. *See also* FP6.

ISTC. Incunabula Short Title Catalogue; a database compiled from 1984 by the British Library, with support from libraries world-wide, of all books printed from moveable type before 1501. Over 28,000 records are held – 85 per cent of known incunabula. In 1996 a CD-ROM *Illustrated Incunabula Short Title Catalogue* was issued, combining ISTC records with 10,000 images of early printed books; each annual update will add further images. *See also* INCIPIT.

ISTIC. *See* Zhong Guo Ke Xue Ji Shu Xin Xi Yan Jiu Suo.

Istituto Centrale per il Catalogo Unico delle Biblioteche Italiane e per le Informazioni Bibliografiche. [Italian Central Union Catalogue] *See* ICCU.

ISUG. *See* International SGML/XML Users' Group.

ISWC. International Standard Work Code; an international standard for identifying and tagging individual parts of copyright works. So far it has been implemented for musical works through ISO/TC46/SC9 Working Group 2 which was responsible for drafting the text of ISO 15707: *Information and documentation – International Standard Musical Work Code (ISWC)*. The ISWC standard was approved for publication in 2001 as International Standard ISO 15707.

IT. Information technology; a generic term that covers the acquisition, processing, storage and dissemination of information of all types – textual, numerical, graphical and sound – and in all application areas – e.g. banking, business, science, technology – not just librarianship and information science. The term is restricted to systems dependent on a microelectronics-based combination of computing and telecommunications technology. Has largely been replaced by 'ICT', Information and Communications Technology.

ital. Abbreviation for italic.

Italian Libraries Association (Associazione Italiane Biblioteche). *See* AIB.

Italian national libraries. *See* Biblioteca Nazionale.

Italian style. *See* Aldine style.

Italic. Sloping type, as distinguished from the normal, upright, roman type, used to emphasize any special point, or for the names of publications, etc. It was first used by Aldus Pius Manutius in 1501, and was originally called Aldine or Chancery, and was based on a humanistic Italian handwriting of a somewhat earlier period. *This is italic* and is indicated in a MS. prepared for the printer by a single underlining. Abbreviated *ital.*

ITC.   *See* International Translations Centre.

Item.   1. (*Archives*) A level of archival arrangement and description. In *MAD* refers to the unit of handling; in ISAD(G) is equivalent to 'file'. 2. (*Information retrieval*) In an index, the reference to the document. Also the document itself, whether a book, serial, abstract, article, photograph or microform, etc. *See also* Compresence, Feature, Term.

Item entry.   In information retrieval, the entry of particulars of a document under a heading or symbol identifying the document.

Ithaka.   <www.ithaka.org> A not-for-profit organization supported by the Hewlett, Mellon and Niarchos foundations with a mission to accelerate the productive uses of information technologies for the benefit of higher education around the world. In pursuing this mission, Ithaka engages in four primary areas of activity: incubating promising projects with a goal of creating sustainable not-for-profit enterprises; providing sharable administrative and technological services; conducting research; and providing advisory services to organizations not directly affiliated with Ithaka.

ITU.   *See* International Telecommunication Union.

ITU-T.   International Telecommunication Union - Telecommunication Standardization Sector <www.itu.int/ITU-T> (Place des Nations, CH-1211 Geneva 20, Switzerland) The ITU-T is one of three Sectors of the International Telecommunication Union and has a mission to ensure the efficient and on-time production of high quality standards (Recommendations) covering all fields of telecommunications. ITU-T was created on 1 March 1993, replacing the former International Telegraph and Telephone Consultative Committee (CCITT). The Recommendations are the result of studies carried out on technical, operating and tariff questions with the aim of ensuring world-wide interconnectivity and interoperability. There are currently over 2,900 ITU-T Recommendations in force.

Ivory board.   A good quality card, made from wood, and used for printing.

IWF.   *See* Internet Watch Foundation.

IYL.   *See* International Youth Library.

J2EE.   Java 2 Enterprise Edition, a technology created by Sun Microsystems that provides support for distributed components and component reuse and which is of particular use in building e-learning environments. See, for example, <www.jisc.ac.uk/elearning_framework.html>. Seen as an alternative to the Microsoft .net framework.

Jacket.   *See* Book jacket.

Jacket band. A strip of paper wrapped round a Book jacket to emphasize some sales aspect.

Jacketed film. Microfilm which has been inserted in a Film jacket. *See also* Microfilm jacket.

Jaconet. Cotton material, glazed on one side, and used to line and strengthen the spines of books.

JANET. <www.ja.net> The UK's education and research network funded by JISC and managed and developed by UKERNA. The network connects UK universities, colleges of further and higher education, research council establishments, regional broadband consortia and organizations that work in collaboration with these bodies. In addition to high-speed access to the Internet, JANET also provides links to other networks in the UK and worldwide that are particularly relevant to the education and research community. *See also* SuperJANET.

JANET User Group for Libraries (JUGL). The Janet User Group for Libraries looked after the interests of librarians, libraries and their users on JANET. As a result of declining participation in the JUGL committee, the changing role of librarians in relation to network issues and the stability of JANET, JUGL was disbanded in 2002 and its interests passed to the JIBS User Group.

JANET User Groups. <www.ja.net/usergroups> The role of these groups is to represent the views and needs of all JANET users, both to the bodies that fund JANET and to the providers of the network. The User Groups are of two types, those representing geographical regions – of which, in 2004, there were eight – and those representing particular interest groups of which there are two: administration; and particle physicists. In addition, there is an overarching JANET National User Group.

Jannon, Jean. A master printer in Paris in 1610, who, due to his Protestant leanings, went to Sedan where he printed for the Calvinist Academy and issued one of the finest and earliest of French specimen books in 1621.

Jansenist style. A very simple binding named after Cornelius Jansen, the seventeenth century Bishop of Ypres, decorated only by a centrepiece (often armorial) and corner fleurons, or devoid of ornamentation on the outside of the covers, but with elaborate Doublures tooled with Dentelle borders.

Janus. 1. <janus.lib.cam.ac.uk> A project to provide a single point of networked access to the descriptions of the archives and manuscript collections held throughout Cambridge. At the outset, the archives are predominantly drawn from the University of Cambridge and its constituent colleges but it is hoped that the database will eventually provide a near comprehensive coverage of archives in the city and surrounding area. 2. Journal of the International Council on Archives.

JAPAN/MARC. MARC for Japan's national bibliography compiled by the National Diet Library and first published in 1978; the format is designed in accordance with UNIMARC. The distinctive characteristic is a processing of Japanese characters (Chinese Kanji and Japanese Kana) and their pronunciations. Japanese characters are represented by JIS (Japanese Industrial Standard) codes, and JAPAN/MARC adopts the Kanji Character Set of JIS codes. A Kanji character has one or more pronunciations, and JAPAN/MARC also shows the pronunciations of words both in Kana and Roman alphabets in the fields of access point block. A CD-ROM version of JAPAN/MARC and JAPAN/MARC Serials has been available since 1988. (Reference: *Toshokan handobukku/Library handbook*, 5th ed. Japan Library Association, 1990, pp. 256–257)

Japan Indexers Association. *See* Nihon Sakuinka Kyokai.

Japan Information Center of Science and Technology. *See* Kagaku Gijutsu Shinko Kiko.

Japan Library Association. *See* Nihon Toshokan Kyokai.

Japan Medical Library Association. *See* Nihon Igaku Toshokan Kyokai.

Japan Patent Information Organization. *See* Nihon Tokkyo Joho Kiko.

Japan Society of Library Science. *See* Nihon Toshokan Gakkai.

Japan Special Libraries Association. *See* Senmon Toshokan Kyogikai.

Japanese paper. A paper, or tissue, in varying substances, having a silky texture; it is handbeaten from the bark fibres of the mulberry tree, or in imitation thereof. Used for printing, etchings, photogravures, books; also used for binding. 'French Japon' is a good imitation, it is less expensive but not so strong.

Japanese style. *See* Chinese style.

Japanese vellum. An extremely costly, strong hand-made Japanese paper with a firm glossy surface, and a creamy tint. It is much used for engravings, and diplomas, or where a very durable paper is required. It will not withstand india-rubber, and must be handled very carefully. An imitation is made by treating thick ordinary paper with sulphuric acid.

JAPIO. *See* Nihon Tokkyo Joho Kiko.

Jason Farradane Award. *See* Farradane (Jason) Award.

Java. An operating system-independent programming language developed by Sun Microsystems designed for use on the Internet and which can be used to create applications that run on one computer or on a network of computers. It can be employed in coding small interactive application modules (applets) used to add interactivity to Web pages. *See also* Applet, J2EE.

JCALT. *See* JISC Committee for Awareness, Liaison and Training.

JCCS. *See* JISC Committee for Content Services.

JCIE. *See* JISC Committee for the Information Environment.

JCLT. *See* JISC Committee for Learning and Teaching.

JCN. *See* JISC Committee for Networking.

JCSR. *See* JISC Committee for the Support of Research.

Jenkins (John H.) Bibliographical Award. This award is offered annually by Union College, Schenectady, New York, for a bibliographical work of unusual merit bearing an imprint date two years before the year of the Award. It is named after John H. Jenkins, bookseller, of Austin, Texas, who returned to Union College the $2,000 reward given him for the recovery of J. J. Audubon's 'elephant folio' of the *Birds of America* which had been stolen from Schaffer Library, Union College, in June 1971, on condition that the College match it and establish a bibliographical prize.

Jenkinson Prize. Established by the Society of Archivists in honour of Sir Hilary Jenkinson, and as a result of an endowment by him.

Jenson. A typeface named after Nicolas Jenson (1420–80), a French printer who went to Venice in 1468 and had his own printing works there. He used his 'perfect roman letter' in *De praeparatione evangelica* by Eusebius, 1470; this served as the model for Morris's Golden type and for Benton's Cloister. The Monotype Centaur, designed by Bruce Rogers, is based on Jenson. The letters are open, dignified, clear and legible, of even colour and perfect harmony. The contrast between thick and thin strokes is slight; the serifs are blunt with very small brackets.

Jessup Report (UK). *A Report on the supply and training of librarians* prepared by the Library Advisory Councils for England and Wales under the chairmanship of F. W. Jessup (HMSO, 1968).

Jeté en moule. ('Cast in a mould') Mould metal type for use in printing. Also called 'Get en mol'.

JETRO. *See* Nihon Boeki Shinkokai.

Jewel case. The plastic container used to hold CD-ROMs and audio Compact discs; also referred to as jewel box.

Jewett's Code. A code of cataloguing rules prepared by Charles Coffin Jewett, Librarian of the Smithsonian Institution, Washington, and published as the second part of *The Smithsonian report on the construction of catalogues of libraries, and their publication by means of separate stereo-titles*, 1852.

Jewish Librarians Association. *See* Association of Jewish Libraries.

Jewish Library Association. *See* Association of Jewish Libraries.

JFR. *See* Joint Fiction Reserve.

JIBS User Group. <www.jibs.ac.uk> A forum by which end-users of networked information resources in the UK's higher education and further education communities can provide feedback to data suppliers and data service providers. It originated as the JISC (assisted) Bibliographic Dataservices User Group (though independent of JISC) but now sees its remit as extending beyond bibliographic material to all electronic content available either via JISC's Information Environment, or delivered independently to institutions by other sources.

JICST. *See* Kagaku Gijutsu Shinko Kiko.

JINI. A technology developed by Sun Microsystems to facilitate the set-up, integration, dynamic configuration and management of distributed service-based applications and which is of particular use in building e-learning environments. See, for example, <www.jisc.ac.uk/elearning_framework.html>.

JIS Kanji character set. The Japanese character set defined by the Japanese Industrial Standard (JIS) Code of the Japanese Graphic Set for Information Interchange. JIS C6226 was established in 1978 and became JIS X0208 in 1983. It consists of the first level characters and second level characters. The 3,489 first level characters include 2,965 Chinese Kanji characters, 83 Japanese own Hiragana, 86 Japanese own Katakana, 10 numerals, 52 Roman, 147 special characters, 48 Greek, 66 Russian, and 32 rule characters. The second level includes 3,388 Kanji characters.

JISC. <www.jisc.ac.uk> (Northavon House, Coldharbour Lane, Bristol BS16 1QD, UK) Joint Information Systems Committee of the UK Higher Education and Further Education Funding Councils. JISC's mission is: 'to help further and higher education institutions and the research community realise their ambitions in exploiting the opportunities of information and communications technology by exercising vision and leadership, encouraging collaboration and co-operation and by funding and managing national development programmes and services of the highest quality'. In line with its 5-year strategy JISC provides: new environments for learning, teaching and research; access to electronic resources; a world-class network – JANET; guidance on institutional change; advisory and consultancy services; regional support for further education colleges. Main sub-committees are: JISC Committee for Awareness, Liaison and Training (JCALT); JISC Committee for Content Services (JCCS); JISC Committee for the Information Environment (JCIE); JISC Committee for Learning and Teaching (JCLT); JISC Committee for Networking (JCN); JISC Committee for the Support of Research (JCSR).

JISC Committee for Awareness, Liaison and Training (JCALT). The JISC sub-committee responsible for addressing the human and organizational issues of deploying communications and information technology within further and higher education in the UK.

JISC Committee for Content Services (JCCS). The JISC sub-committee with responsibility for building a collection of scholarly and educational online resources to support the further and higher education and research communities and the management of the systems that facilitate the delivery of these materials to users.

JISC Committee for Learning and Teaching (JCLT). The JISC sub-committee responsible for supporting the learning and teaching community by helping institutions to promote innovation in the use of information and communications technology to benefit learning and teaching, research and the management of institutions.

JISC Committee for Networking (JCN). The JISC sub-committee charged with providing a pervasive, leading edge, network infrastructure in the UK (JANET).

JISC Committee for the Information Environment (JCIE). The JISC sub-committee with responsibilities for the development of a coherent

Information Environment to support online resources of all types by determining appropriate standards, promoting interoperability of content, specifying appropriate shared services and promoting inter-working and collaborations with other organizations.

JISC Committee for the Support of Research (JCSR). The JISC sub-committee responsible for ensuring that JISC provides appropriate infrastructure and services to support the needs of researchers. In addition to the necessary networking infrastructure, this includes ensuring that key issues such as authentication and data storage/retrieval are addressed.

JISC infoNET. <www.jiscinfonet.ac.uk> A web site providing resources to help improve the support for, and quality of, learning and teaching in UK further and higher education institutions. The core resources are a series of infoKits covering key topics relating to the planning and implementation of information systems but additionally there is a directory of external resources and lists of upcoming events. Case studies on issues such as Information strategies are available.

JISCmail. <www.jiscmail.ac.uk> In November 2000, took over from Mailbase as the primary electronic Mailing list service for UK higher and further education and the research communities. The service is free, being funded by JISC. It uses the World Wide Web and E-mail to enable groups of academics and support staff to talk to each other and to share information. There are over 4,000 lists covering many categories and new ones are easy to establish.

JLA. *See* Nihon Toshokan Kyokai.

JMLA. *See* Nihon Igaku Toshokan Kyokai.

JMRT. *See* Junior Members Round Table.

JNT. <www.ukerna.ac.uk/company/history> The Joint Network Team established in 1979 and given the task of running the JANET network and managing the networking programme for universities and the Research Councils in the UK. From 1 April 1994 known as UKERNA.

JNT Association. *See* UKERNA.

Joanna. A light roman type designed by Eric Gill in 1930. It is remarkable for its small capitals which do not reach the height of the ascenders, themselves not tall.

Job audit. *See* Staff appraisal.

Job description. *See* Job specification.

Job press. A small platen printing press which is used for producing small items such as handbills.

Job printer. One who prints small items such as labels, leaflets, forms, stationery, handbills, etc., in small quantities.

Job sharing. A system whereby a vacant job may be offered to two people who will divide the hours of attendance between them. Administratively the post remains one full-time job, but the system encourages the employment of people who would be unable to consider full-time employment. Job sharing confers contractual rights on each employee.

Job specification. A detailed paper laying down objectives for a post, with criteria for achieving them, and suggesting methods of evaluating success. A less specific outline may be termed a job description. *See also* Personnel specification.

Jobber. In the US, a wholesale bookseller who stocks many copies of various kinds of books issued by different publishers and supplies them to retailers and libraries. There are two types of jobber (i) those who stock mainly current text-books, trade, and technical books, and (ii) those who stock only remainders.

John Campbell Trust. *See* Campbell (John) Trust Award.

John Carter Brown Library. *See* Brown (John Carter) Library.

John Rylands University Library. <rylibweb.man.ac.uk> (Oxford Road, Manchester M13 9PP, UK) The magnificently endowed John Rylands Library, Manchester, with its special collections of books including those of incunabula, manuscripts, and rare books, was merged administratively in 1972 with the existing large research library of the University to form the University Library with this title. The collection now comprises over 2,000,000 books; some 8,000 periodical titles are currently taken, and over 300,000 titles are on microfilm. The extensive holdings of MSS., early printed and rare books are housed in the superb Deansgate building,the home of the original John Rylands Library. Future plans include repairs to the original building together with a new entrance wing. From 1 October 2004 a new 'University of Manchester' came into being through the merger of UMIST and the Victoria University of Manchester and the libraries of the constituent organizations were combined to form a new library service known as the John Rylands University Library, University of Manchester.

Joho Kagaku Gijutsu Kyokai. [Information Science and Technology Association (INFOSTA)] <www.infosta.or.jp> (Sasaki Bldg., 2-5-7 Koishikawa, Bunkyo-ku, Tokyo 112-0002, Japan) Founded in 1950, INFOSTA promotes research and development in information management and technology. Activities include promotion of UDC, administration of the Database Searcher's qualifications for the Science and Technology Agency. Publishes *Joho no Kagaku to Gijutsu* [*Journal of INFOSTA*] (m.).

Joho Shori Gakkai. [Information Processing Society of Japan] <www.ipsj.or.jp> (7th fl Shibaura-Maekawa Bldg., 3-16-20 Shibaura, Minato-ku, Tokyo 108-0023, Japan) Established in 1960, IPJS aims to encourage research and development and education in the field of standardization of computerized information processing in Japan, through conferences, seminars, and publications. With some 30,000 members, it represents Japan as a member of IFIP and FID. Publishes *Joho Shori* [*Information Processing*] (m.), *Transactions* (m.), and *Journal of Information Processing* (q.).

Joined hand. Handwriting in which the letters are all joined to one another. The opposite of Disjoined hand.

Joiner's press.   The name given to the earliest hand printing presses which were introduced about 1440. Made of wood, they were similar to wine presses, the pressure needed to press the paper on to type being applied by means of a screw turning on to a flat platen.

Joint.   1. One of the two parts of the covering material that bend when the covers of a book are opened.   2. The strips of cloth, leather or other material that are used to reinforce the end-papers.   3. The grooves, formed by the backing process, which are made to receive the boards when binding a book. *See also* Hinge.

Joint Academic Network.   *See* JANET.

Joint author.   One who writes in collaboration with another, or several other writers. The parts written by each are not always indicated; in fact, the contribution of each is usually not distinguishable.

Joint board.   Two or more UK library authorities which are authorized by an order of the Secretary of State made after consultation, and with the agreement of the authorities concerned, to be a library authority and provide a library service covering the areas of the separate library authorities before the formation of the joint board. Provision for their formation is made in Section 5 of the Public Libraries and Museums Act, 1964. *See also* Library Authority.

Joint catalogue.   One containing entries for the books in two or more libraries.

Joint Fiction Reserve.   A (UK) scheme whereby a number of libraries agree to hold novels permanently. The authors are allocated according to alphabetical sequence amongst the co-operating libraries by agreement. The first scheme of this kind was started in London and included the keeping of all copies which were redundant in Metropolitan libraries as well as buying all new titles by the allocated authors. In 1962 a Provincial Joint Fiction Reserve scheme (abbreviated PJFR) which is a co-operative effort of all regional bureaux outside London and the South-Eastern area began to operate. Each region is responsible for a certain section of the alphabet. This scheme provides only for the purchase and retention of new publications and is not retrospective. Allocation by author amongst the regions is as follows:

A–C	North-Western	K–M	West Midlands
D–F	Northern	N–S	Yorkshire
G–J	East Midlands	T–Z	South Western

Compare Inter-regional subject coverage scheme.

Joint Funding Councils' Libraries Review Group: Report.   *See Follett Report.*

Joint Information Systems Committee.   *See* JISC.

Joint Network Team.   *See* JNT.

JOIS.   *See* Kagaku Gijutsu Shinko Kiko.

Jordan Report (UK).   A survey: *Working conditions in libraries*, edited by

P. Jordan, and published by the Association of Assistant Librarians, 1968. *See also* Tighe Report.

JORUM. <www.jorum.ac.uk> JISC Online Repository for Learning Materials, a project that undertook a scoping and technical appraisal study in 2003, with a view to informing the procurement in 2004 of a repository system to facilitate the deposit, re-use and sharing of learning content in UK tertiary education. Part of the JISC X4L programme. *See also* Learning object.

Joseph W. Lippincott Award. *See* Lippincott (Joseph W.) Award.

Journal. 1. A newspaper or periodical. Particularly a periodical issued by a society or institution and containing news, proceedings, transactions and reports of work carried out in a particular field. *See also* Electronic journal. 2. A record of a person's activities day by day.

Journalese. Words and phrases commonly used by journalists. Hackneyed phrases.

Journalism. The profession of compiling, writing for and editing newspapers, periodicals, etc.

Journalist. One who edits or contributes to a newspaper or periodical.

JPEG. Joint Photographic Experts Group, a consortium of hardware, software and publishing interests, that has given its name to a standard for the compression of non-moving images in computer systems. Designed to be used on photographs it produces better results than GIF though is less effective on line art and black and white illustrations. Pronounced 'jay-peg'; sometimes abbreviated to jpg. *See also* MPEG.

JST. *See* Kagaku Gijutsu Shinko Kiko.

JSTOR. <www.jstor.org> The Scholarly Journal Archive was formed in 1995 as a not-for-profit organization to create digital back runs of journals. The database, which now holds complete runs of over 600 titles, is located at the University of Michigan and mirrored at Princeton University and at MIMAS for UK users. JSTOR has also contributed to methodologies for collecting usage statistics for e-journals and journals in digital format. *See also* ARTstor, Metrics.

JUBILEE. <online.unn.ac.uk/faculties/art/information_studies/imri/rarea/im/hfe/jub/hfjubilee.htm> JISC User Behaviour in Information Seeking: Longitudinal Evaluation of EIS, a programme of qualitative and longitudinal monitoring of the use of electronic information services, contracted to the University of Northumbria.

Judicial writ. One issuing from a Court of Law.

JUGL. *See* JANET User Group for Libraries.

Jukebox. 1. A device which holds multiple Optical discs and allows the insertion and withdrawal of these to and from drive units as required.

Jumbled type. *See* Pie (3).

Junior assistant. A library assistant who does not supervise the work of other assistants.

Junior book. A book for children.

Junior department. *See* Children's library.

Junior librarian. One who works with children, or in a children's library.

Junior library. *See* Children's library.

Junior Members Round Table (JMRT). A group of the American Library Association.

JUSTEIS. <www.dil.aber.ac.uk/dils/research/justeis/JISCTop.htm> JISC Usage Surveys: Trends in Electronic Information Services, a project to measure and evaluate the overall awareness, uptake, usage and usefulness of information technologies and information services in higher education in the UK, operated by the Department of Information and Library Studies at the University of Wales, Abcrystwyth.

Justification. 1. (*Cataloguing*) The provision of data, especially in the form of a note, introduced into an added entry, cross-reference, or subject heading for the sole purpose of making clear why the particular entry was provided. An entry treated in this way is said to be justified. 2. (*Printing*) In typesetting, equally spacing out letters and words to a given measure, so that each line will be of the same length.

Just-in-case management. A style of management in which policy and operations focus on undifferentiated possibilities that might occur. An example in the library context would be a holdings policy which did not take into account the changing needs of End users or changing methods of access to materials. *See also* Just-in-time management.

Just-in-time management. A system of organizational management whereby goods or services are taken in at the moment they are required, but without causing delays. Such a system avoids paying in advance for materials, and storing them against possible future needs, which would be termed 'just-in-case' management. JIT promotes rapid and efficient production methods and support mechanisms. Accurate, complete and up-to-the-minute information on the whole of the business cycle is a prerequisite.

Jute. A plant which contains weaker and less durable fibres than flax or hemp and which are somewhat easily rotted by water. Jute paper was originally made from old rope, burlap, jute or manilla clippings, but is now usually made from sulphite stock (woodpulp used for making Kraft paper) and is the material from which heavy wrapping paper and large bags for such materials as cement are made. 'Jute tissue' is made from old sacks and similar material and is used for tailors' patterns.

Jute board. A strong, light-weight board, made from jute fibres, and used for binding books.

K. Abbreviation for *kilo*; i.e. 1000. *See* Byte.

K20 Initiative. <k20.internet2.edu> An Initiative of Internet2 that brings together member institutions, primary and secondary schools, colleges and universities, libraries, and museums to make new technologies – advanced networking tools, applications, Middleware, and content – available to innovators, across all educational sectors in the US, as quickly and as 'connectedly' as possible.

Kagaku Gijutsu Shinko Kiko. [Japan Science and Technology Agency (JST)] <www.jst.go.jp> (Library address: 2-8-18 Asahi-cho, Nerima-ku, Tokyo 179-0071, Japan) The library (Japan Information Center for Science and Technology; JICST) holds major collections on science and technology, including 13,600 Japanese and 14,700 English periodical titles. The JOIS (JST Online Information System) gives electronic access to over 1 million citations on science and technology, plus English translations in the J-EAST file <j-east.tokyo.jst.go.jp>. Also publishes printed thesauri and holdings lists.

Kaiser index. *See* Kaiser's system.

Kaiser's system. A method of subject indexing propounded by J. Kaiser in his *Systematic indexing*, 1911.

Kate Greenaway Medal. *See* Greenaway (Kate) Medal.

Kaula (Professor P. N.) Gold Medal. A major international award, started in 1975, and presented to outstanding figures in the world of librarianship and documentation for lifetime achievement. Awarded by the International Awards Committee of the Professor Kaula Endowment for Library and Information Science. Professor Kaula was head of the library school at Benares Hindu University for many years. Recipients of the medal include Bernard Palmer, Jesse Shera, Preben Kirkegaard and Emilia Curras.

KB. *See* Koninklijke Bibliotheek.

KC. The Kyle Classification. *See* Classification for Social Sciences.

KDD. *See* Knowledge Discovery in Databases.

Keep down. (*Printing*) To use capitals sparingly.

Keep in. (*Printing*) 1. To set matter closely so that it does not take up more space than necessary. 2. Type matter with narrow openings between the words. *See also* Drive out.

Keep out. (*Printing*) To set matter widely spaced so that it takes up as many lines as possible.

Keep standing. An order not to distribute the type after running off, pending possible reprinting.

Keep up. (*Printing*) To use capitals freely.

Keepsake. 1. A lavishly printed and ornately bound gift book, often consisting of poetry; many such books were issued annually in the first half of the nineteenth century. 2. Printed commemorative publications issued by clubs or other organizations for special occasions. 3. Before the end of the seventeenth century it was the custom in some English printing establishments to honour visitors by printing their names and the date in an ornamental style – usually in a framework of flowers and rules – and present it to them as a memento. The guest witnessed the setting of the type and pulled the press. The practice became more general during the eighteenth century but declined in the last quarter; it was reserved for distinguished persons in the nineteenth century, for the most exalted of whom the printing was done on silk or satin.

Kelmscott Press. A private press founded and directed by William Morris between 1891 and his death in 1896, although the Press continued until 1898. The three fonts of type used (Golden, 1890; Troy, 1891; Chaucer, 1892) were designed by Morris and cut by E. P. Prince in the years stated but not used until 1892. The books issued were excellent examples of book production. The Golden Typeface was named after Caxton's *Golden legend* in which it was to have been used first. It was, however, used for six books before the *Golden legend* was printed. *See also* Jenson.

Kennedy Report. *Learning works: widening participation in further education*; the report of the Kennedy Committee, published by the Further Education Funding Council (UK) in 1997. The Report sees several opportunities for public, school and college libraries.

Kent (Tony) Strix and Public Sector Awards. Two awards made by UKOLUG (Group of CILIP) to commemorate Tony Kent who had been very active in the Institute of Information Scientists (IIS) and who died in 1997. The Tony Kent Strix Award is given for an outstanding information retrieval initiative (Strix was a retrieval package created by Tony Kent), and the Public Sector Award is given for innovative use of electronic resources in the public sector.

Kenyon Report. The *Report on public libraries in England and Wales* by the Public Libraries Committee (Chairman: Frederic G. Kenyon), presented by the Board of Education to Parliament in 1927 (HMSO, 1927) (Cmd. 2868). The Committee had been asked to enquire into the adequacy of library provision under the Public Libraries Acts, and the means of extending and completing such provision.

Kerfs. Shallow saw-cuts, about $1/32$ inch deep, made between $1/4$ and $1/2$ inch from the ends of the gathered sections of a book. The loops of the kettle stitches formed by the sewing of the section, or the cords, fit snugly into the kerfs and leave the back of the sewn sections smooth.

Kern. (*Printing*) Any part of the face of a type letter which extends over the edge of the Body and rests on the Shoulder of the type adjacent to it, as *fi, fl.* As a verb used to signify the act of 'kerning', reducing the space between letters to improve aesthetics and readability.

Kerned. Said of a type letter which has part of the face projecting beyond the metal body on which it is cast.

Kettle stitch. The stitch made at the head and tail of a book in hand sewing, by which the thread of one section is fastened to the thread of the one on each side. The term is frequently regarded as being a corruption of 'catch up stitch', but it may be derived from the German *Ketten-stich* (chain stitch) or *Kettel stich*, (the stitch that forms a little chain). Also called 'Catch stitch'.

Key. 1. The block or Forme in letterpress printing, and the plate or stone in lithography, which acts as a guide for position and registration of the other colours. Also called Key plate. 2. A binder's tool for securing the bands when sewing. 3. An explanation of the conventional signs or symbols used on a map or diagram.

Key in. The action of inserting a note in the margins of the typescript of a book to indicate the exact or approximate position where illustrations, or other items not incorporated in the text, are to appear.

Key plate. 1. The plate of maximum detail in a set of colour plates to which other plates in the same set are registered during the printing process. 2. Any printing plate that is used to get others into register. Also, Key.

Keyboard. 1. (*Noun*) Device containing typewriter-style keys for adding text and data directly to a computer. 2. (*Verb*) To type (or otherwise record by depressing keys) data or information, usually for direct computer input and processing.

Key-Letter-in-Context. *See* KLIC.

Keyword. (*Information retrieval*) Grammatical element which conveys the signficant meaning in a document. Word indicating a subject discussed in a document. In a Permuted title index, the word considered to be most indicative of the title is to be used as an Access point, and therefore is the keyword of the subject content of the document. *See also* Catchword, KWAC.

Keyword-and-Context. *See* KWAC.

Keyword-in-Context. *See* KWIC.

Keyword-out-of-Context. *See* KWOC.

Kiddult fiction. Fiction that appeals to both children and adults irrespective of the audience the author had in mind when writing the work, or of the marketing adopted by the publisher. The most popular example in recent years is the series of Harry Potter books.

Kier. The part of paper-making machinery used to boil the raw material (e.g. rags, esparto) especially under steam pressure. Also called 'Boiler'.

Kilgour (Frederick G.) Award. *See* OCLC/LITA Frederick G. Kilgour Award.

Kill. (*Printing*) Direction to the printer to melt down, or distribute, composed type matter which is no longer wanted. *See also* Dead matter, Live matter.

Kilobyte. *See* Byte.

KIM. Knowledge and information management. A little-used variant term for Knowledge management.

Kinderbox. A box about 2 feet square and 8 inches deep, divided into four compartments and standing on short legs. It holds large-page books for young children. Called in the USA a 'Cart'.

Kinetic relation. (*Information retrieval*) A phase relation expressing motion, e.g. a person can move to, from, into, out of, through, off, onto, etc. *See also* Phase.

Kinetica. <www.nla.gov.au/kinetica> The bibliographic and library network in Australia. It grew from the Networked Services Project of the National Library of Australia, and replaced the earlier Australian Bibliographic Network (ABN) in 2000.

King (Coretta Scott) Awards. Annual awards, established 1970, given for the most outstanding text, and most imaginative illustrations by a black author and illustrator for children's books. Presented by the American Library Association.

King Report.   1. The report of a committee of which Dr. Gilbert W. King was chairman, set up in 1961 to survey the application of automatic devices to the work of the Library of Congress and other general research libraries. The Report *Automation and the Library of Congress: a survey sponsored by the Council on Library Resources, Inc.* was published by the Library of Congress in January 1963. The MARC (Machine Readable Cataloguing) project was a result of this. *See* MARC.   2. The report *Keys to success: performance indicators for public libraries: a manual of performance measures and indicators*, developed by King Research Ltd., and published by HMSO in 1990 (Library Information Series no. 18).

KISTI.   *See* Han'guk Kwahak Kisul Chongbo Yongu-won.

KLIC.   Acronym of Key-Letter-In-Context, a method which was developed for producing permuted term lists wherein all terms are sorted on each letter in every term with the balance of the term displayed. This method is useful for selecting truncation fragments.

Klischograph.   A German electronic photoengraving machine for producing plastic, zinc, copper or magnesium half-tone plates. Blocks can be engraved for monochrome and for three- and four-colour printing. The machine was invented by Dr. Rudolph Hell of Kiel and is also known in Great Britain as the 'Clichograph'.

KM.   *See* Knowledge Management.

KM Forum.   <www.knowledgeboard.com> An EU-funded project 2003–2006 to build a critical mass of 'knowledge' to ensure that Europe meets its target to be the world's most competitive knowledge-based economy by 2010. Five member states are involved, with some 5,000 KM practitioners and experts. The project will establish and maintain a support infrastructure to aid in the co-ordination of research within the Sixth Framework Programme (*See* FP6), providing a platform for integrated projects and networks of excellence.

Knife-folder.   A folding machine which has a blunt-edged knife parallel with and above the slot formed by two parallel and constantly revolving rollers. When a sheet of paper is placed above these with an edge against a stop the knife descends and presses the sheet between the rollers which carry it away, the fold being made where the knife made contact. *See also* Buckle-folder.

Knockout.   In colour printing, a method of ensuring that the correct colour is reproduced when an image or text is overprinted on a background of a different colour. To achieve this, the knockout is not printed on the background colour separation plate, leaving a stencil effect to take the overprinted image.

Knowbot.   Knowledge robot, an electronic information retrieval tool that permeates networks and systems in its search for relevant information, and then returns and presents it to the user. *See also* Web crawler.

Knowledge classification. A classification used for any branch of knowledge, but which cannot be adapted for classifying books until a generalia class, form classes and divisions, a notation, and an index have been added.

Knowledge Discovery in Databases (KDD). The whole process of taking low-level data and turning it into a form that is more useful,of which Data mining is the core technique.

Knowledge Industry Publications, Inc. Award for Library Literature. A cash award made to an individual for an outstanding contribution to the literature of librarianship. Administered by the American Library Association Awards Committee.

Knowledge Management (KM). The process of collecting, organizing, storing and exploiting the information and data that is held within an organization, particularly information known to individuals (*tacit knowledge*), as well as the general store of known information and data (*explicit knowledge*). The process depends on electronic storage and access, typically through an Intranet. KM is concerned with human resource development, information development, and knowledge creation. It recognizes that knowledge resides in people and is a product of their ability to make connections between factual data, context, and previous experience. It is supported by trusted relationships of partners, and can pose difficulties when implemented within hierarchical organizations. *See also* Content management.

Knowledge Organization Systems/Services (KOS). A range of systems such as classifications, gazetteers, lexical databases, ontologies, taxonomies and thesauri that model the underlying semantic structure of a domain and which, when embodied as Web-based services, can facilitate resource discovery and retrieval. The systems act as semantic road maps and make possible a common orientation by indexers and future users (whether human or machine). New networked KOS (NKOS) services and applications are emerging, drawing on technologies such as information science approaches to automatic indexing and vocabulary mapping, search systems and interfaces. Protocols for distributed use are expected to emerge in the near future. (Reference: Issue of *Journal of Digital Information* devoted to New applications of KOS, vol.4, no. 4: <jodi.ecs.soton.ac.uk>)

Knowledge-based economy. A term intended to convey a vision of the Information society extended fully into skills, employment and human resources; use of Information management competencies would cause the national and global economy to expand and involve larger numbers of workers with appropriate Information literacy skills.

Knowledge-based system. *See* Expert system.

Kokuritsu Johogaku Kenkyujo. [National Institute for Informatics (NII)] <www.nii.ac.jp> (2-1-2 Hitotsubashi, Chiyoda-ku, Tokyo 101-8430, Japan) NII is an inter-university research institute developed by the Ministry of Education, Culture, Sports, Science and Technology

(MEXT) in April 2000, and was formerly NACSIS, established 1986. Its function is to gather, organize and disseminate scholarly information and related systems. It operates an online shared cataloguing system (NACSIS-Cat/Webcat-Plus), an online supply of secondary information (NACSIS-IR), an online interloan and copy service (NACSIS-ILL), electronic document delivery of Japanese academic journal articles (NACSIS-ELS), and the Science Information Network (SINET), and since 2002 Super SINET, an ultrahigh-speed network based on 10 Gbps optical communication technology. NII is now constructing the platform GeNii (Global Environment for Networked Intellectual Information) <ge.nii.ac.jp> to integrate the contents of the services and link them to scientific information resources in and outside Japan. Among NII publications are user manuals, *NII News* (6 p.a.), *NII Journal* (2 p.a.) and *NACSIS Bulletin* (available in English and in Japanese), plus brochures and videos.

Kokuritsu Kobunshokan Naikaku Bunko. [National Archives of Japan] <www.archives.go.jp/index_e.html> (3-2 Kitanomaru Koen, Chiyoda-ku, Tokyo 102-0091, Japan) The National Archives gathers historically important official documents concerning national policies from the various ministries and agencies, and carries out related surveys, research and exhibitions. Among the major collections is the Cabinet Library [Naikaku Bunko] which contains many Chinese and Japanese classics, ancient documents and manuscripts. Publishes *Kitanomaru* (a.), *Arkaibu* (irreg.), an annual report, plus guides to use of the collections (in Japanese).

Kokuritsu Kokkai Toshokan. [National Diet Library (NDL)] <www.ndl.go.jp> (1-10-1 Nagata-cho, Chiyoda-ku, Tokyo 100-8924, Japan) Established in 1948 under the National Diet Library Law, its origins lie in the collections of the Diet and of the Imperial Library, the latter the existing legal deposit library since 1872. It provides services for both the government and for the public, and is open to all over 20 years of age. Since 2003, the WARP [Web Archiving Project] collects website and e-journal content. It publishes *Nihon Zenkoku Shoshi* [*Japanese National Bibliography*] weekly and annually, distributing the data in JAPAN/MARC format on tape since 1981, and on CD-ROM since 1988. Also *Biblos*, an e-only journal, and a wide range of subject guides, indexes and bibliographies, e.g. *Index to Japanese Laws and Regulations* (a.) and *General Index to the Debates*.

Koninklijke Bibliotheek (KB). <www.kb.nl> (Prins Willem Alexanderhof 5, 2501 CN The Hague, Netherlands) The national library (Royal Library) of the Netherlands, founded in 1789.

Korean Library Association. *See* Han'guk Tosogwan Hyophoe.

KOS. *See* Knowledge Organization Systems/Services.

Kraft paper. A strong calendered brown paper of medium colour and with prominent chain-lines (*see* Laid paper) used specially for wrapping purposes. It is sometimes strengthened with hessian or tar to make waterproof wrapping paper of great strength. *See also* Bleached Kraft.

Kungliga Biblioteket. <www.kb.se> (Humlesgården, Box 5039, 102 41 Stockholm, Sweden) The Swedish national library (Royal Library), founded in 1661.

Kungnim Chungang Tosogwan. [National Library of Korea] <www.nl.go.kr> (3-60-1 Panpo-dong, Seocho-gu, Seoul, 137-702, S. Korea) Founded in 1945, the library moved to its present purpose-built premises in 1988. It contains nearly 5 million items, including some 660,000 foreign items, 2,500 newspaper titles, and 17,000 journal titles. It publishes the *Korea National Bibliography*, providing the data in KORMARC format on CD-ROM.

Kuopio University Virtual Library. <www.uku.fi/kirjasto/ virtuaalikirjasto> Part of the Finnish Virtual Library, the Kuopio University Virtual Library covers the subject areas of clinical nutrition, environmental health, molecular medicine and gene therapy, neuro-sciences, nursing and health care, and pharmacy.

Kursiv. *See* Cursive.

Kurzweil reading machine. A combination of a camera, computer and voice synthesizer which converts the printed word into spoken word for the benefit of blind and visually-impaired people.

KWAC. Keyword-and-Context. An index of titles of documents permutated to bring each significant word to the beginning, in alphabetical order, followed by the remaining words which follow it in the title, and then followed by that part of the original title which came before the significant word. *See also* KWIC, KWOC.

KWIC. Keyword-in-Context. A method of Permutation indexing which uses a computer to permute automatically words in periodical article titles, and to group titles in which the same words occur. When the index is printed, the keywords in each index line are printed at the middle of the type measure and thus appear under one another in alphabetical order in a column. The full measure of the line is filled by printing as much of the title immediately before and after the keyword as can be accommodated.

KWOC. Keyword-out-of-Context, a refinement of KWIC. Titles are printed in full under as many Keywords as the indexer considers useful; these may be chosen from a thesaurus or list of standard headings as well as from the title, and there is no limit to the source of Keywords. The Keywords are separated from the title on a line of their own and act as subject headings. *See also* WADEX.

Kyle Classification. *See* Classification for Social Sciences.

LAA. Library Association of Australia. *See* Australian Library and Information Association.

Label. 1. A small strip of leather, usually of a different colour to that used for the binding of a book, placed on the spine and displaying one or more of the following: title, author's name, volume number, date. Also called 'Lettering pieces'. When two labels are used they are described as 'double lettering pieces'. Labels of paper were used on books bound in boards covered with paper. 2. (*Information retrieval*) In a machine-readable record, one or more characteristics which are written or attached to a set of data which contains information about the set, including its identification. *See also* Tag.

Label title-page. The title and author's name printed near the top of an otherwise blank page, or protecting leaf, at the beginning of a book. Often called 'Label title', the name is given to the first form of title-page in early printed books (1470–1550). The earliest extant example is a Papal Bull of Pius II, printed in 1463 at Mainz, probably by Fust and Schöffer.

Labelled notation. The style of the notation used in the Colon Class-ification. Each main class is labelled with a letter, and each facet is first symbolized by combining the main class letter with a facet indicator; simple terms are represented by numerals.

Laboratory collection. *See* Departmental library.

LACA. *See* Libraries and Archives Copyright Alliance.

LACAP. Latin America Co-operative Acquisitions Program. Organized in 1960 as a result of the extension of the Farmington Plan to Latin America. *See also* SALALM.

Lace border. *See* Lacework (2).

Laced on. *See* Lacing-in.

Lacework. 1. A border decoration on bindings, done by tooling, to represent lace. *See also* Dentelle. 2. Borders framing whole-page illustrations in nineteenth-century French books, the border-decoration consisting of punching the pattern out of the paper as in paper doyleys.

Lacing-in. (*Binding*) Attaching the boards by the operation of passing the slips or cords on which the book is sewn, and after they have been splayed out and moistened with paste, through holes pierced in the boards.

Lacuna. (*Pl.* Lacunae) A gap in the stock of a library, which awaits filling.

LAD. *See* Office of Information Programmes and Services.

LAI. *See* Library Association of Ireland.

Laid in. Used in a note to a catalogue entry to indicate the inclusion in a sound recording or musical publication, of a leaflet or pamphlet relating to the music and its performance.

Laid paper. Paper which, when held up to the light, shows thick and thin lines at right angles. They are caused by the weave of the dandy roll, or in hand-made paper by the mould having long thin wires placed very close together and fastened to thicker ones at intervals of about one inch. The horizontal thin ones are called 'wire-lines' or 'wire-marks' and the vertical thick ones 'chain-lines', 'chain-marks' or 'wide-lines'. To obtain the best impression when printing, the wire-lines should run across the page and the chain-lines down it. *See also* Watermark.

LAMA. *See* Library Administration and Management Association – division of American Library Association.

Lambert (Nancy Stirling) Scholarship. Established by Blackwell's, the Oxford booksellers, to encourage the investigation of matters of common concern to libraries and the book trade.

Lambskin. A bookbinding leather with a smooth finish; it is similar in appearance to calf but less durable.

LAMDA. <lamdaweb.mcc.ac.uk> An electronic document delivery service that draws on the journal collections of 10 leading academic libraries in the UK. The service utilizes Ariel scan send-and-receive software to transmit documents electronically. The service grew out of London and Manchester Document Access, a UK eLib project which went live in October 1995.

Laminated. A sheet of paper to which a sheet of clear plastic has been permanently adhered on one or both sides. Book jackets, leaves of books, or paper covers are treated in this way to strengthen them.

Lamination. A method, similar to encapsulation, for protecting fragile leaves by enclosing them between sheets of stiffened, chemically stable polyester, and sealing the edges by heat. The result is a firm but flexible protection for damaged or fragile material. *See also* Silking.

Lampblack. Pure carbon deposit; formerly the most important black pigment used in manufacturing printing inks. It was produced by burning pitch resin in a vessel in a tent made of paper or sheepskins. The smoke was deposited on the inside of the tent which was then beaten to cause the black to fall on to the floor. Impurities were removed by heating it several times until red-hot in an iron box with a small aperture at the top.

Lampoon. A satirical attack generally of a scurrilous but humorous character, upon a person, and written in prose or verse.

LAN. *See* Local area network.

Landscape. A book or document that is wider than its height; one that is designed to be read with its longer edges towards the reader. More often called 'Oblong'.

Landscape binding. A type of binding which has landscape views on its covers, the landscape views being drawn freehand with Indian ink or acid and later coloured, or printed by some means. They date between 1777 and 1821.

Landscape page. A page on which graphs, tables, illustrations, etc. are printed so that their foot is parallel to the fore-edge of the page. Also called 'Broadside page'. *See also* Turned.

Language number. A facet which may form part of a Book number in the Colon Classification. It is obtained by translating the name of the language in which the book is written into appropriate symbols in accordance with the language schedule given in Chapter 5 of the Schedules. *See also* Ethnic numbers.

Language of the text. The language in which the text of a book is printed and which is not determinable from the title, e.g. *Faust*. In such a case the cataloguer may (1) add a note, e.g. 'Text in German and English'; (2) integrate a translator statement, e.g. 'Tr. into English by...'; (3) augment the heading, e.g. 'Goethe, Johann Wolfgang von. Faust. English'.

Language sub-division. (*Classification*) Sub-division of a subject according to the language in which it is written, or sub-division of a language division in the philological class of a scheme of classification.

Lanston. *See* Monotype.

Lapidary type. A font of capital letters similar to those on Roman monumental inscriptions. Examples were cut by Erhard Ratdolt at Augsburg in 1505. *See also* Square capitals.

Laptop. Portable Personal computer, usually battery-operated for use on-the-move, but with the capability for being connected to mains power and Peripherals. Also known as 'notebook'.

Large folio. A general term to indicate a large-sized folio book. *See also* Folio (3).

Large paper copy, or edition. An impression of a book printed on larger and better quality paper than the usual trade edition, thus having wider margins. *See also* Fine paper copy, Limited edition, Small paper copy.

Large post. A sheet of printing paper measuring $16^{1}/_{2} \times 21$ inches.

Large print. Books for partially-sighted readers, printed in a clear, large point typeface.

Large Royal. A sheet of printing paper measuring 20×27 inches.

LASER. The London and South Eastern Library Region was a library co-operative formed in the 1930s and which flourished successfully until 2001. It had been active in the VISCOUNT Programme, in CILLA, and was the base for EARL. With the creation of the London Library Development Agency and other initiatives, the moment came for LASER to be wound up; its funds were placed in the LASER Foundation – formed as a grant-making trust which is intended to target projects on e-content for public libraries, and lifelong learning initiatives.

Laser printer. A printer which uses a laser beam to form a high quality image on paper. Since its introduction as one of the key components of Desktop publishing, and as a result of significant price reductions, it has become the standard printer for most offices, including libraries and information services. Has advantages over the cheaper Inkjet printer in lower page output costs and greater robustness and longevity. Also known, less frequently, as a Page printer. *See also* Page description language.

LaserDisc. An Optical disc format which combines analogue video with digital sound normally in 12-inch formats and now all but replaced by DVD. Pioneer Entertainment, the long-time champion of LaserDisc, abandoned production in the US in June 1999 although the company continued to release small runs in Japan until 2001. LaserDisc still fills niches in education, training, and video installations, but these will also be replaced by DVD in time.

Last fold.   *See* Bolt.

Later cursive.   A Latin manuscript handwriting which came in sequence between Uncial and Half uncial. Its main characteristics are ligatures (joined letters) and the uneven height of the letters, some of which ascended or descended beyond the normal letter limits – which had not previously occurred. This distinction between tall and small letters marked the first stage in the development of minuscules (lower-case letters).

Lateral filing.   Equipment which consists of pockets of tough paper, or linen, which are suspended (and usually move laterally within limits) from two rails placed one behind the other and running from left to right. They are made into fittings which will rest on shelves or as a complete filing cabinet.

Laterally reversed.   In documentary copying, reflecting the original as in a mirror. Also called 'Left-to-right-reversed'. *See also* Right reading.

Lattice stamp.   (*Binding*) A decorative ornament, the distinguishing feature of which is a central diamond formed of lattice or criss-cross work.

Laura Ingalls Wilder Medal.   *See* Wilder (Laura Ingalls) Medal.

Law binding.   *See* Law calf.

Law calf.   A leather binding using plain uncoloured calf or sheepskin. Mainly used for law books but now largely superseded by buckram cloth. Also called 'Fair calf', 'Law sheep'.

Law of scattering.   A 'law' deduced by Dr. S. C. Bradford (and later corrected by B. C. Vickery) who found that about a third of the articles on a subject are printed in the journals devoted to that subject, a further third appear in a larger number of journals devoted to related subjects, and the remaining third in an even larger number of journals in which such articles would not normally be expected to be published. According to the law of scattering, if Tx represents the number of journals having x references, T_2x the total number of journals having $2x$ references, etc., then: $Tx:T_2x:T_3x = 1:n:n^2$ where n may be any number depending on the value chosen for x.

Law sheep.   *See* Law calf.

Lay edges.   The edges of a sheet of paper which are laid against the front and side lay gauges of a printing or folding machine. The front edge is known as the 'gripper edge'.

Layout.   1. A plan, prepared for or by a printer, to show the arrangement of the matter, typefaces, sizes of type, position of illustrations and captions, for a piece of printing.   2. The plan of an entire book.

Laystool.   A stool on which white paper and printed sheets were laid close to the printing pressman's hand. By the nineteenth century a 'horse' with a sloping top had been evolved to take the paper and make it easier to pick sheets off the heap.

Lazerow (Samuel) Fellowship for Research in Acquisitions or Technical Services. An award of the Association of College and Research Libraries.

LC. *See* Library of Congress.

l.c. Abbreviation for lower case. *See* Lower case letters.

LCF. *See* Librarians' Christian Fellowship.

LCLA. *See* Lutheran Church Library Association.

LCSH. Library of Congress Subject Headings; *see* Subject heading.

LDAP. Lightweight Directory Access Protocol, a series of Internet-standard specifications from the Internet Engineering Task Force for a lightweight version of the X.500 global directory service which supports TCP/IP. A typical LDAP server is a simple network-accessible database in which an organization stores information about its authorized users and their privileges.

Le Gascon style. Modified Fanfare bindings of the early seventeenth century, in which the strapwork is retained, the enclosed spaces differentiated by inlaid leather of different colours, and the sprays lighter. Fine dotted scrolls are frequently enclosed in the geometrical compartments and often extended into lines and curves of remarkable lustre and elegance. These scrolls and other ornaments are given dotted lines known as pointillé, instead of unbroken lines. Not practised after about 1660.

Leab (Katherine and Daniel) American Book Prices Current Award. An award for bibliographic catalogues to exhibitions, administered by the Association of College and Research Libraries.

Lead. (*Verb*) To insert leads between type or re-set on a larger body. A page of printed matter where the lines are well spaced out is said to be 'well leaded'.

Lead moulding. A process for making electros or half-tone plates in which the base is lead instead of wax. Soft lead is forced into the forme under great (hydraulic) pressure and a mould of fine quality obtained. A copper shell is then deposited on the mould in the same manner as in wax moulding.

Leaded matter. Having the lines of type separated by 'leads', or cast on a larger body, as 8 pt. type on 9 pt. body, to achieve the same effect. In the latter case, the type is called 'Longbodied'. Type without 'leads' is said to be 'set solid'. 'Double-leaded' means a double space (usually 4 points) between lines of type. *See also* Em, Leads, Pica, Solid matter.

Leader. 1. A short newspaper article expressing views or comments, and usually indicating the policy or editorial views of the proprietors of the paper. Fully, a leading article. 2. A portion of film at the beginning of a roll of film, and which is used for the threading of the film in a camera, processing machine, or projector. 3. (*Information retrieval*) In machine-readable records, the part of the record which precedes the information content, and which carries data needed to manipulate, identify or locate the information content.

Leader writer. The writer of newspaper editorials, or leaders.

Leaders. A sequence of dots or hyphens to lead the eye from one word to another as in tabular work, or across a page as in a table of contents.

Leads. Thin strips of lead which are less than type high, used to separate lines of type or to space them further apart. Type set on a larger body, such as 8 point on a 9 point body to give the same effect without the use of separate leads between each line, is called *long-bodied type*. Leads are usually made 1, 1½ (thin), 2 (middle) which is the usual leading, 3 (thick), and 4 points – known as 'double leaded' thick; when 6 point or more they are called 'clumps' and may be of wood or metal. When clumps are made of wood they are called 'reglets'. Spacing material of greater dimensions than 18 point is known as 'furniture'. *See also* Leaded matter, Solid matter.

Leaf. 1. A sheet of paper, printed, and folded once forms a section of two leaves or four pages, and is called folio; folded twice, it forms a section of four leaves or eight pages and is called quarto. A leaf consists of two pages, one on each side, either of which may or may not be printed on. Usually the recto has an odd number, and the verso the subsequent number, but in reprints this may not be the case. Books with un-numbered leaves or pages may be described in a catalogue or bibliographical entry as containing a specific number (ascertained by counting) of pages or leaves – preferably the latter if the book was published before pagination was general – in the form '320 l'. *See also* Foldings, Foliation, Plate, Section. 2. LEAF <www.leaf-eu.org> Linking and Exploring Authority Files, an EU-funded project 2001–2004 working on a model architecture for distributed search systems to harvest existing name authority records to create a pan-European common name authority file.

Leaf moulding. A technique of document repair. When a damaged document (usually paper or parchment) is laminated, the differences in thickness caused by the damaged sections can be made up by inserting material moulded to the shape of the damaged areas. Conservationists often use simple technology to construct leaf moulding machines.

Leaflet. A small sheet of paper folded once and printed on to make two to four pages following in the same sequence as in a book, but not stitched or bound. Often used to indicate a small, thin Pamphlet.

League of European Research Libraries. *See* LIBER.

Lean matter. *See* Matter.

Lean-face type. Type, the stems and other strokes of which have not their full width.

learndirect. <www.learndirect.co.uk> A UK network of online learning and information services, government sponsored and contributing to the vision of a Learning society. It was developed by the University for Industry (UfI) for workforce development and lifelong learning. A range of public and private providers are involved, and delivery methods are normally online or other electronic means. Three areas are currently targeted: skills for life; business and management; IT skills. There are centres throughout the UK.

Learned journal. A Journal with an academic or research-based target readership; often the product of a Learned society and containing its transactions or proceedings. Also termed 'scholarly journal'.

Learned society. A professional or academic organization founded to serve as a focus for the interchange of information and opinion within a discipline; such a body is often a major journal publisher in its subject field.

Learner support. A term particularly used in the Fielden Report (UK) and defined as 'the activities within library/information services that exist to support individual learners'. It incorporates User education in library and information skills, Mediated access to databases, tailored navigational support, help with study packs and computer-based teaching materials, and tutorial support.

Learning Age. A UK government green paper published in February 1998; *The Learning Age: a Renaissance for a New Britain* (Cm 3790). The paper deals with Lifelong learning, and has received substantial attention in the UK professional press. *See* Lifelong learning.

Learning and Teaching Support Network. *See* LTSN.

Learning object. Any entity, digital or non-digital, which can be used, re-used or referenced during the process of technology-supported learning and in an environment such as a VLE. Examples of learning objects include multimedia content, instructional content, learning objectives, instructional software and software tools, and persons, organizations, or events referenced during technology-supported learning. *See also* Learning Object Metadata.

Learning Object Metadata (LOM). <ltsc.ieee.org/wg12> A standard from IEEE which specifies the syntax and semantics of the attributes required to fully and adequately describe a Learning object. The specification of the standard will help to enable learners or instructors to search, evaluate, acquire, and utilize learning objects, enable the sharing and exchange of learning objects across any technology-supported learning systems, and enable the development of learning objects in units that can be combined and decomposed in meaningful ways. *See also* CanCore, IMS, SCORM.

Learning resources. An umbrella term used in educational contexts to include library services, audio-visual services, computing facilities and other support facilities needed by students to provide a location and essential materials for their taught courses and self-programmed work. Control of such an amalgamation of services – a 'learning resources centre' or 'Information commons' – may be in the hands of a librarian, or other manager.

Learning society. The concept that individuals and organizations should seek constantly to develop skills and understanding. In the UK the term Lifelong learning is similarly used to express this ongoing commitment. *See* Lifelong learning.

Leather. The cured and dyed hide of goat, pig or sheep. Used extensively for binding books.

Leather bound. A book bound in leather, either Full, Half, Quarter, or Three-quarter.

Leather joints. Leather inner joints affixed (usually stuck in but sometimes sewn) to the endpapers of large hand-bound books to give greater strength. They were occasionally used in the seventeenth century in Europe; between 1750 and 1800 they were a fairly common feature of the best English Morocco and Russia bindings, and were usually heavily decorated with fillets, rolls and small tools.

Leathercloth. A fabric or plastic material which has been finished to simulate leather.

Leatherette. Paper or cloth having a surface in imitation of leather.

Leaves of plates. *See* Plate (1).

LEC. *See* London Education Classification.

Lectern. A sloped wooden ledge on which books were laid flat and chained, and at which they were consulted, in mediaeval libraries.

Ledger catalogue. *See* Page catalogue.

Ledger charging. An antiquated method of recording books on loan by entering book numbers against names or ticket numbers in adjacent vertical columns on loose sheets or in a bound ledger.

Ledger weight. (*Reprography*) Photographic paper of moderately heavy weight; used when greater body and mechanical durability are required. 'Duplex ledger' is coated on both sides for reproducing books; the paper used may have a wood, fibre or rag (linen ledger) base.

Left-to-right reversed. *See* Laterally reversed.

Legacy systems. The generic term used to describe obsolete computer systems that must be considered when installing replacement software and systems.

Legal deposit. A method whereby certain libraries are entitled by law to receive one or more copies of every book or other publication which is printed or published in the country. In the UK, the Legal Deposit Libraries Act 2003 clears up long-standing confusion over terminology (*see* Copyright deposit, Copyright library) and extends legal deposit to non-print, electronic and Web resources. An advisory panel is currently working on the details for implementation of the Act; offline, CD-ROM and DVD resources are likely to be covered first and in the interim the British Library is operating a voluntary scheme. Secondary legislation likely in 2006 or 2007 will recommend complete harvesting of all UK-based websites annually and more regular scanning of key sites. The British Library is expected to appoint a Head of Web Archiving. *See also* UK Web Archiving Consortium.

Legal file. A collection of material relating to law cases; it may include briefs, decisions, or histories of cases.

Legend. 1. The title or short description printed under an illustration or engraving, or on a coin or medal. Also called 'Caption' and 'Cut-line'.

2. An explanation of symbols on a map or diagram.   3. A story based on tradition.

Legislative history.   A chronological account of the stages through which a particular bill (*see* Bill (2)) has passed before enactment as a law. This would include all 'readings', committee debates and decisions, and 'floor' debates in both houses. The events leading to the bill, the efforts of organizations concerned in furthering it, any evidence given, and any history subsequent to enactment are also sometimes included.

Leighton Library.   The library of Robert Leighton, Bishop of Dunblane and later Archbishop of Glasgow (1611–84), founded in Dunblane in 1688 for the benefit of local clergy under the term of Leighton's will, and still housed in its original building. In 1734 the library was reconstituted as one of the earliest public libraries in Scotland. A British Library grant to Stirling University has aided production of a catalogue of the collection, and grants have also been given by the Pilgrim Trust and the Historic Buildings Council for Scotland.

Lemma.   The argument or subject written at the head of a literary composition.

Lemonnier style.   A style of book decoration practised by Jean Christophe Henri Lemonnier, who worked for Count Hoym in France in the eighteenth century. It is characterized by pictorial mosaics of landscape, bouquets, etc.

Lending department.   The department of a library containing books for home-reading. Called a 'Circulation department' in the US.

Lending desk.   *See* Circulation desk.

Lending library.   *See* Lending department.

Lenin Library.   *See* Russian State Library.

Lesbian and Gay Librarians Group.   An informal group for all grades of UK library staff; re-established 1985 after several years of inactivity. *See also* Sexuality Issues in Libraries Group.

Let-in note.   *See* Incut note.

Letter book.   A book in which correspondence was copied by some means resulting in a facsimile copy. This was often done by writing the original letter with copying ink, placing it against a dampened sheet of thin paper (leaves of which comprised the book) and applying pressure. Such books were sometimes known as letterpress copybooks. Also, a book of blank or ruled pages on which are written letters, either drafts written by the author or fair copies made by the author or by clerks. The term is also used for a book comprising copies of letters which are bound together, or of one into which such copies are pasted onto guards or pages.

Letter spacing.   The insertion of spaces between the letters of a word or words to lengthen the Measure, improve the appearance of the setting, or in special instances emphasize a word or sentence. *See also* Tracking.

Letter writer.   1. One who writes letters for illiterates.   2. A writer who has become famous for the letters he has written and possibly published.

Lettera rotonda. *See* Antiqua.

Letter-by-letter. *See* Alphabetization.

Lettered proof. The proof of an engraving in which the title and the names of the artist, engraver, printer, etc. are printed under the illustration.

Lettering. The emplacement of the library Call number on the spine of a book.

Lettering on the spine. When the lettering on the spine of a book or book jacket does not go across it, the direction may be up or down according to the choice of the publisher with consequent inconvenience to library users. In 1926 the Publishers Association and the Associated Booksellers of Great Britain and Ireland recommended that 'when a volume stands on the shelf the lettering reads from bottom to top', but in 1948 reversed their decision, recommending that the lettering should be downward so that the title can be easily read when the book lies flat, face upward. *Periodicals of reference value* ... (BS 2509:1970 now withdrawn) recommends that the lettering of periodicals should be 'across the spine if the title is short enough; otherwise along the spine in such a way as to be readable when the publication is lying flat with the *front* cover uppermost'.

Lettering piece. A piece of leather secured to the spine of a book to receive its title. *See also* Label.

Letterpress. 1. The text of a book as distinguished from its illustrations. 2. Matter printed from type as distinct from plates. 3. A method of relief printing as opposed to intaglio or planographic.

Letterpress copybook. *See* Letter book.

Letters close. Letter addressed usually by the sovereign to some individual or group of individuals and closed with a seal.

Letters patent. An open letter issued generally under the great seal of the sovereign or some other magnate as a guarantee to the person or corporation named therein.

Lettre bâtarde. *See* Gothic type.

Lettre de forme. *See* Gothic type.

Lettre de somme. *See* Gothic type.

Lettre ronde. *See* Antiqua.

Levant. A high-grade Morocco leather used for binding books, and made from the skin of the Angora goat.

Level. (*Classification*) A measure of the degree of complexity or generality of a concept, term or class.

Level small caps. *See* Even small caps.

Levels of arrangement. (*Archives*) The groupings into which component parts of archival groups are divided, in which the divisions and order created in the originating system are reflected. *MAD* provides a defined taxonomy of levels, numbered 0–5. *See* Class, Group, Item, Management group, Sub-group.

Levels of description. (*Archives*) In *MAD*, the descriptions corresponding to levels of arrangement. They are subject to the Multi-level rule.

Lever press.   Any printing press on which the impression is made by moving a lever, but the term is usually applied to the type of press used for proofing, etc., in which the lever is pulled down.

Levigator.   A heavy steel disc which is rotated by hand over a lithographic stone when preparing its surface, sand and water being used as the abrasive.

Levin Award.   An award of the Society of Indexers, made to recognize services to the Society.

Lexeme.   A word, particle or stem which denotes the meaning.

Lexicographer.   The compiler of a dictionary.

Lexicography.   The act, or process, of compiling a dictionary.

Lexicology.   The branch of knowledge which is concerned with words, their history, form and meaning.

Lexicon.   A dictionary of the words of a language, the words being arranged in alphabetical order; especially one giving the meaning in another language. It is chiefly applied to a dictionary of Greek, Syriac, Arabic or Hebrew but is also used for encyclopaedias and subject dictionaries.

LFF.   *See* Libraries for the Future.

Liability slip.   A slip recording the loan of a book for use on the library premises. It is cancelled, or returned to the reader, when the book is returned.

LIAC.   *See* Library and Information Assistant's Certificate.

LIANZA.   <www.lianza.org.nz> The Library and Information Association of New Zealand/Te Herenga o Aotearoa was founded in 1910, incorporated by Act of Parliament in 1939; the Maori version of its title was added in 1993, and the current name adopted in 2002. LIANZA is the principal professional association for librarians and information managers, and works for its members and the development of services. Publishes *New Zealand Libraries*.

LIASA.   *See* Library and Information Association of South Africa.

LibDex.   <www.libdex.com> The Library Index, a worldwide directory of library homepages, web-based OPACs, Friends of the Library pages, and library e-commerce affiliate links.

LIBER.   <www.kb.dk/liber> (PO Box 2149, DK-1016 Copenhagen K, Denmark) Ligue des Bibliothèques Européennes de Recherche (League of European Research Libraries). This Association was founded in March 1971 by a steering group set up through the National and University Libraries Section of IFLA at the Council of Europe's headquarters in Strasbourg. Its purpose was to bring together the large libraries of Austria, Belgium, Cyprus; Denmark, Finland, France, Germany, Greece, Holy See, Iceland, Ireland, Italy, Luxembourg, Malta, Netherlands, Norway, Portugal, Spain, Sweden, Switzerland, Turkey and the UK, and thereby to establish close co-operation between European research libraries, particularly national and university libraries, and also to help in finding practical ways of improving the quality of the services these libraries provide. Also, to organize research into librarianship on a European scale, and set up working parties in well-defined and circumscribed subjects. *See also* Conspectus, European Register of Microform Masters.

Liberate roll.   A record of the writs authorizing delivery of money out of the Treasury. Chancery Liberate are rolls of letters issued, and the Exchequer series rolls of letters received; both are copied from the same originals.

LIBEX.   <www.cilip.org.uk/jobs_careers/libex> The International Library and Information Jobs Exchange; a clearinghouse helping to arrange job exchanges. From 2003 based at CILIP; previously located at the Thomas Parry Library, University of Wales, Aberystwyth.

Librarian.   One who has care of a library and its contents; the work includes selection of stock, its arrangement and exploitation in the widest sense, and the provision of a range of services in the best interests of all groups of users. Co-ordination of activities, setting of priorities, evaluation and other managerial tasks are an essential part of the work. Involvement in the community served, whether public, academic, private or any other context is also of great importance.

Librarian-in-charge.   The librarian placed in charge of a particular department.

Librarians' Christian Fellowship.   <www.librarianscf.org.uk> (34 Thurlestone Avenue, Seven Kings, Ilford, Essex IG3 9DU, UK) Formed 1973; it operates as an Organization in Liaison (OiL) with CILIP. An inter-denominational group aiming to bring together Christians, to discuss issues relating to librarianship, and to exert a positive influence on professional affairs. Publishes *Christian Librarian* (a.) and *Newsletter* (3 p.a.).

Librarianship.   The profession of the librarian. *See also* Library science.

Librarianship and Information Work Worldwide (LIWW).   *LIWW* was an annual series of volumes, in which overview chapters examined international developments in all aspects of libraries and the information world. Copious references were cited after each contribution. Published 1991–2000 by Bowker-Saur.

Libraries and Archives Canada/Bibliothéques et Archives Canada.   <www.lac-bac.gc.ca> or <www.nla-bnc.ca> The Canadian national body overseeing strategic development in the archives and libraries sector. At present it is the base for the Association of Canadian Archivists.

Libraries and Archives Copyright Alliance (LACA).   <www.cilip.org.uk/laca> Originally the Copyright Committee of the Joint Consultative Council, it became an independent body when the JCC ceased to function and was known as the Library Association Copyright Alliance. Although technically still independent it was administered by the Library Association and included several representatives of groups of the Association. When the Library Association merged to form CILIP the Alliance retained its acronym (by then well known in copyright circles) and became the Libraries and Archives Copyright Alliance. It has been expanded to include some independent experts, the Royal National Institute for the Blind, the British Library and ARLIS. It has produced a number of guidelines on copyright topics.

Libraries and Information Services in the United Kingdom and Republic of Ireland. The principal directory of UK libraries, published annually by Facet Publishing (CILIP) and previously by Library Association Publishing (30th ed., 2004).

Libraries Change Lives Award. <www.cilip.org.uk> A high-profile award made annually by CILIP to recognize an innovative library or information project that centres on community involvement or development.

Libraries Directory. <www.jamesclarke.co.uk> The oldest established directory of UK libraries, published by James Clarke and Co. since 1897 (49th ed., 2004).

Libraries for the Future (LFF). <www.lff.org> A US-based advocacy group that is working to improve awareness of libraries and their potential roles; the group undertakes research, runs workshops and discussion groups, collaborates with other interested groups representing library users, and promotes a model of a library service that links under-served communities with educational and information resources.

Libraries Online! A scheme of the Microsoft Corporation with the American Library Association to assist in bringing Internet access to public libraries in deprived areas of the USA. *See* Gates Library Foundation.

Librarii. Used in mediaeval times to signify scribes.

Library. 1. A collection of books and other literary material kept for reading, study and consultation. 2. A place, building, room or rooms set apart for the keeping and use of a collection of books, etc. 3. A number of books issued by one publisher under a comprehensive title as the 'Loeb Classical Library', and usually having some general characteristic such as subject, binding, or typography. 4. A collection of films, photographs and other non-book materials, plastic or metal tapes and disks, computer tapes, disks and programs. All of these, as well as printed and manuscript documents, may be provided in departments of one large library or they may be in collections restricted to one type of material. 5. (*Computer programming*) A set of routines stored in a file. More generally applied to any collection of Applications software gathered for a particular purpose or any collection of data files.

Library Acts. *See* Library law.

Library Administration & Management Association (LAMA). A division of the American Library Association. Aims to encourage the study of administrative theory, and improve management practice. Responsible since 1974 for the Library Technology Program. Publishes *LAMA Newsletter* (q.), proceedings, bibliographies.

Library Advisory Councils. The formation of national advisory councils, one for England (excluding Monmouthshire) and the other for Wales and Monmouthshire, was provided for by Section 2 of the Public Libraries and Museums Act 1964. In 1981 they were merged, and retitled the Library and Information Services Council. Subsequently the role of this body passed to the Library and Information Commission (LIC) and now to the Museums, Libraries and Archives Council (MLA). However, in 2003 a 'new' Advisory Council on Libraries was formed by DCMS.

Library Agreement. *See* Net Book Agreement.

Library and Information Assistant's Certificate (LIAC). A sub-professional qualification intended for unqualified library assistants; operated by the City and Guilds of London Institute.

Library and Information Association of New Zealand. *See* LIANZA.

Library and Information Association of South Africa (LIASA). <www.liasa.org.za> (PO Box 1598, Pretoria 0001) Formed 1998, replacing two earlier associations: ALASA (African Library Association of South Africa) and SAILIS (South African Institute for Librarianship and Information Science). A third organization – LIWO (Library and Information Workers Organization) – is expected to continue its separate existence. LIASA means 'dawn' in several African languages. A number of formerly separate associations for the 'independent homelands' have now been absorbed into LIASA.

Library and Information Commission (LIC). The Commission was established in 1995 to provide the UK Government with a national focus of expertise in the field of library and information services. In 2000 the LIC merged with related bodies to form Re:source, which in 2004 was renamed the Museums, Libraries and Archives Council (MLA).

Library and Information Co-operation Council (LINC). Set up in 1989 to replace the National Committee on Regional Library Co-operation, and to continue and develop its work. With the creation of Re:source (*see now* Museums, Libraries and Archives Council (MLA)) LINC had no further role and disbanded in 2001. Two of its programmes continue to function: NEWSPLAN, and HELICON which replaces the LINC Health Panel.

Library and Information History Group (LIHG). A membership group of CILIP; formed in 1962 as the Library History Group to encourage work on the history of librarianship. In 2003 the name was extended to include *information* to take account of a newly emerging field. Publishes *Library History* (2 p.a.). (Reference: A. Black. Information history and the information professional. *Library History*, vol. 20, (March) 2004, pp. 3–6)

Library and Information Plans. *See* LIPs.

Library and Information Research Group (LIRG). <www.lirg.org.uk> (School of Information Management, Leeds Metropolitan University,

Priestley Hall, Beckett Park, Leeds LS6 3QS, UK) Founded in 1977 to bring together those interested in library and information research, this formerly independent professional body has now become a membership group of CILIP. It awards the Daphne Clark Prize, Elsevier/LIRG Award, and various student prizes; issues *Library and Information Research* and the *LIRG Directory of Current Research*. Operates an e-mail discussion list <www.jiscmail.ac.uk/lists.LIS-LIRG.html>.

Library and information science (LIS).   The study and practice of professional methods in the use and exploitation of information, whether from an institutional base or not, for the benefit of users. An umbrella term and used to cover terms such as library science, librarianship, information science, information work etc.

Library and Information Science Abstracts (LISA).   An extended and enlarged form of *Library Science Abstracts*; it commenced publication in January 1969 by the (UK) Library Association jointly with Aslib, which organization withdrew in 1980. The title was sold to Bowker-Saur in 1990, and then in 2002 to CSA <www.csa.com/csa/journals>. Online and CD-ROM versions are available from various vendors, and a printed version from the publisher.

Library and Information Services Council.   The Library Advisory Council (England) was set up by the 1964 Public Library Act; by the late 1970s it was clear that some revision of structure and function was necessary. In 1980 the House of Commons Select Committee on Education, Science and the Arts produced a report *Information storage and retrieval in the British library service* (HMSO, 1980) chaired by Christopher Price, MP, and sometimes referred to as the *Price Report*, which sought machinery to co-ordinate library and information policy on a national basis, and recommended a standing commission representing a wide range of interests concerned with the provision of information. In April 1981 the British Government responded in a white paper *Information storage and retrieval in the British library service* (Cmnd. 8237) (HMSO, 1981) which agreed to treating libraries and information together and in accepting the need for a committee, considered that the Library Advisory Council (England) would suffice, but should be reformed and redesignated the Library and Information Services Council (LISC). LISC(E), covering England, was a statutory body, and similar status was given to LISC(W) covering Wales; LISC(NI) for Northern Ireland was not a statutory body; neither was the Scottish LISC. In 1995 the functions of these bodies passed to the Library and Information Commission (LIC) and then to Re:source (*see now* Museums, Libraries and Archives Council (MLA)).

Library and Information Statistics Unit (LISU).   <www.lboro.ac.uk/departments/dils/lisu> (Loughborough University, Leicestershire LE11 3TU, UK) Set up in 1987 and funded until 1991 by the British Library. Continues the work of CLAIM; publishes *Library and Information Statistics Tables* (a.).

Library and Information Technology Association (LITA). Division of the American Library Association. Founded 1966. Concerned with the development and application of automated systems, electronic data processing techniques, communications technology; promotes research and organizes standards. Publishes *Information Technology & Libraries* (q.), *LITA Newsletter* (irreg.).

Library and Information Workers Organization. *See* LIWO.

Library, Archives and Documentation Services (LAD). *See* Office of Information Programmes and Services.

Library Assistant's Certificate. *See* Library and Information Assistant's Certificate.

Library Association. *See* CILIP.

Library Association of Australia. Founded in 1949, being re-constituted from the Australian Institute of Librarians which had been founded in 1937. In 1989 the name was changed to the Australian Library and Information Association.

Library Association of Ireland (LAI). <www.libraryassociation.ie> (53 Upper Mount Street, Dublin 2, Ireland) Founded in 1928 and incorporated in 1952, the Association represents the profession in the Irish Republic. There are 12 special interest groups. The Association awards the professional qualification (FLAI). Membership is open to all engaged in, or interested in, the profession of librarianship in Ireland or elsewhere. With the March 1972 issue (NS vol. 1, no 1) of *An Leabharlann* (q.), it became the joint journal of the LAI and of the Northern Ireland Branch of the Library Association (now CILIP) with the title *An Leabharlann: The Irish Library*. Conferences of the two bodies have been held since 1961, and there is a standing liaison committee between them.

Library associations. Professional organizations formed to bring together librarians who share common interests in subjects, types of services, or other factors. Especially national associations, such as CILIP or the American Library Association, and of these there are examples in most countries of the world (*see* entries under the titles of major associations or under country names).

Library authority. The local government or other public agency responsible for the operation of a public library service.

Library Bill of Rights. The American Library Association's basic policy on intellectual freedom. First adopted in 1939, a completely revised version was adopted in 1948, with amendments in 1961, 1967, and 1980. Affirms the librarian's right to purchase and provide appropriate materials without restriction, and the user's right of access. In 1984 further interpreted to cover films and video materials.

Library binding. A specially strong binding to enable library books to withstand considerable use. This is achieved by a number of means, but particularly by guarding sections, sewing the sections on tapes and using specially durable cloth.

Library boards. *See* Trustees.

Library/Book Fellows Program. A system of grants to place US library and publishing professionals in working situations overseas; jointly administered by the American Library Association and USINFO.

Library Campaign. <www.librarycampaign.co.uk> (22 Upper Woburn Place, London WC1H 0TB, UK) A UK pressure group which seeks to increase awareness of the importance of library services, monitor local campaigns, and oppose financial constraints. In 1988 a part-time paid Campaign Director was appointed to develop activities and lobby more extensively. Holds an annual conference; issues *The Library Campaigner* (3 p.a.).

Library clerk. One who performs duties involving simple tasks related to library functions but limited to strict adherence to specific routines and procedures. The work is carried out under close supervision of a librarian or Library technical assistant (US).

Library collection. The total accumulation of material of all kinds assembled by a library for its clientele. Also called 'Library holdings', 'Library resources'.

Library committee. The committee responsible for the provision of a library service.

Library consultant. An individual offering a range of professional skills and advice relevant to the operation of libraries. Usually these skills will be marketed on a commercial basis by a Freelance self-employed person who is not directly employed by the library concerned, but who may be retained on contract for a fee. The term Information consultant is loosely used to cover this and other types of consultancy occupations.

Library co-operation. *See* Co-operation.

Library corner. (*Binding*) The turning in of cloth at the corners of books so as to take up the excess in two diagonal folds, one under each turn-in. In this way the cloth is not cut, and the corner given additional strength. *See also* Mitred, Square corner.

Library Council/An Chomhairle Leabharlanna. <www.iol.ie/ ~libcounc> (53–54 Upper Mount Street, Dublin 2, Ireland) A Republic of Ireland body set up in 1947 by the Public Libraries Act; in 1997 the Local Government (The Library Council) Regulations list its function as: to advise and assist local authorities in the improvement of the public library service, to make recommendations to the Minister for the Environment and Local Government in relation to the public library service, to maintain and operate the Central Library (*see* Irish Central Library), and to promote and facilitate library co-operation. The Council carries out research, collects data and statistics, and provides the secretariat for COLICO.

Library discount. Discount on the cost of books purchased for a library.

Library economy. The practical application of library science to the founding, organizing and administering of libraries.

Library edition. 1. A vague term indicating the edition of a book, series or set of books, often all the works of an author, in a substantial and uniform format to distinguish it from another less substantial edition, possibly in paper covers. Sometimes called 'Cabinet edition'. 2. An edition printed on good paper and in a specially strong binding for library use.

Library hand. A handwriting used by librarians with the object of achieving uniformity and legibility in manuscript catalogues and other records. The formation of letters and the slope were determined with clarity in mind, and many librarians used this handwriting before the use of typewriters became common.

Library History Group. *See* Library and Information History Group.

Library holdings. *See* Library collection.

Library Improvement Act. 1988 United States legislation. *See* Library law.

Library Information Technology Centre (LITC). <rigel.soi.city.ac.uk/litc> LITC provided independent advice and information on all aspects IT in libraries, and issued well-regarded publications such as *VINE* and *Library & Information Briefings*. In 2002 it moved from its base at South Bank University, London to City University; its current role is unclear.

Library instruction. *See* User education.

Library law. The legal framework that establishes and governs libraries, especially public libraries, in any given country or state. In the UK, public library legislation began with the *Public Library Act 1850* which was adoptive, and covered England and Wales; this was extended to Scotland in 1853. Improved provision came with the Act of 1855, and amendment Acts of 1866 and 1867. Legislation in 1887 replaced all previous Acts for Scotland, and the position in England and Wales was consolidated by the *Public Libraries Act 1892*, with amendment in 1893, *Public Libraries Act 1908*, *Public Libraries Act 1919*; in 1964 the *Public Libraries and Museums Act* replaced earlier legislation and remains the current Act covering England and Wales. (For preliminary work on this Act *see* Baker Report, Bourdillon Report, Roberts Report.)

In the USA, the *Library Services and Technology Act* (*LSTA*) of 1996 renews and reorganizes provisions contained in the earlier *Library Services and Construction Act* and the *Higher Education Act* (Title II); the new Act controls public library activities, state library services, and interlending; it also authorized an Institute for Museum and Library Services (IMLS). The *Elementary and Secondary Education Act* Title II School Library Resources, and the *Medical Library Assistance Act* are other important statutes. The 1988 *Library Improvement Act* sought to increase library impact on education and learning, especially to the disadvantaged and handicapped, and promote resource sharing and research support (*See also* NCLIS). Each State also has its own legislation covering libraries.

Library Literature. <www.hwwilson.com> An index to the literature of librarianship and information science, published by the H. W. Wilson

Company. *Library Literature* first appeared in 1934, produced by the American Library Association's Junior Members Round Table, and covered 1921–32. H. W. Wilson Company took it over thereafter. It covers 300 periodicals with online access to material from 1984 onwards. Full text indexing was introduced in 1997, and there is a Web version as well as other formats.

Library management. Libraries and information services have become more involved in management practices as their parent organizations have adopted systematic approaches to management. This has applied through the whole range of services – local authorities, educational institutions, industrial, commercial and professional firms, and voluntary bodies. The general starting point will be the overall objectives of the parent body, particularly in respect of the community that it serves. As the environment of most organizations has changed in response to political and financial pressures, clarity of aims has improved, and libraries and information services must relate closely to those aims. Library management will therefore involve implementation of strategies in line with those of the organization, and will cover setting of priorities, justification of resources, and evaluation of risk and performance. These will be achieved by demonstrating understanding of user needs, by budgeting for efficient practice, and by motivation of staff. Management of staff and good leadership will include human resource planning, recruitment and selection of staff, training and development, supervision and interpersonal skills. Understanding of problems, resolving difficulties, and ensuring the smooth running of the infrastructure are also important aspects of management.

Library of Congress (LC). <www.loc.gov> (101 Independence Avenue, Washington, DC 20540, USA) The Library of Congress provides library and information services by authority of Congress, is responsible to Congress for giving priority in its services to Congress, and although not officially a national library provides services appropriate to a national library, and at a higher level than most other specifically designated national libraries. Aims to develop a comprehensive national collection of printed literature, maps, films, music, audio-visual materials and manuscripts. It is responsible for the production of the national bibliography. LC has no interlending role, nor any role in library co-ordination although much has been achieved through voluntary co-operation. LC developed machine-readable cataloguing (MARC) databases for bibliographical records, is the national centre for the exchange of MARC data, and the national agency for CIP, ISBNs and ISSNs.

The Library contains some 128 million items (of which there are 29 million books and 57 million manuscripts) as well as extensive collections of photographs, sound recordings and maps. It operates the US Copyright Office, the Program for Co-operative Cataloging (*see*

PCC), the National Digital Infrastructure and Preservation Program (usually known as the Digital Preservation Program) to collect, archive and preserve digital content, and the THOMAS legislative information system <thomas.loc.gov>.

Library of Congress card. A printed catalogue card on which a full catalogue entry is given, also notes, tracings, and Dewey and L. of C. classification numbers. Such cards have been issued by the Library of Congress since 1901, and are available for purchase. Each card bears a serial number which is used by libraries when ordering printed cards for their catalogues. These numbers are printed in the respective books if published in the USA, usually on the back of the title-page. *See also* Cataloguing in Publication.

Library of Congress Classification. The scheme of classification used in the Library of Congress. The outline of the scheme was drawn up by Dr. Herbert Putnam, in 1897, and is based in some respects on the Dewey Decimal and Cutter's Expansive schemes, the schedules being worked out by specialists in the various subjects. The main tables have been published, each with its own relative index, as completed, and revised from time to time. The result is a series of special schedules of greater detail than any other scheme. The outline, which is purely arbitrary, is as follows:

A	General Works, Polygraphy
B	Philosophy, Religion
C	Auxiliary Sciences of History
D	Universal and Old World History [and Topography] (*except* America)
E–F	American History
G	Geography, Anthropology. Folklore. Manners and Customs. Sports and Games
H	Social Sciences. Economics. Sociology
J	Political Science
L	Education
M	Music
N	Fine Arts
P	Language and Literature
PN–PZ	Literary History. Literature
Q	Science
R	Medicine
S	Agriculture. Plant and Animal Industry. Fish Culture and Fisheries. Hunting. Sports
T	Technology
U	Military Science
V	Naval Science
Z	Bibliography and Library Science.

The scheme does not conform to the theoretical rules for classification, being compiled to meet the needs of the library's huge collection of books. It typifies the enumerative method of classification and retains all powers of growth in the hands of the compiler. It is too detailed and complex for use in any but the largest library but the subject schedules are most useful for special and university libraries. There are no tables for sub-division by form or place which can be used in any part of the scheme. The notation is mixed, consisting normally of two letters and four figures used arithmetically, blanks being left in the alphabet and in the numbers for future insertions. The schedules are undergoing constant amendments and updating.

Library of Congress Subject Headings. *See* Subject headings.

Library orientation. *See* User education.

Library privilege. A non-legal term to describe the various privileges enjoyed by libraries that are allowed to copy copyright material for various purposes without either a licence or the permission of the copyright owner.

Library purchasing consortia. Following the abandonment of the Net Book Agreement in the UK, many libraries formed consortia as a cost effective means of extending their purchasing capabilities and achieving economies of scale in book and periodical acquisition.

Library rate. The amount of money per unit of currency of rateable value of a local authority area which is required to provide a public library service.

Library Research Round Table (LRRT). A group within the American Library Association.

Library school. An expression used loosely to designate Schools or Departments of Information Studies, Information management and/or Librarianship, offering an organized course, or courses, attended by full-time and/or part-time students. It may be a separately managed institution in its own building but is usually a department of an institution for higher education, or a faculty within a university.

Library science. A generic term for the study of libraries and information units, the role they play in society, their various component routines and processes, and their history and future development.

Library Science Abstracts. *See Library and Information Science Abstracts.*

Library science classification. A fully faceted scheme, prepared in draft by members of the Classification Research Group (UK) and entitled *Classification of library science*, was published in 1965. An amended version of this scheme was used in *Library & Information Science Abstracts* until December 1992. A later version with the title *A classification of library and information science* was published in 1975.

Library service. The facilities provided by a library for the use of books, electronic and other materials and the dissemination of information.

Library Services and Construction Act. *See* Library law.

Library Services and Technology Act. *See* Library law.

Library stamp.   A rubber stamp bearing the name of the library; this is used to indicate the ownership of books, periodicals and other publications.

Library statistics.   The measurement of the success of library services. The evolution of digital and electronic services has led to a need for new systems for collection and analysis. NISO has been active in revising Z39.7 *Standard on Library Statistics* <www.niso.org/stats-rpt>; ICOLC and ARL has been similarly engaged. *See also* Metrics.

Library supplier.   A bookseller specializing in the supply of materials to libraries, and offering related Processing services.

Library technical assistant.   One whose duties are based on skills required by a library clerk, but, in addition, possesses a proficiency developed in one or more functional areas or in certain limited phases of library services. Such an assistant works under the supervision of a librarian, and may supervise and direct library clerks or clerical staff. *See also* Library clerk, Para-professional, Technician.

Library Technology Centre.   *See* Library Information Technology Centre.

Library Technology Program (LTP).   Established 1959 as the Library Technology Project, based at the American Library Association headquarters, and financed by grants from the Council on Library Resources. Promoted standardization of equipment, an evaluation programme, a research and development programme, and provided a technical information service. Retitled Library Technology Program in 1966; dissolved in 1972 and the staff and its publication *Library Technology Reports* transferred to the Library Administration and Management Association – a division of the American Library Association.

Library ticket.   One indicating membership of a library and serving as the authority for borrowing books.

Library trustees.   *See* Trustees.

Library Week.   A week designated by the principal library associations in a country, state, region, or internationally, for the promotion of public awareness of libraries and library services, by exhibitions, tours, events, media coverage, etc. *See also* National Libraries Week, National Library Week.

Librettist.   The author of the text of an opera or other extended choral composition.

Libretto.   The text to which an opera or other lengthy musical composition for voices is set.

Libri.   <www.libri.org.uk> (14 Basing Hill, London NW11 8TH, UK) A UK-based charity devoted to the improvement of public library services. In 2004 its report *Who's in charge* was highly critical of the current position and received wide media coverage.

Libri manuscripti.   Books written by hand, as were all books before the invention of printing.

LIBRIS.   <www.libris.kb.se> Library Information System; a bibliographic network serving some 70 Swedish research libraries, and responsible for the Swedish National Bibliography. Based in Stockholm, and established in 1972.

LIBTRAD. Abbreviation for the Working Party on Library and Book Trade Relations which was formed in London in 1965 to investigate and report on matters of common concern to publishers, booksellers and librarians. Biennial conferences, known as 'Holborn' conferences (after the place where they were held), have been organized to consider a problem area of general concern to libraries and the book trade.

Licence leaf. *See* Imprimatur (1).

Lichtdruck. A kind of Collotype.

Liddell Hart Centre for Military Archives. Opened 1964 at King's College, London, to provide a repository for military papers requiring confidentiality.

Lieferung. *See* Fascicle.

Lifelong learning. The process whereby people continue their own education by formal or informal means – training courses, academic courses, reading, evening classes, work-based activity, discussion groups etc. – which will be increasingly essential in an age of technological advance and an employment situation in which short-term contracts, self-employment and teleworking are expected to be common. In the UK, the government has placed great emphasis on lifelong learning <www.lifelonglearning.co.uk> and made it the centrepiece of its vision of a Knowledge-based economy and emerging Information society. The Museums, Libraries and Archives Council (MLA) has similarly stressed that libraries should highlight lifelong learning in their aims and strategies.

Lifelong Learning Sector Skills Council (LLLSSC). Proposed new base for ISNTO; employer consultation is taking place in 2004.

Lifted matter. Type or blocks removed from the forme and put on one side for use in other pages or in another job.

Ligature. Two or more letters joined together, or differing in design from the separate letters, and cast on one type body, as fi, fl to save space, avoid the unsightly juxtaposition of fi, fl, and to reduce the risk of damage to kerned letters; available as a compound character in Desktop publishing systems. The term also refers to the joining stroke which connects the characters. Also called 'Double letter', 'Tied letter'. *See also* Logotype.

Light face. The weight of Typeface which is lighter than medium – the ordinary book weight – having thinner strokes. The opposite of Bold face. Most type families are made in varying weights, usually called light, medium, bold, extra bold; but 'medium' is normally understood when referring to a typeface and is therefore only expressed when it is essential to distinguish it from the other weights.

Light-pen. A pen or stylus with a light sensor connected to a PC and used to capture the data on Bar-codes, particularly in library circulation control systems.

Lightweight paper. Sensitized photographic paper between 0.0044 and 0.0059 inches inclusive. *See also* Photographic papers.

Ligue des Bibliothèques Européennes de Recherche. *See* LIBER.

Likeness. The quality of similarity or alikeness which is used in classification in order to group together objects or ideas according to their likeness.

Lilliput edition. *See* Miniature book.

Limitation notice. The statement in a book published in a Limited edition indicating the number of copies printed which comprise the edition, or part of the edition. The statement would define the special character of the edition, such as printed on 'large paper' or hand-made paper, and provide for the number of the individual copy to be written in.

Limited cataloguing. A term used by the Library of Congress for the standard of descriptive cataloguing which began to be applied in 1951 by the Library of Congress to certain categories of books in order to speed up cataloguing processes. Limited cataloguing is practised in order to reduce the work and time involved in recording more details than are required to identify and locate works which are not of sufficient bibliographic and reference utility to compensate for the time expended.

Limited edition. An edition, printed on special paper and often with a special binding, which is printed in limited numbers (seldom more than 1,500, usually about 200 to 500, but often as few as ten) and sold at a higher price. Each copy bears a printed certificate (usually facing the title-page) indicating the size of the edition on which is written the actual copy number. Sometimes copies are signed by the author.

Limited Editions Club. A US subscription book club, founded in 1929 by George Macy, which produced well-designed and well-printed books.

Limp binding. Said of a book which is not bound in boards but with flexible cloth or leather.

Limp cloth. A term used to describe a style of publisher's binding. *See also* Limp covers.

Limp covers. Thin flexible book covers made of plastic, or of other material, without boards and covered with cloth or leather.

Limp leather. A full leather binding made without using stiff boards and therefore flexible. Often used for Bibles.

LINC. *See* Library and Information Co-operation Council.

Lindisfarne Gospels. *See* Bibles.

Line. 1. The imaginary base-line of a piece of movable type, running set-wise on or about which all the characters are positioned. *See also* Set (2). 2. A row of printed or written characters extending across a column or page. *See also* Measure. 3. A Fillet used in bookbinding. 4. Reproduction of a drawing which prints only solid areas and lines, there being no tones.

Line art. Graphics – freehand drawings, geometric shapes – that are created in black and white with no grey or colour. *See also* Line drawing.

Line block.   A metal printing block made photographically direct from a black and white drawing without any intermediate tones other than tints, and mounted type-high for letterpress printing. *See also* Zincograph (zinco).

Line copy.   A copy of a document which has no tone values. Also called 'Line reproduction'. *See also* Line original.

Line cut.   *See* Line engraving.

Line division mark.   A mark, usually a vertical or oblique line, used in bibliographical transcription to indicate the end of a line of type in the original.

Line drawing.   A black ink drawing made in line or stipple with Indian ink, pencil, crayon, or brush, from which a line block may be made. An impression of grey is achieved by using a tint.

Line end stroke.   *See* Line division mark.

Line engraving.   1. Engraving in which the effects are produced by lines of different width and proximity, cut into copper, steel, zinc or other similar material.   2. A plate produced by the line engraving process. 3. A picture printed from a line engraving.

Line etching.   *See* Etching.

Line management.   Line managers are those within an organization who have authority to take decisions affecting the organization. The antitheses are *staff* posts which have an advisory, data-collecting, information giving role, but cannot take decisions.

Line original.   An original document for copying, and having no tone values. A copy of such an original may be called a 'Line copy' or 'Line reproduction'.

Line printer.   A printer that produces output one line at a time, compared with one character at a time for Dot-matrix printers or one page at a time for Laser printers.

Line reproduction.   *See* Line original.

Lineale.   Styles of Typeface where the characters have no serifs. Such faces were formerly known as Sans serif. They may be sub-divided into Grotesque, Neo-grotesque, Geometric and Humanist.

Line-by-line-index.   An entry in an index, with its page or other reference, which is printed on a single line. Also known as an 'entry-a-line-index'. Where the entries consist of titles which are similarly confined to one line, it is known as a 'title-a-line index'.

Line-casting machine.   A type-casting machine which casts a line of type in one slug. Intertype and Linotype are machines of this kind.

Lined.   Said of a book which has a piece of material (strips of parchment which overlapped the joints and were pasted down under the end-papers of seventeenth- and eighteenth-century bindings) lining the spine to give it strength.

Line-ending.   1. Term used to indicate the last letter of a line of type when giving an exact bibliographical description of a title-page, the ending of each line being indicated by a vertical or oblique stroke or two such strokes.   2. An ornament (of which there are a great variety) filling the space at the end of a line in a mediaeval illuminated manuscript. Also called 'line-filling'.

Line-filling.   *See* Line-ending (2).

Linen.   A cloth made from flax for covering books.

Linen faced.   Paper with a linen finish on one or both sides.

Linen finish.   Paper, the surface of which is made to resemble linen by placing it between plates of zinc and sheets of linen under pressure. *See also* Crash finish.

Linen grained.   A book-cloth which is patterned to resemble linen.

Linen paper.   1. Paper made from rags; originally from linen rags. 2. Linen faced.

Linguistic numbers.   *See* Ethnic numbers.

Lining.   A piece of material, usually mull, placed in the spine of a book when binding to give it strength. Also called 'Back-lining'. *See also* First lining, Second lining, Triple lining.

Lining, ornamental inside.   *See* Doublure (1).

Lining figures.   (*Printing*) Arabic numerals which do not have ascenders or descenders, but which are the same size as capital letters, stretching from base-line to cap line thus: 1234567890. Also called 'Ranging figures'. *See also* Hanging figures.

Lining paper.   1. That portion of an endpaper which is pasted down on the inner cover of a book. The other portion of the endpaper is known as the 'free endpaper'. *See also* Endpaper.   2. Coloured or marbled paper used as an Endpaper.

Lining-up table.   *See* Register table.

Link.   The connection between Web pages established through HTML permitting the exploration of related material.

Link checker.   A program that tests and reports on the validity of hypertext links on Web pages, particularly those links that have been made to external Web sites. It may be a separate, specialized, program, part of a larger program that provides a range of Web services, or provided periodically as a service from a remote application server. *See also* Persistence.

Link resolver.   *See* OpenURL, Resolver.

Linked books.   Separately bound books where the relationship is indicated in various ways, such as collective or series title-pages; continuous paging, series or signatures; mention in contents or other preliminary leaves.

Linocut.   1. A piece of linoleum engraved by hand, mounted on a wooden block at type height and printed from as if from a woodcut. Linocut blocks are very durable and can be electrotyped. Illustrations comprising broad flat masses and bold lettering are suitable for this method.   2. The impression made from a linocut block.

Linofilm.   A photo-composing machine built by the Mergenthaler Linotype Co. of New York and first demonstrated in 1954.

Linoleum block. An engraved piece of linoleum from which a Linocut is made.

Linoleum drypoint. An impression made from a linoleum block on which the design has been made with a drypoint tool.

Linotype. A typesetting machine casting a line of type in a slug. It was invented by Ottmar Mergenthaler (1854–99). The machine carries a large number of single matrices in a magazine; these are released as the keyboard is operated and assembled in sequence with double-wedge spaces separating the words. The spaces are used to justify the completed line as it is brought to the orifice of a mould, and there cast in a type-high slug. Linotype machines have been in use since 1890, and were the kind most used for printing newspapers.

Linson. The trade name for a particularly tough variety of paper used extensively for publisher's casing. It can be embossed to represent linen and is available in a wide variety of colours and finishes. It is used as an alternative to cloth, being much cheaper.

Lint. Dust, or loose fibres, which separate from the raw material during paper-making.

Lippincott (Joseph W.) Award. Donated by Joseph W. Lippincott in 1937, this annual Award is made to a librarian for distinguished service in the profession of librarianship, such service to include outstanding participation in the activities of professional library associations, notable published professional writing, or other significant activity on behalf of the profession and its aims. The Award is administered by the American Library Association Awards Committee.

LIPs. Library and Information Plans are a UK series of surveys and analyses of regional library and information service provision, and provision in specified subject areas. There are over 20 geographic LIPs, and subject-based LIPs in music, law, visual arts.

LIRG. *See* Library and Information Research Group.

LIS. *See* Library and information science.

LISA. *See Library and Information Science Abstracts*.

LISC. *See* Library and Information Services Council.

Lis-link. A general-purpose UK-based library and information science Mailing list where information and discussions relating to all aspects of the subject are posted. It is managed by staff at BUBL and delivered via JISCmail.

List. (*Archives*) The most common type of archival description, containing a short entry for each item within a Class.

List, publisher's. A list of books published by one publisher and still in print.

List of contents. A contents-list or list of 'preliminaries'. *See* Contents.

List of illustrations. This follows the 'Table of contents' and indicates the position in the book of the illustrations, both full-page and 'in the text'. *See also* Preliminaries.

List of signatures. *See* Register (2).

List price. The price of a book as quoted by the publisher in a catalogue.

Listserv. <www.lsoft.com/products/default.asp?item=listserv> A widely used, US-originated, mail server program frequently used when setting up Mailing lists. It allows users to create and maintain e-mail lists on their corporate network or on the Internet and supports newsletters, moderated and unmoderated discussion groups and direct marketing campaigns. List sizes can range from a few participants in a discussion group to several million in a newsletter. *See also* JISCmail.

LISU. *See* Library and Information Statistics Unit.

LITA. Library and Information Technology Association – a division of the American Library Association.

LITA/Library Hi Tech Award. An annual award made by the Library and Information Technology Association (LITA) of the American Library Association and sponsored by Pierian Press; the award recognizes outstanding communication for continuing education in library and information science.

LITC. *See* Library Information Technology Centre.

Literacies. *See* Literacy.

Literacy. The ability to read and write. More recently, the term 'literacies' is used to indicate a range of practical skills associated with information. *See* Information literacy; *compare* Competencies.

Literacy decade. *See* United Nations Literacy Decade.

Literal. An error made in setting type, usually through confusion of similar letters or an unclear manuscript, and involving no more than a letter-for-letter correction, such as a full point for a comma, or a transposition.

Literal mnemonics. *See* Mnemonics.

Literary agent. One who arranges the sale and publication of authors' work with publishers of books, newspapers and periodicals, and who negotiates subsidiary rights such as dramatic, broadcasting, and film rights. An agent also acts for publishers by arranging for the writing of scripts which they need. The author pays the agent on a commission basis.

Literary Guild. One of the original American book clubs; it manufactured its own editions.

Literary manuscript. A record or document produced by hand and indicating literary rather than textual excellence. Also called 'Textual manuscript'. *See also* Artistic manuscript.

Literary property. The product of an author's creative effort in the form of manuscripts or published work which have an existing or potential financial value. *See also* Intellectual property.

Literary warrant. 1. The volume of books which have been written on any topic. 2. (*Classification*) The quantity of expressed and embodied knowledge in any given field, waiting to be organized.

Literary work. A work, other than a Sacred work, written in a literary form, e.g. a poem, drama, novel, etc. and having outstanding qualities such as beauty of form, emotional or intuitive appeal.

Literature review.   A survey of progress in a particular aspect of a subject area over a given period (e.g. one, five, or ten years); it may range from a bibliographical index or mere list of references, to a general critical review of original publications on the subjects covered.

Literature search.   A systematic and exhaustive search for published material on a specific subject, together with the preparation of annotated bibliographies or abstracts for the use of the researcher. This is an intermediate stage between reference work and research, and is differentiated from both. It is often the first step in a research project, patent search, or laboratory experiment and sometimes reveals that the proposed action is unnecessary, having been carried out previously by others; if this is not the case the search usually gives valuable information on similar or identical work previously undertaken.

Literature survey.   1. A bibliography relating to a specific subject and listing material either in a given collection, or in more than one library, or literature on the subject.   2. A listing, with full bibliographical references, of recently published books and articles on a given subject. It serves to keep those to whom it is circulated up-to-date in the literature of the subjects with which they are concerned. Brief annotations are often provided.

Litho crayon.   A special crayon for drawing on lithographic plates.

Litho papers.   Papers made especially for lithographic printing. Made basically from esparto, they have dimensional stability to ensure correct register, and are usually placed the narrow way across the printing machines, for any stretch must be the narrow way of the sheet.

Lithograph.   A print or illustration produced by Lithography.

Lithographic press.   A press for printing from a lithographic stone or plate. It is similar in appearance to a Stop-cylinder press used for bookwork, and operates in much the same way.

Lithographic printing.   A planographic printing process whereby the areas of the printing surface (the non-image areas) are hydrophilic (i.e. have an affinity for water) and the printing (image) areas are hydrophobic (i.e. repel water and attract grease). *See also* Lithography.

Lithography.   The process of drawing designs on stone with a special greasy crayon, chalk, paint or ink, and of producing printed impressions therefrom; also any process based on the same principle in which a thin flexible metal plate or plastic is used instead of stone. The stone is saturated with water, the printing ink is then applied and adheres only to those portions covered by the crayon or other drawing medium. A separate drawing is required for each colour in the resulting print. In direct lithography the drawing is in reverse; in offset lithography the drawing is first made the right way round on transfer paper, printed on to a rubber-covered cylinder and 'offset' on to the paper. Lithography was invented by Aloys Senefelder, a Bavarian, in 1798. From the Greek *Lithos* = stone. *See also* Auto-lithography, Offset lithography, Offset printing, Photo-lithography, Photo-offset.

Lithogravure. A process of photo-engraving on stone.

Litho-offset. *See* Lithography, Offset printing.

Lithophotography. *See* Photo-lithography.

Lithoprint. *See* Offset printing.

Lithotint. An obsolete method of lithography by which the effect of a tinted drawing was produced. Also a picture so produced.

Litterae Venetiae. *See* Bolognese letters.

Live matter. A form of letterpress or illustrations, ready for printing, electrotyping or stereotyping. It may be held for future use. *See also* Matter, Standing type.

Livres à vignettes. Books printed in the eighteenth century which were illustrated by vignette copper-plate engravings. The kind of engraving used was a mixture of etching with some gravure work.

LIW. Library and information work; employment in the area of Library and information science.

LIWO. Library and Information Workers Organization. South African librarianship organization; unlike SAILIS and ALASA, LIWO has not merged into the newly formed Library and Information Association of South Africa (LIASA).

LIWW. *See Librarianship and Information Work Worldwide.*

ll. Abbreviation for leaves of a book, lines of type, *leges* (laws).

LLDA. *See* London Library Development Agency.

Llyfrgell Genedlaethol Cymru. *See* National Library of Wales.

Loaded paper. *See* Coated paper.

Loading. The adding of clay, chalk, or similar materials to Stuff when in the beater of a paper making machine, or flowed into the stock as it goes through the sluice-gate of the Fourdrinier machine. It fills the spaces between fibres and so imparts solidity to the paper and provides a better printing surface.

Loan. A book, or a number of books, on loan to an individual, a group of persons, an institution or a library.

Loan collection. A collection of books, prints or pictures which are available for use at home as distinct from a collection which may only be referred to on the premises.

Loan period. The period which is allowed for reading a book away from a library.

loc cit. Abbreviation for *loco citato* (Lat. 'in the place already cited'). Used in a footnote reference to avoid using the title or short title of the periodical referred to.

Local area network (LAN). A data transmission system linking computers and other devices within a particular spatial or geographical area to enable the communication between all users and the sharing of Applications and Peripherals such as printers. *See also* Metropolitan area network, Wide area network.

Local authority. The unit of administration in Britain which is responsible for providing, either on its own behalf and as it is entitled to do by law, or on behalf of the central government, certain services within the area of its geographical boundaries. Not all of the various services may be provided by each kind of local authority. A local authority with power to provide public libraries is called a Library authority.

Local bibliography. A bibliography of books and other forms of written record relating to a limited geographical area. It normally includes books by and about people born in, or who have resided in, the area, as well as books relating strictly to the geography, natural history, architecture and social history of the area.

Local collection. A collection of books, maps, prints, illustrations and other material relating to a specific locality, usually that in which the library housing the collection is situated. *See also* Local Government (Records) Act, 1962.

Local directory. A directory relating to a specified locality; it may be limited in scope, but usually includes particulars of residents and businesses, the entries being arranged in street order with 'trade' entries in classified order in addition.

Local Government Act, 1966. This UK Act is known particularly for its Section 11, which is the legislation concerned with projects dealing with ethnic populations in the UK, including multicultural library and information provision.

Local Government Act, 1972. (*Archives*) This UK Act governs the management of archives of local authorities in England and Wales, repealing for this purpose the Local Government Act 1933. 'Principal councils' are required to make 'proper arrangements' for 'any documents which belong to or are in the custody of the council'. Provision is also made for the custody of parish archives. Relevant text is published in *Archivum* XXVIII, pp. 388–391.

Local Government (Records) Act, 1962. (*Archives*) This UK Act empowers certain local authorities to undertake responsibilities in acquiring and managing archival accumulations relating to their areas. Normally these are counties; other authorities must have authorization from the Secretary of State for the Environment. The powers given are to promote use of archives, to acquire on deposit or by purchase, to set up supervising committees, and to spend funds on the maintenance of archives relevant to the area. The main provisions are assumed in subsequent general Local Government legislation. The text of this Act is published in *Archivum* XVII, pp. 195–198.

Local Government Standards Body. <www.localegov-standards.org> Set up in the UK in 2003 to provide access to authoritative best practice on local service interoperability standards; it works on the analysis and development of standards, and scrutiny of e-government projects.

Local list. 1. A list of places which may be used to permit sub-division by place in a scheme of classification. 2. A list of books relating to a particular locality.

Local Public Records. Records subject to the (UK) Public Records Acts which were created and held in local areas, e.g. the records of Crown Courts, or Health Authorities. The Lord Chancellor may appoint special places of deposit for these, but normally local record offices are appointed for this purpose.

Local Studies Group. A membership group of CILIP, formed in 1977 and concerned with the furtherance of local history libraries, staff development, and conservation issues. Publishes *Local Studies Librarian* (2 p.a.).

Location. 1. The place on the shelves or elsewhere in which required material may be found. It is indicated on records by the Location mark. 2. That part of an index entry which enables the user to locate the document, or part of a document, to which the entry refers. It may be a book, line, column, page, abstract, patent, report, accession number, classification number, or a more or less complete bibliographic citation.

Location mark. A letter, word, group of words or symbols used on a catalogue entry, book list or bibliography, sometimes in conjunction with the Call number, to indicate the collection, library or position at which the book or item in question is shelved. Also called 'Location symbol'.

Location register. A collection, or list, of records of books, documents, or other items, which are arranged by the Fixed location method or in a Closed access library. The arrangement of the items on the register may be by author, title, or accession number.

Location symbol. *See* Location mark.

Locative abstract. *See* Abstract (3).

Locking up. (*Printing*) Tightening up a forme of type matter in the metal frame known as a chase, preparatory to putting it on the press.

locus sigilli. (Lat. 'the place of the seal') Usually abbreviated LS and printed within a circle at the place for a signature on legal documents.

LOEX. <www.emich.edu/public/loex/loex.html> Library Orientation Exchange, a self-supporting, non-profit educational clearinghouse for library instruction information that began in 1971 through the Conference on Library Orientation. The Exchange provides information on all aspects of instruction to libraries and librarians who are institutional members via a collection of print materials, instructional video and audio tapes, CD-ROMs and Internet sites. Over 600 member libraries in the United States, Canada, the Caribbean, Europe, Australia, the Middle East, and South Africa.

Loft-dried. Hand- or mould-made papers which are dried by suspension in a dry, airy loft.

Log. A registry of items, e.g. on an accession list.

Log off. *See* Login.

Log on. *See* Login.

Log out. *See* Login.

Logical arrangement. (*Cataloguing*) A departure from the normal alphabetical order so as to arrange entries by principles associated with the subject matter or type of the entries, e.g. chronological, hierarchical, numerical.

Logical notation. One in which each symbol of a classification scheme may be divided without limit by a sequence of similar symbols, each having the same value but representing a further step in the sub-division of the subject as represented by the preceding symbol or group of symbols.

Logical sequence. *See* Logical arrangement.

Login. Also, Log on, the act of gaining access to a computer or network, usually requiring the entering of Username and Password. The closing operation or routine is termed 'log off' or 'log out'. *See also* Remote access, Remote login.

Logo. Shortened form of 'logotype', a symbol, design or organization name set in a special Typeface and intended for easy identification of the organization and its products and to be used on stationery and packaging. *See also* Masthead.

Logogram. An initial letter or number used as an abbreviation.

Logograph. A symbol that stands for a whole word.

Logographic writing. The earliest form of picture writing in which a single symbol was used to represent an entire word.

Logography. A method of casting logotypes. It was first patented by Henry Johnson in 1780 who had a font of 3,500 words and syllables, but the idea never developed owing to opposition from compositors of the time.

Logotype. Several letters, or a word, cast on one type, or as a single matrix. Used in the printing of directories or other works in which such combinations are frequently repeated. *See also* Ligature.

LOM. *See* Learning Object Metadata.

Lombardic handwriting. An offshoot of the Italian semi-cursive minuscule which was derived from the roman cursive style used throughout Italy in the seventh to ninth centuries. *See also* Cursive, Handwriting.

London Declaration. The Unesco World Congress on Books held in London, 7–11 June 1982 and attended by representatives of 86 countries issued a declaration under the heading 'Towards a Reading Society', and endorsed a series of recommendations which seek to create an environment in which the role of the book is reinforced. The text of the Declaration is given in the *Library Association Record* vol. 84, no. 6, (June), 1982, page 213.

London Education Classification (LEC). A faceted classification scheme designed for use in the library of the University of London Institute for Education in 1962. The second edition, 1974, referred to as LEC 2, is a thesaurus/classification and was used as the basis for the EUDISED Multilingual Thesaurus.

London Library. <www.londonlibrary.co.uk> (14 St. James's Square, London SW1Y 4KG, UK) Founded in 1841 as a private subscription library to serve the needs of scholars by lending books for use at home; Thomas Carlyle was a principal figure in its conception, as he with others was dissatisfied with the library of the British Museum. The library is still a private institution, entirely self-supporting, and its members are mainly individuals. It is incorporated by Royal Charter. It has occupied its present building since 1845; substantial extensions are in progress, and a computerized catalogue is being introduced.

London Library Development Agency (LLDA). <www.llda.org.uk> A body first proposed in the report *London: Library City* (Comedia, 1996) to improve co-operation and networking between the huge number and variety of libraries within the London area. A feasibility study was carried out on behalf of the Association of London Government, and appeared late in 1998. (Vision Research Consortium. *Feasibility Study to Establish a London Library Development Agency.* BLRIC Report 142) LLDA acts as a co-ordinator for the strategic vision of libraries in the London area, and operates a Gateway to library provision throughout the city. In 2001 it collaborated with the London Museums Agency and the London Regional Archives Council to form London Museums, Archives and Libraries – renamed 2004 as ALM London (*see* Museums, Libraries and Archives Council (MLA)).

London Metropolitan Archives. Formerly Greater London Record Office, responsible for the archives of the Greater London Council, and for the collections previously held by the GLRO.

London Union Catalogue. The union catalogue of the (London) Metropolitan Public Libraries. From 1 November 1934 until the reorganization of the London boroughs on 1 April 1965 it was controlled by the Metropolitan Boroughs Standing Joint Committee, and administered by the Association of Metropolitan Chief Librarians on behalf of the MBSJC. It was maintained at the premises of the National Central Library, and although not strictly a regional bureau, functioned as one, arranging for the loan of books between the London libraries and other libraries throughout the country.

Long. *See* Broad, Oblong.

Long descender. Letters g, j, p, q and y with extra long descenders; these are available as alternatives in some faces as, for example, Linotype Caledonia and Times Roman. *See also* Ascender, Descender.

Long elephant. *See* Elephant.

Long grain. Paper in which the fibres lie in the longer direction of the sheet. *See also* Grain direction, Short grain.

Long letter. A character, such as f, j or k, which has either Ascender or Descender or both. *See also* Short letter, which has neither.

Long page. A page of a book with more lines of type than most of the others. *See also* Short page.

Long primer. An old name for a type size, about 10 point.

Long ream. 500 or 516 sheets of paper. *See also* Ream, Short ream.

Long-bodied type. Type which is cast on bodies larger than usual, e.g. 10 point on 12 point. This avoids the use of Leads.

Look-through. The examination of paper by holding it up against strong light. By this means, the dispersion of fibres can be seen, and consequently the strength of the paper judged; it is also a means of seeing whether the paper is laid or wove, and if its texture is marred by impurities. *See also* Wild look-through.

Loose.   A book, the sections of which are badly loosened from the case, the sewing having broken.

Loose back.   *See* Hollow back.

Loose leaf binding.   A binding which permits the immediate withdrawal and insertion of pages at any desired position, as in a ring binder.

Loose leaf catalogue.   *See* Sheaf catalogue.

Loose-leaf service.   A serial publication which is revised, supplemented, cumulated, and indexed by means of new replacement pages inserted in a loose-leaf binder; such publications are used where the latest statements and revisions of information are important. *See also* Serial service.

Los Alamos Eprint Archive.   Started in August 1991 at the Los Alamos National Laboratory of the US Department of Energy as a fully automated electronic archive and distribution server for research papers in the areas of physics and related disciplines, mathematics, non-linear sciences, computational linguistics, and neuroscience. The arXiv.org domain name was registered in December 1998 and is now used for all but historical purposes. *See* ArXiv.

Lower case letters (l.c.).   Minuscules or 'small' letters such as a.b.c.; those other than capitals. The name originated from the fact that printers kept their type in two large cases, one above the other, each divided into sections containing one Sort. The upper case contained the capital letters, majuscules, and the lower one the others. *See also* Capitals, Small capitals, Upper case letters.

Lower cover.   *See* Reverse cover.

Lower edge.   The Tail of a book. Also called 'Bottom edge', 'Tail edge'.

Lower margin.   *See* Tail margin.

Loxodrome.   *See* Portolan chart.

Lozenge.   (*Binding*) A diamond-shaped figure, or a square figure, placed on one of its corners; it is usually decorated.

l.p.   Abbreviation for Large paper copy or Edition.

LRRT.   *See* Library Research Round Table.

LS.   1. Abbreviation for Library Science.   2 *See locus sigilli*.   3. *See* A.L.S.

LSA.   *See Library and Information Science Abstracts.* ·

LSCA.   Library Services and Construction Act (US). *See* Library law.

LTP.   *See* Library Technology Program.

LTSN.   <www.ics.ltsn.ac.uk> The Learning and Teaching Support Network was set up in 2000 by the UK Higher Education funding bodies to promote high quality learning and teaching. There are 24 subject centres and a generic learning and teaching centre. The Information and Computer Sciences (ICS) centre is split between the University of Ulster for computer science and the University of Loughborough for information and library science. As of 1 May 2004, became part of the Higher Education Academy <www.heacademy.ac.uk>.

Lubetzky Code. A draft, issued in 1960, under the title of *Code of Cataloguing rules, author and title entry.* This was written on entirely fresh lines (but firmly grounded in the Panizzi and Cutter traditions) under the direction of the (US) Catalog Code Revision Committee. Seymour Lubetzky was at the time the specialist in bibliographic and cataloguing policy at the Library of Congress.

Ludlow. A machine which casts slugs for display work. Composing is done by hand, a special composing stick being used; when the characters are all in position, the stick is placed into the machine which casts a line as a slug. It is frequently used in conjunction with the Elrod machine which casts rules, leads, borders and plain slugs.

Lumbecking. The Perfect, or flexible, method of binding whereby the separate sheets are not kept together by sewing but by adhesive only.

Luminotype. The original name for the Ühertype photocomposing machine.

Lumitype. A method of Filmsetting.

Lurk. To view, without contributing, to electronic Mailing lists, Chat rooms or Usenet Discussion groups.

Lutheran Church Library Association (LCLA). <www.lclahq.org> Founded in 1958 in the USA 'to promote the growth of church libraries in Lutheran congregations by publishing a quarterly journal, *Lutheran Libraries*, furnishing booklists, assisting member libraries with technical problems, providing meetings for mutual encouragement, assistance and exchange of ideas among members'.

Lux. The metric measurement of light value, one lumen or foot-candle being equal to 10.76 lux. An illumination of 300–500 lux is appropriate for library study areas and for the use of PCs in libraries.

Luxury binding. *See* De luxe binding.

l.v. Abbreviation for *locis variis* (Lat. 'various places').

Lyonese (Lyonnaise) Style. A style of binding with broad interlaced geometrical strapwork usually painted, lacquered, or enamelled in different colours; so called because it appeared on books bound at Lyons in the latter part of the sixteenth century. Also a style in which the binding is decorated with large corner ornaments and with a prominent centre design, roughly lozenge shaped, the all-over background being filled in with dots.

M. 1. Abbreviation for *million* in computing terminology. 2. Roman figure for 1000 used as an abbreviation by printers.

M25 Consortium of Higher Education Libraries. <www.M25lib.ac.uk> Formed in 1993 to promote co-operation and co-ordination into the complex variety of higher education provision – large universities, specialist institutions, international research centres, medical schools, new multi-site universities etc. – situated within an area defined for convenience by London's M25 orbital motorway. In 2002 the Consortium launched CPD25 – a training and staff development initiative for members.

M25 Link.   An eLib Clump project that developed into the InforM25 virtual union catalogue.

MAAS Media Online.   <www.bufvc.ac.uk/maas> Managing Agent and Advisory Service for Moving Pictures and Sound, a national body formed by the British Universities Film and Video Council and the Open University which is acquiring moving pictures and sound for delivery to the UK higher and further education community. Initially content is being provided through Education Media OnLine.

McColvin Medal.   <www.cilip.org.uk> Part of the CILIP/Nielsen Bookdata Awards series; the awards recognize outstanding reference materials in print and electronic formats.

McColvin Report.   The report: *The Public library system of Great Britain*, including proposals for post-war development, by L. R. McColvin (Library Association, 1942).

Machine coated.   (*Paper*) Paper which has been coated with clay or a similar substance during the actual making of the paper to give it a smooth printing surface. When the coating is applied as a separate and later operation, it is called 'brush coated'.

Machine code.   Information in the physical form that a computer can handle. Also known as machine language.

Machine direction.   The direction in which paper travels through a paper-making machine. Most of the fibres lie in this direction; therefore paper folds more easily along the machine direction (said to be 'with the grain'), and a sheet of paper when wetted expands mainly across this direction, with a corresponding shrinkage of the paper on drying. *See also* Against the grain, Grain direction.

Machine dried.   *See* Cylinder dried.

Machine finish (MF).   Paper which has been made smooth, but not glossy, by receiving the normal finish of a Fourdrinier paper-making machine: this passes the paper over heated drums and through steel calendering rollers. This is the normal paper for letterpress printing where half-tones are not to be used. *See also* Paper finishes.

Machine glazed (MG).   Said of a paper in which the 'glaze' or polish is produced on the paper-making machine, and not by means of super-calenders or a glazing machine. The only paper-machine which glazes in the process of making is the single-cylinder machine or 'Yankee' in which the web of paper is dried on the one large steam-heated cylinder with a highly polished surface. Machine-glazed papers are identified by being glazed on only one side (the under), the other being in the rough condition to which it comes from the wet end of the machine. Papers made on such machines are very varied in character and uses, for example manillas for envelopes, litho, poster, kraft and sulphite bag papers and cheap wrappings and tissues.

Machine indexing. A process whereby the indexing processes are accomplished by mechanized means.

Machine language. *See* Machine code.

Machine made paper. The continuous web, or roll, of paper made on cylinder machines or on the Fourdrinier machine.

Machine proof. A proof taken when corrections which were marked on galley and page proofs have been made, and the forme is on the printing machine. This proof affords the last opportunity for correcting mistakes before machining takes place. Also called 'Press revise'.

Machine readable. Information in a form that can be directly interpreted and used by a computer.

Machine revise. A proof printed when the forme is on the printing machine, in order that a comprehensive revise may be made of the whole of the details of workmanship, including those which the reader has not had an opportunity of verifying. Also called 'Machine proof'.

Machine translation. Automatic translation by computer from one natural language to another. *See also* Mechanical translation.

Machine wire. *See* Wire.

Machining. (*Printing*) 1. That part of printing concerned with actually printing on the paper. The other major processes in producing a book are composition and binding. Called 'Press work' in the US. 2. The actual process of printing by running the forme through the machine to give the paper an impression from the printing surface.

Mackle. A printed sheet with a blurred impression, owing to some mechanical defect in the printing.

Macro. (*Computing*) A group of individual operations combined into a single sequence and which can be called into play with a single keystroke. Facilities are incorporated into some Applications such as Spreadsheets and Word processors and 'stand alone' packages exist.

Macro-appraisal. (*Archives*) Techniques developed in the US whereby Appraisal of large quantities of records can be carried out by a management process involving the analysis of the functions of the creator organization.

Macro-description. (*Archives*) In *MAD* terminology, a description of an archival entity at a higher level, usually Group or Series, dealing with the entity as a whole, and governing a more detailed case-by-case description of the levels below, usually Item.

MAD. *See Manual of Archival Description.*

Made-up copy. A book which has had imperfections made good by the insertion of portions from other copies of the same edition.

Made-up set. A work in a number of volumes which is made up by assembling volumes of more than one edition. It is catalogued as a regular set except that the various editions are specified in a note unless they can be mentioned in the body of the entry.

Magazine. 1. A periodical publication as distinct from a newspaper, separate issues being independently paginated and identified by date rather than by serial number. 2. A receptacle above the keyboard of a Linotype, or similar type-casting machine, for containing the matrices ready for assembling into lines of type or slugs. 3. A container for the automatic projection of photographic slides. 4. A container for roll microfilm which both protects the film and facilitates its loading into a reader.

Magazine case. A cover for periodicals, usually having some contrivance for holding the magazine – cord, rod, etc. Also called 'Periodical case' and 'Reading case'.

Magazine rack. A fitting for displaying magazines.

Magnetic disk. *See* Disk.

Magnetic storage. A storage device that utilizes the magnetic properties of materials to store data, the most common implementation being floppy disks and hard disks.

Magnetic tape. Plastic tape coated with a magnetic material on which information can be recorded and identified by computers and other machines. *See also* DAT.

Mail merge. The automatic production of personalized letters incorporating personal name, address and other details from a standard letter and a database of clients. Mail merge features are integral to many Word processors.

Mailbase. <www.mailbase.ac.uk> A Mailing list service for UK higher education which began in 1989 at the University of Newcastle and from which all lists were migrated to JISCmail in November 2000.

Mailing lists. Co-ordinated electronic lists permitting exchange of ideas and views in subject-based open forums. End users must subscribe to the individual groups of interest, from which all communications then take place via E-mail. A list normally has a list owner who manages the list and generally steers its direction and usage, and moderators who read messages sent to the list to decide whether or not they should be posted. Contrasts with Usenet where prior 'registration' is not a pre-requisite for taking part in discussions. Also known as 'discussion lists'. *See also* JISCmail, Listserv.

Main card. The catalogue card bearing the Main entry.

Main class. The principal division of a scheme of classification, e.g. in Brown's Subject Classification: Matter, Life, Mind, Record; or Dewey's General works, Philosophy, Religion, Social Sciences, Language, Pure science, Technology, The Arts, Literature, History. These are divided into 'Divisions' which are divided into 'Subdivisions' which are in turn divided into 'Sections', each division proceeding by gradual steps, and each new heading becoming more 'intense'.

Main entry. 1. The basic catalogue entry; the main entry has the fullest particulars for the complete identification of a work. In card catalogues – especially dictionary ones – the main entry bears the Tracing. It may bear in addition the tracing of related references and a record of other pertinent official data concerning the work. For music, the entry under the composer's name.   2. The entry chosen for the basic entry, whether it be a personal or corporate name, or the title of an anonymous book, collection, composite work, periodical or serial, or a Uniform title.

Main heading.   1. (*Indexing*) A description sometimes used (for a heading) in contra-distinction to a subheading.   2. (*Cataloguing*) The first part of a composite heading which includes one or more subheadings. That part of a heading which precedes a subheading.

Main stroke.   The principal stroke, heavy line, or stem of a type letter.

Main subject.   A book may treat of several subjects, or may be considered by classifier or cataloguer to need cross references from a subsidiary to the one most important subject. The subject which is given priority and to which references are made is the 'main subject'.

Main title.   That part of the title which precedes the Sub-title.

Main title-page.   The title-page from which the details for a catalogue entry are taken. *See also* Added title-page, Half-title.

Mainframe.   A term indicating a computer with substantial processing power, generally the major one in an organization supporting hundreds of users running a variety of different programs simultaneously. With the distribution of computing and the increased processing power of minicomputers and PCs, mainframes are used less frequently; now needed only for the very largest applications.   A large, very fast mainframe used especially for scientific computations is a Supercomputer.

Maioli style.   The style of book decoration executed for Thomasso Maioli or Mahieu, (actually Thomas Matthieu a Frenchman) a contemporary of Grolier, in the middle of the sixteenth century. A distinguishing characteristic is that the Arabic ornaments are frequently in outline, whereas those of Grolier are ajuré, and of Aldus, solid. The style is generally composed of a framework of shields or medallions, with a design of scrollwork flowing through it, portions of the design usually being studded with gold dots.

Majuscule.   Large letter whether capital (upper case) or Uncial. *See also* Minuscule.

Make-ready (Making-ready).   The process of preparing a forme ready for printing. Levelling up and lining up by patching with paper, or cutting away on the impression cylinder or platen Bed and by underlaying or interlaying the blocks so that the impression from type and blocks on paper will be clear, clean and of uniform colour. The amount and position of make-ready is determined by a trial pull. The time which this process takes is an important item in every printing bill. It is upon the care with which a job is made-ready that the quality of the printing depends. Make-ready is of paramount importance in colour and half-tone work. *See also* Overlay, Underlay.

Make-up.   (*Printing*) 1. A general term for taking the type from the galleys, putting it into page form, insetting illustrative cuts, dividing the matter into page lengths, and adding running heads, titles of sub-divisions, folios, footnotes, etc., and securing with page-cord. The pages of type are then ready for locking in the Chase. 2. Sometimes used instead of 'layout' to indicate the dummy showing the desired arrangement of letterpress and illustrations. 3. A list of the contents of a book supplied by the publisher to the binder to serve as an instruction as to the positioning of plates, plans, folded leaves, map endpapers, etc. 4. (*Archives*) The particular method and order in which the leaves or membranes of a document are fastened together to constitute a complete volume or document, or the manner in which a single leaf or membrane is folded. *See also* Make-up copy, Publisher's binding.

Make-up copy. A set of folded sheets, plates, plans, etc. in correct order and sent by the publisher as an instruction to the binder. *See also* Make-up.

Making available right. A new (2003) right introduced to allow performers to control putting recordings of their performances on the Internet.

MALVINE. <www.malvine.org> Manuscripts and Letters via Integrated Networks in Europe; a multilingual EU project started in 1998 to search for modern manuscript holdings in European libraries. The co-ordinating partner is the Staatsbibliothek zu Berlin.

MAN. *See* Metropolitan area network.

Man Booker Prize. <www.themanbookerprize.co.uk> A high-profile UK literary prize for contemporary fiction, first awarded in 1969. The prize is currently £50,000 and is for the 'best novel of the year' from a British, Commonwealth or Republic of Ireland citizen.

Managed Learning Environment. *See* MLE.

Management. *See* Library management.

Management buyout. The process whereby the existing management of an organization purchases and takes over operation of that organization on the privatization of a public service, the sale of the company, or the financial failure of the previous ownership.

Management by Objectives. *See* Objectives.

Management group. (*Archives*) A set of Groups within a Repository that are described or managed together because they have some common feature. Holdings of repositories, for example, are often divided into management groups such as Public records, official archives, ecclesiastical archives, etc. Level 1 in *MAD* taxonomy of levels of description.

Management information system (MIS). A system designed to use all data collected by an organization to provide management with the inform-ation needed for decision making. *See also* Decision support system.

Managing Agent. In UK higher education, the name given to the intermediary appointed by JISC and who works on behalf of the community to secure a national deal with journal publishers, particularly in the case of electronic materials. Now called Negotiation Agent. *See also* NESLi2.

Manière criblée. A fifteenth-century 'relief' method of producing illus-trations by means of a plate of soft metal such as copper, pewter or zinc in which the drawing was made with a graver and which, being sunk below the level of the plate, would appear as white lines on a black ground when printed. Intermediate tones were produced by punching dots in the surface of the plate at more or less regular intervals. Also called 'Schrotblatt'.

Manilla paper.   A superfine tough quality of wrapping and label paper made from manilla hemp; also applied to cheap imitations made from wood pulp.

Mann (Margaret) Citation.   Instituted in 1950, and administered by the Cataloging and Classification Section of the Resources and Technical Services Division (now ALCTS) of the American Library Association, this citation is made to a librarian in recognition of distinguished contributions to librarianship through publication of significant professional literature, participation in professional cataloguing associations, or valuable contributions to practice in individual libraries.

Manorial courts.   Administrative and legal courts concerned with matters affecting a particular manor. The *Court Customary* was principally concerned with the agricultural organization of the township, while the *Court Leet* had a minor criminal jurisdiction.

Manorial documents.   Documents relating to manors and the management of estates. Manorial Documents Rules were made in 1926 (S. R. & O. 1926, No. 1310) to implement the provisions of the Law of Property Act, 1922, as amended, by which the Master of the Rolls has power to transfer manorial documents to the Public Record Office or a public library, museum, or historical or antiquarian society.

Manual.   *See* Handbook.

Manual input.   (*Information retrieval*) The insertion of data by hand into a machine or other device. *See also* Keyboard (2).

***Manual of Archival Description* (*MAD*).**   Cataloguing (description) guidelines for archives, originally prepared by the Archival Description Project at the University of Liverpool, 1986–1989. The third edition (2000) includes formats for the description of specialized archives such as sound archives and electronic archives, and incorporates a dictionary in line with the definitions agreed by the International Council on Archives in 1999.

Manuale.   A case to protect a Volumen. *See also* Capsa.

Manuscript (MS.).   (*Pl.* MSS.) A document of any kind which is written by hand, or the text of a music or literary composition in hand-written or typescript form, and which, in that form, has not been reproduced in multiple copies. An *illuminated manuscript* is one which has been decorated as described under Illuminated book.

Manuscript catalogue.   One written by hand.

Manuscript librarian.   A librarian who has charge of a collection of manuscripts of all kinds, i.e. unprinted materials (whether written by hand or typed) other than books written by hand before the invention of printing (*libri manuscripti*).

Manuscript music book.   A book of Music paper.

Manuscript note.   A handwritten note in a book.

Manuscript Society.   <www.manuscript.org> The Society was founded in 1948 as the National Society of Autograph Collectors, and has grown to an international membership of over 1,400, including dealers, private collectors, scholars, authors, and caretakers of public collections, such as librarians, archivists, and curators. There are also many institutional members, such as historical societies, museums, special libraries, and academic libraries. Publishes *Manuscripts* (q.), and a newsletter.

Map.   A plane representation of the earth's surface, or a part of same, indicating physical features, political boundaries, etc. Also a similar representation of the heavens, showing the position of the stars, planets, etc. Also called an 'Astronomical map'. The first book to contain a printed map or diagram of the whole world was Isidore of Seville's *Etymologiarum sive Originum libri XX*, Augsburg, 19 November 1472. The earliest and most important maps to be printed from engraved copper plates in England were those of Christopher Saxton, who issued county maps between 1574 and 1579. An 'early map' is considered to be one made before 1825.

Map Curators Group.   <www.cartography.org.uk> (Map Library, Edinburgh University Library, 43 George Square, Edinburgh EH8 9LJ, UK) The group is part of the British Cartographic Society and promotes good practice in its field. An Organization in Liaison (OiL) with CILIP.

Map endpapers.   Endpapers on which maps are printed. *See also* Endpaper.

Map file.   A sequence of sheet or folded maps arranged in classified order, or alphabetically by place name. Sheet maps are kept in shallow drawers, often with hinged fronts which fall down and so reduce wear when consulting the maps, or in specially made vertical cabinets. *See also* Plan cabinet.

Map paper.   *See* Plan paper.

Map projection.   The arrangement of parallels and meridians so as to enable part, or the whole, of the spheroidal surface of the earth to be represented on a plane-surface.

Map room.   A room devoted to the storage and consultation of maps.

Mapping.   *See* Information mapping.

MAPS.   MicrogrAphic Preservation Service. *See* Preservation Resources.

Marbled edges.   The three edges of a book cut solid, and stained to resemble marble. *See also* Edges, Sprinkled edges, Stained edges, Stippled edges.

Marbled paper.   Surface-colour paper used by bookbinders. Marbling is done by floating white paper, or dipping the edges of a sewn book before inserting into the cover, on a bath of gum tragacanth, the surface of which has been sprinkled with various colours, and combed out to a desired pattern.

Marbling.   The process of colouring the endpapers and edges of a book in imitation of marble.

Marbling under gilt.   Marbled edges of a book overlaid with gold. Usually the marbling is not very noticeable until the edges are fanned out. The style was first used in France in the seventeenth century, its invention being accredited to Le Gascon. Sometimes it is found in English bindings of the middle of the eighteenth century and later. *See also* Gilt on the rough, Rough gilt edges, Solid gilt.

MARC. <www.loc.gov./marc> The MARC format was developed to provide an internationally acceptable standard for the exchange of bibliographic data in machine-readable form. *M*achine-*R*eadable *C*ataloguing began in 1966 as a pilot scheme operated by the Library of Congress. Bibliographic records on machine-readable tape were distributed weekly to sixteen US libraries who then used their own computing facilities to process them. At this stage the most usual form of output was the conventional catalogue card. By 1967 the MARC II format had been introduced and the service extended to some fifty libraries. The original MARC format had revealed certain limitations which the MARC II format was specifically designed to overcome. Each record can accommodate a large quantity of bibliographic data in machine-readable form. In addition to a full AACR 2 description, the record may contain Dewey Decimal Classification numbers, Library of Congress Classification numbers, and subject headings. Any of these individual elements may be used to access the MARC file of bibliographic records. Subsequently the British National Bibliography began to develop UKMARC and by 1969 tapes were being distributed to British libraries. Development of MARC has been in the hands of the Library of Congress, National Library of Canada, and the British Library and versions such as USMARC, CANMARC and UKMARC have appeared. The current emphasis is on merging of these formats. In 1999 with the integration of CANMARC and USMARC, a new revision MARC 21 was issued; this offers better coverage for non-book resources and the likely introduction of metadata. In 2001 the British Library began moves to adopt MARC 21 after working with the other partners to bring the versions closer together.

MARC AMC. A MARC format for Archives and Manuscripts Control; a USMARC version was published by the Society of American Archivists in 1985, and is extensively used in North America.

Margin. 1. The unprinted area between printed or written matter and the edges of a page. The proportional width of the margins is a very important element in a properly balanced book-page. A good ratio is: head (top) margin 2; fore-edge (outside) 3; tail, also called 'lower' or 'bottom' (bottom) 4; back (inside) 1½. 2. The area of a map, drawing or print, between the line enclosing the information area and the edge of the paper. 3. On microfilm, the area of background between the line enclosing the information area and the edge of the film frame.

Marginal costs. *See* Costs.

Marginal figure. A figure printed in the margin of a book to indicate the number of a line of type for purposes of easy reference. *See also* Runners.

Marginal heading. A heading printed at the side of the type area.

Marginal note. A note or Gloss written or printed on the margin of a page opposite the portion of text to which it refers. Notes are called *footnotes* when printed at the bottom of the page, and *Shoulder-notes* when printed at the top corner of the page. Also called 'Marginal heading', 'Marginalia'. *See* Side note.

Marginal-hole punched cards. Cards which have rows of holes punched round the margins or over a large part of the card's area. These holes are notched or slotted to record information which is obtained, when required, by inserting needles in the holes and allowing cards on which the required information is recorded to fall away. *See also* Dequeker system, Edge-notched cards.

Marked proof. *See* Proof.

Marking-up. In book-binding, dividing the spine into equal portions and marking the position of the cords.

Marks of omission. *See* Omission marks.

Marks of reference. *See* Reference marks.

Markup. The process of indicating how a document will be formatted in printed or electronic form, usually by inserting non-printing, non-visible characters. The most common use of Markup is in the use of HTML for documents published on the World Wide Web where, for example, the tags used to indicate a heading may be of the form <H1> to begin and </H1> to turn off and resume normal text. Other markup languages are SGML and XML.

Martin (Allie Beth) Award. An annual award to recognize outstanding bibliographic knowledge and ability to communicate that knowledge; made by the Public Library Association of the ALA.

Maschler (Kurt)/Emil Award. Administered by the Book Trust, an annual UK award for 'a work of imagination in the children's field in which text and illustration are of excellence and so presented that each enhances, yet balances the other'.

Masking. (*Printing*) The placement of an opaque cut-out overlay or a transparent overlay on which lines have been lightly drawn, over a photograph or drawing, or lines drawn on the back thereof, in order to indicate areas at the sides which are not to be reproduced.

Mass book. *See* Missal.

Master. 1. The plate, or stencil in duplicating processes, from which copies are made. 2. <www.cta.dmu.ac.uk/projects/master> Manuscript Access through Standards for Electronic Records; an EU project started in 1999 to develop and test a standard for electronic description of manuscripts.

Master file. (*Information retrieval*) 1. A file containing relatively permanent information. 2. A main file of information.

Masthead. The statement of the title, ownership, address and frequency of publication, printer's name and address, and sometimes postage and subscription rates of a periodical publication. It is usually on the last or the editorial page of a newspaper, and on the editorial or contents page of a magazine. Also called 'Flag' and 'Logo'.

Material bibliography. *See* Historical bibliography.

Mathematical order. (*Classification*) Used by E. C. Richardson to indicate a possible order for terms in an Array which forms a series of co-ordinate classes. Order by means of a Notation. Synonymous with S. R. Ranganathan's Canonical order.

Matrix. (*Pl.* Matrices) (*Printing*) 1. The mould from which a stereotype (stereo) or electrotype (electro) is made. The mould is made by placing wet flong (a material, about 1/16 inch thick, made of alternate layers of tissue paper and blotting paper) over the type of which an impression is needed and then beating it with a stiff brush. It is then subjected to pressure, removed and dried. 2. A mould from which type is cast in a typesetting machine. 3. A copper mould which has been struck with a punch and from which individual type letters are cast. Also called a 'strike'. *See also* Electrotype, Stereotype. 4. (*Information retrieval*) A rectangular array of elements used to facilitate the study of problems in which the relation between these elements is fundamental.

Matt art. *See* Art.

Matter. 1. Type, whether in the process of setting up, or standing. It may be *live* matter (not yet printed from) or *dead* matter (awaiting distribution), *open* matter (leaded) or *solid* matter (without leads); *good* matter is that kept standing in case of re-use. The ancient terms, *fat* and *lean* matter, may still be used to indicate the proportion of open spaces or break lines. 2. Manuscript of copy to be printed.

MB. Megabyte. *See* Byte.

MbO. *See* Objectives.

MBone. Multicast backbone, a high-speed channel for the distribution of live video and audio over the Internet. *See also* Multicasting.

Mbps. Mega (million) bits per second, a measure of data transfer rate.

Mbyte. Abbreviation for megabyte. *See* Byte.

MCPS. *See* Mechanical Copyright Protection Society Ltd.

Mean line. (*Printing*) An imaginary line running along the top of all x-height letters, i.e. those without ascenders, a, c, e, etc. *See also* Ascender line, Base line, Cap line, Superior figures (letters).

Mearne style. The style of book decoration used during the seventeenth and early eighteenth centuries in England. This style is named after Samuel Mearne, the stationer and binder to Charles II and is a development of the Fanfare and Le Gascon styles. Red and black inlay was used with great effect, and the centre panel was often in the Cottage style. The All-over style was also often used. Also called 'Restoration style'. *See also* Rectangular style.

Measure. The width to which printed matter is set, i.e. the length of line. It is usually counted in 12 point ems. *See also* Didot system, Em, Point.

Mechanical overlay. *See* Chalk overlay.

Mechanical tints. *See* Tint.

Mechanical translation. A generic term for language translation by computer. *See also* Machine translation.

Mechanical wood. The lowest grade of wood pulp used in the manufacture of paper, and prepared by the purely mechanical process of grinding. This method produces a higher yield than the chemical process but the resulting pulp is less pure. It is suitable only for newsprint: it has good printing qualities and is opaque but impermanent. Also called 'Groundwood pulp'. *See also* Chemical wood.

Mechanical wood pulp. *See* Semi-chemical pulp.

Mechanical Copyright Protection Society Ltd (MCPS). <www.mcps.co.uk> (Elgar House, 41 Streatham High Road, London SW16 1ER, UK) MCPS represents thousands of composers and music publishers whenever their music is recorded; it negotiates agreements on behalf of members, ensures that copyright owners are rewarded for the use of their music, and distributes royalties generated from the recording of copyright music onto various formats – CDs, cassettes, videos, multimedia, audio-visual and broadcast material. Founded in 1924 from the merger of two earlier bodies – Mechanical Copyright Licences Company Ltd (established 1910 in anticipation of the Copyright Act 1911) and the Copyright Protection Society Ltd; from 1976 it has been wholly owned by the Music Publishers Association.

Mechanization. *See* Automation.

Media. 1. A generic term to denote methods of public communication – the press, radio, television etc. 2. A loosely defined term for non-print items held by a library: for example, audio-visual materials, software and possibly maps.

Media centre. Sometimes used for a school library, or learning resources centre in a school, where a range of print and audio-visual media, necessary equipment, and the services of a media specialist, are accessible to students and teachers.

Media file. Information prepared for buyers of advertising space in newspapers and periodicals, and giving particulars of circulation, column and type sizes and rates. Also termed 'media pack'.

Mediaan System. A Belgian system of line measurement used in conjunction with the Fournier system of measuring type bodies; 12 point equals 0.1649 inch or 4.18 mm.

Mediated searching. Information retrieval carried out by library staff or information professionals on behalf of End users, the databases or services in use being 'mediated' by the library staff.

Medical Library Assistance Act. *See* Library law.

Medical Library Association (MLA). <www.mlanet.org> (65 East Wacker Place, Suite 1900, Chicago IL 60601-7298, USA) Founded in the USA in 1898 to foster medical and allied scientific libraries, and exchange medical literature among its institutional members; to improve the professional qualifications and status of medical librarians; to organize efforts and resources for the furtherance of the purposes and objects of the Association. Publishes *Bulletin of the Medical Library Association* (q.), *MLA news* (q.), *Directory of the Medical Library Association* (a.).

Medium. 1. The weight of Typeface midway between light and bold. This is the kind normally used for periodicals and book work. 2. An alternative name for Ben Day tint. *See* Ben Day process. 3. The liquid, usually linseed oil, in which the pigment of printing ink is dispersed and by means of which it leaves an impression on paper. 4. A standard size of printing paper, 18 x 23 inches. 5. A finish given to paper that is neither highly calendered nor antique, but intermediate between the two extremes. Also called 'Medium finish'. 6. In music, the means (instrument/s or voice/s) by which musical sounds are produced, as indicated in the score. *See also* Media.

Medium face. The weight of Typeface half-way between light and bold. Also called 'Half-dark type'. *See* Medium (1).

Medium finish. *See* Medium (5).

Medium weight paper. Sensitized photographic paper between 0.0084 and 0.0111 inches inclusive. *See also* Photographic papers.

MEDLARS. <www.nlm.nih.gov/pubs/factsheets/intlmedlars> Medical Literature Analysis and Retrieval Service, a collection of databases operated and maintained by the National Library of Medicine. MEDLARS operates through a global network of international centres.

Megabyte. *See* Byte.

Meilleur Report (UK). The report *MEILLEUR: Mobility of Employment International for Librarians in Europe*, prepared by Anthony Thompson (Library Association, 1977).

Mellon Microfilming Project. A project funded 1988–1998 by the Andrew W. Mellon Foundation to encourage microfilming of important historical collections. It operated under the aegis of the European Commission on Preservation and Access (ECPA).

Melody edition. *See* Score.

Melvil Dewey Medal. *See* Dewey (Melvil) Medal.

Membrane. A single skin of parchment or vellum either forming part of a roll, or complete in itself. Skins of goats, sheep or calves are used; they are scraped free of hair and reduced in thickness, soaked, stretched, smoothed and dried. This produces a thin, smooth and white parchment, the flesh side being whiter and shinier than the hair side, which is known as the Dorse.

Memoir. 1. A biography of a person written by someone else. 2. A monograph, or dissertation, on some noteworthy subject.

Memoirs. 1. A narrative of events based on the observations, experiences and memories of the writer; an autobiographical record. 2. A collection of researches and accounts of experiments, or dissertations on a learned subject, published by a learned society, especially in the form of a record of proceedings or transactions.

Memoria Mundi. <portal.unesco.org/ci> The Memory of the World International Register is a programme announced in 1993 as part of the

Unesco General Information Programme, and with the support of IFLA, to preserve the most endangered manuscript, documentary and archival heritage by creating a high-quality photographic and computerized 'memory'. A second objective is to preserve the originals in optimum conditions. Specific targets so far identified include items in eastern Europe, Latin America, and the Middle East. In 2005 a committee of international experts will be considering new nomination proposals.

Memorial. 1. A written statement of views in the form of a petition for submission to an authoritative body. 2. Usually in plural, a chronicle or document containing a historical narrative.

Memorial volume. A publication, often consisting of contributions by several writers, in memory of a person or event. Also called 'Festschrift'.

Memorialist. A person presenting, or signatory to, a memorial.

Memory. The storage capacity of a computer system and, while sometimes considered to include hard Disks, is preferably used in relation to RAM. *See also* ROM.

Memory of the World International Register. *See* Memoria Mundi.

Mending. Minor repairs to the leaves of a book not involving the replacement of any material or separation of the book from the cover. Not to be confused with Repairing.

Mentefacts. (*Classification*) A group of 'artificial' entries, i.e. those which do not occur naturally, and which are abstract, e.g. systems of belief and products of the imagination. The other group is said to be Artefacts.

Mentor. One who offers advice and encouragement to the less experienced; mentoring can teach skills, recognize strengths, offer support by example, and helps to develop sound judgement and the gaining of confidence. Enthusiasm can be communicated, and personal growth effected. Formal schemes are becoming more popular, but it is necessary to choose the mentor by agreement, and schemes need time, recognized boundaries, and adequate training for the mentors.

Menu. *See* Pull-down menu.

Mercator's Projection. A chart enabling a mariner to steer a course by compass in straight lines; invented by Gerardus Mercator, all the meridians are straight lines perpendicular to the equator and all the parallels are straight lines parallel to the equator. It was first used by Mercator in a world map in 1569, and made navigation by dead reckoning easier. Edward Wright made its use practicable by publishing a set of tables for constructing the network of charts, and this development has made it possible to use Mercator's projection for all nautical charts.

Mercurius Intelligence. *See* Newsbook.

Merge. (*Information retrieval*) (*Verb*) To combine two files, already in sequence, into a single file.

Merovingian handwriting. The style of handwriting used in France from the sixth to the eighth centuries; a national style of cursive minuscule script which developed from the Latin cursive after the dissolution of the Roman Empire. *See also* Cursive, Handwriting.

Merrill alphabeting (book) numbers. A scheme devised by W. S. Merrill (1866–1969) for arranging books in rough alphabetical order. The table was reprinted in the Introduction to Brown's Subject Classification (1906) and later published in *Public Libraries* (1912). It consists of three tables designed respectively for names, periodical titles and dates. The numbers are treated as decimals and can be further expanded.

Merrythought. (*Binding*) A finisher's stamp in the form of a merrythought, or wishbone, usually decorated with cusps or foliage ornament.

MeSH. Acronym for Medical Subject Headings, the 'vocabulary' of the (American) National Library of Medicine; it is used in connection with MEDLARS, the Library's catalogue and the *Index Medicus*.

Message pad. *See* Personal digital assistant.

Metabolic map. A map which shows the inter-relations and correlations of biochemical reactions in metabolic sequences.

Metadata. 1. Data describing a resource, or data about data. A MARC record is metadata, describing a book or other item through pre-defined elements or attributes but the term is generally understood to mean structured data about digital resources that can be used to help support a wide range of operations. These might include, for example, resource description and discovery, the management of information resources (including rights management) and their long-term preservation, and 'descriptive metadata' that provides more detailed descriptions of resources based on the concepts of book indexes and publishers publicity. Initiatives include the Dublin Core Metadata Element Set, IAFA/whois++ templates, GILS, IMS, indecs, Metadata Object Description Schema, MPEG-21, RDF, Text Encoding Initiative. An extensive resource can be found at: <www.ukoln.ac.uk/metadata>. 2. (*Archives*) The technical information required to put an electronic archive into its context, and to enable it to be retrieved and used even after migration to later systems. Also used more generally to mean contextual data needed in order to interpret archival materials when they have become long non-current.

Metadata Object Description Schema (MODS). <www.loc.gov/standards/mods> A schema for a bibliographic element set developed and maintained by the Network Development and MARC Standards Office of the Library of Congress together with interested experts. As an XML schema, MODS is intended to be able to carry selected data from existing MARC 21 records as well as to enable the creation of original resource description records. It includes a subset of MARC fields and uses language-based tags rather than numeric ones, in some cases regrouping elements from the MARC 21 bibliographic format.

Metal furniture. *See* Furniture.

Metallography. A lithographic process in which metallic plates are used instead of stone.

Metalwork. (*Binding*) A decorative ornament which is an imitation of wrought and curved ironwork.

Methodical catalogue. *See* Systematic catalogue.

Metric book sizes. The following are the metric book sizes recommended in *Page sizes for books* (BS 1413:1989):

	Trimmed sizes in mm	Untrimmed sizes in mm	'Quad' Paper sizes in mm
Metric Cr. 8vo.	186 x 123	192 x 126	768 x 1008
Metric Lge. Cr. 8vo.	198 x 129	204 x 132	816 x 1056
Metric Demy 8vo.	216 x 138	222 x 141	888 x 1128
Metric Royal 8vo.	234 x 156	240 x 159	960 x 1272
A5	210 x 148*	215 x 152.5	860 x 1220*

The trimmed and untrimmed sizes of case-bound books are those of a folded sheet after and before trimming 3 mm from the edges of a page (head, tail and foredge). The measurements followed by a * are ISO sizes.

Metrics. Systems of measurement, particularly assessment of the usability and efficiency of electronic resources. Although earlier terms such as 'bibliometrics', 'scientometrics', 'informetrics' have had limited currency from time-to-time, metrics is becoming the key term for all aspects of evaluation of digital libraries and services, intranets, extranets, websites and all forms of electronic publications. Factors include accessibility, ease of use, functionality, design, speed of navigation. *See also* Performance, Standards for library services, Statistics for library services.

Metropolitan area network (MAN). A high Bandwidth network designed to link together sites within a city and its environs.

METS. <www.ukoln.ac.uk/metadata/resources/mets> Metadata Encoding and Transmission Standard, a standard schema for encoding descriptive, administrative, and structural metadata about digital library objects and the complex links between these types of metadata within a repository. It provides an XML document format for encoding metadata necessary for both management of digital library objects within a repository and exchange of such objects between repositories (or between repositories and their users). METS is being developed as an initiative of the Digital Library Federation and is being maintained in the Network Development and MARC Standards Office of the Library of Congress.

Mezzotint. 1. A process of engraving on copper or steel in which the entire surface of the plate is slightly roughened, after which the drawing is traced and the plate smoothed in places by scraping, burnishing, etc., to produce the desired light and shade effect. 2. An engraving so produced.

MF. (*Paper*) Abbreviation for Machine finish.

MG. (*Paper*) Abbreviation for Machine glazed. *See also* Paper finishes.

Michel style. The style of book decoration practised during the nineteenth century by Marius Michel and his son in France. The designs are often based on natural forms and the ornament is generally expressed in colour, outlined in blind, and very often without the use of gold.

Michigan Library Consortium. *See* MLC.

Micro description. (*Archives*) In *MAD* terminology, a description of an archival entity at a lower level, usually Item, giving a detailed case-by-case description of the material, in a way that will demonstrate its dependence upon the relevant higher levels (usually Group or Series).

Microcard. 1. A term, trademark of the Microcard Corporation and covered by a US patent, which refers exclusively to 5 x 3 inch cards with images arranged in a specific manner. 2. The term is more generally used to indicate an opaque card of varying size on which microcopies have been reproduced photographically. A microcard resembles a Microfiche in that the microcopies are arranged in rows and catalogue details, readable with the naked eye, are at the top of the card. It differs from other microforms in that the prints are positive as well as being opaque, and cannot be directly reproduced. A microcard is not readable without optical aid in the form of a specially-made reader.

Microchip. *See* Chip.

Microcomputer. A computer whose central processing unit is a Microprocessor (*see* Chip). With increased computing power so have capabilities been extended – ranging from simple word-processing to sophisticated library housekeeping routines – and the preferred term is now PC (for personal computer).

Microfiche. A flat sheet of photographic film standardized (BS 4187:1981 and 1978 [2 parts]) at 105 x 148 mm (nominally 4 x 6 inches) and 75 x 125 mm (nominally 3 x 5 inches), displaying at the top a catalogue entry, or title, readable with the naked eye, and bearing in horizontal and vertical rows micro-images of the text of a publication. The standard size of a frame is 11.25 x 16 mm (single) and 23 x 16 mm (double). Where a document is too long to be recorded on one microfiche, each subsequent one is called a 'Trailer' microfiche. Microfiche can be (a) a positive copy printed from strips of microfilm, (b) an actual frame cut from microfilm (usually 70 mm film), or (c) made directly with a step-and-repeat camera. Such sheets may be stored vertically like catalogue cards but require envelopes to protect them from damage. BS/ISO 9923:1994 specifies the characteristics of A6-size microfiche, arranged in formats of 49 and 98 frames, 270 and 420 frames (for COM), and single-frame format. *See also* COM, Ultra-microfiche.

Microfilm. A microphotograph on cellulose film. It may be negative or positive and may be 16 or 35 mm wide and of any length, depending on the number of exposures thereon. For special purposes, e.g. copying newspapers, or engineering drawings, or the preparation of Microfiche, film of 70 mm width may be used.

Microfilm flow camera. A flow camera for taking microcopies automatically, usually on film. *See also* Continuous flow camera.

Microfilm jacket. A transparent holder into which individual strips of film may be inserted for protection.

Microfilm print. An enlarged print made, normally on paper, from microfilm.

Microfilm reader. Apparatus for the reading of micro-records by means of their enlarged projection on an opaque or transparent ground-glass screen; printing facilities may be included.

Microform. A generic term indicating any form of micro-record, whether on flat or roll film, paper or other material.

Micrograph. 1. A graphic record of the image, formed by a microscope, of an object. 2. An instrument constructed for producing extremely small copies of writing, printing or engraving, or for executing minute writing or engraving.

MicrogrAphic Preservation Service. *See* Preservation Resources.

Micrographics. The science and technique of reproducing documents in so small a scale that enlargement is necessary to make them legible. *See also* Microfiche, Microfilm.

Micro-opaque. A copy of the whole, or part, of a book or other document made by means of microphotography, the print being on opaque paper or card. May be made solely by photographic means or by a printing method. Also called 'Opaque microcopy'. *See also* Microcard.

Microphotography. Photography on so reduced a scale that a visual aid is required to discern the features of the resulting microphotograph; 16 mm or 35 mm cellulose film is used, and the final form of the micro-copy may be Microfiche, or Microfilm.

Microprocessor. *See* Chip.

Microscopic edition. *See* Miniature book.

Microsecond. One millionth of a second. *See also* Nanosecond.

Microsoft .net framework. A technology created by Microsoft that provides support for distributed components and component reuse and which is of particular use in building e-learning environments. See, for example, <www.jisc.ac.uk/elearning_framework.html>. Seen as an alternative to the J2EE.

Mid-Atlantic Preservation Service. *See* Preservation Resources.

Middle space. *See* Quad.

Middleware. The software for managing access to Intranet and Internet resources and applications requiring sophisticated security facilities and the means to administer them. This can apply at an organizational level but there are increasing requirements for middleware to handle the more complex access issues at an inter-institutional level. Core middleware functions are considered to be Authentication, Authorization, Identity management, and Information lookup. *See also*

Core middleware (2), Middleware Initiative, NMI-EDIT, NSF Middleware Initiative.

Middleware Initiative. <middleware.internet2.edu> An Initiative of Internet2 working toward the deployment of core Middleware services at Internet2 universities.

Midwest Inter-library Center. *See* Center For Research Libraries.

Miehle. (*Printing*) The commonest type of Two-revolution machine. Robert Michle, a young Chicago machine-minder (d. 1932), made an important contribution to printing machine design by controlling the momentum of the bed (with the forme on it) at the instant of reversal by means of an enlarged star wheel and rack.

Migration strategy. A procedure to ensure that the contents of digitized objects, texts etc, remain accessible as the technology on which they were originally prepared becomes obsolete.

MILC. Midwest Inter-Library Center. *See* Center for Research Libraries.

Mildred L. Batchelder Award. *See* Batchelder (Mildred L.) Award.

Millboard. A kind of strong Pasteboard but made from old rope, sacking, wood pulp, and paper. Used for the covers of books which are heavy or have to stand hard wear. Also called 'Binder's board'.

Millennium bug. *See* Year 2000 crisis.

MIMAS. <www.mimas.ac.uk> Manchester Information and Associated Services, a JISC-supported national data centre providing the UK higher education, further education and research community with networked access to key data and information resources to support teaching, learning and research across a wide range of disciplines. *See also* EDINA.

MIME. Multipurpose Internet Mail Extensions, a standard defined in 1992 by the Internet Engineering Task Force for formatting a non-text (i.e. non-ASCII) Attachment dispatched or received as part of an E-mail message. Non-text files include graphics, spreadsheets, formatted word-processor documents and sound files. In addition to e-mail programs, Web browsers also support various MIME types.

MINERVA. <www.minervaeurope.org> Ministerial Network for Valorising Activities in digitization, a network of EU Member States' Ministries whose objective is the harmonization of activities carried out in the digitization of cultural and scientific content. Due to the high level of commitment assured by the involvement of EU governments, it aims to co-ordinate across national programmes. Under FP6, the MINERVA network has been extended to 'MINERVA Plus' and includes the new EU member states.

Miniature. 1. A coloured initial letter or picture in an illuminated manuscript. 2. A greatly reduced copy of a document which is usually read or reproduced by means of optical aids. 3. A small highly-detailed drawing, painting, or portrait, especially on ivory or vellum.

Miniature book. A very small book, generally 3 inches (10 cm) or less in height, conceived as a whole on a tiny scale, printed with small type on suitable paper, bound in a binding which is tooled delicately, and, if illustrated, having drawings or reproductions which are in keeping with the size of the book. Many distinguished printers and publishers have issued such books. They include Bibles, books of devotion, almanacs, the poets, the classics, books for children, etc. Also called 'Lilliput edition', 'Microscopic edition'.

Miniature painter.   A painter of miniatures. Also called a Miniaturist.

Miniature score.   *See* Score.

Minicomputer.   A mid-level computer capable of handling complex processes efficiently. Minicomputers may be used in Stand-alone mode, linked with other minis to provide a centralized computing resource in an organization, or as a 'front-end' system controlling communications between remote terminals and a Mainframe.

Minim.   Single downstroke of a pen.

Minion.   An out-of-date name for a size of type equal to about 7 point.

Minitel.   *See* Teletel, Videotex.

MINITEX.   <kinglear.minitex.umn.edu> (Andersen Library, University of Minnesota, Minneapolis, Minnesota 55455-0439, USA) A network consortium of libraries in the US states of Minnesota, South and North Dakota. An OCLC Network Affiliate.

Mint.   A book which is in the same condition as when it came from the publisher.

Minuscule.   1. A small type of writing developed from cursive.   2. Lower case letters.

Minute classification.   *See* Close classification.

Minute mark.   A printer's symbol ' to represent feet (measurement) and minutes; it is also placed after a syllable on which the stress falls.

MIPS.   Millions of instructions per second, a measure of computer processor speed.

Mirror.   In large-scale networking, such as on the Internet, mirror sites hold copies of resources that originate from one or more distant sites. Users wishing to access these resources are able to access the mirror site, thus reducing network costs but also at a saving of their time through improved availability and responsiveness. *See also* Cache.

MIS.   *See* Management information system.

Misbound.   A Leaf, leaves or a Section which has been folded wrongly or misplaced by the binder.

Miscellany.   A collection of writings by various authors or on a variety of subjects. Also called 'Miscellanea'.

Misleading title.   One which does not indicate the subject-matter, or the form, of the work.

Misprint.   A typographical error.

Missal.   A book containing the service for the celebration of the mass throughout the year. Sometimes loosely used for any book of devotions. Before the invention of printing, the writing of missals was a branch of art which reached a high state of excellence in the monasteries. The books were written upon vellum in the most beautiful style of penmanship, and were adorned with the utmost magnificence. Also called 'Mass book'. *See also* Book of Hours.

Misses. (*Information retrieval*) Relevant documents which were not retrieved in a search.

Mistletoe tool. (*Binding*) A finisher's tool which appears to have been first used on Irish bindings in about 1766; it is particularly common on the panels of spines of Irish bindings about 1780. In some forms it is embossed, and seems to be a feather rather than a mistletoe leaf.

Mita Toshokan Joho Gakkai. [Mita Society of Library and Information Science] <wwwsoc.nii.ac.jp/mslis> (c/o School of Library and Information Science, Keio University, 2-15-45 Mita, Minato-ku, Tokyo 108-8345, Japan) Established in 1963 as the Mita Society of Library Science, the Society now has a membership of over 860 individuals and 315 institutions, and holds conventions and seminars on developments in the field. Publishes *Library and Information Science* (2 p.a.).

Mitred. (*Binding*) A junction of lines at an angle of 45 degrees such as is necessary at the turn-in of covering material on the inside of the covers. Lines, in finishing, which meet each other at right angles without over-running. The connection at the angles of an outer Frame (2) to an inner frame of Panel (1) by the diagonal use of Fillets (1), or a Roll. *See also* Library corner, Square corner.

Mixed notation. *See* Notation.

Mixed subject heading. (*Indexing*) A subject heading which, in addition to being followed by a number of entries or references, refers (by means of *see also* references) to other subject headings. *See also* Indirect subject heading.

MLA. *See* 1. Museums, Libraries and Archives Council. 2. Medical Library Association. 3. Music Library Association.

MLAC. *See* Museums, Libraries and Archives Council.

MLAJ. *See* Ongaku Toshokan Kyogikai.

MLC. <www.mlcnet.org> (1410 Rensen Street, Suite 1, Lansing, Michigan 48910-3657, USA) Michigan Library Consortium; a network consortium of libraries mainly in the US state of Michigan, but with connections into Minnesota, Wisconsin, New York, Illinois, Missouri, and Canada. An OCLC Network Affiliate.

MLE. Managed Learning Environment, the totality of information systems and processes of a university or other learning institution that contribute directly and indirectly to learning and the management of that learning. The MLE will include the VLE, the student record system, and learning resources.

MLNC. <www.mlnc.org> (8045 Big Bend Boulevard, Suite 202, St. Louis, Missouri 63119-2714, USA) Missouri Library Network Corporation; a network consortium of libraries in the US state of Missouri and the general Midwestern region. An OCLC Network Affiliate.

MmIT. *See* Multimedia and Information Technology Group.

MMS. Multimedia Messaging Service, a messaging service for the mobile environment and an extension of Short Message Service (SMS). It provides automatic, immediate delivery of personal multimedia messages from phone to phone or from phone to E-mail. In addition to the familiar text content of text messages, multimedia messages can contain images, graphics, voice, and audio clips.

Mnemonics. A desirable but non-essential quality of the notation of a classification. It means that the same, similar or analogous concepts, when they re-occur in a schedule, should be denoted by the same digits. When they are drawn from lists of divisions, tables or parts of schedules they are called by Ranganathan 'scheduled mnemonics'. Related ideas or 'associations' as used by Ranganathan in classifying, are called 'seminal mnemonics' to distinguish them from 'scheduled mnemonics'. Mnemonics may be *constant*, i.e. always denoting the same aspects or form wherever used throughout a scheme of classification, or *variable*, i.e. occasionally alternated or altered to suit the special needs of a specific subject. Dewey's common form divisions now called 'Standard subdivisions' are variable whereas the form marks of the Universal Decimal Classification are constant. *Systematic* mnemonics are those which reflect a consistent order; they are mainly a result of synthesis. *Literal* or *alphabetical* mnemonics depend on the use of letters in notation in such a way that the symbol for a class is the initial letter of the same class. Library of Congress classification abounds in the use of literal mnemonics.

Mobile librarian. A librarian whose duties are mainly carried out in a travelling or mobile library.

Mobile library. A vehicle equipped and operated to provide a service comparable to a part-time branch library. *See also* Container library service, Travelling library.

Modelled initial. In a mediaeval illuminated manuscript, an initial letter given a rounded or three-dimensional aspect.

MODELS. <www.ukoln.ac.uk/dlis/models> MOving to Distributed Environments for Library Services, a UKOLN initiative that ran 1995–2000 motivated by the need to develop an applications framework to manage the rapidly multiplying range of distributed heterogeneous information resources and services becoming available.

Modem. Modulator-demodulator; a device that converts a digital signal from a computer to an audible sound that can be transmitted on an analogue telephone line, and similarly decodes replies into digital form to input into the computer. Standards relating to the specification of modems have been produced by the ITU-T as the V series.

Modern face. Printers' types, French in origin dating from 1698; but not popular until after the Revolution when Didot (France), Bodoni (Italy), Figgins, Thorne and Fry (England) cut various versions. 'Modern' were popular throughout the nineteenth century. They are characterized by vertical emphasis, there being a considerable difference between thick and thin strokes and curves thickened in the centre. The fine bracketed serifs are at right angles to the strokes. Examples are: Bodoni (most foundries); Walbaum (Monotype). It is characteristic of modern typefaces that the numerals stand on the Base line, but in some typefaces the numerals are available in both forms, e.g. Bookprint. The term 'Didone' has superseded 'Modern face' for this category of typefaces. *See also* Arabic figures, Old face, Transitional.

Modern Public Records (UK). *Modern public records: the Government response to the Report of the Wilson Committee.* A white paper presented by the Lord Chancellor's Department to Parliament in March 1982 (Cmnd. 8531. HMSO, 1981). *See also* Wilson Committee.

Modern Records Centre. <modernrecords.warwick.ac.uk> Title of the archives department at the University of Warwick, specializing in the archives of labour and employment, and managed in association with the archives of BP plc.

Modification. *(Cataloguing)* Variation in the presentation of information in catalogue entries by, for example, inversion of the initials of a manufacturing firm to bring the last name to the front, the omission of the first part of a geographic name if it indicates a type of governmental administration, the use of a uniform title (perhaps a translation from an original 'foreign' form) to bring all entries for the same work together. *(Indexing)* A word or phrase(s) inserted after a heading to indicate an aspect or character of the information given in the text at the place referred to, to limit its meaning or subdivide the entries.

MODS. *See* Metadata Object Description Schema.

Modular planning. Planning a building so that it consists of a number of modules (units), having no permanent internal walls dividing the floor area into rooms. Each floor is supported by pillars at regular intervals and these pillars can accommodate plumbing, cabling and air conditioning ducts. Except for core service areas (lifts, staircases, etc.) which are enclosed by permanent walls, the whole of the floor area can be subdivided into rooms and departments by placing free-standing bookcases, partitions and furniture where desired, to be varied according to service requirements.

Modularization. The teaching of a subject or discipline by 'modules', particularly in higher education. Such a method means that students do not have to commit themselves to their choice of subject at the beginning of a course of study but can change depending on the credits accumulated and the pre-requisites for subsequent modules. Such a scheme can also make it easier for students to move between institutions. Can have implications for academic libraries if the length of modules is less than the traditional academic year, by stimulating demand for set texts in a shorter time scale.

Modulation of terms. A phrase used to indicate the development of terms, or headings, of a classification. A term should modulate into the term following it.

Mohonk Statement.   A summary of an international conference on the Role of Books and other Educational Materials in meeting the educational and economic goals of developed and developing countries, held 10–13 December 1972 at Mohonk Mountain House, New Paltz, New York. It is reproduced in *IFLA News*, no. 43, (March), 1973, pp. 12–13.

Monitor.   The device on which images generated by a PC, DVD or video cassette recorder can be viewed. Flat panel displays are increasingly being connected to PCs and the term less used.

Monk.   An ink blot or splash on a printed sheet; the term originated in the days when formes were inked with ink balls. *See also* Friar.

Monochrome.   Any illustration in one colour.

Monograph.   A separate treatise on a single subject or class of subjects, or on one person, usually detailed in treatment but not extensive in scope and often containing bibliographies. Frequently published in series. In cataloguing, any publication which is not a Serial.

Monograph series.   A series of monographs with a series title as well as individual titles; often issued by a university or society. *See also* Series (3).

Monographic publication.   A non-serial publication, consisting of text and/or illustrations, either complete in one volume or intended to be completed in a specified number of volumes.

Monoline.   A Typeface in which all the strokes of the characters appear to be of the same thickness. Most Lineale and Slab Serif types are of this kind. *See also* Geometric.

Monophoto.   Trade name for a photo-typesetting, or film-setting, machine manufactured by the Monotype Corporation which produces characters on films instead of metal. *See also* Filmsetting.

Monotype.   Separate paper-perforating and type-founding machines invented by Tolbert Lanston for composing and casting single types. Individual types are cast on the casting machine from paper rolls perforated on the perforating machine in which a keyboard is incorporated.

Montage.   The combination of several photographs, drawings, or parts of pictures, blended to form a single illustration for decorative, display or advertising purposes. *See also* Photo-montage.

Monthly.   A periodical which appears once a month.

Moon type.   A system of reading for the blind in which the letters are formed by raised lines based on a greatly modified form of roman capital letters. It is more easily learned than Braille and is consequently used by adults who have become blind late in life and find it difficult to master Braille. It is named after Dr. William Moon, a blind clergyman.

Moral defence.   (*Archives*) A term coined by Sir Hilary Jenkinson in the *Manual of Archival Administration* (1922) to describe the archivist's duty to preserve the integrity of archival holdings by preserving evidence of their provenance and original order.

Moral rights.   Rights enjoyed by authors irrespective of who owns copyright in a work. Basically the author has the right to be named whenever a work is published or performed or exhibited in public; not to be falsely named as author of a work; not to have the content of a work tampered with. Moral rights are very weak in the UK and virtually non-existent in the USA, but are paramount in Continental European law.

Mordant. Acid or other corrosive, used in etching plates.

Morgue. A collection of obituary notices of famous living people kept up to date in newspaper offices.

Morocco. 1. Leather manufactured from the skins of goats and largely used in bookbinding. 'Niger' Morocco is tanned with a vegetable tannin, and being durable, flexible and relatively thin, is suitable for bookbinding. 'Persian' Morocco lacks strength and durability and is unsuitable for bookbinding. 2. Leather made from sheepskin and lambskin but finished to look like goatskin.

Mortice (Mortise). An open space cut out of a printing plate or block so that type may be inserted in it. A block so prepared is said to be 'pierced'.

Mosaic. (*Printing*) A book decoration formed by inlaying or onlaying small pieces of leather of various colours to form a pattern. The technique is particularly associated with the work of the eighteenth-century French binders Padeloup le Jeune and Le Monnier.

Mosaic map. A photographic representation of the earth's surface and the buildings, etc. thereon, made from two or more aerial photographs placed side by side.

Mother Goose Award. An award given to the most exciting newcomer to British Children's book illustration. Instituted by the specialist firm of booksellers 'Books for Children'. The award was first made in March 1979.

Motion Picture Licensing Corporation (MPLC). <www.mplc.com> An independent US copyright licensing service authorized to grant umbrella licenses to groups, institutions, etc. for public performances of videotapes recorded off-air.

Motorized shelves. A form of compact shelving in which the bookcases are moved by electrical, or mechanical, power.

Mottled calf. A calf binding which has been mottled with colour or acid dabbed on with sponges or wads of cotton.

Mottled finish. A paper with a variegated colour surface produced by mixing two slightly different dyed shades of fibres, or by a drip of colour on the wet pulp.

Mould. 1. (*Paper*) A rectangular wooden frame over which brass wires or wire cloth is stretched to serve as a sieve in order to permit water to drain away from the pulp fibres to form a sheet of paper. A wooden frame called a Deckle fits round the edges of the mould and forms a tray with raised edges; this keeps the required thickness of pulp fibre on the wires until the excess water has drained away. 2. (*Printing*) A device in two parts used for casting movable type.

Mould-made paper. An imitation hand-made paper made from rag Furnish on a machine.

Mount. A card or paper on to which something is pasted to protect, preserve, or display it.

Mounted. A cutting, print, photograph, page, or similar item which is pasted on a mount.

Mounted plate. An illustration printed on a separate sheet of paper and pasted to a page of a book.

Mouse. Handheld device, rolled across a mousemat on the work surface, which causes a pointer to move to a required point in a document or to a folder or file on the 'desktop' on a computer display screen. Part of the WIMPS interface.

Movable location. *See* Relative location.

Movable type. (*Printing*) Type cast as single units as distinct from slugs or blocks on which are a number of characters. It was the use of movable type towards the end of the fifteenth century, instead of engraved blocks, which led to the rapid development of printing. *See also* Incunabula, Slug, Xylography.

Moving History. <www.movinghistory.ac.uk> A research guide to the United Kingdom's twelve public sector moving image archives containing over 100 selected film clips browsable by theme or by archive, guidelines for research and examples of past research, and links and contact points for further information. *See also* Film Archive Forum.

MPEG. <www.chiariglione.org/mpeg> Motion Picture Experts Group, a working group of the International Organization for Standardization/ International Electrotechnical Commission in charge of the development of standards for coded representation of digital audio and video. Established in 1988, the group first produced MPEG-1, the standard on which such products as Video CD and MP3 are based. MPEG1 for audio defines three operational modes – Layers I, II, and III – offering different levels of compression for different applications, MPEG1 Layer III being well known as the MP3 music format. Other specifications are MPEG-2, the standard on which such products as Digital TV set-top boxes and DVD are based, MPEG-4, the standard for multimedia for the fixed and mobile web, and MPEG-7, the standard for description and search of audio and visual content. Work on the new standard MPEG-21 *Multimedia framework* started in June 2000.

MPEG-21. <www.chiariglione.org/mpeg/standards/mpeg-21/mpeg-21.htm> A comprehensive standard framework for networked digital Multimedia designed by MPEG. Unlike other MPEG standards that describe compression coding methods, MPEG-21 describes a standard that defines the description of content and also processes for accessing, searching, storing and protecting the copyrights of content. It is anticipated that the open framework defined by the standard will provide content creators, producers, distributors and service providers with equal opportunities in the MPEG-21 enabled open market. The standard includes the following parts: Digital item declaration; Digital item identification; Intellectual property management and protection; Rights expression language; Rights data dictionary.

MPLC. *See* Motion Picture Licensing Corporation.

MPRC. *See* Music Performance Research Centre.

MS. Abbreviation for Manuscript (*Pl*. MSS.).

MS-DOS. Microsoft Disk Operating System, the Operating system used as a standard on IBM PCs and their compatibles until the introduction of Windows.

MT. *See* Machine translation.

Mudéjar Bindings. Spanish bindings in Cordovan leather, done between the thirteenth and fifteenth centuries by Moorish inhabitants of Spain known as mudéjares who were allowed religious freedom and to practise their crafts, of which bookbinding was one. The main design was a blind-tooled pattern of double outline interlacings with stamped strips of dots, curves, rings, etc. to form a background.

Mudge (Isadore Gilbert) Citation. Instituted in 1958, and administered by the Reference Services Division (now Reference and User Services Association) of the American Library Association, this Citation is given annually to a person who has made a distinguished contribution to reference librarianship.

Muehsam (Gerd) Award. *See* ARLIS/NA.

Mull. A thin loosely woven cotton cloth glued on to the backs of books to help hold the sections together, also termed 'crash'. Known as 'super' in the US.

Multicasting. A bandwidth-conserving technology that can reduce traffic by transporting single streams of information across the network backbone to regional and local distribution points where the data is replicated for simultaneous delivery to multiple users. Some applications that can take advantage of multicast include videoconferencing, video serving and news distribution.

Multicounty library. A library established by the joint action of the governing bodies, or by vote of the residents, of the counties concerned, and governed by a single board of library directors (US).

Multicultural librarianship. The provision of library and information services to all ethnic communities in a public library area. Provision may be needed in several languages, and user encouragement and education are key components. *See also* Diversity.

Multi-dimensional classification. The characterization of each document from more than one point of view. This can be accomplished for the physical placing of documents only when there are as many copies as there are classificatory points of view. *See also* Rigid classification.

Multi-layer paper. *See* Furnish layer.

Multi-level access. (*Information retrieval*) A form of access to files in which entries or blocks of entries are arranged in a definite order of subject symbols. The symbols can arrange the entries systematically as effectively as in an alphabetical index.

Multi-level description. (*Archives*) Technique of description following the multi-level rule established by *MAD* and by the international standard ISAD(G), whereby archival entities are described in a hierarchical way from whole Groups down through Series to Items.

Multi-level indexing. The indexing of a document by the appropriate broader generic terms as well as the narrower term.

Multi-level rule. *See* Multi-level description.

Multimedia. 1. The integration of any combination of text, video, animations, graphics, and sound into an interactive environment delivered via CD-ROM, DVD or over the Internet to PCs or similar consumer hardware. Also seen to be a convergence of computing technology, telecommunications and television leading towards Virtual reality. *See also* Hypermedia, Multimedia publishing. 2. A collection, or the record of a collection, of materials in various Media, including non-book material, audio-visual material and non-print material, with or without books and other printed material.

Multimedia and Information Technology Group. A membership group of CILIP, formed in 1999 by the merger of two earlier groups: the Multimedia Group which was previously known as the Audio-Visual Group, and the Information Technology Group which was formed in 1983.

Multimedia publishing. The production and delivery of information, educational, training and entertainment products incorporating Multimedia techniques.

Multi-platform. Application software designed for use on more than one Platform.

Multiple approach, principle of. A fundamental fact that books may be approached from the points of view of author, title, subject, series, etc.; this always has to be borne in mind by cataloguers. *See also* Cataloguing, principles of.

Multiple entry. (*Information retrieval*) The filing of as many descriptors (terms, entries) in an Item entry system as have been made in respect of a document.

Multiple meaning. *See* Polysemy.

Multiple reference. *See* General reference.

Multiplexer. A device that combines several telecommunications signals into a single channel or line for their more efficient transmission; a similar unit at the other end 'unscrambles' the signals into their original configuration. Multiplexers maintain the Integrity of individual signals by separating by frequency, time or space, thus there is frequency-division multiplexing, time-division multiplexing, and space-division multiplexing. Statistical multiplexers are more sophisticated versions of time-division systems.

Multi-processing. A method of computer design utilizing two or more equal processors that work on computing operations in a linear fashion. *See also* Parallel processing.

Multi-tasking. The ability to carry out several tasks at once e.g. searching the Internet while Word processing, originally applied to computers but increasingly to human beings.

Multi-tier stack. A self-supporting metal framework extending from basement to roof and designed to carry the weight of the deck floors and the book load. The columns are placed close together and permit the use of thin slab concrete or metal plate floors as well as shelf supports.

Multivalued words. (*Information retrieval*) Words which have different meanings in different contexts, whether they be Homographs or Homophones.

Multi-volume publication. A non-serial publication issued in a number of physically separate parts known to have been conceived and published as an entity; the separate parts may have differing authorship and their individual titles as well as an inclusive title.

Municipal library. A public library serving an urban area; the use of the word 'municipal' is becoming less common, and has no legal meaning or connection. In America, one which may also be similarly provided by a village or school district. In Australia, a public library.

Muniment room. A room in which archives are kept.

MUSE. *See* Project MUSE.

Museums, Libraries and Archives Council (MLA). <www.mla.gov.uk> (16 Queen Anne's Gate, London SW1H 9AA, UK) The Council was formed in 2000 under the title Resource (or Re:source) and amended its title in 2004; the acronym MLA is preferred over MLAC. MLA is the national development agency for museums, libraries and archives in England, advising government on policy and priorities. Recent key publications include *Investing in knowledge* and *Inspiring learning for all*. MLA has a devolved infrastructure of nine regional agencies, each of which is independent but core-funded by MLA: ALM London, EEMLAC (East of England), EMMLAC (East Midlands), MLA North West, MLA West Midlands, NEMLAC (North East), SEMLAC (South East), SWMLAC (South West), YMLAC (Yorkshire & Humberside).

Music Libraries Trust. <pages.britishlibrary.net/iaml.uk.irl/mlt> A body which exists to provide modest funds to assist UK music librarians to attend national and international music librarianship events. It awards the E. T. Bryant Memorial Prize in collaboration with the UK branch of the International Association of Music Libraries, Archives and Documentation Centres (IAML).

Music library. A library specializing in music; the stock will comprise printed music and musical reference works, catalogues, textbooks, biographies of composers and general instructional and historical works relating to the subject. Such a library may also stock sound recordings of music.

Music Library Association (MLA). <www.musiclibraryassoc.org> (8551 Research Way, Suite 180, Middleton WI 53562, USA) Founded in the USA in 1931; the purposes of the Association are to promote the establishment, growth, and use of music libraries; to encourage the collection of music and musical literature in libraries; to increase the effectiveness of music library services; and to further studies in music bibliography. Publishes *Notes* (q.).

Music Library Association of Japan. *See* Ongaku Toshokan Kyogikai.

Music paper. Paper ruled with staves of five lines for the writing of music. When made up into a book it is called a manuscript music book.

Music Performance Research Centre. <www.musicpreserved.org> Initiated by the Musicians' Union, the Centre has been recording non-broadcast concerts and opera since 1987 to preserve British performance heritage. Personal conversations with performers are also made. The Centre also holds some 1,500 recordings from the 1930s onwards, and has opened listening facilities at the Barbican Library and Trinity College of Music in London.

Music score. *See* Score.

Musical description. A description of the separate parts for instruments or voices used *simultaneously* during a musical performance. To be distinguished from a Bibliographical description which is only concerned with *successive* parts and/or volumes (i.e. the various editions) of a musical composition.

Musical work. A composition to be played by one or more musical instruments or to be sung by one or more human voices.

Musicology. The study of music as a branch of knowledge or field of research.

Mutton. *See* Em quadrat

NACO. Name Authority Co-operative Program. *See* PCC.

NACSIS. *See* Kokuritsu Johogaku Kenkyujo.

NAG. *See* National Acquisitions Group.

NAHSTE. <www.nahste.ac.uk> Navigational Aids for the History of Science, Technology and the Environment, a project based at the University of Edinburgh and funded by the Research Support Libraries Programme designed to open up a variety of outstanding collections of archives and manuscripts held at the three partner institutions, and to make them fully accessible on the Web.

Naikaku Bunko. *See* Kokuritsu Kobunshokan Naikaku Bunko.

Naked forme. Pages of type secured by page-cord. *See also* Dressed forme, Forme.

NAL. *See* 1. National Agricultural Library. 2. National Art Library.

Name authority file. The list of name headings used in a given catalogue, and the references made to them from other forms. *See also* Authority list, Subject authority file.

Name catalogue.   A catalogue arranged alphabetically by names of persons or places, or both, whether used as authors or subjects.

Name entry.   In indexing, an entry under the name of a person, place, or institution.

Name index.   An index of names of authors or other persons.

Name pallet.   *See* Binder's ticket.

Name reference.   Where alternative forms of names are available, a reference to the one adopted for the heading in a catalogue.

Namespace.   A unique name that identifies an organization that has developed an XML schema; it is identified via a URI (Uniform Resource Identifier). A controlled vocabulary such as the Library of Congress Subject Headings, a set of metadata elements such as the Dublin Core Metadata Element Set, or the set of all URLs in a given domain can be thought of as a namespace that is managed by the authority that is in charge of that particular set of terms.

Nancy Stirling Lambert Scholarship.   *See* Lambert (Nancy Stirling) Scholarship.

Nanosecond.   A billionth of a second, a unit of measurement used to represent the speed at which computers operate. *See also* Microsecond.

NAPLIB.   *See* National Association of Aerial Photographic Libraries.

NARA.   *See* National Archives and Records Administration.

Narration.   *See* Relation (1).

Narrow.   A book whose width is less than two thirds its height.

Narrower term.   (*Information retrieval*) A term which denotes a concept which is narrower than that of a term with a broader, more general, meaning, e.g. *Chairs* is narrower than *Furniture*. *See also* Broader term, Related term.

NASIG.   <www.nasig.org> North American Serials Group, formed 1985 to discuss, resolve and communicate issues relating to serials management. The Group seeks to bring together educators, librarians, publishers and agents and is independent of any other bodies.

NASL.   *See* National Art Slide Library.

National Acquisitions Group.   <www.nag.org.uk> (12 Holm Oak Drive, Madeley, Crewe CW3 9HR, UK) Formed in the UK in 1986 and now has 400 members in libraries, publishing, bookselling, etc. Seeks to bring together those concerned in acquisitions work (production, selection, purchase, supply of books and other printed materials, equipment and software for use in libraries and information units) and to act as a pressure group. Holds an Annual Conference, and issues a *Newsletter* (q.), *Directory* and various reports.

National Advisory Council on Preservation.   A US organization set up in 1987 and representing 20 bodies in the academic, scholarly, archival and library communities. Worked closely with the Commission on Preservation and Access.

National Agricultural Library (NAL).   <www.nalusda.gov> (10301 Baltimore Bvd, Beltsville MD 20705, USA) Formed as a result of the

Organic Act of 1862 which placed upon the Department of Agriculture the duty of 'acquiring and preserving all information concerning agriculture', the nucleus of the library being the transfer of the book and journal collection amounting to 1,000 volumes from the Agricultural Division of the Patent Office. The library was designated the National Agricultural Library in 1962. Services are provided to personnel of the Department of Agriculture in Washington, state agricultural agencies, agricultural colleges and universities, research institutions, industry, individual scientists, farmers and the general public in every part of the world. The Library's database – AGRICOLA – is available online and on CD-ROM, and a co-operative agreement is in operation with OCLC.

National archives. The central archives service of a country, established by legislation to manage the archives of central government and to provide leadership and co-ordination to other archives services. Models are provided by the International Council on Archives, which publishes abstracts of relevant legislation world-wide and also maintains a directory: <www.ica.org>. There is also a model for national archives in the European Union, published by the European Commission.

National Archives (UK). <www.nationalarchives.gov.uk> In 2003 the Public Record Office (PRO) and the Historical Manuscripts Commission (HMC) were merged. Both bodies continue to exist, and the functions of both will continue to be performed. The new organization includes a Digital Preservation Department which has started a digital archive – a long-term depository for electronic government records ranging from e-mails to audio and video files. A web archive is intended to collect and preserve the content of 53 selected central government websites. *See also* UK Web Archiving Consortium.

National Archives and Records Administration (NARA). <www.archives.gov> (700 Pennsylvania Avenue, Washington DC 20408, USA) A grouping of five co-ordinate offices: the Office of Federal Records Centers, the Office of the Federal Register, the Office of the National Archives, the Office of Presidential Libraries, and the Office of Records Management. It supersedes the National Archives Establishment, founded in 1935, and is responsible for identifying, preserving and making available to the federal government of the USA and to the public all forms of government record not restricted by law, which have sufficient historical, informational or evidential value to warrant preservation.

National Archives for Scotland. <www.nas.gov.uk> (General Register House, Edinburgh EH1 3YY, UK) Formerly the Scottish Record Office. Active in managing the records of the government offices of Scotland, of the Scottish Parliament, and those of local authorities. It is the base of the National Register of Archives (Scotland). Online access is not yet available.

National Archives of Australia. <www.naa.gov.au> A Commonwealth budget-funded agency, established as the Australian Archives under the

Archives Act 1983; its name was changed to the National Archives of Australia in 1998. The Archives plays a leading role in the management of Commonwealth records, makes available to the public non-exempt Commonwealth records over 30 years old, encourages and facilitates the use of archival resources of the Commonwealth, and provides leadership in developing and co-ordinating the preservation and use of the archival resources of Australia. Offices are located in Canberra, all States and the Northern Territory.

National Archives of Canada. <www.archives.ca> (395 Wellington Street, Ottawa, Ontario K1A 0N3, Canada) Formerly the Public Archives of Canada. Reconstituted by a new statute in 1980 to operate as the Federal Archives. Headquarters in Ottawa, with branches in provincial capitals. Each Province also maintains an archives service. *See also* Libraries and Archives Canada.

National Archives of India. <www.nationalarchives.nic.in> (Janpath, New Delhi 110001, India) Established in Calcutta in 1891 as the Imperial Record Department, and containing public records from 1748, it became the Archives of India in 1919, moved to Delhi in 1936, and after Independence in 1947 was retitled the National Archives of India. In addition to holdings of public records, maps, papers, books and manuscripts, it possesses records from several Indian states, and the private papers of many eminent Indians. The Government of India adopted an Archival Policy in 1972, and since that date the Archives service advises government departments and state governments on records management. There is a School of Archival Studies, and well-equipped conservation laboratory. A Regional Office is based in Bhopal, and Record Centres in Chennae [Madras], Jaipur, Pondicherry and Bhubaneswar. Publishes *Indian Archives* (bi-annual), *Archeion* (q.).

National Archives of Ireland. <www.nationalarchives.ie> The Act of 1986 united what had until then been the Public Record Office of Ireland and the State Paper Office in Dublin Castle to form the national archives of the republic. The SPO was originally founded in 1706, and the PROI in 1867. Situated in the Four Courts, much of the PROI was destroyed during the civil war of 1924. The National Archives are now based in new buildings in Bishop Street, Dublin, opened in 1992.

National Archives of Japan. *See* Kokuritsu Kobunshokan Naikaku Bunko.

National Archives of New Zealand. <www.archives.govt.nz> (10 Mulgrave Road, Wellington, New Zealand) Headquarters in Wellington, and branch offices in Auckland and Christchurch. The title Archives New Zealand is now preferred.

National Archives of Pakistan. <www.pakistan.gov.pk/cabinet-division/departments/nap> (Pak Secretariat, N Block, Islamabad, Pakistan) Established at Independence in 1947 to administer the archives of government and to provide for continuing administrations within the new country. New legislation in 1992 followed the construction of a new building in Islamabad.

National Art Library (UK). <www.nal.vam.ac.uk> (Victoria and Albert Museum, South Kensington, London SW7 2RL, UK) The library of the Victoria and Albert Museum – the National Museum of Art and Design – is designated as the National Art Library of the UK. The Library is currently being re-organized to become a more central information gateway to the Museum; this process should be complete in 2006.

National Art Slide Library (NASL). <www.library.dmu.ac.uk/services> (De Montfort University, Leicester LE1 9BH, UK) Founded originally in 1898 as a collection of lantern slides, NASL currently has over 500,000 items.

National Assembly Library, Republic of Korea. *See* Taehan Minguk Kukhoe Tosogwan.

National Association of Aerial Photographic Libraries (NAPLIB). <www.rspsoc.org/activities/naplib> A special interest group of the Remote Sensing and Photogrammetry Society; formed 1989 in the UK to safeguard and preserve aerial photographs, and raise awareness of the value of such photographs for archaeological, land use and social purposes.

National Association of News Librarians. *See* Association of UK Media Librarians.

National bibliography. A bibliography which lists all the books and other publications published, or distributed in significant quantity, in a particular country. Sometimes the term is used in respect to the new publications published within a specific period, and sometimes in respect to all those published within a lengthy period of many years. It is also used to indicate a bibliography of publications about a country (whether written by its nationals or not) and those written in the language of the country as well as those published in it.

National biography. A publication containing biographies of nationals of one country.

National Book Awards. Major US literary prizes, presented annually since 1950. The awards are currently made by the National Book Foundation. There are four genres: fiction, non-fiction, poetry and young people's literature.

National Book Committee. A UK organization founded in 1975, representing a wide range of bodies concerned with the place of books in society, which aims to further the use of books and to oppose reductions in library funding. It publishes an annual analysis of spending on books in public libraries, and examines provision in school libraries.

National Book Development Council. At a series of regional meetings convened by Unesco, it was recommended that a council or similar body should be established by every nation with the following objectives: to (a) serve as an intermediary between the book professions and the government so as to ensure the integration of book production and distribution into overall economic and social plans; to act as spokesman for the industries in questions of finance, taxation, customs regulations involving the government; (b) initiate measures that would help prevent or correct conditions prejudicial to book development and to promote activities and plans for national book development; (c) encourage the formation of professional associations relating to reading material where none exist and to strengthen such as are already in being; (d) promote, assist, and, where necessary, co-ordinate plans for concerted action on such questions as the training of personnel; (e) establish suitable machinery for promoting the reading habit and conduct research essential to the full development of book industries; (f) provide information related to the book trade and practices which can serve the development of books and reading generally; (g) undertake such additional activities as would ensure the balanced production and distribution of books and reading materials. The Unesco Secretariat has drawn up a model constitution for such a council.

National Book Foundation. <www.nationalbook.org> The US organization responsible for the National Book Awards.

National Book League. *See* Book Trust.

National Braille Association. *See* NBA.

National catalogue. A list of books in a number of libraries in a country. *See also* National bibliography.

National Cataloguing Unit for the Archives of Contemporary Scientists (NCUACS). <www.bath.ac.uk/ncuacs> (Claverton Down, Bath BA2 7AY, UK) Originally founded in 1973 as the Contemporary Scientific Archives Centre at Oxford, NCUACS was reformed in 1987 at the University of Bath, UK, under the auspices of the Royal Society, and funded by charitable trusts. It aims to locate and catalogue the archives of distinguished British scientists and engineers. It is not an archive, but a processing centre; papers identified are passed to other repositories. The Unit has a wide range of publications and progress reports.

National Center for Accessible E-learning Online Clearinghouse. <easi-elearn.org> A US project database, initiated by Equal Access to Software and Information to collect and disseminate resources on e-learning.

National Central Library (NCL). Formerly the Central Library for Students; this was the (UK) national centre for lending books for study, and the clearinghouse for loans of books and periodicals between public, university and special libraries of all types, working in co-operation with Regional Library Bureaux, and with special libraries known in this connection as Outlier Libraries. The Library ceased to exist as an independent organization on its absorption into the British Library, and thereby lost its identity. *See also* Regional bureaux.

National Centre for Information Media and Technology. Formerly National Reprographic Centre for Documentation (NRCd); name revised 1984. *See* CIMTECH.

National Centre for Text Mining. A UK centre announced in April 2004 to be led by UMIST in Manchester and run by a consortium comprising

UMIST, the Victoria University of Manchester, the University of Liverpool, the University of Salford and involving core international partners: the University of California Berkeley, the University of Geneva, the San Diego Supercomputing Centre, and the University of Tokyo, with the European Bioinformatics Institute having presence on the Technical Directorate. The Centre will be initially focused on biological and biomedical science, the area of science with the largest user community and the fastest growing literature, and the area where most applications research in text mining is being undertaken.

National Centre Libraries for Overseas Periodicals. Nine university libraries in Japan are assigned as centres of academic journals to collect, deposit and supply overseas periodicals according to subject area coverage, within the guidelines of the Science Information System. The system started in 1977, and was based on existing good holdings; some 20,000 additional titles have been collected since that date.

National Centres for Library Services. Organizations of various types which offer a range of services to libraries within a country or region. The term is used probably only for convenience in the IFLA *Round Table of National Centres for Library Service* (ROTNAC).

National Children's Book Week. (Book Trust, 45 East Hill, London SW18 2QZ, UK) An annual UK event to promote wider use and appreciation of reading and libraries; the Young Book Trust provides material for book events in schools and libraries.

National Commission on Libraries and Information Science. *See* NCLIS.

National Committee of Inquiry into Higher Education (UK). *See* Dearing Report.

National Council for Educational Technology (NCET). Formed in the UK in 1988 from the union of the earlier Council for Educational Technology (CET) and the Micro-electronics Education Support Unit (MESU). In 1998 it was restructured, and retitled BECTa.

National Council on Archives (UK). <nca.archives.org.uk> Established in 1988 as a forum in which the interests of owners, custodians and users of archives in the UK could be represented, matters of common concern brought to the attention of the public at large, and co-ordination achieved between the constituent bodies. These are the Association of County Archives, British Association for Local History, British Records Association, Business Archives Council, Federation of Family History Societies, the Historical Association, the Royal Historical Society, Scottish Records Association, Society of Archivists, and SCONUL. It has issued *Rules for the construction of personal, place and corporate names*, as a result of which the National Name Authority File (NNAF) was set up in 1998. *See also* National Archives (UK).

National Diet Library. *See* Kokuritsu Kokkai Toshokan.

National Digital Infrastructure and Preservation Program. <www.digitalpreservation.gov> Operated by the Library of Congress, this programme seeks to collect, archive and preserve digital content. Often known by the abbreviated title 'Digital Preservation Program'.

National Discography. A centralized online database of all commercially recorded UK audio materials, both current and deleted. A joint project of the National Sound Archive and the Mechanical Copyright Protection Society.

National Electronic Library for Health (NeLH). <www.nelh.nhs.uk> Launched in 2000, NeLH is an e-library targeted at healthcare professionals to support knowledge-based diagnosis and decision making, but is also accessible to patients and the public. Its content includes many specialist libraries and clinical resources. The service was receiving over 200,000 visits per month early in 2004.

National Electronic Site Licence Initiative. *See* NESLi2.

National Endowment for the Humanities (NEH). <www.neh.fed.us> A US funding body founded in 1965, which aims to support research, education, and public understanding of the humanities through grants to individuals, organizations, and institutions – many of these being library-related.

National Federation of Abstracting and Information Services (NFAIS). <www.nfais.org> (1518 Walnut Street, Philadelphia, PA 19102, USA) An association for organizations that aggregate, organize and facilitate access to information. Founded in the USA in 1922 and incorporated in January 1958 as the National Federation of Science Abstracting and Indexing Services to encourage and improve the documentation (abstracting, indexing, and analysing) of the world's scientific and technological literature so as to make it readily available to all scientists and technologists. Its foundation was supported by the publishers of many key secondary services (for example, *Biological Abstracts*, *Chemical Abstracts*, *Engineering Index*) and other bodies such as the National Academy of Sciences, National Science Foundation, and Unesco. The scope of activities was enlarged to include the social sciences and the humanities, and the word 'science' was consequently omitted from its name on 1 October 1972. 'Indexing' was changed to 'Information' in 1982. Aims are to help improve members' services and operations and to advance their prestige nationally and internationally; to undertake specific projects on behalf of members that would be broadly useful to most of the member services but which they could not undertake alone; to act as a national spokesman for the member services. Publishes *NFAIS Newsletter* (bi-m.). In 2003, NFAIS appointed a new director and announced a revitalization and new focus.

National Film Archive. *See* British Film Institute.

National Foundation for Educational Research (NFER). <www.nfer.ac.uk> (The Mere, Upton Park, Slough SL1 2DQ, UK) The leading independent educational research institution in the UK; it provides a range of information services to local education authorities in England, Wales and Northern Ireland.

National Grid for Learning. <www.ngfl.gov.uk> The UK Government's plan to develop an infrastructure to network all schools by 2002, outlined in the report *Connecting the Learning Society: the National Grid for Learning* which was published by the Department for Education and Employment in 1997. The plan was compatible with the similar scheme proposed in *New Library: the People's Network*. In 1998, follow-up proposals were issued in the report *Open for Learning, Open for Business: the Government's National Grid for Learning Challenge*. The Grid now functions as a gateway to networked educational resources – a network of selected links to websites for high-quality content and information.

National handwriting. *See* Handwriting.

National Heritage Act, 1980. UK legislation which established a National Heritage Fund, administered by trustees appointed by the Prime Minister, from which grants or loans may be made to assist in the purchase of collections of manuscripts or other 'heritage objects'.

National Information Infrastructure (NII). Plan put forward in the USA by the first Bush administration and continued by the Clinton administration to build a national digital superhighway/information infrastructure, taking advice from all interested parties and keeping in mind the basic aims for wide access, security, and sound regulation. *See also* Global Information Infrastructure, Internet, Internet2, Next Generation Internet.

National Information Policy. *See* National Information Strategy.

National Information Standards Organization (NISO). *See* Z39.

National Information Strategy. Many countries have developed frameworks of policies to steer their transition into information societies; most that do not yet have such a policy are engaged in consultation towards such a framework. The policy would normally be based on an investigation of the changes in information and communication technologies, an assessment of the country's weaknesses and strengths, and the opportunities offered, leading to a vision of the kind of society and economy towards which the country could aim. Factors for inclusion would be social, organizational, and industrial; education, competencies, quality, access, IT, information markets, human resources, legislation and regulation would be covered.

National Information Transfer Centres (NITCs). *See* ISORID.

National Institute of Adult Continuing Education (England and Wales). <www.niace.org.uk> (Renaissance House, 20 Princess Road West, Leicester LE1 6TP, UK) Founded in 1921, NIACE promotes understanding and awareness of adult and continuing education, liaises with overseas organizations, encourages co-operation, and holds meetings and conferences. It is composed of representatives of local authorities, universities, colleges, broadcasting organizations, and voluntary bodies. It organizes Adult Learners Week and the associated New Learning Opportunities Awards.

National Jazz Foundation Archive. <www.jazzservices.org.uk> (Loughton Central Library, Traps Hill, Loughton, Essex IG10 1HD, UK) Founded 1988 and relaunched 1993, the Archive contains books and periodicals, letters, posters and memorabilia. It complements the activities of the National Sound Archive and the British Institute of Jazz Studies.

National Learning Network (NLN). <www.nln.ac.uk> A national partnership programme in the UK designed to increase the uptake of Information Learning Technology (ILT) across the learning and skills sector in England. Supported by the Learning Skills Council and other sector bodies, the NLN provides network infrastructure and a wide-ranging programme of support, information and training, as well as the development and provision of ILT materials for teaching and learning. Initially for the benefit of further education and sixth form colleges – 'post-16 education' – the NLN programme of work is now being rolled out to workplace learning and adult and community learning.

National Lending Library for Science and Technology (UK). Founded (as a consequence of a recommendation in the *Eighth Annual Report* of the Advisory Council on Scientific Policy, 1955) in 1962 and based on the library of the Department of Scientific and Industrial Research with stock from the Science Museum Library and other sources. This library ceased to function as an independent organization, and also lost its identity, on its absorption into the British Library in 1973, becoming a major part of the Document Supply Centre.

National Libraries Committee. *See* Dainton Report.

National Libraries Week (UK). Various events have been organized over the years to celebrate the role of libraries in society; from 1966 professional associations have collaborated to hold such events but not on an annual basis. *See also* National Library Week.

National library. A library maintained out of government funds and serving the nation as a whole. Usually, books in such libraries are for reference only. They usually receive material through legal deposit legislation. The function of such a library is to collect and preserve for posterity the published record of the country's cultural heritage, usually in printed form but increasingly in multimedia formats as well. This is best done by a law requiring publishers to deposit copies of all publications issued by them, and by purchasing books published in other countries. National libraries usually collect comprehensively material published in their own country and material about their own country published outside it. A legal deposit law normally has penalty clauses to enable the act to be enforced. *See also* Legal deposit. The functions of national libraries vary considerably. They may compile union catalogues, produce a national bibliography, publish a retrospective national bibliography, or act as a national bibliographical centre. Most countries have a national library, in fact if not in name. Some more significant ones in international terms are listed amongst the entries that appear on the subsequent pages, or under individual country names.

National Library for the Blind (NLB). <www.nlbuk.org> (Far Cromwell Road, Stockport, Cheshire SK6 2SG, UK) Britain's principal source of general reading in Braille and Moon, the library provides for the blind as nearly as possible what the public library does for the sighted. Its service is completely free and open to all who need it. Begun in 1882, it now houses a third of a million volumes in a specially-adapted modern building. Publishes catalogues, and *NLB Bulletin* (6 p.a.).

National Library for Women. *See* Women's Library.

National Library of Australia. <www.nla.gov.au> (Parkes Place, Canberra, ACT 2600, Australia) Established as a statutory authority under the National Library Act of 1960, the Library was formerly part of the Commonwealth Parliamentary Library. The Act was last amended in 1991. The Library is one of Australia's leading research and reference libraries. Its collections include more than 8 million books, journals, newspapers, microforms, manuscripts, maps, music, pictures, photographs, films, videos and oral history tapes. The Library houses the largest collection in Australia of rare books and books printed before 1800. In addition to Australian items, it has a large collection of materials published overseas with particular emphasis on Asia.

National Library of Canada/Bibliothèque Nationale du Canada. <www.nlc-bnc.ca> (395 Wellington Street, Ottawa, Ontario K1A ON4, Canada) Established in 1953, this Library together with the Public Archives were accommodated in a new building in Ottawa in 1967. The Library is concerned mainly with material in social and behavioural sciences and the humanities, the sciences being served by the Canada Institute for Scientific and Technical Information (CISTI). A new National Library Act came into force on 1 September 1969; amongst other provisions, this assigned co-ordinating powers to the National Library and enabled it to provide active and effective leadership to the libraries of the federal government. The National Library of Canada has a three-fold mandate: to gather, preserve and make known the Canadian literary and musical heritage; to promote the development of library services and resources in Canada; and to support resource sharing among Canadian libraries. There are three operating branches: Public Services; Acquisitions and Bibliographic Services; and Information Technology Services. The National Library produces *Canadiana*, the national bibliography, which provides full English and French cataloguing copy for current Canadian publications and foreign publications of Canadian interest. There is an extensive programme of publishing, and cultural events.

National Library of China. *See* Zhong Guo Guo Jia Tu Shu Guan.

National Library of Education (NLE). <www.ed.gov.nle> (400 Maryland Avenue, SW, Washington DC20202, USA) Founded 1973, the National Library of Education holds materials on the federal role in education, the history of education in the USA, management, psychology and the social sciences, as well as educational statistics. In 2002 the Bush administration created the Institute of Education Sciences, of which NLE should become a component.

National Library of Iran. <www.nli.ir> Currently active with the Iranian Library Association in helping Afghan librarians improve collections and equipment. It has also operated a library science refresher course for Afghan librarians and is trying to re-launch the Afghan Library Association.

National Library of Ireland. <www.nli.ie> (Kildare Street, Dublin 2, Ireland) Originally the library of the Royal Dublin Society, a semi-public, grant-aided institution; it became known as the National Library of Ireland in 1877. It benefits from Irish legal deposit, and is controlled by the Irish government. It is the principal centre for research into Irish literature and history and contains 500,000 books, as well as collections of periodicals, newspapers, maps, prints, drawings, manuscripts, films and photographs, all relating to Ireland.

National Library of Korea. *See* Kungnim Chungang Tosogwan.

National Library of Medicine (NLM). <www.nlm.nih.gov> (8600 Rockville Pike, Bethesda, MD 20894, USA) Founded in 1836 as the Library of the Surgeon General's Office, United States Army, re-named the Army Medical Library in 1922, again re-named the Armed Forces Medical Library in 1952 and finally re-named in 1956 when it became a part of the Public Health Service of the Department of Health, Education and Welfare. The NLM is the world's largest research library in a single scientific and professional field. The Library collects materials exhaustively in all major areas of the health sciences and to a lesser degree in such areas as chemistry, physics, botany and zoology. Lending and other services are provided through a Regional Medical Library Network consisting of 4,000 'basic unit' libraries (mostly at hospitals), 125 Resource Libraries (at medical schools), 7 Regional Medical Libraries (covering all geographic regions of the US), and the NLM itself as a national resource for the entire Network. *See also* MEDLARS.

National Library of New Zealand. [Te Puna Matauanga o Aotearoa] <www.natlib.govt.nz> (PO Box 1467, Wellington 6001, New Zealand) Founded by Act of Parliament in 1965, bringing together various elements previously existing as units of the National Library Service including Country Library Service (1938), School Library Service (1942), New Zealand Library School (1946), and the National Library Centre (bibliographic utilities). It also brought into the National Library the Alexander Turnbull Library (a rich heritage collection of national literature, manuscripts, paintings, etc., with rare books and special collections from other fields, founded 1920). There have been several reorganizations of structure and services. Current emphases relate to heritage matters in national and Pacific literature; policy advice to the government on the availability of, and access to, information; the facilitation of access to information in partnership with other libraries.

In 1985 collections were moved from various locations into a new building; in 1988 the Library became an autononous government department. The National Film Library became part of the National Library in 1990.

National Library of Québec/Bibliothèque Nationale du Québec. <www. bnquebec.ca> (125 Sherbrooke O, Montréal, Québec, H2X 1XA, Canada) Formed in 1967, this Library performs all the modern functions of a national library, including legal deposit and the compilation of current and retrospective bibliographies relating to the Province of Québec. Based on the Library of Saint Sulpice, founded 1915 and acquired by the government of Québec in 1941.

National Library of Scotland (NLS). <www.nls.uk> (George IV Bridge, Edinburgh EH1 1EW; NLS Lending Services: 33 Salisbury Place, Edinburgh EH9 1SL, UK) Founded as the Advocates' Library in 1682, it became the National Library of Scotland by Act of Parliament in 1925 when the Faculty of Advocates transferred to the nation all but its legal collection. The Library has held the British Legal Deposit Privilege since 1710. Its collections of printed books and MSS., augmented by gift and purchase, are very large, and it has an unrivalled Scottish collection. A new building was opened in 1956. In 1974 the Scottish Central Library was incorporated to become Lending Services (NLSLS), and is the Scottish counterpart of the Document Supply Centre of the British Library. A new building to house the Scottish Science Library opened in 1989. Publications include: *Bibliography of Scotland* (annually), *Directory of Scottish newspapers* (1984), *Catalogue of manuscripts* (7 vols.), *General catalogue of printed books on microfiche* (1988).

National Library of South Africa. <www.nlsa.ac.za> (P O Box 990, 0001 Pretoria, South Africa) Formerly known as the South African Library; originally founded in 1818. The Library also incorporates the Centre for the Book (P O Box 15254, Vlaeberg, 8018 Cape Town, South Africa) which promotes the writing, publishing, reading, marketing, and distribution of South African books.

National Library of Wales/Llyfrgell Genedlaethol Cymru. <www.llgc.org.uk> (Aberystwyth, SY23 3BU, UK) A government-financed library which was founded in 1909 following the granting of a Royal Charter in 1907. It specializes in manuscripts and books relating to Wales and the Celtic peoples, and has a stock of over 3 million printed books, 30,000 manuscripts, 3.5 million deeds and documents, and numerous maps, prints and drawings. It is a Legal Deposit Library in respect of books in the Welsh language or dealing with Wales.

National Library Week. National Library Weeks have been held in the USA for over 30 years. Their object has been to attempt to reduce illiteracy and increase interest in books, reading and libraries but their effectiveness was dependent on the extent to which state library associations and agencies and individual libraries organized and developed programmes for their own purposes. From 1975 the (US) National Library Week is organized by the American Library Association. For similar UK activities, *see* National Libraries Week.

National Literacy Association. <www.nla.org.uk> (235 Fairmile Road, Christchurch, Dorset BH23 2LQ, UK) Formed in 1993, the Association is a campaign group to promote literacy. It is gaining a high profile with several celebrity supporters.

National Literacy Trust. <www.literacytrust.org.uk> (Swire House, 59 Buckingham Gate, London SW1E 6AJ, UK) An independent charity, launched in the UK in 1993, to improve reading and writing standards. The Trust works closely with other agencies, for example in the adult literacy field, and aims to build contacts, establish a database of best practice, encourage media interest and generally support literacy promotion. The Trust was responsible for managing the National Year of Reading.

National Manuscripts Conservation Trust. <www.bl.concord/nmct-about> (British Library, 96 Euston Road, London NW1 2DB, UK) Established in 1989 by the British Library and the Royal Commission on Historical Manuscripts, the Trust is intended to assist record offices, libraries, owners of archives, manuscripts, and documents accessible to the public, where a need can be shown for financial support beyond the applicant's normal resources. Grants are made for the preservation of papyri, parchment rolls, paper, maps, files, letters and manuscripts.

National Micrographics Association. Founded in the United States in 1943 as the National Microfilm Association (the name being changed in 1975); it is now the Association for Information and Image Management (AIIM).

National Name Authority File. *See* NNAF.

National Preservation Office (NPO). <www.bl.uk/services/npo> (British Library, 96 Euston Road, London NW1 2DB, UK) Established 1984 by the British Library to initiate research in the area of document and book conservation and preservation; security issues are also now a part of its work. *See also* Enright Report, Ratcliffe Report.

National Reference Library of Science and Invention (NRLSI). Formed by amalgamating the Patent Office Library which was transferred to the British Museum in May 1966, with books on science in the British Museum in separate buildings apart from the British Museum. When the British Library was formed in 1973 this Library was re-named the Science Reference Library and became part of the Reference Division. *See* British Library.

National Register of Archives. <www.nationalarchives/gov.uk/archon> Established in 1945 by the Royal Commission on Historical Manuscripts to collect and disseminate information about manuscript and archival sources for British history outside the Public Records. The NRA now holds more then 40,000 unpublished lists and catalogues drawn from all types of archive service in the UK and other countries.

Information about these is now available online through the service ARCHON.

National Register of Microform Masters (NRMM). First proposed in 1936, the NRMM was established in 1965 after a study conducted for the Association of Research Libraries (ARL). The Library of Congress (LC) took the lead and collated reports of masters sent by libraries, historical societies, and publishers between 1965 and 1983; annual volumes were published. In 1986, with funding from the National Endowment for the Humanities and the Andrew W. Mellon Foundation, ARL and LC began discussion on the creation of machine-readable records; the conversion contract was awarded to OCLC in 1990 and completed in 1997. NRMM is now accessible via OCLC's WorldCat and the RLIN database, and contains 579,000 records for monographic and serial preservation microform masters.

National Reprographic Centre for Documentation. *See* CIMTECH.

National Science Digital Library. *See* NSDL.

National Science Foundation Middleware Initiative. *See* NSF Middleware Initiative.

National Science Foundation Network. *See* Internet.

National Serials Data Program (NSDP). <www.loc.gov/issn> Established on 17 April 1972 in the US as Phase 3 of a co-ordinated effort to implement a system for identifying and controlling serial publications. Its immediate concern was to develop a corporate authority file (a serials data base); to take into consideration the various authorities used by the three National Libraries (Library of Congress, National Library of Medicine, National Agricultural Library); the assignment of ISSNs to prospective periodical titles published in the USA. (Phase 1 resulted in the identification of data elements needed for the control of serials by machine methods and the development of the MARC serials format. Phase 2 was the creation of a machine-readable file of live serial titles in science and technology and the production of a variety of listings.) It is now the US national centre for ISDS and is located within the Library of Congress. *See also* ISSN.

National Sound Archive (UK). Formerly the British Institute of Recorded Sound, the Archive was absorbed within the British Library in 1983. It is now the Recorded Sound special collection in the British Library.

National Technical Information Service. *See* NTIS.

National Television Standards Committee. *See* NTSC.

National Training Organization (NTO). *See* ISNTO.

National Translations Center (NTC). An international depository and referral centre for helping users locate unpublished translations of foreign-language literature in scientific, technological, and social science fields. Located at the Library of Congress 1989 onwards, after a move from the University of Chicago.

National union catalogue. 1. A Union catalogue covering the whole of a country, and giving information on location and availability of books or other materials. *See also* UKNUC.   2. *National Union Catalog (NUC)* Contains holdings data for the collections of the Library of Congress; several sequences have been issued since 1948 when the first set of 167 volumes covering pre-1942 material was issued. Music, recordings and motion pictures are also included in separate volumes.

National Union Catalog of Manuscript Collections (NUCMC). A large-scale US co-operative project to bring together data on some 24,000 manuscript collections in over 90 participating libraries and archives, and some 3,000 collections in the Library of Congress.

National Union Catalogue of Alternative Formats (NUCAF). *See now* RevealWeb.

National Year of Reading (NYR).   September 1998–July 1999 was designated in the UK as the National Year of Reading; the co-ordinators of the Year were the National Literacy Trust. Limited funding was made available for 28 associated projects, of which seven had library involvement.

Natural classification.   One in which qualities which are either inborn/ intrinsic or are essential to the existence of the thing or things to be divided are adopted as the 'difference' (*see* Predicables, five) or characteristic of arrangement, e.g. dividing 'living creatures' into invertebrates and vertebrates. One which exhibits the inherent properties of the things classified, and which groups or separates them according to their natural likeness or unlikeness. *See also* Artificial classification, Characteristic of a classification.

Natural language.   (*Information retrieval, Indexing*) 1. A language the rules of which reflect current usage without being specifically prescribed. 2. The language of the documents indexed. *See also* Artificial indexing language; Indexing language.

Natural Sciences Library of Russian Academy of Sciences. <www.gpntb.ru> (11 Znamenka, Moscow, 119890 Russia) The lead organization of the Academy's 300 libraries throughout Russia; as well as holding an enormous stock the Library is a centre for interlibrary lending, and a scientific institution in the fields of informatics and librarianship.

Natural Selection.   <nature.ac.uk> A subject gateway providing access to Internet resources in the natural world; part of the BIOME Hub of the (UK) RDN.

Nautical almanac.   A publication which tabulates the position of the sun, moon, planets and navigational stars for each date at any time of day or night.

Navigation.   Commonly used to indicate methods of searching and examining online databases and the Web, particularly noting the logical arrangement and the ease of moving around the site or database. A more formal term than Net surfing.

NBA.   1. <www.nationalbraille.org> National Braille Association, a non-profit-making American organization founded in 1945, which exists to produce and distribute Braille and large type publications and tape recordings for blind and partially sighted readers in the USA, particularly students in elementary and secondary schools, colleges and universities. This material is produced by volunteers. The Association also operates the Braille Book Bank, the prime source of current college textbooks in Braille for blind students. 2. *See* Net Book Agreement.

NBL. National Book League. *See* Book Trust.

NBM. *See* Non-book materials.

n.c. Abbreviation for 'not catalogued'; relates usually to a volume of miscellaneous pamphlets which are not individually catalogued.

NCeSS (UK). <www.ncess.ac.uk> National Centre for e-Social Science, funded by the Economic and Social Research Council and established in April 2004 to promote and facilitate e-science within social science research. A broader aim is to stimulate the uptake and use by social scientists of new and emerging Grid-enabled computing in quantitative and qualitative research. Based at Manchester University with support from the UK Data Archive, NCeSS consists of a co-ordinating hub and a set of research-based nodes distributed across the UK.

NCET. *See* National Council for Educational Technology.

NCL. *See* National Central Library.

NCLIS. <www.nclis.gov> (1110 Vermont Avenue, Washington DC 20005, USA) National Commission on Libraries and Information Science, a permanent and independent agency of the federal government charged with advising Congress and the President on matters relating to libraries and information services. Established 1970 it has the primary responsibility for developing and recommending overall plans for providing library and information services adequate to meet the needs of the people of the USA. Aims to: (a) ensure that all local communities are provided with basic, adequate library and information services; (b) provide adequate suitable services to special user constituencies; (c) strengthen existing statewide resources and systems; (d) develop the human resources required to implement a national programme; (e) co-ordinate existing federal library and information programmes; (f) make the private sector a more active partner in the development of a national programme. Current activity includes issues such as copyright, public information, surveys of the use of electronic resources. After concern in 2002 about its funding, NCLIS was re-vitalized in 2003/2004 by the appointment by the Bush administration of several new councillors.

NCR. *See Nihon Mokuroku Kisoku.*

NCUACS. *See* National Cataloguing Unit for the Archives of Contemporary Scientists.

n.d. *See* No date.

NDL. *See* Kokuritsu Kokkai Toshokan.

NDLTD. <www.ndltd.org> Networked Digital Library of Theses and Dissertations, an initiative sponsored by the US Department of Education's Fund for the Improvement of Post-secondary Education with the aim of constructing a global digital library of electronic theses and dissertations.

Near letter quality.   Output from a dot-matrix or Inkjet Printer of a superior quality to the fastest draft printing and supposed to approach the quality of Laser printers.

Near print.   A general term for substitute printing processes, the basic techniques being typewriter composition and offset printing.

Nearest neighbour.   Online searching that involves a match between document and query terms with weights included to indicate relative importance. A measure of similarity is calculated and the retrieved items are arranged in order of decreasing similarity, the most relevant items presented first. *See also* Boolean logic, Proximity indicator.

Neat line.   A line, usually a Grid or Graticule bounding the borders of a map.

NEBASE.   <www.nlc.state.ne.us/netserv/nebase> (1200 N Street, Lincoln NE 68508, USA) The Nebraska Library Commission is a network consortium of libraries, situated in the US state of Nebraska. An OCLC Network Affiliate.

Neck.   *See* Bevel.

Nederlandse Vereniging van Bibliothecarissen, Documentalisten en Literatuur Onderzoekers (NVB).   *See* Dutch library associations.

Need to know.   A basic principle of security which restricts access to classified documents and information to those whose duties make such access essential, no person being permitted to have access merely by virtue of rank or appointment.

Needlework binding.   *See* Embroidered binding.

Negative.   1. In photographing with a camera, a negative image normally results when a film is developed; in this the tones are reversed black being white and vice versa. A positive print, in which the tones are again reversed and then seen as with the naked eye, can be produced from the negative either by contact or by enlargement.   2. In printing, reversed image and light values appear on half-tone blocks of illustrations, and these stand in the same relationship to the resulting print as do negatives in the ordinary photographic process.

Negative selection.   *See* Weeding.

Negotiation Agent.   *See* Managing Agent.

NEH.   *See* National Endowment for the Humanities.

Neighbourhood information centre.   A local service point offering residents advice, information or referral on the whole range of social and welfare topics. Such a centre may be based in, or share premises with, a local public branch library.

NeLH.   *See* National Electronic Library for Health.

NELINET, Inc.   <www.nelinet.net> (153 Cordaville Road, Suite 200, Southborough, MA 01772-1833, USA) New England Library Information Network, a large regional network of diverse membership in Connecticut, Maine, Massachusetts, New Hampshire, Rhode Island and Vermont. An OCLC Network Affiliate.

NEMLAC. *See* Museums, Libraries and Archives Council (MLA).

Neo-caroline. *See* Humanistic hand.

Neo-grotesque. A group of Lineale typefaces derived from the Grotesque group compared with which they have less contrast in the thickness of the strokes, and are more regular in design. The ends of the curved strokes are usually oblique and the 'g' often has an open tail. Of such are Edeh/Wotan, Helvetica and Univers.

NEPHIS. Nested Phrase Indexing System, a computer-assisted system for the production of printed indexes. The indexer decides on appropriate subject descriptions and translates them into input strings. The NEPHIS program then generates the required permutations.

NESLi2. <www.nesli2.ac.uk/index.htm> The UK's national initiative for the licensing of electronic journals on behalf of the higher and further education and research communities for the period 2003–2006. NESLi2 is a product of the JISC and underwritten by the Higher Education Funding Council for England. It follows the three year Pilot Site Licence Initiative (1995–1997) and the original NESLI (National Electronic Site Licence Initiative, 1998–2001), which introduced the concept of a Managing Agent and piloted the use of a model licence for use in negotiating agreements with publishers.

Net Book Agreement. UK agreement drawn up in 1929 (and revised in 1957) between the Publishers Association, the Booksellers Association, and the Library Association. Under the Standard Conditions of Sale, a book could not be sold at less than the 'net' price stated by the publisher except in certain circumstances; for example, it enabled rate-supported libraries and other libraries admitting the public without charge throughout the usual opening hours to receive a discount of 10 per cent on all new books purchased, provided the library applied for a licence. After pressure from large bookselling firms in 1994 and 1995 various legal challenges were made; discounting was becoming common particularly around the Christmas period. Following actions in the Restrictive Practices Court the Agreement fell into abeyance in 1997 and is now abandoned.

Net surfing. Browsing or searching the World Wide Web, Usenet Discussion groups and any other electronic services that can be found on the Internet.

Netcasting. *See* Webcasting.

Netiquette. Network etiquette, the informal code of manners to be observed when using the Internet, particularly when contributing to Usenet groups and Mailing lists. In particular, one is advised not to react quickly to messages that have caused annoyance, to avoid cross-posting to inappropriate forums and to refrain from commercial messages outside business lists.

Netskills. <www.netskills.ac.uk> (University Computing Service, University of Newcastle, Newcastle-upon-Tyne NE1 7RU, UK) Provides Internet training services to facilitate the effective use of internet and Intranet technologies for teaching and learning, research, administration, marketing and other business activities. This is achieved through hands-on workshops delivered at regional centres throughout the UK, the development of a comprehensive range of training materials available under licence, and the provision of online, self-paced tutorials.

Network. 1. A bookbinding design made of intersecting lines forming squares set lozenge-wise. 2. A system of physically separate computers with telecommunication links, allowing resources such as Software and Peripherals to be shared by either commercial or informal arrangement. *See also* Internet, Local area network, Metropolitan area network, Value added network, Wide area network. 3. An informal, personal group of one's colleagues with whom regular contact is maintained for mutual professional support. 4. The Network <www. seapn.org.uk> 'The Network' is a UK network of public libraries, archives, museums, other organizations and individuals in partnership with the Museums, Libraries and Archives Council (MLA) committed to tackling social exclusion in libraries etc. There are courses, conferences and newsletters.

Network computer. *See* Thin client.

Network news. A generic term for the information transmitted in subject-oriented Discussion groups, particularly via Usenet.

Network of Information Professionals (NIP). <www.foi-uk.org> A subscription-based virtual community set up in the UK to help public-sector bodies cope with freedom of information legislation when it is fully implemented in 2005. It is operated by the organization Public Partners.

Neural network. An interconnected system of processing elements which models the neurons in the nervous system and which, through Artificial intelligence techniques, can learn by association and recognition.

Neutrality. In subject cataloguing, a situation in which user preference cannot influence one course over another because it is unascertainable or because it does not exist. Catalogues of general libraries are mostly neutral in this sense whereas those in special libraries may reflect the viewpoints of a homogeneous clientele.

New edition. An issue of a book in which misprints noticed in an earlier edition have been corrected. Reprints which are made a substantial number of years after the original edition may be regarded as new editions, but such cases are best described as '2nd (etc.) edition re-printed'. *See also* Edition, First edition, Impression, Issue, Reprint, Revised edition.

New impression. *See* Impression.

New Learning Opportunities Awards. *See* Adult Learners Week, National Institute of Adult Continuing Education (England and Wales).

New Library: the People's Network. <www.peoplesnetwork.gov.uk> A report commissioned from the (UK) Library and Information

Commission (LIC) by the Department for Culture, Media and Sport (DCMS). The report, which was published in 1997, is a visionary expression of how UK public libraries could re-engineer to prepare for the information society and economy of the twenty-first century; it was described by the Secretary of State as a 'defining moment for the public library service'. The report outlines networking of all service points, training of staff, and potential roles for the revitalized service. The Department made a response in 1998, and at the end of that year published a follow-up report *Building the New Library Network* which contains the practical details and costed implementation proposals, explains how this approach is compatible with the process developed by the National Grid for Learning (NGfL), proposes a framework for creating and managing resources, and outlines a programme of training for all 27,000 UK public library staff. *See now* People's Network.

New Opportunities Fund (NOF). <www.nof.org.uk> A funding source provided from the UK National Lottery and directed at health, education and the environment; late in 1998 a consultation document *New Links for the Lottery: Proposals for the New Opportunities Fund* proposed that the infrastructure of the public library network should be funded from this source. NOF has now become a major funding source for the People's Network (along with the Bill and Melinda Gates Foundation; *see* Gates Foundation), and for public library staff training. Funds are also directed towards digitizing learning materials to provide content <www.enrichuk.net>.

New Zealand Library and Information Association Inc./Te Rau Herenga o Aotearoa. *See* LIANZA.

Newark charging system. An American method of recording book issues whereby the book cards are inscribed with the borrower's number and dated, so becoming the time record.

Newberry Library. A free reference library established in Chicago, Illinois, USA, in 1887 and maintained by a moiety of the estate of Walter Loomis Newberry (1804–68), a Chicago merchant. This bequest is supplemented by subsequent gifts and by the continuing programme of the Newberry Library Associates. The stock totals 900,000 volumes on many subjects but mainly the humanities; the Library is particularly strong on Americana, American Indians, history of printing, Western Europe, Great Britain until the early twentieth century, Latin America, Portuguese discoveries and music, and there are treasures in each of the subject divisions. The first Librarian (1887–95) was William Frederick Poole, compiler of *Poole's index to periodical literature, 1802–81*.

Newbery (John) Medal. The Newbery medal has been awarded annually since 1922 under the auspices of the Association for Library Services to Children of the American Library Association. Donated by the Frederic G. Melcher family, the award is made to the author of the most distinguished contribution to children's literature published in the United States during the preceding year. Winner must be citizen of or resident in the United States. Named after John Newbery (1713–67) the famous British publisher of St. Paul's Churchyard who was the first to publish books for children; he was part-author of some of the best of those he published. The medal was first awarded (in 1922) to Hendrik Willem Van Loon for *The story of mankind. See also* Caldecott (Randolph) Medal.

News feed. The content of electronic news groups, when transmitted over the Internet for use at remote locations. *See also* RSS, Usenet.

News group. *See* Discussion group, Usenet.

Newsbook. A publication printed in a small quarto volume of up to twenty-four pages, and containing news. Newsbooks were first published in 1622, being dated and numbered, and although calling themselves 'weekly', were published at irregular intervals and never on a fixed day of the week. They contained all kinds of news from all over the world but were strictly forbidden to print home news. They were not numbered until 1641 and dealt almost exclusively with the Thirty Years War. Their publication was considerably diminished after the outbreak of the Great Rebellion towards the end of 1641, and ceased in 1642. At first they comprised one sheet of quarto, and later two. Variously called Diurnall, *Mercurius Intelligence. See also* Coranto, Relation.

Newsletter. 1. A manuscript report of current happenings, written for special subscribers and issued irregularly or weekly in the sixteenth and seventeenth centuries. 2. A similar report published in the seventeenth century and sometimes set in script-like type and imitating the appearance of the earlier manuscript newsletter. 3. A brief publication conveying news. Frequently issued by societies or business organizations.

Newspaper. A publication issued periodically, usually daily or weekly, containing the most recent news. The word 'newspaper' was first used in 1670. Previously the word was Coranto and later Newsbook.

Newspaper library. 1. A collection of reference books, pamphlets, reports, press cuttings, government publications etc. provided to serve the needs of the staff of a daily newspaper. 2. The British Library Newspaper Library. *See* British Library, NEWSPLAN.

Newspaper Licensing Agency (NLA). <www.nla.co.uk> (Lonsdale Gate, Lonsdale Gardens, Tunbridge Wells, Kent TN1 1NL) An agency set up in the UK in 1966 to license the use of copyright material which appears in newspapers. It licenses cuttings agencies for multiple distribution of copies to clients and issues licences for almost any kind of organization. It includes all national and an increasing number of regional newspapers. After a recent major court case with Marks and Spencer plc, the remit of the NLA needs clarification as to whether it can license the content or only the typography of newspapers.

Newspaper rod/stick. *See* Stick (2).

NEWSPLAN. <www.newsplan.co.uk> Originally started in 1986 as a national research project, funded by the British Library, to assess the condition of newspapers throughout the UK and Ireland, and establish priorities for microfilming. Ten regional reports appeared locating files and recommending action. For several years the scheme operated as a panel of the Library and Information Co-operation Council (LINC), but now functions independently after the closure of that body. Funding and grants have been forthcoming from the British Library and the LASER Foundation. A database of 2,500 local newspapers is available. The NEWSPLAN 2000 project received £5 million from the Heritage Lottery Fund to microfilm a further 17,000 local newspapers, and follow-on funding will be sought when the first stage ends in 2004. Digitization – which would allow searchability – is being investigated.

Newsprint. The lowest grade of paper: it is made mostly from wood pulp and used for newspapers.

Newsroom. The department of a library which stocks current newspapers.

Next Generation Internet (NGI). <www.ngi.gov> A multi-agency US federal research and development program to develop advanced networking technologies, develop revolutionary applications that require advanced networking, and demonstrate these capabilities on high-speed testbeds. The NGI program was successfully completed and the focus for co-ordinating advanced networking research programmes was expected to transfer to a Large Scale Networking (LSN) Co-ordinating Group. *See also* Internet2.

NFAIS. *See* National Federation of Abstracting and Information Services.

NFER. *See* National Foundation for Educational Research.

NFF. <www.kcl.ac.uk/projects/srch> Non-Formula Funding of Specialised Research Collections in the Humanities, an initiative that provided some £50 million from the UK Higher Education Funding Councils. Completed in July 2000 and work continued via the Archives Hub.

NGfL. *See* National Grid for Learning.

NGI. *See* Next Generation Internet.

NiAA. *See* Northern informatics.

NIACE. *See* National Institute of Adult Continuing Education (England and Wales).

NIC. *See* Neighbourhood Information Centres.

Nick. The groove which is cut on the Belly of a piece of movable type. Its purpose is to enable the compositor to set type the right way up without looking at the face of the type, and also (by reason of the position and number of nicks for each type size and face) to know immediately when a wrong Sort has come to hand. Also called 'Groove'. *See also* Body.

Nickel-faced stereo. A Stereo which is given a facing of nickel in order to lengthen its effective life.

Nickname. A fanciful appellation given by others, in addition to, or in place of, a proper name, as, for example, Scaramouche to Tiberio Fiorella. Also called 'Byname', 'Sobriquet'.

Nickname index. A list of 'nicknames', or popular names, for places, persons, official reports, laws or organizations and giving the full, proper, or official names or titles. It is usually arranged alphabetically.

NICT. New Information Society Technologies: an expression increasingly used within EU reports in place of IST.

Nielsen Bookdata Reference Awards. *See* CILIP/Nielsen Bookdata Reference Awards.

Niger Morocco. Leather produced on the banks of the River Niger from native-tanned goatskin. Often abbreviated to 'Niger'.

Nigerian Library Association (NLA). <nla.bravehost.com> Founded as the West African Library Association in August 1953 as an outgrowth of the Unesco Seminar on the Development of Public Libraries in Africa; this was superseded by the Ghana Library Association, and the Nigeria Library Association in 1963. Publishes *Nigerian Libraries* (3 p.a.), *NLA Newsletter* (members only).

nihil obstat. (Lat. 'nothing hinders') Sanction for publication given by a Roman Catholic censor and usually found on the verso of the title-page or the following leaf.

Nihon Boeki Shinkokai. [Japan External Trade Organization (JETRO)] <www.jetro.go.jp> (Kyodo Tsushin Kaikan Bldg. 6th fl, 2-5 Toranomon 2-chome, Minato-ku, Tokyo 105-8466, Japan) JETRO, established in 1958, is a non-profit, Japanese government-related organization, reorganized in 2003 to provide information on both foreign and domestic trade and investment. It maintains a major collection of research reports, directories and statistics on foreign and overseas trade, and publishes a wide range of freely available electronic materials.

Nihon Igaku Toshokan Kyokai. [Japan Medical Library Association (JMLA)] <wwwsoc.nii.ac.jp/jmla> (Gakkai Center Bldg 5th fl, 2-4-16 Yayoi, Bunkyo-ku, Tokyo 113, Japan) Originally founded in 1927 by five government medical schools, it now has 114 members plus international affiliations, and aims to promote co-operation, good practice and training. it holds conferences and publishes *Igaku Toshokan* [*Medical libraries*] (q.), union lists of foreign medical materials, and *Medical subject headings*.

Nihon Jusshin Bunruiho. [*Nippon Decimal Classification (NDC)*] A standard classification used in Japanese libraries, compiled by the Japan Library Association. The current edition is the ninth (1995); the first edition was compiled in 1929. *NDC* adopts the mechanism of the Dewey Decimal Classification, but the arrangement of the classes is based on Cutter's Expansive Classification.

Nihon Mokuroku Kisoku. [*Nippon Cataloguing Rules (NCR)*] First issued by the Japan League of Young Librarians, [later Japan Library Association] in 1943, these are the standard rules used in Japan. The 1987 edition and its 1994 and 2001 revisions conform to the MARC format and ISBD. The 2001 revision also includes a revised 'Chapter 9: Computer files,' devised according to ISBD(ER).

Nihon Sakuinka Kyokai. [Japan Indexers Association] (c/o Nichigai Associates, Dai 3 Shimokawa Bldg, 1-23-8 Omori-kita, Ota-ku, Tokyo 143-8550, Japan) Established in 1977 to protect the rights of bibliographers and indexers, and to encourage good practice. It has over 260 members, and holds conventions, liaises with similar bodies overseas, and publishes monographs and *Shoshi Sakuin Tembo* (q.).

Nihon Tokkyo Joho Kiko. [Japan Patent Information Organization (JAPIO)] <www.japio.or.jp> (Sato Daiya Bldg, 6th floor, 4-1-7 Toyo, Koto-ku, Tokyo 135-0016, Japan) Founded in 1985 on a non-profit-making basis, JAPIO collects and disseminates information relating to Japanese and overseas industrial property patents, making it available online via PATOLIS-e <www.patolis.co.jp/e-index.html>, on CD-ROM, and by monthly abstracts. Research and translation services are offered, and exchanges are made with US and European patent offices.

Nihon Tosho Code. [Nippon Book Code] The Japanese standard book number system, controlled by the Japan ISBN agency. In general use since 1981, it has been largely superseded by the ISBN.

Nihon Toshokan Gakkai. [Japan Society of Library Science] <www.soc. nacsis.ac.jp/slis> (c/o Department of Library Science, Toyo University, 5-28-20 Hakusan, Bunkyo-ku, Tokyo 112-0001, Japan) Established in 1953 by the integration of various local organizations, current membership is 525 individuals and some 60 organizations. It holds seminars, publishes books, etc. plus *Toshokan Nenpo* [*Annals of the Society*] (a.).

Nihon Toshokan Kyokai. [Japan Library Association (JLA)] <www.jla.or.jp> (1-11-14 Shinkawa, Chuo-ku, Tokyo 104-0033, Japan) Founded in 1892, and adopting its present name in 1908, the association has over 6,700 individual members and 2,800 institutional members (Dec 2003). It aims to enhance the quality of library services and to encourage professional development and research. It adopted statements on 'Intellectual Freedom in Libraries' in 1979 and on 'A Code of Ethics for Librarians' in 1980. Publications are *Toshokan Zasshi* [*Library journal*] (m.), and *Gendai no Toshokan* [*Modern libraries*] (q.), both in Japanese only.

NII. 1. *See* National Information Infrastructure. 2. *See* Kokuritsu Johogaku Kenkyujo.

Nijhoff (Martinus) International West European Specialists Study Grant. An award administered by the Association of College and Research Libraries.

Ninety-one Rules. A cataloguing code comprising 91 rules which was compiled at the instigation, and with the guidance, of Sir Anthony Panizzi, as a guide to cataloguing the printed books in the British Museum. It was the first major code for the consistent cataloguing of books, and set the pattern for good cataloguing practice. It was approved by the Trustees of the British Museum in 1839 and was published in 1841.

NIP. *See* Network of Information Professionals.

Nipper. *See* Bumper.

Nippon Book Code. *See* Nihon Tosho Code.

Nippon Cataloguing Rules. *See Nihon Mokuroku Kisoku.*

Nippon Decimal Classification. *See Nihon Jusshin Bunruiho.*

NISO.   National Information Standards Organization; *see* Z39.

NISS.   National Information Services and Systems, a JISC-funded service that provided online information services for the UK education and research community. Combined with CHEST in 1999 to form EduServ with most of the services being provided by Eduserv Internet except the NISS gateway to library OPACs which is available from the HERO site.

NITC.   Acronym for National Information Transfer Centres. *See* ISORID.

NKOS.   *See* Knowledge Organization Systems/Services.

NLA.   *See* Newspaper Licensing Agency.

NLB.   *See* National Library for the Blind.

NLC.   *See* National Library of Canada.

NLE.   *See* National Library of Education.

NLL(ST).   Acronym for National Lending Library (for Science and Technology).

NLM.   *See* National Library of Medicine.

NLN.   *See* National Learning Network.

NLQ.   *See* Near letter quality.

NLS.   *See* National Library of Scotland.

NLSLS.   National Library of Scotland Lending Services. *See* National Library of Scotland.

NMA.   *See* National Micrographics Association.

NMAP.   <nmap.ac.uk> A guide to quality Internet resources in nursing, midwifery and the allied health professions; part of OMNI and the BIOME Hub of the (UK) RDN.

NMI.   *See* NSF Middleware Initiative.

NMI-EDIT.   <www.nmi-edit.org> Enterprise and Desktop Integration Technologies Consortium, comprising Internet2, Educause and the Southeastern Universities Research Association. Part of the NSF Middleware Initiative, NMI-EDIT is working towards the deployment of interoperable core Middleware services to improve the productivity of academic scientists and higher education, particularly by facilitating multi-institutional collaboration.

NNAF.   (*Archives*) National Name Authority File. Based on the *Rules for the construction of personal, place and corporate names* issued by the National Council on Archives in 1998.

No.   Abbreviation for number (It. 'numero'). *Pl.* Nos.

'No conflict' policy.   The policy of adopting new cataloguing rules only when they do not conflict with existing headings in the catalogue. Also called 'Superimposition' policy.

No date.   Abbreviation: n.d. Indicates that the date of publication is not known. If the book bears no indication of date of publication but this has been obtained from bibliographical or other sources, it is expressed in a bibliographical or catalogue entry within [ ].

No more published.   A phrase used in a note to a catalogue entry for a work which was intended to be published in several volumes but the publication of which was not completed.

Node.   1. A central switching point in a telecommunications network.   2. A branching point in a Hypertext or Hypermedia system.

NOF.   *See* New Opportunities Fund.

Noise.   In general terms, any interference that affects the working of a device or an operation. Thus, in information retrieval, items selected in a search which do not contain the information desired, and in telecommunications, random signals that degrade the quality of the transmission and change its output.

Nom de plume.   *See* Pseudonym.

Nomenclature.   A system of names for a system of classes, or classification; its terms.

non seq.   Abbreviation for *non sequitur* (Lat. 'it does not follow logically').

Non-book materials.   Those library materials which do not come within the definition of a book, periodical or pamphlet and which require special handling, e.g. audio-visual materials, vertical file materials, microforms or computer software.

Non-current records.   (*Records management*) Those that are no longer in full daily use in current business, and can therefore be retired from current information systems, transferred to a Records centre and appraised.

Non-distinctive title.   One that is common to many serials, e.g. *Bulletin, Journal, Proceedings, Transactions.*

Nonesuch Press.   A publishing house founded in 1923 in London by Miss Vera Mendel, with Francis Meynell to supervise book production, and David Garnett, to publish fine editions of scholarly works to be sold at modest prices through normal trade channels. After a period of inactivity production was resumed in 1953 with the Nonesuch Shakespeare in four volumes. Nearly all the books were machine set by various printers but were designed by Meynell. Many 'Monotype' matrices were specially designed for this Press.

Non-expressive notation.   *See* Notation.

Non-fiction.   Books that are not prose fiction.

Non-lining figures.   (*Printing*) Arabic numerals which have ascenders and descenders. Also called Hanging figures, Old Style figures.

Non-net.   A book, usually a school text, likely to be sold in large numbers at one time which was not subject to the minimum selling price of the Net Book Agreement. *See also* Net Book Agreement.

Nonpareil.   1. An out-of-date name for a type size of about 6 point.   2. A 6 point Lead.

Non-Parliamentary Publications.   UK Government publications that do not fall into the definition of Parliamentary Publications. Prior to about 1925 when this heading began to be used in HMSO catalogues, such publications were known as 'Official Publications' or 'Stationery Office Publications'. These can be roughly grouped into (a) Statutory Instruments, (b) Reports, (c) other publications. Statutory Instruments are government orders or regulations made by a Minister under the authority of a specific Act of Parliament. They are numbered according to the calendar year in which they are made, a new sequence beginning each year. Prior to 1948 they were known as Statutory Rules and Orders. 'Reports' include a variety of departmental, committee and working party reports which are prepared for submission to, or for the information of, Parliament. 'Other publications' include the huge range of documents, reports, books etc. that are produced by government departments and agencies.

Non-periodical.   A publication which is published at one time, or at intervals, in complete, usually numbered, volumes, the total number of volumes being generally determined in advance.

Non-print materials.   *See* Non-book materials.

Non-relief type.   Engraved or incised type in which the printing surface is not the character but the typeface around the incised character. This results in a white letter on a printed background.

Non-semantic code.   In information retrieval, one in which the notation does not carry meaningful information beyond that which is inherent in the spelling of the word in the source language for which it stands as the equivalent. *See also* Semantic code.

Non-structural notation.   *See* Structural notation.

Nordic Federation of Research Libraries Association.   <www.dpb.dpu.dk/ df/nvbf_eng> The Federation includes members in Denmark, Iceland, and throughout Scandinavia.

Norsk Bibliotekforening.   *See* Norwegian library associations.

Norsk Fagbibliotekforening.   *See* Norwegian library associations.

Norsk Samkatalog.   <www.nb.no/baser/sambok> Norwegian bibliographic network operating a union catalogue; founded 1983 and has 300 members. Based at the University of Oslo.

Northern informatics.   <www.nets.co.uk/publications> Formerly Northern Informatics Applications Agency Ltd (NiAA), this is a multi-sectoral body set up with the involvement of Information North to initiate, encourage, and co-ordinate bids to the European Commission and other sources to secure funding for practical applications of new technologies.

Northern Libraries Colloquy.   *See* Polar Libraries Colloquy.

Northern Poetry Library.   <www.northumberland.gov.uk/services> (Morpeth Library, The Willows, Morpeth, Northumberland NE61 1TA, UK) Established in 1968, the library aims to obtain all newly published poetry in English produced in the UK; it holds about 13,000 items including a range of poetry magazines.

Northover (Alison) Bursary.   An annual award of CILIP's University, College and Research Group; made to support conference or course attendance.

Norwegian library associations.   The major professional association is Norsk Biblioteksforening (Norwegian Library Association) <www. norskbiblioteksforening.no>, originally founded in 1913, which in 1972 combined with other associations to form a general organization: it has

3,800 members. There is also Norsk Fagbibliotekforening (Norwegian Association of Special Libraries) <www.biblioteknett.no/nff> which supports the technical library community: it has 554 members.

Not. A Finish given to good quality rag papers – not glazed or hot pressed. Those with no finish are called 'rough'; 'not' is less rough but 'not-smooth'. *See also* Hot-pressed, Machine glazed, Rough.

Notation. The symbols which stand for the divisions in a scheme of classification. The purposes of notation are (a) to mechanize the chosen order of classes in a scheme of classification, (b) to serve as a short-hand sign for the easy arrangement of documents on shelves or in drawers or files, and also for entries in respect of them in catalogues and indexes and (c) to provide easily memorized links between catalogues and the storage position of documents. Notation must be brief and Hospitable. If the notation consists of two or more kinds of symbols it is called a 'mixed notation'; if of one kind only, a 'pure notation'. The notation may be expressive or non-expressive. Expressive notation reveals the hierarchical structure of the classification scheme, in addition to mechanizing the order of the classes. The notation must be (a) hospitable, i.e. enable symbols for additional subjects to be added at any position, (b) easily comprehensible, i.e. consisting only of roman letters and/or arabic numbers, and (c) easily memorized, written and spoken. A 'flexible notation' is one which expands with the classification, and permits the insertion of new subjects without any dislocation. *See also* Facet indicator, Faceted notation, Hierarchical notation, Labelled Notation, Pronounceable notation, Retro-active notation, Structural notation, Syllabic notation.

Notch. The process of cutting parallel grooves into the spine of a text block prior to binding. The grooves go across the binding edge (back margin) and serve to increase the amount of surface area on the spine that comes into contact with the adhesive, thus strengthening the binding.

Note. 1. An explanation of the text of a book or additional matter, appearing usually with other notes at the foot of a page, at the end of a chapter or at the end of the book. Where numbers are not used to separate and distinguish the notes, Reference marks are used in a recognized sequence. Also called Footnote. 2. A concise statement, following particulars of collation in a catalogue or bibliographical entry, giving added information such as the name of the series, contents, or bibliographical information.

Notebook. Another name for a Laptop computer.

Nothing before something. Alphabetizing 'word by word', counting the space between one word and the next as 'nothing'. A word files before another word having the same letters plus additional ones, these additional ones being considered 'something'. *See also* Alphabetization.

Noun order. (*Information retrieval*) An order of nouns in a compound heading, the order being determined by rules, by using Operators or by using facet citation chains.

Novel.   A long fictitious story of imaginary people and events.

Novelette.   A short novel.

Novelist.   One who writes novels.

Novella.   A short prose narrative, generally with a structural centre represented by a surprising event.

Novelty.   (*Copyright*) The quality of a new Intellectual work. *Compare* Originality.

NoWAL.   <www.nowal.ac.uk> A consortium of UK academic libraries in the area of Manchester and north-west England. Formerly CALIM.

n.p.   1. Abbreviation for no place of publication, no printer's name, no publisher's name.   2. Abbreviation for 'new paragraph'; an instruction to the compositor that a new paragraph is to be begun. It is indicated in a manuscript or proof by the letters 'n.p.' in the margin and [or // in the text before the first word of the new paragraph.   3. Also used in book reviews and elsewhere as an abbreviation for 'no price'.

NPO.   *See* National Preservation Office.

NRCd.   *See* CIMTECH.

NREN.   National Research and Education Network, a generic term used to indicate the networks established for educational and research interests. Also, specifically, the NASA Research and Education Network <www.nren.nasa.gov>. *See also* GÉANT.

NRLSI.   *See* National Reference Library of Science and Invention.

NRMM.   *See* National Register of Microform Masters.

NSA.   *See* National Sound Archive.

NSDL.   <www.nsdl.org> National Science Digital Library, a (US) digital library of quality resource collections and services organized to support science, technology, engineering and mathematics education at all levels. The NSDL mission is to both deepen and extend science literacy through access to materials and methods that reveal the nature of the physical universe and the intellectual means by which it is discovered and understood.

NSDL Scout Reports.   <scout.wisc.edu/Reports> Since 1994, a weekly electronic publication of the Internet Scout Project offering an annotated selection of new and newly discovered Internet resources of interest to researchers and educators chosen by librarians and subject specialists. The Reports for *Life Sciences* and *Physical Sciences* alternate with the Report for *Math, Engineering and Technology*.

NSDP.   *See* National Serials Data Program.

NSF Middleware Initiative (NMI).   <www.nsf-middleware.org> A programme that addresses a critical need for software infrastructure to support scientific and engineering research. Begun in late 2001, NMI funds the design, development, testing, and deployment of Middleware, a key enabling technology upon which customized applications are built. Specialized NMI teams are defining open-source, open-architecture standards that are creating important new avenues of online collaboration and resource sharing. *See also* GRIDS, NMI-EDIT.

NSFNET. *See* Internet.

NSSN. <www.nssn.org> A National Resource for Global Standards (formerly National Standards Systems Network); a web-based service providing information on approved industry standards, approved international standards, approved US Government standards in addition to standards in development. A co-operative partnership between the American National Standards Institute, US private-sector standards organizations, government agencies, and international standards organizations.

NTBL. Nuffield Talking Book Library for the Blind (UK), established in 1935 as the Talk Book Library for the Blind, the name being changed in 1954. The Library is administered by the Royal National Institute for the Blind and St. Dunstan's through their joint Sound Recording Committee, and maintained by the funds of these two voluntary charities. Membership is free and open to blind persons over the age of 21 who are registered with their local Blind Welfare Authority. The 'books' are specially recorded in the Committee's own studio; they are mainly fiction but a number of recordings of biographies, travel books and other non-fiction subjects are also produced. The 'books' are lent free and played on special recording machines which are non-commercial and rented from the Library. Now known as the British Talking Book Service for the Blind.

NTC. *See* National Translations Center.

NTIS. <www.ntis.gov> (Springfield, VA 22161, USA) The National Technical Information Service was formed in 1970 by the US Department of Commerce to simplify and increase public access to federal publications and data files of interest to the business, scientific and technical communities. It is the US clearinghouse for the collection and dissemination of scientific, technical, and engineering information. Previously known as the Office of Technical Service (OTS), it is a central source for the public sale of government-sponsored research, development and engineering reports and other analyses, information being brought together from hundreds of federal sources.

NTO. *See* ISNTO.

NTSC. National Television Standards Committee. The colour television standard used in the US, Japan and parts of South America; the videotape standard used in the US. *See also* PAL, SECAM.

NUC. See National Union Catalog.

NUCAF. See National Union Catalogue of Alternative Formats.

NUCMC. See National Union Catalog of Manuscript Collections.

NUD*IST. Non-numerical, Unstructured, Data: Indexing, Searching and Theorizing, a software package for analyzing textual documents which facilitates the indexing of components of these documents, is able to search for words and phrases, and supports theorizing by enabling the retrieval of indexed text segments and text and index searches.

Nuffield Talking Book Library for the Blind. *See* NTBL.

NUKOP. New UK Official Publications; *see now* BOPCAS.

Number. 1. A single numbered or dated issue of a periodical or serial publication. 2. One of the numbered fascicules of a literary, artistic or musical work issued in instalments, ordinarily in paper wrappers, and called 'number' by the publisher. 3. In extended vocal works such as cantatas, oratorios and operas (especially the latter), one of the distinct and separate sections into which the composition is divided, each of which is complete in itself and in a specific form, such as aria, duet, chorus. 4. Any item in the programme of a concert or other entertainment. *See also* Opus number.

Number building. (*Classification*) The process of making a number more specific by adding segments taken from other parts of the classification; synthesis of numbers.

Numbered and signed edition. An edition of a work the copies of which are numbered, and signed by the author. *See also* Limited edition.

Numbered column. Where the text of a book is printed in two or more columns to a page, and these instead of the pages are numbered consecutively. Where this is done a note to this effect normally appears at the head of the index.

Numbered copy. A copy of a limited edition of a book which bears the copy number, usually on the page facing the title-page.

Numbered entry. One of the entries in a printed bibliography or catalogue in which the entries are numbered consecutively.

Numbered System. *See* Vancouver Style.

Numbering. Placing the call number on the spine or outer cover/board of a book. *See also* Processing (1).

Numeral. A graphic symbol or character to represent a number or a group of numbers. A figure. *See also* Arabic figures, Hanging figures, Ranging figures, Roman numerals.

Numerals. The correct printer's term for figures and fractions.

Numeration. (*Cataloguing*) A number, roman or arabic, appearing in a heading, indicating the sequence of the person (as e.g. monarchs bearing the same forename) or another element in the heading (e.g. chemical formulae), and so affecting the filing sequence. *See also* Character significance sequence, Logical arrangement.

Numeric Style. *See* Vancouver Style.

Nut. *See* En quadrat.

NVB. Nederlandse Vereniging van Bibliothecarissen, Documentalisten en Literatuur Onderzoekers. *See* Dutch library associations.

Nylink. <nylink.suny.edu> (SUNY Plaza, Albany, NY 12246, USA) An education and research network based at the State University of New York. An OCLC Network Affiliate.

n.y.p. Abbreviation for 'not yet published'.

NYR. *See* National Year of Reading.

NZLIA. *See* LIANZA.

OAI. *See* Open Archives Initiative.

OAI-PMH. *See* Open Archives Initiative Protocol for Metadata Harvesting.

OAIster. <oaister.umdl.umich.edu> A project of the University of Michigan Digital Library Production Services, originally funded through a Mellon grant whose goal is to create a collection of freely available, difficult-to-access, academically-oriented digital resources harvested using the Open Archives Initiative Protocol for Metadata Harvesting.

OAL. Office of Arts and Libraries. *Now see* DCMS.

OASIS. <www.oasis-open.org> Organization for the Advancement of Structured Information Standards, a not-for-profit, international consortium focusing on the development, convergence, and adoption of e-business standards. The consortium produces standards for Web services, security and e-business, and contributes to standardization efforts in the public sector and for application-specific markets.

Obelisk. Alternative name for the dagger (†) reference mark. Similarly a double dagger (‡) is also called a 'Double obelisk'. *See also* Reference marks.

Oberly Award for Bibliography in Agricultural Sciences. Established in 1923, this Award is made by the Oberly Memorial Award Committee of the ACRL Division of the American Library Association every two years to the American citizen who compiles the best bibliography in the field of agriculture or the related sciences.

Objectives. A set of specific aims or targets established as desirable that a given service or system should achieve. *Management by Objectives* (MbO) functions as a management technique by constantly re-defining and monitoring the achievement of agreed objectives in a participative environment.

Object-oriented technology. Any technology that supports the use of 'objects' which store not only data but also the routines that operate on that data.

Oblique. The sign / commonly found on alphanumeric keyboards for computer and viewdata systems. More commonly now termed 'slash'.

Oblong. 1. Of a book that is wider than its height. Hence oblong folio, oblong quarto. This is the result of folding a sheet of paper across the long way (i.e. halving the short side). Also called 'Cabinet size', 'Landscape', 'Long'. The opposite of Broad. *See also* Narrow, Size (1), Square. 2. Applies to a Broad sheet of paper halved lengthways. A quarto size used with the longest dimension at the foot of the page, or sheet, is termed 'oblong quarto' and is the reverse of 'upright'.

Obverse cover. The upper cover of a book. Also called 'Front cover', 'Upper cover'. *See also* Reverse cover.

OCLC. <www.oclc.org> (6565 Frantz Road, Dublin, OH 43017-3395, USA) Online Computer Library Center, Inc. a non-profit membership, computer library service and research organization. The acronym originally stood for Ohio College Library Center, established 1967 to share resources and reduce costs of academic libraries in the state of

Ohio. In 1973 members were admitted from outside Ohio, and a rapid expansion ensued. The new name was adopted in 1981. Currently its computer network and services link over 45,000 libraries in 84 countries; services include WorldCat which is claimed to be the world's most comprehensive database of bibliographic information (55 million entries in May 2004), and numerous projects and initiatives centring on electronic or digital libraries in a global context. Many US consortia are OCLC Network Affiliates. *See also* Preservation Resources.

OCLC/LITA Frederick G. Kilgour Award for Research in Library and Information Technology. First presented in 1998, an award made by the Library and Information Technology Association (LITA) and sponsored by OCLC to commemorate its first President.

OCLCPICA. <www.oclcpica.org> Formed in 2001 when the Dutch library bibliographic network PICA merged with OCLC. The new co-operative provdes access to substantial bibliographical resources from the merged networks. *See also* OCLC, Pica (2).

OCR. *See* Optical character recognition.

Octave device. In classification, the name given by Ranganathan to a method of extending the decimal base of arabic numerals to infinity, by setting the figure 9 as an extender or repeater digit to bring in a further eight figures at the end of the first eight. The series thus reads: 1, 2, 3, 4, 5, 6, 7, 8, 91, 92, 93, 94, 95, 96, 97, 98, 991, 992, and so on, the figure 9 never being used unsupported. The figure 9 is known as the Octavizing Digit. This device, which was first used by Ranganathan in his Colon Classification, and adopted by the Universal Decimal Classification in 1948, can be extended to letters, z (or any last letter of any other alphabet) being used in the same way. By this means the octave device is used for extrapolation in an array. Also known as 'sectorizing device'.

Octavo. (8vo) 1. A sheet of paper folded three times to form a section of eight leaves, or sixteen pages. The following sizes (in inches) of printing papers are usually used to produce an octavo page:

		Double	*Quad*	*Size of 8vo*
Foolscap	13$\frac{1}{2}$ x 17	17 x 27	27 x 34	6$\frac{3}{4}$ x 4$\frac{1}{4}$
Crown	15 x 20	20 x 30	30 x 40	7$\frac{1}{2}$ x 5
Large post	16$\frac{1}{2}$ x 21	21 x 33	33 x 42	8$\frac{1}{4}$ x 5$\frac{1}{4}$
Demy	17$\frac{1}{2}$ x 22$\frac{1}{2}$	22$\frac{1}{2}$ x 35	35 x 45	8$\frac{3}{4}$ x 5$\frac{5}{8}$
Medium	18 x 23	23 x 36	36 x 46	9 x 5$\frac{3}{4}$
Royal	20 x 25	25 x 40	40 x 50	10 x 6$\frac{1}{4}$
Super royal	20$\frac{1}{2}$ x 27$\frac{1}{2}$	27$\frac{1}{2}$ x 41	41 x 55	10$\frac{1}{4}$ x 6$\frac{7}{8}$
Imperial	22 x 30	30 x 44	44 x 60	11 x 7$\frac{1}{2}$

2. A book having sections of eight leaves, or sixteen pages. 3. Any book whose height is between 6$\frac{1}{4}$ and 10 inches. *See also* Book sizes, Paper sizes.

Octodecimo. (18mo) *See* Eighteen-mo.

Odd folios. The page-numbers which come on the first, or recto, side of each leaf, the right hand of each Opening, 1, 3, 5, 7, 9, 11, etc.

Odd page. The page of a publication bearing an odd number; the right-hand page of an Opening, and the recto of a Leaf.

Odd sorts. Characters not normally included in a standard font of type. Also called 'Side sorts'.

Oddments. 1. The items of a printed book which precede and follow the text. These are known as the Preliminaries and the End-matter. 2. When the pages of a book make an exact multiple of sixteen (or thirty-two if the sections are of 32 pages) it is said to make an even working. If an odd eight pages or so are needed to complete the printing it is termed 'uneven working' and the additional pages are said to be oddments.

O.E. Abbreviation for Old English.

OeBF. *See* Open eBook Forum.

OEM. Original Equipment Manufacturer, a company that manufactures products which may be sold or distributed by others, sometimes under other names.

'Off its feet'. Type which has been cast in such a way that its base is not true, with the result that it does not stand firm in the galley.

Offcut. 1. That part of a sheet which has to be cut off after 'imposition', as in the case of a 12mo., so that the sheet may be correctly folded, the cut off piece being folded and inserted in the larger piece after folding. The cut off piece is then called an 'inset' and usually bears a signature mark to indicate its proper place in the gathering. 2. A piece cut off a sheet of paper to reduce it to the size required for a particular job. 3. Remainders of reams which have been cut down to a smaller size.

Office collection. *See* Departmental library.

Office for Library and Information Networking. *See* UKOLN.

Office for Scientific and Technical Information. *See* OSTI.

Office information systems. Generic term for all types of administrative processes carried out using new information technologies – includes word processing, records management, executive information systems, and networks.

Office of Arts and Libraries (UK). *See now* DCMS.

Office of Information Programmes and Services. <www. unesco.org> A Unesco directorate set up in 1988 by the merger of the General Inform-ation Programme (PGI) and the Library, Archives and Documentation Services (LAD). It comprises four divisions: General Information Programme (IPS/PGI); Software Developments and Applications (IPS/SDA); Unesco Information Services (IPS/UIS); Operational Activities (IPS/OPS). There is currently a low level of activity.

Official gazette. A periodical publication issued by, or on behalf of, a government or university to convey official news, statements or decisions.

Official name.   The legal name of a corporate body, office or government department.

Official publication.   One issued by a government or government department, it may be in a series or isolated. The Unesco Convention Concerning the Exchange of Official Publications and Government Documents between States, 1958, considered the following, when they are executed by the order and at the expense of any national governmental authority, to be official publications: Parliamentary documents, reports and journals and other legislative papers; administrative publications and reports from central, federal and regional governmental bodies; national bibliographies, State handbooks, bodies of law, decisions of the Courts of Justice; and other publications as may be agreed.

Off-line equipment.   Peripheral computer equipment, or devices, not in direct communication with a computer.

Off-line operation.   The accomplishment of functions which cannot be carried out when a computer is undertaking standard, Online operations. Thus, some Integrated library systems require files to be updated and Utility programs to be run in off-line mode.

Off-line print.   Printing of search results after the searcher has disconnected from the computer; in Online searching, the results printed and forwarded to the searcher by mail.

Offprint.   *See* Separate.

Offset.   1. The printing process in which the impression is transferred from a litho stone or plate to a rubber-covered cylinder, and thence offset by pressure on to the paper. *See also* Offset printing.   2. Sometimes erroneously used to describe the unintentional transfer of ink from one sheet to another; this is correctly called 'set-off'. *See also* Slip sheet.

Offset foil.   A printing plate used for making prints (copies of documents) by the offset process.

Offset lithography.   A method of printing in which a drawing is made on transfer paper the right way round, printed on to a rubber-covered cylinder and 'offset' on to paper. *See also* Transfer.

Offset paper.   Paper especially made for use on an offset press. It should lie flat, be free from lint, and stretch as little as possible.

Offset printing.   An adaptation of the principles of stone lithography, in which a text or design is drawn or reproduced on a thin, flexible, metal plate which is curved to fit one of the revolving cylinders of the printing press. This text or design is then transferred ('offset') to the paper by means of a rubber blanket which runs over another cylinder and takes the impression from the plate.

Offset-photo-lithography.   *See* Photo-offset.

Oghamic scripts.   Inscriptions, peculiar to the Celtic population of the British Isles, usually found on wooden staves but sometimes also on shields or other hard material. They are also found on tombstones. Used for writing messages and letters. The alphabet consisted of twenty letters which were represented by straight or diagonal strokes varying from one to five in number and drawn, or cut, below, above or through, horizontal lines, or to the left, or right, of, or through, vertical lines. *See also* Runes.

OGSA. *See* Open Grid Services Architecture.

Ohio College Library Center. *See* OCLC.

OHIONET. <www.ohionet.org> (1500 West Lane Avenue, Columbus, OH 43221, USA) A US network consortium of libraries in the state of Ohio. An OCLC Network Affiliate.

OHP. *See* Overhead projector.

OII. *See* Oxford Internet Institute.

OiL. 1. *See* Organization in Liaison. 2. OIL *See* Ontology Inference Layer.

OIS. *See* Office information systems.

OKI. *See* Open Knowledge Initiative.

Ola books. Books made in Sri Lanka from olas, or strips of young leaves of the Talipat or Palmyra palm which are soaked in hot water and pressed smooth. They are cut into strips about 3 inches wide and from 1 to 3 feet long. A cord is passed through holes pierced at the ends of each so as to secure the leaves between two lacquered wooden boards. Writing is done with an iron stylus, and the incisions made more easily readable by rubbing in a mixture of charcoal and oil. The aromatic and preservative nature of the oil is believed to have enabled the books to survive from pre-Christian days. Buddhist monks still make ola books in Sri Lanka. Also called 'olla books'.

Old English (OE). An angular type of the Black letter group.

Old face. The majority of book types in England belong to this family of types. Its origin is generally attributed to Garamond (Paris, first half of sixteenth century) who modelled his design on the roman types of the Venetian printer Aldus Manutius which were actually cut in 1495 for Aldus by Francesco Griffo who also cut the famous Aldine italic. The Old Face group of letters is characterized by oblique emphasis, lightness of colour, comparatively small differences between thick and thin strokes and fairly substantial bracketed serifs. The capitals are slightly lower than the ascending lower case letters and the descenders are long. The modern versions of Old Face have a comparatively small X-height and a narrow set. Examples are, Caslon Old Face (Stephenson Blake and others); Bembo, Fournier, Imprint, Plantin, Van Dijck (Monotype); Garamond (Monotype and Intertype). The figures of Old Face do not all stand on the line. The term 'Garalde' has superseded 'Old face' for this category of typefaces. *See also* Arabic figures, Hanging figures, Modern face, Ranging figures, Transitional.

Old style. A modification of Old face, the ascenders and descenders being shorter. Examples are: Old Style (Stephenson Blake); Old Style Antique (Miller & Richard); Bookprint (Linotype); Bookface (Intertype).

Old style figures. (*Printing*) Numerals, three of which are of x-height, the others having ascenders and descenders. Also called 'Non-lining figures'. *See also* Arabic figures, Modern face.

Oldman Prize. An annual prize awarded by the UK Branch of the International Association of Music Libraries for the best British book on music librarianship or bibliography. Commemorates C. B. Oldman (1894–1969), Principal Keeper of Printed Books in the British Library 1947–59.

Oleograph. A reproduction of an oil painting, printed by lithography, mounted on canvas, sized and varnished, the irregularities of the oil painting and canvas being reproduced by an embossing process.

Olin Book Number. An author number from a scheme devised by Charles R. Olin in 1893. The use of Olin Numbers enables collective biography to be separated yet to be brought into close relation at the same class number. They convert all authors' or compilers' surnames into the letter 'A' followed by figures, thus enabling collective biographies to be arranged before the individual biographies bearing Cutter Author Marks. Olin Book Numbers and Biscoe Time Numbers were printed in the 11th, 12th and 13th editions of the Dewey Decimal Classification.

OMB. *See* One Man Band.

Omissible. Something which may be omitted if required, necessary or desirable.

Omission marks. Three dots, thus …, used on the Base line in quoted text, or a catalogue entry, to indicate that something in the original has been omitted. Also called 'Ellipsis'.

OMNI. <omni.ac.uk> A subject gateway providing access to Internet resources on health and medicine; part of the BIOME Hub of the (UK) RDN.

Omnibus book. A volume containing reprints of short stories by various authors or of novels or other works by one or more authors.

On approval. Applied to a transaction whereby a customer may have the opportunity of examining goods before deciding whether to purchase them, and to return them within a short specified time if it is decided not to keep them. Abbreviated: on appro. 'On approbation' has the same meaning.

On sale. Books supplied to a bookseller under an agreement that they may be returned if unsold. Also known as 'On sale or return'. *See also* Half see safe, See safe.

On-demand publishing. The availability of material at the time it is required by the End user. In most cases on-demand publishing systems have as their base an electronic archive which can be viewed over a network and printouts taken as required, subject to copyright. The term can also refer to 'customization' of texts to suit the demands of individuals or groups, and also to 'bespoke books': anthologies from a variety of sources.

ONE Association. <www.oneassociation.org> Formed in 2003, the Open Network in Europe Association follows up the ONE-2 project; the consortium of seven European national libraries (including the British Library) aims to facilitate searching and retrieval across different systems to give wider access to their collective bibliographical resources.

One man band (OMB).   An Aslib membership group for those employed as the sole member of staff in special libraries and information units.

One person library.   A library or information service having only one member of staff. *See also* One man band.

One place index.   *See* Specific index.

One sheet on.   *See* All along.

One shot.   1. The reprinting in one issue of a periodical of the full text, or an abridgement, of a book, as distinct from a serialized reprint.   2. A magazine of which only one issue has been published.   3. Single issue rights, where the whole of a literary work or an abridgement of it, appears in a periodical.

One side coloured.   Paper or board which has been intentionally coloured during manufacture.

ONE-2.   <www.one-2.org> An extension of the ONE (Open Network in Europe) project and supported by the European Union's Fourth Framework Programme. The 13 partners, who included a number of national libraries across Europe, aimed to exploit the results from the earlier project but also extend those into value added services such as item ordering, inter-library lending, copy cataloguing and update, and electronic document delivery. Technical focus was on Z39.50 and ISO/ILL (ISO 10160/10161). The project ended in October 2001 and contributed significantly to relevant international standardization activities within the ZIG and elsewhere. *See also* ONE Association.

One-stop-shop.   An information agency that can offer all types of support and advice at the same point of service; it is assumed that clients will be more encouraged to use the facility if they have confidence that they will receive co-ordinated and efficient support without having to deal with various disparate bodies.

Ongaku Toshokan Kyogikai.   [Music Library Association of Japan (MLAJ)] <www.mlaj.gr.jp> (c/o Library, Kunitachi College of Music, 5-5-1 Kashiwa-cho, Kunitachi, Tokyo 190-8520, Japan) Established in 1972, the association promotes co-operation between music libraries both domestic and overseas, collates a *Union List of Periodicals in Music*, and issues *MLAJ newsletter* (q.).

Onion skin.   A thin, glazed, transparent paper.

Onlay.   A decorative panel of paper or other material glued to the cover of a book without preparing the cover to receive it. *See also* Inlay.

Online.   1. A general term for devices and Peripherals which are interacting directly and simultaneously with a computer in real time.   2. A reference to, or the act of undertaking, Online information retrieval.

Online Community Award.   <www.cilip.org.uk> An award made annually by CILIP and FreePint to recognize an online community project in any sector.

On-line Computer Library Center.   *See* OCLC.

Online information retrieval. A means whereby a searcher at a remote terminal can access and interrogate databases containing bibliographical or other data. Such databases, produced by commercial firms, government departments, research organizations, academic institutions etc, may be accessed via a Network or a Hub, or directly from a publisher, or may be mounted on the Internet.

Online public access catalogue (OPAC). The catalogue of a library or information centre made available to users online and generally providing a variety of additional facilities such as loans information, online reservations, and library news. With the demise of the Card catalogue, the need for stressing the 'online public access' part has disappeared and they are now frequently just 'catalogues'.

Online searching. *See* Online information retrieval.

Ontology. A common set of terms and their precise relationships used to describe and represent a knowledge area in such a way that communications between computer systems are independent of individual system technologies, information architectures and application domains. Ontologies can be used by automated tools to power advanced services such as more accurate Web search, intelligent software agents and knowledge management.

Ontology Inference Layer (OIL). A modelling language to enable Web-based information to be represented in such a way that it can be understood by machines, thus developing the Semantic Web. Also 'Ontology Interchange Language'. For more information, see <www.ontoknowledge.org/oil>. *See also* Ontology.

Onymous. The exact opposite of Anonymous.

O.P. Abbreviation for Out of print.

op. cit. Abbreviation for *opere citato* (Lat. 'in the work cited'). Used in a footnote reference to avoid using the title or short title of the work referred to. It should not be used if there is more than one book by the author concerned, and preferably not if another book has been referred to since the first citation.

Op. no. Abbreviation for Opus number.

OPAC. *See* Online public access catalogue.

Opacity. The quality of non-transparency in book papers. Creamy or off-white papers are more opaque than bright white ones, and a matt finish gives a greater opacity than a glazed finished.

Opaque copy. A copy of a document on opaque, or non-transparent, material.

Opaque microcopy. A microcopy made on opaque, or non-transparent, material, usually paper or card. Also called 'Micro-opaque'.

Opaque projector. A projector which can project small opaque printed images such as maps, post-cards, illustrations, photographs, pages of books, etc. on to screens or walls.

Opaquing. Painting a negative with an opaque liquid to block out pin-holes and other defects, or render certain parts unprintable.

Open access. 1. Used, in particular, in relation to the movement to make peer reviewed journal literature freely accessible online without restriction. The Budapest Open Access Initiative includes the following statement: 'By open access to this literature, we mean its free availability on the public internet, permitting any users to read, download, copy, distribute, print, search, or link to the full texts of these articles, crawl them for indexing, pass them as data to software, or use them for any other lawful purpose, without financial, legal, or technical barriers other than those inseparable from gaining access to the internet itself. The only constraint on reproduction and distribution, and the only role for copyright in this domain, should be to give authors control over the integrity of their work and the right to be properly acknowledged and cited.' A similar statement is included in the Berlin Declaration. Open access can be supported in two main ways: i) publishing in a suitable Open access journal; or ii) publishing in a suitable Toll access journal and Self archiving. 2. Applied to a library where readers are admitted to the shelves.

Open access journal. A journal that uses a funding model that does not charge its users for access. The funding models developed so far require a one-off publishing charge – paid by author or research funding body – to cover organization, peer review and technical infrastructure, but papers are then freely available to all from the journal's web site. Examples include BioMedCentral and Public Library of Science.

Open Archives Initiative (OAI). <www.openarchives.org> An initiative to develop and promote interoperability standards – via the Open Archives Initiative Protocol for Metadata Harvesting – to facilitate the retrieval and searching of digital content on a global scale. The OAI sprang from a means to improve the availability of scholarly communication by enhancing access to Eprint archives, though the technological framework and standards are independent of the type of content.

Open Archives Initiative Protocol for Metadata Harvesting (OAI-PMH). <www.openarchives.org/OAI/openarchivesprotocol.html> The protocol which provides an application-independent interoperability framework for the Open Archives Initiative to enable the automatic gathering of metadata across multiple repositories. Used in EPrints software; see Eprints (2).

Open back. *(Binding) See* Hollow back.

Open back case. *See* Slip case.

Open back file. A box file for holding pamphlets and similar material, consisting of a five-sided box the shape of a book. The sixth side (the back) is open to allow the easy insertion – and more easy removal – of material.

Open eBook Forum (OeBF). <www.openebook.org> (302A West 12th Street, #304, New York, NY 10014, USA) An international trade and standards organization for the electronic publishing industries whose membership comprises hardware and software companies, print and digital publishers, retailers, libraries, accessibility advocates, authors and related organizations whose common goals are to establish specifications and standards and to advance the competitiveness and exposure of the electronic publishing industries.

Open edge. Any edge of a section of a book which is open and not enclosed by a Bolt.

Open ended. Being possessed of the quality by which the addition of new terms, subject headings, or classifications does not disturb the pre-existing system.

Open ended term list. A list of terms to which, in contrast to a Controlled term list, terms may be added as required, provided that the terms in the existing list are not altered. Also called 'Open indexing system'. *See also* Closed indexing system.

Open entry. A catalogue entry which leaves room for the addition of information concerning a work which is in course of publication, or of which the library does not possess a complete copy or set, or concerning which complete information is lacking. Open entries usually occur in respect of serials still in course of publication, the date of the most recent issue and last volume number being omitted in the case of works in several volumes which are still in course of publication; or of living authors, in catalogues in which birth and death dates are given. *See also* Closed entry.

Open for Learning. *See* British Association for Open Learning.

Open for Learning, Open for Business. *See* National Grid for Learning.

Open Grid Services Architecture (OGSA). <www.globus.org/ogsa> An evolution towards a Grid system architecture based on Web services concepts and technologies being developed by the Globus Alliance and managed by the Global Grid Forum.

Open Knowledge Initiative (OKI). <web.mit.edu/oki> Based at MIT, a collaboration among leading universities and specification and standards organizations to support innovative learning technology in higher education. The result is an open and extensible architecture that specifies how the components of an educational software environment communicate with each other and with other enterprise systems. OKI provides a modular development platform for building both traditional and innovative applications and is designed for broad adoption in the higher education domain.

Open learning. A process of teaching and learning by which students study in their own homes or local centres using materials mailed or broadcast from a central unit. Tutorial work may be handled via the central unit, or on a regional basis. The emphasis is on opening up opportunities by overcoming barriers of geographical isolation, personal or work commitments, and conventional course structures, which have often prevented certain categories of people from gaining access to educational and training facilities. British examples include the Open University, Open College; many traditional educational institutions are moving rapidly into the field. The term *distance learning* is practically synonymous.

Open letters.   Jobbing and display type which have the centres of the strokes of the characters incised, and so beyond the reach of the inkers; this gives the impression of white areas rather than black. Also called 'Outline letters'. *See also* Inline letters.

Open matter.   Type which has been generously 'leaded'. *See also* Leaded matter.

Open Network in Europe.   *See* ONE Association, ONE-2.

Open order.   In book acquisition, for two types of order: (1) those made up of items listed individually, some or all of which have not been supplied, hence the orders are not closed or completed; (2) those which approximate to open requisitions, as they ear-mark sums of money with booksellers to be spent on a particular subject or category.

Open score.   The printed or written music for two or more voices or parts each of which is separately displayed one above another. Also called 'Extended score'. *See also* Score.

Open shelf library.   *See* Open access (2).

Open Society Institute.   <www.soros. org> (400 W 59th St, New York, NY 10019, USA) Founded in 1993 and promotes the development of open societies around the world. Undertakes regional and country-specific projects relating to education, media, legal reform and human rights aimed at encouraging debate and disseminating information.

Open source software (OSS).   <www.opensource.org> Software that provides access to the source code, does not restrict any party from selling or giving away the software and whose license does not require a royalty or other fee and permits the creation of modifications and derived works to be distributed under the same terms as the license of the original software. *See also* Free software, Public domain software, Shareware.

Open Systems Interconnection (OSI).   Work on OSI began in 1977, and its aim is to enable all types and sizes of computers to exchange information across communications networks. OSI specifies international standards to which most major equipment manufacturers are committed. ISO 7498, the *Basic Reference Model of OSI,* was issued in 1983 and has been followed by many standards and recommendations; principally these emanate from the International Organization for Standardization and from ITU-T; see, for example, ISO/IEC 10731:1994 *Information technology – Open Systems Interconnection – Basic Reference Model – Conventions for the definition of OSI services.* The OSI model uses seven layers, or levels, of specification: application (the highest layer); presentation; session; transport; network; data-link; and physical.

Opened.   A book of which the top, fore, and sometimes bottom, edges have not been cut in manufacture but opened with a paper knife before being read.

Opening.   Two pages facing one another. *See also* Conjugate, Double-spread.

Open-letter proof.   A proof of an engraving with the caption engraved in outline letters, whereas the finished engraving has solid letters.

OpenSAML.   <www.opensaml.org> Open Source Security Assertion Mark-up Language, software developed in the NMI-EDIT programme for managing access to web resources with particular emphasis on privacy protection. Used by Shibboleth.

OpenURL.   <www.exlibrisgroup.com/sfx_openurl.htm> A protocol for interoperability between an information resource and a service component, referred to as a link server, which offers localized services. The underlying concept of the OpenURL standard is that links should lead a user to appropriate resources, e.g. to the 'most appropriate' copy when searching for a journal paper. The selection of such a copy is based on user and organizational preferences regarding the location of the copy, its cost, and agreements with information suppliers, and similar considerations. This selection occurs without the knowledge of the user and is made possible by the transport of metadata from the source citation to a Resolver which stores the preference information and the links to the appropriate material. One of the original developers was Ex-Libris who have a version known as SFX. OpenURL is a NISO standard Z39.88, full details available at: <library.caltech.edu/openurl>. *See also* CrossRef, Digital Object Identifier.

Operating system.   The software that provides the End user with a range of general purpose facilities for interacting with a computer. It controls the execution of computer programs and may also provide other features such as scheduling, debugging, input-output control, storage assignment and data management. The operating system provides a uniform and consistent means for all Applications to access the same machine resources. Also referred to as 'system software'. *See also* MS-DOS, Windows.

Operators.   (*Classification*) Categories of relation, indicated by symbols, to mark steps of progression in analyzing complex subjects. An analysis set down in this way is called an 'Analet'. *See also* Relational indexing.

Opisthographic.   Applied to early-printed books printed on both sides of the paper and to manuscripts or parchments with writing on both sides. *See also* Anopisthographic printing, Block books.

Optical character recognition (OCR).   A technique for machine recognition of characters by their images, whereby printed characters are read directly by light-sensitive devices so that text on paper can be transferred into a word processed document. With the falling cost of Scanners, software became available for the reasonably accurate implementation of the technique on desktop PCs. The output from such a system is dependent on the quality of the original and invariably needs manual checking before use as word processed text.

Optical coincidence.   *See* Uniterm concept co-ordination indexing.

Optical copying. 1. Making a copy of a document on photographic material in the same scale, or one different from the original. 2. A print made by such a means may be called an 'optical copy'. 3. A term used in Reprography for a photograph made by means of an optical system. *See also* Contact copying.

Optical disc. A range of discs with the common feature that they all utilize a laser beam in the playback system. Read-only analogue optical discs ('videodiscs' or 'LaserDiscs') were developed as a consumer product; *WORM* (Write once, Read many) discs permit data to be written to optical discs but not changed thereafter and *erasable* optical discs offer the full flexibility of floppy disks and hard disks. CD-ROM and DVD are the most widely-adopted optical discs and the vocabulary has change to take account of this. Thus, CD-R are WORM discs and CD-RW are erasable discs.

Optical fibre. *See* Fibre optics.

Option. The privilege to buy rights in a manuscript or book if required.

Opus Anglicanum. A form of split-stitch embroidery on satin; used as a decorative binding in the fifteenth century. *See also* Fabric binding.

Opus number (Op. no.). A number assigned to a musical work or collection of works, usually in the order of composition. The numbers are assigned by the composer or by the publisher. An opus number may refer to one work or to a group of works of similar form and for the same medium.

Opuscule. (*Pl.* Opuscula) 1. A lesser or minor literary or musical work or composition. 2. A small book or treatise.

OR. 1. Abbreviation for Original. 2. Operational requirement; the specification of the required features of an automated system, given to the computer manufacturer by the client.

ORACLE. The Teletext service provided by the Independent Broadcasting Authority (UK). Originally probably an acronym for Optical Reception of Announcements by Coded Live Electronics. *See also* Videotex.

Orange Book. The specification developed by Sony and Philips for the recordable CD format (CD-R).

Orange Prize for Fiction. <www.orangeprize.co.uk> A UK prize for outstanding fiction by women authors. Runs alongside the Orange Reading Groups Initiative which aims to promote literacy, lifelong learning, and the enjoyment of books and reading, and which is funded by the Association for Business Sponsorship of the Arts with Orange, the Book Trust, NIACE, and Waterstones Booksellers. First awarded in 1996.

Orchestral score. *See* Score.

Order card. The card used for recording orders placed, and later, the delivery of the material and payment for it: the official record of each individual order.

Order department. The department of a library which deals with the ordering and sometimes processing of books and periodicals. Also called 'accession department', 'acquisition department'.

Order file. The file containing records of the books on order from booksellers.

Order information. Data concerning the placing of orders for books and other library materials, and also of their receipt. It includes (1) entering an order, order number, date of order, name of supplier, and fund to which cost will be charged, and (2) after delivery of the goods, date of receipt, cost, and date of invoice.

Order slip. *See* Order card.

Ordered file. (*Information retrieval*) In mechanized systems, one in which the contents are arranged in a predetermined manner to facilitate reference.

Ordinal notation. (*Classification*) One which merely provides order and does not express hierarchical relations. Also called 'Non-expressive notation'. *See also* Hierarchical notation, Notation.

Ordnance Survey (OS). <www.ordnancesurvey.co.uk> Founded in 1791 by the British Government to make an accurate map survey of the British Isles. Many editions have appeared in various scales; maps of Ireland were included until 1922. Current metric series are produced by state-of-the-art computerized mapping techniques. Since 1999 the OS, although still a government agency, has functioned with 'Trading Fund' status – allowing commercial activity to be normal.

Organization for the Advancement of Structured Information Standards. *See* OASIS.

Organization in Liaison (OiL). A network of associated bodies allied with CILIP.

Organ-vocal score. *See* Score.

Origin. *See* Client/server.

Original. 1. Finished art work (drawing, painting or photograph) as completed by the originator, and ready for reproduction. 2. In the author's own words or other original medium. 3. In the author's own language. 4. A first copy. 5. A process block (half-tone or line) as distinct from a duplicate block (stereotype or electrotype). 6. In documentary reproduction, an object, or document, to be reproduced. Abbreviated: Or. or Orig.

Original binding. The binding that was first put on a specific book.

Original order, principle of. *See Respect des fonds*.

Original parts. A first edition of a work which appeared serially in a number of parts, each provided with a paper wrapper, and numbered.

Original sources. *See* Primary sources.

Original writ. One issuing from the Chancery.

Originality. (*Copyright*) The quality of an intellectual work which seems to be significantly different from any other work, either in form or in content. A work may possess originality even when not dealing with new material.

Orihon. 1. A book composed of a continuous, folded, uncut sheet or of small single sheets, folded but uncut. It is held together by cords laced through holes stabbed down one side. This form is used in China and Japan where the paper is so thin that it can only be printed on one side. 2. A 'stabbed binding' of Oriental origin. 3. A manuscript roll on which the text was written in columns running the short way of the paper; the roll was not cut but folded down the margins between the columns of text. *See also* French fold.

Ornamental initial. *See* Initial letter.

Ornamental inside lining. *See* Doublure (1).

Ornaments. Little designs used to decorate printed matter. They are often arranged as borders, headpieces, tail-pieces, etc. Also called 'Printer's ornament'.

Orthography. Spelling correctly, or according to accepted usage.

O.S. *See* Ordnance Survey.

Osborne Collection. A collection of Early English Children's Books which was assembled by Mr. E. Osborne, a former County Librarian of Lancashire, UK. It is owned by the Toronto Public Libraries, Canada.

OSI. *See* Open Systems Interconnection.

Osmosis, method of. The classification by a newly adopted scheme of all literature received after a given date, and the reclassification of the older literature in stock, as and when able to do so.

OSS. *See* Open Source software.

OSS Watch. <www.oss-watch.ac.uk> Funded by JISC to provide the UK further and higher education community with neutral and authoritative guidance about free and Open source software, and about related open standards. Specifically, it offers a web-based clearinghouse for up-to-date information, conferences and workshops, focused assistance for institutions and software projects considering open source, and investigative reports.

Österreichische Nationalbibliothek [Austrian National Library]. <www.onb.ac.at> (Josefsplatz 1, 1015 Vienna, Austria) Founded in the sixteenth century, the Library consists of 9 major collections and other departments. Holdings include almost 3 million books, 8,000 incunabula, and large collections of music manuscripts, maps, papyri, Austrian Literature Archive, International Esperanto Museum. *See also* ÖZZDB.

OSTI. The Office for Scientific and Technical Information; set up by the UK Department of Education and Science to handle funds for research and development into information and information science. Later absorbed into the Research and Development Department of the British Library, later the Research and Innovation Centre.

Oustinoff System. A method devised by Helen Oustinoff, Assistant Director of the University of Vermont Library, to reduce work and ensure accuracy in the ordering of books. By using a Polaroid Camera, copies of bibliographical entries in books or catalogues, are made; these are passed to ordering clerks for making up orders and subsequently filed with the orders.

Out of print.   A book is out of print when the publisher has no more copies for sale and no intention to reprint. Abbreviation O.P.

Out of stock.   Not available from the publisher (although in print) until the stock has been replenished. Abbreviated: O.S.

Outcomes.   *See* Impact.

Outer form.   *See* Form divisions.

Outer forme.   The forme for the side to be printed first; it bears the Signature mark. *See also* Inner forme.

Outline.   1. Usually a popular treatment of an extensive subject, e.g. H. G. Wells' *The outline of history.*   2. (*Printing*) A typeface in which the shape of the character is outlined in a continuous line of more or less consistent width. *See also* Inline letters.

Outline fonts.   Fonts used in PCs which exist as mathematical definitions and from which all type sizes are scaled to produce precise and accurate output; PostScript fonts are an example.

Outline letters.   *See* Open letters.

Output.   The product of a process, that is, the information transferred from the internal storage of a computer to Output devices for external use.

Output devices.   Computer Peripherals which convert the result of the computer's activities into a comprehensible form, e.g. a VDU or Printer.

Output measures.   *See* Performance.

Outreach.   The process whereby a library service investigates the activities of the community it serves and becomes fully involved in supporting community activities, whether or not centred on library premises.

Outsert.   An extra double leaf placed round the outside of a printed section of a book, and forming part of it. *See also* Wrap rounds.

Outside margin.   *See* Fore-edge margin.

Outside source.   An idiom used, often by special librarians, to indicate a source of information outside their own organization which may be drawn upon when the resources of the library are inadequate to deal with enquiry needs.

Outsourcing.   The use of external contractors to provide specialist activities within an organization; in particular it is becoming common for IT facilities to be passed to external companies to manage. Such arrangements allow the organization to concentrate on its core functions, but security and confidentiality of information can be compromised if personnel from outside the organization have unlimited access. Contracts need to be carefully negotiated and monitored.

Ovals, in.   A binding with an oval arabesque centrepiece impressed in the centre of the top and lower covers. A common style in the late sixteenth and early seventeenth centuries, and found both in gold and blind.

Over matter.   Matter set ready for printing but held over through lack of space.

Overcasting.   *See* Oversewing.

Overdue.   1. Colloquialism for an overdue book and also for an Overdue notice.   2. *Overdue* <www.demos.co.uk/overdue> A report subtitled

'How to create a modern public library service', issued by the Demos 'think tank' in the UK in 2003.The report notes the shortage of management talent, and proposes a national library development agency.

Overdue book.   A library book which has been retained longer for home reading than the period allowed.

Overdue notice.   A request to a reader asking for the return of a book which has been kept beyond the time allowed.

Overhead projector.   A device for projecting images written or printed on transparent material on to a screen in front of an audience. The transparency is known as an 'overhead transparency'. *See also* Overlay (2), Presentation software.

Overhead projector panel.   A flat optical panel that rests on top of an Overhead projector and takes the output from a PC for projection onto a screen for demonstrations to groups.

Overheads.   Background costs which are incurred in the provision of a service but which are not specifically attributable to that service; for example, the cost of purchase or lease of a building or recruitment and training of staff required for several different service functions.

Overlay.   1. The placing of pieces of paper on the tympan or impression cylinder of a printing machine, by manipulation of which an even impression is obtained from the matter after it has been levelled as far as possible by Underlay.   2. A group of transparent or translucent prints or drawings which can be superimposed on one another to form a composite print or slide. This method is often used in Overhead projectors.

Overplus.   *See* Overs.

Overprint.   1. To revise printed matter by blocking out unwanted matter and printing a revision above it.   2. To print over matter which has already been printed whether blocked out or not.   3. To add information in a space, or in a Box, on something which has already been printed. This frequently occurs with circulars, catalogues and advertising leaflets where a name and address are inserted to give the impression that the printed matter appears to originate from this source. *See also* Separate. 4. More copies printed than needed, or ordered.   5. In colour printing, to obtain required colours by printing with one colour superimposed over another. *See also* Overprinting.

Overprinting.   1. Printing in a primary colour over printing already carried out in a different colour in order to obtain a compound shade. 2. Application of a varnish or lacquer to matter printed from type or by a litho process, by means of a brush, spray or roller.   3. In blockmaking, superimposing one negative over another on the coated metal plate before developing. *See also* Overprint.

Over-run.   (*Printing*) 1. To turn over words from one line to the next for several successive lines as necessary after an insertion or a deletion. 2. Copies printed in excess of the number ordered.

Over-running.   Re-adjusting a paragraph of type which has been set up, due to corrections affecting the length of a line or poor Make-up, or to avoid a River or the unsatisfactory division of words. Words set in one line are carried forward or backward to adjacent lines as necessary.

Overs.   1. Extra sheets issued from the paper warehouse to the printing room, to allow for make-ready, testing colour, and for spoilt sheets, so that on completion of a job the number ordered is available.   2. Sheets or copies of a work printed in excess of the number ordered to make up spoiled copies, and to provide review and presentation copies. Also called 'Overplus'.

Oversewing.   A method of attaching the leaves of a book to each other before casing or recasing. The leaves are initially separated, by milling or by hand, then clamped in the sewing machine at an angle of 45°. Holes are then punched at intervals of 2.5 cms (1 inch), and threaded needles link the sections together vertically while horizontal shuttle needles form successive lock stitches up the spine of the book. The major advantages of oversewing are versatility and strength; the disadvantage is the perforation of pages which will damage poor quality paper. Called 'whip-stitching' in the US.

Oversize book.   One which is too large to be shelved in normal sequence.

Ownership mark.   A rubber-stamp impression, perforation, embossment, or other mark of ownership in a book.

Oxford corners.   In book finishing, border rules that cross and project beyond each other.

Oxford Decimal System.   A scheme of classification based on the Universal Decimal Classification. It was devised at the School of Forestry of Oxford University and is restricted to the field of forestry.

Oxford Folio.   *See* Bibles.

Oxford hollow.   A tube-like lining which is flattened, and one side stuck to the folded and sewn sections of the book and the other to the inside of the spine of the cover.

Oxford India Paper.   An India Paper about 8lb demy (480) used by the Oxford University Press mainly for Bibles and prayer books, and made from selected rag stock according to a secret formula at their Wolvercote Mill since 1857. It is similar to an India paper first brought to Oxford in 1841, being very thin and opaque (one thousand sheets making less than an inch in thickness), and is a proprietary article. *See also* Bible paper, Cambridge India Paper.

Oxford Internet Institute (OII).   <www.oii.ox.ac.uk> Launched in September 2002, the Institute is a research centre focusing on the social impact of the Internet and the Web, and integrating the findings into European Internet policy.

Oxford rule.   A rule with one thick and one thin line running parallel with each other.

Oxford Text Archive.   <ota.ahds.ac.uk> The Oxford Text Archive hosts AHDS Literature, Languages and Linguistics. It works closely with members of the arts and humanities academic community to collect, catalogue, and preserve high-quality electronic texts for research and teaching.

Oxford University Library. *See* Bodleian Library.

Oxidation. The action which occurs when air contacts the unprotected areas of a lithographic plate which has been inadequately gummed. *See also* Gumming up.

ÖZZDB. <www.onb.ac.at/ausb> Österreichische Zeitungs - und Zeitschriften Datenbank, a library bibliographic network based at the Austrian National Library, Vienna, and specializing in handling serials records of scientific libraries. Founded 1984; members include all Austrian universities, colleges, museums, and state libraries, and numerous special libraries.

p. Abbreviation for page; pp., pages.

P2P. *See* Peer to peer.

PA. *See* Publishers Association.

PAC. 1. Public access catalogue; *See* Online public access catalogue. 2. *See* Preservation and Conservation.

Pacific Rim Digital Library Alliance (PRDLA). <www.prdla.og> Based at the Library of the University of Hong Kong since its formation in 1997, the PRDLA is an alliance of 22 large academic libraries. It crosses the political, linguistic, and technical boundaries of the Pacific Rim and aims to provide cost-effective and efficient methods to maximize access to these significant library collections for the interchange of scholarly information. The Alliance supports new and traditional library functions through the sharing of electronic and hardcopy data, co-operative collection development, personnel exchange, and other activities. Specific actions include the development of multilingual online library catalogue access, document delivery of journal articles via the Internet, and remote access to local online databases. The first major project is the creation of the Pacific Explorations Archive.

Packet device. The symbol used in building classification numbers to connect class numbers from two parts of the classification schedules, the second one being used to show an aspect of the subject indicated by the first number.

Packet notation. The use of a connecting symbol, e.g. in the Colon Classification a bracket, or in the Universal Decimal Classification square brackets, to divide an isolate number by a number drawn from another schedule. Such a digit can be used as an octavizing digit (*See* Octave device) to extend the hospitality of an array.

Packet switching. A method of dividing data into small packets for transmission between computers, terminals, networks; each packet is separately routed, and thus large quantities of data can be transmitted simultaneously by various routes. Data is split either at an initial stage, or at an exchange point, and needs reassembling by the receiving device.

PAD. Packet assembler-disassembler. A device for making up packets from data, and converting the packets back to data in a Packet switching system.

Padding. Blank leaves added at the back of a thin pamphlet when binding it to form a sizeable volume.

Padeloup style. A style of book decoration practised by the Padeloup family in France in the 18th century. It is mainly characterized by its inlays of coloured leathers of diapered simple geometrical form, devoid of any floreation.

Page. *See* Leaf.

Page break. The point in the text of a book where one page ends and the next begins.

Page catalogue. One in which only a few entries are made on a page at first, with spaces left for the insertion of subsequent entries in correct order. Also called 'Guard book catalogue', 'Ledger catalogue'.

Page cord. A cord which withstands water, specially made for printers, and used to tie up pages of type prior to imposition or distribution.

Page description language (PDL). Software utilized when transmitting the contents of a computer file (text and graphics) to a high quality output device such as a Laser printer. In contrast to other printers which receive instructions from the computer one line at a time, laser printers receive one page at a time and the PDL sets this up. Many page description languages are device independent so that a document in this format can be transferred from machine to machine without loss of quality. The 'industry standard' PDL is PostScript, from Adobe Systems.

Page headline. A summary of the contents of a page, or an Opening, or of the main topic of a page or opening, appearing on both left- and right-hand pages, or on one side only in conjunction with a section headline on the other page. Also called 'Page head'. *See also* Headline, Running title, Section headline.

Page printer. Any printer that produces output one page at a time such as a Laser printer. *See also* Page description language.

Page proof. *See* Proof.

Page reference. In bibliographies, the number of the page on which the article, etc., indexed is to be found in a particular volume or volumes.

Pagination. 1. That part of a catalogue entry or bibliographical description specifying the number of pages in a book. 2. The system of numbers by which consecutive pages of a book or MS. are marked to indicate their order. Pagination is rare until 1500 and not really common until 1590.

Painted edges. *See* Fore-edge painting.

PAIS. <www.pais.org> Public Affairs Information Service. Based in New York City, PAIS is a not-for-profit educational corporation founded in

1914 by librarians, chartered in 1954 by the Board of Regents, Education Department, State of New York, and dedicated to providing better access to the literature of public affairs – current issues and actions that affect world communities, countries, people and governments. OCLC took over responsibility for the service in 2000.

Pakistan Library Association. <www.isisnl.org/lamb/plahpg.htm> (Box 1091, Islamabad, Pakistan) The principal professional association in that country.

Pakistan National Scientific and Technical Documentation Centre (PANSDOC). This organization was established in Karachi in 1957, with the technical assistance of Unesco. *See now* APIN.

PAL. Phase Alternate Line, the international colour television standard with the exception of France, the US, and Japan; similarly the format of the international videotape standard. *See also* NTSC, SECAM.

Palaeography. The study and description of ancient and mediaeval manuscripts, documents and systems of writing, including the knowledge of the various characters used at different periods by the scribes of different nations and languages, their usual abbreviations, etc.

Palimpsest. Manuscript in which a second writing has been superimposed upon the original text, which has been wholly or partially obliterated.

PALINET. <www.palinet.org> (3401 Market Street, Philadelphia, PA 19104-2801, USA) A US network consortium of libraries in the states of New Jersey, Delaware, Washington DC, and Eastern Pennsylvania. An OCLC Network Associate.

Pallet. 1. A tool used to decorate the panels on the spine of a bound book. Pallets are usually used to make straight lines (sometimes decorative) but are also used to impress a whole word such as the author's name or title. 2. A bookbinder's typeholder.

Palm leaf book. Manuscript books consisting of strips of Palmyra or Talipat palm leaf from 16 to 36 inches long and from $1^{1}/_{2}$ to 3 inches broad. Writing was done by scratching with an iron stylus and ink prepared from oil and charcoal rubbed over the surface to fill the incisions. The strips were then bound by piercing a hole in the middle of each and stringing them on cords or a piece of twine, and attaching them to a board. They were made in India, Myanmar (Burma) and Sri Lanka. Sacred works were written on Talipat palm leaves in Thailand, the edges of the leaves being gilded, or painted with vermilion, and the leaves threaded on strings and folded like a fan.

Palmtop. *See* Personal digital assistant.

PALS. <www.palsgroup.org.uk> Publisher and Library/Learning Solutions, an ongoing collaboration between UK publishers (ALPSP and the Publishers Association) and higher/further education (JISC). PALS aims to foster mutual understanding and work collaboratively towards the solution of issues arising from electronic publication.

Pamphlet. A non-periodical publication of at least five but not more than 48 pages, exclusive of the cover pages. (General Conference of Unesco,

1964). *See also* Book. It usually has an independent entity, not being a Serial, but it may be one of a series of publications having a similarity of format or subject matter.

Pamphlet binding. 1. Binding done by, or for, a printer, in which the sheets as they come from the press, are wire-stitched. The term applies both to pamphlets and to magazines. 2. The manner in which such publications are bound when they come from the publisher, being Wire stitched, Side-stitched or Saddle stitched.

Pamphlet box. A box, usually of cardboard covered with cloth, or of steel, or plastic, for holding pamphlets and other unbound material. *See also* Box file, Solander case, Transfer file.

Pamphlet style library binding. A style of binding for a thin pamphlet or a group of thin pamphlets which are expected to be used infrequently.

Pamphlet volume. A volume consisting of a number of pamphlets bound together with or without a title-page or table of contents.

Pan American Standards Commission. *See* COPANT.

PANDAS. <pandora.nla.gov.au/manual/pandas/index.html> PANDORA Digital Archiving System, developed and tested by the National Library of Australia and its partners for archiving Australian websites. PANDAS can be set to automatically tag, gather and prepare pages for public display. If pages are not suitable for immediate public access, due to commercial, cultural or privacy reasons, PANDAS can manage appropriate access restrictions.

PANDORA. <pandora.nla.gov.au> Preserving and Accessing Networked Documentary Resources of Australia, the Australian national Web Archive developed by the National Library of Australia to ensure long-term access to selected online publications. The work began in 1996 when it had become clear that an increasing amount of Australian information was being made available via the Web instead of in print publications. *See also* UK Web Archiving Consortium.

Panel. 1. A compartment of the external cover of a book enclosed in a Border (2) or Frame (2). 2. The space between two bands on the back of a book. 3. The list of books 'by the same author' facing the title-page. This is more for bibliographical than for advertising purposes and may include out-of-print titles and those issued by other publishers.

Panel back. In hand binding, a volume finished with panelled borders between the raised bands on the shelf-back.

Panel stamp. A large piece of metal, engraved intaglio, used for impressing a design on the sides of book covers. Some of the stamps used for the early leather bindings were of quarto and folio size, but often book covers of these sizes were impressed two, three, four or more times with small panel stamps. A popular form of ornamentation in the early sixteenth century. *See also* Blocking.

Pan-European Book Industry Group. *See* EDItEUR.

Panizzi Club. Founded in 1914 'to provide opportunities for social intercourse between the Senior Officers of Reference and Research Libraries and to promote all measures tending to their higher efficiency'. Librarians of all kinds of library were admitted to membership. It is not known when the Club ceased to function, but it was the foundation on which the Circle of State Librarians was built.

Panoramic catalogue. The endless chain principle adapted for displaying catalogue entries.

PANS. Pretty amazing new stuff, i.e. ISDN communications when compared to POTS, plain old telephone services.

PANSDOC. Pakistan National Scientific and Technical Documentation Centre. *See* ΛPIN.

Pantone. 1. A photo-engraving method of printing from a flat (planographic) plate with letterpress equipment, having the advantage over letterpress half-tone in that it can print from a screen up to 400 lines on antique paper and other rough surfaces. It is based on the principle that a printing plate bearing an image that is not in relief can be made to repel ink in the bare parts by treating them with mercury, while the printing parts will take up ink. 2. A standard system of colour specification used in printing and adopted by many Desktop publishing programs; full name Pantone Matching System.

Paper. 1. A fibrous material made by breaking down vegetable fibres, purifying them, interweaving them into a compact web and pressing them into thin sheets. Book papers are made from Mechanical wood pulp (used for the cheapest publications and newspapers), Chemical wood pulp (for most books), Esparto or rags, which make the best quality hand-made papers (for fine books). 2. A contribution to scholarly knowledge appearing in a periodical or presented at a conference. *See also* Article, Work. 3. Contraction for newspaper. 4. To insert the end papers and fly-leaves of a book before inserting in its cover.

Paper backed. *See* Paperback, Paper bound.

Paper boards. *See* Boards.

Paper bound. Bound with a paper cover. Also called 'Paper backed'. A book so bound is called a Paperback.

Paper covered. A pamphlet or small book which is not bound in boards, but covered with a stiff paper which is usually pasted on to the book or sewn through. If the paper covers are pasted down on to thin boards, cut flush at the head and tail, flaps turned over, the style is called 'Stiffened paper covers'.

Paper finishes. *Antique*: a rough uneven surface. *Eggshell*: slightly finished surface, having the appearance of the shell of an egg. *Machine*: smoother than antique with a slight gloss, but not suitable for half-tone illustrations, excepting those of coarse-screen finish. *Smooth antique*: an antique slightly rolled. *Super-calendered*: smooth finish without lustre; this will print half-tone blocks up to 100-screen. *American*: a finish with medium gloss and suitable for half-tone illustrations up to 100-screen. *Enamel* or *coated*: has a very high gloss, being coated in the making with china-clay, satin white, and casein which fills in the pores; takes illustrations of the finest screen. *Dull coated*: has the coating as on a coated paper, but is calendered for smoothness only, not for gloss; it has a perfect surface of mellow softness for the finest cuts.

Paper sizes. The dimensions of a sheet of paper or board (generally rectangular shape) as supplied by the manufacturer, the width (the smaller dimension) being given first. The British Standards Specification for writing and printing paper is as follows:

	millimetres	inches
Foolscap	343 x 432	13½ x 17
Foolscap, Double	432 x 686	17 x 27
Foolscap, Oblong Double	343 x 864	13½ x 34
Foolscap, Quad	686 x 864	27 x 34
Pinched Post	368 x 470	14½ x 18½
Post	387 x 483	15¼ x 19
Post, Double	483 x 775	19 x 30½
Large Post	419 x 533	16½ x 21
Large Post, Double	533 x 838	21 x 33
Demy	445 x 572	17½ x 22½
Demy, Double	572 x 890	22½ x 35
Demy, Quad	890 x 1144	35 x 45
Medium	457 x 584	18 x 23
Medium, Double	584 x 914	23 x 36
Medium, Quad	914 x 1168	36 x 46
Royal	508 x 635	20 x 25
Royal, Double	635 x 1016	25 x 40
Crown	391 x 508	15 x 20
Crown, Double	508 x 762	20 x 30
Crown, Double Quad	1016 x 1524	40 x 60

Crown, Quad	762 x 1016	30 x 40
Imperial	559 x 762	22 x 30
Imperial, Double	762 x 1118	30 x 44

Other sizes are:

	millimetres	*inches*
Pott	318 x 394	12½ x 15½
Pott, Double	394 x 635	15½ x 25
Post, Small	400 x 495	15¾ x 19½
Royal, Large	508 x 686	20 x 27
Royal, Super	521 x 698	20½ x 27½

A sheet of 'quad' gives four times the number of sections as a sheet of ordinary size, a 'double' sheet twice the number. Papers for other purposes differ in size. *See also* Book sizes, Octavo.

The American practice is not to use names but to specify the size of paper by inches and its weight per ream. The ordinary sizes (in inches) of book papers in the USA are:

22 x 32	28 x 44	34 x 44	44 x 56
24 x 36	29 x 52	35 x 45	44 x 64
25 x 38	30½ x 41	36 x 48	
26 x 39	32 x 44	38 x 50	
26 x 40	33 x 44	41 x 51	
28 x 42	33 x 46	42 x 56	

The German DIN A series of paper sizes is widely used in Europe. DIN stands for Deutsche Industrie Normen, and indicates standards agreed by Deutscher Normenausschuss (Committee for Standards), a similar body to the British Standards Institution. The A is to distinguish this standard from others known as B and C which apply to related poster and envelope sizes. The chief features of the DIN A series are that they apply to all types of paper, and that the proportions of a sheet remain constant when it is cut or folded in half across the long side. The letters A0 indicate a basic size of 1 square metre. A sheet of paper half this size is indicated by A1, half this size by A2 and so on. A larger sheet than A0 is indicated by 2A. The following table shows 7 trimmed sizes in the DIN A series which correspond to the British sizes from 8-demy to demy 8vo.

	Millimetres	Inches (approx.)	Demy sizes
2A0	1189 x 1682	$46^{13}/_{16}$ x $66^{3}/_{16}$	45 x 70
A0	841 x 1189	$33^{1}/_{8}$ x $46^{13}/_{16}$	33 x 45
A1	594 x 841	$23^{3}/_{8}$ x $33^{1}/_{8}$	$22^{1}/_{2}$ x 35
A2	420 x 594	$16^{9}/_{16}$ x $23^{3}/_{8}$	$17^{1}/_{2}$ x $22^{1}/_{2}$
A3	297 x 420	$11^{11}/_{16}$ x $16^{9}/_{16}$	$11^{1}/_{4}$ x $17^{1}/_{2}$
A4	210 x 297	$8^{1}/_{4}$ x $11^{11}/_{16}$	$8^{3}/_{4}$ x $11^{1}/_{4}$
A5	148 x 210	$5^{7}/_{8}$ x $8^{1}/_{4}$	$5^{5}/_{8}$ x $8^{3}/_{4}$
A6	105 x 148	$4^{1}/_{8}$ x $5^{7}/_{8}$	
A7	74 x 105	$2^{15}/_{16}$ x $4^{1}/_{8}$	
A8	52 x 74	$2^{1}/_{16}$ x $2^{15}/_{16}$	
A9	37 x 52	$1^{1}/_{2}$ x $2^{1}/_{16}$	
A10	26 x 37	1 x $1^{1}/_{2}$	

Series B is intended for posters, wall charts and other large items, and C for envelopes, particularly where it is necessary for an envelope in the C series to fit into another envelope. The International Organization for Standardization (ISO) adopted the A series for trimmed sizes for administrative, commercial and technical uses, and printed matter such as forms, professional periodicals and catalogues; the sizes do not necessarily apply to newspapers, published books, posters, continuous stationery or other specialized items. These sizes are sometimes referred to as 'ISO-A' sizes. The B sizes have also been adopted by ISO and are sometimes referred to as 'ISO-B' sizes, but, unlike the A series, have not been adopted by the British Standards Institution. The ISO recommends that these sizes are intended for use in exceptional circumstances, when sizes are needed intermediate between any two adjacent sizes of the A series. The C sizes have not been adopted by the ISO. *See also* Periodical, Untrimmed size.

Paperback. A book bound in heavy paper or light card covers trimmed to the size of the pages. Originally used for novels in the late nineteenth century. In 1935 Allen Lane founded Penguin Books in England and began publishing large editions of paperbacks at a very low price. Paperbacks now form the bulk of the personal book buying market.

Paper-less office. A concept fashionable in the 1980s based on the assumption that all communications could be handled via non-traditional means using information technology. Never universally accepted as a result of user resistance and a lack of adequate systems, although communications via E-mail and the Internet have made it more of a possibility. Also referred to as 'electronic office'.

Papers. (*Archives*) A generic and broad term to indicate personal and/or family archives.

PAPI. <papi.rediris.es> A system for providing access control to restricted information resources across the Internet. It intends to keep authentication as an issue local to the organization the user belongs to, while leaving information providers full control over the resources offered.

Papyrology. The study of ancient documents and literary manuscripts on papyrus.

Papyrus. 1. A giant water-reed from the stem of which the Egyptians made a writing material. 2. The material itself. 3. A manuscript written on papyrus.

Paragraph indention. Setting the first line of a paragraph one em or so in from the margin. Also called 'Paragraph indentation'. *See also* Hanging indention.

Paragraph mark. 1. The reversed or 'blind' P sign (¶) used in a MS. or proof to indicate the commencement of a new paragraph. 2. The sixth reference mark for footnotes, coming after the parallel. *See also* Reference marks.

Parallel. (*Information retrieval*) Pertaining to the simultaneous handling of all the elements in a group. *See also* Serial (3). (*Printing*) The printer's sign ‖; it is used as the fifth reference mark. *See also* Reference marks.

Parallel arrangement. Separating books of varying sizes to economize shelf space by arranging larger books by one of the following methods: (a) in a separate sequence on the bottom shelves of each tier; (b) in a separate sequence at the end of each class; (c) in a complete separate sequence of the whole classification.

Parallel classification. Material classified by the same scheme is said to be placed in parallel classification when it is again divided by size, character, etc., e.g. there may be four perfectly classified sequences for octavos, folios, pamphlets and illustrations; thus giving four parallel classifications.

Parallel edition. A publication in which different texts of the same work are printed side by side, e.g. the Authorized and Revised versions of the Bible, or an original and a translation into another language, or two or more versions of a work.

Parallel index. A system of indexing books by providing index terms or cross references in small type at the side of a page to give a lead into or onwards from the main text of the page.

Parallel mark. (‖) The fifth reference mark for footnotes, coming after the section mark. *See also* Reference marks.

Parallel processing. A method of computer design utilizing two or more processors that work on a number of computing operations simultaneously, dividing the tasks among the processors available. *See also* Multi-processing.

Parallel publishing. The production of publications simultaneously in print-on-paper and electronic formats.

Parallel rule. A Rule having two lines of the same thickness. *See also* Double rule.

Parallel text. *See* Parallel edition.

Parallel title. The title proper, given in a publication, but in another language, or in another script, than that used for the text. *See also* Added title-page.

Parallel translation. A text, with a translation into another language, both printed in parallel columns.

Parallel transmission. The simultaneous transmission of a group of bits over separate wires. *See also* SCSI.

Paraph. A mark or flourish after a signature, made often as a protection against forgery, and especially used by notaries. Also called a 'Flourish'.

Paraphrase. 1. An arrangement, transcription or imitation of a vocal or instrumental work in a form for voices or instruments other than was originally intended. 2. An abridgement of a literary work.

Para-professional. A member of library staff who has not obtained professional qualifications in librarianship but has administrative responsibilities for some aspects of library management. Para-professionals may fill roles such as branch library supervisor or senior library assistant; career paths to professional status are often available through professional associations.

PARBICA. Pacific Regional Branch of the International Council on Archives.

Parchment. 1. Sheepskin or goatskin dressed with alum and polished. It is not so strong as vellum (calfskin) which it resembles, and from which it can be distinguished by its grain. It is used for documents of a permanent nature and for binding large and heavy volumes. The term is now sometimes applied to fibrous imitations. 2. In the paper trade, wrapping paper with a high resistance to grease and atmospheric humidity.

Parchment-paper. *See* Parchment (2).

Parentheses. Curved lines ( ) used to include words inserted parenthetically. Used in cataloguing to enclose explanatory or qualifying words or phrases to set off some item in the entry, such as a series note. Also called 'Round brackets' or 'Curves'. *See also* Square brackets.

Parenthesis (paren). A short explanatory clause inserted in a sentence, usually between parentheses.

Paris Principles. (*Cataloguing*) The twelve principles on which an author/ title entry should be based. So named as the International Conference on Cataloguing Principles (ICCP), at which they were drawn up, was held in Paris in October 1961. The Conference, which was organized by IFLA, was intended to serve as a basis for international standardization in cataloguing. Since these principles were formulated, at least twenty cataloguing codes have been drawn up which have these principles as their common basis; one of these is AACR 2.

Parish library. One which was provided by a parish council.

Parity bit. A Bit used in checking for errors when data is transmitted between computers.

Parliamentary Papers (UK). A term which when used in the scholars' narrow sense means a particular group of Parliamentary Publications, e.g. (a) House of Lords Papers and Bills, (b) House of Commons Bills, (c) House of Commons Papers, (d) Command Papers, and not all the publications issued by Parliament. *See also* Parliamentary Publications, Sessional Papers.

Parliamentary Publications (UK). Papers printed for parliamentary purposes and made available to the public; these include House of Lords Papers, Bills, Debates, etc., House of Commons Papers, Bills, Debates, Votes and Proceedings, etc., Command Papers, Public General Acts, Local and Private Acts. Also included are documents ordered to be presented to either House by statute; these carry the phrase 'ordered to be printed' and the sessional number on the title page. The official verbatim reports of debates – 'Hansard' – are issued separately for Lords and Commons and published daily while Parliament is sitting. (These are named after Luke Hansard, 1752–1828, and his descendents who printed these reports from 1811–1891. An officially authorized edition began in 1892, and HMSO assumed responsibility in 1909.) Votes and Proceedings of the House of Commons, and Minutes of Proceedings of the House of Lords are issued daily while either House is sitting, and are the agenda and minutes for each day. Journals of the House of Commons and the House of Lords are a complete record of each session, and are published at the end of the session. After the privatization of HMSO, most of the foregoing documents remain the responsibility of The Stationery Office. New publication series cover the Scottish Parliament, the Welsh Assembly, the Northern Ireland Assembly etc.

Parliamentary Session (UK). A parliamentary year which begins with the opening of Parliament and normally ends with its prorogation. It usually begins in the first week of November, immediately after the old session, and does not correspond either with the calendar year or with the government's financial year. Also called a 'Session'. *See also* Sessional papers.

Parochial Registers and Records Measure, 1978. UK provision for the care and custody of parish registers and archives, and for diocesan record offices in the Church of England. Repeals the Parochial Registers and Records Measure, 1929.

Parry Report (UK). The *Report of the Committee on Libraries* (HMSO,

1967) which was set up in 1963 by the University Grants Committee; so named after Dr. Thomas Parry, Principal of the University College of Wales, Aberystwyth, who was the chairman. It surveys libraries in British universities and makes recommendations on their improvement.

Part. 1. A portion of a work in one or more volumes issued by a publisher as the work is completed for publication. Parts may be issued at frequent, regular intervals, as fortnightly, or at monthly, yearly, or irregular intervals, according to the nature of the work and its compilation. It usually has a separate title, half-title, or cover title, and may have separate or continuous paging. It is distinguished from a Fascicle by being a unit rather than a temporary portion of a unit. 2. A division of Work according to its content. 3. The music for any one of the participating voices or instruments of a musical composition. 4. The manuscript or printed copy of the music for such a participant. *See also* Volume (1). 5. A separately published number of a Serial. Parts usually have paper covers bearing the title of the serial, the volume numbers (if any), issue number and date of issue. This information usually appears also on the first page of the text if the cover does not have textual matter on it, and nowadays often at the foot of each page in addition, the title usually being in an abbreviated form.

Part publications. Long works which are issued in separate parts at regular intervals.

Part title. *See* Divisional title.

Partial bibliography. One in which a limit has been put on the material included; e.g. periodicals only, books or articles of a certain period or in a certain country or library. *See also* Select bibliography.

Partial contents note. A note which gives only the more important items in the contents.

Partial title. One which consists of only a secondary part of the title as given in the title-page. It may be a Catchword title, Sub-title or Alternative title.

Partition. A logical section of a hard disk that is dedicated to a particular operating system, application or user and accessed as a single unit.

Partnering. *See* Partnerships.

Partnerships. Alliances formed to enhance efficiency and cost-effectiveness; they may be between public sector and private sector organizations, or strategic alliances made by companies whose products or markets are complementary. Proposals for projects supported by the European Commission usually specify that tenders should come from partnerships of organizations based in different members countries.

Password. The combination of generally alpha-numeric characters that identifies a user or group of users as being authenticated to use stand-alone or networked resources following the keying-in of the related Username. The password is invariably hidden from view by the system which substitutes asterisks or similar symbols in place of the alpha-numeric characters. *See also* Single sign-on.

Pasteboard. The material, made by pasting sheets of brown paper together, and lined on both sides with paper, which is used for printing and also for the covers of books. *See also* Millboard, Strawboard.

Paste-down. That part of an endpaper which is pasted down to the inner surface of the cover or boards of a book. Also called 'Board paper'. The free half of the endpaper forms a fly-leaf.

Paste-down endpaper. *See* Endpaper.

Paste-grain. Split sheepskin hardened by coating with paste and given a highly polished surface.

Paste-in. 1. A correction or addition to the text supplied after the sheets have been printed, and tipped into the book opposite the place to which it refers. *See also* Corrigenda. 2. A separately printed illustration or map, cut to the size of the book, and the inner edge pasted into the text before gathering.

Paste-up. An arrangement on sheets of paper of proofs of a number of pages in order to plan the positioning of blocks, legends, illustrations and text.

Pastiche. A musical or artistic composition consisting of a medley of passages or parts from various sources; usually satirical.

Pasting down. The action of attaching a sewn book to its case or cover.

Pastoral. A book relating to the cure of souls.

Pastoral letter. A letter from a spiritual pastor, especially from a bishop to the clergy or people of his diocese.

Patent. 1. A specification concerning the designs or manufacture of something which is protected by letters patent and secured for the exclusive profit of the designer or inventor for a limited number of years which varies in different countries from fifteen to twenty years. The department which controls the registration of patents is called a 'Patent Office'. 2. A publication, issued by such an office, which gives details of designs and processes. 3. In the field of patents, a 'provisional specification' is a patent application which is merely to establish a date for disclosure of an inventive concept to a Patent Office. It does not include a claim to the monopoly sought; this is made in a 'complete specification' which describes at least one preferred way in which the invention may be performed, and which sets out a claim or claims for the protection sought.

Patent and Trademark Group. A membership group of CILIP; formerly a special interest group of the Institute of Information Scientists.

Patent base. A device for raising the level of the bed of a printing press so that the electrotypes or stereotypes need not be mounted on wood.

Patent file. Patent specifications and drawings which may be arranged by country and number, name of patentee or subject, or an index of such material similarly arranged.

Patent Information Users Group, Inc. <www.piug.org> A US-based, not-for-profit, international society for those concerned with patent information. It encourages the development of patent research and analysis systems.

Patent of addition. A patent which represents an improvement in, or modification of, the invention of another patent in the same name, and for which no renewal fees are necessary to keep it in force. It expires when the other patent expires. *See also* Convention application.

Patent Office Library. Founded in London in 1855 to stimulate developments in the field of invention by making relevant information on applied science freely and readily available to all. On incorporation within the British Museum Library to form the National Reference Library of Science and Invention, its scope was widened to include developments and discoveries in any branch of the natural sciences and technology. Incorporation within the British Library took place in 1973.

Patent roll. A parchment roll upon which royal letters patent were enrolled at the Chancery.

Patentee. The person or persons entered on the register of patents as grantee or proprietor of a patent according to the appropriate national procedure.

PATRA. Abbreviation for Printing, Packaging and Allied Trades Research Association. *See* PIRA.

Patristics. A publisher's series on the writings of the Fathers of the Christian Church, e.g. *The Library of Christian classics* and *Ancient Christian writers*.

Pattern. A specimen volume, or rubbing, sent to a binder to indicate the style of lettering to be used. *See also* Rub.

Pattern board. A board maintained by a binder on which is mounted a specimen of the covering material to show titling layout, colour, size, etc., to ensure uniformity in the binding of a series.

Pattern rubbing. A rubbing made to ensure that subsequent volumes in a series are lettered in the same style. *See also* Rub.

Paulin Report (UK). The Report of the (Library Association) Working Party on the Future of Professional Qualifications (L.A., 1977); Chair Miss L. V. Paulin.

Payne style. The style of book decoration practised by Roger Payne in England in the eighteenth century. It consisted of the repetition of small floral forms in borders or radiating corners, the background being formed with dots and circles.

PBFA. *See* Provincial Booksellers' Fairs Association.

PC. Personal computer, a desktop machine comprising display and Central Processing Unit – separate or integrated – with computing power sufficient for the small business or home user. The increasing power of PCs, coupled with their competitive price, has been responsible for the move of computing away from the large Mainframe to a Distributed provision.

PCC. <www.loc.gov> Program for Co-operative Cataloging; formed in 1995 after deliberations of the Co-operative Cataloging Council, PCC is an international co-operative programme co-ordinated by the Library of

Congress with participation of libraries world-wide. The purpose is to expand access to collections by cataloguing to a level that meets mutually-accepted standards. In 1997 PCC merged with CONSER. NACO (the Name Authority Co-operative Program) and SACO (Subject Authority Co-operative Program) are associated in PCC.

PCMCIA. <www.pcmcia.org> (2635 North First Street, Suite 218, San Jose, CA 95134, USA) Personal Computer Memory Card International Association, an international standards body and trade association with over 200 member companies that was founded in 1989 to establish standards for integrated circuit cards and to promote interchangeability among mobile computers where ruggedness, low power, and small size were critical. The Association promotes the interoperability of PC Cards not only in mobile computers, but in digital cameras, cable TV, set-top boxes, and automobiles and is developing standards for small form factor cards and SmartMedia.

PDA. *See* Personal digital assistant.

PDF. *See* Portable document format.

PDL. *See* Page description language.

PE Notes. In an attempt to speed up decisions on extensions to the Universal Decimal Classification, the International Commission sends out *PE notes* (*Projets d'extensions*) which invite criticisms to be submitted within four months, and *PP notes* (*Projets provisoires*) which are intimations of provisional 'revolutionary suggestions'.

Peacock roll. (*Binding*) A finisher's roll which includes a peacock in its ornamentation. It is characteristic of some English Restoration bindings, and also appears on eighteenth century Irish bindings.

Pear Tree Press. A private printing press, begun in Essex in 1899 by James Guthrie. It moved to Flansham in 1907.

Pearl. An out-of-date name for a size of type equivalent to 5 point.

Pearson Gallery of Living Words. Exhibition area at the British Library's London premises.

Pebbling. *See* Stippling.

Peer review. The process of obtaining impartial opinions from the research and academic community in order to ascertain whether papers submitted for publication in journals or at conferences are of a suitable standard. The opinions are sought by publishers and conference organizers, and are requested from those whose expertise and stature are similar to the author's. *See also* Referee.

Peer to peer (P2P). A network architecture which does not have fixed clients and servers but a number of peer nodes that function as both clients and servers to the other nodes on the network.Thus, all computers have broadly equal abilities and tasks and may share hard drives, CD-ROM drives, and other storage devices with other computers on the network. Also, a commonly used protocol that has been used for downloading software, MP3 music or other files to share them across the Internet. *See also* Client/server.

PELICAN.   <www.lboro.ac.uk/departments/dils/disresearch/pelican> A project to develop charging algorithms for publishers giving licences to higher education institutions to allow digitization and dissemination of individual book chapters and similar items. Funded by JISC 2000–2001. *See also* HERON.

Pellet's process.   A blueprint process suitable only for the reproduction of line drawings whereby the prints have blue lines on an almost white background. It was introduced in 1877.

P.E.N. International.   <www.internationalpen.org.uk> or <www.pen.org> An international fellowship open to all writers of standing, which aims to promote freedom of expression and understanding between nations. Founded in 1921, the acronym originally stood for Poets, Playwrights, Editors, Essayists, Novelists, but creative writers of any genre are eligible for membership. There are 130 centres worldwide; P.E.N. aims to encourage intellectual co-operation and understanding, to emphasize the central role of literature in culture, and defend literature against threats.

Pen-based computing.   *See* Personal digital assistant.

Pen-name.   *See* Pseudonym.

Penny-dreadful.   A thrilling story magazine for children sold at a very low price. A morbidly sensational story.

People's Network (PN).   <www.peoplesnetwork.gov.uk> In the UK, a government-led initiative to bring Internet access and online services to the whole of the population by installing personal computers with broadband connections throughout the public library service. The main categories of use foreseen include learning, finding work, developing personal identity, community enrichment, social inclusion, culture and creativity. PN runs parallel to UK government e-service initiatives. Partners in the scheme are UKOnline (England), Digital Scotland, Cymru Ar-lein (Wales) and ELFNI (Northern Ireland). The scheme started in 2000 and has been supported by the National Lottery New Opportunities Fund and by the Bill and Melinda Gates Foundation (*see* Gates Library Foundation). There is an associated People's Network Excellence Fund to support the development of facilities and resources.

Pepys (Samuel) Medal.   *See* Ephemera Society.

Perfect.   (*Binding*) A method of binding by which the folds of the sections forming the back of the book are cut away; the edges of the loose sheets so formed are then coated with a very flexible but strong adhesive and covered with paper, mull or other material. The book is then inserted into covers by ordinary methods employed when sections are not sewn on tapes. Also called 'Lumbecking'. *See also* Caoutchouc binding.

Perfect copy.   A sheet of paper which has been printed on both sides from an 'inner forme' and also from an 'outer forme'.

Perfecter.   A printing machine which prints on both sides of the paper at the same time whereas stop-cylinder presses and two-revolution machines print on one side only. Also called a 'Perfecting machine' or 'Perfecting press'. The first machine of this kind was made in 1816 by Koenig and Bauer and was called by the maker a 'completing machine'.

Perfecting. Printing the second side of a sheet. A perfecting press is one that prints both sides of a sheet in one operation. Also called 'Backing up'.

Perfecting machine. *See* Perfecter.

Perforating stamp. A punch or stamp which perforates a mark of ownership through the page of a book.

Performance. The success of an organization in doing the job for which it was set up; earlier schemes for examining performance tended to be based on *input* and *throughput* statistics, whereas a more convincing picture can be obtained from the analysis of *output*. Performance can be measured in a regular review of systems, procedures, instructions, policies, standards, objectives, complaints, feedback, legislation, codes of conduct, indicators, audits, inspections etc. *Performance assessment* should be coherent and comprehensive; *performance appraisal*, which tends to be used more as a term relating to staffing, examines context and activities related to objectives. *Performance measures* should be hard and capable of informing judgements; *performance indicators* may be at a higher level, bringing together several measures. Output measures should be selected as part of a framework allowing the choice of suitable indicators. Guidelines for performance measures might cover input standards, a planning/review process, and output measures, and might relate to targeted, goal areas – such as management, finance, human resources, physical facilities, collections, users, or technical services. *See also* Metrics, Public library indicators, Public library standards, Standards for library services, Statistics for library services.

Performing Arts Data Service. *See* AHDS.

Period bibliography. One limited to a certain period of time.

Period division. 1. A division of a classification scheme for works covering a limited period of time. 2. A sub-division of a subject heading in a catalogue which indicates the period covered.

Period printing. Producing books in a style which is similar to that used when they were first published.

Periodical. A publication with a distinctive title which appears at stated or regular intervals, without prior decision as to when the last issue shall appear. It contains articles, stories or other writings, by several contributors. *Newspapers*, whose chief function is to disseminate news, and the *memoirs, proceedings, journals*, etc. of societies are not considered periodicals under some cataloguing rules. *See also* Serial. At the General Conference of Unesco, held at Paris on 19 November 1964, it was agreed that a publication is a periodical 'if it constitutes one issue in a continuous series under the same title, published at regular or irregular intervals, over an indefinite period, individual issues in the series being numbered consecutively or each issue being dated'. In statistical records, a periodical publication with a single system of numeration whether or not the title has changed. Where a change of numeration occurs, a new sequence starting at no. 1, irrespective of any change of title, is considered to be a separate unit.

Periodical bibliography. One which is published in parts and revised or extended by the cumulative method. *See also* Closed bibliography, Current bibliography.

Periodical case. *See* Magazine case.

Periodical index. 1. An index to one or more volumes of a periodical. 2. A subject index to a group of periodicals; usually issued at short intervals and cumulated.

Periodical Publishers Association (PPA). <www.ppa.co.uk> (Queens House, 28 Kingsway, London WC2B 6JR, UK) A professional and trade association of specialist publishers.

Periodical rack. A fitting for accommodating current and possibly a few recent issues of periodicals, either horizontally or perpendicularly without displaying the covers. Each compartment has a label bearing the title of the periodical. *See also* Periodical stand.

Periodical stand. A piece of furniture for displaying periodicals so that much of the cover is visible. Sometimes the display fitting on which current issues are placed is constructed at an angle of 15 to 30° and is hinged to accommodate back numbers on a shelf immediately behind the slope.

Periodicals collection. A library collection of periodicals, newspapers, and other serials whether bound, unbound, or in microform; usually kept as a collection and separate from other library materials.

Peripherals (Peripheral units). A general term for the various devices that can be attached to computers to provide Input, Output and storage.

Permanent paper. Paper, coated or uncoated, which conforms to the American standard ANSI Z39.48. The standard sets requirements for pH, alkaline reserve, addresses the retention of original colour and paper strength. The maximum allowable percentage of lignin is 1 per cent. The international standard ISO 9706 – *Information and document-ation: paper for documents: requirements for permanence* includes identical requirements for pH value and alkaline reserve, but the requirements for tear resistance, and resistance to oxidation differ slightly from Z39.48. Paper which meets the requirements of either standard can be identified by the symbol of compliance consisting of an infinity sign in a circle. The use of permanent paper is recommended for the publication of materials with a known enduring value.

Permanent record film. Photographic material made and treated in such a way that both the image and the base will have the maximum archival quality when stored in ordinary room conditions.

PERMIS. <sec.isi.salford.ac.uk/permis> Privilege and Role Management Infrastructure Standards Validation, part of NMI-EDIT to implement an Authorization (or privilege management) environment. PERMIS has validated the use of Privilege Management Infrastructures based on the use of attribute certificates conforming to the X.509 (2000) standard.

Different applications have been built in the cities of Salford, Bologna and Barcelona that have validated the use of attribute certificates for policy-based privilege management.

Permission. Authority from the owner of copyright to quote passages or reproduce illustrations from a work.

Permutation indexing. Indexing by selecting as entry headings words, phrases or sentences which the author has emphasized as important by using them in the title, introduction, section headings, conclusion, summary, etc. This method became a technique of machine indexing; each entry in the index being a cyclic permutation of all the words in the original titles, each term being brought to a predetermined position for alphabetizing. *See also* KWIC.

Permuted title index. The result of a method of indexing, which can be carried out by a machine, whereby entries are made for every important word in a title. The document identification code follows each entry. Types of such indexes are KWIC, KWOC and WADEX.

Permuterm. An indexing procedure which provides permitted pair combinations of all significant words within titles to form all possible pairs of terms. 'Permuterm' is a contraction of the phrase 'permuted terms'.

Perpetua. Eric Gill's typeface (named after St. Perpetua, a female saint who was martyred at Carthage in A.D. 203). Cut in 1929, it is one of the most distinguished types, being not only used effectively for books, where dignity, repose and stateliness are required, but also for book jackets where the related Bold, and Bold Titling, are specially useful. The serifs are small, firmly pointed, sharply cut and horizontal.

Persian Morocco. A badly-tanned leather derived from Indian goat and sheep. It is an inferior leather unsuitable for binding books, being fairly strong but not durable.

Persistence. In a Web-based environment, the ability to create stable Links irrespective of changes in URLs, thereby increasing the confidence of the end-user when accessing information. If Metadata about an item is registered centrally, any changes to the URL by the content owner have only to be reported once for all existing links to continue to operate. The Digital Object Identifier (DOI), for example, resolves to metadata about the identified object in a manner that persists over changes in location, ownership, description methods, and other changeable attributes. If the object ceases to be available, the DOI at minimum indicates a valid but now defunct identifier. *See also* PURL.

Persistent Uniform Resource Locator. *See* PURL.

Person specification. In personnel work, the setting out of the ideal qualifications, personality, experience etc. to be sought in a candidate for a post. *See also* Personnel specification.

Personal authorship. Authorship of a work in which its conception and execution is entirely the responsibility of an individual and carried out in a personal capacity, not by virtue of any paid or voluntary office held within a corporate body.

Personal catalogue.   A catalogue in which entries are made under an individual's name for books both by and about him or her. *See also* Name catalogue.

Personal computer.   *See* PC.

Personal digital assistant (PDA).   Hand-held electronic personal organizer that appeared on the market from 1993. One of the characteristics of early versions was the non-keyboard, pen-based input but models with keyboards of varying size are available. Functionality can be improved through the use of PC Cards, and data can be synchronized with desktop PCs. Also referred to as 'palmtop'.

Personal name.   *See* Forename.

Personal papers.   (*Archives*) The private documents accumulated by, and belonging to, an individual, and subject to that person's disposition.

Personnel specification.   A statement of the qualities, abilities and responsibilities considered to be necessary in a person who might be appointed to a job. The specification is prescriptive, and concentrates more on personal attributes of staff than on the technical requirements of the job – these would be detailed in a job description or job specification.

Personnel Training and Education Group (PTEG).   A membership group of CILIP; previously known as the Training and Education Group (formed 1983), and prior to that the Library Education Group (formed 1970).

Petabyte.   1,024 Terabytes; colloquially, 1,000 Terabytes or one million Gigabytes.

pf.   Abbreviation for portfolio.

PGI.   *See* General Information Programme.

pH value.   Measurement of the acid and alkaline content of paper, as recorded on a scale. pH7 is neutral; a figure lower than 7 indicates acid quality, higher than 7 indicates alkaline quality, the strengths being indicated by the respective distances from 7 and extending from 1 to 14. The measurement is determined by an electrical apparatus called an ionometer. pH is an abbreviation for *potential of Hydrogen* and indicates hydrogen ion concentration. The scale is logarithmic. *See also* Permanent paper.

Phase.   In classification, that part of a complex subject (i.e. a sub-class representing the interaction of an original subject on another separate subject, e.g. the influence of the Bible on English literature) derived from any one main class of knowledge: that part of a complex subject derived from one distinct field of knowledge: any one of two or more classes brought into relation to one another in a document. The interaction of two or more normally distinct subjects is called a Phase Relation. So far six kinds of phase-relation have been isolated: (1) General phase (the method of presentation); (2) Bias phase (one subject presented for the requirements of another); (3) Comparison phase (one subject compared with another); (4) Difference phase (one subject contrasted with another); (5) Tool phase (one subject used as a method of expounding another); (6) Influence phase (one subject influenced by another). *See also* Classifying, Facet, Focus. Where relations occur between foci in the same facet, these are called 'Intrafacet relations'; relations between two foci in the same array are called 'Intra-array relations'.

Phase Alternate Line. *See* PAL.

Phase box. A rigid box which opens at the hinges, used to protect damaged books from further deterioration.

Phase relation. *See* Phase.

Philosophical classification. *See* Knowledge classification.

Phloroglucin. A chemical which is used in conjunction with hydrochloric acid and alcohol as a test solution to detect Mechanical wood in paper, which it turns red.

Phoenix Award. An award made by the Children's Literature Association; it is given to the author, or estate of the author, of a book for children published twenty years previously, which did not win a major award at the time of its publication, but which from the perspective of time is deemed worthy of special recognition.

Phoenix schedule. (*Classification*) A completely new development of the schedule for a specific discipline. Unless by chance, only the basic number for the discipline remains the same as in earlier editions, all other numbers being freely re-used.

Phonetic writing. A form of writing in which the signs or symbols represent sounds or groups of sounds, rather than objects or ideas as they did in earlier forms of writing such as ideography or pictography. Each element corresponds to a specific sound in the language represented. Phonetic writing may be syllabic or alphabetic, the latter being the more advanced of the two.

Phonogram. A symbol used to express a sound or idea; it can represent a complete word, a syllable, or the sound which a syllable represents.

Phonograph. An obsolete instrument for recording sounds on cylindrical wax records and reproducing them.

Phonograph record. *See* Gramophone record.

Phonorecord. Any object on which sound has been recorded.

Phonoroll. A perforated roll, usually of paper, which is used to activate a player-piano, or player-organ.

Phonotape. *See* Audiotape.

Photo CD. Format developed by Kodak to enable photographs to be transferred to CD-ROM for displaying on television or computer screen. Once in this format the digitized photographs may be viewed and manipulated in the same way as other computer graphics. The Photo CD format can be read by most CD-ROM players.

Photocharging. A charging system which records on film details of the book borrowed, the reader's identification card and a transaction card which is then placed in the book and taken by the reader.

Photo-composing machine. (*Printing*) A machine for setting text by photographic means, as distinct from metal-type composition. *See also* Imagesetter.

Photocopy. The reproduction of the information on a sheet of paper or the page of a book etc. by various types of photographic process or Xerography, etc.

Photo-engraving. Any photo-mechanical process for reproducing pictures or the like in which the printing surface is in relief, as distinguished from photo-lithography and photo-gravure. It includes the half-tone process, zinc etching and other processes for making line cuts, the swelled-gelatine process, etc. *See also* Electronic photo-engraving machines.

Photo-gelatine process. Any of the gelatine processes of photo-mechanical printing, as Collotype, Lichtdruck, Phototype, Albertype, Artotype, Heliotype, etc.

Photographic papers. These are graded in thickness as follows:

Ultra thin (also called 'Extra lightweight')	between 0.0023 and 0.0031 inches inclusive
Extra thin	between 0.0032 and 0.0037 inches inclusive
Thin	between 0.0038 and 0.0043 inches inclusive
Lightweight	between 0.0044 and 0.0059 inches inclusive
Single weight	between 0.0060 and 0.0083 inches inclusive
Medium weight	between 0.0084 and 0.0111 inches inclusive
Double weight	between 0.0112 and 0.0190 inches inclusive

Photography. A basic printing process in which the normal principles of photography are used at some stage, e.g. photo-engraving, photo-offset, photo-lithography.

Photogravure. 1. Any of the various processes for producing prints from a plate prepared by photographic methods. Also called 'Heliogravure'. 2. A print so produced. *See also* Rotogravure.

Photo-lithography. The process of reproducing a picture or design photographically on to metal for lithographic printing.

Photo-mechanical process. *See* Process engraving.

Photo-montage. A picture made by the combination of several photographs or portions of photographs into one large composite photograph, or parts of photographs cut out and pasted together to achieve a particular effect. Other methods are to make a number of exposures on the same negative, or to project a number of negatives to make a composite print.

Photomosaic. An assembly of parts of aerial photographs joined together to form a map.

Photo-offset. Offset printing in which the image is reproduced on a metal plate by photography. Also called 'Photo-litho-offset', and 'Offset-photo-lithography'.

Photosetting. (*Printing*) The setting of type by a photographic means. The equipment is also referred to as a 'phototypesetter', though since the appearance of Desktop publishing the term Imagesetter has also come into (preferred) use. *See also* Computer typesetting, Filmsetting.

Phototype. A form of collotype, being a plate with a printing surface usually in relief, obtained from a photograph.

Phototypesetter. *See* Imagesetter, Photosetting.

Photo-typography. Any photo-mechanical process in which the printing surface is produced in relief so that it can be used with type. *See also* Computer typesetting.

Photo-zincography. A method of reproducing pictures, drawings, etc., by using a zinc plate on which the design has been produced by photographic means.

Phrase-pseudonym. A pseudonym consisting of a phrase, as 'A gentleman with a duster'.

Phylactery. A narrow band or scroll on which a name or a speech was inscribed. Sometimes seen in block books, illuminated manuscripts or incunabula where they are drawn as if issuing from the mouths of characters, or held in the hand. They also appear in contemporary comics and comic strips as 'balloons' coming from the mouths of characters.

Physical bibliography. *See* Descriptive bibliography.

pi. 1. (*Bibliography*) The Greek letter π used to denote an unsigned gathering or leaf which precedes signed gatherings, and in respect of which no signature can be inferred. *See also* Chi. 2. (*Printing*) (*Verb*) To mix up type. (*Noun*) Type which has been mixed up (US). *See also* Pie (3).

Piano reduction. An arrangement for piano of the voice parts of a work for unaccompanied voices for use as an accompaniment during rehearsal, such accompaniment not being intended by the composer for performance. Such music may be indicated by some such designation at the head of the score as 'Piano, for rehearsal only'.

Piano score. *See* Score.

Pica. 1. A standard of typographic measurement, approximately 1/6 inch; in the Point System 0.166 inch, equal to 12 point. *See also* Em. 2. PICA (Centrum voor Bibliotheek Automatisering) <www.oclcpica.org> (Schipholweg 99, PO Box 876, 2300 AW Leiden, The Netherlands) Originally a Dutch library bibliographic network formed in 1969, PICA expanded into a pan-European library co-operative and merged into OCLC in 2001. As well as metadata management, library systems and digital preservation resources, OCLCPICA operates the European Index of National Union Catalogues, and the iport portal <iport.pica.nl>. *See also* OCLC, OCLCPICA.

Pick up.   Type which has been kept standing since first used, ready to be 'picked up' for further use when required.

PICS.   <www.w3.org/PICS> Platform for Internet Content Selection, a specification used for enabling users and systems administrators to Filter out unwanted Internet resources, particularly pornography. PICS associates labels (Metadata) with Internet content and while these labels can be used for filtering in the originally intended manner, the specification also facilitates other uses for labels, including code signing and privacy. The PICS platform is one on which other rating services and filtering software have been built.

Pictogram.   *See* Pictography.

Pictography.   The most primitive stage of true writing, in which a picture or sketch represents a thing, or a sequence of pictures, drawings or symbols (each of which is termed a 'pictogram') tells a narrative. Pictography is a semantic representation, not a phonetic one. *See also* Alphabetic writing.

Pictorial map.   A map which contains pictures indicating the distribution of physical and biological features, and social and economic character-istics, etc.

Picture book.   A book consisting wholly or mostly of pictures.

Picture collection.   A collection of pictures, or of reproductions of pictures. *See also* Illustrations collection, Picture file.

Picture file.   A collection of illustrations, prints, reproductions of pictures, and possibly cuttings; small enough to be filed rather than needing to be displayed. They may be arranged by subject, artist, etc. *See also* Illustrations collection, Picture collection.

Picture-writing.   *See* Pictography.

Pie.   1. A table, or collection, of ecclesiastical rules used before the Reformation in England to determine (from each of the 35 possible variations in the date of Easter) the proper service or office for the day. Also called 'Pye'.   2. An alphabetical index or catalogue, to Court rolls and records (obsolete); usually called a 'pye book'.   3. (*Printing*) Type matter that has been mixed accidentally.

Piece.   (*Archives*) In *MAD*, the single, indivisible unit in a set of archival materials; usually a single document, which may be detachable or bound in with others to form an item.

Piece fraction.   (*Printing*) A fraction that is made by using two or more pieces of type due to the fraction on one piece of type not being available. A Solidus is used between the two groups of figures as 43/50.

Pierced.   *See* Mortice.

Piercy (Esther J.) Award.   Established by the Resources and Technical Services Division (now ALCTS) of the American Library Association to honour the late editor of *Library Resources & Technical Services.*

The Award is given annually 'to recognize the contribution to librarianship in the field of technical services by younger members of the profession', and consequently it is restricted to those with not more than ten years of professional experience.

Pierpont Morgan Library. <www.morganlibrary.org> (29 East 36th Street, New York, NY 10016, USA) Assembled by John Pierpont Morgan (1837–1913), inherited by his son J. P. Morgan, Jr. (1867–1943), who expanded it and in February 1924 conveyed it to six trustees to administer as a public reference library for the use of scholars. Subsequently the State of New York incorporated the collection and dedicated it to 'the advancement of knowledge and for the use of learned men of all countries'. The collection comprises about 55,000 books and manuscripts, and in addition, cuneiform tablets, drawings, prints, Italian medals, and Greek and Roman coins. The collection of mediaeval illuminated manuscripts is unique for its geographical and linguistic coverage.

Pigeonhole classification. *See* Rigid classification.

Pigskin. A strong leather made from the skin of a pig; it has good lasting qualities and is used for covering large books.

PII. Publisher Item Identifier; used to identify specific published items within books and serials. *See also* BICI, Digital Object Identifier.

PILA. *See* Publishers International Linking Association.

Pin holes. 1. Minute and almost imperceptible pits in the surface of art papers, due to frothy coating material. 2. Minute holes in paper, caused by fine particles of sand, alum, etc., being crushed out during the calendering process, leaving a hole. 3. Tiny transparent dots which appear in a litho plate after development and which, unless covered with an opaque medium, will appear in resulting prints.

Pin mark. A small depression on one side of the body of a piece of movable type. It is made by the pin which ejects the types from the moulds of certain casting machines and sometimes bears the number of a body-size of the font.

Pin seal. A binding leather from the skin of a very young, or baby, seal, having much finer grain and a more lustrous finish than ordinary Sealskin. Used for expensive bindings.

Pineapple. (*Binding*) An ornament bearing some likeness to a conventional pineapple, and used in the same position as a Fleuron. *See also* Twisted pineapples.

Pipe roll. A parchment roll upon which a record of the audit at the exchequer was kept.

PIRA. <www.pira.co.uk> (Randalls Road, Leatherhead KT22 7RU, UK) The activities of the former British Paper and Board Industry Research Association (BPBIRA) and of the Printing, Packaging and Allied Trades Research Association (PATRA) are now undertaken by PIRA, the Research Association for the Paper and Board, Printing and Packaging Industries. The PIRA database, holding abstracts of over

500,000 research, technical and business reports, combines PIRA expertise with partner institutes in France, Finland, and Sweden.

Piracy. (*Copyright*) The publication in a foreign country of a copyright work without the permission of, or payment to, the author or original publisher. Piracy is now a major problem for the publishers of audio tapes, compact discs, and multimedia products.

Pirated edition. *See* Unauthorized edition.

Pittsburgh Regional Library Center. (103 Yost Boulevard, Pittsburgh PA 15221, USA) A US network consortium of 100 libraries, covering the states of Maryland, West Virginia and Western Pennsylvania. The Center is now part of PALINET.

Pivoted bookcase. *See* Swinging bookcase.

Pixel. Abbreviation for picture element; the individual dots generated by a computer and which make up the picture on the display screen.

PJFR. *See* Joint Fiction Reserve.

PKI. *See* Digital certificate.

pl. (*Pl.* pls.) Abbreviation for Plate (illustration), also place.

PLA. *See* 1. Private Libraries Association. 2. Public Library Association.

Placard. A large, single, sheet of paper, usually printed, but sometimes written, on one side with an announcement or advertisement, for display on a wall or notice board. Also called a 'Poster'.

Placard catalogue. A list of books displayed on a large sheet, or sheets, and hung up for consultation.

Place of printing. A bibliographer's or cataloguer's term for the name of the town in which a book is printed.

Place of publication. A bibliographer's or cataloguer's term for the name of the town or other locality in which the office of a publisher who issues a book is situated.

Plagiarism. Using another person's work and publishing it as one's own without payment or acknowledgement. Although plagiarism has always been a difficulty in publishing, the greatest problems now occur with the unauthorized re-use of material found on the Internet.

Plain text. An edition of a classic without notes, or possibly even an introduction, and intended for study in a class or with a tutor.

Plan. The representation of anything drawn on a plane, as a map or chart; the representation of a building or other structure, landscape design, arrangement of streets or buildings, or arrangement of furniture in a room or building, in horizontal plane.

Plan cabinet. A piece of furniture designed to accommodate plans, architectural drawings, or reproductions, either suspended or resting in a pocket vertically, or flat in shallow drawers. Also called 'Plan file'.

Plan file. A container for filing plans and maps either vertically or horizontally. Also called 'Plan cabinet'.

Plan paper. A thin, tough, paper which is made specially for printing maps, plans, etc. It is subject to much wear by constant handling and folding. Also called 'Map paper'. *See also* Chart paper.

Planes. (*Classification*) In the Colon Classification these are three in number: Idea, Notation (or Notational) and Words (or Verbal); within which the designing or application of a scheme has to be done.

Planetary camera. A camera used for photocopying in which the document being copied and the film are stationary during exposure. After each exposure the document is changed manually and the film is moved on one frame automatically. Also called a 'Flat-bed camera' or 'Stepwise operated camera'.

Planograph. *See* Offset printing.

Planographic process. 1. A generic term for all printing which depends on chemical action, and in which the printing surface is a plane, merely transferring its image, as in lithography, collotype and offset. 2. The method of printing from flat surfaces, the parts to be printed accepting ink from the rollers while the non-printing areas reject it. The printing, or image, areas are greasy, the rest moist. Printing is by even pressure of a hand-roller or cylinder over the flat plate, or by offsetting the image from a curved plate on to a rubber roller and so to the paper. It is one of the six basic principles of printing, the others being relief, intaglio, stencil, photography and xerography. Also called 'Surface printing'.

Planography. Printing processes which are dependent on the antipathy of oily ink and water, using methods of printing from flat surfaces other than stone. *See also* Planographic process.

Plantin. A typeface designed by Christopher Plantin (1514–89) one of the world's most distinguished printer–publishers, whose house and printing equipment now form the Plantin-Moretus Museum at Antwerp. This Old face is characterized by the thickness, and consequent black appearance, of all the strokes.

Plaquette. A small metal relief, like a classical cameo, which is inlaid into Italian book bindings of the sixteenth century.

Plaster of Paris mould. One made by placing a thin film of plaster of Paris mixed with water to a fluid consistency on a sheet of paper which is then transferred face downwards to the forme and subjected to moderate pressure after several sheets of an absorbent type of paper are placed on the paper-backed plaster of Paris. It is used for reproducing illustrations by half-tone and three- and four-colour half-tone processes.

Plastic binding. A type of binding used for pamphlets, commercial catalogues, etc. which are printed on unfolded leaves. These leaves and the separate front and back covers are kept together by means of a piece of curved plastic which has prongs, or combs, which pass through slots punched near the binding edge of the leaves and curled within the cylinder thus formed by the plastic. *See also* Spiral binding.

Plasticizer. (*Archives*) A substance added to, for example, a synthetic resin, to increase its flexibility. If the plasticizer is in some measure chemically combined with the resin, it is said to be an 'internal' plasticizer.

Plasticizing. Putting a plastic cover or sleeve on to a book or Book jacket, either by securing a loose cover or by laminating the plastic using heat.

Plat.   A map or chart, such as a precise and detailed plan, showing the actual or proposed divisions, special features, or uses of a piece of land, e.g. a town or town site (US).

Plate.   1. An illustration, often an engraving taken from a metal plate, printed separately from the text of the book with one side of the leaf blank, and often on different paper. Plates may be bound into a book or they may be loose in a portfolio. They are not generally included in the pagination. *See also* Figure.   2. A flat block of wood or metal, usually of copper, nickel or zinc, on the surface of which there is a design or reproduction of a type forme, to be used for printing, engraving, embossing, etc. The method of printing may be relief, intaglio, or planographic.   3. To make an electrotype or stereotype from printed matter. *See also* Illustrations, Leaf.

Plate cylinder.   The roller of an offset printing machine which bears the printing plate. *See also* Offset printing.

Plate guarded and hooked.   An illustration printed on a separate piece of paper and stuck to a narrow strip of paper or linen to form a guard which is then placed around, or hooked-in, a section before sewing. *See also* Hooked on own guard.

Plate line.   *See* Plate mark.

Plate mark.   A line marking the boundary edge of a plate used in making an engraving; it is caused by the pressure used to make the impression on the sheet of paper. The part of the paper on which the plate rested is depressed and more smooth than the surrounding portion.

Plate number.   One or more figures, or a combination of letters and figures, assigned serially to each musical composition on preparation for printing, being copied by the engraver at the bottom of each page and sometimes on the title-page also. If on the title-page only, it is better designated as 'Publisher's number'.

Plate paper.   A superfine soft rag paper of good substance, made for steel-plate or photogravure printing. Of recent years cheaper esparto qualities have been introduced.

Platen.   The flat part of a printing press which presses the paper on to the forme. *See also* Platen press. (*Reprography*) A mechanical device which holds the film in position in a camera, or copying apparatus, and holds subject material accurately in the focal plane during exposure.

Platen press.   A printing press which has a flat impression, not a cylindrical one. The type is normally fixed on the bed in a vertical or almost vertical position, and the platen bearing the paper is swung up and pressed against the type. Such machines are usually used for jobbing work. *See also* Cylinder press.

Plates volume.   In a work of several volumes, the one which consists of illustrations to the text, and has no printed matter other than that relating specifically to the illustrations.

Platform.   A computer hardware system such as the IBM PC or Apple Macintosh, usually incorporating the appropriate Operating system.

Platform for Internet Content Selection. *See* PICS.

Plating. The process of pasting book plates and other labels in library books.

Plea roll. A parchment roll on which a record of cases heard in the King's Court was entered.

Plenum Publishing Corporation Award. Offered by the Corporation 'to a member of the Special Libraries Association for an outstanding original paper, not previously published or presented, covering any aspect of special libraries or special librarianship'. The Award was first made in 1977.

PLG. *See* Public Libraries Group.

PLoS. *See* Public Library of Science.

Plotter. An Output device used for the printing of charts, engineering drawings and other large-scale graphics.

Plough. The tool used for cutting the edges of a book.

PLR. *See* Public Lending Right.

PLRG. *See* Public Libraries Research Group.

PLS. *See* Publishers' Licensing Society.

Plug and play. At its basic level, a phrase indicating that a PC can be unpacked, plugged into the power supply and used immediately. This contrasts with most systems in the real world which require considerable initial setting up. Spelt with initial capitals – Plug and Play – it represents an officially defined framework (initially proposed by Microsoft and Intel) to incorporate the basic concept into hardware and software. As such, Plug and Play has three immediate goals: to make PCs easier to set up and configure; to ease the task of installing new hardware and software; to provide PCs with entirely new features such as the ability to respond dynamically to configuration events such as the connection of Peripherals. *See also* Hot pluggable.

Plug-in. A software utility that provides additional functionality to an Application by, for example, enabling the importing of non-standard file formats. A term particularly used by the designers of Web browsers to indicate that certain file formats can be displayed directly within the browser itself.

PLUS. *See* Cipfa.

PMEST formula. Ranganathan's five Fundamental Categories – Personality, Matter, Energy, Space, Time – or facets, which, in this order, are arranged by decreasing concreteness; a general citation order of facets in a compound subject.

PN. *See* People's Network.

Pochoir. French for 'stencil'. A hand-coloured illustration process which, although dating from the eighteenth century, is still used in France, and is similar to Silk screen except that paper, celluloid or metal stencils are used and the colour is dabbed through, rather than drawn across, the stencil. It is an expensive method, and is used for editions de luxe. 2. A method of reproducing gouache paintings. The design, necessarily simplified, is preprinted by collotype and the ink applied with stencil and brush.

Pocket.   A wallet-like receptacle made from linen or stiff paper inside a cover of a book (usually the back cover) to hold loose music parts, diagrams, maps, microfiche, floppy disks, etc. Also called 'Cover pocket', 'Book pocket'.

Pocket card charging.   The recording of loans of books by using a card kept in a corner pocket stuck to the inside of the cover of a book. The best-known method is the Browne Book Charging System.

Pocket edition.   A small edition of a book, already printed in an octavo edition, of $6^3/_4$ x $4^1/_4$ inches or less. Sometimes these are paperbound but they are then usually called 'paperbacks'.

Pocket part.   A separate publication which is issued to bring a book up-to-date, and is usually kept in a pocket on the inside of the back cover.

Pocket score.   *See* Score.

Poetry Library.   <www.poetrylibrary.org.uk> (Level 5, Royal Festival Hall, London SE1 8XX, UK) The Poetry Library, housing the Arts Council Poetry Collection is a UK national collection of poetry, comprising some 80,000 volumes published in the English language since 1912. Also stocks journals, cassettes, photographs and cuttings; opened in new premises at the Royal Festival Hall, London, at the end of 1988. A small theatre, known as the Voice Box, is available for poetry readings.

Poetry Society.   <www.poetrysociety.org.uk> (22 Betterton Street, London WC2H 9BU, UK) A literary society formed in 1909 which now has 4,000 members – teachers, librarians, booksellers, journalists, readers and writers; it operates a series of awards, and organizes the Annual National Poetry Day. Publishes *Poetry Review* and *Poetry News*.

Point.   1. The unit of measure for printer's type: approximately 1/72 (0.013837) of an inch. Thus 12 point type is 12/72 or 1/6 of an inch in the body. One inch equals 72.25433 points and 72 points equal 0.9962 of an inch. Each body size is an exact multiplication of the point size. Type bodies are measured in points. The width of a line of type (or 'measure') is determined in pica (12 pt.) ems – called 'picas' in the US. The depth of a page of type is similarly measured in ems or picas. After a fire at the typefoundry of Marder, Luse & Co. in Chicago in 1872, this firm began to supply type the bodies of which were multiples of 1/12 part of a typical Pica measuring 0.166 inch. The United States Type Founders' Association recommended this system to its members in 1886, and British typefounders conformed to the American point system in 1898. The standard measurements according to the British-American Point System are:

5-point	0.0692 in.	14-point	0.1937 in.
6-point	0.0830 in.	16-point	0.2213 in.
7-point	0.0968 in.	18-point	0.2490 in.

8-point	0.1107 in.	24-point	0.3320 in.
9-point	0.1245 in.	30-point	0.4150 in.
10-point	0.1383 in.	36-point	0.4980 in.
11-point	0.1522 in.	48-point	0.6640 in.

| 12-point | 0.1660 in. |

See also Didot system.   2. Any mark of punctuation. A full point (full stop).

Point and click.   A popular description of WIMPS or GUI for PCs, being the operation of using the Mouse to point at information or an Icon on screen and then clicking to implement a task.

Pointillé.   A binding decoration in gold done with tools with a dotted surface.

Points.   1. Small holes made in the sheets during the printing process which serve as guides in registering when the sheets are folded by machinery. 2. The bibliographical peculiarities of a printed book, the absence or presence of which determine whether the book is a first or other edition, or a particular issue of an edition, or a variant, etc.

Polaire.   The leather case or satchel in which monks placed their books. Polaires were usually made without decoration although exceptionally they bore a design stamped in relief.

Polar Libraries Colloquy.   <www.acs.ucalgary.ca/~tull/polar> (Scott Polar Research Institute, Lensfield Road, Cambridge CB2 1ER, UK) An international group of librarians, archivists and information specialists representing libraries and institutions of all kinds either located in the Arctic or Sub-Arctic or located elsewhere but whose interests are wholly polar. Formed in 1971 as the Northern Libraries Colloquy; name changed in 1996.

Pollard and Redgrave.   *See STC.*

Polydecimal.   A classification developed by L. Melot, which uses both letters and numbers in the notation.

Polyester film.   A clear, stable, chemically inert film used to encapsulate fragile, damaged or heavily-used documents.

Polyglot.   A book giving versions of the same text in several languages, generally arranged in parallel columns. The first of the great Polyglot bibles was the so-called *Complutensian Polyglot.* The second of the famous polyglot Bibles was printed between 1569 and 1573 by Christopher Plantin, with the patronage of Philip II of Spain. It was in eight folio volumes, the text being in Hebrew, Greek, Latin, Chaldaic, and Syriac. The Paris Polyglot Bible, 1654, in nine volumes edited by G. Michel Le Jay and others added Arabic and also Samaritan to Plantin's text. The *Biblia sacra polyglotta* published in six volumes in London between 1655–57 was in nine languages. *See also* Bibles.

Polygraphic.   Written by several authors.

Polygraphy.   Books consisting of several works or extracts from works by one or a number of authors.

Polyhierarchic.   (*Classification, Information retrieval*) Pertaining to an organizational pattern involving a multiplicity of facets or aspects.

Polynomial.   A work by several authors.

Polyonymal.   Having several, or different, names.

Polyonymous.   Possessing many names.

Polyptych.   *See* Codex.

Polysemy.   (*Information retrieval*) The quality of a term having two or more independent or overlapping meanings; sometimes written *polysemia*. Also called 'Multiple meaning'.

Polyvinyl acetate adhesive.   *See* PVA.

POP.   Post Office Protocol, the protocol used by e-mail programs to obtain E-mail from a mail server. Messages are downloaded to the desktop machine when the user logs on.

Popular copyrights.   Used at the beginning of this century to denote books published by firms specializing in low-priced editions, who used, with the permission of the copyright owners, the plates made for the original editions.

Popular edition.   An edition of a book published on poorer paper, possibly without illustrations, and in a paper cover or a less substantial cloth binding than the normal edition, and sold at a cheaper price.

Popular library.   A department containing books of general interest for home-reading, those of special interest, or of an advanced character being placed in Subject departments.

Popular name.   An abbreviated, shortened, or simplified form of the name of a government department, society or other corporate body, by which it is usually known.

PORBASE.   <www.porbase.org> Base Nacional de Dados Bibliographicos; Portuguese bibliographic network established in 1988. Based at the National Library, Lisbon.

Porcelain.   A sheet of paper consisting of a sheet of blotting-paper pasted to one of coated stock (US).

Pornography.   Sexually explicit material published in any format, and likely to be regarded as obscene or licentious. In catalogues of conventionally published printed works, the euphemistic term 'Erotica' may appear. Pornography is now a major problem on the Internet where huge amounts of such material are present, and could be chanced upon by children.

Porphyry, tree of.   A device for abstracting the qualities of terms. It is, in a rough sense, a sub-dividing of the term Substance, by adding differences at different steps; thus Substance, by the addition of the difference Corporeality, divides into Corporeal and Incorporeal Substance; then (neglecting the Incorporeal), to corporeal is added the difference 'Body' which results in Animate and Inanimate. This method of division is known as bifurcate (or division in pairs, positive and negative). *See* Predicables, five.

Port.   1. port. (*Pl.* ports.) Abbreviation for Portrait.   2. A location for passing data into and out of a computer, e.g. for connecting peripherals such as printers, modems and external hard disks.

Portable computer.   *See* Laptop.

Portable document format (PDF).   A format developed by Adobe Systems that enables documents to retain their Integrity when transferred across networks and hardware platforms, requiring only free or cheap 'reader' software to read them. The advantage is that full page formatting is retained, with type styles, diagrams and charts represented exactly as they would be in the original.

Portal.   An access point to all the electronic services that an End user will need to carry out the full range of tasks associated with a particular organization, disipline or interest. The resources made available are typically brought together from more than one source and additional advantages such as Single sign-on can be offered. As an example, a university portal will provide a personalized, single-point of access to the online resources that support members of the institution in all aspects of their learning, teaching, research and other activities. Access will be provided to the institutional VLE for course materials, e-mail, chat, to finance and room bookings, and to information resources and library data such as books on loan and fines. The portal is personalized to the extent that undergraduate students will see a different view to postgraduates who will see a different view to academic staff. Subject portals provide services across multiple heterogeneous content providers within a specific subject area. *See also* Hub.

Portfolio (pf).   A case for holding loose paintings, drawings, illustrations, diagrams, papers or similar material. Usually made of two sheets of strawboard, covered with paper or cloth with a wide cloth joint to form the 'spine', often with cloth flaps attached at the edges of one board to turn in and so protect the papers, and with tapes at fore-edges to secure the contents.

Portico Prize.   <www.theportico.org.uk> A prize established in 1985 for a work of fiction, non-fiction or poetry set wholly or partly in the North-West of England. The prize is sponsored by Manchester's Portico Library, a subscription library founded in 1806, and is awarded bienially.

Portolan chart.   An early type of chart produced, often in MS., between the thirteenth and seventeenth centuries to guide mariners in coastwise sailing. Such charts were based on estimated bearing and distances between the principal ports or capes. They are believed to have been first produced by the admirals and captains of the Genoese fleet during the second half of the thirteenth century and maybe earlier, and are sometimes called 'Compass maps' or 'Loxo-dromes', but wrongly so, as they were used before compasses. Originally a harbour book or written sailing instructions, but the name has come to be used for a sea chart. In England a portolan became known as a 'ruttier' or 'rutter of the sea' (from 'route'). Also called 'Portolan', 'Portulan', 'Portolano'.

Portrait. 1. A representation of a person, made from life, especially a picture or representation of the face. 2. When portraits are a feature of a work they are indicated in the collation part of a catalogue entry as *ports*. Otherwise they are subsumed. *See also* Illustrations. 3. (*Publishing*) An illustration, or a book, is referred to as 'portrait' when its height is greater than its width. 4. (*Printing*) A table is said to be 'set portrait' when set upright on the page with the bottom of the table parallel with the bottom edge of the page. *See also* Landscape.

Portuguese Association of Librarians, Archivists and Documentalists. *See* Associação Portuguesa de Bibliotecários, Arquivistas e Documentalistas.

Portuguese National Library. *See* Biblioteca Nacional (1).

Portulan. *See* Portolan chart.

Positive. In photography and documentary reproduction, the film or print which has the same tones as the original. It is sometimes made from a Negative in which the image and the tones are in reverse compared with the original.

Positive microfilm. A film bearing microcopies with tone values corresponding to those of the originals.

Positive process. A documentary reproduction, or copying, process, in which the tones and the image are the same as in the original.

Post. 1. In co-ordinate indexing, to put the accession number of a document under each entry representing a co-ordination term. 2. (*Networking*) The act of posting, or sending, an item to an electronic Bulletin board, Mailing list, Usenet Discussion group or similar.

Post octavo. A book size, 8 x 5 inches. *See also* Book sizes.

Post-co-ordinate indexing system. One in which the indexer or cataloguer is concerned only with simple concepts as headings with a number of entries under each, providing a device or devices whereby the user can combine them to create compound subjects. The Batten and Uniterm systems are of this kind. *See also* Pre-co-ordinate indexing system.

Post-dated. A book which bears a date of publication which is later than the actual date. The opposite of 'Ante-dated'.

Poster. *See* Placard.

Posthumous work. One which is first published after the death of the author.

Posting. An item dispatched to an electronic Bulletin board, Mailing list, Usenet Discussion group or similar.

Postings. The number of records retrieved by a search statement.

Postings list. (*Information retrieval*) An alphabetical list of descriptors with the identification numbers of documents using the descriptor posted against it.

Post-print. The electronic Full text of a peer-reviewed journal article after refereeing and final changes but not usually including publishers mark-up. It is this version that is being increasingly deposited by authors in Eprint archives. *See also* Pre-print.

PostScript. A Page description language marketed by Adobe Systems which utilises scalable Outline fonts and permits accurate re-sizing of graphics.

Pot cassé **device.** A device consisting of a broken jar, or urn, pierced by a wimble (Fr. *toret*) and usually accompanied by the motto '*non plus*'. It was used by Geoffrey Tory the French printer on his title-pages. It was also used as part of the design for decorating book covers.

POTS. Plain old telephone services, used when referring to analogue, non-ISDN lines. *See also* PANS.

Pott. An obsolete name of a size of paper varying from 15 x 12½ inches to 17¼ x 14¼ inches, and being the smallest of the original (uncut) hand-made papers; the name is probably derived from a water-mark design of a pot. *See also* Paper sizes.

Pounce. (*Binding*) An adhesive used under gold or colours.

Powder. (*Binding*) An heraldic term signifying a diaper design of small figures (sprays, flowers, leaves, etc.) frequently repeated by the use of one to three small tools at regular intervals over the greater part of a binding, producing a powdered effect. Sometimes there is a coat of arms, or some other vignette, in the centre, or even at each corner; there may be a lightly tooled fillet around the side of the cover. Also termed *semé, semée* or *semis*.

Power press. A printing press in which the operation of the machine was done by some form of power other than the human being. It was introduced in the nineteenth century and superseded the Hand press for rapid operation.

pp. 1. Plural of pages. 2. Abbreviation for Privately printed (strictly p.p.).

PPA. *See* Periodical Publishers Association.

PPBS. Planning Programming Budgeting System; a management and financial system that requires identification of goals, examination and costing of alternative means of securing those goals, specifying necessary activities for each alternative, and overall evaluation. The emphasis of PPBS is on planning, and improvement of the decision making process.

PPRG. *See* Publicity and Public Relations Group.

Practile. (*Information retrieval*) The percentage of useful documents retrieved per search.

Praeses. The person or persons who open an academical disputation by propounding objections to some tenet or proposition, usually moral or philosophical, as distinguished from the Respondent who defends it.

Prague Declaration. <www.nclis.gov> A declaration 'Towards an information literate society' that proposes basic information literacy principles and associated policy recommendations to create a global

Information Society. The declaration was promulgated by the 40 participants from 23 countries attending the Information Literacy Meeting of Experts, organized by the US National Commission on Library and Information Science (NCLIS) and the National Forum on Information Literacy with the support of UNESCO. The meeting was held in Prague, Czech Republic, September 20–23, 2003.

Prebound. *See* Pre-library bound.

Precedent epithet. An epithet which both in common usage and in cataloguing practice precedes a person's forename(s), e.g. 'Mrs', 'Sir'.

PRECIS. PREserved Context Index System, a subject indexing system in which the initial string of terms, organized according to a scheme of role-indicating operators, is computer-manipulated so that selected words function in turn as the approach term. Entries are restructured at each step in such a way that the user can determine from the layout of the entry which terms set the appropriate term into its context and which terms are context-dependent on the approach term. This system was developed initially in the British National Bibliography and was used in its publications. *See also* Pre-co-ordinate indexing system.

Precision ratio. (*Information retrieval*) The ratio of retrieved relevant documents to the total number of retrieved documents. *See also* Relevance ratio.

Pre-co-ordinate indexing system. (*Information retrieval*) A system by which terms are combined at the time of indexing a document, the combination of terms being shown in the entries. This is the system known as PRECIS. Such a system co-ordinates terms to form compound classes at the indexing stage, and is used with classification schemes, the classified catalogue and the alphabetical subject catalogue. *See also* Post-co-ordinate indexing system.

Predicables, five. A series of logical terms and notions, first explained by Porphyry in his treatise on Aristotle's *Topics*, and forming the basis of the science of classification. They are: 1. Genus – a main class, or group of things, which may be divided into sub-groups called 2. Species, the groups into which the genus is divided. 3. Difference – a characteristic which enables a genus to be divided, e.g. add to the genus 'books' the difference 'method of production' and the species 'MS. books', and 'printed books' result. 4. Property – some quality of a thing or group of things which, although common, is not exclusive to them, e.g. 'jealousy' is common to 'human beings' and 'animals'. 5. Accident – a quality which is incidental to a class, which may or may not belong to it, and which has no effect on the other qualities of the class. *See also* Porphyry, tree of; Bifurcate classification.

Preface. The author's reasons for writing, and afterthoughts. It indicates the scope, history, and purpose of the book and the class of readers for whom it is intended, and expresses thanks to helpers. It is usually written by the author, follows the Dedication, and precedes the Introduction. It is usual to write a new preface to a new edition, outlining the extent of changes and additions. Sometimes called 'Foreword'.

Preface date.   The date given at the beginning or end of the preface.

Preferred order.   The order in which the facets in a faceted classification schedule are arranged. Once this preferred order has been decided it is invariable. The purpose of preferred order is to display the relations between the terms to the best advantage.

Preferred term.   In a thesaurus, a preferred term is used to gather in one place other nearly synonymous terms that would lead to scattered entries in a catalogue, etc.

Pre-library bound.   Books bound in a Library binding before being sold. Called 'prebound' for short.

Preliminaries (prelims).   Those parts of the book which precede the first page of the text. The order should be: half-title, frontispiece, title, history of book (date of first publication, dates of subsequent reprints and revised editions) and imprint, dedication, acknowledgements, contents list, list of illustrations, list of abbreviations, foreword or preface, introduction, errata. All except the frontispiece, which faces the title-page, and the history and imprint which are on the verso of the title page, should begin on right-hand pages, but the errata may be placed on the left-hand or be printed on a separate slip and pasted in. Preliminaries were usually printed last on a separate sheet or sheets, and paged separately, usually in Roman figures. Sometimes abbreviated to 'prelims'. When they are printed on leaves conjugate with leaves bearing part of the text, it is often an indication in very old books of an issue later than the first. Also called 'Front matter', 'Preliminary matter'. *See also* Subsidiaries.

Preliminary cataloguing.   The making of preliminary catalogue entries by clerical officers or junior assistants. These entries are examined with the books by the cataloguer, who is thus saved clerical work, being enabled to concentrate on professional work requiring judgment and decision. *See also* Searching.

Preliminary edition.   An edition issued in advance of the ordinary edition. This is sometimes done in order to obtain criticisms of the text before the final edition is published. Also called 'Provisional edition'.

Preliminary leaf.   One of the unnumbered leaves, printed on one or both sides, which appear before the numbered leaves at the beginning of a book.

Preliminary puff.   *See* Puff.

Prelims.   Abbreviation for Preliminaries.

PREMIS.   <www.oclc.org/research/projects/pmwg> Preservation Metadata: Implementation Strategies, a joint OCLC/RLG expert working group aimed at the development of recommendations and best practices for implementing preservation metadata. The group sought to define a core set of preservation metadata elements applicable to a broad range of digital preservation activities and develop a data dictionary to provide recommendations and guidelines for applying, populating, and managing the core elements; also to identify and evaluate alternative strategies for encoding, storing, managing, and exchanging preservation metadata within a digital preservation system.

Pre-natal cataloguing. *See* Cataloguing in Publication.

Pre-natal classification. Classifying material before it is published, classification numbers (L. C. and Dewey) being printed on the back of the title-pages of books. This is carried out by a centralized agency at the national level. *See* Cataloguing in Publication.

Pre-print. An academic paper or a portion of a work printed and issued before the publication of the complete work. A paper submitted at a conference which is published prior to the holding of the conference. *See also* Eprints, Post-print.

Pre-processed book. One which is delivered by the book supplier with all the necessary processing completed.

Pre-publication. The practice of disseminating small numbers of duplicated copies of scientific or technical papers or documents, etc., prior to publication by normal routines in printed serial publications.

Pre-publication cataloguing. Cataloguing books at a national library or national bibliographic centre from gathered and folded sections or review copies of books which are submitted for the purpose by the publishers. *See also* Cataloguing in Publication.

Pre-publication price. The price at which a book would be sold if ordered prior to a specified date (which is before the publication date) after which the book would cost substantially more.

Prescribed books. Those which are prescribed for a course of reading.

Prescribed library. In UK copyright law, a library funded from the public purse or established solely for academic study and not conducted for profit. Prescribed libraries may enjoy certain privileges under copyright law. *See also* Library privilege.

Presentation copy. 1. A copy of a book bearing a presentation inscription, usually by the author. 2. A copy of a book presented by the publisher. Only a book that is spontaneously presented properly qualifies for this description; one that is merely autographed at the request of the owner should be called an 'inscribed copy'.

Presentation software. Software which can be used to create material to support a lecture or presentation. Most packages are flexible in the output that can be produced, from lecture notes and handouts on paper to Overhead projector sheets and 35mm Transparencies. Alternatively, the presentation can be made directly from the presentation software on a PC via a Data projector. A typical example is PowerPoint.

Preservation. According to IFLA, all the managerial and financial considerations including storage and accommodation provisions, staffing levels, policies, techniques and methods involved in preserving library and archive materials and the information contained in them. Digitization is increasingly used as a technique to allow access to content without risk to original materials. Current issues in the preservation field include questions of access to originals where surrogates are available, bibliographic control of digitized content, and copyright protection of such content.

Preservation and Conservation. <www.ifla.org/VI/4/pac.htm> (Bibliothèque Nationale de France, Quai François Mauriac, 75706 Paris 13, France) PAC is an IFLA core programme introduced at the 1984 meeting in Nairobi, and officially launched in Vienna in 1986. The aim of PAC is to encourage and promote the development of preservation efforts in the world's libraries. The international focal point for PAC is the Bibliothèque Nationale de France and there are regional centres in Tokyo (for Central and East Asia), Canberra (for South East Asia and the Pacific), Moscow (for Eastern Europe and the CIS), Washington (for North America) and Caracas (for Latin America and the Caribbean). Paris serves this purpose for Western Europe, Africa and the middle East. Publishes *International Conservation News* (3 p.a.).

Preservation metadata. In the same way that a master copy of a microfilm made for preservation purposes needs content information and data on date of filming and equipment used, similarly digital files made for preservation purposes need descriptive metadata to ensure that the file structure, date of creation, resolution, bit-depth, etc. are known from the file header. This information will be essential as files will need to be refreshed and migrated to new systems and platforms as older equipment and software becomes obsolete. For further information see <www.oclc.org/research/projects/pmwg/background.htm>. *See also* Digital preservation, PREMIS.

Preservation microfilming. A process of preserving the contents of a document by microfilming them. A policy for preservation microfilming will involve selecting and preparing the materials, filming, checking quality, storage of master negatives, cataloguing and registering.

Preservation Resources. <www.oclc.org/preservation> A non-profit organization, originally founded 1985 by Columbia, Cornell and Princeton Universities, with New York Public Library and the New York State Library, and called the Mid-Atlantic Preservation Service (MAPS). In 1990 the Board of Trustees transferred control of MAPS to OCLC. To reflect the transition from a regional to an international base, the name was changed to MAPS – The MicrogrAphic Preservation Service. In 1994 MAPS was re-organized as a division of OCLC and was known as Preservation Resources; in 2003 it was re-named OCLC Preservation Service Center. Housed in a purpose-built facility at Bethlehem, PA, USA, the service offers a full range of storage, workshops and consultation resources.

Preserved Context Index System. *See* PRECIS.

Presidential Libraries. <www.archives.gov/presidential_libraries> The papers of US presidents from Herbert Hoover onwards are placed in a separate research library; ten such collections are currently administered by the National Archives and Records Administration (NARA) and are sited throughout the US in the home territory of the president. Each library is a repository for preserving and making available papers and other records on the presidency, and each incorporates a museum. When a president leaves office, NARA establishes a Presidential Project until a new presidential library is built and transferred to government. Papers of earlier presidents are held in fragmentary collections in the Library of Congress.

Press. 1. A double-sided bookcase of not less than four tiers (i.e. two each side), called in the US, a 'Range'. In the US a single-sided bookcase with more than two tiers placed end to end; formerly, a 'Bookcase'. 2. The machine, or apparatus, used to press the paper on to the type, plate, engraving or block. In printing there are three methods of imparting this pressure: (a) by the Platen press; (b) by the Flat-bed cylinder press; (c) by the Rotary press. *See also* Printing press. 3. A simple piece of machinery, possibly a 'screw press', used to keep a book or books in position under pressure to effect adhesion of pasted or glued surfaces, or for some other purpose, during the binding process. 4. A popular name for the trade, and craft, of writing for, and publishing, newspapers and periodicals.

Press à un coup. A hand printing press on which the operator could lower the platen on to the type in a single movement. It was invented by François Ambroise Didot (1720–1804), the elder son of François Didot (1689–1759).

Press agent. One who arranges for editorial publicity in the press (*see* Press (4)) for individuals, institutions, etc.

Press book. One issued by a private press.

Press copy. *See* Review copy.

Press cutting. A piece cut from a newspaper or periodical. Also called 'Clipping' (US), 'Cutting'.

Press errors. Errors made by a compositor when setting type. These are corrected at the printer's cost. Also called 'Printer's errors'.

Press mark. The symbol given to a book to indicate its location. Used in old libraries to indicate the *press (see* Press (1)) in which the book is shelved, not the book's specific place. This is not so precise as the Call number. Press marks are usually written on the spine of a book (often on a label or tag), on the endpaper, on the front or back of the title-page and against the entry in the catalogue. *See also* Class number, Fixed location.

Press notice. A short statement of specific information in a newspaper – including an 'obituary notice' – announcement of a death, notice of an engagement, birth or marriage, or a reference to, or a review of, a new book, or a criticism or commentary on an artistic performance.

Press number. A small figure which in books printed between 1680 and 1823 often appears at the foot of a page, sometimes twice in a gathering (once on a page of the outer forme and once on a page of the inner), the page on which it appears being apparently a matter of indifference, though there is some tendency to avoid a page bearing an ordinary Signature. The press number is believed to have been used to indicate on which press the sheet was printed. Sometimes termed 'Working with figures'.

Press photographer. One who takes and supplies photographs for publication in the press.

Press proof. The final proof passed by the author, editor, or publisher for printing.

Press queries. Obscurities in a MS. referred to the author by the printer's proof reader.

Press ready. Sometimes used as a synonym for Make-ready but also to indicate other machine preparations than that of the forme, such as of the inking, paper-feed, and paper delivery mechanisms.

Press release. An official statement giving information for publication in newspapers or periodicals.

Press revise. An extra proof taken from type in which corrections marked on earlier proofs have been made, and when machining is about to take place. The press revise is submitted to the machine reviser who finally passes it for press. Also called 'Machine proof'.

Press run. The number of copies to be printed rather than the number ordered: it is usually larger than the number ordered to allow for spoilage.

Presswork. Making an impression on paper from matter set up in type; in modern usage, the care and attention devoted to this as indicated by the quality of the result. It includes the preparation of the printing surface for even printing and the control of inkflow during the running of the press. *See also* Machining.

PrestoSpace. <www.cordis.lu/ist/directorate_e/digicult/presto.htm> Preservation towards storage and access: standardised practices for audio-visual contents in Europe, an FP6 project whose objective is to provide technical solutions and integrated systems for digital preservation of all types of audio-visual collections.

Presumed author. *See* Supposed author.

Prima. 1. The first word of the next page, sheet or slip being read, and printed (repeated) at the right hand of the measure immediately below the last line. 2. A mark made on copy where reading is to be resumed after interruption.

Primary access. (*Information retrieval*) Access to a particular entry (or block of entries) in a file; it may be simultaneous, sequential, fractional or random access. *See also* Secondary access.

Primary bibliography. 1. An original, 'extensive' or 'general' bibliography dealing with books unrelated in subject matter. 2. One which is the original record of the whole, or part of, a publication. *See also* Secondary bibliography.

Primary binding.   The style of binding used for a book when it is first published.

Primary distribution.   The initial despatch of a document from its originator, or publisher, to more than one destination, especially in accordance with a mailing or distribution list.

Primary name heading.   (*Cataloguing*) An author heading which is provided for an entry where one person or body has primary intellectual responsibility for the existence of a work.

Primary publication.   A publication which contains mainly original (new) matter, e.g. papers describing the results of original research, as distinct from Secondary publication. Also called 'Primary journal'.

Primary sources.   Original manuscripts, contemporary records, or documents which are used by an author in writing a book or other literary compilation. Also called 'Source material' and sometimes 'Original sources'. *See also* Secondary sources.

Primer.   A simple introduction, of an elementary nature, to a subject, possibly intended as a school class book. *See also* Introduction (2), Long primer.

Principles of classification.   The rules formulated by logicians and classifiers by which a scheme of classification is made.

Print.   1. (*Noun*) A reproduction of a picture or drawing by any printing process. Generally applied to etchings, engravings, mezzotints, etc. 2. (*Verb*) To apply ink and then paper to blocks, plates or types to make an 'impression' or a 'print' of the image.

Print collection.   A collection of prints such as engravings, etchings, etc.

Print film.   A fine grain, high resolution film which is used primarily for making contact film copies.

Print room.   A room in a large library in which the collection of prints is kept.

Print run.   The number of copies printed.

Print server.   A computer and associated software that provides users with shared access to networked printers.

Printed.   Broadly, any representation of characters which are reproduced on any material by mechanical or electostatic means.

Printed as manuscript.   *See* Printed but not published.

Printed book.   A book produced from type or by a similar process. *See also* Book, Publication.

Printed but not published.   Printed, but not put on sale, and therefore not published. This fact may be so noted on the title-page. Also called 'Printed as manuscript'.

Printed catalogue.   A catalogue, printed and issued in book form as distinct from a card, or other, form of catalogue.

Printed edges.   Matter which is printed by means of rubber type on the cut edges of books. This is done on the fore-edge in order to aid speedy reference to the contents, but also here and on the top and bottom edges for the purposes of advertising.

Printed matter. Any form of literary composition, text or document (regardless of stylistic or literary merit) which has been set up in type or by any other means and printed on paper.

Printer. 1. The person or firm responsible for printing a book or other publication, as distinguished from the publisher or bookseller. Of considerable importance in cataloguing rare books, where the printer statement, even when it includes a number of names, is given in the imprint. Added entries may be given under printers' names. When no publisher's name is given on the title page, the printer's may be given in the imprint. 2. Equipment for producing computer Output in paper copy. The main types in current use are Inkjet, and Laser. *See also* Imagesetter, Plotter.

Printer's copy. An earlier text or manuscript used by a printer as the basis for setting a work. *See also* Copy-text.

Printer's device. *See* Device.

Printer's devil. An apprentice to the printing trade, especially to a compositor. The origin of the term is said to be that in 1561 a monk published a book called *The Anatomy of the Mass*, and although it had only 172 pages, fifteen more were needed to correct the many typesetting mistakes. These were attributed to the special instigation of the devil, but they turned out to be the work of an apprentice learning the trade.

Printer's errors. *See* Press errors.

Printing. *See* Impression.

Printing and Allied Trades Research. *See* PIRA.

Printing block. A general term for any kind of Block used in printing.

Printing Historical Society. <www.printinghistoricalsociety.org.uk> (St Brides's Institute, Bride Lane, Fleet Street, London EC4Y 8EE, UK) Founded in 1964 'to encourage the study of, and foster interest in, the history of printing; to encourage the preservation of historical equipment and printed matter; to promote meetings and exhibitions; to produce publications in connection with these aims'. Publishes *Printing History News*.

Printing press. A machine for making impressions from a plate, block or type which has been inked, on paper or some other material. *See also* Cylinder press, Flat-bed press, Intaglio, Letterpress, Lithography, Offset, Platen press, Rotary press.

Printings. A general term for papers which are specially suitable for printing as distinct from other purposes.

Print-on-demand. A system whereby titles from publishers' backlists which would have become out-of-print can be printed from digitized files in single, paperback format copies as required. Costs are low, and delays are few. *Compare* Electronic publishing.

Printout. Output of any size directed to a Printer or Plotter from a Stand-alone or networked PC.

Priority date. The date when the basis of the claim was first disclosed to a patent office; it is usually the date on which a provisional or complete specification was filed, or a convention date. It is the date on which a patent claim relies if it is challenged. *See also* Convention application, Patent of addition.

Prison Libraries Group. A membership group of CILIP; formed 1984, and prior to that a sub-group of the Medical, Health and Welfare Libraries Group (from 1975).

Prison library. A library maintained in a prison for the use of prisoners.

Privacy. *See* Data protection.

Private Bills. Bills published by their promoters for submission in the House of Commons.

Private Libraries Association (PLA). <www.the-old-school.demon.co.uk/pla.htm> An international society of authors, publishers, booksellers, librarians and private book collectors – collectors of rare books, fine books, single authors, reference books on special subjects, and above all collectors of books generally for the simple pleasures of reading and ownership. Its functions include the organizing of lectures on subjects of bibliographical interest and visits to famous libraries, printing works, binderies, etc; running an Exchange Scheme enabling members to dispose of surplus material and advertise for desiderata; issuing publications of interest to members. Publishes a *Newsletter, Exchange List* and *The Private Library* (q.). An Organization in Liaison (OiL) with CILIP.

Private library. One which is owned by a private individual. Also a library owned by a society, club or other organization, to which members of the public have no right of access.

Private mark. Some indication of ownership, usually the name of the library impressed with a rubber stamp, which is always placed in a particular part of a library book.

Private press. A printing establishment which undertakes only the work of the owner, or of publishing clubs who may be supporting it financially, or prints only those books (usually not first editions) which the proprietor fancies. Private presses are usually small establishments using hand presses or small letterpress machines, and producing well-printed books in limited editions on hand-made paper. Examples are the Kelmscott, Essex House, Doves, Vale, Gregynog, Ashendene, Cuala, Eragny, and Pear Tree.

Private publisher. One who has works printed at their own expense, and publishes them mainly to ensure the publication of work which might not otherwise be published and/or to achieve a high standard of physical production.

Privately printed (p.p.). This term is given to books printed for the author or a private individual, usually for distribution *gratis*. It is also applied to books printed on a Private press. When printed on a public press it is often described as being printed at the author's expense, or by private subscription.

PRO. *See* Public Record Office.

Probable association, principle of. The principle that the heading chosen for a catalogue entry (whether for a person, subject, place, organization, etc.) should be one most users of the library are likely to look under. *See also* Cataloguing, principles of.

Procedure manual. Generally synonymous with Staff manual except that it may be more detailed, and personnel matters are omitted. Also called 'Work manual'.

Proceedings. The published record of meetings of a society or institution, frequently accompanied by the papers read or submitted, or by abstracts or reports. *See also* Transactions.

Process. (*Verb*) 1. To manipulate data by mechanical means.   2. To prepare books and other documents for a collection, especially physical preparation such as labelling and giving marks of ownership.

Process block. A metal printing surface produced with the aid of photography and a chemical or mechanical process.

Process camera. One used for the production of a photographic intermediate (usually film – either negative or positive) necessary for making an image on a material from which prints can be made, e.g. an offset-litho plate.

Process colour printing. *See* Colour work.

Process embossing. *See* Embossing.

Process engraving. Any of the processes for reproducing pictures, print, etc. that use plates or blocks prepared by photographic, mechanical or chemical action rather than by hand. Also called 'Photo-mechanical process', and 'Process work'.

Process photography. The reproduction of line copy as distinct from continuous tone copy, e.g. a line drawing compared with a photograph. Materials of great contrast are used with this method.

Process record. Usually a card record of a book or other item received at a library and in process of being added to library records.

Process slip. A slip or card bearing author's name, title, imprint, collation, tracings, and allocations of copies to libraries or departments. It accompanies the book through the cataloguing department. Called also, Accession slip, Copy slip, Guide slip, Routine slip, and in the US Rider slip.

Process stamp. A rubber stamp impression on the back of the title-page of a book to give the library history of the book.

Process work. *See* Process engraving.

Processing. 1. Strictly, the carrying out of the various routines such as stamping, labelling, numbering, etc., before a book or other item is ready for the shelves, but it may include *all* the processes involved in such preparation.   2. Preparation of index entries for manual or mechanized systems from books, journal articles or other items of information.   3. In photography and documentary reproduction, the carrying out of such processes as are necessary after the projection of the image to be copied on to the sensitized material.   4. (*Archives*) The actions connected with the description, arrangement and preservation of archival material, and undertaken with a view to facilitating use. 5. The manipulation of data by a computer. *See also* Central processing unit, Multi-processing, Parallel processing.

Processing center.   In the US, a building in which the Processing (1) for a number of libraries is carried out. Such centers have developed by co-operation of librarians in adjoining areas.

Processing department.   1. A combined ordering (or acquisition) and cataloguing department.   2. A department in which the work of preparing items for circulation, other than cataloguing and classification, is carried out. *See also* Cataloguing department, Technical services department.

Processor.   *See* Central processing unit.

Proctor Order.   The system of classification of incunabula named after the order used by R. G. C. Proctor in his *Index of early printed books in the British Museum*, 1897–1903.

Professional assistant.   A member of the professional staff performing work of a nature requiring training and skill in the theoretical or scientific parts of library work as distinct from its merely mechanical parts.

Professional associations.   Groups of qualified personnel which are formed to protect professional standards of service, supervise qualification routes, assist members in professional matters and other support roles. *See also* Library associations.

Professional Ethics, Code of.   A document setting out the norms of professional conduct and behaviour required of members of a professional association. The American Library Association has adopted such a document, and in the UK CILIP is currently working towards a new Code. (The Library Association adopted a Code in 1983 but this required re-working after the formation of CILIP.) The corresponding code for archivists was adopted by the Society of Archivists in 1997: <www.archives.org.uk>. The International Council on Archives also issues a Code: <www.archives.ca/ica>.

Professionalism.   The character and conduct of those working in a profession. *See also* Professional Ethics, Code of.

Profile.   1. A biographical account combined with a description and assessment of the subject's achievements.   2. (*Information retrieval*) A set of indexing terms which characterize the interests of an individual or a group using a selective dissemination of information service. Also called an Interest-profile, this is matched with the terms by which each document is indexed in the system.   3. A sub-set from an Attribute set such as Bib-1 that acts as a group of preferred or designated access points to a Z39.50 target database.

Pro-forma invoice.   1. An invoice received for checking and approval prior to receiving the formal invoice.   2. An invoice provided to facilitate payment before the despatch of materials, to avoid the cost of chasing outstanding payments.

Program.   (*Noun*) An outline giving the schedule of actions to be followed or the order and arrangement of such a schedule. A sequence of steps or coded instructions to be executed by a computer: Software. (*Verb*) To determine the steps and plan the procedures necessary for a computer to solve a problem.

Program for Co-operative Cataloging.   *See* PCC.

Programmer.   A person who is skilled in the writing, developing and Debugging of computer Software.

Programming language.   The Code used to write instructions (a 'program') that tell a computer what to do.

Progressive proof.   A proof showing the sequences and effect at each stage of a colour-printing process as each colour is added. *See also* Flat proof.

PROI.   *See* National Archives of Ireland.

Project Counter.   *See* Counter (3).

Project Gutenberg.   <gutenberg.net> Launched on July 4 1971 with an electronic version of the US Declaration of Independence, the project is re-publishing digitally literature that is in the public domain, and making it available for free downloading over the Internet. There are some 10,000 works now available, and music scores have been added.

Project management.   The planning and co-ordination of a project from inception to completion aimed at meeting the requirements of both customer and sponsor and ensuring completion on time, within cost and to required quality standards. The method is being increasingly used in libraries for piloting new services and changes to existing ones before fully implementing them across the whole customer base. An important element is a regular reporting process which can keep track of any unforeseen changes to schedules and agree the necessary steps to be taken. A 'Project Group' or 'Steering Group' is normally created to oversee progress and includes as members customers and key stakeholders. The industry-standard PRINCE2 methodology can be used as the basis for running projects though this can be seen as heavyweight at times and is often slimmed down and adapted to the needs of an organization or group of projects.

Project MUSE.   <muse.jhu.edu> Launched in 1995 by the Johns Hopkins University Press, in 1999 MUSE expanded to become a partnership of not-for-profit publishers, increasing its ability to offer essential periodicals in the humanities, arts, and the social sciences. It offers 250 quality journal titles from 40 scholarly publishers and covers the fields of literature and criticism, history, the visual and performing arts, cultural studies, education, political science, gender studies and economics.

Project Quartet.   Based on the work of BLEND, this project examined further potentials of electronic publishing, networking, CD-ROM, and Optical discs. The UK Universities of Birmingham, Loughborough and Hertfordshire, and University College London were partners in the Project. The investigation centred on the use of new technology to improve information exchange within the academic research community.

Project teams. Workplace groups formed to examine tasks and services, plan strategies, and implement action; current management practice is to involve all levels of staff in such teams.

Project WiLL. *See* WiLL.

Projected books. Microfilmed books intended for projecting on to a ceiling, wall or screen for the benefit of physically handicapped people.

Projection. The method used by a cartographer for representing on a plane the whole, or part, of the earth's surface; for example, Mercator's Projection.

Projection print. In documentary reproduction, a copy having a larger scale than the original: an enlargement. Also called a 'Blow-up'.

Projection printing. A method of obtaining a photographic copy by exposing a photosensitive surface to the projection of an image through an optical system.

Prompt. Symbol on a computer display screen; an indication that the user should make a response.

Prompt book. *See* Prompt copy.

Prompt copy. The copy of a play used by a prompter, showing action, cues, movements of actors, properties, costumes, and scene and light plots.

PRONI. *See* Public Record Office of Northern Ireland.

Pronounceable notation. (*Classification*) A notation, which for ease of memorizing consists of letters which as a group can be pronounced. Also called Syllabic notation.

Proof. 1. In bookbinding: the rough edges of certain leaves left uncut by the plough are proof that the book is not cut down. 2. An impression made from type before being finally prepared for printing. Proofs are made on long sheets of normal page width (Galley or Slip proof) for the author's inspection and correction but not until after a *First proof* has been made, corrected by the printer's reader and returned to the compositor. When the printer has made the corrections the type is divided up into pages, the page numbers inserted, and a further proof submitted to the author. This third proof is called the *Page proof.* A *Marked proof* is one marked by the printer's reader, corrected by the author and again read by the printer's reader, and a *Revise* or *Revised proof* is a further one embodying corrections made by the author/or reader to the first proof. *See also* Author's proof, Clean proof. 3. A preliminary impression taken from an engraved plate or block, or a lithographic stone. Usually called 'Trial proof'. 4. An impression taken from a finished plate or block before the regular impression is published and usually before the title or other inscription is added. Also called 'Proofprint' or 'Proof impression'.

Proof before letters. A proof of an engraving, etching or other illustration process made before the addition of title, artist's and engraver's name, date, dedication or other matter.

Proof corrections.   Signs used by proof readers on printers' proofs to indicate corrections to be made in the typesetting. These have become established over the centuries. *See also* Standard Generalized Markup Language.

Proof press.   A small or medium-sized press operated electrically or by hand on which proofs from type or other relief surfaces are made.

Proof reader.   A person who reads printers' proofs to discover errors in type, punctuation, statement and so forth, and marks the corrections on the proof.

Proof reader's marks.   *See* Proof corrections.

Proof reading.   The process of reading a printer's proof and comparing it with the MS. or Copy in order to detect errors in typesetting. Errors are marked on the proof in accordance with generally accepted signs and the resulting 'corrected proof' is returned to the printer so that the necessary corrections may be carried out. *See also* Proof, Proof corrections.

Proof sheet.   A sheet of paper on which a proof of type-matter, plate, or block, is made by a printer. *See also* Proof.

Proper name.   A name used as the designation of a single person, place or thing, e.g. Leonard, Wimbledon, Festival Hall.

Property.   *See* Predicables, five.

Proprietary information.   Information which is owned by reason of discovery or purchase, and is private or confidential to a firm or organization.

Prospectus.   1. A leaflet or pamphlet issued by a publisher and describing a new publication.   2. A publication written to inform, arouse interest in, and encourage the reader to take some action concerning, a book about to be published, a school or other education institution, or the issue of stock or shares of a company, etc.

PROSPO.   Public Record Office of Ireland. *See* National Archives of Ireland.

Protection.   (*Copyright*) The legal guarantee of Copyright in an Intellectual Work which is given by the law of a country. This protection is usually given either from the date of its deposit with a national organization or its date of publication.

Protocol.   Agreement on methods of coding data to permit its transfer between computers without loss of Integrity. *See also* IP (2), Open Systems Interconnection, TCP/IP.

Provenance.   1. A record or indication of previous ownership of a book or manuscript. A special binding, book plate, or inscription may indicate previous owners, collections or libraries through which a particular book has passed.   2. (*Archives*) In archival theory, the principle that the archives of a given records creator must not be intermingled with those of different origin.   3. (*Archives*) In general archival usage, the originating entity which created or accumulated the records; also the source of Personal papers and manuscript collections.   4. Information concerning the successive changes of ownership or custody of a particular document.

Provincial Booksellers' Fairs Association (PBFA). <www.pbfa.org> (Old Coach House, 16 Melbourn Street, Royston SG8 7BZ, UK) Founded 1974, now the largest association of antiquarian and secondhand booksellers in the UK with over 670 members. Operates a nationwide series of book fairs and a monthly Hotel Russell Fair in London.

Provincial Joint Fiction Reserve (UK). *See* Joint Fiction Reserve.

Provisional edition. A book which is published in a small edition and circulated to selected individuals or sold in the ordinary way, so that observations, criticisms and suggestions may be submitted and considered before a final edition is published. Also called 'Preliminary edition'.

Provisional specification. *See* Patent, Specification (4).

Proximity indicator. A Code used in Online or CD-ROM searching which enables the relationship between two or more search terms to be defined. Thus, one symbol might indicate that two key words should be adjacent, another that they should appear in the same sentence and a third that they can be anywhere in the citation. *See also* Nearest neighbour.

Prussian Instructions. The German cataloguing code; an English translation was published by the University of Michigan Press in 1938.

Psalm-book. A Psalter.

Psalter. The Book of Psalms in which the Psalms are arranged as in the Book of Common Prayer for use in a religious service, whether to be spoken or sung; in the latter case they may be in a metrical version. Notable early examples are the *Arundel Psalter* (two illuminated manuscripts bound together; one probably by a fourteenth century court artist, the other of the East Anglian school and probably earlier; now in the British Library); the *Luttrell Psalter* (British Library) is also East Anglian and was copied about 1340 for Sir Geoffrey Louterell of Lincolnshire. The *Mainz Psalter*, in Latin, was printed by Johann Fust and Peter Schoeffer in Mainz, and is dated 14 August 1457; this is the first printed book to give the name of the printer and the date of printing.

Pseudandry. The use by a woman author of a masculine name as a pseudonym. *See also* Pseudonym.

Pseudepigraphy. The attributing of false names to the authors of books.

Pseudo abstract. An abstract that was written in anticipation that an article, or 'paper' would be written in the future, but has not been, and might never be, written. Such an abstract is written by a speaker invited to address a meeting of a professional association and is published prior to the delivery of the full 'paper' which may, in the event, be spoken extempore and never published or otherwise recorded.

Pseudograph. A literary composition falsely attributed to a particular writer.

Pseudonym. A name used by an author, which is not his or her real name. Also called a 'Pen name' or '*Nom de plume*'. *See also* Syncopism, Telonism, Titlonym.

Pseudonymous works. Those written by persons who have used a name other than their real name on the title-page in order to conceal their identity. *See also* Pseudonym.

Pseudo-weeding. *See* Weeding.

PSIGate. <www.psigate.ac.uk> A Hub – the Physical Sciences Gateway – of the (UK) RDN offering access to high quality Web resources in the physical sciences: astronomy; chemistry; earth sciences; materials science; physics; and science history and policy.

PSTN. Public switched telephone network, the standard system used for connecting domestic and commercial telephones.

PTEG. *See* Personnel Training and Education Group.

PTT. Postal, Telephone and Telegraph Administration, a general term used to denote a government-supported, national supplier of telecommunications services.

Public Access to Science Act. Proposed US legislation initiated by Congressman Martin Sabo and currently (2004) moving through the political system. The Act would make all research funded by the US federal government exempt from copyright protection, safeguarding its availability to the public.

Public Affairs Information Service. *See* PAIS.

Public catalogue. A catalogue made available for public rather than staff use. *See also* Online public access catalogue.

Public documents. The regular official publications of a government, containing reports, statistics, etc.

Public domain. Material not copyrighted, or for which copyright has expired. *See also* Public domain software.

Public domain software. Software placed in the 'public domain' by its authors and which may be used and distributed without payment. *See also* Free software, Open Source sofware, Shareware.

Public goods. An expression that encompasses a range of essential information that should be easily and freely available to the public as a basic human right. *Compare* International commons.

Public key cryptography. *See* Digital certificate.

Public key infrastructure (PKI). *See* Digital certificate.

Public Lending Right. A subsidy paid out of public funds to authors whose works are lent out from public libraries. Such schemes have operated in the Scandinavian countries for many years, and PLR was introduced in the UK in 1983. An annual report is issued <www.plr.uk.com> and in 2002 a quinquennial review was published <www.dcms.gov.uk/heritage.plr>.

Public Libraries Acts. *See* Library law.

Public Libraries Group (PLG). A membership group of CILIP; formed 1974 after the cessation of the Library Association's County Libraries Group.

Public Libraries Research Group (PLRG). <chieflib.org.uk> Originally established in 1970 as part of the Library Association's London and

Home Counties Branch, PLRG is now an independent body carrying out research relevant to the public library field. Although its current profile is low, it has recently been closely identified with the Society of Chief Librarians.

Public Libraries Review (UK). The report *Reading the Future: a Review of Public Libraries in England* was issued early in 1997 by the then Department of National Heritage; it had been awaited for many months after the document published by Aslib Consultants in 1995 (*Review of the Public Library Service in England and Wales for the Department of National Heritage*) and the subsequent consultation process. It was expected to be a key document on the development of public library policy. The report indicated that public libraries would get funding to provide Internet access, and the Library and Information Commission was asked to investigate how libraries should respond to the challenge of new technology.

Public library. A library provided wholly or partly from public funds, and the use of which is not restricted to any class of persons in the community but is freely available to all.

Public Library Association (PLA). A Division of the American Library Association under this name since 1958; originally organized in 1951, it is 'concerned with the improvement and expansion of public library services to users of all ages and in all types of communities, and with increasing professional awareness of the social responsibilities of the library to its public'. Publishes *PLA Newsletter* (q.).

Public Library Indicators. Standard statistics collected from public libraries in order to ensure that the service provided fulfils certain minimum criteria. In the USA an annual public library survey is conducted by the National Center for Education Statistics (NCES) through the Federal-State Co-operative System for Public Library Data <nces.ed.gov/pubsearch/getpubcats>. In the UK, the Audit Commission has prepared similar indicators <www.audit-commission.gov.uk>. *See also* Metrics, Performance, Public library standards, Standards for library services, Statistics for library services.

Public Library Manifesto. <www.unesco.org/webworld/libraries/manifestos> A document published by Unesco first in 1949, revised in 1972 and published in all the major languages of the world for wide distribution, particularly in developing countries. It sets out the basic services which public libraries should provide, how they should be provided, administered and financed. A third revision was agreed in 1994.

Public Library of Science (PLoS). <www.plos.org> A non-profit organization of scientists and physicians supported by a $9 million grant from the Gordon and Betty Moore Foundation and in-kind support from the Howard Hughes Medical Institute which, in 2003, launched a publishing venture to provide scientists with high-quality, high-profile Open access journals. *See also* BioMedCentral, PubMed Central.

Public Library Plans (UK). From 1998 each public library authority in the UK must submit an annual plan to the Department for Culture, Media and Sport (DCMS); the plans are to cover various performance indicators relating to efficiency, access and usage. The scheme was announced in the report *Reading the Future: a Review of Public Libraries in England*.

Public library standards. In the UK, the central government Department of Culture, Media and Sport (DCMS) routinely collects various measures of performance from public library services. The strategic paper *Framework for the Future* (2003) did not mention standards, leading to doubts about their future; in 2004 DCMS confirmed that PLSs would still be collected in a slimmed-down set of input and output service standards based around current practice – these are to be titled 'Service Public Library Standards (SPLSs)' – with the addition of impact standards to be developed. Internationally, IFLA and UNESCO have issued *Guidelines and Standards for Public Libraries* (2001) based on the 1994 Public Library Manifesto. *See also* Metrics, Performance, Public library indicators, Standards for library services, Statistics for library services.

Public Record Office (UK). <www.nationalarchives.gov.uk> The body responsible for the management of the archives of central government in England and Wales, the PRO was founded in 1838. In 2003 it was merged with the Historical Manuscripts Commission to form the National Archives (UK).

Public Record Office of Ireland. *See* National Archives of Ireland.

Public Record Office of Northern Ireland (PRONI). <proni.nics.gov.uk> (66 Balmoral Avenue, Belfast BT9 6NY, UK) Formed in 1924 in Belfast to provide for the reception and safe keeping of the records of the Northern Ireland Government, the Courts of Justice, the local authorities and other public bodies. The Office also encourages the depositing of documents by private individuals and institutions so that the public may have access to all material of social, economic and historical interest.

Public Records (UK). Records subject to and defined by the Public Records Acts 1958 and 1967. Essentially these are records created and used by central government and its agencies. Some non-government institutions, such as the nationalized railways and mines, are included, others not. Public Records are regulated by the Lord Chancellor, and may not be disposed of except under orders from his Department. Records include material held in any format, including electronic.

Public Sector Award. *See* Kent (Tony) Strix and Public Sector Awards.

Public Sector Information (PSI). A generic term for all kinds of information collected by public administrations – central and local government, schools, colleges, transport data, geographic data, statistics on all aspects of life, commercial activity, etc., and which is severely underused. In 1999 the European Union published a Green Paper titled

Public Sector Information: a key resource for Europe which proposed legislation on harmonization of policies on the use by the private sector of data collected from public sources (higher education organizations have particular problems with this aspect). A Draft Directive was issued for consideration by the EU in 2003 <europa.eu.int/eur-lex/psi>; a portal <www.epsigate.org> has been established to encourage awareness of PSI. A major international policy conference was scheduled for November 2004.

Publication. 1. A work issued to the public in the form of a document or book. 2. The act of issuing a book to the public. 3. As defined in Article VI of the Universal Copyright Convention 1971, 'the reproduction in tangible form and the general distribution to the public of copies of a work from which it can be read or otherwise visually perceived'.

Publication date. *See* Date of publication.

Publication day. 1. The day of the week or month on which a periodical is issued. 2. The first day on which a book may be sold to the public.

Publication right. A right existing in Europe to give exclusive rights to anyone who first publishes a work which is out of copyright. It is similar to typographical right, and in the UK will not come into force for practical reasons until 2039.

Publicity and Public Relations Group (PPRG). A membership group of CILIP; formed 1984.

Publish. 1. The action of a publisher in issuing and offering for sale to the public, a book or print produced on some kind of printing, copying or photographic reproducing machine. 2. The action of an author, artist, or composer of music, in creating something, and arranging for it to be reproduced in quantity and offered for sale.

Published. A document which has been reproduced in a number of copies and made available to the public to whom it may be sold or distributed free of charge and whether or not it is intended to have a restricted readership such as to members of a learned, professional or political organization.

Published price. The retail price at which a book is published.

Publisher. A person, firm, or corporate body responsible for placing a book on the market, as distinguished from the printer. Publisher and printer may be the same, but in modern books usually not. Relates also to publication of music, reproduction of works of art and of maps and photographs. A firm which undertakes publishing is sometimes referred to as a 'Publishing house'.

Publisher colours. *See* ROMEO.

Publisher's binding. The binding in which a publisher issues a book.

Publisher's case. *See* Publisher's cover .

Publisher's catalogue. A list of books issued for sale by a publisher.

Publisher's cloth. Used to indicate a book as issued by the publisher in a cloth binding.

Publisher's cover.   The cover for a book that is provided by a publisher for the normal trade edition of a book. Also called 'Publisher's case'. *See also* Case, Edition binding.

Publisher's device.   *See* Device.

Publisher's dummy.   A Dummy book made up of the right number of sections of plain paper, and sometimes cased, to indicate the size of a proposed book.

Publisher's imprint.   *See* Imprint.

Publisher's list.   A list of books published by one publisher and still in print.

Publisher's mark.   *See* Device.

Publisher's number.   *See* Plate number.

Publisher's reader.   One whose work is the reading, judging and criticizing of manuscripts offered for publication.

Publisher's series.   The name given to a series of books which usually have been published previously, and comprising standard or current books on related or unrelated subjects, issued in a uniform style and at the same price, and bearing a series title such as *World's Classics*, or *Everyman's Library*. Each volume contains one or more distinct works, and some series include books published for the first time. Also called 'Trade series'. Series which comprise only books previously published are sometimes called 'Reprint series'.

Publishers Association (PA).   <www.publishers.org.uk> (29 Montague Street, London WC1B 5BW, UK) A trade association which was founded in Britain in 1896. Membership is open to any publisher in the United Kingdom whose business, or an appreciable part of it, is publishing books, journals or electronic publications. The PA offers information to members on developments in copyright, publishing law, finance, taxation, employment and environmental legislation; international developments affecting publishing; market statistics; notice of training opportunities, seminars and conferences; advice on topics of current concern. Market development is a core priority of the Association. There are four major sub-groups: Academic and Professional Publishers Council (CAPP), Educational Publishers Council (EPC), Electronic Publishers Forum (EPF), and the General Books Council (GBC).

Publishers International Linking Association (PILA).   <www.crossnet.org> A non-profit, independent organization formed at the beginning of 2000 by major scholarly publishers which operates the CrossRef service. The Board of Directors comprises representatives from AAAS (Science), AIP, ACM, APA, Blackwell Publishers, Elsevier Science, IEEE, Kluwer, Nature, OUP, Sage, Springer, and Wiley.

Publishers' Licensing Society (PLS).   <www.pls.org.uk> (37–41 Gower Street, London WC1E 6HH, UK) Formed in the UK in 1981, the directors of PLS together with the Authors' Collecting and Licensing Society (ACLS) make up the board of the Copyright Licensing Agency (CLA). PLS and ACLS secure mandates from rights owners; CLA offers licences to institutions and individuals who want to copy copyright works. Money thus collected is shared between PLS and ACLS who distribute it to rights owner members. There are currently plans to extend coverage to digitization. PLS deals with over 1,500 publishers; its board is constituted from the Publishers Association, the Periodical Publishers Association, and the Association of Learned and Professional Society Publishers. *See also* Authors' Licensing and Collecting Society; Copyright Licensing Agency.

Publishing. The trade of publishing books; this includes negotiations with authors or their agents, design of books in conjunction with printers, book production, publicity and sales through book wholesalers and retailers. In addition to books it relates to music, reproduction of works of art and of photographs and maps. *See also* Desktop publishing, Multimedia publishing.

PubMed Central. <www.pubmedcentral.gov> A digital archive of life sciences journal literature, developed and managed by the National Center for Biotechnology Information at the US National Library of Medicine. Access to the archive is free and unrestricted. PubMed Central differs in two ways from Public Library of Science and BioMedCentral: i) it is not a publisher, and ii) some journals do not supply their contents to the archive until some months or even years after paper publication.

Puff. A term, in use since the seventeenth century, for exaggerated praise for a book, used in advertisements and on the book's jacket. *See also* Blurb.

Pugillares. From two to eight small wooden writing tablets of ivory, wood, or metal and covered with wax on one side upon which writing could be scratched with a stylus. Sometimes the tablets were hinged together with rings or leather cords down one side to form a tablet book. Notebooks of this sort were known as *pugillaria*. *See also* Codex.

Pull. A trial print taken from type of a block before an edition is printed.

Pull service. An online service that responds by matching particular requests with items in a database, only at the time of the request being made. In contrast to Push technology.

Pull-down menu. Part of a GUI or WIMPs system whereby a vertical listing of available grouped commands appears when a pointer is Clicked on one of several broad terms displayed horizontally. The horizontal display is known as the 'menu bar'.

Pulled. In bookbinding, a book the cover of which has been removed and all the sheets separated. *See also* Take down.

Pulled type. Type letters which have been pulled out of the forme by inkballs.

Pulling. (*Binding*) Stripping the old covers off a book, separating the sections and removing any old glue prior to rebinding.

Pullout. (*Book production*) *See* Throw out.

PULMAN. <www.pulmanweb.org> Public Libraries Mobilising Advanced Networks, an EU-funded project focusing on the important role

Europe's public libraries have to play in the implementation of key policies central to the development of e-Europe. The final conference was held in Oeiras, Portugal, with 200 high level policy representatives from over 36 European countries and issued a manifesto setting out the goals for the development of public library services, and helping drive forward the next phase of innovation amongst public libraries and other local public cultural institutions in Europe. *See also* CALIMERA.

Pulp. The mechanically or chemically prepared mixture made from vegetable fibres which becomes paper when passed over wire and dried. *See also* Chemical wood, Hand-made paper, Mechanical wood. 2. A cheap magazine printed on newsprint.

Pulp board. Board manufactured in one thickness, or by bringing two or more thicknesses of board or paper together into a single structure on a multiple-wire machine, as distinct from boards made by laminations of paper pasted together and called 'Pasteboard'. Sizes are:

	inches		
Imperial	22	x	30
Postal	22½	x	28½
Pulp Royal	20½	x	25

Punch. A piece of steel on which a type character is engraved. After hardening it is used as a die to strike the matrices from which type is cast.

Punch engraving. A method of book illustration which had previously been used by goldsmiths and ornament engravers. The tools used consisted of a dotting punch, a small pointed punch set in a wooden handle and used by hand pressure, and larger punches with either grained or plain striking surfaces intended for use with a hammer.

Punched card. A lightweight card which has holes punched in certain positions either round the edges (edge-punched) or in the body of the card (body-punched) to represent specific pieces of information. Edge-punched cards were sorted manually with the aid of a 'needle' and body-punched cards usually by machine.

Punctuation. *See* Dash, Filing code, Quotes.

Purchasing consortia. *See* Library purchasing consortia.

Pure bibliography. The type of bibliography which treats of the value of the contents of books, including textual criticism.

Pure notation. *See* Notation.

PURL. <purl.oclc.org> Persistent Uniform Resource Locator, a methodology for maintaining viable, long-term access to Internet resources in the face of URLs that can alter with changes in hardware configuration, file system re-organization or changes in organizational structure leaving users stranded and without access to resources. A PURL is a URL, but instead of pointing directly to the location of the resource it points to an intermediate resolution service which it has been agreed will be unchanging. If the actual URL moves, this change still has to be notified to the PURL service but all original pointers will remain intact. *See also* Digital Object Identifier, Persistence, Resolver.

Push technology. In knowledge management and information management, the process whereby information is selected and delivered ('pushed') to users direct to the desktop based on pre-set criteria and agreed schedule parameters. Also known as Webcasting, the process was initially criticized for overloading users with irrelevant material and becoming a conduit for advertising. Later technology is more closely and successfully programmed and has become commonplace; many commercial services are available.

Pustaka. A book consisting of long strips of the thin bark of trees or of a kind of paper made from tree bark; it may deal with magic medicine, domestic remedies, or 'the art' of destroying life. The Sanskrit word 'pustaka' is used for this kind of book in North Sumatra, Java and other countries, but in South Sumatra 'pustaha' is used; here such books were used as divination texts, for codes of law and for legends. Pustakas were written in a brilliant ink on long strips of writing material, folded concertina-fashion and tied together with a string of woven rushes.

Put to bed. *See* Bed.

Putnam (Herbert W.) Award. An award made to a US librarian for the purpose of travel or writing to further the library profession. Administered by the American Library Association Awards Committee and presented at irregular intervals.

Putwiths. Acknowledgements and other consequential papers such as corrigenda and addenda relating to documents already filed in a correspondence or similar file, and which in themselves are of no significance from a filing or indexing point of view.

PVA. Polyvinyl acetate adhesive, a white synthetic resin glue which dries clear or water white. It is not easily reversible so it should not be used for repairs in all situations, but it is strong and flexible and recommended for procedures like 'tipping-in' loose leaves.

Pye. An alternative spelling of Pie.

Pye book. *See* Pie.

Pyes. A kind of ecclesiastical calendar. *See* Pie (1).

QA. Quality assurance, or Quality assessment. *See* Quality.

q.v. Abbreviation for *quod vide* (Lat. 'which see'); *Pl. qq.v. (quae vide).*

Quad. Abbreviation for Quadrat. 1. A piece of metal, lower in height than type, and used for spacing:

> An em quad (mutton), the square of the body.
> An en quad (nut), $1/2$ the body or 2 to an em.
> A thick space, $1/3$ the body or 3 to an em.
> A middle space, $1/4$ the body or 4 to an em.
> A thin space, $1/5$ the body or 5 to an em.
> A hair space, $1/12$ the body approximately.

See also Em quadrat, En quadrat, Paper sizes. 2. Prefix to standard paper-size names to indicate a sheet four times the size of a single and twice the size of a double, sheet. *See also* Octavo, Paper sizes.

Quad mark. *See* Back mark, Black step, Collating mark.

Quadrat. A term which is never used in its full form, but in the abbreviated version Quad.

Quadrata. An early style of Latin manuscript writing; it was practised from the second to the fifth century A.D. and was characterized by a square capital letter based on formal inscriptions cut with a chisel in stone. Also called 'Square capital' hand.

Quadrigesimo-octavo. *See* Forty-eightmo.

Quadrille. Paper ruled so as to form a very large number of small squares; it is used for graphs, etc.

Qualification. The addition of one or more words in parentheses to a subject heading, usually in dictionary catalogues, indicating the sense in which the heading is being used. Also used in indexes to the scheme of classification. Chiefly used to distinguish homonyms.

Qualified heading. A heading followed by a qualifying term which is usually enclosed in parentheses, e.g. Composition (Art), Composition (Law).

Qualified list. Produced by deleting False and Unsought links of the chain (when using the Chain procedure to produce subject index entries) and adding qualifiers to the remaining terms. It is the second stage of the conversion of a classification symbol to a verbal subject heading, the first being Basic analysis.

Qualifier. A sub-heading in a subject index which has been constructed by Chain procedure. (*Indexing*) A word, or words, added to a heading, after punctuation or within parentheses, in order (a) to distinguish it from identical headings which have different meanings, or (b) to identify the heading, e.g. by using an epithet or honorific title. *See also* Access point.

Quality. 'Quality is the totality of features and characteristics of a product or service that bear on its ability to satisfy stated or implied needs' (BS 4778:1991). The achievement of a quality service in librarianship and information work may involve many factors: fitness for purpose, conformity to standards, customer satisfaction, reliability, economy, efficiency, effectiveness may all be a part of the quality process. *Quality assurance* or *quality assessment* (QA) are the systems and structures used to achieve a quality service; they must be dynamic, so that development is not frozen, and they should take account of the purpose of the organization to avoid simple mechanical checklists. The base standard is BS EN ISO 9000. *Quality audit*, *quality control* and *customer charters* are other frequently found terms; *quality circles* are groups specially formed to consider and implement quality strategies. *Total Quality Management* (TQM) is a whole organization approach which embraces all activities involved in providing a service to the users and the community, and includes efficiency and cost-effectiveness by maximizing the potential of employees in the process of improvement. TQM needs the motivation of all staff, a QA system, and an implementation phase.

Quality of service. A concept introduced with Internet2 to ensure that the network can successfully meet demand whenever an intensive application – for example, media integration, interactivity, real time collaboration – requires high speed, high performance connectivity. Being investigated via the End-to-End Performance Initiative.

Quarter binding. A binding in which the spine and a very small part of the sides is covered with a stronger material than the rest of the sides. 'Half-binding' has the corners covered with the same material as the spine. In 'three-quarters binding' the material used on the spine extends up to half the width of the boards.

Quarter bound. *See* Quarter leather .

Quarter leather. A term used to describe a book with a leather spine and cloth sides. *See also* Half leather, Leather bound, Three-quarter leather.

Quarterly. A periodical published once every quarter, four times per year.

Quartet. *See* Project Quartet.

Quarto. 1. A sheet of paper folded twice to form a section of four leaves. The sheets given under the definition Octavo are folded twice to give the quarto book sizes, in inches, presented below. Double size sheets folded three times would give the same size sections but would be described bibliographically as octavos, not quartos. Abbreviated 4°, 4to. 2. A book having sections of four leaves, or eight pages. 3. A book over 10 and under 13 inches high (the popular, or book trade, definition).

Foolscap	$8^{1}/_{2}$	x	$6^{3}/_{4}$
Crown	10	x	$7^{1}/_{2}$
Large post	$10^{1}/_{2}$	x	$8^{1}/_{4}$
Demy	$11^{1}/_{4}$	x	$8^{3}/_{4}$
Medium	$11^{1}/_{2}$	x	9
Royal	$12^{1}/_{2}$	x	10
Large Royal	$13^{1}/_{2}$	x	10
Super Royal	$13^{1}/_{2}$	x	$10^{1}/_{4}$
Imperial	15	x	11

Quarto edition. One issued in Quarto form.
Quarto shelving. Shelves to accommodate quarto books.

Quasi-facsimile bibliography.   One which attempts to reproduce the kind of type used in the original – roman, italic or gothic, etc.

Quaternion.   Paper or vellum folded into a section of four leaves.

Query.   The symbol ? written in the margin of a proof by the printer's reader to indicate to the author that some detail needs checking. Sometimes 'Qv' is used.

Question mark.   *See* Interrogation mark.

Questioned document.   A document, the origin or authorship of which has been challenged and is in doubt.

Quick-reference books.   Books which are essentially of a reference character, such as directories, dictionaries and gazetteers. *See also* Ready reference.

Quinternion.   A Gathering of five sheets folded once to form ten leaves or twenty papers.

Quire.   1. 24 sheets of paper and one 'outside', making 25; the twentieth of a ream; 25 copies of a newspaper or periodical.   2. A gathering, section or signature, especially when unfolded. Books in sheets, unbound, are said to be 'in quires'. *See also* Section. For 'Cording quires', *see* Cassie.

Quoins.   Wedges of metal or wood, used to lock the matter in the Chase.

Quotation marks.   *See* Quotes.

Quotations.   (*Printing*) Very large quads, used for filling up large areas of space in printed matter: they are usually hollow, simply four walls, sometimes strengthened by one or more internal girders. Also called 'Quotes'.

Quotes.   The inverted commas " " placed at the beginning and end of quotations. *See also* Quotations. Sometimes called 'Double quotes' to distinguish them from 'Single quotes': '...'. *See also* Double quotes, Duck-foot quotes, Single quotes, Turned comma. In Germany and Austria they are printed thus „...“ although some German printers now prefer the French guillemets but pointing inwards (»...«). Spanish printers prefer the guillemets («...») pointing outwards.

Qwerty.   The standard typewriter keyboard arrangement used in the UK and USA, placing the letters q.w.e.r.t.y. from the left on the top row. *See also* Azerty.

Rack.   A shelf, or group of shelves, or a case, usually built on to a wall or into a piece of furniture, for displaying books, magazines or periodicals, and distinguished as Book rack, Magazine rack, according to the special use of the fitting.

RAD.   *Rules for Archival Description*, issued by the Bureau of Canadian Archivists, 1990–1997. *RAD* is the national standard for Canadian archivists.

Radial routeing.   *See* Routeing. Also called 'controlled circulation'.

Radiating stacks.   Island stacks arranged like a fan, the point being towards the staff area thus enabling all readers on both sides of every stack to be visible to the staff.

Rag paper. Paper made from rags, especially cotton rags.

Ragged. In typesetting, uneven layout or lack of justification; left or right-hand margins may be ragged, or both.

Raised bands. When the cords, on which the sections of a book are sewed, are not embedded in their backs and consequently show as ridges, they are called raised bands. The opposite of Sunk bands.

Raised floor. *See* Suspended floor.

Raised-letter printing. *See* Thermography .

RAM. Random Access Memory; computer memory in which data stored at any point can be accessed without delay regardless of its position and which is *volatile*, i.e. it can be written to as well as read. *See also* ROM.

Ramage List. The *Finding-list of English books to 1640 in libraries of the British Isles (excluding the national libraries and the libraries of Oxford and Cambridge)* compiled by D. Ramage and published by the Council of the Durham Colleges in 1958. It gives locations for 14,000 books in 144 libraries, based on the 1st edition of *STC* and using STC numbers.

Ramean tree. *See* Porphyry, tree of.

Ramie. China (Chinese) grass which has been used for paper making in China since the third century A.D. In Europe it is normally used only for textiles and banknotes.

Ramifying classification. *See* Branching classification.

RAMP. *See* Records and Archives Management Programme.

Randolph J. Caldecott Medal. *See* Caldecott (Randolph J.) Medal.

Random access. (*Information retrieval*) A storage device not restricted to sequential scanning. Book indexes, card catalogues, optical discs, and photographic strips are all of this kind. With this method, access to any location in the file is equally rapid; it is also quicker than sequential scanning. *See also* RAM.

Random access memory. *See* RAM.

Ranfurly Library Service. *See* Book Aid International.

Ranganathan Award for Classification Research. On the sponsorship of the DRTC (Bangalore), this award was offered by the Committee on Classification Research of the International Federation for Document-ation (FID/CR) in honour of Dr. R. S. Ranganathan (1892–1972), the Indian classificationist. It was first awarded in 1976 to Derek Austin in recognition of his achievement in designing PRECIS.

Range. A US term for a bookcase, equivalent to the English 'Press'.

Ranging figures. The numerals of modern typefaces which do not have ascenders or descenders but extend from the base line to the cap line, e.g. the Times figures 1234567890. Also called 'Lining figures'. *See also* Hanging figures.

Rank. 1. (*Information retrieval*) A measure of the relative position in a series, group, classification or array. (*Classification*) 2. (*Noun*) A measure of the relative position of terms in a series, group, classification, or array.   3. (*Verb*) To arrange terms in an ascending or descending series according to importance.

Ranked output.   *See* Nearest neighbour.

Rare book.   A book so old, scarce or difficult to find that it seldom appears in the book markets. Among rare books may be included: incunabula, sixteenth to eighteenth century imprints, first editions, limited and deluxe editions, specially illustrated editions, books in fine bindings, unique copies, books of interest for their associations (local, regional, subject etc.).

Rare Books Group.   A membership group of CILIP, formed in 1967 to bring together members concerned with collections of rare books and similar materials.

RASCAL.   <www.rascal.ac.uk> Research and Special Collections Available Locally, an electronic gateway to research resources in Northern Ireland. The Directory consists of comprehensive descriptions of collections held in libraries, museums and archives available to researchers in the humanities and social sciences.

Ratcliffe Report.   *Preservation policies in British Libraries; report of the Cambridge University Library conservation project*, (BLRDD Library and Information Report 25, 1984) Chairman Dr. F. W. Ratcliffe. The report revealed a very unsatisfactory national picture of preservation, and led to the establishment of the National Preservation Office.

Rate, library.   *See* Library rate.

Rattle.   The sound produced by shaking or snapping a sheet of paper; it is indicative of hardness (due to the degree of wetness or hydration) and, generally speaking, of quality. Called 'crackle' in the USA. Linen rags will give a toughness and rattle to papers which is distinctive from those made from cotton.

Raw data.   (*Information retrieval*) Data, in machine-readable form or otherwise, which has not been processed.

Raw paper.   *See* Body paper.

RDF.   <www.w3.org/RDF> Resource Description Framework, an infrastructure that enables the encoding, exchange and re-use of structured Metadata. It is an XML application and the result of a number of metadata communities bringing together their needs to provide a robust and flexible architecture for supporting metadata on the Internet and WWW. RDF provides a uniform and interoperable means for exchanging metadata between programs, between sectors and particular interest groups, and across the Web. A key component of the Semantic Web. *See also* RSS.

RDN.   <www.rdn.ac.uk> Resource Discovery Network, a UK collaboration of over seventy educational and research organizations that gathers resources which are carefully selected, indexed and described by subject specialists as being particularly relevant to learning, teaching and research. The RDN builds upon the foundations of subject gateway activity carried out under the eLib Programme and is a co-operative network consisting of a central organization, the RDNC (Resource Discovery Network Centre) and a number of independent service providers, each known as a Hub: ALTIS; Artifact; BIOME; EEVL; GEsource; Humbul; PSIgate; and SOSIG.

RDNC. <www.rdn.ac.uk/about/#RDNC> Resource Discovery Network Centre, the central co-ordinating organization of the RDN, responsible for the overall development of the service. The RDNC sets service standards, creates the network collection development policy, promotes the RDN, develops strategic partnerships and supports the Hubs.

Reader. 1. A person employed by a printer to read through proofs with the 'copy' to make sure that corrections have been properly made. *See also* Publisher's reader. 2. A person who makes use of literary material in a library; a member of a lending library is frequently called a Borrower. 3. In a US special library or information department, the member of staff who scans current publications to select articles, news items, etc., pertinent to the work of individuals and departments of the organization of which the library is a part, for subsequent dissemination. 4. In a newspaper library, the member of the library staff who scans the several editions of the paper and marks articles for cutting and filing. *See also* Dissemination of information. 5. In reprography, a device for projecting a readable image of a microcopy on to a screen within the device or on to a separate portable screen or suitable surface which may be opaque or translucent. *See also* Microfilm reader. 6. In an educational institution, a member of the faculty whose role is primarily in research.

Reader area. That portion of the total floor space of a library which is allocated for use by readers.

Reader development. Schemes and initiatives that aim to improve the reading skills of the population (adults and children) and enhance their enjoyment of reading. Many organizations may support such schemes; in the UK, The Reading Agency (TRA) has been prominent with its Summer Reading Challenge and its Reading for Enjoyment Toolkit. Book clubs, the BBC Big Read series, and book prizes are attracting much publicity.

Reader for the press. A printer's reader. *See* Reader (1).

Reader services. A part of a library's establishment devoted to the provision of assistance, advice, and other services to the library's users. Usually found in tandem with a Technical services unit.

Reader-interest classification. A very simple and broad classification, intended to reflect the special interests of readers rather than the subject contents of books as such.

Reader-printer. In documentary reproduction, a microform reader which can also be used to make prints.

Reader's card. The card issued to a reader when registering to use a library.

Reader's proof. The first proof which is made from composed type; it is read by the printer's reader and sent to the compositor who makes any necessary alterations before the second proof is pulled and which is the first one sent to the author.

Reader's set.   A set of proofs in which corrections are to be made, usually so marked on the proofs by the printer's reader.

Reader's ticket.   The membership card or some form of identification, or ticket issued to a reader on joining a library.

Readers' adviser.   An experienced and tactful member of the staff who is detailed for advising readers on their choice of books, interesting casual readers in more systematic reading, recording results of interviews, maintaining a close touch with local educational agencies and generally furthering the use of the library service.

Reading Agency (TRA).   <www.readingagency.org.uk> The Reading Agency (TRA) was formed in 2002 by the merger of three earlier bodies – the Reading Partnership, LaunchPad and Well-Worth Reading. TRA works to improve services to readers by inspiring, challenging and supporting libraries; its role is to influence, innovate and encourage training, dissemination and networking. It works closely with the Society of Chief Librarians, ASCEL and CILIP.

Reading case.   *See* Magazine case .

Reading circle.   A group of people who meet regularly to read, study or discuss books.

Reading copy.   A copy of a book offered for sale in poor condition, the text being complete and legible. Also called 'Binding copy'.

Reading file.   (*Archives*) A file containing copies of documents arranged in chronological order. Also known as 'chronological file', 'continuity file'.

Reading list.   A list of recommended books and/or periodical articles in some special order and on a particular subject, often with guidance as to their purpose and features. *See also* Resource list, Source list.

Reading room.   A room set aside for the reading of periodicals or books.

Reading shelves.   Examining books to see that they are in correct order on the shelves. Also known as 'Shelf tidying', 'Shelf checking' and in US practice as 'Shelf reading' and 'Revising shelves'.

Reading the Future: a Review of Public Libraries in England.   *See* Public Libraries Review.

Read-only memory.   *See* ROM.

Ready reference.   Reference work concerned with questions of a factual nature which can be answered readily, often from Quick-reference books which in many libraries are shelved together with standard reference books, sometimes in a separate area reserved for dealing with questions of this nature.

Real time.   A computing term indicating that the computer response to commands is closely related to the input of data. *See also* Online.

Realia.   Three-dimensional objects such as museum materials, dioramas, models and samples which may be borrowed or purchased by a school library and used in connection with class lessons.

Realization. In music, the written expression, by an editor, on music staves of a full harmonization which is indicated by a figured bass on the original score. The realization may also be made in performance from the Figured bass.

Really Simple Syndication. *See* RSS.

Ream. A pack of 500 identical sheets of paper. A ream contains twenty quires. In the UK, packs of 480 sheets for special classes of papers, such as wrapping papers and blotting paper, are recognized. A ream of hand-made and drawing papers may contain 472, 480 or 500 sheets. Originally a ream contained 516 sheets. A 'short ream' has 480 sheets, a 'long ream' 500 or 516 sheets.

Re-back. To repair a book by providing a new spine without re-covering the sides or re-sewing. *See also* Backed (3).

Re-bound. Said of a book the original binding of which has been replaced with another, usually after re-sewing the sections.

Rebus. 1. A form of riddle, in which words or their syllables, names, mottoes, etc., are represented by objects or by a combination of objects, letters or words. 2. An enigmatical representation of a name, word or phrase by figures, pictures, arrangement of letters, etc., which resemble the intended words or syllables in sound. 3. REBUS <www.rebus. unibe.ch> Réseau des Bibliothèques utilisant SIBIL; users of SIBIL are grouped into the REBUS bibliographic network. (SIBIL – Système Informatisé pour Bibliothèques is a record format most used for shared cataloguing.) Five centres are at present involved: Lausanne, St. Gallen and Basle (Switzerland), Montpellier (France) and Luxembourg.

Recall. 1. (*Verb*) To request the return to the library of a book or other item which is on loan. 2. (*Noun*) The retrieval of a required document or reference from an information store.

Recall notice. A notice sent to a reader requesting the return of a book or other item which is overdue or required for use by someone else. *See also* Overdue notice.

Recall ratio. In information retrieval, the number of documents actually recalled from an index in response to a question on a given theme, in proportion to the number of documents on that theme which are known to be indexed. Also called 'Sensitivity'. *See also* Relevance ratio.

Recase binding. A method of rebinding suitable for any previously bound volume where the sewing is intact, but the case is damaged or detached. The original case is removed and a new one attached without disturbing the original sewing. Old end papers are removed and new ones added.

Re-casing. The re-insertion of a book into its original cover, with or without re-sewing.

Receiving desk. *See* Circulation desk.

Recension. A revision. Used to indicate a scholarly edition of a work, for instance of a classic, in which the existing text is thoroughly re-edited, revised and re-examined by collation with all known sources of textual emendation. *See also* Redaction (1).

Recess printing. Intaglio, photogravure and other processes whereby the ink is obtained from cavities or recesses in the printing plate or cylinder.

Recommendation card. *See* Suggestion card.

RECON. Abbreviation for *remote control* or for *retrospective conversion* (e.g. of records in a card catalogue to an automated form).

Record. 1. A document preserving an account of fact in permanent form, irrespective of media or characteristics. 2. The data relating to a document on which a catalogue or other entry is based. 3. A unit of information preserved in writing, typescript or coded form. A set of data elements forming a unit. Records are combined to form files. 4. In automatic data processing, a collection of related items of data, which for the purpose of operating systems, is treated as representing a unit of information. 5. A Gramophone record. *See also* Records.

Record mark. (*Information retrieval*) A character which is used to terminate each record within a machine-readable file. Also called 'Record terminator'.

Record Office. In the UK, the generic term normally used for an archives service of any kind, but particularly one run by local government. Under the Local Government (Records) Act 1962, it has become established that most 'principal Councils' should run such a service.

Record Repositories in Great Britain. A directory of some 250 UK archive repositories – local and national government, academic and corporate – giving details of holdings, facilities and web addresses. Published periodically by the National Archives (11th ed., 1999) and previously by the Historical Manuscripts Commission.

Recordable CD. See CD-R.

Records. (*Archives, Records management*) All created information, irrespective of date or medium, created, used and kept by an organization or person, in pursuance of their normal business and legal obligations. In Britain, colloquially used also to cover Archives.

Records and Archives Management Programme (RAMP). <www. unesco.org/webworld/public_domain/archives> Set up in 1979 as one of the functions of the General Information Programme of Unesco. Over the period since then RAMP has published many monographs, guidelines and standards covering all aspects of archives and records management, intended for free distribution world-wide. The programme is particularly concerned to raise awareness of the value of archives, and assist in establishing infrastructures through standards, legislation, training and the debating of issues.

Records centre. (*Records management*) An institution or building that provides storage for, and reference service to, records transferred from current administrative systems for medium or long-term retention. Ideally, records centres are low-cost, high-density storage facilities. Also sometimes termed *intermediate storage*.

Records management. The discipline concerned with the control and use of information-bearing media within an organization. Nowadays it is usually considered to be an essential part of information management, and it is naturally connected also to archive management. The term denotes the handling, efficient storage, and effective use of records, on paper or in other formats including electronic records, from their creation through the management of current and non-current records to the archival stage. The term is often used loosely; recent developments have highlighted the importance of good records management for health and safety reasons in complex areas of industry, for compliance with regulatory factors in the pharmaceutical industry, and for the competitiveness gained by rapid implementation of new intelligence retrieved from databases.

Records Management Society (RMS). <www.rms-gb.org.uk> (Woodside, Coleheath Bottom, Speen, Princes Risborough HP27 0SZ, UK) Established in 1983, provides a forum for all whose work is concerned with the control or use of records, irrespective of level or qualification. Publishes *Records Management Bulletin* (6 p.a.).

Re-covering. The process of making a new book cover and affixing it to a volume without re-sewing the sections.

Rectangular style. Bindings executed for Charles II while Samuel Mearne was the Royal Bookbinder. Their design consists of a simple three-line gilt rectangular panel with a crown or similar emblem at each corner. Crimson Morocco was mostly used.

Recto. 1. A right-hand page of an open book or manuscript, usually bearing an odd page number. Sometimes called an uneven page. Abbreviated 'ret'. 2. The first side of a printed or ruled sheet of paper when folded and bound, as distinct from the 'verso' which is the reverse side. *See also* Verso.

Red edges. The edges of a book cut, coloured red, and burnished.

Red ochre. A powder used by type casters to coat the inner surface of their moulds when casting very small sorts to make the metal flow more easily.

Red printing. Printing in a second colour (usually red) for headings, capitals, etc. This is usually performed on a separate machine after the text has been printed.

Red under gold edges. The three edges of a book cut, coloured red, and then gilt. *See also* Edges.

Redaction. 1. The editing, arranging, or revision for publication of a literary work which was left by the author incomplete or in a state unsuitable for publication. *See also* Recension. 2. A new, or revised, edition of a work.

RedLightGreen. <www.redlightgreen.com> A service from Research Libraries Group developed with funding from the Andrew W. Mellon Foundation. Using 120 million records from the RLG Union Catalog, RedLightGreen is optimized with specific tools to help undergraduates locate relevant and legitimate works for their research, check availability through a link to their local online catalogue, and create citations in standard formats. The pilot for the service was launched in September 2003.

Reduction. 1. In documentary reproduction, a copy the scale of which is reduced compared with the Original. 2. In music, an arrangement of a musical work for a smaller group of instruments than for which it was originally written.

Reduction of numbers. (*Classification*) Dropping by the classifier of one or more digits at the end of a notation number given in the schedules or tables. This results in a shorter number with a more inclusive meaning, and thus in broader classification. *See* Broad classification.

Reduction of schedules. (*Classification*) Dropping by the editors of some or all of the previous subdivisions of a number in a classification scheme with resultant classification of these concepts in a higher number. This results in notation for the topic that is one or more digits shorter than it was in the immediately preceding edition.

Redundancy. (*Information retrieval*) The use of more words or symbols than are necessary to convey a meaning (thought, word or idea). It may be planned repetition in order to overcome Noise in the system.

Redundant indexing. The use of more than one term, the meanings of which are not clearly distinguishable, for indexing the same information in a document.

Re-edition. A publication which is distinguished from previous editions by changes made in contents (revised edition) or layout (new edition).

Reel fed. A printing press which prints on paper in a reel instead of single sheets.

Reel to reel. The playback or projection from one reel or spool of film or audiotape to a separate take-up reel or spool.

'Refer from' reference. An indication, in a list of subject headings, of the headings from which references should be made to the given heading; it is the reverse of the indication of a 'See' or 'See also' reference.

Referee. An independent expert who assists the editor of a journal in evaluating the acceptability of contributions submitted for publication. *See also* Peer review.

Reference. (*Cataloguing*) 1. A direction from one heading to another. References may be *general* to indicate a class, giving an individual heading only as an example, as

Animals, *see also* under the names of animals as Lion.

or *specific* by stating the exact heading to which reference must be made, as

Animals, *see* Lion.

Clemens, S. L., *see* Twain, Mark.

They may be made between (a) synonymous headings – 'see' references, and (b) related headings – 'see also' references. 2. A partial record of an item, under subject or title, referring to the main entry. 3. (*Information retrieval*) An indication referring to a document or other item.   4. An indication of where to find specific information mentioned in a text. *See also* References.

Reference and User Services Association (RUSA).   A part of the American Library Association, RUSA aims to stimulate and support in every type of library the delivery of reference and information services to all groups regardless of age, and of general library services and materials to adults. It facilitates the development and conduct of direct services to library users, the development of programmes and guidelines for service to meet the needs of those users, and assists libraries in reaching potential users. Formerly known as the Reference and Adult Services Division. Publishes *RUSA Update* (q.), *RUSQ* (q.).

Reference card.   A catalogue card bearing a cross-reference. *See also* Cross references.

Reference code.   A set of symbols, usually alphanumeric, to identify documents within an accumulation of archives. *MAD* provides a standard which includes symbols for each level of description used.

Reference department.   The department of a library containing Reference materials for consultation in the library only.

Reference edges.   The left-hand and bottom limits of a microfiche grid.

Reference interview.   The initial discussion between an enquirer and the library or information service staff to determine exactly what level and quantity of information would be appropriate as a response to the query made.

Reference librarian.   A librarian in charge of, or undertaking the work of, a reference library.

Reference library.   A library or department containing Reference materials which may not normally be used elsewhere than on the premises.

Reference linking.   Methods of improving the flow of scholarly communication by seamless navigation between full-text and bibliographic databases; cited items found during reading can be speedily presented to the user without further searching or delay. Organizations such as NFAIS are currently exploring the technology to support this. *See also* CrossRef, OpenURL.

Reference management software.   Software used to record Bibliographical references in a personal Database which can then form the foundation of citations in published papers. The software permits customizable Fields to be created, and the automatic formatting of references into the layouts required by publishers. Some packages work in association with word processors so that the references can be accessed directly in formatted form by the word processor itself; some also enable Downloaded records from Online or CD-ROM searches to be saved in a compatible format.

Reference marks.   1. Printers' marks used to indicate references to other books or passages or to footnotes on the page. Where more than one reference is given on a page the order of the marks is as follows: * (asterisk or star), † (dagger or obelisk), ‡ (double dagger or double obelisk), § (section mark), ‖ (parallel mark), ¶ (paragraph mark). If more than six notes are required to a page, these signs are given first in single, then double and afterwards in treble sequence. Letter and figures in alphabetical or numerical order are more often used for the same purpose. 2. A set of suitable marks, usually fine line crosses, which provide reference points for registration in printing of art work, image location etc.

Reference material. Sources of information (databases, abstracts, journals, books, etc.) which are used for answering enquiries in a library. Such items are not normally lent, but consulted only on the premises. Related sources, such as collections of supporting literature, notes of valuable web sites, particular subject expertise of staff, may also be included in this expression.

Reference matter. *See* Subsidiaries.

Reference service. The provision and organization by a library of Reference work.

Reference source. Any material, published work, database, web site, etc. which is used to obtain authoritative information.

Reference work. 1. That branch of the library's services which includes the assistance given to users in their search for information on various subjects. 2. The work of the Reference library. 3. Any authoritative Reference source – database, web site, publication etc. – compiled to be referred to rather than for continuous reading.

References. A list of publications to which an author has made specific reference; usually placed at the end of an article or chapter, or at the end of a book, sometimes in chapter order.

Referral centre. An organization for directing researchers for information and data to appropriate sources such as libraries, agencies, document-ation centres and individuals.

Reflex copying. A process for reproducing photographically copies of documents which are opaque or printed on both sides. The light-sensitive emulsion on the paper is placed against the document: light is passed through the sensitized paper and reflected back from the light parts of the document – not from the dark or printed parts. The reversed negative which results may then be used to print a positive by transmitted light on the same kind of paper.

Refresh rate. The number of times a second the display on a computer monitor is re-drawn to keep the display visible. Normally expressed in hertz (Hz), low values indicate a slower refresh rate which gives rise to more flicker on screen.

Regional agencies. *See* Museums, Libraries and Archives Council (MLA).

Regional bibliographic center. A clearinghouse for regional co-operation among library groups in the USA, locating books required and facilitating their loan between libraries, directing research workers and students requiring materials on particular subjects and possibly compiling complete or partial union catalogues.

Regional bibliography.   *See* National bibliography.

Regional bureaux (UK).   The offices which act as clearinghouses for requests for particular books which are not in stock where asked for, and pass on the requests to other libraries in their own regional areas. *See* Regional library co-operation (UK).

Regional catalogue.   1. A catalogue of the books in libraries situated in a given geographical region.   2. A catalogue of books relating to, or written by, people living in a given geographical region.

Regional headquarters.   Premises from which are administered the library service points in its region but at which the public may or may not be served directly. It provides the control, bookstock, administrative services and other facilities which are normally available from head-quarters in a centralized system.

Regional library co-operation.   Regional Library Systems in the UK, which are not statutory bodies, were first formed in the 1930s; nearly all public and university libraries and large numbers of other public and private sector libraries are now members of regional schemes. With the formation of the regional structure of the Museums, Libraries and Archives Council (MLA), the role of the regional schemes is unclear and adjustments are expected. *See* CONARLS, Unityweb.

Regional library system.   *See* Regional bureaux, Regional library co-operation.

Register.   1. The ribbon attached to a volume to serve as a bookmarker.   2. A list of signatures attached to the end of early printed books, or printed above the colophon or on a separate leaf, for the guidance of the folder or binder. A 'registrum'.   3. In printing, a term used when the type area on the recto coincides exactly with that on the back of the verso. The adjustment of colour blocks so that the colours are superimposed with absolute accuracy. Register is of tremendous importance in multi-colour process work. When properly adjusted the work is said to be 'in register', when not, 'out of register'.   4. A catalogue or bibliography; particularly, an official list or enumeration.

Register of Preservation Microforms (RPM).   <www.bl.uk/about/collectioncare/rpmintro> RPM is a database containing descriptions of preservation microforms created by the National Preservation Office when the original is in danger of deterioration. Locations are given; updated as a co-operative project between the national libraries of the UK and the Republic of Ireland. The database itself is at <www.eromm.org>.

Register table.   A table with an opaque-glass top and a box-like interior fitted with lights and painted white. It is used to position negatives on positives together with any accompanying type matter, on a layout sheet. It is also used for other purposes, e.g. register work in colour printing. Also called a 'Lining-up table', 'Shining-up table'.

Registered archivist.   An Archivist who by training and experience has conformed to the standards required by the Society of Archivists, and has been admitted to the professional register. The Register is regulated by the body of Registered Archivists.

Registered reader. One who has become a member of a library, and is entitled to borrow books and other material.

Registration. 1. The process of examining readers' application forms and making out membership cards or tickets. This may be done at one library in a system (centralized registration) or at each branch. 2. The entering of particulars of books and other items added to a library in the Accessions register.

Registration card. A membership, or identity, card which is issued to members entitling them to use, or borrow items from, a library.

Registration department. The unit which is concerned with maintaining records of membership and issuing membership cards or tickets.

Registration marks. (*Printing*) Pairs of marks, usually in the form of a cross, to show the relative position and exact orientation of two pieces of artwork that are to be superimposed in printing.

Registration period. The period during which a Registered reader is entitled to use library services before being required to re-register.

Registrum. *See* Register (2).

Registry. An office or system charged with the management of incoming and outgoing documents, filing systems, and the movement of documents through the department. Registries are typical of civil service procedures, and the selection of government records for transfer to the Public Record Office is an aspect of their work.

Reglet. A strip of wood, about the height of leads, used to separate lines of type, thus saving leads, lightening the forme and making it easier to handle. They are chiefly used in poster work. *See also* Leads.

Regnal numbers. In Brown Classification, the first divisions of each block of numbers devoted to a country relate to the country's historical development, by reigning monarch or other ruler. These numbers provide for all royal biographies, State papers, histories and special monographs, or any event of a historical nature.

Regular folio. *See* Folio (2).

Rehearsal score. *See* Score.

Reimposition. The rearrangement of pages of type matter in a forme, consequent upon the addition of new matter to type already arranged in pages, or to the use of a different type of folding machine.

Reinforced binding. Publisher's binding strengthened by a library book-binder, usually by adding a cloth strip to the Hinge and resewing with strong thread.

Reinforced union paper. Union paper which has a lining between the two sheets of which it is made, in order to increase its mechanical strength.

Reinforcing-piece. (*Binding*) The paper or parchment, on which for greater strength, the backs of some or all of the sections are sewn, and part of which shows under the paste-downs. *See also* Paste-down.

Re-issue. A re-publication at different price, or in a different form, of an impression, or edition, which has already been issued, usually from standing type or plates.

Rejection slip. A printed acknowledgement sent out by a publisher or magazine editor, when returning a MS. to an author informing him or her that the MS. has not been accepted for publication.

Rejects. Copies of printed matter which are rejected by publisher or customer because of inferiorities.

Related term. (*Information retrieval*) A term which is co-ordinate (i.e. equal in status or specificity) to another. *See also* Broader term, Narrower term.

Related title. A title which has a relationship to another by being a subsequent book in a series, or a commentary on, or a 'reply to' an earlier work. In the eighteenth century many anonymous pamphlets of this kind were published.

Related work. (*Cataloguing*) A work which has some relationship to another. It may be a continuation, supplement, index, concordance, manual, sequel, scenario, choreography, libretto, special number of a serial, collection of extracts from serials, a work produced by the editorial staff of a serial, or a work in a subseries.

Relation. 1. A non-periodical pamphlet published in England and describing a battle or some other event. A forerunner of the newspaper. Also called a 'Discourse' or a 'Narration'. *See also* Coranto, Newsbook. 2. (*Information retrieval*) Relationship between two concepts or between class numbers of a classification.

Relation marks. Symbols used in an agreed order when building up the classification numbers of the Universal Decimal Classification in order to separate the various parts and also to indicate their meaning.

Relational database. A database in which a wide range of characteristics for objects (or people) can be recorded and which, via search and report systems, can extract information relating to specific criteria.

Relational indexing. (*Facet analysis, Indexing*) 1. Any system which involves a formal statement of the relationship between terms and in particular one in which complex subjects are represented by terms connected by symbols indicating their notational relations. 2. Such a system in which the structure of complex subjects is represented by the inter-position of symbols between terms to denote particular relations. The symbols are known as 'relational symbols' or 'operators'.

Relative classification. Classification which shows, as most modern schemes do, the relationships between subjects. It is the opposite of Fixed location systems prevalent prior to the Dewey Decimal Classification (1876).

Relative humidity. The percentage of the quantity of water in a volume of air in relation to the maximum quantity it can hold at a given temperature. Correct relative humidity is essential for the preservation of paper: if too low, so that the air is dry, paper becomes embrittled; if too high, dampness causes fungal moulds to grow. BS 5454:1977, paragraph 9.2, recommends a level of RH for a library of between 55 per cent and 65 per cent, where the temperature is between 13° and 18°C.

Relative index.   An alphabetic index to a classification scheme in which all relationships and aspects of the subject are brought together under each index entry. An index to a scheme of classification also translates a natural language term into a class number; this it does by putting the class number after the natural language term. Such an index is provided for the Dewey Decimal Classification and collocates subjects at one place which in the Schedules are scattered by discipline. A selective index is complementary to the schedules. *See also* Specific index.

Relative location.   An arrangement of books according to their relation to each other and regardless of the shelves or rooms in which they are placed and allowing the insertion of new material in its proper relation to that already on the shelves. Also called 'Movable location'. The opposite of Fixed location.

Relative relief map.   One which shows the relative height of land areas by colour or shading, but not the steepness of slope: this is shown by an Average slope map.

Relativity.   That property of the index to a scheme of classification which reverses the subordination of subject to discipline, thus bringing together from all disciplines the various aspects of individual subjects.

Relator.   (*Cataloguing*) A word or words in a heading indicating the relationship of the person named in the heading to the work specified in the remainder of the entry, e.g. editor, illustrator.

Relevance ratio.   In information retrieval, the number of documents which are actually wanted in proportion to the number of documents retrieved in response to a question on a given theme. *See also* Recall ratio, Precision ratio.

Relevant characteristic.   *See* Characteristic of a classification.

Relief.   (*Binding*) Said of a finisher's tool which is made in such a way that the design, when impressed on the leather, appears in relief.

Relief map.   One which represents elevations of the earth's surface by various methods.

Relief model.   (*Cartography*) A scaled representation in three dimensions of a section of the earth's crust or of another heavenly body. Usually the vertical scale is exaggerated compared with the horizontal in order to accentuate mountains and plateaus. Known in the USA as a 'terrain model'.

Relief printing.   Printing from characters or designs that are raised above their surrounding surface, such as type, plates, etc., as distinguished from Intaglio printing. It includes woodcuts, wood engravings, zinc etchings, and half-tones.

Remainders.   When books have ceased to sell well, the publisher's stock remaining is sold off by auction or at a reduced price, to a wholesaler or bookseller. Such books are then known as remainders.

Remake.   To re-page a book, either partly or completely. To re-arrange typographic elements in a page or publication.

Remarque proof.   *See* Artist's proof.

Remote access.   The use of online services from a remote computer; often applied to the use of an organization's networked services when working from home or other remote location. *See also* Remote login.

Remote login.   Used in the early days of online bibliographic searching to indicate a facility that allowed queries to be made to a remote computer Host and information or data to be obtained directly without necessarily downloading to the local machine. Only the databases provided by the remote host could be used and no access was provided to a range of networked services. One method of Remote login was via Telnet. *See also* Remote access.

Remote storage.   Locating storage facilities for library stock in sites that are less expensive to maintain than the main library premises; remote storage is typically considered for older or infrequently used materials, but may be advantageous for other purposes such as controlled climate for vulnerable items or improved access through a specialized centre. *See also* Repository library.

Removable storage.   A hard disk in which the disk itself, in the form of a cartridge, is removable; much like a high capacity floppy disk. Capacities generally range from 100 MBytes to 2 Gigabytes. The advantages of portability, the facility for readily transferring large files e.g. from user to bureau, and for file Back-up have become less obvious with the appearance of high-capacity/low weight portable hard discs and the predonderance of CD-R.

Removes.   Quotations, passages or notes set, usually at the foot of a page, and in smaller type than that of the text.

Renaissance ornament.   (*Binding*) Conventional decorative ornament, apparently suggested by columns, urns, vases, beasts, birds, garlands and foliage which appear in Renaissance architecture.

RENARDUS.   <www.renardus.org> A project funded by the European Union to work towards building an academic subject gateway service in Europe. There are 12 partners, including the UK, France, Germany and the Netherlands. It is envisaged that it will be possible to search and browse via a single interface a range of existing gateways with top-quality metadata. The system would be Z39.50 compliant.

Render.   In computer graphics, to apply shading or texture to three-dimensional objects to increase their realism.

Renew.   To extend the period (a) for which a book or other item is on loan; (b) during which a library membership ticket is valid; (c) for supplying a periodical on subscription.

Repairing.   The repair of a worn binding including restoring the cover and reinforcing the joints. Not to be confused with Mending.

RePEc.   <repec.org> Research Papers in Economics, a volunteer-driven initiative to create a public-access database that promotes scholarly communication in economics and related disciplines. The heart of the project is a decentralized database of working papers, journal articles and software components. All RePEc material is freely available. *See also* WoPEc.

Répertoire Internationale des Sources Musicales. *See* RISM.

Repertory catalogue. A catalogue of books in more than one library.

Repetitive strain injury (RSI). Injury that can occur at any joint such as the wrist, elbow or shoulder, as a result of work requiring the repetitive movement of fingers, hands and arms. Particularly associated with keyboarding work on PCs and terminals.

Replacement. 1. A book bought to take the place of a worn-out copy of the same title. 2. The routine involved in substituting a volume for one which has been withdrawn.

Replevin. (*Archives*) 1. The recovery of property such as archives, documents, manuscripts, by an institution or organization which claims ownership. 2. The writ and legal action by which a person or institution secures such property. *See also* Estray.

Replica. A copy or reproduction of a work of art, especially one made by the artist, and assumed to be of equal quality to the original. A doublette. A facsimile or nearly exact copy.

Report. A publication giving a formal or official record, as of the activities of a committee or corporate body, or of some special investigation, or the proceedings of a governmental body. *See also* Technical report.

Report literature. A general term which includes reports of all kinds, which give the results of research or development work, and which are associated with the name of the sponsor within a numbered sequence. The publications may include technical notes and memoranda, preprints, conference proceedings and papers, research and development reports, as well as formal reports.

Repository. 1. A network-accessible server used as a store for digital content, e.g. in Self archiving or for an Eprint archive, and which can disseminate those contents by exposing metadata to harvesters such as the Open Archives Initiative Protocol for Metadata Harvesting. Where the server holds the eprints for a whole university or similar institution, the phrase *institutional repository* is frequently used. 2. (*Archives*) A generic term for that part of an archives service that is concerned with the physical custody and preservation of archival materials.

Repository library. A storage facility for books or other library stock, operated generally by a group of libraries in a geographical area, or nationally in a subject field, with the intention of saving costs and improving access. Such facilities may imply a measure of collaborative acquisition, willingness to interlend, co-operative cataloguing etc. Electronic repositories allow centralized access to digitized collections; there are considerations of copyright and licensing to be addressed.

Representative fraction. The ratio between distance measured on a map and the corresponding distance on the ground. Thus a map on the scale

1 inch to 1 mile has a representative fraction of 1 : 63,360 there being 63,360 inches in a mile.

Reprint. 1. A copy of a book, made from the same type or stereotype as the original, with which it is identical except for possibly a new title-page and a note on the verso of the title-page of the number and date of reprinting and the correction of minor errors. *See also* Edition, Facsimile reprint, First edition, Impression, Issue, New edition, Revised edition, Separate. 2. Setting up type and printing again, using a previous printing as 'copy' as distinct from manuscript 'copy'. 3. A contribution to a periodical, afterwards issued separately, though not necessarily from the same type as the original. Sometimes called a Separate. 4. A British Standard (BS 4719:1971, now withdrawn) defined a reprint as 'All those copies of an edition reproduced at an interval after the original printing of the edition. In current practice this term is frequently preferred to impression'. In recent years, arrangements have been made between publishers to print copies of out-of-print books which are in demand, but which the original publisher does not wish to reprint, or by firms specializing in the reproduction of very old and/or scarce books. Photographic reproduction methods are used, and the original text remains unchanged.

Reprint series. A series of books, which have been published previously by one or more publishers, now issued in the same format by one publisher and bearing a series name. The books need not be related in either subject matter or treatment. *See also* Publisher's series.

Reprinted article. One which has been reprinted, but with its own pagination. *See also* Separate.

Reproduction proof. A proof copy of a work of art, photograph, tabulation, etc., of the highest quality which may be used for reproduction purposes by means of a printing block or plate.

Reprographic marking. The reprographic transfer of workshop drawings directly on to the materials, e.g. sheets of metal, to be fashioned.

Reprography. The reproduction in facsimile of documents of all kinds by any process using light, heat or electric radiation – photocopies, microcopies, blueprints, electro-copies, thermo-copies, etc.; also reproduction by methods of duplicating and office printing.

Republication. 1. The re-issuing of a publication by a publisher other than the original, without changes in the text. Sometimes used of reprints made in another country. 2. Broadly, re-issuing a work, with or without textual changes, or as a new edition.

Request card. *See* Suggestion card.

Request form. A form, or card distributed to the users of a special library to request information or material from the library. It can be so designed as to show the progress of steps taken to meet the request, record the borrowing of material from another library and record the loan of material to the user.

Requisition card. *See* Suggestion card.

Requisition form. *See* Call slip.

Research and development report. A document which formally states the results of, or progress made with, a research and/or development investigation, which, where appropriate, draws conclusions and makes recommendations, and which is initially submitted to the person or body for whom the work is done. A report is usually one of a series and commonly carries a report number which identifies both the report and the producing, disseminating or sponsoring organization.

Research book. In film studio research libraries, a scrapbook made up of sketches, abstracts, and other information relating to the settings, architecture, costumes, etc., which are gathered in advance of the production of a particular picture in order to ensure that the presentation is historically and artistically accurate.

Research carrel. *See* Carrel.

Research librarian. A title often used in respect of the librarian in a special library who undertakes the work of a Research service as distinct from one who undertakes the work normally carried out in a reference library. *See also* Information officer.

Research Libraries Group. *See* RLG.

Research Libraries Information Network. *See* RLIN.

Research Libraries Network (RLN). Announced in July 2004, the RLN was planned to transform the way research information is collected, organized, preserved and accessed across the UK. The RLN will bring together the UK's four higher education funding bodies, the British Library, the National Libraries of Scotland and Wales and the eight members of Research Councils UK to develop the UK's first national framework aimed at addressing the information needs of researchers. The RLN was set up following the recommendations of the Research Support Libraries Group and endorsed by the House of Commons Select Committee on Education and Skills. It will: (i) provide strategic leadership for collaboration between publicly-funded research information providers and their users to develop effective, efficient and integrated information resources and services to support UK research; (ii) co-ordinate action to propose and specify solutions to meet researchers' changing needs; and (iii) act as a high-level advocate for research information across the UK and internationally. The RLN will be set up initially for three years, up to the end of July 2007. It will be led by an executive unit, with a budget of up to £3 million, which will be based at the British Library and take strategic guidance from an advisory board.

Research library. A library consisting of specialized documents and information sources, and providing facilities for undertaking exhaustive investigation. It may also provide referral services in support of studies in subject fields connected with development, testing and evaluation as well as research. *See also* Centre, Referral centre, University research library.

Research Papers in Economics.   *See* RePEc.

Research room.   *See* Search room.

Research service.   A service rendered by special librarians by examining, appraising and summarizing information obtained from various sources and from individuals and organizations considered to be authorities in the appropriate fields. This implies giving the solutions to problems, providing statistics and other information as distinct from supplying publications from which the information may be obtained. The information assembled is usually presented in tabular, report or memorandum form. Also called 'Search service'. *See also* Literature search.

Research stall.   *See* Carrel.

Research Support Libraries Group (RSLG).   <www.rslg.ac.uk> A strategic advisory group established by the four UK higher education funding bodies in collaboration with the British Library and the national libraries of Wales and Scotland to advise on the development of a national strategy to ensure that UK researchers have access to world class information resources. Chaired by Sir Brian Follett, it recommended the establishment of the Research Libraries Network (RLN).

Research Support Libraries Programme (RSLP).   <www.rslp.ac.uk> A national initiative, funded by the four higher education funding bodies in the UK. The Programme brought together both traditional and new forms of access to library information, with specific reference to support for research. While the principal beneficiaries have been researchers and their postgraduate research students in UK higher education institutions, there have also been significant benefits for other groups. It started in the academic year 1999–2000 and finished on 31 July 2002, with funding totalling almost £30m awarded during the lifetime of the Programme.

Réseau Romand.   Swiss library bibliographic network, founded 1982, with 40 members – mainly university and special libraries. Based in Lausanne; a member of REBUS.

Réseau SIBIL France.   French library bibliographic network; founded 1987 as a part of REBUS.

Reservation.   A request for a specific book or other item to be reserved for a reader as soon as it becomes available on completion of processing, or on its return from the binder or another reader.

Reserve card (form, slip).   A card on which borrowers enter particulars of books to be retained for them when available for borrowing.

Reserve collection.   1. Library material for which there is infrequent demand and which consequently is not kept on open shelves, but individual items of which are obtained on request.   2. In academic libraries, material which is in great demand because of being placed on reading lists and which might be re-located to a dedicated area of the library and assigned restricted loan periods. Also known as Short-loan collection, Course reserve collection. *Compare* Electronic course reserve collection.

Re-set edition. One printed from newly set type but without revision of the text.

Re-setting. Setting type again, because of corrections, additions, changes of layout, etc.

Resist. A coating of glue, enamel or shellac used to protect a plate from acid corrosion during the etching process.

Resolution. 1. In documentary reproduction, the measure of the ability of an emulsion to record fine line detail or of a lens to record minute lines or points clearly, distinctly and separately. Also called 'Resolving power'. 2. In photography, a measure of the sharpness or visibility of an image; it is usually measured in line pairs per mm. 3. The measurement of the number of onscreen dots that a monitor or VDU can accommodate; the greater the number, the clearer the image.

Resolver. Software that enables links to Internet resources to be automatically re-directed when changes in systems and URLs would otherwise result in failed attempts at access. A 'link resolver' with more complex functionality is used in OpenURL systems. *See also* Persistence, PURL.

Resource. Resource (also Re:source) was established in 2000 as the key UK strategic agency for museums, libraries and archives. In 2004 the name was changed to Museums, Libraries and Archives Council (MLA).

Resource centres. Collections of books and non-book materials of all kinds, which are relevant sources of information and instruction in schools and colleges.

Resource Description Framework. *See* RDF.

Resource Discovery Network. *See* RDN.

Resource Discovery Network Centre. *See* RDNC.

Resource list. A Reading list which provides direct Links to the electronic Full text of recommended readings and which provides context by indicating relevance at particular points in the course being studied. Resource lists can link to any digital object – to animations, audio files, e-books, graphics files, individual journal papers, Web sites – as well as to the library OPAC.

Resources and Technical Services Division. *See* Association for Library Collections and Technical Services.

Respect des fonds. (*Archives*) The principle, promulgated in France in about 1840, governing the treatment of archives. It states that the archives accumulated by one organization should be treated separately from those of all other organizations, and that archivists should aim to protect or restore the original order and system under which the archives were created. Also known as the *Principle of provenance*, and the *Principle of original order*.

Response time. The time taken by a computer to respond to and complete a command.

Restoration. According to IFLA, those techniques and judgements used by technical staff engaged in the making good of library and archive materials damaged by time, use or other factors. Current practice indicates that any restoration work should attempt to return the damaged item to as close to its original state as possible.

Restoration style.   *See* Mearne style.

Restricted loan.   A loan of library material with some form of limitation, as on period of loan, or number of volumes allowed at one time.

Ret.   Abbreviation for Recto, the second side of a sheet of paper. *See also* Verso.

Retention schedule.   In Records management an officially authorized list of record series, in which each series is allocated a retention period and an instruction as to its disposal. The concept is used both in government and in private sector organizations.

Retired Members Guild.   A membership group of CILIP, formed in 2000 for those members who have retired from the profession.

Retouching.   1. Hand etching or improvements carried out to a photographic print or negative used in Process engraving.   2. The hand-correcting of colour separations used in the photo-engraving and photo-lithographic processes. Called 'Dot-etching' in the US.

Retree.   Slightly defective sheets of paper. Derived from the French *retiré*, 'withdrawn'.

Retrieval.   1. The action of searching a database, catalogue, or physical store in order to locate a document, other form of record, or item of information, and the actual recovery of the required item. *See also* Retrieval device.

Retrieval device.   A record of documents or information which is consulted in order to obtain what is needed and recorded as being in the Store. An abstracts journal, a text-book, a library catalogue, or a database used to select documentary information, are all retrieval devices.

Retrieval system.   A sequence of actions which result in obtaining (retrieving) required information. The system requires such components which enable the information to be identified in the Store.

Retro-active notation.   (*Classification*) 1. A Notation in which Facet indicators and intra-facet connectors are eliminated by using one species of characters indicating the construction of the notation (and thereby the subject matter of the material) in reverse order to the schedules.   2. A notation in which compounds are specified merely by adding earlier numbers to later ones. The notation to the Dewey Decimal Classification is of this kind, where, e.g. the form number 08 is used as a facet indicator to indicate the literary form in which a work is presented.

Retrospective bibliography.   A bibliography which lists books published in previous years as distinct from a 'current' bibliography which records books recently published. Also called 'Closed bibliography'. *See also* Bibliography.

Retrospective conversion.   The partial or complete conversion of an existing catalogue into machine-readable form, as opposed to converting records created currently. Also known as RECON, retro-conversion.

Return key. A key on a terminal keyboard that is used at the end of each command or entry procedure to indicate the end of inputting. Use of this key causes the computer to accept the input and make a response.

Returns. Unsold publications which are returned by a bookseller to the publisher. Also called 'Crabs'.

Reusable learning object. *See* Learning object.

Re-use of numbers. (*Classification*) A total change in the meaning of a given number as between one edition and another.

rev. Abbreviation for revise, revised, revision. *See also* Revised edition.

RevealWeb. <www.revealweb.org.uk> Reveal is the UK national database of resources in alternative formats (formerly National Union Catalogue of Alternative Formats (NUCAF)) and contains over 100,000 books held by some 250 organizations.

Revenue stamps. Stamps which were stuck on English newspapers in accordance with the Stamp Act, 1712. The paper had to be stamped before printing. The duty was the same irrespective of the size of the newspaper, and the Act, which was repealed in 1855, consequently had the effect of increasing the size of newspapers. *See also* Stamp Acts.

Reversal process. Developing in such a manner that the material exposed in the camera shows a positive instead of a negative image. The reversal process is used extensively in colour photography, and for producing duplicate negatives.

Reverse Browne. A method of issuing books which is similar to the Browne book charging system but which uses a pocket book-card and a card ticket.

Reverse cover. The lower cover of a book, i.e. that nearest to the last leaf. Also called 'Back cover', 'Lower cover'. *See also* Obverse cover.

Reverse left to right. (*Printing*) To reverse a design, etc., so that it prints as if a mirror image.

Reverse out. (*Printing*) When making a plate or block, reversing black to white so that the final appearance of the print is of white printed on black (or another colour) instead of the normal black on white.

Reverse Polish Notation (RPN). A method for defining Boolean expressions without the need for parentheses and widely used by computers and pocket calculators. Polish Notation was devised in 1951 by the Polish logician Jan Lukasiewicz as a parenthesis-free notation for logic. By placing the operators in a Boolean or algebraic expression before their operands, the need for parentheses is eliminated. Reverse Polish Notation similarly dispenses with the need for parentheses but the operators appear as a suffix rather than prefix. Z39.50 clients and servers communicate in RPN.

REVIEL. <www.cerlim.ac.uk/projects/reviel> Resources for Visually Impaired Users of the Electronic Library. Originally a British Library-funded project which aimed to develop electronic library services for users who are blind or visually impaired. After research into such issues as standards and copyright, it carried out research into the concept of a virtual library for visually impaired people. This has resulted in the development of an online catalogue of materials held in formats such as Braille, Moon, large print and audio. Major contributors are the (UK) Royal National Institute for the Blind and the National Library for the Blind.

Review. 1. A periodical publication which is devoted largely to critical articles and reviews of new books. Also called 'review journal', 'reviewing journal'. 2. An evaluation of a work published in a periodical or newspaper.

Review copy. A copy of a book sent by the publisher to a newspaper or magazine for the favour of a review. Sometimes called 'Press copy'.

Review of the Public Library Service in England and Wales for the Department of National Heritage. *See* Public Libraries Review.

Revise. *See* Proof.

Revised edition. A new edition of a book in which errors have been corrected, and possibly new material added. Sometimes wrongly called 'Enlarged edition'. *See also* Edition, First edition, Impression, Issue, New edition, Reprint.

Revised proof. *See* Proof.

Revising shelves. *See* Reading shelves.

Revived copyright. When copyright protection was extended from 50 to 70 years after the author's death, some works were already out of copyright because the author's death exceeded 50 years but was less than 70 years. Such works were again protected under revived copyright.

Revolving bookcase. One having shelves on four or more sides; built around a central cylinder it rotates in either direction on a spindle.

REWERSE. <www.rewerse.net> Reasoning on the Web with Rules and Semantics; an EU network of excellence project (2004–2008) bringing together 27 institutions from 14 European countries with funding from the Information Society Technologies (IST) priority of the Sixth Framework Programme (FP6). The project will develop and test a collection of coherent and complete reasoning languages for advanced Web systems and applications.

RFC. Request For Comments; documents that are the written definitions of the protocols and policies of the Internet. Details can be found at: <www.rfc-editor.org>.

RFID. Radio Frequency Identification, an alternative to the Bar code that uses tiny microchips in tags to hold and transmit detailed data about the item tagged. RFID has advantages over bar codes such as the ability to hold more data, the ability to change the stored data as processing occurs, it does not require line-of-sight to transfer data and is very effective in harsh environments where bar code labels may not work. However, a lack of standardization, particularly in the commercial sector, is currently delaying take-up.

RGB. Red, green, blue, the 'key' or 'main' colours that are combined in an additive colour system to produce all intermediate shades. In an additive system, mixing percentages of the three main colours produces the desired result; adding no colour produces black, and adding 100 per cent of all three colours produces white. *See also* CMYK.

Ribbon arrangement. A method of arranging books in a public library with non-fiction on upper shelves and novels on lower shelves, or vice versa, or novels on middle shelves and non-fiction above and below, the object being to disperse the readers around the library and avoid congestion at the fiction shelves.

Rice paper. Paper made from the pith of a small tree, *Aralia* (also *Fatsia*) *papyrifera*, grown in Taiwan.

Rich Site Summary. *See* RSS.

Rich Text Format (RTF). A format developed by Microsoft to enable computer files to be moved across networks and between different Applications and Platforms while retaining full formatting information.

Rider. An additional note appended to a text.

Rider slip. *See* Process slip.

Ridge. One of the two projections along the sides of a rounded and backed volume against which the board is fitted. Also called 'Flange' or 'Shoulder' (US). *See also* Binding edge.

RIDING. <riding.hostedbyfdi.net/riding/index.html> A Z39.50-based Gateway to the catalogues of academic libraries and selected public libraries in Yorkshire, Humberside and the North East (UK). Began as an eLib Clump project.

Right. The printer often needs to know which is the right side of a sheet of paper owing to differences in surface, and the undesirable effect of using sheets laid one way mixed with those laid another way in the publication. Flat papers are usually packed with the right side uppermost; if folded, the right side is outside. In handmade papers, the right side touches the wire cover of the mould; the 'wire' side is therefore known as the right side. In blue and azure papers the right side is usually darker than the other. In machine-made papers, it is the upper side which is the right side, i.e. the one on which the Couch roll acts and not the Wire. A Watermark , in both hand-made and machine-made paper is read from the right side. Thus, it can be taken that in hand-made papers, the 'wire' side is the right side, but the opposite is the case in machine-made papers.

Right reading. (*Reprography*) An image which is legible in a normal reading position as opposed to being a mirror image, i.e. Laterally reversed.

Rights. A generic term to describe the exclusive control which owners enjoy over works of creativity. They include copyright, database right, lending and rental, rights of performance and 'neighbouring' rights in sound recordings, films, and videos. They also include moral rights to protect the paternity and integrity of a work.

Rigid classification. 1. The classification of books referring to their positions on shelves rather than their subjects. Such methods of classification were used before the formation of modern schemes of bibliographical classification, and resulted in the allocation of numbers to books according to the shelf, in a given tier of a particular press, or alcove, in a specific room. Another form of rigid classification is the arrangement of books in broad subjects according to size and accession number. These were known as Fixed location systems. 2. The characterization of each document from a single point of view and thereby the allocation of only one classification symbol to it. When a document is shelved or stored, and only one copy is available, one single physical location must be provided: this is indicated by a symbol representing one point of view, usually the most important, or major, one. Sometimes called a 'Pigeonhole classification'. *See also* Multi-dimensional classification.

Ring fence. The procedure whereby funding for certain activities is protected, and may not be diverted to other uses. *Compare* Top slicing.

Ring network. A topology for a Local area network in which all devices are connected in a closed loop or ring. More suitable for long distances than Bus or Star networks.

RIP. 1. Rest in proportion; an instruction in reprography or printing to enlarge or reduce material by an agreed amount. 2. Raster image processor, a unit that, when attached to an Imagesetter, enables the processing of PostScript output, making the Imagesetter available to Desktop publishing systems.

RISC. Reduced Instruction Set Computer/Computing, a microprocessor designed with a simple instruction set to optimize performance and provide rapid computing.

Rising space. *See* Work up.

Rising type. Type which rises up in the forme, usually in the centre, when locked up too tightly. Spaces and quads rise and print due to poor justification or loose lock-up.

Risk management. The concept that control and governance of any organization in the private or public sector should anticipate possible disruption and formulate strategies to minimize potential damage. Threats include failure of systems, sabotage, terrorist activity, etc. The concept has similarities to Information management in that the processes of identification of risk, analysis, evaluation and monitoring require understanding of management models and an appreciation of the value of information and ways by which it flows.

RISM. <www.rism.org.uk/publications> Répertoire Internationale des Sources Musicales; published under the auspices of the International Musicological Society, and the International Association of Music Libraries. Aims to list all available bibliographies of musical works, writings about music and textbooks on music published up to 1800, with locations. Publication started in 1960 and eventually some 30 volumes are envisaged; several of the earlier volumes have now been revised. Series A(1) covers the printed music of single composers; series A(11) (available in electronic format) covers manuscripts; series B consists of catalogues of self-contained groups of material; series C is a multi-volume directory of music research libraries.

Ritblatt (John) Gallery.   Exhibition area at the British Library, London.

River.   What appears to be a streak of white running vertically or diagonally through printed matter. It is caused by spaces between words occurring almost one below the other in several lines of type. Rivers are avoided by re-setting the type and varying the spacing or placing a very short word on a line above or below.

RLG.   <www.rlg.org> (1200 Villa Street, Mountain View, CA 94041, USA) Research Libraries Group, Inc., a consortium of major universities and research institutions mainly in the United States. It was formed in 1974 by New York Public Library, and the Universities of Harvard, Yale and Columbia. Over 150 members collaborate in operating a set of ongoing programmes and developing new initiatives to enhance access to research information. RLG's programmes and technical resources focus on collecting, organizing, preserving, and providing information necessary to education and scholarship. *See also* RLIN.

RLG Conspectus.   *See* Conspectus.

RLIN.   <rlin21.rlg.org> Research Libraries Information Network; formed by RLG members in 1974 and originally an outgrowth of BALLOTS. RLIN is now used by libraries world-wide, and contains records for several million items held in over 200 of the world's leading research institutions, including bibliographic descriptions of monographs, serials, archival materials, musical scores, sound recordings, maps, photographs, films and computer files. Work is currently in progress to introduce a new infrastructure, known as RLIN21.

RLN.   *See* Research Libraries Network.

RMS.   *See* Records Management Society.

RNL.   *See* Russian National Library.

Roan.   A thin sheepskin used for binding books.

Roberts Report.   Popular name for the Report of the 'Roberts Committee' which was set up by the Minister of Education in September 1957 under the chairmanship of Sir Sydney Roberts, 'to consider the structure of the Public Library Service in England and Wales, and to advise what changes, if any, should be made in the administrative arrangements, regard being had to the relation of public libraries to other libraries'. The Report is entitled *The Structure of the Public Library Service in England and Wales*, 1959 (Cmnd. 660). This Report resulted in the setting up of working parties by the Minister of Education in 1961. *See also* Baker Report, Bourdillon Report.

Robinson Medal.   <www.cilip.org.uk> An award made by CILIP to recognize innovation in library administration suggested by para-professional staff.

Robot. Any program which follows hypertext links and accesses Web pages but is not directly under human control. Examples are Web crawlers, Harvesting programs which extract e-mail addresses and metadata from web pages, and intelligent web searching programs.

Roll. 1. A bookbinder's tool consisting of a brass wheel about 3 inches in diameter secured in a long handle which rests against the shoulder when being used. The edge of the wheel is engraved so as to impress a continuous line or repeating pattern as it revolves under pressure. Also called 'Fillet'. 2. The design impressed by the tool referred to. *See also* Scroll (3), Tooling.

Roll cassette. A light-proof container for roll film on a spool. Also called a 'Roll magazine'.

Roll microfilm. Micro-copies on roll film as distinct from those on sheet microfilm, as Microfiche.

Rolled edges. Edges of book covers decorated with a Roll, or Fillet.

Roller shelves. Deep shelves which rest on a series of rollers or ball bearings and are drawn out so that folio volumes such as bound volumes of newspapers can be lifted off instead of being dragged off with possible damage to the binding. Also a series of rollers placed horizontally behind one another and which support large books; they revolve on their spindles as the volumes are pushed on and off.

Rolling bookcase. A bookcase suspended from overhead tracks or running on rails let into the floor enabling cases to be placed very close together and moved to permit consultation of the books. *See also* Compact storage.

Rolling press. A hand press, for printing from incised or etched plates. Power is applied by passing the plate and paper, covered by thick blankets, between oak rollers held in a rigid frame. The upper roller which is turned by a capstan, carries the plate through the press.

Rom. 1. Abbreviation for Roman. 2. ROM Read-Only Memory, computer memory from which data can be retrieved, but which cannot be altered or up-dated. *See also* CD-ROM, RAM.

Romains du Roi. A series of roman and italic types made for use in the Royal Printing Office of Louis XIV in the Palace of the Louvre, Paris, between 1694 and 1745. They were based on drawings which accompanied a report made to Louis XIV, and are characterized by being condensed letters with thin, flat, unbracketed serifs. Designed by Philippe Grandjean, they were first used in 1742 for *Médailles sur la événements du règne de Louis-le-Grand*.

Roman. Ordinary type as distinct from italic, being vertical instead of sloping and having graduated thick and thin strokes and serifs. It is based on the Italian Humanistic or Neo-Caroline hand of the fifteenth century and was first used by Adolf Rusch in Strasbourg in 1464, and perfected by Johannes da Spira, a German who used roman type for the first book to be printed in Venice, in 1469, and by Nicholas Jenson, a Frenchman, also in Venice, 1470. The use of roman types was greatly expanded in Italy in the last quarter of the fifteenth century; they may be divided into three main groups, Venetian Type, Old Face and Modern Face. Written in full, or in its abbreviated form 'Rom', the word 'Roman' is used on printer's copy or on a proof to indicate that the matter is to be set up in roman, i.e. not italic type. *See also* Antiqua, Egyptian, Italic, Roman numerals, Transitional, Typeface.

Roman à clef. A novel in which one or more characters are based on real people but are given fictitious names.

Roman Index. *See* Index Librorum Prohibitorum.

Roman numerals. Capital letters which are used as numbers in books for chapter headings and for the designation of part numbers, appendixes, on title-pages for date of publication, etc., and in lower-case form for the pagination of preliminary pages. The roman capitals most commonly in use as numerals are:

1	5	10	50	100	500	1000
I	V	X	L	C	D	M

A complete sequence to 20 in capitals is: I, II, III, IV, V, VI, VII, VIII, IX, X, XI, XII, XIII, XIV, XV, XVI, XVII, XVIII, XIX, XX, and in tens from 30 to 100: XXX, XL, L, LX, LXX, LXXX, XC, C. The numerals from x to xx indicate the method of building numbers. Italic figures 1 to 20 are: *i, ii, iii, iv, v, vi, vii, viii, ix, x, xi, xii, xiii, xiv, xv, xvi, xvii, xviii, xix, xx.* Combinations of numbers are made up by addition and subtraction, e.g. XX = 20; XIX = 19; XXIV = 24; MCMLVII = 1957. Roman numerals were used by the earliest fifteenth-century printers because they had no arabic figures, and were normally used in early printed books. *See also* Chronogram.

Romanization. The representation of 'picture writing' characters, such as Chinese, Japanese and Korean in the Roman alphabet. *See also* Transliteration.

Romantic style. A bookbinding decoration with an informal, non-classical style in which fancy predominates.

ROMEO. <www.lboro.ac.uk/departments/ls/disresearch/romeo> Rights Metadata for Open Archiving, a project funded by JISC for one year to investigate the rights issues surrounding the Self archiving of research in the UK academic community. The project introduced four 'colours' for publishers, depending on their responses to self archiving: a white publisher does not formally support self archiving; a yellow publisher permits the archiving of a Pre-print; a blue publisher permits the archiving of the Post-print; and a green publisher permits self archiving of both pre-print and post-print. The project ended in July 2003 and the searchable database of publishers' responses is now managed and made available via the SHERPA project.

Ronde. An upright angular form of script type. Being based on French manuscript it has the appearance of upright handwriting.

Roquade. <www.roquade.nl> A project instigated in 1999 by Utrecht University Library, Delft University of Technology Library and the Netherlands Institute for Scientific Information Services to provide an alternative view of the traditional scientific journal and consider ways of moving towards electronic publishing. In particular, the project aimed to create an infrastructure that focuses on rapid publication by removing some of the delays introduced via traditional peer review. Continued as part of the FIGARO initiative.

Rotary camera. *See* Continuous flow camera.

Rotary card file. A filing cabinet in which cards are placed on their edges in a wheel- or drum-like container. The container revolves on an axle in the side of the drum in such a way that the cards are always on their edges, those in the lower half being prevented from falling out by a fixed retaining strap of webbing or other material. Another type consists of large round trays which revolve on a pivot, each tray being divided up so as to provide several rows of cards side by side.

Rotary gravure. *See* Rotogravure.

Rotary press. A style of press that prints from curved electrotype or stereotype plates held on a cylinder, the paper being fed from a continuous roll and passing between this cylinder and another one which makes the impression. It is used for printing newspapers, periodicals or large editions and occasionally for books of a large run. There are also 'sheet-fed rotary presses'. All printing presses are rotary in principle except the flat-bed press and the platen press which are largely used in letterpress work. Where printing is done from the original flat forme on an endless web of paper, this is called a 'flat-bed web press'. Also called a 'Web press' when the paper is fed from a continuous reel. *See also* Cylinder press, Flat-bed press, Platen press.

Rotated catalogue. A classified catalogue in which entries are made under each integral part of the classification symbol, instead of making an entry under the class number with merely references from headings or parts comprising the composite symbol. Also called 'Cyclic classified catalogue'.

Rotated entry. An entry in an index to documents, or a classified catalogue, where full information and not merely a reference is given under each heading.

Rotated indexing. The indexing of documents classified by a faceted classification whereby a full entry, and not a reference, is made under each heading representing, or being, a part of the classification symbol. Also called 'Cyclic indexing'.

Rotational indexing. The making of a Correlative index wherein each term is 'rotated' so as to file in the first position.

ROTNAC. *See* Round Table of National Centres for Library Services.

Rotogravure. 1. An intaglio or photogravure printing process for rotary presses, in which the impression is obtained from an etching made on a copper cylinder which is automatically inked as it revolves.   2. An illustration produced by this process.

Rotunda.   *See* Gothic type.

Rough.   Rag paper that has not been given a finish. *See also* Finish, Hot-pressed, Not.

Rough calf.   A calf skin prepared with a nap similar to suede leather; used for bookbinding from the seventeenth century.

Rough edges.   A widely used term to indicate paper with rough edges whether because they are Uncut or a result of the way the paper was made. *See also* Deckle edge.

Rough gilt edges.   A book which has been 'cut rough' and the edges gilded, or which has been cut solid and gilded before sewing so that when the book is later sewn the edges are slightly uneven. This method has been widely used by English binders, specially by non-trade binders who dislike the solid-block-of-metal appearance of solid gilding. *See also* Gilt on the rough, Marbling under gilt, Solid gilt.

Rough pull.   *See* Flat pull.

Roulette.   *See* Fillet.

Round back.   1. The back of a thin booklet of which the folded sheets have been inserted inside each other and wire-stitched, sewn, or corded to the cover from the centre.   2. A book which has been rounded during the binding process and so given the familiar round back. The opposite of 'Flat back'. *See also* Backing, Flat back, Rounding.

Round brackets.   *See* Parentheses.

Round letter.   *See* Antiqua.

Round table.   A group of members of an organization having a similar area of interest. Round tables are opportunities for informal meetings and discussions and are unlikely to be an administrative part of the parent body.

Round Table of National Centres for Library Services (ROTNAC).   An IFLA group, for co-operative organizations serving a range of libraries in individual countries and termed for this purpose 'National Centres'.

Round Table on Archives (CITRA).   The International Conference of the Round Table on Archives is an annual meeting of heads of national archives services, held under the auspices of the International Council on Archives.

Rounded corners.   In library bookbinding the sharp corners of the boards are sometimes cut and slightly rounded as a preventative against wear.

Roundel.   (*Binding*) A decoration consisting of a double ring, usually with a centre dot.

Rounding.   The bookbinding process which gives the book a convex spine – and consequently concave fore-edges. It is achieved by a forwarder hammering the spine of a book, after it has been sewn and had its first coat of glue, with a round-headed hammer while gripped between backing boards at the same time as the book is backed. This operation can be done by machine. In the UK and US books are backed (to provide joints) as well as rounded. In most European countries backing is seldom done, with the result that there are no joints. *See also* Backing, Flat back, Round back.

Roundlet. A small circle in gold used by bookbinders' finishers as part of a book's decoration.

Routeing. The systematic circulation of periodicals or other printed material among the staff of a library or organization in accordance with their interests in order to keep them informed of new developments. *Automatic routeing* is the sending of each issue as soon as it is received to a pre-arranged list of persons. *Selective routeing*, or *selective circulation*, is sending articles and publications selected on the basis of an individual's known interests, usually with an Attention note. *Circular routeing* (also called *uncontrolled circulation*) is the sending of a periodical to all who need it before it is returned to the library: this is achieved by sticking to the cover a slip with the names of persons and/or departments for rapid perusal; such slips may bear a space for the insertion of the date of onward transmission. *Radial routeing* (also called *controlled circulation*) ensures that the periodical is returned to the library by each reader before it is passed on, enabling the librarian to keep better control of loans. *See also* Routeing slip, Selective routeing.

Routeing slip. A slip pasted on to the cover of a periodical and bearing the names of the persons (possibly with space for dates of sending) to whom it is to be circulated. *See also* Attention note, Routeing.

Routes to Knowledge (RTK). The current strategic project of the (UK) Museums, Libraries and Archives Council (MLA). RTK is the follow-up phase to WILIP, and is being planned during 2004/2005 for action 2005 onwards. *See* WILIP.

Routine. A set of coded instructions used to direct a computer to perform a desired operation or sequence of operations; a sub-division of a Program.

Routine slip. *See* Process slip.

Routing. (*Printing*) Cutting away mechanically the non-printing areas of a half-tone or line block.

Roxburghe Binding. A book with plain black leather back, without raised bands, lettered in gold near the top within a border, having cloth or paper sides, and leaves gilt at top otherwise untrimmed. So named after the third Duke of Roxburghe (Scotland), a famous book collector who adopted this style for the books in his library.

Royal. A sheet of printing paper measuring 20 x 25 inches.

Royal Commission on Historical Manuscripts. *See* National Archives (UK).

Royal Library. The description used for several national libraries including Denmark, Sweden, Netherlands, Belgium.

Royalty. Payment made to an author by the publisher of a book, the basis being calculated as an agreed percentage of the retail price of the book, and paid in respect of every copy of the book sold.

R.P. Indicates that a book is not available from the publisher but is 'reprinting'. If R.P. is followed by a date as 'R.P. Jan.' it indicates when a reprint will be ready.

RPM. *See* Register of Preservation Microforms.

RPN. *See* Reverse Polish Notation.

RSI. *See* Repetitive strain injury.

RSL. *See* Russian State Library.

RSLG. *See* Research Support Libraries Group.

RSLP. *See* Research Support Libraries Programme.

RSS. <web.resource.org/rss/1.0/spec> RDF Site Summary, a lightweight multipurpose extensible metadata description and syndication format. RSS is an XML application, conforms to the W3C's RDF Specification, and is extensible via XML-namespace and/or RDF based modularization. Developed initially by Netscape but now widely used to exchange headline metadata between news content providers and portals, thereby delivering news headlines on the Web. Also known as Really Simple Syndication, Rich Site Summary.

RTF. *See* Rich Text Format.

RTK. *See* Routes to Knowledge.

RTSD. Resources and Technical Services Division (of the American Library Association). *See now* Association for Library Collections and Technical Services.

Rub. A representation of the back or sides of a book showing the lettering, bands, decoration, etc. It is done by firmly holding a piece of paper or tracing linen over the part of the binding of which an impression is to be made, and rubbing with a cobbler's heel-ball, lead pencil or soft crayon all over it until a recognizable copy of all details of the back or sides of the volume is obtained; often used as a master pattern in journal binding.

Rub off. Printing ink which has rubbed on to the fingers from a printed sheet which has not dried sufficiently.

Rubber back binding. A binding in which the folds of the sections are cut off and the spine dipped in rubber solution before insertion in the cover.

Rubbing. *See* Rub.

Rubric. 1. The heading of a chapter, section or other division of a book, and catchwords or marginal index words printed or written in red (the remainder of the text being in black), or otherwise distinguished in lettering, as a guide to the contents of pages. 2. A particular passage so marked.

Rubricated. A book in which rubrics have been used.

Rubrication. The carrying out of rubrics.

Rubrisher. One who carried out rubrication, or the plain painting of the large initial letters at the commencement of chapters of MSS. or early printed books, in red and blue. *See also* Rubric.

RUDI. <www.rudi.net> Resource for Urban Design Information; based at Oxford Brookes University, RUDI developed from a joint eLib research project with the University of Hertfordshire 1996–1998. Its success led to the formation of a limited company, RUDI Ltd, which started trading in March 2001.The new company offers a limited amount of high quality public domain information, but the bulk of its content is available only by subscription.

Rule. A strip of metal used to print lines; it is of type height of varying thickness (hair, fine, medium, 1½, 3, 4, 6, 12 point) with a face finished to a continuous line or lines. Rules which are placed at right angles to form frames or borders are said to be abutted or mitred according to whether the ends of the rules are square or mitred at an angle of 45°. A rule may also be designed to print dots or patterns. A Swelled rule is a line which is wide in the middle and tapers to a fine point at each end. *See also* Dotted rule, Double rule.

Rule border. (*Printing*) A frame, made up of rules, fitted around a page of type. Also called 'Rule frame'. *See also* Box.

Run. A machinist's term for a number of impressions taken from a forme, or plate, at one time. On completion, the job is said to be 'run-off'.

Run on. 1. A term, used in manuscripts and proof reading, to indicate to the printer that printed matter must be continuous and not broken up into paragraphs. This indication is marked by a line joining the end of one piece of matter to the beginning of the next and the writing of 'run on' in the margin. 2. To let a printing press continue to print sheets after the printing order has been completed. Sheets so printed 'run on cost' and involve little more than charges for paper and machine time.

Run out and indented. A style of typesetting where the first line is set to the full measure, and the second and subsequent lines of the paragraph are indented.

Run over. The continuation of matter on to another page.

Run-around. Variation of length of lines of type to fit around blocks.

Run-on card. A catalogue card which bears the continuation of an entry on the previous card. The heading is usually repeated on successive cards which are numbered 'Card 1', 'Card 2', etc. Also called 'Extension card'.

Run-on chapters. Chapters which do not start on a new page but run on at the end of the previous chapter. This is a style used in cheap bookwork.

Run-on style. In book indexes, the typographical style which allows the subheadings to be printed continuously (with their relative page references) instead of being arranged under one another, and indented, under the heading to which they relate. Called in the US 'Run-in style'. *See also* Indented style.

Run-up gilt book. In Extra binding, used to describe the running of gold lines by a fillet so that the gilt panel lines are not mitred at each band. *See also* Bands.

Runes. 1. The earliest Scandinavian and Anglo-Saxon alphabet. Some letter forms continued in use in English documents until the seventeenth century and even later. A notable example is the 'y' form th, which has given rise to the pseudo-archaic form 'ye' for 'the'. 2. The name given to the characters which were cut or carved on metal, stone or wood by the ancient Teutons, usually as memorial inscriptions, but also for divination and for messages, and for carving the name of the artist or for the owner of weapons or ornaments. Runic characters were used for secular documents; amongst the more important runic manuscripts are: the old Danish legal MS., *Codex Runicus* (end 13th century), *Fasti Danici* (*c.* 1348), *Codex Leidensis* at Leyden, the *Codex Sangallensis* (878) at St. Gallen, and the *Codex Salisburgensis* (140). The Runic alphabet is also known as 'Futhark', from the sequence of its first seven letters.

Runners. Figures or letters printed for reference purposes at regular intervals down the margins of a book and against lines of type to indicate the particular number or position of any given line. This is usually done in long poems or in school texts of plays or of texts in foreign languages.

Running headline (Running head). *See* Running title.

Running number. One, such as an accession number, which is given from a consecutive sequence to a book or other object.

Running title. The title that runs through a book or section of a book, repeated at the head of each page or at the top of the left-hand pages, with the chapter heading or the subject contents of both open pages on the right-hand page. Also called a 'Running head'. *See also* Drop-down title, Headline, Page headline, Section headline.

RUSA. *See* Reference and User Services Association (of the American Library Association).

Russia. A variety of calf leather used for bookbinding. It is specially tanned, and finished with birch oil which gives it a characteristic spicy odour. 'American Russia' is cowhide.

Russian Information Library Consortium (RICL). <www.ribk.ru> A consortium of the five largest libraries in Russia with the National Library of Scotland; the consortium will create a joint virtual catalogue of the five libraries and encourage exchange of experience and best practice. The consortium is funded by the European Union under its Tacis Institution Building Partnership Programme to support the development of non-profit organizations in the former Soviet Union <europa.eu.int/comm/europeaid/projects>.

Russian library associations. The Russian Federation has a number of library associations, but the most important is the Russian Library Association <www.rba.ru> (18 Sadovaya Street, 191 069 St. Petersburg, Russia) which was founded in 1994 by the merger of a number of smaller rivals. There are over 30 regional and national organizations involved, and the Association has 31 sections, round tables and committees.

Russian National Library (RNL). <www.nlr.ru> (18 Sadovaya Street, 191 069 St. Petersburg, Russia). Formerly the Saltykov-Shchedrin Public

Library, RNL is one of the world's largest libraries; it has especially rich collections of incunabula. Current work features co-operative developments with the Mayakovsky Central City Library on the creation of a St Petersburg database.

Russian National Public Library for Science and Technology. <www.gpntb.ru> (12 Kuznetsky Most, 103919 Moscow, Russia) The major scientific and technical library in Russia with the state repository of science publications, the union catalogue of scientific and technical literature, and a role in research, international information provision, and a centre for online facilities. Stock of over 8 million books and periodicals; there are 14 reading rooms in the main building and 8 Moscow branches.

Russian State Library (RSL). <www.nlr.ru> (3/5 Vozdvizhenka, 101000 Moscow, Russia) Dating in part from 1795 and including the private collection of Count N. P. Rumiantsev, the library was organized in 1862 into the first free public library in Moscow. It was named the Lenin Library in 1924 and functioned as the national library of the USSR until 1991. In 1992 it was reorganized on the basis of a Presidential decree as the Russian State Library. Several programmes are in progress to provide electronic access to manuscript, rare book, theses, and newspaper collections. The stock totals over 32 million items.

Rustic capital. 1. An upper case letter with a design engraved on the face, or an ornamentally designed letter. 2. The form of roman capital letters used by early scribes as a book hand between the second and sixth centuries A.D. The letters were less formal and not so heavy as the Quadrata or Square capitals from which they were derived, giving a thinner, and more condensed appearance to the page. Also called 'Scriptura actuaria'.

Rustica. A freely-written, rather elegant fourth- and fifth-century writing used in Roman manuscripts. This style seems to have been influenced by Greek artistry and craftsmanship; it was displaced as a manuscript letter by the Uncial, but used as initials or for emphasis in the line, in the same way that italics or small capitals are used by modern printers, in manuscripts until the eleventh century.

Ruthven Press. An iron printing press, patented in 1813 by John Ruthven, an Edinburgh printer. In this, the bed which carried the type remained stationary while the platen was moved over it on a wheeled carriage. Springs kept the platen raised until the moment of impression, when power was applied through a series of levers which were worked by depressing a bar at the side of the press.

Rutland. Trade name for a fine-quality sheepskin used for bookbinding.

Ruttier. *See* Portolan chart.

Rylands (John) Library, Manchester. *See* John Rylands University Library of Manchester.

s.a. Abbreviation for *see also*.

SAA. *See* Society of American Archivists.

SAB. Sveriges Allmänna Biblioteksförening. *See* Swedish Library Association.

SABINET. <www.sabinet.co.za> Established in 1983 as a not-for-profit organization dedicated to improving the information infrastructure of South Africa; became an OCLC international distributor in 1995. In 1997 a replacement organisation – SABINET Online – took over the operational activities. SACat, South Africa's union catalogue, resides on the SABINET Online system and contains some 3 million records. In 1998 links with OCLC were further enhanced.

SACO. Subject Authority Co-operative Program. *See* PCC.

Sacred work. A basic writing of a religion, such as the *Bible, Koran, Talmud, Upanishads* which is generally accepted as such by those who follow that religion. In classification, it is often treated as if it were a class or a subject.

Saddle stitching. Binding a pamphlet by placing it on the saddle-shaped support of a stitching machine where it is automatically stitched with wire or thread through the centre of the fold. *See also* Flat stitching, Side-stitch.

Safari. <ltssolweb1.open.ac.uk/safari/signpostframe.htm> Skills in Accessing, Finding, and Reviewing Information, a generic Web-based resource from the Open University (UK) designed to be used by students to meet a broad range of Information skills outcomes.

SAILIS. South African Institute for Librarianship and Information Science. *See* Library and Information Association of South Africa (LIASA).

SAILS. <sails.lms.kent.edu> Standardized Assessment of Information Literacy Skills, a project developed at Kent State University (US) to create a tool to measure Information literacy and assess its impact on student learning. The aim is the development of a tool that is standardized, easily administered, valid, and reliable. The three-year grant involves testing at a range of institutions, building to the projected participation of 100 libraries in 2004/2005.

Sakai. <www.sakaiproject.org> A community source software development project founded by the University of Michigan, Indiana University, MIT, Stanford, the uPortal Consortium, and the Open Knowledge Initiative with support from the Mellon Foundation to produce open source collaboration and learning environment software with the first release in July 2004. An Educational Partners' Program extends the project to other academic institutions around the world.

SALALM. <www.library.cornell.edu/colldev/salalmhome> Seminars on the Acquisition of Latin American Library Materials. The first Seminar was held in 1956 'to consider the problems involved in finding, buying and controlling library materials relating to Latin America'. A seminar has been held each year since (Ann Arbor, Michigan, 2004). *See also* LACAP.

Salami slicing. The custom of publishing the results of research in small pieces with the aim of increasing the number of publications attributable to the authors and gaining greater coverage for the work.

Salle. A well-lit room in a paper-mill where the paper is examined sheet by sheet, sorted, counted and arranged in reams. Also called 'Finishing house' or 'Finishing room' in a machine paper mill.

SALSER. <edina.ed.ac.uk/salser> Scottish Academic Libraries Serials, a World Wide Web-based virtual union catalogue of the serials holdings of research and university libraries in Scotland, including the National Library of Scotland. Hosted by EDINA.

Sample pages. Selected pages of a proposed book, set by the printer as a specimen and model for the whole book.

Sampleback. A strip of leather, cloth or other material made up to represent the back of a book and used as a sample for matching colour, material, lettering, etc.

SAN. <www.isbn.org/standards> or <www.niso.org/standards/resources/Z39.43> Standard address number; a set of unique codes for every UK publisher and library supplier. The scheme was pioneered by the Publishers Association, developed by Whitakers, and is now operated by Book Industry Communication. Z39.43 is the US equivalent (*See* Z39).

Sanding. Rubbing down the edges of a book with sand-paper, or a sand-wheel machine, so as to remove as small an amount of paper as possible.

Sans serif. A type without Serifs. The best known is 'Gill Sans' designed by Eric Gill; other well-known sans serif types are Futura and Vogue. The first sans serif type, designed by William Caslon, was named Egyptian; it was afterwards re-named Sanserif.

SARBICA. South-East Asian Regional Branch of the International Council on Archives; it was inaugurated in Kuala Lumpur in July 1968 as the first branch of the International Council on Archives.

Sarum use. In the fifteenth century, certain Parisian presses specialized in books of Hours of the Virgin (the layman's prayer book) which were similar in format but differed slightly according to the locality in which they were to be used. To prevent the printer and binder mixing the various editions, abbreviations such as *Sar* for *secundum usum Sarum* or *Par* for *secundum usum ecclesiae Parisiensis* were placed after the signature letter. The version used mostly in England, particularly in the southern part, and in Scotland, was that of Salisbury or 'Sarum', the York use being confined to the north. Their use was discontinued after the Reformation. Sarum books were largely produced in Paris and Rouen.

SATIS. Socially Appropriate Technology Information System. A clearinghouse for information and referral in the fields of alternative and appropriate technology. Set up in 1982 by 25 organizations mainly from the non-government sector. There are now 300 organizations in membership; a user survey was carried out in 2003 – the results can be seen at <web/idrc.ca/en/ev-37609-201-1-DO_TOPIC>.

Saunders Report. *Towards a unified professional organization for library and information science and services*; prepared by Professor Wilfred Saunders and published by the (UK) Library Association in 1989. The report urges the merger of the Library Association, Aslib and the Institute of Information Scientists. It was received positively by all the bodies concerned but the proposal did not come to fruition at this time. *See* CILIP.

Sawcuts. Grooves made in the back of a book with a saw to take the cords used in sewing.

Sawing-in. Sawing grooves in the back of a book for the reception of the cord in sewing.

Sayers Memorial Prize (UK). This Prize takes the form of professional books, and was created from the royalties of the *Sayers memorial volume*, and donated by the editors D. J. Foskett and B. I. Palmer. The volume was produced as a tribute to the late W. C. Berwick Sayers, Chief Librarian of the Croydon Public Libraries for many years, a former President of the Library Association, and particularly noted for his teaching and writing on classification.

SBN. 1. *See* Standard Book Number. 2. <opac.sbn.it> National Library Service (Servizio Bibliotecario Nazionale), the network of national services including 800 Italian state, regional, and university libraries contributing to the creation of the online national union catalogue run by ICCU. SBN is a network which aims to provide services to end-users.

s.c. Abbreviation for (1) small capitals; (2) super-calendered paper.

sc. Abbreviation for *scilicet* (Lat. 'namely').

Scale. The ratio of the distance on an architectural drawing, map, globe, model or vertical section, to the actual distances they represent.

Scaling. The process of calculating the area by which an illustration block must be altered to fit a given layout.

Scan. 1. To examine every reference or every entry in a file routinely as part of a retrieval scheme. To examine periodicals and other materials to determine the usefulness of the information contained to the library's users, especially to the interests and work of individuals served by a special library. 2. SCAN <www.scan.org.uk> Scottish Archive Network Project; an electronic network to link every Scottish archive and make archival heritage accessible to all over the Internet. The project received funding late in 1998 from the Heritage Lottery Fund. 3. To digitize an image or a text file by using a scanner. *See* Scanner.

Scan plates. A generic term for plates made by an electronic photo-engraving machine.

Scanner. A computer Peripheral that can convert images on paper – or any object that can be placed flat on its platten – into digital form for use in, or manipulation by, a computer. Colour scanners are now cheap enough to be purchased by libraries with internal publishing programmes. They produce acceptable output for both line art and photographs where high-end, high-cost, Drum scanners are unaffordable or unavailable. Coupled with Optical character recognition software, scanners can be used to produce Machine-readable text for utilization in word processors.

SCANUL-ECS. *See* SCECSAL.

Scatter. The separation of entries in an index for the same topic or concept caused by entry under both singular and plural forms, or variant forms of name, or entry in one instance under a broad heading and in another under a specific heading, or by the imprecise use of terms, or by lack of control of synonymy. *See also* Bibliographical scatter.

Scattering. *See* Law of Scattering.

SCECSAL. <www.scecsal.org.za> Standing Conference of Eastern, Central and Southern African Libraries. The organization was formerly known as the Standing Conference of African National and University Libraries – Eastern, Central and Southern (SCANUL-ECS) and dates from 1964. It promotes contact and co-operation between academic libraries in the region.

SCENAA. <www.scenaa.net> The Standing Committee of European National Audiovisual Archives; an initiative of Swedish and UK institutions (including the British Library). The network now has 13 institutional partners; it lobbies on heritage issues, promotes collaboration, co-operation, preservation, and standards for access.

Scenario. 1. The outline of a film plot. 2. Any abbreviated presentation of the personages, plot, and outline of a dramatic work, such as a play, dramatic oratorio, cantata or opera. In cataloguing music, the term is also used for a ballet plot, directions for a dance composition, etc.

Schedule. 1. A statement of the sub-divisions of a classification along with their class number as set out on paper so as to show hierarchical and other logical relationships. *See also* Summum Genus. 2. A series of serial classifications, arranged in one series of co-ordinate classes, with sub-classes, if there are any, arranged in secondary series, or columns, indented to show the subordination. These secondary series may be sub-divided successively, resulting in tertiary and quaternary series. These forms are equivalent to Tabular classification of three or more dimensions. 3. In information retrieval, any list of terms used in constructing a file. *See also* File (3). 4. An appendix to an Act of Parliament or other document; an annex or supplement. 5. (*Archives*) A document attached to another document, especially in amplification. 6. (*Records management*) A list of classes of records, allocating to each a life span and a disposal instruction, formally adopted or authorized by an organization. *See also* Destruction schedule.

Scheduled mnemonics. *See* Mnemonics.

Scheme. *See* Bill of type.

Scheme of classification. The schedules, index, and apparatus of a classification; the complete classification tables.

Scholarly journal. *See* Learned journal.

Scholarly publishing. Those activities of the publishing industry whose products are targeted at an academic or research-based readership.

Scholarly Publishing and Academic Resources Coalition. *See* SPARC.

Scholars Portal. <www.arl.org/access/scholarsportal> A Portal that integrates end-user searching of diverse resources, launched in May 2002 and developed by a consortium of seven Association of Research Libraries members working with a commercial vendor. The project seeks to provide software tools for an academic community to have a single point of access on the Web, to find high-quality information resources, and to deliver the information and related services directly to the user's desktop.

Scholium. (*Pl.* Scholia) An explanatory marginal note or comment, or interpretative remark, especially an annotation on a classical text by an ancient grammarian.

School district library. A free public library established and financially supported by action of a school district for the use of residents of the district. Such a library is supervised by a local board of education or by a separate library board appointed by a board of education (US).

School edition. An edition of a book especially prepared for use in school.

School librarian. A professionally qualified librarian employed to organize and operate a library within a school. *See also* Teacher-librarian.

School libraries department. A section of a public library service, or local education service, which administers a system of school libraries. Also called Education library service/department.

School Libraries Group. A membership group of CILIP, formed in 1980 to unite and represent members interested in librarianship in schools, to develop the role of the qualified librarian in schools, and emphasize the contribution made to education by the school library or resource centre.

School library. An organized collection placed in a school for the use of teachers or pupils, but usually for pupils. It may comprise books and other materials, electronic resources and PCs, and be in the care of a professional librarian, teacher, or teacher-librarian. Variously called *Instructional materials center, Learning resources centre*, *Media centre*.

School Library Association (SLA). <www.sla.org.uk> (Unit 2, Lotmead Business Village, Lotmead Farm, Wanbrough, Swindon SN4 0UY, UK) Formally constituted in 1937, strengthened in 1945 by the adhesion of the former School Libraries Section of the Library Association, and incorporated in 1955. This Association aims to promote development of the school library as an instrument of education in schools of all kinds; to encourage efficient methods of administration and routine; and to provide opportunities for interchange of experience among school librarians and others interested in the aims of the Association. *See also* International Association of School Librarianship.

School library supervisor. The US term for a librarian who supervises and co-ordinates the work of several other school librarians. The American

Association of School Librarians recommends one for every system having five or more schools. Duties and responsibilities vary but usually include: consulting with school administrators, providing leadership, guidance and knowledge in school librarianship to stimulate improvement in the service. Also called 'Adviser', 'Consultant', 'Co-ordinator', 'Director', 'District-librarian', 'Head Librarian', 'Specialist'.

School of Librarianship. *Synonymous with* Library School.

Schrotblatt. *See Manière Criblée.*

Schwabacher. 1. An early variety of Gothic type used in Germany. 2. A type used in Germany today, based on early Gothic designs.

Schweizerische Landesbibliothek. <www.snl.ch> (Hallwylstr. 15, 3003 Berne, Switzerland). The national library of Switzerland, founded in 1895.

Schweizerische Vereinigung für Dokumentation. The Association Suisse de Documentation. *See* ASD.

Science fiction. Imaginative fiction describing life and adventure in the future, life on other worlds, interplanetary travel, etc. It usually has a scientific or prophetic background.

Science Fiction Foundation Collection. <www.liv.ac.uk/~asawyer/sffhome> The Collection is the largest resource of science fiction material in Europe, and one of the most important outside the USA; it was established as the research library of the Science Fiction Foundation, created in 1970 by George Hay with Arthur C. Clarke and Ursula LeGuin as patrons. It is housed in the Special Collections Department in the Sydney Jones Library at the University of Liverpool, UK and holds some 25,000 books and magazines with a large stock of critical works.

Science Reference and Information Service (SRIS). Former name of a specialized service at the British Library.

Science-Technology Division. A division of the (US) Special Libraries Association. Often abbreviated Sci-Tech.

Scientific and Technical Information Centre of Russia (VNTIC). <www.vntic. org.ru> (14 Smolnaya Street, Moscow, 125493 Russia) The Centre is a federal information institution responsible for the maintenance of the complete All-Russia (before 1991 All-Union) fund for scientific research and development reports, projects, and dissertations. For all state-funded research, documents must be presented to VNTIC for incorporation in its databases.

Scientific Publications: Free for all? *See* House of Commons Science and Technology Committee.

SCIP. <www.scip.org> Society of Competitive Intelligence Professionals; founded in 1986, the Society has a membership of over 5,000 professionals from companies and consulting firms in the USA and 63 other countries. There are 75 chapters around the world. Members are involved in the ethical gathering of information and its analysis in the competitive environment. In 2003 SCIP and AIIP announced that they would form a strategic alliance.

SCL. *See* 1. Scottish Central Library.   2. Society of Chief Librarians.

SCOBI. Standing Committee on Business Information; a part of the Information Services Group of CILIP. Formed in 1972 the Committee is concerned with the provision of commercial and business resources in libraries.

Scoggin Memorial Collections. From 1970, notable books of the year for children and young adults are selected by the Association for Library Service to Children (American Library Association) and formed into collections. They were begun by the Children's Book Council, of New York City, to honour Margaret Scoggin, an authority on books for the young. They are a project of the US Section of the International Board on Books for Young People and are presented each year to repositories in parts of the world where publishing either does not exist or is not fully developed; one collection also is given to the International Youth Library in Munich.

SCOLE. *See* Standing Committee on Library Education.

SCOLMA. <www.lse.ac.uk/library/scolma> Standing Conference on Library Materials on Africa. This organization was set up at a meeting held in Chatham House in 1962. Its aims are: to facilitate the acquisition and preservation of library materials needed for African studies; to assist in the recording and use of such materials; to sponsor the publication of bibliographies and the organization of conferences.

SCONUL (UK). <www.sconul.ac.uk> (102 Euston Street, London NW1 2HA, UK) The Standing Conference of National and University Libraries was founded in 1950 to represent the interests of the libraries of member institutions by providing a forum for the exchange of information and the marshalling of collaborative effort. The Standing Conference, in promoting the aims of national and university libraries, also represents their interests to government, official and semi-official bodies as the need arises. The Conference holds plenary meetings twice yearly at which each member institution is represented by its chief library officer. There are a number of Advisory Committees. In 1993 the Council of Polytechnic Librarians (COPOL) was merged into SCONUL. *See also* Seven Pillars.

SCONUL Library Design Awards. An irregular series of awards for UK universities made to recognize outstanding new or remodelled buildings that put user needs first. The most recent awards were made in 2002.

SCOOP. <nurcombe@cix.co.uk> (42 Moors Lane, Darnhall, Winsford CW7 1JX, UK) Standing Committee on Official Publications. Took over the functions of the (UK) Library Association/HMSO Services Working Party in January 1983; working groups were formed to examine certain topics, and SCOOP keeps the profession aware of work and developments in British official publishing. Electronic developments are especially monitored, and government websites are evaluated. The Committee is a part of the Information Services Group of CILIP.

Scope note. 1. In information retrieval, a statement giving the range of meaning and scope of a subject heading or descriptor and usually referring to related or overlapping headings. 2. In co-ordinate indexing, a symbol appended to a term or term number to narrow the definition of the term rather than designate the role of a word in its context.

Score. A printed or written version of a musical work in notational form which shows the parts for the participating voices or instruments on two or more staves ('staffs' in the US), one above the other. The term is not usually applied to music for one performer. A *Full score* shows the music for each participating voice or instrument on separate staves one above the other, with the music for each solo voice, each choral part and each instrument being set out on a separate stave one above another. A *Miniature score* has the same music as a full score but is reduced considerably in size by photographic reproduction. Miniature scores are usually so described on the title-page, but if not, can be considered to be such if the music is smaller than normal and the page size is not more than 20 cms. An *Orchestral score* is the full score of an orchestral work. A *Piano score* is an orchestral or vocal work reduced to a piano version. A *Piano-conductor score* (violin-conductor score, etc.) is a piano (or violin, etc.) part in a concerted work, with cues to indicate when vocal or instrumental performers 'come in', i.e. begin to perform. The pianist (or violinist, etc.) performs and conducts at the same time. A *Vocal score* shows the music for voices on separate staves but the orchestral parts reduced to a piano version. This is the common version for members of choirs, of the music of cantatas, operas, and oratorios. Also called 'Piano-vocal score'. A *Close score* has the music for more than one part or instrument on one stave. Also called 'Compressed score', 'Short score'. An *Open score* has the music for each voice or part on a separate stave, each being placed above one another, as in a full score. Also called 'Extended score'. A *Small full score* is a photographic reduction of a *Full score*. *Pocket score* is synonymous with *Miniature score*. A *Study score* is musically identical with a *Full score*. A *Part* shows the individual instrumental or vocal lines and states the nature of the part, e.g. Chorus part, Tenor part, Violin part. A *Short score* is one showing all the parts on the smallest possible number of staves; also called a 'Compressed full score'. A *Full music edition* is a fully harmonized version of a vocal work, especially a collection of hymns or of songs. A *Melody edition* is the melody line only of a vocal work; it is used mainly of collections of songs and hymns. A *Chorus score* is one showing all the chorus parts, with the accompaniment, if any, arranged for keyboard. *See also* Realization, Reduction. A *Rehearsal score* is a compressed version of a full score, in many respects similar to a 'Short score' but with sufficient cues to be of practical use at rehearsals. An

Organ-vocal score is a score of a work for chorus and/or solo voices and organ, the accompaniment being a reduction of the music originally composed for an instrumental ensemble. A *Piano-vocal score* is a similar work to an organ-vocal score, but for piano instead of organ. *See also* Transcription (2).

Scoring. Compressing the fibres of heavy paper along a line, to facilitate either folding or tearing. Scoring with a dull rule increases folding endurance. The use of a sharp rule however partially breaks the paper fibres and has a similar effect to perforating.

SCORM. <www.adlnet.org> Shareable Content Object Reference Model, a collection of specifications adapted from multiple sources to provide a comprehensive suite of e-learning capabilities that enable Interoperability, accessibility and reusability of Web-based learning content; a product of the US Government's initiative in Advanced Distributed Learning. Previously known as Shareable Courseware Object Reference Model. *See also* IMS (1), Learning object, Learning Object Metadata.

Scottish Archive Network. *See* SCAN.

Scottish Book Trust. <www.scottishbooktrust.com> (Sandeman House, Trunk's Close, 55 High Street, Edinburgh EH1 1SR, UK) Formed 1997 after the transfer to the new organization of initiatives and resources developed by the Scottish branch of the Book Trust. Maintains a library of the previous year's UK books published for children; publishes a newsletter, *Shelf Life*.

Scottish Central Library (SCL). Now incorporated in the National Library of Scotland, it was the Scottish counterpart to the National Central Library; formed in 1952. It was founded in Dunfermline in 1921 as the Scottish Central Library for Students. As from 1953 it absorbed the Regional Library Bureau of Scotland (founded in 1945) and became responsible for the Scottish Union Catalogue from the same date. In 1974 this Library was incorporated within the National Library of Scotland, becoming the NLS Lending Services (NLSLS).

Scottish Cultural Resources Access Network. *See* SCRAN.

Scottish Libraries Across the Internet. *See* SLAINTE.

Scottish Library and Information Council. *See* SLIC.

Scottish Library Association. *See* CILIPS.

Scottish Poetry Library. <www.spl.org.uk> (5 Crichton's Close, Canongate, Edinburgh EH8 8DT, UK) An independent and free public lending and reference library for poetry. The Library was founded in 1984, and in 2000 moved into an award-winning new building.

Scottish Record Office. *See* National Archives for Scotland.

Scottish Science Information Service. <www.nls.uk/collections/sciencetech> (Causewayside Building, 33 Salibury Place, Edinburgh EH9 1SL, UK) A part of the National Library of Scotland; opened in new premises in 1989 to act as a national library and information resource for the scientific and technical community, with particular emphasis on those researchers working in industry and commerce. Incorporates the Scottish Business Information Service.

Scottish style. An eighteenth-century style of book decoration resembling the Harleian Style, but which has for a centre-piece a straight stem from which short sprays branch at regular intervals on either side, or else consists mainly of a large wheel pattern.

Scottish University Special Collections and Archives Group. *See* SUSCAG.

Scout Reports. *See NSDL Scout Reports.*

SCRAN. <www.scran.ac.uk> The Scottish Cultural Resources Access Network is a project funded by the Millennium Commission to build a networked multimedia resource base for the study, teaching and appreciation of history and material culture in Scotland. There are currently over 1 million resources available, including 300,000 images, movies and sound files. All this material is copyright-cleared and available to licensed users at home, in schools, colleges and universities. CILIP members can have access at low cost.

Scraperboard. 1. A method of drawing for reproduction. It utilizes a 'board' coated with a chalk surface and covered with a black wash which the artist scrapes away to reveal the white lines and areas of his drawing. Black lines may be drawn in afterwards if desired. 2. A drawing made by this method. It is similar in appearance to a wood engraving.

Scratchboard. US term for paper coated with black ink which is scratched away to show the white paper underneath. The picture drawing so produced. A scraperboard.

Screamer. The printer's term for exclamation marks used for display purposes.

Screen. 1. A grid of opaque lines cut in glass (used in making half-tone blocks) crossing at right angles, and producing transparent square apertures between the intersections which split up the image into dots; these dots are distinctive of the half-tone process. The number of lines to the inch varies from forty for a coarse screen for use with rough or poor quality paper to 250 for a fine screen for use with art paper. *See also* Half-tone. 2. (*Reprography*) A surface of any material on to which, or if translucent, through which, an image is projected. 3. A computer monitor or Visual display unit (VDU).

Screen saver. Software Utility that automatically loads after a pre-determined period of inactivity on the computer monitor. The intention is to prevent 'burn-in', a ghost image caused by the destruction of screen phosphor when the screen has been left on for an extended period of no-use. A popular and cheap utility with many variations that enable user customization.

Screw press. A press used by bookbinders to flatten paper or books in process of binding, especially after pasting or glueing. It is operated by turning a wheel or lever attached to the upper end of a large-dimension screw placed perpendicularly which has at its lower end a heavy iron plate below which, and on the bed of the press, are placed the papers or books to be pressed. *See also* Press (3).

Scrim. *See* Mull.

Scrinium. A cylinder-shaped container with movable lid used by the Romans to hold a number of scrolls.

Script. 1. A form of printer's cursive type resembling handwriting. 2. Any typeface which is cut to resemble handwriting. 3. Handwriting, as opposed to printed characters. 4. A typescript, specially of a play, film scenario, or text of spoken matter for broadcasting.

Script writing. *See* Disjoined hand.

Scriptores. Writers who copied books by hand in Roman times.

Scriptorium. The room in a mediaeval monastery or abbey which was set aside for the copying of manuscripts, and for writing and studying generally.

Scriptura actuaria. *See* Rustic capital.

Scroll. 1. Movement of the display in a Window on a VDU to view other parts of a document. 2. A roll of paper or parchment, usually containing writing and rolled onto rollers. This was an early form of manuscript, called by the Romans *volumen* (roll) from which the word *volume* is derived. The scroll (or 'roll') comprised a number of sheets of papyrus or parchment glued together to form a 20- or 30-feet long strip which was wound on a cylinder with projecting ornaments or knobs in ivory or colours, and was finished with a coloured parchment cover, fastened with laces and identified with a 'sittybus', or title label. The text was written in rather narrow columns on the recto of the material, where, if papyrus, the fibres run horizontally. 3. (*Binding*) A scroll-shaped stamp used for bearing an inscription, or an ornament of similar shape, and generally used between Flowers on a roll.

SCSI. Small Computer Systems Interface, an out-dated high-speed Parallel interface for connecting Peripherals such as hard disks and scanners to PCs. Pronounced 'scuzzy'. Superceded by Firewire and USB.

sculpt. Abbreviation for *sculpsit* (Lat.). Indicates on an engraving the name of the engraver, and on sculpture the name of the sculptor. *See also del.*, *fecit*.

Scumming. A fault in the lithographic process usually caused by plate wear, in which the water-accepting layer becomes inefficient.

SCURL. <scurl.ac.uk> Scottish Confederation of University and Research Libraries, a body comprising the chief librarians of the thirteen Scottish Universities, Edinburgh and Glasgow public libraries and the National Library of Scotland.

Scuzzy. *See* SCSI.

SD Classification. The scheme of classification, used by the US government's Superintendent of Documents who is responsible for the centralized control and distribution of US government documents. It is not a systematic scheme in that there is no visible subject relationship between the various parts. The notation consists of a combination of letters and numbers.

SDI. Selective dissemination of information; a system, usually automated, whereby literature items are matched against the interest profiles of individual or corporate users of an information service and relevant documents or abstracts are supplied to the user immediately. *See also* Current awareness.

SDSL. Symmetric Digital Subscriber Line, telecommunication services that offer the same Broadband speed for uploading and for downloading information, in contrast to ADSL. SDSL services are designed to be particularly suited to organizations that regularly need to send and receive large amounts of data.

Seal print. A woodcut with blind embossing around the picture, the embossing being done after the printing. Practised in the fifteenth century. Also called 'Gypsographic print'.

Sealskin. Binding leather made from the skin of the seal; it has a coarse grain, but is soft to the touch. *See also* Pin seal.

Seamless UK. <www.seamless-uk.info> A consortium of 9 UK local authorities and 14 national information providers (led by Essex County Council), funded by the New Opportunities Fund; the consortium developed a national citizens' gateway to local and national information sources. Out of this has come a community information thesaurus of 2,300 terms.

Search and retrieve. *See* SR.

Search engine. Software produced by any publisher or data provider to enable detailed access – via, for example, author, title, keyword – to their information, usually held in a database. On the World Wide Web, third party search engines are based on Web crawlers that traverse the Web following links between pages and copying relevant information to create a database which is then indexed to form searchable keywords.

Search record. A record which shows the publications, organizations, and individuals consulted in answering an enquiry or obtaining information.

Search room. 1. A room associated with an archives or record centre in which people may carry out their searches in the documents. 2. A room in which volumes of indexes to periodicals, volumes of abstracts, and similar bibliographical and search tools are provided for users to conduct literature searches. *See also* Archives.

Search statement. An individual search consisting of one search term or several terms linked.

Search strategy. The plan adopted for answering a particular enquiry, or more specifically, the search statements used to answer an enquiry.

Search term. A word or phrase input by the user to find those records on the database that contain that term.

Searching. The act of checking a book against the catalogue to determine whether it is a duplicate, another edition of a book already in stock, or a new title (to be) added to the library. The term is also applied to the discovery of material in electronic resources. *See also* Literature search, Online information retrieval.

SECAM.   Système Electronique Couleur Avec Memoire. The colour television standard used in France and the countries of the former Soviet Union. Similarly, the videotape standard used by these nations. *See also* PAL, NTSC.

Second half-title.   A repetition of the title of a book between the preliminaries and the text.

Second lining.   A strip of brown paper the full size of the back of a book which is glued into position after the First lining has been affixed.

Secondary access.   (*Information retrieval*) Access from one entry to related entries in a File. *See also* Primary access.

Secondary bibliography.   1. An 'intensive' or special bibliography dealing with books and other materials relating to one subject for the compilation of which primary bibliographies have been used.   2. A bibliography in which material is rearranged for convenience of research (US). *See also* Bibliography, Primary bibliography.

Secondary entry.   An entry in a catalogue other than the Main entry; an Added entry. *See also* General secondary.

Secondary publication.   1. A document such as an abstract, digest, index to periodicals, current awareness journal, or popularization, which is prepared in order to disseminate more widely information which has already appeared in another form, particularly in a Primary publication.   2. The act of publishing such material.

Secondary service.   *See* Abstracting service.

Secondary sources.   Books or unpublished literary material in the compilation of which Primary sources have been used.

Secondary title.   An addition to the main title of a serial to distinguish an independent section.

Second-hand book.   One which has previously been owned by another person. A bookseller who deals in such books is called a 'Second-hand bookseller'.

Secret literature.   *See* Clandestine literature.

Secret press.   *See* Clandestine press.

Section.   1. The unit of paper which is printed, folded and sewn and which, together with other sections, goes to make up a printed book. It usually consists of one sheet of paper, but may be one and a half or two sheets, or even one sheet and an extra leaf pasted in. Also called 'Signature', 'Gathering', 'Quire', 'Stave'. Each section of a book bears a different Signature. *See also* Foldings.   2. All the shelves arranged between two uprights. *See* Tier.   3. A sub-division of an administrative unit or department of a library, e.g. 'Processing section'. Sometimes called a 'Division' or 'Department'.   4. In the Dewey Classification a sub-division of a 'division'.   5. One of the separately folded parts of a newspaper, such as the 'Business section'.   6. A portion of a text of a book which can logically be divided into separate parts or sections.

'Section 11'. *See* Local Government Act, 1966.

Section headline. One which consists of whatever sub-divisions (chapters, books, parts, etc.) the book may have. *See also* Headline, Page headline, Running title.

Section mark. 1. The sign § used before a numeral thus: §6, to refer to a section. 2. The fourth reference mark for footnotes, coming after the double dagger. *See also* Reference marks. It is sometimes also used in quantity for borders. *See* Borders (3).

Section title. A half title which introduces a section of a book.

Sectional brace. *See* Brace.

Sectionalized index. An index to a periodical split into sections such as (a) long articles of importance, (b) short paragraphs and brief news items, (c) literature abstracts, and similar well-defined groups.

Sections. *See* Section. For use in classification, *see* Main class.

Sector Skills Councils (SSCs). A UK government-sponsored network of organizations created to identify skills needs in particular areas of employment, and take steps to overcome deficiencies and ensure adequate training facilities for the workforce. SSCs have taken over from National Training Organizations (NTOs) and cover wider fields of employment. The Information Services NTO (ISNTO) is likely to be merged with others to form a new Lifelong Learning SSC in 2004/2005.

Sectorizing device. A digit such as the Octave device for extending the capacity of a numerical base in the Colon Classification.

Security. *See* Computer security.

Security system. *See* Book detection system.

Sedanoise. The smallest size type of the early seventeenth century, designed by Jannon at Sedan. *See also* Jannon, Jean.

SEDIC. <www.sedic.es> (c/o Santa Engracia 17, 28010 Madrid, Spain) The Sociedad Española de Documentación e Información Científica is active in the field of information management and is developing international links.

SEDODEL. <www.snv.jussieu.fr/inova/publi/ntevh/secure> Secure Document Delivery was an EU funded project to develop a secure electronic environment within which materials can be delivered in any format required for use by visually impaired people. It uses COPYSMART technology, based on the CITED model.

See. (*Cataloguing*) A reference from a heading under which no entries are placed, to one or more which contain them.

See also. (*Cataloguing*) A reference often found in dictionary catalogues – and sometimes in classified ones – from one heading with entries under it, to related ones.

See copy. An instruction written on a proof to a printer to refer to the 'copy' in order to correct a typesetting error.

See safe. Said of books bought from a publisher by a bookseller, and paid for, but with the understanding that at some future date the publisher may be asked to exchange unsold copies for copies of another title. *See also* Half see safe, On sale.

SEEREN. <www.dante.net/server/show/nav.00100f007> South East European Research and Education Networking project to establish connectivity to GÉANT in the countries in South East Europe that were not already connected: Albania, Bosnia-Herzegovina, Bulgaria, the former Yugoslav Republic of Macedonia, and Serbia and Montenegro. The SEEREN infrastructure provides connections at between 2 and 34 Mbps.

Segal (Judy) Trust. Established in 1990 in memory of the former chief conservator at the Bodleian Library, the Trust promotes the training of manuscript and archive conservators in less developed countries by awarding travel bursaries.

SEKT. <sekt.semanticweb.org> The Semantically Enabled Knowledge Technologies project is funded by the European Union Information Society Technologies priority of FP6, 2004–2007. There are 12 partners, public and private, from a range of countries co-ordinated by BT Exact in the UK. The project focuses on the method by which electronic information is described and annotated; development of more sophisticated metadata extraction will be followed by international standards and languages for the Semantic web.

Select bibliography. One which gives only a selection of the literature of a subject, the selection having been made with a view to excluding worthless material or to meeting the needs of a special class of people. Also called 'Selective bibliography'. *See also* Bibliography (1), Partial bibliography.

Select list of references. A partial list of references for material for further reading, the selection having eliminated items which for one reason or another are not particularly appropriate in the circumstances. The details included in the entries may be similar to those provided in a bibliography, although some items of a bibliographical nature may not be included, and the subject coverage would not be so great.

Selectasine. A process in silk screen printing; the term implies that one screen only is used for all the colours of a design.

Selected term co-ordination. (*Indexing*) The co-ordination of significant terms in titles with other selected title terms.

Selection section. The division of a cataloguing, accessions, or order department, which deals with the selection of books.

Selective abstract. *See* Abstract.

Selective bibliography. *See* Select bibliography.

Selective cataloguing. The omission of certain types of entry, or of entries for little-used books, or of parts of an entry (as for example some items in collations), in order to reduce the bulk and cost of a catalogue without impairing its efficiency.

Selective circulation. *See* Routeing.

Selective classification. The arrangement of large groups of little-used books either alphabetically or chronologically rather than by specific subject in order to save the expense of cataloguing and classifying.

Selective dissemination of information. *See* SDI.

Selective listing in combination. *See* SLIC index.

Selective record service. A procedure that enables libraries to select individual catalogue records to suit their requirements from the bibliographic databases of host organizations.

Selective routeing. Routeing to only a selection of the staff of a library or organization.

Selector. The component in a Retrieval system which enables the information required to be identified in a Store. It may consist of, or comprise, recording media, code symbols or reading devices.

Self archiving. The depositing of journal papers in an Open access, Open Archives Initiative-compliant, Eprint archive to provide immediate access to the Full text of research findings. *See also* Budapest Open Access Initiative.

Self archiving colours. *See* ROMEO.

Self-charging system. Any system for recording book loans in which the borrower makes part or all of the record. Also known as self-issue system.

Self-cover. A pamphlet in which the same paper is used for cover and text.

Self-ends. Endpapers which are leaves forming part of the end sections of a book.

Self-financing. Services of a library, information unit or other organization that are operated on the basis of charging fees that cover the cost of the operation.

Self-positive. In documentary reproduction, a positive print which is prepared without the use of an intermediate negative. Also called 'Direct positive'.

Self-renewing library. A phrase popularized by the Atkinson Report. The principle of self renovation is that a library should remain at a constant overall size, in terms of stock, by discarding material at an equal rate to its acquisition, thereby maintaining the currency of its collections, and relying on document supply agencies for materials seldom required.

Self-wrapper. The paper cover of a pamphlet or book which is an integral part of the sheet or sheets comprising the publication. It may or may not be printed.

Semanteme. The ultimate, smallest irreducible element or unit of meaning, such as a base or root which contains and represents the general meaning of a word or group of derivatives. *See also* Truncation.

Semantic code. 1. A linguistic system developed for use on machines designed to detect logically defined combinations; a symbol representing the concept of a word. 2. In information retrieval, one in which the notation carries meaningful information in addition to that which is carried by the source word. *See also* Non-semantic code, Descriptor.

Semantic factoring. US term for Facet analysis.

Semantic relation. (*Information retrieval*) A general term used to indicate all types of relationship between language descriptors in a thesaurus. *See also* Relation.

Semantic Web. <www.w3.org/2001/sw> A common framework that allows data to have well-defined meaning and thus to be shared and re-used automatically by machines across application, enterprise, and community boundaries. It is a collaborative effort led by W3C with participation from a large number of researchers and industrial partners and is based on the RDF which integrates a variety of applications using XML for syntax and URIs for naming. Reference: Tim Berners-Lee, James Hendler, Ora Lassila, The Semantic Web, *Scientific American*, May 2001 (available from the web address above).

Semantics. The study of the relations between linguistic symbols (words, expressions, phrases) and the objects or concepts to which they refer. Semantics relates a symbol to its meaning. *See also* Syntax.

Semé, Semis. *Synonymous with* Powder.

Semi-annual. A periodical which is issued at six-monthly intervals. Also called 'Half yearly'.

Semi-chemical pulp. The product of an intermediate process between Mechanical wood pulp (merely ground wood without the addition of chemicals or heat) and Chemical wood pulp which is obtained by the action of chemicals on wood chips.

Semi-current records. (*Records management*) Records retired from current systems because they are no longer needed for every-day use. They may be transferred to a Records centre.

Semi-monthly. *See* Fortnightly.

Seminar collection. *See* Departmental library.

Semi-pulp. A term applied to the product of the grinding process in paper making, the ground wood still containing impurities and large fragments of wood.

Semi-rag. Paper made partly of rags.

Semi-weekly. A serial publication issued twice a week. Also called 'Twice weekly'.

SEMLAC. *See* Museums, Libraries and Archives Council (MLA).

Senior assistant. An assistant librarian who supervises of the work of junior assistants but does not have the responsibility for a department.

Senmon Toshokan Kyogikai. [Japan Special Libraries Association] <www.jsla.or.jp> (c/o Japan Library Association Bldg. Fl 6, 1-11-14 Shinkawa, Chuo-ku, Tokyo 104-0033, Japan) Established in 1952 to facilitate co-operation between member libraries (c.625 institutions) concerning library administration, training, and international liaison. Publishes *Senmon Toshokan* [*Bulletin*] (6 p.a.) and *Senmon Joho Kikan Soran* [*Directory of special libraries, Japan*] (a.).

Sensing mark. (*Reprography*) A mark on film or paper which activates an electrical device to carry out automatically a function such as cutting paper.

Sensitive paper.   A paper which has been treated with light-sensitive chemicals for photographic purposes. *See also* Sensitized paper.

Sensitivity.   *See* Recall ratio.

Sensitized paper.   Paper used in documentary reproduction which is coated with an emulsion sensitive to light or heat.

Separate.   A copy of an article published in a periodical, specially reprinted for the author's use, but retaining the numbering of the issue from which it was taken. It may or may not have a title-page. Sometimes called 'Extracted article', 'Off-print', 'Overprint', or 'Reprint'. *See also* Reprinted article.

Separation negatives.   Individual negatives for each colour used in colour reproductions. *See also* Colour separation.

Separator.   (*Classification*) A symbol (e.g. a point, bracket, colon) used to separate parts of a lengthy notation.

Separatrix.   The diagonal stroke / , used in proof correction to mark and separate alterations.

Separatum   (*Pl.* Separata) A reprint of one of a series of papers. An offprint or Separate.

seq.   (*Pl. Seqq.*) Abbreviation (in singular) of Latin *sequens* 'the following', *sequente* 'and in what follows', *sequitur* 'it follows' and (in plural) of *sequentes, -tia* 'the following', *sequentibus* 'in the following places'. *See also* entry for *et seq.*

Sequel.   A literary work, usually a novel, which is complete in itself, but continues an earlier work.

Sequence of signs.   The use of recognized signs in notes (*see* Reference marks) and especially of 'Relation marks' in the Universal Decimal Classification to separate the different components of a classification number and at the same time indicate their meaning.

Sequential camera.   One which produces a sequence of images in column form on one film from items which are fed into the camera in a predetermined sequence.

SERENATE.   <www.serenate.org> A European Union study into European research and educational networking, as targeted by e-Europe. Funded 2002–2004 by the Research Network Technologies priority of FP6.

Serial.   1. Any publication issued in successive parts, appearing at intervals, usually regular ones, and, as a rule, intended to be continued indefinitely. The term includes periodicals, newspapers, annuals, numbered monographic series and the proceedings, transactions and memoirs of societies. Not to be confused with Series.   2. A book consisting of parts or volumes published successively with a common title and intended to be continued indefinitely, not necessarily at regular intervals. (In the USA the term 'serial' is used to mean a periodical, regular or irregular.)   3. (*Adj.*) The handling of data in a sequential fashion. *See also* Parallel, Serial transmission.   4. A long story published in instalments.   5. As defined by the International Serials Data System (ISDS): for the purpose of allocating an International

Standard Serial Number (ISSN) 'a publication in print or in non-print form, issued in successive parts, usually having numerical or chronological designations, and intended to be continued indefinitely'.

Serial catalogue. An official, or a public catalogue of serials in a library.

Serial Item and Contribution Identifier. *See* SICI.

Serial number. 1. The number indicating the order of publication in a series. 2. One of the consecutive numbers appearing in front of an entry in a bibliography or catalogue.

Serial publication. *See* Serial.

Serial record. A record of a library's holdings of serials.

Serial rights. An author's rights in the publication of work by instalments.

Serial section. A division of an order, or an acquisition, department that has charge of the acquisition of serials; or a sub-division of a preparation division where responsibility is taken for the cataloguing of serials.

Serial service. A serial publication which is revised, accumulated or indexed by means of new or replacement pages. *See also* Loose-leaf service.

Serial transmission. The linear transmission of data, one bit at a time, over a single wire. *See also* Firewire, USB.

Serials department/section. The administrative unit in charge of handling serials; this may include ordering, checking, cataloguing, preparation for binding, etc.

Serials librarian. One who is responsible for the receipt of serials and for the maintenance of the relative records.

Series. 1. Volumes usually related to each other in subject matter, issued successively, sometimes at the same price, and generally by the same publisher, in a uniform style, and usually bearing a collective 'series title' on the Half title or the cover, or at the head of the Title-page. 2. Succeeding volumes of essays, etc., issued at intervals or in sequence. 3. A type of serial publication (*See* Serial (1)) in which the parts (a) have, in addition to a constant title, a distinctive title for each part; (b) consist of a single work; (c) are not issued at predetermined intervals. The successive parts may, or may not, be given systematic or sequential numbering. This type of series is also called 'Monographic Series', 'Monograph Series'. 4. (*Archives*) A Folder holding documents related to a particular subject or function, or documents arranged in accordance with a filing system. 5. (*Archives*) A level of archival arrangement and description recognized by ISAD(G), and corresponding, generally, to the PRO 'class'. 6. A number of articles or stories of a similar nature or by the same author published in succession. *See also* Publisher's series, Reprint series. 7. (*Classification*) A succession of classes, or terms, in some relation.

Series authority file. A list of series entries used in a given catalogue together with the references made to them from other forms.

Series entry. In a catalogue or bibliography, a brief entry under the name of the series to which the publication belongs. *See also* Series.

Series note. In a bibliography or in a catalogue, a note following the collation, and giving, in parentheses, the name of the series to which a book belongs.

Series number. The number assigned by a publisher to an individual book or piece of music published in a series. The series may contain titles which are unrelated, or they may be related to one another by subject, musical form, medium of performance (musical), or the titles may be unrelated. *See also* Publisher's series.

Series statement. 1. The information on a publication which names the series to which it belongs and gives the number, if any, of the publication in the series. 2. (*Cataloguing*) The statement in a catalogue entry, of the name of the series to which the document belongs, and the number, if any, of the publication in the series. This usually appears within curved brackets at the end of the entry.

Series title. The title of a series to which a book belongs. It may appear on the half-title page, title-page, or a page following the title-page.

Serif. A fine finishing stroke or grace, drawn at right angles to, or obliquely across, the ends of stems or arms of a letter. Letters without serifs are usually described as 'sans serif'.

Serigraphy. *See* Silk screen.

Serrated square. (*Binding*) A stamp, more or less square with concave serrated sides, and usually a cruciform centre; often used in a group and giving the effect of a number of circles with serrated inner edges.

Server. *See* Client/server.

Service contract. *See* Contract (2).

Service points. Places at which the public are served, including branches (inclusive of mobile branches and travelling libraries, each halt to count as a separate service point), centres, school libraries, hospital libraries, youth clubs, prisons, etc. The characteristic denoting a service point is that provision is intended to be permanent and/or continuous, is of a relatively wide subject range, and is located at a definite place. Does not include the supply of collections of books to adult classes, choral and dramatic societies, and for other similar purposes where the use of the collection is intended to be limited in duration and where the books cover a relatively narrow subject range.

Service provider. *See* Internet Service provider.

Service Public Library Standards (SPLSs). *See* Public Library Standards.

Servizio Bibliotecario Nazionale. [(Italian) National Library Service] *See* SBN (2).

Session. *See* Parliamentary session.

Sessional Papers. Two series (*House of Commons Sessional Papers* and *House of Lords Sessional Papers*) of Parliamentary Papers arranged (and probably bound) in sessional sets. The *House of Commons Sessional Papers* consist of the *House of Commons Bills,* the *House of Commons Papers* and the *Command Papers*. The *House of Lords Sessional Papers* consist of the *House of Lords Papers and Bills.*

Set. 1. A series of publications associated by common publication or authorship, and which form one unit, being issued in a uniform style. They may be by one author, or on one subject, or they may be a file of periodicals or be unrelated but printed and bound uniformly. 2. (*Printing*) The distance between the left- and right-hand sides of a piece of movable type. Type is said to have a wide or narrow set according to the width of the Body; a figure is used to indicate the comparative width of a Monotype design, e.g. 12 point 10½ set, is narrower than 12 point 12 set.   3. To compose type.   4. A range of items retrieved from a single search statement. *See also* Boolean logic.

Set flush.   1. An instruction to the typesetter to set the type right up to the left-hand margin, avoiding indentions at the beginning of paragraphs. 2. Matter so composed.

Set hand.   Writing which conforms to definite rules, such as styles of abbreviations. Not generally applied to hands later than the seventeenth century.

Set of a font.   (*Printing*) The measurement of the widest letter, described by the point system, as e.g. 12 point 11¼ set.

Set of a letter.   (*Printing*) The width of a piece of type across its shank (i.e. the piece of metal bearing the face, or printing-surface).

Set solid.   Type matter with no leads between the lines.

Set-off.   1. The accidental transfer of ink from one printed sheet to another. 2. Any kind of paper placed between a sheet after printing to prevent the ink from one sheet soiling another. Also called 'Slip sheet'. *See also* Offset.

Setting rule.   *See* Composing rule.

Setting type.   Composing type either by hand or by machine so that it is ready for printing.

Seven Pillars.   <www.sconul.ac.uk/activities/inf_lit/seven_pillars.html> Fully, the Seven Pillars of Information Literacy, designed by SCONUL in 1999 to be a practical working model which would facilitate further development of ideas amongst practitioners in the field, and would hopefully stimulate debate about the ideas and about how those ideas might be used by library and other staff in higher education concerned with the development of students' skills. The model combines ideas about the range of skills involved, with both the need to clarify and illustrate the relationship between information skills and IT skills, and the idea of progression in higher education embodied in the development of the curriculum through first-year undergraduate up to postgraduate and research-level scholarship.

Seventy-twomo (72mo).   A sheet of paper folded into seventy-two leaves, making 144 pages.

Sewed.   In cataloguing, a pamphlet stitched without covers.

Sewing.   When the sections of a book have been gathered and collated, they are sewed together, one by one, with thread, usually by machine. In job binding they are usually sewed by hand. *See also* All along, Stabbing, Stitching, Thread stitched, Wire stitched.

Sewing frame. The frame on which the cords or tapes are attached and stretched taut, and to which the sections of a book are sewn by hand.

Sewing on tapes. When the sections of a book are sewn together and two or more tapes are used to secure the book to the covers, some of the loops pass over the tapes thus also securing the sections to them. In Library binding and hand-sewing, each section is sewn to every tape.

Sewn. A book is said to be sewn when the sections are fastened together with linen threads passing round tapes or cords.

Sexagesimo-quarto. *See* Sixty-fourmo.

Sexto (6to). A sheet of paper folded three times to form a section of six leaves or twelve pages; a half-sheet of twelves.

Sexto-decimo (16mo). A sheet of paper folded four times to form a section of sixteen leaves (thirty-two pages); a half-sheet of thirty-two. Now called foolscap 8vo. Also called 'Sixteen-mo'.

Sexuality Issues in Libraries Group (SILG). (Regents College, Inner Circle, Regent's Park, London NW1 4NS, UK) An organization for lesbian, gay and transgendered workers in public and academic libraries; formerly the Burning Issues Group. An Organization in Liaison (OiL) with CILIP.

s.f. Abbreviation for *sub finem* (Lat. 'towards the end').

SfB. Classification system for trade literature, periodicals, and information concerning the building industry. The letters are the initials of the Swedish committee which originated it, Sanarbetskommittèn för Byttnadsfrågor.

SFX. *See* OpenURL.

SGML. *See* Standard Generalized Markup Language.

Shackleton Report (UK). *Report of the Committee on University Libraries*, 1966, after R. Shackleton, the Chairman of the Committee which examined the structure of the three different types of library in Oxford: direct grant (Bodleian, Ashmolean and Taylorian); those financed by the General Board (mainly faculty libraries); college libraries. Recommendations were made on buildings, administration and services.

Shaded tools. (*Binding*) Finisher's tools partly in outline and partly solid.

Shadow. A typeface which gives a three-dimensional effect.

Shagreen. A type of leather with a rough, granular surface. When used for bookbinding it is usually prepared from sharkskin.

Shaken. A cataloguing term used in the US to describe copies of books which have loose leaves and/or binding.

Shank. The rectangular body of a type letter, on which are the Nick, or nicks, Pinmark, Belly and Back. Also called Body and Stem. The piece of metal on which the shoulder bearing the Face or printing surface of a type-letter is supported. *See also* Shoulder.

Shape. Books which are not of normal proportions are described as 'oblong' or 'landscape' when the width of the page exceeds its height, 'narrow' when the width is less than $3/5$ of the height, and 'square' if more than $3/4$. *See also* Size (1).

Share the Vision. <www.visugate.org.uk/contributors/stv> (National Library for the Blind, Far Cromwell Road, Bredbury, Stockport SK6 2SG, UK) A partnership organization to improve information delivery, especially through public libraries, for visually impaired people. The goal is to make public libraries the single point of information delivery and access for visually impaired people in any location. The partnership includes the British Library, CILIP, Museums, Libraries and Archives Council (MLA), Society of Chief Librarians and independent advisors.

Shareable Content Object Reference Model. *See* SCORM.

Shared authorship. A work which is produced by the collaboration of two authors, compilers, editors, translators, collectors, adapters, etc.

Shared cataloguing. A form of cataloguing undertaken by the Library of Congress and other agencies responsible for national bibliography. The Library, under the United States Higher Education Act, 1965 was charged with '(a) acquiring so far as possible, all library materials of value to scholarship currently published throughout the world; and (b) providing catalogue information, for such materials promptly after receipt …' and in order to achieve these objects arranged with other national agencies to send catalogue entries for all works published in their country. *See also* Co-operative cataloguing.

Shareware. Copyrighted software distributed freely but subject to a small payment if the end user wishes to retain for future use and have access to documentation and updates. *See also* Free software, Open Source software, Public domain software.

SHARP. <www.sharpweb.org> (PO Box 30, Wilmington, North Carolina 28402-0030, USA) Society for the History of Authorship, Reading and Publishing. Formed in 1997 to promote research into the creation, dissemination and uses of the printed and written word including the history of printing, publishing, bookselling, copyright, libraries, literary criticism. Holds annual conferences, maintains an electronic bulletin board, and publishes *Book History* (2 p.a.) and *SHARP News* (q.).

Sharpness. In photography, the density-gradient at an edge of an image.

Shaved. A book which has been trimmed by the binder so closely that the lines of print have been grazed, without actually being cut into. *See also* Cropped.

Sheaf binder. A case or binder to hold a sheaf of papers to form a loose-leaf catalogue or other record. The sheets of paper are punched with holes to go over posts which keep the sheets in position, and there is some form of locking device to keep the covers and the sheets securely in position.

Sheaf catalogue. A catalogue made on slips of paper, as distinct from one made on cards, and fastened into a sheaf binder which permits the insertion of new material in correct order.

Sheepskin. The skin of a sheep prepared as a bookbinding material. Such skins have been used for bookbinding in the United Kingdom since about 1400. The boards they covered were usually of oak. *See also* Alaska seal, Law calf, Roan, Rutland, Skiver, Smyrna Morocco.

Sheet.   1. A large piece of paper as manufactured. Also used of the sheet after it has been printed and folded to form a section of a book or pamphlet; to avoid confusion, a folded sheet is best called a Section. Sheets of paper bearing the same size name can be in double ('double') or quadruple ('quad') size. *See also* Octavo, Paper sizes.   2. An individual map printed (usually) on one side of a sheet of paper. Also called 'Sheet map'.

Sheet index.   (*Cartography*) An index, usually based on an outline map, showing the layout, numbering system, etc. of map sheets which cover an area.

Sheet map.   A map printed on one side of a sheet of paper. Also called a 'Sheet'.

Sheet music.   Printed music which is not bound into stiff covers. There is no limit on the number of pages. *See also* Score.

Sheet stock.   A stock of unbound printed sheets of a block which are kept in stock by the printer until the publisher orders them to be bound up. This method of binding books as required to meet orders, is done to spread the cost of production.

Sheet work.   Printing one side of a sheet of paper from an 'inner forme' and the other from an 'outer forme'. Also called 'Work and back'. When both sides have been printed, the sheet is known as a 'Perfect copy'. By this method, one sheet is used to print one copy using two formes. *See also* Half-sheet work.

Sheet-feed.   Said of a printing press which takes paper cut into sheets instead of paper in a continuous roll.

Sheets.   The printed pages of a book, either flat or folded, but unbound. *See also* In sheets.

Sheetwise.   A method of printing in which a separate forme is used for printing each side of a sheet of paper. *See also* Work and turn.

Sheffield Local Co-operation Scheme.   Library Co-operation in Sheffield (UK) has a long history; the Sheffield Interchange Organization (*see* SINTO) was formed in 1932. The Sheffield Libraries Co-ordinating Committee was very active in the 1980s, and was then replaced via a LIP initiative.

Shelf.   A flat piece of wood, steel or other material, which is placed horizontally between two uprights, or supported on brackets, to hold books. Shelves may be constructed of rollers to save wear on the binding of very heavy and large books. The normal length of shelves is 3 feet or 1 metre from centre to centre of the uprights supporting them.

Shelf capacity.   The capacity of a library for storing books on shelves; it is generally expressed by the total number of books which can be so accommodated or by the number of linear feet or metres available for housing books or other library materials.

Shelf checking.   *See* Reading shelves.

Shelf classification.   A classification which is designed for use in arranging books on shelves rather than for minute precision in designating subject areas and relationships.

Shelf department.   The administrative unit of a library responsible for the care of books on the shelves, and sometimes for other work such as classification and shelf-listing.

Shelf dummy.   A piece of wood or cardboard placed on a shelf to indicate a specific book which is shelved out of sequence.

Shelf guide.   A guide placed on the edge of a shelf to indicate its contents. Also called 'Shelf label'.

Shelf height.   The vertical distance between two shelves.

Shelf life.   The length of time which sensitized materials used in photo-copying or documentary reproduction may be kept before exposure without loss of efficiency.

Shelf list.   A list of the books in a library, the entries being brief and arranged on cards or computer printout in the order of the books on the shelves, and forming, in effect, in a classified library, a subject catalogue without added entries, analytics and cross-references. Useful in a Stock check.

Shelf mark.   *See* Shelf number.

Shelf number.   With Fixed location, a number given to a shelf to assist in the finding of books by indicating the one on which any individual book will be found. This number is incorporated in the Book number. *See also* Call number.

Shelf reading.   *See* Reading shelves.

Shelf register.   *See* Shelf list.

Shelf support.   1. The upright part of a book stack which holds the shelves, either directly or by means of a bracket.   2. The small fittings which fit into slots in the uprights and actually support the shelves. These may be pins, studs or brackets.

Shelf tidying.   *See* Reading shelves.

Shelf-back.   *See* Spine.

Shell.   (*Printing*) The electro plate before it is backed with metal.

Shelving.   1. All the shelves in a library.   2. The act of putting books away in their proper places on the shelves of a library.

Shera (Jesse H.) Award for Research.   An award made by the Library Research Round Table for the best paper presented by an author at an LRRT meeting.

SHERPA.   <www.sherp.ac.uk> Securing a Hybrid Environment for Research, Preservation and Access, a project in the JISC FAIR programme investigating issues associated with the future of scholarly communication and publishing. In particular, it is initiating the development of openly accessible institutional digital repositories of research output, created through Self archiving, in a number of research universities in the UK. *See also* Eprint archive, Repository (1), ROMEO.

Shibboleth. <shibboleth.internet2.edu> A project of Internet2/MACE which is developing architectures, policy structures, practical technologies, and an Open source implementation to support inter-institutional sharing of web resources subject to access controls. In addition, Shibboleth is developing a policy framework that will allow inter-operation within the higher education community.

Shiner. A mineral impurity seen as a shining speck on the surface of paper, sometimes due to mica in the china clay which is used as Loading being compressed into a translucent spot during passage through the calenders. Hard, brittle materials fall out and leave 'pinholes'.

Shining-up table. *See* Register table.

Shoes. (*Binding*) Metal attached to the edges only at the corners of the covers of books, and sometimes at the base of the spine, to protect the leather binding.

Shooting stick. A tool of metal or hardened wood used to hammer wooden quoins into position against the side of a chase when locking up a forme.

Short and. *See* Ampersand.

Short cataloguing. The style of cataloguing in which the entries give author, main title, and date only.

Short descenders. Lower case letters with descenders (g, j, p, etc.) which are shorter than usual; these can be obtained with certain fonts of type.

Short form cataloguing. *See* Short cataloguing.

Short grain. Paper in which the fibres lie in the shorter direction of the sheet. *See also* Grain direction, Long grain.

Short letter. A character, such as a, o, s, which has neither ascender nor descender. *See also* Long letter.

Short page. A page of type matter with fewer lines of type than there is room for, or than has been specified. In bookwork the space at the foot is left blank or it may be filled with a decorative piece. *See also* Long page, Type page.

Short ream. 480 sheets of paper. *See also* Long ream, Ream.

Short score. *See* Close score, Score.

Short story. A complete story, generally fewer than 10,000 words in length.

Short title. 1. The abbreviated title by which an Act of Parliament is known and officially designated. 2. Enough of the title of a book to enable it to be identified in a catalogue or bibliography.

Short-loan collection. *See* Reserve collection (2).

Shorts. 1. The copies of different sheets needed to complete an imperfect edition. 2. Books ordered from, but not delivered by, a bookseller owing to their not being in stock.

Short-title system. A system of bibliographical references in publications which uses a shortened form of the title of a book or periodical article after the first full mention.

Shoulder. The top of the shank of a piece of movable type; parts are the Bevel (or neck), Beard, Line and Side bearing. The Face is above the bevel.

Shoulder-head.   A short descriptive heading, which precedes a paragraph; it is set in large or small capitals, or in italics, flush to the left-hand margin occupying a separate line and with a line of leading between it and the following paragraph. It marks the second division of text within the chapter, subsidiary to the Cross-head and superior to the Side head. *See also* Marginal note.

Show through.   Printed matter which shows through from the other side of a printed leaf, due to ink penetration because of the paper being insufficiently opaque or to improper pressure during machining. *See also* Strike through.

S.I.   *See* Statutory Instruments.

SIBIL.   Système Informatisé pour Bibliothèques. *See* REBUS.

SIBMAS.   <www.theatrelibrary.org/sibmas> Société Internationale des Bibliothèques et des Musées des Arts du Spectacle; this international association was formed during the tenth international congress of the IFLA Section of Libraries and Museums of the Theatre Arts, held in Brussels in October 1972 during the annual IFLA Council, when the former International Society for Performing Arts Libraries and Museums restructured itself in this way. SIBMAS is concerned with all matters relating to performing arts collections in libraries, archives and museums. An International Council is held every two years. There are several active national branches. *See also* International Society for Performing Arts Libraries and Museums.

sic.   (Lat. 'so, thus, in this manner') Usually printed in [ ] to indicate that an exact reproduction of the original is being made.

SICI.   Serial Item and Contribution Identifier (NISO Z39.56-1996); based on the ISSN standard, SICI identifies serial items (issues) and the articles or other contributions contained in them. *See also* BICI, Digital Object Identifier.

Side.   1. The right hand or left hand of a piece of type when the printing surface is uppermost and facing the viewer. The front is called the 'belly' and the back the 'back'.   2. The front or back cover of a bound book.

Side bearing.   The amount of 'shoulder' on either side of a piece of movable type; it controls the amount of white space left between characters when composed into lines.

Side head (Side heading).   A short descriptive sub-heading dividing sections of a chapter, indented one em and usually printed in italics (but maybe in caps, large and small, or in bold), not occupying a separate line, and placed at the beginning of a paragraph with the matter running on. It is the third division of text within a chapter, subsidiary to the Shoulder-head. *See also* Cross-head, Heading (4).

Side lettering.   *See* Side title.

Side note.   A marginal note outside the type page, and usually set in narrow measure in type several sizes smaller than the text of the page. *See* Marginal note. Also called 'Hanging shoulder note'. Sometimes it is a substitute for a Cross-head, but more usually provides a gloss on the text, or running commentary, which does not interrupt the argument; if read with continuity, side notes give an abstract of the whole book.

Side sewing.   *See* Side stitch.

Side sorts.   *See* Odd sorts.

Side stick.   *See* Chase.

Side stitch.   (*Binding*) To stitch a booklet or pamphlet of two or more folded signatures from back to front through the leaves or sections (not through their folds), and near their binding edges, using thread or wire. Also called 'Flat stitching', 'Side sewing', 'Stab-stitch'. When wire is used the process is called 'Wire-stabbing'. *See also* Saddle stitching, Singer sewing.

Side title.   A title impressed on the front cover, or side, of a bound book.

Side wire.   To side-stitch a pamphlet with wire staples.

Siderography.   The process of producing steel engravings and making prints therefrom.

SIG.   *See* Special Interest Group.

Sigil.   A chronological Coden in which the first characters would represent the date of publication followed by those representing the title.

Sigillography.   The science or study of seals, being a branch of diplomatics. Also called 'Sphragistics'.

Sigla.   Symbols; it is sometimes printed at the head of a table of these.

SIGLE.   *See* System for Information on Grey Literature in Europe.

Sign manual.   A signature written with the person's own hand, especially the signature of a sovereign or head of state, to give authority to a state document.

Signature.   1. A folded printed sheet, forming part of a book; a section. 2. The letter or number, or combination of letters and numbers, printed at the foot of the first page, and sometimes on subsequent leaves of a section, as a guide to the binder in arranging them in their correct order. These were written or stamped in until 1472 when Johann Koelhoff of Cologne, printed a signature as the last line of a text page. The binders of MSS. usually cut off the signature letters. Each section has a different signature and when letters are used, as is usual, they progress in alphabetical order, J, V and W usually being omitted to avoid confusion. There is also a historical reason for the omission of these letters: MSS. and early printed books were usually written in Latin, in which alphabet I stands for both I and J, and V for both U and V, and there is no W. When the alphabet has been used up a lower case sequence or a new sequence of double letters followed by one of treble letters, or sequences combining capital and lower case letters are used. If the same sequence is used again it is known as a duplicated or triplicated signature. Signatures are usually omitted in US books. Also called 'Signature mark'. *See also* Collation, Collating mark, Designation mark, Direction line, Section, Title signature, Volume signature.   3. The name or initials, written in a person's own hand to authenticate a document.   4. (*Networking*) Lines appended to E-mail communications providing contact details for the sender: name, address, telephone number; alternatively (or also) incorporating some pithy saying or graphic that the sender finds amusing or meaningful.

Signature and catchword line.   The line of type which in an old book bears both the signature and the catchword. It is usually below the lowest line of text. Also called 'Direction line'; should the signature and catchword be on separate lines, the lower is called the direction line.

Signature mark.   The letter or number, or a combination of both, placed at the left of the tail margin of the first page of each section of a book. *See also* Signature (2).

Signature title.   *See* Title signature.

Signatures, list of.   *See* Register (2).

Signed edition.   *See* Autographed edition, Limited edition.

Signed page.   The first page of a section – the one bearing the Signature (2).

Significant punctuation.   *See* Filing code.

Significant words.   In permutation indexing, words which are permitted to be indexed by reason of their absence on a Stop list.

SIIA.   <www.siia.com> (1090 Vermont Avenue NW, Washington, DC 2005, USA) The Software and Information Industry Association was formerly the Information Industry Association (IIA); the Association serves the interests of those involved in online business, e-publishing standards, digital rights etc. Divisions include: software, content, education, financial, global, research.

SILG.   *See* Sexuality Issues in Libraries Group.

Silhouette.   1. To remove non-essential background from a half-tone to produce an outline effect.   2. A print, illustration, drawing, or other form of artistic reproduction from which background has been removed.

Silicon chip.   *See* Chip.

Silk paper.   Produced at Baghdad in the Middle Ages and famous through-out Persia. It was prepared from linen. The term is also used for papers containing a quantity of short, coloured silk fibres, or even one or more strands of silk or metal running through the sheet; this is used for bank notes, and is difficult to counterfeit.

Silk screen.   A stencil process for multiplying an original design and for lettering in colours which is used for posters and other jobs requiring short runs and for which lithography would be too expensive. Bolting silk, organdie, phosphor bronze or steel gauze are tightly stretched over a wooden frame. A stencil bearing the design is fixed to the underside of the silk or other material and paint is forced through the silk at the open parts of the stencil with a rubber squeegee on to the paper, silk, metal, glass, wood or other material to be printed.

Silked.   A leaf of a book which has been repaired by silking.

Silking.   The application of silk chiffon to one or both sides of a sheet of paper as a means of repairing or preserving it. *See also* Lamination.

Silver halide paper.   A paper used in lensless copying machines. It is necessary to use the traditional photographic developing processes of making negatives (i.e. developing, rinsing, fixing, washing, drying) before making positive copies.

Silver processes.   A group of processes using silver halide sensitized materials for document copying.

Silvered.   The edges of a book which are treated with silver instead of gold.

Simplex.   A communications link between a computer and a remote terminal operating in one direction only. *See also* Duplex.

Simplified cataloguing.   The elimination of some of the information normally given in full catalogue entries to reduce the work involved in cataloguing and thereby the cost, or to make the catalogue simpler to use. *See also* Full cataloguing, Limited cataloguing, Short cataloguing.

Simplified filing.   A method of filing cards in a catalogue or entries in an index of any type, that deliberately ignores detailed rules of filing in the interests of greater speed of filing or ease of access.

Simulation.   In the examination of operational or organizational problems, or solutions to problems, or alternative paths of action, simulation is the construction of a fictional model system, which may be computer-based, on which experiments can be carried out to plot likely outcomes of particular decisions.

sine loco.   (Lat. 'without a place') Used in a catalogue entry, in the abbreviated form (*s.l.*) for no place of publication.

sine nomine.   (Lat. 'without a name') Used in a catalogue entry, in the abbreviated form (*s.n.*) for no known publisher.

SINET.   Science Information Network.   <www.sinet.ad.jp> The Japanese academic computer network, providing networking services for academic research purposes since 1986, under the auspices of the National Institute for Informatics, formerly NACSIS. It consists of a packet switching network using a communication infrastructure for virtual networks such as N1net (an older proprietary network), JAIN (TCP/IP-based university network), WIDE (funded by corporate users), and TISN (used by physicists and chemists), plus the internet backbone network (SINET) which interconnects campus LANs via TCP/IP, and which since 2002 has been integrated within Super SINET, an ultrahigh-speed network based on 10 Gbps optical communication technology. It links over 230 universities and 340 research institutes in Japan, and is linked to research networks in the USA and Europe.

Singer sewing.   Side stitching with thread, the sewing extending the full length of the volume. *See also* Sewing, Stabbing, Thread stitched.

Single look-up.   An index to items embracing bibliographical references which give full bibliographical details, thus avoiding the need to refer to another section of the index.

Single quotes.   Superior commas used to indicate quoted matter already within quoted matter. '...' So named to distinguish them from double quotes "...", the more common form of quotation mark. *See also* Double quotes.

Single revolution machine. A letterpress printing machine in which the continuously running cylinder, having a diameter twice that of the Two-revolution Machine, runs at a constant speed. During the first half-rotation the bed moves forward and the impression is made; during the second half-rotation the bed returns. Some makes of this type of machine have varying speeds for the bed and/or cylinder.

Single sign-on. The mechanism whereby the Username and Password for a user on a network need only be added once, at first entry, and from that point on access is provided to all available resources without further authentication.

Single weight paper. Sensitized photographic paper between 0.0060 and 0.0083 inches inclusive. *See also* Photographic papers.

Sinkage. Space left at the top of a printed page in excess of the normal margin, for example at the beginning of a new chapter.

SINTO. <extra.shu.ac.uk/sinto> (The Adsetts Centre, Sheffield Hallam University, Pond Street, Sheffield S1 1WB, UK) Sheffield Interchange Organization. This is the earliest UK scheme of local library co-operation, having been commenced in 1932 to promote and develop library and information services, initially in Sheffield, but more recently taking in South Yorkshire, North Derbyshire and the surrounding area.

SISO. A Dutch 'scheme for the classification of the subject catalogues in public libraries' which was published in 1958 by the Central Association of Public Libraries of Holland. It is basically Dr. Greve's 'Hague Scheme' first published in 1931; it has a decimal notation, and the schedules resemble the Universal Decimal Classification and Dewey Decimal Classification.

Site librarian. The librarian in charge of one of a number of libraries within a multi-site system.

Sittybus. A title label which identified papyrus rolls. *See also* Scroll (2).

Sixteen-mo. *See* Sexto-decimo.

Sixth Framework Programme (EU). *See* FP6.

Sixty-fourmo (64mo). A sheet of paper folded six times to form a section of sixty-four leaves, making 128 pages. Also called 'Sexagesimoquarto'.

Size. 1. (*Cataloguing*) The size of a book is measured by its height; a book is called 'narrow' if the width of the cover is less than $3/5$ of the height; 'square' if more than $3/4$; and 'oblong' or 'landscape' if the width of the cover is greater than the height. Width is usually given only when unusual, or for old books. When both height and width are given, the height is given first. Measurements are usually given in centimetres in bibliographies and catalogues, although often in inches in the latter. The fold symbol (e.g. f°, 4°, 8°, 12°) is often used as an indication of approximate size. *See also* Book sizes, Fold symbols, Foldings, Type size. 2. (*Paper*) A mixture of gelatine, alum and formaldehyde through which paper is passed, after coming from the paper-making machine, in order to produce a better surface and to repel water. 3. (*Binding*) A bonding material placed between binding material and lettering.

Size copy.   *See* Dummy (1).

Size letters.   The symbols (F, Q, O, etc. i.e. Folio, Quarto, Octavo, etc.) used to indicate the size of books. *See also* Fold symbols, Foldings.

Size notation.   The method of indicating the size of a book: it may be by measurement in centimetres or inches, by Fold symbols or by Size letters.

Size rule.   A rule graduated in inches and/or centimetres with fold symbols and corresponding Size letters marked at the proper places; it is used for measuring books.

Sized paper.   Paper which has been treated to make it less receptive to water. Blotting paper is unsized: writing paper is hard-sized. The treatment consists of adding resin to the Stuff in the Breaker or to the surface of the paper or board (surface sizing) so that the finished paper will be non-absorbent. Animal glue, starch or casein may be used as alternatives. *See also* Size (2).

Sizing.   1. The act of applying size. *See* Size (2).   2. (*Book production*) Marking the reduction, or final, size on the original of an illustration as an instruction to the block maker.

Skeleton.   The cross-bars which separate the pages of type in a forme, the 'furniture' (pieces of wood or metal) which form the page margins, and the running titles, which are left in position when the pages of type have been removed after printing for breaking up, ready for the emplacement of the next pages of the same volume.

Skeleton abstract.   (*Information retrieval*) An abbreviated stylized abstract.

Sketch.   1. A drawing.   2. A brief description of a person or event.   3. A short musical or dramatic play.

Skinner (Constance Lindsay) Award.   *See* Women's National Book Association.

Skiver.   A leather made from the hair or grain side of split sheepskin; it is often embossed and finished in imitation of various leather grains.

Skiver label.   A paper-thin skiver used for a title panel on the spine of a book.

Skolnik Award.   An annual award recognizing outstanding contributions to and achievements in the theory and practice of chemical information services. The Herman Skolnik Award is presented by the Division of Chemical Information of the American Chemical Society.

s.l.   Abbreviation for *sine loco* (Lat. 'without a place'). Used in cataloguing entries when the probable place of publication cannot be ascertained.

SLA.   1. *See* School Library Association.   2. Scottish Library Association. *See* CILIPS.   3. *See* Special Libraries Association.

Slab serif.   (*Printing*) A serif consisting of a plain horizontal stroke which is not bracketed to the upright stroke of a letter.

SLAINTE. <www.slainte.org.uk> Scottish Libraries Across the INTErnet; an information service on Scottish cultural events, organizations and publications. Maintained by CILIPS and SLIC.

Slanted abstract. An abstract giving emphasis to a particular aspect of the contents of a document so as to cater for the interests of a particular group of readers.

Slash. The signs / (forward slash) and \ (back slash) commonly found on alphanumeric keyboards for computer systems; also called 'oblique'.

Sleeve. 1. A transparent, plastic jacket made to fit over a Book jacket to protect the book from wear and at the same time preserve the information printed on the book jacket. 2. A plasticized, printed case made of thick card (*see* Boards (3)) to slip over and so protect a Gramophone record.

SLIC. <www.slainte.org.uk/slic> The Scottish Library and Information Council reviews, monitors, evaluates and promotes all types of library and information service in Scotland; it updates standards for all sectors, and promotes good practice. It reports to, and advises, the Secretary of State for Scotland on library and information matters. Grants are available for projects and specific initiatives. SLIC liaises widely with other bodies and is involved in networking on information issues through working groups and a programme of seminars and conferences. An electronic newsletter is issued. For many years, the directorship of SLIC has been a combined role with the directorship of CILIPS (previously Scottish Library Association). *See also* SLAINTE.

SLIC index. An index compiled on the principle of Selective Listing In Combination. It consists of deriving every combination of terms from the set of alphabetically ordered terms assigned by the indexer, selecting from these combinations only those which do not form the beginnings of longer combinations, and listing these selected groups in alphabetical order.

Slide. A visual positive image on transparent material, usually film, mounted in rigid format designed for projection. Also called 'Transparency'.

Slide box. *See* Slip case.

Slide case. *See* Slip case

Slide-tape. *See* Tape-slide presentation.

Sliding shelves. Large shelves for the flat storage of Folios; designed so that they may be pulled forward to facilitate handling and save wear and tear on the bindings.

Slip. (*Verb*) 1. To discharge a book. *See* Book card, Discharge. 2. To list books on separate slips of paper, one for each book. (*Noun*) A small piece of paper, usually of standard 5 x 3 inches size, used to record briefly author and title, etc., as part of the book-preparation processes, or for some temporary recording purpose.

Slip case. 1. A cardboard box made to fit one or more volumes published together, and open at the front to show the titles. Also called 'Open-back case', 'Slide box', 'Slide case', 'Slip-in case'. 2. (*Archives*) A box usually open-fronted, sometimes with a soft fabric lining, used to protect a book or set of books.

Slip catalogue. *See* Page catalogue.

Slip proof. *See* Proof.

Slip sheet. A sheet of paper which is placed between sheets as they come from the printing machine to prevent offset. *See also* Set-off.

Slipcancel. A small piece of paper bearing a printed correction and pasted over the incorrect matter in a printed book.

Slipping books. The US term for Discharge of books.

Slipping desk. *See* Circulation desk.

Slips. 1. The pieces of sewing cord or tape which project beyond the back of the book after it is sewn, and which are afterwards attached to the boards. Also called 'Tabs'. 2. The paper slips on which are written the instructions to the binder. *See* Slip (2). 3. Applied to matter not set up into pages, but pulled as proofs, on long slips of paper called galley proofs. *See also* Proof.

Slotted shelving. A form of adjustable steel shelving whereby the shelves slide into slots running through the uprights from back to front.

Slug. A line of type set solid on a composing machine.

Slug-casting machine. A machine for setting up type in the form of cast lines or slugs. These include Intertype, Italtype, Linotype, Ludlow and Typograph.

Slugset. Type which has been set in slugs, e.g. lines of type cast in one piece.

Slur. A letterpress machine printing fault caused by an irregular movement of the paper while the impression is being taken, and resulting in the distortion of dots in a half-tone or a double impression of the type characters.

Small and Medium-sized Enterprises. *See* SMEs.

Small capitals. The smaller capital letters (as distinct from the full capitals) of which they are about 2/3 the size, thus: A, B, C; the same size as the X-height of a letter. Indicated in a MS. or proof by two strokes underneath. Abbreviated s.c., s.cap., sm.cap., s.caps., small caps. *See also* Capitals, Lower case letters, Upper case letters.

Small Computer Systems Interface. *See* SCSI.

Small demy. *See* Demy.

Small full score. *See* Score.

Small paper copy. A copy, or an edition, of a book which is printed on paper of a smaller size than a Large paper copy or large paper edition. Also called 'Small paper edition'.

Small pica. An obsolete size of type, about 11 point.

Small type (s/t). (*Printing*) Strictly, type which is intermediate in size between that used for the main text of a book and that used for the footnotes. Colloquially, type of any size except large.

Smalt. A species of glass, usually deep blue through the use of oxide of cobalt, and finely pulverized for use as a colouring medium in paper making. It is usually used as a 'loading', and as it is resistant to acids, alkalis, heat and moisture, it is a very permanent colouring material. As it has a low colouring power it is expensive, and is used mainly for hand-made and the better machine-made azures for writing. Having a high specific gravity, it usually sinks through the pulp and colours one side more than the other.

Smartcard. A credit card with integrated circuit to provide limited digital storage and memory and enable financial transactions. *See also* SmartMedia.

SmartMedia. <www.ssfdc.or.jp/english> A PC Card about one-third the area of a conventional card and only 0.76mm in thickness that is expected to help electronic devices such as the digital still camera and various forms of portable information equipment become even smaller in size. *See also* PCMCIA, Smartcard.

Smasher. *See* Bumper.

Smashing machine. A machine used in binderies for compressing folded signatures to render them more compact for binding by expelling the air from between the pages.

SMDL. *See* Standard Music Description Language.

SMDS. Switched Multimegabit Data Service, a public data network operating at speeds of up to 34 Mbits per second.

SMEs. Small and Medium-sized Enterprises are those businesses employing relatively few staff, and which generally have no information facilities of their own; as they are specifically identified as a growth area in employment terms, their information needs are a priority activity for many information provision organizations.

Smilies. Character combinations used in e-mail and network communications intended to signify smiling or frowning faces and all manner of variants in-between. The most common smiley (tilt your head) is :-).

Smooth antique. *See* Paper finishes.

SMS. Short Message Service, a service for sending messages of 160–224 characters to mobile phones that use Global System for Mobile (GSM) communication. GSM and SMS services are primarily available in Europe. The technology does not require the mobile phone to be active and within range because messages will be held for a number of days until they can be retrieved. SMS messages can be sent to digital phones from a Web site or from one digital phone to another. Use of SMS is known colloquially as text messaging or texting.

Smyrna Morocco. A sheepskin finished with a grain to imitate Morocco. *See also* Sheepskin.

Smyth sewing. Sewing through the sections of a book; done by a Smyth sewing machine. The usual kind of sewing in Edition binding, usually without tapes (US). *See also* Case (1).

s.n. Abbreviation for *sine nomine* (Lat. 'without a name'). Used in catalogue entries when the name of the publisher is unknown.

Snail mail. Traditional postal mail seen from the perspective of E-mail.

SOAP. A lightweight XML-based protocol intended for exchanging structured information in a decentralized, distributed environment. Originally an acronym for Simple Object Access Protocol but this has been largely dropped as development has moved away from the initial intention.

Sobriquet. A nickname: a fanciful appellation. As these names are usually better known than the real names, books by or about them are often entered in catalogues under the sobriquet. *See also* Nickname.

SOCCEL. *See* Society of County Children's and Education Librarians.

Social exclusion. A general term for all types of barriers and hurdles that might deter members of a community from accessing and using public services. The term covers social disadvantage, racial or ethnic discrimination, educational handicaps, and other factors that prevent involvement. Strategies to combat social exclusion will include positive measures to identify and assess problems, ensure organization-wide awareness, and provide training in attitude and competencies.

Sociedad Española de Documentación e Informatión Científica. *See* SEDIC.

Société Internationale des Bibliothèques et des Musées des Arts du Spectacle. *See* SIBMAS.

Society for the History of Authorship, Reading and Publishing. *See* SHARP.

Society of American Archivists (SAA). <www.archivists.org> (527 S. Wales Street (5th. Floor), Chicago IL 60607, USA) Founded in 1936, this is the world's largest professional association of those individuals and institutions interested in the preservation and use of archives, manuscripts, and current records. The Society's membership includes over 4,000 persons serving in government, academic institutions, historical societies, businesses, museums, libraries, religious organizations, professional associations, and numerous other institutions. There are professional affinity and regional groups. SAA publishes *The American Archivist* (q.) and several monographs.

Society of Archivists. <www.archives.org.uk> (Prioryfield House, 20 Canon Street, Taunton TA1 1SW, UK) Formed in 1947 as the Society of Local Archivists and renamed in 1954 to recognize an expanding membership, the Society is the professional body for archivists, archive conservators and records managers in the UK and Ireland. It promotes the care and preservation of archives, the better administration of record repositories and aims to advance the training of its members. Membership consists of registered members, members, student members and institutional affiliates, and is open to all concerned or qualified in archive administration, conservation and records management.

Society of Authors. <www.societyofauthors.net> (84 Drayton Gardens, London SW10 9SB, UK) A UK body that gives advice to members on business matters, publishes guides to contracts, copyright, VAT, etc., administers a trust fund for authors, organizes special interest groups and pursues campaigns on behalf of the profession. Operates in collaboration with many other literary, copyright and library organizations.

Society of Chief Librarians (SCL). <chieflib.org.uk> A professional association representing the heads of services of public libraries in England and Wales, formed in the mid-1990s to replace FOLACL (the Federation of Local Authority Chief Librarians) which had itself replaced the Association of London Chief Librarians, which retains a certain independent existence, the Association of Metropolitan District Chief Librarians, and the Society of County Librarians. The Society aims to take a leading role in the national development of public libraries, and represents its members to government, professional and advisory bodies. The Public Libraries Research Group is associated with the Society.

Society of Competitive Intelligence Professionals. *See* SCIP.

Society of County Children's and Education Librarians (SOCCEL). SOCCEL was a self-help group reporting to the UK Society of County Librarians; in 1995/96 it agreed to merge with AMDECL and YELL to form the Association of Senior Children's and Education Librarians (ASCEL).

Society of County Librarians. *See* Society of Chief Librarians.

Society of Indexers. <www.indexers.org.uk> (Blades Enterprise Centre, John Street, Sheffield S2 4SU, UK) Founded in 1957, the Society's objectives are: to promote improved standards and techniques in all forms of indexing; to provide and promote facilities for initial and further training of indexers; to establish criteria for assessment of conformity of indexes to recognized standards; to establish procedures for conferring professional status on members; to conduct and promote relevant research; to publish and disseminate guidance, information and ideas on good practice; promote among indexers, authors, publishers and other interested persons and organizations relationships conducive to the advancement of good indexing and the professional status of indexers; to enhance awareness and recognition of the role of indexers in the analysis, organization and accessibility of recorded knowledge and ideas. The Society presents the Carey Award, the Levin Award, and the Wheatley Medal. An Organization in Liaison (OiL) with CILIP.

Society of Information Technology Management. *See* SocITM.

Society of Public Information Networks (SPiN). <www.spin. org.uk> The Society has 300 members from local authorities, health agencies, libraries, museums, central government departments, voluntary organizations and private sector companies. Its aims include representing and promoting the joint interests of public information network providers in the UK, acting as a forum for ideas and advice on how to use electronic public information technologies, and encouraging the advancement of those technologies. The Society presents the 'Better Connected Websites Awards', based on assessments by SocITM.

Society publication. An official publication issued by, or under the auspices of, a society, institution or association.

SocITM. <www.socitm.gov.uk> The (UK) Society of Information Technology Management was formed in 1986 to further the interests of ICT managers in the public sector, including local authorities, police services, fire services, housing etc. There are currently 1,600 members from over 450 organizations, and SocITM has become a respected forum especially in assessment of progress towards e-government. It is associated with the 'Better Connected Websites Awards' given by the Society of Public Information Networks (SPiN).

SOCRATES. <www.socrates-uk.net> The overall programme of various (EU) actions aiming to improve the quality and strengthen the European dimension in education. The programme includes Comenius (schools and colleges), Erasmus (higher education), Gruntvig (lifelong learning), Lingua (foreign languages) and Minerva (ICT, distance learning). The first phase of SOCRATES ended in 1999; the second phase runs 2002–2006.

Soda pulp. (*Papermaking*) Chemical wood pulp which is prepared by digesting the wood fibres under pressure with a solution of caustic soda. This process is usually applied to straw and soft or deciduous trees such as aspen, poplar, etc., which cannot be treated by the sulphite process (*see* Sulphite pulp) usually confined to coniferous woods.

Soft cover. *See* Paperback, Paper-bound.

Soft hyphen. *See* False hyphen.

Soft-ground etching. One in which the ground commonly used is softened by mixing with tallow, the design being made with a pencil on a piece of fine-grained paper stretched over the ground. This, when etched with acid, gives the effect of pencil or chalk lines in the printed impression.

Software. A generic term for computer programs (both Operating systems and Applications). Supplied on disk, CD-ROM, or downloadable over the Internet. *See also* Hardware.

Software and Information Industry Association. *See* SIIA.

Solander case. A book-shaped box for holding a book, prints, pamphlets or other material, named after its inventor, Daniel Charles Solander (1736–82). It may open at the side or front with hinges, or have two separate parts, one fitting over the other. Its most developed form has a rounded back, projecting Squares like a book, and possibly one or more spring catches. Also called 'Solander', 'Solander box', 'Solander cover'.

Solid filing. *Synonymous with* letter-by-letter filing. *See* Alphabetization.

Solid gilt. A book the edges of which have been gilded 'in the round', i.e. after the book has undergone Rounding. *See also* Gilt on the rough, Marbling under gilt, Rough gilt edges.

Solid matter. Type which has been set without 'leads'. Matter so set is said to be 'Set solid'. *See also* Leaded matter, Leads.

Solidus.   An oblique stroke used for various purposes, e.g. to indicate line endings in a bibliographical description of a title-page, as An/address/to the/… Also called 'Virgule'.

SOLINET.   <www.solinet.net> (1438 West Peachtree Street NW, Atlanta, GA 30309, USA) Southeastern Library Network, Inc., a network consortium formed in 1973 to enable members to improve access to information and effectively address the region's needs for education and economic development; 2,500 member libraries in the states of Alabama, Florida, Georgia, Kentucky, Louisiana, Mississippi, North Carolina, South Carolina, Tennessee, Virginia, Puerto Rico and the Virgin Islands. An OCLC Network Affiliate.

Sombre.   A binding with both Blind and coloured Tooling.

Sort.   A single type-letter. The complete assemblage of sorts, made up in the correct proportion of characters, is called a 'font'. Also called 'Character'. *See also* Code, Digit, Special sorts.

Sort of symbol.   (*Information retrieval*) A constituent part of a symbol, e.g. in the symbol ABA 553 there are six digits but only four sorts or characters (A, B, 3 and 5).

SOSIG.   <www.sosig.ac.uk> The Social Sciences Information Gateway, a Hub of the (UK) RDN providing a trusted source of selected, high quality Internet information for researchers and practitioners in the social sciences, business and law. Based at the University of Bristol.

Sound card.   An Expansion card which gives a PC audio capabilities; other hardware will usually be required for recording and playback.

Sound library.   A collection of audio recordings such as Compact discs, Gramophone records, tape, and sound film.

Source.   1. Any document which provides the users of libraries or of information services with the information sought.   2. Any document which provides information reproduced in another document.   3. The data or records providing the basis for an informational search.

Source document.   (*Information retrieval*) A document from which data is extracted. *See also* Source.

Source index.   An index to sources of unusual and elusive information. This is usually built up in the process of dealing with enquiries.

Source language.   The natural language in which a document is originally written. *See also* Code.

Source list.   A list of references appended to a treatise to show the sources used by the author. *See also* Reading list.

Source material.   *See* Primary sources.

Sous Direction des Bibliothèques et de la Documentation.   <www.sup.adc. education.fr/bib> The department of the French Ministry of Education responsible for libraries and information services within the general education system.

South African Institute for Librarianship and Information Science (SAILIS).   *See* Library and Information Association of South Africa (LIASA).

South African Library. *See* National Library of South Africa.

South-East Asian Regional Branch of the International Council on Archives. *See* SARBICA.

Southeastern Library Network, Inc. *See* SOLINET.

Space. 1. (*Printing*) A small rectangular block of metal not bearing a character, which is used between letters or words to provide spacing. Spaces are less than type height, cast in point sizes and smaller than an em quad (mutton), the square of the body. The usual sizes are:

en quad (nut), $1/2$ body or two to the em;
thick space ($1/3$-em space), $1/3$ body or three to the em;
middle space ($1/4$-em space), $1/4$ body or four to the em;
thin space ($1/5$-em space), $1/5$ body or five to the em;
hair space ($1/12$-em space), $1/12$ body or twelve to the em.

2. To remove from one place to another according to a prescribed format, e.g. to remove horizontally to the right, or vertically, on a printed page. 3. (*Information retrieval*) A unit of area on a record, i.e. an area that may contain only one printed character.

Space dot. *See* Centred dot.

Space lines. Strips of brass which are often used in place of Leads.

Spacebands. Wedge-shaped pieces of metal used in line-casting machines such as Linotype and Intertype to separate words and at the same time automatically justify lines of type.

Spacing. The distribution of printed matter on a printed page or pair of pages so that it is aesthetically satisfactory. It relates to the space between letters, words, lines, and any decorative or illustrative matter.

Spam. Unrequested, junk E-mail usually of a promotional nature and which is received as part of mass mailouts. In mid-2004 it was estimated that 50–70% of all e-mail was spam and Internet Service Providers were investigating improved Filters and other techniques to reduce the nuisance. Said to derive from the Monty Python Spam Song. *See also* Cloaking.

Spanish. The best grade of esparto grass. Cheaper grades grown in North Africa are known as Tripoli.

Spanish calf. A light-coloured calf on which brilliant effects can be obtained by staining.

Spanish Federation of Archives, Documentation, Libraries and Museums Societies. *See* FESABID.

Spanish library associations. *See* FESABID, SEDIC.

Spanish National Library. *See* Biblioteca Nacional (2).

SPARC. <www.arl.org/sparc> Scholarly Publishing and Academic Resources Coalition; an initiative of the Association of Research Libraries (ARL) in affiliation with the Association of College and Research Libraries (ACRL) and the Canadian Association of Research Libraries (CARL). Its goal is to reduce the risks to publishers of entering markets 'where the prices are highest and competition is needed most – primarily in the science, technical and medical areas – with alternatives to existing high-priced journals'. The initiative grew from a meeting of 45 ARL institutions in 1997; its first agreement was in 1998 with the American Chemical Society. There are now over 200 coalition members – research institutions, libraries and other organizations seeking to encourage competition in the scholarly communications market. A European equivalent – SPARC Europe – has been formed with the support of LIBER, SCONUL, JISC and other organizations.

Special bibliography. *See* Bibliography.

Special classification. A scheme of book classification which is applied to a single section of knowledge.

Special collection. A collection of books connected with local history, celebrities, industries, etc., or on a certain subject or period, or gathered for some particular reason, in a library which is general in character.

Special edition. 1. An edition of a work or works, re-issued in a new format, sometimes with an introduction, appendix, or illustrations, and having a distinctive name. 2. An edition which differs from the normal edition by some distinctive feature, such as better paper and binding or the addition of illustrations. 3. An extra or enlarged number of a newspaper or periodical, such as an anniversary, Christmas, or souvenir number.

Special Interest Group (SIG). A group of members of an organization formed to represent a focus on a specific area of activity; probably more applicable to a small area than a 'division' or 'section'.

Special issue. *See* Special number.

Special librarian. One who is in charge of, or is employed in, a Special library; should have a knowledge of the literature of the field covered by the library (not necessarily a special knowledge of the field itself) and also of the means of organizing it for use.

Special librarianship. The branch of librarianship which is concerned with selecting, administering, and evaluating books and non-book materials in specific and limited fields of knowledge, and disseminating the information contained therein to meet the needs of the particular institution or its clientele.

Special Libraries Association (SLA). <www.sla.org> (1700 18th Street NW, Washington, DC 20009, USA) Founded in the USA in 1909, the aims of this not-for-profit organization are to serve the interests of innovative information professionals and their strategic partners who, as special librarians, 'collect, analyze, package and disseminate information to facilitate decision-making in corporate, academic and government settings'. There are 58 regional chapters representing 12,000 members in 83 countries, 24 special interest divisions and several caucuses including information futurists, non-traditional careers and women's issues. The vision, mission and core value statements were revised in 2003; there is an extensive publishing programme.

Special library.   1. (a) A library or information centre, maintained by an individual, corporation, association, government agency or any other group; or, (b) a specialized or departmental collection within a library. 2. A collection of books and other printed, graphic or record material dealing with a limited field of knowledge, and provided by a learned society, research organization, industrial or commercial undertaking, government department or educational institution. It may also be a special branch of a public library serving certain interests or occupational groups, such as a technical library; or a subject library meeting the needs of all enquirers on a given subject, such as a music library. Broadly, a library which is neither academic, commercial, national nor public. It is intended to serve the needs of a portion of the community requiring detailed information respecting a limited subject field.

Special number.   A special issue (usually enlarged in size) of a periodical devoted to a special subject or occasion. More routine occasions to which issues of periodicals are wholly or partly devoted are: (a) directory issue containing a directory of the trade or group served by the periodical; (b) membership list containing a list of members; (c) proceedings issue containing papers read at a conference, or a summary of the same; (d) an annual review, or annual report, issue surveying the past year and giving tables of statistics, possibly with forecasts relating to the following year; (e) yearbook (handbook, or almanac) issue combining any or all of the foregoing types, together with general data kept up to date by annual revisions. *See also* Special edition.

Special sorts.   Type characters which are not usually included in a Font, and are supplied on request, such as fractions, musical signs, superior and inferior letters and figures, etc.

Special title-page.   A title-page, usually with imprint, preceding a single part of a larger work. Also one preceding the normal title-page of a complete work which is issued or re-issued as part of a collection, series, or serial publication.

Species.   In classification, the groups into which a genus is divided. *See also* Predicables, five.

Specific cross-reference.   A reference in a catalogue to a specific heading or headings.

Specific differences.   Differences which characterize some individuals as a *specific* sub-class within a more comprehensive *generic* class.

Specific entry, principle of.   An entry in a catalogue under the actual subject, as distinct from one under some broader heading embracing that subject. It should be as specific as, but not more specific than, the content of the document. This is the principle for entry of subjects in a dictionary, subject or classified catalogue. *See also* Cataloguing, principles of.

Specific index.   An index such as that to Brown's Subject Classification, which has one entry only to each subject. Also called 'One-place index'. *See also* Relative index.

Specific reference. (*Cataloguing*) One which states the exact heading to which reference must be made as (in a dictionary catalogue): Automobiles *see* Motor cars, whereas a general reference would be: Animals *see also* under the names of individual animals, as Antelope. In the subject index to a classified catalogue references are usually specific as: Religion 200, Methodists 287. *See also* General reference.

Specific subject. (*Classification*) The most precise, and therefore least general, subject heading that is appropriate for a particular document. *See also* Close classification.

Specification. 1. Instructions prepared for a binder, printer, equipment supplier or builder setting out the details of work to be carried out. 2. (*Information retrieval*) The cataloguing, bibliographical, or similar description, of a document. *See also* Unit record. 3. (*Classification*) Definition by Specific difference in characters. 4. In the field of patents, a concise statement of a set of requirements to be satisfied by a product, a material or a process, indicating, whenever appropriate, the procedure by means of which it may be determined. A *provisional specification* is a specification filed with a patent application merely to establish a date for disclosure of an inventive concept to the Patent Office; it does not include a claim to the monopoly sought. A *complete specification* is a patent specification which describes at least one preferred way in which the invention may be performed, and which sets out a claim or claims for the protection sought. 5. (*Book production*) A book designer's specification listing typeface and size, style for headings, margins, illustration type and position, etc.

Specificity. (*Information retrieval*) In the testing of an information retrieval system, a measure expressing the ratio of the number of relevant or non-relevant documents retrieved to the total number of documents in a file.

Specificity rule. (*Cataloguing*) This rule provides that an entry in a subject catalogue should be made under the specific subject of a document, not under a more general one which includes that specific subject.

Specimen pages. Printed pages which are submitted by the printer to show the proposed style of setting. They usually include a chapter opening with any sub-headings.

Speckled sand edge. A bound book of which the top-, fore-, and bottom-edges have been rubbed down with sandpaper and sprinkled or sprayed with colour.

SPECTRUM. <www.ala.org/spectrum> A programme of the American Library Association (ALA) to encourage black and ethnic minority people to enter the librarianship and information professions. There is a bursary scheme for students, and mentoring and leadership support for those later in their careers. CILIP consulted its membership in 2003/2004 on the introduction of a similar scheme.

Spell checker. Software, commonly available as part of an application such as a word processor, used to check, in either batch mode or while-you-write, the spelling of words and to suggest alternatives when errors are identified. Most implementations have the facility for creating custom dictionaries for those terms or spellings excluded from general purpose spell checkers.

Sphragistics. *See* Sigillography.

Spider. *See* Web crawler.

SPIN. *See* Society of Public Information Networks.

Spine. The part of the cover of a book which conceals the folds of the sections. It normally bears the title, author and (when in a publisher's case) the publisher's name. Also called 'Back', 'Backbone', 'Shelf-back', 'Backstrip'.

Spine title. The title which appears on the spine of a book. It is often shorter than the title as given on the title-page.

Spiral binding. A type of binding used for pamphlets, art reproductions, commercial catalogues, and occasionally books, printed on separate leaves, usually of art paper. These leaves are drilled or slotted near the binding edge to take a spiral-twisted wire or strip of plastic, which is drawn through the apertures. A tendency for the wire to be torn through the holes makes this style unsuitable for publications likely to be subject to much, or to careless, handling. Also called 'Coil binding', 'Spirex binding'. *See also* Plastic binding.

Splice. A join made by cementing or welding together two pieces of film or paper so that they will function as one when passing through a camera, processing machine, projector or other apparatus. Lap splices are those in which the two pieces overlap and are cemented together. Butt slices are those in which the two pieces are placed together without overlapping and welded.

Split boards. The boards normally of Millboard forming the covers of a book, which are split to receive the ends of the tapes on to which the sections are sewn.

Split catalogue. A library catalogue in which the different varieties of entry – e.g. subject, author, title – are filed in separate alphabets. *See also* Divided catalogue.

Split fractions. Type for setting fractions cast in two parts which when combined make the complete fraction. The upper half contains the upper figure and the lower half the dividing line and the lower figure. Fractions may be set vertically with a horizontal dividing line, e.g. $\frac{3}{8}$ or diagonally, e.g. ³/₈ or 3/8.

Split leather. Leather which has been divided into two or more thicknesses.

SPLSs. Service Public Library Standards. *See* Public library standards.

Spoiled letter. *See* Damaged letter.

Spoiled sheets. Printed sheets which bear imperfections; it is to allow for such that additional sheets, called 'overs', are issued by the printer. Often called 'Spoils'.

Spoken Word Publishing Association (SWPA). <www.swpa.co.uk> SWPA is a UK trade association for the spoken word industry, reflecting the growing market for tapes and CDs of classics, comedy, novels, poetry, drama, and children's subjects. Publishes *SWPA Resources Directory* (a.).

Spongy paper.   *See* Featherweight paper.

Sponsorship.   A financial arrangement whereby an individual or a company will contribute to, or subsidize, the cost of the operation of a service or the production of a book; the sponsor's name is associated with the resulting service or production, and goodwill is generated by the encouragement of projects that would otherwise not be possible.

Sports and Recreation Information Group.   *See* SPRIG.

Spot colour.   A technique of colour printing in which each colour within a document requires a separate pass through the printer and in which just that colour is applied to the output.

Spread.   A pair of facing pages.

Spreadsheet.   An Application program devised for the manipulation of numerical data. Based on the concept of *cells*, which hold discrete values (numerical or alphabetic), and which are arranged in *columns* and *rows*, the spreadsheet is used to calculate the result of certain effects – 'what if' calculations. Especially useful when handling large amounts of tabular data and can equally be applied to textual data where no calculations are required.

SPRIG.   <www.sprig.org.uk> (English Sports Council North West, Astley House, Quay Street, Manchester M3 4AE, UK) The Sports and Recreation Information Group serves the interests of information workers in the fields of leisure, tourism, sport, recreation and hospitality management. An Organization in Liaison (OiL) with CILIP.

Sprinkled edges.   The three cut edges of a book which have been finely sprinkled with colour to prevent them becoming, or appearing to be, soiled. *See also* Edges.

SQL.   Structured Query Language, a standard language for interrogating relational databases.

Squabble.   A printing fault caused by one or more letters being pushed into an adjacent line.

Square.   1. Said of a book the width of a cover of which is more than three-quarters its height. *See also* Narrow, Oblong.   2. (*Binding*). The boards of a book are cut slightly larger than the bound sections after trimming so as to leave an even projection over the Head, Tail, and Fore-Edge. This projection of the boards is called the 'square'.

Square back.   *See* Flat back.

Square brackets.   Signs [ ] used in a catalogue or bibliographical entry to indicate that whatever appears within them does not appear in the original, but has been supplied by the copier. Not to be confused with Parentheses.

Square capitals.   The alphabet used as a book hand from the third to the fifth centuries, being adapted from the Roman lapidary capitals. The letters had square serifs instead of being sharply pointed as were those cut in stone. Also called 'Capitales quadrata' and 'Quadrata'. *See also* Lapidary type, Rustic capital.

Square corner. (*Binding*) Folding the covering material over the boards in such a way that after cutting a wedge-shaped piece at the corner, one turn-in may neatly overlap the other. *See also* Library corner, Mitred corner.

Square up. To trim, or adjust, illustrations so that all corners are right angles.

Squared up half-tone. *See* Half-tone.

Squares. The portions of the boards of a bound book which project beyond the paper on which it is printed.

S.R. 1. Abbreviation for the Register of the Stationers' Company. 2. SR Search and retrieve, the original name used by ISO standards 10162 and 10163. In March 1997 the US NISO Z39.50 version 3 was accepted as an ISO standard and numbered 23950. *See* Z39.50.

S.R. & O. Statutory Rules and Orders. *See* Statutory Instruments.

SRIS. *See* Science Reference and Information Service.

SRO. Scottish Record Office. *See* National Archives for Scotland.

SRS. *See* Selective record service.

SRW. Search/Retrieve Web Service, a protocol bringing together Z39.50 experience with developments in web technologies which aims to integrate access to various networked resources, and to promote inter-operability between distributed databases. A part of the ZING initiative.

S/S. Abbreviation for same size; an instruction, written on the illustration, to the blockmaker to make a block the same size as the copy.

SSCs. *See* Sector Skills Councils.

SSL. Secure sockets layer, an approach to World Wide Web security developed by Netscape.

s/t. Abbreviation for Small type.

Staatsbibliothek zu Berlin – Preussischer Kulturbesitz. <www.staatsbibliothek-berlin.de> (Unter den Linden 8, 10117 Berlin/Potsdamerstr. 33, 10785 Berlin, Germany) Founded in 1661 the Library now contains over 10 million books (including 4,400 incunabula), 38,000 periodical titles and many important special collections including the manuscripts of compositions by J. S. Bach, Beethoven and Mozart.

Stab marks. Punctures made in folded sheets of printed paper preparatory to sewing.

Stab stitch. *See* Side stitch.

Stabbed. *See* Stabbing.

Stabbing. Binding together one or more sections of a book with wire or thread passed through holes stabbed through the back edge of the folded sheet. This method prevents the book from lying flat when open. A book so bound is said to be 'stabbed'. Piercing the Boards with a bodkin for the Slips to pass through is sometimes termed 'stabbing'. *See also* Stitching.

Stack.   1. A piece of furniture containing at least four tiers of shelves back to back.   2. The space equipped for the storage of books on one or more floors; more properly, the self-supporting structure of steel book cases, often extending for several floors, or decks, and independent of the walls of the building. For other terms used in connection with book stack equipment, *see* Bay, Compartment, Deck, Press, Range, Section (2).   3. A stack room usually adjoining a public department, containing lesser-used books, and to which only the staff have access.

Staff.   US spelling for a Stave in music. *Pl.* Staffs.

Staff and line management.   *See* Line management.

Staff appraisal.   The technique of monitoring the performance of individual members of staff, having agreed objectives and criteria with the individuals at the outset, and discussing the findings with them during and after evaluation. Staff appraisal is a continuous process, and is usually used as a basis for staff development programmes, promotion opportunities, etc. Can be used to reconcile the individual's view of the job with the organization's view: such a use is sometimes termed *job audit*.

Staff development.   The continuing and wide-ranging process of improving the performance, efficiency, morale, and job satisfaction of all members of an organization's staff; methods include individual counselling, in-service training, the encouragement of qualification attainment, and other support facilities. *See also* Continuing professional development, Training.

Staff enclosure.   That part of a public department of a library which is restricted to the use of the staff. *See also* Circulation desk.

Staff manual.   A guide book indicating the correct procedures and processes to be followed by the staff in the various departments or branches of a library system. Called in the US a Procedure manual.

Staff training.   *See* Training.

Stained edges.   The edges of a book which have been stained with colour. Where only the top edges have been stained the term 'stained top' is used. *See also* Edges.

Stained label.   A coloured panel painted or printed on the spine of a book as a background for lettering, and to simulate a leather label.

Stained top.   *See* Stained edges.

Stalls.   In old libraries, combined book shelves and reading desk, or Lectern, the books being stood upright on shelves (of which there were three) above the reading desk. The fore-edges of the books faced outwards, and the books were chained. This type of shelving was first used by Sir Thomas Bodley at the Bodleian Library, Oxford, and replaced the mediaeval lectern.

Stamp.   *See* Blocking, Panel stamp, Tooling.

Stamp Acts.   Towards the end of the seventeenth century in the UK duties were imposed on certain legal documents, and paper, vellum and parchment. The Stamp Act of 1712 added to the list of dutiable articles, e.g. essay periodicals like the *Spectator*, and from time to time the list increased. The notorious Stamp Act of 1765 ordered a stamp to be applied to all legal documents in the colonies; it met with great opposition in North America, and was repealed the following year. The subsequent history of the duties is of innumerable variations, generally increasing in the eighteenth, and declining in the nineteenth and twentieth centuries. *See also* Revenue Stamps.

Stand-alone. Any device that operates on its own without connection to other devices; usually refers to computers when not connected to a network.

Standard Address Number. *See* SAN.

Standard author. An author whose writings have sufficient literary merit to justify a place in the literature of the country, and which, it is hoped, will not become out of print.

Standard Book Number (SBN). The UK forerunner of the International Standard Book Number system (*see* ISBN). The system was prepared by the Publishers Association of Great Britain and came into operation in 1968; in 1969, after a meeting sponsored by ISO, the ISBN system was developed. During 2005–2007 major changes will take place to the ISBN systems, which will be extended to 13 digits.

Standard Book Numbering Agency. A company which is formed in each participating country to operate the International Standard Book Number system. Its duties are to allocate where necessary, verify, record and publish International Standard Book Numbers and maintain master files. In the UK, the Standard Book Numbering Agency Ltd. was jointly sponsored by J. Whitaker & Sons Ltd., the Council of the British National Bibliography Ltd. (later incorporated within the Bibliographic Services Division of the British Library) and the Publishers Association. In the USA the R. R. Bowker Company performs this function. *See also* ISBN, Standard Book Number.

Standard edition. The edition of an author's books, so called by the publisher, to suggest a good quality of book production which is better than that used for a cheaper edition. It may contain notes and an introduction but need not be a Critical edition nor a Definitive edition. *See also* Uniform edition.

Standard for Record Repositories. <www.nationalarchives.gov.uk/advice/standards> Issued at intervals by National Archives (UK) and previously by the Historical Manuscripts Commission, as a supplement to BS 5454:2000 *Recommendations for the Storage and Exhibition of Archival Documents*. The current standard is 3rd edition, 2001; it consists of guidelines covering the constitution, finance, staffing, and access policies for repositories.

Standard Generalized Markup Language (SGML). An encoding scheme adopted by the International Organization for Standardization as ISO 8879 (1986) for the definition of device-independent, system-independent methods of representing texts in electronic form. This representation is achieved through the definition of document hierarchy and the use of text Markup which ensures that every element in a document fits into a logical structure. Hytime is a version for particular use with Multimedia documents and XML is a derivation for use on the World Wide Web. *See also* International SGML/XML Users' Group.

Standard Music Description Language (SMDL). <xml.coverpages.org/gen-apps> A standard developed for ISO/IEC CD 10743:1995 as an architecture for the representation of music information, either alone or in conjunction with text, graphics or other information needed for publishing or business purposes.

Standard title. The title under which copies of a work, or musical composition, appearing under different titles, is entered in a catalogue. Also called 'Conventional title', 'Uniform title'.

Standard work. A book recognized as of permanent value.

Standards. Agreed targets for performance, or an accepted format for the operation of a system etc. Especially Standards for library services (*see* entry below), or, in the context of technical standards, commonly agreed methods and procedures for complex operations. *See also* American National Standards Institute Inc., British Standards Institution, COPANT, DIN, International Organization for Standardization, Z39.

Standards for library services. A statement of the criteria by which a given type of library service can be evaluated; such statements may be specific in quantitative detail, or may be intended as a stimulus towards an ideal, in which case they may be rather entitled *guidelines* or *mission statements*. In some areas of work, standards as such are being replaced by the concept of planning procedures and output measurement as better indicators of efficiency and effectiveness. Quality of provision is a key concept in recent standards. *See also* Metrics, Public library standards, Statistics for library services.

Standing Committee on Business Information. *See* SCOBI.

Standing Committee on Library Education (SCOLE). A Standing Committee of the American Library Association concerned with the development of professional education.

Standing Committee on Official Publications. *See* SCOOP.

Standing committees. Committees which local authorities and other bodies may set up to carry out particular and continuing functions, or manage departments, or provide services.

Standing Conference of National and University Libraries. *See* SCONUL.

Standing Conference on Library Materials on Africa. *See* SCOLMA.

Standing formes. *See* Standing type.

Standing order. 1. An order to supply each succeeding issue of a serial, periodical or annual publication, or subsequent volumes of a work published in a number of volumes issued intermittently. 2. One which is to be acted upon until countermanded. Also called 'Continuation order' and (in the US) a 'Till-forbid order'.

Standing press.   A larger press than a Bench press. It stands on the floor and is used to press cased books. Pressure is applied by a platen which is screwed down with a crow bar. *See also* Building-in machine, which dries and presses books in a few seconds.

Standing type.   Type from which a book has been printed, and which is kept 'standing' exactly as it came from the machine, to be used again if further copies are made. Also called 'Live matter', 'Standing formes'.

Stanhope Press.   The first all-iron printing press introduced in 1800 by Charles Mahon, 3rd Earl Stanhope (1753–1816). The platen, which covered the whole forme, was operated by a screw which had several levers thus enabling a satisfactory impression to be obtained with less physical effort than with previous machines.

Star.   *See* Asterisk, Reference marks.

Star map.   A map of the heavens. Also called an 'Astronomical map'.

Star network.   A topology for a Local area network in which each device is connected to the central controller or hub in a Star-shaped arrangement. *See also* Bus network, Ring network.

Star signature.   A signature indicating an off-cut (part of a sheet) and distinguished by an asterisk placed with the signature letter or figure of the main part of the sheet. This part of a section is usually placed inside the part bearing the plain signature.

Starch.   The original material for sizing paper. It is now used in addition to other sizing agents as a loading agent in order to give a hard 'rattle' and an improved 'finish' to paper.

Starch paste.   An adhesive made of wheat and rice starch added to water. Easily reversible so that it can be used in conservation and restoration work.

Starr.   A Hebrew deed, covenant, contract, or obligation, anciently required to be filed in the royal exchequer, and invalid unless so deposited. The name was applied to all agreements between Jews and Christians and, occasionally, to other Jewish documents before the expulsion of the Jews from England in 1290. Starrs were written in two languages, Latin or Norman-French, with an acknowledgement in Hebrew at the foot.

Start.   Leaves of a book are said to 'start' when the sewing is defective, causing the leaves to become loose.

Starter.   (*Classification*) The first curve, used in the Colon Classification to enclose the Subject device number. The second, or closing, curve is called the 'Arrester'. *See also* Brackets, Curves.

State.   An impression of an engraving taken from a plate at any stage in the perfecting process. Various states include *open letter proof* and *publication state*. An *early impression* is one of the first copies to be taken; it is consequently sought after by collectors as representing a print taken when the plate is in its best condition.

State document centre.   A library that has the responsibility of collecting, preserving and organizing as complete a file as possible of the public documents of the state in which it is situated.

State library. In Australia, the United States, etc., a library maintained by state funds, which preserves the state records and provides books for the use of state officials, books relating to the history of the state, books published by authors living in the state, and newspapers published in the state. In many states, all classes of books are purchased in order to supply any resident's needs for books or information. *See also* National library.

State Library Administrative Agency. A term used in the (US) Library Services Act, 1961, to mean the official State agency charged by State law with the extension and development of public library services throughout the State.

State library agency. A state organization existing to extend and improve library services in the state. It should be free from partisan politics and political interference of all kinds, led by professional librarians, supported by law, and adequately financed. Functions include the planning of a state-wide public library service, promotion of the development of these libraries supervising library provision with a view to improving services by formulating and enforcing minimum standards.

State library associations. In Australia, the United States, etc., each state has a local library association. The standard and size of these organizations vary enormously. Most issue a newsletter, and some produce more substantial journals.

State Paper Office of Ireland. *See* National Archives of Ireland.

Stationarii. Men commissioned by universities in mediaeval times to attend to the production and distribution of books.

Stationer. From Lat. *stationarius* 'one who stands' (i.e. at a stall). One who sells stationery. Originally used to mean a bookseller.

Stationers' Company. The authority which regulated and organized printing and the book trade in England. It was established by a Royal Charter from Queen Mary in 1557, created a livery company in 1560, and until the passing of the Copyright Act in 1842 had an absolute monopoly, as all apprentices to the printing trade were obliged to serve a member of the Company, and every publication was required to be 'Entered at Stationers' Hall' as proof of registration. The *Registers* which commenced in 1554 are of great value in the history of English literature.

Stationery Office (TSO). *See* Her Majesty's Stationery Office, Parliamentary Publications.

Statistical bibliography. 1. The assembling and interpretation of statistics relating to books and periodicals in order to: (a) demonstrate historical movements; (b) determine the national or universal research use of books and journals; (c) ascertain in many local situations the general use of books and journals. 2. To shed light on the processes of written communication and of the nature and course of development of a discipline by means of counting and analyzing the various facets of written communication.

Statistical multiplexer. *See* Multiplexer.

Statistics for library services. Collection of data on the operation of library services to demonstrate effectiveness and efficiency, value for money, impact on the community etc. Traditional statistics have tended to focus on inputs (budget, stock) and outputs (issue figures, number of visits etc.) without addressing questions of performance or user satisfaction. Professional organizations collect data to prove the need for government or institutional support for services, and bodies such as Cipfa and the Library and Information Statistics Unit at the University of Loughborough in the UK have adopted more innovative approaches. Internationally, ISO 2789 *Information and Documentation – International Library Statistics* offers guidance on the collection of data for electronic information resources and e-delivery as well as traditional services, and advice on performance indicators. ANSI/NISO Z39.7 *Standards on Library Statistics* is currently under review. Collection of data on electronic resources has been under urgent discussion by many organizations including ARL, IFLA, CLIR, NCLIS, ICOLC and the STM Association. *See also* Metrics, Performance, Standards for library services.

Statutory Instruments (UK). Documents by which the power to make, confirm, or approve Orders, Regulations, or other subordinate legislation, conferred by an Act of Parliament on Her Majesty in Council or on a Minister of the Crown, is exercised. Prior to 1 January 1948, when the Statutory Instruments Act, 1946, came into operation, they were known as *Statutory Rules and Orders*. Although Statutory Instruments are frequently required to be laid before Parliament, they rank as Non-Parliamentary Publications.

Statutory reference. In the British patents field, a reference placed at the end of a patent specification as a statutory act by the Comptroller to direct attention to another specification.

Stave. 1. The five horizontal lines on which musical notation is written or printed. Spelt 'staff' in the US. 2. *See* Section (1).

STC. Abbreviation for *A short-title catalogue of books printed in England, Scotland, and Ireland, and of English books printed abroad, 1475–1640*, by A.W. Pollard and G.R. Redgrave (London, Bibliographical Society, 1926). A second edition appeared from the same publisher in 3 vols. 1976–1991; this is an author list of 37,000 items in 500 locations, with an index (vol. 3) to printers and publishers, etc. It retains the original numbering system – STC numbers. Records are included in the *English Short Title Catalogue (ESTC)*.

STC-Wing. Abbreviation for *A short-title catalogue of books printed in England, Scotland, Ireland, Wales and British America and of English books printed in other countries, 1641–1700*, compiled by D. G. Wing and originally published 1945–1951. A second edition appeared in 1972–1988 (Index Committee of the Modern Language Association of America). Continues *STC* above, and contains 120,000 entries. *See ESTC*.

Steel engraving. *See* Engraving.

Stem. 1. The outline of the design of a type letter; the bare lines apart from the serifs, which indicate most clearly the character and height of the letter. The main stroke of a letter. 2. The body of a type letter between the face and the foot. Also called the Shank or Body. 3. A string of letters which occur at the beginning of several related words, e.g. 'libr' for library, libraries, librarians, etc.

Stencil. 1. The basic principle of printing, in which a wax, silk or other stencil is used. The ink is applied to the back of the printing image carrier (i.e. the stencil) and reaches the front through the image areas which are porous and open. *See also* Silk screen. 2. The 'master' or image area which carries the image, and by means of which the printing is done. 3. A thin cut metal plate which allows the transfer of a design, etc., to paper when an ink roller or brush is passed over its surface.

Step-and-repeat camera. A microfilm camera which provides a series of latent image frames in a predetermined pattern on a single sheet of film.

Step-and-repeat machine. A machine for multiple copying (on offset plates, etc.), with devices for the adjustment of each copy. Intended specially for reproduction in colour in which the printing plates for each colour must be superimposed precisely when printing.

Stepwise operated camera. *See* Planetary camera.

Stereo. *See* Stereotype.

Stereoscopic slide. A pair of positive photographic prints made from negatives taken from two slightly different viewpoints to give a three-dimensional effect when viewed through a specially made viewer.

Stereotype (Stereo). A metal printing plate carrying a printing surface in relief, made by pouring stereotype metal into a papier-mâché (called 'flong'), or plaster of paris, mould of the original type, line block or very coarse half-tone. Future printings are made from the resulting 'stereos'. The whole process is known as stereotyping. Curved stereos are used on rotary presses for high-speed work, particularly newspaper printing. The process was patented in 1725 by William Ged, a Scottish printer, who was commissioned by Cambridge University to stereotype prayer books and bibles. *See also* Matrix (3).

Stereotype metal. An alloy of tin, antimony, and lead; used for casting stereos.

stet. (Lat. 'let it stand') Written in the margin of printer's copy or proof to denote the cancelling of any correction marked thereon. Dots under the words indicate the correction to which the 'stet' refers.

Stick. 1. The tool used by the compositor for setting or forming into lines the types selected from the Case. It usually contains about twenty lines of 8 point type. 2. A device like a small-diameter walking stick divided down its length, used for holding from one to about six copies of a newspaper. Also called 'Newspaper rod', and 'Newspaper stick'.

Stiff back. *See* Tight back.

Stiffened and cut flush.   *See* Cut flush.

Stiffened paper covers.   *See* Paper covered.

Stigmatypy.   The use of small type-units to design and print a picture or portrait.

Stigmonym.   Dots instead of the name of the author. Used on the title-page and elsewhere in a book. Where the authorship of such books cannot be traced, they are catalogued under their titles.

Still frame.   A single image on a videotape held on the display screen.

Stipple.   A printing surface of a copper plate used for making illustrations; it consists of dots, instead of lines. The process is to cover the plate with ordinary etching ground, and through this to sketch the contours and lightly indicate the main shadows with dots by means of the etching needles and a roulette. The portions of the plate thus uncovered are bitten with acid, after which the drawing is completed and given brilliance by flicking or dotting directly on to the surface of the plate with a specially curved graver or roulette. The dots may be fine or coarse, to give effects of light and dark. Although this method was used by W. W. Ryland (1732–83) the Royal engraver, it was first made popular in the eighteenth century by Francesco Bartolozzi, an Italian painter and engraver who came to London in 1764 from Venice and worked for the publisher John Boydell. Half-tones are a kind of stipple engraving.

Stippled edges.   The edges of a book which have been spotted irregularly with colour to prevent them appearing to be soiled. *See also* Edges, Marbled edges, Sprinkled edges, Stained edges.

Stippling.   1. (*Paper*) A roughened finish, also called 'Pebbling'.   2. (*Printing, Art*) A gradation of light and shade produced by dots.

Stitching.   The operation of fastening a pamphlet consisting of a single section, with wire or thread passed through the centre of the fold. *See also* Sewing, Stabbing, Thread stitched.

STM.   Scientific, technical and medical; an abbreviation for a field of publishing in which there is substantial revenue, high prestige, and where the development of new methods of electronic publishing and document delivery has been especially active.

STM Association.   <www.stm-assoc.org> (Prins Willem Alexanderhof 5, PO Box 90407, 2509 LK The Hague, Netherlands) An association formed to discuss ideas, pass information and support the interests of the STM publishing community – large and small companies, non-profit organizations, learned societies, primary and secondary publishers and 'new players'. The Association has been active in developing usage statistics for electronic products.

Stock.   1. (*Printing*) Paper or other material for printing upon.   2. (*Paper*) The material (rags, waste-paper, esparto, ropes, etc.) used for making paper; the term is applied at any stage of manufacture, whether to untreated materials or the finished paper. *See also* Half-stuff, Pulp, Stuff, Whole-stuff. Also, the printing trade term for paper.   3. All the books and other items in a library. 4. All the books available for sale by a bookseller or publisher.

Stock book. *See* Accessions record/register (1).

Stock check. *See* Stocktaking.

Stock editor. A member of the staff of a library who is responsible for maintaining the stock in good physical condition and for ensuring that the latest and most useful titles are available in adequate quantities.

Stock revision. A part of the stock management process; the stock of a particular library or a total library system is examined by subject area on a regular basis with regard to its adequacy to meet user needs, and is improved by the purchase of new material, or extra copies, or by discarding old material as appropriate.

Stockholding bookseller. A retail bookseller who keeps a varied and large stock of books.

Stockholm Challenge. <www.challenge.stockholm.se> A set of awards organized by the city of Stockholm to recognize ICT initiatives that benefit society. In 2004, there were over 900 entries for the awards from 100 countries worldwide, including projects in e-government, e-business, culture, health and education. The Challenge was set up in 1994 by Martin Bangemann, then European commissioner responsible for ICT, and was formerly called the Bangemann Challenge.

Stocktaking. The process of taking stock by checking records of items possessed with copies on the shelves and records of loans and making appropriate changes to catalogue and any other related records. Also known as stock check.

Stone. Usually a steel-top table (originally it was stone) on which the imposing work – that is, the assembling of the various parts of a printing job – is done. It is on the stone that the type, blocks, etc., are locked in the chase and levelled with mallet and planer. *See also* Imposition.

Stone engraving. Engraving on blue or grey lithographic stone (fine-grained, compact limestone); a hand process which is used chiefly for script and line drawings in which sharpness and precision of line are more important than artistic expression. The outline is traced and then deeply scored with a steel or diamond pen. As the number of copies which can be made on a hand press is small, it is usual for a stone engraving to be made as an original for transferring to a plate for use on a printing press. Also used to indicate a print made from an engraved stone.

Stone proof. One made after the forme has been locked up for press, but before it has been put on the press.

Stop list. (*Indexing, Information retrieval*) A list of words or terms, or roots of words, which are considered to be meaningless or non-significant for purposes of information retrieval, and which are excluded from indexing. The opposite of Go list.

Stop-cylinder press. A type of printing machine in which a cylinder (which is placed over a reciprocating bed on which rests the forme) revolves once during which the impression is made on paper fed underneath the cylinder, and stops until the forme is again in position for printing the next sheet. Often called a 'Wharfedale' press. *See also* Miehle, Perfecter, Single-revolution machine, Two-revolution machine.

Stopping out. Painting with varnish such parts of an etching plate as are not to be further etched by acid during repeated dipping in the acid bath. In blockmaking, painting out of the screen or the negative, parts of the subject which are not required to be printed.

Stopword. A word which cannot be used as a search term on a particular database.

Storage. A source from which documents or information of specified descriptions may be supplied. A receptacle for information. *See also* Memory.

Storage centre. A library or library agency in which co-operating libraries store little-used library materials, and which are readily available on request. Also called 'Deposit library', 'Reservoir library' (US), Repository library.

Storage devices. Any device used to store digital data such as a hard Disk. When used in the context of an overall computer system, *primary* storage refers to the main memory, which is usually the internal store of the computer (RAM) and *secondary* includes hardware such as Disk drives.

Story hour. A definite period set aside for telling stories to the youngest members of a junior library. The stories are told by members of the staff, particularly the children's librarians.

Straight matter. Text uninterrupted by illustrations, tables or any special settings.

Straightening. The task of arranging tidily books in correct classified order. *See also* Reading shelves.

Straight-grain leather. A leather that has been dampened and rolled, or 'boarded', to make the grain run in straight lines. An innovation credited to Roger Paine.

Straight-grain Morocco. Morocco leather in which the natural grain has been distorted by elongated lines or ridges all running in the same direction.

Strap binder. A binder fitted with thin steel strips which pass through the staples of the periodicals.

Strapwork. (*Binding*) Interlaced double lines, usually forming a geometrical pattern.

Strawberry Hill Press. The private press on which Sir Horace Walpole, fourth Earl of Orford, printed his own and other books. The Press functioned between 1757 and 1789, and the printers included William Robinson, Thomas Kirgate, Benjamin Williams, and others. The Press was situated at Walpole's estate at Strawberry Hill, Twickenham, Middlesex, UK.

Strawboard. A coarse yellow board, made from straw and used for the covers of books.

Streamer. A printed poster used in shop or window advertising.

Streaming. A process whereby data – particularly audio and video – is transferred in Real time, in a stream rather than in a complete package for subsequent playback. This requires technologies that match the bandwidth of the audio or video signal to the viewer's connection, so that the data is always delivered at the designed frame rate. *See also* Webcasting.

Stress. The thickened part of a curved stroke or letter.

Strike. *See* Matrix (3).

Strike through. A fault in printing when ink printed on one side of a sheet penetrates to the other. *See also* Show through.

Strip film. A length of microfilm which is too short to be conveniently wound on a reel.

Strip in. To combine one photographic record with another, or a photograph and lettering, preparatory to using them together in making a printing plate. In lithography the operation of stripping is analogous to the operation of imposing in letterpress.

Strip index. A form of Visible index in which entries are made on strips of card which take only one line of typewriting. These strips are placed in a metal frame and the surface of the whole of each strip is visible.

Striped film. Cinematograph film edged with a narrow band of magnetic coating for carrying sound.

Stripping. The removal, and subsequent destruction of documents of no further importance, from files which it is decided to preserve.

Strix Award. *See* Kent (Tony) Strix and Public Sector Awards.

Strong. (*Printing*) A term used by some printers to indicate a printed page with too many lines of type on it.

Structural notation. A notation to a classification which indicates the hierarchy or structure of the scheme. A non-structural notation does not do this. *See also* Hierarchical notation.

Structured indexing language. The use of words in non-literary order to construct succinct meaningful subject headings (e.g. 'libraries, university', for university libraries; 'Greenhouses: heating, natural gas-fired', for natural gas-fired heating of greenhouses). *See also* Artifical indexing language, Natural language.

Structured query language. *See* SQL.

Stub. 1. The part of an original leaf which is left after most of it has been cut away to insert a correct one (*see* Cancel). 2. A narrow strip of paper or linen sewn between sections of a book for attaching folded maps or other bulky items. *See also* Compensation guards, Guard.

Student charter. *See* Charter.

Study pack. A collection of core journal papers and chapters from books gathered together as a unit in accordance with prevailing copyright regulations and distributed to students (either via the library or the academic department) for a section of their course. Also known as course pack.

Study score.   A musical score, similar to a Miniature Score but of a somewhat larger size due to the work being fully scored, i.e. having music for so many instruments that it would be difficult to read if reduced to the normal miniature score size. *See also* Score.

Stuff.   The pulp in the paper-maker's vat prior to its being removed to the mould. *See also* Half-stuff, Pulp, Stock (2), Waterleaf, Whole-stuff.

Sturt (Ronald) Foundation. *See* Talking newspapers.

Style book.   *See* Style manual.

Style manual.   A set of rules drawn up by a printing establishment for the guidance of its staff to ensure that details of typography, spelling, capitalization, punctuation and other matters about which opinions and customs differ, are in accordance with the prevailing practice of that establishment. Such rules are known as the 'style of the house'. *Rules for compositors and readers of the Oxford University Press* are a standard set followed by many printers and authors.

Style sheet.   1. A guide to a printer's House style.   2. A list of types and their sizes, style of setting, etc., proposed for a given publication. *See also* Style manual.   3. (*Desktop publishing*) A comprehensive list of the paragraphs and their characteristics used in a document which ensures consistency throughout. A style sheet for a paragraph will include such information as the Typeface, size, any indentations, space before and after, and the style of the following paragraph. Style sheets have the advantage that should one decide to change a particular characteristic towards the end of a project, the change can be applied quickly to the complete document. *See also* Cascading Style Sheets.

Stylus, Style.   A writing instrument, pointed at one end, which was used in ancient and mediaeval times for writing on wax or clay. *See also* Electric stylus.

Subaltern genera.   The intermediate classes of a classification between the Summum genus and the Infima species.

Sub-branch.   A small branch library open a few hours each day. A part-time library. *See also* Branch library.

Sub-committee.   A committee formed from members of a larger committee to consider one or more matters on behalf of the larger committee to which it reports its deliberations.

Subdivision.   1. The word commonly used to denote the process of dividing a scheme of classification into its parts.   2. The result of such subdivision.

Sub-entry.   In indexing, the part of the entry following the entry-word or heading which is used to subdivide a large number of references into a group of related items, i.e. the whole entry minus the entry-word or heading.

Sub-group.   (*Archives*) In *MAD*, a level of archival arrangement and description, corresponding to sub-fonds in ISAD(G).

Subheading. 1. A secondary heading, used in the subdivision of a subject. In a verbal heading it is the second or subsequent word, separated from the preceding by punctuation. 2. A word or group of words added to a heading and designed to delimit a particular group of entries under the heading, or to designate a part of the entity named in the heading. Subheadings may be subjected to modification, and if there is more than one modification of a subheading, each of the modifications is then known as a sub-subheading. Each group of sub- and sub-subheadings is indented in printing to make the meaning clear. The terms sub- and sub-subheadings are often abbreviated to 'subhead' and 'sub-subhead'.

Sub-index. An index within an index.

Subinfeudation. The granting or sub-letting of lands by a feudal vassal to an undertenant on the same terms as he held them from his overlord. Abolished in England in 1290, but the principle still survives in Scotland.

Subject. 1. The theme or themes of a book, whether stated in the title or not. 2. (*Indexing*) A unit concept found in, or derived from, manuscript or published literary material. It may be found, or expressed, as a theme, name, date, first line of a poem, title of a book, or be an expression coined to convey the gist of the material indexed, etc.

Subject analytic. *See* Analytical entry.

Subject arrangement. Books arranged in order of subject, either alphabetically or according to some scheme of classification.

Subject authority file. The list of subject headings used in a given catalogue, and the references made to them. Also the entries made for the classified list of class symbols or numbers and the appropriate subject index entries made when first allocating a book to a particular position in the classification. An entry is made for each step taken when indexing by the chain indexing method. *See also* Authority list, Chain index, Name authority file.

Subject bibliography. A list of material about a particular subject or individual.

Subject catalogue. Any catalogue arranged by subjects, whether in alphabetical or classified order. Alphabetico-classed catalogue.

Subject cataloguing. That part of cataloguing which involves the allocation of subject headings to entries for specific books or other documents. *See also* Descriptive cataloguing.

Subject Classification. The scheme devised in 1906 by J. D. Brown (1862–1914), in which the main classes in the evolutionary order are Matter and Force, Life, Mind, and Record. The notation is mixed (letter and figure) and does not permit of easy extension although the Categorical Tables enable a certain amount of subdivision. The third edition (1939) was edited by J. D. Stewart. After that it has not been revised and is now a dead classification. Also known as 'One-place' classification.

Subject concepts. (*Classification*) The terms which result when a subject is divided by a single characteristic. The group of terms which so results is called a 'Facet'.

Subject department. A department in a large general library in which are located resources on a particular subject, e.g. science, whether intended for reference or for home-reading. Also called 'Departmentalized library'.

Subject device. Ranganathan's term for the process of further dividing a given number by any other number from the schedules. It is one of the distinctive principles of the Colon Classification for Hospitality and number synthesis and is used in the Dewey Decimal Classification when a subject such as 016 Subject Bibliography is divided by any other number from the schedules.

Subject entry. 1. In a catalogue, an entry under the heading adopted to indicate a book's subject. In a subject catalogue it is the basic unit, and includes the description of the document, and its location. In the classified file of the Classified catalogue the heading may also be the Location mark. Subject entries for music are entered under the medium of performance (*see* Medium (6)) or the form (*see* Form (2)) in which the music is written. They may also be given under the subject described in the music. 2. In an index, an entry relating to a subject as distinguished from one beginning with the name of a person.

Subject guide. A guide to the shelves of a library, showing where books on particular subjects may be found. Also called 'Topic guide'.

Subject heading. The word or group of words under which books and other material on a subject are entered in a catalogue in which the entries are arranged in alphabetical order. The heading may include punctuation to which an arranging significance may be assigned. In a Classified catalogue the subject heading consists of a classification symbol with or without its verbal meaning. It may also include entries for all material on the same subject in an index or bibliography, or arranged in a file. Lists of headings are used by some cataloguers to aid them in their choice of appropriate subject headings and to achieve uniformity. A standard listing is the *Library of Congress Subject Headings*.

Subject heading language. The terms used as subject headings and under which entries are made, as well as those from which references are merely made to other subject terms.

Subject index entry. An entry in the subject index of a classified catalogue which directs to the class number under which entries for books on the required subject will be found.

Subject libraries. *See* Subject department.

Subject reference. A reference from one subject to another whether a synonym or a related heading.

Subject series. A number of books published in a named series by one publisher and dealing with different phases of a single subject or with a particular field of knowledge. The books are usually written by different authors, are not usually reprints, and are uniform in textual and physical characteristics. Similarly, a number of musical compositions dealing with different phases of music, media of performance, form, etc.

Subject specialization.   A scheme of co-operation whereby libraries in a restricted geographical area purchase books on a specific subject. In some schemes the libraries act as depositories for preserving little-used books on their particular subject which might otherwise be discarded.

Subject-word entry.   Entry in a catalogue under a word of the title of a book indicative of its subject matter.

Sub-librarian.   In UK academic libraries, a senior librarian with managerial responsibility for main sections of work, e.g. Reader services, or for major branch libraries. Responsible to either the Deputy Librarian or the Librarian.

Subordination.   The allocation of a subject term to its right place in the classification schedules; its order of precedence in the Hierarchy. In a Faceted classification the placing of a term belonging to one Facet after a term belonging to another facet, in a Citation order.

Subscriber.   A person who pays a subscription to receive a periodical as published, or to be a member of a society, or of a private library. *See also* Subscription library.

Subscribers' edition.   An edition prepared for circulation only to persons who have agreed to purchase on announcement and before publication. It may differ from the ordinary 'trade edition' by the inclusion of a list of subscribers, by being printed on hand-made or other special paper and having larger margins, or by being sumptuously bound.

Subscript.   1. An indexing notation.   2. A small letter or figure put below the level of the foot of a full-size lower case character as in H_2O. Usually called an 'Inferior' character. *See also* Superscript.

Subscription agent.   A firm or organization which arranges, at the order of an individual or library, for the regular delivery of serials as published, and handles the financial records. *See also* Managing Agent.

Subscription books.   1. Those published at intervals by societies and issued to subscribing members.   2. Individual books of limited appeal, the publication of which depends to some extent on subscriptions promised prior to publication, and the price of which is raised after publication. Also called Subscription edition.

Subscription library.   A commercial lending library the members of which pay subscriptions entitling them to borrow books during the period of the validity of their subscription. They were first formed in England in the late seventeenth and early eighteenth centuries. *See also* Circulating library.

Subscription price.   The price at which books are sometimes offered for sale before they are published. The price is usually lower than the after-publication price. This is done to give the publisher some guidance as to the potential sales of the book and therefore of the number to be printed.

Subseries.   A series of publications, the title of which is distinctive and is dependent on the title of another series.

Subsidiaries.   The parts of a book in addition to the text and including notes (whether placed in the pages or massed at the end of a book), bibliographies, appendices, glossaries, plates, indexes, imprint, colophon, blank leaves, end-papers and book jackets. Sometimes called 'Reference matter'. Also called 'End-matter', 'Back matter'. *See also* Preliminaries.

Subsidiary rights.   Rights enjoyed by authors to allow works to be made into films, broadcasts, serials or sound recordings.

Subsidy publishers.   *See* Vanity publishers.

Substance.   The weight of paper expressed in terms of weight per ream of sheets of a given size; the weight of a ream of a particular size and number of sheets is known as the 'substance number'. The 'substance' of the paper is the product of the density, i.e. the degree of dilution of the Stuff flowing on to the machine wire, and the speed at which it is permitted to flow, plus the speed of the machine wire.

Subtitle.   A secondary or subordinate title, usually explanatory, and often following a semicolon, 'or', 'an', or 'a'.

Suggestion card.   A printed card which is filled in by a reader with particulars of a book suggested for addition to a library. All appropriate bibliographical information is entered, and in some libraries it subsequently serves as an Order card. Also called 'Recommendation card', 'Request card', 'Requisition card', 'Suggestion slip'.

Sulphate pulp.   (*Papermaking*) Chemical wood pulp which has been prepared by cooking wood chips under pressure and high temperature in a solution consisting mainly of sulphate of soda (Glauber's salt). The resulting paper is strong, and is often used unbleached, but it can be bleached white. The process was introduced by Dahl in 1883–4. *See also* Soda pulp.

Sulphite pulp.   (*Papermaking*) Chemical wood pulp which has been prepared by submitting the wood fibres to the action of sulphurous acid and its acid salts (bisulphite of lime, magnesia, or soda) at high pressure and in closed vessels. The process was invented by B. C. and R. Tilghmann in 1863–6 and is usually used with coniferous woods. *See also* Soda pulp.

Summum genus.   The first, comprehensive class from which the division of a classification commences. The terminology of schedule construction, as used by Ranganathan is: *universe* (= *summum genus*) an aggregate of *entities* (things or ideas) under consideration which is *divided* by a succession or *train* of *characteristics* each of which gives rise to an *array* of classes. The *order* of a class is the number of characteristics used to divide it out of the universe; the *rank* of a class is its position in its array. A *chain* is a series of classes in successive subordination, each one being subordinate to the preceding one. *See also* Infima species, Subaltern genera.

SUNCAT. <www.suncat.ac.uk> Serials UNion CATalogue for the UK, a project arising from the UKNUC which received funding from the JISC and the Research Support Libraries Programme to develop a key tool for locating serials held in UK libraries and a central source of high-quality bibliographic records. The project commenced in February 2003 and a pilot service containing records from 22 leading research libraries was expected to be launched in September 2004.

Sunk bands. (*Binding*) Cords or bands (in old books, often of leather) which are placed in grooves sawn into the backs of sections of a book to give a smooth back or spine. The sewing of the sections passes round the bands. The opposite of Raised bands. Also called 'Sunk cords'.

Suomen Kirjastoseura. *See* Finnish library associations.

Super. *See* Mull.

Super Royal. A sheet of printing paper measuring $20^{1/2} \times 27^{1/2}$ inches.

Super-calender. A machine, separate from the paper-making machines, which consists of a stack of from five to sixteen rolls. Paper is passed through under pressure to be given a highly glazed finish; it is then known as 'Super-calendered'. *See also* Calendered paper.

Super-caster. An instrument for casting large sizes of type for hand-composition.

Supercomputer. A computer that performs at or near the currently highest operational rate for computers. Primarily used for scientific and engineering applications with intensive computational requirements, and simulations such as nanoscale electronics, quantum chemistry, computational chemistry, aerodynamics and the molecular modeling of proteins.

Superimposed coding. A system of coding which uses more than one code symbol per concept, the combination of code symbols being such that the number of random combinations is minimal.

'Superimposition' policy. *See* 'No Conflict' policy.

Superior figures (letters). Very small characters aligning with the top of the next text type, usually as reference marks to footnotes or notes at the end of the chapter or text, or in a margin. They are cast on the mean line, and often on the same body as the type with which they appear. Also called 'Superiors', 'Superscript'. *See also* Inferior characters, Mean line, Reference marks.

SuperJANET. <www.ja.net> The broadband high speed part of JANET. The name was coined in 1989 for a new initiative aimed at providing an advanced optical fibre broadband network for UK higher education. SuperJANET was envisaged as a network of networks formed by a national network complemented by a number of regional MANs. The SuperJANET project has transformed the JANET network from one primarily handling data to a network capable of simultaneously transporting video and audio in real time, enabling users and researchers to use Multimedia tools such as videoconferencing. In March 2001 SuperJANET4 was launched with a 2.5 Gbps core backbone from which connections to regional network points were made at speeds ranging between 155 Mbps to 2.5 Gbps. In 2002 the core SuperJANET4 backbone was upgraded to 10 Gbps. SuperJANET4 also saw an increase in userbase with the inclusion of the further education community and the use of the backbone to interconnect schools networks. The contract UKERNA holds for the provision of SuperJANET4 ends in December 2005 and SuperJANET5 is planned. *See also* Abilene.

Superordinate class. (*Classification*) A class which is of more general extension or higher grade, or rank: a more general class. *See also* Co-ordinate classes.

Superscript. (*Printing*) A small character aligning with the top of a full-size lower case character; superscripts are usually used as reference marks to footnotes or notes at the end of the chapter or text. Usually called 'Superior' characters. *See also* Subscript, Superior figures (letters).

Supplement. 1. Additional matter continuing, or adding new matter to that already published. It is usually issued separately. 2. An extra sheet, section, or number accompanying a normal issue of a newspaper or periodical. *See also* Addendum.

Supplementary publication. *See* Auxiliary publication.

Supplied title. The title composed by the cataloguer to indicate the nature and scope of a monographic work with a very brief or a misleading title.

Supposed author. One to whom is attributed by some authoritative source the authorship of a work published anonymously or of which the stated authorship is doubted. Also called 'Attributed author', 'Presumed author'. Such a book is catalogued under the name of the supposed author which phrase appears after the name to qualify it. The authority for the supposition is given in a note.

Supposititious author. One who is substituted for the genuine author with intent to defraud.

Suppressed. 1. Withheld from publication or circulation by author, publisher, government, or ecclesiastical authority because of unreliability, inaccuracy or moral tone. 2. (*Bibliography*) Of a leaf which has been cancelled because of some inaccurate, imperfect, or objectionable feature.

supra. (Lat. 'above') Used in footnotes and sometimes in the text to refer to an item previously mentioned. *See also* infra.

SureStart (Children's Centres). In the UK, an early-years concept encouraging the educational development of children from the most disadvantaged families. For the involvement of libraries in this initiative, *see* BookStart.

Surface paper. *See* Coated paper.

Surface printing. *See* Planographic process.

Surface sizing. The addition of resin or other materials to the surface of a sheet of paper or board to render it more resistant to liquids, especially writing ink. *See also* Engine-sizing.

Surfing.　*See* Net surfing.

Surname.　A family name which a person uses in conjunction with his or her personal names. It is the name used as a heading for entries in a catalogue or bibliography.

Surname indexing.　The allocation of symbols to surnames so that they may be arranged in order other than by strict alphabetization.

SUSCAG.　<www.archives.gla.ac.uk/suscag> Scottish University Special Collections and Archives Group, established to foster co-operation and discuss issues of common concern; it is involved in funding plans and in development of information strategies and policies.

Suspended floor.　Removable panels laid on a metal grid with space below for runs of data and power cables, providing maximum flexibility for cabling expansion. A common feature of computer rooms that has been implemented in some modern library buildings.

Suspension file.　Loops of tough manila, the full width of a filing cabinet drawer, which are attached to, and suspended from, rigid metal or plastic bars which at their extreme ends rest on a cradle, or framework, contained in the drawer. Into these loops are placed files or wallets containing documents, papers, photographs, etc.

Suspension shelving.　Shelves affixed to, or between, shelf-ends having lugs which engage in slots in uprights fixed to the wall. No support other than the shelf-end is provided at the front of the shelves. The shelf-ends are the full depth of the shelf and serve as book supports. Also called 'Bracket shelving'. *See also* Cantilever shelving.

SUTRS.　Simple Unstructured Text Record Syntax, describing the lack of formatting that is applied to records extracted from databases with this syntax: they are presented as a simple text string.

SVD.　Schweizerische Vereinigung für Dokumentation/Association Suisse de Documentation. *See* ASD.

SWARBICA.　South and West Asian Regional Branch of the International Council on Archives.

Swash Letters.　Italic capitals and lower-case letters with tails and flourishes.

Swedish binding.　*See* Cut flush.

Swedish Institute for Children's Books.　<www.sbi.kb.se> (Odengatan 61, SE-113 22 Stockholm, Sweden) Opened in 1967; aims at acquiring literature which is unobtainable, or rarely found, in Swedish Libraries. It also serves as a documentary centre for children's books built up on an international basis; and to supply individuals and libraries with the information and material they need.

Swedish Library Association (Svensk Biblioteks Förening).　<www.biblioteksforening.org> (Saltmätargaten 3A, PO Box 3127, 103 62 Stockholm, Sweden) Founded in 1915, one of the association's principal tasks is to act as a gathering agency, a common platform for Swedish library co-operation. Publishes *Biblioteksbladet* (18 p.a.).

Swedish national library.　*See* Kungliga Biblioteket.

Swelled rule.   *See* Rule.

Swinging bookcase.   A form of compact book storage whereby two presses consisting of hinged three-foot tiers are placed one on each side of one fixed press. When the books on either side of the fixed press or on the inner sides of the two outside presses are to be consulted, the hinged tiers are swung out into the gangways. Also called 'Pivoted bookcase'.

Swiss library associations.   *See* ASD, Association of Swiss Librarians.

Swiss national library.   *See* Schweizerische Landesbibliothek.

Switched Multimegabit Data Service.   *See* SMDS.

Switching.   The process of connecting machines, terminals, users, etc., via a telecommunications link that is established at the time it is required, rather than being a permanent connection of wires. Switching in networks is required whenever a signal moves between carriers (e.g. Ethernet to X.25) or changes speed (e.g. 10 Mbits per second Ethernet to 100 Mbits per second FDDI). There are two primary categories of switching: packet and circuit.

SWMLAC.   *See* Museums, Libraries and Archives Council (MLA).

SWOT analysis.   An evaluative procedure based on four facets – strengths, weaknesses, opportunities and threats.

SWPA.   *See* Spoken Word Publishing Association.

Swung dash.   A curved dash ~ similar to a Tilde.

Syllabic notation.   A notation using the letters A–Z to produce pronounceable syllables, each of which signifies a Concept. The three symbol letter notation is used in D. J. Foskett's London Education Classification, e.g. Jip = Assessment; Mob = Sciences; Ser = Further education. Such class marks are easy to say and remember. Also called Pronounceable notation.

Syllabic writing.   The middle stage in picture writing in which a symbol was used to represent each syllable or vowel when this constitutes a syllable in the spoken language; thus, a combination of signs representing a group of syllables conveys a spoken word. A syllabic form of writing is known as a syllabary. *See also* Phonetic writing.

Syllabification.   The action or method of dividing words into syllables. Also called 'Syllabication'.

Symbol.   A substitute or representation of characteristics, relationships, or transformations of ideas or things.

Symposium.   1. A volume of the papers or addresses originally presented at a conference.   2. The conference itself.   3. A collection of articles specially written on a given theme.

Synchronous.   In user and citation studies, referring to changes that reflect the influence of age as shown in observations made on a single occasion. *See also* Diachronous.

Syncopism.   Applied to a pseudonym where dots take the place of certain letters. Such books are catalogued under their titles when the author's full name cannot be ascertained, with added entries under the leading initials of the syncopism. *See also* Pseudonym.

Syndetic.   Having entries connected by cross references. In information retrieval, co-ordination of two or more related documents.

Syndetic catalogue.   A dictionary catalogue that connects entries by a scheme of cross-references to form a co-ordinated whole. References are made from broad subjects to those that are less broad, and from these to still more subordinate subjects, and sometimes *vice versa*.

Syndetic index.   An index in which relationships between headings are provided, e.g. by the indexing sequence (classified or other subject arrangements), the use of subheadings and cross-references.

Synecdoche.   A figure of speech in which a species is used for the whole genus (e.g. 'bread' for food in general) or the genus for a species.

Synopsis.   1. A brief outline of the plot, setting, or important points of a play, book or serial.   2. A factual summary of an article or paper contributed to a learned journal, suitable for use as an abstract published in accompaniment with the article, presumed to be prepared by the author of the article but in any case subjected to the same editorial scrutiny and correction which is given to the full article.

Synoptic journal.   A journal which publishes brief resumés, abstracts, diagrams, etc., of full articles, which are not themselves published, but made available if requested.

Synoptic table.   A classification 'map' showing relationships between terms.

Syntactics.   A theory dealing with the formal relations between signs or expressions and the formal properties of language, distinct from their meaning or interpreters.

Syntax.   Concerned with the relations between symbols without reference to their meanings. *See also* Semantics.

Synthetic classification.   *See* Faceted classification.

Synthetic indexing.   *See* Co-ordinate indexing.

Synthetic indexing language.   A list of subject terms used as headings together with rules for the construction of headings for composite subjects. *See also* Enumerative indexing language.

System for Information on Grey Literature in Europe (SIGLE).   <www.cas.org/online/dbss/sigle> SIGLE provides access to reports and other grey literature produced in Europe. It was established in 1980 and is managed by EAGLE – the European Association for Grey Literature Exploitation. All subject areas are covered. The SIGLE database is available at <stneasy.org>.

System software.   *See* Operating system.

Systematic auxiliary schedules.   Twenty schedules provided in Bliss' Bibliographic Classification to serve as tables of common subdivision. Only the first three – form divisions (*see* Anterior numeral classes), geographical subdivision, subdivision by language – are of general application throughout the scheme, the remainder being applicable to groups of classes, to single classes, or to sub-classes. Symbols from these schedules are added to those from the main tables of the classification which indicate subject matter. Auxiliary tables are also provided in the Universal Decimal Classification.

Systematic bibliography. The enumeration and classification of books. The assembling of bibliographical entries into logical and useful arrangements for study and reference.

Systematic catalogue. A classified catalogue. One in which the classes and subjects are arranged in a logical order according to some scheme of classification.

Systematic file. *See* Classified file.

Systematic mnemonics. *See* Mnemonics.

Systematic schedules. *See* Systematic auxiliary schedules.

Système Electronique Couleur Avec Memoire. *See* SECAM.

Systems analysis. The examination and investigation of routines and administrative processes with the aim of bringing about improvements.

Systems librarian. One responsible for the day-to-day operation of the Integrated library system and possibly other library Automation, and charged with maintaining the Integrity and security of files, loading of new data, the setting of parameters in accordance with the needs of the library, and the downloading of data for use in external applications.

T1. (US) A leased line of 1.544 Mbps.

T3. (US) Specification for a 45 Mbps communication line.

Tab. (*Binding*) A small piece of paper, card, plastic or fabric attached to the outer edge of a card, or leaf of a book, and bearing one or more characters to serve as a guide or index.

Tabbed. A Guide card which has tabs projecting from the upper edge.

Table. 1. An arrangement of written words, numbers or signs, or of combinations of them, in a series of separate lines or columns. 2. A synoptical statement or series of statements; a concise presentation of the details of a subject; a list of items. *See* File (3).

Table book. 1. An ancient writing book comprised of wax-covered tablets of metal, ivory or wood and fastened together at the back by rings or thongs of leather. The writing was done with a stylus. 2. An obsolete name for a note-book. 3. An elaborately decorated edition of a book, often covered in velvet or silk, for display on a drawing-room table. Popular in the nineteenth century. *See also* Coffee-table book.

Table of contents. *See* Contents.

Table of precedence. (*Classification*) A statement of the correct citation order under a subject that the schedules subdivide according to several characteristics.

Tablet. 1. An ancient writing material made of clay (used when moist and afterwards baked), stone, lead, wood or ivory and covered with wax. Also called 'Tabula'. 2. A flat PC Peripheral with a stylus used primarily for the creation and inputting of graphics material. The stylus is said to convey the feel of traditional artists tools (i.e. pen, pencil) more so than a mouse, thereby aiding control over the finished image.

Tabular classification.   A classification or table consisting of several columns and several horizontal series, some of which may not be of equal numbers of terms. The terms need not recur as in cross-classifications. A tabular classification may be less regular and less complete than a cross-classification. *See also* Columnar, horizontal.

Tabular work.   (*Printing*) Figures and other matter arranged vertically in columns, with or without rules.

Tachygraphy.   A system of shorthand invented by Thomas Shelton and used by Samuel Pepys when writing his *Diary* (14 January 1660 – 31 May 1669).

Tack marks.   Small dots incorporated in imposing schemes for sheets printed by the Work And Turn method. One dot is used for the first side printed and two for the second.

Taehan Minguk Kukhoe Tosogwan.   [National Assembly Library, Republic of Korea] <www.nanet.go.kr> (1 Yeoido-dong, Yeongdeungpo-gu, Seoul 150-703, S. Korea) Founded in 1952, the library's principal role is to provide information to members of the National Assembly, and more recently, to the public. Since the new copyright laws of 1999, the Digital Library has enabled remote access to bibliographical and other databases and to the full-text databases of parliamentary proceedings. The Library moved to its present location in 1987, and currently holds over 1.8 million books and over 150,000 other items: periodical titles, newspapers, microform, audio-visual, and CD items. Publishes *Library Bulletin* (m.), *Kukhoe Tosogwanbo* [*Library Review*] (6 p.a.).

Tag.   (*Information retrieval*)   1. A character or digit which is attached to a record, or to a Field in a record, as a means of identification.   2. An identification label ('identifier') to signal to the computer what is coming next.   3. In a machine-readable record, one or more characters attached to a set of data that contains information about the set.   4. (*Desktop publishing, Text processing*) The use of codes to indicate formatting changes. *See* Markup.

Tag Image File Format.   *See* TIFF.

Tagged (Tagging).   (*Cataloguing, Information retrieval*)   1. With Variable field coding (*see* Fixed field coding), the use of symbols to indicate what part of an entry is about to follow.   2. Attaching characters or digits to a record, or to a field in a record, as a means of identification.

Tail.   1. The bottom or lower edge of a book. The term is applied both to the margin below the text and to the cover of the book.   2. In typography, the lower portion of letter *g* and the projection on the *Q*.

Tail edge.   *See* Lower edge.

Tail fold.   *See* Bolt.

Tail margin.   The space below the bottom line of a page of type matter. Also called 'Lower margin'. *See also* Margin.

Tail ornament.   An ornament appearing at the foot of a page or the end of the matter occurring on it, especially at the end of a section, chapter or book. It is sometimes called a 'Tail piece'. *See also* Head ornament.

Tail piece. *See* Tail ornament.

Tailband. A decorative band similar to a Headband but at the tail of a book.

Tailcap. The fold of leather at the foot of the spine of a book to protect the Tailband.

Tailed letter. A digraph consisting of a letter and a full stop, which gives the impression of being a letter with a horizontally tailed last stroke. *See also* Swash letters.

Take. The amount of copy taken at one time by a compositor to set up in type. *See also* Break-line, End a break, End even.

Take down. (*Binding*) To take a book to pieces and reduce it to its original sections. *See also* Pulled.

Taking out turns. Inserting the correct type character where the twin black footmarks (as ■■) on a galley proof indicate that the correct one was not available. *See also* Turned sort.

Talbotype. *See* Calotype.

Talking book. A 'book' for the blind recorded on tape. *See also* NTBL.

Talking newspapers. Cassettes containing news and short magazine articles; they are prepared locally and circulated amongst visually handicapped persons; in the UK there is a National Association of Talking Newspapers. In 1995, the Association set up the Ronald Sturt Foundation to organize new groups and assist in the training of volunteer helpers.

Tall copy. A book that has lost nothing of its original height in binding

Tally. (*Information retrieval*) 1. The form of a record, or unit, on which may be made one or more entries. *See also* Entry (5), File (3) 2. Notched piece of wood used as a receipt for money or goods, both public and private, from the early Middle Ages until about the third decade of the nineteenth century.

Tape. 1. A plastic strip coated or impregnated with magnetic or optically sensitive substances, used for data input, memory or output; being a linear medium, tape does not permit random access to data held on it, in comparison to Disks. 2. Loosely for Audiotape or Videotape.

Tape cassette. Audiotape wound onto two spools in an enclosed plastic case; this format protects the tape, and is easy to insert into playback equipment. *See also* DAT.

Tapes. The pieces of tape to which the sections of a book are sewn, the ends being pasted to the boards or between the split boards which form the covers.

Tape-slide presentation. A co-ordinated and synchronized programme of transparencies and audiotape.

TAPPI. <www.tappi.org> (15 Technology Parkway South, Norcross, GA 30092, USA) Technical Association for the Pulp and Paper Industry (US); a body concerned in the development of permanent/durable paper and deacidification processes. Has a large-scale publishing programme producing books, reports, conference proceedings and CD-ROM-based training products.

Target.   *See* Client/server.

Tarred brown paper.   Wrapping paper consisting of one or more sheets of paper coated or impregnated with coal- or wood-tar or bitumen and so given some degree of waterproofing. *See also* Union paper.

TASI.   <www.tasi.ac.uk> Technical Advisory Service for Images, a JISC-funded service that provides advice and guidance to the UK further and higher education community on the creation of digital images, their use to support teaching, learning and research and the management of digitization projects.

Tauber Report.   A report, *Resources in Australian libraries*, written by Maurice F. Tauber, Melvil Dewey Professor of Library Service at Columbia University, New York, of a systematic survey of the total library resources of Australia. It was published in 1963.

Taxonomy.   The science of classification. Also, the study of the names and naming of items in generic assemblies. The term has been revived in the discussion and development of standards for metadata; in this context the plural taxonomies has been used almost as a synonym for classification schemes.

TCP/IP.   Transmission Control Protocol/Internet Protocol, the standard that enables all connected computers, irrespective of manufacturer, to communicate in a single language over the Internet. It is an open, non-proprietary protocol. *See also* IP (2).

TDF.   Transborder Data Flow. *See now* Universal Dataflow and Telecommunications.

Teacher-librarian.   A title indicating a member of a school's staff with specific teaching commitments, but who is allocated a number of hours per week to organize and maintain a school library. *See also* School librarian.

Teacher's book.   An explanatory handbook issued with a series of textbooks or a single textbook for the use of teachers. It sometimes has a 'key' or answers to questions and problems.

Team.   Small collaborative groups of professional and assistant staff, established in libraries and information services to plan and operate activities and to examine specific problems. Team structures aid communication, encourage participation, and increase job satisfaction and commitment. The team leader will probably be a member of a more senior team, and by such means several teams will have interlocking, co-operative relationships.

Team librarianship.   The organization of professional staff into small groups responsible for various service functions or for several functions, within a certain geographical area or over the whole of a library system. Team librarianship removes professional staff from the daily routine of responsibility for a service point, thereby providing opportunities for organizational and individual development through joint setting of priorities and solving of problems. *See also* Team.

Tear sheet.   A sheet of paper torn from a publication; when the item consists of more than one sheet, it is called a 'clipped article' or 'clipping'. *See also* Cutting.

TechDis.   <www.techdis.ac.uk> The JISC TechDis service aims to improve provision for disabled staff and students in the UK further, higher and specialist education sectors through technology. TechDis provides an advice and information resource via extensive web-based databases and an e-mail helpdesk.

Technical abstract bulletin.   A periodical containing indicative and/or informative abstracts of newly published or released technical literature. The abstracts are usually arranged in subject order, and alphabetical subject and/or author indexes are provided.

Technical Association for the Pulp and Paper Industry.   *See* TAPPI.

Technical information centre.   An organization for acquiring, processing and disseminating technical information. Such a centre usually has a library and a staff of scientists and engineers for extracting, evaluating and indexing technical literature.

Technical information system.   A network of information services providing facilities for the processing of information and data, and its communication to users.

Technical journal.   A journal which is devoted to a particular branch of technology. Also called a 'Technical periodical'.

Technical library.   A library containing mostly books of a technical nature. When connected with a public library, it may be a section of the reference library or a separate department.

Technical processes, Department of.   *See* Processing department, Technical services department.

Technical report.   A scientific paper, article, translation, probably recording the current position of scientific research and development in a subject field. *See* Report literature.

Technical services.   All the activities and processes concerned with obtaining, organizing and processing library material for use.

Technical services department.   A department of a library where the functions of book acquisition, cataloguing, classification and processing are carried out. Also called 'Technical services division'.

Technician.   A sub-professional grade in libraries; technicians may hold a qualification relating to audio-visual, computing equipment etc. and be graded more highly than unqualified library staff, or they may be unqualified support staff.

Teenage libraries.   Libraries intended to serve young adult readers who are not attracted to adult libraries, but have outgrown libraries for children.

t.e.g.   Abbreviation for top edge gilt. *See* Gilt top.

TEI.   *See* Text Encoding Initiative.

TEL.   *See* European Library.

Telecommunications.   The means of communication over long distances, as by telephone or fax, and the broadcast methods of radio, television, or satellite. Electronic facilities such as the Internet and World Wide Web depend on telecommunications to link networks and computers.

Teleconferencing. Networked collaboration between colleagues communicating in real time using text messages, voice and screen. Users may share a joint view of a piece of work on screen. *See also* Videoconferencing.

Telematics. The converged technologies of computing, telecommunications and broadcasting. This has become one of the general terms used to describe features of the Information Society, Electronic commerce, networking etc. It has been particularly mentioned in the context of the European Union's programmes. *See* FP6.

Teleordering. A process whereby booksellers store orders daily, usually identified by ISBN, which are overnight automatically communicated to a central computer and thence directed to the terminals of participating publishers. Other publishers receive orders in the post. Confirmation or errors are reported back to the bookseller.

Telescoped notation. (*Classification*) The assignment of more than one facet to a single notation sequence, in an otherwise expressive notation.

Teletel. The French videotex service. The terminals are called minitels. *See* Videotex.

Teletext. The generic term for broadcast Videotex. British examples are Ceefax and Oracle.

Teletypesetting (TTS). The process of setting type with a teletypesetter apparatus, consisting essentially of a separate keyboard that perforates a tape which is fed into an attachment to the slugcasting machine, or into a sender that transmits electrical impulses telegraphically to any number of re-perforators, with the perforated tape causing the slugcasting machine to set type.

Teleworking. A general term used to describe a method of working in which the employee is not based in the employer's premises or office, but works at home or in another location, using computer and telecommunications technology to communicate with the employer. In the information field, data entry and online cataloguing are typical of the work that might be available. Although many such workers are employed by one employer on a permanent basis, it is a system that is also very suitable for the self-employed.

Telnet. A terminal emulation protocol for use over the Internet. Also, the name given to the software that uses the protocol and enables Remote login to networked computer systems.

Telonism. Terminal letters of an author's name used as a pseudonym, as N. S. (John Austis). *See also* Titlonym.

Template. A baseline document that can contain pre-assigned formatting features and text appropriate to a particular need – e.g. letter writing; report writing – and which can be used many times with appropriate additions and modifications. A range of standard templates are frequently provided in Word processing and other Applications software but customized versions are easily created for specific requirements. *See also* Wizard.

TEN-155. <archive.dante.net/ten-155.html> The European research network running at 155Mbps and which connected 20 national and one regional research networks between 11 December 1998 and 30 November 2001. Replaced by GÉANT.

Tendering. *See* Competitive tendering.

Tera. Prefix denoting one million million, as in terabyte, abbreviated TB or TByte.

Terabyte. 1,024 Gigabytes; colloquially, 1,000 Gigabytes.

TERENA. <www.terena.nl> (Singel 468-D, NL-1017 AW Amsterdam, The Netherlands) Trans-European Research and Education Networking Association formed in October 1994 to 'promote and participate in the development of a high quality international information and telecommunications infrastructure for the benefit of research and education'. Produces technical reports and other documents which are available from the web site.

Term. (*Information retrieval*) In an index, the subject heading or Descriptor. (*Indexing*) A heading consisting of the word(s) or symbol(s) selected from, or based on, an item in the text of a document, and used as an indexing unit, identifying an item in a classification scheme, or catalogue, or any form of information retrieval. *See also* Heading (2), Indirect subject heading, Mixed subject heading. Also (in patents literature) a word, phrase or sentence which is descriptive of the subject-matter content, or part of the subject-matter content, of a document. *See also* Authority list (1), Controlled term list, Open-ended term list.

Term indexing. Choosing words used in the text as headings of the index to the text. *See also* Concept indexing.

Terminal. A combination of VDU and Keyboard, often a microcomputer, used to contact a remote computer or network.

Terminal digit posting. Arranging and recording serial numbers of documents on the basis of the last digit of the serial number.

TERMNET. *See* INFOTERM.

Ternion. Three sheets folded together in folio.

Terrain model. *See* Relief model.

Tetraevangelium. A book containing the four Gospels.

Tetralogy. A set of four related dramatic or literary compositions, said especially of three Greek tragedies and a satyric comedy.

T$_E$X. A mark-up language, compiler and output software developed by Donald Knuth of Stanford University to facilitate the typesetting of mathematical and scientific expressions. A Type encoding program.

Text. 1. The body of a work following the Preliminaries. 2. The type matter on a page as distinct from the illustrations. 3. In the conservation of documents, that part of a sheet of paper or membrane of a document covered by writing, printing or drawing.

Text area.   *See* Type area.

Text block.   The leaves of a volume after they have been fastened together by stitching, glueing, stapling etc. The block is then cased in some way to form a book.

Text comparator.   A machine that presents the images of two documents so that they appear to lie exactly on top of each other. Tiny discrepancies in apparently identical pages thus become noticeable.

Text Encoding Initiative.   <www.tei-c.org> An international and interdisciplinary standard that helps libraries, museums, publishers, and individual scholars represent all kinds of literary and linguistic texts for online research and teaching, using an encoding scheme that is maximally expressive and minimally obsolescent. It is sponsored by the Association for Computers and the Humanities, the Association for Computational Linguistics, and the Association for Literary and Linguistic Computing and is hosted by four universities: University of Oxford Research Technologies Service; Brown University Scholarly Technology Group; University of Bergen Department of Culture, Language, and Information Technology; and the University of Virginia Electronic Text Center and the Institute for Advanced Technology in the Humanities. *See also* Type encoding program.

Text hand.   A style of writing employed for books, treatises and the headings of business documents from about 1100 to 1500.

Text mining.   A technology that looks for patterns in natural language text and, by applying techniques from natural language processing, data mining, and information retrieval, attempts to discover new, previously unknown information. Text mining can be used to identify and gather relevant textual sources, to analyze these to extract facts involving key entities and their properties, and to combine the extracted facts to form new facts or to gain valuable insights. *See also* National Centre for Text Mining.

Text title.   *See* Caption title.

Text type.   Type used for setting the text of a book or periodical, or other large amounts of copy. It is seldom larger than 14 point.

Textbook.   A book written specifically for use by those studying a subject, especially for academic purposes.

Textile binding.   An ornate style of binding using fabrics. It was popular in France and England during the Renaissance. Coloured satin and velvet, often embellished with many-coloured silk embroidery and gold and silver threads, were frequently used.

Texting.   *See* SMS.

Textual bibliography.   The study and comparison of texts and their transmission through different printings and editions.

Textual manuscript.   *See* Literary manuscript.

Textual records.   (*Archives*) Manuscript or typescript documents as distinct from cartographic, audio-visual, and machine-readable archives.

Textura.   *See* Gothic type.

Thames board.   A British-made board used in Edition binding. Each side is covered with brown Kraft paper to give equal tension, and thus rigidity.

Theatre Library Association.   <tla.library.unt.edu> (149 West 45th Street, New York, NY 10036, USA) The Association is a non-profit organization established in 1937 to advance the interests of all those involved in collecting and preserving theatrical materials and in utilizing those materials for purposes of scholarship. The membership is international and includes public and private institutions as well as librarians, curators, private collectors, historians, professors, theatre designers, writers, and other interested persons. Publishes *Broadside* (q.), *Performing Arts Resources* (a.); awards the George Freedley Memorial Award, and the Theatre Library Association Award for an outstanding American book in the field of recorded performance (established 1974).

Theatre Museum Library   <theatremuseum.vam.ac.uk> (c/o Theatre Museum, 1 Tavistock Street, London WC2E 7PA, UK) A branch collection of the (UK) National Art Library, at present housed in the Theatre Museum in Covent Garden; co-ordinates publication of *Directory of Theatre Resources*.

Thematic catalogue.   One containing a list of one or more composers' works and the opening themes or passages of each composition, or for each section of lengthy musical compositions. Entries are usually arranged in chronological order, or by categories.

Theme.   *See* Topic.

Thermal process.   A process for copying documents without the use of liquid chemicals. Heat sensitive paper is used to make copies from an original having carbon or metallic writing or printing inks.

Thermography.   1. Any printing process which involves the use of heat; specifically that method of printing from ordinary type or plates on an ordinary press and in which a special ink is used, the type impression being sprinkled while still wet with a special powder and then subjected to a heating process which causes the particles to adhere to the printed surface and fuse together to give the printing a raised effect. Also called 'Raised-letter printing', 'Imitation embossing' and 'Virkotype process'. 2. The Thermal process of document copying.

Thermoplastic binding.   A method of binding a book without sewing. The folds are cut off, the edges roughened and glued and the covers stuck on.

Thesaurus.   1. Literally, a storehouse, or treasury, of knowledge. A term which is best known through its use in the title *Thesaurus of English words and phrases* by P. M. Roget, first published in 1852 and frequently revised.   2. A lexicon, more especially where words are grouped by ideas; a grouping or classification of synonyms or near synonyms; a set of equivalence classes of terminology.   3. A compilation of groups of words, consisting of the links between words used in documents and words used as Descriptors, prepared for consultation in information retrieval. They display relations within the vocabulary based on semantics, not on orthography. A number of thesauri of the most commonly used terms in various subject areas have been published in order to achieve a unity of indexing terminology in their respective fields. 4. A thesaurus may be defined either in terms of its function or of its structure. In terms of function, it is a terminological control device used in translating from the natural language of documents into a more constrained system language (documentation language, information language). In terms of structure, a thesaurus is a controlled and dynamic vocabulary of semantically and generically related terms which covers a specific domain of knowledge.

Theses alive! <www.thesesalive.ac.uk> A two-year project begun in 2002 based at the University of Edinburgh and part of the JISC FAIR initiative to promote the adoption of a management system for electronic theses and dissertations in the UK.

Thesis. A report or treatise prepared as a part of an academic course for a higher degree or diploma. *See also* Dissertation.

Thick space. (*Printing*) A space whose width is one-third of its own body.

Thickness copy. *See* Dummy (1).

Thin client. A Client/server model where the client has the minimum amount of code possible, and the intermediate servers handle much of the processing load. This approach centralizes the complexity of a Middleware application to a few servers that are easily maintained. By contrast, in fat-client implementations, the client does most of the processing. In hardware terms, the thin client machine is frequently referred to as a network computer.

Thin paper. Sensitized photographic paper between 0.0038 and 0.0043 inches inclusive. *See also* Photographic papers.

Thin space. (*Printing*) A space whose width is one-fifth of its own body.

Thirty-sixmo. (36mo) A sheet of paper folded to form 36 leaves, making 72 pages. Also called 'Trigesimo-sexto'.

Thirty-twomo. (32mo) A sheet of paper folded five times to form a section of 32 leaves (64 pages) each leaf being one thirty-second of the sheet. Also called 'Trigesimo-secundo'.

THOMAS. <thomas.loc.gov> The US legislative information system operated by the Library of Congress.

Thorough-bass. *See* Figured-bass.

Thread. A group of linked discussions on a Usenet Discussion group.

Thread stitched. A booklet that is fastened with thread through the section fold. *See also* Sewing, Side-stitch, Wire stitched.

Three dots. Used on the type Base line thus ... in quoted text, or a catalogue entry, to indicate that some part of the original has been omitted. Called 'Omission marks', 'Ellipsis'.

Three-colour process. Printing by photo-mechanical colour separation in half-tone, which will reproduce colour in the copy in three printings of yellow, red and blue. *See also* Two-colour process, Two-colour reproduction.

Three-decker.   A novel published in three volumes during the latter half of the nineteenth century.

Three-quarter binding.   *See* Quarter binding.

Three-quarter leather.   A book bound similarly to one in Half leather, but with the leather of the spine projecting across a third of the sides. *See also* Leather bound, Quarter leather.

Thriller.   A novel of a sensational character, usually dealing with crime and criminals.

Throughput.   The volume of work that flows through an organization; this can be a useful basis on which to monitor performance.

Throw out.   Maps, tables, or diagrams likely to be much consulted during the reading of a book, are sometimes 'thrown out' by the binder. This is done by making the 'guard' the size of the page, or printing the map on extra large paper, and pasting it at the end of a book or beyond the text which refers to it, so that the whole of the map, etc., when opened out, may remain in view during reading.

Thumb book.   *See* Bibelot.

Thumb index.   A series of rounded notches cut into the fore-edges of a book, with or without tabs let in and bearing in progressive order from top to bottom the letters or words showing the arrangement. Usually provided for Bibles and dictionaries.

Tied down.   (*Binding*) Where the fillets which flank the bands of the spine are carried on to meet at a point near the hinge.

Tied letter.   *See* Ligature.

Tied up.   Said of type-matter that has been made up into pages and tied up with page-cord to secure it until imposition.

Tier.   A set of shelves one above another between two uprights and reaching from the floor to the top of the shelving: a section of a Press. *See also* Bay, Book press, Book stack, Bookcase.

Ties.   1. Silk, leather, cord, tape, ribbon or other slips attached, usually in pairs, to the outer edges of boards of books for a decorative purpose, or to prevent sagging by holding the covers together.   2. Terminations to tooled lines on each side of projecting bands on the spine of a bound book and carried over on to the covers to form ornamental features.

TIFF.   Tag Image File Format, particularly used when saving scanned documents for their use in Applications and Image manipulation software. Variants of the format exist.

Tighe Report.   A report by F. C. Tighe and based on a national survey of the conditions of service of assistant librarians in UK public libraries. The *Recommendations on welfare and working conditions of public library staffs*, based on this report, were approved by the Council of the Association of Assistant Librarians and adopted by the Council of the Library Association in May 1953. *See also* Jordan Report.

Tight back.   A binding in which the cover of leather or other material is pasted or glued to the spine, so that it does not become hollow when open. The pages do not lie flat when the book is open unless the paper used is thin and not stiff, as e.g. India paper. This is therefore a less satisfactory form of binding than either Flexible or Hollow. Also called 'Fast back', 'Stiff back'. *See also* Flexible sewing, Hollow back.

Tight joint.   *See* Closed joint.

Tilde.   (*Printing*) An accent in the form of a wavy line as used over letters in Spanish and Portuguese: – ñ; õ. Also used in mathematics.

Till-forbid order.   *See* Standing order.

Tilted shelves.   The bottom or lower two or three shelves of a bookcase which are arranged in a sloping position to render the examination of titles easier.

Time numbers.   A series of numbers or letters designed to facilitate the arrangement of books in chronological instead of author or alphabetical order. *See also* Biscoe time numbers, Merrill alphabeting numbers.

Time-division multiplexing.   *See* Multiplexer.

Times Europa.   A new type, designed by Walter Tracy for *The Times*, to replace Times New Roman which had been in use for forty years. Tracy was manager of the typographic department of the Linotype Co. and designed five newspaper text faces: Jubilee (1954); Adsans (1958) a 4³/₄ pt. sans serif face; Maximus; Linotype Modern (1961) and Times–Europa, first used by *The Times* on 9 October 1972.

Times New Roman.   A Typeface designed under the direction of Stanley Morison by the Monotype Corporation for *The Times* newspaper in 1932 and later extensively used in book work. Usually called 'Times Roman'.

Time-schedule.   *See* Time-sheet.

Time-sharing.   The ability of a computer system to handle different users carrying out different tasks during the same time period. Each user is provided with processing capability in turn but the speed of change is intended to simulate continuous operation. Time-sharing systems, at one time common, have fallen into disuse as a result of the wide availability of low-cost, high performance PCs.

Time-sheet.   A schedule showing the exact hours each day that each member of staff is scheduled to be on duty. Also called 'Time-schedule'.

Tint.   (*Printing*) 1. A ready-made dotted, hachured or other pattern, available in various densities, which can be applied by a draughtsman, block-maker or printer to an illustration in order to give an impression of grey to a line drawing. Usually called 'Mechanical tint'.   2. A solid panel in a second colour.

Tipped in.   A single leaf, errata slip or illustration, inserted in a book at the inner edge with a narrow edge of paste against the following page.

Tipping machine.   A bookbinding machine for the gluing of single plates and end-papers on to folded sheets or sewn sections. Some models also glue paper covers on to the folded and sewn sections.

692

Tips.   Very thin millboards used for book-binding.

TISA.   Towards an Information Society for All; a series of annual conferences operated by the British Council from 2001 (Bologna). Subsequent meetings have been in Berlin (2002), Paris (2003), Bucharest (2004). The theme of the conferences has been to address the digital divide and encourage the launch of accessible services in the developing world. *See also* World Summit on the Information Society (WSIS).

TISN.   Todai International Science Network. *See* SINET.

Tissued plate.   An illustration in a book which has a thin tissue placed between it (either loose or pasted to the inner margin) and the text page to protect it from Set-off. Sometimes the tissue bears the caption relating to the illustration or an appropriate quotation. *See also* Interleaf.

Tissue-papers.   Sheets of superfine thin paper placed in front of illustrations to protect them from Set-off while the ink is fresh. These are often removed after the ink has dried, but sometimes they are to be found Tipped-in, and they frequently bear a typographical description of the illustration.

Tithe documents.   Documents relating to tithes. In the UK, the Tithe Act, 1936, as amended, provides that copies of tithe documents shall be transferred to the National Archives (UK) or to any public library or museum or historical or antiquarian society willing to receive them. On the transfer of such documents the governing body of the library, museum or society assumes responsibility for their proper preservation. The Tithe (Copies of Instruments of Apportionment) Rules were made in 1946 (S. R. & O., 1946, No. 2091) to implement the provisions of the Act.

Title.   The word or words by which an intellectual work is designated on its Title-page, and distinguished from any other work. In its fuller sense, it includes any sub-title, alternative title, or associated descriptive matter, but excludes the name of the author and/or editor, translator, etc. (unless the name forms a grammatically inseparable part of the title) and the edition, but not the imprint. *See also* Back title, Binders title, Collective title, Cover title, Short title, Spine title.

Title analytic.   *See* Analytical entry.

Title area.   (*Reprography*) The portion of a Microfiche which is specifically allotted for title and other bibliographical information.

Title backing.   The material, or treatment, applied to the back of the title area (i.e. the area extending the full width of the film and above the micro-images) of a microfiche so that the title can be more easily read by reflected light.

Title card.   A catalogue card bearing an entry under the title of a work.

Title catalogue.   A catalogue consisting only of title entries.

Title entry.   A record in a catalogue, bibliography or index, usually under the first word of a title not an article.

Title index.   *See* KWIC.

Title leaf. The leaf at the beginning of a book, the recto of which is the Title-page. The verso usually bears bibliographical details of printer, copyright date, the ISBN, etc. and any earlier editions. The BS 4719: 1971 *Title leaves of a book* defined title leaves as 'The initial printed leaves of a book. They normally consist of two leaves, the half-title leaf followed by the title leaf, but there may be only one leaf or more than two title leaves'. This BS, now withdrawn, listed 15 items of bibliographical and other information which should be given on the title leaves.

Title piece. A leather label, sometimes coloured, pasted on the back of a binding, and bearing the title of the book.

Title proper. The title appearing on the Title-page, or elsewhere in a publication which does not possess a title-page, but which is obviously the chief title. It is the chief title of a publication and includes any Alternative title but excludes parallel titles and any other title.

Title sheet. The first printed sheet of a book containing the title-page and other preliminary matter.

Title signature. The title (often abbreviated to initial letters) placed on the signature line of signed pages to prevent the binder mixing up the sheets of various books. Also called 'Direction line'. *See also* Signature and catchword line.

Title space. The area specifically allotted on a microfiche or microcard for title information. *See also* Title backing.

Title wrap-around. A feature of the KWIC index whereby unused space is filled by allowing the remainder of the imprinted title at the end of the type-line to appear at the beginning of the same line, providing space is available there. Also called 'Title recirculation', 'Title snap-back'.

Title-a-line catalogue. A catalogue in which the entries occupy only a single line of type.

Title-a-line index. *See* Line-by-line index.

Title-cut. *See* Framed-cut.

Title-page. Usually the recto of the second leaf which gives the title in full, sub-title (if any), author's name in full together with particulars of qualifications, degrees, etc., edition, publisher's name and address, and date of publication. The verso may give particulars of edition, printer's name and sometimes address, binder's name, details of type and paper used in making the book, owner of copyright, and CIP information. If there is more than one page giving particulars of the title, the title-page is that which gives the fullest information. *See also* Double title-page, Engraved title-page, Second half-title, Section title, Title leaf.

Title-page border. A frame, at first a woodcut, and later made of heavy type ornaments, surrounding the matter on the title-page.

Title-page title. The title of a book as it appears on the title-page. It is the authority for the correct reference to the book; other versions of the title as given on the spine, cover, half-title, top of the pages or jacket may vary slightly.

Titling. Capital letters of modern roman type which are cast 'fullface' on the body ; there are thus no Beard or Lower case letters. They are used for headlines, titles, jackets or posters.

Titlonym. A quality or title used as a pseudonym, as 'A Barrister'. If the author's name cannot be determined, such books are catalogued as if they were anonymous, entry being made under the title. An added entry is made under the titlonym. *See also* Telonism.

T.L.S. *See* A.L.S.

TNT. <www.cordis.lu/ist/directorate_e/digicult/tnt.htm> Fully TNT – The Neanderthalers, an FP6 project with the subtitle 'Transforming representational cultural heritage into digital media popular scientific content and developing a visual simulation engine for collaborative real-time exploration'. The intention is to develop advanced services and applications to improve access to Europe's cultural heritage, particularly to collections and artefacts of the Neanderthal species.

TOCS. Table of Contents Service, whereby the contents pages of journals are used to alert End users on a regular basis to articles of interest; can be commercial or produced in-house. *See also* ETOCs, Zetoc.

Toggle press. The Albion press which was introduced in 1823 and allowed the platen to be lowered and given great pressure by means of a toggle-jointed lever instead of the screw method. A toggle-jointed lever is one with an elbow-shaped joint with two arms known as the chill and the wedge. When the joint is straightened so that chill and wedge form a straight line, great endwise pressure is produced.

Token charging. A system of issuing books whereby the borrower is given a token which is exchanged for a book on leaving.

Token ring. A Local area network which uses a method of data transmission by which devices insert data or messages into tokens circulating on a ring.

Toll access journal. A journal, normally from a commercial publisher or professional society, that funds itself using the 'traditional' model of charging subscriptions to individuals and institutions, thereby limiting access to these subscribers to the spread of research literature. In contrast to the newer model of the Open access journal.

Tome. A volume, or book, especially a heavy one.

Tony Kent Strix and Public Sector Awards. *See* Kent (Tony) Strix and Public Sector Awards.

Tool phase. In classification, where one discipline is used to assist the investigation of another, the document is classified under the thing investigated, not under the tool of investigation. It is one of Ranganathan's six 'phase relations'.

Toolbox. A software package for converting data.

Tooled edges. The edges of a book which have been impressed with designs. *See also* Edges.

Tooling. The impressing of designs – by means of finishing tools such as rolls – into a leather or cloth binding. The tools used may be 'embossed' in which case there is modelling on the top surface (i.e. the bottom of its impression), 'outline', 'shaded' or 'azured'. When this is done through gold leaf it is called 'gold tooling', when neither leaf nor pigment is used it is called 'blind tooling'. When the entire cover design is a single piece, it is called a 'stamp'. Gold tooling is believed to have been introduced by Thomas Berthelet, royal binder to Henry VIII. *See also* Azured tool, Block (3), Edge-rolled.

Top edges gilt (t.e.g.).   The top edges of a book cut smooth and gilded. Also called 'Gilt top'.

Top margin.   The space between the top line of type of a book or periodical, and the edge of the page. *See also* Margin.

Top side.   *See* Felt side.

Top slicing.   The procedure, particularly in universities, whereby the funding of service departments such as libraries is deducted from the total available before the remainder is split among academic departments.

Topic.   In co-ordinate indexing, a group of terms describing a given subject. Also called 'Information item' and 'Theme'.

Topic guide.   A shelf guide; it may include the subject and class number, placed on the shelf at the beginning of the books on the subject. Also called 'Subject guide'.

Topic map.   <www.topicmaps.org/xtm> A model and grammar in XML for representing the structure of information resources used to define topics, and the relationships between topics. Can be thought of as a combination of the techniques of traditional indexing, library science and knowledge representation, with automated technologies of linking and addressing.

Topographical catalogue.   A catalogue of books relating to places.

Topographical index.   An index of places arranged in alphabetical order.

Topographical map.   One which shows physical or natural features of an area.

Topology.   The configuration formed by the connections between devices on a Local area network; thus Bus network, Ring network, Star network.

Tory style.   A style of binding executed in the sixteenth century for Geoffroy Tory the famous French printer, wood-engraver and designer. Distinguished by arabesque panels, borders and ornaments.

Total quality management (TQM).   TQM applies concepts of quality assessment across the whole of an organization; it may function as a programmed approach to organizational change more than as a simple quality control mechanism. It encourages inter-departmental co-operation based on customer-orientated services. *See also* Quality.

Town plan.   A map of a town showing the organized arrangement of streets, open spaces, etc. *See also* Plat.

Toyo Bunko.   [Oriental Library] <www.toyo-bunko.or.jp> (2-28-21 Honkomagome, Bunkyo-ku, Tokyo 113-0021, Japan) The principal library and research institute for Asian Studies in Japan, the collections of the Toyo Bunko were originally based on part of the library of

George Morrison, and since 1948 it has been closely associated with the National Diet Library. It now contains some 880,000 items, and publications include *Toyo Gakuho* [*Journal of the research department of the Toyo Bunko*] (2 p.a.), *Memoirs*, (a.) and many research monographs in both Japanese and other languages.

TPI. Abbreviation for Title-page, Index. Used to refer to the separately published title-page and index to a volume of a serial which may often have to be separately ordered for insertion in a bound volume.

TQM. *See* Total quality management.

Tr. (trans) Abbreviation for Transactions, translated, Translation, Translator.

Tracing. An indication on the front or back of a main entry catalogue card showing under what additional headings added entries appear. Also, the record (on the main entry card, or on an authority card) of all the related references made. Specially important in a dictionary catalogue in order to ensure that in case of change, correction or removal, all the cards referring to a given book may be traced and the change applied to all of them. In co-ordinate indexing, a list of descriptors, Uniterms, etc., applied to a specific document.

Tracing paper. Paper treated with a coating of Canada balsam in turpentine, or a solution of castor oil or linseed oil in alcohol. The papers chosen for this treatment must have excellent transparency, high tearing strength, and be resistant to erasure; they must contain no loading and be engine-sized. Tracing papers cockle readily on absorbing moisture from the atmosphere and must therefore be wrapped in waxed or other waterproof paper.

Tracking. The spacing between a group of selected letters. Tracking can be adjusted in Desktop publishing software to help match a section of text to the space available and also to provide specific effects. *See also* Kern, Letter spacing.

Tract. 1. A pamphlet containing a short propagandist discourse, especially on a religious, political or social subject. 2. A pamphlet printed on a single sheet and imposed in pages.

Trade bibliography. *See* Bibliography (1), Trade catalogue (1).

Trade binding. 1. The binding in which a publisher issues a book. Also called 'Publisher's binding'. 2. Plain calf or sheep bindings which were used in England by publishers from the fifteenth to the eighteenth centuries; only rarely did they carry lettering on the spines. Until the nineteenth century, purchasers usually bought books unbound or enclosed in wrappers, and had them bound to order.

Trade book. A common US publishing term for a book intended for general readership. It is neither a children's book, a textbook, nor a technical treatise, but a book which would interest anybody, and be published by a commercial publisher as distinct from one published by a society, institution, governmental agency or other non-commercial group.

Trade catalogue. 1. A list of the books in print published in a country, and frequently of books published abroad, for which the home publishers are agents. 2. A publication containing particulars of goods manufactured by, or sold by, a firm; frequently illustrated and containing prices.

Trade directory. A Directory which is concerned with one trade or a group of related trades.

Trade edition. Copies of a book which are regularly printed and supplied to booksellers by publishers at the appropriate wholesale rates, especially such an edition contrasted with a de luxe, paperback, library-bound, or book club edition. *See also* Large paper copy, or edition, Subscribers' edition.

Trade information. *See* Bibliographical information.

Trade journal. A periodical restricted to the interests of a trade or industry and including all or some of the following: news items, articles and descriptions of goods, products and manufactured articles, lists of new publications, statistical data, patents, personal notes, legislative activities, etc. Also called 'Trade paper'.

Trade list. A list of publications in print, which is issued by a publisher for the information of the bookselling trade, often providing space for ordering the various titles and giving particulars of the terms under which the books are sold to booksellers.

Trade paper. *See* Trade journal.

Trade series. *See* Publisher's series.

Trade terms. The provision of facilities for retailers to obtain goods at a discount for re-sale to the public. In the book trade, the discounts may vary according to the kind of book. Export terms are usually different from those for the home market.

Trade Union Information Group (TUIG). <u.coxhead@unison.co.uk> (Policy and Research Department, UNISON, 1 Mabledon Place, London WC1H 4DT, UK) Set up in 1980 to stimulate and encourage the development of information services to serve trade unionists. An Organization in Liaison (OiL) with CILIP.

Trademark. The name or other symbol used to identify a product made by a particular manufacturer or distributed by a particular dealer, and which distinguishes that product from similar items from competing manufacturers or dealers. Most countries operate a central registry of trademarks, often associated with a patent office, which provides substantial legal protection to the owner of the mark. Also spelt trade mark. The terms trade name and brand name are practically synonymous.

Traditional format. The format of oriental books, consisting of double leaves with folds at the fore-edge and with free edges sewn together to make a Fascicle. Usually several fascicles are contained in a cloth-covered case.

Trailer. A portion of developed but unexposed copying material, such as film strip, at the end of a sequence of exposures, which is not cut off; it serves to protect the exposed portion and assists projection.

Trailer record. A record which follows a group of similar records and contains pertinent data related to the group of records.

Training.   The process of developing the skill, awareness or expertise of staff, both professional and non-professional. Training may consist of induction into a system or routine, organization of new skills or attitudes, or development of existing skills towards greater efficiency, job satisfaction, commitment, interchangeability, co-operation, or promotion. It is important that training should be carefully prepared in response to needs, and its effectiveness monitored. Libraries may join *co-operative training* groups to reduce costs and spread expertise. Training specifically aimed at promotion opportunities may be termed *staff development. See also* Continuing professional development.

Training co-operative.   *See* Co-operative training.

Transaction card charging.   Book issue methods in which the records of loans are kept in the order in which they are made, transactions being given numbers in consecutive order. At the time of recording the loan a numbered 'transaction card' is inserted in the book and remains there until the book is returned to the library. Abbreviated T-card charging.

Transactional analysis.   The scientific study of the behaviour of individuals or groups of individuals in the process of communication with other individuals or groups.

Transactions.   The published papers read at meetings of a society or institution, or abstracts of the same. Also sometimes synonymous with Proceedings. A general distinction made between Transactions and Proceedings is that the Transactions are the papers presented and the Proceedings the records of meetings.

Transborder Data Flow.   An IFLA project established in 1985 to promote the electronic transfer of data between libraries across national boundaries. *See now* Universal Dataflow and Telecommunications (UDT).

Transcribe.   (*Information retrieval*) To copy from one external storage medium to another.

Transcript.   1. A copy made from an original, particularly of a legal document.   2. Also, a written record of words usually spoken, e.g. of court proceedings, or of a broadcast. In the archives field, an exact reproduction, so far as the resources of script or typography allow, of an original document, with the single exception that abbreviations may be extended providing their interpretation is unquestionable.

Transcription.   1. An expression in one notation that is equivalent to an expression in another.   2. In music, the arrangement for one musical medium of music originally composed for another, e.g. an organ piece from an orchestral overture.   3. An arrangement in which some liberty is taken by way of modification or embellishment. *See also* Version.

Transfer.   A chemically prepared paper for transferring drawings direct on to lithographic stone or a rubber-covered cylinder used in offset lithography.

Transfer file.   1. A container of some kind (box-like or folder) of a less sturdy type and cheaper, to contain older material which must be filed but which is seldom referred to and encumbers current files.   2. The material itself which is removed from current files.

Transfer list.   (*Records management*) A list of records transferred from current administrative systems to a Records Centre; also termed 'transmittal list'.

Transfer printing.   *See* Decalcomania (Decal).

Transitional.   A name sometimes given to the typeface designed about 1760 by John Baskerville, and those based on it. Transitional types retain the bracketed serifs of old face and suggest by their precision the engraved quality of modern face types. The faces are more angular, with sharper contrast between the thick and thin strokes. Bell is a 'transitional' typeface, as are also Fournier, Caledonia and Columbia. *See also* Egyptian, Modern face, Old face, Typeface.

Translated title list.   A periodically issued bulletin which lists, usually in a systematic order, the translated titles of periodical articles and documents which are likely to be of interest to its readers.

Translation.   1. The act of turning a literary composition from one language into another.   2. The work so produced. *See also* Machine translation.

Translation rights.   The right to allow or refuse the publication of any literary production in another language is a part of Copyright.

Translator.   One who translates from one language into another.

Transliteration.   The representation of the ordinary characters of a language by those of another, as from Arabic, Cyrillic, or Greek into Roman, each digit or letter being transcribed independently of the others.

Translucent copy.   In documentary reproduction, a copy on translucent material.

Translucent screen.   A sheet of glass treated in some way (ground, opal, coated, etc.), or of plastic, on to which an image is projected in a microfilm reader.

Transmission copying.   In documentary reproduction, making a photocopy by passing light through a one-sided original which is in contact with sensitized paper. Included in this method are blue-print and Diazo or dyeline processes and the use of silver halide paper in contact with a single-sided document which is thin enough to permit light to pass through it.

Transmission printing.   The making of contact prints by passing light through the original and on to the material of reproduction. *See also* Contact copying, Transmission copying.

Transparency.   An image, in black and white or colour, on transparent base-stock, usually film, which may be viewed by transmitted light, usually with the aid of a projector. Also called 'Slide'.

Transparent vellum.   A method (patented in 1785) used by Edwards of Halifax which rendered the vellum to be used in bookbinding transparent. A painting or drawing was done on the underside and the whole then lined with white paper.

Transpose.   To change over the positions of letters, words or lines of type. This is marked on a proof by putting a loop round the characters to be changed and writing 'trs.' in the margin.

Trapping.   In colour printing, a slight overlapping of objects to prevent gaps which could appear as a result of misalignment or movement in the final output.

Travelling Librarian Award.   *See* Wrench (Sir Evelyn) Travelling Librarian Award.

Travelling library.   A motor vehicle equipped with shelves, which visits districts where there is no other library service, at specified times on a certain day or days of the week. In the UK there is a tendency to describe such a vehicle as a 'Mobile Branch Library' or 'Mobile Library' and to use the term 'Travelling Library' for a small vehicle which is shelved or otherwise equipped to provide a service to villages, and isolated farms and houses, with short stops for issuing books. *See also* Mobile library.

Travelling mould.   *See* Wire.

TRC MARC.   MARC for Japanese books, first published in 1982, and compiled by Toshokan Ryutsu Center (TRC) <www.trc.co.jp> which is a joint stock company developed from the Technical Services Department of Nihon Toshokan Kyokai (Japanese Library Association). TRC via TOOLi offers bibliographical data for all new books, available via TRCD (TRC MARC on CD-ROM) and RLIN. TRC MARC is also one of the referral MARCs for the NACSIS-Cat online shared cataloguing system, with Japan MARC, UKMARC and USMARC and China MARC.

Treatment of correspondence.   *See* Correspondence management.

Tree calf.   A calf binding which has had acid poured on it in such a way as to form stains resembling a tree-like pattern.

Tree of Life.   <tolweb.org/tree> A collaborative web project producing an encyclopedic resource on phylogeny and biodiversity with contributions from biologists from around the world. On more than 2,600 Web pages the resource provides information about the diversity of organisms on Earth, their history, and characteristics.

Tree of Porphyry.   *See* Porphyry, tree of.

Tree structure.   An hierarchical system used in database construction to organize material from general (root) to specific (leaf) concepts. Searching in such a structure proceeds via only one path subdividing at a series of branches.

Trial binding.   A sample of the proposed cover for a book submitted by the binder or casemaker to the publisher.

Trial issue.   A few copies of a book printed for circulation to critical friends prior to the printing of the edition for publication which is printed without re-setting of the type. If re-setting occurs then the preliminary edition is known as a 'trial edition'.

Trial proof.   *See* Proof (3).

Trigesimo-secundo.   (32mo) A sheet of paper folded five times to form a section of 32 leaves (64 pages). Also called 'Thirty-twomo'.

Trigesimo-sexto.   *See* Thirty-sixmo.

Trigger.   The colloquial name for the device fitted to library books so that they can be detected when passing through a Book detection system.

Trilogy.   A set of three related dramatic or literary compositions.

Trimmed.   1. Paper which has been trimmed on one or more sides to ensure exactness of corner angles and to reduce to the size required. 2. (*Binding*) The top edge untouched, and only the inequalities removed from the others, the folds not being opened. *See also* Edges.

Trimmed page size.   The size of a sheet after folding and trimming.

Trimmed size.   The final dimensions of a sheet of paper. British paper-makers may interpret this term as 'guillotine trimmed'. *See also* Paper sizes, Untrimmed size.

Trinity College Library, Dublin.   <www.tcd.ie/library> (College Street, Dublin 2, Ireland) The oldest library in Ireland; it was founded in 1657 (the College was founded by Elizabeth I in 1591) and much enlarged by the addition of Archbishop Usher's Library. In 1801 it was granted the right to receive a copy of every publication issued in the United Kingdom. It is rich in manuscripts, its best-known treasure being the *Book of Kells*.

Triple lining.   A method of Lining used to give added strength. It is used in better-quality cased books and consists of providing a strip of crêpe manila lining, with head-and-tailbands if desired. All the lining processes used can be carried out mechanically.

Triplex paper.   *See* Duplex paper.

Tripoli.   The cheaper grades of esparto grass, grown in North Africa. *See also* Esparto.

Tripper.   (*Reprography*) A device, operated mechanically or electronically, to control lights, film advance, or the beginning or end of the operation.

TRIPS.   <docsonline.wto.org/gen_search.asp> Trading of Intellectual Property Rights; a system of international interchange of intellectual property rights negotiated by the World Trade Organization (WTO) in 1995 and which is slowly moving into effect with full implementation due in 2005. The new system is likely to have serious implications for the information world. *See also* GATS.

Triptych.   *See* Codex.

TRIS.   <www.trisweb.org/tris> A scheme of the European Union to co-ordinate a series of trial projects whereby libraries, museums and archive services from all over Europe collaborated in the testing of ICT applications and implementation of innovative products and services in the cultural heritage sector. The scheme ran 2001–2003.

Trojan horse.   A program inserted into a computer system that masquerades as a legitimate program but acts towards malicious ends, e.g. the copying of otherwise confidential information or for the destruction of data. *See also* Virus, Worm.

Troy type. A type cut by William Morris in 1892; it was an 18 point Gothic type based on the early types of Schoeffer, Mentelin and Zainer. *See also* Chaucer type, Golden type.

trs. Abbreviation for Transpose; in proof correcting it is written in the margin to indicate that the position of the words, letters or lines around which a loop is drawn are to be exchanged.

True anonyma. Books which could be catalogued under the author's name if their authors were known. These are catalogued in the Library of Congress and some other libraries with the author line left blank so that it can be entered should the authorship be discovered. *See also* Formal anonyma.

Truncation. 1. The process of shortening or cutting off part of a keyword or a title in a Permuted Title Index. A truncated title lacks one or more words or syllables at the beginning or end. 2. Shortening of a search term so that it will match related terms starting with the same stem, e.g. 'libr': will match library, libraries, librarian, etc. *See also* Wildcard.

Trunking. A method of distributing power and data cables in a modular way around a building. The type of trunking most used in modern library buildings consists of three compartments – one for power, one for Local area network cables, one for telephones – in particular to ensure that data transmission does not suffer degradation from interference.

Trustees. A Board of Library Trustees is the Committee responsible for the control of a library system in the US. Also known as 'Library Board', 'Board of Directors', 'Library Trustees', and occasionally 'Library Commission'.

T.S. Abbreviation for typescript and tub-sized. *See also* Tub-sizing.

TSO. The Stationery Office (UK); *see* Her Majesty's Stationery Office.

TTS. Abbreviation for Teletypesetting.

Tub-sizing. Dipping sheets of Waterleaf into a tub of animal glue, gelatine, a prepared starch, or a combination of these, drying on cow-hair ropes or hessian, and then glazing them. Tub-sized paper (abbreviated 'T.S.') is strong and has a high resistance to moisture. Also called 'Animal Tub-sized' (abbreviated 'A.T.S.'). *See also* Engine-sizing.

TUIG. *See* Trade Union Information Group.

Tumbler scheme. The method of perfecting sheets to be printed from a forme imposed in the oblong, or landscape, manner. In order to obtain correct page sequence, the sheet must be turned or tumbled, in its short direction. *See also* Work and turn.

Turabian Style. *See* Chicago Style.

Turn over. 1. Printed matter extending beyond the allotted space. 2. The part of an article continued from a preceding page. Also called Run over. 3. The second and subsequent lines of a paragraph.

Turned. (*Printing*) A printed impression of a graph, table or illustration, etc., which is turned at right angles so that its foot is parallel to the fore-edge of the page. *See also* Landscape page.

Turned comma.   A comma which is used upside down and in a superior position, i.e. on the Mean line; it is used at the beginning of quoted matter '...' and in the abbreviation of the Scottish 'Mac', as in M'Gregor.

Turned letter.   A letter used upside down such as a 'u' for an 'n'.

Turned sort.   A type letter used foot uppermost for one not known or not available. This is very conspicuous in galley proof. When turned sorts are replaced with the correct letters, the process is called 'taking out turns'.

Turn-in.   1. That portion of the material covering the boards of a book which overlaps the head, tail and fore-edges of the boards and is turned-in over these edges of the boards.   2. To make use of type matter which is already set.   3. The turned-over end of a book jacket which is folded around the cover.

Turnkey system.   A computer system supplied complete for a specific purpose. No preparation is required on the part of the purchaser other than to turn the key to commence (theoretically!).

Turnover lines.   The second or subsequent lines of type in a paragraph. Called 'Run-in lines' in the US.

Turns.   *See* Taking out turns.

Tutor librarian.   A librarian in an educational institution who has a teaching and liaison role with students on the library and how to make the best use of it, as well as having responsibility for the administration or functioning of the library.

Twelvemo.   *See* Duodecimo.

Twenty-fourmo.   (24mo) A sheet of paper folded to form a section of 24 leaves (48 pages). Also called 'Vicesimo-quarto'.

Twentymo.   (20mo) A sheet of paper folded into 20 leaves, making 40 pages.

Twice weekly.   A periodical which is published twice a week. Also called 'Semi-weekly'.

Twin wire paper.   A Duplex paper made by bringing the two wet webs together, Wire sides innermost, to form a single sheet with two top or Felt sides and no wire side or 'underside'. Such paper is particularly suitable for offset printing. *See also* Right.

Twisted pair.   A cable constructed from two separately insulated strands of wire twisted together. One wire carries the sensitive signal, the other is grounded to absorb potential radio interference and protect the signal.

Twisted pineapples.   (*Binding*) The form of ornament used on a number of English and French finishers' rolls, and consisting of twisted stems with conventional pineapples at intervals. *See also* Pineapple.

Two on.   Printing two sheets, jobs, pages, etc., at the same time. The printing of small jobs in duplicate is done to facilitate the work and economize in time and costs.

Two sheets (sections) on.   The method of sewing books when two sections are treated as one. In hand-sewing two sheets at a time are placed on the sewing-frame; the thread is passed from the kettle stitch of the lower section, and brought out at the first tape or cord, when it is inserted in the upper section, and so on. Thus, two sections receive only the same number of stitches one would do by the All along method. Although a weaker method than the all along, it helps to reduce the swelling in the back in the case of very thin books.

Two sides coloured.   Paper or board both sides of which have been coloured intentionally during manufacture.

Two-colour half-tones.   Two half-tone plates in which one of the plates is made with the line of the screen as in a one-colour half-tone, and the other with lines at a different angle, usually about 30⁰. The colours tend to blend into one another in different tones.

Two-colour press.   A machine which prints in two colours at one operation. The principle is applicable to letterpress, lithography and offset machines. Most offset printing is carried out on two-colour presses.

Two-colour process.   A photo-mechanical process in which the printing is done in two colours.

Two-colour reproduction.   Printing in two colours instead of the more usual four. The colours used are normally green or blue, and orange; subjects have to be carefully chosen or the resulting prints may be not true to the original, or they may be crude.

Two-layer paper.   *See* Furnish layer.

Two-line letter.   (*Printing*) A capital letter having a depth of body (or height of letter on the printed page) equal to double that of the size specified, as 'two-line pica'. Three- and four-line letters are used similarly. They are often used as the initial letter for the first word of a chapter.

Two-page spread.   *See* Double spread.

Twopenny library.   A circulating library, usually in shop premises, for which the charge for borrowing a book was twopence a week. The charge became much greater but the name persisted.

Two-revolution machine.   A printing machine in which the cylinder, over which the paper is fed, does not stop after traversing the Forme but continues to revolve, rising slightly during its second revolution so that it cannot come into contact with the type, and descending when the forme is again in position for printing. During its second revolution, the bed with the forme returns and the sheet is delivered. The earliest machine of this kind was made by Koenig in 1814. *See also* Miehle, Perfecter, Single-revolution machine, Stanhope press, Stop-cylinder press.

Two-up.   1. Printing two texts, or duplicate stereos made from the same forme, side by side on the same sheet of paper. It is an economical way of machining short runs.   2. The processing of two books as a single unit from the forme through all the binding processes until they are separated by the trimmer. A method which is sometimes used for mass-producing Paperbacks.

Two-way paging.   The system of page numbering used for a book with the texts in two languages, one of which reads from left to right (as

English) and the other from right to left (as Hebrew or Arabic); the texts being in two sections with page sequences from opposite ends of the book.

Tying-up. The tying of a volume after the cover has been drawn on, so as to make the leather adhere better to the sides of the bands; also for setting the headband.

Tympan. A kind of leaf consisting of a thin frame of metal over which is stretched parchment or cambric, and which is hinged to the carriage bearing the forme of a printing press in such a way that it places the paper resting on it in the exact position for printing.

Type. 1. *See* Characteristic of a classification. 2. (*Printing*) A small rectangular block of metal or wood, having on its upper end a raised letter, figure, or other characters. *See also* Typeface, Type size. For purposes of nomenclature, a single movable type character has always been considered as a human being standing erect, and having a Body (but no head), a Face, Beard, Neck, Shoulder, Back, Belly, Feet. Type letters are formed within three imaginary lines: the 'base line' on which the bases of capitals rest, the 'mean line' running along the top of the lower-case letters which are without ascenders, the 'cap line' which runs across the top of the capital letters. *See also* Body (1), X-height.

Type area. The area, or part, of a page of a book, periodical or other publication which will be, or has been, filled with printed matter.

Type code program. *See* Type encoding program.

Type encoding program. Typesetting programs that employ special codes embedded in the text itself to govern the formatting of that text e.g. the position and style of characters, graphics and rules. Examples are Standard Generalized Markup Language and T$_E$X. The alternative approach is WYSIWYG.

Type facsimile. A reprint in which a printed original is copied exactly.

Type flowers. Conventional designs cast in type metal of type height and used to decorate a book as an alternative to using blocks. *See also* Flowers.

Type gauge. A rule marked off in ems, points and inches and used for measuring width of type, page depths, etc.

Type height. 1. The standard height to which type bodies are cast. In the UK and the USA this is 0.918 of an inch from the feet, on which the type rests, to the printing surface, except for the Oxford University Press which works to 0.9395 inches. On the continent of Europe the standard height is 'Didot Normal' (0.9278 inches). 2. The height to which a printing plate is mounted for use in letterpress work; it must be the same height as the letterpress.

Type metal. (*Printing*) An alloy of tin, lead, antimony and sometimes copper which is used for casting type.

Type ornaments. Conventional designs cast in type metal, being larger than Type flowers and used to ornament chapter heads and tails, and title-pages.

Type page.   The part of a page that is printed upon; i.e. the type area, the margins being excluded.

Type size.   The measure of the dimensions of type, taken from the body of the individual type rather than the actual printing area. Also called 'Body size'. The following are the type sizes normally used in book work:

	Old Name
5 point	Pearl
6 point	Nonpareil
7 point	Minion
8 point	Brevier
9 point	Bourgeois
10 point	Long Primer
11 point	Small Pica
12 point	Pica
14 point	English
16 point	Columbian
18 point	Great Primer
22 point	Double Pica

Larger sizes exist, but these are used for display and not book work. Other, mostly discarded, sizes with their names are:

	Old Name
3½ point	Minikin (or Brilliant)
4 point	Brilliant
4 point	Gem
4½ point	Diamond
5½ point	Ruby (or Agate)
6½ point	Emerald
16 point	Two-line Brevier
20 point	Paragon
24 point	Two-line Pica
28 point	Two-line English
36 point	Two-line Great Primer
40 point	Two-line Paragon
44 point	Two-line Double Pica
48 point	Four-line Pica (or Canon)
60 point	Five-line Pica
72 point	Six-line Pica

Type-casting machine.   Originally, one which cast single type units which were then set up in a stick by hand. Later machines such as *Monotype, Linotype* and *Intertype* both set and cast.

Typeface.   1. The printing surface of the upper end of a piece of type which bears the character to be printed.   2. The style, or design, of characters on a set of pieces of type, comprising all the sizes in which the particular design is made. There are four classes of typeface: Abstract, Cursive, Decorative, Roman, and they may also be divided in the following nine categories: Humanist, Garalde, Transitional, Didone, Slab serif, Lineale, Glyphic, Script and Graphic.

Type-high. A printing block or plate which has been mounted on wood or metal to the same height as type for use on a printing machine.

Typescript (T.S.). Typewritten matter; a typed manuscript.

Typesetter. 1. One who sets type; a compositor. 2. A bureau that offers Computer typesetting or Desktop publishing services, particularly output from an Imagesetter. 3. *See* Imagesetter.

Typesetting. The arrangement of printing types in order for printing, including the operation of machines. *See also* Computer typesetting.

Typesetting machine. A machine for selecting, assembling and spacing typefounders' letterpress printing types which are arranged in channels instead of cases. *See also* Type-casting machine.

Typical characteristic. *See* Characteristic of a classification.

Typical class. *See* Characteristic of a classification.

Typo. Abbreviation for Typographical error.

Typograph. Trade name for a typecasting, setting and distributing machine which casts a slug or line of type, similar to the Linotype machine.

Typographer. One who is responsible for the lay-out and appearance of printed matter.

Typographical copyright. A right found chiefly in the UK giving the publisher of a work exclusive rights over the typography (as distinct from the content) of the published work. *See also* Publication right.

Typographical error. A mistake made by the typesetter; a mistake in any printed matter. Commonly called 'typo'.

Typography. 1. Printing, or taking impressions from movable letter-units or 'types'. The art of printing. 2. The character and appearance of printed matter.

Typometer. A gauge for measuring the body and thickness of type and comparing them with a standard.

UAP. *See* Universal Availability of Publications.

UBC. *See* Universal Bibliographic Control.

UBCIM. Universal Bibliographic Control and International MARC. *See* Universal Bibliographic Control.

UCAID. <www.ucaid.edu> The University Corporation for Advanced Internet Development, a non-profit consortium that oversees the Abilene and Internet2 projects and that now appears to have been re-badged to Internet2.

UCC. Universal Copyright Convention. *See entry under* Copyright, International.

UCISA. <www.ucisa.ac.uk> (UCISA Administration, University of Oxford, 13 Banbury Road, Oxford OX2 6NN, UK) Universities and Colleges

Information Systems Association. UCISA exists to promote excellence in the application of information systems and services in support of teaching, learning, research and administration in UK higher education. Its aims are: to identify best practice and to spread its use through the organization of conferences, seminars and workshops; the promotion and support of collaboration between institutions; the publication, including electronic publication, of material; the promotion of development and research; and to inform and support policy making processes within institutions and nationally on the cost effective application of information systems and services.

UCR. *See* University, College and Research Group.

UDC. *See* Universal Decimal Classification.

UDDI. Universal Description, Discovery and Integration protocol, a specification for maintaining standardized directories of information about Web services, recording their capabilities, location and requirements in a universally recognized format.

UDT. *See* Universal Dataflow and Telecommunications.

UFC. Universities Funding Council. *See now* Higher Education Funding Councils.

UfI. *See* University for Industry.

UGC. University Grants Committee. *See now* Higher Education Funding Councils.

Übertype. A photo-composing machine built in 1928 by Edmund Üher, a Hungarian. It was first called Luminotype.

UK Council for Health Informatics Professions (UKchip). <www. ukchip.org.uk> Set up in 2002 and fully launched in June 2004, UKchip operates a voluntary online register for those in the health informatics professions who agree to work to clearly defined standards. As the use of ICT in the health sector has become so widespread, the role of such professionals is most important in managing information and protecting patient interests. UKchip will collaborate with other organizations to promote a code of conduct and establish a framework for Continuing professional development.

UK Data Archive. <www.data-archive.ac.uk> A national resource centre founded in 1967 that acquires, disseminates, preserves and promotes the largest collection of digital data in the social sciences and humanities in the UK. Its primary aim is to support secondary use of quantitative and qualitative data for research and learning. Funded by the Economic and Social Research Council, JISC and the University of Essex where it is located. *See also* NCeSS.

UK Electronic Information Group. *See* UKOLUG.

UK Libraries Plus. <www.uklibrariesplus.ac.uk> A co-operative venture between higher education libraries in the UK to enable part-time, distance, and placement students to borrow material from other libraries. In addition, there is provision for full-time students and staff to use other libraries on a reference-only basis. Membership is open to any higher education institution which is funded by one of the UK Higher Education Funding Councils, and over half are members.

UK LOM Core. <www.cetis.ac.uk/profiles/uklomcore> A UK-specific application profile of the Learning Object Metadata standard.

UK Mirror Service. <www.mirror.ac.uk> A large collection of freely available software and data from around the world that is copied or 'mirrored' to be made available to higher and further education institutions in the UK; previously known as HENSA, the Higher Education Software Archive. The material includes software for several platforms, textual and numerical data, audio material, static and moving pictures and Web-based information. This information is provided free of charge without restrictions. Provided by Lancaster University and the University of Kent; it was announced that from 1 August 2004 a new contract was to be funded by JISC.

UK Online User Group. *See* UKOLUG.

UK Serials Group (UKSG). <www.uksg.org> (114 Woodstock Road, Witney, Oxford OX8 6DY, UK) Formally established in 1978, the UK Serials Group is an autonomous organization which brings together all parties interested in serials. It is not exclusively a group for librarians – membership is open to any organization or individual having an interest in serials. The current membership includes representatives from publishers, agents, industry and many different types of libraries and information units. The aims of the Group include promoting discussion about serials and related areas between interested parties; developing and maintaining links between the producers and users of serials; encouraging research in the field of serials management. The Group seek to achieve these aims by holding meetings and conferences, by the issuing of publications and by encouraging exchange of information. European involvement is increasing. An International Research Award was instituted in 2002. Publishes *Serials* (3 p.a.).

UK Web Archiving Consortium (UKWAC). A group comprising The British Library, JISC, The National Archives, The National Library of Wales, the National Library of Scotland and the Wellcome Trust that aims to expand the lifespan of website materials from around 44 days to a century or more. Launched in June 2004 UKWAC will run for an initial period of two years and work, with the permission of rights holders, on an experimental system for archiving selected key UK websites ensuring that invaluable scholarly, cultural and scientific resources remain available for future generations. Each consortium member will select and capture content relevant to its subject and/or domain with, for example, the British Library archiving sites reflecting national culture and events of historical importance. PANDAS archiving software will be used.

UK Web Focus. <www.ukoln.ac.uk/web-focus> A national web co-ordinator post, funded by JISC and the Museums, Libraries and Archives Council (MLA), and based at UKOLN.

UKBorders. <edina.ac.uk/ukborders> A service providing digitized boundary datasets of the UK available in many GIS formats for teachers and researchers in higher and further education to download and use in their work.

UKchip. *See* UK Council for Health Informatics Professions.

UKDA. *See* UK Data Archive.

UKeIG. UK Electronic Information Group. *See* UKOLUG.

UKERNA. <www.ukerna.ac.uk> (Atlas Centre, Chilton, Didcot, Oxfordshire, OX11 0QS, UK) The United Kingdom Education and Research Networking Association that manages the operation and development of the JANET and SuperJANET networks for UK higher and further education under a Service Level Agreement from JISC. UKERNA is the trading name of the company whose legal title is The JNT Association. Publishes *UKERNA News* (3 p.a.).

UKLA. *See* United Kingdom Literacy Association.

UKLight. An advanced global network facility which provides the ability to interconnect collaborating sites around the world, and within the UK, with high capacity switched network circuits. The facility is provided to enable and advance any application areas which can potentially develop new ways of working through the use of such connections. These developments will radically transform the landscape of the information economy and present new facilities and opportunities to the UK academic community. UKLight is funded by HEFCE and the facility is managed by UKERNA.

UKMARC Format. *See* MARC.

UKNUC. <www.uknuc.shef.ac.uk> UK National Union Catalogue, the acronym used for the Feasibility Study into a National Union Catalogue for the UK funded jointly by JISC, RSLP and the British Library and led by the University of Sheffield. The Final Report was submitted in 2001 and recommended that a physical (rather than a distributed) architecture be pursued, that a National Union Serials Catalogue be developed, and that further research and development be undertaken into distributed union catalogues; the report is available from the web site. *See now* CC-Interop, SUNCAT.

UKOLN. <www.ukoln.ac.uk> (Library, University of Bath, Bath BA2 7AY, UK) Formerly the UK Office for Library and Information Networking, UKOLN was formed in 1992 from the Centre for Bibliographic Management and the UK Office for Library Networking. UKOLN is a centre of expertise in digital information management, providing advice and services to the library, information, education and cultural heritage communities by influencing policy and informing practice, promoting community-building and consensus-making by actively raising awareness, advancing knowledge through research and development, building innovative systems and services based on Web technologies, and acting as an agent for knowledge transfer. Hosts and provides mirrors for a number of electronic journals and project materials (e.g.

Ariadne; *D-Lib*). UKOLN is funded by the Museums, Libraries and Archives Council and JISC as well as by project funding from the JISC and the European Union.

UKOLUG. <www.ukolug.org.uk> (The Old Chapel, Walden, West Burton, Leyburn DL8 4LE, UK) The UK Online User Group was formed in 1978 as a special interest group of the Institute of Information Scientists (IIS), but was always open to all. With the merger of IIS to form CILIP, UKOLUG has become a membership group of CILIP but continues to have a high profile national and international presence. The Group organizes the Kent (Tony) Strix and Public Sector Awards. The Group intends to change its name to UKeIG – UK Electronic Information Group – at the start of 2005.

UKOnline. The English partner with Digital Scotland, Cymru Ar-lein and ELFNI in the People's Network (PN).

UKOP. <www.tso.co.uk/ukop> United Kingdom Official Publications; Website hosted by The Stationery Office (TSO) (*see* Her Majesty's Stationery Office) from 2003, and previously by Chadwyck-Healey/ Proquest. UKOP is a comprehensive catalogue of all UK official publications and is recognized as such by the British government. As well as the entire TSO catalogue, the website contains all departmental publications (covering all the non-TSO output).

UKRA. *See now* United Kingdom Literacy Association (UKLA).

UKSG. *See* UK Serials Group.

UKWAC. *See* UK Web Archiving Consortium.

ult. Abbreviation for *ultimo* (Lat. 'last'). Used for 'last month'. *See also inst.*

Ultimate class. The class of the smallest extension admitted by the scheme of classification, into which a document can be placed.

Ultra thin paper. Sensitized photographic paper between 0.0023 and 0.0031 inches inclusive. Also called 'Extra light-weight'. *See also* Photographic papers.

Ultra-microfiche. A Microfiche with such small images that 3,000 page-images can be accommodated on one 4 x 6 inch fiche. Also known as 'Ultrafiche'.

Ulverscroft/IFLA Libraries for the Blind Section Award. <www. foundation.ulverscroft.com> An award made by the Ulverscroft Foundation to support a visit by anyone working in the field of library services for visually-impaired people to another service anywhere in the world for help or expertise to develop their own service.

U-Matic. ³/₄ in. video-cassette format marketed by the Sony Corporation now largely replaced by VHS for the domestic market and by Betacam for professional recording.

UN Literacy Decade. *See* United Nations Literacy Decade.

Unauthorized edition. An edition issued without the consent of the author, his or her representative or the original publisher. The responsibility to the author would be moral, not legal. A pirated edition is an unauthorized reprint involving an infringement of copyright.

Unbacked. Printed on only one side of the paper.

Unbleached paper. Special paper made from unbleached Stuff. Such papers do not usually have a good colour; they retain the colour of the original white rags, no bleaching during the process of manufacture having taken place. The paper is consequently stronger as bleaching weakens the pulp.

Unbound. A publication the leaves or sections of which have not been fastened together.

Uncial. Style of majuscule writing, resembling capitals in some letter forms, but with rounder curves. This was a more flowing cursive form of Latin manuscript handwriting and was used for commercial and everyday writing. In use generally from the fourth to the eighth centuries.

Uncut. A book is described as being 'uncut' when the edges have not been trimmed or cut by a guillotine, thus leaving 'bolts' which have to be opened with a paper knife. Until this has been done the book is described as being unopened. Also called 'Unploughed', 'Untrimmed'. *See also* Edges.

Undergraduate library. In academic libraries, pressure on space and the disturbance caused by large numbers of users, may be alleviated by providing separate facilities in an undergraduate library for students who require access primarily to a core collection and space and facilities to work.

Underground literature. *See* Clandestine literature.

Underground press. A printing press which secretly prints leaflets, pamphlets, periodicals or books which have as their object the overthrow of the government, or of authority, or the propagation of subversive or generally unconventional political views.

Underlay. Work done on the printing machine by placing paper, thin card, etc., under the matter in the forme so as to level it up as much as possible for printing, before the final touches are put on by means of Overlay.

Underline. A line or series of lines placed under parts of 'copy' or proof to indicate style of type to be used: a single line indicates italic; a double line, small capitals; a treble line, capitals; a wavy line (which can be placed under any of the aforementioned) bold face. Called 'Underscore' in the US. *See also* Caption (2).

Underrun. A shortage in the number of copies printed.

Underscore. *See* Underline.

Unesco. <portal.unesco.org> (7 place de Fontenoy, 75700 Paris, France) United Nations Educational, Scientific and Cultural Organization, an international body which exists to further the development of emerging nations. Constituted 16 November 1945 in London by representatives of 44 governments; an agreement between the United Nations and Unesco was approved by the General Assembly of the UN in New York at its October–December 1946 session. It is financed by Member States of the UN who are eligible for membership. The Unesco Press was established in 1974 to continue the publishing and distribution functions of the former Office of Publications. Unesco has formed a Libraries Portal giving access to library websites, events, calendars, and an 'information observatory' <www.unesco.org/webworld/portal_bib> and an associated archives portal <www.unesco.org/webworld/portal_ archives>. *See also* General Information Programme, ISORID, Office of Information Programmes and Services, Public Library Manifesto, UNISIST.

Unesco coupons. A form of international currency enabling foreign payments to be made for education, scientific and cultural materials without the procedures of making payments through the normal machinery of banks, and the involvement of currency control regulations. The currency is entitled 'Unum' (Unesco Unit of Money).

Unesco Public Library Manifesto. *See* Public Library Manifesto.

Uneven pages. Those which bear the odd page-numbers. The right-hand, or recto, pages.

Uneven working. *See* Even working.

Unexpurgated edition. An edition of a work in which the full text is given, including any objectionable material which normally would be omitted. *See also* Expurgated edition.

Ungathered. The printed sheets of a book which have not been gathered, or collected, into order.

Unicode. <www.unicode.org> A character coding system designed to support the worldwide interchange, processing, and display of the written texts of the diverse languages and technical disciplines of the modern world. In addition, it supports classical and historical texts of many written languages.

Uniform edition. The individual works of an author published in an identical format and binding. *See also* Standard edition.

Uniform heading. The form of a heading adopted for use in the catalogue for an author (personal or corporate), title, or for any other heading.

Uniform Resource Identifier. *See* URI.

Uniform Resource Locator. *See* URL.

Uniform Resource Name. *See* URN.

Uniform title. The distinctive title by which a work, which has appeared under varying titles and in various versions, is most generally known, and under which catalogue entries are made. Also called 'Conventional title', 'Filing title', 'Standard title'.

UNIMARC. Universal machine-readable catalogue – a standard format developed under the auspices of a Working Group set up by IFLA. Its primary purpose was to facilitate the international exchange of bibliographic data in machine-readable form between national agencies. *See also* Universal Bibliographic Control, MARC.

Union catalogue. A catalogue of stock in the various departments of a library, or of a number of libraries, indicating locations. It may be an author or a subject catalogue of all the books, or of a selection of them, and may be limited by subject or type of material. *See also* Centralized cataloguing, Clump, Co-operative cataloguing, National union catalogue (1).

Union list. A complete record, usually printed, of holdings of material in a certain field, on a particular subject, or of a given type such as of periodicals or annuals, for a group of libraries.

Union of International Associations. <www.uia.org> Founded in Brussels in 1907 as the Central Office of International Associations and became a federation under its present name at the first World Congress of International Organizations in 1910. Serves as a documentation centre on international governmental and non-governmental organizations, their activities and meetings. It now functions as a clearinghouse for over 40,000 international bodies.

Union paper. Two sheets of wrapping paper stuck together with tar, bitumen, or some similar material with a waterproofing property. *See also* Reinforced union paper, Tarred brown paper.

Unique entry, principle of. (*Cataloguing*) The entry for a book under a heading chosen (from more than one alternative) for person, subject, organization, place, etc., cross-references being provided from the other words which might have been used as alternatives. *See also* Cataloguing, principles of.

UNISIST. <unesdoc.unesco.org/images/0013> United Nations Information System in Science and Technology, resulting from a feasibility study undertaken by Unesco and the International Council of Scientific Unions (ICSU), and approved by the 17th session of the General Conference of Unesco in November 1972. It comprises five main objectives: '(a) improving tools of systems interconnection; (b) improving information transfer; (c) developing specialized information manpower; (d) developing science information policy and national networks; (e) special assistance to developing countries'. UNISIST's most embracing and far-reaching activity is the establishment of a standardization programme for all phases of information handling, the ultimate goal being the evolution of a world-wide science information system. UNISIST National Committees have been formed in many Member States and governmental agencies nominated to act as national focal points for questions relating to the UNISIST programme. Recent activity has been modest. Publishes *UNISIST Newsletter* (q.). *See also* BSO, General Information Programme, INFOTERM, ISDS, ISSN.

Unit bibliography. A bibliography of different editions of a book with the same title.

Unit card. *See* Unit entry.

Unit Concept Co-ordinate Indexing. (*Information retrieval*) A system based on a combination of the Colon Classification structure with the techniques of the Uniterm system.

Unit entry. A basic catalogue entry which gives the fullest information – a Main entry – and which is used for all Added entries, usually with the addition of appropriate headings (subject, author, title, series, editor, illustrator, translator, etc.).

Unit record. The records comprising a descriptor file. Each consists of (a) descriptors (e.g. subject headings or class numbers) appropriate to the subject of the documents, (b) specifications of the documents (e.g. author, title, publisher, date, pagination, etc., plus possibly an annotation or abstract), (c) a document address, i.e. class number, call number, shelf number, file number, accession number or other indication of its whereabouts in the Store.

United Kingdom Education and Research Networking Association. *See* UKERNA.

United Kingdom Literacy Association (UKLA). <www.ukla.org> A non-profit professional organization, formed originally in 1963 as the United Kingdom Reading Association (UKRA) and adopting its current title in 2003. The Association encourages research and good practice in reading and literacy, networks teachers and researchers, encourages training, debates issues and acts as a clearinghouse for literacy information.

United Kingdom Office for Library and Information Networking. *See* UKOLN.

United Kingdom Reading Association (UKRA). *See now* United Kingdom Literacy Association (UKLA).

United Nations Information System in Science and Technology. *See* UNISIST.

United Nations Literacy Decade. 2003–2012 has been so designated; information literacy may be added to the targets.

United States Government Printing Office (USGPO). <www.gpo.gov> Created by a Congressional Joint Resolution on 23 June 1860, the Government Printing Office executes orders for printing and binding placed by Congress and the departments, independent establishments, and agencies of the federal government; it distributes government publications as required by law, and maintains necessary catalogues and a library of these publications; it also prints, for sale to the public, documents which are of a non-controversial nature.

United States Information Agency (USIA). *See now* USINFO.

United States Information Service. *See now* USINFO.

United States of America Standards Institute. *See* American National Standards Institute, Inc.

Uniterm concept co-ordination indexing. With this system, invented by Mortimer Taube in 1953, periodical articles or other documents to be indexed are scanned to see their subject contents, expressed in one or two simple basic words called 'keywords' (which are to be found in the *Thesaurus* containing all the keywords likely to be used in the literature of the subject) and the accession number of the document recorded on cards by punching holes in numbered squares. The information is retrieved by placing the cards several at a time over an illuminated glazed frame so that the light shines through the holes showing which documents have all the required terms. 'Uniterm' was the trademark of the developer of the system. *See also* Batten system, Co-ordinate indexing.

Uniterm index. A method of indexing which involves the selection of keywords to represent the content of the record or document that is being indexed. The keywords must be predicted when analyzing a question in order to provide searching clues.

Unityweb. <www.thecombinedregions.com> The web-based service founded as the Unity Combined Regions Database, a bibliographic tool managed by CONARLS on behalf of eight of the ten regional library co-operatives in the UK ('The Combined Regions') with the British Library and Share the Vision. Unityweb contains 9 million records and 30 million locations.

Universal Availability of Publications (UAP). <www.ifla.org/VI/2/uap> A programme initiated by IFLA and supported by Unesco to ensure the widest possible availability of published materials in any format to users in any location as a basic human right. The programme made substantial achievements in international interlending. In 2003 its base at the British Library closed, although some activities will continue elsewhere.

Universal Bibliographic Control and International MARC (UBCIM). <www.ifla.org/VI/3/ubcim> The Universal Bibliographic Control (UBC) programme was set up in 1974 by IFLA to encourage international conformity in the exchange of bibliographic data, following activity from 1969 by cataloguing experts. The International MARC Programme was amalgamated with UBC in 1986 to form UBCIM. Much was achieved, and the programme had become redundant; it was closed in 2003. The UNIMARC format, which had been one of the major projects of UBCIM, is to be continued by the National Library of Portugal. Other aspects of the programme will be continued by ICABS.

Universal Copyright Convention. *See* Copyright, International.

Universal Dataflow and Telecommunications (UDT). An IFLA core programme established in 1985, and hosted by the National Library of Canada. It aimed to promote electronic transfer of data between libraries, nationally and internationally. The programme became redundant and was closed in 2003. Many aspects are continued by ICABS.

Universal Decimal Classification (UDC). <www.udcc.org/about.htm> (UDC Consortium, PO Box 90407, 2509 LK The Hague, The Netherlands) UDC (French abbreviation: CDU; German abbreviation: DK) is a sophisticated indexing and retrieval tool, adapted by Paul Otlet and Senator Henri La Fontaine in Brussels from the Decimal Classification of Melvil Dewey. It was first published (in French) between 1904 and 1907. It has been extensively revised and developed and has become a flexible and effective system for organizing bibliographic records for information resources in any medium. New developments and new fields of knowledge can be readily incorporated. A core version of UDC (Master Reference File – held at the Royal Library, The Hague) with over 65,000 subdivisions is available in database format, and the UDC Consortium maintains and reviews the scheme, initiating revisions and extensions. Printed and electronic versions are available from UDCC in several languages; the latest English-language version of the abridged Pocket Edition (PD 1000) was issued in 2003.

Universal Information System in Science and Technology. *See* UNISIST.

Universal Standard Bibliographic Code. *See* USBC.

Universities and Colleges Information Systems Association. *See* UCISA.

Universities Funding Council. *See now* Higher Education Funding Councils.

University, College and Research Group (UCR). A membership group of CILIP, formed originally in 1927. The Group represents the interests of national, university and research librarians.

University Corporation for Advanced Internet Development. *See* UCAID.

University for Industry (UfI). <www.ufi.com> Part of the UK government's vision for lifelong learning, UfI was proposed in the early 1990s and embodied in a report from the Institute for Public Policy Research *The University for Industry: creating a National Learning Network* (1996); in 1998 the Department for Education and Employment published the *UfI pathfinder prospectus*. The scheme is a way of brokering learning, connecting individuals and companies with courses to meet their needs; libraries of all types have a major role to play as the resource base for non-traditional learners. Services are delivered by learndirect <www.learndirect.co.uk>.

University Grants Committee (UK). *See now* Higher Education Funding Councils.

University library. A library or group of libraries established, maintained, and administered by a university to meet the needs of its students and members of the academic staff.

University research library. A Research library differing from other university libraries by virtue of the size, range, depth and quality of its collections, necessary general background stock to support its special areas, and large-scale holdings amassed over a long period of time to form a concentration of materials important enough to attract scholars world-wide.

UNIX. A multi-user, multi-tasking operating system developed in 1969 at AT&T Bell Laboratories for use on minicomputers. It exists in various forms and implementations and was very important in the development of the Internet, many networked tools being developed for it.

Unjustified. (*Printing*) Type which is set with equal word spacing resulting in text lines of different length. *See also* Justification (2).

Unlettered.   A book without the title or the author's name on the spine.

Unopened.   When the 'bolts' or folded edges of the sections of a book, have not been opened with a paper-knife. Not be confused with Uncut.

Unpaged.   Pages of a book which do not bear page numbers. These usually occur amongst the Preliminaries; if referred to in a catalogue or bibliography, the total number, or the page numbers which the individual pages would have been given, are entered within [ ].

Unprocessed paper (or board).   Paper or board in sheets or reels as supplied to the printer or stationer.

Unscheduled mnemonics.   *See* Mnemonics.

Unscheduled records.   (*Archives*) Those for which no final decision has been made as to their disposition.

Unsewn binding.   *See* Perfect.

Unsigned.   A book, the sections of which bear no signature letters or figures, and are therefore 'unsigned'.

Unsought link.   (*Classification*) In chain indexing, a step in a notational hierarchy which is unwanted for indexing purposes, either because no enquirer is likely to search under the appropriate verbal term, or because of faulty subordination in the classification scheme itself. *See also* Chain index, False link, Subordination.

Untrimmed page size.   The size of a sheet after folding and before trimming.

Untrimmed size.   The dimensions of a sheet of paper, untrimmed and not specially squared, sufficiently large to allow a trimmed size to be obtained from it as required. British papermakers may interpret this term as 'not guillotine trimmed'. *See also* Paper sizes, Periodical, Trimmed size.

Unum.   Unesco Unit of Money. *See* Unesco coupons.

Updated version.   A Derivative work resulting in modifying an Intellectual work by removing items of information and substituting for them, or adding, new or more up-to-date knowledge.

Upper case letters.   Capital letters, i.e. those contained in the upper of the two cases of printer's type. Their use is indicated in a MS. or proof by underlining with three lines. Abbreviation: u.c. *See also* Capitals, Lower case letters, Small capitals.

Upper cover.   *See* Obverse cover.

Upright.   1. A book that is taller than its width.   2. A sample of print or a printing job, that is set to an upright size. *See also* Broad.

UPS.   Uninterruptible power supply, a device connected between power source and a computer to ensure continuation of power in the event of failure of the mains supply.

Upward reference.   A direction from a less to a more comprehensive subject heading in an alphabetico-specific subject catalogue. The reverse of Downward reference.

Urban Libraries Council.   <www.urbanlibraries.org> (1603 Orrington Avenue, Suite 1080, Evanston, IL 60201, USA) ULC is open to public libraries serving populations of 50,000 or more, or situated in areas defined as metropolitan for statistical purposes, and to library-related corporations; it is a not-for-profit organization for mutual support and information dissemination. Publishes *Urban Libraries Exchange* (m.), and many surveys.

URI. <www.w3.org/Addressing> Uniform Resource Identifier, a short string that identifies resources – documents, images, downloadable files, services, electronic mailboxes – on the World Wide Web. Both URL and URN are URIs: the URL identifies a resource via a representation of its primary access mechanism (e.g., its network location); while the URN is a namespace identifier. Further clarification can be found at <http://www.w3.org/TR/uri-clarification>.

URL. Uniform Resource Locator, the standardized method of encoding location and access information to resources across multiple information systems across the Internet. The URL consists of four parts: protocol <http:> or <ftp:>; Internet name and port <www.shef.ac.uk>; document path <inf/rec>; filename <xxx.html>. *See also* PURL, URI, URN.

URN. Uniform Resource Name, intended as a way of referencing an object on the World Wide Web that is not dependent on location (as is the URL). Software processing of the name would locate the object using a name lookup service. *See also* Digital Object Identifier, Persistence, PURL, URI, URL.

US Internet Service Provider Association (USISPA). <www.usispa.org> A group of the largest Internet service providers in the United States who joined forces to form a lobbying group and address policy matters of direct concern. The Association serves as the ISP community's representative during policy debates and as a forum in which members can share information and develop best practices for handling specific legal matters.

US National Standards Association. A co-ordinating body for United States government standards and specifications. *See* American National Standards Institute, Inc.

USA Standards Institute. *See* American National Standards Institute, Inc.

USASI. United States of America Standards Institute. *See* American National Standards Institute, Inc..

USB. Universal Serial Bus, a specification for connecting Peripherals to computers at speeds of up to 12 Mbps and developed by a group that included Intel, Microsoft, Compaq, Digital Equipment, IBM, NEC and Nortel. USB began to be used in quantity in 1998/99 and, being Hot pluggable, had definite advantages over the outdated SCSI standard. USB 2.0 offers data transfer speeds of 480 Mbps. *See also* Firewire.

USBC. Universal Standard Bibliographic Code was the subject of a feasibility study undertaken for the British Library by the University of Bradford; it aimed to eliminate the duplication of bibliographic records when large files are merged. USBC is a fixed length code unique to each item recorded and is derived by computer algorithm directly from bibliographic details.

Usenet. A global network of discussion groups enabling participation in, or simply the viewing of, arguments, discussions, news reports, on a wide-ranging variety of topics. Usenet is divided into categories covering broad areas such as recreational activities, the sciences, computing, and social issues. These are further subdivided hierarchically until groups dealing with very specific subjects (e.g. music; jazz) can be identified. The feed for all Usenet groups taken by an institution is controlled by the network administrator and the contents are all held on the local Usenet computer for a specified time. Google Groups <groups.google.com> contains the entire archive of Usenet discussion groups dating back to 1981 and the database containing more than 845 million posts is searchable. Contrasts with Mailing lists which use E-mail for communications and which also require prior registration. *See also* FAQs.

User education. A programme of information provided by libraries to users, to enable them to make more efficient, independent use of the library's stock and services. A programme of user education might include tours, lectures, workshops and the provision of support materials. Also termed *library instruction* and *library orientation. See also* Information literacy.

User group. Users of a Host system or of particular computer or software systems may band together to share experiences, pass on hints, and provide feedback to the host or manufacturer.

User interface. That part of an Application or Operating system through which the End user interacts with the software. First generation PCs used Command-driven interfaces which have now been replaced by WIMPS and GUI systems in all general-purpose computers. User interface design in applications software must take account of usability, orientation (particularly in web-based systems), the use of colour, the need for online help, the skills of all potential user groups (naïve or experienced), and requirements for the disabled. Also known as Human computer interface.

User relevance. The appropriateness of information retrieved for a user even if it is not exactly what was requested.

User satisfaction. A measure of performance based on the user's perception of the adequate delivery of a service, or of a required item or piece of information in an acceptable period of time.

User studies. Research projects, surveys or questionnaires carried out to determine what users want from a service, how they seek information, whether existing services provide adequate responses, and how improvements or new services could best be targeted.

User-friendly. Used to describe a software Application or computer system designed to be very easy to operate, even by untrained users. GUIs and WIMPS interfaces exemplify such systems. *See also* User interface.

Username. The combination of generally alpha-numeric characters that identifies a user or group of users as having the right to access stand-alone or networked resources. In many systems a Password is used to authenticate the username and provide access. *See also* Single sign-on.

User-profile. *See* Interest-profile.

USGPO. *See* United States Government Printing Office.

USINFO. <usinfo.state.gov> The US government information service set up in 1999 when the previous United States Information Agency (USIA) and United States Information Service (USIS) merged into the Department of State to form the Bureau of International Information Programs. USINFO runs three offices: geographic liaison, thematic programs, and technology services.

USMARC. The version of the MARC format operated by the Library of Congress. *See* MARC.

USNARA. *See* National Archives and Records Administration (NARA).

USNP. <www.neh.gov/projects/usnp> The US Newspaper Program is funded by the National Endowment for the Humanities with technical assistance from the Library of Congress. Fifty states have participated in the Program and catalogue records are passed to OCLC. The Program also funds cataloguing at eight national newspaper repositories.

ut infra. Lat. 'as below'.

ut sup. Abbreviation for *ut supra* (Lat. 'as above').

Utilities. Software Applications used for a range of support and maintenance purposes, e.g. the recovery of accidentally deleted files, optimizing hard disk space, and converting file formats.

v. Abbreviation for verse, *versus* (against), *vide* (see), *vice* (in place of), *violino* (violin), *voce* (voice), and Volume.

V series. <www.itu.int/itudoc/itu-t/rec/v> A total of over 80 recommendations of the International Telecommunication Union (ITU-T) on Data communication over the telephone network, including specifications for modems of different speeds.

V.3 Online/V.3 CD/V.3 Web. *See* VISCOUNT.

Vacuum drying. A method for drying books, loose papers and newspapers. The materials are placed in a chamber where a vacuum is created by lowering the temperature. Hot air is introduced until a predetermined temperature is reached; the moist air is then pumped out and the cycle is repeated if necessary. *See also* Desiccant drying, Freeze drying.

Vade mecum. A guide, handbook, or manual which can be conveniently carried for reference.

VADS. *See* Value added network.

VALE. <www.valenj.org> Virtual Academic Library Environment; provider of online access to universities and other educational institutions throughout New Jersey, USA.

Validation. *See* Data validation.

Value added network (VAN).   A network which leases telecommunications links from a public utility, and supplements these with additional services, specialized features, etc. and markets the 'improved' network to customers. Also known as 'Valued Added Data Services' (VADS).

VAN.   *See* Value added network.

Van Gelder paper.   A brand of good-quality paper which is produced in Holland and used mainly for fine paper copies. A variety with an Antique Finish is used by artists for drawings, sketches and water-colour paintings. Also called 'Dutch paper'.

Vancouver Style.   A citation method in which each paper is given a running number at the point it is cited in an article (presented in parentheses or as a superscript), the full references being arranged in numerical order at the end of the article. The items making up a reference are as follows: (i) author's name and initials – if there are up to 6 authors they should all be named; (ii) full title of the paper; (iii) title of the journal; (iv) date of publication; (v) volume number; (vi) part number in parentheses; (vii) page numbers. The use of punctuation between items can vary, e.g.

1. Weng, C. G., Tam, M. T. and Lin, G. C. Acoustic emission characteristics of mortar under compression. Cement and Concrete Research 1992; 22(4): 641–652.

Also known as Numbered System, Numeric Style. *See also* Chicago Style, Harvard Style.

Vanity publishers.   Firms who publish and market books at authors' risk and expense. Also called 'Subsidy' or 'Co-operative' publishers.

Vapourware.   Software promoted and demonstrated but which is extremely late in being delivered, if it ever is.

VAR.   Value Added Reseller, a company that takes products from an OEM, adds value in the form of maintenance, training or other enhancements and sells on at an increased price.

Variable field coding.   (*Cataloguing, Information retrieval*) *See* Fixed field coding.

Variable mnemonics.   *See* Mnemonics.

Variant.   A term given to corrections inserted in later printings of a book. These are frequent in hand-printed books and are accounted for by the fact that mistakes were noticed and the type altered during printing, the sheets already printed remaining untouched.

Variant edition.   The edition of a work which gives the author's variations, textual changes and alterations in the text, possibly from their first composition to their final appearance in a Definitive edition.

Variorum.   Abbreviation of the Latin *cum notis variorum* 'with notes by various editors'.

Variorum edition.   An edition of a work composed from a comparison of various texts which have been published previously, variations being given in footnotes, and including the notes of various commentators. In the USA, publishers tend to use this term for Definitive edition, Textual variant or Variant edition.

Various dates (v.d.).   Used to describe a volume containing several works of different date or a work consisting of several volumes published at different dates.

Vat.   The tank containing beaten pulp from which hand-made sheets of paper are made.

Vat paper.   Another name for Hand-made paper.

Vatican Code.   The Vatican Library's *Rules for the catalog of printed books* (American Library Association, 1931; 2nd ed., 1948, tr. from the 2nd Italian ed. published in 1938) were drawn up to provide a new general catalogue of the Library.

Vatican Library.   <www.vatican.va> Founded in the mid-1440s by Pope Nicholas V, the Library possesses an extrordinarily rich collection of rare books and documents, illustrated manuscripts, and coinage. It holds the four oldest surviving manuscripts of Virgil's poems, and has acquired many notable collections such as the Palatine Library of Heidelberg, the Cerulli collection of Persian and Ethiopian manuscripts, the libraries of the Duke of Urbino, Queen Christina of Sweden, the Barberini, the Ottoboni, and the Chigi. There are over 150,000 manuscripts and 2 million printed books, including 8,000 incunabula.

Vat-sized.   Said of paper when the size is added to the pulp before the pulp is used to form a sheet.

Vaughan Williams Memorial Library.   <www.efdss.org/library> The English national folk-music archive and resource centre, located at the headquarters of the English Folk Dance and Song Society, London.

vCUC.   <www.nlc-bnc.ca/resource/vcuc> Virtual Canadian Union Catalogue, a project to use Z39.50 for searching Canadian library catalogues, either individually or as a distributed virtual union catalogue. Co-ordinated by the National Library of Canada.

VCR.   *See* Video cassette recorder.

v.d.   Abbreviation for Various dates.

VDU.   *See* Visual display unit.

Vegetable parchment.   A partially transparent wrapping paper. *See* Parchment (2).

VEL.   *See* CIC.

Vellum.   Calf skin dressed with alum and polished, and not tanned like leather. A smooth, fine parchment.

Vellum parchment.   A very strong hand-made vellum paper, similar in appearance to animal parchment, but almost indestructible and not as easily affected by heat, mildew and insects as are skins. Called 'art parchment' in the USA.

Vendor.   *See* Host (1).

Venetian type.   A roman type which is characterized by heavy slab serifs, thick main strokes, and a slightly oblique calligraphic emphasis in the round forms. The bar of the small 'e' is tilted. The roman types of

Nicholas Jenson are the finest examples of this kind of type. *See also* Humanistic hand.

Venn diagrams. Graphic methods of sorting out the simple logical relationships between objects or classes of objects. They are named after the English logician John Venn (1834–1923).

verbatim et literatim. (Lat. 'word for word' and 'letter for letter'.) A literal translation or transcription.

Verbatim report. A word for word version of a speech, lecture, or debate.

Verein Deutscher Bibliothekare (VDB). [Association of German Librarians] <www.rdb-online.org> (Postfach 8029, 48043 Münster, Germany) A major German library association, founded in 1900 and reformed in 1948. A member of Bundesvereinigung Deutscher Bibliotheksverbande (BDB).

Vereinigung Schweizerischer Bibliothekare. *See* Association of Swiss Librarians.

Verenigung Openbare Bibliotheken. [Netherlands Public Library Association] *See* Dutch library associations.

Verification. (*Information retrieval*) The process of checking the data input to a computer.

Vernacular. The language of a country. When it is directed that a name shall be given in the vernacular, it means the form which is customary in the country concerned.

Version. 1. A rendering in graphic art form, or sequence of words, of a record, publication, or document, especially a translation of the Bible. 2. One of several intellectual forms taken by the same work. (These may be an original text and its translation, or various texts in one language based on the same original work.) 3. In music, a Transcription in which the original work is so changed as to be virtually a new work, either in the same or in a different medium.

Verso. The left-hand page of an open book or manuscript, usually bearing an even page number. The reverse, or second, side of a sheet of paper to be printed. *See also* Recto.

Vertical file. 1. A drawer, or number of drawers, in a case, in which papers or similar material may be filed on their edges. 2. A collection of pamphlets, cuttings, correspondence, or similar material arranged on their edges in a drawer or box.

Vertical filing cabinet. A cabinet of two, three or four drawers, each of which is wide enough to take quarto or foolscap files resting on their spines.

Vertical press. A printing press in which the flat forme moves up and down instead of to and fro horizontally.

VETGATE. <vetgate.ac.uk> A subject gateway providing access to Internet resources on animal health; part of the BIOME Hub of the (UK) RDN.

VHS. Abbreviation for video-home-system; half inch videotape format manufactured by JVC and aimed mainly at the consumer market.

Vicesimo-quarto. (24mo) *See* Twenty-fourmo.

vid.   Abbreviation for *vide* (Lat. 'see').

vide.   (Lat. 'see ') Used in footnotes to refer to an item mentioned elsewhere in a text, especially in the combinations *vide ante* ('see before'), *vide infra* ('see below'), *vide post* ('see after') and *vide supra* ('see above').

Video cassette recorder (VCR).   Video recording and playback equipment which uses videotape cassettes.

Video CD.   Name given to the format which enables, through MPEG compression, video to be delivered via compact disc. *See also* DVD.

Video library.   A collection of video-recordings, often available for hire to the public as a commercial venture.

Video on demand.   The system that allows End users to choose what they see on television, when they see it, and to pay for it on demand. Early implementations included 'movies on demand' distributed to hotels and hospitals. The large-scale take-up of the concept in the home requires the availability of low cost set-top boxes which will act as interactive decoders.

Videoconferencing.   A means of holding discussions or conferences by linking together remote sites by telecommunications systems; people at each location are enabled to see and hear all other participants. Techniques are developing rapidly, and many commercial companies are offering videoconferencing bases for hire; several vendors are now offering equipment for companies to set up permanent links to scattered sites. *See also* Teleconferencing.

Videodisc.   *See* Optical disc.

Videotape recording.   An electronic recording of sound and vision on magnetic tape; usually marketed in an enclosed plastic box as a 'video cassette'.

Videotex.   A generic term for a system whereby computer based information is made available on an adapted television monitor. There are two main types: *interactive* in which information is carried by telephone line and the user can request any page from a theoretically limitless databank, and *broadcast* in which information is carried by radio waves and the user may only select from a comparatively limited number of pages (e.g. in the UK CEEFAX and ORACLE). Interactive videotex is also known as *Viewdata*.

Videotext.   Strictly, a German teletext service; however this term is often confused with Videotex.

Viditel.   Dutch videotex system.

Viewdata.   *See* Videotex.

Vignette.   A small illustration or ornament used principally in book production at the beginning and ends of chapters, not having a definite border but the edges shading off gradually.

Vignetted half-tone.   *See* Half-tone.

Vinculum.   In mathematics a straight, horizontal line placed over two or more numbers of a compound quality to join them. An old name for a Brace.

Viniti. <www.viniti.ru> Vsesoyuznyi Institut Nauchnoi i Tekhnicheskoi Informatsii [All-Russia Institute of Scientific and Technical Information] Viniti was established in 1952 in Moscow and had as its main tasks: (a) the preparation of abstracts in the natural and applied sciences, excluding architecture, building, medicine and agriculture; (b) the organization of instruction in scientific information in universities and institutes at undergraduate and postgraduate levels; (c) the organization and co-ordination of research into the rational organization of information activities, and the mechanical and automatic means of processing and retrieving scientific information. Publishes *Abstract Journal (Referativnyi Zhurnal; Rzh)* in 41 series covering the main fields of natural, exact, and technical sciences, and taken from the VINITI database of over one million documents in 66 languages; from 1995 there have been CD-ROM and Web versions. VINITI is the focal point for many international collaborative programmes.

VIPs. *See* Visually Impaired People.

Virgule. An oblique stroke, /, used typographically for a number of purposes, e.g. 14/18 as an alternative to 14–18; and/or; in bibliographical descriptions to indicate line-endings. Usually called 'Solidus'.

Virtual catalogue. *See* Clump (1).

Virtual communities. Groups of people coming together to network and discuss topics of mutual interest. Communication between members is totally electronic. Such communities may be formed for professional purposes or for social reasons.

Virtual Electronic Library Initiative. A project of the Committee on Institutional Co-operation; *see* CIC.

Virtual Learning Environment. *See* VLE.

Virtual library. Techniques of virtual reality – sophisticated computer simulations – could be used to provide users with library and information services by electronic means, with network document delivery and access, as if from a 'real' library but without a physical entity actually being necessary. The term is often used loosely for networked access to conventional library resources. *See also* Digital library.

Virtual organization (VO). An organization created by collaborating institutions which allows shared use of computational and data resources, particularly in relation to Grid facilities. Amongst other considerations, a VO requires that efficient access control mechanisms to the shared resources by known individuals are in place.

Virtual Private Network. *See* VPN.

Virtual Reference Desk (VRD). <www.oclc.org> or <iis.syr.edu> A series of conferences operated since 1999 by OCLC and the Information Institute at Syracuse University to discuss changes in the fields of reference work, reference systems, standards and practices.

Virtual reality. A computer system that gives the impression of transporting a user to another environment through accurate simulations of that environment, usually using helmets and gloves to provide tactile and visual feedback. The main application is considered to be in computer games and entertainment software, but the technique offers ways of simulating systems that would otherwise be dangerous to research.

Virtual union catalogue. *See* Clump.

Virus. A program that, once admitted to a computer system, has the ability to replicate itself and infect other programs. *See also* Trojan horse, Worm.

VISCOUNT. <www.oclcpica.org> Originally Viewdata and Interlibrary Systems Communication Network. Funded 1985–87 by the British Library with participation of several British regional co-operative schemes. LASER operated the network for several years, introducing new facilities V.3 Online and V.3 CD. In 2003 the network passed to OCLCPICA; a further facility – V.3 Web – was introduced. There are now over 5 million bibliographic records with locations and the service is used by 70 public library systems in the UK.

Visible cloth joint. A cloth joint used to fasten the sections of a sewn book to its covers, and visible when the book is bound.

Visible index. 1. A frame, or series of frames, usually of metal, for holding cards or strips of card, on which records are entered. They are made so that all the headings contained in the frame are visible at the same time and so that entries may be added or extracted at will whilst maintaining the alphabetical, or other, sequence. 2. A record, as of periodicals or a list of subjects, contained in such a device.

Visigothic handwriting. A Spanish form of handwriting, being a national adaptation of the Latin cursive after the dissolution of the Roman Empire. It was used in Spain in the eighth and ninth centuries, and also spread to Italy. *See also* Cursive, Handwriting.

VISION project. <www.rlg.org/vision.html> A joint project of the Research Libraries Group (RLG) and the Visual Resources Association (VRA); announced in 1997 and aiming to bring more visual resources information online, test standards for creating and sharing such information, and evaluatie new data in the context of existing RLG databases.

Visual aids. Film strips, films, and other illustrative material used as an adjunct to teaching or lecturing.

Visual Arts Data Service. *See* AHDS.

Visual display unit. A monitor used for the display of data from a computer.

Visual Resources Association (VRA). <www.vraweb.org> The Association furthers research and education in the field of visual resources and promotes co-operation among the members of the profession. Committees: Data Standards; Intellectual Property Rights; Joint VRA/ ARLIS Taskforce on professional issues. Publishes *VRA Bulletin* (q.).

Visually Impaired People (VIPs). The term now generally used for people who are blind or who have limited vision. In the UK there has been much activity to ensure that copyright regulations do not unnecessarily disadvantage such people, making exceptions to allow copying of material into formats such as large print that are more accessible, but protecting rightsholders.

viz. Abbreviation for *videlicet* (Lat. 'namely').

Vlaamse Vereniging voor Biblioteek- Archief en Dokumentatiewezen. *See* Belgian library associations.

VLE. Virtual Learning Environment, the information system that facilitates online interactions between learners and tutors providing, for example, controlled access to curriculum content, student tracking facilities, online assessment systems, access to learning resources, and communication facilities between learner and tutor. The VLE is a part of the wider MLE within a learning institution.

VNTIC. *See* Scientific and Technical Information Centre of Russia.

VO. *See* Virtual organization.

Vocabulary. *See* Index language.

Vocal music. Music written to be sung by one or more persons: if for many people, it is known as choral music, and in its larger concerted forms of cantata, oratorio, or opera is accompanied by an orchestra, otherwise it may be unaccompanied, or a piano or organ used.

Vocal score. *See* Score.

Voice mail. Storage of voice messages for retrieval by the addressee; similar to E-mail, as the messages are stored digitally and reconstituted only when the addressee accesses the system to collect mail.

VoIP. Voice over Internet Protocol, the use of the Internet for making telephone calls. The main advantage for users of VoIP connections is that they generally only have to pay their normal (local) Internet connection charges regardless of where they are calling anywhere in the world. VoIP telephony hence threatens the traditional distance and even time-based pricing model upon which all major voice line telephone services are currently based.

vol. (*Pl.* vols) Abbreviation for Volume.

Vol-Info. <groups.yahoo.com/group/vol-info> Voluntary Sector Information Workers Network. Set up in 2003 to continue the earlier VOLSIF; there are now 120 members. Operates as a forum for those involved in information services in the voluntary sector, charities and non-profit organizations.

Vollans Report. *Library co-operation in Great Britain*, 1952, the report on the working of the national interlending system which R. F. Vollans wrote at the request of the joint working party set up by the National Central Library in 1949. The recommendations, together with other proposals, were incorporated in a joint memorandum, *Recommendations on library co-operation*, issued by the joint working party in 1954, and measures to implement them were taken by the National Committee on Regional Library Co-operation.

VOLSIF. Voluntary Sector Information Workers Forum. *See now* Vol-Info.

Volume. 1. A book distinguished from other books or from other volumes of the same work by having its own title-page, half-title, cover title or portfolio title, and usually independent pagination, foliation, or register. It may be designated 'part' by the publisher, and it may have various title-pages, paginations, or include separate works or portfolios, etc. The volume may be as originally issued or as bound subsequently; in this sense 'volume' as a physical, or material, unit, may not be the same as 'volume' as a bibliographical unit. A volume of music may consist of a score, of loose parts, or of a score with loose parts in pockets. 2. Whatever is contained in one binding. 3. A document or part of a document bound or intended to be bound in one cover and, normally, having its own title-page. 4. For library statistical purposes, any book, pamphlet, or document, in whatever form it exists which has been separately published and is separately catalogued and accessioned. In a catalogue entry the statement of the number of volumes relates to the physical, not the bibliographical, number, e.g. 1 *vol in* 2; 2 *v. in* 1; 8 *vols. in* 6. 5. (*Computing*) Another name for a storage device such as a hard Disk or tape unit. Large hard disks may be Partitioned into smaller, more manageable volumes dedicated to particular tasks or users.

Volume capacity. *See* Shelf capacity.

Volume number. A number used to distinguish certain volumes of a work, set or series.

Volume signature. The number of the volume, as 'Vol. I', or simply 'I', or a letter, placed on the same line as the signature (*see* Signature (2)) to prevent the binder mixing the sections of various volumes.

Volumen. (Lat. 'a thing rolled up') The papyrus roll used in ancient Egypt, Greece and Rome, which was written on one side in ink with a reed pen, the text being in columns, the lines of which ran parallel with the length of the roll. The last sheet of the papyrus was rolled round a stick which had knobbed ends and served as a handle. The rolls were kept in boxes (Capsa) or on shelves, and for purposes of distinction when placed in this position had a vellum label attached to the end of the roll. This label bore the title of the work, and was sometimes coloured. A wooden case (*Manuale*) was sometimes used to protect the edges of the roll from being frayed by the owner's toga or cloak. *See also* Scroll (2).

Voluntary Sector Information Workers Forum (VOLSIF). *See* Vol-Info.

Voluntary Sector Information Workers Network. *See* Vol-Info.

Volute. (*Binding*) An ornament consisting of a large curl in the form of a Corinthian volute, and at the opposite end a small curl turning the other way. Found in pairs in sixteenth-century finishers' rolls of the heads-in-medallions type.

Vormelker (Rose L.) Award. An annual prize awarded by the Special Libraries Association.

Vosper (Robert) Fellowships. A series of annual awards funded by the Council on Library and Information Resources to encourage involvement in the IFLA core programmes. First awards were made in 1989.

Vowel-ligatures. The ligatures æ or œ are used in Old English and French words (Ælfric, Cædmon, hors d'œuvre, etc.), but the combinations *ae* and *oe* are printed as two letters in Latin, Greek and English words (Aetua, Boeotia, larvae, etc.).

v.p. Abbreviation for 'various places' or 'various publishers'. *See also l.v.*

VPN. Virtual Private Network, a network constructed by using public wires to connect nodes, set up solely for the users of a single institution. The networks so created use encryption and other security mechanisms to ensure that only authorized users can access the network and that data cannot be intercepted.

VRA. *See* Visual Resources Association.

VRD. *See* Virtual Reference Desk.

VRML. Virtual Reality Modelling Language, a standard language that permits the creation of three-dimensional objects and virtual worlds that can be delivered across the Internet.

Vulgate. The Latin Bible translated by St. Jerome in the fourth century and authorized by the Roman Catholic Church. *See also* Bibles.

W3. *See* World Wide Web.

W3C. <www.w3.org> The World Wide Web Consortium, founded in October 1994 to develop the full potential of the World Wide Web via common protocols that promote its evolution and ensure its interoperability. W3C is jointly hosted by the Massachusetts Institute of Technology Laboratory for Computer Science, ERCIM (host for Europe) and the Keio University Shonan Fujisawa Campus (host for Asia). W3C's long term goals for the Web are: to make the Web accessible to all by promoting technologies that take into account the vast differences in culture, language, education, ability, material resources, access devices, and physical limitations of users on all continents; to develop a software environment (the Semantic Web) that permits each user to make the best use of the resources available on the Web; and to guide development with careful consideration for the novel legal, commercial, and social issues raised by the technology.

WADEX. Abbreviation for Word and Author Index. A computerized indexing system which uses authors' names as well as titles, printing authors and significant words from titles on the left-hand margin, using them as headings and following them with the full author and title. *See also* KWIC, KWOC.

w.a.f. With all faults. An abbreviation used in booksellers' and auctioneers' catalogues to indicate that a book is, or may be, faulty and is offered for sale in this condition and therefore not subject to return because of defects.

WAGUL. <www.library.uwa.edu.au/affiliations/wagul> Western Australian Group of University Librarians, WAGUL promotes the provision of quality services to enhance and expand access for staff and students of publicly-funded universities in Western Australia; projects have included a serials overlap study, collaborative purchasing of expensive monograph titles, and feasibility of collaborative cataloguing.

WAIS. Wide Area Information Server, a Client/server application which allows the searching and retrieval of information from world-wide databases. WAIS was developed by Thinking Machines Corporation of Cambridge, Massachusetts in collaboration with Apple Computer, Dow Jones, and KPMG Peat Marwick. WAIS databases may be accessed by WAIS and World Wide Web clients. WAIS supports the Z39.50-1988 (version 1) protocol.

Walford Medal. <www.cilip.org.uk> An award made by CILIP to recognize sustained and continual contributions to bibliography and the profession. Named after Dr John Walford, whose *Guide to Reference Materials* was first published in 1959; he was compiler of the Guide for many years, and remained closely associated with the work until his death, over 40 years later.

Wall shelving. Shelving placed against walls.

Wallis (Helen) Fellowship. An annual award made by the British Library to recognize outstanding international work derived from the Library's cartographic collections; Helen Wallis was the Library's Map Librarian 1967–86.

Walter press. A rotary press which was first used in 1866 for printing *The Times*. It was constructed by J. C. MacDonald and J. Calverlye for J. Walter, owner of *The Times*. By 1880 this kind of press was in use throughout Europe.

WAN. *See* Wide area network.

Wanting. This word when followed by details of parts or volumes of a publication in a catalogue entry, indicates that those items are not possessed.

Wants list. A list of books wanted, which is issued by a librarian or second-hand bookseller.

WAP. Wireless Application Protocol, the standard for accessing the Internet with wireless devices such as mobile phones.

WARBICA. West African Regional Branch of the International Council on Archives.

WARP. [Web Archiving Project – Japan] *See* Kokuritsu Kokkai Toshokan.

Warwick Framework. <www.ukoln.ac.uk/metadata/resources/wf.html> A container architecture for aggregating metadata objects for interchange proposed at a workshop on Metadata, held at Warwick University, UK in 1996. An object may be described by different metadata formats (e.g. Dublin Core, MARC) and the Warwick Framework allows these to be brought together and appended to the document.

Wash drawing. An illustration, usually in sepia or black or white, done with a brush.

Washing. When developing photographic negatives, or making prints on sensitized paper, the materials are thoroughly washed in clean running water after they have been in the fixing solution so as to remove all traces of the developing or fixing solutions.

Washington Library Network.   *See* Western Library Network.

Washington Press.   The American counterpart of the Albion Press. It was invented in 1827.

WATCH project.   <tyler.hrc.utexas.edu> The Writers and Their Copyright Holders (WATCH) project ran 1994–96 and aimed to create a file of copyright holders for authors so that this information would be freely available via the Internet. Initially a project of the Harry Ransom Humanities Research Center at the University of Texas, with later collaboration from the University of Reading, UK. The first phase was completed in 1996, and work continues on a routine level.

Waterleaf.   Hand-made paper in its initial stage of manufacture, consisting of pulp spread and evened by shaking in the hand mould, and pressed between felts. It is semi-absorbent, being unsized, and must be sized before it is suitable for use as writing paper. *See also* Engine-sizing, Tub-sizing.

Waterleaf paper.   Body paper which has been prepared for surface sizing or impregnation.

Watermark.   A paper-maker's device which can be seen on any sheet of good paper when held up to the light. In handmade paper this is caused by twisting or soldering wire into the mould on which the paper is made; in machine-made paper, by a special roller called a 'dandy', which revolves over the moving pulp on the mould, impressing the mark at every revolution. The watermark is usually placed in the centre of one-half of the sheet. *See also* Countermark, Digital watermarking, Impressed watermark.

Wave-border.   (*Binding*) An eighteenth-century finisher's roll border incorporating an undulating line with other conventional ornament. Found in both English and Irish bindings.

Wavy line.   A line placed underneath words in 'copy' or proof to indicate that bold-faced type is to be used.

Wax engraving.   A method of making electros from which to print maps in letterpress work. The outline is drawn on a wax mould and the lettering impressed by hand. On this a copper shell is then deposited.

Wayzgoose.   An annual outing or party held in summer by employees of the printing industries. Originally an entertainment given by a master-printer to mark the return to shorter hours of daylight and the necessity to re-light candles. The derivation of the word is unknown.

WDSL.   *See* Web Services Description Language.

Web.   1. A large roll of paper which is fed into a printing machine. 2. Abbreviation for World Wide Web.

Web accessibility.   In evaluation of a website, the consideration of how readily the site can be accessed by users who have special needs. In the UK, disability legislation now makes it essential to conform to certain basic standards, such as the W3C guidelines <www.w3c.org/WAI>. The

Disability Rights Commission has also investigated accessibility <www.drc-gb.org>.

Web browser. The software used for navigating the World Wide Web that handles the protocols, translates HTML documents to be displayed on screen and utilizes Plug-ins or helper applications to handle a variety of text and multimedia formats. Because of the ubiquity of the web, browsers have become the primary access point for large numbers of library applications such as OPACs, bibliographic databases, electronic books and journals and other user-focused services.

Web crawler. A software Robot that traverses the World Wide Web following links between pages and copying relevant information – in some cases metadata, in others the whole web page or set of pages – to create a database which is then indexed to form searchable keywords for use by web search engines. Also known as Web robots, Web spiders though, strictly, a spider is just that part of the process that follows the links. *See also* Cloaking.

Web harvesting. The regular sampling and retention of information published on selected websites. In efforts to preserve information that is published only on the Web, national libraries are regularly carrying out such harvesting as a part of their conservation and preservation role. The choice of sites to be harvested will depend on criteria that need careful consultation. *See also* Harvest, UK Web Archiving Consortium.

Web log. *See* Blog.

Web pages. Any information made available in electronic form on the World Wide Web marked up using HTML and often incorporating graphics. There is no real technical limit to the size of an individual web page and this varies tremendously moving from one set of pages to another. Most designers attempt to divide their content into easily digestible chunks and bring these together using the HTML 'link' command. A group of web pages combined in this way under a subject or organizational banner is known as a 'web site'. The entry point to a site – the first page on which can normally be found indexes, a description of content, or search boxes – is referred to as the 'home page'.

Web portal. See Portal.

Web press. A printing machine on which the paper is fed from a continuous reel. A 'web perfecting press' prints consecutively on both sides of a continuous reel of paper. Also called 'Web machine'.

Web Services. A modular collection of web protocol-based applications that improve interoperability and can be combined to provide automated added-value services on behalf of users. Web services are based on four sets of standards: XML for data, SOAP for message packaging, UDDI for registering, publishing and finding appropriate services and Web Services Description Language for describing services.

Web Services Description Language (WDSL). An interface description language for XML-based Web Services. It can describe information such as the access point (URL), protocol (SOAP, Http, or MIME) and message format (such as XML Schema) of the Web service. See, for example, <www.w3.org/TR/wsdl20>.

Web site.   A set of web pages with a particular focus, e.g. organizational, personal or subject. *See also* Blog, Web pages.

Webcasting.   A combination of Push and Pull technologies that enables users to subscribe to individual Web pages or entire Web sites and allows for the broadcast delivery of information via Streaming audio and video. An emergent technology in 1997, webcasting was developed to provide users with customized content – e.g. sports, news, stocks, weather – that can be updated regularly and automatically. Webcasting gives users the ability to specify the type of content they want to see, and it gives content providers a means of delivering such information directly to the desktop. Also known as Netcasting. *See also* RSS.

WebDAV.   <www.webdav.org> World Wide Web Distributed Authoring and Versioning, a Working Group of the Internet Engineering Task Force that has given its name to a specification to define extensions to the Hypertext Transfer Protocol (Http) that allows users to collaboratively edit and manage files on remote web servers.

Webpac.   Web OPAC, a library OPAC made available to users via a Web browser.

Webring.   A collection of Web sites that fit together through a common theme and which are joined by Links allowing Internet users to navigate quickly through them.

Weeding.   Discarding from stock books which are considered to be of no further use. Pseudo-weeding is transferring from one department to another, from stack to shelf and *vice versa*, or from files to bound form. Also, examining documents in an archives depository in order to discard items which appear to lack permanent value. *See also* Stripping.

Weekly.   A newspaper or periodical published once a week.

Wei T'o.   A non-aqueous deacidification system for books, developed in Canada in the 1970s. Books are vacuum dried in a chamber, then a 5 per cent solution of methoxy magnesium carbonate is pumped in and the pressure increased so that the books are saturated. The solvent is removed by a second drying period. The entire cycle takes about one hour. A spray version is available for treating single sheets.

Weigendruck.   The German term for Incunabula.

Weight.   'The degree of blackness of a typeface' (BS2961:1967). The types in a Family vary in weight from extra-light to ultra bold.

Weight of face.   Comparative colour value of typefaces when printed, as light, medium, bold.

Welsh Books Council.   [Cyngor Llyfrau Cymru] <www.cllc.org.uk> (Castell Brychan, Aberystwyth, SY23 2JB, UK) A marketing and promotional organization for authors and publishers in Wales, assisting in editing, design and distribution. Supports reading and literacy; funded by the Welsh Assembly.

Welsh Music Information Centre. <www.tycerdd.org/eng/wmic> (15 Mount Stuart Square, Cardiff CF10 5DP, UK) Founded in 1973 and re-established in 2000 after financial collapse. Funded by the Arts Council Wales, the Centre supports archiving, publication and performance of the works of Welsh composers.

WERTID. The West European Round Table on Information and Documentation. An informal group of members of national associations in the field of information and documentation from Belgium, France, Germany, Portugal, Spain and the UK. *Now see* European Council of Information Associations.

Wesermael (Guust van) Prize. Established in 1991 by IFLA to commemorate Guust Van Wesermael who was Professional Co-ordinator/Deputy Secretary General from 1989 to 1991. Awarded to a public or school library in a developing country to purchase books to improve literacy.

Western. An adventure story set in the 'Wild West' of America.

Western Library Network (WLN). <www.wln.com> A consortium network, originally titled the Washington Library Network. Over 350 current members primarily in Washington, Oregon, Idaho, Montana, Alaska, Arizona, British Columbia, with extensions internationally, especially to the Australian and New Zealand bibliographic networks. WLN merged with OCLC in 1999 and is now more correctly titled OCLC Western Service Center.

Wet end. The part of the paper-making machine where the wet pulp is formed into a web of paper, up to the first drier. The other end is known as the 'dry end'.

Wet flong. *See* Flong.

w.f. *See* Wrong font.

WfMC. *See* Workflow Management Coalition.

Wharfedale. *See* Stop-cylinder press.

Whatman paper. A brand of fine grade English hand-made wove drawing paper which was originally made by James Whatman from *c.* 1770 at Turkey Mill near Maidstone, Kent. Sometimes used for limited editions and privately-printed books.

Wheatley Medal. <www.cilip.org.uk> or <www.indexers.org.uk> An award made annually for an outstanding index first published in the UK. The medal, which is named after Henry B Wheatley (author of *How to make an index*, 1902) is jointly administered by CILIP and the Society of Indexers.

Whig Bible. *See* Bibles.

Whip-stitching. The American term for Oversewing.

Whitbread Book Awards. <www.whitbreadbookawards.co.uk> An annual series of awards presented in the UK, and backed by CILIP, the Booksellers Association and other organizations. The categories of awards are: novel, first novel, biography, poetry, and children's.

White Book. An official report published by the German government, so-called because issued in a white paper cover. *See also* Blue Book.

White edges.   Edges of books which have been cut but not coloured or gilded. *See also* Edges.

White House Conferences.   <www.imls.gov/pubs/whitehouse> The first White House Conference on Library and Information Services was held in 1979, and its report (US Government Printing Office, 1979) was submitted to Congress in full by President Carter, with 25 major resolutions for discussion. The planning and organizing body for the event was NCLIS; preparation for the first conference extended over five years and involved 100,000 people in pre-conference activities and meetings. One of the recommendations of the first conference was that similar events should be held every decade, and a second conference took place in 1991. In June 2002 a White House Conference on School Libraries was hosted by First Lady Laura Bush.

White letter.   'Roman' type as opposed to Black letter or Gothic type.

White line.   (*Printing*) A line of space the same depth as a line of printed characters.

White Pages.   Electronic Directory services for locating information about individuals. In spite of considerable efforts there is no single White Pages directory service for the entire Internet. *See also* LDAP, Whois, Whois++, Yellow Pages.

White Paper (UK).   A term often used to denote a Report, Account or other Paper ordered by the House of Commons to be printed, or prepared primarily for debate in the House, and printed in the parliamentary series of official publications. There is a growing tendency, however, to apply the term to similar official publications not required by Parliament and published accordingly in the non-parliamentary series. *See also* Blue Book, Parliamentary Publications.

White publisher.   A publisher, as defined by the ROMEO project, that does not support the Self archiving by authors of their academic papers.

White-line method.   *See* Wood engraving.

White-out.   To space out composed matter, as in displayed or advertisement work.

Whitford Committee.   The Committee under the chairmanship of Mr. Justice Whitford that produced the *Report on copyright and design law* (HMSO, 1977). *See* Copyright.

Whitney-Carnegie Awards.   Award administered by the American Library Association to support the preparation of bibliographic aids to research.

Whois.   A networking directory facility which began as a White Pages for the ARPAnet community, listing around 70,000 people working on the Internet and those carrying out network research. Information about networks, networking organizations, domain names, and the primary contacts associated with them can be located by searching databases using Internet entities, such as domains, networks, and hosts. Whois search is available from InterNIC <www.internic.net>. *See also* Directory services, Whois++.

Whois++. A simple Client/server search and retrieve protocol based upon extensions to the Whois information model and which, through a distributed indexing facility, offers the possibility of searching across multiple servers. *See also* Common Indexing Protocol.

Whole bound. Books bound entirely in leather.

Whole number. The number given by a publisher to an issue of a periodical or serial publication, and continuing from the first issue. It is distinguished from the numbers assigned for volume and part of volume, and from those assigned for series and volume.

Whole-stuff. The pulp used in making paper after it has been thoroughly beaten and bleached, and is ready for the Vat or the paper machine. *See also* Half-stuff.

Who's who file. *See* Biography file.

Wickersham quoins. Expanding steel Quoins which are inserted with Furniture at the side and foot of a Chase. They are adjusted with a key to lock and unlock pages of type in the chase.

Wide. 1. Any material, such as a map or illustration that is wider than the type pages. 2. WIDE, Widely Interconnected Distributed Environment. *See* SINET.

Wide Area Information Server. *See* WAIS.

Wide area network (WAN). A data transmission system linking several organizations; may be national or international in scope. WANS are the inter-organization equivalent of Local area networks (LANs).

Wide lines. *See* Laid paper.

Widener Library. <hcl.harvard.edu/widener> A special collection of some 3,300 volumes, mainly nineteenth-century English literature, Shakespeare, and Extra-illustrated books assembled by Harry Elkins Widener (1885–1912) who lost his life in the sinking of the Titanic. His mother gave funds for the building of a magnificent Memorial Library (opened 1915) which houses the collection as well as the college library.

Wider Information and Library Issues Project. *See* WILIP.

Widow. An incomplete line of type at the top of a column or page, usually the last line of a paragraph, and avoided in good typography because of its unsightliness.

Width. Typefaces are of varying widths in the same Family, and are distinguished by the following (in progressive order): ultra-condensed, extra-condensed, condensed, semi-condensed, medium, semi-expanded, expanded, extra-expanded, ultra-expanded. 'Medium' is the width usually used and indicates the width which the manufacturer determines is the one representing the design and from which variants in the family have been, or may be, derived. *See also* Font, Typeface (2), Weight.

Wiener Library. <www.wienerlibrary.co.uk> (4 Devonshire Street, London W1W 5BH, UK) Founded in Amsterdam by Dr Alfred Wiener in 1933, and brought to London in 1939. After financial difficulties in the late 1970s which threatened the future of the collection, some material was sent to Tel Aviv in return for support from Israel, but all such material was microfilmed first. The Collection comprises material on Nazi Germany and the immediate post-war years.

Wi-Fi.   Wireless Fidelity, the consumer name for IEEE 802.11b. It is a trade term promulgated by the Wireless Ethernet Compatibility Alliance (WECA). 'Wi-Fi' is used in place of 802.11b in the same way that Ethernet is used in place of IEEE 802.3. Products certified as Wi-Fi by WECA are interoperable with each other even if they are from different manufacturers.

Wiki.   A website or other hypertext document collection that allows any user to add content and permit that content to be edited by others. Wikis use simplified hypertext markup language. The first wiki was established by Ward Cunningham in 1995 <c2.com/cgi/wiki?WikiWikiWeb> and named after the 'wiki wiki' or 'quick' shuttle buses at Honolulu Airport. (Reference: Lamb, Brian (2004) Wide open spaces: wikis, ready or not. *EDUCAUSE Review*, vol. 39, no. 5 (September/October) <www.educause.edu/ir/library/pdf/ERM0452.pdf>)

Wild look-through.   Look-through which is irregular and cloudy.

Wildcard.   A character used in keyword searching which can assume the value of any alphanumeric character and so permit wider search options (e.g. alternative spellings) to be achieved quickly. *See also* Truncation (2).

Wilder (Laura Ingalls) Medal.   A bronze medal designed by Garth Williams, awarded by the Association for Library Service to Children (Division of the American Library Association) to an author or illustrator whose books, published in the US, have over a period of years made a substantial and lasting contribution to children's literature. First awarded (to Laura Ingalls Wilder) in 1954, and now offered every three years.

WILIP.   The Wider Information and Library Issues Project was an initiative of Resource (now the Museums, Libraries and Archives Council (MLA)) to clarify the role of libraries in the economic, educational, social and cultural life of the UK. Consultation took place in 2002/2003; the Project sought to find a framework linking information strategies in various sectors, to identify evidence of impact, to highlight workforce and leadership development, and to investigate funding sustainability. It is now continued by Routes to Knowledge (RTK).

WiLL.   <www.londonlibraries.org.uk/will> Project WiLL – What's in London Libraries – is an accessible public interface to the catalogues of 33 London borough libraries. It was developed with support from the London Library Development Agency (LLDA) and the People's Network Excellence Fund, and launched in 2003.

William L. Clements Library.   *See* Clements (William L.) Library.

Williams (Raymond) Community Publishing Prize.   An annual UK award by the Arts Council in memory of the cultural historian, novelist and teacher who stressed the importance and interest of the community;

founded in 1990, the prize recognizes the activities of small publishers rooted in their communities and reflects 'the values of ordinary people and their lives'.

Willow. A machine consisting mainly of two rotating drums inside which spikes are fixed to tear out the raw material (rags, esparto, waste paper, etc.) for paper-making. Also called a 'Devil'. Often combined with a 'duster' which removes unwanted dust from the material.

WILS. <www.wils.wisc.edu> (728 State Street, Madison, WI 53706, USA) Wisconsin Library Services is a network consortium formed in 1972 and having 500 members in the US state of Wisconsin. An OCLC Network Affiliate.

Wilson Committee (UK). The Committee appointed by the Lord Chancellor in 1978 to inquire into the working of those provisions of the Public Record Acts of 1958 and 1967 which have a bearing on the selection of Public records for transfer to the Public Record Office, and public access to them. The Chairman was Sir Duncan Wilson and the Report was published in 1981. *See also* Modern Public Records.

Wilson Library Periodical Award. An award offered annually by the H. W. Wilson Company in respect of a periodical published by a local, state, or regional library, library group, or library association in the United States or Canada which has made an outstanding contribution to librarianship.

WIMP. Acronym for either *windows, icons, menus and pointer* or *windows, icons, mouse and pull-down menus*, the PC User interface that dispensed with command line strings. The acronym became popular with the Apple Macintosh computer but with the introduction of the Windows Operating system, the term has been generally superseded by GUI.

Window. 1.(*Archives*) An opening made in repair paper or parchment to expose a small portion of text. 2. Part of a GUI or WIMP interface which enables the computer display to be adapted to suit the needs of individual users and the Application files with which they are working.

Windows. A Graphical User Interface developed by Microsoft which makes the computer interface user friendly by removing the necessity for inputting command line strings.

Wing Short Title Catalogue. *See STC-Wing.*

WIPO. <www.wipo.int> (34 Chemin des Colobettes, 1211 Geneva 20, Switzerland) Acronym of the World Intellectual Property Organization; it was established in Stockholm in July 1967 and became operative in April 1970 when it continued the work of the United International Bureaux for the Protection of Intellectual Property (BIRPI). Aims to: (a) promote the protection of intellectual property throughout the world through co-operation among States and, where appropriate, in collaboration with any other international organizations; (b) ensure administrative co-operation between the Unions created by certain international conventions or agreements dealing with various subjects of intellectual property. WIPO is the only intergovernmental organization specializing in all aspects of intellectual property, and currently has 171 states in membership. It administers 15 international treaties on industrial property and the six intergovernmental copyright Unions, the most important of which are the International Union for the Protection of Industrial Property created in 1883 at the Paris Convention, and the International Union for the Protection of Literary and Artistic Works (including scientific works) created in 1886 at the Berne Convention. This last is basically concerned with copyright and works jointly with the IGC. The Secretariat of WIPO, called the International Bureau of Intellectual Property, functions also as the secretariat of the various organs of the Union. WIPO is not only the administrative centre but also the international organization responsible for the promotion of such property throughout the world through co-operation between the States. The special organ for this purpose is its Conference consisting of all member states party to the WIPO Convention. In 1994 an arbitration centre was established to help the resolution of intellectual property disputes between private parties. WIPO has also set up a dispute resolution mechanism for domain names on the Internet. *See also* Berne Copyright Convention, Copyright, International, IGC.

WIPO Copyright Treaty.   Adopted in Geneva in December 1996 but still awaiting ratification by the minimum number of states to come into force. The Treaty, which updated the Berne Convention, covered the following areas: computer programs to be regarded as literary works; compilations of data (databases) to be eligible to be literary works; rental and communication to the public rights were both introduced; photographs enjoy greater protection. The Treaty is of most significance for the library community as it specifically recognizes the importance of balancing authors rights with the greater public interest.

Wire.   The endless band of plain brass or bronze, tinned or leaded, or of nickel or stainless steel wires, which forms the moulding unit of a paper-making machine and carries the pulp from the breast box to the couching rolls and so felting it into a sheet, or web of paper. The mesh of the wire varies from fifty to ninety wires per inch according to the quality of paper made. Also called 'Machine wire', 'Wire-cloth', 'Wire-gauze', or 'Travelling mould'.

Wire lines.   *See* Laid paper.

Wire mark.   *See* Laid paper.

Wire sewing.   Sewing the sections of a book with wire staples driven through the folds of the sections and through tapes, canvas or muslin to which the staples are clinched. Also called 'Wire stitching'. *See also* Saddle stitching, Sewing, Stitching, Thread stitched.

Wire side.   The side of a sheet of paper which has come in contact with the Wire of the paper-making machine during the course of manufacture. *See also* Felt side, Right, Twin wire paper.

Wire stabbing. Securing a number of leaves or sections by inserting one or more wire staples, usually from back to front (i.e. not through the fold of sections). This work is done on a stapling machine. Also called 'Side stitching'. *See also* Saddle stitching.

Wire stitched. The fastening of a single section with wire driven through the centre of the fold and clinched (saddle stitched) or through the inner margin of the section (side stitched).

Wire-cloth. *See* Wire.

Wired. *See* Wire stitched.

Wire-gauze. *See* Wire.

Wireless systems. Originally used to indicate radio systems, the term now encompasses what is seen to be the second wireless revolution, that of cellular communications. *See also* Wi-Fi.

Wisconsin Library Services. *See* WILS.

Wiswesser Line Notation. A method of representing structural details of chemical compounds by a string of characters, suitable for handling along with ordinary text material.

With the grain. Said of paper which has been folded in the direction in which the fibres tend to lie. *See also* Against the grain.

Withdrawal. The process of altering or cancelling records in respect of items which have been withdrawn from the stock of a library.

Witt Library. <www.courtauld.ac.uk/sub_index/photographic/witt> The Library was founded in the 1890s by Sir Robert and Lady Witt who began to collect photographs of works of art; their collection was willed to the University of London in 1944 and is now a part of the Courtauld Institute. The Library is an internationally renowned collection of 1.6 million photographs, reproductions and cuttings of paintings and drawings by over 75,000 Western artists. The Witt Computer Index enables in-depth searching, including subject access.

Wittenborn (George) Award. *See* ARLIS/NA.

Wizard. Features in an Application that assist in the production of a range of documents by automating common tasks, particularly related to formatting. For example, in a word processing program, a wizard might help in the preparation of a business-style letter by prompting for common elements and automatically positioning these at what the program designer feels are the most appropriate locations within the document while still allowing a limited degree of customization. *See also* Template.

WLN. *See* Western Library Network.

WNBA. *See* Women's National Book Association.

Women's Art Library. The Library was originally titled Women Artists Slide Library and was housed in Battersea Arts Centre in South London; it opened in 1982 and comprises 30,000 slides, journals, theses, books, newsletters, photographs and other documentation on women artists whether well-known or obscure. Publishes *Women's Art* (6 p.a.). After a number of temporary locations the Library is now housed at Goldsmiths' College, University of London, and a website is reported to be in preparation.

Women's Library (The). <www.thewomenslibrary.ac.uk> (Old Castle Street, London E1 7NT, UK) A major UK women's history collection comprising over 60,000 books, archives and artefacts which chart women's changing role in society. Founded in 1926 as the library of the London Society for Women's Service (a non-militant movement for universal suffrage led by Dame Millicent Fawcett), and later given the name Fawcett Library. The library has been in several locations and funding has been difficult; however more secure financial support has now been organized and the collection is located in refurbished premises under the control of London Metropolitan University.

Women's National Book Association (WNBA). <www.wnba-books.org> (2166 Broadway, Suite 9F, New York, NY 10024, USA) The only professional organization in the book trade that covers a national cross-section of women engaged in all phases of the American book industry. Founded in 1917. Membership is open to all women in the world of books – booksellers, critics, editors, librarians, literary agents, writers, illustrators, those engaged in publishing, book production or other activities allied to the book trade. There are ten chapters in the USA, and affiliated groups in Japan and India. It offers the Constance Lindsay Skinner Award, as a tribute to an author and editor who was for a long time active in the affairs of the Association, to a woman for distinguished contributions to the book world. It was first awarded in 1940 to Anna Carroll Moore. Publishes *The Bookwoman* (2 p.a.).

Wood block. A wood-engraving block of wood, usually box-wood, on which a design for printing has been cut in relief.

Wood engraving. 1. The art or process of cutting designs in relief with a graver or burin upon the end-grain of a block of box-wood, leaving the black areas of the design raised for printing and the cut areas white; this has caused the process to be known as the 'white-line' method. This technique was introduced by Thomas Bewick. *Compare* Woodcut which is rougher and cut along the grain. 2. A print from a wood engraving. *See also* Etching.

Wood letter. A large type-letter of wood; used in poster printing.

Wood pulp. Wood reduced to a pulp by mechanical or chemical means for subsequent paper-making.

Wood type. Wood letters above 72 point used in poster work, because they are lighter and cheaper than metal.

Woodcut. An illustration made by pressing a sheet of dampened paper on a block of soft wood such as beech or sycamore which has been cut away to leave a design at the surface, so that when the block is inked an impression will be left on the paper, the cut-away parts showing white. The side-grain of a block of softer wood, such as pear or sycamore, is used for woodcuts rather than for wood engravings, and the design is executed with a knife whereas a variety of gravers are used for wood engravings. The design of a woodcut is of black lines or masses on a white background whereas that of a wood engraving is the reverse; woodcutting is therefore known as a *black-line* method whereas wood engraving is a *white-line* method. Before the invention of movable type, books (text and illustrations) were printed in this way; these are called Block books. When movable type came into use, only borders, capitals and illustrations were printed from wooden blocks. *See also* Florentine woodcuts.

Woodcut title-page with panel.   *See* Framed-cut.

Wooden boards.   Said of books made before the sixteenth century which had covers made of thick wooden boards. By 1550 they had been replaced almost completely by pasteboards in England, although these had been used in the East for centuries. Leather was stretched over the boards and secured.

WoPEc.   <netec.mcc.ac.uk/WoPEc.html> Working Papers in Economics, a service for finding and downloading the latest research results in economics. Between 1996 and 1999 WoPEc was supported by the UK eLib programme. *See also* RePEc.

Word.   In information retrieval, a spoken or written symbol of an idea. In computer terminology, the contents of a storage location. *See also* Filing code.

Word break.   (*Printing*) Splitting a word at the end of a line.

'Word by word'.   *See* Alphabetization.

Word indexing.   A form of indexing which is the simplest to apply as it assumes on the part of the indexer a minimum knowledge of the subject-matter background and the least amount of technical skill. Such a type of indexing can be performed with precision by machines. *See also* Concordance, KWIC, Permutation indexing and Uniterm index which are of this kind, and Controlled indexing, Index, Uniterm concept co-ordination indexing.

Word processing.   The use of Application software running on a PC to produce textual documents of all sizes and types: letters, memoranda, notices, reports. The software enables direct inputting of the text, provides sophisticated facilities for formatting the text, incorporating and editing graphics, and carrying out Mail merges. When coupled with a Laser printer is capable of producing high quality documents, though if additional facilities are required the file from the work processor can be imported into Desktop publishing software.

Word recognition test.   Usually a standardized test of the ability to read single words aloud. The words are graded in difficulty and the tests yield scores which can be converted into reading ages (the measure most commonly employed when standards of reading are being discussed).

Word-book.   A lexicon, or dictionary.

Words authority file.   *See* Thesaurus.

Work.   Any expression of thought in language, signs or symbols, or other media for record and communication [i.e. a work before printing or other publication]. After publication it becomes a 'published work'. *See also* Document. A work is now generally taken to mean a published document varying in extent from a single paper (*see* Paper (2)) or Article to a contribution to knowledge written by one or more persons and published in several volumes, or even all the published writings by one person. It is also used to include a series of related but separate series (*see* Series (1), (2), (3)) or Periodicals.

Work and back.   *See* Sheet work.

Work and tumble.   The method of printing the second side of a sheet of paper by turning it over in its narrow direction and feeding it into a printing machine to print the reverse side.

Work and turn.   To print from a forme in which the pages have been so imposed that when a sheet has been printed on both sides and cut in half it will provide two copies. *See also* Sheetwise, Tumbler scheme.

Work manual.   *See* Procedure manual.

Work mark.   As the last part of a book number, it is a letter indicating the title, edition, etc., of a work. This is added to the normal author mark to distinguish several titles by one author, giving each a definite location. It usually consists of the letter of the first word not an article of the title, plus, in the case of later editions, the edition number, and/or in the case of other titles beginning with the same letter and having the same class number, a figure (consecutively for each title). *See also* Author mark, Book number, Call number, Volume number.

Work off.   To print the paper; to finish printing.

Work slip.   A card, or other form of record, that accompanies a document throughout the cataloguing and preparation processes and on which the cataloguer notes directions and information necessary to prepare full catalogue entries, cross-references, etc.

Work up.   A smudge or mark on a printed page caused by a letter or piece of spacing material in an improperly locked forme working up into a printing position during a press run. Also called 'Black', 'Rising space'.

Workflow.   The automation of procedures within an organization so that documents, information or tasks 'flow' from one participant to another in a manner that is governed by rules and protocols; there are many software products to support the process. Key benefits include improved efficiency, better control, improved customer service, flexibility and business process streamlining. Often introduced in parallel with Information management.

Workflow Management Coalition (WfMC).   <www.wfmc.org> Founded in 1993 the Coalition is a not-for-profit, international organization of workflow vendors, users, analysts, and university/research groups. It promotes and develops the use of workflow through the establishment of standards for software interoperability and connectivity between products. There are over 200 members.

Workgroup computing. *See* Groupware.

Working party. A group of members of an organization having similar interests, formed to meet a particular need without establishing a permanent committee or other body.

Working Party on Library and Book Trade Relations. *See* LIBTRAD.

'Working with figures'. *See* Press number.

Workplace Libraries. An alternative term to Special Libraries, indicating library services operating in the commercial, industrial, voluntary, and healthcare sectors. Such libraries are most likely to be involved in Information management techniques, and to be keen to demonstrate their efficiency in financial terms.

Workstation. 1. A powerful personal computer usually running the UNIX Operating System. 2. Occasionally used to indicate the specialized furniture on which Personal computers and their Peripherals are placed.

World Book Capital. A Unesco scheme to choose a city annually to be a centre for promotional activity for books. The inaugural city was Madrid in 2001; in 2002 the capital was Alexandria, in 2003 New Delhi, in 2004 Antwerp, and in 2005 Montreal. The programme, highlighting culture, literacy and reading begins each year on April 23 – World Book Day.

World Book Day. April 23 is the chosen date for the annual, international World Book Day held under the auspices of Unesco; the date is significant for the births or deaths of several literary names – Shakespeare, Cervantes, Nabokov – and the event is apparently founded on a Catalan festival (Dia del Libro) held on St. Jordi's/St. George's Day – Jordi being the patron saint of Catalonia. The date of April 23 is however not always observed; for example in the UK the date selected for the high-profile media and online celebration is now early March (in 2005, March 3). The UK event is organized by the People's Network, CILIP, MLA, and The Reading Agency: <www.worldbookday.com>.

World Intellectual Property Organization. *See* WIPO.

World Metal Index. <www.sheffield.gov.uk/in-your-area/libraries/central-library/world-metal-index> A metallic materials identification service giving chemical, mechanical and physical properties of grades of metals both ferrous and non-ferrous. Items are identified from national, foreign and international standards and an extensive collection of world-wide trade literature. Over 200,000 metals are covered.

World Summit on the Information Society (WSIS). <www.itu.int/wsis> Following recommendations from the International Telecommunication Union (ITU) in 1998, the United Nations and ITU have organized a sequence of conferences at governmental level to address problems of inequality of access to information. The first conference was held in Geneva in December 2003; business included a political declaration and a plan of action to investigate the Digital divide and the role of electronic resources in civil society, in the private sector, and in government and international organizations. The second conference will be held in Tunis in 2005 to review progress and refine objectives.

World Wide Web (WWW). A networked information retrieval and communication tool characterized particularly by its use of Hypertext Links to other documents and its ability to handle non-textual information such as graphics and video. Credited to Tim Berners-Lee of CERN, the European Particle Physics Laboratory in Geneva, Switzerland, the World Wide Web has become virtually synonymous with the Internet. Also referred to as 'the Web'. *See also* Portal, W3C, Web browser, Web pages.

World Wide Web Consortium. *See* W3C.

Worm. 1. A computer program that replicates itself, is self-propagating and spawns in network environments, in contrast to a Virus which causes problems on local systems. 2. WORM: Write Once, Read Many. *See* Optical disc.

Worm-bore (Wormhole). A hole or series of holes bored into, or through, a book by a book worm. A book containing such holes is said to be 'wormed'.

Wove paper. Paper which, when held up to the light, shows a faint network of diamonds. This is caused by the weave of an ordinary Dandy Roll (machine-made paper) or mould (hand-made paper). James Whatman was probably the first manufacturer of wove paper, and it was first used by John Baskerville in 1757 when he printed his Virgil on it. Not to be confused with Laid paper.

Wrap rounds. Units of four pages of illustrations, or multiples of four, wrapped around a section of a book and sewn with it. Also called 'Outserts'.

Wrap-around gathering. A book in which one or more leaves at one end are printed on paper forming part of a section at the other end. This practice was used most in the seventeenth and eighteenth centuries.

Wrapper. *See* Book jacket.

Wrench (Sir Evelyn) Travelling Librarian Award. Originally set up in 1965 by the founder of the English-Speaking Union, this Fellowship is now run jointly by CILIP and the ESU which is an independent organization founded to foster good relations between the USA and the Commonwealth by a programme of educational exchanges. The award is now often referred to simply as the Travelling Librarian Award.

Writ. King's precept in writing under seal commanding an official to perform or abstain from some action.

Write protect. To prevent the copying of data onto magnetic storage, by physical means or by configuring software. For example, on a 3.5" floppy disk, moving the plastic tag to the open position will protect the disk.

Writing masters. In the fifteenth century professional writers, no longer needed for literary works because of the invention of printing, became writing masters. The increase of reading led to a general demand to learn the art of writing, and these masters found employment in the universities, schools, Courts, and houses of the wealthy. 'Writing masters' books' giving examples of the various hands, appeared in the sixteenth century.

Wrong font (w.f.).   A letter of a different face or size from the rest of the text. This is caused in hand-set printing by placing type in a wrong case of type when 'distributing' after a printing job.

Wrong side.   (*Printing*) There is a wrong side and a right side to paper and this is important for many printing purposes. *See* Right.

WSDL.   *See* Web Services Description Language.

WSIS.   *See* World Summit on the Information Society.

WWW.   *See* World Wide Web.

WYSIWYG.   (pronounced 'wizzy-wig') What You See Is What You Get, a phrase introduced with Desktop publishing to indicate that the paper or film output from the system would exactly match the screen display. This in comparison to the limited display facilities of older Visual display units and to the limitations in display of some Type encoding programs.

X series.   <www.itu.int/itudoc/itu-t/rec/x> A total of approximately 400 recommendations of the International Telecommunication Union (ITU-T) on Data networks and open system communication.

X Windows.   A windows operating system developed at Massachusetts Institute of Technology for networked UNIX applications; also available on PCs.

X4L.   <www.x4l.org> Exchange for Learning, a UK programme to explore the re-purposing of existing and forthcoming JISC-funded content suitable for use in learning. The programme encompasses content created by other bodies and agencies where intellectual property rights allow for educational use in further or higher education. Part of the activity is to explore the process of integration of Learning objects into VLEs and MLEs.

Xerography.   A method of making copies by the use of light and an electrostatically charged plate. It was invented by Chester F. Carlson, patented by him in 1937 and developed in the Graphic Arts Research Laboratory at the Battelle Memorial Institute. Rank-Xerox Limited, a joint company formed by the Haloid Company and Rank Organization (Rank-Xerox), exploits this process throughout the world. Smaller and larger copies than the original can be made, as also can offset plates on a paper base. This is a dry method of positive reproduction of drawn or written material (whether in ink, pencil or colour) and of printed or typewritten matter, or the representation of objects, directly on to ordinary paper which does not need a coated or emulsified surface. The process depends on the ability of static electricity to attract particles of black powder to un-exposed areas of the image.

X-height. The height of that part of a lower case letter between the Ascender and the Descender, i.e. the height of a lower case x. Used to describe the apparent height of a type which may vary within the same point size according to the design of the typeface, e.g. in 12 point type from 0.056 to 0.08 inches. Centaur, Egmont, Perpetua and Walbaum have small x-heights, Plantin and Times Old Roman big.

XHTML. <www.w3.org/MarkUp> Extensible HyperText Markup Language, a family of current and future document types and modules that reproduce, subset, and extend HTML, reformulated in XML. XHTML is the successor of HTML, and a series of specifications has been developed. XHTML 1.0 is the first major change to HTML since HTML 4.0 was released in 1997 and will enable the provision of richer Web pages on an ever increasing range of browser platforms including cell phones, televisions, cars, wallet sized wireless communicators, kiosks, and desktops.

XML <www.w3.org/XML> Extensible Markup Language, a flexible text format developed by W3C to enable the use of SGML on the World Wide Web. XML is extensible because it is not a fixed format like HTML and it therefore allows much greater control and flexibility over the way in which documents are displayed on the Web. XML is not a single Markup language, it is actually a metalanguage based on SGML which enables users to design their own customized, markup language for many classes of document. XML has been designed for ease of implementation, and for interoperability with both SGML and HTML.

Xylograph. 1. A block book. 2. A wood engraving.

Xylographic book. *See* Block books.

Xylography. The art or process of engraving on wood. *See also* Woodcut, Wood engraving.

Xylotype. Wood engraving, or a print from a wood engraving.

Y2K. *See* Year 2000 Crisis.

YALSA. *See* Young Adult Library Services Association.

Yankee machine. A machine on which machine-glazed papers are made. Its chief characteristic is one large steam-heated cylinder with a highly polished surface in place of the usual drying rolls. Machine-glazed papers are glazed on only one (the under) side, the other being in the (rough) condition in which it comes from the Wet end of the machine.

Yapp edges. *See* Circuit edges.

Year 2000 Crisis (Y2K). In the late 1990s it was widely feared that older computer systems would be unable to function when year identifiers changed to '2000'. Despite high-profile warnings, the date change passed with minimal problems. Also termed the 'Millennium Bug'.

Year book. A volume often called an *annual*, containing current information of a variable nature, in brief descriptive and/or statistical form, which is published once every year. Often year books review the events of a year.

Year number. A symbol used to represent the year in which a book was published. This forms a central part of the Book number, as used with the Colon Classification, and is obtained by translating the year of publication into the appropriate symbols in accordance with the Scheme's General Time Schedule, or a special chronological table for this purpose.

Year of Reading. *See* National Year of Reading.

YELL. *See* Youth and Education Librarians of London Group.

Yellow Book. 1. An official report published by the French government, so called because issued in a yellow paper cover. *See also* Blue Book.

Yellow Pages. Electronic Directory services for locating information about services and service providers (including, for example, OPACs). *See also* White Pages.

Yellow Press. A popular name for sensational newspapers and periodicals.

Yellow publisher. A publisher, as defined by the ROMEO project, that permits authors to Self archive only the pre-print of their academic paper.

Yellowback. A cheap popular novel, usually not of the first quality. So named from the fact that such books were published in shiny yellow paper covers with a picture on the front.

YMCK. *See* CMYK.

YMLAC. *See* Museums, Libraries and Archives Council (MLA).

Young adult book. One intended for adults but suitable for adolescents. *See also* Kiddult fiction.

Young Adult Library Services Association (YALSA). A division of the American Library Association; established in 1957 as the Young Adult Services Division (YASD). It is concerned with development of services to young people in all types of library, and particularly evaluates and selects media materials.

Young Book Trust. A specialist section of the Book Trust.

Younger Committee (UK). The Committee on Privacy set up by the British Government in 1970 under the chairmanship of Kenneth Younger. The Committee reported in 1972. *See* Data protection.

Youth and Education Librarians of London Group. YELL was an informal group set up by the Association of Chief Librarians of London, and known until 1992 as the Senior Children's Librarians of London Group. In 1995/96 YELL, the Association of Metropolitan District Education and Children's Librarians (AMDECL), and the Society of County Children's and Education Librarians (SOCCEL) agreed to merge as the Association of Senior Children's and Education Librarians (ASCEL).

Youth Libraries Group. A membership group of CILIP, founded as the Work with Young People Section in 1946, changing its name in 1963. It is concerned to develop and encourage literacy and the use of books for children and young people.

Z39. <www.niso.org/standards> (P.O. Box 1056, Bethesda, MD 20827, USA) Abbreviation for National Information Standards Organization (Z39) which develops standards for the American National Standards Institute, Inc. (ANSI) in the areas of library science, information sciences and related publishing practices. NISO (Z39) represents the major professional organizations, principal commercial agencies in the field, and US Government Departments; the Council of National Library and Information Associations serves as its secretariat. The Standards are all based on voluntary consensus. The Standard with the widest international impact is Z39.50 (see below). Information on current Standards is available on the website.

Z39.50. <www.loc.gov/z3950/agency> A retrieval protocol which allows client applications to query databases on remote servers, to retrieve results, and to carry out some other typical retrieval-related functions. The standard, *Information Retrieval (Z39.50): application service definition and protocol specification*, is represented as both ANSI/NISO Z39.50 and ISO 23950. Z39.50 corresponds to the Client/server model of computing with the client known as the 'origin' and the server as the 'target'. The Z39.50 Maintenance Agency provides information pertaining to the development and maintenance of Z39.50 (existing as well as future versions) and the implementation and use of the Z39.50 protocol. *See also* ZING.

Z39.88. *See* OpenURL.

ZeeRex. Z39.50 Explain, Explained and Re-Engineered in XML, an XML schema used to describe the configuration and capabilities of Z39.50 and SRW servers; a part of the ZING initiative.

Zero-based budgeting (ZBB). A management and financial system that requires an organization to identify priorities and justify activities from 'point Zero', that is without any prior assumptions. This may lead to a re-ranking of traditional goals, and examination of hidden costs.

Zetoc. <zetoc.mimas.ac.uk> Z39.50-compliant access to the British Library's Electronic Table of Contents of around 20,000 current journals and around 16,000 conference proceedings published annually. The database covers 1993 to date, and is updated on a daily basis. It includes an e-mail alerting service, so that users can receive notification of relevant new data. Free to use for members of JISC-sponsored UK higher and further education institutions. *See also* ETOCs, TOCS.

Zhong Guo Guo Jia Tu Shu Guan. [National Library of China] <www.nlc.gov.cn/english.htm> (39 Bai Shi Qiao Road, Beijing 100081, P. R. China) Founded in 1909, and based on parts of the Imperial collections of the Song, Yuan, Ming and Qing dynasties, the library moved in 1987 to its new premises, thought to be the largest single library building in the world, with 170,000 square metres of floor space, 22 storeys and additional basements. There are 1,600 staff, stock exceeds 22 million items, and there are 3,000 study spaces in 33 reading rooms. It is a comprehensive research library, the national repository of domestic publications, the national bibliographic centre, the national centre of library information networks, and the library research and development centre. The Library serves the central legislature, key government institutions, education, business and the general public. The Library is responsible for implementing official cultural agreements and conducts communication and co-operation with libraries at home and abroad. Publishes *Journal* (q.).

Zhong Guo Jiao Yu Huo Ke Yan Ji Suan Ji Wang. [China Education and Research Network (CERNET)] <www.edu.cn/index.shtml> CERNET was the first nationwide education and research computer network in China, established in 1993. It is government-funded, directly managed by the Ministry of Education, and operated by Tsinghua and other leading universities. CERNIC (China Education and Research Network Information Center) provides network resources and information services and is an important platform for China's remote learning initiative. It acts as the nation-wide Internet Registry, responsible for the academic network edu.cn. Publishes *CERNET Dao Bao* [*CERNET news*] (q.).

Zhong Guo Ke Xue Ji Shu Xin Xi Yan Jiu Suo. [Institute for Scientific and Technical Information of China (ISTIC)] <www.istic.ac.cn> (15 Fuxing Road, Beijing 100038, P. R. China) Established in 1956 under the Ministry of Science and Technology, ISTIC carries out the collection, storage and service of scientific and technological documents, database building, information analysis and research, information service network infrastructure construction, information professionals training and media publishing etc. The Engineering and Technology Library is the authoritative center for document resources collection and services.

Zhong Guo Tu Shu Guan Xue Hui. [China Society for Library Science (CSLS)] (c/o National Library of China, 39 Bai Shi Qiao Road, Beijing 100081, P.R. China) Founded in 1925 as the Library Association of China, it aims to promote library science and encourage professional communication among its 10,000 members through conferences and symposia. Publishes *Tu Shu Guan Xue Tong Xun* (*Journal of Library Science in China*) (q.).

ZIG. <lcweb.loc.gov/z3950/agency/zig/zig.html> Z39.50 Implementors Group; founded in the US in 1990 from a group of manufacturers, vendors, consultants and information providers to develop the Z39.50 standard for information searching and retrieval.

Zigzag fold. *See* Accordion fold, Concertina fold.

Zinc etching. *See* Zincograph.

Zinco. 1. Abbreviation for Zincograph. 2. A block made of zinc and used as an alternative to a Binder's brass. It is less durable, and the impression made with it lacks sharpness.

Zincograph (zinco). 1. A zinc plate which is etched and mounted for use as a line block for printing book illustrations and diagrams in black and white. The printing method is known as Zincography. 2. A print or design made from such a block.

Zincplate litho. *See* Lithography.

ZING. <www.loc.gov/z3950/agency/zing> Z39.50-International: Next Generation, a number of initiatives by Z39.50 implementors to make the intellectual/semantic content of Z39.50 more broadly available and to make the protocol more attractive to information providers, developers, vendors, and users by lowering the barriers to implementation while preserving the contributions that have accumulated over nearly 20 years. ZING initiatives include SRW, CQL and ZeeRex.

Zipf's Law. Formulated by George K. Zipf in 1949. Zipf studied the word counts of linguistic samples and observed that if the words appearing in a piece of text (one of reasonable length) are counted and ranked in order of frequency, this frequency is proportional to the rank order. *See also* Law of Scattering.

Zoomorphic initial. In a mediaeval illuminated manuscript, an initial letter formed by the bodies of beasts.

Zurich Index. *See Concilium Bibliographicum.*

Zweig (Stefan) Programme. 1987 was the inaugural year of the British Library Stefan Zweig Programme. This annual series of concerts and lectures was set up by the Library in response to the gift to the nation, in May 1986, of the enormously important collection of autograph musical and literary manuscripts formed by the Austrian writer Stefan Zweig.